D0071705

COMMUNICATION YEARBOOK 10

edited by

MARGARET L. McLAUGHLIN

an Annual Review Published for the
International Communication Association

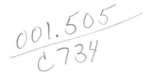

SAGE PUBLICATIONS
The Publishers of Professional Social Science
Newbury Park   Beverly Hills   London   New Delhi

For information address:

SAGE Publications, Inc.
2111 West Hillcrest Drive
Newbury Park, California 91320

SAGE Publications Inc.
275 South Beverly Drive
Beverly Hills
California 90212

SAGE Publications Ltd.
28 Banner Street
London EC1Y 8QE
England

SAGE PUBLICATIONS India Pvt. Ltd.
M-32 Market
Greater Kailash I
New Delhi 110 048 India

Printed in the United States of America

Library of Congress: 76-45943
ISBN 0-8039-2939-0

FIRST PRINTING

CONTENTS

Selection Committees, Divisions, and Interest Groups

Information Systems

George Barnett, *State University of New York at Albany*
James Dillard, *University of Wisconsin—Madison*
Kathy Kellermann, *University of Wisconsin—Madison*

Interpersonal Communication

Janis F. Andersen, *San Diego State University*
Joseph Folger, *Temple University*
Sally Jackson, *University of Oklahoma*
Michael E. Roloff, *Northwestern University*
Sally Planalp, *University of Illinois at Urbana-Champaign*

Mass Communication

James Anderson, *University of Utah*
William G. Christ, *Trinity University*
Roger Desmond, *University of Hartford*
Gina Garramone, *Michigan State University*
Chin-Chuan Lee, *University of Minnesota*
Roy L. Moore, *Georgia State University*

Organizational Communication

George Cheney, *University of Illinois*
Beverly Davenport-Sypher, *University of Kentucky*
Eric Eisenberg, *University of Southern California*
Linda Putnam, *Purdue University*

Intercultural and Development Communication

Robert L. Nwanko, *Howard University*
Josep Rota, *Howard University*
William Starosta, *Howard University*
June Ock Yum, *State University of New York at Albany*

Political Communication

Gina Garramone, *Michigan State University*
Kathleen E. Kendall, *State University of New York at Albany*
Michael W. Mansfield, *Baylor University*
Roy Miller, *Southern Illinois University*

Instructional and Developmental Communication

Dave Buller, *Texas Tech University*
William Todd Mancillas, *California State University at Chico*
Judy C. Pearson, *Ohio University*
Timothy Plax, *Rockwell International*
Robert Stewart, *Texas Tech University*

Health Communication

Paul Arntson, *Northwestern University*
Elizabeth Kunimoto, *University of Hawaii*
Peter Northouse, *Western Michigan University*
Eileen Berlin Ray, *University of Kentucky*
David Smith, *University of South Florida*

Philosophy of Communication

Martin Allor, *Concordia University*
Jackie Byars, *University of Wisconsin—Madison*
David Eason, *University of Utah*
Norman Elliot, *University of Utah*
Fred Fejes, *Florida Atlantic University*
Lawrence Grossberg, *University of Illinois at Urbana-Champaign*
Michael Hyde, *Northwestern University*
Astrid Kersten, *LaRoche College*
Richard Lanigan, *Southern Illinois University*
David Miller, *Purdue University*
Barbara O'Keefe, *University of Illinois at Urbana-Champaign*
John Stewart, *University of Washington*
Ellen Wartella, *University of Illinois at Urbana-Champaign*

Human Communication Technology

John Bowes, *University of Washington*
Donald Case, *University of California, Los Angeles*
Milton Chen, *Harvard University*
David Dozier, *San Diego State University*
Rick Ducey, *National Association of Broadcasters*
Andrew Finn, *AT&T Communications*
Maureen Germano, *AT&T Marketing Research*
Andrew Hardy, *General Motors Corporation*
Glen Hiemstra, *Antioch University*
Kimberly Neuendorf, *Cleveland State University*
Amy Phillips, *North Hollywood, California*
Joey Reagan, *Washington State University*
Ronald E. Rice, *University of Southern California*
Jessica Severn, *San Diego State University*
Charles Steinfield, *Michigan State University*
Sharon Strover, *University of Texas at Austin*

Popular Culture

Jim Combs, *Valparaise University*
Dennis Corrigan, *University of Iowa*
James Fee, *University of Akron*
Steve Smith, *University of Arkansas*

Public Relations

Vince Hazelton, *Illinois State University*
Gay Wakefield, *Southern Illinois University*
Emma Oshagan, *San Diego State University*
Bonita Dostal Neff, *Purdue University at Calumet*

THE INTERNATIONAL COMMUNICATION ASSOCIATION

Communication Yearbook is an annual review. The series is sponsored by the International Communication Association, one of several major scholarly organizations in the communication field. It is composed of 2,500 communication scholars, teachers, and practitioners.

Throughout its 37-year history, the Association has been particularly important to those in the field of communication who have sought a forum where the behavioral science perspective was predominant. The International Communication Association has also been attractive to a number of individuals from a variety of disciplines who hold communication to be central to work within their primary fields of endeavor. The Association has been an important stimulant to the infusion of behavioral concepts in communication study and teaching, and has played a significant role in defining a broadened set of boundaries of the discipline as a whole.

The International Communication Association is a pluralist organization composed of ten subdivisions: Information Systems, Interpersonal Communication, Mass Communication, Organizational Communication, Intercultural and Development Communication, Political Communication, Instructional and Developmental Communication, Health Communication, Philosophy of Communication, and Human Communication Technology.

In addition to *Communication Yearbook*, the Association publishes *Human Communication Research*, the *ICA Newsletter*, and *ICA Directory*, and is affiliated with the *Journal of Communication*. Several divisions also publish newsletters and occasional papers.

PREFACE

This tenth volume in the *Communication Yearbook* Series conforms to the established format of a series of essays, reviews, and commentaries followed by a selection of the best offerings from ICA's 1986 divisional paper competitions. Each of the 40 papers in *Communication Yearbook 10* was reviewed by at least 2 of the 57 members of the *CY* Editorial Board; the divisional selections were reviewed first by paper selection committees in each of ICA's 10 divisions and 2 interest groups. More than 70 people were involved in this blind reviewing process at the divisional level.

Many people contributed to the preparation of *Communication Yearbook 10*. Thanks are due again this year to Paul Bohannon, Dean of the Division of Social Sciences and Communication, and Kenneth Sereno, Chairman of Communication Arts and Sciences, for providing me with the released time as well as the clerical and material support needed to finish the project. Thanks are also due to Editorial Assistant Joan Cashion and to Communication Arts and Sciences staff members Gwen Brown, Lindoria Horn, and Carla Francis for their many services.

—*Margaret L. McLaughlin*

OVERVIEW OF THE COMMUNICATION YEARBOOK SERIES

This is the tenth in a series of annual volumes providing yearly reviews and syntheses of developments in the evolution of the science of communication. Each volume in the series provides (1) disciplinary reviews and commentaries on topics of general interest to scholars and researchers no matter what their specialized interest in communication studies, (2) current research on a variety of topics that reflect the scholarly concerns of persons working in designated areas, and (3) subject and author indexes that offer convenient reference for each volume. Reviews and commentaries for this volume were solicited by the series editor; chapters presenting current research were selected through processes of competitive judging. Final acceptance of all chapters was based upon refereeing processes established by the editor.

Reviews and Commentaries

Review and Commentary chapters are general discussions and critiques of substantive and methodological matters of generic interest and relevance that transcend the more specialized concerns of scholars working in the highly diversified discipline of communication science. This section provides a unique outlet for discussions of issues and ideas not readily adaptable to more restrictive journal formats.

Selected Studies

Communication Yearbook is also an outlet for edited versions of representative current research that has been selected competitively for presentation at annual conferences of the International Communication Association. *Yearbook 10* presents studies selected for the 36th Annual Conference held in Chicago in May 1986. These studies represent the papers chosen by competitive evaluation by each of ICA's divisions and interest groups; and by the *Yearbook's* editor and editorial board. The papers represent research from the following divisions and interest groups: Information Systems, Interpersonal Communication, Mass Communication, Organizational Communication, Intercultural and Development Communication, Political Communication, Instructional and Developmental Communication, Health Communication, Philosophy of Communication, Human Communication Technology, Popular Culture, and Public Relations.

I ● COMMUNICATION REVIEWS AND COMMENTARIES

1 ● Speech Accommodation Theory: The First Decade and Beyond

HOWARD GILES ● ANTHONY MULAC ●
JAMES J. BRADAC ● PATRICIA JOHNSON

*University of Bristol ● University of
California—Santa Barbara ● University of Bristol*

THE first publications concerning "speech accommodation theory" (SAT) emerged in 1973. Giles (1973) not only demonstrated the phenomenon of interpersonal accent convergence in an interview situation, but also introduced his "accent mobility" model in the context of a critique of some aspects of the Labovian (1966) paradigm (see also Bell, 1984). This was a blueprint for subsequent formulations addressing a greater diversity of speech levels (Giles & Powesland, 1975). To this end, and in that same year, Giles, Taylor, and Bourhis (1973) published a paper that confirmed empirically some fundamental ideas inherent in what subsequently was to be labeled *SAT*. In a bilingual context, they found that the more effort in convergence a speaker was perceived to have made, the more favorably that person was evaluated and the more listeners would converge back in turn. Moreover, a plethora of convergent strategies was discovered even in what for some would be described as a socially sterile

AUTHORS' NOTE: The authors are very grateful to Nikolas Coupland, Margaret McLaughlin, Richard L. Street, Jr., John Wiemann, and two anonymous referees for their comments on an earlier draft of this chapter.

Correspondence and requests for reprints: Anthony Mulac, Department of Communication Studies, Ellison Hall, University of California—Santa Barbara, Santa Barbara, CA 93106 laboratory setting. Since then, empirical and theoretical developments and consequences have been somewhat profuse, and particularly so in the 1980s (for example, Ball, Giles, & Hewstone, 1985; Giles, 1984). Hence, the aim of this state-of-the-art chapter is to present a concise overview of SAT achievements to date, to renovate some of its propositional components in the light of recent thinking, and to lay down some priorities for future research.

SAT, developed by Giles and associates, focuses on the social cognitive processes mediating individuals' perceptions of the environment and their communicative behaviors. Its theoretical framework developed out of a wish to demonstrate the value and potential of social psychological concepts and processes for understanding the dynamics of speech diversity in social settings. It purports to clarify the motivations underlying, as well as the constraints operating upon, speech shifts during social interactions and the social consequences of these. Specifically, it originated in order to elucidate the cognitive and affective processes underlying speech convergence and divergence, although other speech strategies (for example, speech complementarity and speech competition) have come into its theoretical purview more recently.

Convergence has been defined as a linguistic strategy whereby individuals adapt to each other's speech by means of a wide range of linguistic features, including speech rates, pauses and utterance length, pronunciations and so on. Divergence refers to the way in which speakers accentuate vocal differences between themselves and others. Both of these linguistic shifts may be either *upward* or *downward,* where the former refers to a shift in a societally valued direction and the latter refers to modifications toward more stigmatized forms.

Beyond these basic distinctions several more specific accommodative forms can be indicated. The complexity level increases. Thus in any interaction, convergence can be mutual (A— > < —B) and if mutual can result in style matching (A— > < —B) or, probably less commonly, style switching (A—— >B; A< ——B). Convergence can be nonmutual (A— > B). Both interactants can maintain their dissimilar styles, neither converging nor diverging (A B). Divergence can be mutual (< —A B— >) or nonmutual (< —A B). And one person can attempt to converge as the other diverges (< —A < —B). Further, convergence can refer to a speaker's attempt to move toward the other's manifest speech style (Seltig, 1983) or to a speaker's attempt to move toward a style suggested by a belief, expectation, or stereotype regarding the other's style. The *response to a manifest* style versus *response to a belief* about other's style, and so on, distinction can be offered for divergence as well. Additionally, the distinction between partial and total convergence or divergence can be offered (Street, 1982). Thus, for example, a speaker initially exhibiting a rate of 50 words per minute can move to match exactly another speaker's rate of 100 words per minute (total convergence) or can move to a rate of 75 words per minute (partial convergence). Finally, we can distinguish between unimodal and multimodal divergence or convergence. The former distinction indicates that a speaker can converge to or diverge from one aspect of the other's speech, for example, rate, whereas the latter distinction indicates convergence or divergence at two or more levels, for example, rate and accent.

The central notion of the framework—its advantages relative to SAT's theoretical competitors have been discussed elsewhere (Street & Giles, 1982)—is that during interaction individuals are motivated to adjust (or to accommodate) their speech styles as a strategy for gaining one or more of the following goals: evoking listeners' social approval, attaining communicational efficiency between interactants, and maintaining positive social identities. In addition, it is the individual's *perception* of the other's speech that will determine his or her evaluative and communicative responses.

But, before proceeding perhaps we should ask: Are the various phenomena encompassed by speech accommodation worth theorizing about? What importance attaches to speech accommodation processes? Briefly, it is clear to us that the various forms of convergence and divergence can have important psychological and communicative consequences. For example, dialect divergence can increase or enhance the diverger's sense of social identity (Bourhis & Giles, 1977). Or, to give another example, convergence to another's dialect can lead persons to attribute to the converger the traits of friendliness, warmth, and so on (Coupland, 1985). And, of course, attributed personality characteristics can affect the attributer's subsequent interactions with the converger. So it seems to us that *understanding* the structures and processes implicated in speech accommodation is a worthwhile goal. And not only are accommodation phenomena potentially consequential, they are ubiquitous; they pervade human interaction.

The theory has been developed via a number of social psychological principles. Speech convergence is considered primarily in terms of similarity attraction (Byrne, 1969), causal attribution (Heider, 1958), and speech divergence with respect to intergroup processes (Tajfel & Turner, 1979). Consideration of these principles allows for explication of both the intentions thought to underlie speech shifts and the evaluations of them. This chapter presents an overview of the two speech strategies, convergence and divergence, with respect to antecedent motives and evaluative consequences. Speech convergence will be considered in terms of desire for social approval, situational constraints on its occurrence and evaluation, observers' causal attributions that may be invoked to account for it, as well as the level of awareness necessary for its inception. Speech divergence, which has been explored empirically less often, is considered in terms of the interactional functions, identity maintenance, and cognitive organization (see Giles, Scherer, & Taylor, 1979). The chapter concludes with a more complete and refined set of SAT propositions than hitherto proposed relating to the determinants, functions, and social consequences of speech shifts. Yet it does more than this, as the latter also are reformulated in such ways as to take into account the theoretical implications of current research in some other relevant but independent areas of inquiry, particularly those of self-presentation and couple identity. Finally, some new theoretical and methodological priorities for the future are proposed.

CONVERGENCE

Convergence and Desire for Social Approval

SAT proposes that speech convergence be considered a reflection (often nonconscious) of a speaker's or group's need for social integration or identification with another. The theory has its basis in research on similarity attraction which, in its simplest form, suggests that as one person becomes more similar to another, this increases the likelihood that the second will like the first. Thus interpersonal convergence through speech is one of many strategies that may be adopted in order to become more similar to another. It involves the reduction of linguistic dissimilarities between two people in terms of most language features from dialects (Coupland, 1980) to nonverbal behaviors (von Raffler-Engel, 1979). Thus, for example, Welkowitz and Feldstein (1969, 1970) reported that dyadic participants who perceived themselves to be similar in terms of attitudes and personality converged durations of internal pauses (those within a conversational turn) and of switching pauses more than did those participants perceiving dissimilarity. Dyadic interactants who perceived themselves to be similar were more able and willing to coordinate and influence one another's speech patterns and timing than other dyads, presumably because these perceived similar dyads were initially more positively oriented and more certain of one another (Byrne, 1971). In addition to pause duration, Welkowitz, Feldstein, Finkelstein, and Aylesworth (1972) found that dyadic participants perceiving themselves as similar converged vocal intensity more than subjects randomly paired.

The language choice of male and female interactants has demonstrated convergence also. Mulac, Wiemann, Yoerks, and Gibson (1983) assigned university students to problem-solving dyads, either same-sex or mixed-sex, with a partner whom they did not know well. Linguistic analyses indicated that a combination of 12 language features predicted interactant gender in same-sex, but not mixed-sex, dyads; in other words, mixed-sex dyadic participants appeared to have met "midway" linguistically. Another interesting example of convergence brought to our attention by Mary

Evans (personal communication) is the tendency some balanced bilingual speakers have in even converging regularly toward the grammatical *errors* made by nonfluent second-language learners acquiring the other's native tongue (Jones, 1984). Needless to say, this nonconscious and doubtless positively intended strategy on the part of the fluent speaker has the effect of retarding the nativelike proficiency of the second-language learner.

Increasing similarity along a dimension as important as communication is likely to increase a speaker's attractiveness (Dabbs, 1969), his or her predictability (Berger & Bradac, 1982), intelligibility (Triandis, 1960), and interpersonal involvement (LaFrance, 1979) in the eyes of the recipient. In view of this, convergence may be best considered as a reflection of an individual's desire for social approval in many instances. For example, Purcell (1984) observed Hawaiian children's convergent shifts in prosodic and lexicogrammatical features depending on the likability of the particular peers present when talking together in small groups, and Putman and Street (1984) reported interviewee shifts in speech rate and duration when intending to sound likable to an interviewer. Similarly, Coupland (1984) found convergent speech shifts in the phonological variations of a travel agent when conferring in her office with clients of different socioeconomic status and education.

A compelling set of illustrations in like manner comes from a large-scale naturalistic study of code-switching in Taiwan by Berg (1985), who examined 8,392 interactions across many markets, department stores, shops, and banks. In general, the most common pattern of communication in these situations was *mutual* accommodation to the other's dialect, the nature of which depended on the particular setting involved. For instance, customers would downwardly converge to salespeople in the market place and would receive upward convergence in return, but in banks (given the sociolinguistic and socioeconomic attributes of the salespeople there) customers would now upwardly converge to the clerks who would downwardly converge to them. Of particular interest to SAT is the continual finding that in many of these settings where customers, of course, hold the relative monetary reins, salespeople converged much *more* to customers than vice versa. Of course in times of commodity scarcity and economic hardship, one might expect the reverse pattern to be operative in view of the social approval (and even survival) motive.

An exception to the convergent style/social approval connection is the case in which a speaker "makes fun of" another by mocking his or her communicative behavior (see Basso, 1979). In this case, the speaker typically will signal the intention to mock the other's style through the use of various meta-communicative devices. Kathryn Shields (personal communication) has observed Jamaican schoolteachers (who usually adopt a standardized form in the classroom) converging/mimicking their pupils' creolized forms when the latter are deemed disruptive, inattentive, or lacking in academic effort. This suggests that one's perception of a speaker's intention is crucial to specifying the consequences of both convergence and divergence.

For affective reasons again, people converge to where they *believe* their partners are linguistically. For example, Bell (1982) reported that New Zealand broadcasters would read the same news phonologically quite differently depending on which socioeconomic bracket they thought their listening audience derived from (see also Seltig, 1985). Often of course we are quite accurate in pinpointing the linguistic attributes of our recipients, yet on other occasions we are quite wrong. Beebe (1981), for instance, found that Chinese Thai bilingual children would use Chinese phonological variants when being interviewed by an objectively sounding Standard Thai speaker who looked ethnically Chinese. Similarly, some Singaporeans' and Australian immigrants' attempts lexically, grammatically, and prosodically to match "upwardly" the speech of native English speakers may miscarry, and in other cases, native English speakers mismanage their *downward* convergent attempts toward what they believe Singaporeans and Aborigines sound like (Platt & Weber, 1984). It also should not escape notice that two of the cultural settings in which accommodative tendencies have been observed above are Oriental; the conviction that these sociolinguistic processes are really quite widespread begins to look viable.

From these examples it can be argued that speech convergence is often cognitively mediated by our stereotypes of how socially categorized others will speak (see Hewstone & Giles, 1986), and "foreigner talk" and speech to certain ethnic minorities and young children can be examplars of this. In the area of gender and communication there is some evidence (Mulac et al., 1983) that observers' ratings of male and female interactants' transcripts suggest a convergence toward a stereotypical, rather than actual, opposite-sex partner's language behavior. In same-sex dyads, in which the effects of individuals' language judged by naive transcript readers was likely to be consistent with the effects of sex-role stereotypes (Mulac, Incontro, & James, 1985), women were rated higher than men on "sociointellectual status" and "aesthetic quality"; no difference was found on perceived "dynamism." However, in mixed-sex dyads, interactants' language use led to stereotype-consistent convergence. No difference was found on sociointellectual status. Moreover, men were rated higher on aesthetic quality and women were rated higher on dynamism.

A vivid demonstration of stereotypical convergence at a different lifespan stage is reported by Caporael, Lukaszewski, and Culbertson (1983), who found that some nurses would use baby talk to the institutionalized elderly, irrespective of the latter's actual capabilities, if these nurses had generally unfavorable views of their charges' functional autonomy (see also, Ryan, Giles, Bartolucci, & Henwood, 1986). Blind persons also often report being the recipients of such stereotyped convergence, as argued by Klemz (1977, p. 8):

The blind are discriminated against in less formal situations. All too often strangers address them as though they were deaf, or mentally deficient; or refuse to address them at all, and talk to their companions instead. Most people are prepared to help the blind, but they are not prepared to accept them as normal colleagues and companions. They *expect* the blind to be helpless and offer them help, whether they need it or not. (emphasis added)

By contrast, in some cases convergence may reflect one speaker's attempt to reciprocate another's *actual* communicative behavior, which may be either consistent or inconsistent with an appropriate stereotype. For example, a student may converge to a particular professor's extremely rapid rate of speech even though the professorial stereotype may dictate cautious and thoughtful utterance. More will be said later about convergence to actual behavior versus stereotypical convergence.

A variety of studies in impression formation support the notion that speech convergence is often positively evaluated. Putman and Street (1984) found that interviewees who converge toward their interviewers in terms of speech rate and response latency (and also complement each other in utterance duration) are reacted to favorably by the latter in terms of perceived social attractiveness. Other research indicates that relative similarity in speech rates, response latencies, language, and accent are viewed more positively than relative dissimilarity on dimensions of social attractiveness (Street, Brady, & Putman, 1983), communicative effectiveness (Giles & Smith, 1979), perceived warmth (Welkowitz & Kuc, 1973), and cooperativeness (Feldman, 1968). Furthermore, professional interviewees' perceptions of student interviewers' competence also has been shown to be positively related to the latter's convergence on speech rate and response latency (Street, 1984).

However, there are differential evaluations of convergence depending on its magnitude and the dimensions on which it occurs. Giles and Smith (1979) presented eight versions of a taped message to an English audience. The taped voice was a Canadian exhibiting varying degrees and combinations of convergence on three linguistic dimensions (pronunciation, speech rate, and message content). Listeners appreciated convergence on each linguistic level, but upgraded the speaker most when he converged on speech rate and *either* content *or* pronunciation. Convergence on all three dimensions, however, was perceived negatively as patronizing. Thus convergence does not seem to be necessarily linearly related to positive evaluations and there appear to be optimal levels, and possibly optimal *rates* in some situations as well (see also Bradac, Hosman, & Tardy, 1978). It seems that listeners have ranges of acceptable or preferred behavior (Cappella & Greene, 1982). For example, Street (1982) found that observers tolerated differences between interviewer and interviewee speech rates of up to 50 words a minute, but beyond those limits the speaker was downgraded.

The "overconvergence" (on all three dimensions simultaneously) in the Giles and Smith study may be seen in other situations as a result of a marked set (Scotton, 1980). That is, the degree of convergence is perceived to be inappropriate for the situation, thereby leading to negative evaluations. Certainly a number of the institutionalized elderly in the Caporael and associates' study above reported irritation at being addressed by baby talk (presumably those who, to use the terminology of Rubin and Rubin [1982], felt contextually young) and those overconverged in the Platt and Weber study expressed amusement at best, irritation at worst. As pointed out by Coleman (1985), being on the receiving end continually of such linguistic phenomena will lead ultimately to the development of a distorted sense of self. Jones, Farina, Hastorf, Markus, Miller, and Scott (1984), more generally, have shown how the use of "child among adults" communicative patterns by the physically "normal" can enforce psychological distance (or even exile) with the handicapped that is not warranted by their actual limitations, but can become internalized and thereby lead to self-stigmatization. The situation becomes exacerbated when so-called normals believe that their abilities and attributes are being compared with those who have been labeled as incompetent (Piner & Kahle, 1984). Self-evaluative processes, so triggered, may well be manifest in "superiority" behavior of the type outlined by Jones and associates (1984), Snyder's (1981) tactic of "behavioral confirmation," and inherent in our notion of "overconvergence." Moreover, our recall of certain events is determined, at least in part, by our expressed descriptions of them accommodated for others (Higgins & McCann, 1984). Thus relating an event to an elderly person may not only produce a stereotypic "talked down" version, but ultimately may result in a simplified, inadequate recall of that same event by the accommodator, the responsibility for which is likely to be attributed negatively to the elderly person.

Yet such a lack of quality communication may not only induce lowered self-esteem for many in the short-term, but can add intolerable psychological burdens in the long run on many of those (for example, the elderly, blind) who are already having to cope with severe physical and or social problems. Under these circumstances, negative social identities emerge, life satisfaction is reduced, physical and mental health goes into decline, and valued social welfare and medical resources are subsequently implicated and reduced.

These important caveats notwithstanding, accepting the notion that people find approval from others satisfying and that speech convergence goes some way toward achieving this, it is likely that there is a tendency for people to converge toward one another in many situations, albeit some people are more "person-centered/receiver-focused" (O'Keefe & Delia, 1985) and "rhetorically sensitive" (Ward, Bluman, & Dauria, 1982) communicators than others. Indeed, Higgins's (1980) "communication games" approach to interpersonal communication, in essence, posits such a conversational rule, and certainly the phenomenon appears ubiquitous in the sense of its early ontogenetic (e.g., Street, Street, & Van Kleeck, 1983), cross-sex (Brouwer, Gerritsen, & De Haan, 1979), and cross-cultural (Scollon & Scollon, 1979) appearances. It follows from this that the greater the speaker's need to gain another's approval or attraction, the greater the degree of convergence there will be, up to a certain optimal level. Interestingly, it could be argued that not only do speakers converge to where they believe others to be, but in some (as yet, unspecified) conditions to where they believe others *expect them* to be linguistically. In any event, factors that may influence the intensity of the social approval need include the probability of future interactions with the other, the extent of their social power over the speaker, capacities for empathy, previous experience of converging toward that person, as well as interindividual variability in the need for social approval. Natale (1975a, 1975b) found that speakers scoring higher on a social desirability scale, designed to measure trans-situational need for social approval, converged more to their partner's vocal intensity and pause length than speakers who scored lower, indicating less need for social approval. Similarly, Street and Murphy (1985) found that males scoring higher on Swap and Rubin's (1983) "interpersonal orientation" measure (which presumably taps an individual's responsiveness to variations in another's behavior) converged speech rate, response latency, and interruption frequency to a greater extent than males who scored lower on this measure. However, the relationship between interpersonal orientation and nonverbal convergence did not hold for females.

There is evidence, then, that convergence may reflect a speaker's desire for social integration or identification. It seems also to be the case that participants in an encounter may display mutual, symmetrical convergences, though often to different degrees, and for different purposes. For instance, Thakerar, Giles, and Cheshire (1982) present data indicating that high-status speakers converge to low-status participants by means of slowing down their speech rates and nonstandardizing their accents for "cognitive" reasons, that is, to facilitate recipients' understanding of the message. In contrast, the latter quicken their speech rates and standardize their accents for mainly affective reasons, that is, to enhance their perceived competence in the eyes of the former. Such (superficially divergent) speech adjustments are only feasible to the extent that speakers have the repertoirial flexibility to make these modifications and maintain them. Trudgill (1981) suggests that lexical shifts probably precede grammatical and phonological convergence and that the latter also may be inhibited by difficulties in restructuring, as well as by a desire to avoid loss of contrast and strongly stereotyped features. Thus different speakers may adopt different convergent strategies as well as having different purposes for so doing. Of course, it is very possible that a particular convergent act will be encoded for both communicational efficiency and affective reasons. Richard Bourhis (personal communication) has exploratory data with Canadian student nurses suggesting that they might feel like "linguistic brokers" between physicians and their patients. The nurses believe that physicians do not converge their medical language to a sufficiently appropriate degree with their hospital patients. Arguably, in order to compensate for the apparent lack of understanding and to promote solidarity and empathy, student nurses report that they make considerable efforts in order to bridge the communicational gaps which if not breached are likely to detract from optimal health care.

Developing the notion of social approval further, the *power* dimension is among the most crucial determinants of the degree to which convergence will be manifest (see Berg, 1985). Thus, for example, Wolfram (1973) reports that in New York City, where both Puerto Ricans and Blacks agree that the latter hold more power and prestige than the former, Puerto Ricans assimilate the dialect of Blacks far more than vice versa. Josiane Hamers (personal communication), using role-taking procedures in a Quebec industrial setting, has demonstrated greater bilingual convergence to a recipient who was an occupational superior than one who was a subordinate; foremen converged more to managers than workers and managers converged more to higher managers than foremen. Similarly, research on the linguistic assimilation of immigrants in alien-dominant cultures suggests that language shifts are typically unilateral (see Giles, 1978), with subordinate groups converging to the dominant group in their use of language far more than vice versa (for example, Taylor, Simard, & Papineau, 1978). From a different perspective, Kincaid, Yum, Woelfel, and Barnett (1983) demonstrated that at the level of culturally held beliefs and values, Korean immigrants in Hawaii "converge" over time toward the equilibrium point of the host society. In terms of Tajfel and Turner's (1979) social identity theory, convergent language shifts have been considered as a tactic for achieving a positive self-image (Giles & Johnson, 1981). Seeking social approval is the main element of the individual mobility strategy that may be adopted by certain members of subordinate groups who perceive their ingroup's social position as legitimate and immutable (see also Albo, 1979; Giles & Bourhis, 1976).

In another study examining Spanish-English code-switching, it was found that bilingual Mexican American women tended to follow the language switches and also the frequency and types of language switches initiated by a male in conversation. Bilingual convergence was notably more limited or nonexistent in speech exchanges between two females (Valdes-Fallis, 1977). These findings confirm the SAT perspective based on the higher values and social power associated with male dominance in Western society (see Kramarae, 1981). This view also may explain the differences in the nonverbal convergence of men and women in problem-solving dyads reported by Mulac, Studley, Wiemann, and Bradac (in press). They measured the simultaneous gaze and talk behaviors of the same interactants in both same-sex and mixed-sex dyads, finding that women, but not men, converged toward their partners' behavior. This study also demonstrated that complete matching of a partner's gaze/talk behaviors was more indicative of women.

A study by Aboud (1976) suggests that awareness and influence of power and status differences in language usage is present at an early age. Six-year-old Chicano and Anglo-American children were asked to explain to two listeners of their own age how to play a game they had just learned; the listeners asked "Tell me how to play the game" in either Spanish or English. Although 71% of the Spanish-dominant Chicanos converged by adopting the language of their English listener, only 17% of the English-dominant Anglos accommodated to the Spanish listener despite the fact that half of them were in a bilingual program. Furthermore, none of the nonconvergers used any alternative forms of accommodation, such as using just a few keywords in Spanish or apologizing for not speaking this language.

As mentioned earlier, convergence may reflect a speaker's desire for social integration or identification. Similarly, it has been shown that the more an individual desires another's approval, the more the latter's voice will sound similar to the individual's own. Thus Larsen, Martin, and Giles (1977) found that speakers who anticipated interaction with an authoritative prestigious figure perceived his or her speech as sounding more similar to their own than did subjects who were told nothing about the speaker and who did not expect to meet him or her. Perceiving fewer language differences may be expected to facilitate the convergence process as well as making the target appear to be more accessible perceptually.

Situational Constraints on Speech Convergence

Convergent behavior will not always be the most appropriate or positively evaluated strategy, however, even in situations in which the speaker is seeking approval. Ball, Giles, Byrne, and Berechree (1984) point out that much of the previous research on SAT has centered around the dynamics of situations where norms are ambiguous or nonexistent, even at the social evaluational level (for example, Bourhis, Giles, & Lambert, 1975; Street, 1982). And perhaps this is not surprising given that SAT arose in part as a reaction against the theoretical bias in sociolinguistic theory favoring normative explanations (Giles & Hewstone, 1982). Indeed, as Scotton (1976) argues, it is a moot point as to when many situations are so normatively constrained that there still does not exist a wide latitude of acceptable communicative behaviors. Moreover, language behaviors are often used negotiatively so as to determine creatively what social norms are operating. Hence, in contexts of social ambiguity, people are likely to converge on others present (usually those with more status or dominance) by social comparison (Suls & Miller, 1977) so as to sound as though they "fit in" and say the "right thing." Admittedly, although this could be just another manifestation of the need for social approval, it does come about by a quite different mechanism and is worthy of elevation into the propositional format of SAT.

Some research has explored the situational boundaries of SAT. For example, Genesee and Bourhis (1982) showed in a Quebec study that situational norms were a strong factor in the evaluative reactions of listeners to a French Canadian salesman who either converged toward an English Canadian customer or maintained his own ingroup language over a sequence of interactive exchanges. For instance, the salesman was *not* upgraded on many dimensions for converging toward the customer. This was so apparently because of the established situational norm "the customer is always right." Space precludes an adequate critique of this factorially complex, two-study paper by Genesee and Bourhis. However, suffice it to say that careful examination of their findings (which are couched heavily in situational preeminence terms) shows that many accommodative tendencies were apparent in their data that were not highlighted by the authors. This was especially the case among those listening groups who could best identify with the target speakers on audiotape. For instance, even given the above mentioned situational norm, the immediately converging salesman was upgraded by monolingual English Canadian observers in terms of how positively they felt the customer would experience that situation. Nevertheless, the Genesee and Bourhis study is a pioneering landmark in its consideration not only of interpersonal accommodation with respect to (actually different, competing) social norms, but also in its attention to ingroup biases, the sociostructural statuses of the languages involved, and the sequential nature of accommodative exchanges. There is a need to explore the ways in which normative and accommodative processes combine and interact *sequentially* (see Bourhis, 1985) during the different trajectories of interpersonal development and their demise.

With some of those initial ends in mind, Ball, Giles, Byrne, and Berechree (1984) conducted a study in which listeners rated an interviewee who was heard outside and inside an interview speaking with either a "refined" or "broad" Australian accent. He either maintained his accent, or converged downward or upward, or diverged downward or upward toward the interviewer who spoke (in a factorial experimental design) with either a "broad" or "refined" accent. The results showed that the perception of the interviewee's speech was markedly affected by the subjects' supposed normative expectations that the interviewee would adhere to social pressures of sounding more refined inside the interview. This was evidenced to the extent that when the interviewee actually maintained his refined accent he was *perceived* to have become more refined in accent. The interviewee was rated as more competent, eager, and determined when using a refined accent, largely irrespective of whether he upwardly diverged or converged to the refined accent. That is, adherence to the sociolinguistic norms for an interview was the valued event, and little judgmental significance was attributed (at least in terms of the traits used therein) for accent shifts in terms of interpersonal accommodation. The study indicates that accommodation processes are indeed relegated in evaluative importance when strong social norms are operative, and has led to more explicit reference to situational constraints in the propositions of SAT (Ball et al., 1984). Berg (1985) also found in certain Taiwanese stores that the social meanings of transacting would dictate to which sociolinguistic norms both customer and salesperson accommodated. Similarly, Bradac and Mulac (1984) found that a speaker's use of a "powerless" verbal style was negatively evaluated even when it matched the "powerless" style of a second speaker. Moreover, a speaker's use of a "powerful" style was evaluated especially favorably when it diverged from a second speaker's "powerless" style.

Thus convergence will not be the most useful strategy to adopt in all contexts, and a passing, situated reliance on social exchange principles, which implies that the strategy should only be enacted when potential social rewards outweigh costs, can be conceptually fruitful (Chadwick-Jones, 1976). In some instances it may incur more costs (such as a decrease in perceived competence when downward) than rewards (such as increased perceived attractiveness; see Giles, 1977). Rewards could include gains in listeners' approval, cooperativeness, and compliance, but the specific rewards would be dependent on the particular speech features involved. Potential costs, on the other hand, could include expended effort, the possible loss of personal or social identity, and, of course, anticipated sanctions accruing from antinormative or nonnormative communications.

Recently, much attention has been afforded social cognitive aspects of language-situation relationships (Forgas, 1983). Certainly, we ought in future to attend to how communicators subjectively define the dimensions of the situation they are in, including its goal structure and the salience of their own identities at the time (Giles & Hewstone, 1982; McKirnan & Hamayan, 1984). One aspect of situational relevance herein that SAT has not until now afforded theoretical salience is that of physiological arousal. This mechanism has been accorded status in other interpersonal theories (for example, Cappella & Green, 1982; Patterson, 1983) and conceded by us as influential in general terms more recently (Giles & Street, 1985). Hence, it is timely for us to reformulate SAT propositions so as to take into account the strong possibility that high levels of physiological arousal—and particularly those that are situated by affective labels—are likely to inhibit the production of socially sensitive convergent strategies; indeed, it is even possible that under extreme conditions communicatively disruptive *divergent* speech patterns are likely. Doubtless the roles of different forms of arousal mediate accommodative processes in ways more complex than this, yet it does provide us with an embryonic blueprint for subsequent empirical explorations.

Speech Convergence, Attributions, and Intentions

Convergence and divergence can be produced, as discussed above, for a number of reasons. It is therefore pertinent for SAT to draw upon research on causal attribution which, in general terms, suggests that we understand people's behaviors, and hence evaluate them, in terms of the motives and intentions we attribute as being the cause of their actions (Heider, 1958). It has been proposed that a perceiver takes into account three factors when attributing motives to an act: the other's ability, effort, and external pressures impelling the person to act in a particular way (Kelley, 1973).

Simard, Taylor, and Giles (1976) examined the implications of attribution principles for the evaluation of convergence. They found that listeners who attributed another's convergence toward them as a desire to break down cultural barriers perceived this act very favorably. When this same shift was attributed externally to situational pressures forcing the speaker to converge, then the convergent act was perceived less favorably. Similarly, when a non-convergent act (that is, maintaining one's speech) was externally attributed to situational pressures, the negative responses were not so pronounced as when the behavior was attributed internally to the speaker's lack of effort. It should be noted, although being cognizant of actor-observer differences in making attributions about the same behavioral events (Farr & Anderson, 1983), that we require far more information as regards what social cues different recipients of accommodative acts utilize *for what attributional purposes*. When, for example, do listeners attribute nonconvergence to a personally-insulting maneuver; a failure to perceive the appropriate situational norm; an inflexible or even decayed speech repertoire; or a successful social rejection of speech characteristic of a particular contrastive group? As the last alternative implies, motives and intentions are attributed often for more *social* than *situational* or *individualistic* reasons as being due to interactants' memberships in various social groups and the historically determined meanings they have for them (see also Hewstone & Jaspars, 1984).

The foregoing has considered speech convergence as an active communicative strategy and has examined a number of social psychological principles that prove useful in understanding the function of the process and its effects. The literature review points to explicit and implicit links between noncontent speech accommodation and speakers' goals and intentions. It should be noted, however, that use of terms such as *strategies* and *intentions* does not necessarily imply that these purposive behaviors are always performed or evaluated consciously with full *awareness*. Behavior is organized by cognitive processes at many levels simultaneously (see O'Keefe & Delia, 1985) and it is unlikely that these ever are all monitored consciously. Berger and Roloff (1980) suggest that much communication is produced and received at low levels of awareness, and that in many instances speech accommodation may be scripted behavior (see Schank & Abelson, 1977). That is, because convergence facilitates interaction maintenance and goals, interactants may automatically apply a convergence script (or schema) to move toward more similar speech. Factors may intervene and bring speech behavior to a state of greater awareness, for example, when there is a discrepancy between expectations and what is encountered, or when a novel situation is presented (Langer, 1978). In Street's (1982) study, subjects were unaware of response latency and speech rate convergence, but were highly aware of divergence of these behaviors. In other situations, speech divergence may be scripted with interactants unknowingly revealing negative attitudes or desire for social dissociation. Norman's (1981) activation-trigger-schema model provides one possible basis for examining how cognitive structures hierarchically organize and regulate behavior at multiple levels, and as such may be usefully applied to SAT in the future.

It seems, then, that one may have intentions and low cognitive processing at the same time, as well as overt and deliberately produced speech adjustments. An interesting study with regard to both scripted and overtly intentionalized behavior is Bourhis's (1983) study in Quebec. The results of a sociolinguistic survey conducted with English Canadians and French Canadians (ECs and FCs, respectively) showed that speakers can be consciously aware of convergence and divergence in language switches as well as the probable reasons for them (Taylor & Royer, 1980). Thus, for instance, ECs reported being more likely to converge to French in Montreal today than in the past, and they also reported that FCs were less likely to converge to them in English today than in the past. Correspondingly, the converse was true for the FCs' reports. However, in a follow-up set of field studies designed to test how well these reports matched actual accommodative *behavior*, Bourhis (1984) found little overlap. FCs were more likely to reciprocate convergence than ECs in intergroup encounters, and ECs were more likely than FCs to maintain their own language. Bourhis suggested that in spite of sociopolitical changes favoring the ethnolinguistic ideals of FCs in Montreal, ECs are still in the habit of maintaining English when interacting with FCs, and FCs are still in the habit of converging to English with ECs. That is, it may be that contrary to their avowed intentions, old habits (or scripts) for intergroup communication "die hard."

Speech Maintenance and Divergence

It may appear from the foregoing, superficially at least, that the absence of convergence, speech maintenance (Bourhis, 1979), is a passive response of a nonattending, or disagreeable, social being. Such an argument might be tendered by some to explain, for example, the failure of men to change their gaze/talk behavior when they interacted with women as opposed to men in the study by Mulac et al. (in press) introduced above. Although this could sometimes be the case, it is far from representative of those other occasions in which people (for example, ethnic minorities) deliberately use their language or speech style as a symbolic tactic for maintaining their identity, cultural pride, and distinctiveness (Ryan, 1979). Moreover, repertoire constraints or certain personality factors might dictate nonconvergence. With respect to the latter, Hart, Carlson, and Eadie's (1980) conception of those individuals who typify their communication attitude of *Noble Selves* would be predicted to maintain their idiosyncratic speech and nonverbal characteristics across many situations. Noble Selves are those straightforward, spontaneous persons who see deviation from their assumed "real" self as being against their personal principles and, thus, intolerable.

It has been suggested further that in certain situations individuals may wish to go beyond this communicative stage and actually *accentuate* the linguistic and social differences between themselves and outgroup members (see also Doise, 1978). Scotton (1985) recently introduced the term *dis-accommodation* to refer to those occasions where people rephrase or repronounce something uttered by their partner so as to maintain their own integrity, distance, or identity. For example, a speaker might say, "OK, man, let's get it together at my pad around 2:30 tomorrow afternoon," and receive the reply, "Fine, sir, we'll relocate, 14:30, at your cottage, tomorrow." Now whether this apparent refusal to converge is a different phenomenon from, or a special, more consciously conceived case of, the general notion of *speech divergence* (Giles, 1973), a term coined for the modification of speech *away from* interlocutors, is a moot point. In any case, an example of divergence is found in Putman and Street's (1984) study in which interviewees who role-played sounding dislikable were found predictably to diverge in noncontent speech features away from their interviewers. Seltig (1985), in an analysis of a German radio program, has indicated how interviewers diverge from supposed experts as a signal of their own identification with the opposing (lay) views of members of the interactive audience.

In many instances, albeit of course not all, divergent strategies are adopted in dyads—or indeed larger groups (see Ros & Giles, 1979)—where the participants are members of different social or ethnic groups (Fitch & Hopper, 1983). Thus Tajfel and Turner's (1979) social identity theory of intergroup relations and social change provides an appropriate framework from which to consider the processes of speech maintenance and divergence (see Giles & Johnson, 1981).

Tajfel and Turner (1979) suggest that people do not always react to others as individuals so much as reacting to them as representatives of different social groups. They proposed that encounters could be seen as lying along an interindividual/intergroup continuum where those at the former extreme would be encounters between two or more people that were fully determined by their interpersonal relationships and individual characteristics, and those at the latter extreme (the intergroup pole) would be encounters determined by certain social categories. The more participants perceive an encounter toward the intergroup end of the continuum, "the more they tend to treat members of the outgroup as undifferentiated items in a unified social category rather than in terms of their individual characteristics" (Tajfel & Turner, 1979, p. 36). Thus Hogg (1985) found that males were judged to sound more "masculine" (by an independent group of observers) when talking to females when gender was made salient than when it was not; in other words, they appeared to be diverging vocally from their opposite sex interlocutors.

Turner (1982) suggests that under these same depersonalizing conditions, ingroup members also take on the characteristics in a *self-stereotyping* manner of their own social group. As a mediating factor, then, the examination of *linguistic* self-stereotyping would seem to be a topic worthy of further empirical inquiry as it holds out the promise of explaining some of the variance in individuals' divergent strategies. It is most likely that people's views of what is prototypical ingroup speech vary considerably, and may often be quite incorrect from an objective standpoint.

Social identity theory is concerned with behavior found at *this* level of extreme prototypicality and enables predictions that the more individuals define situations in intergroup terms and desire to maintain or achieve a positive ingroup identity, the more likely it will be that speech divergence will occur. The precise psychological climate necessary for, and the extent of, such divergence, Giles and Johnson (in press b) claim in their ethnolinguistic identity theory, is a function of a number of intergroup variables, most prominently individuals' perceptions of (1) the social structural forces operating in their own group's favor (see Bourhis & Sachdev, 1984) and (2) the legitimacy, as well as the stability, of their ingroup's position in the intergroup status hierarchy (see Giles & Johnson, in press b).

The sequence of processes central to social identity theory (social categorization-identification-social comparison-psychological distinctiveness) suggest that when one of an individual's social group memberships is construed as situationally salient, he or she will attempt to differentiate from relevant outgroup individuals on dimensions that are valued as core aspects of their group identity. Should language be a salient dimension of that group membership, as it so often is for ethnic groups (see Taylor, 1976), then differentiation by means of speech or nonverbal divergence (see also LaFrance, 1985) will ensue (on one or more of the following dimensions: language, dialect, slang, phonology, discourse structures, isolated words and phrases, posture, and so on) in order to achieve a positive psycholinguistic distinctiveness (Giles, Bourhis, & Taylor, 1977).

A demonstration of speech divergence was provided by Bourhis and Giles (1977) with Welsh people in an interethnic context. Welsh people who placed a strong value on their Welsh group membership and who were learning the Welsh language took part in a survey on the techniques of second-language learning. In a language laboratory setting they heard questions presented verbally to them individually in their language booths by a Standard English speaker who at one point challenged their reasons for learning what he called "a dying language with a dismal future." These Welsh subjects, in contrast to a control group who did not value the Welsh language in any integrative sense (Gardner & Lambert, 1972), broadened their Welsh accents in their replies compared with earlier emotively neutral questions. In addition, some used Welsh words and phrases, and one simply conjugated particular Welsh verbs in response! Previously, in response to a neutral question, many of the subjects had emphasized their Welsh group membership to the English-sounding speaker in terms of the *contents* of their responses. The study demonstrates that psycholinguistic distinctiveness can occur (see however Cacioppo & Petty, 1982), like convergence, in many different linguistic forms. Other studies have shown that many social groups positively evaluate representative ingroup speakers on audiotape who diverge in speech style when interacting with members of relevant outgroups (Bourhis, Giles, & Lambert, 1975; Doise, Sinclair, & Bourhis, 1976). Conversely, and not surprisingly, divergence from an outgroup member is often viewed as insulting, impolite, or downright hostile (Deprez & Persoons, 1984; Sandilands & Fleury, 1979).

An interesting example of divergence is provided by Escure's (1982) study of interactional patterns of Belize Creole, in which choice of dialect by Creoles fulfills identity maintenance functions. She showed that a speaker's speech act is often defined as a power relationship with the interlocutor (see above), and that the interlocutor's ethnic membership narrows the Creole speaker's choices. In interaction with Caribs, the selection of the mesolect is determined by a combination of linguistic insecurity (the stigma attached by outgroups and some ingroup members as "raw" Creole) and of social dominance relative to the neighboring Carib group. The Caribs often respond by sneers and asides delivered in neutral tones in their own language, incomprehensible to the Creoles, but understood and responded to by other Carib bystanders.

It is likely that there is a hierarchy of strategies for psycholinguistic distinctiveness varying in the degree of social dissociation that they indicate (Hewstone & Giles, 1986). These may range from a few pronunciation and content differentiations, through forms of accent and dialect divergences to verbal abuse and naming, abrasive humor, and the maintenance or switch to another language in response to an outgroup speaker. Clearly, the degree of linguistic divergence that can be manifested will depend also on the verbal repertoires of the speakers.

A study by Bourhis, Giles, Leyens, and Tajfel (1979) investigated the last of these strategies, namely language divergence. Trilingual Flemish students (Flemish-English-French) were recorded in a language laboratory in "neutral" and "ethnically threatening" encounters with a Francophone Walloon outgroup speaker. Many Flemish and Francophone students speak English together as an emotionally neutral compromise (Scotton, 1979) between asserting linguistic distinctiveness and conforming to pressures to use the other's language. In this study the Francophone spoke in English, although revealing his Walloon identity by distinctive French pronunciations. When the speaker asked a threatening question, listeners rated him as sounding more French (a process termed *perceptual divergence*) and themselves as feeling more Flemish than when a neutral question had been asked. The listeners' cognitive dissociations were observed at covert levels as whispered disapproval as the Walloon spoke and were shown more overtly by divergent shifts to the ingroup language of Flemish. This divergence occurred only in specific conditions (and only by half of the subjects) when the subjects' own group membership had been emphasized by the experimenter, and when the speaker was known from the outset to be hostile to Flemish ethnolinguistic goals. In a follow-up study reported in the same chapter, the Walloon speaker himself diverged into French in his threatening question and language divergence was now shown by all subjects in their response, given the same preconditions as in the first study.

Another study (Taylor & Royer, 1980) examining divergence was carried out in Quebec with FC students who anticipated meeting a speaker they heard on audiotape. Those who heard an Anglophone who was in complete disagreement with their own ethnolinguistic values anticipated speaking more French than did a matched group of FCs who expected to meet an Anglophone who was in complete agreement with their language goals. Furthermore, this anticipated divergence was accentuated after the former group of subjects had discussed together their probable language strategies towards the EC in the context of group discussion. This *linguistic polarization* (see also Myers & Lamm, 1976) was attributed by the FCs themselves to their feelings of ingroup belongingness and the need to assert their positive ethnic identity (see also, Giles & Johnson, in press a).

It should be noted that there might well be a societal norm favoring the use of the ingroup language in Quebec among FCs (Bourhis, 1983). In the context of Wales, however, there does appear to be a fairly strong societal norm among most bilingual Welsh that English is the appropriate medium for conversation with Anglophones even inside Wales. Hence, Giles and Johnson (in press a), using essentially the same Taylor and Royer paradigm in a series of two experiments in this culture, showed that for anticipated language divergence to transcend the normative demands of English usage in response to an outgroup speaker, the latter had to threaten directly core elements of Welshpersons' ethnic identity to which they were strongly committed. In other words, the dimensions of inter-group salience, the nature and strength of communicational norms, and the degree of commitment to social identification are all likely crucial, inter-acting variables not only in determining whether or not divergence occurs, but also the form it takes. Indeed, SAT propositions (not to mention those of ethnolinguistic identity theory) require some modest extension to take account of the prevalence of societal norms as illustrated in Giles and John-son (in press b). Interestingly enough, Giles and Byrne (1982) have argued that the same factors that facilitate the production of ethnolinguistic dif-ferentiation, or divergence, often can be important contributing factors among those ethnic minority individuals who display an apparent lack of proficiency in dominant forms (see also Hildebrandt & Giles, 1984).

Divergence and Cognitive Organization

As with speech convergence, divergence has been examined empiri-cally, as well as theoretically, more from the perspective of the (affective) identity maintenance function than in terms of cognitive organization (Giles, Scherer, & Taylor, 1979). However, divergence may function not only as an expression of attitudes but also to put order and meaning into the interaction and to provide a mutually understood basis for communica-tion. For example, the accentuation of accent, as well as content differen-tiation in certain contexts, or other forms of divergence, may serve to indicate that speakers are not members of the host community or familiar with the current situation in which they find themselves. This kind of self-handicapping tactic (Weary & Arkin, 1981) thereby increases the proba-bility that any norms inadvertently broken can be attributed externally and that a greater latitude of acceptance will be made available for the speaker; divergence here has some social utility (Ryan, personal communication). This divergence, moreover, acts as a form of self-disclosure to indicate that certain norms and spheres of knowledge and behavior may not be shared and intersubjectivity is at a premium (see also Rommetveit, 1979).

In other situations speech divergence may be a strategy employed to bring another's behavior to an acceptable level or to facilitate the coordina-tion of speech patterns. Two studies have indicated that sometimes inter-actants (for example, therapists and adults) may diverge in the amount they talk in order to encourage their partners (that is, clients and children) to talk more (Matarazzo, Weins, Matarazzo, & Saslow, 1968; Street, Street, & Van Kleeck, 1983). Anecdotally, it is common for people to slow down their speech rate with extremely fast-talking others in order to "cool them down" to a more comfortable communicative and cognitive level. Albeit in a different theoretical context, Ickes, Patterson, Rajecki, and Tan-ford (1982) showed that when males were expecting to talk via an intercom system to a "cold" rather than a "warm" woman they sounded far more warm in the former than the latter conditions, presumably to enhance the projected warmth of their interlocutor.

In yet another domain, Gottman's (1982) research provides us with another illustration of divergence for cognitively instrumental reasons, and this time in *longer-term* relationships. His data show, notwithstanding Lederer and Jackson's (1968) quid pro quo principle that posits that successful marriages are built on the reciprocation of positive remarks, that marital satisfaction more likely has the communicative foundation of so-called negative affect deescalation. That is, an unfavorable remark made by one spouse will be greeted with a more positive "defusive" reply from the other. This is a useful example as it also implies the difficulty in construing identity maintenance and cognitive organization as mutually exclusive. As Thakerar, Giles, and Cheshire (1982) proposed, it is most profitable to consider these as two orthogonal dimensions and, in the case of Gottman's research, negative affect deescalation might be divergence (or perhaps disaccommodation, to adopt Scotton's [1985] terminology) when both identity maintenance *and* cognitive organization are deemed salient.

In other situations, dissimilarities between interactants' speech may not only be acceptable, but even expected (Grush, Clore, & Costin, 1985). Ball et al. (1984) showed in their study that an interviewee maintaining his standard accent with an interviewer who spoke with a broad accent was more positively evaluated than when he converged "down" to the interviewer. In this case, it seems that situational norms override other evaluative considerations such as convergence as a strategy for increased similarity and attraction. Other contexts also typically involve differential speech behavior (Miller & Steinberg, 1975; Watzlawick, Beavin, & Jackson, 1967) yet do maintain a similar or complementary pattern of speech. For example, in interviews, the speech behaviors of interviewer and interviewee differ but the speakers may adjust their speech to maintain complementary speech patterns (Matarazzo & Weins, 1972; Putman & Street, 1984). That is, speakers may diverge or maintain dissimilar speech patterns in dyads when a role or power discrepancy exists. These speech differences may indicate optimal sociolinguistic distances and be psychologically acceptable and comfortable for both participants. This analysis may explain the finding (Mulac et al., in press) that women failed to converge toward men's lower level of gaze while silent in mixed-sex dyads, although women, unlike men, otherwise displayed convergence in same- and mixed-sex settings. Further instances where so-called speech complementarity is likely to occur are interactions between doctor-patient, employer-employee, teacher-pupil, parent-child, as well as in young, male-female romantic encounters. Indeed, those physicians who subscribe to possessing a patient-oriented (rather than to a doctor-oriented) communicative style (Tate, 1983) may well be competent in their

capacities to converge and complement either sequentially or simultaneously with their clientele. As Giles (1980) argued, it is not entirely impossible to concoct instances in which people may wish to converge, diverge,
and complement each other with regard to various verbal, vocal, and nonverbal forms *simultaneously*.

TOWARD A REFORMULATED SAT

We argue that SAT presents a broad and robust basis from which to
examine mutual influences in communication, taking account of social and
cognitive factors, and having the scope to cover the social consequences of
speech shifts as well as their determinants and the motivations underlying
them. Furthermore, it is applicable to a broad range of speech behaviors,
and nonverbal analyses potentially, with the flexibility of relevance at both
interpersonal *and* intergroup levels. In this epilogue section, we present a
reformulated and elaborated SAT based on the foregoing as well as relevant research and theory in the area of impression management, to be
introduced briefly below. The chapter concludes with some theoretical and
methodological priorities for the future.

The most recent version of SAT propositions can be found in a joint
examination of Beebe and Giles (1984) and Ball et al. (1984), but the
work and ideas reviewed herein suggest the need for a reformulation of
these most recent propositions. To this end, we highlight convergence and
divergence as situational definers, as possessing optimally received rates,
as well as being constrained by contextual norms. Yet, given recent ideas
on relational identities and self-presentation, we believe that our propositions could be extended profitably along these lines also. Before so doing,
let us briefly overview work in these independent research traditions.

Relational Identity and Self-Presentation

In a recent *Handbook* chapter, Giles and Wiemann (in press) argue for
the need to consider social comparison processes as a central element of
our understanding of how language behaviors are produced and received.
Moreover, they highlight the roles of relational identity and self-presentation in their theoretical framework.

Our estimates of self-worth come to a certain extent from our own private observations, attributions, and projected consequences of our
actions, cognitions, and feelings. These subjective yardsticks that are constructed largely idiosyncratically may be termed *intraindividual comparisons* and are a feature of a self-reflexive model of the human being (Farr,
1980). Yet, given we exist in a social world where our reality is socially constructed anyway (Berger & Luckmann, 1966), from a symbolic inter-

actionist perspective, our conceptions of our value come also from appraising how *others* see us (Mead, 1934). Hence, we make social comparisons for self-evaluative purposes and especially so in contexts where norms are subjectively ill-defined and or where no objective criteria for self-worth are available. Tajfel (1974) extended this essentially interindividual comparison process to the *intergroup* level for application when individuals wished to assess the affect associated with their *social* identities.

Giles and Fitzpatrick (1984), however, argued for the need in relational situations to make so-called couple comparisons. In this context it is worth underlining Berger and Bradac's (1982) notion that the development and dissolution of relationships are fraught with stressful uncertainties and ambiguities. A reliance on couple comparisons, and those of course chosen for their particular appropriateness, are useful templates for judging our own relationship status, be it romantic heterosexual, or even parental. Thus it would seem useful, as Giles and Wiemann (in press) advocate, to reformulate Tajfel and Turner's (1979) bipolar interindividual/intergroup continuum to constitute tridimensional space wherein self, group, and relational situations could be construed as high-low. Indeed, it is possible to conceive of a romantic heterosexual relationship as on some occasions being high on all three dimensions; that is, "I'm me, but I'm a feminist, although I am us." Which type of identity assumes salience when is, of course, a matter for further research.

At this juncture let us introduce notions of self-presentation (Goffman, 1963). Tedeschi (1974) has argued that the acquisition and maintenance of social power and influence is a fundamental social motivation. He sees this desire as mediating our self-presentations, most of which are manifest linguistically (see also, Tedeschi, Lindskold, & Rosenfeld, 1985). Hence, we strategically and tactically wish to establish and create a positive impression along the dimensions desired in socially influential others. Having managed such a social construction allows us considerable social power over others. Obviously, on other occasions, we do not have the luxury of asserting ourselves as we have to protect or defend our spoiled identities and save face (see, for example, Goffman, 1959). Tedeschi provocatively suggests that feelings of positive self-esteem are not autonomous, they are barometers as to how much social influence we are having and the degree of interpersonal power we hold. Conversely, embarrassment, guilt, and shame (that is, negative esteem) are really affective responses to an awareness that we have lowered our social influence and power.

An important aspect of self-presentation theory is that we do not sit idly and passively accept others' evaluations of us; the social comparison process is far more creative. By communication (Baumeister, 1982) we attempt to manage others' impressions of us, thereby being active in formulating our own individual, group, and relational esteems. Thus, as Giles and Wiemann (in press) propose, impression management research needs to be extended to acknowledge explicitly the role of group *and* relational presentations. Although there is some appreciation of this in the literature (for example, Wiemann & Kelly, 1981), empirical work has not attended much to the possibility and theoretical consequences of the *relationship* being a unit of analysis. When we are talking in couples, very often we do not treat others in terms of their individual contributions but rather construe their conversations as "couple talk" (Giles & Fitzpatrick, 1984). In the same way that speech divergence can be considered an exemplar of self-stereotyped, *group presentation,* so too we can envisage *couple presentations.* The latter might include *couple-disclosures* (for example, we did . . . our feelings. . . .) and various nonverbal signals of expressed affection, obviously private, intimate codes.

Our self-, group-, and relational-identities are mediated by language attitudes. In other words, the social knowledge that deep pitch, fast speech rate, standard dialect, and dynamic style are associated with perceived competence is used in order to construct a self-presentation of this ilk. Sometimes of course these self-presentations can be measured and conceptualized *artifactually* as convergence or even as divergence depending on the linguistic attributes of the recipients (see Coupland, 1984). Although there is minimal work on this issue, we also hold relational stereotypes (Giles & Fitzpatrick, 1984) and therefore strategically we might use these to mediate an *independent* couple type presentation (see Fitzpatrick, 1984), or even perhaps a dissatisfied couple image (see Gottman, 1979). Furthermore, we can utilize couple presentations even in the absence of our partner and therefore it is instructive theoretically to open up the possibility of couple convergence and divergence.

In sum then, much of what is apparently convergence and divergence may be motivated by desires to extend our social influence through individual self-presentations. On other occasions when our relational identities come to the fore, we may wish to construct couple identities through language that sometimes converges on those present, and on other times we wish to distance ourselves relationally from them. This type of analysis, which will be reflected in SAT propositions below, now begins to yield the true complexity of so-called interpersonal communication wherein our manifold identities can be expressed in a multitude of convergences and divergences both simultaneously sometimes, and sequentially oftentimes.

SAT: Reformulated Propositions

Regarding *antecedents* for convergence and divergence:

(1) People will attempt to converge toward the speech and nonverbal patterns *believed* to be characteristic of their message recipients, be the latter defined in individual, relational, or group terms, when speakers:
(a) desire recipients' social approval (and the perceived costs of acting in an

approval-seeking manner are proportionally lower than the perceived rewards);

(b) desire a high level of communicational efficiency;

(c) desire a self-, couple-, or group-presentation shared by recipients;

(d) desire appropriate situational or identity definitions;

when the recipients'

(e) actual speech in the situation matches the belief that the speakers have about recipients' speech style;

(f) speech is positively valued, that is, nonstigmatized;

(g) speech style is appropriate for the speakers as well as for recipients.

(2) The magnitude of such convergence will be a function of

(a) the extent of speakers' repertoires, and

(b) individual, relational, social, and contextual factors that may increase the needs for social comparison, social approval, and or high communicational efficiency.

(3) Speakers will attempt to maintain their communication patterns, or even diverge away from their message recipients' speech and nonverbal behaviors when they

(a) desire to communicate a contrastive self-image;

(b) desire to dissociate personally from the recipients or the recipients' definition of the situation;

(c) define the encounter in intergroup or relational terms with communication style being a valued dimension of their situationally salient in-group or relational identities;

(d) desire to change recipients' speech behavior, for example, moving it to a more acceptable level;

when recipicients:

(e) exhibit a stigmatized form, that is, a style that deviates from a valued norm, which is

(f) consistent with speakers' expectations regarding recipient performance.

(4) The magnitude of such divergence will be a function of

(a) the extent of the speakers' repertoires, and

(b) individual, relational, social, and contextual factors increasing the salience of the cognitive and affective functions in (3) above.

Several points about these propositions, which pertain to antecedents for convergence or divergence, merit discussion. Under many circumstances, speakers must realize that they are using a given style and that they are accordingly converging to, or diverging from, the recipients' style. For this realization to exist, speakers must have beliefs or other cognitive structures, for example, various schemata, that indicate just how speech *can* be similar to or different from that of others. That is, a "naive taxonomy" of speech must exist and this presumably enters into perception and performance at some level. This naive taxonomy may bear little resemblance to the taxonomies of linguists, sociolinguists, and so on.

Implicit in the four propositions are the ideas that (1) speakers have beliefs about and schemata regarding situations and message recipients;

(2) they have beliefs about the "goodness" and "badness" of particular styles; (3) they have beliefs about the "goodness" and "badness" of convergence/divergence; (4) they have perceptions of situations and message recipients' language performance in these situations; and (5) speaker beliefs, schemata, and perceptions combine to affect his or her situated language performance.

These ideas point to the many complexities associated with accommodation. For example, it allows a particular case in which the desire to adhere to a valued style will be in conflict with the desire to converge or diverge, and an interesting question here is what factors are implicated in the resolution of this conflict; in other cases, the desire to adhere to a valued style and the desire to converge or diverge will supplement or reinforce each other. In the latter case, the production of a particular style—the one that is valued and corresponds to the convergent or divergent desire—is relatively likely. On the other hand, speakers will be relatively unlikely to exhibit a style that departs from a valued norm and deviates from the desire to converge or diverge. But, as usual, things are even more complex. For example, conflicts can exist at other levels, say, when the style generally favored is not favored in this particular situation. Or there may be a conflict in which one desires to adhere to a valued style that conflicts with the particular, perhaps idiosyncratically negotiated situational expectation regarding convergence or divergence but which is consistent with the generalized expectation for convergence or divergence in a situation of this type.

Regarding now *consequences* of convergence/divergence:

(5) Convergence will be positively evaluated by message recipients, that is, will lead to high ratings for friendliness, attractiveness, and solidarity when recipients perceive
  (a) a match to their own communicational style;
  (b) a match to a linguistic stereotype for a group in which they have membership;
  (c) the speaker's convergence to be optimally distant sociolinguistically, and to be produced at an optimal rate, level of fluency, and level of accuracy;
  (d) the speaker's style to adhere to a valued norm;
  especially when
  (e) perceived speaker effort is high;
  (f) perceived speaker choice is high;
  (g) perceived intent is altruistic or benevolent.
(6) Divergence will be negatively rated by recipients when they perceive
  (a) a mismatch to their own communicational style;
  (b) a mismatch to a linguistic stereotype for a group in which they have membership;
  (c) the speaker's divergence to be excessively distant, frequent, fluent, and accurate;
  (d) the speaker's style to depart from a valued norm;

especially when
(e) perceived speaker effort is high;
(f) perceived speaker choice is high;
(g) perceived intent is selfish or malevolent.

The preceding propositions indicate through an additive logic the evaluative extremes: when 5a through 5g obtain, evaluations will be maximally positive and when 6a through 6g obtain, evaluations will be maximally negative. It should be noted, however and for example, that when 6a and 6b obtain but 6d does not—a speaker mismatches a message recipient's style but does *not* depart from a valued norm—negative evaluations will be attenuated; in some cases this sort of divergence that adheres to a valued norm would be expected to produce *positive* evaluations in fact. Similarly, convergence that departs from a valued norm should produce attenuated positive or even negative evaluations. Thus the most accurate prediction regarding a message recipient's evaluative reaction will be made when all of the components suggested by propositions 5 and 6 are examined simultaneously. In particular situations some of the components may be weighted more heavily than others in the production of evaluative reactions, but a lack of pertinent data allows us to say nothing more about this here.

Two additional points need to be made. First, perceptions of low effort and low choice can attenuate positive ratings for convergence and negative ratings for divergence. Thus perceived effort and choice can be viewed as intensifying variables, variables that serve to polarize ratings. Second, as suggested previously in this essay, much hinges on the recipients' perceptions of speaker intent. It seems likely that the attribution of a malevolent intent will override style matching, adherence to a valued norm, high perceived effort, and so on, to produce a negative solidarity rating. Conversely, attribution of a benevolent intent may well override effortful divergence, deviation from a valued style, and so on, to produce a positive rating for solidarity. Convergence and divergence seem likely to have the greatest impact upon solidarity when speaker intent is ambiguous or unknown.

All of the above suggests that perceptions can be in conflict and this conflict will affect solidarity judgments. For example, recipients may perceive that the communicator is matching recipients' in-group stereotype but mismatching recipient's actual behavior in the situation or vice versa. Or recipients may perceive that the communicator is adhering to a valued norm but is also mismatching recipient's behavior. The extent to which each of the conflicting variables will affect judgments of solidarity cannot be specified at this time. That is, if there is mismatched behavior but adherence to a valued norm, *which* will affect solidarity ratings more? It is clear from the above that there are cases in which adherence to a valued norm will override accommodation processes, but surely there will be many exceptions to this pattern. For example, when ingroup/outgroup issues are the topic of an interpersonal exchange between members of competing social groups, we would predict that similarity or dissimilarity of style would be more important than adherence to or divergence from a valued norm.

One can extend discussion by focusing upon two variables that typically are not discussed in the context of accommodation consequences, although we discussed one of them previously; these are self-perception and judgments of communicator status. With regard to the former, the converging or diverging communicator may view him- or herself differently as a result of this convergence or divergence than will the recipient of this action. For example, convergence may increase a recipient's feelings of friendliness but may decrease a converger's parallel feelings. The latter mentioned effect may occur as a consequence of projected guilt created by the nonadherence to an ingroup style, for example. This suggestion of encoder/decoder differences reflects the more general suggestion of attribution theory that observers and actors may view events dissimilarly (see Street, 1985). Moreover, a recent study by Street and Wiemann (in press) underlines the potency of this perspective for people experiencing together the same communicative acts in a naturalistic setting. They found that physicians' self-reports of their communications did not correlate with, and were significantly different from, patient perceptions of those same acts.

Regarding the status variable, it is worth noting that solidarity alone has been the focus of most discussion of accommodation consequences (see however, Putman & Street, 1984; Street, 1984). But because status/intellectual competence attributions are a primary type of judgment that persons make of communicators (Zahn & Hopper, 1985), questions regarding the consequences of convergence or divergence for status/competence attributions are worth raising. For example, it appears that adherence to a valued norm under circumstances in which a communicator diverges from another's *nonadhering* style will enhance judgments of the former person's sociointellectual status (Bradac & Mulac, 1984). We speculate that this effect will be heightened in a situation in which the communicator's adherence is perceived to be a product of low effort and where accuracy is high (although perhaps not extremely high). It may be heightened even more when the communicator who adheres to the valued norm also matches the stereotype representing the other person's expected style (and diverging from the other's actual performance).

Future Directions

Although SAT research and theory has come a long way in the first decade, it is apparent—and particularly so from the last section—that an enormous amount of research has yet to be done. One obvious direction is a programmatic test of the above propositions across the life span and in different social and cultural contexts. In addition, we are in dire need of specifying the acoustic, nonverbal, sociolinguistic, *and discourse* features that make up convergent, divergent, and other communicative strategies in different social settings (Coupland, 1985; Seltig, 1985), as well as exploring the relationships between accommodative processes and comforting messages on the one hand (Burleson, 1985) and expressed *empathy* (Bavelas, Black, Lemery, & Mullett, in press) on the other. Furthermore, we should be sensitive to the fact that our complex Speaker-Hearer sequentially dovetails convergent and divergent strategies from moment to moment in order to express different personae and interactional functions (see Coupland, 1985). One interesting challenge that might have to be met if significant progress in these empirical and theoretical directions is made, is whether or not SAT can be expanded comfortably to accommodate more and more complexity in its propositional format. At the same time another challenge that will have to be met involves *explaining* this increased propositional complexity in terms of a parsimonious and unique set of integrative principles. Paralleling these developments, we would advocate priority be afforded new analytical/methodological procedures. For instance, to what extent can simultaneous behavior of two or more interactants through computer entry and alignment of data inform SAT? To what extent can stochastic and lag sequential procedures achieve the same ends? Finally, an SAT perspective might have applied relevance for situations rife in potential miscommunication and misattribution (for example, blind-sighted, stutterer-nonstutterer). Indeed, Rutter (1985) has argued, on the basis of empirical data, that the communicative problems associated with schizophrenic speech may not arise so much because of any cognitive deficiencies on the part of schizophrenics so much as their *social* inability to take account of the role of their interlocutors.

It is hoped that this chapter might intrigue the scholar new to SAT (which perhaps ought now to be relabeled more appropriately, *Communication* Accommodation Theory) as to the value of its framework for understanding a modest range of communicative behaviors, cognitions, and processes, and at the same time provide a cohesive state-of-the-art overview that integratively points the way forward.

REFERENCES

Aboud, F. E. (1976). Social development aspects of language. *Papers in Linguistics, 9,* 15-37.

Albo, X. (1979). The future of the oppressed languages in the Andes. In W. C. Cormack. & S. Wurm (Eds.), *Language and society: Anthropological issues* (pp. 309-330). The Hague: Mouton.

Ball, P., Giles, H., Byrne, J. L., & Berechree, P. (1984). Situational constraints on the evaluative significance of speech accommodation: Some Australian data. *International Journal of the Sociology of Language, 46,* 115-130.

Ball, P., Giles, H., & Hewstone, M. (1985). Interpersonal accommodation and situational construals: An integrative formalisation. In H. Giles & R. St. Clair (Eds.), *Recent advances in language, communication and social psychology* (pp. 263-286). London: Lawrence Erlbaum.

Basso, K. H. (1979). *Portraits of "The Whiteman."* Cambridge: Cambridge University Press.

Baumeister, R. F. (1982). A self-presentation view of social phenomena. *Psychological Bulletin, 91,* 3-26.

Bavelas, J. B., Black, A., Lemery, C.R., & Mullett, J. (in press). Motor mimicry as primitive empathy. In N. Eisenberg & J. Strayer (Eds.), *Empathy and its development.* Cambridge: Cambridge University Press.

Beebe, L. (1981). Social and situational factors affecting communicative strategy of dialect code-switching. *International Journal of the Sociology of Language, 32,* 139-149.

Beebe, L., & Giles, H. (1984). Speech-accommodation theories: A discussion in terms of second-language acquisition. *International Journal of the Sociology of Language, 46,* 5-32.

Bell, A. (1982). Radio: The style of news language. *Journal of communication, 32,* 150-164.

Bell, A. (1984). Language style as audience design. *Language in Society, 13,* 145-204.

Berg, M. E. van de (1985). *Language planning and language use in Taiwan.* Dordrecht: ICG Printing.

Berger, C. R., & Bradac, J. J. (1982). *Language and social knowledge.* London: Edward Arnold.

Berger, C. R., & Roloff, M. E. (1980). Social cognition, self-awareness, and interpersonal communication. In B. Dervin & M. J. Voight (Eds.), *Progress in communication sciences* (Vol. II, pp. 1-50). Norwood, NJ: Ablex.

Berger, P., & Luckmann, T. (1966). *The social construction of reality: A treatise in the sociology of knowledge.* New York: Doubleday.

Bourhis, R. Y. (1979). Language in ethnic interaction: A social psychological approach. In H. Giles & B. Saint-Jacques (Eds.), *Language and ethnic relations* (pp. 117-141). Oxford: Pergamon.

Bourhis, R. Y. (1983). Language attitudes and self-reports of French-English usage in Quebec. *Journal of Multilingual and Multicultural Development, 4,* 163-179.

Bourhis, R. Y. (1984). Cross-cultural communication in Montreal: Two field studies since Bill 101. *International Journal of the Sociology of Language, 46,* 33-47.

Bourhis, R. Y. (1985). The sequential nature of language choice in cross-cultural communication. In R. L. Street, Jr., & J. N. Cappella (Eds.), *Sequence and pattern in communicative behavior* (pp. 120-141). London: Edward Arnold.

Bourhis, R. Y., & Giles, H. (1977). The language of intergroup distinctiveness. In H. Giles (Ed.), *Language, ethnicity and intergroup relations* (pp. 119-135). London: Academic Press.

Bourhis, R. Y., Giles, H., & Lambert, W. E. (1975). Social consequences of accommodating one's style of speech: A cross-national investigation. *International Journal of the Sociology of Language, 6,* 55-72.

Bourhis, R. Y., Giles, H., Leyens, J. P., & Tajfel, H. (1979). Psycholinguistic distinctiveness: Language divergence in Belgium. In H. Giles, & R. St Clair (Eds.), *Language and social psychology* (pp. 158-185). Oxford: Blackwell.

Bourhis, R. Y., & Sachdev, I. (1984). Vitality perceptions and language attitudes. *Journal of language and Social Psychology, 3,* 97-126.

Bradac, J. J., Hosman, L. A., & Tardy, C. H. (1978). Reciprocal disclosures and language intensity: Attributional consequences. *Communication Monographs, 45,* 1-17.

Bradac, J. J., & Mulac, A. (1984). Attributional consequences of powerful and powerless speech styles in a crisis-intervention context. *Journal of Language and Social Psychology, 3,* 1-19.

Brouwer, D., Gerritesen, M., & De Hann, D. (1979). Speech differences between men and women: On the wrong track? *Language in Society, 8,* 33-50.

Burleson, B. R. (1985). The production of comforting messages: Social-cognitive foundations. *Journal of Language and Social Psychology, 5,* in press.

Byrne, D. (1969). Attitudes and attraction. *Advances in Experimental Social Psychology, 4,* 35-89.

Byrne, D. (1971). *The attraction paradigm.* New York: Academic Press.

Cacioppo, J., & Petty, R. (1982). Language variables, attitudes, and persuasion. In E. B. Ryan & H. Giles (Eds.), *Attitudes towards language variation: Social and applied contexts* (pp. 189-207). London: Edward Arnold.

Caporael, L. R., Lukaszewski, M. P., & Culbertson, G. H. (1983). Secondary baby talk: Judgments by institutionalized elderly and their caregivers. *Journal of Personality and Social Psychology, 44,* 746-754.

Cappella, J. N., & Greene, J. (1982). A discrepancy-arousal explanation of mutual influence in expressive behavior for adult-adult and infant-adult interaction. *Communication Monographs, 49,* 89-114.

Chadwick-Jones, J. (1976). *Social exchange theory.* London: Academic Press.

Coleman, L. (1985). Language and the evolution of identity and self-concept. In F. Kessel (Ed.), *The development of language and language researchers: Essays in tribute to Roger Brown.* Hillsdale, NJ: Lawrence Erlbaum.

Coupland, N. (1980). Style-shifting in a Cardiff work-setting. *Language in Society, 9,* 1-12.

Coupland, N. (1984). Accommodation at work: Some phonological data and their implications. *International Journal of the Sociology of Language, 46,* 49-70.

Coupland, N. (1985). "Hark, hark the lark": Social motivations for phonological style shifting. *Language and Communication, 5,* 153-171.

Dabbs, J. M., Jr. (1969). Similarity of gestures and interpersonal influence. *Proceedings of the 77th Annual Convention of the American Psychological Association, 4,* 337-338.

Deprez, K., & Persoons, K. (1984). On the identity of Flemish high school students in Brussels. *Journal of Language and Social Psychology, 3,* 273-296.

Doise, W. (1978). *Groups and individuals.* Cambridge: Cambridge University Press.

Doise, W., Sinclair, A., & Bourhis, R. Y. (1976). Evaluation of accent convergence and divergence in cooperative and competitive intergroup situations. *British Journal of Social and Clinical Psychology, 15,* 247-252.

Escure, G. (1982). Interactional patterns in Belize Creole. *Language in Society, 11,* 239-264.

Farr, R. (1980). Homo loquiens in social psychological perspective. In H. Giles, W. P. Robinson, & P. M. Smith (Eds.), *Language: Social psychological perspectives* (pp., 409-413). Oxford: Pergamon.

Farr, R., & Anderson, T. (1983). Beyond actor-observer differences in perspective: Extensions and applications. In M. Hewstone (Ed.), *Attribution theory: Social and functional extensions* (pp. 45-64). Oxford: Blackwell.

Feldman, R. E. (1968). Response to compatriots and foreigners who seek assistance. *Journal of Personality and Social Psychology, 10,* 202-214.

Fitch, K., & Hopper, R. (1983). If you speak Spanish they'll think you are a German: Attitudes towards language choice in multilingual environments. *Journal of Multilingual and Multicultural Development, 4,* 115-128.

Fitzpatrick, M. A. (1984). A typological approach to marital interaction: Recent theory and research. In L. Berkowitz (Ed.), *Advances in experimental social psychology* (Vol. 18, pp. 1-47). New York: Academic Press.

Forgas, J. (1983). Language, goals, and situation. *Journal of Language and Social Psychology, 2,* 267-293.

Gardner, R. C., & Lambert, W. E. (1972). *Attitudes and motivation in second language learning.* Rowley, MA: Newbury House.

Genesee, F., & Bourhis, R. Y. (1982). The social psychological significance of code-switching in cross-cultural communication. *Journal of Language and Social Psychology, 1,* 1-28.

Giles, H. (1973). Accent mobility: A model and some data. *Anthrological Linguistics, 15,* 87-105.

Giles, H. (1977). Social psychology and applied linguistics. *ITL: Review of Applied Linguistics, 33,* 27-42.

Giles, H. (1978). Linguistic differentiation between ethnic groups. In H. Tajfel (Ed.), *Differentiation between social groups* (pp. 361-393). London: Academic Press.

Giles, H. (1980). Accommodation theory: Some new directions. *York Papers in Linguistics, 9*, 105-136.

Giles, H. (Ed.). (1984). *The dynamics of speech accommodation* [Special issue]. *International Journal of the Sociology of Language, 46*.

Giles, H., & Bourhis, R. Y. (1976). Black speakers with white speech—a real problem? In G. Nickel (Ed.), *Proceedings of the 4th. International Congress on Applied Linguistics* (Vol. 1, pp. 575-584). Stuttgart: HochschulVerlag.

Giles, H., Bourhis, R. Y., & Taylor, D. M. (1977). Towards a theory of language in ethnic group relations. In H. Giles (Ed.), *Language ethnicity, and intergroup relations* (pp. 307-348). London: Academic Press.

Giles, H., & Byrne, J. L. (1982). An intergroup model of second language acquisition. *Journal of Multilingual and Multicultural Development, 3*, 17-40.

Giles, H., & Fitzpatrick, M. A. (1984). Personal, group and couple identities: Towards a relational context for the study of language attitudes and linguistic forms. In D. Schiffrin (Ed.), *Meaning, form and use in context: Linguistic applications* (pp. 253-277). Georgetown: Georgetown University Press.

Giles, H., & Hewstone, M. (1982). Cognitive structures, speech and social situations: Two integrative models. *Language Sciences, 4*, 187-219.

Giles, H., & Johnson, P. (1981). The role of language in ethnic group relations. In J. C. Turner, & H. Giles (Eds.), *Intergroup behavior* (pp. 199-243). Oxford: Blackwell.

Giles, H., & Johnson, P. (in press a). Perceived threat, ethnic commitment, and interethnic language behavior. In Y. Y. Kim (Ed.), *Current studies in interethnic communication*. Beverly Hills, CA: Sage.

Giles, H., & Johnson, P. (in press b). New directions in language maintenance: A social psychological approach. *International Journal of the Sociology of Language*.

Giles, H., & Powesland, P. F. (1975). *Speech style and social evaluation*. London: Academic Press.

Giles , H., & Street, R. (1985). Communicator characteristics and behavior. In M. L. Knapp & G. R. Miller (Eds.), *Handbook of interpersonal communication* (pp. 205-261). Beverly Hills, CA: Sage.

Giles, H., Scherer, K. R., & Taylor, D. M. (1979). Speech markers in social interaction. In K. R. Scherer & H. Giles (Eds.), *Social markers in speech* (pp. 343-381). Cambridge: Cambridge University Press.

Giles, H., & Smith, P. M. (1979). Accommodation theory: Optimal levels of convergence. In H. Giles & R. St. Clair (Eds.), *Language and social psychology* (pp. 45-65). Oxford: Blackwell.

Giles, H., Taylor, D. M., & Bourhis, R. Y. (1973). Towards a theory of interpersonal accommodation through language: Some Canadian data. *Language in Society, 2*, 177-192.

Giles, H., & Wiemann, J. (in press). Language, social comparison, and power. In S. Chaffee & C. R. Berger (Eds.), *Handbook of communication*. Beverly Hills, CA: Sage.

Goffman, E. (1959). *The presentation of self in everyday life*. New York: Doubleday.

Goffman, E. (1963). *Stigma*. Princeton: Prentice-Hall.

Gottman, J. (1979). *Marital interaction*. New York: Academic Press.

Gottman, J. (1982). Emotional responsiveness in marital conversations. *Journal of Communication, 32*, 108-120.

Grush, J. E., Clore, G. L., & Costin, F. (1975). Dissimilarity and attraction: When difference makes a difference. *Journal of Personality and Social Psychology, 32*, 783-789.

Hart, R. P., & Burks, D. M. (1972). Rhetorical sensitivity and social interaction. *Speech Monographs, 39*, 75-91.

Hart, R. P., Carlson, R. E., & Eadie, W. F. (1980). Attitudes toward communication and the assessment of rhetorical sensitivity. *Communication Monographs, 47*, 1-22.

Heider, F. (1958). *The psychology of interpersonal relations*. New York: John Wiley.

Hewstone, M., & Giles, H. (1986). Social groups and social stereotypes in intergroup communication: Review and model of intergroup communication breakdown. In W. B. Gudykunst (Ed.), *Intergroup communication* (pp. 10-26). London: Edward Arnold.

Hewstone, M., & Jaspars, J. (1984). Social dimensions of attribution. In H. Tajfel (Ed.), *The social dimension* (Vol. 2, pp. 379-404). Cambridge: Cambridge University Press.

Higgins, E. T. (1980). The "communication game": Implications for social cognition and persuasion. In E. T. Higgins, C. P. Herman, & M. P. Zanna (Eds.), Social cognition: The Ontario symposium (pp. 343-392). Hillsdale, NJ: Lawrence Erlbaum.

Higgins, E. T., & McCann, C. D. (1984). Social encoding and subsequent attitudes, impressions, and memory: "Context-driven" and motivational aspects of processing. Journal of Personality and Social Psychology, 47, 26-39.

Hildebrandt, N., & Giles, H. (1984). The Japanese as subordinate group: Ethnolinguistic identity theory in a foreign language context. Anthropological Linguistics, 25, 436-466.

Hogg, M. (1985). Masculine and feminine speech in dyads and groups: A study of speech style and gender salience. Journal of Language and Social Psychology, 4, 99-112.

Ickes, W., Patterson, M. L., Rajecki, D. W., & Tanford, S. (1982). Behavioral and cognitive consequences of reciprocal and compensatory responses to pre-interaction expectancies. Social Cognition, 1, 160-190.

Jones, E. E., Farina, A., Hastorf, A. H., Markus, H., Miller, D. T., & Scott, R. A. (Eds.). (1984). Social stigma: The psychology of marked relationships. New York: Freeman.

Jones, G. E. (1984). L2 speakers and the pronouns of address in Welsh. Journal of Multilingual and Multicultural Development, 3, 17-40.

Kelley, H. H. (1973). The process of causal attribution. American Psychologist, 28, 107-128.

Kincaid, D. L., Yum, J. O., Woelfel J., & Barnett, G. A. (1983). The cultural convergence of Korean immigrants in Hawaii: An empirical test of a mathematical model. Quality and Quantity, 18, 59-78.

Klemz, A. (1977). Blindness and partial sight. Cambridge: Woodhead-Faulkner.

Kramarae, C. (1981). Women and men speaking. Rowley, MA: Newbury House.

LaFrance, M. (1979). Nonverbal synchrony and rapport: Analysis by the cross-lag panel technique. Social Psychology Quarterly, 42, 66-70.

LaFrance, M. (1985). Postural mirroring and intergroup relations. Personality and Social Psychology Bulletin, 11, 207-217.

Labov, W. (1966). The social stratification of English in New York City. Washington, DC: Center for Applied Linguistics.

Langer, E. J. (1978). Rethinking the role of thought in social interaction. In J. H. Harvey, W. Ickes, & R. F. Kidd (Eds.), New Directions in attribution research (Vol. 2, pp. 36-58). Hillsdale, NJ: Lawrence Erlbaum.

Larsen, K., Martin, H. J, & Giles, H. (1977). Anticipated social cost and interpersonal accommodation. Human Communication Research, 3, 303-308.

Lederer, W. J., & Jackson, D. D. (1968). The mirages of marriage. New York: Norton.

Matarazzo, J. D., Weins, A. N., Matarazzo, R. G., & Saslow, G. (1968). Speech and silence behavior in clinical psychotherapy and its laboratory correlates. In J. Schlier, J. D. Matarazzo, & C. Savage (Eds.), Research in psychotherapy (Vol. 3). Washington, DC: American Psychological Association.

Matarazzo, J. D., & Weins, A. W. (1972). The interview: Research on its anatomy and structure. Chicago: Aldine-Atherton.

McKirnan, D. J., & Hamayan, E. V. (1984). Speech norms and attitudes towards outgroup members: A test of a model in a bicultural context. Journal of Language and Social Psychology, 3, 21-38.

Mead, G. H. (1934). Mind, self and society. Chicago: Chicago University Press.

Miller, G. R., & Steinberg, M. (1975). Between people: A new analysis of interpersonal communication. Chicago: Science Research Associate.

Mulac, A., Incontro, C. R., & James, M. R. (1985). A comparison of the gender-linked language effect and sex-role stereotypes. Journal of Personality and Social Psychology, 49, 1099-1110.

Mulac, A., Studley, L. B., Wiemann, J., & Bradac, J. J. (in press). Male/female gaze in same-sex and mixed-sex dyads: Gender-linked differences and mutual influence. Human Communication Research.

Mulac, A., Wiemann, J., Yoerks, S., & Gibson, T. W. (1983, July). Male/female language differences and their effects in like-sex and mixed-sex dyads: A test of interpersonal accommodation and the gender-linked language effect. Paper delivered at the 2nd International Conference on Social Psychology and Language, Bristol.

Myers, D. G., & Lamm, H. (1976). The group polarization phenomenon. *Psychological Bulletin, 83,* 606-627.

Natale, M. (1975a). Convergence of mean vocal intensity in dyadic communications as a function of social desirability. *Journal of Personality and Social Psychology, 32,* 790-804.

Natale, M. (1975b). Social desirability as related to convergence of temporal speech patterns. *Perceptual and Motor Skills, 40,* 827-830.

Norman, D. A. (1981). Categorization of action slips. *Psychological Review, 88,* 1-15.

O'Keefe, B. J., & Delia, J. G. (1985). Psychological and interactional dimensions of communicative development. In H. Giles & R. St. Clair (Eds.), *Recent advances in language, communciation and social psychology* (pp. 41-85). London: Lawrence Erlbaum.

Patterson, M. (1983). *Nonverbal behavior: A functional perspective.* New York: Springer-Verlag.

Piner, K. E., & Kahle, L. R. (1984). Adapting to the stigmatising label of mental illness: Foregone but not forgotten. *Journal of Personality and Social Psychology, 47,* 805-811.

Platt, J., & Weber, H. (1984). Speech convergence miscarried: An investigation into inappropriate accommodation strategies. *International Journal of the Sociology of Language, 46,* 131-146.

Purcell, A. K. (1984). Code shifting in Hawaiian style: Children's accommodation along a decreolizing continuum. *International Journal of the Sociology of Language, 46,* 71-86.

Putman, W., & Street, R. (1984). The conception and perception of noncontent speech performance: Implications for speech accommodation theory. *International Journal of the Sociology of Language, 46,* 97-114.

Robinson, W. P. (1972). *Language and social behavior.* Harmondsworth: Penguin.

Rommetveit, R. (1979). On the architecture of intersubjectivity. In R. Rommetveit & R. M. Blakar (Eds.), *Studies of language, thought, and communication* (pp. 93-107). London: Academic.

Roloff, M., & Berger, C. R. (Eds.). (1982). *Social cognition and communication.* Beverly Hills, CA: Sage.

Ros, M., & Giles, H. (1979). The language situation in Valencia: An accommodation framework. *ITL: Review of Applied Linguistics, 44,* 3-24.

Rubin, A. M., & Rubin, B. (1982). Contextual age and television use. *Human Communication Research, 8,* 228-244.

Rutter, D. R. (1985). Language in schizophrenia: the structure of monologues and conversations. *British Journal of Psychiatry, 146,* 399-404.

Ryan, E. B. (1979). Why do low-prestige language varieties persist? In H. Giles & R. St. Clair (Eds.), *Language and social psychology* (pp. 145-175). Oxford: Blackwell.

Ryan E. B., Giles, H., Bartolucci, G., & Henwood, K. (1986). Psycholinguistic and social psychological components of communication by and with the elderly. *Language and Communication, 6,* 1-22.

Sandilands, M. L., & Fleury, N. C. (1979). Unilinguals in des milieux bilingues: Une analyse des attributions. *Canadian Journal of Behavioral Science, 11,* 164-168.

Schank, R., & Abelson, R. P. (1977). *Scripts, plans, goals, and understanding.* Hillsdale, NJ: Lawrence Erlbaum.

Scollon, R., & Scollon, S. B. (1979). *Linguistic convergence: An ethnography of speaking at Fort Chipewyan, Alberta.* New York: Academic.

Scotton, C. M. (1976). Strategies of neutrality: Language choice in uncertain situations. *Language, 52,* 919-941.

Scotton, C. M. (1979). Codeswitching as a "safe choice" in choosing a lingua franca. In W. C. McCormack & S. Wurm (Eds.), *Language and society: Anthropological issues* (pp. 71-83). The Hague: Mouton.

Scotton, C. M. (1980). Explaining linguistic choices as identity negotiations. In H. Giles, W. P. Robinson, & P. M. Smith (Eds.), *Language: Social psychological perspectives.* Oxford: Pergamon.

Scotton, C. M. (1985). What the heck, sir: Style shifting and lexical coloring as features of powerful language. In R. L. Street, Jr. & J. N. Cappella (Eds.), *Sequence and pattern in communicative behavior* (pp. 103-119). London: Edward Arnold.

Seltig, M. (1983). Institutionelle Kommunikation: Stilwechsel als Mittel strategischer Interaktion. *Linguistische Berichte, 86,* 29-48.

Seltig, M. (1985). Levels of style-shifting exemplified in the interaction strategies of a moderator in a listener participation programme. *Journal of Pragmatics, 9,* 179-197.

Simard, L., Taylor, D. M., & Giles, H. (1976). Attribution processes and interpersonal accommodation in a bilingual setting. *Language and Speech, 19,* 374-387.

Shatz, M., & Gelman, R. (1973). Development of communication skills. *Monograph of the Society for Research in Child Development, 152.*

Snyder, M. (1981). On the self-perpetuating nature of social stereotypes. In D. L. Hamilton (Ed.), *Cognitive processes in stereotyping and intergroup behavior.* Hillsdale, NJ: Lawrence Erlbaum.

Street, R. L., Jr. (1982). Evaluation of noncontent speech accommodation. *Language and Communciation, 2,* 13-31.

Street, R. L., Jr. (1984). Speech convergence and speech evaluation in fact-finding interviews. *Human Communication Research, 11,* 139-169.

Street, R. L., Jr. (1985). Participant-observer differences in speech evaluation. *Journal of Language and Social Psychology, 4,* 125-130.

Street, R. L., Jr., Brady, R. M., & Putman, W. B. (1983). The influence of speech rate stereotypes and rate similarity on listeners' evaluations of speakers. *Journal of Language and Social Psychology, 2,* 37-56.

Street, R. L., Jr., & Giles, H. (1982). Speech accommodation theory: A social cognitive approach to language and speech behavior. In M. Roloff & C. R. Berger (Eds.), *Social cognition and communication* (pp. 193-226). Beverly Hills, CA: Sage.

Street, R. L., Jr., & Murphy, T. M. (1985, November). *Interpersonal orientation and speech behavior.* Paper delivered at the Speech Communication Association Annual Meeting, Denver.

Street, R. L., Jr., Street, N. J., & Van Kleeck, A. (1983). Speech convergence among talkative and reticent three-year-olds. *Language Sciences, 5,* 79-86.

Street, R. L., & Wiemann, J. (in press). Patient satisfaction with physician interpersonal involvement, expressiveness, and dominance. In M. McLaughlin (Ed.), *Communication Yearbook 10.* Beverly Hills, CA: Sage.

Suls, J. M., & Miller, R. L. (1977). *Social comparison processes.* New York: John Wiley.

Swap, W. C., & Rubin, J. Z. (1983). Measurement of interpersonal orientation. *Journal of Personality and Social Psychology, 44,* 208-219.

Tate, P. (1983). Doctors' style. In D. Pendleton & J. Hasler (Eds.), *Doctor-patient communication* (pp. 75-85). London: Academic.

Tajfel, H. (1974). Social identity and intergroup behavior. *Social Science Information, 13,* 65-93.

Tajfel, H., & Turner, J. C. (1979). An integrative theory of intergroup conflict. In W. G. Austin & S. Worchel (Eds.), *The social psychology of intergroup relations* (pp. 33-47). Monterey, CA: Brooks/Cole.

Taylor, D. M. (1976). Ethnic identity: Some cross-cultural comparisons. In J. W. Berry & W. J. Lonnev (Eds.), *Applied cross-cultural psychology.* Amsterdam: Swets and Zeitlinger.

Taylor, D. M., & Royer, E. (1980). Group processes affecting anticipated language choice in intergroup relations. In H. Giles, W. P. Robinson, & P. M. Smith (Eds.), *Language: Social psychological perspectives* (pp. 185-192). Oxford: Pergamon.

Taylor, D. M., Simard, L., & Papineau, D. (1978). Perceptions of cultural differences and language use: A field study in a bilingual environment. *Canadian Journal of Behavioral Science, 10,* 181-191.

Tedeschi, J. T. (Ed.). (1974). *Perspectives on social power.* Chicago: Aldine.

Tedeschi, J. T., Lindskold, S., & Rosenfeld, P. (1985). *Introduction to social psychology* (Ch. 3, pp. 65-96). New York: West.

Thakerar, J. N., Giles, H., & Cheshire, J. (1982). Psychological and linguistic parameters of speech accommodation theory. In C. Fraser & K. R. Scherer (Eds.), *Advances in the social psychology of language* (pp. 205-255). Cambridge: Cambridge University Press.

Triandis, H. C. (1960). Cognitive similarity and communication in a dyad. *Human Relations, 13,* 175-183.

Trudgill, P. (1981). Linguistic accommodation: Sociolinguistic observations on a sociopsychological theory. In *Papers from the Parasession on Language and Behavior, Chicago Linguistics Society.* Chicago: Chicago University Press.

Turner, J. C. (1982). Towards a cognitive redefinition of the social group. In H. Tajfel (Ed.), *Social identity and intergroup behavior.* Cambridge: Cambridge University Press.

Valdes-Fallis, G. (1977) Code-switching among bilingual Mexican-American women: Towards an understanding of sex-related language alternation. *International Journal of the Sociology of Language, 17,* 65-72.

von Raffler-Engel, W. (1979). The unconscious element in inter-cultural communication. In R. St. Clair & H. Giles (Eds.), *The social and psychological contexts of language* (pp. 101-130). Hillsdale, NJ: Lawrence Erlbaum.

Ward, S. A., Bluman, D. L., & Dauria, A. F. (1982). Rhetorical sensitivity recast: Theoretical assumptions of an informal interpersonal rhetoric. *Communication Quarterly, 30,* 189-195.

Watzlawick, P., Beavin, J. H., & Jackson, D. (1967). *Pragmatics of human communication.* New York: Norton.

Weary, G., & Arkin, R. M. (1981). Attributional self-presentation. In J. H. Harvey, M. J. Ickes, & R. Kidd (Eds.), *New directions in attribution theory and research* (Vol. 3). Hillsdale, NJ: Lawrence Erlbaum.

Welkowitz, J., & Feldstein, S. (1969). Dyadic interaction and induced differences in perceived similarity. *Proceedings of the 77th Annual Convention of the American Psychological Association, 4,* 343-344.

Welkowitz, J., & Feldstein, S. (1970). Relation of experimentally manipulated interpersonal perception and psychological differentiation to the temporal patterning of conversation. *Proceedings of the 78th Annual Convention of the American Psychological Association, 5,* 387-388.

Welkowitz, J., Feldstein, S., Finkelstein, M., & Aylesworth, L. (1972). Changes in vocal intensity as a function of interspeaker influence. *Perceptual and Motor Skills, 35,* 715-718.

Welkowitz, J., & Kuc, M. (1973). Inter-relationships among warmth, genuiness, empathy and temporal speech patterns in interpersonal attraction. *Journal of Consulting and Clinical Psychology, 41,* 472-473.

Wiemann, J., & Kelly, C. W. (1981). Pragmatics of interpersonal competence. In C. Wilder-Mott & J. H. Weakland (Eds.), *Rigor and imagination: Essyas from the legacy of Gregory Bateson.* New York: Praeger.

Wolfram, W. (1973). Sociolinguistic aspects of assimilation: Puerto Rican English in East Harlem. In R. W. Shuy & R. W. Fasold (Eds.), *Language attitudes: Current trends and prospects.* Washington, DC: Georgetown University Press.

Zahn, C. J., & Hopper, R. (1985). Measuring language attitudes: The Speech Evaluation Instrument. *Journal of Language and Social Psychology, 4,* 113-124.

2 ● Mass Communication Research in Japan: History and Present State

YOUICHI ITO

Keio University

J APANESE communication studies, like the communication studies of any other country, cover a vast variety of subjects. Not only subjects but also approaches and methods are varied. In order for a review of such diverse studies to be possible, criteria for the selection of representative literature must be utilized.

The first criterion for selection is a study's historical value. The section entitled *Early History* describes how and by whom Japanese communication studies were started. The second criterion is the importance of the study as a component of one of the major schools. An academic *school* usually refers to a cluster of studies that share similar research questions, theories, and methods. It is suggested in this article that there are four major schools of Japanese communication studies: (1) environmentalist school, (2) American school, (3) Marxist school, and (4) information society school. In the section entitled *Major Schools,* priority was given to studies that represent or were influential in each school.

By using the criteria mentioned above, we should accomplish three purposes: (1) present a comprehensive, bird's-eye view of Japanese communication studies from past to present, (2) contribute to the study of the relationship between the social sciences and sociocultural characteristics of a country, and (3) present an evolutionary model of communication studies useful to communication scholars in academically developing countries. The implications of this synthesis of Japanese communication studies in terms of the above purposes, particularly the second and the third, will be discussed in the article's last section entitled *Implications for Communication Studies in Non-Western Countries — Conclusions.*

AUTHOR'S NOTE: The author would like to acknowledge Alex S. Edelstein of the University of Washington and Rebecca Rice of the American University for helpful comments on an earlier draft.

Correspondence and requests for reprints: Youichi Ito, Institute for Communications Research, Keio University, Mita, Minato-Ku, Tokyo, 108, Japan.

EARLY HISTORY

It is not easy to tell exactly when the study of journalism and mass communication started in Japan because it depends upon what we mean by *study*. For example, many outstanding journalists and newspaper publishers in the late 19th century such as Shunzo Yanagawa (1832-1870), Yukichi Fukuzawa (1835-1901), Shigenari Yasukawa (1839-1906), Genichiro Fukuchi (1841-1906), Soho Tokutomi (1863-1957), and others wrote many essays on newspapers and journalism. In addition, books were written on newspapers in England (Yasukawa, 1875), theories and history of the freedom of the press in Europe (Amano, 1887), and the duties of journalists (Tokutomi, 1891).

Koike (1882) described the history of Japanese newspapers and government oppression of journalists in early textbooks on newspapers. *Shimbungaku,* written by Matsumoto (1889), dealt with the idea of the freedom of the press in the West, organizations and practices of major American newspapers, and the techniques of writing and editing. Other books on newspapers or journalism were published by Kuroiwa (1912), Sugimura (1915), Onose (1915), Goto (1915), Yoshino (1916), and others. In 1919 three series of books entitled *Shimbungaku Zensho* were published (Dainihon Shimbun-kai, 1919). This series is a collection of articles written by first-rate scholars and journalists of the time. The articles cover a wide range of subjects including history, law, management, organizations, policies, newspapers in foreign countries, news agencies, editing, and even mass psychology. In 1930, 12 series of books entitled *Sogo Jahnarizumu Kohza* were published. This collection of articles also covered a wide range of topics. The strong influence of Marxism in this series reflects the intellectual atmosphere of the time. According to Wada (1969, p. 70), this publication made the term *janarizumu* (journalism) popular in Japan, and stimulated journalism studies. The English term *journalism* became Japanized at around this time as *janarizumu.*

Although these works contained useful information, analyses, insights, and suggestions, their primary value today are as historical documents. However, the following scholars are usually referred to as the *founding fathers* of the study of journalism and mass communication in Japan: Nyozekan Hasegawa (1875-1970), Hideo Ono (1885-1977), Jun Tosaka (1900-1945), and Ikutaro Shimizu (1907-). The achievements of Ono and Tosaka will be examined in depth as their work is held in the highest regard.

Hideo Ono (1885-1977)

Hideo Ono began his academic career with the study of German literature at the University of Tokyo. After graduation, he worked for two newspaper companies as a journalist. Later, he returned to his academic roots and traveled to Germany to study *Zeitungswissenschaft* and *Publizistik* (both roughly mean the study of journalism). His first book, entitled *Nihon Shimbun Hattatsu-shi,* was published in 1922 following his return to Japan. This book, together with another published in 1960 (Ono, 1960), was highly respected by journalism scholars and practitioners. Unlike other books on the history of Japanese newspapers, the book related the history of newspapers to popular culture, society, and the life of the masses. Ono related the development of newspapers to the development of culture. This approach influenced later studies on the history of mass media.

In 1925 Ono organized a study group called the *Shimbungaku Kenkyu-kai.* In addition, he edited Japan's first academic journal on journalism, entitled *Shimbungaku Kenkyu,* in January 1926. In that same year, he began teaching a course called the "Comparative History of Newspapers" at the University of Tokyo. In 1929 he created the *Shimbungaku Kenk-yushitsu* (Program for the Study of Journalism) at the University of Tokyo. Ono assisted in the establishment of Japan's first Department of Journalism at Tokyo's Jochi University in 1932. In 1936 he started teaching a course named "Journalism" at the University of Tokyo. The Program for the Study of Journalism was expanded to the *Shimbun Kenkyujo* (Institute of Journalism) in 1949. Ono became the first director of the institute. He also became the first president of the Japan Society for Journalistic Studies (its name was changed to the Japan Society for Studies in Journalism and Mass Communication in 1966) created in 1951. Ono retained the president's position for the first 16 years of the society's existence.

Ono was a prolific scholar. He authored or coauthored 21 books and edited 4 others. Most of his books described the history of newspapers and journalism not only in Japan but in other countries. One of his most highly regarded books is *Kawaraban Monogatari* (1960). The literal translation of *kawaraban* is a tile engraving. *Kawaraban* prints during the Tokugawa period (1603-1867) are treated as the forerunner of the modern newspaper.

Kawaraban provided the masses with news and entertainment beginning with its first publication in 1615. Basically, the function of *kawaraban* was similar to the "extras" of modern times. They were sold and often read aloud on the street. *Kawaraban* covered all types of sensational news— civil war, riot, murder, satire, humor, suicide, seduction, and rape. Some titles included "An Eight-Year-Old-Girl Gives Birth to a Baby Boy," "Tatsumi's Love and Suicide," "A Lie Contest in Yedo (old name for Tokyo)," "A Monster Attacks a Mountain Village," and "A Huge Whale Sinks a Ship."

Ono's study ascertains that the concept of *news* understood by *kawaraban* printers and the masses in the Japanese traditional society was very similar to the modern Western concept of news. Most news printed in *kawaraban* can be easily explained by the definitions and components of news described in contemporary textbooks on journalism. The study of *kawaraban* contributed a great deal to understanding the characteristics of modern Japanese newspapers. Although modern Japanese newspapers are far more complicated and sophisticated than *kawaraban,* they still continue some *kawaraban* traditions.[1]

Oyama and Nixon (1961, pp. 92-93) evaluate Ono's research in a book review in *Journalism Quarterly.* Their review concludes:

> The greatest value of the book is Prof. Ono's keen insight in relating Kawaraban to the political, social and cultural progress of the Japanese people.
>
> One section critically presents the remarkable functions played by Kawaraban with regard to national and international affairs in both news and editorials, and its effects on the development of the political, social and moral behavior of the Japanese people. (p. 93)

Ono's only theoretical work is *Shimbun Genron,* published in 1947, in which he discusses the definitions, political roles and functions of the newspaper. His understanding of *theory* was derived from the early 20th-century German idea of *Kulturwissenschaft* (cultural science), which is quite normative in nature. For example, most definitions concern ideas of what should be rather than what actually is.

Theories were then developed based upon these normative definitions. Ono's view of Japanese newspapers was always "critical."[2] However, this kind of approach no longer is favored by contemporary Japanese communication scientists. This diminished his theoretical contribution to present-day Japanese communication studies. Nevertheless, he played a vital intellectual role in studies of Japanese journalism and newspapers.

Jun Tosaka (1900-1945)

The influence of Marxism or communism on journalism in Japan increased in the mid-1920s. As examples, Hayasaka (1926) and Aono (1926) rejected "bourgeois" newspapers and planned and advocated the inauguration of "proletariat newspapers." Fukumoto (1926) and Kadoya (1929) advocated Lenin's views of propaganda, education, agitation, and organization. These views, as a whole, were called *proletariat journalism* and carried considerable weight with Japanese journalists and intellectuals of the 1920s and 1930s. For example, articles based upon proletariat journalism occupied a sizable portion of the *Sogo Jahnarizumu Kohza* (1930). This early dogma claimed that commercial newspapers (bourgeois newspapers) represented the interests of the ruling capitalist class. On the other hand, newspapers published by workers (proletariat newspapers) represented the interests of the working class. As the working class became stronger, the proletariat newspapers would become more influential and help to transform the society from capitalism to socialism.

Although Tosaka is generally classified as a Marxist scholar, he considered this view too superficial. He asserted that the nature of journalism could not be determined simply by the form of ownership. Tosaka conceded that the contents of commercial newspapers often reflected the interests of the capitalist class, but he emphasized also the autonomous and independent functions of journalism. He saw functional similarities between journalism and academism of two kinds: They both created and diffused "ideology" to the society, and they both examined reality and tried to find "truth" in it. The relative independence of journalism and academism permitted them to pursue truth, create and advocate criticisms, ideologies, and new ideas.

Tosaka studied philosophy at Kyoto University and started his career in that field. Like Ono, he also was prolific. He wrote his first book, *Kagaku Hohoron* in 1929 at the age of 29. Before he was arrested and sent to jail as a political dissident in 1938, he had completed 14 books. He died in jail at the age of 44 on August 9, 1945, only a week before Japan's surrender. As a philosopher he covered a wide range of subjects including science, literature, ideology, epistemology, ethics, and even technology. His theories on journalism are outlined in two books, *Ideorogi no Ronrigaku* (1931) and *Ideorogi Gairon* (1932).

Tosaka combined and tried to synthesize Marxism and the German *Zeitungswissenschaft*. He learned the nature of journalism from the German study of journalism and the role of ideology in social change from Marxism. His approach was basically normative in contrast to the value-free approach adopted by most contemporary communication scholars, and his studies remained at a highly abstract theoretical level. His failure to apply his theory to practical ends placed limitations on the adoption of his ideas. But Ono published his masterpiece in his 60s while Tosaka was imprisoned at 38 and died at the age of 44. Perhaps he died too young.

Tosaka nonetheless strongly influenced postwar Marxist journalism studies. The tendency to consider journalism in capitalist societies in terms of the strain between capitalist ownership and individual journalists' conscience and critical spirit continues to be strong among Japanese Marxists. In part this is because Marxists in Japan have always been less dogmatic and more flexible than other Marxists. Two factors might account for this tendency. One is disappointment with actual practices of journalism in socialist countries; another is the influence of Tosaka, who had emphasized the importance of the independent critical mind of journalists struggling under the capitalist system.

MAJOR SCHOOLS

Many scholars followed Ono and Tosaka. Their work ranged from the history and theory of communication and mass media, to public opinion, propaganda, collective behavior, interpersonal communication, effects of communication, diffusion, political communication, rural communication, mass media management, economic analysis of mass media industries, mass communication laws, advertising, communication policy, telecommunications, and others.

In a review of postwar Japanese communication studies, Takizawa (1972, p. 71; 1976, p. 258) writes that postwar studies were indebted to three outstanding scholars; Ikutaro Shimizu (1907-   ), Hiroshi Minami (1914-   ), and Rokuro Hidaka (1917-   ). This writer would add Tadao Umesao (1920-   ). These four scholars represented the four major "schools" of contemporary Japanese communication studies.

Environmentalist School

Environmentalist refers to the studies that construct theories using concepts such as *pseudoenvironment* and *pseudoevent*. In this article, however, this term will be used in a broader sense. *Environmentalism* or *environmentalist theories* in this article refers to the theories having the following characteristics:

(a) The primary concern is the influence of mass communication as a whole on the whole society rather than the influence of a specific message on individual attitudes or behavior.
(b) The contents of mass media, at any given time, are assumed to be basically homogeneous rather than heterogeneous. The variance in content among different mass media is not relevant.
(c) Receivers of given messages are assumed to be homogeneous. Demographic or psychological variations among media receivers are minimized.
(d) The theories are not based on Marxist ideology.
(e) Mass media's ability to provide the public with logic, explanations, and excitement (called the environment creative ability) is emphasized.
(f) The method used to prove theory is empirical but descriptive. Usually, various facts, episodes, and statistical data, including opinion survey data, are used to support theory. The case study is the most commonly employed research method.[3]

The basic assumptions of environmentalists are that humans are creatures reacting and trying to adapt to their environment; however, people have two kinds of environment. One is the direct environment that a person can contact directly through his or her sensory organs. The indirect environment, however, may be contacted only through other people's sensory organs (that is, through mass communication media).

This conceptualization was first proposed by Lippmann (1922) in *Public Opinion*. It distinguished between the "real environment" and the "pseudo-environment." Using this conceptualization, Shimizu (1949) analyzed the nature of modern journalism and later (1951) coined the phrase *domination by copies* (which became quite popular among Japanese communication students). He warned that the masses in the modern age are surrounded by dubious, contracted copies of originals inaccessible to direct contact by most people.

Fujitake (1968), one of Shimizu's disciples, used concepts and theoretical frameworks developed by Lippmann and Shimizu. He first did a thorough review of literature on the relationship between people's perceptions and the environment, discussing Lippmann (1922), Koffka (1935), Shimizu (1951), Znaniecki (1952), Lasswell (1948), Boulding (1956), and Boorstin (1961). Then he focused on the process of the pseudo-environment (created by the mass media) becoming the real environment. He proposed that journalism as a daily activity defined or gave meaning to the changing environment. Most people accepted the "definitions of situations" provided by the media and acted as if they were, in fact, their "real environment." This is how mass media created and changed our environment or society.

Fujitake (1974) analysed rumor and panic using this model: that is, collective behavior, in many cases, resulted from people's reactions to inappropriate definitions of situations provided by the pseudo-environment (that is, mass media, false information, or rumor). Fujitake (1975) supported his theory with a collection of examples and many social events for which the mass media were responsible.

Most examples of work by scholars of this school concern the following matters:

(a) National events such as the Olympics (Fujitake, 1967; Fujitake and Akiyama, 1967), General MacArthur's parade (Lang and Lang, 1960), and the landing on the moon (Katz, 1980; Katz, Dayan, & Motyl, 1981).
(b) Journalism or campaigns during wartime such as Japanese journalism before and during World War II (Kakegawa, 1972; Toriumi, 1973). Kate Smith's campaign for the promotion of war bonds (Merton, 1946).
(c) Mass hysteria such as McCarthyism (Boorstin, 1961).
(d) Diplomatic problems involving vital national interests such as the demand for the reversion of occupied territories (Tsujimura, 1976a, 1981) and Sadat's visit to Jerusalem (Katz, 1980).

According to environmentalist theory, mass media define the situation, forming the pseudo-environment, which dominates individual perception, attitude, and behavior, thus forming the real environment. This process creates actual social change. However, questions arise as to what extent the assumption of homogeneous mass media is realistic. It is true that even in democratic societies where freedom of speech is guaranteed, there are occasions on which the major mass media of the country take the same stand (therefore providing identical definitions of the situation). There also are persistent arguments in many democratic countries that the contents of major mass media are basically the same and differences are only superficial.

Marxists long have insisted that the mass media in capitalist societies represent the interests of the ruling class; although commercial mass media sometimes carry antigovernmental editorials and articles, they do so only in an established framework, and although they sometimes contribute to a change of administration or social, political, and economic reform, they never act as catalysts for the fundamental change of the system. Therefore, differences in commercial media are superficial and actually reinforce capitalist values. For this reason Japanese Marxists have been sympathetic to the environmentalist approach.

Among non-Marxists there are also many scholars who think that mass media rationales are basically the same, as expressed in the following frequently quoted statement: The mass media "are the cultural arm of the industrial order from which they spring" (Gerbner, 1972, p. 51). Using concepts like "news frame" and "media frame," Goffman (1974), Tuchman (1978, 1981), and Gitlin (1980) discussed how the masses are conditioned by basic (industrial, capitalist) "frames" provided by mass media.

Although American and British non-Marxist communication scholars have criticized their mass media for being biased to the right (or the establishment), Japanese and German non-Marxist scholars have criticized their media for the opposite reason. After World War II, in reaction to the prewar nationalistic and totalitarian ideology, the Japanese intellectual climate became very susceptible to Marxist ideas and sympathetic to claims of the Eastern bloc. Leading intellectuals in the 1950s and 1960s were antigovernment, anticapitalism, and anti-American. Their views on Japanese history, tradition, culture, customs, and sociopolitical systems were all negative. Such views were reflected in mass media and even in school textbooks.

However, a backlash against this postwar intellectual climate occurred in the early 1970s. The two major reasons were China's opening to the West and Japan's economic success. China's change in domestic and foreign policies was the most serious blow to the leftists, for their support depended on the guilt feelings of the Japanese.[4] This had resulted in a nation sensitive and sympathetic to Chinese affairs. On the other hand, such sentiment did not exist toward the Soviet Union. The new political environment in China freed conservative Japanese intellectuals to identify with the new policies and at the same time attack the leftists who had supported Maoist policies.

One of their major targets was the leading Japanese newspapers, particularly the *Asahi Shimbun,* the most prestigious newspaper in Japan. The first severe attack was directed toward the reporters and correspondents who had extolled the Chinese Cultural Revolution and Lim Piao. In this volatile atmosphere a book entitled *Everything About Newspapers* (translation), published in 1975, sold more than 150,000 copies, rare for this kind of book. It cited numerous examples of the leftist bias of the major Japanese newspapers.

Shichihei Yamamoto is a social critic and not a communication scholar. However, he raised interesting discussions in his book entitled *A Study of Kuuki (kuuki* roughly means atmosphere) published in 1977. In his criticism against the biased Japanese mass media he gave many examples in which not only reasonable opinions but even scientific facts (regarding, for example, the relationship between certain chemicals and a disease as well as safety standards for pollution) were not seriously considered due to the "unreasonable and abnormal" *kuuki* created by the mass media. Yamamoto called such social phenomena "domination by *kuuki*" and argued that it had always existed in Japanese modern history. According to him, before and during the war, the *kuuki* was in favor of militarism and ultranationalism but after the war it turned to Socialism and Communism.

When American and British communication scholars discussed news frame or media frame, they meant to caution against the conservative nature of mass media. However, when Tsuruki (1982) discussed the frame imposing function of mass media, he apparently had in mind the leftist-biased Japanese mass media, particularly newspapers. Comparing this function with the agenda-setting function, he stated that "whereas the agenda setting function concerns merely the emphasis of certain issues, the frame imposing function concerns the underlying logic or rationale behind stands taken by mass media" (p. 33). According to Tsuruki, mass media "not only select the issues which should be reported or should not be reported, but also decide the guidelines from which the issues are reported" (p. 36). Thus the mass media provide society with a particular logic or way of thinking (usually based upon a chosen ideology) regarding issues.[5]

Another problem for environmentalist theories is that several cases have been reported in which editorials of all the major mass media were very similar, but public opinion did not agree with them. Tsujimura (1976a, 1976b, 1981) persistently pursued the relationship between newspaper editorials and public opinion polls for a long period of time and collected many interesting cases. According to his survey, all major newspapers were against the government drafts for the San Francisco Peace Treaty in 1952 and the Japan-Korea Normalization Treaty in 1964, but public opinion polls supported the government in both cases. Japanese newspapers persistently have campaigned against the Self Defense Forces, and public opinion polls have always endorsed it. Major Japanese newspapers have always been sympathetic to big strikes, but opinion polls have always been negative about strikes.

According to Tsujimura, the reasons for the gap between mass media and public opinion polls are (a) the consciousness gap between the elites (journalists) who tend to be leftist-oriented and the masses (public opinion polls) who are more conservative, (b) time lag, and (c) the influence of government policy. Tsujimura's case studies (1976b, 1981) made it clear that government policy, even when major mass media are all against it, plays a crucial role in the formation and change of public opinion, particularly in international affairs. Even if the mass media strongly object to a certain government policy, the public has a tendency to support government policy when the issue is not familiar to them. Therefore, public opinion, particularly that regarding international affairs, cannot be completely understood without considering government policy as a determining factor.

These arguments indicate that even when the contents of major mass media are basically the same, the formation and change of public opinion cannot be explained or predicted as easily as some environmentalist theories claim. It seems that there is still a long way to go until the mechanisms of public opinion change and social change become satisfactorily explained.

As long as there exist occasions on which contents of the major mass media become identical or homogeneous for some reason, this approach maintains validity. However, when we consider the situation in which variance in media contents and variations among media receivers count, the American school described in the following section has greater validity.

American School

As perceived by Japanese scholars, the *American school* refers to mainstream American communication studies. This does not mean, of course, that all studies by American researchers belong to this category. However, a conception of a so-called American school seems to be internationally shared. It usually refers to studies that have the following characteristics:

(a) The primary concern with regard to mass media influence is individual change rather than social change.[6] Similarly, the primary concern in terms of the function of mass media is the functions for individuals (uses and gratifications) rather than those for the whole society.
(b) The standard methods to prove theory are surveys and experiments.
(c) Intensive attention is paid to demographic, cognitive, and personality differences among individuals as explanatory variables.

Before World War II, Japanese communication studies were based upon German *Zeitungswissenschaft* or *Publizistik* and Marxism. In 1947, Iguchi (1947) introduced Lasswell's paradigm to Japan. According to Yamada (1975), this was the first occasion for Japanese scholars to be exposed to American communication studies. Influenced by this article, books by Minami (1949) and Iguchi (1949) systematically introduced American mass communication studies.

Hiroshi Minami (1914-) is particularly regarded because of the number of books he published and his influence on Japanese social psychologists. The books were widely used as college textbooks. According to Takizawa (1972, p. 73), Shimizu analyzed society through mass communication whereas Minami analyzed human attitudes and behavior through mass communication. This same difference can be said to symbolize the difference between the environmentalist and the American schools.

In 1954, the Japanese translation of Schramm's *Mass Communication* (1949) further stimulated interest in American communication studies. Furthermore, until around the mid-1960s the United States government was quite generous about giving scholarships to Japanese students. As a result, many Japanese scholars trained in American universities joined Japanese universities in the late 1950s and early 1960s. They introduced to Japan most of the major theories and methods developed in the United States.

Minami (1949, 1954), Ikuta (1957, 1968), Kato (1957), Tanaka (1969), Kawanaka (1971), and Iwao (1966) all studied in the United States before the early 1960s and brought back American theories and methods. These were incorporated in textbooks and eventually became common learning for communication scholars and students. Many scholars did research based on those American models. Their major achievements are summarized or reviewed in Kato (1974), Yamada (1975), Tokinoya (1984), Takeshita (1983), and Yoshida and Yamanaka (1983).

The American approach has various strengths in comparison to the other approaches. First of all, the American model is more general than the environmentalist or Marxist approaches. For one thing, it does not assume homogeneity of media contents as do the environmentalist and Marxist schools. On the other hand, however, the American school has been criticized for being too narrow, too microscopic, and sometimes too trivial. This deficiency is a result of the limited methodology used by this school— surveys and experiments. Surveys and experiments must be planned, but important social events or phenomena (except elections) cannot be predicted. These problems have been recognized by Japanese scholars and attempts have been made to overcome them. One of the remedies was to conduct social surveys when important events or phenomena occur or soon after.

When a run on a bank took place in a small Japanese town in 1973 due to a rumor, several research teams were dispatched to investigate. This case was unusual because the local police were able to detect the entire route of the rumor. Ito, Ogawa, and Sakaki (1974a, 1974b), Fujitake (1974), and Kinoshita (1977) described in detail the route of the rumor from the very first innocent conversation by local high school girls to the bank panic. Several hostile and vicious rumors directed to minority groups (Koreans and the lowest caste people segregated in old Japan) were recorded (Ito, Ogawa, & Sakaki, 1974a, 1974b). Two questionnaire surveys were conducted. According to Kinoshita (1977), most people heard the rumor either near home from neighbors or at their work place from colleagues. Ito, Ogawa, and Sakaki (1975) found that the most important factors that drove people to the bank were past experience (of financial fraud that had occurred in that area several years before) and the amount they had in the bank.

Iwao and Pool (1983) surveyed American reactions to the 12-hour television program *Shogun* because it recorded extremely high ratings (32.6% in the lowest city and 69% in the highest city, San Francisco). The researchers thought that this series (broadcast in the United States by NBC in 1980) would have a strong impact on American images of Japan. The researchers' first discovery was that most American viewers were most strongly impressed by the enormous cultural differences. But, the most significant question was that concerning American opinions regarding the Japanese formed after watching *Shogun*. Although some people developed a greater respect for the traditional Japanese culture and were impressed with Japanese cleanliness, politeness, and quietness, others thought the Japanese were very cruel, untrustworthy, and savage, and felt that "the culture of the Far East closely resembled that of Africa." Reactions of American viewers were sharply polarized. Iwao and Pool found that the crucial factor that determined the directions of their attitudes (favorable or unfavorable) was prior contact with Japanese people and culture. Those viewers who had prior contact with Japanese people and culture developed favorable images of Japan after they watched *Shogun*.

Another way to overcome the weaknesses of the American approach is called in Japan the *omnibus method*. This method combines different research methods to test the same hypothesis. A combination of quantitative and qualitative methods is most commonly used. Opinion survey and aggregate data analysis, content analysis and opinion survey, opinion survey and psychological experiment, and so on are often combined. In this way the scientific rigor of the American school and the width, depth, and social relevance of other schools may be secured at the same time.

Tsujimura, Kim, and Ikuta (1982) divided their research team composed of Japanese and Korean researchers into three groups—the opinion survey group, psychological experiment group, and content analysis group. Each group was to pursue the same research purpose; that is, the analysis of communication gaps between Japan and Korea. The opinion survey revealed psychological obstacles between the two nations. The content analysis pointed out the historical, political, economic, and social problems between the two countries. And the psychological experiment group made suggestions based on experiments on how the attitudes of the two peoples toward each other might be improved. By combining these three methods the study assured width, depth, and social relevance. This is often said to be lacking in American studies. Considering Japanese group-mindedness, the omnibus method may be very well suited to the Japanese research environment.

The strength of the American school is that it provides information about intervening variables to media effects. Although the consideration of intervening variables sometimes makes media effect studies complicated and too microscopic, information about them is very important for the actual practice of propaganda, advertising, publicity, or persuasion. Without information about intervening variables, it is extremely difficult to plan effective propaganda, advertising, publicity, or persuasion. Therefore, practitioners of persuasion owe very much to achievements by this school.

The American school also has made Japanese communication studies more rigorous and scientific. They also have contributed to the standardization of the style of academic writing. Before the American influence, the distinction between academic writing and essays or critiques was sometimes not very clear. In such writing personal opinions often mingled in the process of proving or testing something. Logic and expression were too dogmatic, emotional, sentimental, vague, or roundabout. Such tendencies still exist in some of the writings of the environmentalist and Marxist schools in Japan.

Although the American approach will not completely satisfy all scholars and students, it will continue to have strong influence on Japanese communication studies.

Marxist School

The Marxist approach to communication studies sharply differs from the American school. Those characteristics are:

(a) The central subject is the influence of mass communication as a whole on the whole society, namely, social change rather than individual change. In this sense this school resembles the environmentalist school.

(b) The method to prove a theory is almost the same as the environmentalists—description of facts, data, and episodes that support the theory.

(c) Mass media are considered to belong to the superstructure of the society. Therefore, mass communication activities and mass media contents are considered to be determined and dominated by the substructure of the society (that is, the production relationship or class relationship of the society). (Environmentalists do not adopt this assumption. This is an important difference between the two schools.)

(d) A natural conclusion drawn from assumption (c) is that the major function of mass media is to reinforce the dominant values of the society by educating the people. A society's mass media are responsible for leading the people to adapt to society. Therefore, the function of mass communication is to preserve the status quo.

Marx and Lenin's views of mass media, propaganda, education, and agitation were introduced in Japan in the 1920s by Hayasaka (1926), Aono (1926), Fukumoto (1926), and Kadoya (1929), and others. Tosaka (1931, 1932) synthesized these views with the German study of journalism introduced by Ono and developed his synthesis into unique theories. However, after Tosaka was arrested and imprisoned in 1938, oppression of Marxists became very severe, and the publication of Marxist studies became impossible.

After the war, the Marxist approach was revived. In a famous article published in 1954, Hidaka (1954) criticized both the environmentalist and American psychological approaches for being superficial. Like Tosaka, he regarded the contents of mass media in capitalist societies as propaganda for the ruling class. He emphasized the role of personal communication and group communication as means to counteract the capitalist propaganda of mass media. Just as there exist historical laws (or historical inevitability) in the evolution of economic systems, Hidaka suggested that there might exist similar laws in the evolution of mass communication systems. Thus he suggested five historical stages or types of communication systems:

(1) absolute monarchy
(2) early modern (in bourgeois elitist societies)
(3) modern (in mass societies)
(4) fascism
(5) socialist

This classification reminds us of the "four theories of the press" (Siebert, Peterson, & Schramm, 1956). The difference is that Hidaka discussed these types as historical stages with the socialist type as the most developed system and emphasized historical laws behind such development.

In the 1950s and early 1960s the Marxist approach to the study of communication became quite popular in Japan. Tosaka's writings were reevaluated by postwar Marxist communication scholars. (See for example, Yamamoto, 1962, 1969.) The Institute of Journalism at the University of Tokyo was the largest intellectual center. Many students who studied under Hidaka (then a professor at this Institute) later joined the faculties of universities all over Japan. These Marxist communication scholars were called *Hidaka school* or *Todai school* (an abbreviation of the University of Tokyo). Later, however, Professor Hidaka, who was involved in a radical leftist movement in the early 1970s, resigned his post. Nevertheless, his disciples still hold important positions in universities in Japan, and this school maintains an influence upon Japanese communication studies.

It is important to note, however, that among leading Marxist communication scholars in Japan, none blindly accepts Lenin's or Soviet official theories of mass communication. There seem to be two factors involved. The first is the influence of Tosaka. Although in large part his theories were based upon Marx's view of history and society, he was by no means a dogmatic Marxist. His way of thinking was flexible; he absorbed and included knowledge and academic achievements from other areas such as German *Publizistik*. Therefore, Tosaka's theories were quite sophisticated and profound. In comparison to Tosaka's works, Lenin's or Soviet official theories on mass communication appear naive and simplistic.

Another reason for the independent thinking of Japan's Marxists was their disillusionment with the actual practice of mass media and mass communication policies in the Soviet Union and other Communist countries. At least in present-day Japan even self-admitted Marxists find it extremely difficult to justify the oppression of dissident opinions, monopoly of communication media, concealment of news, and so on, as practiced in Communist countries. Various justifications or excuses for these actions have been given by some Marxists, but such excuses have been criticized by other Marxists. For example, Yamamoto (1980), an authority on the study of Tosaka, writes, "Considering the present situation, we can not be as naive as to accept such excuses" (p. 47). Yamamoto (1980) writes that the "monolithic solidarity between the party and people" is nothing but a fable. He further states:

> Some people make a distinction between bourgeois newspapers and proletariat newspapers, and think that only the latter report truth. However, if we see newspapers in Socialist countries such as *Pravda* or *People's Daily*, we soon realize that such a view is absolutely ridiculous. (p. 47)

On the other hand, as a disciple of Tosaka, Yamamoto believed that mass media in capitalist societies represented, in principle, the ruling class ideology; however, the ruling class was not monolithic but suffered internal competition, friction, and disagreement. The mass media in modern capitalist countries have not always been on the side of monopolistic capitalists. Capitalists have sometimes been criticized by the mass media to benefit smaller businesses, consumers, and even the most suppressed underprivileged people. Further, competition and friction exist within the ruled class, as well. In other words, contradictions exist everywhere; the structure of modern capitalist societies is not as simple as classical Marxists imagine. But through complicated processes and mechanisms that have not yet been sufficiently clarified, mass media have contributed to the continuation of capitalist regimes.

It is easy to condemn contemporary mass media [in capitalist countries] by giving many examples and episodes. However, I am reluctant to completely deny them because I cannot think of any ideal type of journalism or mass communication system to replace them. As mentioned before, conformism and lack of freedom in the journalism of Socialist countries cannot be the "proletarian freedom beyond bougeois democracy." We cannot rely upon party organs or radical political newspapers since they are ignored by ordinary citizens. Furthermore, although present mass media represent the ruling class ideology, they are certainly not party organs of the ruling class, and contradictions exist not only between the ruling class and the ruled class, but also in the ruling class as well as in the ruled class. (Yamamoto, 1980, p. 55)

Therefore, he concluded, in the present situation "what is necessary is criticism and not total denial or rejection" (Yamamoto, 1980, p. 56). Yamamoto (1980) suggested that the role of the Marxist approach in capitalist countries was for criticism rather than denial. It would not be wrong to conclude that Yamamoto's reformist view well represents the views of most other Marxist communication scholars in present-day Japan.

Information Society School

Of the four schools represented in Japanese communication research, this is the newest. Although the roots of the other three schools are in Europe and the United States, the information society school is rooted in Japan and the United States. Although there are many important American studies which contributed a great deal to the formation and development of this school, it is Japan that took the lead in evolving it as a new approach to communication studies. The word "information society" itself is a direct translation of the Japanese word *johoka shakai* which was coined in Japan in 1967.[7] The characteristics of this school are:

(a) The central concern is the Japanese concept *johoka* (informationization). *Informationization* is a process of social change to a state characterized by abundant information in terms of both stock and flow, quick and efficient distribution and transformation of information, and easy and inexpensive access to information for all members of society.
(b) Regarding informationization, the following questions must be answered scientifically.
   (i)   How can we measure the amount of information flow and stock in a society?
   (ii) How can we measure and compare the degrees of informationization internationally and longitudinally?
   (iii) What kind of influence does informationization have on society as a whole as well as individual lives?
   (iv) Why does informationization occur in advanced industrial countries?
   (v)   What do people do with information, and what does information do to

people? (Rather than what do people do with media, and what do media do to people?)

(c) The methods used by this school are varied. In addition to all the methods used by the other three schools, aggregate data analyses including macro-economic and econometric methods are often used.

(1) Basic Ideas and Theories

Tadao Umesao (1920-   ) published an economic-stage theory in which he discussed the development of industries in terms of the stages of agriculture, material industries, and information industries (Umesao, 1963). At this time, the formula sounds commonplace, but in the early 1960s, Umesao's idea was considered unique because the developmental stage theories widely known were just those of Marx (1939), Clark (1940), and Rostow (1960). Daniel Bell's concept of the *post-industrial society* had just been presented at a seminar held in 1962.

Umesao specialized in zoology and anthropology, so his views on economic development were seen as bold and unique. Umesao suggested dividing industries into three categories: endoderm, mesoderm, and ectoderm. Major endoderm organs in animals including human beings are the digestive organs and lungs. The muscles, bones, and the genital organs are the major mesoderm organs. The principal ectoderm organs are represented by the brain and nervous system as well as the sensory organs. Roughly speaking, the major function of endoderm organs is the maintenance of life in the individual. The major functions of mesoderm organs are movement, reaction to the outer world, and reproduction. The ectoderm organs' major function are the control of all other organs, therefore, the control of the individual's behavior. In the case of human beings thought and creativity are added to the mere control of behavior.

According to Umesao, the functions of endoderm organs in a biological organism are equivalent to the functions of agriculture, fishery, and cattle breeding in human society. These industries Umesao called *endoderm industries*. Similarly, the functions of mesoderm organs in a biological organism are the equivalent of the transportation, construction, and manufacturing industries in human society. Umesao called these industries *mesoderm industries*. Finally, the functions filled by ectoderm organs in a biological organism are similar to what he called *intellectual or spiritual industries* which consist of the information, communication, culture, and education industries. He called these industries *ectoderm industries*.

Umesao suggested that the degree of evolution of any animal is closely related to the proportional development of each kind of organ. If one compares an amoeba, a horse, and a human being, one can understand what he meant. Generally speaking, the less evolved the animal is, the larger the proportion of endoderm organs, particularly digestive organs, are. The more evolved the animal is, the larger the proportion of mesoderm and ectoderm organs, particularly the brain, become. Although the above can be said using a rough macroscopic description, it cannot be applied to individual species to rank them as to their degree of evolution.

Just as the proportions of mesoderm and ectoderm organs increase according to the evolution of the animal, Umesao thought that the proportions of mesoderm industries (transportation, construction, and manufacturing industries) and ectoderm industries (information, communication, culture, and education industries) must increase with the development of a society. In other words, he suggested that the development of a society can be measured by changes in the proportions of these three kinds of industries.

The analogy with animal evolution suggests several conclusions. Umesao emphasizes, for example, that even those animals considered most primitive have some form of mesoderm and ectoderm organs. Similarly, even in the kind of society said to be least developed, some form of mesoderm and ectoderm industries or elements exist. Without them the society cannot survive or maintain its integrity. The degree of development is only a matter of emphasis and proportion.

Umesao also emphasized that just as a human being, the most highly intellectually evolved creature on earth, cannot survive and properly function without endoderm and mesoderm organs, our society would not and could not exist without endoderm and mesoderm industries. The industrial evolution (not revolution) does not mean a complete metamorphosis, but is only a matter of change in proportion of the three types of industries. Although Umesao himself did not explicitly state the following natural conclusions, readers of his article have done so. The industrial revolution caused a drastic increase in the proportion of mesoderm industries (that is, the transportation, construction, and manufacturing industries). According to Umesao's theory, the information revolution logically follows next and results in a drastic increase in the proportion of information, communication, culture, and education industries. This change has come to be called *johoka* or informationization.

What characterizes industrialization is a drastic increase in the momentum of society as a whole. This momentum includes an increase in offensive and defensive strength and a great increase in the mobility of individual members of the society. On the other hand, *johoka* involves a drastic increase in capabilities in communication, data processing, and various cultural and intellectual activities. Furthermore, as a result of *johoka*, various components of the society become closely connected to each other by elaborate feedback systems, like the nervous system in the human body. In addition, many social activities become better controlled and more orderly in comparison to the *pre-johoka* age. On an individual level, people come to enjoy not only high mobility plus affluence in food, material, and energy, but also affluence in cultural and intellectual activities.

As the concept of informationization gained prominence, some scholars began to think about the role of information per se (rather than media) in society. Researchers began to attempt to restructure conventional communication studies to answer questions regarding the meaning of information to man.

For example, Kitamura (1970) criticized conventional communication models that basically stem from the stimulus-response model. He emphasized individual autonomy and suggested that communication should be understood in terms of individuals interacting with their environment. According to him, people receive or extract meaning from their environment. Kitamura called this phenomenon *information behavior.*

Both Kato (1972) and Nakano (1980) regarded information as one of the major components of the environment and defined information behavior as man's action on his environment to extract meaning and pleasure. Particularly important to Nakano was the direct interaction between information as an element of our environment and an individual as an acting unit. Nakano (1980, p. 19) criticized conventional communication models whose focus was on the interactions between individuals or between the media and individuals. Conventional studies have dealt with these subjects separately, like the study of interpersonal communication, the study of people's exposure to television, and so on. According to Nakano (1980, p. 19), these constitute only a small portion of people's information environment and information behavior. He recommends directly studying the interaction between people and information (in our information environment) instead of studying the interaction of people and the media. The research question derived from this conceptualization of information behavior becomes: What kind of individuals have what kind of needs for what kinds of information? Japanese research on this question will be introduced in the section "micro empirical research."

(2) Macro Empirical Research

Some early macro empirical research of the information society school took ideas directly from Umesao's article. For example, Umesao's article, discussed in the previous section, referred to Engels' ratio, namely, the proportion of household income spent on food.

Engels' ratio was devised in the middle of the 19th century when the mesoderm industry was rapidly expanding. One of the uses of Engels' ratio was to show the proportion of endoderm elements (digestive elements) in a household budget. This ratio certainly had some meaning in those days. However, now we need a new index which will show the proportion of ectoderm elements (information, communication, cultural, and educational elements) in a household budget. (Umesao, 1963, p. 56)

Umesao's suggestion was operationalized by the Research Institute of Telecommunications and Economics (RITE) (1968, 1970) and Sanuki (1970). The researchers formulated a ratio of expenditure for various kinds of information-related activities within the total expenditure of a household and called it the *information ratio*. These studies compared Engels' ratio and the information ratio in Japan longitudinally. According to Sanuki's calculation, the information ratio in Japan surpassed Engels' ratio in 1958. Sanuki (1970, p. 212) suggested defining an information society as a society in which the information ratio exceeds 50%. The information ratio values are different between RITE (1968, 1970) and Sanuki (1970) as a result of a difference in the method of calculation. However, all three studies confirmed that as personal income increased the information ratio became higher and Engel's ratio lower. Society became "informationized" as it became more affluent.

However, just as the French and Chinese spend a larger portion of their income for eating than many other nations do, the propensity to consume information goods and services may be different from one nation to another even if the income levels are the same. Thus RITE (1968, 1970) calculated the information ratio of various countries. This study revealed that the information ratio (after income differences were adjusted) was high in the United States, Canada, and Japan, but relatively low in Western European countries.

As mentioned above, Sanuki suggested that the information ratio may be used as an index to show the degree of informationization of society. Strictly speaking, however, the information ratio only indicates the propensity to consume information goods and services in households and may not accurately show the degree of informationization of the whole society. Thus RITE (1968, 1970) and Sanuki (1970) independently developed a new index called the *johoka* (informationization) index to compare the degrees of informationization of various societies. According to RITE (1968, 1970), as of 1966, the United States was the most highly informationized society, followed by England, Japan, West Germany, and France. The Ministry of Posts and Telecommunications (MPT) borrowed the measurement method developed by RITE and continued international comparisons for several more years. According to MPT's latest data, as of 1973, the rank order of informationization in the world was as follows: (1) U.S.A., (2) Japan, (3) West Germany, (4) France, and (5) U.K. (MPT, 1975, pp. 30-31).

Sanuki (1970) used his informationization index to compare the degrees of informationization of 46 prefectures in Japan.[8] The informationization gap between the most informationized prefecture, Tokyo, and the least informationized prefecture, Kagoshima, (4.11 times) was found to be much larger than the income gap between the most wealthy prefecture, Tokyo, and the poorest prefecture, Kagoshima (2.89 times). The informationization index was found to be highly correlated with per capita income and the urbanization index. Furthermore, the regression lines were found to be slightly upwardly curvilinear in both cases, which indicates that the speed of informationization increases as per capita income and the degree of urbanization increases.

American economist Fritz Machlup (1962) had a strong impact on Japanese researchers. Five research groups conducted United States-Japan comparisons using Machlup's method. According to their calculation using Machlup's method, the percentage of the information industry against the gross national product (GNP) in the United States as of 1963 was about 34%. The figure of Japan for the same year was 21% (Asahi Shimbun, 1965, 1967), 16% (Nippon Electric Co., 1966), and 16.7% (Nomura Research Institute, 1969).

Asahi Shimbun (1965, 1967) and Nippon Electric Co. (NEC) (1966) both noted that the percentage of the information industry against GNP was increasing both in Japan and the United States, which means that the information industry then was growing more rapidly than the whole economy. Asahi Shimbun (1965, 1967) also noted that the growth rate of the Japanese information industry exceeded that of the American counterpart.

Marc Porat (1976) also had a significant impact on Japanese researchers. RITE (1982) calculated the scale of the Japanese information industry and its percentage against GNP for 20 years since 1960 using Porat's method. According to Porat's calculation, the percentages of the information industry against GNP as of 1960, 1970, and 1974 were 39.2%, 43.1%, and 44.6% in the United States. In comparison, and, according to the calculation by RITE using the same method, the figures for 1960, 1970, and 1979 were 29.5%, 29.5%, and 35.4% in Japan. (The method of calculation is different between Machlup and Porat.) If the percentage of the information industry against GNP indicates the degree of informationization, Japan is not yet as informationized as the United States.

Although importing the Machlup-Porat method from the United States, Japan exported to the United States the "information flow census" method. This method originally was proposed in a research report by a think tank called the Association for Economic Planning (1969). The idea was adopted, developed and refined by researchers at the Ministry of Posts and Telecommunications (MPT) and RITE. This is a method to convert all forms of information into words and measure the amount of information flow by a single unit, words. The amount of information (words) sent from various media and the amount of information actually consumed by receivers was calculated. Thus the consumption rate of information (the amount of words supplied divided by the amount of words consumed) was calculated over time. Furthermore, the distance of information flow was computed and multiplied by the amount of flow.

The cost to move one word one kilometer was calculated for various communications media to explain media users' choice behavior. It was found that there was a clear negative correlation between the per-word, per-kilometer transmission cost and the amount of information flow. Furthermore, longitudinal comparison of these costs across various media revealed that this cost accounted for the increase or decrease of information flow by various media. In other words, cost explains the rise and fall of various communications media (see Figure 2.1).

The standard method for measurement of information flow was established in 1975 by researchers at MPT. Surveys using this method have been conducted every year. The results have been published in MPT's annual White Paper.

MPT (1982a) calculated the amount of information production *or origination* and consumption in the 47 prefectures in Japan. It was found that 84.7% of total information supplied in Japan was produced in *or originated from* Tokyo, followed by Osaka (7.8%) and Aichi, where Nagoya City is (1.5%). In other words, 94% of all the information supplied in Japan was produced in (or originated from) these three urban prefectures. The per capita information supply in Tokyo was found to be eight times higher than the national average and the per capita information consumption 1.6 times higher. These figures were found to be highly correlated with the degree of urbanization and per capita income of the prefecture, which supports the aforementioned high correlation between the informationization index and per capita income (and the degree of urbanization) found by Sanuki (1970). Interestingly, however, the per capita consumption of electric media is slightly negatively correlated with the degree of urbanization because of the rural population's heavy dependence on television.

In this study by MPT "information flow matrices" were made for various media to show how much information flows from which prefecture to which prefecture. It was found that only Tokyo and Osaka provide information on a nationwide scale. Other urban prefectures were represented as just regional centers in the pattern of information flow. Most prefectures were found to receive more than 80% of their information from Tokyo.

Pool, Inose, Takasaki, and Hurwitz (1984) compared the amount of information flow in the United States using the "information flow census method." The American data supported the negative correlation between the per-word transmission cost and the amount of information flow. The average annual growth rates of information flow in the United States and Japan are shown in Table 2.1.

The volume of words supplied to the American and Japanese public has been growing about two and a half times as fast as the volume consumed. "As a result, the volume of words consumed, which in 1960 in the U.S. had been 1.3% of the total words supplied, by 1975 amounted to only 0.5% of those words supplied and by 1980, just 0.4%. In Japan the volume con-

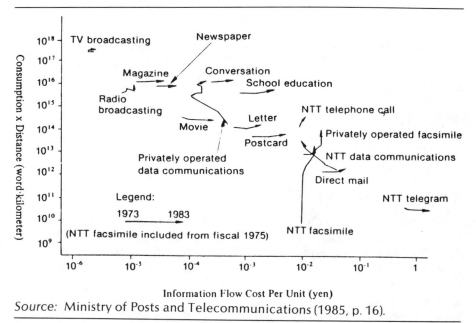

Source: Ministry of Posts and Telecommunications (1985, p. 16).

Figure 2.1 Longitudinal trends in information flow amount-distance (consumption x distance) and information flow cost per unit (flow cost/consumption x distance).

sumed was 3.8% of the volume supplied in 1960 and 1.6% in 1975" (Pool et al., 1984, p. 42). The comparison of the information consumption rates in the United States and Japan revealed that the rate is lower in the United States than in Japan. This may be an indication that the United States is more informationized than Japan.

MPT (1982) revealed that information emanated from Tokyo to other parts of Japan. In other words, an "unbalanced information flow" exists within Japan. Given Japan's example, there is reason to believe that an unbalanced flow may occur among different societies. What are the factors that determine the amount of information flow from one society to another? Ito and Kochevar (1983, 1984) tackled this question in international communication. Using international flow data for films, television programs, and satellite communication, they examined determining forces of 20 independent variables. It was found that economic (such as trade) and political relationships (symbolized by the number of treaties) account for a large portion of the import of information in all three media. Compared with political and economic factors, geographical, cultural, and historical factors such as distance, cultural affinity, common language, and religion were not as important as determining factors of the international flow of information.

Table 2.1
Annual Growth Rate in Per Capita Supply and Consumption
of Information in the United States and Japan (in percentages)

	Supply		Consumption	
	U.S.A.	Japan	U.S.A.	Japan
1960-1965	9.9	7.4	1.8	3.1
1965-1970	6.1	8.0	1.2	0.7
1970-1975	6.3	9.4	2.1	3.0
1975-1980	4.6	NA	1.5	NA

Source: Pool, Inose, Takasaki, & Hurwitz (1984, p. 42).

(3) Micro-Empirical Research

The micro studies of the information society school are usually called the "study of information behavior." As previously mentioned, Kitamura (1970), Kato (1972), and Nakano (1980) suggested analyzing the information environment as a whole. One of the implications of this suggestion is that an important task of the study of information behavior is to explain and predict information flow patterns (information ecology) or media distribution patterns (media ecology). If such patterns change, reasons must be provided. In order to deal with such ecological questions, the approach has to be more holistic than conventional approaches.

Maejima (1973) conducted a questionnaire survey (effective sample size 935), in which she divided people's information needs into "information transmission needs" and "information collection needs." She examined to what degree each need is or is not satisfied, and how the degree of satisfaction or dissatisfaction is affected by personal attributes such as sex, age, education, and profession. The major findings of this survey were as follows: (1) The content of information including entertainment that individuals collect (mainly from mass media) is basically the same as the content of information that they transmit to, or talk about with, other people. (2) There is a high correlation between an individual's information collection needs and his or her expected social role. (3) The degree of satisfaction of an individual's information transmission needs decreases as the level of informational content shifts from family and local community to national affairs.

Fujiwara (1980) conducted a nationwide survey called "The Japanese Information Behavior Survey" (effective sample size 2,786). According to Fujiwara, the purpose of this research was to find out what kind of information people are exposed to, based on what kind of needs, in what kind of situations, and through what kind of media. He also asked how he or she used information, what meaning an individual gave to, and what gratifications were acquired from his or her information behavior (Fujiwara, 1978, p. 11). The last few questions remind us of conventional studies of media exposure and its uses and gratifications. However, like Nakano, Fujiwara also emphasized that exposure to the media or uses of the media constitutes only a small part of an individual's information behavior. Therefore, Fujiwara devoted a considerable portion of his questionnaire items to personal conversation. He also stated that another purpose of this survey was "to classify the Japanese information behavior as a whole, without neglecting any element of it, into a relatively few clusters, and study the interrelationships of these clusters" (Fujiwara, 1980, p. 11; see Ito, 1983, for details on Fujiwara's cluster analysis).

Joho Shakaigaku Kenkyu-jo (Research Institute for Information Sociology) conducted a questionnaire survey on information behavior in 1980 in Yamagata City (effective sample size 847) and in 1981 in Kumamoto City (effective sample size 707). Hirose (1982), who was one of the members of the research team, wrote about the background motivations inherent in these two surveys. One of the motivations is essential to the Japanese study of information behavior, and deserves to be quoted at length:

> Nowadays, typical mass communication research intends to provide detailed analyses of specific and limited aspects of human communication behavior. In newspaper readership surveys, for example, researchers treat people only as newspaper readers and ignore all other aspects of their information behavior. Of course, such an approach is sometimes necessary, and such analyses can have some significance.

> Actually, however, people in their daily lives do not exist just as newspaper readers. They watch television, write letters, talk with their family and friends, and attend meetings. In fact, people are the agents of extremely varied "information behaviors." Therefore, we thought it necessary and natural to grasp people's daily information behavior from a holistic viewpoint.

Thus the researchers at the Research Institute for Information Sociology listed 37 different types of information behavior including personal conversation. Then they asked respondents to rate, by five category scales, the extent to which they practiced each of these behaviors. Their findings were quite similar to those indicated by Maejima (1973) and Fujiwara (1980, 1981). For example, national newspapers were read by well-educated males, managers, specialists, and students, whereas local newspapers were read by farmers, fishermen, merchants, and shopkeepers. Women, particularly housewives, spent more time than men in personal communication, including telephone conversation. Here again, the researchers found that social role expectations and utility strongly influenced people's information behavior.

The researchers classified their 37 types of information behavior into three categories: (1) mass communication, (2) medio communication

(communication on the level of local community, in groups and circles), and (3) interpersonal communication. Then they computed respondents' average amount of time spent on each of the 37 types of information behavior. The order of mean values was (1) interpersonal communication, (2) mass communication, and (3) medio communication. This order was the same for the two cities, Yamagata and Kumamoto. Furthermore, the researchers computed the mean scores of respondents' time spent in the 37 information behaviors in the 2 cities and called these scores the "general information behavior index." According to them, "by computing such information behavior indices for various parts of Japan, we would be able to determine the levels of informationization in various parts of Japan" (Hirose, 1982).

RITE (1981) studied information behavior by using a secondary analysis of existing data, particularly time budget surveys and media exposure surveys. In this study, information behavior was first classified into two categories: (1) media information behavior and (2) direct information behavior (without using media). Furthermore, these two types of information behavior were divided into categories according to the place where they occurred: (a) home, (b) workplace, and (c) other places. The same information behavior, for example, telephone conversation was divided into telephone conversation at home, at the work place, and at other places, such as a public telephone on the street. In the end, all kinds of information behavior were placed in one of the six categories.

By using existing data for 39 different types of information behavior, the researchers at RITE computed how many minutes per day one Japanese individual spends on average for each of the 39 types of information behavior. Taking telephone conversation as an example, the average Japanese spends 10.1 minutes on telephone conversation at home, 19.4 minutes at the work place, and 1.5 minutes (using public telephones) at other places each day. Using various statistical models, the researchers projected predictions for 10 to 20 years in the future for each of the 39 types of information behavior.

(4) Organizations Representative of the Information Society School

The information society school in Japan has been developed mainly by researchers at private research institutes, think tanks, and government agencies rather than by university researchers. Most university researchers have been conservative and have stood aloof from new developments. In 1983, however, a new academic association named "The Japan Society of Information and Communication Research" (JSICR) was created (in addition to the existing Japan Society for Studies in Journalism and Mass Communication).

JSICR consists of the following five divisions: (1) Division on the Problems of Information Societies, which deals with legal problems in information societies such as privacy, consumer protection, computer software protection, computer crime, and so on; (2) Division on the International Flow of Information, which deals with subjects like free and balanced flow of information among nations, cultural exchange, and international language policies in Asia; (3) Division on the Information and Communication Industries, which deals with the economic structure of information and communication industries and policies for them; (4) Division on Information Resources, which deals with data base, libraries, and transborder data flow; and (5) Division on Quantitative Analysis of Information Societies, which includes the macro and micro empirical research of the information society school. JSICR's membership as of September, 1985, is about 1,200.

A new foundation called "The Telecommunications Advancement Foundation" (TAF) was created in 1984. According to their prospectus, one of their purposes is to promote healthy development of an information society by subsidizing legal, economic, social, and cultural research on telecommunications. Together with the existing two large foundations in this area, the Hoso Bunka (Broadcasting Culture) Foundation and the KDD Engineering and Consulting, TAF will be an important financial source for information society research.

Stimulated by such incentives and activities, the number of university researchers entering this field is steadily increasing. Considering all these conditions, Japan, together with the United States, will probably continue to take the lead in organizing and developing the information society school as a new approach to communication studies.

IMPLICATIONS FOR COMMUNICATION STUDIES IN NON-WESTERN COUNTRIES — CONCLUSIONS

In this chapter, we have reviewed Japanese communication studies from the 1920s to the present. Major works by two of the four "founding fathers" and the major four schools of present Japanese communication studies were introduced.

One of the characteristics of Japanese communication studies may be said to be their strong concern with the environment. In the "environmentalist school," environment has been the key concept. However, as we have already discussed, Tosaka and his followers have emphasized that ideology is ubiquitous and journalism is a day-to-day expression of various ideologies of the society. Thus for most Japanese Marxist communication scholars, people are surrounded by and immersed in ideologies of the society: Ideology is the environment.

It was also noted that environment is an important concept in the "information society school" as well. Nakano (1980) used the term information environment, and Kato (1972, pp. 41-42) wrote that people's environment consisted of information. The only school among the major four schools in which the concept of environment does not play a particularly important role is the "American school."

Generally speaking, except for scholars in the American school, Japanese prefer the idea that people are surrounded by and affected by information flow to the individualistic models such as the "sender — message — receiver — effects" model. Although many individualistic models such as the Shannon-Weaver model, Sebeok model, and the Gerbner model were introduced in Japan, they were not well accepted.[9] The reason might be that Japanese think the influence on people's attitudes and behavior by abstract and comprehensive matters such as the environment, atmosphere, climate, groups, and so on, is more decisive and important than the influence of specific message(s) from specific individual(s). This belief reflects the structure of Japanese culture and society. In Japan, a competent leader usually refers to someone who can create a consensus-oriented atmosphere which most people cannot resist rather than someone who gives an eloquent speech and leads people by using logic.

The second characteristic of Japanese communication studies is a stronger emphasis on information than communication. This characteristic is emphasized in the "information society school." However, this is by and large true of the other schools (again except the American school). There are probably two reasons for this. The first is that there is no indigenous Japanese word for *communication. Komyunikeishon* is used in Japanese to mean *communication.* However, this term is not frequently used in daily conversation among nonspecialists. Publishers, government agencies, and even universities often try to avoid the term *komyunikeishon* because it is a borrowed term and not familiar to ordinary people. On the other hand, *joho,* which is the equivalent to *information,* is an indigenous word, thus easily understood.[10] Although the writer has never calculated which of the two terms is more frequently used in Japanese literature, it is certain that in Japan the terms *information* and *information flow* are often used in situations where *communication* would be used in English-speaking countries.

Because the needs or problems are different from one society to another, social science also should differ from one country to another. Even when we import foreign theories and methods, needs of the importing country should be reflected at least in the selection of theories and methods imported. Ono, Tosaka, Shimizu, and Umesao are respected in Japan not only because they were prolific writers but also because the needs of the Japanese society at that time were reflected in their works. Mere translation or importation of foreign theories and methods are less worthwhile. By fostering and developing a country's unique theories and methods based on its individual needs, a country or a region can encourage similar patterns of development of communication studies in the rest of the world.

However, it has not been easy to foster and develop unique characteristics of Japanese research. It was not until the 1960s that the individual characteristics of Japanese communication studies began to emerge. Despite Tosaka's and Shimizu's notable contributions, the 40 to 50 years between the 1920s and the 1960s were spent introducing and digesting American and European studies. During these 40 to 50 years, there appeared several original and outstanding scholars. Some of them proposed important and original ideas. Unfortunately, however, these ideas did not develop in Japan nor have they had any influence themselves on foreign academics.

One reason has been the language barrier. Although any Japanese scholar can read at least one foreign language (usually English), most of them cannot write an article or a book in a foreign language. Therefore, many good articles and books have never been published in any language other than Japanese. This made it impossible for any good ideas to be accepted, fostered, and developed outside Japan.

Another factor has to do with Japanese academicians themselves. Many Japanese university researchers have studied and been trained abroad. As young scholars they were strongly influenced by some famous foreign researchers and subsequently identified themselves with foreign academic schools. After returning home, these people taught foreign methods and theories, translated the articles and books by their former teachers and colleagues, and made efforts to transplant foreign methods and theories in Japan. Of course, the significance of such efforts cannot be denied, for they have raised the academic level of Japan. On the other hand, these scholars have not paid enough attention to the ideas, methods, and theories created and proposed by fellow Japanese scholars.

Finally, until the 1960s research activities in Japan were confined to university campuses and highly specialized academic circles. Only universities and the Ministry of Education could provide funds for research. Research funds were not available in the private business sector (including private foundations who would support academic research). Thus there were numerous discrepancies between academics and the real world. The needs of the Japanese society, economy, and culture were not well reflected. Research, in those days, was done solely for academic purposes. Before the 1960s the Japanese government and private industries were trying to catch up with more advanced countries. Because of this goal, the need for original research did not come out. In the 1960s, however, Japan began to catch up in many areas. Japanese government agencies and private companies began to spend more money on research to create new models. Research institutes attached to government agencies, public corporations and large private companies, independent think tanks, private

research companies, and private foundations were created and their numbers were increased. The number of experts and researchers who worked
for such research institutions outside university campuses steadily
increased.

Most of these nonuniversity researchers were more "Japanese" or
"domestic" in many respects than university researchers. In some cases
this characteristic caused defects in their research. Many were not as
sophisticated in understanding methodologies and theories as university
researchers. Often they were too concerned with the practical utility of their
research results. Nevertheless, they had their own strengths. One of these
was that they were more sensitive to the research needs of the real world.
Another was that they were often bolder in methods and theory than university researchers. They often failed because of such boldness, but when
they succeeded, they created innovative methods and theories. In late
1960s university researchers' sophisticated methods, theories, and other
techniques began to merge with nonuniversity researchers' bold, original,
and innovative ideas reflecting the needs of Japanese society, culture, and
economy. As a result of this blending of styles of research, authentic "Japanese communication studies" were born.

The importance of indigenous research was reinforced upon the writer
during his visits to South Korea in 1979 and 1980. The high quality of university researchers and well-organized curriculum for journalism and communication education was quite impressive. However, the number of
communication experts outside the universities was far smaller than in
Japan. As a result, the number of communication researchers as a whole
seemed to be only about one-eighth that of Japan. (Korea's total population is
about one-third that of Japan.) In addition, research funds available from
sources other than universities or the Ministry of Education appeared to be
far less than in Japan. This situation is similar to Japan's in the late 1950s
and early 1960s. Under such conditions, although some outstanding
scholar could develop unique theories or methods, it would still be difficult
to establish an authentic Korean school based on the real needs of the
Korean society and culture.

Every academically developing country will not necessarily follow the
same development path as Japan. However, the writer hopes that the
description of the Japanese experience will be of help to communication
experts outside Japan, particularly in academically developing countries,
in creating research, theories, and policies to solve their particular society's
problems.

NOTES

1. For example, most Japanese newspapers, even quality ones, carry serial stories
every day, and once a week (usually on Sundays) many newspapers offer *haiku, waka*
(serious short poems), and *senryu* (humorous short poems) contests. These customs are

said to have come from *kawaraban* or other similar publications during the Tokugawa period (1603-1867).

2. Politically or ideologically, Ono was a middle-of-the-roader. In the 1930s the influence of Marxism was very strong among Japanese intellectuals. However, Ono never accepted Marxism. On the other hand, he never cooperated with the militaristic government. In addition, despite his strong ties with Germany and many friends in the German academy, he was against Nazism. In 1938 he severely criticized two famous German journalism professors for having accepted Nazism in a lecture entitled "Nazi Theories on Journalism." The content of this lecture was published in 1941, the year the Pacific War began.

3. A criticism of this school can be that only supportive data and facts are adopted and nonsupportive ones are ignored. Some of the studies using this approach can also be criticized as "episodic."

4. The Chinese claim that about 15 million Chinese were killed during Japan's invasion of China between 1931 and 1945.

5. Although in a different context, Horie (1965) also emphasized mass media's function of providing "logic" to society. According to Horie (1965, p. 77), "Mass media provide the public with materials they select. The public reacts to them emotionally and in disorganized ways, which mass media change to well-structured, consistent logic."

6. Some people argue that individual change naturally leads to social change. This process, however, is not that simple. Besides, most of the subjects used to test theory in this school have little to do with social change. Typical subjects are attitudes toward cigarettes, political candidates, a certain kind of toothpaste, and the like.

7. According to the writer's investigation through literature and interviews, the term *johoka shakai* was coined in 1967 by a group of scholars who belonged to *Kagaku Gijutsu to Keizai no Kai* (A Study Group for Science, Technology and Economics).

8. Okinawa Prefecture was not included in this research because Okinawa at that time was still under the American occupation.

9. Lasswell's model is an exception. The reason is that Lasswell's model clarifies the structure of early communication studies.

10. Strictly speaking, from an etymological viewpoint, the word *joho* is *not* indigenous to Japan either. We can say, however, that the concept *joho* has been almost completely Japanized, whereas *communication* has not.

REFERENCES

English Language Literature

Boorstin, D. J. (1961). *The image*. London: Weidenfeld & Nicolson.

Boulding, K. E. (1956). *The image*. Ann Arbor: University of Michigan Press.

Clark, C. (1940). *The conditions of economic progress*. London: Macmillan.

Edelstein, A. S., Bowes, J. E., & Harsel, S. M. (Eds.). (1978). *Information societies: Comparing the Japanese and American experiences*. Seattle: University of Washington Press.

Fujitake, A. (1967). Tokyo Olympics and the Japanese public. *Studies of Broadcasting, 5*, 49-109.

Gerbner, G. (1972). Mass media and human communication theory. In D. McQuail (Ed.), *Sociology of mass communications* (pp. 35-58). London: Penguin.

Gitlin, T. (1980). *The whole world is watching: Mass media in the making & unmaking of the new left*. Berkeley: University of California Press.

Goffman, E. (1974). *Frame analysis: An essay on the organization of experience*. Harmondsworth, Middlesex: Penguin.

Ito, Y. (1981). The "johoka shakai" approach to the study of communication in Japan. In G. C. Wilhoit & H. de Bock (Eds.), *Mass communication review yearbook* (vol. 2) (pp. 671-698). Beverly Hills, CA: Sage.

Ito, Y. (1983a). *The "johoka shakai" approach to the study of communication in Japan — micro studies —*. Paper presented at the Conference for the Comparison of the Information Society Studies and Informationalization Policies in Japan, the United States, and Europe, Tokyo.

Ito, Y. (in press). Mass communications in Japan. In A. S. Tan (Ed.), *Alternative mass communication system: The third world, China and Japan*. Hillsdale, NJ: Lawrence Erlbaum.

Ito, Y., & Kochevar J. (1983). Factors accounting for the flow of international communication. *Keio Communication Review, 4*, 13-37.

Ito, Y., & Ogawa, K. (1984). Recent trends in johoka shakai and johoka policy studies. *Keio Communication Review, 5*, 15-28.

Iwao, S., & Pool, I. de Sola. (1983). International understanding via TV programmes: The case of *Shogun. Keio Communication Review, 4*, 3-12.

Kato, H. (1959). *Japanese popular culture*. Tokyo: Charles Tuttle.

Kato, H. (1974). *Japanese research on mass communication: Selected abstracts*. Honolulu: The University Press of Hawaii.

Katz, E. (1980). Media events: The sense of occasion. *Studies in Visual Communication, 6*, 84-89.

Katz, E., Dayan, D., & Motyl, P. (1981). In defense of media events. In R. W. Haigh, G. Berber, & R. B. Byrne (Eds.), *Communication in the twenty-first century* (pp. 43-59). New York: Jonn Wiley.

Katz, E., & Szecskoe, T. (1981). *Mass media and social change*. Beverly Hills, CA: Sage.

Koffka, K. (1935). *Principles of Gestalt psychology*. London: Kegan, Paul, Trench, & Trubner.

Lang, K., & Lang, G. E. (1960). The unique perspective of television and its effect: A pilot study. In W. Schramm (Ed.), *Mass communications* (pp. 544-560). Urbana: University of Illinois Press.

Lang, K., & Lang, G. E. (1968). *Politics and television*, Chicago: Quadrangle Books.

Lasswell H. D. (1948). The structure and function of communication in society. In L. Bryson (Ed.), *The communication of ideas*. New York: Harper.

Lippmann, W. (1922). *Public opinion*. New York: Harcourt.

Marx, K. (1939). *Grundrisse der Kritik der politischen Oekonomie*. Moscow: Marx-Engels-Lenin-Institut.

Machlup, F. (1962). *The production and distribution of knowledge in the United States*. NJ: Princeton University Press.

Masuda, Y. (1980). *The information society*. Tokyo: Institute for the Information Society.

Merton, R. K. (1946). *Mass persuasion: The social psychology of a war bond drive*. New York: Harper & Row.

Ministry of Posts and Telecommunications (1978). *Information flow census in Japan: A quantitative study of information societies*. Paper distributed at an OECD conference.

Ministry of Posts and Telecommunications (1985). *Report on present state of communications in Japan: Fiscal 1984*. Tokyo: The Japan Times.

Oyama, H., & Nixon, R. (1961). Ono, Hideo; A tale of kawara-ban: A history of mass communication during the Yedo period (1590-1868). *Journalism Quarterly, 38*(1), 92-93.

Pool, I. de Sola (1983). Tracking the flow of information. *Science, 221*, 609-613.

Pool, I. de Sola, Inose, H., Takasaki, N., & Hurwitz R. (1984). *Communications flows: A census in the United States and Japan*. Tokyo: University of Tokyo Press.

Pool, I. de Sola, Wang, S., Fryling, R., Hurwitz, R., & Duffy, G. (1982). *Communications flows in the United States: A census, with comparisons to Japan*. Monograph. Massachusetts Institute of Technology, Research Program on Communications Policy.

Porat, M. U. (1976). *The information economy*. Palo Alto, CA: Stanford University.

Rostow, W. W. (1960). *The stages of economic growth: A non-Communist manifesto*. England: Cambridge University Press.

Schramm, W. (1949). *Mass Communications*. Urbana: University of Illinois Press.

Siebert, F. S., Peterson, T. A., & Schramm, W. (1956). *Four theories of the press*. Urbana: University of Illinois Press.

Takasaki, N., & Ozawa, T. (1983). Analysis of information flow in Japan. *Information Economics and Policy, 1*(2), 177-193.

Tsuruki, M. (1982). Frame imposing function of the mass media as seen in the Japanese press. *Keio Communication Review, 3,* 27-37.

Tuchman, G. (1978). *Making news: A study in the construction of reality.* New York: Free Press.

Tuchman, G. (1981). Myth and the consciousness industry: A new look at the effects of the mass media. In Katz, E. & T. Szecskoe (Eds.), *Mass Media and Social Change* (pp. 83-100). Beverly Hills, CA: Sage.

Znaniecki, F. (1952). *Cultural sciences: Their origin and development.* Urbana: University of Illinois Press.

Japanese Language Literature

Akuto, H. (1972). *Komyunikeishon* (Communication). Tokyo: Chikuma Shobo.

Amano, C. (1887). *Taisei shimbun-ron* (Newspapers in the West). Tokyo: Maruzen.

Aono, S. (1926, July). Musan kaikyu no shimbun ni tsuite (Newspapers for the proletariat). *Kaiho,* 73-77.

Ariyama, T. (1984, October). Fukuzawa Yukichi no janarizumu-ron (Yukichi Fukuzawa's theory on journalism). *Mita Hyoron,* 24-32.

Asahi Shimbun, Department of Advertising. (1965, March). Chishiki sangyo eno kanshin to nihon no chishiki sangyo (Concern with the information industry: Present state of the Japanese information industry). *Kokoku Geppo,* 4-8.

Asahi Shimbun, Department of Advertising. (1967, March). Chishiki sangyo eno kanshin to nihon no chishiki sangyo (Concern with the information industry: Present state of the Japanese information industry). *Kokoku Geppo,* 2-9.

Association for Economic Planning (1969). *Johoka shakai no keisei* (The formation of information societies). Monograph.

Association for Economic Planning (1970). *Johoka shakai no hatten: Kokusaika suru joho nettowahku* (The development of information societies: Internationalization of information networks). Monograph.

Chinone, H. (1969). Fukuzawa Yukichi no komyunikeishon-ron (Yukichi Fukuzawa's theory on communication). *Shimbungaku Hyoron, 18,* 145-154.

Dainihon Shimbun-kai (Ed.). (1919). *Shimbungaku zensho* (Handbook of the study of newspapers). Tokyo: Dainihon Shimbun-kai.

Fujinuma, S. (1970). Waga kuni ni okeru hoso kenkyu no shiten (A perspective for the study of broadcasting in Japan). In NHK Hosogaku Kenkyu-shitu (Eds.), *Hosogaku josetsu* (pp. 427-484). Tokyo: Nihon Hoso Shuppan Kyokai.

Fujitake, A. (1968). *Gendai masu komyunikeishon no riron* (Contemporary mass communication theories). Tokyo: Nihon Hoso Shuppan Kyokai.

Fujitake, A. (1974). *Panikku* (Panic). Tokyo: Nihon Keizai Shimbun-sha.

Fujitake, A. (1975). *Jiken no shakaigaku* (Sociology of events). Tokyo: Chuo Koron (Chuko shinsho).

Fujitake, A. (1985). *Terebi media no shakairyoku* (Social force of television). Tokyo: Yuhi-kaku (sensho).

Fujitake, A., & Akiyama T. (1967). *Tokyo orimpikku* (Tokyo Olympics). Tokyo: NHK Hoso Yoron Chosa-jo.

Fujiwara, N. (1980). Shichosha no ruikeika (Categorization of viewers. *Bunken Geppo,* August, 11-26; October, 20-37; November, 27-41.

Fujiwara, N. (1981). Bangumi sentaku wo kiteisuru shichosha tokusei (Attributes of viewers as determinants of program choice). *Bunken Geppo,* August, 1-12; October, 13-32; December, 6-11.

Fujiwara, N., & Okita, K. (1979). Nihonjin no joho kodo (Information behavior of the Japanese people). *NHK Hoso Bunka Kenkyu Nempo, 24,* 169-225.

Fukuda, T. (1975). *Shimbun no subete* (Everything about newspapers). Tokyo: Takagi Shobo.

Fukumoto, K. (1926, August). Zen musan kaikyu no tame no shimbun (Newspaper for the entire proletariat). *Marukusu Shugi,* 102-112.

Goto, K. (1984). Johoka shakai-ron no genjo to kadai (The present state and problems of information society studies). *Shimbungaku Hyoron, 33*, 2-12.
Goto, M. (1915). *Shimbun oyobi shimbunkisha* (Newspaper and journalists). Tokyo: Nishohdoh.
Goto, T. (1926). *Shimbunshi kowa* (Lectures on newspapers). Tokyo: Dobunkan.
Hayakawa, Z. (1967). Masu komi kenkyu no hattatsu to genjo (The development and present state of mass communication research). In R. Hidaka, T. Sato, & M. Inaba (Eds.), *Masu komyunikeishon nyumon* (pp. 211-229). Tokyo: Yuhikaku (sosho).
Hayakawa, Z., & Ogawa H. (1971). Wagakuni no masu komi kenkyu no genjo ni tsuite (The current state of mass communication studies in Japan). *Hosogaku Kenkyu, 22*, 5-46.
Hayasaka J. (1926). Shakai soshiki to shimbun zasshi (Social organizations and the press). In *Shakai mondak kohza, 6*, (15), (pp. 1-48). Tokyo: Shinchohsha.
Hidaka, R. (1954). Masu komyunikeishon gairon (Theories of mass communication). In I. Shimizu, M. Kido, H. Minami, & R. Hidaka (Eds.), *Masu komyunikeishon kohza* (Vol. 1). Tokyo: Kawade Shobo.
Hirose, H. (1982, August 17). "Chiiki juumin no joho kodo" chosa (A survey on "information behavior of local populaces." *Shimbun Kyokai-ho*.
Horie, F. (1969). Sasebo ni okeru gensen i joh hoshano jiken to kokumin yoron (National public opinion on the abnormal radioactivity incident by a nuclear submarine in Sasebo). In Nihon Kokusai Seiji Gakkai (Ed.), *Kokusai Seiji, 41*, 77-97.
Iguchi, I. (1947). Komyunikeishon josetsu: Lasswell kyoju no hohoron ni tsuite (Introduction to communication: on the methodology of Professor Lasswell). *Shiso no Kagaku, 2*(2), 391-399.
Iguchi, I. (1949). *Komyunikeishon no kagaku* (Science of communication). Tokyo: Taiyo Tosho.
Iguchi, I. (1951). *Masu komyunikeishon* (Mass communication). Tokyo: Kobun-sha.
Ikuta, M. (1957). *Masu komyunikeishon no shomondai* (Problems of mass communication). Tokyo: Keio Tsushin.
Ikuta, M. (1968). *Masu komyunikeishon no kenkyu* (Studies of mass communication). Tokyo: Keio Tsushin.
Inaba, M. (1969, September). Joho dokusen no hiningensei to dakkyaku no hoko (Dehumanization caused by information monopoly: Suggestions for remedy). *Keizai Hyoron*, 45-54.
Inaba, M. (1976). *Gendai masukomi-ron* (Contemporary mass communication theories). Tokyo: Aoki Shoten.
Ito, Y. (1983b). Johoka shakai ron no shintenkai (New perspectives of information society studies). *Keio Daigaku Hogaku Kenkyu, 56*(8), 29-51.
Ito, Y., & Kochevar J. (1984). Terebi bangumi no kokusaikan no nagare no kitei youin ni kansuru kenkyu (A study on the determinant factors of international flow of television programs). *Kenkyu Hokoku: Hoso-Bunka Foundation, 8*, 98-102.
Ito, Y., Ogawa, K., & Sakaki, H. (1974a). Dema no kenkyu: Aichi-ken Toyokawa Shinyokinko "torituke" sawagi no genchi chosa (A study of rumor: A field survey of a bank panic at the Toyokawa Saving Bank in Aichi Prefecture.) *Sogo Janarizumu Kenkyu, 69*, 70-80; 70, 100-111.
Ito, Y., Ogawa, K., & Sakaki, H. (1974b, April). Aru dema no issho (A life of a rumor). *Bungei Shunju*, 178-188.
Ito, Y., Ogawa, K., & Sakaki, H. (1975). *Panikku no kenkyu* (A study of panic). Unpublished report of a questionnaire survey at Kozakai-machi.
Iwao, S. (1966). Komyunikeishon no jikkenteki apurochi (Experimental approach to communication). *Nenpo Shakai Shinrigaku, 7*, 5-17.
Joho Shakaigaku Kenkyujo (1981). Chiiki jumin no joho kodo ni kansuru sogo chosa: Yamagata-shi wo taisho ni shite (A comprehensive survey on information behavior of local populaces: at Yamagata City). Monograph.
Joho Shakaigaku Kenkyujo (1982) Chiiki jumin no joho kodo ni kansuru sogo chosa: Kumamoto-shi wo taisho ni shite (A comprehensive survey on information behavior of local populaces: at Kumamoto City). Monograph.

Kadoya, H. (1929). Puroretaria shimbun-ron (Proletariat journalism). In Seiji Hihan-sha (Ed.), *Marukusushugi Kohza* (Vol. 1) (pp. 237-302). Tokyo. Marukusushugi Kohza Kanko-Kai.

Kakegawa, T. (1972). Masu media no tohsei to taibei roncho (Control of mass media and editorials on the United States). In C. Hosoya, M. Saito, S. Imai, & M. Royama (Eds.), *Nichibei kankei-shi 4: Kaisen ni itaru 10 nen (1931-1941)*. Tokyo: Tokyo Daigaku Shuppan-kai.

Kato, H. (1957). *Masu komyunikeishon* (Mass communication). Tokyo: Kodan-sha (shinsho).

Kato, H. (1972). *Joho kodo* (Information behavior). Tokyo: Chuo Koron (Chuko shinsho).

Kawanaka, Y. (1971). *Gendai komyunikeishon* (Modern communication). Tokyo: Veritasu.

Kinoshita, T. (1977). Ryugen (Rumor). In H. Ikeuchi (Ed.), *Kohza: Shakai shinrigaku* (pp. 11-86). Tokyo: Tokyo Daigaku Shuppan-kai.

Kitamura, H. (1970). *Joho kodo ron* (Information behavior). Tokyo: Seibundo Shinko-sha.

Koike, Y. (1882). *Nihon shimbun rekishi* (The history of newspapers in Japan). Tokyo: Gengendo.

Kuroiwa, R. (1912). *Shimbunshi-ron* (On newspapers). Tokyo.

Maejima, M. (1973, July). Joho yokkyu no jittai to kozo (The state and structure of information needs). *Bunken Geppo,* 10-38.

Matsumoto, K. (1889). *Shimbungaku* (Study of Newspapers). Tokyo: Hakubunkan.

Minami, H. (1949). *Shakai shinri gaku* (Social psychology). Tokyo: Kobun-sha.

Minami, H. (1954). *Gendai no masu komyunikeishon* (Modern mass communication). Tokyo: Kaname Shobo.

Ministry of Posts and Telecommunications (1975). *Tsuushin hakuso* (White paper on communications). Tokyo: Seifu Kankobutsu Sentah.

Ministry of Posts and Telecommunications (1982a). *Teijuu koso suishin no tameno joho ryutsuryo no chiiki kakusa ni kansuru chosa hokokusho* (A research report on information flows among different areas in Japan: A project for the promotion of land reallocation plans). Monograph.

Ministry of Posts and Telecommunications (1982b). *Shouwa 55 nendo joho ryutsu sensasu* (Information flow census: Fiscal 1980). Monograph.

Ministry of Posts and Telecommunications (1985). *Shouwa 59 nendo joho ryutsu sensasu* (Information flow census: Fiscal 1984). Monograph.

Naigai-sha (Ed.). (1930-1931). *Sogo jahnarizumu kohza* (Handbook of the study of journalism) (12 volumes). Tokyo: Naigai-sha.

Nakano, O. (1980). *Gendaijin no joho kodo* (Information behavior of modern man). Tokyo: Nihon Hoso Shuppan Kyokai (NHK bukkusu).

Nakano, O., & Hayakawa, Z. (Eds.). (1981). *Masukomi ga jiken wo tsukuru* (Mass media create events). Tokyo: Yuhikaku (sensho).

Nippon Electric Co. (1966). Internal report. Quoted in Research Institute, the National Association of Broadcasters in Japan (p. 278) (1969).

Nomura Research Institute (1969, April). Waga kuni ni okeru joho kiki sangyo no tembo (Prospect of information equipment industries in Japan). *Zaikai Kansoku,* 51-53, 55-58.

Okada, N. (1970). "Johoka shakai" no shakaigakuteki shakaishinrigakuteki mondaiten (Sociological and social psychological problems of "information societies"). *Shimbungaku Hyoron, 19,* 6-8.

Okada, N. (1981). Jiken to nyusu no aida (Between events and news). In O. Nakano & Z. Hayakawa (Ed.), *Masukomi ga jiken wo tsukuru* (pp. 19-41). Tokyo: Yukikaku (sensho).

Ono, H. (1922). *Nihon shimbun hattatsu-shi* (The history of Japanese newspapers). Osaka: Osaka Mainichi Shimbun.

Ono, H. (1947). *Shimbun genron* (Theories of Journalism). Tokyo: Tokyo-do.

Ono, H. (1960). *Kawaraban monogatari* (A tale of tile prints). Tokyo: Yuzankaku.

Onose, F. (1915). *Saishin jissai shimbungaku* (New practical studies of journalism). Tokyo: Uetake Shoin.

Research Institute, National Association of Broadcasters in Japan (Ed.). (1969). *Joho sangyo no shorai* (Future of information industries). Tokyo: Gendai jahnarizumu shuppan-kai.

Research Institute of Telecommunications and Economics (1968). *Sangyoka igo no shakai ni okeru joho to tsushin* (Information and communication in a post-industrial society). Monograph.

Research Institute of Telecommunications and Economics (1970). *Sangyoka igo no shakai ni okeru denki tsushin no yakuwari* (The roles of telecommunications in a post-industrial society). Monograph.

Research Institute of Telecommunications and Economics (1976). *Joho no nagare kara mita chiiki kaihatsu koka no bunseki* (An analysis of local development effects as viewed from information flow). Monograph.

Research Institute of Telecommunications and Economics (1981). *Joho tsushin niizu no kodo kagakuteki bunseki to chouki yosoku* (A behavioral scientific analysis of information and communication needs and long-term predictions). Monograph.

Research Institute of Telecommunications and Economics (1982). *80 nendai ni okeru johosangyo no kozo bunseki* (Structural analysis of information industries in the 1980s). Monograph.

Sanuki, T. (1970). Johoka shakaido no keiryo bunseki (Quantification of the degree of informationization). In Z. Katakata & T. Sanuki (Eds.), *Nihon no chishiki sangyo.*Tokyo: Daiyamondo-sha.

Shibata, S. (1969, September). "Johoka shakai-ron" no hihan (Criticism of information society studies). *Keizai Hyoron*, 55-70.

Shimizu, I. (1937). *Ryugen Higo* (Rumor). Tokyo: Nihon Hyoron-sha.

Shimizu, I. (1949). *Jahnarizumu* (Journalism). Tokyo: Iwanami Shoten.

Shimizu, I. (1951). *Shakai shinrigaku* (Social psychology). Tokyo: Iwanami Shoten.

Sugimura, K. (1915). *Saikin shimbunshi-gaku* (Contemporary journalism). Tokyo: Keio Gijuku Shuppan-kyoku.

Takeshita, T. (1983). Media gidai settei kasetsu no jisshoteki kento (Empirical considerations of the agenda-setting hypothesis). *Tokyo Daigaku Shimbun Kenkyujo Kiyo, 31,* 101-143.

Takeuchi, I. (1984). Terebi chukei wo meguru kozairon (Pros and cons regarding on the spot TV broadcasting). In T. Mizuhara & A. Tsujimura (Eds.), *Komyunikeishon no sha-kaishinrigaku* (pp. 113-128). Tokyo: Tokyo University Press.

Takizawa, M. (1972). A report at a symposium "Mass communication studies in Japan: Reviews and prospect." *Shimbungaku Hyoron, 21,* 71-75.

Takizawa, M. (1976). *Komyunikeishon no shakai riron* (Sociology of communication). Tokyo: Shinhyoron.

Tanaka, Y. (1969). *Komyunikeishon no kagaku* (Science of communication). Tokyo: Nihon Hyoron-sha.

Tokinoya, H. (1984). 1970 nendai iko no nihon ni okeru masu komyunikeishon no riron-teki jisshoteki kenkyushi (The history of theoretical and empirical studies on mass communication in Japan since the 1970s). *Shimbungaku Hyoron 33,* 179-190.

Tokutomi, S. (1891). *Shimbunkisha no san shokubun* (Three duties of journalists). Tokyo.

Toriumi, Y. (1973). Taigai kiki ni okeru shimbun roncho (Newspaper editorials at national crises). In Nihon Bunka Kaigi (Ed.), *Nihon ni okeru jahnarizumu no tokushitsu* (pp. 4-23). Tokyo: Kenkyu-sha.

Tosaka, J. (1929). *Kagaku hohoron* (Methodology of science). Tokyo: Iwanami Shoten.

Tosaka, J. (1931). *Ideorogi no ronrigaku* (Logics of ideology). Tokyo: Tetto Shoin.

Tosaka, J. (1932). *Ideorogi gairon* (On ideologies). Tokyo: Riso-sha.

Tsujimura, A. (1976a). Yoron to seiji rikigaku (Public opinion and political dynamics). In Nihonjin Kenkyu Kai (Ed.), *Nihonjin kenkyu, No. 4: Yoron towa nanika.* Tokyo: Shiseido.

Tsujimura, A. (1976b). *Shimbun yo ogoru nakare* (Warnings to newspapers). Tokyo: Ta-kagi Shobo.

Tsujimura, A. (1981). *Sengo nihon no taishu shinri* (Mass psychology in postwar Japan). Tokyo: University of Tokyo Press.

Tsujimura, A., Kim, K., & Ikuta, M. (1982). *Nihon to kankoku no bunka masatsu* (Cultural frictions between Japan and Korea). Tokyo: Idemitsu Shoten.

Tsurumi, S. (1965). Jahnarizumu no shiso (Ideology of journalism). In *Gendai nihon shiso taikei* 5. Tokyo: Chikuma Shobo.

Umesao, T. (1963, March). Joho sangyo-ron (On information industries). *Chuo Kohron*, 46-58.

Wada, Y. (1969). Meiji-Taisho-ki no jahnarizumu-ron (Journalism studies during the Meiji and Taisho periods). *Shimbungaku Hyoron, 18,* 70-75.

Wada, Y. (Ed.). (1980). *Shimbungaku wo manabu hito no tameni* (Introduction to journalism studies). Tokyo: Sekai Shiso-sha.

Yamada, M. (1975). Sengo nihon ni okeru masu komyunikeishon kenkyu no doko (Trends of mass communication research in postwar Japan). *Sogo Jahnarizumu Kenkyu,* 48-56, 73-74.

Yamamoto, A. (1962). Ideorogi toshite no jahnarizumu (Journalism as an ideology). *Doshisha Daigaku Jimbungaku, 61,* 25-44.

Yamamoto, A. (1969). Nihon jahnarizumuron-shi no ichi dessan (A historical sketch of Japanese journalism theories). *Shimbungaku Hyoron, 18,* 61-75.

Yamamoto, A. (1970). Comments at the symposium "Critical Review of Journalism." *Shimbungaku Hyoron, 19,* 124-129.

Yamamoto, A. (1974, March). Gendai shakai ni okeru nyusu no kinou (The functions of reporting in modern societies). *Shimbun Kenkyu,* 33-37.

Yamamoto, A. (1980). Idorogi (Ideology). In Y. Wada (Ed.), *Shimbungaku wo manabu hito no tamani* (pp. 45-47). Tokyo: Sekai Shiso-sha.

Yamamoto, S. (1977). *"Kuuki" no kenkyu* (A study of "kuuki"). Tokyo: Bungei Shunju-sha.

Yasukawa, S. (Ed.). (1875). *Eikoku shimbunshi kaimei kanki* (Newspapers in Great Britain). Tokyo: Shikoh-doh.

Yoshida, F. & Yamanaka, H. (1983). 1970 nendai ni okeru nihon no jisshohteki masukomi kenkyu no jokyo (The state of the art of empirical mass communication research in Japan during the 1970s). Unpublished paper delivered at the annual convention of the Japan Society for Studies in Journalism and Mass Communication held at Matsuyama City, Japan.

Yoshino, S. (Ed.). (1916). *Shimbun* (Newspapers). Tokyo: Minyu-sha.

3 ● Perceived Control: Foundations and Directions for Communication Research

DAVID A. BRENDERS

Indiana University

THE perception that one has some measure of personal control over the important areas of his or her physical and social situation has emerged as a fundamental prerequisite of psychological well-being and social adjustment (see Garber & Seligman, 1980; Langer, 1983; Lefcourt, 1973, 1981, 1982). More than two decades of research supports the proposition that the expectation that important life outcomes are attainable through personal effort is psychologically adaptive, and a belief in the primacy of fate, powerful others, or "the system" leads to maladaption and is characterized by various cognitive, motivational, and behavioral deficits (see Lefcourt, 1982). Although one's perception of personal control may or may not correspond to an objective appraisal of the way things actually are (see Langer, 1983) even a specious sense of control is in many situations more life enhancing than its absence. This state of affairs has prompted Lefcourt (1973) to remark that even if personal control or freedom of choice has been relegated to the status of "illusion" by the doctrines of modern behavioral science, it is nonetheless an *important* illusion in terms of its consequences.

Perceived control promises to be an important concept for the communication scholar as well. Many of the significant events in our lives are mediated by interpersonal interaction, and one's perceived control over the process and outcomes of interaction promises to be a powerful determinant of the quality and nature of one's interpersonal behavior. A theoretically coherent and empirically valid conception of perceived control of interpersonal interaction will add greatly to the theory, research, and praxis of human communication.

This chapter will review critically some promising evidence for a link

AUTHOR'S NOTE: I would like to thank Robert Norton, Brant Burleson, Joseph Rychlak, and Phillip Tompkins for helping to refine my thinking on these issues.

Correspondence and requests for reprints: David A. Brenders, Department of Speech Communication, 809 E. 7th St., Indiana University, Bloomington, IN 47405.

between perceived control and interpersonal behavior. Because the terms control and perceived control inhabit many psychological theories (see Bochner & Krueger, 1979; Collins, Martin, Ashmore, & Ross, 1973) and may be said to motivate any or all behaviors on some theoretical level of abstraction, no claim of exhaustiveness is made for this review. However, the following general claims can be supported in the literature of perceived control and should find greater support and elaboration within studies of the control of interpersonal interaction.

Perceived interpersonal control influences an individual's sense of psychological well-being. Situations that deny the application of interpersonal skills are demoralizing. Those who perceive little or no contingency between their behavior and interactional outcomes may be likewise demoralized (Garber & Seligman, 1980). Situations that promote expectancies for interpersonal control or the learning of outcome contingent interpersonal behaviors are in and of themselves "remoralizing" or therapeutic (Dweck, 1975; Lefcourt, 1973; Silver & Wortman, 1980).

Expectations for interpersonal control need not correspond with "objective" assessments of one's control over the behavior of another. How much verbal influence a person has exerted over the thoughts and feelings of another outside of the confines of the actor's mutual perceptions of influence may be a formally undecidable question (Bateson, 1968; Watzlawick, Beavin, & Jackson, 1967). This does not mean that individuals do not make assessments of how much they control the other or are controlled interpersonally, or the extent to which they are able to mobilize or restrain personal and environmental forces toward the end of influencing another (see Cialdini, Braver, & Lewis, 1974; Cialdini & Mirels, 1976). Given the formally undecidable nature of interpersonal causality and the ease with which persons may create illusions of control or incompetence (see Langer 1975, 1979), assessments of interpersonal control may be especially susceptible to the influence of contextual cues and the implicit control ideologies of the culture.

Interpersonal expectancies and outcomes become self-reinforcing cognitive/behavioral patterns. The social realities of those with various control expectancies become real in their consequences for future learning and performance. That is, those with positive expectancies for control of the interpersonal situation discover, through their efforts, the contingencies that make a difference in this situation. Those taking a more fatalistic or helpless orientation will chronically avoid the sort of encounters that would disconfirm their belief or behave in such a passive, defensive, or apprehensive manner that their belief is confirmed (Bateson, 1968; Jones, 1974; Watzlawick, 1984). Unless this expectancy-behavior-outcome pattern is strategically or serendipitously interrupted or undermined by outside forces, a style of interpersonal behavior will be maintained consistent with the initial "prophecy."

Expectancies for control via interpersonal interaction are an important component in the development and maintenance of competent communication patterns. Differential control expectancies will imply differential strategies for interpersonal goal attainment. Control expectancies should therefore correspond to characteristic patterns of interpersonal behavior. If one lacks the expectancy for interpersonal control, one may exhibit less proactive behavior and more reactive or self-debilitating behavior in situations where proactive involvement is usually rewarded. However, there may be a curvilinear relationship between perceptions of interpersonal control and social meshing. At one extreme, those with grandiose control beliefs may be personally effective but socially irritating. On the other end of the continuum, those experiencing a sense of social helplessness will be both psychologically depressed and socially withdrawn (see also Parks, 1985).

Despite converging areas of interest between the literatures of control and communication, the concept of perceived interpersonal control marks an area of reciprocal deficiency in the literatures of psychology and communication science. Although communication study can profit from the psychological literature of perceived control (see Berger & Metzger, 1984), the interpersonal sphere of behavior has received insufficient attention and elaboration in perceived control research (see Paulhus & Christie, 1981).

The current chapter is an initial step toward rectifying this deficiency. Toward this end, relevant issues in the literature of perceived control will be reviewed critically. This review will begin by identifying general issues concerning control as a culturally defined construct, trace the evolution of the construct of perceived control from the early social learning approach to locus of control, through multidimensional, multisituational, and multiattributional studies of control, to the more recent self-report and experimental work specifically concerned with the relationships between perceived control and interpersonal behavior. Future directions for communication research are then offered.

THE CONCEPT OF CONTROL

The concept of control pervades the vocabulary of psychology and communication study (Bochner & Krueger, 1979; Lefcourt, 1982). When currently used, the term *control* can mean practically anything from the ability to avoid electric shocks (see Garber & Seligman, 1980) to the "mindful process of mastering" (Langer, 1983). Control has been seen as an objective feature of the environment, a subjective feature of our experience, a proactive judgment that influences future behavior, or a culturally derived motive. The lack of personal control has been linked to a host of cognitive and behavioral deficits and embodies or contributes to the conditions of helplessness, powerlessness, alienation, anomia, and other social/psychological ills (see Lefcourt, 1982; Perlmuter & Monty, 1979).[1]

Because control is a highly variegated construct in everyday usage as well as in the vocabulary of social science, we will begin by examining the various cultural senses of the word control. As we shall see, perceived or ascribed control of interaction has active and passive aspects that more or less correspond with social benchmarks on various levels.

Cultural Senses of the Word Control

Psychologists Arnkhoff and Mahoney (1979) assert that persons commonly mean one of four things when they speak of personal control: skill, power, regulation, or restraint. We will want to add choice and autonomy to this list (see Langer, 1983; Sennett, 1980; Steiner, 1979). Some of these terms denote active manipulation of the environment and others denote the mastery of self, some refer to external resources and some refer to inner capabilities.

Although both power and skill refer to one's ability to change or manipulate one's environment, the term *control* also commonly refers to the ability to master the self (see Rothbaum, Weisz, & Snyder, 1982). This ability to control the self is often termed *restraint, reserve,* or *personal autonomy* (Arnkhoff & Mahoney, 1979; Sennett, 1980). These senses of the word are important because if they are neglected, one's definition of control is skewed toward overrepresenting extroversion or dominance and neglecting the ways that individuals seek external rewards by controlling the self. Personal restraint also may be viewed as a tactic in the active control of others. Control as restraint put to the service of modifying or neutralizing the behavior of others may be called *control by autonomy* (Sennett, 1980). Therefore, strategically withholding or restraining responses can serve the function of neutralizing the social power others potentially have over us and reasserting our dominance.

Sometimes even "giving in" to one's environment can be perceived as control. "Going with the flow" or "waiting for a lucky break" may sometimes be interpreted as mastering an otherwise intractable situation, at least from the actor's point of view, and not identical with "giving up" or relinquishing control. Rothbaum, Weisz, and Snyder (1982) have argued that when the usual primary methods of control by "changing the world" are ineffective, a person may achieve secondary control by "changing the self" to capitalize on the rewards that are available, and that this secondary control is preferable to personal helplessness. One asserts secondary control when he or she is able at least to predict the occurrence of disappointing events (predictive control), conform his or her reinforcements to the workings of chance (illusory control), identify self with powerful others (vicarious control), or render the situation understandable or meaningful (interpretative control) (Rothbaum, Weisz, & Snyder, 1982, p. 11). These directive aspects of otherwise "inward" behaviors describe ways that individuals manage to control reinforcements in situations of diminished opportunities, and persons may persist in them even when the environment permits greater active control (Rothbaum et al., 1982, p. 7). Thus such seemingly ill-advised behaviors as waiting for one's luck to change, surrendering oneself to some cause or leader, or expecting and preparing for the worst may be the cultural manifestations of the quest for secondary control of one's life, and preferable to the perception of no control at all.

Culturally speaking, personal control is a function of both the acquisition and utilization of social resources and the mastery of personal behavior. Beliefs regarding skill, power, regulation, restraint, and autonomy influence our self-perceptions and our perceptions of the competency of others. Those who lack sufficient skills are socially deficient, those who lack power are helpless, and those who lack restraint are either inadequately socialized or mentally ill. Those who perceive that they can and do manipulate these social and personal resources perceive that they are in control, and are usually perceived by others as being in control. The implicit cultural standard concerning control, a standard that makes these judgments possible, will be reviewed in the next section.

The Ideology of Control

Various authors have called attention to the difference between personal assessments of one's own ability to control events and the belief in the possibility or perceived normative ability to control these events. The former belief has been called a belief in *personal control* and the latter one's *control ideology*. A survey of these arguments reveals that the term *control,* whether personal or extrapersonal, has been used to refer to any one of four separate facets of the construct: 1) individual differences in terms of how much a person is influenced by personal versus environmental causes (PROACTION versus REACTION), 2) individual differences in persons' assessments of their personal control (PERSONAL SKILL, POWER, or EFFICACY expectancies or attributions), 3) individual differences in beliefs regarding the potential controllability of events across persons (BELIEFS IN INTERNAL VERSUS EXTERNAL CONTROL or that individual's CONTROL IDEOLOGY), and 4) differences in terms of one's assimilation of the culturally derived standards regarding control (CULTURAL CONTROL IDEOLOGY) (see Arnkhoff & Mahoney, 1979; Collins et al., 1973; Gurin, Gurin, Lao, & Beattie, 1969; Renshon, 1979). These four senses of the term form a kind of hierarchy of control beginning at the level of personal behavior, moving through levels indicating various beliefs, and ending with a superordinate cultural standard. In terms of beliefs, people may differ in terms of how skillful they perceive themselves to be, how much control they believe others can or do possess, and how much they subscribe to what their culture promotes as a normal or veridical belief regarding control.

There are also psycho-social states of affairs associated with the distance or lack of correspondence between the various levels of the hierarchy. Regarding control, the less distance there is between level 1 and 2, the more receptive or self-aware a person may be said to be. The greater the correspondence between level 2 and 3, the more a person will see himself or herself as competent, and a significant disparity between these levels will lead to self-perceptions of personal deficiency, incompetence, or personal disadvantage. The less distance between level 3 and 4, the more socially congruent or adjusted the person's beliefs will be.

The Salience of Control Beliefs

Despite the plethora of control-related terms and the variety of directions the concept of control may take, we are wise to consider how often persons are actually likely to utilize attributions of control in the determination of their attitudes or behavior. Berger and Metzger (1984) have remarked that in developing highly variegated personality variables we run the risk that "our verbal descriptions of these alleged processes may make persons seem to be more rational, active, and purposive than they actually are" (p. 289). Although there appear to be no firm answers to these issues, various control researchers have established general predictions concerning the salience of control beliefs.

Julian Rotter (1982) has hypothesized that two important factors influencing the salience of post hoc attributions of causality and expectancies for future control are the unexpected nature or novelty of the event, and whether or not strong reinforcements are associated with the event. That is, when we lack previous experience with an event, we are more concerned with issues of causality and control than when we are confronted with a familiar event (Rotter, 1982, p. 316). The impact an event has on us, especially when the effect is strongly negative, is also likely to provoke the generation of causal explanations. Taken together, the strength and novelty of a reinforcement provokes the search for causal reasons. Rotter (1982) also speculates that the formation and expression of causal attributions is mediated through our culture.

Ellen Langer (1983) has observed that to control events without the awareness of personal control is the same as the experience of no control. An individual who attends to the process of manipulating events in an active way experiences more of the facilitative effects of personal control than someone who achieves his or her ends through a stereotyped routine or mindless habit. Langer (1983) posits that personal control involves the "mindful process of mastering" rather than the uninvolved and/or totally uneventful production of outcomes.

According to this approach, persons are more likely to make control attributions or expectancies when habitual routine breaks down or there is some particularly important and uncertain challenge to be met. Control perceptions are salient in those relatively rare situations where important outcomes are met with less than certain methods of goal attainment. How much one can influence the process and outcomes of such situations becomes an important aspect of the nature of the event, and therefore a salient predictor of future behavior and of an individual's felt sense of mastery (Chanowitz & Langer, 1980, p. 107).

According to Langer (1983), one experiences the salutory effects of perceived control the more one 1) actively involves himself or herself in the task, 2) focuses on the *processes* involved in achieving a goal rather than merely executing stylized, outcome-centered behaviors, and 3) concerns herself or himself with situations not completely mastered, tasks that supply a challenge to one's skill.

To say that attributions of or expectancies for control are not always salient to an individual is not to say that they are unimportant. Over one thousand studies confirm that one's belief or lack of belief in personal control profoundly influences his or her attitude toward the self and the environment (see Lefcourt, 1982). To appreciate the potential relevance of personal control beliefs in determining behavior, we will examine the theory and research regarding a generalized expectancy for internal/external control as one aspect of the more general theory of human behavior that prompted it, the social learning theory of Julian Rotter (1954, 1966, 1975). Rotter's (1966) locus of control construct is the most theoretically elaborated and empirically verified conception of perceived personal control to date (see Lefcourt, 1982, p. 32). Therefore, we will use this formulation extensively in the sections to come.

SOCIAL LEARNING THEORY AND LOCUS OF CONTROL

Most of the research on perceived control has used the locus of control construct as the empirical vehicle of perceived control (see Lefcourt, 1982). However, the originators of this approach have warned that some of the research has misapplied the construct (Lefcourt, 1980; Rotter, 1975). Therefore, this section will be devoted to understanding the locus of control construct from within the general explanatory framework of social learning theory (Rotter, 1954; Rotter, Chance, & Phares, 1972). As many excellent reviews of the locus of control literature exist (Lefcourt, 1982; Phares, 1973) this material will be covered briefly.

In its most general formulation, social learning theory posits that, from within a specific psychological situation, a person's behavior is a joint function of how much an individual values various outcomes and his or her expectancy that certain behaviors will bring about these outcomes (Rotter, 1954). These two factors vary independently. One may not pursue a valued reinforcement if the expectancy of obtaining it is low. Likewise, outcomes that are not valued are not pursued even if one's expectation of producing them is high (Phares, 1973, p. 3). Thus for any particular situation, our behavior is determined both by the desirability of the outcome (need or reinforcement value) and our general estimation that we will be successful in our attempt (freedom of movement).

However, the perceived probability of success is not the only determinant of whether or not a person will pursue a valued goal. The forces to which a person attributes success and failure help explain the nature of the situation and how he or she should expect personal behavior and outcomes to be linked. Previous success attributed to luck leads to a different sort of future expectancy than does success due to skill. Therefore, freedom of movement is complemented by generalized expectancies for rewards in situations perceived as similar to the present one (GE), expectancies based on experience in the present situation (E'), amount of experience one has had in the situation (N), and one's expectancy for internal versus external control of the reinforcement, or "the extent to which [a person] believes that he controls the occurrence of such rewards (GE.E)" (Phares, 1973, p. 3).

Although freedom of movement deals with one's expectation for success, locus of control highlights a differential expectancy for control of the reinforcement.

> Perceived control is defined as a generalized expectancy for internal as opposed to external control of reinforcements. Like freedom of movement, it is an abstraction derived from a series of specific expectancy-behavior-outcome cycles. However, where freedom of movement concerns the likelihood of success, the generalized expectancy of internal versus external control of reinforcements involves a causal analysis of success and failure. (Lefcourt, 1982, p. 33)

Just as one's evaluation of specific encounters generalizes to become a more or less abstract expectancy for success or failure in certain need areas, one develops a generalized expectancy that these outcomes are related or unrelated to one's behavior. To the extent that a person does not perceive responsibility for the occurrence or nonoccurrence of some event, then it must be attributable to environmental factors such as natural forces, powerful others, fate, luck, or the like. Locus of control helps to shape one's expectancies for success in a particular situation by specifying the probable impact of personal effort or voluntary behavior on the eventual outcome.

Two observations are important for understanding the predictive role of locus of control within the framework of social learning theory. First, persons utilize both specific and generalized expectancies for control in determining the nature of the situation. If situational cues are explicit, they may override one's generalized expectancy for the control of reinforcements. Experience in the particular situation (E') helps to increase the relevance and explicitness of these cues (see Phares, 1973).

A second important consideration is that locus of control, like freedom of movement, does not predict behavior independently of need potential or reinforcement value. Locus of control is an expectancy variable rather than a motivational variable (see Lefcourt, 1966). Therefore, one needs to know the value of the outcome for the person as well as his or her probability for success and control to predict his or her behaviors (see Rotter, 1975). Behaviors may be inhibited because the reinforcement value of the outcome is low or one's freedom of movement is low as well as because the outcome is perceived to occur outside of the person's control.

Generalized expectancies, including expectancies for control, are most influential when specific expectancies are absent, as in novel or ambiguous situations. The more experience one has with a situation, the more one's specific expectancies for that situation overwhelm one's generalized expectancies. However, assuming that outcomes are determined by chance often results in self-fulfilling prophecies that preclude learning the "real" nature of the situation.

In general, studies of the I-E construct (see Phares, 1973, pp. 12-14) have indicated that internals are more willing to delay gratification (Zytkoskee, Strickland, & Watson, 1971), get more satisfaction from skilled rather than chance-related achievements (Schneider, 1972), adjust their expectancies in a more rational way after failure (upward after success and downward after failure) (Ducette & Wolk, 1972; Feather, 1968), suffer less from debilitative anxiety (Joe, 1971; Phares, Ritchie, & Davis, 1968), and display greater achievement motivation (Crandall, Katkovsky, & Crandall, 1965; Hersch & Scheibe, 1967; Strickland, 1972).

LOCUS OF CONTROL AS A MULTIDIMENSIONAL CONSTRUCT

There is an inevitable reflexive relationship between the theoretical rationale of the locus of control construct and instruments designed to assess individual differences in control orientation. Since the development of the Rotter I-E scale (see Rotter, 1966), a great deal of research has been done regarding the precise outlines of the construct domain of locus of control. Much of this research concerns the potential number and nature of various subdimensions of control. These subdimensions usually highlight one of three persistent issues in locus of control research: the type of reinforcement involved, the specification of agents of external control, and generalizability across reinforcement areas (Lefcourt, 1982, p. 171).

As Rotter (1966) conceptualized locus of control as a unidimensional construct, the I-E scale was designed to assess control beliefs over a wide variety of situations, but provide low predictability about control beliefs in any particular situation. Subsequent research has provided evidence for a variety of external "beliefs" as well as outcome dependent and situation specific locus of control expectancies (Collins, 1974; Collins et al., 1973; Lefcourt, 1976, 1979; Phares, 1979), often using as evidence factor analyses of modified versions of the Rotter scale. As these psychometric developments inevitably have affected subsequent research on locus of control, the findings of these and other researchers will be examined in detail.

Defensive Externality

Previous research on locus of control in success and failure situations (Davis & Davis, 1972; Gregory, 1978; Phares, Ritchie, & Davis, 1968; Phares, Wilson, & Klyver, 1971), has demonstrated that internals differ from externals in the ways that they handle the effects of successful and unsuccessful performance (Phares, 1973, p. 13). Internals tend to adjust their aspirations upward after success and downward after failure and externals do the opposite (Feather, 1968). Internals are less likely to blame others for failure (Phares, Wilson, & Klyver, 1971) and show a greater preference for skilled rather than chance tasks (Rotter & Mulry, 1965). This research suggests that internals should be more likely to show effort and motivation toward success than externals.

However, the relationship between locus of control and motivation is not a simple one. Phares (1973, 1979) contends that for some individuals, *avowed* external beliefs may serve a defensive function that is unrelated to an individual's motivation for success. That is, "defensive externality" may serve to attenuate the aversive effects of failure. Research thus far has demonstrated that defensive and congruent externals (those whose behavior is "congruent" with an external orientation) (DEs and CEs) differ in their level of interpersonal trust (Hochreich, 1968, in Phares, 1979) with defensive externals scoring lower on trust than congruent externals. Lloyd and Chang (1977, in Phares, 1979) found that defensive externals accept responsibility for success, but not for failure. Defensive externals are more likely to attribute their failure to the nature of the task, and prefer to perform tasks that easily permit such interpretations (see Phares, 1979).

The most satisfying explanation for the difference between defensive and congruent externality concerns differences in goal valuation coupled with expectancies for goal achievement. Therefore, the value of the goal in question may interact with one's expectancy for success in determining defensive versus congruent externality. The congruent external does not place a particularly high value on certain goals and therefore shows little motivation toward goal achievement. The defensive external either highly values the goal in question or expects to be evaluated on his or her performance on a socially valued goal. Given that he or she does not expect to be successful, the defensive external seeks a rationalization for failure and at the same time the attractiveness of the goal in question motivates him or her to attempt success.

Sources of External Control

One aspect of the dimensionality controversy surrounding locus of control involves the various potential sources of external control. In Rotter's (1966) original conceptualization, the various sources of external control (luck, chance, fate, powerful others, the world's complexity) are treated as if they were functionally equivalent. Research subsequent to the Rotter monograph has shown that respondents do indeed differentiate between the sources of external control (Lefcourt, 1976; Phares, 1979) and do vary their behavior based on the perceived source of external control.

Hersch and Scheibe (1967) compared locus of control to other personality constructs and concluded that although internals were fairly homogeneous with regard to their beliefs about control, externals were less so. As they state, "This finding suggests a diversity in the psychological meaning of externality" (p. 612). A good deal of subsequent research (Lefcourt, 1982) provides further evidence for the variability of external beliefs.

Much of the research conducted to assess the potential varieties of external control beliefs draws a distinction between the control of personal events and the control of political or social processes. The first attempt to distinguish between personal versus social control was conducted by Gurin et. al. (1969). These researchers distinguished between "personal control" and a person's "control ideology" or attitudes about how the society at large distributes rewards and how many of these rewards were under an average person's control. Gurin et al. contended that black and white Americans were likely to differ in their "control ideology," and stated that blacks were more likely to perceive that the societal reward process for blacks differed from that of whites. However, these differences in control ideology may not affect how individuals of different races perceive the contingencies inherent in strictly personal rather than socially mediated events.

Mirels (1970) has made a similar distinction between "personal" and "social system control," although this latter factor concerns the control of strictly political events. Reid and Ware (1973, 1974) incorporated the social system control factor into a tripartite distinction among system control, personal control, and self-control, or the control of inner desires and impulses. Reid and Ware found that such attitudes as political cynicism were predictable given the social system control factor but unrelated to either personal or intrapersonal control (Lefcourt, 1976, p. 133).

Although Reid and Ware (1974) and others distinguished between "the system" and the person in delineating control beliefs, Levenson (1973) distinguished among the self, chance, and powerful others as agents of control (Levenson, 1981). Levenson (1973) found that schizophrenics as well as those involuntarily admitted to mental hospitals were more likely to believe that powerful others controlled their lives than neurotic and depressed patients. Levenson speculated that "control by powerful others and control by chance forces dimensions reflect rather stable, meaningful orientations for maladjusted persons" (p. 403). Of potentially greater interest is the supporting finding that although a patient's internal control score increased after a period of hospitalization, his or her "chance" and "powerful others" scores tended to remain constant. This latter finding suggests that therapy under these conditions may increase a person's "personal efficacy" or "coping ability" without changing his or her overall beliefs about the nature of the social world. This finding is also supported by the work of Gilbert (1976), who found that, as a result of treatment, "clients regained control over their environment as opposed to having learned a different generalized perception of their world" (p. 308).

The most ambitious attempt to explicate the underlying dimensionality of the I-E scale has been conducted by Collins and his associates (Collins, 1974; Collins et al., 1973). Collins et al. (1973) contend that the Rotter locus of control scale confounds some useful distinctions posed by attribution theory. Specifically, a person may be consistently inner or outer directed independently of his or her locus of control orientation. The outer directed person need not also believe in fate or luck but may perceive and deftly manipulate environmental contingencies. From the analysis of their data, the authors concluded that "inner direction" and "other direction" were independent aspects of personality, and could therefore coexist in determining behavior. The two other factors uncovered were labeled "belief in the predictability of behavior" and "lack of socially imposed direction" (p. 490). The authors contend that persons with an internal locus of control correspond to specific *combinations* of these factors.

In another analysis of the Rotter scale, Collins (1974) describes further dimensions of the internal/external control concept. Factor analysis of this modified version of the Rotter scale uncovered four distinct control beliefs: (1) belief in a difficult/easy world, (2) belief in a just/unjust world, (3) belief in a predictable/unpredictable world, and (4) belief in a politically responsive world (pp. 385-386). Although there is some interdependence among the four control beliefs (that is, a person who believes the world is difficult and complex may be more likely to believe the world is unjust), these factors are relatively independent and combine to create various control beliefs.

Thus an internally oriented person not only attributes his successes to skill or perseverance but assumes that the environment consistently rewards the successful application of skill or perseverance. An internally oriented person can nonetheless lack the motivation to change an unjust or politically unresponsive world, and may be identified as external on measures that stress the control of political institutions. According to this analysis, a person may possess a sense of political or institutional cynicism and yet strive for success in daily affairs, or may even be motivated to change the system. In like manner, an externally oriented person may believe that the world possesses some sort of hypothetical order or lawfulness, but that this order is too complex or difficult to analyze and thus is out of the individual's control. This differs from a belief in luck in that although "complexity" and chance are functionally equivalent, belief in luck precludes the possibility of a better understanding of the situation in the future.

Multidimensional, Goal Specific Approaches

The research of Lefcourt, Von Baeyer, Ware, and Cox (1979) has attempted to integrate the attribution theory concepts of Weiner (1974) within a multidimensional, goal specific approach to locus of control. Their approach is operationalized in an instrument called the *Multidimensional-Multiattributional Causality Scale (MMCS)*. This scale has been shown to afford greater predictability of attitude and behavior within the goal areas that it specifically measures (Lefcourt, 1979; Lefcourt, 1981; Lefcourt, Von Baeyer, Ware, & Cox, 1979).

The most apparent difference between the MMCS and other locus of control scales is that the items on the MMCS differentiate between stable and variable attributions of causality (Weiner, Heckhausen, Meyer, & Cook, 1972), as well as between internal and external sources of control. As the term implies, stable attributions of causality are those that are resistant to change over time or do not vary from situation to situation. Thus a person's overall intelligence, because it does not vary from situation to situation, may provide a "stable" causal reason for a person's academic success or failure. On the other hand, the effort that one applies to an academic task may vary from situation to situation and thus supplies a variable attribution of causality for academic achievement. Both intelligence and effort are internal attributions, but attributing one's past failures to a variable cause such as insufficient effort may supply more motivation for future changes in performance than to attribute this failure to a stable and thus unchangeable cause (see Dweck, 1975). In order to utilize this distinction, the MMCS contains items relating to each of the four possible causal pairs of attributions: stable/internal, stable/external, unstable/internal, and unstable/external (Lefcourt et al., 1979, pp. 287-288).

Another important feature of the MMCS is that it is a goal-specific locus of control measure. In contrast to the Rotter I-E scale (1966), which was designed as a global measure of control beliefs (generalized expectancies), the MMCS samples control beliefs within a limited content area (specific expectancies). This specificity should increase the predictive power of the scale within predetermined content areas of interest (Lefcourt, 1980, p. 251; Lefcourt et al., 1979, p. 288). Currently, scales that measure control attitudes in academic achievement and social affiliation situations have been constructed and tested successfully for construct validity (see Lefcourt et al., 1979). Content specific measures are not new, and previous research attests to the utility of health-related and other specialized control measures (Reid & Zeigler, 1977; Wallston, Maides, & Wallston, 1976). However, the combination of goal specificity and varied attributional focus is unique to the MMCS.

A third factor incorporated into the MMCS is that items are balanced in their treatment of success and failure experiences. As previous research has shown that individuals may make different causal attributions for success and failure (Crandall, Katkovsky, & Crandall, 1965; Phares, 1973; Phares, 1979), the MMCS treats each situation separately. As the Collins et al. (1973) research reviewed previously supported the idea that internal and external attributions are relatively uncorrelated and therefore independent, the MMCS provides separate scores for internality and externality.

Another promising multidimensional approach to perceived control has been developed by Paulhus and Christie (1981) (see also Paulhus, 1983). These authors apply a "person × situation interactionistic" perspective to perceived control that highlights differential control expectancies given different "spheres of behavior." The sphere specific factors of their multidimensional inventory assess control of the nonsocial environment (personal efficacy), interaction with others (interpersonal control), or conflicts with the political or social system (sociopolitical control). Given that different expectancies for control may be associated with these spheres of activity, an accurate "control profile" for an individual would differentiate among these domains. For example, Paulhus and Christie (1981) provide evidence to suggest that Machiavellianism (Christie & Geis, 1970) combines sociopolitical cynicism with high expectations for interpersonal control (p. 170).

These authors also propose an intriguing facet analysis of the conceptual domain of perceived control (Paulhus & Christie, 1981, pp. 181-184). The facets included in this analysis are (1) *source,* whether control originates from the self or chance, fate or powerful others, (2) *sphere of behavior,* such as the efficacy, interpersonal, or sociopolitical spheres discussed above, (3) the *target* of control, whether self, other, or mankind, and (4) the *valence* of the situation, whether a success or a failure. Paulhus and Christie argue that the more focused multidimensional or multifactor control work to date has sought to elaborate one or more of these proposed facets.

This analysis also facilitates the parsimonious referencing of statements regarding perceived control into a mapping sentence containing the above four parameters and taking the general form X controls Y in situation Z (Paulhus & Christie, 1981, p. 182). This mapping sentence is composed as follows:

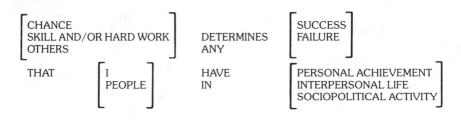

The mapping sentence generates 36 potential control statements that characterize a particular facet of the individual's control beliefs (p. 183).

LOCUS OF CONTROL IN INTERPERSONAL SITUATIONS

A great deal of research supports the notion that those who expect a measure of control over their environment behave in much more active, controlling, and rationally goal directed ways than those who do not possess this expectancy. "Internals"[2] both exert greater influence over their environment and are themselves less vulnerable to indiscriminate influence by others (Lefcourt, 1982, pp. 42-59; Phares, 1973, pp. 10-11). Although the influence of perceived control on interpersonal interaction has yet to be investigated fully, studies using both the Rotter scale (1966) and various goal specific measures have confirmed that perceived control does influence interpersonal behavior. Various measures of an expectancy for interpersonal control have appeared, either as components of multidimensional measures such as the Lefcourt MMCS (1979, 1981) or the spheres of control battery (Paulhus, 1983; Paulhus & Christie, 1981) discussed earlier, or as unidimensional measures of control in interpersonal interaction among adults (Deysach, Ross, & Heirs, 1977; Dudley, 1977; Lewis, Cheney, & Davies, 1977) or children (Dahlquist & Ottinger, 1983). Attribution researchers (Girodo, Dotzenroth, & Stein, 1981; Kelley, 1972) also have begun to explain how various causal attributions of self and other behavior affect the person's sense of control of interpersonal encounters and how these attributions influence his or her subsequent interpersonal style.

To date, research concerning perceived control and interaction has focused mainly on the areas of control and interpersonal influence, interpersonal assertiveness, and social sensitivity. Each of these areas will receive attention in subsequent sections.

Control and Interpersonal Influence

A good deal of research has shown that locus of control is an important variable in predicting a person's resistance to outside influence attempts (Biondo & McDonald, 1971; Crowne & Liverant, 1963; Doctor, 1971; Getter, 1966; Lefcourt, 1967; Lefcourt & Wine, 1969; Ritchie & Phares, 1969). From an integrated view of this research it is evident that the externally oriented person tends to comply in influence situations, and an internally oriented person resists influence in various and complex ways.

Gore (1962, cited in Lefcourt, 1982, p. 48) found that internal subjects resisted attempts at subtle persuasion by an experimenter who attempted to vary their responses to TAT (thematic aperception test) cards. Gore attempted to vary the length of the stories respondents produced in response to the cards by verbal suggestions that were in one condition "overt" and in the other condition "subtle." She found that although internals and externals did not differ in the length of their stories in the overt suggestion condition, in the subtle suggestion condition, internally oriented persons rebelled and produced the opposite of what was being subtly suggested by the experimenter. Lefcourt (1976) hypothesizes that these results suggest that although an internally oriented person does not mind being cooperative, he or she will respond negatively to attempts to manipulate him or her.

> If an experimenter conveys his expectations to a subject he may, in effect, be perceived as sharing his hypothesis with the subject, thus inviting the subject to join him in a curious objective attitude toward the criterion behaviors. This shared attitude would be one that expresses respect for the subject as a person rather than as an object to be manipulated and influenced. In contrast the "subtle coercion" described above pits experimenter against subject . . . [and] the internal resists being placed in positions where he is the pawn or "put down" so to speak. (Lefcourt, 1976, p. 42)

Other studies have confirmed and enlarged on this basic finding. Research by Getter (1966) and Strickland (1970) has shown that internals are more resistant than externals to experimenter control in verbal conditioning experiments. Those subjects who were both internally oriented and aware that the experimenter was attempting to reinforce certain behaviors resisted learning the proper response. However, during extinction trials these individuals did exhibit the "conditioned behavior," as if to indicate that they were not unteachable, merely uncooperative. Externals were more likely to cooperate consistently with the experimenter, whether aware of the conditioning or not (see also Brownell, 1982; Cravens & Worchel, 1977).

Ritchie and Phares (1969) found that externals were more influenced by the status of a source of information than were internals. Spector (1983) provides some correlational evidence to suggest that externals are more influenced by normative pressures to conform and internals rely on the information provided by the other. The findings of Lefcourt, Lewis, and Silverman (1968) seem to indicate that internals prefer their own interpretations of a task to those given by the experimenter. A study by Lefcourt and Wine (1969) produced similar results (see also Baron, Cowan, Ganz, & McDonald, 1974).

Not only do internals resist influence attempts from the outside more rigorously, they also appear to take more active participation in exerting influence over events in the world. Seeman and Evans (1962) found that internal patients in a tuberculosis hospital knew more about their condition and actively sought out more information from the staff than did externals. Seeman (1963) also found this link between information-seeking and internality among prison inmates. Gore and Rotter (1963) and Strickland (1965) found a positive relationship between internality and social activism among blacks. Phares (1973) interprets these findings to mean that internals are more active in determining their own outcomes.

> From the foregoing it seems clear that internals are more actively involved in influencing their world . . . those who score more toward the internal end of the dimension consistently adopt a more active, alert, and calculating posture with respect to their world. (p. 10)

A person's control orientation may also determine how he or she explains successful and unsuccessful attempts at influence. Cialdini and Mirels (1976) found that internals attributed higher intelligence to those who yielded rather than resisted their persuasive appeals, and externals made the opposite assessment. Thus internals and externals were moved to attribute characteristics to compliant and noncompliant others "consistent with [their] existing perception of personal competence" (p. 396). These results are consistent with a study by Levine and Uleman (1979) that suggests that internals and externals differ in their causal attributions for success and failure, externals being more likely than internals to attribute success to the workings of the environment and failure to the self.

However, internal locus of control does not generally equate with indiscriminate influence or verbal dominance. Preliminary research does suggest that perceived control performs an intervening role in determining when and how individuals assert themselves.

Locus of Control and Assertiveness

Available evidence suggests that internals are more confident in their ability to handle the contingencies that may occur in interpersonal encounters. Conversely, externals see themselves as more dependent on the good will of others and view their interpersonal situations as more mercurial and precarious.

Internals appear to be more trusting than externals. This increased trust has been linked to their greater belief in a just world (Nowicki & Blumberg, 1975), but may also correspond to their superior confidence in their own interpersonal abilities. Duke and Nowicki (1974) have shown that externals desire more distance between themselves and a stranger, and Rajeck, Ickes, and Tanford (1981) have shown that externals become more concerned about the intrusion of a stranger in unstructured settings and spend more time soliciting information from them. Rajeck, Ickes, and Tanford speculate that because externals have a low expectancy for control of this ambiguous situation, they solicit information in order to make the situation more predictable. A study by Lowe, Gormanous, and Kersey (1978) has shown that externals also report more social anxiety than internals.

Studies with uncooperative children (Bugental, Caporael, & Shennum, 1980) and untrained dogs (Valentine, 1978) have shown that persons with low expectancies for interpersonal control experience these situations as more unmanageable or uncontrollable and display fewer assertive paralinguistic cues than internals.

Although Hartwig, Dickson, and Anderson (1980) have reported that internals score higher on various measures of assertion than do externals, the link between perceived control and assertiveness is not a simple one. Bugental, Henker, and Whalen (1976) supported the hypothesis that given a low confidence in the outcomes of interaction, externals would indiscriminately employ more coercive power tactics than internals.

Of greater potential interest, Bugental, Henker, and Whalen (1976) revealed that internals and externals display characteristic patterns of verbal and vocal assertiveness. Externals, although verbally assertive, "leak" their lack of interpersonal confidence through low levels of vocal assertiveness. Conversely, internals show their social self-confidence through (paralinguistic) vocal cues of assertiveness. Although externals proved to be more verbally assertive in both unstructured and interpersonal influence tasks, internals proved to be more vocally assertive even when less verbally assertive. Thus internals send vocal cues congruent with their expectations but vary their verbal tactics to the requirements of the task. Externals, although more verbally assertive, betray a lack of confidence in the vocal channel.

A study by Emery and Axley (1982) provides some evidence that a person's locus of control orientation is reflected in his or her behavioral patterns of relational control. Married couples were shown to "vary their structuring of relational control statements depending upon the particular 'blend' of loci of control represented in the dyad" (p. 500). As married couples, internals and externals were shown to occupy congruent dominant and submissive roles in complementary (see Millar & Rogers, 1976) interaction patterns. This congruence between expectancies and relational behavior holds heuristic promise in light of the Heins (1978) contention that the marriages of depressed persons are often characterized by a struggle for interpersonal control, and the finding by Norton (1985) that ineffective marriages are marked by perceptions that one's spouse controls the relationship communicatively.

Doherty and Ryder (1979) have revealed that among newlyweds in a marital conflict situation, locus of control and interpersonal trust influenced the amount of assertiveness displayed. Specifically, internal husbands were more assertive than externals, and high trust external husbands were the least assertive, whereas low trust internal wives were the most assertive. In light of the Emery and Axley (1982) study, it is also interesting to note that "husband-wife locus-of-control combinations were not associated with differential levels of assertive behavior" (p. 2218).

Interpersonal Control: Extroversion and Shyness

In terms of desirability for long-term relationships, Nowicki and Blumberg (1975) have shown that both internals and externals find others with internal characteristics more attractive. Internals disclose personal information more easily, display more facilitative listening cues, and appear to be less daunted by a partner's unresponsiveness (Lefcourt 1981, pp. 257-265).

Perceived control of interpersonal situations also aids in minimizing the effects of negative life events, possibly acting as a buffer for debilitating anxieties and depression (Johnson & Sarason, 1978; Lefcourt, 1981). How persons attribute causes for social success and failure also influences their social self-esteem and subjective probability for success in heterosexual encounters (Girodo, Dotzenroth, & Stein, 1981). High levels of social self-esteem are associated with attributions of success to internal, stable causes like ability and failures to external unstable causes. Those with low social self-esteem show the opposite pattern, although they often report effort, an internal variable cause, as a reason for success.

The characteristic attribution style of the shy person helps keep him or her in a self confirming negative cycle.

> We might predict that if a shy person enters into a heterosexual social transaction with the expectation that he will not do well, should the outcome be successful, the chances are that it will be attributed to a variable cause, either effort or luck. While an effort attribution might increase self esteem, it would do little to increase self-confidence and reduce social avoidance. (Girodo, Dotzenroth, & Stein, 1981, p. 336)

The attribution style of the shy person with low social self-esteem leads him or her to develop low estimations of social success which, if disconfirmed, are attributed to causes other than personal ability. Therefore, success does not necessarily beget increased self-confidence.

All of the above research indicates that the locus of control variable has considerable construct validity and relevance to communication study (see also Berger & Metzger, 1984). Locus of control is a reliable indicator of various and important psychological and environmental variables, some of them (information seeking, compliance-gaining, and resistance to persuasion) directly relevant to interpersonal communication. In the following sections we will explore the implications of perceived control for communication research.

IMPLICATIONS OF PERCEIVED CONTROL FOR COMMUNICATION RESEARCH

The possible research directions open to the communication scholar interested in the relationships between perceived control and communication are multiform. As we have seen, expectancies for internal control characterize the discriminating receiver and producer of influence. In general, these findings suggest that perceptions of control help the person to act in proactive, goal directed ways as opposed to reactive, self-limiting, and self-diminishing ways.

Research has yet to uncover fully the *developmental antecedents, situational influences, behavioral correlates,* and *differential outcomes* associated with the expectancy for control in interpersonal situations. Specifically, a person by situation interactionist approach (Lefcourt, 1981, 1982; Naditch & DeMaio, 1975), one that incorporates personal goals and expectancies with salient environmental factors, will help to elaborate the necessarily reflexive relationships between control expectancies and communication behaviors. Such an approach will begin to answer such questions as how developmental factors influence a sense of interpersonal control, how situational cues reinforce moment-to-moment control expectancies, how ongoing control expectancies help to define and circumscribe communicative possibilities, and how these expectancies produce differential interaction styles and goal-directed verbal strategies (see also Berger & Metzger, 1984).

Previous sections have outlined the work already conducted in the areas of scale construction, interpersonal influence, communication "style" (that is, assertiveness), resistance to influence, and social sensitivity. This final section will highlight emerging or provocative areas of convergence between the construct of perceived control and communication research.

The Assessment of Interpersonal Control

As is evident from earlier sections, locus of control can be conceived as a global construct that summarizes an individual's overall control orientation with regard to multiform life goals and outcomes, a situation specific expectancy, or as a "sphere specific" expectancy (see Paulhus & Christie, 1981). Situation specific and sphere specific expectancies differ in that a situation specific orientation assesses expectancies for control in particular contexts, for example, work versus political participation (see Lefcourt, 1981); and a sphere specific approach assesses expectancies for control as they relate to particular spheres of activity, for example, activities that require interpersonal skills as opposed to those that require individual effort and concentration (Paulhus & Christie, 1981; Paulhus, 1983). Early work by Lefcourt (1979, 1981) with situation specific questionnaires, and by Paulhus and Christie (1981) with sphere specific assessments of control, provide evidence that both approaches may be valid for assessing an individual's specific expectancies for interpersonal control.

These approaches will be important to the communication scholar interested in interpersonal control because parsing out the contribution of locus of control in determining communicative outcomes will require assessment techniques appropriate to those outcomes. As situation specific control measures require validation and refinement (see Lefcourt, 1981, 1982), an opportunity exists for linking the special strengths of communication research with an undertaking that promises to uncover important determinants of psychosocial well-being.

A *caveat* is also in order. Given that situation specific or sphere specific techniques should yield more accurate predictive relationships than a generalized expectancy for control (see the section of this chapter on social learning theory), researchers in the area of communication and control should be aware that studies attempting to establish relationships between locus of control and communicative variables using global assessments such as the Rotter I-E scale (Rotter, 1966) may yield equivocal or misleading results. For example, because the Rotter scale places a great deal of emphasis on the individual's assessment of his or her perceived potential for political and societal input as an indicator of his or her locus of control orientation (Phares, 1973; Reid & Ware, 1974), variables such as political alienation or apathy become potential sources of internal invalidity when this scale is used to measure expectancies for control in other contexts (see Rotter, 1975).

Also, because the Rotter scale was designed to assess generalized expectancies for control, correlations derived between locus of control and communicative outcomes using this scale may be deceptively low. Such results need not discourage the communication researcher because, although the relationship between a generalized expectancy for control and a particular communicative variable may be low, this does not necessarily indicate that situation specific expectancies for control of the particular outcome may not yield a stronger and more interpretable relationship.

Interpersonal Influence

As research reviewed earlier has illustrated, a person's expectancy for control influences his or her preferred tactics for interpersonal influence. Perceived control in general and perceived interpersonal control in particular should help to further unravel differences in compliance gaining or power strategy selection (see Berger, 1985; Wheeless, Barraclough, & Stewart, 1983). For example, although it appears that externals use more coercive approaches (see the previous section on locus of control and assertiveness), we may find internals to be both more interpersonally flexible and more willing to persist in employing risky or socially undesirable behaviors. Internals may also be less daunted by early setbacks (see Lefcourt, 1981, pp. 257-265), the social power of the other, or situational cues suggesting comformity.

Previous research also has shown that internals and externals differ in the ways in which they accept or resist outside influence. This research suggests that a person's control orientation may influence his or her selection of strategies to resist the compliance-gaining attempts of others (McLaughlin, Cody, & Robey, 1980). Attention to the subtleties of control and influence (Lefcourt, 1982) and factors influencing perceptions of the other's control potential (Langer, 1975, 1983) will aid this investigation.

For example, Stewart, Kearney, and Plax (1985) hypothesized that internals and externals differ in their perceptions of the amount and type of classroom control exercised by teachers and their reported likelihood of resisting teacher influence. They found that "externally oriented students perceived their teachers engaging in significantly more control attempts in the classroom than did internally oriented students" (p. 701), but failed to find a difference between internals and externals in their reported likelihood of resisting teacher "behavior alteration tactics." This work indicates that internals and externals see the teacher-student interpersonal situation differently, at least in terms of teacher behavior. There are many intriguing reasons why this may be so (see previous sections on assertiveness and extroversion; also see Sandler, Reese, Spencer, & Harpin, 1983).

The failure to find differences between the internals' and externals' likelihood of resisting teacher directives is also interesting if not surprising given previous research in this area (see Lefcourt, 1982, p. 51). This work indicates that internals are not motivated to resist influence they consider legitimate or reasonable. Given that the "behavior alteration tactics" used in the Stewart et al. study are all legitimate teacher behaviors in at least some circumstances, there may be no *a priori* reason for internals to resist them.

Expectancies for control influence how individuals perceive various situations (see Lefcourt, 1982). This influence should generalize to the perception of interactive situations. Cody and McLaughlin (1985) have remarked that "individuals actively select situations that foster and encourage the behavioral expression of their own characteristic dispositions" and that locus of control should be one cognitive determinant of situation selection (pp. 268-269). Research on locus of control and situation structure and information utilization generally supports a *congruence* hypothesis (see Sandler et al., 1983). Therefore, internals should be motivated to seek out, exert greater effort in, and derive greater satisfaction from situations allowing personal control, while externals may seek more structured but less opportune environments. A person's control orientation also has been linked to greater receptivity to messages congruent with that orientation (see Sandler et al., 1983). Perceived control should influence the perceived situational appropriateness of various verbal behaviors as well. For example, Marston, Baaske, and Cody (1985) have demonstrated links between perceived control situation perception and selection of social influence tactics.

Situational and contextual cues also influence the potential salience of control expectancies and/or how much ongoing personal control is perceived (see Langer, 1983). This is especially true of novel or ambiguous situations. Because interpersonal behavior often produces ambiguous cues regarding causality (Bateson, 1968), one's perceptions of control may be both salient and nonveridical. Under these conditions, one's stable expectancy for interpersonal control can be expected to influence significantly how the situation is perceived, evaluated, and acted upon. Thus interpersonal control promises to become a key component in the formation of positive and negative interpersonal self-fulfilling prophecies (see Watzlawick, 1984), especially in unrepresentative or novel interpersonal encounters (that is, job interviews, conflicts, loss, or separation).

Situational cues indicating personal causality and interpersonal control also may be important factors in achieving unobtrusive influence or "spontaneous compliance" (Strong & Claiborn, 1982). As Strong and Claiborn (1982) note, "the key to effective relationship control is to induce the other to try to control us as we wish to be controlled" (p. 33). Creating variable impressions of autonomy and dependence, as well as selectively making the partner's behavior control-enhancing or control-diminishing, seem to be keys to this process.

Communicator Characteristics

Interpersonal control also promises to become a key predictor of a person's ongoing style of communicative behavior (see also Berger & Metzger, 1984). As we have seen, the evidence suggests that those with an expectancy for internal control can be expected to be more strategically dominant, socially self-confident, relaxed, attentive, and trusting than externals. These characteristics should result in different profiles on such characteristics as communicator style (Norton, 1983), predisposition to verbal behavior (Mortensen & Arntson, 1974), Machiavellianism (Christie & Geis, 1970; see Hunter, Gerbing, & Boster, 1982; Paulhus & Christie 1981, p. 170), rhetorical sensitivity (Hart, Carlson, & Eadie, 1980) and the like in ways that influence others' perceptions of the person's interpersonal competence, attractiveness, and credibility. Further work should refine the relationships between perceived control and variables affecting self-presentation.

The connections between individual expectancies for control and patterns of relational control (Millar & Rogers, 1976) deserve additional research scrutiny as well. Interpersonal control should be especially salient in marriages and other long-term relationships that incorporate reciprocal expectations for outcome and agenda control. Differential expectancies for the control of the marital relationship itself may influence partner communication behaviors and reflexively enhance or reduce relational satisfaction (see Doherty, 1983; Miller, 1981, in Lefcourt, 1982).

There are also important researchable links between interpersonal control and such impediments to communication as unwillingness to communicate, communication apprehension, and reticence (see Kelly, 1982; Leary, 1983a).[3] Social learning concepts such as reinforcement value and freedom of movement, as well as general and specific expectancies for control, may help to explicate and differentiate between these constructs (see also Leary, 1983a; Naditch & DeMaio, 1975).

A growing body of research supports the utility of a self-presentational approach to communication apprehension (Leary, 1983b; Schlenker & Leary, 1982). Self-presentation is both a product of interpersonal control and an influence on the number and kind of strategies available for interpersonal control. A deficient sense of control over some important social outcome will lead to anxiety, and the anticipation of a significant level of social anxiety may limit one's control options to defensive, "secondary," or image-protecting schemes (see Schlenker & Leary, 1982; Snyder, Smith, Augelli, & Ingram, 1985).

Interpersonal control should influence larger ongoing patterns of interaction as well. Given the Rothbaum, Weisz, and Snyder (1982) "two-process" model of control, those expecting little control over the events of their lives rarely develop the severe affective and motivational deficits associated with learned helplessness (Seligman, 1975) but rather pursue a life path based on "secondary" (that is, predictive, illusory, vicarious, and interpretative) strategies and goals. Persons expecting little primary control over their lives and/or interpersonal situations may have a different ongoing "interpersonal agenda" and expend more effort toward capitalizing on lucky breaks, seeking the aid and approval of powerful others, developing defensive explanations for potential social failures, or otherwise pursuing interpersonal strategies that permit some limited mastery of the situation. One's choice of primary or secondary, active or reactive paths to control may be determined by both personality and cultural factors (see Weisz, Rothbaum, & Blackburn, 1984). Because interactions between persons with discrepant control expectations are based on incompatible goals for the situation (for example, taking responsibility and changing the situation versus blaming the world or saving face), these "crossed" interactions may create their own sorts of misunderstandings.

Communication Competence

Given the potential role of perceived control in determining interpersonal influence strategies, communication style, and social self-presentation, perceived interpersonal control promises to occupy a central position in theories of communication competence. As Parks (1985) has stated, competence judgments are fundamentally involved with "cognitive and behavioral activities associated with personal control" (p. 175), and at the highest level of integration, involve the person's *assessment* of his or her control; therefore, Parks (1985) asserts that "any of a wide variety of measures that tap the individual's evaluation of his or her ability to exert control (e.g. self-esteem, communication apprehension, perceived control, satisfaction, and helplessness) should also measure communicative competence to some degree" (p. 186). Although the exact relationships of generalized and interaction-specific expectancies for control and competence have yet to be determined precisely, it is interesting to note that some hallmarks of Parks's conception of the competent communicator, such as "the ability to react to failure in a way that promotes satisfaction in the future" (p. 187), are also fundamental characteristics of those with an internal locus of control (Ducette & Wolk, 1972).

In general, perceived control should both influence and be influenced by how students learn communication skills. The student's characteristic control profile should prove to influence what is learned in communication classes and/or generalized to behavior. Likewise, teaching communication skills effectively may necessarily involve reinforcing the perceived control and efficacy enhancing potential of the material for students.

As may now be apparent, the construct of perceived control has a broad and as yet untapped potential for enriching the theory, research, and practice of interpersonal communication. Interpersonal control may be especially relevant in educational and health care settings. Future research is likely to yield results of great theoretical and practical significance.

NOTES

1. In the interest of brevity, the extensive literature of learned helplessness, powerlessness, alienation, and anomia will not be reviewed here. For an insightful review of the various facets of learned helplessness, see Garber and Seligman (1980). The attributional approach to helplessness is applied to communication problems in Parks (1985).

2. As Rotter (1975) and Lefcourt (1980) have pointed out, locus of control is not a typology. Therefore, it is not entirely accurate to refer to persons as "internals" or "externals." When the terms are used in this essay, please read them as a shorthand expression for "those espousing internal/external beliefs that are noticeably beyond the norm."

3. See Parks (1985) for a learned helplessness approach to communication apprehension.

REFERENCES

Arnkhoff, D., & Mahoney, M. (1979). The role of perceived control in psychopathology. In L. Perlmuter & R. Monty (Eds.), *Choice and perceived control* (pp. 155-174). Hillsdale, NJ: Lawrence Erlbaum.

Baron, R. M., Cowan, G., Ganz, R. L., & McDonald, M. (1974). Interaction of locus of control and type of performance feedback: Considerations of external validity. *Journal of Personality and Social Psychology, 30,* 285-292.

Bateson, G. (1968). Conventions of communication: Where validity depends upon belief. In J. Ruesch & G. Bateson (Eds.), *Communication: The social matrix of psychiatry* (pp. 212-227). New York: Norton.

Berger, C. R. (1985). Social power and interpersonal communication. In M. L. Knapp & G. R. Miller (Eds.), *Handbook of interpersonal communication* (pp. 439-499). Beverly Hills, CA: Sage.

Berger, C., & Metzger, N. (1984). The functions of human communication in developing, maintaining, and altering selfimage. In C. Arnold & J. Bowers (Eds.), *Handbook of rhetorical and communication theory* (pp. 273-337). Boston: Allyn & Bacon.

Biondo, J., & MacDonald, A. P. (1971) Internal-external locus of control and response to influence attempts. *Journal of Personality, 39,* 407-419.

Bochner, A., & Krueger, D. (1979). Interpersonal communication theory and research: An overview of inscrutable epistemologies and muddled concepts. In D. Nimmo (Ed.), *Communication Yearbook 3* (pp. 197-211). New Brunswick, NJ: Transaction Books.

Brownell, P. (1982). The effects of personality-situation congruence in a managerial context: Locus of control and budgetary participation. *Journal of Personality and Social Psychology, 42,* 753-763.

Bugental, D. B., Caporael, L., & Shennum, W. A. (1980). Experimentally produced child uncontrollability: Effects on the potency of adult communication patterns. *Child development,* 51, 520-528.

Bugental, D. B. Henker, B., & Whalen, C. (1976). Attributional antecedents of verbal and vocal assertiveness. *Journal of Personality and Social Psychology, 34,* 405-411.

Chanowitz, B. & Langer, E. (1980). Knowing more (or less) than you can show: Understanding control through the mindlessness-mindfulness distinction. In J. Garber & M. Seligman (Eds.), *Human helplessness: Theory and applications* (pp. 97-129). New York: Academic Press.

Christie, R., & Geis, F. (1970). *Studies in Machiavellianism.* New York: Academic Press.

Cialdini, R. B., Braver, S. L., & Lewis, S. K. (1984). Attributional bias and easily persuaded other. *Journal of Personality and Social Psychology, 30,* 631-637.

Cialdini, R. B., & Mirels, H. L. (1976). Sense of personal control and attributions about yielding and resisting persuasion targets. *Journal of Personality and Social Psychology, 33,* 395-402.

Cody, M. J., & McLaughlin, M. L. (1985). The situation as a construct in interpersonal communication research. In M. L. Knapp & G. R. Miller (Eds.), *Handbook of interpersonal communication* (pp. 263-312). Beverly Hills, CA: Sage.

Collins, B. (1974). Four separate components of the Rotter I-E scale: Belief in a just world, a predictable world, a difficult world and a politically responsive world. *Journal of Personality and Social Psychology, 29,* 381-391.

Collins, B., Martin, J., Ashmore R., & Ross, L. (1973). Some dimensions of the internal external metaphor in theories of personality. *Journal of Personality, 41,* 471-492.

Crandall, V. C., Katkovsky, W., & Crandall, V. J. (1965). Children's belief in their control of reinforcements in intellectual-academic achievement situations. *Child Development, 36,* 91-109.

Cravens, R. W., & Worchel, P. (1977). The differential effects of rewarding and coercive leaders on group members differing in locus of control. *Journal of Personality, 45,* 150-168.

Crowne, D. P., & Liverant, S. (1963). Conformity under varying conditions of personal commitment. *Journal of Abnormal and Social Psychology, 66,* 547-555.

Dahlquist, L. M., & Ottinger, D. R. (1983). Locus of control and peer status: A scale for children's perceptions of social interaction. *Journal of Personality Assessment, 47,* 278-287.

Davis, W. L., & Davis, D. E. (1972). Internal-external control and attribution of responsibility for success and failure. *Journal of Personality, 40,* 123-136.

Deysach, R., Ross, A., & Hiers, T. (1977). Locus of control in prediction of counselor effectiveness within a therapeutic camp setting. *Journal of Clinical Psychology, 33,* 273-278.

Doctor, R. (1971). Locus of control of reinforcement and responsiveness to social influence. *Journal of Personality, 39,* 542-551.

Doherty, W. J. (1983). Locus of control and marital interaction. In H. M. Lefcourt (Ed.), *Research with the locus of control construct, Vol. 2: Developments and social problems* (pp. 155-183). New York: Academic Press.

Doherty, W. J., & Ryder, R. G. (1979). Locus of control, interpersonal trust and assertive behavior among newlyweds. *Journal of Personality and Social Psychology, 37,* 2212-2220.

Ducette, J., & Wolk, S. (1972). Locus of control and extreme behavior. *Journal of Consulting and Clinical Psychology, 39,* 253-258.

Dudley, G. (1977). Predicting interpersonal behavior from a measure of expectancy for interpersonal control. *Psychological Reports, 41,* 3, 1223-1230.

Duke, M. P., & Nowicki, S. (1974). Locus of control and achievement—the confirmation of a theoretical expectation. *Journal of Psychology, 87,* 263-267.

Dweck, C. S. (1975). The role of expectations and attributions on the alleviation of learned helplessness. *Journal of Personality and Social Psychology 31,* 674-685.

Emery, D., & Axley, S. R. (1982). Marital interaction: Perceptions and behavioral implications of control. In M. Burgoon (Ed.), *Communication Yearbook 6* (pp. 489-505). Beverly Hills, CA: Sage.

Feather, N. T. (1968). Valence of outcome and expectations of success in relation to task difficulty and locus of control. *Journal of Personality and Social Psychology, 7,* 372-386.

Frank, J. D. (1974). *Persuasion and healing: A comparative study of psychotherapy.* New York: Schocken.

Garber, J., & Seligman, M. E. P. (1980). *Human helplessness: Theory & applications.* New York: Academic Press.

Getter, H. (1966). A personality determinant of verbal conditioning. *Journal of Personality, 34,* 397-405.

Gilbert, L. (1976). Situational factors and the relationship between locus of control and psychological adjustment. *Journal of Counseling Psychology, 23,* 302-309.

Girodo, M., Dotzenroth, S., & Stein, S. (1981). Causal attribution bias in shy males: Implications for self esteem and self confidence. *Cognitive Therapy and Research, 5,* 325-338.

Goodstadt, B. E., & Hjelle, L. A. (1973). Power to the powerless: Locus of control and the uses of power. *Journal of Personality and Social Psychology, 27,* 190-196.

Gore, P. S., & Rotter, J. B. (1963). A personality correlate of social action. *Journal of Personality, 31,* 58-64.

Gregory, W. L. (1978). Locus of control for positive and negative outcomes. *Journal of Personality and Social Psychology, 36,* 840-849.

Gurin, P., Gurin, G., Lao, R., & Beatie, M. (1969). Internal-external control in the motivation dynamics of negro youth. *Journal of Social Issues, 25,* 29-53.

Harré, R. (Ed.). (1976). *Life sentences: Aspects of the social role of language.* New York: John Wiley.

Hart, R. R., Carlson, R. E., & Eadie, W. F. (1980). Attitudes toward communication and the assessment of rhetorical sensitivity. *Communication Monographs, 47,* 1-22.

Hartwig, W. H., Dickson, A. L., & Anderson, H. H. (1980). Locus of control and assertion. *Psychological Reports, 46,* 1345-1346.

Heins, T. (1978). Marital interaction in depression. *Australian and New Zealand Journal of Psychiatry, 12,* 269-275.

Hersch, P. D., & Scheibe, K. E. (1967). On the reliability and validity of internal-external control as a personality dimension. *Journal of Consulting Psychology, 31,* 609-613.

Hill, D. J., & Bale, R. M. (1981). Measuring beliefs about where psychological pain originates and who is responsible for its alleviation: Two new scales for clinical researchers. In H. Lefcourt (Ed.), *Research with the locus of control construct; Vol. 1, Assessment methods* (pp. 281-320). New York: Academic Press.

Hunter, J. E., Gerbing, D. W., & Boster, F. J. (1982). Machiavellian beliefs and personality: Construct invalidity of the machiavellian dimension. *Journal of Personality and Social Psychology, 43,* 1293-1305.

Joe, V. C. (1971). A review of the internal-external control construct as a personality variable. *Psychological Reports, 28,* 619-640.

Johnson, J. H., & Sarason, I. G. (1978). Life stress, depression, and anxiety: Internal-external control as a moderator variable. *Journal of Psychosomatic Research, 22,* 205-208.

Jones, R. A. (1974). *Self fulfilling prophecies: Social, psychological, & physiological effects of expectancies.* New York: Halsted.

Kelley, H. H. (1972). *Causal schemata and the attribution process.* New York: General Learning Press.

Kelly, L. (1982). A rose by any other name is still a rose: A comparative analysis of reticence, communication apprehension, unwillingness to communicate, and shyness. *Human Communication Research, 8,* 99-113.

Langer, E. (1975). The illusion of control. *Journal of Personality and Social Psychology, 32,* 311-328.

Langer, E. (1979). The illusion of incompetence. In L. Perlmuter & R. Monty (Eds.), *Choice and perceived control.* Hillsdale, NJ: Lawerence Erlbaum.

Langer, E. (1983). *The psychology of control.* Beverly Hills, CA: Sage.

Larsen, K. S., Triplett, J., Brant, W. D., & Langenberg, D. (1979). Collaborator status, subject characteristics and conformity in the asch paradigm. *Journal of Social Psychology, 108,* 259-263.

Leary, M. R. (1983a). The conceptual distinctions are important: Another look at communication apprehension and related constructs. *Human Communication Research, 10,* 305-312.

Leary, M. R. (1983b). *Understanding social anxiety: Social, personality and clinical perspectives.* Beverly Hills, CA: Sage.

Lefcourt, H. M. (1966). Internal-external control of reinforcement: A review. *Psychological Bulletin, 65,* 206-220.

Lefcourt, H. M. (1967). The effects of cue explication upon persons maintaining external control expectancies. *Journal of Personality and Social Psychology, 5,* 372-378.

Lefcourt, H. M. (1973). The functions of the illusions of control and freedom. *American Psychologist, 28,* 417-425.

Lefcourt, H. M. (1976). *Locus of control: Current trends in theory and research.* Hillsdale, NJ: Lawrence Erlbaum.

Lefcourt, H. M. (1979). Locus of control for specific goals. In L. Perlmuter & R. Monty (Eds.), *Choice and perceived control* (pp. 209-220). Hillsdale, NJ: Lawrence Erlbaum.

Lefcourt, H. M. (1980). Personality and locus of control. In J. Garber & M. Seligman (Eds.), *Human helplessness: Theory and applications* (pp. 245-259). New York: Academic Press.

Lefcourt, H. M. (Ed.). (1981). *Research with the locus of control construct: Vol. 1, Assessment methods.* New York: Academic Press.

Lefcourt, H. M. (1982). *Locus of control: Current trends in theory and research* (2nd ed.). Hillsdale, NJ: Lawrence Erlbaum.

Lefcourt, H. M., Lewis, L. E., & Silverman, I. W. (1968). Internal versus external control of reinforcement and attention in decision-making tasks. *Journal of Personality, 36,* 633-682.

Lefcourt, H. M., & Wine, J. (1969). Internal versus external control of reinforcement and the deployment of attention in experimental situations. *Canadian Journal of Behavioral Science, 1,* 167-181.

Lefcourt, H. M., Von Baeyer, C., Ware, E. E., & Cox, D. (1979). The multidimensional-multiattributional causality scale. *Canadian Journal of Behavioral Science, 11,* 286-304.

Levenson, H. (1973). Multidimensional locus of control in psychiatric patients. *Journal of Consulting and Clinical Psychology, 41,* 397-404.

Levenson, H. (1981). Differentiating among internality, powerful others and chance. In H. Lefcourt (Ed.), *Research with the locus of control construct: Vol. 1, Assessment methods* (pp. 15-63). New York: Academic Press.

Levine, R., & Uleman, J. S. (1979). Perceived locus of control, chronic self-esteem, and attributions to success and failure. *Personality and Social Psychology Bulletin, 5,* 69-72.

Lewis, P., Cheney, T., & Davies, A. S. (1977). Locus of control of interpersonal relationships questionnaire. *Psychological Reports, 41,* 507-510.

Lowe, W. C., Gormanous, G. K., & Kersey, R. (1978). Self-consciousness and locus of control. *Perceptual and Motor Skills, 46,* 801-802.

Marston, P. J., Baaske, K., & Cody, M. J. (1985). *Locus of control and the social influence process.* Unpublished manuscript, University of Southern California.

McLaughlin, M. L., Cody, M. J., & Roby, C. S. (1980). Situational influences on the selection of strategies to resist compliance-gaining attempts. *Human Communication Research, 7,* 14-36.

Millar, F. E., & Rogers, L. E. (1976). A relational approach to inter-personal communication. In G. Miller (Ed.), *Explorations in interpersonal communication* (pp. 87-103). Beverly Hills, CA: Sage.

Mirels, H. C. (1970). Dimensions of internal versus external control. *Journal of Consulting and Clinical Psychology, 36,* 40-44.

Mortensen, D., & Arntson, P. (1974). The effects of predispositions toward verbal behavior on interaction patterns in dyads. *Quarterly Journal of Speech, 61,* 421-430.

Naditch, M., & DeMaio, T. (1975). Locus of control and competence. *Journal of Personality, 43,* 541-559.

Norton, R. W. (1983). *Communicator style: Theory, applications, and measures.* Beverly Hills, CA: Sage.

Norton, R. W. (1985). *Perceived interactive behaviors of a quality marriage.* Unpublished manuscript, Purdue University.

Nowicki, S., & Blumberg, N. (1975). The role of locus of control of reinforcement in interpersonal attraction. *Journal of Research in Personality, 9,* 48-56.

Parks, M. R. (1985). Communication and the quest for personal competence. In M. L. Knapp & G. R. Miller (Eds.), *Handbook of interpersonal communication* (pp. 171-201). Beverly Hills, CA: Sage.

Paulhus, D. (1983). Sphere-specific measures of perceived control. *Journal of Personality and Social Psychology, 44,* 1253-1265.

Paulhus, D., & Christie, R. (1981). Spheres of control: An interactionist approach to assessment of perceived control. In H. Lefcourt (Ed.), *Research with the locus of control construct: Vol. 1, Assessment methods* (pp. 161-188). New York: Academic Press.

Perlmuter, L., & Monty, R. (1979). *Choice and perceived control.* Hillsdale, NJ: Lawerence Erlbaum.

Phares, E. J. (1973). *Locus of control: A personality determinant of Behavior.* Morristown, NJ: General Learning Press.

Phares, E. J. (1979). Defensiveness and perceived control. In L. Perlmuter & R. Monty (Eds.), *Choice and perceived control* (pp. 195-208). Hillsdale, NJ: Lawrence Erlbaum.

Phares, E. J., Ritchie, D. E., & Davis, W. L. (1968). Internal-external control and reaction to threat. *Journal of Personality and Social Psychology, 10,* 402-405.

Phares, E. J., Wilson, K. G., & Klyver, N. W. (1971). Internal-external control and the attribution of blame under neutral and distractive conditions. *Journal of Personality and Social Psychology, 18,* 282-289.

Rajeck, D. W., Ickes, W., & Tanford, S. (1981). Locus of control and reactions to strangers. *Personality and Social Psychology Bulletin, 7,* 282-289.

Reid, D. W., & Ware, E. (1973). Multidimensionality of internal-external control: Implications for past and future research. *Canadian Journal of Behavioral Science, 5,* 264-271.

Reid, D. W., & Ware, E. (1974). Multidimensionality of internal versus external control: Addition of a third dimension and non distinction of self versus others. *Canadian Journal of Behavioral Science, 6,* 131-142.

Reid, D. W., & Zeigler, M. (1977). A survey of the reinforcement and activities elderly citizens feel are important for their general happiness. *Essence, 2,* 5-24.

Renshon, S. (1979). The need for personal control in political life: Origins, dynamics, and implications. In L. Perlmuter & R. Monty (Eds.), *Choice and perceived control* (pp. 41-63). Hillsdale, NJ: Lawerence Erlbaum.

Ritchie, E., & Phares, E. J. (1969). Attitude change as a function of internal-external control and communicator status. *Journal of Personality, 37,* 429-433.

Rodin, J., & Langer, E. (1977). Long term effects of a control-relevant intervention with the institutionalized aged. *Journal of Personality and Social Psychology, 35,* 897-902.

Rothbaum, F., Weisz, H., & Snyder, S. (1982). Changing the world and changing the self: A two process model of perceived control. *Journal of Personality and Social Psychology, 42,* 5-37.

Rotter, J. B. (1954). *Social learning and clinical psychology.* Englewood Cliffs, NJ: Prentice-Hall.

Rotter, J. B. (1966). Generalized expectancies for internal versus external control of reinforcement. *Psychological Monographs, 80,* (Whole No. 609).

Rotter, J. B. (1975). Some problems and misconceptions related to the construct of internal vs. external control of reinforcement. *Journal of Consulting and Clinical Psychology, 48,* 56-67.

Rotter, J. B. (1982). *The development and applications of social learning theory: Selected papers.* New York: Praeger.

Rotter, J. B., Chance, J. E., & Phares, E. J. (1972). *Applications of a social learning theory of personality.* New York: Holt, Reinhart & Winston.

Rotter, J. B., & Mulry, R. C. (1965). Internal versus external control of reinforcements and decision time. *Journal of Personality and Social Psychology, 2,* 598-604.

Sandler, I., Reese, F., Spencer, L., & Harpin, P. (1983). Person x environment interaction and locus of control: Laboratory, therapy, and classroom studies. In H. M. Lefcourt (Ed.), *Research With The Locus of Control Construct: Vol 2, Developments and Social Problems* (pp. 187-251). New York: Academic Press.

Schlenker, B. R., & Leary, M. R. (1982). Social anxiety and self-presentation: A conceptualization and model. *Psychological Bulletin, 92* (3), 641-669.

Schneider, J. M. (1972). Relationship between locus of control and activity preferences: Effects of masculinity, activity, and skill. *Journal of Consulting and Clinical Psychology, 38,* 225-230.

Seeman, M. (1963). Alienation and social learning in a reformatory. *American Journal of Sociology, 69,* 270-284.

Seeman, M., & Evans, J. W. (1962). Alienation and learning in a hospital setting. *American Sociological Review, 27,* 772-783.

Seligman, M. E. P. (1975). *Helplessness: On depression, development, and death.* San Francisco, CA: Freeman.

Sennett, R. (1980). *Authority.* New York: Vintage.

Silver, R. L., & Wortman, C. B. (1980). Coping with undesirable life events. In J. Garber & M. E. P. Seligoran (Eds.), *Human helplessness: Theory and applications* (pp. 279-340). New York: Academic Press.

Snyder, C. R., Smith, T. W., Augelli, R. W., & Ingram, R. E. (1985). On the self-serving function of social anxiety: Shyness as a self-handicapping strategy. *Journal of Personality and Social Psychology, 48,* 970-980.

Spector, P. E. (1983). Locus of control and social influence susceptibility: Are externals normative or informational conformers? *The Journal of Psychology, 115,* 199-201.

Steiner, I. (1979). Three kinds of reported choice. In L. Perlmuter & R. Monty (Eds.), *Choice and perceived control* (pp. 17-27). Hillsdale, NJ: Lawerence Erlbaum.

Stewart, R. A., Kearney, P., & Plax, T. G. (1985). Locus of control as a mediator: A study of college students' reactions to teachers' attempts to gain compliance. In M. L. McLaughlin (Ed.), *Communication Yearbook 9* (pp. 691-704). Beverly Hills, CA: Sage.

Strickland, B. R. (1965). The prediction of social action from a dimension of internal-external control. *Journal of Social Psychology, 66,* 353-358.

Strickland, B. R. (1970). Individual differences in verbal conditioning, extinction, and awareness. *Journal of Personality, 38,* 364-378.

Strickland, B. R. (1972). Delay of gratification as a function of race of the experimenter. *Journal of Personality and Social Psychology, 22,* 108-112.

Strong, S. R., & Claiborn, C. D. (1982). *Change through interaction: Social psychological processes of counseling and psychotherapy.* New York: John Wiley.

Sullivan, C. F., & Reardon, K. K. (1985). Social support satisfaction and health locus of control: Discriminators of breast cancer patients' styles of coping. In M. L. McLaughlin (Ed.), *Communication Yearbook 9* (pp. 707-722). Beverly Hills, CA: Sage.

Valentine, M. (1978). Actual and perceived control during canine-human interactions. *Journal of Social Psychology, 106,* 25-36.

Valins, S., & Nisbett, R. E. (1971). *Attribution processes in the development and treatment of emotional disorders.* Morristown, NJ: General Learning Press.

Wallston, K. A., Maides, S., & Wallston, B. S. (1976). Health related information seeking as a function of health related locus of control and health value. *Journal of Research in Personality, 10,* 215-222.

Wallston, K. A., & Wallston, B. S. (1981). Health locus of control scales. In H. M. Lefcourt (Ed.), *Research With The Locus of Control Construct: Vol. I, Assessment Methods* (pp. 189-243). New York: Academic Press.

Watzlawick, P. (Ed.). (1984). *The invented reality.* New York: Norton.

Watzlawick, P., Beavin, J., & Jackson, D. (1967). *The pragmatics of human communication.* New York: Norton.

Weiner, B. (1974). Achievement motivation as conceptualized by an attribution theorist. In B. Weiner (Ed.), *Achievement motivation and attribution theory* (pp. 3-48). New York: General Learning Press.

Weiner, B., Heckhausen, H., Meyer, W., & Cook, R. E. (1972). Causal ascriptions and achievement behavior: A conceptual analysis of locus of control. *Journal of Personality and Social Psychology, 21,* 239-248.

Weisz, J. R., Rothbaum, F. M., & Blackburn, T. C. (1984). Standing out and standing in: The psychology of control in America and Japan. *American Psychologist, 39,* 955-969.

Wheeless, L. R., Barraclough, R. A., & Stewart, R. A. (1983). Compliance-gaining and power in persuasion. In R. Bostrom (Ed.), *Communication Yearbook 7* (pp. 105-145). Beverly Hills, CA: Sage.

Zytkoskee, A., Strickland, B. R., & Watson, J. (1971). Delay of gratification and internal versus external control among adolescents of low socioeconomic status. *Developmental Psychology, 4,* 93-98.

4 ● Some Footnotes on the Role of Public Communication in Incumbent Politics

RODERICK P. HART

University of Texas — Austin

WHEN *Time* (1984) magazine published a story on the 1984 campaign entitled "Facing the Fatigue Factor," it was a sign of the presidential times. Evermore, challengers as well as incumbents are finding it wise or necessary, expected or demanded, that they travel the length and breadth of the land and speak to the American people. If they are leading in the polls they must travel the rally circuit to ensure that their campaign workers do not slacken their efforts. If they are running neck and neck with their opponents, the candidates must out-travel and out-talk each other to demonstrate that they have the stamina to fight the good fight. And if they trail their opponents, they must redouble their efforts by including two shopping malls in Joplin rather than one, three party fund-raisers in Kansas City instead of two. Somehow, candidates, reporters, and voters have come to equate electoral success with rhetorical energy and no political mathematician dares question this postulate.

The irony, of course, is that this scurrying about has intensified during an era featuring the miracles of mass communication. Even though political remarks can now reach the ears of tens of millions of Americans simultaneously, their authors still insist on delivering the messages personally as well. Part of the explanation for these "talkathons" lies in tradition—the color and drama of a presidential campaign is a quadrennial expectation, a kind of political olympics. Another explanation lies in the psychodrama of American politics: Long consecutive days spent on a heated campaign trail supposedly "harden" the candidates in the blast furnace of media scrutiny so that they are transformed into tempered presidential steel. This latter explanation is reinforced by the *Time* (1984, p. 37) article as it describes the Democratic candidate in the primaries as moving "at a ferocious pace, running an electoral marathon at sprinter's speeds."

Correspondence and requests for reprints: Roderick P. Hart, Department of Speech Communication, University of Texas—Austin, Austin, TX 78712

The tremendous amount of coverage offered to candidates by *Time* and the other media outlets are clearly sufficient to offset the physical and mental rigors of campaigning. Weekly interviews, full-color pictures from the campaign, occasional re-presentations of the candidates' best remarks, and the media's own ability to provide enthusiastic descriptions of election-year hoopla are real allies to the candidates, especially if the candidates are comparatively bland (as they were in 1984). Moreover, as *Time* (1984, p. 39) revealingly notes, "a bushed candidate is more prone to mistakes and misstatements." Because of this, the candidates are shadowed by the media as they travel their routes delivering their oratory. With campaign speeches being as formulaic as they are, the media are naturally attracted to the odd indiscretion, the misdelivered line, the inverted fact. In any event, the effect of extensive media coverage of campaigns is clear: The modern presidential campaign has become a blizzard of political discourse, some of it repetitious, much of it acquiring the status of pseudo-event, but all of it pursued with both vigor and intensity.

My purpose in this chapter is modest. I wish to comment on certain incidental features of political discourse in modern election campaigns, features that throw an interesting light on political phenomena presumably already well understood. The trends I shall mention here are not in themselves earth-shattering; they form but a small portion of the larger mosaic known as the modern election campaign. But these trends are signs of the times and should, I contend, cause us to reexamine some of the assumptions we make about modern politics. Specifically, I shall argue (1) that mass media institutions shape political speech but in ways normally overlooked; (2) that *rhetorical* decisions, not just economic or demographic or power-based decisions, best characterize a political campaign; (3) that federal elections require candidates to speak about fundamental matters in fundamental ways, thereby serving as a kind of intellectual housecleaning for the nation; and (4) that influential though the mass media have become in political life, they have *not* served to replace certain powerful, region-based variables in the American political equation.

Individually, none of these propositions may seem particularly noteworthy. Collectively, however, they invite us to reconsider what we think we know about politics in the United States and what we think we know about public life in a mediated age. Moreover, they invite us to reexamine the role of traditional speech-making in political campaigns, a phenomenon that many researchers have treated as outdated and have relegated to the field's conceptual attic. Collectively, the propositions advanced here urge us to rethink what we think we know about political communication and to tarry a bit longer in the curio shop of public oratory.

My approach in this essay is suggestive, not probative. I shall advance the four propositions mentioned above but only have space sufficient to adumbrate their substance and implications. Moreover, I shall operate as an essayist and shall claim the licenses of the essayist: Although I will present certain facts here, I will comment upon them only in passing, spending the majority of my time discussing the importance of those facts for the American polity. For taking such an approach I ask the reader's indulgence. Those interested in the evidentiary status of the data referred to are urged to consult the larger work from which these brief remarks are extracted, a work entitled *The Sound of Leadership: Presidential Communication in the Modern Age* (in press). My hope is that the present chapter, limited in scope though it is, will cause the reader to think anew about what politicians say and why they say such things.

The facts upon which this essay is based were collected over a period of six years and deal exclusively with U.S. presidential politics. The datapoints consist of the 8,887 speeches appearing in the *Public Papers of the Presidents* between 1945 and 1982. (These years encompass the Truman through Reagan administrations. The study began with Truman because his presidency coincided with the rise of the electronic media.) During data collection, each speech was tagged with an identifying number and then entered by date into a computerized data bank so that various statistical patterns could be examined. In addition, each speech was coded with the following information: (1) president, (2) year in office, (3) general location of the speech (for example, domestic, international, and so on), (4) regional location (Northeast, Midwest, and so on), and (5) state. The general and specific topics (for example, science and agriculture, economics, international conflict) also were recorded, as was the audience being addressed (for example, government employees, invited guests, and so on). Attention was paid to the timing of the speech during the president's administration, to its timing during the political year (for example, fall versus summer), and to its timing on the day of delivery (was it the only speech given? one of several?). The social setting of the speech was catalogued, with discriminations being made among ceremonies, briefings, political rallies, and so on; moreover, the political setting was noted, with distinctions being made, for example, between speeches delivered in small, partisan states and those in large, nonpartisan states (*partisanship* being defined by historical vote totals). Finally, a range of collateral measurements was made for each speech, with its date of delivery linked to presidential popularity, national unemployment, party control of Congress, legislative success rates, and density of mass media coverage.

The majority of these factors will not be treated here, but they are mentioned in passing to give the reader an idea of the scope of the larger project. Moreover, I shall not attempt here to explicate the complete analytical protocol employed in the study nor will I provide operational definitions for the markers used to discriminate among the message-situations. By way of methodological commentary, however, it is worth noting that my data base consisted of speech acts, not just messages. That is, the specific content of the speeches was treated as important *in light of the more basic social/political decision to speak*—in a particular locality, at a particular time, about a particular topic, by a particular president. Thus my data were generated more by categorical analysis than by content analysis; they reflect macro-rhetorical trends, not micro-rhetorical peculiarities. In a sense, my data base bears more resemblance to the pages of a daily appointment calendar than to transcripts of tape-recorded conversations. It tells us only who said what to whom, when, and where. But, as we shall see, patient inspection of such a large and comprehensive data base can tell us much about *why* who spoke to whom then and there.

Proposition One:
The Mass Media Shape the
Rhetorical Decisions of Incumbents

Proposition One is deceptively self-evident. So is Table 4.1. It reveals that every recent American president spoke more frequently during election years than during nonelection years. Interestingly, these increases involved not just campaign speeches but also ceremonies and briefings. Lately, international speaking also has increased during election years, signaling that the modern president becomes rhetorically omnivorous when votes are to be had. From the chief executive's standpoint the modern campaign is less political than presidential because he brings all of his office to bear on the election.

There is another way of looking at Table 4.1 and that is to note how comparatively modest the nonelection/election year changes have been. Yes, presidents speak more frequently during election campaigns but they also speak a good deal all the time, as if the American people voted each day. In some senses, the voters do—via the Roper and Gallup polls, through telegrams to their representatives in Congress, and by saving or spending their money or by hoarding or flaunting their gasoline supplies (depending upon the president's current request of them). The American mass media also vote every day and so the White House now houses a full-time rhetorical manufacturing plant. It is therefore not surprising that the president's best known aides are often his most skilled communication advisors—Ted Sorensen, Dick Goodwin, Ron Ziegler, Gerald Rafshoon, Michael Deaver. Modern presidents have become true rhetorical insurgents—grabbing at persuasive opportunities before others notice them, constructing the persuasive ground rules before their opponents or the media have a chance to do so, injecting rhetorical solutions into situations that would have been previously dealt with privately. Thus although presidents do increase their speech-making during elections, they do so only by intensifying, not by redefining, their speaking schedules.

Given the pressures placed upon them by the mass media, it might seem

Table 4.1
Presidential Speaking in Nonelection versus Election Years

President	Average # Speeches nonelection years	Average # Speeches election years
Truman	122.2	244.8
Eisenhower	108.0	123.3
Kennedy	236.5	298.0
Johnson	280.0	347.1
Nixon	182.3	203.3
Ford	396.0	542.1
Carter	281.5	379.5
Reagan	212.0	343.0

Note: Nonelection years = odd-numbered years (1945-1981); election years = even-numbered years (1946-1982).

surprising that presidents do not pursue their reelections even more vigorously than they do. One of the favorite games played by the media is speech-baiting, an operation in which reporters play the role of White House booking agent. The game, of course, is played in public, so that all participants know that an invitation to speak has been made. Sometimes, the matchmakers even go so far as to suggest the proper arrangements. During his September 18, 1980, news conference, for example, Jimmy Carter (1980a, p. 1829) was confronted with the following question: "Mr. President, the big debate really concerns who will occupy this place next January 21. [Here, the reporter essentializes a complex political environment so that the President will not be tempted to wander when giving his answer.] And since presidential elections are now federally funded [Don't think you're going to escape our scrutiny, Mr. President.], I was just wondering [Actually, I've planned this question very carefully. This is hardly a spontaneous thought on my part.] whether you might consider [Note my qualifications. I'm being appropriately deferential in front of 20 million television viewers.], as President [You *are* the president after all. You're not a coward, are you?] inviting your chief opponent, Ronald Reagan, to a debate here in the White House. [This place has nice lines. The paintings and the balustrades will photograph well.]" The presumptuousness of this particular brand of speech-baiting is heightened when one recollects that, as of this date, Mr. Carter had already accepted three invitations to debate Ronald Reagan in other contexts. Essentially, the reporter's query dealt with staging and lighting.

In earlier days, the game was played less audaciously. When he inquired about Dwight Eisenhower's plans for electioneering, for instance, Robert Clark of the International News Service asked simply, "Can you tell us how much more speechmaking you now plan to do than you originally intended and whether you feel that your health places any limitation on the extent of your campaign activities?" (Eisenhower, 1956b, p. 806). After commenting about the current state of his health, Mr. Eisenhower (1956b, pp. 806-807) asserted in part: "I would say, yes, I am probably doing a little bit more than I originally planned in my own mind; but I will tell you one thing: I am not doing one-tenth of what a lot of people want me to do." Eisenhower's full reply was 75% shorter than that supplied by Jimmy Carter to the inquiry posed above. By 1980, a president could not be cavalier about anything asked by the press, especially if it even remotely dealt with presidential valor. The press treats electoral speaking as akin to manhood because they and their readers like to think of politics as a form of civilized combat. If presidents fail to respond fully to such duels in behalf of Dame Politics, the press reminds them gently that nothing less than Honor itself is at stake.

Sometimes not so gently. The October 14, 1976, transcript of Gerald Ford's news conference contains the following remarkable exchange:

> Q. Mr. President, a review of your travel logs from this fall and last fall shows that for a comparable period last fall you spent exactly as much time on the road — 15 days last fall — when there was no campaign and no election than you have this fall when there is a hotly contested Presidential election. Doesn't this lend a little bit of credence to Governor Carter's charge that you've been kind of hiding in the White House for most of this campaign?
>
> *The President.* Tom [Tom De Frank, *Newsweek*], didn't you see that wonderful picture of me standing on top of the limousine with, I think, the caption "Is he hiding?" The truth is, we are campaigning when we feel that we can be away from the White House and not neglect the primary responsibilities that I have as President of the United States. I think you are familiar with the vast number of bills that I've had to sign. We've done that. That's my prime responsibility, among other things.
>
> We do get out and campaign. We were in New York and New Jersey earlier this week. We're going to Iowa, Missouri, and Illinois between now and Sunday. We will be traveling when we can. But my prime responsibility is to stay in the White House and get the job done here. And I will do that, and then we will campaign after that. (Ford, 1976a, p. 2526)

This question was asked of Gerald Ford, a president who gave 682 speeches in 1976, over half of which were campaign speeches. On 38 different days that year Ford gave between 4 and 6 speeches; on 24 other days he gave 7 or more. Mr. Ford spoke in 44 of the continental United States during his abbreviated presidency as well. What is truly remarkable about the exchange above is that Ford's election-year behavior was contrasted by reporter De Frank to the President's activities during 1975 — the busiest nonelection year for any president since 1945 (and, presumably, since 1789) and the second busiest year *of any sort* during that time (only Lyndon Johnson's 1964 total of 471 speeches surpassed Mr. Ford's). In other words, as far as the press is concerned, a president can never speak often enough. If we are a "presidential nation," as some have claimed, we are so because the mass media now seem incapable of thinking beyond the occupant of the White House. With the Chief Executive providing copy for virtually every newspaper's front page every day and visuals for the first three minutes of virtually every televised newscast, the president is nothing less than their Great Provider and his speeches their daily bread.

Proposition Two:
Rhetorical Decisions
Characterize Political Campaigns

Although many have attempted the task, nobody has yet written the definitive treatise on how to be elected president of the United States. Every four years, presidential staffs try to write this book, but the advice they give is largely ad hoc. At times, of course, even such situational advice is bad advice. Of the last seven chief executives who sought reelection, four won by comfortable margins but used substantially different strategies; one barely managed to hold onto his job; and two lost despite the unprecedented amount of money spent on their campaigns. A quick retrospective of these campaigns points up the different (rhetorical) routes to the White House.

Table 4.2 reveals two of these routes. What appears to be a Democratic/Republican difference in audience preference is, in actuality, an artifact of two different campaigns—those of Harry Truman and Gerald Ford. Mr. Truman hit the open road, bringing his message of a recalcitrant, "do-nothing" Congress to the attention of every American within earshot of an engineer's whistle. He doubled the number of rallies Gerald Ford held in the 24 smallest states and spoke 5 times more often in such places than any of the other presidents seeking reelection. Only Harry Truman could have accomplished such an intensive, protracted rhetorical feat: almost 400 political rallies in less than 6 months without the benefit of either extensive air travel or a sympathetic press. Moreover, many local Democrats were understandably reticent about being associated with what appeared to have been a doomed candidacy. Circumstances like these prompted his open-ended campaign and they also required him to become his own best press agent. His speeches on the campaign trail had a raucous, at times bumptious, quality to them. The identifications Truman (1948c, p. 892) sought to build were more gemeinschaft than gesellschaft ("Providence—a great Democratic city in a great Democratic state. Rhode Island shows them the way!") and they allowed Mr. Truman to reach out to potential supporters in almost primitive ways ("It certainly is a pleasure to be here tonight in your wonderful city of Vinitia [Oklahoma]. I have been here many a time. I was driving out here at one time and stopped here at 5

Table 4.2
Use of "Open" versus "Closed" Rallies by Modern Presidents

President's Political Affiliation	% usage with Truman and Ford		% usage without Truman and Ford	
	open rallies (N = 874)	closed rallies (N = 376)	open rallies (N = 186)	closed rallies (N = 257)
Republican	29.2	67.3	48.4	44.7
Democratic	70.8	32.7	51.6	55.2

Note: Open = events open to the public; closed = an organization-sponsored event or one employing a restrictive guest list.

o'clock in the morning to get breakfast. And I got a good one, too.") (Truman, 1948d, p. 627).

These "open" rallies (that is, rallies without a prearranged guest list) permitted Truman to speak a political language that seems quaint by modern standards. Mr. Truman did not have to contend with the kind of strategy-sensitive press facing a contemporary chief executive. As a result, Truman (1948b, p. 358) could, without compunction, use the hoary ploy of contrasting the taste of his immediate audience with that of another, more removed grouping: "I can't tell you [citizens of Butte, Montana] how overwhelmed I am at the welcome you gave me this afternoon on the streets. In Kansas City, which is a suburb of my old hometown, I have never had such a welcome." Used with some discretion, this strategy could be used by Truman (1948b, p. 358) profitably in virtually any locality: "I thought I had seen nearly all the people in New Mexico at Gallup. Then when I got to Albuquerque, it looked as if the people had come in from all the other states. The Mayor of Albuquerque told me it was the biggest crowd that had ever been out in Albuquerque. And now it looks as if Las Vegas has shown them all how."

The sounds of 1976 were distinctly different. Jerry Ford spoke often to specialized (closed) groups of voters and toured the country on the other side of Truman's railroad tracks: the Governor's Mansion of South Carolina on October 23, 1976, the Huntington-Sheraton Hotel on October 24, the Grossmont Shopping Center later that day, Allstate Insurance Company Headquarters on the 26th, the New Jersey School Boards Association the day after. The presidential stopping places of 1948—Afton, Holdenville, Claremore, Marshfield—became more exclusive as well as more Republican in 1976: West Palm Beach, Ocean Ridge, Briney Breezes, Coral Springs. In contrast to 1948, the American people in 1976 did not wander into a presidential rally sociologically neutered. If geography was the key to Harry Truman's campaign, demography was the watchword to Gerald Ford's. One of Mr. Ford's (1974, p. 23) speeches to the Veterans of Foreign Wars exemplified this. After making the obligatory introductory remarks ("As a proud member of Old Kent Post VFW 830, let me . . ."), Ford hastened to add: "Speaking of national unity, let me quickly point out that I am also a proud member of the American Legion and the AMVETS." Later in the speech, Mr. Ford (1974, p. 24) steered his vessel in the direction of other ports ("As a lawyer . . .," "As a former naval reservist . . .," "As a former Congressman . . ."), tacking in each case to particularized political winds.

Mr. Ford's targeted campaign was born not just from Republican loins but from a more general sense that organized groupings of voters were far more dependable than the crowds that heard Harry Truman on a hit-or-miss basis three decades earlier. Truman traveled to 40 states in 1948 and Ford to 37 in 1976 but, when there, they talked to fundamentally different persons who had gathered for fundamentally different reasons. Their campaigns had different textures and they evoked different kinds of emotions. On election eve, for example, Jerry Ford (1976b, pp. 2839, 2840) used his national address to recompartmentalize his campaign. His speech is a pastiche of the appeals he had made to the business community ("When I became President, inflation was over 12%"), to religious constituencies ("When I took the oath of office in August of 1974, I said I had not been elected by your ballots, but I asked that you confirm me by your prayers."), to the young people of America ("We have restored confidence and trust in the White House itself, and America is at peace."), to conservatives ("Some people have wanted to cut the defense budget. That would be a big gamble."), and to liberals ("We will do a better job in meeting some of the problems of our major metropolitan areas.").

Harry Truman's nationwide address on election eve was more whole because the Truman experience in 1948 had been, in reality, more a social movement than a political campaign. His speech is less mechanistic than Ford's, more a statement of political philosophy than a listing of his stands on the issues. When he spoke he had little fear of crisscrossing his special interest groups because he rarely had faced them in his campaign. The result is a speech rich in bathos but also a speech reflecting the emotional unity of his protracted campaign:

> During the past 2 months the Senator and I have been going up and down the country, telling the people what the Democratic Party stands for in government. I have talked in great cities, in State capitals, in county seats, in crossroad villages and country towns.
>
> Everywhere the people showed great interest. They came out by the millions. They wanted to know what the issues were in this campaign, and I told them what was in my mind and heart.
>
> I explained the meaning of the Democratic Party platform. I told them that I intend to carry it out if they will give me a Democratic Congress to help.

From the bottom of my heart I thank the people of the United States for their cordiality to me and for their interest in the affairs of this great Nation and of the world. I trust the people, because when they know the facts, they do the right thing. I have tried to tell them the facts and explain the issues.

Now it is up to you, the people of this great Nation, to decide what kind of government you want—whether you want government for all the people or government for just the privileged few.

Tonight I am at my home here in Independence—Independence, Missouri—with Mrs. Truman and Margaret. We are here to vote tomorrow as citizens of this Republic. I hope that all of you who are entitled to vote will exercise that great privilege. When you vote, you are in control of your Government.

Tomorrow you will be deciding between the principles of the Democratic Party—the party of the people—and the principles of the Republican Party—the party of privilege.

Your vote tomorrow is not just a vote for one man or another; it is a vote which will affect you and your families for years to come. (Truman, 1948e, p. 939)

When they ran for reelection, the other presidents also presented distinctive rhetorical profiles. Indeed, Dwight Eisenhower did not really run for reelection; he walked. With good reason, Eisenhower fancied himself as being above politics and he nursed this image throughout his presidency. At some point early in 1956, Mr. Eisenhower and his advisers must have counted the votes and decided to wage their campaign by not waging one. Ike gave only 31 regional speeches that year (compared to Harry Truman's 336 eight years earlier) and virtually none of these occurred in Republican states. By husbanding his political energy in this way, Eisenhower provided few, if any, targets for Adlai Stevenson. In October of 1956, a month when other presidents would be busily fighting the political wars from coast to coast, Mr. Eisenhower did not speak at all on 13 of those 31 days. He visited only 11 states (normally for one or two speeches per state). Such antipolitical politics is indeed rare from the vantage point of the mediated 1980s.

Lyndon Johnson's campaign in 1964 was certainly a busy one in contrast. His election-year October produced 89 speeches even though LBJ enjoyed an Eisenhower-sized lead over his opponent, Barry Goldwater. But Lyndon Johnson loved politics and he loved political oratory even more. In fact, Mr. Johnson never really stopped running for the presidency even after he had been reelected to it. Presidents like Dwight Eisenhower and Richard Nixon abandoned the small states after achieving reelection, and Harry Truman, Gerald Ford, and Jimmy Carter largely ignored them until their electoral votes were needed. John Kennedy and Ronald Reagan visited such places only during the off-year elections. Lyndon Johnson, in contrast, toured the United States incessantly and it seemed comparatively unimportant to him whether the states he visited had many or few electoral votes. Throughout his life, LBJ had run for some office or other and he carried a campaigner's attitude into the White House. In nonelection years, for example, he sought out audiences favorable to his course in Vietnam just as avidly as he sought votes in 1964. For Johnson, politics was not something one did every four years but something one was—always. His 1964 campaign for reelection required only minimal adjustments in a personal schedule and personal mind-set that prized political opportunities over all other opportunities.

As one might suspect, Richard Nixon's reelection campaign was as tightly controlled and as given to expediency as Mr. Nixon was himself controlled and expedient. Table 4.3 indicates how carefully the Nixon campaign counted votes, with almost all of his speech-making occurring in the 12 most populous states. No other president's rhetoric was nearly this "concentrated." Strategist that he was, Mr. Nixon did both politics and rhetoric by the numbers. Indeed, during one of the few token speeches he gave in one state of modest electoral value, Nixon (1972d, p. 1107) justified his doing so neither philosophically nor politically but more as a way of settling a quantitative score he had intended to settle for some years: "As I stand here in Rhode Island, it just occurred to me that while in those elections to which I referred, in '60 and '68, I have at one time or another carried most of the States, Rhode Island is a State that I have never carried. Let me say, the third time will be a charm. This is the year when we take Rhode Island."

Richard Nixon was an awkward man—awkward with people, awkward with his own emotions—and this came through most clearly in political settings. Some of Nixon's advisers thought him his own worst enemy on the hustings because he could not make small talk comfortably nor show genuine warmth when shaking the hands of ordinary Americans. His campaign speeches reveal how ill-suited he was to the grimy aspects of day-to-day politics and why his lieutenants sought to keep him in the Rose Garden as often as they could. When he should have been self-effacing he was self-congratulatory ("In checking my notes, I find that I have a proud distinction today: the first President of the United States ever to visit Prospect [Illinois])" (Nixon, 1970b, p. 993). When he should have been subtle he was obvious ("I want you to know how very grateful I am for this enormous crowd. . . . I think that all of you inside the hangar should know that there are at least twice as many outside the hangar.") (Nixon, 1970c, p. 999). Instead of allowing the audience to draw its own conclusions and thereby persuade itself, Mr. Nixon heaped data upon them ("I want to thank the *San Jose Mercury* for their very nice editorial providing the red carpet treatment.") (Nixon, 1970d, p. 1020) or mentioned items that would have been more impressive if left implicit ("I want to express appreciation for the fact that in hotel after hotel, there were signs out. 'Welcome

Table 4.3
Richard Nixon versus Other Presidents on Speaking in Various States

State Population (Mainland only)	% Nixon speeches		% other presidents' speeches	
	Reelection year (N = 43)	Other years (N = 207)	Reelection year (N = 1142)	Other years (N = 1354)
Most populous states (N = 12)	83.7	55.5	63.5	51.9
Large states (N = 12)	7.0	22.2	19.1	23.6
Small states (N = 12)	7.0	14.4	12.8	13.3
Least populous states (N = 12)	4.7	7.7	4.6	11.2

President Nixon.'") (Nixon, 1970a, p. 1047). Naturally, the egos of all politicians are hardy, but Nixon had a special need to provide the color commentary and to evaluate the success of his game plan as he executed it.

Jimmy Carter's reelection bid was hampered by the Iranian crisis (during which Mr. Carter retreated to the Rose Garden), but in September and October of 1980 the President came roaring back, delivering more speeches (118) during those months than any previous chief executive except Harry Truman. Carter's days in the presidential Rose Garden were hardly spent cultivating the shrubbery, however. He utilized ceremonies and formal briefings to keep his face and thoughts prominently displayed before the American people. Oftentimes, these events were political in content if not in form. His remarks during the inauguration ceremonies for the new Department of Health and Human Services on May 14, 1980 were both tear-stained ("I was raised by a registered nurse, my mother, who for a lifetime has devoted her talents and her commitments to caring for other people.") and programmatic ("We must have a coordinated effort between government at all levels.") (Carter, 1980b, pp. 908, 910), precisely the style one might expect during an election-year stump speech. The ceremonial ribbons he cut that day did not prevent Mr. Carter (1980b, p. 909) from using either political jabs ("Compared to the last budget of my predecessor in the White House, Federal aid to education, for instance, in our 1981 request is 73% higher.") or an almost unseemly kind of political preening ("We've increased aid to mass transit programs by two-thirds; doubled economic development aid grants; increased spending for subsidized housing."). His conclusion also employed the motifs one might expect to hear on the campaign trail: "We still have a long way to go, and we face more years of hard work. . . . I both congratulate you on this day and pledge that together you and I will redouble our efforts to meet that noble challenge" (Carter, 1980b, p. 910).

In this and in many other of his speeches during 1980, Carter camouflaged his partisan rhetoric with the trappings of ceremony, thereby experiencing some of the pleasures of campaigning without the stricture of a campaign regimen. No doubt, this restraint produced some amount of frustration for an aggressive politician like Jimmy Carter. Still, Carter's approach reveals how everything a president touches turns to politics during a reelection year. For Jimmy Carter, as well as for his predecessors, speech often becomes a solution when the fall elections roll around. The forms they choose will vary—badgering for Truman, pontificating for Johnson, ritualizing for Carter—but most presidents find the voice that suits them and they use it when their job is threatened. In doing so, they are responding to instincts both political and primordial.

The importance of the rhetorical distinctiveness traced here cannot be gainsaid even though many observers would have us believe that the mass media have so homogenized electoral politics that candidate-specific factors no longer obtrude. My findings suggest the contrary: Whom an incumbent president decides to talk to and how he decides to talk to them are every bit as distinctive today as they were prior to the advent of the mass media. This is not to say, of course, that the mass media have failed to *accelerate* these normal political processes (something we have already suggested in Proposition One above). But it is to say that modern political campaigns still develop distinctive profiles resulting from an amalgamation of socio-demographic variables, political calculations, and the rhetorical mind-sets of the persons running for office. Even more intriguing is that these profiles are revealed at the primitive level of the speech act itself, suggesting perhaps that nobody—neither pauper nor prince nor president—can hide when he or she speaks. Such a conclusion should be heartening to the student of political communication, for it suggests that even in an era of daily political polling, saturation advertising, focus-group testing, automated mailings, and PAC-controlled fund-raising, much of a political campaign consists of people talking to people, just as it always has.

Proposition Three:
National Elections Return
Candidates to Rhetorical Essentials

When examined in the large, the federal elections waged between 1946 and 1982 tell an interesting story. Generally speaking, these campaigns have returned the American political process to its essentials. They have served as a means of reconnoitering, a way of determining what is truly native to the political terrain in the United States. They also have broadened the perspectives of presidents. Table 4.4 makes this point especially

Table 4.4
Specific Topical Foci in Presidential Speeches during
Nonelection and Election Years

Topic	# Speeches nonelection years	# Speeches election years
Science	293	369
Economics	271	390
Government	213	796
Human services	336	374
Human values	485	617
International cooperation	878	828
International conflict	199	295
Multiple topics	676	1303
Other	260	301

clear. Elections encourage not only more discussion but also more discussion about more matters. With the exception of the topic of international cooperation, presidents increased their rhetorical efforts across the board during elections. American elections appear to reward the centrist, the candidate who can address the full range of issues affecting the nation's constituencies. These topical patterns probably point up institutional forces at work. During elections, both progressives and conservatives become Americans above all else, the former bowing to industry, the latter to the blue-collar worker. Elections shape presidential discourse by suggesting appropriate, traditional themes and it is the sounding of these themes, more than their specific manifestations, that is important.

Presidents thus pay homage to all of the nation's deities even if they do so more from a sense of obligation than from one of personal conviction. Dwight Eisenhower's genuflections were particularly noteworthy in 1956:

Take labor. The opposition say that they alone truly care for the working men and women of America and that the Republican Party is really a vague kind of political conspiracy by big business to destroy organized labor and to bring hunger and torment to every worker in America.

This is more than political bunk. It is willful nonsense. It is wicked nonsense.

Let's see what the record shows about this.

The record shows: Organized labor is larger in numbers and greater in strength today—after these years of Republican Administration—than ever in our Nation's history.

The record shows: Not under the opposition's leadership, but under the leadership of this Administration, the workers of America have received the greatest rise in real wages—the kind of wages that buys groceries and cars and homes—the greatest rise in 30 years.

The record shows: We—not they—have made the most successful fight to stop inflation's robbery of every paycheck.

The record shows that this check upon inflation is most vital—not for the few who are rich—but for the millions who depend upon salaries or pensions, those who are old, those who are sick, those who are needy. (Eisenhower, 1956a, pp. 835-836)

Eight years later, Lyndon Johnson, he of the Great Society, visited Mr. Eisenhower's home state of Kansas to establish his responsibility in fiduciary matters:

This tax cut that I put into effect when I signed the bill this year giving back $12 billion to American taxpayers—this tax cut put money into Kansas pocketbooks, $22 million more in the State of Kansas alone. That tax cut is helping to create more jobs. It is helping to put more Americans to work.

Here in Wichita where we meet today, there are 13,000 more jobs than there were 3 years ago. The unemployment rate was 4.6% 3 years ago. Today it is down to 3%, well below the national average for the other States. When the tax cut is fully effective it will mean 22,000 more jobs for Kansas workers. Yes, responsibility is serving America, and I think and I hope, and I believe that you people in Kansas want it to continue next Tuesday. (Johnson, 1964c, p. 1521)

Democrats as Republicans, Republicans as Democrats. The presidential election brings a variety of political instincts to the fore, probably justifying the Marxists' charges that institutional politics in the United States is one-dimensional, a seamless amalgamation of economic interests. Incumbent presidents from both political parties become especially aware during election years that every political topic, each piece of proposed legislation, attracts the (oftentimes) frenzied interest of large and powerful groups. Thus elections cause presidents to stretch, to reach out for every issue they can possibly embrace and to pull it to their political bosoms.

When examining presidential speeches during election years, one senses a returning, a returning of the presidency to its essential purpose (preservation of the commonwealth); a returning from the chief executive's complex political agenda to the simpler concerns of the everyday voter; and a returning of the federal government to localized issues, localized control. There is a literal returning too. In the average president's first year in office, less than 17% of his speeches were delivered in *regional* contexts. That number jumps to 28.8% in the second year, to 37.2% in the third year. If the president's fourth year in office was a "normal" (that is, reelectoral) fourth year (as it was for Eisenhower, Nixon, and Carter), regional speaking often increased even more. A national election makes any American byway a powerful political magnet, slowly drawing the president and his speeches toward it. In this limited sense at least, the presidential election serves exactly the purpose the Founding Fathers intended for federal governance—ensuring that the president remains the nation's first citizen—one's neighbor, not one's lord.

Elections become an apt time to affirm that no matter how vigorously Americans may disagree about certain social or philosophical matters, they still appreciate their heritage: the freedom to strive for material comfort. Largely, then, presidents blow the economic and technological trumpet during their political rallies. They emphasize the importance of family farms, mass transportation, scientific research and development, small business initiatives, and lower interest rates for housing. About these things Americans often have agreed, no matter how they have argued about prayer in the schools, racial integration, or affirmative action. Naturally, these latter topics are discussed during elections, but they are clearly relegated to secondary status by the president especially when he tours the nation, as can be seen in Table 4.5.

The pragmatic themes found in presidential campaign speaking are essential to maintaining some level of interdependence for several hundred million Americans who are variously skilled, variously educated, variously churched, and varied, too, in ethnic composition. Thus it is not surprising that this effect is increased fourfold when the president tours the hinterlands, there where the bottom-liners dwell. No matter what the watchwords of the president's previous three years might have been (the Peace Corps, Medicare, Detente), the watchwords of American elections—jobs, profits, prosperity—do not change. Residents of the Third World may call it crass materialism or economic imperialism but presidents called it basic Americanism when they are among basic Americans. It is revealing that no matter how hard Walter Mondale tried in 1984 to accuse Ronald Reagan of militaristic jingoism that the American people had difficulty seeing beyond Mr. Reagan's "economic recovery." And it is also revealing that even though the Republican platform's social agenda was radical by many standards (strong philosophical opposition to busing, abortion, and women's rights), Mr. Reagan himself largely ignored these themes when campaigning.

Although it would be reductionistic to suggest that American elections are solely pragmatic, that is certainly their direction. Lyndon Johnson's case is an interesting one. Although he spoke about "humanistic" matters more often than other presidents, Johnson's systemic speaking still dominated his agenda in 1964 (roughly 60% of his speeches were of this sort), was reduced during the off-year elections of 1966 (50%), and reduced even further during his last year in office (40%). That is, the gross national product, not his projected social programs, became the focus of a great many of his campaign speeches when he sought reelection. But as he approached the end of his administration, as he became more and more committed to Vietnam and more enamored of his Great Society, and as he became less and less encumbered by thoughts of another reelection cam-

Table 4.5
General Topical Foci for Presidential Speeches During
Election and Nonelection Years

Topic	"N" Nonelection year speeches	"N" Election year speeches	% increase
All speaking			
systemic	777	1557	100.4
humanistic	818	992	21.3
Regional speaking only			
systemic	162	808	398.8
humanistic	166	277	66.9

Note: Systemic = speeches focusing on the economic, technological, or political aspects of domestic governance; humanistic = speeches lionizing abstract human values or discussing human welfare and services.

paign, Mr. Johnson slipped further and further away from the earnest, albeit pedestrian, macroeconomic theories he espoused in 1964:

> If you can get the businessman, the big company, the big corporation, and the people that work for them, if you can get them to understand that what is good for one of them is good for the other, and we can have understanding instead of harassment—and I am just foolish enough to think that somehow or other we can do that, and I have been promoting it for 11 months, I have been bringing them in and talking to them.
>
> If business puts everything that it has and all it can muster into the pot, and you put, as workers, everything you have into that pot, and then you take a spoon and scoop it up and make a big pie out of it, the bigger that pie is the more you will get and the more they get if we divide it reasonably equitably.
>
> I will tell you something else that is important: After business gets a return on their investment and their machinery and their management, and the worker gets a return on his sweat and what he did all day long, then Uncle Sam, the Government, I come in and I take my knife, and the bigger the pie is the more I get for Government because I get 52% of all that is left.
>
> So it just seems to me that it is good sense for all of us to try to have peace at home and try to get along. That is why you don't hear me talking about economic royalists, big business, big labor, racketeers, profitmakers, and things like that.
>
> We have laws that determine what is equitable and what is just, and we follow those laws. The laws will be just. There are some people who don't want to follow the laws, but the laws, in the end, will be just. If we will follow those, and try to all work together, in the end we will have peace at home. (Johnson, 1964b, pp. 1553-1554)

Presidential elections do more than get presidents elected. They do, in fact, broaden the national dialectic. They do, in fact, lure the president out among the people. They do, in fact, cause the chief executive to abandon many of his particular, philosophical notions in favor of the more general and more practical concerns for nationwide prosperity. Viewed collectively, this breadth, this sociability, and this pragmatism contribute to what has come to be known as modern politics. Elections, those special choosing times, remove from politics all but its politicalness. Perhaps that is what was always intended.

Proposition Four:
The Mass Media Have Been Unable
to "Deregionalize" American Politics

As anyone who has traveled in the United States knows, Americans have a sense of place or, perhaps, a sense of places. Vast though the land mass is, Americans have grouped themselves into various localities and these localities have taken on political features—conservative Mormons building a nation within a nation beside their great Salt Lake; ruddy-faced Irish in South Boston instinctively pulling the Democratic lever; well-to-do Evanston banking executives taking the scenic lake route to the Loop; Mexican Americans laboring next to rutted roads in the South Texas valley. These Americans distinctively flavor the places they inhabit. When would-be presidents run for office, they must reckon carefully with these subcultural facts and find a rhetoric capable of reaching Americans where they live. And they must do so despite their unprecedented opportunities to broadcast mass messages to mass constituencies.

Table 4.6 is altogether unremarkable, which is itself remarkable. No matter how one looks at the regional speaking patterns of presidents, the totals are isomorphic with population figures. Table 4.6 also reveals an almost perfect "democratization" of rhetoric—one person, one vote, one speech. No matter where one looks—at region, at population, at party affiliation, or at a combination of these variables—it is clear that voter density drives presidential speech-making.

It must be kept in mind, of course, that this is a 40-year picture of regional speaking and that it somewhat blurs the twists, turns, and personalities of recent presidential history. In some ways, however, that history makes these parallel trends all the more interesting. We have been led to believe that American politics has been completely nationalized by the mass media, that speech-as-regional-flattery has thereby been rendered passé. We also have been led to believe that political power is distributed unequally in the United States. We have been led to believe that, for example, the Northeast's money, education, and media outlets make it the nation's political soul and that the other sections of the country need be attended to only when expediency (that is, electioneering) dictates.

But Table 4.7 shows that all four regions in the United States play an important role in presidential politics, during election year and nonelection year alike. The Northeast clearly does not dominate and the other areas of

Table 4.6
Regional Speechmaking by American Presidents: 1945-1982

	Population[a] (in thousands)	% U.S. Population (N = 192,039,000)	% Presidential Speaking (N = 2746)
State's Location			
Northeast	51,550	26.8	24.6
Midwest	56,495	29.4	29.8
South	52,739	27.4	26.5
West	31,255	16.3	19.1
State's Population			
most populous	115,579	60.2	57.5
large	44,370	23.1	21.3
small	24,044	12.5	13.0
least populous	8,046	4.2	8.1
State's Politics			
partisan Democratic	58,650	30.5	27.2
partisan Republican	23,291	12.1	16.1
neutral	110,098	57.3	56.7
State's Significance			
dense/neutral	89,881	46.8	43.0
medium/neutral	17,977	9.4	10.9
dense/partisan	53,980	28.1	26.7
sparse/neutral	2,240	1.7	2.6
sparse/partisan	27,961	14.6	16.8

a. Based on 1967 figures (roughly the midpoint of this study); Alaska and Hawaii not included.

the country are obviously visited with great frequency even when the polling booths are empty.

All of these data tell a similar story. Political oratory is no affaire de coeur, no sudden, uncontrolled moment of passion with the audience assembled. The political orator is a strategist above all else, one who knows that the Midwest may not have the physical endowments of the mountain states but that its many millions of inhabitants make campaign visits there rewarding nonetheless. Politics is a studied courtship and speech-making a carefully selected dowry (because presidents have little else to offer. Members of Congress, after all, are more prone to regional pork-barreling than is the president). So the president travels and speaks, and his speech often becomes a major local event whose sectional impact both precedes and follows it. Such a speech is spectacle for the townspeople. The president becomes a potential source of exciting disclosures; he travels in an imposing and slightly mysterious entourage; and he impresses even the cynical because he has risen to a station grander than that of the audience.

From the president's standpoint, such speaking is also attractive because it allows him—especially during an election year—to depend upon certain stock themes having virtually automatic regional appeal. Often, these themes are so rich in tradition, so rhetorically suggestive, that the president can speak for a considerable period of time without once entering into

Table 4.7
Regional Speaking by Presidents in Nonelection versus Election Years
(reported in percentages)

Location	Nonelection year speeches (N = 646)	Election year speeches (N = 2088)
Northeast	27.7	23.6
Midwest	22.2	32.1
South	32.2	24.8
West	18.0	19.5

politically dangerous territory. Consider, for example, Richard Nixon's campaign speaking in 1974. In a speech in Atlanta on October 12, 1972, he made the following brave declaration:

> I do not believe in dividing this Nation—region against region, young versus old, black versus white, race versus race, religion versus religion. I believe this is one country. I believe this is one Nation. And I believe that while we are all proud of our backgrounds—some are westerners, some are southerners, some are northerners, some are black, some are white, some are Italian background, some are of American stock, as they call it—but whatever we may be and whatever our backgrounds may be, we are Americans first, and that is what we must always remember. (Nixon, 1972c, p. 976)

Immediately after making this statement, Nixon denounced those who had charged him with having a Southern strategy for the campaign. "It is not a Southern strategy; it is an American strategy" Mr. Nixon declared. Then, he (Nixon, 1972c, pp. 976, 979, 980) went on to talk of his training at Duke University ("a fine law school"), the exploits of Robert E. Lee ("the best general produced on either side"), the cultural hallmark of the South ("a deep religious faith"), and then ended his speech by quoting the views of a southern Southerner (Richard Russell) and a northern Southerner (Woodrow Wilson).

Mr. Nixon carried his regionless rhetoric to other areas of the country that year. In the East, Nixon (1972b, p. 1013) was pleased to be in a place "with so much history, with so much character, with so much to offer America" and he spoke with a fondness for the region ("My wife's father was born in Connecticut," "Our two girls went to camp in Vermont") seemingly unmatched anywhere in the nation. Except in Oklahoma. There he noted "that out here in the middle of this country there are a people—a people who are strong, a people who have backbone, a people who will stand up for America" (Nixon, 1972e, p. 1104). And except in New Mexico, a state with "a great tradition, a background of Spanish-speaking Americans" who especially had impressed this president-of-all-the-people-but-you-in-particular early in life:

I remember, however, that when we, in English, say we want to welcome somebody someplace, we say, "Make yourself at home." But those who speak Spanish have a much warmer way of saying it. They say, "Estan ustedes en su casa"—you are in your own home—and that's the way we feel today. (Nixon, 1972a, p. 1122)

Although Richard Nixon's rhetoric was unusually transparent (and his emotions unusually contrived), his expediency seems fairly typical of presidential politics. Using other research techniques, researchers have found similar regional trends. Whether they called it "coalition building" and based their results on the 1980 race (West, 1983), or they studied campaign logs from 1932 to 1976 (Tatalovich, 1979), researchers agree that population, not ideology or personal preference or geographic proximity, is the single best predictor of where presidents campaign. This rhetorical census-taking often has interesting consequences. When concluding a 1982 campaign speech in job-needy Pennsylvania, for example, Ronald Reagan concluded with a quotation from James Russell Lowell's poem, "Columbus." Mr. Reagan set up the poem exquisitely:

Lowell wrote of that momentous voyage across the Atlantic. The crew had been told again and again that they would soon see land on the horizon, and they saw only water. They were tired, hungry, lonely, desperate, and ready to mutiny. But as Lowell wrote, "Endurance is the crowning quality and patience all the passion of great hearts." (Reagan, 1982b, p. 637)

It is hard to determine how comforting Reagan/Lowell were for Pennsylvanians in May of 1982 because that state was experiencing extraordinary economic distress at the time. How different Mr. Reagan spoke when he ventured into Texas the next month, a state whose booming population and booming economy removed the constrictions from his voice and allowed him to conclude on a booming rhetorical note: "What you've created here has captured the imagination of the world. Entrepreneurs, laborers, and men and women looking for opportunity are flocking here not expecting a handout, but knowing that with hard work they can improve their lives. That's what Texas is and, I hope, will always be about" (Reagan, 1982a, p. 783).

Population plus voter directionality predicts most precisely whom the chief executive talks to when the chips are down. Harry Truman badgered New Yorkers in 1948; Lyndon Johnson did the same to Pennsylvanians in 1964; Jimmy Carter dramatically increased his speaking to Floridians in 1980. In other words, *electoral diffidence* best assures the attention of the president of the United States. In contrast, the political loyalty found in such states as Maryland, Massachusetts, Georgia, and Kansas may be appreciated by presidents but does not result in very many election-year speeches. Such data accent the expediency of politics but make it a double expediency because we are here talking about human *speech,* normally thought of as a gift freely given to another. Political speech is thus not speech at all but more a kind of mechanical interfacing between machine parts resulting in a political widget carefully adapted to market forces. This is a metaphor for the times because this is speech for the times.

Nowhere is this love-'em-and-leave-'em attitude better shown than in the state of Ohio, a state bulging with electoral votes but one in which the upstate, urban, Democratic voters are counterbalanced by downstate, rural, Republicans. There is an eloquence of brevity to Table 4.8, with Ohio being virtually ignored by the presidents during nonelection years but avidly pursued when votes were being cast. Harry Truman spoke there only when campaigning. Lyndon Johnson spoke there 14 times during election years but only twice otherwise. Neighbor Jerry Ford spoke in Ohio only 3 times in 1975 but 28 times in 1974 and 1976. Apparently, Ohio is the sort of state that only an acquisitive politician can love.

Perhaps even more interesting than this crass politicalness is what the presidents actually said when they arrived in Ohio. They spoke not as if they were long-lost relatives looking for a political handout but as if they knew the people of Ohio down to the sinews of their beings. Said Dwight Eisenhower in 1956:

> When they [the naysayers] visit a city like Cleveland, let them look around at the hustle and bustle; talk to, and especially listen to, the people here. Let these politicians absorb some of the spirit that animates Clevelanders, all of them—whether they work in banks, in factories, in orchards and fields or in kitchens. Their worries.and fears of the future of America should begin to sound foolish—even to them. (Eisenhower, 1956a, p. 830)

Said Lyndon Johnson in 1964:

> I think I know something about the people of Ohio. I think they are good, patriotic Americans. Some of them are Republicans and some of them are Democrats and some of them are Independents. Nearly all of them are pretty independent. But I believe when the chips are down, whether it is when the draft calls them or Uncle Sam summons them, I believe that most of them do what they think is best for their country, regardless of their party, and that is what I want you to do. (Johnson, 1964a, p. 1259)

Said Jerry Ford in 1976:

> If I might add a special observation and comment—us Michiganders look at people from Ohio and, you know, we have nothing but great, great respect for you.

Table 4.8
Presidential Speaking in Ohio versus Other States

State	# Nonelection year speeches	# Election year speeches	% increase
All other states	634	1963	209.6
Ohio only	12	125	941.7

The thing that impresses me about the many people I see here and what I saw on each side of the street is that you have so many wonderful traditions, such distinctive and delicious food, a uniquely spirited way of life, a very special place in this great American family. Through your support for people [like] Frank Lausche, Jim Rhodes, Bob Taft, myself, we want to make certain that what we do politically preserves these unique things that each and every one of you represent. (Ford, 1976b, p. 2757)

Ohio, it seems, brings out the sociologist in a president. Ostensibly, it is a state presidents know so well that they need visit it only when the spirit moves them. That spirit has moved powerfully during election years.

Table 4.9 records the workings of a kindred spirit, one which brings presidents home differentially. For a politician, a home state is not just an emotional haven but also a political launching pad. A speech there is virtually guaranteed to produce colorful banners, smiling faces, an enthusiastic band, and an ocean's roar of applause. Thus presidents returned home twice as often during election years as during nonelection years, an imbalance repeated by all of the presidents except John Kennedy (who, of course, was assassinated before a possible reelection bid.) The rhetorical advantages inherent in such speeches are prodigious, especially in a mediated age. These talks abruptly remove the president from the lockstep formulas of the typical campaign address. They also extend an invitation to an unusual visitor in a campaign—genuine emotion. They discourage use of election-year clichés in favor of plain, highly specific language adapted to local surroundings. They encourage a president to feel like the human being he rarely feels like and to speak in a neighborhood sort of way. Gerald Ford's return to Michigan just before election day in 1976 possessed all of these features. The timing of his address, the presence of the national media, and his own, earnest style made for a vignette Charles Kuralt would have been proud of.

I have made a lot of speeches, and this is the hardest one to make, because as I look out in this audience and as I saw so many people as we came down Monroe Avenue—Democrats, Independents, Republicans—people that Betty and I lived with, that Betty and I love, that I tried to help over the years when I had the honor of representing this great congressional district, I could

Table 4.9
Presidential Speaking in Home States in Election and Nonelection Years

	Truman	Eisenhower	Kennedy	Johnson	Nixon	Ford	Carter	Reagan[a]
"N" speeches	40	22	8	90	39	34	23	20
Nonelection year %	20.0	36.4	100.0	33.3	48.7	14.7	47.8	25.0
Election year %	80.0	63.6	0.0	66.7	51.3	85.3	52.2	75.0

a. Through 1982 only.

tell you some stories about how the tough problems came to our office. And we never asked the person that walked in that office whether he or she was a Democrat or a Republican. We said, what can we do to help you, and that is the way I want to be your President.

You know, those wonderful experiences over a period of time, of taking that trailer down through Ottawa County, Ionia County, Kent County, and sitting and listening to wonderful people who had a problem, who wanted to give me a little trouble, give me a hard time—and they did—but also we had a couple of friends that might come in and say nice things about us. But the wonderful experience of representing the Fifth Congressional District will be something that I will never forget, and I thank you for the opportunity.

You know, I had a speech I was going to make, but I threw it away.

As we came off the expressway, we went down College Avenue and Betty said, "I went to Fountain School." We went right by it. Then we went by Central High School, but then, you know, I said to her, "Well, South High, that was a great school, too."

But anyhow, Grand Rapids, Kent County, Ottawa County, Ionia, well, all of them—western Michigan can make the difference and this is what I want you to know and what I think it is all about tomorrow. (Ford, 1976d, pp. 2835-2836)

To examine such regional speaking patterns is an invitation to cynicism. Hometown becomes photo-opportunity. Voters become audiences, if there are enough of them. Place becomes scene. Nowhere are these patterns better noted than in the American South, a region that has grown steadily in importance during the 40 years examined in my study. Table 4.10 shows how presidential speaking has increased considerably in what might be thought of as the "industrialized" South (as opposed to the more rural South of Alabama, Mississippi, Kentucky, South Carolina, and Arkansas which also experienced similar, but less dramatic, increases). The political partisanship and cultural provincialism earmarking that region for so many years has given way to manufacturing plants, financial centers, and, inevitably, to presidential speeches. Jerry Ford averaged almost 90 speeches a year in the South, an area in which Harry Truman and Dwight Eisenhower rarely spoke. Ford's average was 3 times higher than that of native son Lyndon Johnson. During his first year in office,

Table 4.10
Alterations in Presidential Speaking in Selected Southern States

State	# Speeches 1945-1957	# Speeches 1958-1970	# Speeches 1970-1982
Florida	15	28	84
Georgia	1	13	39
Louisiana	3	8	19
North Carolina	6	12	34
Tennessee	2	12	29
Texas	28	104	95
Virginia	6	16	35

Ronald Reagan spoke in the South more often than in any other region of the United States. Because the favor of a presidential speech carries both cultural as well as political significance, these trends may signal a permanent deregionalization of the American South.

Contrary to much popular commentary about electronic politics in the United States, about the "massification" of corporate, religious, and political life, about the depersonalization of a media-crazed citizenry, presidents continue to travel when they talk, in part because of traditions continuing to work themselves out and in part because even the nation-spanning, nation-shrinking mass media cannot completely remove sectional tribalism. It must be said, of course, that only the introductions and conclusions of these campaign speeches bear geographical markings, perhaps signaling that America is growing up, if not growing together.

CONCLUSION

A presidential election strips an incumbent presidency bare of all but its essential, political soul. Rhetoric is used to reclothe the presidency, to make it seem that even the crassest form of campaigning is nothing less than an institutional mandate. During election years presidents barnstorm the country, trying on a new hat in each locale and extending their coattails, if they have them, to those who share their political worldviews. Each of the last eight presidents has found a unique campaign style and the rhetoric they produced signals what the presidency meant to them and what they were willing to do to keep their jobs. As we have seen, the modern campaign has certain benefits for the American people because it forces presidents, again and again, back to socioeconomic basics and away from the rarefied atmosphere of political ideology. We also have seen that there is nothing particularly subtle about political geography, that there is almost a perfect fit between what a particular constituency can do for a president and what he is willing to do for them (or to them) rhetorically. There is something refreshingly honest about the patterns observed here, for they have focused us repeatedly on the realities of power in the United States. When they speak, presidents do not like to use words like power, but it is the only concept available to explain why they speak when they speak.

Some of the facts commented upon here seem trivial at first—who uses closed rallies, who speaks of economics, who visits Ohio—and not at all suitable to the modern, social scientific study of political processes. Simply to ask who says what to whom when and where seems too primitive a set of questions to ask in an era that has produced psychographic testing of voters, double-blinded attitude sampling, and computer simulations of political campaigns. My argument, of course, is that these are indeed primitive questions and, hence, among the most important to be answered. Although space does not permit it, I think that the case could be made that only by coming to grips with the *facts* of a speech act (as opposed to its message content) can we ever gain a sufficiently rich understanding of human communication. After all, by choosing to utter words to another, a speaker makes at least these decisions: to speak to A and not to B or C or D; to speak now and not then or never; to speak here and not there; to speak about this matter and not about all other matters; and to speak for this period of time, not longer or shorter. These rhetorical decisions contain "information" for the discerning student of communication, even before he or she begins to explore what was said and how it was said. Thus although the brief observations made here may constitute only footnotes to the text of modern politics, they may be footnotes without which the text of modern politics would be inexplicable.

Ultimately, of course, the importance of such data lie in their implications for public policy. In a penetrating analysis of contemporary politics, Paul Corcoran has argued that turning politics over to media moguls has undermined the very essence of political intercourse. He deplores the media-packaging of "candidate images" and the increasing disuse in politics of "actual persons" sharing dialogue. Noting how "electronic" modern campaigning has become, Corcoran (1981, p. 171) asks rhetorically, if despondently: "Why risk an awkward moment or a disastrous slip of the tongue in live appearances when these elements can be eliminated in the studio?" Corcoran (1981, p. 199) also observes that because of the media, "political rhetoric virtually has lost its standing as a separate technique of communication, and that oral performance in its surviving manifestations is an archaic, subsidiary method in comparison with electronic technology." Finally, Corcoran (1981, p. 139) opines that politicians are now less orators than actors, that instead of facing "attentive masses, the image emerges of a speaker sitting in a bare cubicle, addressing not a throng, but merely a microphone and a camera lens."

Corcoran may well be correct that eloquence in politics has declined because of the mass media but he is quite wrong about the facts in the case.

The last 40 years have witnessed an unprecedented surge in the amount of presidential speaking—in television studios as well as in localities—precisely *because of* the corresponding rise of the electronic media. The speeches of presidents have become the raw materials of much political reportage, however these materials are reprocessed by the network studios prior to being shown in America's homes. Radio and television constantly intrude into the campaigns of presidents, goading them to find one more audience for one more speech in the hope that it will produce something important, or, if not important, at least something novel. A modern president now spends much of his time trying to out-think the media by out-scheduling them. The result is the most plentiful and most skillfully choreographed speech the nation has known.

Media strategist David Garth (1984, p. 12) has observed that "Most people believe what they see in the unpaid media." Raymond Strother (1984, p. 12), another media guru, echoes him: "The messages in free media and paid media have to be the same. The free media has far greater impact in a presidential primary." The "free media," for the uninitiated, is what used to be called the news. Perhaps the most distressing aspect of this "mediazation" of the presidency is how preoccupied with image reporters and presidents have become. And this self-absorption has consequences. What responsibility, for example, does the press have when voters are able to discourse knowingly about their president's golf handicap but unable to explain nuclear freeze legislation or trade import barriers? To whom must the president answer when he finds himself making a speech to steelworkers in Pittsburgh on a Tuesday night in lieu of investigating new ways to limit nuclear weaponry or to increase the fluidity of international markets? In the modern age, questions like this seem naïve. "The people get what they ask for," responds the press. "The people need to touch their leaders," responds the president. These answers seem so right, so definitive, as to end discussion. But it is also worth asking what is *best* for the people, what might be the highest function served by electoral campaigns and political journalism, or how the president could most perfectly meet his Constitutional mandate to be the nation's leader, not its most canny follower (or its most clever strategist). Were standards of this sort to be seriously invoked, contemporary American politics would be revised on a massive scale. Campaigning presidents and news commentators behave as they do because, on balance, it is convenient for them to do so. Only discerning voters, which now means discerning students of political communication, could cause them to behave otherwise.

REFERENCES

Carter, J. (1980a). The President's news conference of September 18, 1980. *Public Papers of the Presidents, 1980: 2*, 1826-1834.

Carter, J. (1980b). Remarks at Inauguration Services for the Department of Health and Human Services, May 14, 1980. *Public Papers of the Presidents, 1980: 1*, 908-911.

Corcoran, C. (1979). *Political language and rhetoric*. Austin: University of Texas Press.

Eisenhower, D. (1956a). Address at a rally in the public square, Cleveland, Ohio, October 1, 1956. *Public Papers of the Presidents, 1956*, 828-837.

Eisenhower, D. (1956b). The President's news conference of September 27, 1956. *Public Papers of the Presidents, 1956*, 806-819.

Ford, G. (1974). Remarks to the Veterans of Foreign Wars Annual Convention, Chicago, Illinois, August 19, 1974. *Public Papers of the Presidents, 1974*, 22-28.

Ford, G. (1976a). The President's news conference of October 14, 1976. *Public Papers of the Presidents, 1976: 3*, 2521-2532.

Ford, G. (1976b). Remarks on the eve of the presidential election, November 1, 1976. *Public Papers of the Presidents, 1976: 3*, 2839-2840.

Ford, G. (1976c). Remarks at a fundraising reception for Senator Robert Taft, Jr., in Cleveland, October 28, 1976. *Public Papers of the Presidents, 1976: 3*, 2756-2759.

Ford, G. (1976d). Remarks at a rally on arrival at Grand Rapids, Michigan, November 1, 1976. *Public Papers of the Presidents, 1976: 3*, 2835-2837.

Garth, D. (1984, April 16). Quoted in M. Schram, The medium isn't the message. *Washington Post National Weekly Edition*, p. 12.

Hart, R. P. (In press). *The sound of leadership: Presidential communication in the modern age*. Chicago: University of Chicago Press.

Hart, R. P. (1984). *Verbal style and the presidency: A computer-based analysis*. Orlando, FL: Academic Press.

Johnson, L. (1964a). Campaign remarks in Ohio, October 8, 1964. *Public Papers of the Presidents, 1963: 2*, 1251-1261.

Johnson, L. (1964b). Remarks at an airport rally in Wilmington, Delaware, October 31, 1964. *Public Papers of the Presidents, 1963: 2*, 1552-1558.

Johnson, L. (1964c). Remarks at an airport rally in Wichita, October 29, 1964. *Public Papers of the Presidents, 1963: 2*, 1520-1523.

Nixon, R. (1970a). Remarks in Las Vegas, Nevada, October 31, 1970. *Public Papers of the Presidents, 1970*, 1047-1054.

Nixon, R. (1970b). Remarks in Mount Prospect, Illinois, October 29, 1970. *Public Papers of the Presidents, 1970*, 993-999.

Nixon, R. (1970c). Remarks at Rockford, Illinois, October 29, 1970. *Public Papers of the Presidents, 1970*, 999-1004.

Nixon, R. (1970d). Remarks in San Jose, California, October 29, 1970. *Public Papers of the Presidents, 1970*, 1020-1027.

Nixon, R. (1972a). Remarks at Albuquerque, New Mexico, November 4, 1972. *Public Papers of the Presidents, 1972*, 1121-1127.

Nixon, R. (1972b). Remarks at a campaign reception for Northeastern supporters in New York State, October 23, 1972. *Public Papers of the Presidents, 1972*, 1011-1015.

Nixon, R. (1972c). Remarks at a campaign reception for Southern supporters in Atlanta, Georgia, October 12, 1972. *Public Papers of the Presidents, 1972*, 975-981.

Nixon, R. (1972d). Remarks at Providence, Rhode Island, November 3, 1972. *Public Papers of the Presidents, 1972*, 1107-1110.

Nixon, R. (1972e). Remarks at Tulsa, Oklahoma, November 3, 1972. *Public Papers of the Presidents, 1972*, 1101-1106.

Reagan, R. (1982a). Remarks at a fundraising dinner for Governor William P. Clements, Jr., in Houston, Texas, June 15, 1982. *Public Papers of the Presidents, 1982: 1*, 778-783.

Reagan, R. (1982b). Remarks at a fundraising luncheon for Governor Richard L. Thornburgh in Philadelphia, Pennsylvania, May 14, 1982, *Public Papers of the Presidents, 1982: 1*, 634-637.

Strother, R. (1984, April 16). Quoted in M. Schram, The medium isn't the message. *Washington Post National Weekly Edition*, p. 12.

Tatalovich, R. (1979). Electoral votes and presidential campaign trails, 1932-1976. *American Politics Quarterly, 7*, 489-497.

Time (1984, April 23). Facing the Fatigue Factor, pp. 37-39.

Truman, H. (1948a). Address at the stadium in Butte, Montana, June 8, 1948. *Public Papers of the Presidents, 1948,* 304-307.

Truman, H. (1948b). Campaign stop at Las Vegas, New Mexico, June 15, 1948. *Public Papers of the Presidents, 1948,* 358-359.

Truman, H. (1948c). Campaign stop at Providence, Rhode Island, October 28, 1948. *Public Papers of the Presidents, 1948,* 892-894.

Truman, H. (1948d). Campaign stop at Vinita, Oklahoma, September 29, 1948. *Public Papers of the Presidents, 1948,* 627.

Truman, H. (1948e). Radio remarks in Independence on election eve, November 1, 1948. *Public Papers of the Presidents, 1948,* 939-940.

West, D. M. (1983). Constituencies and travel allocations in the 1980 presidential campaign. *American Journal of Political Science, 27,* 515-529.

5 ● The Role of Theory in Broadcast Economics: A Review and Development

BENJAMIN J. BATES

University of California, Santa Barbara

T HERE is a wide area of research across several disciplines under the general rubric of media economics. Some of this work has dealt with the development and investigation of theory; a great deal more has addressed the social and economic effects of various features of the media marketplace. I propose to survey the status of theory, and then extend its consideration and use in one specific aspect of this field, the economics of broadcasting.

The economics of broadcasting has attracted a fair degree of attention from both traditional economists and communication scholars. To the economist, the field of broadcast economics has deserved attention as a result of several distinctive features. First, it is a heavily regulated industry, which has led to the creation of certain features deemed worthy of intellectual perusal, including the issues of special rents due to regulation and the social welfare implications of regulation in the provision of public goods in the form of programming. Another feature of the industry lies in its unusual production of "dual" goods; that is, it produces one physical product, programming, which is then traded for another nonphysical product, viewers per minute of time, to which it then sells access in order to generate revenue. To the communication scholar, the study of broadcast economics is of interest largely due to the recognition that broadcasting in the United States is commercial, and thus that the primary motivating factors for broadcasters' behavior are economic. And to be able to understand and predict behavior, then, it is useful to understand the economic structure of the industry.

In general, what scholars mean by the *economics of* some field is a delimiting of a specific approach to the understanding of a specific type of behavior within that field. To a large degree it refers to the use of the tech-

Correspondence and requests for reprints: Benjamin J. Bates, Communication Studies Program, 1832 Ellison Hall, University of California, Santa Barbara, CA 93106.

niques and theories of microeconomics to understand, explain, and model the economic behavior of actors in that field or industry. Economic behavior is influenced by several factors related to structure, production, and distribution of goods of one sort or another. The various factors influencing broadcaster behavior can be integrated into specific models, which can then be examined and/or analyzed in order to determine or predict such behavior.

Economic theory, or models, are largely self-contained once a set of basic assumptions is made with regard to the nature of the marketplace and the actors contained therein. I will first discuss the status of theory in the study of broadcast economics, both as described directly and as it exists in the statement of the basic assumptions generated by prior work and general experience. Then, consideration of the use of that theory within applied research will be made. Finally, some ideas for the integration of theory into the study of broadcast economics will be attempted.

In order to maintain consistency in this review, I will define the confines of broadcasting, or the broadcast industry, as that segment of commercial telecommunications whose signal is broadcast unscrambled to the general public over the standard radio and television bands. As such, the industry includes normal broadcast stations and networks. Excluded from this definition are cable, program networks available exclusively over cable, noncommercial networks and stations, and pay TV. In essence, this paper will restrict its concept of broadcasting to the standard, advertiser-supported broadcast media.

THE STATE OF THEORY
IN BROADCAST ECONOMICS

Not a single mass medium . . . sells its product or services according to the principles involved in the laws of supply and demand, or in the calculation of different cost factors. (Landau & Davenport, 1959, p. 291)

The literature on broadcast economics is extensive and ranges from considerations of pure theory to the quantitative cranking out of limited models independent of theory. It is thus somewhat surprising to find so little integrated theory expounded. In spite of the existence of a series of books on the economics of broadcasting, and of television in particular (Levin, 1980; Noll, Peck, & McGowan, 1973; Owen, 1975; Owen, Beebe, & Manning, 1974), the emphasis of research seems to have been on the study of impact and policy concerns rather than the development and integration of theory. This focus on the features of broadcasting has resulted in the mass of applied research being essentially theory-less, resulting in calls such as those by Gerald (1958), Landau and Davenport (1959), Smythe

(1981), and Babe (1983) for continued research into the economics of mass media as well as the integration of theory and application in research (Smith, 1983).

Perhaps the lack of a strict statement and use of theory in applied research results from a perception that the basic theory of broadcast economics is so simple that it is not necessary to state it explicitly. In fact, one can infer from an examination of most of the impact and policy studies a basic model of economic behavior that might be considered an underlying theory: that the broadcaster, in order to make the biggest profits possible, goes after the largest audience possible. Thus, for instance, economic impact is sometimes stated in terms of impact on audience (Park, 1971b, 1972).

Most of the applied research appears to be based on fairly simplistic assumptions, such as seeking to maximize audience, rather than any explicit theoretical model(s). However, this approach is simplistic at best; in fact, it is quite likely to be dead wrong, particularly with regard to the current state of broadcasting.[1] It is time to attempt to bridge the gap between theory and applied research by specifying both theory and assumptions in the building of a firm theoretical basis for research in the economics of broadcasting, such as is offered by standard market analysis of supply and demand.

Building upon this tradition, the study of broadcast economics can be seen as essentially consisting of three parts. First, there is "structural" research into the assumptions of the model such as industry structure and likely behavior patterns. Then there is research into the factors influencing the development of the supply and demand functions themselves, which can be considered as the study of "value" in broadcasting. Finally, there is research into the application of the supply and demand market model to real or potential changes in the industry or marketplace, which could be termed *output analysis*. This last area covers the study of economic impacts in broadcasting. In building toward an integrated framework for future analysis, I will consider first structure, then value, and finally, what is known about impact.

The Good

The quotation opening this section was taken from a paper by Landau and Davenport (1959) criticizing the use of economic models without proper theoretical development. Although working from that reasonable basis, much of the potential impact of their paper was muted by an improper consideration of what the products of mass media were, and thus a misconception of the results of the application of economic analysis. Specifically, they ignored the role of advertising in most of the mass media. It is interesting to note, though, that the only published response to the Landau and Davenport study was a paper by Currier (1960) which restricted itself to newspapers; there was apparently little initial reaction to the assertion that the product of the broadcast industry was its signals and programs, and broadcast good's consumers the general public.

Even in the study of economic theory this concept of program as good was reinforced. Early consideration was given to television as an example of what Samuelson (1958) referred to as a pure public good. Here again the perceived product of television was its signal, and the consumers of that product were the audience. And although the merits of Samuelson's definition and example were debated in the economics literature (Buchanan, 1967; Minasian, 1964, 1967; Samuelson, 1964, 1967), the conception of the signal/program as product remained unchallenged. This debate focused on the relative efficiency of pay versus "free" television.

This focus on social welfare criteria and broadcast signals as the product of the broadcast industry by economists was furthered in the considerable literature on program diversity (Beebe, 1977; Braunstein, 1979; Greenberg & Barnet, 1971; Hall & Batlivala, 1971; Levin, 1971b, 1980; Litman, 1978, 1979a, 1979b; Manning & Owen, 1976; Noll, Peck, & McGowan, 1973; Owen, 1978; Owen, Beebe, & Manning, 1974; Steiner 1952, 1979; Steiner & Wiles, 1963). Here, the good which was considered in examinations of social efficiency and welfare criteria was once more the programs (and signals) produced by broadcasters. Most of the research on program diversity focused on the question of the relation of the structure of the broadcast industry to the production of a diversity of programming options.

In these diversity studies, it was implicitly assumed that, as profit-maximizers, broadcasters would automatically seek the largest audience possible. Economic behavior was generally simplified to the seeking of the greatest possible audience under the limitations of various structural market constraints. Similarly, the presumption underlying the conceptualization of social welfare was that it could be measured by the diversity of programming available for consumption, particularly the availability of what was termed *minority-interest* programming. If any consideration was given to the economic value of advertising, it was usually expressed as a straight return per viewer-hour (Owen, Beebe, & Manning, 1974).

Most of the basic questions and results of this period of intensive research on the issue of diversity in television can be found in a pioneering 1949 dissertation by Steiner (1979; also see Steiner, 1952) examining the nature of competition in radio. Examining the radio industry under the dominance of networks, Steiner developed both the methodology used in later studies and the insights into the development of networks and the limiting structure of the industry which seemed to define the allowable degree of competition and diversity as evidenced in programming of that period. Although focusing on the program as his variable of interest, Steiner

(1979, p. 8) did state that in the functioning of the industry "the program is often only a by-product." There is present in Steiner's work, then, the roots of the concept that the true economic product of the industry was time; specifically, broadcast time that could be used to reach an audience.

Although it has long been recognized that the broadcast industry was largely financed by advertisers (FCC, 1938), early considerations of the output of that industry focused on an examination of programming. However, the beginnings of a shift in theory from a focus on programming can be found in considerations of the impact of the economic (structure) of broadcasting upon policy formation by Coase (1966) and Kahn (1974). Both studies argued that the broadcast industry was financed by the advertiser, and thus the consumer of programming was barred from direct participation in the determination of either the type or amount of programming offered. Although there can still be seen in this argument the perception that programming is the product, there is also the concept that advertising was itself a product of the broadcasting industry.

This beginning shift was further evidenced by Borchadt's (1970) affirmation that television as an industry was dependent upon advertising for financing. Finally, with Melody, (1973, p. 12) and Owen, Beebe, and Manning (1974, p. 4) came the explicit statement that TV stations were in the business of producing audiences, not programs, and that the product of television was therefore measured in terms of people and time. The concept of advertising (or audience) as the economic output of broadcasting, or its product, has been affirmed in more recent research (Larson, 1980; Long, 1979; Parkman, 1982), which noted that the direct participants in the market were stations and advertisers. Similarly, Singleton and Gwyn (1983, p. 77) noted that advertising by local merchants "was the financial mainstay of small market radio." Recently, Harwood (1984) began to measure the productivity of radio and television broadcasting in terms of advertising dollars.

The conception of program as an economic product, however, proved to be tenacious. In one of the earliest books on the economics of broadcasting, Noll, Peck, and McGowan (1973) still asserted that a distinctive feature of the industry was that TV gave away its product, that is, its signal and programs. More recently, Levin (1980) stated that the basic function of networks was to act as a middleman, exchanging the products of program for audience. This notion is somewhat traceable to Wiles's (1963, p. 198) assertion that broadcast programming was a new kind of product: specifically, "the mere vehicle for the advertisement of another product." That concept flows through both Noll, Peck, and McGowan's (1973) and Owen, Beebe, and Manning's (1974) treatments of the economics of broadcasting, although the primary focus remained upon the program as the product of broadcasting. Thus in some areas the focus of research remained upon the more visible good produced by broadcasters, despite the recognition of the existence of economically more important products.

It should be clear, however, that as far as the economics of broadcasting is concerned, the proper, final, product to be considered is the access to audience provided to advertisers. Although programs and signals are in fact products of broadcast stations and networks, as noted by Landau and Davenport (1959) and Noll, Peck, and McGowan (1973), such product is given away: no price is charged and no revenue is collected. Changes in signal and programming will thus have no economic impact except as inputs in the determination of audience (directly through attractiveness or reach or indirectly through cost considerations). The motivating factor in economic behavior is the generation of profit; thus the appropriate factor for consideration must be that through which profit is generated. For broadcasting, that implies consideration of the basic source of funding, advertising.

There is another way to look at this disparity in perception as to the product of the broadcast industry. Clearly, the final product of broadcasting, the good which is bought and sold in the marketplace, is the access to audience. There remains, however, the question of how that audience is produced. It is clearly not produced directly, but through an exchange of intermediate goods. Members of the audience exchange their time and their attention (advertisers hope) to the broadcaster in exchange for the programming the broadcaster provides for that audience member's consumption. As stated, somewhat colloquially, by Melody (1973, p. 12): "The bait for attracting an audience is a program." Thus the program can be seen as an intermediate good in the production of the audience for the advertising-supported broadcaster.

Thus it is not denied that the signals or programs are goods in and of themselves, or that they might have impact upon the economics of broadcasting. In fact, both the signal and the programs it carries can be seen as important input factors influencing the production of the final good of access to audience. The end result, and the focus of study, however, must remain upon that which generates revenues and profits for most broadcast enterprises.

For the immediate purposes of this study, then, the central concept upon which the framework of theory and application of broadcast economics is based is the notion of the audience as the product of broadcasting; the good for which supply and demand functions are appropriately defined and toward which economic behavior is directed within the marketplace. To be precise, it is access to audience for a period of time via the broadcast signal which is the good in question; a good which is represented by the broadcast segment.

Features of the Broadcast Good

There are several features of audience access through the provision of broadcast time to advertisers that make its economic treatment distinctive.

First is an expansion of the issue of time, in particular the length of the broadcast segment: There are the short (15 to 60 seconds) drop-in spots called announcement time, and the longer segments (5 minutes or longer), generally called program time, that requires the presentation of programming (Peterman, 1965). To maintain uniformity in treatment, this report will concentrate on a consideration of broadcast spots, with the presumption that blocks would be treated in essentially the same manner.

A second feature of this good, as epitomized by the broadcast spot, is its perishability. Access to an audience, at a particular time, is a classic example of a perishable good: once that time has passed, the good no longer exists or has value. Further, such access cannot be transferred to other markets: The particular audience in question is immobile. This feature has been commented on in several works addressing the nature of broadcast advertising (French & McBrayer, 1979; Peterman, 1965), although recognition of the perishability of broadcast time does not seem to have been incorporated in the mainstream literature, at least explicitly.

Another important aspect of broadcast spots is the existence of substitutes for that good. Access to an audience can be achieved through a variety of channels. And although neither competing stations nor alternative media can be considered perfect substitutes, as they reach different audiences with differing effectiveness, their presence has a significant impact upon the demand for advertising. Economists have noted that the more (and better) substitutes there are available for a good, the greater its price elasticity (Ferguson, 1972, p. 105). Noll, Peck, and McGowan (1973), in considering the broadcast industry, have noted that the demand for broadcast spots was highly elastic. That is, the advertiser will quite likely switch out of television should the price rise, or into it with a fall in price, relative to the cost of access to the audience through other media. This substitutability is reflected in early research by Kinter (1948a, 1948b) and McCombs (1972), which suggested that spending on advertising tends to be constant in any market, and that the various media in that market compete for shares of that total. This notion is further supported by current work on the economic theory of advertising, which suggests that the total demand for advertising is determined by factors independent of the media used (Ehrlich & Fisher, 1982).

Using an approach derived from ecological theory, Dimmick and Rothenbuhler (1984) have attempted to measure the degree of this competition among major advertising media. Although finding competition, they also noted that the various media occupy distinct "niches," or degrees to which they make use of various advertising resources. Thus although other media compete for the advertising dollar, they are not perfect substitutes for broadcast advertising, having different features and degrees of effectiveness (Ehrlich & Fisher, 1982; Hileman, 1968; Levin, 1960; Manning & Owen, 1976), which tends to mitigate somewhat the influence of the presence of close substitutes.

Finally, a further important aspect of broadcast spots is that the supply is essentially fixed. In a consideration of network television advertising, Bowman (1975) found that the supply of broadcast advertising time was highly inelastic, that price had an insignificant effect on the quantity supplied. This may be due in part to the fact that the economic good of broadcast spots is comprised of two fixed inputs: audience and time. Time is of fixed supply, setting an upper limit as to the availability of broadcast spots (of whatever duration). This absolute upper limit, however, is never approached, as other forces act to further restrict the supply of these spots.

These forces could be called, collectively, *enlightened self-interest*. Fundamental to these restrictive forces are the requirements and policies of the FCC. The Federal Communications Commission imposes certain conditions upon broadcast license holders in the form of required announcements and an obligation to "serve the public interest." These conditions require preemption of a segment of the broadcast schedule, thereby restricting the supply of broadcast advertising. In addition, the FCC has commented upon the amount of broadcast time devoted for advertising purposes on several occasions (Kahn, 1978), and has twice cited "over-commercialization" as a rationale for license revocation (Sterling, 1984).[2]

There is another force that acts to restrict the potential supply of broadcast advertising, involving a special feature of some entertainment programming. In large part this force arose from the National Association of Broadcasters' Codes, which used to set precise limits upon the amount of commercial advertising available in any time period. Before these codes were revoked, the major networks and most stations had agreed to abide by the restrictions imposed by the codes, and programming was produced with those Codes in mind.

This meant that "holes" of specific length and position were left in the programs delivered to the networks and/or individual stations, especially in television. As the networks, for the most part, kept to firm schedules, and affiliation and syndication agreements limited the abilities of individual stations to cut programming, stations could not readily adjust the amount of time available to them for sale to potential advertisers. In the short run, then, broadcasters in television, whether stations or networks, were presented with a largely fixed fraction of broadcast time for sale.

There remained some control over supply, through the expansion or contraction of operating hours, or through the expansion or contraction of scheduled commercial breaks in locally produced programming. This latter form of control is evidenced most clearly in radio, where most of the programming is locally produced, and where the supply of broadcast advertising time can therefore more easily be manipulated. There was also some concern expressed that the revocation of the Codes by the courts would result in a flood of additional commercials, but that fear has not yet been realized. The need for preproduced nonlocal programming in television should keep the supply of commercial time restricted in this manner for the foreseeable future.

In addition, Noll, Peck, and McGowan (1973, p. 34) found that "the value of advertising to the advertiser is sensitive to [both] the total amount and proportion of advertising in the medium," providing additional pressure on the broadcaster to restrict the amount of advertising spots supplied. When all is considered, it would seem that the factors described above act to restrict the amount of time that broadcasters can make available for advertising, particularly in television. In fact, it would appear that these forces act to severely restrict not only the total amount of the supply of broadcast advertising in television, but also act to restrict individual broadcasters' control over the determination of that amount.

The Players

In economic analysis there are two primary "players": economic actors (individuals or firms) whose behavior is fundamental for both theory and application. There are those who produce (or supply) the product (or good) and those who consume (or demand) it. Clearly, one of these players is the broadcaster, either a station or a network, depending upon the level of analysis. The perception of the identity of the second player, however, has been tied to the perception of what constituted the good.

In Owen, Beebe, and Manning (1974, p. 7), a figure was presented that identified the principal actors in the television industry and characterized their interrelationships. Named as the players in commercial broadcasting were viewers, stations, advertisers, networks, the Federal Communications Commission (FCC), and program producers and syndicators. The "players" were linked in essentially three markets: the market for programs as input goods, the market for programs as output, and the market for audiences. As the first market is for an input to the production of broadcast goods, it lies outside of the scope of this work and will therefore not be here addressed.

As noted above, early considerations stated that the (programmed) signal was the good, and thus the general public who might be expected to consume it provided the second player. As an important intermediate consumer, as well as a component of the good in question, the general public remains an influencing factor. With the shift to the concept that the appropriate good for analysis was the audience itself came the rise of the definition of the advertiser as the second basic economic force (actor) in the marketplace (Long, 1979; also implicit in Korn, 1977; Webbink, 1973; White, 1977).

There is yet another actor in the economics of broadcasting. Although not usually considered a direct participant in the marketplace, the government, or more appropriately government regulation, has proved to be a significant force in the marketplace (Besen, 1974; Besen & Hanley, 1975;

Borchadt, 1970; Crandall, 1971, 1974; Long, 1979). Government policy and regulation has been noted as influencing not only the structure of the market and the industry itself (Besen, Krattenmaker, Metzger, & Woodbury, 1984; Smythe, 1960), but the basic behavior of the two principal players (Comaner & Mitchell, 1972; Levin, 1980). Further, the federal government has been known to intercede directly in the broadcast marketplace, as with the 1971 ban on cigarette advertising.

In broadcast economics, therefore, there are essentially four players in a two player game of supply and demand. Two of these, the broadcaster and the advertiser, are the direct players: the ones whose behavior (moves) determine the outcome of this economic game. There are two other groups, however, who can be said to influence both the structure and the rules of this game, and must therefore be taken into account. Both the government and the general public are involved in the economics of broadcasting, although in most instances as a presumed state or context, rather than as active participants.

As an example, consider some of the broadcast diversity articles (Beebe, 1977; Park, 1975; Spence & Owen, 1977), which took as assumptions various sets of programming preferences (audience behavior). Others (Besen, 1975; Braunstein, 1979) examined the influence of policy alternatives. Even in such articles, in which the public, as economic agents, were treated as variables, they are perceived of as variable states rather than active participants in the broadcast marketplace. Thus even in that portion of the research on the economics of broadcasting that claims programming as its principle economic good, the consumer of that good, the general public, is not treated as an active participant in the marketplace.

Therefore, the researcher interested in understanding and/or predicting economic behavior within broadcasting is left with two active participants in the marketplace: those who seek to sell access to an audience (the broadcaster), and those who seek to purchase that access (the advertiser). It is the interaction of these two forces in the derivation of economic surplus (that is, profits) that provides the basis for the economics of broadcasting.

The Market

Economic behavior and theory exist within the context of a market, at one level or another. Alternatively, one could state that goods are supplied and sold within markets. Markets are not defined by geopolitical boundaries, but rather by the specific good being examined and those who are interested in, or able to, supply or purchase that good. Further, various characteristics of the market can have profound effects upon the workings of that market, making consideration of the market and its structure of prime importance to any economic analysis.

What is the marketplace for broadcasting? Conceptually, the marketplace for broadcasting is variable, governed by the nature of the particular product in question. That is, there is no single broadcast marketplace; rather, there are likely to be a number of ranges, or levels, of markets to be considered for both radio and television. Early studies within the FCC (1938, p. 39) indicated that markets for regional and local radio stations were different: "National advertisers preferred stations of high power, and local advertisers utilized stations in their own communities." Similarly, Steiner (1952, 1979) and Levin (1980) argued that the U.S. broadcasting system was composed of several related market segments rather than distinctive, separate components.

Whether the product of broadcasters is considered to be programs or advertising, the key to the broadcast marketplace is the range and reach of the signal: the potential audience for that broadcast. In the market for programs, the potential consumers are those capable of receiving the program, whereas the demand for broadcast time is created by advertisers in search of access to that audience of program consumers. In either case, it is clear that the market in which those who supply and those who demand seek to trade is determined by the size and scope of the potential broadcast audience.

Thus the market for broadcast time can be seen to operate on several levels, governed by the reach of the broadcast signal. At the local level there are the stations and advertisers seeking to trade in (access to) local audiences. At the highest level, the major networks and national advertisers similarly deal in national audiences. Intermediate level markets exist whenever local markets are aggregated in search of more broadly defined audiences, through regional networks or special interconnects.

Although there may be, in fact, many kinds of broadcast markets, the development of theory in broadcast economics is aided by the fact that these markets are fundamentally similar. That is, although different levels of aggregation exist, the structure of the market and the behavior of the agents within it remain essentially the same. Thus this analysis and development of theory will focus on an abstract conception of the broadcast marketplace, one which should be equally valid at all levels of economic analysis. Only where differences resulting from the level of aggregation become important will they be noted and discussed in depth.

There are several features of the broadcast marketplace that must be addressed for the proper application of economic theory. Key among these are issues of structure. Economic analysis started with the concept of perfect competition, where there were sufficient numbers of both buyers and sellers in the marketplace that neither exercised any control over the functioning of that market. Markets are seldom perfect, however, resulting in market structures that force alteration of the basic economic theories and approaches through the influences of the number and relative size of the market participants and the uniformity of the product involved.

For the most part, it is widely recognized that broadcast markets are not "perfect." The number of suppliers (broadcasters) is restricted, for the most part due to technical and policy limitations. This results in a limited number of suppliers in any market (and significantly fewer television than radio signals), which can result in one of three basic economic structures on the supply side. First is the case of monopoly, where only one supplier exists. In broadcasting, such a supply structure is limited to a few local markets, with little overall impact. For example, recent Nielsen studies estimate that only 3% of U.S. television households could receive three or fewer stations.

A second kind of market structure, which is likely to be of greatest interest in the consideration of television markets, is termed *oligopoly*. Oligopoly exists when a small number of firms supply most or all of the product in a market. The national TV market for advertising is an excellent example of oligopoly. Although there are a sizable number of alternatives, the three major networks, at any given time, control access to 70% to 80% of the broadcast television audience, and can supply that audience to advertisers. With such dominance, the major networks, singly or collectively, can be seen to have the capacity to exercise a degree of control over the market.

A third basic structure is called monopolistic competition, in which a number of firms compete to supply a somewhat differentiated product. Each firm can influence the market somewhat, but not to the degree exercised by the oligopolist or the monopolist. Further, this influence results in large part from the differentiation of the firm's product. This structure can be seen in many of the larger radio markets, in which the presence of a moderate number of stations, and the targeting of audience through program differentiation, reduces levels of concentration.

Most broadcast markets can be classified as either examples of oligopoly or monopolistic competition, depending upon the level of concentration and the degree of program differentiation in the particular marketplace being considered. Within the literature, television markets have generally been treated as oligopolistic (Flynn, 1970; Levin, 1980; Long, 1979; Noll, Peck, & McGowan, 1973; Pearce, 1980; Peterman, 1971) with a 70% or higher share for the top three firms in almost all markets (Fournier & Martin, 1983). Further, the early studies made the presumption that some degree of market power existed in broadcasting resulting from both concentration in markets (Blake & Blum, 1965) and vertical integration within the industry (Litman, 1979c). Some recent studies (Fournier & Martin, 1983; Woodbury, Besen, & Martin, 1983), however, have questioned the validity of that assumption. Not so much attention has been granted radio; currently, the larger numbers of stations in most markets, the greater product differentiation, and the absence of major program suppliers suggests that monopolistic competition may be the more appropriate market structure. This possibility was, in fact, raised in Steiner's (1952, 1979) pioneering study of the structure of the radio industry in the 1940s.

The possible influence of concentration among advertisers upon the broadcast industry also was addressed in what became known as the "Tonypandy" debate in the 1960s. Some policy researchers (Blake & Blum, 1965; Leonard, 1969) argued that large advertisers were able to extract significant discounts in their purchase of advertising time from the television networks. As this presumption was incorporated into antitrust litigation, other researchers, principally Blank (1968, 1969), argued that the effect of volume discounts on actual (rather than published) rates was small, and was being obliterated by the shift in emphasis from program sponsorship to spot rates.

One study by Larson (1980) examined the question of concentration in both the U.S. television and advertising industries directly. Examining only the national market, he found that the networks were highly concentrated, but that on a national basis, stations were not. This last is hardly surprising, considering the number of commercial television stations and the FCC's ownership limitations. Larson did note, however, that local market concentration was likely to be higher than the national measures.

Larson also examined another aspect of market structure: buyer concentration. Crandall (1972) had suggested that there appeared to be an "unexplored" degree of monopoly power not in advertising markets, but among the buyers. Concentration among buyers, as with sellers, can influence the economic functioning of the marketplace. Outside of competition, there are two basic "buyer" structures, monopsony and oligopsony, which mirror the seller structures of monopoly and oligopoly.

Larson (1980, pp. 34-35) found that, for total advertising billings, the industry was mildly oligopsonistic, with the eight largest advertising agencies controlling between 25%-40% of the total purchases. Network advertising was more concentrated, with the eight largest firms again purchasing 40%-60% of the supply. Although figures were not available for local markets, it is likely that local advertising is less concentrated. As noted by Crandall (1972), however, fewness does not necessarily imply power or control.

There remains one more aspect of concentration to be considered: whether or not the current levels are by any means necessary. That is to say, can one expect drastic changes in the basic structure of broadcast markets? By and large, it can be stated that broadcast television markets are, and will remain, oligopolistic. This result derives primarily from various technical and legal restraints imposed by the FCC, which limit the number of available television stations in markets, and thus the capacity for a fourth competitive network (Crandall, 1974; FCC Network Study Staff, 1958; Noll, Peck & McGowan, 1973; Park, 1975).

First, FCC policy set aside a limited bandwidth for television signals, and fixed output power limits. In doing so, that agency fixed certain technical limits to the number of stations available. Then, to promote their stated goal of local service, the FCC assigned those available stations to cities and towns across the United States. Thus in any area, there are only a fixed number of licenses available. Researchers have argued that such policies had the effect of restricting competition (Crandall, 1974; Levin, 1971a; Long, 1979) and of generating scarcity "rents" to broadcasters (Levin, 1962, 1971a, 1975).

The actual number of signals available is dependent upon economic considerations as well as federal regulation. Broadcasting in the United States is a private, commercial enterprise, and requires the generation of enough revenue, over time, to cover both operating and investment costs. Smythe (1960) argued that the heavy initial investment in broadcast television was one barrier to entry. Other studies (Besen & Hanley, 1975; Greenberg, 1969; Korn, 1977; Webbink, 1973) have found that a certain minimum audience must be served in order to generate sufficient revenue for private investment in television properties.

Another factor, in some degree independent of the number of signals actually available, is programming. Recall that oligopoly exists when a few firms control a significant proportion of the supply of the product. Historically, the three commercial television networks have generated the bulk of the programming available for television broadcasts, garnering between 60% and 100% of the viewers during their broadcast hours in local markets through their affiliates. Several studies have been commissioned by the FCC over the years as to the viability of additional networks, with the general conclusion that the high program costs and the lack of stations available for affiliation have made such a venture economically unworkable (Crandall, 1974; FCC Network Study Staff, 1958; Noll, Peck & McGowan, 1973; Park, 1975). There was even doubt as to the initial viability of three networks, although Litman (1979b) concluded recently that the three major networks now compete on roughly an equal footing.

Although the programming market has loosened considerably over the last few years, most (nonmovies) programming is still generated for the major networks, giving the national marketplace an oligopolistic look. Thus it seems that both legal and economic constraints have acted to provide the television industry with its basically oligopolistic structure. However, with technical changes and the advent of cable and low-power television, it is not clear that the structure need remain so. As with radio, the opening of new technologies and general expansion could well result in a shift of structures, perhaps to the monopolistic competition that seems to be becoming more prevalent, or at least appropriate, in considerations of the radio industry.

Summary

In contrast to the quotation opening this section, it would appear that the broadcasting industry *does* sell its product according to the principles involved in the economic laws of supply and demand. That is, of course, accepting the conclusion that the proper product of broadcasting for economic analysis is the access to audience it offers through the sale of broadcast time. Discussions in this section regarding access to the audience as the product of the broadcasting industry also have noted several features that will, in fact, influence the application of these laws. Specifically, it was noted that broadcast time is a perishable good with several close, but not perfect, substitutes. Further, certain forces act to restrict the supply of that good that can be made available in any market.

It also was found that the principal economic actors, the broadcasters and the potential advertisers, operate in a variety of markets. It was argued that although these markets could vary in both size (from local to national) and medium (radio as distinct from television), the basic elements of these markets remained consistent throughout the various market forms. It was noted, though, that there was one aspect of broadcast markets that varied: its structure, or degree, of concentration, which ranged from monopolistic structures in some small communities to oligopolistic or monopolistic competition structures in many of the larger markets. It was argued that radio markets tended toward monopolistic competition, and television markets evidenced oligopolistic structures.[3] It was noted further that national markets evidenced a degree of oligopsonistic structure, and local markets were generally more competitive.

Although these properties do tend to preclude broadcasting from the standard considerations (examples) of supply and demand under perfect competition, they by no means invalidate that approach. In fact, the unique features of broadcasting and its economic good make such an approach even more useful, in that they render questionable the standard economic behaviors and outcomes that may have been used in place of a more rigorous theoretical analysis.

VALUE IN BROADCASTING

The true value of any good lies in its usefulness, or potential usefulness, to its owner. As such, value is individually variable: Each person or entity has an individual value for any good. Value in this sense is called *utility* by economists and is considered to be subjective, and thus largely unknown. Adam Smith, to facilitate analyses, differentiated between the use value of a good, and its exchange value (Rima, 1972) or price. From such a beginning, modern economic theory has used the price of a good as a measure of its aggregate, or average, value. Following this, most of the studies reported here have used price as an indicator of value.

There have been a number of studies that have attempted to determine what factors influence the value of various facets of the broadcast industry. Primary to this study are those that have focused on the basic good of the broadcasting industry, the access to an audience through broadcast time. As would be expected, the major factor is usually some aspect of audience, real or potential. The recognition of the influence of audience size upon advertising rates and revenues occurred quite early in American broadcasting. For example, an early FCC report (1938) noted that station revenues were related to community size, network affiliation, and the power of stations.

In work originally published in the late 1940s, Reinsch and Ellis (1960) and Steiner (1979, 1952) found that the value of radio time was based upon the size and the characteristics of the audience for that time, although noting that market relationships, such as the amount and nature of competition, also influenced the value of such time. Later, Ripley (1959) found that market size was an important factor influencing the revenues generated by a radio station, but not its profitability, and Deutschmann and Emery (1961) identified audience, market prosperity, and advertising time prices as factors influencing the value of radio stations. Levin (1964, 1971a), however, asserted that for radio stations, class and broadcast power might be more important factors than community size in explaining variations in time sales and profit margins. In a recent dissertation, Yadon (1983) incorporated such concerns into a model of entry into radio market, using the retail sales in a market as a measure of market size.

Turning to television, both Ogden (1961) and Owen, Beebe, and Manning (1974) referred to the value of television time in terms of households delivered, indicating the importance of audience in the determination of prices. Virtually all considerations of the value of broadcast time have cited some measure of audience or market size and characteristics as the primary influence in the determination of that value. This link also emerged in studies examining television stations' viability (Webbink, 1973) and the supply and demand curves for network TV advertising (Bowman, 1975).

Audience size and characteristics were not the only factors identified in the various studies looking at the influences of the price, or value, of television time. Ogden (1961), for example, also had noted that market conditions, both in economic terms and with respect to competition, affected the value of broadcast time. Competition, considered primarily in terms of the number of competing stations, was mentioned by a number of researchers (Besen, 1976, 1978; Blau, Johnson, & Ksobeich, 1976; French & McBrayer, 1979; Kelley, 1967; Levin, 1975; Park, 1978; Peterman, 1971), although some also noted that the presence of alternative media restricted the range of possible prices (Kelly, 1967; Peterman, 1965,

1971). Market economic conditions also were mentioned as possible influences by Kelly (1967) and French and McBrayer (1979).

Measures of relative competition also were mentioned by a number of studies as having an impact upon the value of broadcast television time. Peterman (1965) had noted differences in value among different dayparts. Blau, Johnson, and Ksobeich (1976) included program spending as an influential factor in the determination of value, and others generalized that factor through consideration of network affiliation (Besen, 1976, 1978; Levin, 1980; Park, 1978; White, 1977). Another measure of relative competition was introduced by Besen (1976), to account for the relative disadvantage of UHF stations, compared with VHF broadcasters. This "UHF handicap" was included in a number of subsequent studies (Besen, 1978; Park, 1978; White, 1977; Wirth & Wollert, 1984), proving to have a significant influence on the price of television time.

Several other factors were included in various studies, including measures of economic concentration (Levin, 1980), cable penetration (Park, 1971a; Wirth & Wollert, 1984), and the size of the advertiser buying the time (Fournier & Martin, 1983). Although some of these studies were strictly analytical (French & McBrayer, 1979; Ogden, 1961; Owen, Beebe, & Manning, 1974) or based on surveys (Kelley, 1967), most studies attempted to derive quantitative models of value, with varying degrees of success. Park (1978) criticized the limiting nature of some of the models used, but a second criticism, that the use of cross-sectional analysis limited the validity of results to a single point in time, was only recently addressed.

In looking at advertising rates over time, Bates (1983, 1986) tended to confirm the basic set of factors offered by previous researchers. As in all cases, measures of audience, directly or indirectly through market size, proved to be the dominant factor influencing the price of broadcast time on television. Other factors, such as network affiliation (or lack thereof), competition, and market characteristics (both economic and demographic) contributed slightly to the explanation of advertising rates. The "UHF handicap" factor noted by Besen (1976) and others did appear, but seemed to lose influence over time, and cable penetration appeared to increase in influence over time.

Some additional supporting evidence for the influence of audience can be found in a series of studies examining the value and/or viability of broadcast stations. In studies attempting to model the value of television stations, Levin (1964, 1971a, 1975) and Blau, Johnson, and Ksobiech (1976) found that the sales price for television properties depended on market size, network affiliation, the age of the station, and the number of competing independent stations. Deutschmann and Emery (1961) had found similar relationships among audience, market characteristics, and the value of radio stations. Looking at the value of television stations indirectly, in terms of revenue generation potential, Fisher and Ferrall (1966) measured the impact of audience size upon station revenues. Similarly, Besen and Hanley (1975), Greenberg (1969), and Webbink (1973), found that the viability of television stations in general (measured in terms of potential profitability) depended primarily upon the size of the market and the number and type of television stations in direct competition. Restricting his consideration to independent television stations, Korn (1977) identified market size, programming expenditures, and coverage handicaps as factors influencing viability for such stations.

The factors identified in these myriad reports and studies can be grouped into three basic influences. First, there are the indicators of potential audience: factors such as market size, average audience, and market rank. Next, there are those factors that influence the exact audience for any particular bit of broadcast time: network affiliation, programming expenditures, media competition, coverage handicaps such as the "UHF" handicap, and cable penetration. Then there are those factors reflective of the nature of the particular audience: demographics, income, and general economic conditions. In conclusion, then, it would seem that the evidence presented by the literature would tend to support the statement that the primary source of value of broadcast time lies in the nature and the size of the audience it attracts.

THE ROLE OF THEORY IN
ECONOMIC IMPACT STUDIES

A great deal of the research in the field of broadcast economics has been related to the question of policy. Specifically, such work has examined the actual or potential impact of policy decisions regarding broadcasting and/ or new technologies upon the (then) current state of the industry. Most of this research was motivated by actual, or proposed, rule-makings of the FCC.

Ideally, such research should proceed according to the standard "scientific" model: A theory is proposed and examined to derive a specific hypothesis regarding the likely impact of the identified independent factor (that is, policy), and then that hypothesis is tested through observation. However, in examining the evidence of such work extant, it appears that a great deal of the analysis performed has not followed this procedure. Specifically, most economic impact studies seem to follow a somewhat ad hoc "a posteriori" model: Actual changes are sought after the implementation of some policy (or technological development) without any explicit development of theory or hypothetical consequences. The standard methodology of these studies seems to be to specify a model that includes a measure of the policy factor and to then fit that model to a selected set of data. Statistical significance of the factor is then interpreted as evidence of impact.

Such a methodology was used in examinations of network behavior and the prime time access rule (Crandall, 1971, 1972; Levin 1980; Owen, Beebe, & Manning, 1974), programming diversity and the possibilities for new networks (Crandall, 1974; FCC Network Study Staff, 1958; Levin, 1980; Noll, Peck, & McGowan, 1973; Owen, Beebe, & Manning, 1974; Park, 1975) the Carroll Doctrine (Levin, 1975; Litman, 1979a; Park, 1971b; Prisuta, 1977), concentration (Levin, 1980; Litman, 1978; Parkman, 1982; Peterman, 1971; Prisuta, 1977), entry restrictions in television markets (Besen & Hanley, 1975; Fournier & Martin, 1983; Greenberg, 1969; Levin, 1980; Webbink, 1973), cross-ownership (Howard, 1974; Parkman, 1982; White, 1977; Wirth & Wollert, 1984), and cable television (Agostino, 1980; Fisher & Ferrall, 1966; Park, 1971a, 1972; Noll, Peck, & McGowan, 1973; Webster, 1983, 1984).

Although the models presented in these studies are of varying degrees of sophistication, and are based upon measures of differing degrees of validity, they share several basic, and limiting, features. First, what theory and/or hypotheses are incorporated in these studies are usually implicit in the specification of the model to be fitted rather than explicitly stated and examined in the body of the work. Second, these analyses are limited in the sense that the statistical procedures used can give little or no information as to the validity, or correctness, of the models; they only indicate whether or not a specific model "fits" a given set of data.[4] Also, such modeling is further restricted in the sense that it can only be employed in the presence of the (potential) impact factor; it cannot properly be used to predict the impact of change in a factor, or the introduction of a new influence.

A prime example of this sort of method is Litman's (1979a) examination of the impact of the FCC's Carroll Doctrine. The rationale behind this doctrine argues that public interest broadcasting is costly and therefore broadcasters must be assured of profits in order to make such programming available. Following this, Litman attempts to fit a series of regression models in which measures of public service programming are "explained" by other, indirect, measures of profitability. The basic models examined by Litman presume that there is a direct, causal, link between profits and public interest programming, and allow for no mitigating factors. And although the actual fitted equations contain no direct measure of a station's profits, Litman's conclusion of the validity of the doctrine is based solely on the finding that such fitted equations are statistically significant. No recourse is made to the economics of broadcasting or any theory of economic behavior in examining this clearly economic impact.

There has been industry impact research based on other basic methodologies. Studies of the impact of cable television upon local broadcasting have been based upon surveys of both stations and audiences (Becker, Dunwoody, & Rafaeli, 1983; Kaplan, 1978, Singleton & Gwyn, 1983). From an analytical and legal approach, Braunstein (1979) examined the likely impact of the proposed Communications Act rewrite upon selected public interest concerns. Policy researchers such as DeVany, Eckert, Meyers, O'Hara, and Scott (1980) and Krasnouw and Longley (1978) have examined policy issues from historical or legal perspectives. Some impact studies have been based strictly on theoretical models (Braunstein, 1984; Park, 1971a; Parker, 1984; Samuelson, 1958).

Like the bulk of empirical studies, though, the above studies and methods also have failed to integrate theory with observation. Yet not all studies have focused exclusively upon one form of analysis or another. Owen (1975), for example, included an examination of theory as applied to the question of diversity in program production in an appendix to his analysis of the impact of policy on the economics of broadcasting. Besen and Mitchell (1975) used several models of audience behavior as the basis for their study of the economic impact of the Watergate hearings upon the television networks. In addition, one historical analysis by Long (1979) of the FCC's impact upon market structure in television did incorporate a theoretical model to predict and explain the emergence of networks in broadcasting, a model similar to that presented by Steiner (1979) for radio.

From the review of this research and an examination of the other research on economic impact in broadcasting, it would seem that theory plays only a small role in such studies, if indeed it plays any part. To a large degree, Levin (1980) can be seen as typifying the field of impact research, as he devoted an entire book to a synthesis of economic studies of television regulation (albeit with a focus on the diversity issue), yet failed to consider theory explicitly or to derive specific hypotheses regarding the nature of any factor's impact that could then be tested. Rather, Levin and the other researchers he cites merely attempted to measure some presumed impact. Little wonder, then, that as late as 1983 there were calls for the integration of theory with practical research (Smith, 1983).

SUMMARY

Although there is a considerable amount of research in the "economics of broadcasting," studies have, for the most part, been narrowly focused and bereft of theory. There has been little attempt to integrate findings, or to base applied research on anything more than the simplest of assumptions regarding the economic behavior of broadcasters and/or advertisers.

The failing of the field to integrate theory and applied research, moreover, cannot be blamed on any lack of knowledge or understanding. It seems plain, on the basis of this review, that enough is known about the nature of the broadcast good (access to audience through time sales), the structure of broadcasting markets, and the factors influencing the value of broadcast advertising time to provide an integrated framework for any further research in this area. Several books attempted to provide overviews of broadcast economics (notably Levin, 1980; Noll, Peck, & McGowan, 1973; Owen, Beebe, & Manning, 1974); their presentations, however, were segmented, dealing with theory and research only within narrow foci. There have been two recent papers, however, which have attempted to gather together what is known about the economics of broadcasting.

The first of these was a paper presented by McFadyen and Hoskins (1985) at last year's ICA meeting, which addressed the economics of broadcasting as it applied to the Canadian system. In the other, I (Bates, 1985) attempted to derive a simple theoretical model that could be used as a basis for much of the applied research in the area of economic impact in broadcasting. This model, based upon a supply/demand analysis, was simple, even simplisitic, although integrating much of what was known about the nature of broadcast goods and markets. Although the simplicity of the model restricted its usefulness, it still provided a start toward the further development of an integrated theory of broadcast economics. And the review of the published research in the field clearly indicates that there is a strong need for further development of theory, and the integration of that theory into applied research.

NOTES

1. Although there is a demonstrable link between audience size and revenues (whether actual or potential), the link with profits is less certain. Further, there is considerable evidence that in the magazine industry, as well as radio, that profits may well be higher with a restricted audience: that going after a selected fragment of audience is more profitable than going after mass audiences.

2. This influence was evidenced in various Commission statements and documents tracing back to the Federal Radio Commission in 1929, culminating in a 1963 attempt to regulate directly the number and frequency of broadcast advertisements (Krasnow & Longley, 1978). This history of concern influenced the development of a series of self-regulating Codes enacted by the National Association of Broadcasters that proscribed various limits on the type and amount of advertising that could be presented. For examples of such statements and Codes, see Kahn (1978).

3. There is some difference in opinion and research, however, as to whether or not the television industry derives, and/or wields, any degree of market power from the demonstrated high levels of concentration. Pearce (1980), for example, asserts that the major television networks wield substantial power, both economically and politically. Some recent empirical studies, however, have failed to find any evidence of such power being exercised (Fournier & Martin, 1983; Woodbury, Besen, & Martin, 1983).

4. Discussion of the limits of mathematical or statistical models can be found in Draper and Smith (1966), Wonnacott and Wonnacott (1970), and Parker (1984).

REFERENCES

Agostino, D. (1980). Cable television's impact on the audience of public television. *Journal of Broadcasting, 24*(3), 347-365.

Babe, R. E. (1983). Information industries and economic analysis: Policy-makers beware. In O. H. Gandy, Jr., P. Espinosa, & J. A. Ordover, (Eds.), *Proceedings from the Tenth Annual Telecommunications Policy Research Conference*. Norwood, NJ: ABLEX.

Babe, R. E. (1984). Comment. In Canadian-U.S. Conference on Communications Policy, *Cultures in collision: The interaction of Canadian and U.S. television broadcast policies*. New York: Praeger.

Bates, B. J. (1983). Determining television advertising rates. In R. N. Bostrom (Ed.), *Communication Yearbook 7*. Beverly Hills, CA: Sage.

Bates, B. J. (1985). *Economic theory and broadcasting*. Paper presented at the 68th Annual Convention of the Association for Education in Journalism and Mass Communication, Memphis, TN.

Bates, B. J. (1986). *Factors influencing the value of television time: An analysis over time*. Unpublished doctoral dissertation, University of Michigan.

Becker, L. B., Dunwoody, S., & Rafaeli, S. (1983). Cable's impact on the use of other media. *Journal of Broadcasting, 27*(2), 127-139.

Beebe, J. H. (1977). Institutional structure and program choices in television markets. *Quarterly Journal of Economics, 91*(1), 15-38.

Besen, S. M. (1974). The economics of the cable television 'consensus.' *Journal of Law and Economics, 17*(1), 39-52.

Besen, S. M. (1976). The value of television time. *Southern Economic Journal, 42*(3), 435-441.

Besen, S. M. (1978). The value of television time: Some problems and attempted solutions: Reply. *Southern Economic Journal, 44*(4), 1016-1018.

Besen, S. M., & Hanley, P. J. (1975). Market size, VHF allocations, and the viability of television stations. *Journal of Industrial Economics, 24*(1), 41-54.

Besen, S. M., Krattenmaker, T. G., Metzger, A. R., Jr., & Woodbury, J. R. (1984). *Misregulating television: Network dominance and the FCC*. Chicago: University of Chicago Press.

Besen, S. M., & Mitchell, B. M. (1975, May). *Watergate and television: An economic analysis*. Rand Corporation report, R-1712-MF.

Besen, S. M., & Soligo, R. (1973). The economics of the network-affiliate relationship in the television broadcasting industry. *American Economic Review, 63*(3), 259-268.

Besen, S. M., & Soligo, R. (1975). The economics of the network-affiliate relationship: Reply. *American Economic Journal, 65*(5), 1037-1038.

Blake, H. M., & Blum, J. A. (1965). Network television rate practices: A case study in the failure of social control of price discrimination. *Yale Law Journal, 74*(8), 1339-1401.

Blank, D. M. (1966). The quest for quantity and diversity in television programming. *American Economic Review, 56*(2), 448-456.

Blank, D. M. (1968). Television advertising: The great discount illusion, or Tonypandy revisited. *Journal of Business, 41*(1), 10-38.

Blank, D. M. (1969). Tonypandy once again. *Journal of Business, 42*(1), 104-112.

Blau, R. T., Johnson, R. C., & Ksobiech, K. J. (1976). Determinants of TV station economic value. *Journal of Broadcasting, 20*(2), 197-207.

Borchadt, K. (1970). *Structure and performance of the U. S. communications industry: Government regulation and company planning*. Boston: Harvard University, Graduate School of Business Administration, Division of Research.

Bowman, G. M. (1975). Network television advertising: Demand and supply. In B. M. Owen (Ed.), *Telecommunications policy research: Report on the 1975 Conference proceedings*. Palo Alto: Aspen Institute.

Braunstein, Y. M. (1979). The potential for increased competition in television broadcasting—Can the market work? In Canadian-U.S. Conference on Communications Policy, *Cultures in collision: the interaction of Canadian and U.S. broadcast television policies*. New York: Praeger.

Buchanan, J. M. (1967). Public goods in theory and practice: A note on the Minasian-Samuelson discussion. *Journal of Law and Economics, 10*, 193-197.

Coase, R. H. (1965). Evaluation of public policy relating to radio and television broadcasting: Social and economic issues. *Land Economics, 41*(2), 160-167.

Coase, R. H. (1966). The economics of broadcasting and government policy. *American Economic Review, 56*(2), 440-447.

Comaner, W. S., & Mitchell, B. M. (1972). The costs of planning: The FCC and cable television. *Journal of Law and Economics, 15*(1), 177-206.

Crandall, R. W. (1971). The economic effect of television-network program ownership. *Journal of Law and Economics, 14*(2), 385-412.

Crandall, R. W. (1972). FCC regulation, monopsony, and network television program costs. *Bell Journal of Economics and Management Science, 3*(2), 483-508.

Crandall, R. W. (1974). The economic case for a fourth commercial television network. *Public Policy, 22*(4), 513-536.

Currier, F. (1960). Economic theory and its application to newspapers. *Journalism Quarterly, 37*(2), 255-260.

Deutschmann, P. J., & Emery, W. B. (1961). Sale and value of radio stations. *Journal of Broadcasting, 5*(3), 219-228.

DeVany, A. S., Eckert, R. D., Meyers, C. J., O'Hara, D. J., & Scott, R. C. (1980). *A property system approach to the electromagnetic spectrum: A legal-economic-engineering study*. San Francisco: CATO Institute.

Dimmick, J. and Rothenbuhler, E. (1984). The theory of the niche: Quantifying competition among media industries. *Journal of Communication, 34*(1), 103-119.

Draper, N. R., & Smith, H. (1966). *Applied Regression Analysis*. New York: John Wiley.

Ehrlich, I., & Fisher, L. (1982). The derived demand for advertising: A theoretical and empirical investigation. *American Economic Review, 72*(3), 366-388.

FCC Network Study Staff (1958). Prospects for a fourth network in television. *Journal of Broadcasting, 2*(1), 3-11.

Federal Communications Commission (1938). *Report on social and economic data pursuant to the Informal Hearing on broadcasting, Docket 4063, Beginning October 5, 1936.* Washington, DC: Government Printing Office.

Ferguson, C. E. (1972). *Microeconomic Theory*. (3rd ed.) Homewood, IL: Richard D. Irwin, Inc.

Fisher, F. M., & Ferrall, V. E., Jr. (1966). Community antenna television systems and local station audience. *Quarterly Journal of Economics, 80*(2), 227-251.

Flynn, P. H. (1970). Countervailing power in network television. *Journal of Broadcasting, 14*(3), 297-305.

Fournier, G. M., & Martin, D. L. (1983). Does government restricted entry produce market power? New evidence from the market for television. *Bell Journal of Economics, 14*(1), 44-56.

French, W. A., & McBrayer, J. T. (1979). Arriving at television advertising rates. *Journal of Advertising, 8*(1), 15-18.

Gerald, J. E. (1958). Economic research and the mass media. *Journalism Quarterly, 35*(1), 49-55.

Graham, D. A., & Vernon, J. M. (1975). The economics of the network-affiliate relationship: Comment. *American Economic Review, 65*(5), 1032-1036.

Greenberg, E., (1969). Television station profitability and FCC regulatory policy. *Journal of Industrial Economics, 17*(3), 210-238.

Greenberg, E., & Barnet, H. J. (1971). TV program diversity—New evidence and old theories. *American Economic Review, 61*(2), 89-93.

Hall, W.C., Jr. & Batlivala, R. B. D. (1971). Market structure and duplication in TV broadcasting. *Land Economics, 47*(4), 405-410.

Harwood, K. (1967). On public broadcasting for private profit. *Journal of Broadcasting, 11*(3), 191-198.

Harwood, K. (1970). On economic productivity in broadcasting. *Journal of Broadcasting, 14*(1), 5-12.

Harwood, K. (1984). Productivity of labor and capital in radio and television broadcasting in the United States. *Journal of Broadcasting, 28*(2), 225-235.

Hileman, D. G. (1968). Changes in the buying and selection of advertising media. *Journalism Quarterly, 45*(2), 279-285.

Howard, H. H. (1974). Cross-media ownership of newspapers and TV stations. *Journalism Quarterly, 51*(4), 715-718.

Kahn, F. J. (1963). Economic regulation of broadcasting as a utility. *Journal of Broadcasting, 7*(2), 97-112.

Kahn, F. J. (1974). The quasi-utility basis for broadcast regulation. *Journal of Broadcasting, 18*(3), 259-276.

Kahn, F. J., Ed. (1978). *Documents of American broadcasting* (3rd ed). Englewood Cliffs, NJ: Prentice-Hall.

Kaplan, S. J. (1978). The impact of cable television service on the use of competing media. *Journal of Broadcasting, 22*(2), 155-165.

Kelley, W. J. (1967). How television stations price their service. *Journal of Broadcasting, 11*, 313-323.

Kinter, C. V. (1948a). How much income is available to support communications? *Journalism Quarterly, 25*(1), 38-42.

Kinter, C. V. (1948b). A case study in the economics of mass communications. *Journalism Quarterly, 25*(4), 360-362.

Korn, A. (1977, March 15). *Economics of new entry of independent stations into television markets*. Staff report to the FCC.

Krasnouw, E. G., & Longley, L. D. (1978). *The politics of broadcast regulation* (2nd ed). New York: St. Martin's Press.

Landau, E., & Davenport, J. S. (1959). Price anomalies of the mass media. *Journalism Quarterly, 36*(3), 291-294.

Larson, T. L. (1980). The U. S. television industry: Concentration and the question of network divestiture of owned and operated stations. *Communication Research, 7*(1), 23-44.

Lees, F. A., & Yang, C. Y. (1966). The redistributional effect of television advertising. *The Economic Journal, 76*, 328-336.

Leonard, W. N. (1969). Network television pricing: A comment. *Journal of Business, 42*(1), 93-103.

Levin, H. J. (1958). Economic structure and the regulation of television. *Quarterly Journal of Economics, 72*(3), 424-450.

Levin, H. J. (1960). *Broadcast regulation and joint ownership of media*. New York: New York University Press.

Levin, H. J. (1962). Federal control of entry in the broadcast industry. *Journal of Law and Economics, 5*, 49-67.

Levin, H. J. (1964). Economic effects of broadcast licensing. *Journal of Political Economy, 72*(2), 151-162.

Levin, H. J. (1971a). *The invisible resource: Use and regulation of the radio spectrum*. Baltimore: Johns Hopkins Press.

Levin, H. J. (1971b). Program duplication, diversity, and effective viewer choices: Some empirical findings. *American Economic Review, 61*(2), 81-88.

Levin, H. J. (1975). Franchise values, merit programming and policy options in television broadcasting. In R. E. Caves & M. J. Roberts (Eds.), *Regulating the product: Quality and variety*. Cambridge, MA: Ballinger Publishing.

Levin, H. J. (1980). *Fact and fancy in television regulation: An economic study of policy alternatives*. New York: Russell Sage Foundation.

Litman, B. R. (1978). Is network ownership in the public interest? *Journal of Communication, 28*(2), 51-59.

Litman, B. R. (1979a). Public interest programming and the Carroll Doctrine: A reexamination. *Journal of Broadcasting, 23*(1), 51-60.

Litman, B. R. (1979b). The television networks, competition and program diversity. *Journal of Broadcasting, 23*(1), 393-409.

Litman, B. R. (1979c). *The vertical structure of the television broadcasting industry: The coalescence of power*. East Lansing: Michigan State University.

Long, S. L. (1979). *The development of the television network oligopoly*. New York: Arno Press.

Manning, W. G., & Owen, B. M. (1976). Television rivalry and network power. *Public Policy, 24*(1), 33-57.

Mansfield, E. (1979). *Microeconomics: Theory and Applications* (3rd ed). New York: W. W. Norton.

McCombs, M. E. (1972). Mass media in the marketplace. *Journalism Monographs, 24*.

McFadyen, S., & Hoskins, C. (1985). The economic factors relating to Canadian broadcasting policy. Paper presented at the Annual Convention of the International Communication Association, Honolulu, HI.

Melody, W. (1973). *Children's television: The economics of exploitation*. New Haven: Yale University Press.

Minasian, J. R. (1964). Television pricing and the theory of public goods. *Journal of Law and Economics, 7,* 71-80.

Minasian, J. R. (1967). Public goods in theory and practice revisited. *Journal of Law and Economics, 10,* 205-207.

Noll, R. G., Peck, M. J., & McGowan, J. J. (1973). *Economic aspects of television regulation*. Washington, DC: Brookings Institution.

Ogden, W. B. (1961). *The television business: Accounting problems of a growth industry*. New York: Ronald Press Co..

Owen, B. M. (1974). Discussion-Economics of the First Amendment. *American Economic Review, 64*(2), 400-402.

Owen, B. M. (1975). *Economics and freedom of expression: Media structure and the First Amendment*. Cambridge, MA: Ballinger.

Owen, B. M. (1978). The economic view of programming. *Journal of Communication, 28*(2), 43-47.

Owen, B. M., Beebe, J. H., & Manning, Jr., W. G. (1974). *Television Economics*. Lexington, MA: Lexington.

Park, R. E. (1971a). The growth of cable TV and its probable impact on over-the-air broadcasting. *American Economic Review, 61*(2), 69-73.

Park, R. E. (1971b). Television station performance and revenues. *Educational Broadcasting Review, 5*(3), 43-49.

Park, R. E. (1972). Cable television, UHF broadcastng, and FCC regulatory policy. *Journal of Law and Economics, 15*(1), 207-232.

Park, R. E. (1975). New television networks. *Bell Journal of Economics, 6,* 607-620.

Park, R. E. (1978). The value of television time: Some problems and attempted solutions: Comment. *Southern Economic Journal, 44*(4), 1006-1015.

Parker, I. (1984). Models of reality and realities of models: A comment. In Canadian-U.S. Conference on Communications Policy, *Cultures in collision: The interaction of Canadian and U.S. broadcast television policies*. New York: Praeger.

Parkman, A. M. (1982). The effect of television station ownership on local news ratings. *Review of Economics and Statistics, 64*(2), 289-295.

Pearce, A. (1980). The economic and political strength of the television networks. In M. Botein & D. M. Rice (Eds.), *Network television and the public interest: A preliminary inquiry*. Lexington, MA: Lexington.

Peterman, J. L. (1965). The structure of national time rates in the television broadcasting industry. *Journal of Law and Economics, 8,* 77-131.

Peterman, J. L. (1971). Concentration of control and the price of television time. *American Economic Review, 61*(2), 74-80.

Posner, R. A. (1972). The appropriate scope of regulation in the cable television industry . *Bell Journal of Economics and Management Science, 3*(1), 98-129.

Prisuta, R. H. (1977). The impact of media concentration and economic factors on broadcast public interest programming. *Journal of Broadcastng, 21*(3), 321-332.

Reinsch, J. L., & Ellis, E. I. (1960). *Radio station management* (2nd ed). New York: Harper & Row.

Rima, I. H. (1972). *Development of Economic Analysis*. Homewood, IL: R. D. Irwin, Inc.

Ripley, J. M. (1959). Which radio stations make better profits? *Central States Speech Journal, 11*(1), 24-26.

Samuelson, P. A. (1958). Aspects of public expenditure theories. *Review of Economics and Statistics, 40*(4), 332-338.

Samuelson, P. A. (1964). Public goods and subscription TV: Correction of the record. *Journal of Law and Economics, 7,* 81-83.

Samuelson, P. A. (1967). Pitfalls in the analysis of public goods. *Journal of Law and Economics, 10,* 199-204.

Singleton, L. A., & Gwyn, R. J. (1983). The safety net examined: The impact of cable technology on small market radio services. In O. H. Gandy, Jr., P. Espinosa, & J. A. Ordover (Eds.), *Proceedings for the Tenth Annual Telecommunications Policy Research Conference*. Norwood, NJ: ABLEX.

Smith, J. R. (1983). Four perspectives on media research in the 1980's. *Journal of Broadcasting, 27*(2), 185-190.

Smythe, D. W. (1960). On the political economy of communications. *Journalism Quarterly, 37*(4), 563-572.

Smythe, D. W. (1962). Time, market and space factors in communications economics. *Journalism Quarterly, 39*(1), 3-14.

Smythe, D. W. (1981). Communications: Blindspot of ecomomics. In W. H. Melody, L. Salter, & P. Heyer (Eds.), *Culture, communication, and dependency: The tradition of H. A. Innes.* Norwood, NJ: ABLEX.

Soley, L., & Hough, G. (1978). Black ownership of commercial radio stations: An economic evaluation. *Journal of Broadcasting, 22*(4), 455-467.

Spence, M., & Owen, B. M. (1977). Television programming, monopolistic competition, and welfare. *Quarterly Journal of Economics, 91*(1), 103-126.

Steiner, P. O. (1952). Program patterns and preferences, and the workability of competition in radio broadcasting. *Quarterly Journal of Economics, 66*(2) 194-222.

Steiner, P. O. (1979). *Workable competition in the radio broadcasting industry.* New York: Arno.

Sterling, C. H. (1984). *Electronic media: A guide to trends in broadcasting and newer technologies, 1920-1983.* New York: Praeger.

Turow, J. (1980). Television sponsorship forms and program subject matter. *Journal of Broadcasting, 24*(3), 381-389.

Webbink, D. W. (1973). Regulation, profits and entry in the television broadcasting industry. *Journal of Industrial Economics, 21*(2), 167-176.

Webster, J. G. (1983). The impact of cable and pay cable television on local station audiences. *Journal of Broadcasting, 27*(2), 119-126.

Webster, J. G. (1984). Cable television's impact on audience for local news. *Journalism Quarterly, 61*(2), 419-422.

White, K. J. (1977). Television market shares, station characteristics, and viewer choice. *Communication Research, 4*(4), 415-434.

Wirth, M. O., & Wollert, J. A. (1984). The effects of market structure on television news pricing. *Journal of Broadcasting, 28*(2), 215-244.

Wiles, P. (1963). Pilkington and the theory of value. *The Economic Journal, 73*(2), 183-200.

Wonnacott, R. J., & Wonnacott, T. H. (1970). *Econometrics.* New York: John Wiley.

Woodbury, J. R., Besen, S. M., & Fournier, G. M. (1983). The determinants of network television program prices: Implicit contracts, regulation, and bargaining power. *Bell Journal of Economics, 14*(2), 351-365.

Yadon, R. E. (1983). *A model of entry into select U.S. radio markets between 1973 and 1978.* Unpublished doctoral dissertation, Michigan State.

6 ● Revised Lag Sequential Analysis

DONALD DEAN MORLEY

University of Colorado, Colorado Springs

COMMUNICATION theorists have long argued that human communication is best studied as a process (for example, Berlo, 1960; Smith, 1972). In recent years communication researchers have made substantial progress toward the process oriented study of communication through the use of interactive coding schemes, Markov analysis, and lag sequential analysis. The extent of the progress and the value of these techniques have been the subjects of some debate (Miller, 1981; Phillips, 1981), and their introduction has been accompanied by such problems as lack of comparability of coding schemes (O'Donnell-Trujillo, 1981), inappropriate analysis of nonstationary Markov data (Jackson & O'Keefe, 1982), an incorrect computer program for lag sequential analysis (Morley, 1984), the application of incorrect statistical tests to lag sequential designs, and failure to control for autodependence in lag sequential designs (Allison & Liker, 1982).

My objective is to offer a relatively nontechnical explanation of the problems associated with lag sequential analysis and to (1) provide an appropriate descriptive statistic for lag sequential designs, (2) provide the correct method for controlling autodependence, and (3) indicate how lag sequential analysis can be used as both a descriptive and inferential statistic.

AN APPROPRIATE DESCRIPTIVE STATISTIC

Determining the most appropriate statistic for a given lag sequential analysis depends on whether the researcher is confronted with a binomial or a hypergeometric probability problem. With both types of probability problems the researcher is trying to determine if the observed or conditional probability of a given behavior is significantly different from the expected probability of that behavior. A critical difference between bino-

Correspondence and requests for reprints: Donald Dean Morley, Department of Communication, University of Colorado, P. O. Box 7150, Colorado Springs, CO 80933.

mial and hypergeometric probabilities is the method used to arrive at the expected probability. If the expected probability was a theoretically derived true probability (for example, a perfectly honest coin is expected to turn up heads 50% of the time), then the binomial distribution would be appropriate for determining if the observed probability differed significantly from the expected probability. If, however, both the expected and observed probabilities were empirically derived from a finite population, then the hypergeometric distribution is appropriate (Marasscuilo & McSweeney, 1977, pp. 97-110).

Although selection of the most appropriate probability distribution for lag sequential analysis depends on how the expected probabilities were derived, it is doubtful that any lag analysis in communication should be based on binomial probabilities or approximations of binomial probabilities. The reason is that the expected probability of any human behavior cannot be known in the same way as the expected probability is known in a coin flipping experiment. In fact, every published lag sequential study in communication has used empirically determined expected probabilities (Dindia, 1982; Ellis, Hamilton, & Aho, 1983; Ellis & McCallister, 1980; Emery, 1982; Hirokawa, 1980; Krueger, 1980, 1983; Krueger & Smith, 1982; McLaughlin & Cody, 1982; Putnam, 1982; Putnam & Jones, 1982; Ting-Toomey, 1983). All of these studies, however, have used a statistic based on the binomial distribution. Specifically, the z statistic used, and advocated by Sackett (1979) is:

$$Z = \frac{p(B|C) - p(B)}{\sqrt{\dfrac{p(B)\,(1 - p(B))}{N_c}}}$$

where $p(B)$ is the unconditional expected probability of the lagged behavior, $p(B|C)$ is the probability of the lagged behavior given the occurrence of the criterion, and N_c is the number of times the criterion occurs. Sackett's z is simply the normal approximation of the binomial (Hays, 1973, pp. 305-309) which if squared is identical to a goodness of fit chi-square (Hays, 1973, pp. 721-727).

Allison and Liker (1982), however, point out that Sackett's z is not appropriate because in actual practice the expected probability ($p(B)$) is empirically derived instead of being a theoretically derived probability. As a result the standard error must be estimated differently. Specifically, Allison and Liker point out that lag sequential analysis is a test for the difference between two proportions in a two by two contingency table where the marginals are the occurrence of the criterion (C), nonoccurrence of the criterion ($\overline{C}$), occurrence of the lagged behavior (B), and nonoccurrence of the behavior ($\overline{B}$). Allison and Liker (1982) therefore demonstrate that a better z statistic is:

$$Z = \frac{p(B|C) - p(B)}{\sqrt{\dfrac{(p(B))(1 - p(B))(1 - p(C))}{(N_t - K)(p(C))}}}$$

where p(B) and p(B|C) are the same as in Sackett's z, p(C) is the probability of the criterion, K is the lag number, and Nt represents the total number of observations in the sample. If squared the z is a chi-square test for independence with one degree of freedom and is simply a large sample approximation of hypergeometric probabilities (Marascuilo & McSweeney, 1977, pp. 192-196).

Even Allison and Liker's proposed chi-square test for independence, however, would only be inferential if all observations were independent. Allison and Liker, however, do not discuss this limitation for any of their significance tests. In fact, they state explicitly that the logit-linear models they propose "conform to conventional practices for statistical inference" (p. 402). However, nothing about the logarithmic transformations used in constructing logit-linear models corrects for lost independence because in a lag sequential design independence was lost in the sampling process when multiple observations were taken from each respondent or dyad.

The confusion and controversy over the issue of independence is not new and has been intensely debated by Lewis and Burke (1949), Pastore (1950), and Peters (1950). Much of the confusion stems from the fact that "independence" has been used to refer to two quite different concepts. One use of the term refers to *statistical independence*. The existence or nonexistence of statistical independence is an empirically testable question. For example, a chi-square test for independence indicates the extent to which two variables are statistically dependent. The second use of independence concerns the *independence of observations*. Such independent observations are necessary in order to use samples to make inferences about population parameters. This requires that the unit of observation that is submitted to statistical analysis be the same as the population parameter that the researcher wishes to generalize to (Bock, 1975, pp. 6-7). Thus if 100 observations are made of a single dyad the only inferences that can be made are limited to that particular dyad. If the researcher wishes to generalize to the population of dyads, then multiple dyads must be observed and the N for the statistical analysis will be the number of dyads.

The obvious solution to the problem of independence would be to make independent observations. However, lag sequential analysis as it is currently understood would then be impossible. Communication lag sequential analyses have not been characterized by independent observations and therefore cannot be generalized to a larger population of individuals or dyads. Instead, the z or chi-square statistics can only be descriptive of the communication behaviors contained in the specific sample (Lewis & Burke, 1949). Sackett (1980) recognizes this limitation for the normal approximation of the binomial and cautions that the z scores and their associated significance levels should be viewed as descriptive indices of sequential dependence.

The major problem with this approach, however, is that the z statistic, chi-square, and significance levels are highly dependent upon sample size and are therefore poor descriptors of relationship strength. In fact, significance levels should not even be reported because they can easily be misinterpreted by readers as inferential. A better descriptive statistic that is insensitive to sample size, does not require the reporting of significance levels, and indicates strength of the criterion-behavior relationship is easily derived by converting the chi-square test for independence to a phi-coefficient with

$$\sqrt{\chi^2/N}$$

Proof that the phi-coefficient is equivalent to the more familiar Pearson correlation is provided by Hays (1973, p. 744).

Although calculating the phi-coefficient from a contingency table that has been collapsed across respondents would be the easiest procedure, this permits more loquacious individuals to contribute disproportionately to, or detract from, the criterion-behavior correlation. A better procedure would be to calculate the correlation between the criterion and behavior for each respondent, dyad, group, or any other unit of analysis the researcher wishes to describe.

Table 6.1 contains coded strings of behavior and the lag one criterion-behavior correlations. The Cs represent occurrences of the criterion, the Bs the behavior of interest, and the Os other behaviors. For example, the first respondent in Table 7.1 has eight coded communication acts. At lag one every act except for the last act will immediately precede another behavior. Therefore we have seven behaviors that can be used in the analysis of lag one and each subsequent lag will reduce the number of acts available for analysis by one. When a behavior immediately precedes another behavior the antecedent behavior occupies the lag one criterion position. At the criterion position one of two possibilities exists. Either the criterion (C) occurs or the criterion is not present ($\overline{C}$). With this three category coding scheme the occurrence of either O or B in the criterion position is an

Table 6.1
Hypothetical Criterion-Behavior Sequences

Subject													r	z
1	O	B	O	0	C	O	C	B					.300	.310
2	C	O	C	B	C	B	O	O					.730	.929
3	O	C	O	C	O	C	B	O					.471	.512
4	C	O	C	B	O	O	C	B					.730	.929
5	O	C	B	C	B	C	O	O					.730	.929
6	O	B	C	B	C	C	B	C	O	C	B	O	.449	.482
7	C	B	B	B	O	C	O	C	B	O	C	O	.214	.217
8	O	C	B	O	O	O	B	C	B	C	O	O	.542	.607
9	C	B	C	O	O	C	B	B	C	B	O	C	.448	.482
10	O	C	B	O	C	B	C	O	C	O	C	B	.912	1.539
11	B	B	C	B	B	O	O	C	O	B	C	O	-.039	-.039
12	O	O	O	C	O	B	C	B	C	B	B	O	.386	.407
13	B	B	O	O	C	O	B	C	C	O	B	O	-.375	-.394

instance of $\overline{C}$. For the subsequent behavior that occupies the noncriterion position two possibilities exist. Either the behavior of interest (B) occurs or does not occur ($\overline{B}$). Therefore, the first two behaviors of respondent one adds one count to the $\overline{C}$, B cell of the two by two contingency table. Assigning the second count to the contingency table is accomplished by allowing the second act in the string to occupy the criterion position and the third act occupies the noncriterion position. In this instance one count is added to the $\overline{C}$, $\overline{B}$ cell. If the analyst proceeds through the string of behaviors in this manner until the string is exhausted he or she will end up with a contingency table from which the Pearson r is calculated.

In the above example the respondent was the unit of analysis because the respondent's own behavior served as the criterion for his or her own subsequent behavior. In the typical application of lag sequential analysis, however, the researcher is attempting to describe the interaction of the dyad and the dyad becomes the unit of analysis. Although the two by two contingency approach still applies, the logic involved in calculating the correlation changes. Specifically, when analyzing dyads a coded behavior from one member of the dyad is designated the criterion and used to predict a behavior of the second member. Unlike calculating the correlation for a single respondent, the second member's behavior will not occupy the criterion position. This means that the lag one N for the contingency table will be equal to one half the total number of coded behaviors.

With group interaction the procedures for calculating the descriptive correlation depends on the research question. For example, if the researcher wished to examine the relationship between management's and labor's messages (for example, Putnam & Jones, 1982), the calculation can be simplified by treating management as one member of a dyad and labor as the other member. If, on the other hand, the research question involved examining the effect of the group leader's behavior on group members, a separate correlation would be calculated between the leader and each group member. When no conceptual basis exists for limiting the number of correlations, then the researcher would probably want to calculate correlations for all possible dyads within the group. These correlations can then be averaged to form an aggregate descriptive index of the group's behavior.

Although correlations from different individuals or dyads cannot be directly averaged to form an aggregate index of their behavior, they can be averaged once transformed with Fisher's (1954) r to z transformation. Specifically, any value of r can be converted to an approximately normally distributed variable with

$$z = \frac{1}{2} \text{Ln}[(1 + r)/(1 - r)]$$

Performing these calculations, however, will not be necessary because tables of the r to z transformation are readily available (for example, Hays, 1973). The average z value can then be converted back to r in order to provide an aggregate index of the criterion-behavior relationship. For example, the columns on the right of Table 6.1 contain the lag one criterion-behavior correlations and z transformations for each respondent. The average z is .532 which translates back into an aggregate correlation of .487.

THE PROBLEM OF AUTODEPENDENCE

Allison and Liker point out that current lag sequential analysis procedures are based on the unrealistic assumption that a person's behavior at a given lag is not dependent on his or her behavior at previous lags. Allison and Liker argue that to control for autodependence the actor's behavior at a given lag should be made conditional on both the criterion and the actor's own behavior at all previous lags. This would involve constructing a three-way contingency table at lag two, a four-way table at lag three, and so on. For example, Table 6.2 was taken directly from Allison and Liker. The husband's behavior at time one (Ht) is the criterion and the wife's response at lag two (Wt + 1) is the lagged behavior. If the wife's behavior at lag one (Wt) is ignored and the table is collapsed we find the criterion is highly predictive of the wife's lag two behavior ($\chi^2 = 27.64$). However, the authors point out that the wife's lag two behavior is highly dependent on her lag one behavior ($\chi^2 = 1,184.7$). To control for this autodependence they suggest that a chi-square be computed for each value of Wt and then summed. The result is a not quite significant chi-square of 5.91 with two degrees of freedom.

Table 6.2
Wife's Lag One and Two Responses to
Husband's Criterion Behavior

Wt	Ht	Wt + 1	
		1	0
1	1	577	139
1	0	222	76
0	1	169	1089
0	0	149	839

Obviously, Allison and Liker's procedure suffers from the practical difficulty of having the number of cells double for each lag analyzed. The greatest difficulty with their technique for controlling autodependence, however, is that it does not do so. Instead the hypothesis tested in their example was that the wife's behavior at lag two was jointly dependent on the criterion and the wife's own lag one behavior. In other words, they are testing a second order Markov process (Markus, 1979, pp. 13-14). This is best illustrated by the highly idealized data in Table 6.3. When the table is collapsed so that only the criterion (Ht) predicts the wife's lag two behavior (Wt + 1) the chi-square is zero. Similarly, when only the wife's lag one behavior is used to predict her lag two behavior the chi-square is again zero. However, when both the criterion and the wife's lag one behaviors are taken into account the result is a significant chi-square of 20.00 with two degrees of freedom.

The correct method for controlling autodependence is most easily understood if the chi-squares are expressed as correlations. At lag one we have the correlation between the criterion and the lag one behavior, and at lag two we have correlations between the criterion and lag two behavior, criterion and lag one behavior, and the lag one and lag two behaviors. Given these three correlations the effect of any autodependence can be removed with part correlation (Kerlinger & Pedhazur, 1973, pp. 92-97). For example, returning to Allison and Liker's data (Table 6.2) we find that the husband's behavior is predictive of the wife's behavior at lag one ($r = .138, p < .0001$) and lag two ($r = .092, p < .0001$). Additionally, the wife's lag one behavior is highly predictive of her lag two behavior ($r = .631, p < .0001$), which indicates autodependence. Part correlation reveals that the husband's behavior is not predictive of the wife's lag two behavior once the effect of the wife's lag one behavior has been removed from her lag two behavior ($r = .006, p = .719$).

The use of part correlation can be extended easily to any number of lags. Fortunately, these need not be hand calculated because they are provided by all multiple regression programs.

In addition to controlling for autodependence, the regression approach also permits researchers to examine the joint influence of two behaviors on

Table 6.3
Data illustrating a second order
Markov process

Wt	Ht	Wt + 1	
		1	0
1	1	15	5
1	0	5	15
0	1	5	15
0	0	15	5

a subsequent behavior. This is accomplished by designating the behavior the researcher wants to predict as the dependent variable and using dummey coding (Cohen & Cohen, 1983, pp. 181-220). For example, in the Allison and Liker data (Table 6.3) Wt + 1 is the dependent variable and can have a value of either 0 or 1. Similarly Wt and Ht are independent variables with values of either 0 or 1. However, Wt and Ht are only main effects predictors of Wt + 1. To predict the interaction or joint influence of Wt and Ht on Wt + 1 we create a third variable by multiplying Wt by Ht (Wt*Ht). Wt and Ht are entered first in the equation followed by Wt*Ht. Once the effects of Wt and Ht have been removed the resulting part correlation between Wt + 1 and Wt*Ht is .035 and we can conclude in the descriptive sense that the relationship between Wt*Ht and Wt + 1 is infinitesimal.

AN INFERENTIAL STATISTIC

In the descriptive analysis the correlations were based on multiple observations from each respondent or dyad. Although descriptively useful, the correlations or z's are not adequate for statistical inference because such multiple observations are not independent. Although communication researchers have generally acknowledged this limitation in their methods section, they soon find themselves faced with the nearly impossible task of discussing the implications of their results without implying inferential conclusions.

The solution to the problem of independence is to condense multiple nonindependent measures into a single aggregate score for each unit of analysis. In communication, for example, we do not hesitate to take multi-item instruments composed of seven interval scales, calculate a mean score for each person, use the individual as the unit of analysis, and then generalize to the larger population of people. However, we are slower to recognize that probabilities, odds ratios, variances, and measures of covariance are also aggregate means that can be subjected to inferential statistical analysis. Selection of the most appropriate aggregate score depends on the extent that the score conceptually captures the phenomenon being studied and on the population to which the researcher wishes to generalize. If the objective is to make inferences about the larger population of dyads, then the dyad needs to be treated as the unit of analysis. Similarly, inferences about groups require that the group be treated as the unit of analysis.

In lag sequential analysis inferential tests are easily derived from the descriptive Fisher z's when the respondents or dyads are independent. Specifically, though the observations that compose each z are not independent (as with any other multiple response measure), the z's across the units of analysis are independent from each other. For example, the mean z for a given group is composed of nonindependent observations because multiple observations are taken from each dyad in the group and group members are observed in more than one dyad. The lack of independent observations, however, presents no problem when calculating an aggregate score for the group. In fact calculating an aggregate score from multiple observations has important statistical and conceptual advantages (Rushton, Brainerd, & Pressley, 1983). Once the aggregate score for a given group has been calculated, the score will be independent from the aggregate score of a different group. Therefore the aggregate scores for a sample of groups constitute independent observations that can be statistically analyzed and used to make inferences about groups.

In terms of the statistical test the null hypothesis is that the expected mean z is zero. Under the null hypothesis the expected mean z will be zero. Therefore, a simple t-test for the difference between a sample mean and the expected population mean of zero will suffice as an inferential test. For the data in Table 6.1 the observed mean z is .532 and is significantly different from the expected mean of zero, t = 3.94, p < .01. At subsequent lags t-tests can be applied to the transformed part correlations.

Additional statistical techniques, such as tests for the equivalence of correlations (Cohen & Cohen, 1983, p. 55), can be used also to compare the sequential communication styles of distressed and nondistressed couples, males and females, high and low communication apprehensives, or any other characteristic of interest. When a large number of lags are analyzed or comparisons made, however, researchers will want to prevent the alpha level from becoming inflated with either traditional post hoc techniques or procedures explained by Larzelere and Mulaik (1977) and Steiger (1980).

CONCLUSION

The application of statistical theory to the analysis of human communication processes is still in its infancy. Understandably, early attempts to extend statistical techniques beyond traditional static designs to more process-oriented designs have been accompanied by misunderstandings and limitations. This chapter's purpose has been to alleviate some of the misunderstandings by demonstrating the use of modified lag sequential procedures in both descriptive and inferential applications.

REFERENCES

Allison, P. D, & Liker, J. K. (1982). Analyzing sequential categorical data on dyadic interaction: A comment on Gottman. *Psychological Bulletin, 91*, 393-403.

Berlo, D. (1960). *The process of communication.* New York: Holt, Rinehart & Winston.

Bock, R. D. (1975). *Multivariate statistical methods in behavioral research.* New York: McGraw-Hill.

Cohen, J., & Cohen, P. (1983). *Applied multiple regression/correlation analysis for the behavioral sciences* (2nd ed.). Hillsdale, NJ: Lawrence Erlbaum Associates.

Dinda, K. (1982). Reciprocity of self-disclosure: A sequential analysis. In M. Burgoon (Ed.), *Communication yearbook 6* (pp. 506-528). London: Sage.

Ellis, D. G., Hamilton, M., & Aho, L. (1983). Some issues in conversational coherence. *Human Communication Research, 9*, 267-282.

Ellis, D. G., & McCallister, L. (1980). Relational control sequences in sex-typed and androgynous groups. *The Western Journal of Speech Communication, 44*, 35-49.

Emery, D. & Axley, S. R. (1982). Marital interaction: Perceptions and behavioral implication of control. In M. Burgoon (Ed.), *Communication yearbook 6* (pp. 489-505). London: Sage.

Emery, D., & Ellis, D. (1980, November). *Relational control in marital dyads: A lag sequential analysis.* Paper presented to the Speech Communication Association, New York.

Fisher, R. A. (1954). *Statistical methods for research workers* (12th ed.). Edinburgh: Oliver and Boyd.

Hays, W. L. (1973). *Statistics for the social sciences* (2nd ed.). New York: Holt, Rinehart & Winston.

Hirokawa, R. Y. (1980). A comparative analysis of communication patterns within effective and ineffective decision-making groups. *Communication Monographs, 47*, 312-321.

Jackson, S. A., & O'Keefe, B. J. (1982). Nonstationary data should not be "corrected." *Human Communication Research, 8*, 146-153.

Kerlinger, F. N., & Pedhazur, E. J. (1973). *Multiple regression in behavioral research.* New York: Holt, Rinehart & Winston.

Krueger, D. L. (1980). Competitive and cooperative decision-making groups: An analysis of differences and communication patterns. *Communication Research, 7*, 457-478.

Krueger, D. L. (1983). Pragmatics of dyadic decision making. *Western Journal of Speech Communication, 47*, 99-117.

Krueger, D. L., & Smith, P. (1982). Decision-making patterns of couples: A sequential analysis. *Journal of Communication, 32*, 121-134.

Larzelere, R. E., & Mulaik, S. A. (1977). Single-sample tests for many correlations. *Psychological Bulletin, 84*, 557-569.

Lewis, D., & Burke, C. J. (1949). The use and misuse of the chi-square test. *Psychological Bulletin, 46*, 433-489.

Marascuilo, L. A., & McSweeney, M. (1977). *Nonparametric and distribution-free methods for the social sciences.* Monterey: Brooks/Cole.

Markus, G. B. (1979). *Analyzing panel data.* Beverly Hills, CA: Sage.

McLaughlin, M. L., & Cody, M. J. (1982). Awkward silences: Behavioral antecedents and consequences of the conversational lapse. *Human Communication Research, 8*, 299-316.

Miller, G. R. (1981). "'Tis the season to be jolly": A yuletide 1980 assessment of communication research. *Human Communication Research, 7*, 371-380.

Morley, D. D. (1984). Corrections to lag sequential results in communication research: An introduction. *Human Communication Research, 11*, 121-123.

O'Donnell-Trujillo, N. (1981). Relational communication: A comparison of coding systems. *Communication Monographs, 48,* 91-105.

Pastore, N. (1950). Some comments on "the use and misuse of the chi-square test." *Psychological Bulletin, 47,* 338-340.

Peters, C. C. (1950). The misuse of chi-square—a reply to Lewis and Burke. *Psychological Bulletin, 47,* 331-337.

Phillips, G. M. (1981). Science and the study of human communication: An inquiry from the other side of the two cultures. *Human Communication Research, 7,* 361-370.

Putnam, L. L. (1982). Procedural messages and small group work climates: A lag sequential analysis. In M. Burgoon (Ed.), *Communication yearbook 5* (pp. 331-350). New Brunswick, NJ: Transaction.

Putnam L. L., & Jones, T. S. (1982). Reciprocity in negotiations: An analysis of bargaining interaction. *Communication Monographs, 49,* 171-191.

Rushton, J. P., Brainerd, C. J., & Pressley, M. (1983). Behavioral development and construct validity: The principle of aggregation. *Psychological Bulletin, 94,* 18-38.

Sackett, G. P. (1979). The lag sequential analysis of contingency and cyclicity in behavioral interaction research. In J. P. Osofsky (Ed.), *Handbook of infant development* (pp. 623-649). New York: John Wiley.

Sackett, G. P. (1980). Lag sequential analysis as a data reduction technique in social interaction research. In D. B Sawin, R. C. Hawkins, L. Olszewski, & J. H. Penticuff, (Eds.), *Exceptional infant volume 4: Psychosocial risks in infant-environment transactions* (pp. 300-340). New York: Brunner/Mazel.

Smith, D. H. (1972). Communication research and the idea of process. *Speech Monographs, 39,* 174-182.

Steiger, J. H. (1980). Test for comparing elements of a correlation matrix. *Psychological Bulletin, 87,* 245-251.

Ting-Toomey, S. (1983). An analysis of verbal communication patterns in high and low marital adjustment groups. *Human Communication Research, 9,* 306-319.

7 ● Assessment of the Use of Self-Referent Concepts for the Measurement of Cognition and Affect[1]

KIMBERLY A. NEUENDORF ● STAN A. KAPLOWITZ
EDWARD L. FINK ● G. BLAKE ARMSTRONG

Cleveland State University ● Michigan State University
University of Maryland ● Marist College

T HE importance of cognition and affect in the consideration of communication issues is widely acknowledged; the measurement of these sets of constructs has been, to say the least, problematic. One technique that has enjoyed a recent history of wide use is multidimensional scaling (MDS), a tool with the potential to measure cognition and affect with a single measurement procedure, and to do so in a relatively unobtrusive manner, by not specifying dimensions for respondents to use in making comparisons among concepts.[2]

To use spatial models to represent both beliefs and attitudes, one must represent *affect* within a spatial model that is typically seen as a structure of cognitions. One approach is suggested by Osgood, Suci, and Tannenbaum (1957), who regard evaluation as one dimension of a three-dimensional space whose other dimensions are activity and potency. Woelfel and his associates, however, reject this approach on the grounds that the three dimensions are not the only dimensions used by respondents when making evaluations, that they are not uncorrelated (orthogonal), and that they may not share a common origin (see Woelfel & Fink, 1980, p. 78 ff.).[3] Instead, Woelfel and his associates propose that an appropriate self-referent concept be included in the space as a *maximum preference* location.

Although affect often has been considered to be postcognitive (that is, occurring only after cognitive operations have taken place), some recent treatments hold that cognition is not a necessary prerequisite for affect. Zajonc (1980), for example, indicates that affective reactions may actually

Correspondence and requests for reprints: Kimberly A. Neuendorf, Department of Communication, Cleveland State University, Cleveland, OH 44115.

exist apart from cognitive content, as in the case of a fond remembrance of a book whose contents one has forgotten (p. 159). Zajonc's conclusion is that "affect and cognition are under the control of separate and partially independent systems that can influence each other in a variety of ways" (p. 151).

On empirical grounds, Cooper (1973) came to a similar conclusion. Asking subjects to make pair-wise judgments of dissimilarity and of preference for a list of soft drinks, he constructed two spaces—a similarity space and a preference space. He found these spaces to contain some significant differences, concluding that it is unlikely that "the characteristics used in the evaluation of preferences will be a subset of the characteristics used in the evaluation of similarity" (p. 270).

We don't, however, regard either Zajonc or Cooper as having shown that we cannot combine preference and evaluation into a single space. Creating a separate preference space, as Cooper does, is not equivalent to measuring preference through the distance between a concept and some "maximum preference" location. To see this, note that if two concepts are equally preferred, the distance between them would be zero in Cooper's preference space. They need not, however, be at the same location in a general cognitive space because they may be equally far from the "maximum preference" location although being at very different locations. (In other words, they may be equally well liked, but for very different reasons).

And, even if we accept Zajonc's argument that affect and cognition sometimes operate independently, there might well be sufficient interdependence so that treating them within the same framework is not only possible, but useful.

Self-Referent Concepts in MDS

The typical approach to measuring preference or affect via MDS is to assume that the *less* preferred something is, the *further* it will be from a "maximum preference" concept or location (Barnett, 1980; Barnett, Serota, & Taylor, 1976; Woelfel & Saltiel, 1978). Typically, a researcher includes a self-referent concept such as "me" or "yourself" within the list of concepts whose interdistances the respondent is to rate. There are, however, obvious grounds for suspecting that proximity between concept *A* and the concept "me" may be measuring something other than favorability—the degree to which the respondent sees him or herself as *similar* to *A*. Further, a number of researchers have interpreted proximity to a self-referent concept as an indicator of how central or important the respondent believes the concept to be (Barnett, Serota, & Taylor, 1976; Reagan, 1978; Serota, Cody, Barnett & Taylor, 1977). Although such various assumptions abound, most reports fail to provide empirical evidence. Only one variable—the amount of time and energy invested in the concept—has been found to covary significantly with closeness to the self-concept in empirical tests (Barnett, 1980; Newton & Buck, 1981; Woelfel, 1976).

That the selection of a referent concept is needed in order to interpret proximities is obvious (Woelfel, Cody, Gilham, & Holmes, 1980; Woelfel & Napoli, 1982). Cody (1980) writes of the use of a "target" concept—the point to which one wishes to move a manipulated concept—in assessing the effectiveness of the implementation of a message strategy. He notes that a variety of concepts have been used as targets, including *the Ideal Credible Source, Me,* and *my vacation* (p. 145).

Barnett (1980) states that "an attitude toward any single object is the measured distance between the object and the self" (Barnett, 1980, p. 5), and posits a relationship between word usage and attitude: "Besides the scaled synonyms, some concept of self, such as 'me' or 'myself,' should be scaled. . . . The symbol which is used more frequently should be closer to the self concept" (p. 13). Although this prediction may hold true, it does not show that closeness to the self is indicative of positive affect. Rather, Barnett has *defined* positive affect as proximity to the self-referent.

The self has been used as an attitudinal referent in a variety of other ways. Woelfel and Saltiel (1978) label the target point the receiver's "'own position,' i.e., the position of the receiver vis-à-vis the source, the position advocated, and other concepts, like good-bad, etc." (p. 2). Barnett et al. (1976) further contend that "The candidate or party closest to 'Me,' the averaged position for self, would be the candidate or party most preferred by the polity" (p. 230). Assuming that preference implies voting behavior, they endorse the desirability of *moving* concepts, by identifying the "vector which will enable the candidate's point to converge with Me" (p. 230).

In a reanalysis of this study, Serota et al. (1977) note that those concepts close to the "me" are the "issue positions that the respondents identified as central to themselves" (p. 479). Again, alternative conceptualizations abound. For example, the authors found the concept of "busing" to be located relatively far from "me." They explain that this means that busing is not central to the respondents' selves. Respondents may, in fact, feel that busing is a very "central" issue, but oppose it strongly. Conversely, the respondents may favor busing but deem it a noncentral issue.

Woelfel (1976), without indicating empirical support, outlines the purported utility of the concept "me":

Careful and extensive research has shown that the distance of any concept from the "me" in the map is strongly associated with the amount of time and energy people invest in that concept. Political candidates closest to the "me" receive the most votes in elections. Products closest to the "me" are bought most frequently; activities in general which are closest to the me are performed more frequently than those far from the me. And most important of all, moving a concept closer to the "me" results in greater favorability toward that concept and increased behavior toward that concept. (p. 4)

Such statements, although encouraging, are in need of close examination. First, although consistency theories (for example, Heider, 1958) contend that similarity to "me" and favorable affect are correlated, MDS research customarily *defines* favorability *as* closeness to "me." Second, even if "activities in general which are closest to the me are performed more frequently than those far from the me," the possible causal mechanisms that bring this about and allow the confounding of affective and cognitive measures remain unspecified. And, although Woelfel's examples certainly suggest that closeness to the self is *associated* with preference or positive affect, this does not mean that it should be assumed to be the most valid measure of affect. Height and weight are positively correlated, for example, yet we would rather measure each directly than use either measure as a surrogate for the other.

In summary, there have been a variety of conceptualizations and usages of self-referent concepts. Yet no effort has been made to validate the use of the self as an attitudinal referent. We hold that empirical inquiry must precede any interpretation of the distance between a given self-referent and any other concept(s).

The Self-Concept

A common perspective on the self-concept is that which acknowledges that an individual has many selves, their number and characteristics depending upon psychological states, social roles, and situational contingencies. The multiplicity of the self is well documented in the areas of clinical and experimental psychology (Kihlstrom & Cantor, 1984). Explanatory models for this differentiation of the self have ranged from Mead's (1934) basic assertion that a person has as many selves as there are social roles for him or her to fulfill, to hierarchical models that suggest a "whole hierarchy of selves . . . gathered together at various levels of abstraction" (Kihlstrom & Cantor, 1984, p. 6), to the view that we think of ourselves in the way that most clearly differentiates each of us from our current surroundings (McGuire & Padawer-Singer, 1976). In the extreme, the symbolic interactionists' view of self assumes that we define ourselves by the ways in which we perceive others to categorize us; when situations are so unproblematic that this reflexive activity does not take place, there may actually be no self-concept (Stryker & Statham, 1985).

A useful alternative to Kihlstrom and Cantor's hierarchical model is Rosch's (1975) "prototype" view. It presents a probabilistic model in which a model concept or prototype is selected by the individual on the basis of characteristics that would with great probability place the prototype in a category of interest. Applied to the *self-concept,* this approach suggests that there exists a "prototype" self, which is an abstraction from the set of selves viewed in a variety of contexts. Further, there may be *several* alternate "exemplars" for the self (Smith & Medin, 1981). Thus multiple summary selves are available to represent the broad category we call "self," and their choice will be influenced by past experiences and the resultant probabilities that various characteristics are representative of the general category of "self" or some subcategory thereof.

From this discussion arise some critical issues for researchers using MDS. Barnett (1980) suggests that concepts used in an MDS procedure should be generated by the population under examination, not imposed by the researcher. It seems that this should be considered for the self-concept also, especially if several distinct exemplars of the self are possible. And if, as Barnett has found, various synonyms of a word have significantly different locations in people's cognitive spaces ("pig," in his research), then the same may be true of different self-referents.

Predictions

Just how does the individual use the self-concept in a measurement situation? Does closeness to "me" indicate preference, perceived similarity to self, or something else? Are alternative self-referents different in the extent to which they tap preference or favorability? We may begin to answer these questions by conducting a study that compares various self-concept terms and validates them against measures of favorability and perceived similarity.

We suggest that different self-referents will allow the measurement of different mixes of similarity and preference. To develop such self-referents for our study, we applied common, ordinary language use interpretation to terms referring to the self. For example, *my preference* and *the ideal me* seem to be terms that would imply an affective response, and *the actual me* seems likely to elicit cognitive judgments of perceived similarity, and *me* could conceivably elicit either judgment. We therefore hypothesize that, in a multidimensional scaling task:

> *H1A:* The self-referent "actual me" will serve as the best indicator of similarity to self; distance of concepts from the "actual me" will be more strongly negatively correlated with judgments of similarity to self than will distance of concepts from other self-referents.
>
> *H1B:* The "actual me" will serve primarily as a measure of similarity to self, and not of favorable affect; after the correlation between similarity and distance of concepts from the "actual me" has been taken into account, the incremental explained variance resulting from favorability will be minimal.
>
> *H2A:* The self-referents "ideal me" and "my preference" will serve as the

best indicators of favorable affect; distance of concepts from the "ideal me" and "my preference" will be more strongly negatively correlated with judgments of favorability than will distance from other self-referents.

H2B: The "ideal me" and "my preference" will serve primarily as measures of favorable affect, and not of similarity to self; after correlations between favorability and distance of concepts from the "ideal me" and "my preference" have been taken into account, the incremental explained variance resulting from similarity will be minimal.

H3: The simple "me" will tap both similarity to self and favorable affect to some extent, and not serve as a primary, strong measure of either; distance of concepts from "me" will correlate with both similarity and favorability to a moderate extent (that is, of a magnitude falling between the correlations of favorability and similarity with distances from other self-referents), and after taking into account the correlation of either favorability or similarity with distance from the "me," there will be a *moderate* incremental effect of the other variable on distance from the "me."

Additionally, this study more generally predicts that *the choice of a self-referent label will make a difference in how meanings are assigned to distances by respondents.* This implies that the multidimensional spaces generated by paired comparisons may differ due to the choice of self-referents affecting the bases upon which respondents differentiate among concepts, and that respondents will discriminate among multiple self-referents, resulting in different locations for these concepts in a common multidimensional space.

METHOD

Questionnaire Design

An instrument was developed that attempted to assess attitudes and beliefs within an MDS format and that also measured, in a non-MDS manner, favorability toward concepts and perceived similarity of those concepts to the self. The subject area of "racial/ethnic attitudes" was chosen; although this choice is to some extent arbitrary, the realm of inquiry is one of wide interest (Condran, 1979; Jackman, 1979; Pavlak, 1973) and one in which the multidimensionality of perceptions and beliefs is already acknowledged (Cantor & Mischel, 1979, cited by Kihlstrom & Cantor, 1984).

Using preliminary procedures recommended by Woelfel and Fink (1980), concepts related to racial and ethnic attitudes were collected from a small sample. In an open-ended questionnaire, respondents were asked to list racial and ethnic groups that "make up a significant part" of the U.S.

population. Subjects also were asked to list concepts for each of a series of racial ethnic groups in the following manner:

> Now we would like you to tell us some of the characteristics or things you think of when you visualize members of various racial or ethnic groups. Please complete the following sentences as completely and honestly as you can. "When I think of a Black American, I think of someone who . . ."[4]

Over 200 concept phrases and 30 racial and ethnic groups were generated in this manner. Those concepts grouped reliably by judges were given labels by the researchers. There were thirteen concepts—seven racial/ethnic groups and six attributes—retained. They were the following:

HARD-WORKING	WHITE AMERICAN
PROUD	ARAB AMERICAN
PUSHY/LOUD	BLACK AMERICAN
UNEDUCATED	HISPANIC AMERICAN
WEALTHY	JEWISH AMERICAN
PROMISCUOUS ("LOOSE")	ORIENTAL AMERICAN
	AMERICAN INDIAN

According to Woelfel and Fink (1980), a "yardstick," presented to respondents as a standard by which to judge paired comparisons, ought to consist of a pair of concepts that are judged to be a distance apart that is (1) moderate and (2) relatively consistent across subjects (that is, having small interindividual variability). Using these criteria, the distance between the paired concepts "Uneducated" and "Hard-working" was chosen as the final yardstick via a test of 25 subjects.[5] "Hard-working" was selected as the yardstick concept for the non-MDS measures of favorability and perceived similarity.[6]

The resultant concept pool was included in a paired-comparison direct magnitude estimation portion of the final questionnaire. This questionnaire was executed in 5 different experimental forms; the experimental groups differed as to which self-referent(s) was/were included. One condition included the simple, unqualified "me" with the 13 racial/ethnic concepts; a second included the concept "the actual me" with the 13; a third, "the ideal me"; a fourth, "my preference"; and a fifth, all three modified self-referents.

Measures of favorability and similarity to self were included for each of the 13 racial/ethnic concepts. Positive *affect* was measured as follows:

> We would like you to indicate how favorable you feel toward several things and ideas. Imagine that 100 is how favorable you feel toward "Hard-

Working," and 0 is not favorable at all. You can give any number you wish. How favorable do you feel toward: (concept list)

A perceived *similarity* measure also was obtained for each concept:

We would like you to indicate how similar some things and ideas are to you. Imagine that 100 is how similar "Hard-Working" is to you, and 0 is not similar at all. You can give any number you wish. How similar are these things and ideas to you: (concept list)

Data Collection

Questionnaires were distributed to students in an introductory sociology class and an introductory communication class at a large midwestern university. Prior to completing the forms, participants received an explanation of the use of magnitude scales. Participants were randomly assigned to experimental conditions. The total N was 160, with 30 to 35 respondents per condition.

Data Transformations

All data were transformed in several ways. First, to eliminate extreme responses, any responses greater than 99,999 were set equal to that number. Second, our questionnaire instructed respondents that all yardstick values were 100, and subsequently were *asked* for the values on measures including the yardsticks. If a respondent gave a response other than 100 to one of these yardsticks, the response was adjusted to 100 while preserving the ratio of all responses to the yardstick. This was accomplished by means of the following rescaling

$$x' \;=\; x \;(100/y)$$

where x is the raw value of a nonyardstick response, x' is the rescaled value, and y is the subject's response for the yardstick.

Third, initial analysis found the distributions for all measures to be highly positively skewed. Because the mean is only a useful measure of central tendency if the data are not highly skewed, we have performed a logarithmic transformation on the data to reduce such skew, and used the transformed data to calculate means.[7] The resultant means subsequently were transformed back to the original units via an antilog function.[8]

RESULTS

Table 7.1 presents correlational analyses that examine the linear relationships between self-referent distances and measures of favorability and similarity. For these analyses, data were pooled across subjects within each experimental group; the unit of analysis for Table 7.1 was the *concept*, rather than the individual subject. For each self-referent ("me," "actual me," and so on), hierarchical (forced-entry) multiple regression procedures were employed to predict distance from that referent. The mean similarity and favorability scores on the 13 concepts served as predictor variables.

In row 1 of Table 7.1 we see, consistent with H1A, that distance from the "actual me" has the highest association with similarity to self (R-squared $= .55, p < .01$). From row 2, we see, consistent with H2A, that distance from "my preference" and the "ideal me" have the highest associations with favorability (R-squared $= .75$ and $.58$, respectively, both $p < .01$). Consistent with H3, we see that distance from "me" is more strongly associated with similarity to self ($.44, p < .05$) than is distance from "my preference" or the "ideal me" ($.24$, ns, and $.34, p < .05$, respectively), but is less strongly associated with similarity than is distance from the "actual me" ($.55$). Also consistent with H3, distance from "me" is more strongly associated with favorability ($.42, p < .05$) than is distance from the "actual me" ($.29$, ns) but less associated with favorability than are distances from "my preference" and the "ideal me" ($.75$ and $.58$, respectively).

H1B and H2B predicted that the increment to the total R-squared added by the second variable (which the distance is purportedly not measuring) will be quite small. Looking at rows 4 and 5 of Table 7.1, these predictions are dramatically borne out for the "ideal me" and "my preference," with an R-squared increment of $.02$ and $.01$ respectively (both ns). The hypotheses also are confirmed for the "actual me"—the R-squared increment is only $.08$ (ns). Consistent with H3, the incremental R-squared for favorability and similarity on "me" ($.11$ and $.12$, respectively, both ns) are each larger than the incremental R-squared for the second predictor of any of the other three self-referents.[9]

Multidimensional analyses were generated by the Galileo computer program.[10] Again, separate analyses were conducted for the four single self-referent conditions, and also in this case for the experimental condition in which respondents were presented with three modified self-referents ("actual me," "ideal me," and "my preference"). Figure 7.1 presents a graph for the "me" condition of the first three real dimensions, which account for 79.8% of the real variance in the space.[11] This graph gives a rough indication of the aggregate structure for subjects presented with racial group labels, adjectives commonly used to describe racial groups, and the concept "me." The concept "me" is located relatively close to most of the racial group concepts, "proud," and "hard-working" and relatively far from "promiscuous" and "Arab American."

Figure 7.2 shows the first three real dimensions for the condition in which all three self-referents ("actual me," "ideal me," "my preference") were presented. Although all three appear within the same general region,

Table 7.1
Predictions of Distances from
Concepts to Various Self-Referents,
from Favorability and Similarity (n = 13)[a]

	ME		ACTUAL ME		IDEAL ME		MY PREF.	
	R^2	F	R^2	F	R^2	F	R^2	F
R^2 SIM only	.44[b]	8.64*	.55	13.44**	.34	5.67*	.24	3.47
R^2 FAV only	.42	7.97*	.29	4.49	.58	15.19**	.75	33.00**
R^2 SIM & FAV	.54	5.87*	.64	8.89**	.61	7.82**	.76	15.83**
Incremental R^2								
adding FAV to SIM	.11	1.36	.08	0.96	.26	3.88	.52	11.82**
Incremental R^2								
adding SIM to FAV	.12	1.50	.35	5.93*	.02	0.22	.01	0.11

Note: Degrees of freedom for all F's in the first two rows are 1, 11; df for all F's in row 3 are 2, 10; df for all F's in the last two rows are 1, 10.

a. N = 13 refers to the 13 mean, aggregated distances from each self-referent to all concepts, and the corresponding 13 mean favorability and 13 mean similarity scores. These 3 sets of means were calculated from responses by 30 to 35 subjects per experimental condition (that is, "me," "actual me," "ideal me," "my preference").

b. All zero-order correlation coefficients (r's, not shown) between self-referent distances and favorability or similarity were *negative,* indicating in all cases that the further away a concept was from a self-referent, the less favorably it was viewed, or the less similar to self it was reported to be.
*p < .05; **p < .01.

the third real dimension (DIM 3) clearly differentiates among them. The "ideal me" and "my preference" are close together in the space, and the "actual me" is relatively far from them. It should be noted that the analysis presented in Figure 7.2 emphasizes somewhat the differences among the three self-referents due to Galileo's translation of the space so that all concepts *other* than the self-referents are assumed to be stable (translated to the centroid of the stable concepts and then rotated to least squares best fit).

The introduction of *three* self-referents into the space does affect the manner in which concepts are discriminated by respondents. Clearly, Dimension 3 in Figure 7.2 is primarily a discriminator among self-referents, a dimension that is impossible for the single self-referent spaces. Introduction of this new source of variance has resulted in a new dimension of inter-concept discrimination.

Complementing Figure 7.1, Table 7.2 presents results of a comparison between the multidimensional space for the group of respondents presented with the simple "me" (Figure 7.1), and that for each of the other three single self-referent groups. Treating the 13 adjective and racial group concepts as stable, the Galileo procedure has rotated each of these three spaces to congruence with the first space ("me" group). Thus the "movement" of these 13 concepts from their locations in space 1 to spaces 2, 3,

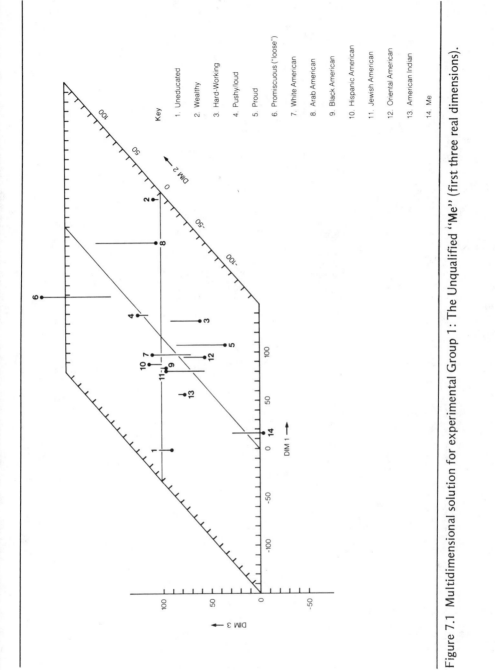

Figure 7.1 Multidimensional solution for experimental Group 1: The Unqualified "Me" (first three real dimensions).

Key

1. Uneducated
2. Wealthy
3. Hard-Working
4. Pushy/loud
5. Proud
6. Promiscuous ("loose")
7. White American
8. Arab American
9. Black American
10. Hispanic American
11. Jewish American
12. Oriental American
13. American Indian
14. Me

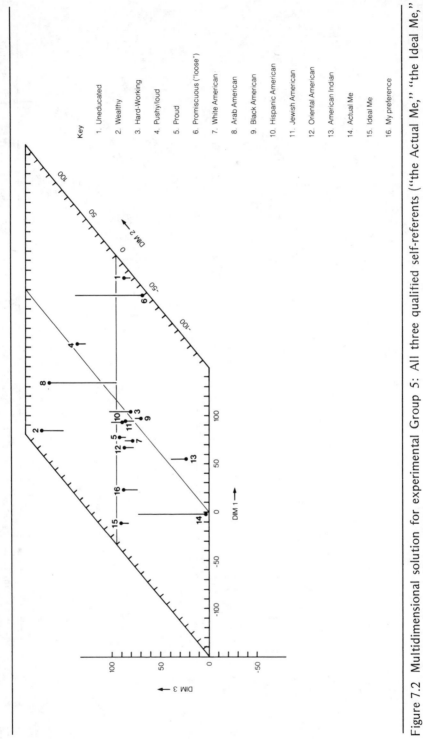

Key

1. Uneducated
2. Wealthy
3. Hard-Working
4. Pushy/loud
5. Proud
6. Promiscuous ("loose")
7. White American
8. Arab American
9. Black American
10. Hispanic American
11. Jewish American
12. Oriental American
13. American Indian
14. Actual Me
15. Ideal Me
16. My preference

Figure 7.2 Multidimensional solution for experimental Group 5: All three qualified self-referents ("the Actual Me," "the Ideal Me," "My Preference") (first three real dimensions).

Table 7.2
Concept "Movement" From Space 1
(Group presented with unqualified "ME")[a]

	Distance "moved" from Space 1 to Space:		
	2 (Actual me)	3 (Ideal me)	4 (My preference)
Concept:			
Uneducated	24.7	−38.0	25.4
Wealthy	2.8	11.4	59.3
Hard-working	17.9	61.3	50.0
Pushy/loud	36.5	18.1	−54.9
Proud	7.1	−20.7	54.2
Promiscuous ("Loose")	−22.5	29.1	42.7
White American	50.5	26.6	37.4
Arab American	48.7	−24.3	85.5
Black American	8.2	29.3	21.8
Hispanic American	−12.8	−31.3	−37.4
Jewish American	65.8	60.6	76.1
Oriental American	13.7	34.4	25.1
American Indian	38.8	50.1	−22.4
Actual me	86.8[b]		
Ideal me		81.1[b]	
My preference			102.4[b]

a. Negative distances are allowed due to the existence of imaginary dimensions in the solutions.
b. Distance from unqualified "me" in Space 1.

and 4 is minimized, and the self-referent concept is allowed to move freely.[12] The results show substantial movement for all self-referents—in all cases, the self-referents experienced greater movement than any other concept (although some concepts did experience substantial movement—for example, Arab American).[13] Thus the discrimination among self-referents displayed in Figure 7.2 is not a contextual artifact resulting solely from forcing respondents to make direct comparisons among the three self-referents.

DISCUSSION

This study has indicated that various self-referents (1) vary in their use as referent concepts for favorability (affect) and/or perceived similarity to self, (2) are not found in the same location in an aggregate multidimensional space, and (3) may affect the dimensionality of the cognitive structure of which each is a part.

Support for the study's predictions was obtained. The "actual me," as predicted, provided the best referent for similarity. "My preference" was the best referent for favorability, and "the ideal me" also served as a strong indicator of favorability. More generally, it is critical to note that the four different self-referent concepts were not treated as equivalent by subjects. Like the porcine concepts in Barnett's (1980) "Pigs in Space," the various self-referents are differentiated in the aggregate cognitive space. The diverse perspectives that an individual may employ for the self, articulated by Mead (1934) and many others, is provided further support by this study. The self can provide exemplars from the category of all possible selves, which are referents for perceived similarity to self and for affective evaluation; other exemplars may be possible.

For those anticipating the need to use a self-referent in an MDS study, at least one major practical recommendation may be derived from this research: Don't use the simple "me." It seems to measure both similarity and favorability to some extent, but is not the best indicator for either. People apparently have a very general conceptualization of "me," and it encompasses both cognition and affect. It is a broad-based exemplar, possibly drawing upon many situations and past experiences, as Mead (1934) has indicated it should. Unfortunately, many studies already have been conducted under the premise that proximity to the "me" implies positive affect.

Important is the general finding that affect may be assessed within a cognitive space. As anticipated, similarity to self and favorability were found to be related but not identical. The multidimensional analyses disclosed no single, purely "good-bad" affective dimension, as Osgood, Suci, and Tannenbaum (1957) have predicted. Rather, support is obtained for the conception of a "maximum preference location" within a cognitive space (Woelfel & Fink, 1980). The caution of Zajonc (1980)—that evaluative judgments may not be captured by cognitive operations—is not supported by this study's results, because the appropriate selection of a self-referent does allow the tapping of affective information. The spaces incorporate the assessment of perceived similarity, allaying Cooper's (1973) concern that affect and cognition may operate in significantly different ways, prohibiting their assessment in a common space. Our findings suggest that one may use the same method to assess both cognition and affect, but may not necessarily do so with the same referent. It may be that out of an aggregate cognitive structure consisting of all dimensions and configurations, only certain parts or points of view are selected by individuals, generated by their consideration of a given self-referent.[14]

Communication researchers need to be aware that the manner in which people view themselves is an integral part of the process of measurement of all cognition and affect. Every time we ask people what they like or what they believe, an implicit self-concept is engaged. In making that self-concept more explicit, researchers may enhance or reduce the validity of their measures; thus a firm grasp of how the self-concept is referenced in a given situation is vital to the valid measurement of cognition and affect. Much of what we know about reactions to persuasive messages, the effects of mass mediated messages, the structure of linguistic meaning—and the list goes on—has relied on the measurement of unobservable constructs tapped by some reference to the self. The multiplicity of this self is a fact that warrants careful attention in the future development of communication theory and research.

NOTES

1. This is a revision of a paper presented to the Annual Meeting of the International Communication Association, San Francisco, 1984.

2. A comprehensive bibliography of communication studies using MDS can be found in Barnett (1986). Discussion of the theoretic assumptions of the measurement model and its application to problems of attitude change may be found in Kaplowitz and Fink (1982, 1983).

3. They also reject Osgood, Suci, and Tannenbaum's use of bounded seven-point semantic differential scales, favoring unbounded continuous scales.

4. Each respondent was presented with two different racial or ethnic labels to which to respond, randomly extracted from the following list: Black American, Mexican American, Asian American, White American, Jewish American. A more detailed description of the preliminary data collections is available from the first author.

5. The standard introduction "If Red and White are 100 units apart, how far apart are ___ and ___?" was given. The chosen yardstick pair had the lowest variance within the set of concept pairs whose mean distances were moderate relative to distance estimates of all pairs of concepts.

6. This selection was made on the basis of the concept's membership in the MDS yard-stick pair, and a seemingly less variable cognitive location than "uneducated." The variances of concept pairs including "hard-working" were generally smaller than the variances of concept pairs including "uneducated," implying greater common agreement on the cognitive location of "hard-working."

7. Lodge (1981) proposes the use of the *geometric* mean as the measure of central tendency for magnitude scaled data. This is equivalent to performing a logarithmic transformation on the data, calculating the mean, and then exponentiating this result. We added .1 to each raw value due to zeros in the raw data. See Bauer and Fink (1983) for a complete discussion of the merits of data transformations of this type.

8. During subsequent regression analyses, a test of residuals disclosed (1) no systematic violations of the homoscedasticity assumption of the distribution of residuals, nor (2) any nonlinearity of the residuals. Thus transformation back to the original units provided consistency with the MDS solution and did not violate assumptions about errors of prediction.

9. The sample size for the correlations is the number of concepts (13) rather than the number of respondents (160).

10. Woelfel and Fink (1980) provide documentation on this program.

11. However, because the Galileo procedure identifies imaginary dimensions as well as real, the 3-dimensional graph does not fully display the richness of the multidimensional structure of the solution. (A total of 83.7% of the real variance in Figure 7.2 is accounted for by the first three real dimensions.)

12. Treating the self-referent concepts as free allows, but does not *require*, the distances between these concepts in Table 7.2 to be large.

13. The average correlation for the consistency in location for the self-referents (the concept vector correlations) is .50, and the average correlation for the consistency of orientations for the first three real dimensions is .87, indicating high stability of the major dimensions across spaces and a lower stability of the self-referents across spaces.

14. The significant effect of concept choice on the dimensionality of cognitive structure is a notion that already has gained some attention. Tversky and Gati (1978), for example, describe a situation in which the similarities between string instruments (banjo, violin, harp, electric guitar) were increased when a wind instrument (clarinet) was added to the set (p. 90).

REFERENCES

Barnett, G. A. (1980). *Frequency of occurrence as an estimate of inertial mass: Pigs in space.* Unpublished manuscript, Rensselaer Polytechnic Institute, Communication Research Laboratory.

Barnett, G. A. (1986). *Bibliography of Galileo research.* Unpublished manuscript, State University of New York at Buffalo, Department of Communication.

Barnett, G. A., Serota, K. B., & Taylor, J. A. (1976). Campaign communication and attitude change: A multidimensional analysis. *Human Communication Research, 2,* 227-244.

Bauer, C. L., & Fink, E. L. (1983). Fitting equations with power transformations: Examining variables with error. In R. N. Bostrom (Ed.), *Communication Yearbook 7* (pp. 146-199). Beverly Hills, CA: Sage.

Cody, M. J. (1980). The validity of experimentally induced motions of public figures in multidimensional scaling configurations. In D. Nimmo (Ed.), *Communication Yearbook 4* (pp. 143-164). New Brunswick, NJ: Transaction Books.

Condran, J. G. (1979). Changes in white attitudes toward blacks: 1963-1977. *Public Opinion Quarterly, 43,* 463-476.

Cooper, L. G. (1973). A multivariate investigation of preferences. *Multivariate Behavioral Research, 8,* 253-272.

Heider, F. (1958). *The psychology of interpersonal relations.* New York: John Wiley.

Jackman, M. R. (1979). The subjective meaning of social class identification in the United States. *Public Opinion Quarterly, 43,* 443-462.

Kaplowitz, S. A., & Fink, E. L. (1982). Attitude change and attitudinal trajectories: A dynamic multidimensional theory. In M. Burgoon (Ed.), *Communication Yearbook 6* (pp. 364-394). Beverly Hills, CA: Sage.

Kaplowitz, S. A., & Fink, E. L. (1983). *Source-message- receiver relations and attitude change: A dynamic multidimensional theory.* Unpublished manuscript, Michigan State University, Department of Sociology.

Kihlstrom, J. F., & Cantor, N. (1984). Mental representations of the self. *Advances in Experimental Social Psychology, 17,* 1-47.

Lodge, M. L. (1981). *Magnitude scaling: Quantitative measurement of opinions.* Beverly Hills, CA: Sage.

McGuire, W. J., & Padawer-Singer, A. (1976). Trait salience in the spontaneous self-concept. *Journal of Personality and Social Psychology, 33,* 743-754.

Mead, G. H. (1934). *Mind, self, and society.* Chicago: University of Chicago Press.

Newton, B. J., & Buck, E. B. (1981, May). *Metric multidimensional scaling of viewers' perceptions of TV in 5 countries.* Paper presented at the International Communication Association Convention, Minneapolis, MN.

Osgood, C. E., Suci, G. J., & Tannenbaum, P. H. (1957). *The measurement of meaning.* Urbana: University of Illinois Press.

Pavlak, T. J. (1973). Social class, ethnicity, and racial prejudice. *Public Opinion Quarterly, 37,* 225-231.

Reagan, J. (1978). *A pilot study comparing the sense of community scale with a Galileo plot of its concepts.* Unpublished manuscript, Michigan State University, Department of Telecommunication.

Rosch, E. (1975). Cognitive representations of semantic categories. *Journal of Experimental Psychology: General, 104,* 192-223.

Serota, K. B., Cody, M. J., Barnett, G. A., & Taylor, J. A. (1977). Precise procedures for optimizing campaign communication. In B. D. Ruben (Ed.), *Communication Yearbook 1* (pp. 475-491). New Brunswick, NJ: Transaction Books.

Smith, E. E., & Medin, D. L. (1981). *Categories and concepts.* Cambridge, MA: Harvard University Press.

Stryker, S., & Statham, A. (1985). Symbolic interaction and role theory. In G. Lindsey & E. Aronson (Eds.), *Handbook of Social Psychology* (3rd ed., Vol. 1, pp. 311-378). New York: Random House.

Tversky, A., & Gati, I. (1978). Studies of similarity. In E. Rosch & B. B. Lloyd (Eds.), *Cognition and categorization* (pp. 81-98). Hillsdale, NJ: Lawrence Erlbaum Associates.

Woelfel, J. (1976). Galileo: *A non-technical introduction*. Unpublished manuscript, Michigan State University.

Woelfel, J., Cody, M. J., Gillham, J., & Holmes, R. A. (1980). Basic premises of multidimensional attitude change theory: An experimental analysis. *Human Communication Research, 6*, 153-167.

Woelfel, J., & Fink, E. L. (1980). *The measurement of communication processes: Galileo theory and method*. New York: Academic Press.

Woelfel, J., & Napoli, N. (1982). *Proposed standards for the measurement of human emotion*. Unpublished manuscript, State University of New York at Albany, Department of Communication.

Woelfel, J., & Saltiel, J. (1978). Cognitive processes as motions in a multidimensional space. In F. Casmir (Ed.), *International and intercultural communication* (pp. 105-130). New York: University Press.

Zajonc, R. B. (1980). Feeling and thinking: Preferences need no inferences. *American Psychologist, 35*, 151-175.

8 ● Gender Differences in Adolescents' Uses of and Attitudes Toward Computers

MILTON CHEN

Harvard University

T he impressive rate of adoption of microcomputers in schools and homes has provoked concern for equity in their availability, uses, and effects (Chen, 1985a; Lepper, 1985; Linn, 1984; Paisley & Chen, 1984). In schools alone, the number of microcomputers increased nearly 20-fold in just three years, from 33,000 in June of 1981 to 630,000 in June of 1984 ("Computer Makers Find Rich Market"). Recent data collected by Dataquest, a market research firm in San Jose, indicate that, as of February 1985, 13.1% of American households possessed a personal computer, with higher-end systems growing in popularity (Dataquest, 1985).

As with previous communication technologies, there is concern that a "knowledge gap" will divide the computer-haves from the have-nots. Recent studies indicate that, predictably, schools and homes with higher socioeconomic status have been earlier adopters of microcomputers (Becker, 1985; Center for Social Organization of Schools, 1983; Rogers, Daley, & Wu, 1982).

However, microcomputers present a new concern about equity that goes beyond the advantages of higher SES. Recent studies have begun to address the nature of sex differences in children's and adolescents' uses of and attitudes toward computers (Hawkins, in press; Hess & Miura, in press; Lockheed, in press). It is common to find more boys than girls taking computer classes, attending computer camps, and indicating greater interest in computers in both home and school settings.

These differences raise new questions for communication research and especially research on media and children. Although much of the research

AUTHOR'S NOTE: The survey from which these data are taken was a project of the Education and Technology Panel of the Study of Stanford and the Schools. Funding was provided by the Lilly Endowment.

Correspondence and requests for reprints: Milton Chen, Harvard Graduate School of Education, Larsen Hall, 4th Floor, Appian Way, Cambridge, MA 02138.

on television and children focuses on the "unintended" and antisocial effects of programming with largely entertainment purposes, computers offer useful skills and knowledge to those who value and seek such learning. Therefore, the differing motivations and values of computer users versus nonusers become important variables for studying the social effects of the technology.

Recent research has begun to investigate the issues posed by the use of microcomputers in schools and homes. However, many of the studies are limited in their sampling and their focus on qualitative description. The study reported here utilized a large random sample of high school students in the Bay Area to study sex differences in their uses of and attitudes toward computers.

REVIEW OF LITERATURE

The literature on gender differences is vast, encompassing diverse areas of physiological, cognitive, and affective functioning. Maccoby and Jacklin (1974), in their landmark compilation of the literature on sex differences, referenced over 1,400 studies. Deaux (1984) documented continued growth in the literature during the 1970s and early 1980s, including the rise of several journals devoted to research on sex roles. In this discussion of previous research, we will focus selectively on studies of gender differences among children and adolescents in both cognitive and social development, with special emphasis on studies in the areas of mathematical and scientific learning. Mathematics and science are often portrayed as allied fields for computer science, requiring similar intellectual skills of abstract reasoning and symbolic representation. In a more practical sense, computer programming courses at the high school level often carry prerequisites in algebra or other basic mathematics courses.

Sex Differences in Achievement in Mathematics and Science

Substantial research has been devoted in the past two decades to investigating sex differences in mathematics achievement. Through the middle elementary grades, few differences are found between girls' and boys' achievement. However, beginning in early adolescence (ages 8 to 12), differences in math achievement and interest emerge. This incipient gap increases through the high school, college, and graduate school years.

During the years 1972-1973 and 1977-1978, the mathematics component of the National Assessment of Educational Progress (NAEP) was conducted with a sample of over 70,000 9-, 13-, and 17-year-olds. Carpenter,

Coburn, Kepner, Lindquist, and Reys (1981) found that the difference in the national mean favoring boys over girls, although minimal for 9-year-olds, increased for 13- and 17-year-olds. For 9- and 13-year-olds, the sex differences widened from the 1972-1973 to the 1977-1978 assessments.

During the five-year period of 1976-1981, average mathematics scores on the Scholastic Aptitude Test (SAT) for male versus female high school students differed by between 48 and 59 points, with males scoring higher (National Center for Education Statistics, 1982). For the same period, verbal scores between the sexes differed by only 4 to 12 points (males also with higher scores). The same pattern persists for the performance of male and female college graduates on the mathematics and verbal tests of the Graduate Record Exam (GRE).

Several researchers have suggested that a major factor in differential levels of mathematics or science achievement may be differential amounts of exposure to the subject matter. This explanation has been termed the *differential coursework hypothesis* (Fennema & Sherman, 1977; Pallas & Alexander, 1983). Some studies have reported that females take fewer courses in mathematics during the junior high, high school, and college years and that, consequently, their achievement scores suffer compared to males. According to this hypothesis, when amount of course work is controlled for, the differences in achievement become minimal.

Sex Differences in Affective
and Attitudinal Factors

Given the influence of experiential factors (including both formal classroom instruction and informal exposure through home or after school activities) in mediating sex differences in mathematics and science, research has focused upon affective and attitudinal variables that motivate boys as opposed to girls to seek out and acquire different types of experiences. Differential motivation and interest in mathematics and science is often reported. In one study, Haertel, Walberg, Junker, and Pascarella (1981) conducted an analysis of NAEP science data with 2,346 13-year-olds sampled for the 1976 assessment. No sex difference in science achievement scores was found. However, a sex difference favoring boys was found for the motivation construct, operationalized as the performance of voluntary science activities (for example, hobbies, lectures, museums).

Socioeconomic status and race showed significant main effects across both learning and motivation outcomes. An SES by sex interaction effect indicated that the family's socioeconomic status had a positive effect on boys' motivation, but not girls'. The investigators suggested that a combination of both a supportive family environment (as measured by SES) and individual expectations were required to motivate performance of such activities.

Further theoretical work has investigated the importance of self-concept in achievement in mathematics, English, and other domains (Eccles, Adler, & Meece, 1984). A traditional theory of self-concept holds that those with a positive conception of their abilities in certain tasks approach those tasks with more confidence, higher expectations, and greater persistence. They consequently outperform those with less confidence, lower expectations, and less persistence.

Sex differences based on self-concept appear to arise most strongly for tasks perceived as "sex-typed." That is, boys and girls may evaluate their own abilities more favorably for tasks thought to be more appropriate for their sex. Mathematics is viewed by children as a "male" subject (Eccles, 1983; Fennema & Sherman, 1978). Reading and English are stereotyped as female domains as early as the sixth grade.

Eccles and her colleagues at the University of Michigan have been the principal proponents of a revision to this traditional view emphasizing the student's beliefs about his or her own abilities in a subject-matter domain (Eccles, 1983; Eccles, Adler, & Meece, 1984; Meece, Eccles-Parsons, Kaczala, Goff, & Futterman, 1982). Their theory, based on recent "expectancy-value" models in psychology, relates motivations not only to perceived ability and chances of success but to the importance or incentive value of the task as well. A theory of "subjective task value" suggests that girls may decline to undertake computer experiences not only based on perceived probabilities of success or failure, but also due to a belief that computers will not return the subjective rewards they seek.

Sex Differences
in Social Behavior

Computer use is not solely a matter of individual cognitive skill but a form of social behavior as well. For children and adolescents, computing occurs in a social environment. The settings can include the school computer lab, the home computer room, the video arcade, the library, and other informal learning environments. The social context involves the preferences and influence of role models, such as parents, siblings, classmates, or friends.

The importance of parental influence in sex-role socialization has been a frequent subject of study. That parents hold differing expectations for the behaviors of their sons and daughters has been well documented in several reviews (for example, Eccles, Adler, & Kaczala, 1982; Parsons, Ruble, Hodges, & Small, 1976). Fathers often exert a strong influence against non-sex-stereotypical play activities for their young children (Maccoby,

1980). This literature suggests that parents may play a strong role in influencing girls' versus boys' interests in computers.

The peer group also has been studied as an important socializer of behaviors and expectations. In reviewing the literature in this area, Maccoby (in press) notes the extent to which boys and girls are raised in separate cultures. Beginning in the preschool years, children seem to gravitate spontaneously toward same-sex clusters, creating a situation she terms as *spontaneous segregation by sex*. Boys' versus girls' cultures engage in their own shared norms and expectations for behaviors.

Those behaviors may affect the relative attractiveness of computers for boys versus girls. Boys' groups orient around issues of dominance and competition through direct commands, and girls adopt more cooperative strategies in directing group behavior through consensus. Most video and computer games have emphasized the former rather than the latter themes. The research suggests that those activities pursued by boys by definition will be of less interest to young girls. To the extent that boys overtly express their enthusiasm for computers and aggressively seek out computer experiences, girls may be disinclined to follow suit.

Sex Differences
in Computer Use

Studies of High School Students
and Older Adolescents

The 1977-1978 National Assessment of Educational Progress contained several computer-related items in its mathematics assessment (Carpenter et al., 1981). The national sample of 13- and 17-year-olds responded to items on their knowledge of and experiences with computers. Less than 15% of the sample reported having some coursework in computer programming, although two-thirds agreed that some knowledge of programming would be useful. In response to the knowledge items, the great majority (at least 75%) of students were unable to read a simple flowchart or complete a simple exercise in BASIC. Lower levels of computer access and ability were found for girls, minorities, rural students, and those in the southeastern states.

A survey of high school students' computer literacy was conducted by the Minnesota Educational Computing Consortium (MECC) in 1979 (Anderson, Klassen, Krohn, & Smith-Cunnien, 1982). The survey sample was composed of 2,535 11th-grade students and 3,615 8th-grade students in Minnesota. The MECC survey found little evidence of sex differences in computer literacy. Girls and boys were roughly equal in overall computer literacy as well as programming test scores. Girls outscored boys for items presented as word problems. These findings held for students at both the 8th- and 11th-grade levels.

Anderson et al. attributed this equality in performance to Minnesota's statewide commitment to computer literacy, in which equal access to computers for all students is mandated. However, the researchers observed that in many other school systems, computers are a scarce resource and courses in computer science are still taught as advanced electives. In these environments, they suggested that the enthusiasm of males in electing and participating in such courses may lead to a loss of motivation on the part of the females.

Most recently, the California State Department of Education conducted a survey of 6th- and 12th-graders' knowledge of and attitudes toward computers (California Assessment Program, 1984). Similar to the NAEP findings, knowledge of computer programming was low, although boys scored higher than girls at both grade levels. The higher scores among males were associated with greater exposure to computer experiences.

A study by Eastman and Krendl (1984) has emphasized the importance of investigating gender differences among different types of computer uses. In their study of 8th-graders' accessing of an online video encyclopedia to write a science essay, few differences were found between male and female abilities with the computer task. In addition, gender differences at pretest in attitudes about boys' versus girls' abilities (boys holding superior beliefs about male abilities) were nonsignificant at posttest. The researchers attributed this change to the beneficial effects of computer experience in reducing students' sex stereotypes.

Studies of College Students

The research group at Carnegie-Mellon University also has focused on sex differences in college students' uses of and attitudes toward computers (Kiesler, Sproull, & Eccles, in press). Female college students at CMU were less likely to have had prior computing experience and to play computer games. Women were more likely to have negative experiences in their first computing course at college. The researchers traced these differences to early experiences with computers in elementary school and video game arcades. They also pointed to anecdotal evidence of boys as early as the preschool age monopolizing the school's computers and restricting the access of young girls.

Several researchers point to the male-oriented culture that prevails in settings where computers are likely to be used, such as video arcades, computer stores, and computer centers in schools. They also note that the majority of computer games available for children favor male themes of action and/or adventure and competition (Kiesler, Sproull, & Eccles, 1983; Lepper, 1985).

Studies of Computer Camps

An interesting development with microcomputers has been the rise of computer camps. Expertise with computers has reached a level of social status similar to talent in music or sports, skills for which summer enrichment camps traditionally have been offered. However, some early studies of computer camps indicate the beginnings of a gender gap.

Hess and Miura (in press) surveyed the directors of 23 computer camps with a total enrollment of 5,533 students. Across camps, differential patterns of enrollment were found for boys versus girls. Girls composed 28% of the beginning and intermediate classes, 14% of advanced programming classes, and only 5% of high-level courses teaching assembly language.

In addition, tuition costs also mediated a sex difference: As the cost of a camp rose, girls' enrollment declined. Hess and Miura interpreted this difference as indicating favoritism of families toward the computer education of their sons. Several camp directors were cited as saying that fathers were actively encouraging use of computers by their sons but not their daughters.

Researchers at the Children's Television Workshop have investigated sex differences in some detail at a single computer camp (Revelle, Honey, Amsel, Schauble, & Levine, 1984). Of the 294 campers ranging in age from 7 to 19, 15% were girls. Boys were more likely to have used computers longer and more frequently at both home and school and to be more proficient in programming at the start of camp.

DESIGN AND METHODOLOGY
OF THE STUDY

The above literature suggested several theoretical guidelines and specific hypotheses for the design of this survey and specific analyses reported here. The first is a fundamental assumption that underlies this study: that gender differences in computer learning are not primarily innate but are based upon a complex pattern of socialization. Therefore, this study is directed toward analysis of socialization factors that differentially affect the computer interests and attitudes of male versus female adolescents.

Second, the research suggests that adolescence is a period in which such differences should be found. Studies of mathematics and science learning cited above suggest that the effects of differential socialization appear as early as the age of eight. Although the literature suggests the expectation of a generally higher level of interest in and experience with computers among males, studies also recommend closer attention to specific types of computer experiences. The similarities and differences between students' perceptions of the learning of mathematics, science, and computers remain important questions for research.

Third, the literature emphasizes the importance of controlling for students' experiences in analyzing gender differences in achievement. Many studies that controlled for experience (either through analysis of subsamples with equivalent amount of course-taking or through selective sampling) find minimal differences between boys and girls.

Fourth, the literature suggests that students' attitudes and motivations be closely studied as predictors of their acquisition of computer experiences. If the notion of boys and girls raised in "separate cultures" is correct, we would expect to find different norms for the perceived attractiveness and benefits of computer use among boys and girls.

With those considerations in mind, this survey was designed to investigate the computer uses and attitudes of a sample of high school students from five Bay Area High Schools. This study was conducted in May and June of 1983 by the Education and Technology Panel of the Study of Stanford and the Schools, a collaborative research effort between Stanford University and high schools in five Bay Area school districts. The five schools surveyed in this study represented each of the five school districts. Prior to the survey, during the 1982-1983 school year, some preliminary data on computer usage and history had been collected through interviews with principals and key teachers.

A survey instrument was designed and pretested with a small sample of high school students from a school district that was not represented in the study. After minor revisions were made, the survey was administered during one class period at each of the five high schools. A systematic random sample of 1,138 students completed the questionnaire.

This report focuses on some basic analyses pertaining to gender differences in computer uses and attitudes. In particular, three different categories of data from the survey are discussed:

(1) Computer experiences of high school students. These include classroom use of computers in elementary, junior high, and high school courses (for both programming and other applications); use of computers in other informal school settings, such as computer clubs; and use of computers in homes, camps, or other out-of-school settings.
(2) Students' attitudes toward computers, such as interest in computers, perceived skill with computers, and belief in gender equality in computer skill and use.
(3) Social influences affecting computer use, such as peer-group interest in and expertise with computers and the family's encouragement of computer use.

Other measures were obtained through the survey instrument, including measures of students' personalities (for example, self-esteem, locus of control), future educational and occupational aspirations, perceptions of school experience (favorite subject, perception of difficulty of school sub-

jects), and students' backgrounds (for example, age, sex, ethnicity, parental education, and occupational level). Further analyses of relationships
among computer experiences, attitudes toward computers, and social
influences can be found in Chen (1985b).

The representativeness of these schools for other American high
schools bears some comment. The five high schools studied here are
located in or near the Silicon Valley area, where many occupations are
related to the computer industries. "Computer consciousness" may therefore be higher in this area than in other regions of the country. One indication of this heightened awareness is the greater percentage of students
reporting the presence of a home computer, compared with national
averages.

However, the advantage in knowledge and uses of microcomputers
among these families may not apply across variations in school settings.
For instance, the five high schools include one with a well-developed computer program, in which computers were used in programming, journalism, special education, mathematics, and science classes. In contrast, one
of the schools offered only a few courses that used computers (that is, in
biology and business classes). Although the home environments of these
students may indicate a higher degree of computer awareness (as indicated
by parents' occupations or the presence of a home computer), the five high
schools present a range of diversity and quality in their computer programs
that is not obviously different from patterns of use in many other high
school districts during the 1982-1983 school year.

RESULTS

Students' Computer Usage in School

Table 8.1 presents data for the total sample and by gender on measures
of computer use before and during high school. These uses include both
classes in computer programming and classes in which some nonprogramming application was taught (for example, word processing, data analysis,
drill and practice in subject areas). Asterisks denote probability levels based
on t and chi-square tests of significance for sex differences.

Computer programming is the one use of computers that most clearly
differentiates males from females. A higher percentage of boys enrolled in
more programming courses both before and during high school than did
girls. The ratio between male and female enrollments rose with the level of
difficulty of the programming course. However, there was no difference
between boys' and girls' enrollment in other courses that utilized computers, either before or during high school.

Data were gathered on students' enrollment in high school courses in
computer programming, mathematics, and science. Although the "differ-

Table 8.1
Students' Use of Computers in Schools

	Total Sample N = 1,138 %	Boys n = 595 %	Girls n = 531 %
Pre-high school use	25.5	27.1	23.7
Pre-high school programming course	16.0	18.6	13.1*
Currently enrolled in a			
high school programming class	6.5	8.3	4.6*
Semesters of high school programming			
One	9.0	9.6	8.4
Two	3.0	4.3	1.5
Three or more	1.7	2.6	0.4**
Enrolled in high school			
nonprogramming class	18.2	17.9	18.6

Notes: Missing cases diminish sample sizes by at most 10%; probability levels for significance tests: *p < .05, **p < .01; significance test for semesters of high school programming reflects three levels of enrollment.

ential course work" hypothesis attributes higher achievement to a greater number of courses taken, these data do not support the hypothesis for boys' versus girls' course enrollments in mathematics and science. There was no gender difference in the average number of mathematics and science courses taken. However, as suggested by data in Table 8.1, a gender difference was found for computer programming.

In a related item, students were asked about their intentions to take computer programming courses in their future high school years. Boys also indicated interest in taking a higher number of programming courses than did girls.

Although males and females differed in their frequency of enrollment in computer programming classes, no gender difference was found on one measure of programming skill. Students who had taken a programming course during high school were asked to report their grade from the most recent programming class taken. Boys' mean grade on a scale of 1 (high) to 7 (low) was 1.89; girls' mean grade was 2.03 ($t = 0.58$, df $= 162$, $p =$ ns).

Students' Home Computer Use

Table 8.2 summarizes data for the availability of six electronic technologies, including home computers, in students' homes. Although the figures on presence of home computers are higher than national averages reported during 1983 (ranging from 8%-10%), these percentages compare favorably with data from another study of home computers in the same locale (Rogers, Daley, & Wu, 1982).

Among the six technologies, the largest gender difference was found for the home computer. Whether parents are favoring boys with computers,

Table 8.2
Presence of Computers and Other Electronic Technologies in Home

	Total Sample N = 1,138 %	Boys n = 595 %	Girls n = 531 %
Home computer	21.0	23.7	18.1*
Computer terminal	6.3	6.3	6.4
Videocassete recorder (VCR)	33.0	34.4	31.5
Video game player	58.3	60.1	56.3
Cable television	52.9	54.6	51.0
Calculator	97.3	95.7	98.7*

Notes: Missing cases diminish sample sizes by at most 10%; probability levels for significance tests: *p < .05, **p < .01.

or boys are more insistent and successful in influencing purchases, is not known. Further multivariate analyses will examine how these figures are affected by SES and other family background variables. For the other technologies, there were no differences between the percentages of boys' versus girls' homes with computer terminals, VCRs, video game players, and cable television. A slightly higher percentage of girls in this sample reported calculators in their homes.

For students with home computers, a further significant difference was found in their amount of use. Boys used their home computers an average of 6.1 hours per week, and girls had an average weekly use of 3.6 hours. Further analyses will investigate whether the amount of use differed by type of use, such as programming, game-playing, word processing, or connecting to computer networks.

Use of Computers in
Other Informal Settings

Data also were gathered on students' use of computers in other informal settings outside the school and home. Because these uses are a sporadic and irregular part of students' lives (for example, use of a computer in a public library, at a friend's house, or parent's office), the precise measurement of the frequency of occurrence of and amount of time spent in such activities is problematic. The item in this survey simply asked students whether or not they had *ever* participated in such computer activities as computer camps or clubs, or used computers in libraries, friends' homes, or parents' offices. Boys again reported more frequent experiences with computers, such as using a friend's computer or belonging to a computer club at school. No differences were found between boys' and girls' use of a computer in the public library or at a parent's office. Figures on computer camp enrollment were too low to enable interpretation of gender differences.

Social Models for Computer Use

The research literature suggests that an important factor in the development of boys' interest in computers may be the stronger presence and encouragement of male adult and peer models. The "culture" in which boys are raised may include more same-sex models who demonstrate, encourage, and legitimize computer use by boys. Young boys may be more likely than young girls to have a father, uncle, neighbor, or other adult male model engaged in computer-related professions. At the high school level, most computer teachers are men, although many elementary teachers introducing computers to children are women. Among their peer group, boys may be more likely than girls to have other same-sex friends interested in computers.

Students responded regarding two dimensions of modeling influence: 1) knowledge about computers on the part of their father, mother, sisters, brothers, and friends; and 2)their encouragement of the students' own computer learning.

The data do not support parents' differential influence on boys' versus girls' computer learning. Similar percentages of boys and girls reported that their fathers and mothers were knowledgeable about computers and had encouraged computer learning, with the exception that girls report a higher percentage of computer-knowledgeable mothers than do boys. As suggested above, these levels of parental experience with computers may reflect employment with Silicon Valley industries. The trend continues with siblings. Both boys and girls report similar percentages of brothers and sisters who are knowledgeable about and have encouraged computer learning.

The major difference is in the influence of peers. Boys report a much higher percentage of friends who know about computers and have encouraged their use. Although this item did not ask for the sex of these friends, other data from the survey indicate that boys and girls have more same-sex than opposite-sex friends. The data suggest that the culture in which boys are raised includes more male peers who demonstrate and encourage computer use. As Maccoby's theory of gender-separate cultures implies, same-sex peer groups appear to play an important socializing role in adolescents' acquisition of experience with computers.

Students' Attitudes Toward Computers

A basic purpose of the survey was to gather data not only on students' experiences with computers but their attitudes regarding these experiences as well. These beliefs and attitudes included students' interest in and liking for computers, their perceived competence and abilities with computers, the importance of equal access to and ability with computers for females and males, and whether or not computer expertise gains respect from parents and peers.

A factor analysis (principal components with varimax rotation) was performed on the 32 attitude items and confirmed the presence of five dimensions of computer attitudes. The five factors were named (1) Interest in Computers (general interest in and attraction toward computer activities); (2) Gender Equality (women and girls can be as skilled with computers as men and boys); (3) Computer Self-Confidence (self's perception of confidence and skill with computers); (4) Computer Anxiety (computers are difficult to master and raise feelings of inadequacy); and (5) Interpersonal Respect (computer skill leads to respect from parents and peers). Based on the factor analysis, additive indexes corresponding to these five dimensions were computed. (Reliabilities for these indexes are given in Note 2.) Each index ranges between one (negative) to five (positive). Table 8.3 presents the results of t-tests of differences between the means for boys and girls on these five indexes.

Boys exhibited more positive attitudes toward computers on four of the five scales: Interest in Computers, Computer Self-Confidence, Computer Anxiety (lower), and Interpersonal Respect. However, the largest difference was for girls' higher levels of agreement with statements of gender equality (for example, agreement with "women can do as well as men in computer careers," disagreement with "the boys in my school are better with computers than the girls"). The findings present a contrast between girls' strong feelings that females are and should be as competent with computers as men and their own more negative feelings and interests regarding computers.

The "differential coursework hypothesis" argues that sex differences in achievement scores are a function of the taking of courses and the acquisition of experience with subject matter. This survey investigated whether or not the above differences in computer attitudes could be explained by experience with the subject, in the form of home and school computer activities. The most substantial computer experience in the study was the high school computer programming course. Table 8.4 contains findings of t-tests between two groups: all boys in the sample and girls with at least one semester of high school programming.

Compared with Table 8.3, data in Table 8.4 show that the original differences in attitudes between all boys and girls in the sample are not found for girls who have had one semester of programming in high school. Although these girls amount to only 10% of girls in the sample, they exhibit more positive attitudes toward computers than girls who have not taken programming. Whether girls who take programming approach these courses with more positive attitudes or such attitudes develop out of the experience cannot be determined on the basis of these analyses. However, these findings do support a clear association between positive attitudes about computers and the acquisition of computer experience and thereby offer indirect support for the differential coursework notion.

Table 8.3
Students' Attitudes Toward Computers

	Boys n = 595	Girls n = 531
Interest in computers (6 items)	3.87	3.76*
Gender equality (5 items)	3.80	4.39***
Computer self-confidence (3 items)	3.00	2.66***
Computer anxiety (4 items)	2.26	2.44***
Interpersonal respect from computer skills (2 items)	2.88	2.56***

Notes: Attitude indexes computed on a five-point scale (5 = high, 1 = low); missing cases diminish sample sizes by at most 10%; *p < .05, **p < .01, ***p < .001.

Table 8.4
Students' Attitudes Toward Computers: Boys
Versus Girls with a Minimum of One Semester of Programming

	Boys n = 595	Girls with Programming n = 54
Interest in computers (6 items)	3.87	3.95
Gender equality (5 items)	3.80	4.29***
Computer self-confidence (3 items)	3.00	3.01
Computer anxiety (4 items)	2.26	2.32
Interpersonal respect from computer skills (2 items)	2.88	2.71

Notes: Attitude indexes computed on a five-point scale (5 = high, 1 = low); missing cases diminish sample sizes by at most 10%; *p < .05, **p < .01, ***p < .001.

DISCUSSION

Consistent with some earlier studies, this survey found several expected gender differences in computer use favoring boys. Boys were more likely to have taken a computer programming course before and during their high school years. Computers were found more frequently in homes of males and were more frequently used by males than females.

However, no difference was found among male and female students who had taken courses using computers for more general applications. Similar percentages of male and female students enrolled in high school courses in which computers were used for nonprogramming application (for example, business classes using word processing or spreadsheet software, classes using computer-assisted instruction in various subjects). There also was no difference in percentages of boys and girls who had taken a class using computers before high school. This finding points to the importance of analyzing gender differences in computing by type of use and age of users.

Boys had more favorable attitudes about computers, based on attitude scales measuring general interest and perceived skill. Boys also felt that computer skill was more valued as a source of respect from others than did girls.

The largest gender difference in attitudes, however, was found for girls' high levels of agreement with the importance of gender equality in computer use. Girls felt strongly that women can and should be as skilled with computers as men. However, their own personal agendas did not match their aspirations for women in general. This finding suggests that although notions of gender equality have become socially accepted and even strongly advocated by girls, their willingness to commit their own personal interests and resources in furthering this goal may still lag behind.

However, those girls who do obtain computer experiences exhibit much the same levels of interest and confidence as boys. The findings for those girls who have completed one semester of high school programming suggest that the "attitudinal barrier" may be based on lack of exposure to computers.

An interesting research question with implications for educational practice asks how to attract those girls and boys who are forming negative attitudes about computers on the basis of little or no experience. Consistent with research cited on the "separate cultures" of boys versus girls, these findings indicate that same-sex peer groups play a powerful role as socializers of computer attitudes. Boys presented more frequent peer models of computer knowledge and encouragement for other boys than did girls.

This differential effect of peer group socialization has been noted by teachers and educators using computers in classrooms. Some advocate introducing computers to children and adolescents through mixed-sex groupings. Others believe that during the early years of exposure, it is crucial that girls be allowed to proceed at their own pace, without the pressure of competition from boys.

Further research can be devoted profitably to investigating differences in the "subjective task values" that females and males attach to their activities. For instance, if girls believe that computer work is necessarily isolating and devoid of collaborative interaction with others, it is possible to structure computer experiences to offer a greater degree of peer interaction. Creative use of peer tutoring arrangements may well contribute to enhancing girls' confidence in their computer abilities.

This study also suggests that subject-matter courses in business, science, math, and English are introducing female high school students to computers in greater numbers than computer programming classes. In these courses, the utility of the computer in the learning of subject-matter content is highlighted. Such courses may provide a more direct avenue to encouraging females' computer interests than the more technical emphasis in programming courses.

Given the current interest of teachers, school administrators, families, computer manufacturers, and state and federal education agencies, it seems likely that computers will continue to be purchased and used in schools and homes in increasing numbers. As employment opportunities for students increasingly require facility with computers, early exposure to the technology and its various applications can enhance a young person's career options. Research into the processes by which students become interested in and develop skills with computers can have both theoretical value and practical implications for the equitable implementation of this important learning technology.

NOTES

1. In this paper, the terms *sex difference* and *gender difference* are used interchangeably. Although in some usages, *sex* connotes more biologically based interpretations and *gender* suggests emphasis on socialization, this subtle distinction largely has been lost in the research literature.

2. Reliabilities for the five attitude indexes were computed using Cronbach's alpha:

Interest in Computers (6 items)	.90
Gender Equality in Computer Use (5 items)	.80
Computer Self-Confidence (3 items)	.73
Computer Anxiety (4 items)	.78
Interpersonal Respect from Computer Skill (2 items)	.88

REFERENCES

Anderson, R. O., Klassen, D. L., Krohn, K. R., & Smith-Cunnien, P. (1982). *Assessing computer literacy: computer awareness and literacy: an empirical assessment.* Minneapolis: Minnesota Educational Computing Consortium.

Becker, H. (1985). How schools use microcomputers: Results from a national survey. In M. Chen & W. J. Paisley (Eds.), *Children and microcomputers: Research on the newest medium* (pp. 87-108). Beverly Hills, CA: Sage.

California Assessment Program (1984). *Computer literacy of California's sixth and twelfth grade students.* Sacramento: California State Department of Education.

Carpenter, T., Coburn, M. K., Kepner, H. S., Jr., Lindquist, M. M., & Reys, R. E. (1981). *Results from the second mathematics assessment of the National Assessment of Educational Progress.* Reston, VA: National Council of Teachers of Mathematics.

Center for Social Organization of Schools (1983, April). *School uses of microcomputers: Reports from a national survey* (Issue No. 3). Baltimore: Johns Hopkins University.

Chen, M. (1985a). A macrofocus on microcomputers: Eight utilization and effects issues. In M. Chen & W. J. Paisley (Eds.), *Children and microcomputers: Research on the newest medium* (pp. 19-36). Beverly Hills, CA: Sage.

Chen, M. (1985b). *Gender differences in adolescents' uses of and attitudes towards computers.* Unpublished doctoral dissertation, Stanford University, Department of Communication.

Computer makers find rich markets in schools. (1984, December 10). *The New York Times,* pp. B1, B9.

Dataquest. (1985). *Survey bulletin: February 1985 Top Line survey data.* San Jose, CA: Author.

Deaux, K. (1984). From individual differences to social categories: Analysis of a decade's research on gender. *American Psychologist, 39*(2), 105-116.

Eastman, S. T., & Krendl, K. A. (1984). *Computers and gender: Differential effects of electronic search on students' achievement and attitudes.* Bloomington: Indiana University, Department of Telecommunications.

Eccles, J. (1983). Sex differences in mathematics participation. In M. Steinkamp & M. Maehr (Eds.), *Women in science* (pp. 80-110). Greenwich, CT: JAI Press.

Eccles, J., Adler, T., & Meece, J. L. (1984). Sex differences in achievement: A test of alternate theories. *Journal of Personality and Social Psychology, 46(1),* 26-43.

Eccles, J., Adler, T., & Kazcala, C. M. (1982). Socialization of achievement attitudes and beliefs: Parental influences. *Child Development, 53,* 310-321.

Fennema, E. (1980). Sex-related differences in mathematics achievement: Where and why. In L. H. Fox, L. Brody, & D. Robin (Eds.), *Women and the mathematical mystique.* Baltimore: Johns Hopkins Press.

Fennema, E., & Sherman, J. (1978). Sex-related differences in mathematics achievement and related factors: A further study. *Journal for Research in Mathematics Education, 9,* 189-203.

Haertel, G. D., Walberg, H. J., Junker, L., & Pascarella, E. T. (1981). Early adolescent sex differences in science learning: Evidence from the National Assessment of Educational Progress. *American Educational Research Journal, 18,* 329-341.

Hawkins, J. (in press). Computers and girls: Rethinking the issues. *Sex Roles.*

Hess, R., & Miura, I. T. (in press). Gender differences in enrollment in computer camps and classes: The extracurricular acquisition of computer training. *Sex Roles.*

Kiesler, S., Sproull, L., & Eccles, J. S. (1983). Second-class citizens? *Psychology Today,* 41-48

Kiesler, S., Sproull, L., & Eccles, J. S. (in press). Poolhalls, chips, and war games: Women in the culture of computing. *Psychology of Women Quarterly.*

Lepper, M. (1985). Microcomputers in education: Motivational and social issues. *American Psychologist, 40(1),* 1-18.

Linn, M. C. (1984). Fostering equitable consequences from computer learning environments. Berkeley: University of California, Berkeley, Lawrence Hall of Science.

Lockheed, M. (in press). Women, girls, and computers: A first look at the evidence. *Sex Roles.*

Maccoby, E. E. (1980). *Social development: Psychological growth and the parent-child relationship.* New York: Harcourt Brace Jovanovich.

Maccoby, E. E. (in press). Social groupings in childhood: Their relationships to prosocial and antisocial behavior in boys and girls. In J. Block, D. Olweus, & M. R. Yarrow (Eds.), *Development of antisocial and prosocial behavior.* New York: Academic Press.

Maccoby, E. E., & Jacklin, C. (1974). *The psychology of sex differences.* Stanford, CA: Stanford University Press.

Meece, J. L., Eccles-Parsons, J., Kaczala, C. M., Goff, S. B., & Futterman, R. (1982). Sex differences in math achievement: Toward a model of academic choice. *Psychological Bulletin, 91,* 324-348.

National Center for Education Statistics, U. S. Department of Education (1982). *Digest of education statistics, 1982.*Washington, DC: Government Printing Office.

Paisley, W., & Chen, M. (1984). The Second Electronic Revolution: The computer and children. In R. Bostrom (Ed.), *Communication yearbook 8* (pp. 106-136). Beverly Hills, CA: Sage.

Pallas, A. M., & Alexander, K. L. (1983). Sex differences in quantitative SAT performance: New evidence on the differential coursework hypothesis. *American Educational Research Journal, 20(2),* 165-182.

Parsons, J. E., Ruble, D. N., Hodges, K. L., & Small, A. W. (1976). Cognitive-developmental factors in emerging sex differences in achievement-related expectations. *Journal of Social Issues, 32,* 47-61.

Revelle, G., Honey, M., Amsel, E., Schauble, L., & Levine, G. (1984, April). *Sex differences in the use of computers.* Paper presented at the annual meeting of the American Educational Research Association, New Orleans.

Rogers, E. M., Daley, H., & Wu, T. (1982) *The diffusion of home computers.* Stanford, CA: Stanford University, Institute for Communication Research.

II ● INFORMATION SYSTEMS

9 ● Exponential Decay and Damped Harmonic Oscillation as Models of the Bargaining Process

FRANK TUTZAUER

Bowling Green State University

BARGAINING and negotiation, first studied from an economic standpoint (Nash, 1950), and later from a psychological standpoint (Siegel & Fouraker, 1960), recently has entered the domain of the communication scientist (Donohue, Diez, & Stahle, 1983; Putnam & Jones, 1982). As the study of bargaining has progressed, different aspects of the negotiation situation have been emphasized in each of the major theoretical approaches. Economic analyses typically have been grounded in game theory, a branch of mathematics devoted to the strategic dimension of conflict, and explicated in the classic works of von Neumann and Morgenstern (1944), Rappoport (1960), and Luce and Raiffa (1957). As a consequence of the game-theoretic emphasis, economists see bargaining as a phenomenon to be explained on the basis of the utility functions of the players and the payoff structure of the situation (Roth, 1979). Psychologists, although not ignoring utilities and payoffs, have tended to incorporate nonstrategic components into their theories. This tendency has led to the investigation of a number of behavioral, motivational, and personality variables in bargaining research (Rubin & Brown, 1975). The present

AUTHOR'S NOTE: The study reported in this chapter is based on the author's doctoral dissertation, and would not have been possible without the help of many people, including Carol Miller-Tutzauer, Michael Roloff, Charles Berger, and Robin Lester.

Correspondence and requests for reprints: Frank Tutzauer, Interpersonal and Public Communication, Bowling Green State University, Bowling Green, OH 43403.

study continues recent trends by taking a communication-oriented approach to bargaining—an approach that gives primacy to the interaction of the bargainers in explanations of outcome. The view presented herein parallels that of McGrath (1966), who sees the process of negotiation as "a fundamental form of human interaction" (p. 101). The explicit assumption of the present analysis is that a communication approach to bargaining will yield valuable insights into an extremely important form of human interaction.

I begin from the premise that it is desirable to examine the dynamical, or time-dependent, characteristics of communication systems (Krippendorff, 1977). Such an assumption is not unusual, and is, in fact, one of the primary advantages of a communication-oriented viewpoint. Communication scholars, since the inception of the field, have "placed strong emphasis on examining communication phenomena that change over time" (Monge, Farace, Eisenberg, Miller, & White, 1984, p. 22), so it seems natural that communication theories of bargaining should possess a dynamical component. Consequently, I adopt a system-theoretic viewpoint in which information exchange is seen as altering the communicative trajectories of bargaining systems. By positing the existence of two fundamental psychological forces, a mathematical description of the system becomes available, and the role of information in altering bargaining dynamics can be explored.

The structure of the chapter is as follows: In the next section, the basic theory is outlined. After narrowing the problem and formalizing the dynamics of concession making, two specific force configurations are introduced—one based on exponential decay, and one on damped harmonic oscillation. Finally, the models are subjected to empirical testing, and the results are considered.

A DYNAMICAL THEORY OF
INTEGRATIVE BARGAINING

The notion that psychological forces underlie bargaining behavior is not a new one (Oliva & Leap, 1981). The most well-known force-based theory is probably McGrath's (1966) tri-polar model, which attributes concession making to three fundamental forces: those impelling the negotiator toward the position of his or her reference group, those moving the negotiator toward agreement with the opposing party, and those in the direction of constructive solutions when viewed from the perspective of society at large. The problem with existing models based on bargaining forces is that such models are invariably verbal formulations lacking the precision of mathematical theories. This situation is lamentable given that the very nature of forces-type models implies that "in addition to English, vector analysis might be used to analyze and/or develop new forces-type models, thereby permitting possible quantification of the magnitude and direction of bargaining factors that were previously described in less operative verbal terms" (Oliva & Leap, 1981, p. 340). It is my purpose in this section to begin such an analysis.

Basic Force Configurations

Narrowing the problem. To formalize the forces at work and their effect on negotiation behavior, it becomes important to examine communication, for negotiation behavior is primarily communicative. However, with few exceptions (Morley & Stephenson, 1977), the communication researcher is usually not interested in studying every instance and kind of communication taking place in a bargaining interaction. The present chapter is no exception, and I will limit the problem by placing primary emphasis on the communication of offers, leaving the dynamical modeling of other communicative behaviors for a subsequent date.

The exchange of offers is one of the four major attributes of the negotiation situation for which communication can be used. Beisecker (1970) argues that during the interaction, a bargainer's communication focuses on the discovery and reevaluation of preferences, the discovery and reevaluation of the interpersonal relationship between the bargainers, the exchange of offers, and procedural matters. And although procedural matters, the bargainers' preferences, and the relationship between the bargainers are not without influence, only through a sequence of offers can a final contract be reached. Ikle (1973), too, lists the transmission and acceptance of offers as the first function of communication in a bargaining setting, and the central importance of offer strategies (Hamner & Yukl, 1977; Tutzauer, 1986) suggests that, in any initial attempt at least, the analysis of offers should be given primacy over an analysis of other forms of communication. It will be impossible to model bargaining dynamics without accounting for the bid/counterbid process. The key role of offers in bargaining communication cannot be overemphasized.

> Inherent within the interaction model [of bargaining] is the assumption that the participants are able to transmit and evaluate offers. Direct verbal communication can provide one channel through which this can be accomplished. Thus used, communication focuses on the outcome of the interaction. Its content pertains to offers made by one participant and his reactions (evaluations or modifications) to offers made by others. (Beisecker, 1970, p. 155)

Despite my conviction that the study of bargaining begins with the study of offers, one must nonetheless keep in mind that only a partial explanation of bargaining phenomena will be possible until other types of communication are integrated into the theory. One drawback of mathematical explanations is that they give an impression of comprehensiveness to whatever theory is being espoused. And although working through the math will quickly dispel this illusion, there is always the risk that the theory will seem more all-embracing than it is or even claims to be. One is cautioned, therefore, to remember that the present formulation applies only to the description and explanation of offer sequences and how these sequences, in turn, contribute to certain outcomes.

Concession paths. To capture the relationship between verbal offers and internal forces, it will prove useful to have a geometric representation of the bargaining problem. A key notion in the study of integrative bargaining (Pruitt, 1981) is that every agreement has a certain benefit for one bargainer as well as a (possibly different) benefit level for the other bargainer. Thus each possible agreement can be represented by two coordinates, and the set of all such agreements—termed the *feasible outcome set* and denoted by the letter F—is a subset of the real plane $\mathbb{R}^2$. The x-coordinate represents the benefit to Bargainer 1, and the y-coordinate is the benefit to Bargainer 2. As elsewhere, I will assume this set to be compact and convex (Nash, 1950). It can readily be seen that any particular point of the set represents a potential demand by one of the bargainers expressed in terms of profits. As the demands change over time (due to internal forces), we think of the points as moving in the plane. The map α_i: $\mathbb{R} \rightarrow \mathbb{R}^2$, associating to each real number t Bargainer i's demand at time t, represents Bargainer i's concession trajectory through time. If $\alpha_i(t) \in F$ then the demand is feasible. The image of α_i is a path in $\mathbb{R}^2$ and the restriction of α_i to $[p,q] \subset \mathbb{R}$ is called a *concession path* with initial demand $\alpha_i(p)$ and final demand $\alpha_i(q)$. The concession path can be thought of as the course over which the point representing Bargainer i's demand moves, given that it starts at $\alpha_i(p)$. Representing as it does internal demands, α_i is not physically observable at every time t; nonetheless, its shape can be inferred from the sequence of offers communicated during the negotiation session. A typical concession path is shown in Figure 9.1.

In the mathematical study of abstract dynamical systems (for example, Hirsch & Smale, 1974; Palis & de Melo, 1982), diagrams similar to Figure 9.1 are called *phase portraits*. They are useful in depicting time-dependent phenomena because we think of points (in our case representing a bargainer's demand) as *moving* in the plane. In this fashion, what happens to *both* components of the bargainer's demand (benefit claimed for self and benefit offered to other) can be visualized simultaneously, rather than individually (which is what would be required if we were to construct separate benefit-time graphs for each component).

Note that at any time $t \in [p,q]$, the point representing the demand of the bargainer (in terms of profits) is somewhere on the concession path. Fur-

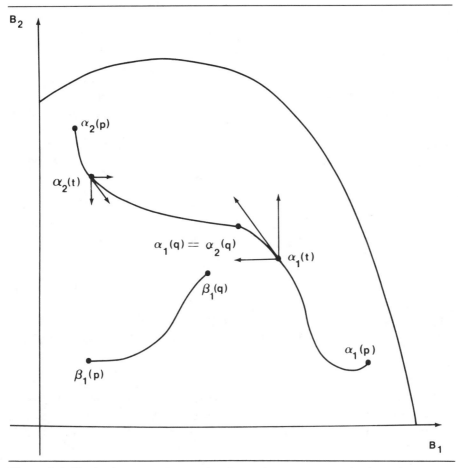

Figure 9.1 Typical concession paths. B_1 and B_2 represent the benefit to Bargainers 1 and 2, respectively.

thermore, this point is moving in a certain direction and with a certain speed. We assume that the motion of the point is produced by two fundamental forces: a *self-oriented force* toward a lowering or raising of the amount of profit demanded by the bargainer for him or herself, and an *other-oriented force* toward lowering or raising of the amount of profit the bargainer is willing to give to the opponent. The names of the forces are arbitrary; the important point is that the bargainer's demand is the product of two orthogonal forces, one parallel to the x-axis, one parallel to the y-axis. The resultant of these two forces has magnitude and direction, and therefore can be considered as a vector attached to the point $\alpha_i(t)$. Thus we can define a function that associates with every point of the concession path the vector indicating the point's direction and speed. Such vector-valued functions are called *vector fields*, and, in our situation, their values are given by the derivative of α_i with respect to time—that is, the instantaneous time-rate of change $\alpha_i'(t)$. Throughout, we shall let X represent the vector field governing Bargainer 1's demands, and Y will denote Bargainer 2's.

By defining X and Y on $\mathbb{R}^2$ (rather than just on the concession path), greater flexibility with respect to initial demand results. Although X and Y act on the points $\alpha_1(p)$ and $\alpha_2(p)$ so as to move them to $\alpha_1(q)$ and $\alpha_2(q)$ at time q, other initial conditions may change the result. The initial demands $\beta_1(p)$ and $\beta_2(p)$ will be moved by X and Y respectively to $\beta_1(q)$ and $\beta_2(q)$ at time q. Whether or not there exists an i such that $\beta_i(q) = \alpha_i(q)$ depends on the particular vector fields under investigation. (In Figure 9.1, for example, $\beta_1(q) \neq \alpha_1(q)$.)

To help illustrate the concepts thus far discussed, look once again at Figure 9.1, and consider the concession paths α_1 and α_2, both restricted to [p,q]. At t = p, Bargainer 1's demand is given by $\alpha_1(p)$. As $\alpha_1(p) \in F$, there are two aspects to this demand, a level of profit for Bargainer 1 and a corresponding level for Bargainer 2. At time t, Bargainer 1's demand is given by $\alpha_1(t)$. As at any other time, this demand is changing. In particular, there is a self-oriented force (represented in the figure by a horizontal arrow) impelling the bargainer to lower the amount of personal profit requested, and an other-oriented force (vertical arrow), tending to make the bargainer yield a higher profit to the opponent. The resultant of these two forces $X(\alpha_1(t))$ is given by the derivative $\alpha_1'(t)$. The process continues until t = q, where the final demand is $\alpha_1(q)$. A similar setup holds for Bargainer 2. By convention, we shall say that the self- and other-oriented forces are positive or negative according to whether they point away from or toward zero.

One advantage of the way bargaining behavior has been defined here is that both distributive and integrative bargaining can be modeled. Integrative bargaining, a situation in which outcomes of high mutual benefit are sought (Pruitt, 1981), is seen to be the result of the interplay between the self-oriented and other-oriented forces. In Figure 9.1, for example, $\beta_1|[p,q]$ represents an integrative concession path; Bargainer 1 begins with a demand of $\beta_1(p)$ and moves to the demand of $\beta_1(q)$, a demand that is more integrative than $\beta_1(p)$. Virtually any type of movement in the profit space can be modeled. Even sequential information is available. In Figure 9.1, for example, $\alpha_1|[p,q]$ represents a concession path where the rate of change is very fast at first, but slows down as time approaches q. The path given by $\alpha_2|[p,q]$ demonstrates the opposite behavior. Small forces close to $\alpha_2(p)$, coupled with the nearness of $\alpha_2(t)$ to $\alpha_2(p)$, imply a slow moving system that speeds up rapidly toward the end. Thus the system can be treated dynamically as communicative patterns change with time.

Simple and oscillatory models. Three theoretical concepts are needed to specify a bargaining system: a feasible outcome set F, which contains every possible agreement, and the vector fields X and Y, which capture the forces acting on the bargainers. Thus far, the only assumption made about the vector fields X and Y is that they be differentiable (otherwise there would exist a point at which the forces acting on the bargainers were undefined). By introducing further assumptions, assumptions based on theoretical suppositions, one can examine the correspondence between theoretical bargaining systems and actual bargaining communication.

As a first theoretical supposition, we begin with the idea that, as seems reasonable, a bargainer's willingness to concede decreases as time passes. Kelley, Beckman, and Fischer (1967) found that as a bargainer approached his or her resistance point, concessions became increasingly difficult to make. For an integrative situation, this assumption is, of course, two-pronged, having meaning in terms of both a bargainer's own profit and the profit he or she is willing to yield to the opponent. The simplest vector fields possessing this theoretical property are those given by

$$X(x) = xA + B \qquad [1]$$

where A is a matrix of the form

$$A = \begin{pmatrix} -a_1 & 0 \\ 0 & -a_2 \end{pmatrix} \qquad a_1, a_2 > 0$$

and $B = (b_1, b_2)$ is a real vector with positive entries. Such vector fields have solutions in which benefits display positive or negative exponential decay as a function of time. For simplicity, vector fields in the form of Equation 1 will be called *simple concession functions*. The matrix A will be called a *concession matrix*, and B will be called the *resistance vector*. A typical phase portrait is sketched in Figure 9.2.

To see that simple concession functions do indeed meet the assumption of decreasing willingness to concede over time, it helps to examine possible solutions. Equation 1 coupled with the initial condition $\alpha(0) = p$ yields a unique solution, namely

$$\alpha(t) = Ke^{tA} - BA^{-1} \qquad [2]$$

where e is the base of the natural logarithm, and $K = (k_1, k_2)$ is based on A, B, and the initial demand p. (For a derivation of Equation 2, see the Appendix.) As t becomes large $\alpha(t)$ approaches $-BA^{-1}$, which can be thought of as a resistance point. The entries of $-BA^{-1}$ are b_1/a_1 and b_2/a_2.

The claim of decreasing concession rates over time is equivalent to asserting $\|\alpha'(t)\| < \|\alpha'(t_0)\|$ for all $t > t_0$. This assertion can be demonstrated by differentiating Equation 2, obtaining

$$\alpha'(t) = KAe^{tA}.$$

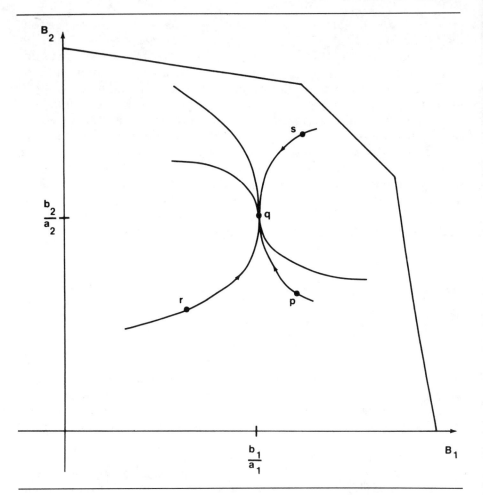

Figure 9.2 Typical concession paths for a simple concession function. B_1 and
          B_2 represent the benefit to Bargainers 1 and 2, respectively.

Because A is a diagonal matrix, e^{tA} is a matrix with e raised to the $-a_i t$ as the
ith diagonal element, and zeroes elsewhere. Also, KA is a 1×2 vector
with entries of the form $-a_i k_i$, $i = 1,2$. So the product of KA and e^{tA} is

$$\alpha'(t) = (-a_1 k_1 \exp[-a_1 t], \; -a_2 k_2 \exp[-a_2 t])$$

where exp denotes the exponential function with base e. Clearly, as t
increases, each of the entries of $\alpha'(t)$ becomes closer and closer to zero,
proving that the norm of $\alpha'(t)$ decreases as well. Consequently, if $t > t_0$
then $\|\alpha'(t)\| < \|\alpha'(t_0)\|$, and we conclude that the willingness to concede

(as measured by the magnitude of the fundamental forces) decreases as time progresses.

Despite its simplicity, the proposed concession function captures a wide range of concessional behavior. For example, suppose Bargainer 1's behavior is governed by forces whose corresponding vector field is as in Figure 9.2. If such a bargainer begins with a demand of p, further demands communicated to the opponent will be along the indicated curve, in the direction of the arrow. Unless a satisfactory agreement is reached, the bargainer will eventually communicate a demand of q, and all further demands also will be q until the opponent relents or time expires. Consider now an initial demand of r. In this instance an integrative path is followed. An initial demand of s is highly counterproductive, hurting both bargainers and becoming less integrative as time progresses. The only parameters needed to determine the behavior of a bargainer having a simple concession function are those related to the strength of the fundamental forces (contained in the concession matrix A) and those related to the resistance point (contained in B, from which we calculate $-BA^{-1}$). Once these parameters are known, the trajectory of any initial demand can be determined. If the trajectories of the bargainers intersect at the same point at the same time, and if such a point is a feasible alternative, then they have reached an agreement.

The appeal of the simple model, however, stems from intuitive notions of bargaining that have been generalized from rather simplistic zero-sum situations. Indeed, most of the research supporting the assumption of decreased willingness to concede over time (for example, Kelley, Beckman, & Fischer, 1967; Pruitt & Drews, 1969; Smith, Pruitt, & Carnevale, 1982) has been conducted using unidimensional tasks in which the frontier of the feasible outcome set was a straight line—not at all like Figures 9.1 and 9.2, possibilities allowed in this chapter. Because it is reasonable that in a complicated bargaining task there may be at least some situations in which a simple concession function is inappropriate, it seems wise to consider alternatives, on an exploratory basis at least. Yet, when postulating the form of such an alternative, one is confronted by a dearth of relevant findings to guide the effort. The largest body of research on multidimensional tasks with nonlinear agreement frontiers is that pertaining to the antecedents of integrative bargaining (Pruitt, 1981, summarizes this research). Unfortunately, offer-time data are rarely (if ever) reported, so it is difficult to speculate on the form of the relevant concession functions. One exception is the study conducted by Oliva, Peters, and Murthy (1981). These researchers were not directly interested in integrative bargaining, and the payoff structure was not reported. Nonetheless, it seems entirely likely that the agreement frontier was nonlinear, given that the researchers employed a complex, multidimensional task involving 20 disputed issues in a union-management scenario. The group of negotiators was divided into 35 union-management teams, and, for illustrative purposes, the authors plotted the motion of 8 teams in the control space of a cusp catastrophe. The actual control factors were union and management bargaining "intensities," not demands—though these intensities "certainly include perceptions regarding demands" (Oliva, Peters, & Murthy, 1981, p. 153). If one examines the plots carefully, it appears that as time progresses most of the management and union bargaining intensities oscillate around an equilibrium (although at least one team exhibited indications of simple motion in union intensities). However, it is difficult to be certain; the intensities must be inferred from two hard to read graphs, and are certainly in no form that can be tested. Furthermore, the intensities are at best crude proxies for offers, and include much that may add to, or obscure, the relevant variation. Still, it seems prudent to build an oscillatory component into any proposed alternative to simple concession functions. I shall do so by examining vector fields based on the differential equation

$$mx''(t) + cx'(t) + kx(t) = F(t).$$

Consider the forces acting on Bargainer 1. Bargainer 2 can be treated similarly. Suppose that at any time t, Bargainer 1's demand is given by

$$\alpha(t) = [Z(\cos(tD)) + C(\sin(tD))]e^{tA} + B. \tag{3}$$

In the above equation, A and B are as before, $Z = (z_1, z_2)$ and $C = (c_1, c_2)$ are real vectors, and D is a matrix having diagonal entries $d_1, d_2 > 0$, and zeroes elsewhere.

Let X be the vector field giving rise to $\alpha(t)$ as a solution. The vector field X is complicated and a phase portrait cannot be sketched easily; we will make greater headway by examining one of the entries of $\alpha(t)$. Figure 9.3 shows the relationship between offer and time for the first component of $\alpha(t)$. As can be seen, the trajectory oscillates around (and in the limit approaches) b_1. Thus b_1 can be thought of as a long-term resistance point, although in the short term resistance varies around b_1. The bargainer begins with an initial demand of $z_1 + b_1$, which is a distance $|z_1|$ from the ultimate resistance point b_1. Variations around b_1 are determined by a_1, the so-called *damping coefficient*. The higher the parameter, the more damped the motion. The parameter d_1 determines the distance between peaks. Finally, c_1 is related to how fast the bargainer's concessions are changing at the outset. Entirely analogous descriptions hold for the parameters of the second component. Due to the nature of X, it will be termed a *damped oscillatory concession function*, or, more simply, an *oscillatory function*.

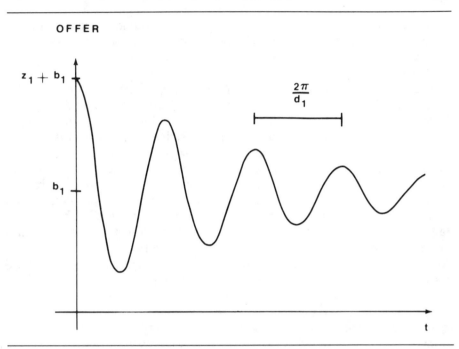

OFFER

Figure 9.3 Offer as a function of time in the damped oscillatory case.

There is an interesting similarity between simple and damped oscillatory concession functions. Let $B(t) = [-ZD(\sin(tD)) + CD(\cos(tD))]e^{tA} - BA$. (The reason for this definition will be apparent shortly.) Differentiating Equation 3 yields

$$\alpha'(t) = [Z(\cos(tD)) + C(\sin(tD))]Ae^{tA} + [-ZD(\sin(tD)) + CD(\cos(tD))]e^{tA}.$$

Adding and subtracting BA, and using the fact that A and e^{tA} commute, we can factor, obtaining

$$\alpha'(t) = \{[Z(\cos(tD)) + C(\sin(tD))]e^{tA} + B\} A \\ + [-ZD(\sin(tD)) + CD(\cos(tD))]e^{tA} - BA \\ = \alpha(t)A + B(t)$$

where the last equality follows by substitution.

As $\alpha(t)$ is a solution of X, we have $X(\alpha(t)) = \alpha'(t)$, and thus for any demand $x = \alpha(t)$ we may write

$$X(x) = xA + B(t).$$

Evidently, then, damped oscillatory concession functions are very similar to simple concession functions. The difference, of course, is the oscillatory behavior induced, apparently, by the rather complicated dependence of the resistance point on time. Following earlier terminology, we will call A a *concession matrix,* and B(t) the *resistance vector* at time t.

The oscillatory function offers a number of advantages as a model of bargaining process. First of all, it can depict a variety of bargaining behaviors. There is, of course, no overriding reason that resistances must remain constant over time. Indeed, a bargainer's resistance point may change in a complex fashion as the negotiation session progresses. The oscillatory function captures this behavior and still allows for a long term equilibrium. Second, although much more complicated than a simple concession function, the oscillatory model is relatively parsimonious. To obtain oscillations, the use of trigonometric functions is almost mandatory, and simplification of Equation 3 usually can be gained only at the expense of losing the equilibrium property. Third, the oscillatory function seems capable of accounting for the Oliva, Peters, and Murthy (1981) data, though, of course, it is difficult to tell given their method of presentation and the way they defined their variables. Finally, the differential equation that forms the basis of the oscillatory model is a common theoretical device. It has been applied, with varying degrees of success, in such diverse contexts as spring vibration (Rainville & Bedient, 1974), attitude change (Kaplowitz & Fink, 1982; Kaplowitz, Fink, & Bauer, 1983), network analysis (Rice & Barnett, 1986), and intercultural communication (Barnett & Kincaid, 1983; Kincaid, Yum, Woelfel, & Barnett, 1983). The oscillatory model is thus a familiar tool, and its incorporation into theories of bargaining should prove easier than competing trigonometric formulations.

Yet, these advantages notwithstanding, we need to determine what variable or variables (if any) give rise to oscillatory behavior on the one hand and simple motion on the other. In this study the hypothesized antecedent of model type is information exchange, a choice based primarily on the form of the various concession functions, but informed by previous research as well. Implicit in the assumption that a bargainer's willingness to concede decreases over time is the idea that the bargainer has enough information to make a reasonable estimate of the opponent's profit schedule. If the bargainer has enough a priori information, or if enough information has been exchanged, then the estimate is not hard to make, and a simple model seems likely. If the information is not readily available, however, the bargainer, in order to find an acceptable agreement, may be forced to vary the amount of profit demanded (within certain limits), decreasing the variation as the bargainer gains more experience with his or her opponent. Thus a pattern of damped oscillation emerges. This argument, of course, is similar to one proposed by Cross (1965, 1977), who sees bargaining as a learning process. The negotiators, hampered by a lack of information about their opponents, vary their concession rates in order to gain information, ultimately converging to a solution. (See also Tracy & Rissen, 1978.) My argument is that when bargainers are deprived of information, they compensate by systematically altering their concessions, but when information is readily available, as in unidimensional tasks or when a large amount of information is exchanged, then there is no need for such search-oriented behavior, and the more parsimonious assumption of decreasing concession rates over time is to be preferred.

Also relevant is the research summarized by Pruitt (1981), who suggests that information about profit levels and issue priorities is the most critical. And although Pruitt is interested in what bargaining processes lead to given outcomes, rather than in whether or not information determines model type, his work nonetheless suggests the importance of information exchange in altering the bargaining process. We thus arrive at our first prediction: When bargainers are instructed to exchange a large amount of information regarding the priority of issues and levels of profit, their subsequent communication will be best described by a simple concession function; when instructed to withhold such information, damped oscillatory functions will be most appropriate.

A second prediction, of course, concerns the influence of model type on outcome. More specifically, it can be hypothesized that the final agreement, as well as the time it takes to reach it, can be predicted accurately on the basis of model parameters and initial condition. Merely note that the vector field X (whether simple or damped oscillatory), coupled with the initial condition $\alpha(0) = p$, yields a unique solution $\alpha: \mathbb{R} \to \mathbb{R}^2$. Let α and β be the solutions for X and Y, respectively. After estimating the parameters empirically, we need only ask if there exists a $t \in \mathbb{R}$ such that

$$\alpha(t) = \beta(t) \qquad [4]$$

with $\alpha(t)$ a feasible agreement. If not, the dyad is classified as deadlocked; if so, solving the above equation for t provides the time to agreement, and substitution into either $\alpha(t)$ or $\beta(t)$ provides the final agreement.

EMPIRICAL EVIDENCE

This section reports the results of a study designed to test the major ideas of the dynamical theory outlined above. The data were collected as part of a larger project; treatments, questionnaire items, and so forth not directly relevant to the present theoretical propositions have been ignored. An abbreviated methods section including relevant aspects of data collection appears below; complete details can be found in Tutzauer (1985).

Method

The participants were 82 undergraduates who negotiated in dyads. The task used was similar to Pruitt's (1981) buyer/seller simulation, although it was modified to fit the constraints of the larger study (see Tutzauer, 1985). The scenario involved a buyer and seller attempting to agree on the wholesale price of three imaginary goods: typewriters, vacuum cleaners, and television sets. Because the goods were not equally valuable to the negotiators, tradeoffs could be developed producing outcomes of high joint benefit. Dyads were randomly assigned to one cell of a 2 by 2 design (high/low information exchange by high/low integrative potential). The integrative potential variable is not relevant here and has been ignored. (See Tutzauer, 1985, for the effects of integrative potential on outcome, as well as for other effects of information exchange not reported here.) Those bargainers in the high information condition were instructed to begin their negotiation by exchanging information regarding priorities and profits; those in the low condition were told to withhold such information. All bargainers were given the value of $2300 as a target point (limit) in the negotiations, and were allowed 20 minutes in which to reach an agreement. Audio tapes of the negotiation sessions provided the data on times and offers used in parameter estimation.

Results

Manipulation checks and reliabilities. Information exchange was manipulated by varying the instructions that the bargainers received. In order to determine if those instructed to engage in a high level of information exchange did in fact do so (at least when compared to bargainers in the low condition) each participant was asked to estimate his or her partner's limit. Those in the high information condition, if the manipulation was successful, should have been able to make such estimates better than low information bargainers. Thus high information bargainers should have answered the question with profit levels that were much closer to the partner's true limit than would have low information bargainers. Phrased differently, the variance of the low information bargainers' estimates should have been significantly greater than the corresponding variance of the high information bargainers. Such was indeed the case: The standard deviation of the low information bargainers' estimates was 0.3779, a value that was significantly greater than the high information bargainers' standard deviation of 0.2836, $F(36,36) = 1.776$, $p < .05$, suggesting that information exchange was manipulated successfully.

A large portion of the data to be analyzed consisted of the bargainers' offers and the times at which they were made. To obtain these data, a single coder monitored audio tapes of the negotiations, and the offers and times were noted for each bargainer. To assess the reliability of this procedure, the offers and times for 16 bargainers (20%) were recoded by a second coder. For offers, there was an 85% agreement between the two coders. Furthermore, the two coders exhibited a correlation of .997, t(99) = 125.068, p < .001, between the times each of the m recorded.

Model fits. The first step in the analysis was to fit the various concession models to the pattern of offers communicated by the bargainers. To do so, without using all of the degrees of freedom, required at least four offers in the simple case and six in the oscillatory case. Consequently, every bargainer making five or fewer offers was deleted from any analysis requiring model fits. This criterion, coupled with the fact that poor equipment caused the offers of two dyads to be inaudible, resulted in the deletion of 18 buyers and 19 sellers—5 in the low/low condition, 15 in the high/high condition, and 11 and 6 respectively in the high integrative potential/low information exchange and high information exchange/low integrative potential conditions. Whenever such severe attrition occurs, it is natural to ask whether or not there is differential mortality across conditions. Of concern in the present study is an apparently high discrepancy between the dropout rates in the high and low integrative potential conditions, where 26 bargainers in the high condition and 11 in the low condition were deleted due to an insufficient number of offers. A binomial test that this proportion was significantly different than $1/2$ revealed a probability level well in excess of .80. Furthermore, an uncorrected chi-square failed to attain a magnitude large enough to question the hypothesis of independence, $\chi^2(1, N = 37) = 0.085, p < .80$. Consequently, one can feel confident that differential mortality does not pose a severe problem.

For each of the remaining 45 bargainers, the nonlinear procedure of the CDC version of SPSS (Robinson, 1981) was used to estimate profit offered to self and profit offered to opponent as functions of time. The particular functions used for the present investigation were

$$y = ke^{-at} + v$$

and

$$y = e^{-at}[z(\cos(td)) + c(\sin(td))] + b$$

where t is time, y is the amount of profit offered to other or self, as the case may be, and a, b, c, d, k, v, and z are the parameters to be estimated, subject to the constraints

$$a,b,d,v \geq 0$$

and

$$v \leq 4$$

Note that, based on Equation 2, the parameter v represents the entries of the matrix $-BA^{-1}$.

Both functions were fit to each of the 45 bargainers' offers to self and to opponent, and a separate R^2 was determined for each. Overall, 820 parameters were estimated and 180 R^2s were calculated. These results are available upon request. In general, however, both models resulted in large R^2s with significant F-ratios, though, as always in nonlinear regression, these F-tests should be considered as approximations only. Statistical tests used in linear regression apply to the nonlinear case only to the extent that the particular model-data set combination has a sum-of-squares surface approaching that of a linear model. Given the extremely large Fs obtained, however, the results should not be too wide of the mark.

On the whole, the simple model fared better than the oscillatory version with 48 of 90 tests showing significance versus 17 for the oscillatory model. The oscillatory model, though usually producing a large R^2, often larger than for the corresponding simple model, was expensive in terms of degrees of freedom, and thus more often failed to reach a .05 significance level.

For each bargainer, a determination had to be made as to whether or not their offers to self and to opponent were best described by a simple or an oscillatory function of time, or perhaps neither. To make this determination, the following rules were utilized: If neither model had a significant R^2, then neither model was chosen. If only one model was significant, then that model was chosen. If both models reached significance, the more parsimonious simple function was retained except in those cases in which the difference in the residual sums-of-squares between the 2 models was significant and favored the oscillatory version. Of the 13 instances in which both models were significant, only twice did the difference in residual sums-of-squares so favor the oscillatory model: the seller component of Bargainer 33's offers, $F(2,5) = 7.628, p < .05$, and the buyer component of Bargainer 35's offers, $F(2,6) = 6.267, p < .05$.

For every model finally chosen, each estimated parameter was divided by its asymptotic standard error to obtain an approximate significance level. Overall, the parameters were fairly well determined, though there were some notable exceptions. For the 46 simple models, k was significant 29 times, the parameter a was significant 24 times, and v was significant 39 times. (Again, the exact results are available on request.) There were few enough oscillatory models finally chosen that the results can be presented conveniently in tabular form. As can be seen (Table 9.1), only a, b, and d were consistently well estimated, with c and z never reaching significance. The implications of these findings will be considered later.

It was predicted that the oscillatory model would be found predominantly among low information bargainers and that high information bargainers could be best described by simple models. Table 9.2 shows the

Table 9.1
Parameter Estimates for Oscillatory Models

y^a	a	b	c	d	z
33S	0.1563*	1.7250*	0.2191	3.2415*	-1.5115
35B	1.3723	2.0273*	-15.8699	4.3969*	13.3576
41B	2.9270*	2.0235*	-5100.8906	3.8751*	-19216.9460
41S	2.0172*	2.1218*	317.2850	3.8616*	1907.1455
59B	1.5214*	2.1394*	-0.8357	1.1394	3.2102

a. Following Pruitt (1981), every offer yields a profit to the buyer and to the seller. The numbers in this column identify the bargainer, and the letters indicate whether the function is being fit to the buyer's or the seller's profit. For example, 33S means that the dependent variable is the profit offered to the seller by Bargainer 33.

*Indicates that the parameter divided by its asymptotic standard error is greater than 1.96, an approximate significance level of at least .05.

appropriate cross-classification. Although a larger percentage of the models in the high information exchange condition were of the simple type, as opposed to the low condition, with the reverse holding for oscillatory models, an uncorrected chi-square was insufficient to reject the hypothesis of independence between rows and columns, $\chi^2(2, N = 90) = 3.893, p < .20$. The low overall frequency of oscillatory models, however, is troubling, and it may be that the hypothesis holds for high information bargainers (who use simple models), and those in the low information condition use some model not considered in the present study. To test this possibility, the "oscillatory" and "no fit" categories were collapsed into a single "other" category, producing a 2 × 2 table. A corrected chi-square of 1.561, on 1 degree of freedom, produced a one-tail probability of .105, following Mantel's rule (Mantel, 1974), a result that approaches but does not attain significance. On the other hand, to get an idea of the degree of association between information exchange and model, a cross-product ratio was calculated, and its value of 0.535 was highly significant, $z = 2.329, p < .01$. This finding suggests that the odds of a model's being simple, given that it comes from a high information bargainer, is only 0.535 that of a low information bargainer. Conversely, the odds are 1.868 times greater that a model is simple given that it comes from a high information bargainer as opposed to a low information bargainer. Thus the likelihood that a high information bargainer will use a simple model is significantly greater than the likelihood that a low information bargainer will use such a model. Taken together, the chi-square and cross-product ratio results suggest that the prediction of information as a determinant of model use receives partial, though not unambiguous, support.

Given the large number of simple fits compared to the relatively small number of oscillatory fits, it is possible that the simple concession formulation simultaneously described all bargainers. That is, given bargainer-to-bargainer variation in parameters, we would like to know if a simple con-

Table 9.2
Frequency of Model Types Classified on the
Basis of Information Exchange

		Model			
		Simple	Oscillatory	No fit	
Information Exchange	Low	17 (42.5)	4 (10.0)	19 (47.5)	40
	High	29 (58.0)	1 (2.0)	20 (40.0)	50
	Total	46 (51.1)	5 (5.6)	39 (43.3)	

Note: N = 90; numbers in parentheses are row percentages.

cession model explained a large portion of the variance in the entire data set. One could attempt to fit a single equation to the data set as a whole, but in so doing it would have to be assumed that the bargainers' parameters were identical, an indefensible assumption given the theory I wish to test. The usual method in such a situation is to introduce a number of design variables, one for each equation, allowing the researcher to combine the smaller equations into one big equation, the parameters of which are estimated and used to produce a single R^2 (Daniel & Wood, 1980). It will be noted, however, that instead of estimating one large equation with design variables, I instead estimated separate equations for each smaller offer-time data set. I chose this procedure because several difficulties—two practical and one conceptual—prevented me from using design variables. First of all, by introducing design variables, the researcher is limited to a relatively small number of equations. Because the computer workspace required is a multiplicative function of, among other things, the number of parameters and the number of cases, the nonlinear algorithm can quickly outstrip the capabilities of most computer systems when too many design variables are used. For example, in the case of simple models, I would have to define 90 design variables, and then attempt simultaneous estimation of literally hundreds of parameters with over a thousand cases.

The second difficulty is that nonlinear estimation procedures are highly sensitive to initial parameter estimates, estimates that have to be provided to the program. In solving a single problem, it is not at all unusual to make several computer runs, each time improving the initial estimates. When the complexity of the problem is increased over a hundredfold, however, the ability to make accurate initial parameter estimates suffers tremendously, and making the necessary computer runs (if they can be undertaken at all) quickly becomes cost prohibitive. It is simply unmanageable unless the problem is split into many smaller subproblems, allowing the researcher to work on poor initial estimates where needed.

The final difficulty with using design variables is conceptual. Testing the theory outlined in previous sections required a separate R^2 for the offer-time data of each bargainer. Without these R^2s, no assignment of model type could be made, and thus neither hypothesis could be tested. When one large equation is estimated, it is difficult to recover these individual R^2s. Because I was interested primarily in the adequacy of individual fits, rather than a global assessment of the adequacy of the models, I chose to fit separate equations.

Still, it would be nice to have some idea of how well the simple model fared on an overall basis. Because I'm unable to use the traditional method advocated by Daniel and Wood (1980), I chose to employ a modification introduced elsewhere (Tutzauer, 1986). The method, which involves comparing squared deviations from variable predictors (that is, the individual equations) to the sum of squared deviations from individual means (rather than the grand mean), produces an R^2 of .609, $F(44,834) = 2.562, p < .01$. This result is conservative in the sense that variable predictors produce a smaller total sum-of-squares than that calculated on the basis of the grand mean, and thus results in an R^2 lower than what would be obtained using design variables.

Finally, it was predicted that time/outcome combinations could be determined on the basis of Equation 4. Unfortunately, analytical solutions to Equation 4 were difficult to find. As an alternative, predictions were generated as follows: Time was incremented from 0 to 20 minutes in steps of 0.1. Substitution into the appropriate equations produced estimates for the profit that each bargainer offered to the seller and to the buyer. The time that produced the smallest value of $\|\alpha(t) - \beta(t)\|$ was taken as the predicted time of agreement. Writing $\alpha(t) = (\alpha_1(t),\alpha_2(t))$ and $\beta(t) = (\beta_1(t),\beta_2(t))$, the predicted final profit for the buyer was taken to be $1/2(\alpha_1(t) + \beta_1(t))$ and the seller's final profit was predicted as $1/2(\alpha_2(t) + \beta_2(t))$, where t was chosen as described above. Using these values, the correlation between predicted and observed times was .99, $t(2) = 17.877, p < .005$. For seller's profit, the corresponding correlation was .87, $t(2) = 5.210, p < .025$, and for buyer's profit, .86, $t(2) = 4.860, p < .025$, indicating a close match between predicted and observed, though care should be exercised in interpreting these findings due to the limited degrees of freedom.

SUMMARY AND IMPLICATIONS

The results of this study are at once encouraging and disappointing. They are disappointing because the hypothesis that model type could be predicted on the basis of information exchange received only partial support. Very few oscillatory models were chosen, and those that were could not be said to occur predominantly among low information bargainers.

Only the existence of simple models could be predicted with any accuracy, and even here the results were mixed. A chi-square test, though close, failed to detect a significant frequency difference between high and low information conditions, but a z-test of the cross-product ratio showed that the odds of high information bargainers using the simple model were higher than the corresponding odds for low information bargainers.

On the other hand, the remainder of the results are extremely encouraging. The inability to predict the occurrence of oscillatory models may mean that a single type of model accounts reasonably well for the diverse types of offer sequences common in integrative bargaining. A number of factors attest to the usefulness of simple models in predicting communicative behavior, regardless of experimental condition. First of all, the simple model is parsimonious. It is among the most elegant of models that one could postulate as underlying bargaining behavior and is certainly much less complicated than the alternative considered in the present chapter, namely, oscillatory models. Second, the simple model is reasonably accurate in describing behavior on both an individual and global level. Individually, over half of the estimated (simple) equations fit the data adequately, with many more possessing large R^2s that failed to attain significance due to the low number of offers made by the bargainer under consideration. On a global basis, the R^2 of .609 indicates that use of the simple model reduces predictive errors by more than 60% when compared to the mean.

Finally, an examination of model parameters lends theoretical support to the simple concession function. The pattern of significance among the parameter estimates clearly indicates that the most important parameter in the simple model is v. This parameter corresponds to the bargainer's resistance point. Concession rate (the a parameter), and whether or not the bargainer followed an integrative path (indicated by the sign of the k parameter), although not unimportant, do not exert as much influence on the estimation of the model as does resistance. This finding dovetails nicely with the results of previous research on integrative bargaining. Although concession rate is of prime importance in distributive situations (see Morley & Stephenson, 1977, for a review), it is the bargainer's limit, or resistance point, that exerts the most profound influence in integrative bargaining, as a number of experimental studies have shown (Kimmel, Pruitt, Magenau, Konar-Goldband, & Carnevale, 1980; Pruitt & Lewis, 1975; Roloff & Tutzauer, 1985). When one considers the oscillatory model (Table 9.1), it is readily seen that the most important parameter is b. Once again, this represents the bargainer's resistance point. The parameters governing the oscillations (c and z) were poorly estimated, again suggesting the importance of the simple model.

The final note of encouragement is that, regardless of model type, it seemed apparent that bargaining outcome could be determined accurately on the basis of initial conditions and model parameters. In particular, it was hypothesized that, given a complete set of model parameters for an arbitrary dyad, the time to agreement and the settlement value could be determined. This hypothesis was tested with extremely low power (both bargainers had to have made a sufficient number of offers, and the dyad had to survive four significance tests at the .05 level in order to remain in the analysis), but nonetheless received substantial support. The correlations between prediction and observation were extremely high (above .86) and easily reached significance despite low power, suggesting that model parameters and initial conditions are sufficient to determine the outcome of the bargaining interaction.

Obviously, it is time to move away from static, unidimensional formulations of bargaining communication toward dynamically based theories allowing for the multidimensional nature of such taken-for-granted concepts as offers, agreements, and integrativeness, as well as other variables. The present investigation, by appealing to the underlying forces governing concession behavior, has taken an initial step in that direction. To the extent that it has illustrated the importance of multidimensional, dynamical concepts, the study should be judged a success.

APPENDIX

Let $K = (k_1, k_2)$, $B = (b_1, b_2)$, and $p = (p_1, p_2)$ be vectors, and consider the matrix

$$A = \begin{bmatrix} -a_1 & 0 \\ 0 & -a_2 \end{bmatrix} \quad a_1, a_2 > 0.$$

Earlier, it was claimed that

$$\alpha(t) = Ke^{tA} - BA^{-1} \qquad [A1]$$

was a solution to $X(x) = xA + B$ given the initial condition $\alpha(0) = p$. It is the purpose of this section to demonstrate the claim.

Let $K = p + BA^{-1}$. We seek $\alpha: \mathbb{R} \rightarrow \mathbb{R}^2$ such that

$$\alpha(0) = p \qquad [A2]$$

and

$$\alpha'(t) = X(\alpha(t)) \qquad [A3]$$

for any $t \in \mathbb{R}$. Clearly, Equation A1 implies

$$\alpha(0) = K - BA^{-1} = p$$

as required by Equation A2. Furthermore, differentiation of A1 yields

$$\alpha'(t) = KAe^{tA}.$$

But

$$
\begin{aligned}
X(\alpha(t)) &= X(Ke^{tA} - BA^{-1}) \\
&= (Ke^{tA} - BA^{-1})A + B \\
&= Ke^{tA}A - BA^{-1}A + B \\
&= KAe^{tA} \\
&= \alpha'(t).
\end{aligned}
$$

So Equation A3 holds as well, showing A1 to be the desired solution.

REFERENCES

Barnett, G. A., & Kincaid, D. L. (1983). Cultural convergence: A mathematical theory. In W. B Gudykunst (Ed.), *Intercultural communication theory: Current perspectives* (pp. 171-194). Beverly Hills, CA: Sage.

Beisecker, T. (1970). Verbal persuasive strategies in mixed-motive interactions. *Quarterly Journal of Speech, 56,* 149-160.

Cross, J. G. (1965). A theory of the bargaining process. *American Economic Review, 55,* 67-94.

Cross, J. G. (1977). Negotiation as a learning process. *Journal of Conflict Resolution, 21,* 581-606.

Daniel, C., & Wood, F. S. (1980). *Fitting equations to data: Computer analysis of multifactor data* (2nd ed.). New York: John Wiley.

Donohue, W. A., Diez, M. E., & Stahle, R. B. (1983). New directions in negotiation research. In R. N. Bostrom (Ed.), *Communication yearbook 7* (pp. 249-279). Beverly Hills, CA: Sage.

Hamner, W. C., & Yukl, G. A. (1977). The effectiveness of different offer strategies in bargaining. In D. Druckman (Ed.), *Negotiations: Social-psychological perspectives* (pp. 137-160). Beverly Hills, CA: Sage.

Hirsch, M. W., & Smale, S. (1974). *Differential equations, dynamical systems, & linear algebra.* New York: Academic Press.

Ikle, F. C. (1973). Bargaining and communication. In I. de Sola Pool, W. Schramm, F. W. Frey, N. Maccoby, & E. B. Parker (Eds.), *Handbook of communication* (pp. 836-843). Chicago: Rand McNally.

Kaplowitz, S. A., & Fink, E. L. (1982). Attitude change and attitudinal trajectories: A dynamic multidimensional theory. In M. Burgoon (Ed.), *Communication yearbook 6* (pp. 364-418). Beverly Hills, CA: Sage.

Kaplowitz, S. A., Fink, E. L., & Bauer, C. L. (1983). A dynamic model of the effect of discrepant information on unidimensional attitude change. *Behavioral Science, 28,* 233-250.

Kelley, H. H., Beckman, L. L., & Fischer, C. S. (1967). Negotiating the division of a reward under incomplete information. *Journal of Experimental Social Psychology, 3,* 361-398.

Kimmel, M. J., Pruitt, D. G., Magenau, J. M., Konar-Goldband, L., & Carnevale, P. J. D. (1980). Effects of trust, aspiration, and gender on negotiation tactics. *Journal of Personality and Social Psychology, 38,* 19-22.

Kincaid, D. L., Yum, J. O., Woelfel, J., & Barnett, G. A. (1983). The cultural convergence of Korean immigrants in Hawaii: An empirical test of a mathematical theory. *Quality and Quantity, 18,* 59-78.

Krippendorff, K. (1977). Information systems theory and research: An overview. In B. D. Ruben (Ed.), *Communication yearbook I* (pp. 149-171). New Brunswick, NJ: Transaction/ICA.

Luce, R. D., & Raiffa, H. (1957). *Games and decisions: Introduction and critical survey.* New York: John Wiley.

Mantel, N. (1974). Comment and a suggestion. *Journal of the American Statistical Association, 69,* 378-380.

McGrath, J. E. (1966). A social psychological approach to the study of negotiation. In R. V. Bowers (Ed.), *Studies on behavior in organizations: A research symposium* (pp. 101-134). Athens: University of Georgia Press.

Monge, P. R., Farace, R. V., Eisenberg, E. M., Miller, K. I., & White, L. L. (1984). The process of studying process in organizational communication. *Journal of Communication, 34,* 22-43.

Morley, I. E., & Stephenson, G. M. (1977). *The social psychology of bargaining.* London: Allen and Unwin.

Nash, J. F., Jr. (1950). The bargaining problem. *Econometrica, 18,* 155-162.

Oliva, T. A., & Leap, T. L. (1981). A typology of metamodels in collective bargaining. *Behavioral Science, 26,* 337-345.

Oliva, T. A., Peters, M. H., & Murthy, H. S. K. (1981). A preliminary empirical test of a cusp catastrophe model in the social sciences. *Behavioral Science, 26,* 153-162.

Palis, J., Jr., & de Melo, W. (1982). *Geometric theory of dynamical systems: An introduction* (A. K. Manning, Trans.). New York: Springer-Verlag.

Pruitt, D. G. (1981). *Negotiation behavior.* New York: Academic Press.

Pruitt, D. G., & Drews, J. L. (1969). The effect of time pressure, time elapsed, and the opponent's concession rate on behavior in negotiation. *Journal of Experimental Social Psychology, 5,* 43-60.

Pruitt, D. G., & Lewis, S. A. (1975). Development of integrative solutions in bilateral negotiations. *Journal of Personality and Social Psychology, 31,* 621-633.

Putnam, L. L., & Jones, T. S. (1982). The role of communication in bargaining. *Human Communication Research, 8,* 262-280.

Rainville, E. D., & Bedient, P. E. (1974). *A short course in differential equations* (5th ed.). New York: Macmillan.

Rappoport, A. (1960). *Fights, games, and debates.* Ann Arbor: University of Michigan Press.

Rice, R. E., & Barnett, G. A. (1986). Group communication networking in an information environment: Applying metric multidimensional scaling. In M. L. McLaughlin, *Communication yearbook 9* (pp. 315-338). Beverly Hills, CA: Sage.

Robinson, B. (1981). *SPSS subprogram NONLINEAR: Nonlinear regression* (SPSS No. 433). Evanston, IL: Northwestern University, Vogelback Computing Center.

Roloff, M. E., & Tutzauer, F. (1985, May). *Looking for the golden needle in the haystack: Two tests of competing theories in integrative bargaining.* Paper presented at the meeting of the International Communication Association, Honolulu.

Roth, A. E. (1979). *Axiomatic models of bargaining* (Lecture Notes in Economics and Mathematical Systems, No. 170). Berlin: Springer-Verlag.

Rubin, J. Z., & Brown, B. R. (1975). *The social psychology of bargaining and negotiation.* New York: Academic Press.

Siegel, S., & Fouraker, L. E. (1960). *Bargaining and group decision making: Experiments in bilateral monopoly.* New York: McGraw-Hill.

Smith, D. L., Pruitt, D. G., & Carnevale, P. J. D. (1982). Matching and mismatching: The effect of own limit, other's toughness, and time pressure on concession rate in negotiation. *Journal of Personality and Social Psychology, 42,* 876-883.

Tracy, B. H., & Rissen, H. (1978). Bargaining as trial and error: The case of the Spanish base negotiations 1963-1970. In I. W. Zartman (Ed.), *The negotiation process: Theories and applications* (pp. 193-224). Beverly Hills, CA: Sage.

Tutzauer, F. (1985). *The dynamics of bargaining in settings with integrative potential.* Unpublished doctoral dissertation, Northwestern University, Evanston, IL.

Tutzauer, F. (1986). Bargaining as a dynamical system. *Behavioral Science, 31,* 65-81.

von Neumann, J., & Morgenstern, O. (1944). *Theory of games and economic behavior.* Princeton: Princeton University Press.

10 ●The Sound of One Mind Working: Memory Retrieval and Response Preparation as Components of Pausing in Spontaneous Speech

John O. Greene ● Sandi W. Smith
Ruth C. Smith ● Joan L. Cashion

Purdue University ● University of Southern California

Pausal phenomena in spontaneous speech, those fleeting periods of silence and nonlexical phonation, have, over the last quarter-century, assumed a conceptual significance roughly inversely proportional to their duration. On one hand, speech hesitations have been shown to play an important role in social perception in that they are associated with judgments of deception (Kraut, 1978; Zuckerman, DePaulo, & Rosenthal, 1981), competence (Brown, Strong, & Rencher, 1973; Lay & Burron, 1968), and social attractiveness (Brown, Strong, & Rencher, 1973; Street & Brady, 1982). Perhaps even more important than the role that pausal phenomena play in social perception, however, are the clues that they provide concerning the processes of behavioral production (see Butterworth, 1980a; Rochester, 1975; Siegman & Feldstein, 1979).

The two most fundamental goals of inquiry in human communication are the prediction and explanation of communicative behavior. With respect to the former, we might ask what information would be needed to predict the behavior of the individual social actor. In answer, two types of information would appear to be necessary: First, we would need to know what the person is thinking; how he or she has construed the situation, what ideas have been formed, and so on. Second, it would be necessary to understand how such cognitive contents are manifested in behavior. The history of social science demonstrates that as long as these elements are lacking, the ability to predict specific behaviors is severely limited (see, Epstein, 1979, 1980, 1983; Liska, 1975; Mischel, 1973; Mischel & Peake, 1982). However, when even rudimentary means of assessing cogni-

Correspondence and requests for reprints: John O. Greene, Department of Communication, Purdue University, West Lafayette, IN 47907.

tive contents are employed, the ability to predict behavior accurately is enhanced markedly (for example, Ajzen, 1985).

If knowledge of cognitive content and the links between such content and specific behaviors is necessary for accurate prediction, then these components become crucial objects of explanation. Thus an explanation of behavioral production would need to focus on two essential issues: (1) the nature of the processes underlying the formation of cognitive content, and (2) the nature of the processes linking such abstract cognitions to behavior.

One recent attempt to address precisely these issues is action assembly theory (Greene, 1984a). This theory specifies the cognitive structures and processes underlying the production of verbal and nonverbal behaviors. At present, however, the theory is probably best considered a potential account of behavioral production because not all of its components have been subjected to empirical test (see, Greene, 1983, 1984b; Greene & Cappella, 1984; Greene, O'Hair, Cody, & Yen, 1985).

Central to action assembly theory is the proposition that long-term procedural memory is comprised of a large number of modular units, termed *procedural records,* which preserve action-outcome relations. According to the theory, two processes are involved in bringing any particular procedural record to bear upon behavioral production. The first of these processes is that of activation, whereby procedural records are, in effect, retrieved from memory. This activation process is held to proceed in parallel and with no demands on central processing capacity. Activation does, however, take time, a point crucial to the investigation reported here. The second process, assembly, involves the organization of activated procedural records to form a coherent representation of action. Unlike the activation process, assembly is serial in nature and makes considerable demands on processing capacity. It, too, takes time.

In summary, action assembly theory addresses the problems of cognitive content formation and behavioral manifestation of this cognitive content in terms of activation and assembly processes. One major aim of the research reported here was to test the plausibility of such an account.

Each procedural record, according to action assembly theory, is characterized at all times by some level of activation. This level of activation is increased under two circumstances. The first of these occurs when the person encounters a goal or desired outcome that matches the outcome stored in that record. Second, situational factors that have proven relevant in past goal pursuits will serve to increase the activation levels of procedural records associated with those goals. This level of activation rapidly decays back to resting levels when goals or situational conditions change. For this reason, we should expect that the time required to begin execution of a response will be increased when a person is not warned of the task in advance such that activation of appropriate procedural records can begin.

Put another way, when a subject is prevented from activating procedural records relevant to some task, response latency should be increased relative to a situation in which those records have been activated prior to some start signal.

By similar reasoning the opportunity to assemble procedural records in advance of behavioral production should result in shorter response latencies than situations involving activation but no prior assembly.

In support of this general line of reasoning, a vast body of literature indicates speeded responses for a variety of cognitive and motor tasks when participants have the opportunity to prepare or plan responses in advance (for example, Doll, 1969; Hayes & Martenuik, 1976; Kerr, 1978). Similarly, advance planning quickens speech production by reducing the frequency and duration of silent and filled pauses (Butterworth, 1980b; Deese, 1978, 1980; Greene, 1984b; Lindsley, 1975; Tannenbaum & Williams, 1968). Such studies, however, are not sufficient to localize temporal effects in the activation or assembly phases, or, indeed, to provide evidence that two distinct processes are involved.

The current investigation sought to separate the effects of these processes by assigning participants to one of three conditions defined by the type of preparation they permitted. All participants began by speaking on an assigned topic. At the conclusion of their monologue, participants in one group were told that they would be asked to speak on the same topic again, but they were given 90 seconds to plan what they were going to say. These participants, then, had the opportunity to activate and assemble information in advance of talk. A second group was asked to speak on the focal topic a second time immediately at the conclusion of their first monologue. Thus, unlike participants in the first group, these participants should find it necessary to decide what to say as they speak. However, although these participants will not have had the opportunity for advance assembly that participants in the planning group have had, they should have some temporal advantage arising from the fact that relevant information will still have some residual activation from the first monologue. Finally, the third group was given a 90 second distraction task at the end of the first monologue that prevented planning and also presumably permitted the activation of procedural records relevant to the monologue task to decay toward resting levels. Notice, then, that if there is no time-consuming assembly process operating in behavioral production, participants in the Planning condition should have little advantage over participants in the No Delay condition. Similarly, if there is no time-consuming activation process operating, then participants in the No Delay condition should have little advantage over people in the Distraction condition.

The dependent variables examined in this investigation involved various types of speech hesitations during the focal monologues. The basic rationale for employing such measures is that they provide an index of the speed with which a response is executed. Cognitive operations that require more time should be expected to result in greater amounts of pausing, and there is considerable evidence in support of this point (for example, Butterworth, 1975; Goldman-Eisler, 1956, 1961; Greene, 1984b; Mackay, 1981, 1982; Sabin, Clemmer, O'Connell, & Kowal, 1979; Siegman, 1979; Taylor, 1969).

Because pausal phenomena are characterized by some degree of "functional equivalence," Siegman (1978, 1979) suggests that investigators examine various types of hesitations in studies of speech production. For this reason, three distinct types of pauses were examined in the study reported here. Speech onset latency was assessed as the length of time from presentation of the speaking task to initiation of a response. Once the participant had begun speaking, two additional measures were employed. Speech rate was used as an index of the amount of silent pausing during speech. This move is justified on the basis of previous studies that have found correlations on the order of .8 to .9 in magnitude between speech rate and the frequency and duration of silent pausing (Goldman-Eisler, 1958; Maclay & Osgood, 1959; Sabin et al., 1979). Finally, filled pause rate (Maclay & Osgood, 1959; Mahl, 1956) was examined in order to investigate the use of nonlexical utterances to delay speech production. In an effort to control for individual differences in characteristic speech latencies, speech rate, and filled pause rate (Goldman-Eisler, 1956; Greene, 1984b), change scores for each of these variables were computed as the difference between monologues 1 and 2.

The use of filled pause rate as an indicant of delayed production merits a cautionary note. On face, it seems reasonable to suggest that filled pauses can be used to slow speech output, and there is evidence that filled pauses are associated with more difficult cognitive tasks (Levin, Silverman, & Ford, 1967; Reynolds & Paivio, 1968; Taylor, 1969). Further, there is evidence of the functional equivalence of silent and filled pauses in that when speakers make an attempt to eliminate silent pauses, the frequency of filled pauses in their speech will increase (Beattie & Bradbury, 1979). However, filled pauses and silent pauses do not appear to be strictly functionally equivalent (Brotherton, 1979; Greene, 1984b; Siegman, 1978). Of particular importance in the context of the study reported here is the fact that filled pauses serve to prevent interruption when speech is delayed (Maclay & Osgood, 1959; see also, Duncan, 1972). For this reason, we should expect to find that filled pauses are relatively more frequent in dyadic interactions than in monologues, and this does appear to be the case (Siegman & Pope, 1966). Thus because the present study involved a monologue speaking task, no strong predictions were advanced concerning the relative frequency of filled pauses.

In summary, action assembly theory leads us to expect that participants given the opportunity to plan speech in advance (Planning condition) will demonstrate fewer speech hesitations than participants who are thinking about the topic but have not planned their talk (No Delay condition). Subjects in this No Delay condition, in turn, should be quicker in executing speech responses than participants who have not been thinking about the monologue topic (Distraction condition). On the basis of this theoretical rationale two research hypotheses and one research question are advanced:

H1: There will be a monotonic trend for change in speech onset latency such that participants in the Planning condition will demonstrate the greatest decrease in onset latency, No Delay condition next, and Distraction condition participants least.

H2: There will be a monotonic trend for change in speech rate such that participants in the Planning condition will demonstrate the greatest increase in speech rate, No Delay condition next, and Distraction condition participants least.

RQ1: Will Planning, No Delay, and Distraction manipulations have any effect upon change in filled pause rate?

In addition to these issues suggested by action assembly theory, the present investigation was designed to explore two other concerns. Studies of pausal phenomena often focus upon hesitations to the exclusion of an examination of the ideational content expressed by the speaker. Yet because of the relationships between pausing and generation of ideas outlined above, it seems desirable to examine what participants have to say in addition to the temporal characteristics of the stream of phonation. Because the current investigation required that participants speak twice on the same topic, it was possible to study content changes from monologue 1 to monologue 2. Such an analysis is potentially valuable because it allows an examination of the effects of speech planning and preparation on the content of talk. This issue is of considerable importance in that the failure to demonstrate content changes would weaken the claim that preparation time is used to generate and plan speech content.

There are two fundamental types of changes in content that we might expect to observe. One of these is the addition of new ideas, and the other is the deletion of ideas previously expressed. With respect to the addition of new ideas, we should expect that the opportunity to plan will result in greater frequency of new ideational content.

H3: Participants given the opportunity for advance planning will introduce more new ideas in monologue 2 than participants in the Distraction condition.

Expectations for the deletion of ideas are less clear-cut. On one hand, participants distracted from the monologue task might forget concepts previously expressed. In this case more ideas should be deleted in the distraction condition than in the other conditions. Conversely, planning might permit the participant to edit out ideas that, upon further rumination, are seen to be flawed or less compelling. Such an editing process would lead us to expect more deletions in the planning condition. A pair of research questions, then, concern the deletion of ideas and the "forgetting" and "editing" accounts for such deletions:

> RQ2: Will type of preparation have any effect upon the deletion of ideas previously expressed?
> RQ3: Will the pattern of deletions indicate support for "editing" or "forgetting" processes in deletion?

The final concern of the present study was to investigate an anomaly revealed in an earlier investigation reported by Langer and Weinman (1981). As noted above, the opportunity for advance planning typically results in more fluent speech. Similarly, familiar material is usually associated with fewer speech hesitations than novel topics, concepts, and sentences (Mackay, 1981, 1982; O'Connell, Kowal, & Hormann, 1969; Sabin et. al., 1979). Thus it is somewhat surprising that Langer and Weinman found that when given the opportunity for planning, participants speaking on a familiar topic were less fluent than those speaking on a novel topic. Apparently, thinking about routine issues disrupted speech, and thinking about unfamiliar topics had a facilitative effect. This unusual pattern of results suggests that replications are necessary in order to substantiate this phenomenon.

The method employed by Langer and Weinman is noteworthy because the study reported here attempted a parallel manipulation. These authors approached people waiting at employment offices in the Boston area, and asked them to speak on one of two topics: "Why it is difficult to find jobs in Boston," or "Why it is difficult to find jobs in Alaska." Following this lead by Langer and Weinman, the current study manipulated topic familiarity as well as type of preparation in order to examine possible familiarity-by-preparation interactions:

> RQ4: Will the speech hesitation phenomena examined in this study reveal a topic familiarity-by-type of preparation interaction of the form of that reported by Langer & Weinman (1981)?

EXPERIMENT

Method

General Procedure. Participants were randomly assigned to one of six experimental conditions defined by type of preparation (Distraction, No

Delay, Planning) and topic familiarity (familiar, unfamiliar). All participants were run individually. Each experimental session began with administration of an informed consent form and a brief description of the experimental procedures. Participants were told that they would be asked to speak on a series of topics and that their monologues would be tape recorded. Each participant was then fitted with a headset microphone.

Following this, the participant was presented with a card, placed facedown, and told that the first topic to be discussed was typed on the reverse of the card. At a signal from the experimenter the participant was to turn the card over, read it aloud, and then speak on the subject for as long as he or she wished. When finished, the participant was advised to signal this fact with the word "finished." Participants then were asked if they had any questions. When the participant indicated that the instructions were understood, the experimenter gave the signal to read the card.

The first card was the same in all conditions and was included as a practice trial. When the participant had finished, the experimenter produced a second card, again placed facedown before the subject. The instructions were the same as for the practice session. At this time half the participants were given a familiar topic and half were given a parallel, but unfamiliar topic.

When finished with this second monologue, participants were given instructions appropriate to their experimental condition. Those in the Distraction condition were given a passage to read that was unrelated to the topic of discussion. Participants in the No Delay condition were immediately asked to read the card aloud again and to discuss the topic a second time. Finally, participants in the Planning condition were told that they would be required to discuss the same topic again, but that they would be given 90 seconds to plan their response. As with the practice monologue and monologue 1, participants spoke as long as they wished and concluded with the signal "finished."

At the end of this second monologue on the focal topic participants were debriefed, cautioned against discussing the experiment, and dismissed.

Participants. Participants were 80 students enrolled in undergraduate communication classes at a Western university.[1] All participants received class credit for participating in the experiment.

Stimulus materials. Three topics of discussion were employed in the experiment: one for the initial practice session, one for the familiar-topic monologues, and one for the unfamiliar-topic monologues. In the practice session all participants were given the following task:

> "Discuss your impressions of Los Angeles. What do you like and dislike about the city?"

For the focal monologues, participants in the familiar topic condition were given the following topic:

"What problems do you think students have in finding housing here at USC?"

Participants in the unfamiliar topic condition were given the following question:

"What problems do you think university students have in finding housing in Tokyo?"

These two topics were chosen to provide a conceptual parallel to the questions posed by Langer and Weinman (1981) in order to provide a close approximation to their topic familiarity manipulation.

At the conclusion of the first monologue, participants in the Distraction condition were asked to read an unidentified but internally coherent passage from *Zen and the Art of Motorcycle Maintenance* (Pirsig, 1974). This passage was selected to be long enough that no participant could complete it during the 90 second distraction period. At the conclusion of this period, the participant was presented with a topic card, placed facedown, asked to read the card and discuss the issue.

In the Planning condition, participants were told that they would be asked to discuss the same issue a second time, but only after they had 90 seconds to plan their talk. This 90 second delay between monologues for participants in the Distraction and Planning conditions was chosen to duplicate the 90 second planning period Langer and Weinman (1981) had employed.

Finally, participants in the No Delay condition were presented with the second issue card immediately upon completion of the first. With the exception of these manipulations in type of preparation, all participants were given the same instructions.

Equipment. Audio recordings of participants' monologues were made using a Shure SM10A unidirectional microphone coupled with a Sanyo RD 7 stereophonic cassette tape recorder. The microphones were attached to the lightweight headsets supplied with the device.

Dependent variables. Speech onset latency was measured as the length of time between the completion of reading the issue card and the first vocalization of the response. This interval was measured by use of a digital stopwatch. Speech rate was computed by dividing the total number of words, not including filled pauses and speech disruptions, by the total duration of the monologue, from onset of speech to the "finished" signal. Filled pause ratio was computed as the total number of "er," "um," and "ah" vocalizations divided by the total duration of the monologue.

In addition to these chronometric measures, each response was coded according to the number of idea units introduced about the topic. The monologues also were scored to ascertain the number of idea units added and deleted in monologue 2.

Data Analysis and Results

Reliability. Data analysis began with transcribing both monologues produced by each of the 80 participants. These transcripts were made by three different individuals. In order to assess the coding reliability for filled pauses, a fourth person independently counted the filled pauses in all 160 monologues. These tallies were then correlated with the number of filled pauses identified in the transcripts. Pearson product moment correlations computed independently for each transcriber were found to be .984, .967, and .950, indicating excellent reliability in coding filled pauses.

Reliability for speech onset latency was established by having two people independently time the response latency for a subset of 40 randomly selected monologues. This procedure produced a correlation coefficient of .991.

Coding reliability for the number of new idea units and number of deleted idea units was assessed by having two people independently code the idea units in both monologues produced by a randomly selected subset of 30 subjects (5 subjects from each of the 6 experimental conditions). The product moment correlation coefficient for number of new idea units was found to be .942, and for number of ideas deleted, $r = .802$.

Speech onset latency. Change scores for this variable were computed by subtracting response latency for the first monologue from that of the second. These change scores then were treated by a 2 × 3 (familiarity-by-type of preparation) analysis of variance (Hull & Nie, 1981). The results of this analysis revealed a significant effect for type of preparation, $F(2,74) = 3.522, p = .035$. Neither familiarity, $F(1,74) = 1.454, p = .232$, nor the interaction of type of preparation and familiarity, $F(2,74) = 1.437, p = .244$, produced significant effects. Decomposing the main effect for type of preparation into monotonic and residual components revealed a significant monotonic trend over the three preparation conditions, $F(1,74) = 6.79, p < .025$, and no significant residual component, $F(1,74) = .25$, n.s. The direction of this monotonic trend can readily be seen from the cell means given in Table 10.1. Consistent with Hypothesis 1, there is a clearly discernible trend toward quicker response latencies as one moves from the Distraction to Planning conditions.

Speech rate. Speech rate for each monologue was computed by dividing the total number of words in the transcript by the duration of the monologue, expressed in seconds. As with speech onset latency, speech rate change scores were then computed and analyzed via a 2 × 3 analysis of variance. Just as in the case of speech onset latency, the analysis of change in speech rate revealed a significant main effect for type of preparation, $F(2, 74) = 3.983, p =$

Table 10.1
Cell Means and Standard Deviations for
Change in Speech Onset Latency

	Type of Preparation		
	Distraction	No Delay	Planning
Familiar topic	.37	-.44	-.68
	(1.28)	(1.14)	(2.11)
Unfamiliar topic	.16	-.30	-3.10
	(6.22)	(2.38)	(2.35)

Note: Standard deviations are given in parentheses. Negative numbers indicate a faster response latency for monologue 2 than for monologue 1.

.023, and no effect for familiarity, $F(1, 74) = .33, p = .566$, or the interaction term, $F(2, 74) = .941, p = .395$. Decomposing the main effect for preparation into monotonic and residual elements revealed a significant monotonic trend, $F(1, 74) = 7.165, p < .01$, and no significant residual component, $F(1, 74) = .797$, n.s. The cell means and standard deviations for change in speech rate are given in Table 10.2. From these it can be seen that, consistent with Hypothesis 2, there is a significant trend toward a greater increase in speech rate as one moves from the Distraction condition to the Planning condition.

Filled pause rate. Change in filled pause rate was analyzed in the same manner as speech rate change and speech onset latency change. Cell means and standard deviations for this variable are given in Table 10.3. The analysis of variance revealed no significant effect for type of preparation, $F(2,74) = 1.850, p = .164$, familiarity, $F(2,74) = .129$, $p = .721$, or their interaction, $F(2,74) = 1.390, p = .255$.

Addition of new ideas. Like the hesitation variables, the content variables were also analyzed by a 2×3 (familiarity-by-type of preparation) analysis of variance. The results of the analysis on the number of new ideas added in the second monologue showed a significant effect for type of preparation, $F(2,74) = 3.656, p = .031$, but no effect for familiarity, $F(1,74) = .775, p = .382$, or the preparation-by-familiarity interaction, $F(2,74) = .199, p = .820$. The cell means for this variable are given in Table 10.4. An exploratory follow-up analysis was conducted by collapsing across levels of familiarity and employing Scheffe's procedure with $\alpha = .05$. This analysis revealed that the only significant pairwise difference in number of new ideas added was between the Distraction condition and the Planning condition. These results, then, indicate support for Hypothesis 3.

Deletion of ideas. The analysis of number of ideas deleted from monologue 1 to 2 produced a pattern of results different from that of all the other variables examined here. In this case there was no significant main effect for type of preparation, $F(2,74) = 1.027, p = .363$, although the effect of familiarity was significant, $F(1,74) = 4.099, p = .047$. There was no significant interaction effect, $F(2,74) = .417, p = .660$. Inspection of Table

Table 10.2
Cell Means and Standard Deviations for Change in Speech Rate

| | Type of Preparation | | |
	Distraction	*No Delay*	*Planning*
Familiar topic	−.12	−.00	.41
	(.47)	(.48)	(.47)
Unfamiliar topic	−.11	−.08	.19
	(.64)	(.46)	(.54)

Note: Negative numbers indicate a slower speech rate for monologue 2 than for monologue 1.

Table 10.3
Cell Means and Standard Deviations for
Change in Filled Pause Rate

| | Type of Preparation | | |
	Distraction	*No Delay*	*Planning*
Familiar topic	.03	.00	−.01
	(.03)	(.05)	(.03)
Unfamiliar topic	.00	.01	.00
	(.04)	(.05)	(.01)

Note: Negative numbers indicate a smaller filled pause rate for monologue 2 than for monologue 1.

Table 10.4
Cell Means and Standard Deviations for
Number of New Ideas

| | Type of Preparation | | |
	Distraction	*No Delay*	*Planning*
Familiar topic	1.21	1.79	1.85
	(.98)	(1.67)	(.69)
Unfamiliar topic	.83	1.50	1.85
	(.94)	(1.09)	(1.14)

10.5 shows that the significant effect of familiarity arose from the tendency to remove more ideas when speaking on the familiar topic than when speaking on the unfamiliar one.

SUMMARY AND IMPLICATIONS

The experiment reported here was developed to address three distinct areas of concern. The primary focus of the investigation was to examine the plausibility of the separate activation and assembly processes identified by action assembly theory. The second concern was with exploring the nature of changes in speech content that accompany the opportunity to

Table 10.5
Cell Means and Standard Deviations for
Number of Ideas Deleted

	Type of Preparation		
	Distraction	No Delay	Planning
Familiar topic	1.50	1.79	2.23
	(1.34)	(1.25)	(1.01)
Unfamiliar topic	1.08	1.43	1.31
	(1.44)	(.94)	(1.38)

plan output in advance of production. Finally, this experiment attempted to replicate an unusual pattern of results reported by Langer and Weinman (1981).

Tests of Action Assembly Theory

Action assembly theory (Greene, 1984a) identifies two distinct processes underlying the production of verbal and nonverbal behavior: activation of procedural records and the assembly of activated procedural records to form an output representation. This notion of two separate processing stages was used to derive Hypotheses 1 and 2 and Research Question 1. Because the activation process takes time, it was assumed that participants distracted from a task would be slower in executing that task than those who had relevant information activated in memory. Further, the opportunity to plan speech in advance should allow preliminary assembly of procedural records, providing a temporal advantage over people with appropriate information activated but not assembled.

Based on this line of reasoning, Hypothesis 1 was that there would be a monotonic trend in change in speech onset latency such that participants in the Distraction condition would show the least increase in quickness, No Delay participants next, and Planning condition participants would benefit most of all. The analysis of speech onset latency provided strong support for this hypothesis in that a significant monotonic trend was found with the condition means in the predicted direction.

The rationale underlying Hypothesis 2 was exactly the same as that for the first hypothesis except that although speech onset latency provides an index of processes occurring before the initiation of a response, speech rate is an indicant of cognitive processing after the beginning of speech. Just as with speech onset latency, the analysis of speech rate change scores revealed strong support for the action assembly formulation in that a significant monotonic trend was discovered, with the condition means in the expected direction.

Although strong predictions were advanced for the speech onset latency and speech rate variables, expectations for filled pauses were less clear-cut.

Previous research suggests that filled pauses are not strictly equivalent with silent pauses as a means of delaying speech production. For this reason, Research Question 1 was posed, reflecting a concern with the relation between filled pauses and monologue preparation. The results of the current analysis revealed no effects for planning or topic familiarity on changes in filled pause rate, a finding that is consistent with previous null results for monologue data (Greene, 1984b).

On the basis of these results, then, it appears that the separate activation and assembly processes identified by action assembly theory are at least plausible. The notion of *plausibility* is of central importance here because any pattern of results in temporal data is always subject to alternative interpretations concerning underlying cognitive processes (Taylor & Fiske, 1981). It is for this reason that the task of cognitive science is held to be the development of sufficient models of the human information processing system, rather than some "true" model that negates all others (Greene, 1984c).

The claims for action assembly theory on the basis of the current data are three-fold (1) the theory has been useful as an heuristic tool in that it suggested the experimental hypotheses and methods, (2) the theory provides a conceptual framework for integrating a range of diverse data, including that reported here, and (3) those aspects of the theory examined in the current study appear plausible as elements of an account of behavioral production.

Content Changes Accompanying Speech Preparation

A unique advantage of the experimental design employed here is that it allows an assessment of changes in narrative content as a result of advance preparation. Such content changes could occur either through the addition of new ideas or through the deletion of ideas previously mentioned. With respect to the former, Hypothesis 3 made explicit the expectation that increased preparation would result in a greater number of ideas. This hypothesis was supported in that a significant main effect for preparation was found in the experiment reported here.

The expectations concerning deletion of ideas previously expressed were less straightforward in that it is possible to identify two distinct mechanisms of deletion: forgetting and editing. If forgetting occurs, then we should expect participants in the Distraction condition to exhibit more deletions than those in the other conditions. Conversely, if editing occurs then participants in the Planning condition should exhibit relatively more deletions. Unfortunately from the standpoint of an investigation of this issue, the analysis of ideas deleted revealed no significant effect for type of preparation. Instead, there was an effect for topic familiarity in that more ideas were deleted when speaking on the familiar issue. It is possible that this occurred because participants produced more ideas when speaking on the familiar topic so that there was simply more opportunity for deletion. This possibility is lessened, however, in that although there was a slight tendency for participants speaking on the familiar topic to produce more ideas in monologue 1 (familiar $M = 3.20$; unfamiliar $M = 2.90$), that difference was not statistically significant, $t(78) = .96$, $p = .34$. Similarly, there was no significant difference in the total number of ideas produced when speaking on a familiar ($M = 2.98$) versus unfamiliar ($M = 3.03$) topic in monologue 2, $t(78) = .17$, $p = .866$. Taken together, these results would seem to indicate that when speaking on a familiar topic participants were more able to be selective in choosing ideas because they deleted more from time 1 to time 2 without providing fewer total ideas at time 2. This notion of selectivity is consistent with the conception of editing developed above.

Although we must be extremely cautious in drawing any conclusions in the face of the null results for type of preparation on deletion of ideas, there is a pattern in the cell means for this variable that merits note simply to make it explicit for future reference. As can be seen in Table 10.5, the direction of means for number of ideas deleted is supportive of an editing rather than a forgetting process. This follows from the fact that, for both familiar and unfamiliar topics, the fewest ideas were deleted in the distraction condition. It seems unlikely, then, that the opposite pattern of results (and, hence, forgetting) is likely to occur with such an experimental design. Future studies of changes in speech content accompanying preparation should attempt to substantiate this tentative conclusion and also to delineate those conditions that will lead to forgetting rather than editing processes.

Replication of Langer and Weinman (1981)

The final aim of this investigation was to attempt a replication of an earlier investigation by Langer and Weinman (1981). These authors discovered a familiarity-by-type of preparation interaction effect for filled pause rate. The analysis of change in filled pause rate reported above failed to produce any evidence of such an effect. Further, no interaction effect was detected in the analysis of the speech onset latency or speech rate variables.

Because these analyses involved change scores, they are not strictly comparable to the results reported by Langer and Weinman. For this reason, a pair of supplementary analyses were undertaken to search for an interaction effect similar to that found in the earlier study. Those follow-up analyses focused upon filled pause rate in each monologue rather than change in filled pause rate.

In the original study by Langer and Weinman, filled pause rate was computed only for the first 15 seconds of the participant's response rather than for the entire monologue. Thus it is possible that this effect emerged due to some factor that occurs early in a monologue, but then is dissipated as talk continues. The first supplementary analysis thus employed filled pause rate over the first 15 seconds of monologue 2. This variable was treated by a 2×3 (familiarity-by-type of preparation) analysis of variance as before. This analysis revealed no significant effects for type of preparation, $F(2,74) = .589, p = .557$, familiarity, $F(1,74) = .333, p = .566$, or their interaction, $F(2,74) = 1.609, p = .207$.

The second follow-up analysis involved two changes designed to ferret out any possible effects. First, the filled pause rate for the entire second monologue was examined. Further, in an effort to increase the power of the design, an analysis of covariance was employed (BMDP, 1983). Because all participants had spoken on the same topic in the practice session, filled pause rate in this monologue was used as a covariate in the statistical analysis of the monologue 2 data. The product moment correlation between filled pause rate in the practice session and monologue 2 was .585, indicating considerable individual stability across different topics of discussion. The inclusion of this covariate resulted in marginally significant effects for familiarity, $F(1,73) = 3.70, p = .058$, and the familiarity-by-type of preparation interaction, $F(2,73) = 2.96, p = .058$. No main effect was found for type of preparation, $F(2,73) = 1.88, p = .159$. Although the interaction term in this analysis did approach significance, inspection of Table 10.6 reveals that the direction of means is opposite that found by Langer and Weinman in that participants speaking on a familiar topic after the opportunity to plan their speech tended to be most fluent.

In summary, then, the analysis of change in speech onset latency, speech rate, and filled pause rate revealed no evidence of a type of preparation-by-familiarity interaction. Analysis of filled pause rate in the first 15 seconds of the second monologue also failed to produce such an effect. Finally, an analysis of covariance produced a marginally significant interaction effect, but one based on a pattern of means precisely opposite that reported by Langer and Weinman (1981). On the basis of these analyses it seems safe to conclude that no effect like that reported by Langer and Weinman was operating in the present data. The reason for this discrep-

Table 10.6
Adjusted Cell Means and Standard Deviations for
Filled Pause Rate in Monologue 2

	Type of Preparation		
	Distraction	*No Delay*	*Planning*
Familiar topic	.12	.10	.07
	(.05)	(.08)	(.05)
Unfamiliar topic	.07	.09	.08
	(.03)	(.06)	(.08)

ancy remains unclear. It is possible that differences in participant populations (people at an employment office versus university undergraduates) may have contributed to this effect. Alternatively, the fact that participants in the present study already had spoken on the issue once may have dramatically changed the direction of effects. At any rate, the phenomenon reported by Langer and Weinman should be regarded as suspect until its replicability is demonstrated.

NOTE

1. Four additional subjects were not included in the final data analysis due to failure to follow instructions or to improper use of recording equipment by the experimenters.

REFERENCES

Ajzen, I. (1985). From intentions to actions: A theory of planned behavior. In J. Kuhl & J. Beckmann (Eds.), *Action control: From cognition to behavior* (pp. 11-39). Berlin: Springer-Verlag.

Beattie, G. W., & Bradbury, R. J. (1979). An experimental investigation of the modifiability of the temporal structure of spontaneous speech. *Journal of Psycholinguistic Research, 8,* 225-248.

BMDP (1983). *BMDP statistical software.* Berkeley: University of California Press.

Brotherton, P. (1979). Speaking and not speaking: Processes for translating ideas into speech. In A. W. Siegman & S. Feldstein (Eds.), *Of speech and time: Temporal patterns in interpersonal contexts* (pp. 179-209). Hillsdale, NJ: Lawrence Erlbaum.

Brown, B. L., Strong, W. J., & Rencher, A. C. (1973). Perceptions of personality from speech: Effects of manipulations of acoustical parameters. *Journal of the Acoustical Society of America, 54,* 29-35.

Butterworth, B. (1975). Hesitation and semantic planning in speech. *Journal of Psycholinguistic Research, 4,* 75-87.

Butterworth, B. (Ed.) (1980a). *Language production: Vol 1, Speech and talk.* London: Academic Press.

Butterworth, B. (1980b). Evidence from pauses in speech. In B. Butterworth (Ed.), *Language production: Vol 1, Speech and talk* (pp. 155-176). London: Academic Press.

Deese, J. (1978). Thought into speech. *American Scientist, 66,* 314-321.

Deese, J. (1980). Pauses, prosody, and the demands of production in language. In H. W. Dechert & M. Raupach (Eds.), *Temporal variables in speech: Studies in honor of Frieda Goldman-Eisler* (pp. 69-84). The Hague: Mouton.

Doll, T. J. (1969). Short-term retention: Preparatory set as covert rehearsal. *Journal of Experimental Psychology, 82,* 175-182.

Duncan, S., Jr. (1972). Some signals and rules for taking speaking turns in conversations. *Journal of Personality and Social Psychology, 23,* 283-292.

Epstein, S. (1979). The stability of behavior: I. On predicting most of the people much of the time. *Journal of Personality and Social Psychology, 37,* 1097-1126.

Epstein, S. (1980). The stability of behavior: II. Implications for psychological research. *American Psychologist, 35,* 790-806.

Epstein, S. (1983). Aggregation and beyond: Some basic issues on the prediction of behavior. *Journal of Personality, 51,* 360-392.

Goldman-Eisler, F. (1956). The determinants of the rate of speech output and their mutual relations. *Journal of Psychosomatic Research, 1,* 137-143.

Goldman-Eisler, F. (1958). Speech production and the predictability of words in context. *Quarterly Journal of Experimental Psychology, 10,* 96-106.

Goldman-Eisler, F. (1961). Hesitation and information in speech. C. Cherry (Ed.), *Information theory* (pp. 162-174). London: Butterworth.

Greene, J. O. (1983). Development and initial tests of an action assembly theory. (Doctoral dissertation, University of Wisconsin-Madison, 1983). *Dissertation Abstracts International, 44,* 2622A.

Greene, J. O. (1984a). A cognitive approach to human communication: An action assembly theory. *Communication Monographs, 51,* 289-306.

Greene, J. O. (1984b). Speech preparation processes and verbal fluency. *Human Communication Research, 11,* 61-84.

Greene, J. O. (1984c). Evaluating cognitive explanations of communicative phenomena. *Quarterly Journal of Speech, 70,* 241-254.

Greene, J. O., & Cappella, J. N. (1984, November). *Cognition and talk: The relationship of semantic units to temporal patterns of fluency in spontaneous speech.* Paper presented at the annual meeting of the Speech Communication Association, San Francisco.

Greene, J. O., O'Hair, H. D., Cody, M. J., & Yen, C. (1985). Planning and control of behavior during deception. *Human Communication Research, 11,* 335-364.

Hayes, K. C., & Marteniuk, R. G. (1976). Dimensions of motor task complexity. In G. E. Stelmach (Ed.), *Motor control: Issues and trends* (pp. 201-228). New York: Academic Press.

Hull, C. H., & Nie, N. H. (1981). *SPSS update 7-9: New procedures and facilities for releases 7-9.* New York: McGraw-Hill.

Kerr, B. (1978). Task factors that influence selection and preparation for voluntary movements. In G. E. Stelmach (Ed.), *Information processing in motor control and learning* (pp. 55-69). New York: Academic Press.

Kraut, R. E. (1978). Verbal and nonverbal cues in the perception of lying. *Journal of Personality and Social Psychology, 36,* 380-391.

Langer, E. J., & Weinman, C. (1981). When thinking disrupts intellectual performance: Mindfulness on an overlearned task. *Personality and Social Psychology Bulletin, 7,* 240-243.

Lay, C. H., & Burron, B. F. (1968). Perceptions of the personality of the hesitant speaker. *Perceptual and Motor Skills, 26,* 951-956.

Levin, A., Silverman, I., & Ford, B. (1967). Hesitations in children's speech during explanation and description. *Journal of Verbal Learning and Verbal Behavior, 6,* 560-564.

Lindsley, J. R. (1975). Producing simple utterances: How far ahead do we plan? *Cognitive Psychology, 7,* 1-19.

Liska, A. E. (Ed.). (1975). *The consistency controversy: Readings on the impact of attitude on behavior.* New York: John Wiley.

Mackay, D. G. (1981). The problem of rehearsal or mental practice. *Journal of Motor Behavior, 13,* 274-285.

Mackay, D. G. (1982). The problems of flexibility, fluency, and speed-accuracy trade-off in skilled behavior. *Psychological Review, 89,* 483-506.

Maclay, H., & Osgood, C. E. (1959). Hesitation phenomena in spontaneous English speech. *Word, 15,* 19-44.

Mahl, G. F. (1956). Disturbances and silences in the patient's speech in psychotherapy. *Journal of Abnormal and Social Psychology, 53,* 1-15.

Mischel, W. (1973). Toward a cognitive social learning reconceptualization of personality. *Psychological Review, 80,* 252-283.

Mischel, W., & Peake, P. K. (1982). Beyond déja vu in the search for cross-situational consistency. *Psychological Review, 89,* 730-755.

O'Connell, D. C., Kowal, S., & Hormann, H. (1969). Semantic determinants of pauses. *Psychologische Forschung, 33,* 50-67.

Pirsig, R. M. (1974). *Zen and the art of motorcycle maintenance.* Toronto: Bantam.

Reynolds, A., & Paivio, A. (1968). Cognitive and emotional determinants of speech. *Canadian Journal of Psychology, 22,* 164-175.

Rochester, S. R. (1975). The significance of pauses in spontaneous speech. *Journal of Psycholinguistic Research, 4,* 51-81.

Sabin, E. J., Clemmer, E. J., O'Connell, D. C., & Kowal, S. (1979). A pausological approach to speech development. In A. W. Siegman & S. F. Feldstein (Eds.), *Of speech and time: Temporal speech patterns in interpersonal contexts* (pp. 35-55). Hillsdale, NJ: Lawrence Erlbaum.

Siegman, A. W. (1978). The telltale voice: Nonverbal messages of verbal communication. In A. W. Siegman & S. Feldstein (Eds.), *Nonverbal behavior and communication* (pp. 183-243). Hillsdale, NJ: Lawrence Erlbaum.

Siegman, A. W. (1979). Cognition and hesitation in speech. In A. W. Siegman & S. Feldstein (Eds.), *Of speech and time: Temporal speech patterns in interpersonal contexts* (pp. 151-178). Hillsdale, NJ: Lawrence Erlbaum.

Siegman, A. W., & Feldstein, S. F. (Eds.) (1979). *Of speech and time: Temporal speech patterns in interpersonal contexts.* Hillsdale, NJ: Lawrence Erlbaum.

Siegman, A. W., & Pope, B. (1966). Ambiguity and verbal fluency in the TAT. *Journal of Consulting Psychology, 30,* 239-245.

Street, R. L., Jr., & Brady, R. M. (1982). Speech rate acceptance ranges as a function of evaluative domain, listener speech rate, and communication context. *Communication Monographs, 49,* 290-308.

Tannenbaum, P. H., & Williams, F. (1968). Generation of active and passive sentences as a function of subject or object focus. *Journal of Verbal Learning and Verbal Behavior, 7,* 246-250.

Taylor, I. (1969). Content and structure in sentence production. *Journal of Verbal Learning and Verbal Behavior, 8,* 170-175.

Taylor, S. E., & Fiske, S. T. (1981). Getting inside the head: Methodologies for process analysis in attribution and social cognition. In J. H. Harvey, W. Ickes, & R. F. Kidd (Eds.), *New directions in attribution research* (Vol. 3) (pp. 459-524). Hillsdale, NJ: Lawrence Erlbaum.

Zuckerman, M., DePaulo, B. M., & Rosenthal, R. (1981). Verbal and nonverbal communication of deception. In L. Berkowitz (Ed.), *Advances in experimental social psychology* (Vol. 14) (pp. 2-59). New York: Academic Press.

11 ● Conservatism in Judgment: Is the Risky Shift-ee Really Risky, Really?

KATHY KELLERMANN ● SUSAN JARBOE

University of Wisconsin—Madison ● *California State University, Fresno*

THAT groups make choices and decisions different from individuals is almost a given in small group theory and research today. However, Stoner's (1961) discovery that groups make riskier choices than individuals took many researchers by surprise, as previous supposition had it that groups were more cautious than individuals in their decision making. Over time, risk and caution in decision-making groups have been assessed in a variety of formats (see, e.g., Chapko & Solomon, 1974; Seeborg, Lafollete, & Belohar, 1980) and in a diversity of situations (see, e.g., Myers & Kaplan, 1976; Teger & Pruitt, 1967). This assessment found the risky shift phenomenon to be a choice shift effect, alternatively labeled *group polarization,* wherein groups become either more risky or more cautious than individuals when making decisions. The increasing maturity and sophistication of research and theory on the group polarization process has generated several promising avenues to explore in the search to refine our understanding of group decision processes; however, most of the attention has continued to focus on risky shift rather than cautious shift effects.

The robustness of the risky shift effect led to the development of numerous explanations and hypotheses attempting to account for the occurrence of the phenomenon. Four explanations were forwarded initially for risky shifts in groups (see, for review, Cartwright, 1971; Dion, Baron, & Miller, 1970; Miller, 1978; Pruitt, 1971a, 1971b). The diffusion of responsibility hypothesis holds that fear of failure is reduced in group settings, enhancing tendencies toward risk-taking by eliminating the ability to make direct attributions of blame to particular group members. Among other criticisms, the diffusion of responsibility hypothesis cannot explain shifts toward caution or shifts toward risk without discussion (Pruitt, 1971a). Although diffusion

Correspondence and requests for reprints: Kathy Kellermann, Department of Communication, Michigan State University, East Lansing, MI 48824.

of responsibility may not explain the choice shift effect completely, recent research suggests that groups do have a sense of responsibility (Cline & Cline, 1980) and make attributions of responsibility (Forgas, 1981). An alternative explanation of risky shifts is provided by the leadership hypothesis which holds that initially high risk-takers are more influential during group discussion than low risk-takers. Although not completely supported in the literature, some versions of the leadership hypothesis are able to explain part of the choice shift effect (Pruitt, 1971a). The familiarization explanation holds that risk-taking is a result of increased familiarity with the issues resulting from group discussion; however, the explanation fails to account for the varying patterns of shifts induced by both familiarization and group process effects (Dion, Baron, & Miller, 1970). The cultural value explanation holds that risk (or caution) is a value related to specific situations that come into play during decision making, promoting shifts in the direction of the operative cultural value. While some researchers believe the value hypothesis is a promising approach for explaining choice shifts (Dion, Baron, & Miller, 1970; Pruitt, 1971a), other researchers disagree (Chapko & Solomon, 1974; Murningham & Castore, 1975; Vinokur, Trope, & Burnstein, 1975).

These four initial explanations have been focused and integrated by scholars, resulting in two overarching approaches to explaining choice shifts in groups. Social comparison theory posits that, during interaction, some group members discover they do not average or exceed other members on socially desirable characteristics related to risk-taking. The discrepancy resulting from this comparison process theoretically motivates members to change responses, thereby producing a choice shift effect. Several assumptions underlie the social comparison explanation: that group members initially overestimate themselves on desired dimensions compared to the rest of the group; that group members want to perceive themselves as equal to or better than the group; and that exposure to others' choices provides a stimulus to change one's position in the desired direction (Lamm & Myers, 1978; Laughlin & Earley, 1982). Social comparison theory has received support from several studies (Jellison & Riskand, 1970; Myers & Lamm, 1976; Sanders & Baron, 1977), particularly for its ability to predict the heightening of the effect with group discussion (Goethals & Zanna, 1979).

The second overarching approach, persuasive arguments theory, focuses on the group discussion process in more detail than social comparison theory. Persuasive arguments theory has three major tenets: that there are a collection of arguments for various choices; that some members have some arguments but not all members have all arguments; and that during discussion various arguments are elicited and weighed. The relative persuasiveness of previously unconsidered arguments theoretically determines the extent of the choice shift (Laughlin & Earley, 1982; Miller, 1978). Persuasive arguments theory has been supported in research that found that merely reading arguments can produce a choice shift (Murningham & Castore, 1975; Vinokur & Burnstein, 1974) and knowledge of others' positions is unnecessary to produce the shift given the existence of the persuasive arguments (Burnstein & Vinokur, 1973). Although the number of majority arguments are not related to group polarization (Alderton & Frey, 1983), the ratio of risk to caution arguments assists in predicting individual shifts (Fischer, McDowell, & Boulanger, 1976).

Several critical tests of the two theories have been undertaken, generally explaining the results by trying to combine the two theoretical approaches. Burnstein, Vinokur, and Trope (1975) found that the number of arguments was more important than the number of others' choices available for comparison in producing the choice shift. Later, Burnstein and Vinokur (1975) posited that knowledge of others' choices yields ideas (arguments) for those choices that may persuade group members to change their opinions. Boster and Mayer (1984a) suggested that people use the judgment of others as a means to check their perceptions of the quality of arguments. Several researchers have thus concluded that both social comparison processes and persuasive arguments contribute to the choice shift effect with neither theory being independently sufficient to explain the data (Boster & Mayer, 1984a, 1984b; Hale, 1984; Lamm & Myers, 1978; Mayer, 1986; Miller, 1978).

Regardless of the approach employed in group polarization research, the constant has been the comparison of the group to individuals acting alone with the assumption that individuals acting alone provide an accurate and adequate standard of comparison. In other words, risk or caution in group decision making has been assessed only in comparison to risk or caution in individual decision making. Thus if individuals are at some optimal level of risk-taking in decision making, groups that make more risky decisions are engaged in "risky shift." However, if individuals were not the optimizers of risk that such comparisons presume, groups may shift in an optimal direction rather than a risky or cautious direction. Thus the claimed inadequacies in social comparison and persuasive arguments theory may stem from an assumption of adequacy in individual decision making as it relates to risk and caution. For example, if individuals were not sufficiently polarized in their personal decision making, it may not be social comparison sparking a shift, but the group discussion acting as a compensatory mechanism for the less than optimal information processing of individuals. Although no work in the group discussion area directly focuses on this issue, research has indicated that the *utility* of various courses of action is focused on during the group discussion (Vinokur, Trope, & Burnstein, 1975) and that new information causes risk polarization by changing the evaluation of the utility of decision outcomes (Zaleski, 1980). The group may be serving an "error-checking" function in terms of the revision of individual opinion.

Within the domain of decision making and judgment research, considerable evidence exists that individuals do not revise their opinions sufficiently when presented with new informatiom (see, for review, Kahneman, Slovic, & Tversky, 1982; Nisbett & Ross, 1980). In particular, the conservatism effect references the willingness of individuals to alter their opinions upon the receipt of new information, with the alteration being in the "right" direction though not "far enough" (Edwards, 1968). Determinations of the conservatism of individual decision making come about by using Bayes' theorem as an objective standard of opinion revision. Bayes' theorem provides a precise means of determining "how far" an opinion should be revised given knowledge of the initial opinion and the new information that sparks opinion revision. Although Bayesian approaches to inference are not universally considered appropriate (see, for debate, Ajzen & Fishbein, 1978; Cohen, 1979, 1980; Fischoff & Lichtenstein, 1978; Navon, 1978, 1981; Shafer, 1976; Williams, 1978), judgment research traditionally has employed Bayes' theorem as a normative standard for optimal opinion revision (Slovic, Fischoff, & Lichtenstein, 1977; Slovic & Lichtenstein, 1971).

Bayes' theorem states that for an hypothesis H and new information D, that $P(H|D) = P(H) * P(D|H)/P(D)$. $P(H)$ represents the *initial* opinion an individual holds about some event and $P(H|D)$ represents the posterior probability (opinion) an individual holds after the receipt of new information. The formula specifies the optimal revision in opinion that should occur upon receipt of any datum. When the new information is irrelevant or nondiagnostic with respect to the hypothesis, $P(D|H)/P(D) = 1$ and assessments of probability should depend only on the prior probability $P(H)$. However, when the new information is correlated or diagnostic with respect to the hypothesis, then $P(D|H)/P(D) \neq 1$ and the prior probability $P(H)$ should be revised according to the diagnosticity of the new information.

The conservatism effect results from insufficient revision of $P(H)$ when new information is presented; individuals act as if the new information is less diagnostic than it actually is. Indeed, several studies have indicated that the more diagnostic the data, the more conservatism is evidenced (see, for review, Slovic & Lichtenstein, 1971). Two to nine presentations of new data are often necessary to create the opinion revision that should occur according to Bayes' theorem with one datum (Peterson, Schneider, & Miller, 1965; Phillips & Edwards, 1966).

As individuals are conservative information processors, it is unknown whether or not groups are cautious or risky in their judgments with respect to an objective standard of optimality such as Bayes' theorem. Groups could easily be offsetting the conservatism of individual decision making by providing enough new information in the form of persuasive arguments to reach an optimal decision. The persuasive arguments theory of group polarization highlights the introduction of new information in the explanation of opinion revision by focusing on the ratio of risk to caution arguments or the presence/absence of arguments. The multiple presentations of new information necessary to create the opinion revision normatively appropriate for one new datum are possibly provided by the group in the form of persuasive arguments. The conservatism effect in individuals provides a reason why a persuasive arguments explanation of the choice shift would occur: to compensate for the insufficient revision of individual decision making due to inadequate attention paid the diagnosticity of data. The purpose of this study is, therefore, to investigate whether or not the choice shift is truly risky/cautious or whether or not the group serves to offset optimally the conservatism of individuals when making decisions.

Generally, the choice shift effect has been demonstrated by comparing the risk a group is willing to assume to the average of the risk each individual in that group is willing to assume; individual measures are completed prior to a group discussion that has as its goal the generation of the group estimate. Defining polarization strictly in terms of differences between the average individual risk and the group risk confounds the information environment available for decision with the decision process itself. If all individuals had the exact same information and that information were complete and exhaustive for making an optimal decision, the information environment would be held constant in the group to individual comparison. However, as explanations of group polarization indicate, considerable argument exists over the influence of group discussion in the occurrence of the choice shift. Many instances of group polarization have been documented in the absence of actual group interaction (Mackie & Cooper, 1984; Murningham & Castore, 1975; Rim, 1982). If new information emerges in the group that individuals had not considered previously, opinion revision should occur to reach an optimal decision according to Bayes' theorem. On the other hand, if all relevant information were directly provided individuals and the group, any differences between their risk assessments cannot be explained within the domain of persuasive arguments theory.

Persuasive arguments theory hinges its rationale on new information arising either in the group discussion or in the minds of the individuals during group interaction. Within the context of human conservatism in information processing and a constant, complete information environment, persuasive arguments theory would imply that polarization would not occur. In Bayesian terms, if the base rate (initial opinion of risk) for some outcome was *provided* (rather than allowed to vary randomly across individuals in the group) and a new datum with specified diagnosticity was *provided* (rather than allowing groups to generate different data with different diagnosticity values than individuals), then individuals should revise the initial base rate to the same extent as groups because the "persuasive arguments" are held constant across both the individuals and the group. Thus a constant information environment in which all relevant data needed for an optimal decision are provided does not lend itself to the choice shift effect within a persuasive arguments perspective.

A choice shift resulting from a constant information environment would suggest the group is serving an error-checking function, offsetting the conservatism of individual decision making; social comparison theory posits exactly this outcome. Social comparison theory implies that even in a constant information environment, group polarization would occur because individuals would still discover they do not average or exceed other members on socially desirable characteristics and alter their opinion accordingly. Past studies of group polarization have not maintained a constant information environment, however, and "critical" tests of these two theories of the choice shift are inadequate for evaluating the power of either approach. Thus the present study investigates the occurrence of the choice shift effect to determine if it is a function of a nonconstant information environment sparking opinion revision or an error-checking function offsetting human conservatism.

In order to investigate causes of group polarization, groups must be brought together and assigned a task(s) that spark what traditionally has been identified as a choice shift. In the present study, groups were provided with five problems, each composed of two parts. The first part of each problem asked for an assessment of the minimum risk that would be acceptable for an individual to undertake an action, a measurement method traditionally employed to identify group polarization effects. The second part of each problem specified an initial assessment of risk (the base-rate for the "initial opinion") and provided new information with a specified diagnosticity for which an estimate of "success" was solicited. Thus it was possible to determine if group polarization in traditional senses occurred and whether or not a constant information environment could eliminate the choice shift effect, respectively. Use of Bayes' theorem allowed investigation of the relative optimality of individual versus group decision making and the extent to which group discussion may serve an error-checking function for human conservatism.

METHOD

Participants

Participants in this study were 219 undergraduates drawn from communication courses at the University of Wisconsin. These participants were placed in 33 groups. Five of the groups had to be deleted from the analysis because one member of the group failed to provide 1 of 10 necessary responses on which to base individual to group comparisons. A total of

180 individuals in 28 groups were used in the analysis. Groups ranged in size from 3 to 10 with a modal group size of 7 persons.

Procedures

As part of a class activity, each group was brought to videotaping facilities and arranged for optimal camera exposure. Participants were told that the activity related to decision-making processes and consisted of two parts: an opinion survey and a group discussion. Participants then completed the opinion survey individually prior to the group discussion. Each survey consisted of 5 brief scenarios with two questions asked per scenario. The first question asked participants to identify the lowest probability they found acceptable for an action to be undertaken; the second question asked participants to estimate the likelihood that a particular action would occur. Verbal instructions explaining the differences in these questions were provided to all participants. After all members of a group had completed the opinion survey, instructions were given for a group discussion. The group was asked to discuss all five scenarios from the survey and to achieve a consensus decision for each question. All groups were told they should not begin their discussion by reporting the individual assessments they had completed, but instead begin as if they were encountering the scenarios for the first time. It was suggested that each group take about six minutes per scenario and no more than 35 minutes overall with an equal amount of time being spent on each scenario. Each group was assigned a timekeeper to make the group aware of its use of time. A recorder was also assigned in each group and this individual kept track of the group's decisions on another copy of the same survey. All groups were videotaped during their discussions and all surveys were collected at the end of the videotaping.

Survey Construction

The survey was designed to permit the assessment of two issues: (1) the occurrence of risky/cautious shift using traditional measurement procedures (the nonconstant information environment) and (2) the effect of a constant information environment on the group decision-making process when compared to individual decision making. To prompt risky and cautious shift, five scenarios that have been found to induce polarization in past research were selected from the Choice Dilemma Questionnaire. These five scenarios are concerned with a job change, an operation, a football game, a POW camp, and a marriage proposal. Typically, the job change, football game, and POW scenarios produce risky shifts in groups and the operation and marriage scenarios produce cautious shifts. All scenarios are hypothetical "real life" situations in which a person has to choose between a risky or cautious alternative. The risky alternative is usually presented as more desirable though with lower chances of success. Thus the job change scenario concerns an electrical engineer faced with a choice between his present, secure job with a modest salary and little chance of upward mobility or a job with a new firm that has an uncertain future but offers substantial salary and other benefits. Persons are asked to determine the lowest odds they would consider acceptable for them to pursue the "risky" option. A choice of 1 in 10 would indicate a strong risk orientation for that scenario whereas a choice of 9 in 10 indicates a cautious orientation. These five scenarios were employed to create the nonconstant information environment that has sparked choice shifts in past research.

To examine the influence of a constant information environment on the occurrence of risky shift, an "addendum" was written to each of the five scenarios. This addendum followed the scenario and the first question. Each addendum included a specified initial opinion $P(H)$ and provided data D with an estimate of its validity given the base rate $P(D|H)$. For example, the job change scenario addendum told participants that newly founded companies have a certain chance of becoming financially sound (the base rate); that a management consultant firm had predicted that the newly founded company offering the engineer the job would succeed in becoming financially sound (the datum); and the accuracy of the management consultant firm in past predictions of this sort (the probability of the prediction given the base rate). The survey then asked participants to assess the chance that the newly founded company offering the engineer the job would prove financially sound. According to Bayes' theorem, all relevant information is provided for opinion revision as $P(D)$ can be estimated from the information given. In mathematical terms, $P(D) = P(D)|H)^{*}P(H) + P(D|not\ H)^{*}P(not\ H)$. In other words, the probability of a prediction of success can be determined by examining the probability of a prediction of success given the base rate (which is provided) and the probability of the prediction given any other base rate (which can be calculated). As the prediction of success is a fact, $P(D|not\ H)$ can be obtained by subtracting $P(D|H)$ from 1. In a like manner $P(not\ H) = 1 - P(H)$.

Five different base rates and five different accuracy estimates were employed in the addendums—1, 3, 5, 7, or 9 chances in 10 of "success." Thus a given addendum might indicate that the general chance of success was 1 in 10 and that the accuracy of the prediction of success was 7 in 10. Participants and groups therefore were forced to integrate the new information and revise the initial opinion. Such procedures are standard in judgment research.

For each scenario and addendum, 25 different versions were constructed from the 5 base rate levels and the 5 accuracy rate levels. Given there were 5 scenarios and addendums on each survey, 25 different *versions* of the survey were constructed such that each survey contained (in one of the scenarios/addendums) each base rate and reliability rate. In other words, each survey permitted the specification of 5 base rates and 5 reliability rates. The surveys were constructed in such a way from the scenarios/addendums that each version presented each base rate level and reliability rate level only once. Furthermore, the correspondence between the base rate and accuracy rate was controlled so that no group could detect a pattern in the two rates. For example, a group would not be given base rates and reliability rates of (1,1), (3,3), (5,5), (7,7), (9,9) or of (1,9), (3,7), (5,5), (7,3), (9,1). Rather, each survey was constructed to disrupt such correspondence in base rates and reliability rates across the scenarios. For example, one survey contained base rate and reliability rates of (1,9), (3,5), (5,1), (7,7), (9,3). Consequently, 25 different versions of the survey were constructed in which each survey had each base rate and reliability rate level. In each survey the order of the scenarios was held constant: job change, operation, football game, POW camp, marriage. However, the base rate and reliability rate varied across the maintained scenario order.

Interaction Indices

The videotapes were analyzed in two main ways: (1) cautious versus risky arguments and (2) social comparison statements. Arguments were defined as any utterance that contained at least two components of traditional models of arguments. For example, most traditional models of argument identify at least four components: (1) name (making the claim), (2) explain (defining, describing), (3) support (offering evidence), and (4) conclude (summarizing, stating implications). Toulmin's model of argument identifies three main components (claim, data, warrant) with several additional "subcomponents," such as reservations. Two *main* components had to be present for an utterance to be considered an argument. Arguments were classified as cautious if their explicit or implicit assumption was a choice of the "less desirable though less risky" alternative in the scenario. Similarly, arguments were classified as risky if their explicit or implicit assumption was a choice of the "more desirable though more risky alternative" in the scenario. Therefore, any arguments in support of the job change, the operation, the two-point football conversion, the escape from the POW camp, or opting for marriage were considered risky and rejection of such actions was considered to be cautious. Agreements with and repeats of arguments were coded also. Agreements were defined as the indication of support by other group members with the argument and usually took the form of "Yeah" or "That's right" or "Exactly." Repeats of arguments were defined as restating a previously offered argument in the same or in synonymous words. The arguments related to both the scenario and its addendum were separately coded. In the case of the addendum, arguments were separated into categories of "higher" and "lower" to represent the speaker's beliefs about what the final estimate size should be. These higher/lower category designations were then reclassified into the analogues of risky/cautious based on the relationship of the base rate and the reliability rate. When arguments occurred that suggested positions closer to the base rate *and* the base rate was higher than the reliability rate, then "higher" arguments were considered conservative as little opinion revision is occurring based on the new datum. For similar reasons, when arguments suggested positions closer to the base rate *and* the base rate was lower than the reliability rate, then "lower" arguments were considered conservative. By contrast, arguments directed at the reliability rate were coded as "non-conservative" as they tended to recognize the diagnosticity of the datum.

Social comparison statements were coded in terms of their *informational* value or their *coercive* value, a separation often found in the social comparison literature. An eight category coding scheme was developed for this purpose. Statements of position were utterances that identified the estimate the individual maintained for the answer. Socioemotional reactions were positive or negative responses to *individual* statements of position. Group norm establishment (demonstration of similarities) involved the group trying to pull opinions together to identify points of agreement. Awareness of group differences meant that the group is cognizant that individuals or coalitions disagree with each other. These four categories are *information* utterances as they all concern the location of individuals in terms of their position on the issue. *Coercive* utterances, by contrast, involve pressuring tactics. Pressure to conform statements involve the group's wanting an individual to agree with a group norm. Admissions of conformity reflect a change in opinion toward the group norm. Refusals to conform are utterances that indicate a change in opinion will not be made, at least not as far as the group norm would require. Awareness of conformity refers to the explicit recognition of pressuring processes and tactics operating in the group. Table 11.1 provides examples of utterances from each of these categories as well as the distribution of utterances that occur across the categories.

One *simultaneous* test of reliability for arguments, repeats, agrees, and the eight social comparison categories was undertaken for 2 coders trained in the coding procedures. Training continued until fewer than 4 errors were made *between* the 2 coders with no category having more than 1 error. As coders were required to *write out* all acts but repeats and agrees, exact equivalence could be determined. For 1 group, across the 5 scenarios and 5 addendums (thus 10 sets of arguments and social comparison coding forms), 267 discrete acts were identified by the 2 coders of which 266 were identical. One coder failed to record one "agreement" to an argument that another coder identified. Thus we were confident that coders were chunking the group interaction and assigning it to categories in a highly reliable manner.

Table 11.1
Social Comparison Coding Sheme

Social Comparison Categories	Scenario %	Addendum %
Information Utterances	(83.98)	(92.25)
Statements of position ("I am high," "I put 7," "I think it should be in the middle," "That's what I put," "Me, too")	52.17	54.64
Socioemotional reactions to individuals positive ("Right on!" "That sounds good")	.17	.00
negative ("Wow!" "Really!" "9 in 10, no!" "Oh, how could you!")	1.85	.50
Group norm establishment/demonstration of similarities ("So we're all high?" "Does everyone agree?" "It's 7 or 9, right?" "So its 9 in 10?" "We did it!" "We're acting as a group!")	27.82	37.19
Awareness of group differences ("You put 9, you put 7, you put 1, you put 3," "I disagree with you," "We all put 5 except for you," "We all see it differently")	1.97	.20
Coercive Utterances	(16.02)	(7.48)
Pressure to conform ("Do you see why we say that?" "Don't you want to change?" "Don't hang us up," "Why wouldn't you do it?" "Chicken!")	4.11	1.20
Admissions of conformity ("All right, I'll go 5 in 10," "I can see going lower," "Now that we talked, I can see 7," "Yes, I'd be willing to change,")	7.17	5.78
Refusals to conform ("I'm sticking with 5," "I won't go higher than 3," "No, I don't want to do that")	4.34	.50
Awareness of conformity ("Peer pressure, huh!" "We're twisting your arm," "You've given in twice, now")	.40	.00
Total Utterances	1729	1003

RESULTS

Manipulation Checks

The creation of the traditional choice shift. In order to investigate the conservatism of decision making on the choice shift effect in information constant environments, groups in the study had to exhibit what traditionally has been determined to be evidence for risky or cautious shift. This determination of choice shift is obtained by comparing the average individual risk group members are willing to assume to the risk the group is willing to assume. Table 11.2 displays the results of this analysis for each of the five scenarios. As predicted, the job change, football, and POW camp scenarios created risky shift and the operation and marriage scenarios created cautious shift. Of the 140 total decisions (5 scenarios for each of 28 groups), only 10 evidenced no shift (see Table 11.2). However, the operation scenario did not solely evidence cautious shifts; 11 of the 28 groups evidenced risky shifts on this scenario. For those groups evidencing risky shift on the operation scenario, the difference in risk assessment was found to mark a significant change in orientation, $t(10) = 3.77, p < .001$. Although the operation scenario did not produce strictly cautious shifts as initially intended, the fact that it did *produce shifts* satisfies the requirements of the research plan. In other words, the creation of both risky and cautious shifts with the operation scenario is acceptable given that the intent was to produce choice shifts and to try to obtain shifts across the scenarios that were not all in the same direction. Thus the creation of choice shifts using traditional methods of determining such shifts was successful.

The creation of an information constant environment. The addendum of each scenario was designed to provide all necessary information for reaching a decision so that the analysis of the results would not be confounded by a nonconstant information environment when comparing individual to group assessments. The total number of arguments for scenarios $(M = 11.39, SD = 6.15)$ was found to be significantly greater than the total number of arguments $(M = 2.50, SD = 2.46)$ made concerning the decision in the addendums, *correlated* $t(139) = 16.08, p < .001$. Furthermore, the average 2.5 arguments made concerning the addendum decision were almost all about how to manipulate the information rather than the provision of new information. Indeed 90% of the arguments related to the decision on the addendum concerned whether the information provided should be added, multiplied, divided, and so on. Thus the creation of an information constant environment for individual to group assessment comparison was successful.

The control of extraneous variables. As groups in the study varied in size and as a "latin square" type of procedure was employed in the survey construction such that the addendum odds were not constant by scenario, statistical analyses were undertaken to determine if group size and scenario content needed to be employed as covariates in analyses related to odds estimates (the addendum). For each base rate and reliability rate a one-way ANOVA was conducted by the scenario topic (job change, operation, football, POW, marriage) on the group estimate of the odds of success and on individuals' estimate of the odds of success. For group estimates of the odds of success, 8 of the 25 ANOVAs indicated significant differences in

Table 11.2
Choice Shift Creation Results

Scenario	Average Individual Risk	Difference Between Group and Average Individual Risk	t Value on Difference	Number of Shifts		
				−	0	+
Job change	5.27 (.94)	.55 (1.09)	2.74	4	5	19
Operation	6.94 (.91)	−.27 (1.26)	−1.25	15	2	11
Football	4.47 (1.09)	.90 (1.16)	4.34	2	1	25
POW camp	4.81 (1.24)	.67 (1.03)	3.43	2	1	25
Marriage	6.75 (.97)	−.75 (1.20)	−3.56	20	1	7

Notes: All t-tests are one-tailed. Critical value for $p < .05$ for 27 df is 1.70.
A "−" indicates cautious shifts, a "0" indicates no shifts, and a "+" indicates risky shifts.

estimates due to the scenario and for individuals' estimates 5 of 25 ANOVAs indicated significant differences. Given the error rate would predict only 1 in 20 tests should be significant, the scenario content was used as a covariate in all analyses of odds estimates. Similarly, group size had a significant influence on odds estimates for 6 of the 25 base and reliability rate levels for group estimates and for 4 of the 25 ANOVAs for individual estimates. Therefore, group size as well as scenario content became a covariate in all other analyses of odds estimates.

Sensitivity to the Diagnosticity of New Information

Revision of opinion upon receipt of new information. When presented with new information in the form of the prediction of success and its associated reliability rate, both individuals and groups revised the initial opinion (the base rate presented them) in trying to predict the success of the "risky" alternative. Table 11.3 presents the results of the analyses of opinion revision upon receipt of new information for each of the five base rates employed in the study. Although individuals and groups differentially revised the individual base rate opinion dependent upon the reliability of the prediction of success, this opinion revision shows marked patterns. The exact reliability rate is less important than the comparison of the reliability rate to the base rate. The mean odds of the revised opinion varied only as a function of whether the reliability rate was less than, equal to, or greater than the base rate. For example, when the base rate was 5 in 10, the mean odds of the revised opinion were *less* than the mean odds estimate for the reliability rate of 5 in 10 when the reliability rate was less than 5 in 10; however, it did not matter whether the reliability rate was 1 in 10 or 3 in 10. Similarly, for this same base rate, the mean odds of the revised opinion were greater than the mean odds for a reliability rate of 5 in 10 when that reliability rate was *greater* than 5 in 10. When the base rate was 3 in 10, the 1 in 10 reliability rate decreased the mean odds of the revised opinion and

Table 11.3
Sensitivity of Individuals and Groups to New Information

Base Rate	F	1 in 10		3 in 10		5 in 10		7 in 10		9 in 10
				Mean Odds for Reliability Rate						
1 in 10										
individuals	23.45 (.001)	1.85	=	2.44	<	3.53	<	4.43	=	5.40
groups	12.48 (.001)	1.29	=	1.56	=	2.92	<	4.58	=	5.40
3 in 10										
individuals	33.14 (.001)	2.75	=	3.49	<	4.24	=	4.50	<	6.70
groups	14.03 (.001)	2.50	=	2.83	<	4.25	=	4.22	<	7.38
5 in 10										
individuals	25.96 (.001)	4.12	=	4.17	<	5.12	<	6.41	=	6.57
groups	9.37 (.001)	4.00	=	4.50	=	5.00	<	7.17	=	6.17
7 in 10										
individuals	14.57 (.001)	4.99	=	5.59	=	5.87	<	6.65	<	7.75
groups	3.62 (.021)	5.33	=	6.00	=	6.26	=	6.80	<	8.10
9 in 10										
individuals	5.60 (.001)	6.71	=	6.42	=	6.87	=	7.42	<	8.33
groups	NS	7.54	=	7.55	=	8.00	=	7.60	=	8.68

Note: For individuals, $df = 4/173$. For groups, $df = 4/21$. For both individuals and groups, group size and scenario content were employed as covariates in the analysis. Newman-Keuls tests of the differences between the mean odds of the opinion as a function of the reliability rate are indicated by $=$, $<$, and $>$ signs.

reliability rates greater than 3 in 10 increased the mean odds of the revised opinion when compared to the odds at the 3 in 10 reliability rate.

Individuals and groups were differentially sensitive to the new information. The mean odds of success of the revised opinion generally required a reliability rate to be *greater* than the base rate before a significant difference between group estimates occurred. To some degree, this finding may be an artifact of the sample size. There were 180 individuals who were fairly equally divided across the reliability rates in contrast to 28 groups being fairly equally divided across the reliability rates. Regardless of this potential artifact affecting the exact point in which sensitivity to new information sets in, the conclusion is still valid that individuals and groups do revise their opinions differentially dependent upon the reliability rate of the new information.

Conservatism in information processing. To examine whether or not groups are truly more polarized than individuals in their decisions, Bayes' theorem was employed to predict the optimal revised opinion given an initial opinion (base rate) and new data with specified diagnosticity (reliability rate). Because each of the addendums was written with dichotomous choices (success/failure), Bayes' theorem reduces to the following:

$$P(\text{Success}|\text{Data}) = \frac{P(\text{Reliability}|\text{Data}) \bullet P(\text{Base Rate})}{P(\text{Reliability}|\text{Data}) \bullet P(\text{Base Rate}) + (1 - P(\text{Reliability}|\text{Data})) \bullet (1 - P(\text{Base}))}$$

Table 11.4 provides the Bayesian optimal final opinion for each base and reliability rate combination.

The average individual estimate was then compared to the Bayesian optimal value to determine if individuals were conservative in opinion revision. This comparison was undertaken with a single-group *t*-test where the theoretic mean was set equal to the value predicted by Bayes' theorem to be optimal. As can be determined from Table 11.4, 23 out of 25 times the estimates produced by individuals for the revised opinion were significantly different than the Bayesian estimates. Figure 11.1 plots the individual revised opinion estimates against the Bayesian optimal opinions. As can be noticed from Figure 11.1, individuals are exhibiting the classic signs of the conservatism effect: they are moving "in the right direction" though "not far enough." For example, when the base rate is 1 in 10 (that is, .1), individuals reduce their final opinion estimates as the reliability of the new datum decreases; however, individuals fail to reduce their estimates as far as they should. Similarly, when the base rate is .5, individuals revise their estimates downward as the reliability rate goes below .5 and upward as the reliability rate goes above .5 though they do not revise their opinions "far enough" to reach the optimal level. These results verify the conservatism of individual information processing.

The average group estimate for each base rate and reliability rate was compared to the Bayesian optimal estimate to determine if group decision making is also conservative or whether groups differ from individuals and approach or exceed the Bayesian optimal estimate. Again, single-group *t*-tests were conducted with the Bayesian estimate employed as the theoretic mean. Table 11.4 indicates that in 16 of 25 instances, groups provided estimates significantly different from Bayesian optimal estimates. Moreover, as can be seen in Figure 11.1, these estimates are *not* risky, which would require *exceeding* the Bayesian estimate. Groups *never* exceed the Bayesian estimate and in 16 of 25 cases they exhibit marked conservatism effects. Finally, the difference between the average individual estimate for the group and the group's estimate was tested to determine if groups make different, *more* optimal decisions than individuals. A *t*-test on the difference between individuals and their group estimate indicated that in only 6 of 25 instances did groups make different decisions than individuals. In 5 of these 6 instances, groups were closer to the Bayesian optimal estimate than were individuals. It is interesting that 4 of the 5 instances in which groups were closer to the optimal estimate occurred with high base rates (.7 and .9). Nonetheless, group decision making operates much like individual decision making, being *conservative* though in the right direction.

Table 11.4
Bayesian Optimality and Individual and Group Estimates

Base Rate	Reliability Rate	Bayesian Optimal	Individuals			Group			Difference Between Average Individual and Group Estimate		
			Mean	SD	N	Mean	SD	N	Mean	SD	N
.1	.1	.011	.185∿	.072	39	.129∿	.060	6	.056	.081	6
.1	.3	.045	.244∿	.056	33	.156	.113	5	.088	.095	5
.1	.5	.100	.353∿	.057	40	.292*	.142	6	.062	.111	6
.1	.7	.206	.443∿	.109	41	.458∿	.128	6	−.016	.092	6
.1	.9	.500	.540	.151	27	.540	.207	5	.000	.081	5
.3	.1	.045	.275∿	.072	31	.250∿	.071	5	.025	.081	5
.3	.3	.155	.349∿	.064	39	.283*	.098	6	.066	.124	6
.3	.5	.300	.424∿	.048	41	.425*	.099	6	−.001	.093	6
.3	.7	.500	.450∿	.054	34	.422	.126	5	.028	.168	5
.3	.9	.794	.670∿	.112	35	.738	.170	6	−.068	.122	6
.5	.1	.100	.412∿	.031	43	.400∿	.089	6	.073∿	.012	6
.5	.3	.300	.417∿	.048	33	.450∿	.050	5	−.032	.040	5
.5	.5	.500	.512	.051	30	.500	.000	5	.012	.051	5
.5	.7	.700	.641∿	.028	34	.717	.103	6	−.076	.098	6
.5	.9	.900	.657∿	.066	40	.617∿	.143	6	.040	.155	6
.7	.1	.206	.499∿	.159	40	.533∿	.150	6	−.034	.145	6
.7	.3	.500	.559∿	.110	36	.600*	.089	6	−.040	.073	6
.7	.5	.700	.587∿	.044	36	.627	.157	6	−.040	.126	6
.7	.7	.845	.665∿	.081	31	.680*	.109	5	−.147∿	.061	5
.7	.9	.955	.785*	.042	37	.810∿	.022	5	−.242∿	.032	5
.9	.1	.500	.671∿	.048	27	.754∿	.105	5	−.083*	.059	5
.9	.3	.794	.642∿	.068	39	.755	.157	6	−.112*	.123	6
.9	.5	.900	.687∿	.143	33	.800	.141	5	−.113*	.092	5
.9	.7	.955	.742∿	.078	40	.760∿	.078	6	−.018	.031	6
.9	.9	.989	.833∿	.073	41	.868*	.082	6	−.035	.040	6

Note: For comparisons of individuals to Bayesian estimate, the critical values for 26 to 42 df range from 1.70 - 1.68 with $p < .05$, 2.47 - 2.42 with $p < .01$, and 2.77 - 2.70 with $p < .005$. For comparisons of groups to Bayesian estimate or for difference scores to Bayesian estimate, the critical values for 4 to 5 df range from 2.13 - 2.02 with $p < .05$, 3.75 - 3.36 with $p < .01$, and 4.60 - 4.03 with $p < .005$. "*" denotes a significant difference at $p < .05$, "∧" denotes a significant difference at $p < .01$, and "∿" denotes a significant difference at $p < .005$.

The conclusion to be drawn from this series of results is that the choice shift effect occurs because of a nonconstant information environment and that when this confound is removed the choice shift, for the most part, is also removed. Moreover, the choice shift occurring in the nonconstant information environment is neither risky nor cautious, instead being *conservative*. In other words, the choice shift occurring in the nonconstant information environment moves the group toward an optimal answer but does *not* achieve the optimal answer.

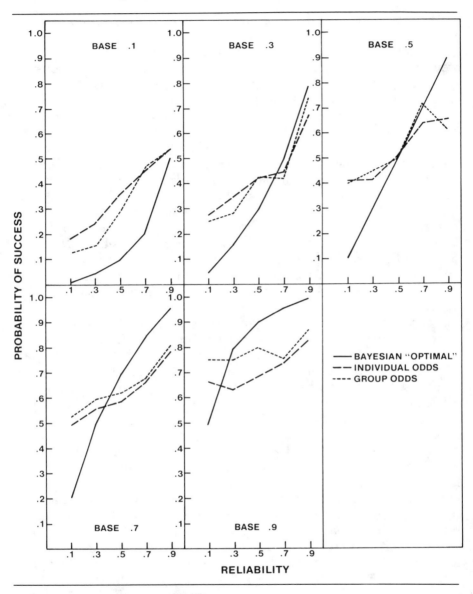

Figure 11.1 Decision optimality.

The Determinants of Choice Shift

The argumentative and social comparative base of the choice shift was explored in analyses designed to understand the influence of a nonconstant information environment on the creation of the shift. This section provides methodological insight into the problem of individual to group comparisons when the design of the study permits the information environment to confound the analyses.

The role of the information environment was examined in numerous ways. First, the constant environment was compared to the nonconstant environment in terms of arguments, repeats of arguments, agreements with arguments, and social comparison statements. As indicated earlier, the total number of arguments was significantly higher for the scenario (nonconstant environment) assessment of risk than for the addendum (constant environment) assessment of probability. The approximate difference between the two environments was 10 arguments, just "1 bit" of new data over that needed to generate the opinion revision specified by Bayes' theorem for "1 bit" (Peterson, Schneider, & Miller, 1965; Phillips & Edwards, 1966). Although the nonconstant environment assessments of risk evidenced more social comparison statements (M = 12.35, SD = 6.70) than the constant environment assessments of probability (M = 7.16, SD = 4.03), *correlated* $t(139)$ = 8.68, p < .001, the nonconstant environment assessments of risk had the same number of arguments (M = 11.39, SD = 6.15) as they had social comparison statements (M = 12.35, SD = 6.70), *correlated* $t(139)$ = -1.72, p < .088. By constrast, the constant information environment assessments of probability evidenced far more social comparison statements (M = 7.16, SD = 4.03) than arguments (M = 2.50, SD = 2.47; *correlated* $t(139)$ = -15.39, p < .001). The type of information environment also affected the type of social comparison statements that were employed, Chi-square(1) = 38.48, p < .001. Coercive social comparison utterances were relatively more likely in the nonconstant environment than in the constant environment and informative social comparison statements were relatively more likely in the constant environment than the nonconstant environment (see Table 11.1 for percentage figures). Thus the nonconstant environment not only confounds analyses with different information between the comparison groups but it differentially affects the kind of information that is exchanged.

If the nonconstant nature of the information environment is ignored, it is possible to reach a variety of conclusions about what "causes" the choice shift—arguments or social comparison statements. A number of regression analyses were performed to isolate determinants of the difference in risk assessment between the average of the individuals in the group and the group's estimate. This risk difference was regressed on (1) the ratio of risk to total arguments and (2) the total number of social comparison statements, as is typical in choice shift research. When a stepwise procedure was employed, only the ratio of risk to total arguments was a significant predictor in the equation, Beta = .51, F = 47.07, df = 136, p < .001, adj r^2 = .25. When the number of social comparison statements was forced into the equation the adjusted r^2 decreased slightly (to .247). These results seem to suggest a conclusion of the influence of persuasive arguments in group decision making. However, it cannot be concluded that persuasive arguments provide new information to individuals that they would not have if they had not been in a group. When a stepwise regression is employed using (1) the ratio of risk to total arguments, (2) the ratio of repeated risky arguments to total repeated arguments, (3) the ratio of agreements for risky arguments to the total agreements for arguments, and (4) the total number of social comparison statements, the ratio of risky arguments to total arguments fails to enter the equation. Instead, repeat and agree ratios are the most important predictors of the difference in risk assessment, Agrees Beta = .33, F = 13.03, df = 122, p < .001; Repeats Beta = .27, F = 8.45, df = 121, p < .004; Adj r^2 for equation = .27. The issue of interpretation of repeats and agreements is problematic. Certainly, such utterances do not provide *new* information in the sense of diagnosticity or arguments. Indeed, such utterances seem to provide social comparison information on where group members stand on the issue. The *lack* of importance of both persuasive arguments and social comparison statements in creating shifts in group choices is provided by a regression analysis conducted on the difference in *odds* assessment (the constant information environment assessment) as a function of argument ratio and social comparison statements. The argument ratio employed was based on the *diagnosticity* of the new information as described in the methodology. Neither variable entered the equation in a stepwise regression procedure for predicting differences in odds assessments and when both were forced into the equation, the adjusted r^2 remained zero.

DISCUSSION

The traditional definition of the choice shift—be it risky or cautious—has relied on a comparison of individual to group risk assessments. This comparison has been made in the face of a nonconstant information environment. When the information environment is held constant, choice shifts tend not to occur. These results imply that the impetus behind traditional choice shifts are persuasive arguments providing new information to individuals. The failure to identify choice shifts from social comparison statements in the constant information environment suggests that the social comparison hypothesis is insufficient to spark opinion revision. However, the choice shifts occurring under traditional methods are neither risky nor cautious; they are *conservative*. Groups process information much like individuals, revising their opinions in the right direction though not to the optimal extent. As 9 "bits" of information are required to create opinion revision that should have occurred with "1" bit of information, the group can serve an error-checking function by creating opinion revision through the provision of additional bits of new information. Indeed, the average number of arguments on a decision is 10, just sufficient to create the revision that should have occurred with only one new bit of information. Consequently, if groups generate a sufficient amount of new information, choice shift will occur. Nonetheless, these *shifts* are still not optimal in that 9 or 10 new arguments should create far more revision of opinion than 1 new argument. Consequently, risky shift is not risky and cautious shift is not cautious; both choice shifts are *conservative* and reflect the same conservatism bias exhibited by individuals.

Groups can serve an error-checking function for individuals *if* they generate sufficient numbers of new arguments that individuals in the group had not previously heard. The number of new arguments generated by a group can be affected by many factors, one of which is the structure of the discussion. The conservatism bias is reduced on simple mathematical tasks in nominal groups as compared to interacting groups (Brightman, Lewis, & Verhoeven, 1983). As nominal groups tend to generate more ideas than freely interacting groups, such a finding is not surprising. Nonetheless, even the nominal groups do not achieve optimal opinion revision. Although nominal groups *approach* more closely the optimal Bayesian opinion, they are doing so by generating more data to reach the opinion revision that should have occurred with the first datum. Thus the reduction in the conservatism bias is a function of the number of arguments introduced rather than an alteration in the actual process by which information is processed.

Although the results strongly support the persuasive arguments explanation of the choice shift under the constraint that this explanation is the embodiment of the conservatism effect in a group setting, social comparison processes may still influence the process. The regression results suggest that repetitions of arguments and agreements to arguments are the strongest predictors of shifts in risk. As these types of utterances provide no new information at an argument level and seem to provide information about the positions of individuals, the social comparison process may be operative *only* after the introduction of arguments. In other words, new information is necessary to create choice shifts and social comparison processes determine the direction of those shifts. Thus the ratio of risk to caution arguments is less important than the ratio of agreements or repeats of risky versus cautious arguments. In Bayesian terms, the new argument would serve as a datum and the agreements or repeats of that argument would determine its reliability. Consequently, initial opinions would be revised in accordance with the number of arguments as well as the support those arguments generated in terms of agreements and repeats. The failure to detect choice shifts in the constant information environment does not dispute this reasoning; rather, the lack of introduction of new data prevents social comparison information from having any impact in terms of assessing reliability of data. Clearly, further research would be useful to test this reasoning.

When the information environment is not constant, individuals can come to the discussion with different initial opinions. Upon the receipt of new information, individuals may revise their opinions, though the revised opinions may still not converge due to different initial opinions. As a result, the same argument may have a different impact for each individual, thereby requiring employment of other tactics to achieve a group decision. The increased reliance on coercive utterances to achieve consensus in decision making may be an indication of the employment of such tactics. When groups made decisions in the nonconstant information environment, they were far more likely to employ coercive utterances than groups who made decisions with an *invariant* initial opinion across group members. Given the differential impact the arguments might have on opinion revision, the increased use of coercive tactics may be the means for achieving group consensus through means other than opinion revision. Many of the admissions of conformity were of the form "O.K., I guess I'll go along" rather than "I've really changed my mind" or "I see your point of view so I'll change." It is possible that when groups have to achieve consensus and initial opinions vary markedly among group members that coercive tactics are employed to reach the decision though individuals' personal opinions are not changed. To test this reasoning, individual odds assessments would have to be obtained after the group discussion as well as prior to the discussion. As the postdiscussion odds were not a focus in this study, they were not collected. Consequently, this reasoning presents a hypothesis that could be tested in future research.

In the few instances in which choice shifts occurred in the constant information environment, these shifts more closely approached the optimal estimate for the revised opinion, though the conservatism effect was still apparent. The concentration of these shifts in the range of the higher base rates may reflect unique information processing biases of groups as compared to individuals. What is interesting is that the more confident the group is of the initial opinion (high base rate), the more accurately they employ new data. This finding is in stark contrast to "group-think" effects in which groups ignore information contrary to their point of view. Given that extremely high cohesiveness is a necessary condition for the occurrence of group-think, groups that are moderately or mildly cohesive may respond to contrary information in much different and more accurate ways. In other words, moderately or mildly cohesive groups better understand the diagnosticity of contrary information and integrate this information into their decisions in contrast to very highly cohesive groups that reject contrary information. (Although no measure of cohesiveness is available in this research, the groups were not zero-history groups; the group members did know each other through normal classroom interaction and were working with each other in a project group.) Again, this ability to integrate the information in ways significantly different than individuals is a function of initial opinions being strongly held.

In conclusion, groups process information in much the same manner as individuals, revising their opinions upon the receipt of new information in a conservative manner. Choice shifts in risk are the likely result of a sufficient number of new arguments being presented in conjunction with support through repetition or agreement indicating the direction of the shifts. However, these shifts do not lead the group to an optimal decision given the information it has at hand. Rather, groups can more closely approach the optimal decision than do individuals if the necessary arguments and supportive statements are provided. Thus risky shift isn't really risky and cautious shift isn't really cautious. The group is serving an error-checking function for the conservatism of individual processing, though the group itself suffers from the same conservatism as individuals. The persuasive arguments explanation of the choice shift is dependent upon the conservatism of human information processing and, if our reasoning is correct, would require a sufficient number of new arguments to be presented to create the shift expected optimally with one new argument. The role of social comparison processes in choice shift effects appears to be a minor one if it exists at all, though it is possible that social comparison processes are important for determining the direction of the shift and for achieving consensus when individuals have varying initial opinions.

REFERENCES

Ajzen, I., & Fishbein, M. (1978). Use and misuse of Bayes' theorem in causal attribution: Don't attribute it to Ajzen and Fishbein either. *Psychological Bulletin, 85,* 244-246.

Alderton, S. M. & Frey, L. R. (1983). Effects of reactions to arguments on group outcome: The case of group polarization. *Central States Speech Journal, 34,* 86-95.

Boster, F. J. & Mayer, M. E. (1984a, May). *Differential argument quality mediates the impact of a social comparison process of the choice shift.* Paper presented at the International Communication Association Convention, San Francisco.

Boster, F. J., & Mayer, M. E. (1984b). Choice Shifts: Argument qualities or social comparisons. In R. Bostrom (Ed.), *Communication yearbook 8* (pp. 393-410). Beverly Hills, CA: Sage.

Brightman, H. J., Lewis, D. J., & Verhoeven, P. (1983). Nominal and interacting groups as Bayesian information processors. *Psychological Reports, 53,* 101-102.

Burnstein, E., & Vinokur, A. (1973). Testing two classes of theories about group induced shifts in individual choice. *Journal of Experimental Social Psychology, 9,* 123-137.

Burnstein, E., & Vinokur, A. (1975). What a person thinks upon learning he has chosen differently from others: Nice evidence for the persuasive arguments explanation of choice shifts. *Journal of Experimental Social Psychology, 11,* 412-426.

Burnstein, E., Vinokur, A., & Trope, Y. (1973). Interpersonal comparison versus persuasive argumentation: A more direct test of alternative explanations for group induced shifts in individual choice. *Journal of Experimental Social Psychology, 9,* 236-245.

Cline, R. J. & Cline, T. R. (1980). A structural analysis of risky-shift and cautious-shift discussions: The diffusion-of-responsibility theory. *Communication Quarterly, 28,*26-36.

Cartwright, D. (1971). Risk taking by individuals and groups: An assessment of research employing choice dilemmas. *Journal of Personality and Social Psychology, 20,* 361-378.

Chapko, M. K., & Solomon, H. (1974). The cross-situational validity of risk as a value. *Memory & Cognition, 2,* 497-500.

Cohen, L. J. (1979). On the psychology of prediction: Whose is the fallacy? *Cognition, 7,* 385-407.

Cohen, L. J. (1980). Whose is the fallacy? A rejoinder to Daniel Kahneman and Amos Tversky. *Cognition, 8*, 89-92.

Dion, K. L., Baron, R. S., & Miller, N. (1970). Why do groups make riskier decisions than individuals? In L. Berkowitz (Ed.), *Advances in experimental social psychology* (Vol. 5., pp. 305-377). New York: Academic Press.

Edwards, W. (1968). Conservatism in human information processing. In B. Kleinmuntz (Ed.), *Formal representations of human judgment* (pp. 17-52). New York: John Wiley.

Fischer, D. G., McDowell, R., & Boulanger, F. (1976). Initial position, ratio of arguments, and individual shifts in decision. *Journal of Social Psychology, 99*, 145-146.

Fischhoff, B., & Lichtenstein, S. (1978). Don't attribute this to Reverend Bayes. *Psychological Bulletin, 85*, 239-243.

Forgas, J. P. (1981). Responsibility attribution by groups and individuals: The effects of interaction episode. *European Journal of Social Psychology, 11*, 87-99.

Goethals, G. R., & Zanna, M. P. (1979). The role of social comparison in choice shifts. *Journal of Personality and Social Psychology, 37*, 1469-1476.

Hale, J. L. (1984, May). *The effect of ambiguity on polarity shift processes.* Paper presented at the International Communication Association, San Francisco.

Jellison, J. M., & Riskand, J. (1970). A social comparison of abilities interpretation of risk-taking behavior. *Journal of Personality and Social Psychology, 15*, 375-390.

Kahneman, D., Slovic, P., & Tversky, A. (Eds.). (1982). *Judgement under uncertainty: Heuristics and biases.* Cambridge: Cambridge University Press.

Lamm, H., & Myers, D. G. (1978). Group-induced polarization of attitudes and behavior. In L. Berkowitz (Ed.), *Advances in experimental social psychology* (Vol. 11). New York: Academic press.

Laughlin, P. R., & Earley, P. C. (1982). Social combination models, persuasive arguments theory, social comparison theory, and choice shift. *Journal of Personality and Social Psychology, 42*, 273-280.

Mackie, D., & Cooper, J. (1984). Attitude polarization: Effects of group membership. *Journal of Personality and Social Psychology, 48*, 575-585.

Mayer, M. E. (1986). Explaining choice shift: A comparison of competing effects coded models. In M. L. Mc Laughlin (Ed.), *Communication Yearbook 9* (pp. 297-314). Beverly Hills, CA: Sage.

Miller, N. (1978). A questionnaire in search of a theory. In L. Berkowitz (Ed.), *Group processes* (pp. 301-312). New York: Academic Press.

Murningham, J. K., & Castore, C. H. (1975). An experimental test of three choice shift hypotheses. *Memory & Cognition, 3*, 171-174.

Myers, D. G., & Kaplan, M. F. (1976). Group-induced polarization in simulated juries. *Personality and Social Psychology Bulletin, 2*, 63-66.

Myers, D. G. & Lamm, H. (1976). The group polarization phenomenon. *Psychological Bulletin, 83*, 602-627.

Navon, D. (1978). The importance of being conservative: Some reflections on human Bayesian behavior. *British Journal of Mathematical and Statistical Psychology, 31*, 33-48.

Navon, D. (1981). Statistical and metastatistical considerations in analysing the desirability of human Bayesian conservatism. *British Journal of Mathematical and Statistical Psychology, 34*, 205-212.

Nisbett, R., & Ross, L. (1980). *Human inference: Strategies and shortcomings of social judgment.* Englewood Cliffs: Prentice-Hall.

Peterson, C. R., Schneider, R. J., & Miller, A. J. (1965). Sample size and the revision of subjective probabilities. *Journal of Experimental Psychology, 69*, 522-527.

Phillips, L. D., & Edwards, W. (1966). Conservatism in a simple probability inference task. *Journal of Experimental Psychology, 72*, 346-357.

Pruitt, D. (1971a). Conclusions: Toward an understanding of choice shifts in group discussion. *Journal of Personality and Social Psychology, 20*, 495-510.

Pruitt, D. (1971b). Choice shifts in group discussion: An introductory review. *Journal of Personality and Social Psychology, 20*, 339-360.

Rim, Y. (1982). Personality and risky shift in a passive audience. *Personality and Individual Differences, 3*, 465-467.

Sanders, G. S., & Baron, R. S. (1977). Is social comparison irrelevant for producing choice shifts? *Journal of Experimental Social Psychology, 13,* 303-314.

Seeborg, I., Lafollete, W., & Belohlav, J. (1980). An exploratory analysis of effect of sex on shift in choices. *Psychological Reports, 46,* 499-504.

Shafer, G. (1976). *A mathematical theory of evidence.* Princeton: Princeton University Press.

Slovic, P., Fischoff, B., & Lichtenstein, S. (1977). Behavioral decision theory. *Annual Review of Psychology, 28,* 1-39.

Slovic, P., & Lichtenstein, S. (1971). Comparison of Bayesian and regression approaches to the study of information processing in judgment. *Organizational Behavior and Human Performance, 6,* 649-744.

Stoner, J. A. F. (1961). *A comparison of individual and group decisions involving risk.* Unpublished Master's thesis, Massachusetts Institute of Technology, School of Industrial Management.

Teger, A. I., & Pruitt, D. G. (1967). Components of group risk taking. *Journal of Experimental Social Psychology, 3,* 189-205.

Vinokur, A., & Burnstein, E. (1974). Effects of partially shared persuasive arguments on group induced shifts: A group problem solving approach. *Journal of Personality and Social Psychology, 29,* 305-315.

Vinokur, A., Trope, Y., & Burnstein, E. (1975). A decision making analysis of persuasive argumentation and the choice shift effect. *Journal of Experimental Social Psychology, 11,* 127-148.

Williams, P. M. (1978). On a new theory of epistemic probability. *British Journal for the Philosophy of Science, 29,* 375-387.

Zaleski, A. (1980). The influence of group cohesiveness, type of communication, and the content of decision tasks on risk polarization. *Rocznitzi Fliozuficzne, 28,* 27-58.

III ● INTERPERSONAL COMMUNICATION

12 ● Communication Network Involvement in Adolescents' Friendships and Romantic Relationships

LEONA L. EGGERT ● MALCOLM R. PARKS

University of Washington

F RIENDSHIPS and romantic relationships are especially important during adolescence for managing self-identity, intimacy, and other developmental issues (Bell, 1981; Douvan & Adelson, 1966; Erikson, 1968; Thornburg, 1975). But, it is not enough to explain friendships and romances solely as functions of identity management; nor is it sufficient to use a two-person model, for these intimate relationships do not develop in a vacuum (Parks, Stan, & Eggert, 1983). They are "set in a nexus of other relationships, and may be influenced by the relationships that each participant has with other individuals" (Hinde, 1981, p. 15). Accordingly, this study considers the role of one social structural phenomenon, *communication networks,* in the development of adolescents' personal relationships. Particularly, it compares the associations between communication network involvement and the dynamics of two types of personal relationships: adolescents' close same-sex friendships vis-à-vis their cross-sex romantic relationships. Its central hypothesis is that the

AUTHORS' NOTE: We are indebted to Jerald R. Herting for his assistance with the LISREL procedures. We would also like to thank Darwin Bullock, Gordon Dickman, Sally Hooper, Barbara Linck, Liela Nicholas, Steffany Raynes, Barbara Velategui, and William Wortman for their assistance in gathering the data. This chapter is based on the doctoral dissertation of the first author, completed under the direction of the second author.

Correspondence and requests for reprints: Leona L. Eggert, Department of Psychosocial Nursing SC-76, University of Washington, Seattle, WA 98195.

dynamics of adolescents' existing friendship and romantic relationships are positively and reciprocally associated with communication network involvement (Duck & Gilmour, 1981b; Parks, Stan, & Eggert, 1983; Ridley & Avery, 1979).

Moreover, the consensus among scholars calls for urgently needed empirical tests of both existing relationship development models, and of their applicability to different life-cycle age groups (Dickens & Perlman, 1981; Kimmel, 1979; Kon, 1981a; Kon & Losenkov, 1978; LaGaipa, 1981; Parks, 1982). For example, Kimmel (1979) asserts that relevant dimensions of personal relationships change with age; yet it is still unclear which dimensions change or remain constant throughout the life cycle and across types of personal relationships (Duck & Gilmour, 1981b; Parks, Stan, & Eggert, 1983). Thus this study pursues two questions: (1) What similarities and differences exist in the nature and evolution of adolescents' close friendships and romantic relationships in social context? (2) How do these two types of relationships compare with existing theories of personal relationship development and network involvement?

It should be stated at the outset that the present study is limited to findings of association between network involvement and relational development. Even though these linkages are likely causal and nonrecursive, the first step in constructing theory, of necessity, is confirming or disconfirming the general pattern found by Parks, Stan, and Eggert (1983). In the present context this means respecifying and testing the model *across relationship types* and *across the life cycle*.

Investigators from interpersonal communication, personal relationship, and network perspectives currently acknowledge the need to link their theories, thereby dealing with both dyadic relationships and their embeddedness in social contexts (Befu, 1977; Duck, 1980; Feld & Elmore, 1982a; LaGaipa, 1981a; Parks & Adelman, 1983; Parks, Stan, & Eggert, 1983; Ridley & Avery, 1979; Wellman, 1981). Hence, in specifying a theoretic model, we integrate these perspectives, progressing in three major sections. We consider first how relational development is defined. Then we define network involvement and identify a set of interrelated factors for further analysis. Finally, we hypothesize how each of the network involvement factors might be linked with the elements of relational development. We draw on the principle of *transitivity* from network theory for bridging the personal relationship and communication network levels of analysis, thus linking micro and macro levels of analysis.

Conceptualizing Relational Development

This dimension requires a broad conceptualization and multiple indicators to overcome past measurement problems of exclusive or narrow foci. Generally, personal relationships become close by moving from nonpersonal interaction, to interpersonal attraction and intimacy, to commitment.

This is congruent with models of social penetration (Altman & Taylor, 1970); social exchange (Braiker & Kelley, 1979; Burgess, 1981; Burgess & Huston, 1979) and developmental models of interpersonal attraction (Berscheid & Walster, 1978; Byrne, 1971), interpersonal communication and uncertainty reduction (Berger & Calabrese, 1975; Miller & Steinberg, 1975). Hence we defined relational development as a global latent variable comprised of three interrelated factors: (1) sociability, (2) intimacy, and (3) commitment. As a set the three elements represent the level of development and strength of adolescents' close relationships; as discrete dimensions they deal with how dyads interact and communicate and with the attributions they make about their feelings for each other and their relationship. These elements were explicated further by multiple indicators.

Indicators of the *sociability* dimension included both the percentages of free time spent together, and the frequency of communication with each other (Dunphy, 1963; Gold & Douvan, 1969; Hinde, 1981; Homans, 1979; Parks & Adelman, 1983). Second, empirical evidence suggests that the *intimacy* dimension should be manifest by levels of perceived similarity (Bersheid & Walster, 1969; Byrne, 1971; Duck, 1980; Gold & Douvan, 1969; Griffitt & Veitch, 1974; Kandel 1978a, 1978b; Levinger, 1979; Murstein, 1976), decreased uncertainty (Berger & Calebrese, 1975), satisfying interactions (Hecht, 1978; Kon, 1981; Larson, 1982), liking, love, and interpersonal solidarity (Bersheid & Walster, 1974; Hill, Rubin, & Peplau, 1976; Rubin, 1970, 1974; Walster & Walster, 1978; Wheeless, 1976). Finally, the *commitment* dimension should be reflected by attributions the pair make of the enduring nature and attachment of their relationship (Hinde, 1981; Levinger, Senn, & Jorgensen, 1970; Parks, Stan, & Eggert, 1983).

In general, then, we should be able to assess the growth of adolescents' personal relationships by a *pattern* of frequent, face-to-face and satisfying interactions—characterized by reductions in uncertainty about each other and repeated exchanges of companionship or shared activities, intimate self-presentation, liking, and love—among persons similar in nature. Further, relational commitment could be reflected by expressed expectations for a continued friendship or dating relationship. We presumed that there would be strong positive associations among the sociability, intimacy, and commitment elements (Berndt, 1982; Bigelow & LaGaipa, 1980; Homans, 1950: La Gaipa, 1981b; Larson, 1982; McCall & Simmons, 1978).

Conceptualizing Network Involvement

This dimension defines the *structure* of the network under study; in the present context, this consists of the adolescent's own network of close family and other close friends, and his or her partner's network of close family and other close friends. Thus it deals with "the delivery system for the giving and receiving of different supports" (La Gaipa, 1981a, p. 82) from these four sectors. We presumed this delivery system was a communication system—that is, that the factors of network involvement would be functions of communication between the dyads and persons in each others' networks. Network involvement was thus defined here by four communication-based factors including (1) levels of attraction, (2) range of communication contacts; (3) levels of expressed support from the partner's network of family and friends; and (4) levels of expressed support from the subject's own network of family and friends. Because these factors were significantly linked with the internal dynamics of relational development in the Parks, Stan, and Eggert (1983) study, they were used to conceptualize communication network involvement here. Multiple indicators were used for each of these four factors.

We also predicted that the four network involvement factors would link positively with each other. Parks, Stan, and Eggert (1983) concluded that "factors like attraction, support, and communication exhibited complex indirect associations with romantic involvement" (p. 128). The interrelatedness of the network factors was explained by interpersonal attraction and communication, reinforcing social exchanges, and cognitive consistency. Similarly, we posit here that adolescents' affiliation and cognitive consistency needs should influence perceived attraction, range of communication contact, and support from the partner's network. Also, support from the adolescents' own parents is expected because they are generally reinforcing of their offspring's friendships and dating relationships to promote autonomy (Campbell, 1975). This, in turn, may serve to bolster the adolescents' confidence or color their perception, fostering positive associations among the factors related to the partners' network. Furthermore, the adolescents' "wishful thinking" may lead to a biased perception of networkwide support because diverging perceptions of support represent conflict and would therefore create cognitive dissonance.

Linking Relational Development and
Communication Network Involvement

The principle of transitivity supplies one answer to the question of how the dynamics of any particular personal relationship are associated with the dynamics of other relationships within the pair's network. Transitivity, a mathematical term, posits that if person A likes person B and B likes person C, then A will come to like C. Thus the AC relationship is a product of the AB friendship and the A< - - >C tie is predicted to be transitive.

Transitivity has been used to explain a wide range of sentiment relationships and network structures (Bishop, 1979; Davis & Leinhardt, 1972; Hallinan & Felmlee, 1975; Holland & Leinhardt, 1970). However, why transitivity occurs at all has not been explained well. Cognitive balance

(Heider, 1946, 1958) is the most popular explanation, but network researchers and others suggest that multiple social processes are more likely causes of transitivity (Davis, 1979; Feld & Elmore, 1982; Granovetter, 1973, 1980; Hallinan, 1982). Parks, Stan, and Eggert (1983), for example, explained transitivity in terms of social reinforcement, uncertainty reduction, information exchanges, satisfaction of social expectations, barrier forces, and opportunities of joint interaction. Moreover, La Gaipa (1981a) claims that dyadic relationships and each of the pair's other personal relationships in their social systems are influenced or constrained by variables at three levels: psychological or individual, interpersonal or behavioral, and cultural-normative. Hence, variables at these three levels can be conceived of as determinants of transitivity; and in the present context, those chosen for inclusion are (1) at the cultural level—bonding and barrier forces such as social norms demanding network interaction and positive sentiments; (2) at the interpersonal level—shared activities and satisfying interactions, shared information, and relational reinforcement; and (3) at the individual level—affiliation needs, personal goals, and cognitive balance. These determinants will thus be used to explain potential linkages between network involvement and relational development.

Hypotheses advanced in this section will link each network involvement factor, in turn, with dyadic relational development. We posit they apply to both adolescents' same-sex best friendships and opposite-sex romantic relationships (hereafter, simply *friendships* and *dating relationships*).

Network attraction and relational development. Transitivity may result, first, from two important individual antecedents: the *affiliation needs* of A's and C's relevant *resources*. Schachter (1974) posits that a person's inclusion and affiliation needs are core motivators of sociability, promoting interpersonal attraction and relationship formation; and friendliness was one substantive explanation for transitivity proffered by Hallinan and Felmlee (1975) and Feld and Elmore (1982a). Transitivity also could arise if C is able to provide relevant resources satisfying A's personal goals (La Gaipa, 1981a, 1981b; Schachter, 1974). From a social exchange framework, transitivity would be a function of the reward/cost ratio in the AC relationship compared with available alternative AC relationships in B's network. Additionally, affiliation and filter theories predict an association between C's attractiveness and similarity between A and C (Burt, 1978; Granovetter, 1973).

Attraction principles and personal motives take on additional meaning when cast in the dyadic AB relationship context. First, B's network members may provide an entrée to an attractive new social circle with potential rewards (Granovetter, 1973, 1980). A could also be attracted to B's friends and family to gain their approval, thereby enhancing the AB relationship. Also, attraction and the notion of transitivity stems from balance or consistency theories (Festinger, 1957; Heider, 1958; Newcomb, 1968). These

theories all posit that unbalanced or inconsistent bonds in sentiment relationships produce psychological distress, creating pressure in individuals to
alter their attitudes toward cognitive consistency. Thus

> *H1:* The elements of relational development and the perceived level of
> attraction for members in the partner's network will be positively
> associated.

Range of network communication and relational development. Transitivity also may occur as a result of satisfying interactions and shared information with network members. It seems logical that as a dyad mutually
invests in their togetherness, this commitment should include meeting a
wider range of network members and interacting with them. Parks (1982)
argued that through interaction with ties, such as those between friends of
friends, opportunities can emerge for social comparison and tangible
resources. And "as the frequency of interaction between two or more persons increases, the degree of their liking for one another will increase and
vice versa" (Homans, 1950, p. 112), contributing to transitivity. Intuitively,
it makes sense that as the friendship or dating relationship develops in
breadth and depth, A will expect to meet B's friends and family. By way of
contrast, when this expectation is not met, uncertainty is likely to become
greater, leading to possible dissolution of the AB relationship. Communicating with an increasing range of contacts in B's network is a potentially
rich source of information exchange, helping A gain more understanding
of B (Berger, 1979, 1982; Parks & Adelman, 1983). Berger's (1979)
theory also predicts that A will communicate more with B's network members because they have the potential to support or oppose the AB relationship, and because of expected future interactions. Hence, we posit:

> *H2:* The elements of relational development and range of communication
> in the partner's network will be positively associated.

Network support and relational development. Possibly one of the most
important causes of transitivity, from a reinforcement or rewards perspective, is the support or nonsupport that network members provide a dyad.
Lewis (1973) found that the more family and friends supported a given
couple, the greater the couple's commitment to each other. It seems logical
that many of these same "bonding" and "barrier forces" also would occur
to support adolescents' friendship relationships. Campbell (1975) contends that parents' initial reservations about their adolescent's friends or
dates may be withheld because of a greater desire to see their offspring
experience close friendships and dating relationships. In fact, Parks, Stan,
and Eggert (1983) found that the partner's family did greet new relationships with neutral or positive support; and Driscoll, Davis, and Lipetz

(1972) speculated that once a pair are committed, more support from family and friends emerges. Thus network support can influence personal relationship development; conversely, committed personal relationships can elicit network support (Parks, Stan, & Eggert, 1983). Milardo (1982) found greater pair involvement associated with an increased number of shared friends who later became close friends. This shared network also can serve as a "barrier force" for a dyad, making dissolution more difficult (Levinger, 1979; Milardo, 1982). Furthermore, network ties may come packaged with norms and family rules or expectations for shared activities and inclusion (Homans, 1979; Wellman, 1981). Thus these reasons for transitivity suggest:

H3: The elements of relational development will associate positively with the levels of support from the adolescent's own network of close family and friends; and

H4: The elements of relational development will associate positively with the levels of support from the partner's network of close family and friends.

Comparing Friendships and Romantic Relationships

In the previous section we advanced four hypotheses predicting the same dynamics between the four network involvement factors and the relational development factors in both relationship types. Here we speculate that differences should occur in the strength of some links between specific elements of relational development (for example, intimacy and commitment) and specific network factors (for example, network support) across the two relationship types.

Given our conceptualization of the internal dynamics of relational development, we would expect commitment to be a function of the rewards and costs of the sociability and intimacy elements—among both close friends and dating partners. But, the *intimacy* and *commitment* factors may be two of the most important dynamics, varying in amount in different relationships (Weiss, 1974). This is because (1) individuals become attached to particular others, in (2) role-identified relationships having specific assumptive bases (McCall & Simmons, 1978, p. 171-172). Although the trajectory in dating relationships is generally conceded to be toward "falling in love," friendships are not necessarily intimacy-bound in the same fashion (Delia, 1980; Kon, 1981). Even though role expectations for emotional attachments are strong and like love in friendships (Kon, 1981), these expectations are typically transferred to heterosexual relationships during late (age 17-18 years) adolescence (Dickens & Perlman, 1981; Douvan & Adelson, 1966; Wright, 1981). This could mean that levels of the intimacy and commitment elements may differentially define the two relationship types, resulting in different measurement models for friendships and dating relationships.

Moreover, dating relationships may have more network involvement influencing the relational elements, thus resulting in different structural associations between the dyadic and network factors. The potential for marriage in dating relationships and its consequences for family structure may be a key determinant. This may mean that social contexts and shared social role expectations, expressed particularly in terms of *network support* and *approval,* may influence especially the links between *commitment and network support.* However, we thought advancing hypotheses at this point was highly speculative because empirical data about bonding in adolescents' friendships versus romances is scarce and contradictory (Kon, 1981). Thus we undertook an exploratory comparison of links between all three developmental factors and network involvement, asking:

> Will the dynamics of relational development and communication network involvement covary in significantly different ways in adolescents' friendships and dating relationships?

In sum, our central hypothesis is that a strong, positive association exists between dyadic relational development and communication network involvement in both adolescents' friendship and dating pairs. First, we defined relational development as three interrelated elements, positing that the same three internal dynamics would exist and define patterns of dyadic development in both adolescents' close friendships and dating relationships. Second, we defined communication network involvement by four factors, positing an interrelated set of factors in both relationship types. Third, we predicted the same positive associations between four elements of communication network involvement and the three elements of dyadic formation in both relationship types. Finally, we suggested that differences might occur across adolescents' friendships and romantic relationships, warranting exploratory comparisons.

METHOD

Subjects

Subjects were drawn from two high schools in a predominantly white, middle-class community. Approximately 400 adolescents were surveyed in 16 different classrooms, tapping a range of college-bound and noncollege-bound students. Available for the present study were 338 (an 85% return) completed questionnaires: 204 about a current best friendship (69 males, 135 females) and 134 about a current dating relationship

(46 males, 88 females). Both friendships and dating relationships were characterized by a wide range of closeness, exclusivity, and relationship growth. For example, the duration of friendships ranged from less than 2 weeks to 156 months, but was positively skewed (Mdn = 13.37 months). In contrast, the average duration of the dating relationships was half that of the friendships, ranging from less than two weeks to 72 months, but also positively skewed (Mdn = 6.25 months). The typical adolescent was 16.77 years (SD = .94) in the friendship group and 17.18 years (SD = .78) in the dating group. They described themselves as Protestant (Friends = 64%; Dating = 43%), Catholic (Friends = 27%; Dating = 29%), or as having no religious preference (Friends = 24%; Dating = 19%).

Procedures

Data were collected by making the survey an integral part of a classroom unit on "Ways of Knowing in the Social Sciences." The adolescents were first instructed in their rights as subjects; then they answered a survey questionnaire as an experiential exercise in understanding how data are collected. The use of any student's questionnaire was voluntary; informed consent was sought from both the students and their parents.

Data collection occurred over three consecutive days to accommodate an extensive five-part questionnaire. First, students were requested to list their four closest family or relatives and their eight closest friends. They were instructed to obtain a similar list of names from their best friend or dating partner. These two lists produced a four-sector, 24-person communication network for each subject: their own and their partner's closest family and nonkin contacts. Students then completed questions measuring the perceived support, and attraction to each known network member, thus also revealing the range of communication in the partner's network. Other parts of the questionnaire measured the affective and cognitive indicators and demographics serving to describe the sample and their personal relationships.

MEASUREMENT

Relational Development

We conceptualized relational development in terms of three unobserved, interrelated elements: sociability, intimacy, and commitment. Ten indicators were used to measure these three elements.

Sociability was observed by two indicators: the percentage of free time the pair spent together (0-100%) in the past two weeks, and the amount of interaction—the number of days—in the past two weeks (0-14) in which face-to-face communication occurred.

Intimacy was measured by six scaled indicators; responses were recorded on five-point Likert items and summed to produce a total scale score for each indicator. Rubin's (1970) love and liking scales (yielding scores ranging from 13-65 for each) were used to assess emotional attachment in the relationships. Wheeless's (1976) interpersonal solidarity scale (ranging from 10-50) was used as a global indicator measuring the general strength of the relational bond. Three additional scales also reflected relational intimacy: Parks, Stan, and Eggert's (1983) scale of perceived similarity (yielding scores ranging from 5-25); Parks's (1978) scale of relational uncertainty (ranging from 5-40); and Hecht's (1978) scale of communication satisfaction (ranging from 19-95). In each scale, higher scores represent greater intimacy in friendship and dating relationships.

Commitment or the extent to which the relationship was expected to continue was measured by two indicators asking the subject to estimate (1) the probability (0-100%) that the relationship would continue for three more months and (2) the probability (0-100%) that the relationship would result in marriage in dating relationships, or being "friends forever" in friendships.

Communication Network Involvement

We conceptualized communication network involvement as four unobserved, interrelated elements: the expressed support from the subject's own network; expressed support from the partner's network; attraction to members of the partner's network; and the range of communication contact with the partner's network. We used 10 manifest indicators to measure these factors of network involvement.

Support from the adolescent's own network was measured by two five-point Likert scales: A response to the first item, "this person does not (or would not) approve of my current best friend" was reversed and added to the response from "this person has often expressed approval or support for my relationship with my best friend." This yielded a scale score ranging from 2 to 10 for each of the 12 network members. Two final measures were derived (1) a mean support score (2-10) created by averaging the four individual scores for family and relatives; and (2) a mean support score (2-10) created by averaging the individual scores from the 8 network friends. Each final score reflected an opposition-support continuum with higher scores indicating greater support.

Support from the partner's network was measured by similar methods used for obtaining the support scores from the adolescent's own network. Subjects responded to the same statements noted above for each person they had actually met in the partner's network. Thus scores were averaged across the appropriate groups to produce two final measures: (1) the average perceived support from known members in the partner's family (2-10), and (2) the average perceived support from known persons among the partner's friends (2-10). Again, higher scores represent greater support.

Attraction to members of the partner's network was assessed in terms of agreement with two items: "I like this person a lot" and "I feel very close to this person." Again, five-point scales were used and subjects responded only to known members in the partner's total network. These responses were averaged to produce two final indicators: (1) the average level of attraction to the partner's known family members (2-10), and (2) the average level of attraction to the partner's friendship network (2-10). Higher scores represent greater levels of attraction.

Range of communication in the partner's network was measured by two indicators: (1) the number of known family members (0-4) in the partner's network, and (2) the number of known friends (0-8) in the partner's network. Again, higher scores indicate a greater range of communication contacts, implying that the subject knew and interacted with more members of his or her partner's network.

RESULTS

Preliminary Analyses

Several preliminary analyses were conducted in preparation for using a confirmatory factor analysis as the essential analytic procedure in this study. First, reliability estimates were obtained for multi-item scales in the model. Almost all indicators appeared to have acceptable internal consistency. Second, distributional analyses served to describe the adolescents' best friendships and dating relationships, and established an acceptable multivariate normal distribution for the model indicators—a necessary condition for proceeding with the LISREL analysis. Third, the zero-order correlation matrices for both relationship types were analyzed and are presented here in Table 12.1. All 18 model indicators are included; they are divided according to the relational development and network factors specified in the theoretic model.

The Confirmatory Factor Analysis

Confirmatory factor analysis, using Joreskog and Sorbom's LISREL V/VI (1983), was the primary analytic procedure. It was used to estimate (1) the measurement model of links between the latent factors and the observed manifest indicators for each factor, and (2) the structural model of associations among the unobserved elements of relational development and network involvement. Hypotheses thus became associations between the dimensions of relational development and communication involvement.

Table 12.1
Zero-Order Correlation Coefficients Among All Indicators: for Both DATING and FRIENDSHIP Groups

Indicator	1	2	3	4	5	6	7	8	9	10	11	12	13	14	15	16	17	18
X1 Percentage of free time spent together	1.00[a]																	
	1.00																	
X2 Communication frequency with partner	.67	1.00																
	.43	1.00																
X3 Perceived similarity	.02	-.00	1.00															
	.18	.08	1.00															
X4 Uncertainty (Parks, 1978)	-.14	-.12	-.27	1.00														
	-.06	-.06	-.21	1.00														
X5 Communication satisfaction (Hecht, 1978)	.08	-.05	.51	-.40	1.00													
	.15	.05	.45	-.40	1.00													
X6 Interpersonal solidarity (Wheeless, 1976)	.19	.13	.44	-.36	.66	1.00												
	.27	.07	.48	-.38	.62	1.00												
X7 Love (Rubin, 1970)	.16	.12	.57	-.34	.59	.73	1.00											
	.18	-.02	.36	-.31	.54	.68	1.00											
X8 Liking (Rubin, 1970)	.06	.05	.68	-.34	.57	.48	.58	1.00										
	.13	-.08	.61	-.34	.58	.55	.55	1.00										
X9 Probability relationship lasts for 3 more months	.18	-.05	.31	-.12	.17	.26	.26	.24	1.00									
	.17	.13	.21	-.28	.27	.28	.17	.16	1.00									
X10 Probability of marriage/ being friends forever	.28	.11	.35	-.28	.14	.32	.27	.27	.47	1.00								
	.02	.03	.17	-.24	.27	.31	.24	.21	.42	1.00								

Variable	Group	Coefficients
X11 Support from own family	Dating	.10 .09 .26 −.14 .27 .27 .11 .13 .21 −.02 .11 1.00
	Friendship	.08 .02 .25 −.20 .27 .30 .29 .34 .23 .22 1.00
X12 Support from own friends	Dating	.23 .17 .33 −.28 .34 .16 .25 .26 .08 .21 .46 1.00
	Friendship	.21 .06 .33 −.20 .31 .31 .35 .40 .25 .23 .62 1.00
X13 Support from partner's family network	Dating	.03 −.07 .27 −.27 .27 .19 .26 .21 .25 .21 .23 .41 1.00
	Friendship	.16 .07 .13 −.29 .19 .16 .17 .07 .23 .27 .35 .37 1.00
X14 Support from partner's friendship network	Dating	.27 .09 .42 −.24 .37 .33 .40 .32 .18 .32 .24 .62 .45 1.00
	Friendship	.18 .14 .32 −.15 .25 .30 .27 .24 .19 .19 .44 .55 .44 1.00
X15 Range of contact in partner's family	Dating	.08 −.02 −.16 .05 −.05 −.01 −.08 −.10 .12 .03 −.00 .13 −.11 .04 1.00
	Friendship	.01 .01 −.09 −.16 −.00 .15 .15 −.08 .12 .16 .24 .10 .15 .01 1.00
X16 Range of contact among partner's friends	Dating	.25 .28 −.02 −.05 .17 .19 .04 .07 .08 .10 .05 .27 −.16 .33 1.00
	Friendship	.19 .22 .09 −.05 .10 .22 .04 −.02 .14 .11 .07 .08 .09 .18 .32 1.00
X17 Attraction to partner's family	Dating	.03 −.06 .41 −.25 .31 .39 .43 .49 .29 .35 .20 .36 .31 .12 .14 1.00
	Friendship	.03 −.07 .14 −.30 .14 .20 .23 .16 .15 .42 .25 .26 .45 .21 .03 1.00
X18 Attraction to partner's friends	Dating	.06 .09 .32 −.15 .28 .26 .21 .30 .23 .22 .18 .42 .43 .08 .36 1.00
	Friendship	.16 .21 .18 −.10 .04 .10 .12 .12 .09 .15 .15 .15 .39 −.00 .13 .22 1.00

a. Dating Group coefficients are listed first, Friendship Group coefficients are listed below; N = 134 for Dating Group; N = 204 for Friendship Group: $p < .05$ if $r > .27$; $p < .05$ if $r > .16$; $p < .01$ if $r > .23$; $p < .01$ if $r > .12$; $p < .001$ if $r > .18$, $p < .001$ if $r > .23$.

Assessment and Respecification Procedures

Fitting the theoretic model to the data from both relationship types, test-ing the adequacy of these fits, and comparing the two models entailed a number of assumptions and procedures. We began by estimating the over-all model with the hypothesized links between the factors and an assump-tion of uncorrelated errors for both groups. Although the hypotheses were generally supported, the models were judged as fitting poorly[1] for both relationship types:

Dating group:	Chi-square = 472.14, df = 161, p = .0001
	GFI = 0.705, AGFI = 0.577, RMR = 0.078
Friendships:	Chi-square = 411.45, df = 161, p = .0001
	GFI = 0.786, AGFI = 0.693, RMR = 0.078

Also, unreasonable values in two of the parameter estimates were present in both models. This meant the estimated models were fundamentally wrong in some parameters and required respecification for both groups (Herting & Costner, 1985; Long, 1983).

These results led to an extensive reconstruction process guided by theo-retic considerations and the diagnostics[2] available from each successive LISREL run. This work progressed in two major steps: first, the relational development and network involvement submodels were respecified sepa-rately for each group; and second, the submodels were merged by adding one network dimension at a time to the relational development submodel.[3] Modifications were made one at a time, determining their appropriateness by single degree-of-freedom chi-square tests (Long, 1976), inspections of the goodness-of-fit index (GFI), its adjustment for degrees of freedom (AGFI), and the root mean square residual (RMR). If the difference in chi-square before and after each modification in nested models was significant (that is, > 3.84), and improved goodness-of-fit indices and residuals were evident, then the modification was adopted.[4] Our goal was to improve the goodness-of-fit by adopting modifications that made sense theoreti-cally and successively reduced the chi-square, the GFI, AGFI, and RMR indices.

The respecification procedures led to friendship and dating final models fitting the data very well as evidenced by all indices presented in Table 12.2. Goodness-of-fit criteria were met with both the standardized correlation and unstandardized covariance matrices. Also, in both groups the normal-ized residuals were all less than two; the Q-plot of these residuals fit a straight line, the slope of which was larger than one, further indications of a good fit.[5]

Achieving good fitting final models led to a number of revisions in each model. For the sake of clarity, we organized our discussion in the next sec-

Table 12.2
Overall Goodness-of-Fit: Dating and Friendship Models

Relationship Type	Chi-Square	df	p	GFI	AGFI	RMR
With Correlation Matrix						
Dating relationships	99.69	85	.132	.886	.795	.053
Friendships	94.39	82	.165	.934	.877	.045
With Covariance Matrix						
Dating relationships	99.64	83	.103	—[a]	—	—
Friendships	94.39	80	.130	—	—	—

a. These values as given in the LISREL output when using the covariance matrix are not interpretable and are, thus, omitted here. The same GFI and RMR indices obtained with the correlation matrix would still generally hold.

tions around the major components of the LISREL confirmatory factor model: (1) The measurement models which include a) the associations between indicators and factors, and b) the links among measurement errors; (2) the structural models—i.e. associations among the unmeasured concepts, representing tests of our hypothesized links; and (3) the comparison tests for equality of parameters across the dating and friendship models.

The Measurement Models:
Friendships and Dating Relationships

Associations between indicators and factors. The standardized Lambda X estimates are displayed in Tables 12.3 and 12.4—for friendships and dating relationships respectively. The estimates indicate links between the indicators and their respective dimensions, and can be interpreted like factor loadings in a conventional factor analysis. In both groups, each indicator was significantly related to its dimension; that is, the parameter estimates were at least twice their standard errors;[6] and the total coefficients of determination were 1.0.[7]

Some notable respecifications occurred in achieving good fitting final models. First, the indicator of communication frequency between pairs required multiple shared paths and correlated error terms with many other indicators; including these led to identification problems. A good fit occurred only when this indicator was omitted. One plausible explanation for this respecification was that communication frequency functioned here as a contextual variable—that is, the other factors of relational development were functions of communication frequency and, in effect, were influenced by how much the adolescents interacted with each other.[8]

Second, in both models the interaction time indicator (X1) and the perceived similarity (X2) indicator exhibited "direction of effect specification errors" (Herting & Costner, 1985). Hence, a more realistic conception treats these indicators as factors in their own right, rather than reflectors of

Table 12.3
Lambda × Matrix of Standardized Estimates for Indicators and Factors: Adolescents' Friendships

	Indicator	Factor: Time	Similarity	Intimacy	Commitment	Support: Own Network	Support: Friends' Network	Range of Contacts	Attraction to Friend's Network
X1	% Time spent together	.800 (.000)**	—	—	—	—	—	—	—
X2	Perceived similarity	—	.800 (.000)**	—	—	—	—	—	—
X3	Uncertainty (Parks, 1978)	—	—	-.499 (.070)*	—	—	—	—	—
X4	Communication satisfaction (Hecht, 1978)	—	—	.768 (.063)*	—	—	—	—	—
X5	Interpersonal solidarity (Wheeless, 1976)	—	—	.755 (.065)*	—	—	—	.351 (.063)*	—
X6	Love (Rubin, 1970)	—	—	.715 (.066)*	—	—	—	—	—
X7	Liking (Rubin, 1970)	—	—	.768 (.059)*	—	—	—	—	—
X8	Prob. relationship lasts 3 more months	—	—	—	.624 (.086)*	—	—	—	—
X9	Prob. friends forever	—	—	—	.677 (.087)*	—	—	—	—

X10	Support from own family network	.718 (.066)*	—	—	—
X11	Support from own friendship network	.852 (.065)*	—	—	—
X12	Support from partner's family network	—	.568 (.072)*	—	—
X13	Support from partner's friendship network	—	.773 (.074)*	—	—
X14	Range of contact in partner's family	—	—	.533 (.100)*	—
X15	Range of contact among partner's friends	—	—	.540 (.090)*	—
X16	Attraction to partner's family	—	—	—	.653 (.130)*
X17	Attraction to partner's friends	—	—	—	.305 (.082)*

Note: Stand errors are in parentheses.

* Loading was at least twice its standard error.

** Loadings were fixed at .800, which assumes some measurement error of these single indicators and approximates their epistemic correlations.

Total Coefficient of Determination for all X-Indicators = 1.00.

Table 12.4

Lambda × Matrix of Standardized Estimates for Indicators and Factors: Adolescents' Dating Relationships

| | Factor: | | | | | | | |
Indicator	Time	Similarity	Intimacy	Commitment	Support: Own Network	Support: Friends' Network	Range of Contacts	Attraction to Friend's Network
X1 % Time spent together	.800 (.000)**	—	—	—	—	—	—	—
X2 Perceived similarity	—	.800 (.000)**	—	—	—	—	—	—
X3 Uncertainty (Parks, 1978)	—	—	-.453 (.086)*	—	—	—	—	—
X4 Communication satisfaction (Hecht, 1978)	—	—	.781 (.075)*	—	—	—	—	—
X5 Interpersonal soliddarity (Wheeless, 1976)	—	—	.833 (.071)*	—	—	—	—	—
X6 Love (Rubin, 1970)	—	—	.832 (.070)*	—	—	—	—	—
X7 Liking (Rubin, 1970)	—	—	.658 (.071)*	—	—	—	—	—
X8 Prob. relationship lasts 3 more months	—	—	—	.660 (.095)*	—	—	—	—
X9 Prob. friends forever	—	—	—	.736 (.096)*	—	—	—	—

		Col 1	Col 2	Col 3	Col 4
X10	Support from own family network	.376 (.091)*	—	—	—
X11	Support from own friendship network	.904 (.111)*	—	—	—
X12	Support from partner's family network	—	.550 (.085)*	—	—
X13	Support from partner's friendship network	—	.860 (.087)*	—	—
X14	Range of contact in partner's family	—	—	.412 (.105)*	—
X15	Range of contact among partner's friends	—	—	.806 (.147)*	—
X16	Attraction to partner's family	—	—	—	.690 (.084)*
X17	Attraction to partner's friends	—	—	—	.653 (.086)*

Note: Standard errors are in parentheses.

* Loading was at least twice its standard error.

** Loadings were fixed at .800 which assumes some measurement error of these single indicators and approximates their epistemic correlations.

Total Coefficient of Determination for all X-Indicators = 1.00.

sociability and intimacy as theoretically specified. Thus both models were substantially improved by respecifying relational development along four dimensions: interaction time, similarity, intimacy, and commitment. What this means is that interaction time and similarity become direct sources of covariation with the other dyadic and communication network involvement dimensions in the models.

Third, one modification involving a shared indicator resulted in a significant improvement, but only in the friendship model. The interpersonal solidarity indicator became a shared indicator of range of communication among the partner's network (see Table 12.3). Thus the number of persons met in the best friends' network also is reflected by the level of interpersonal solidarity among the pairs.

Associations among measurement errors. The overall models for both friendships and dating relationships were substantially improved by also dealing with spurious association specification errors (Herting and Costner, 1985); that is, correcting for omitted paths between error terms of measured variables.[9] Each error path permitted improved the overall fit of the respective models.

The significance of the correlated errors lies in what they mean conceptually. Hence, three patterns of error paths were examined: those among the dyadic indicators, those among network indicators, and those between the dyadic and network involvement indicators. A rather global mind set or response bias seems to explain the first two patterns of correlated errors in both groups adequately. For example, the errors for love and interpersonal solidarity can be explained by conceptually overlapping measures that were physically close in the questionnaire. Further, error terms in the network set correlated most strongly between support from the partner's network and attraction to these members. Thus perceptions of support may have been colored by how much adolescents liked these people and/or vice versa. The third pattern of correlated errors—between the network and dyadic development indicators—can be explained by similar theoretic reasons accounting for the hypothesized links among the unobserved factors. That is, given substantive associations among the major factors in the model, one would also expect to find some correlated errors among their respective indicators. Hence, we discuss next the major associations found between the dyadic and network factors in the structural models.

The Structural Models:
Friendships and Dating Relationships

The hypotheses in this study were expressed as associations among the factors in our analysis. They were viewed as comprising a system of links between communication network involvement and dyadic relational development. The covariations between these eight dimensions thus compose the *factor structure* in each final model. Table 12.5 presents the Phi matrices for the two relationship types; it shows the standardized associations found between the factors. These estimates (correlations) are also visually portrayed in Figures 12.1 and 12.2 for dating and friendship relationships respectively.

Associations between relational development and communication network factors. The majority of the hypotheses connecting relational development factors with communication network factors were supported. As Table 12.5 shows, most of the associations were far more than twice their standard errors in both groups. However, some paths also were nonsignificant (see also Figures 12.1 and 12.2).

Attraction to the partner's network associated strongly and positively with all of the relational development dimensions in both groups—with one exception. The link between dyadic interaction time and attraction to the partner's network was nonsignificant (r = .13 friends; r = .14 dates). The strongest link in the friendship group was between attraction and commitment (r = .80); and in the dating group, between attraction and similarity (r = .69) and attraction and intimacy (r = .68). This means that attraction to the partner's network is strongly and positively related to (especially) commitment in friendships and to similarity and intimacy in dating relationships. Thus H1 was accepted for three of the four associations posited.

Range of communication correlated in different ways with the dyadic factors across relationship types: It linked significantly with interaction time in both relationships (r = .29 friends; r = .32 dates), and nonsignificantly with intimacy in both groups (r = .01 friends; r = .14 dates). Otherwise, the associations were opposite in the two groups: significant between range of communication and similarity among friends (r = .30), but not so among dates; and significant between range of communication and commitment among friends (r = .33), but not so among dates. Thus H2 was accepted and rejected in a divergent pattern across the two relationship types.

Support from the adolescents' own network associated positively with all dyadic factors in friendships and dating relationships. The strongest correlation in the friendship group was between the intimacy factor and support (r = .54); in the dating group, it was between the similarity factor and support (r = .42). Thus H3 was accepted for both friendships and dating relationships.

Support from the partner's network also correlated positively with all dyadic factors in both relationship types. The strongest link here in both groups was with perceived similarity (r = .46 friends; r = .62 dates). Thus H4 was also accepted in both groups.

Table 12.5
Phi Matrix of Standardized Estimates Among Factors: Friendships and Dating Relationships

Factor		KSI 1	KSI 2	KSI 3	KSI 4	KSI 5	KSI 6	KSI 7	KSI 8
KSI 1 Time spent together	D	1.000[a]							
	F	1.000							
KSI 2 Similarity	D	.069 (.129)	1.000						
	F	.280* (.101)	1.000						
KSI 3 Intimacy	D	.221 (.112)	.802* (.064)	1.000					
	F	.269* (.091)	.672* (.069)	1.000					
KSI 4 Commitment	D	.429* (.119)	.575* (.104)	.455* (.095)	1.000				
	F	.160 (.112)	.395* (.101)	.471* (.086)	1.000				
KSI 5 Support from subject's network	D	.318* (.116)	.421* (.109)	.352* (.097)	.232* (.115)	1.000			
	F	.283* (.093)	.455* (.082)	.541* (.068)	.438* (.091)	1.000			
KSI 6 Support from partner's network	D	.360* (.115)	.624* (.094)	.548* (.083)	.429* (.107)	.796* (.106)	1.000		
	F	.263* (.101)	.463* (.090)	.400* (.082)	.437* (.101)	.807* (.064)	1.000		
KSI 7 Range of contact in partner's network	D	.322* (.128)	-.080 (.124)	.139 (.111)	.152 (.127)	.389* (.122)	.085 (.122)	1.000	
	F	.295* (.110)	.300* (.128)	.007 (.116)	.332* (.115)	.144 (.109)	.194 (.111)	1.000	
KSI 8 Attraction to partner's network	D	.137 (.131)	.686* (.101)	.678* (.083)	.561* (.110)	.620* (.108)	.525* (.095)	.436* (.128)	1.000
	F	.131 (.121)	.397* (.124)	.352* (.113)	.803* (.180)	.502* (.123)	.330* (.114)	.230 (.130)	1.000

Note: Standard errors are in parentheses; Friendships: Overall chi-square = 94.39, df = 82, p = .165; Dating Relationships: Overall chi-square = 99.69, df = 85, p = .132.

a. Coefficients are listed according to the following code: D = Dating; F = Friendships.

* Correlation is significant—i.e., it is at least twice its standard error.

DATING RELATIONSHIPS

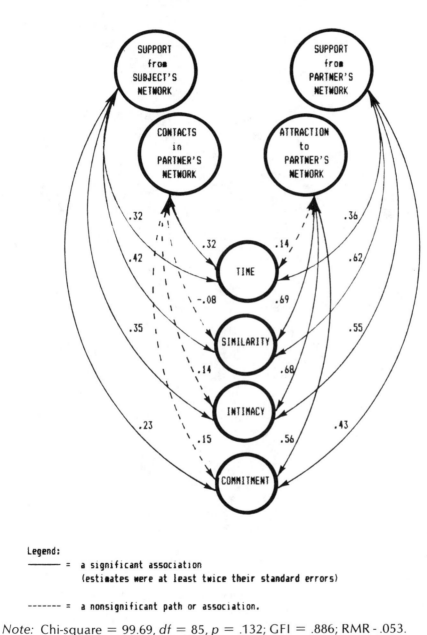

Legend:

――――― = a significant association
        (estimates were at least twice their standard errors)

------- = a nonsignificant path or association.

Note: Chi-square = 99.69, *df* = 85, *p* = .132; GFI = .886; RMR - .053.

Figure 12.1 Final model for adolescents' dating relationships: linking dyadic development and network factors.

FRIENDSHIP RELATIONSHIPS

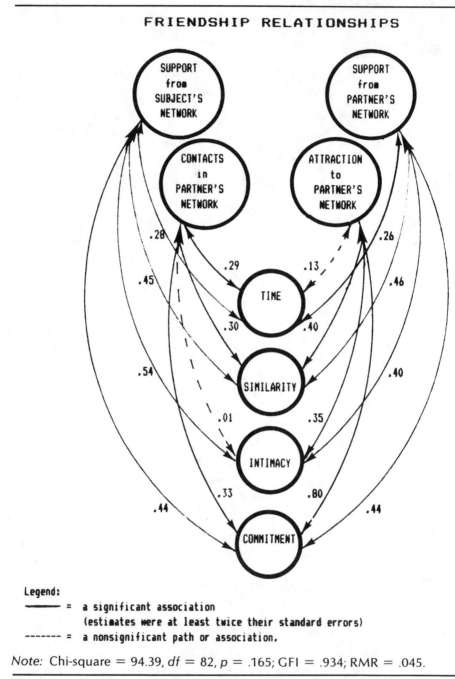

Legend:
———— = a significant association
(estimates were at least twice their standard errors)
------- = a nonsignificant path or association.

Note: Chi-square = 94.39, *df* = 82, *p* = .165; GFI = .934; RMR = .045.

Figure 12.2 Final model for adolescents' friendships: linking dyadic development and network factors.

Comparing support from the adolescents' own network versus the partner's network across relationship types revealed a rich picture: Support from the adolescents' own network linked equally or stronger with friendship development than did support from the partner's network. The antithesis occurred in dating relationships; support from the partner's network had stronger links with relational development than did support from the adolescents' own network. Taken together, these findings suggest an egocentric network connection in best friendships versus a more sociocentric network connection in dating relationships.

Associations in the dyadic submodels only. For the most part, the dyadic factors were tightly interrelated in both dating and friendship submodels as was posited (Figure 12.3 presents a visual summary); however, similarities and differences are evident across the two relationship types. The intimacy of the relationships is strongly and positively associated with perceived similarity in both groups (r = .80 dates; r = .67 friends). Conversely, interaction time linked strongly and positively with relational commitment in dating relationships (r = .43), but not so in friendships. Also, interaction time and similarity were significantly linked in friendships (r = .28), but not so in dating relationships. Further, the majority of these associations had stronger positive correlations in dating relationships than in best friendships, indicating tighter connections among the dyadic factors in dating relationships.

Associations in the network submodels only. The network factors were not as strongly interrelated as was predicted; positive, direct links did not occur among all factors, as Figure 12.4 shows. The strongest associations occurred between the two support dimensions in both groups (r = .81 friends; r = .80 dates). Also in both groups, support from the adolescents' own network linked strongly and positively with attraction to the partners' network (r = .50 friends; r = .62 dates), as did support from the partners' network and attraction to these same persons (r = .33 friends; r = .52 dates). This suggests that the adolescents are taking their cues for liking the partners' network members more from their own network than from the partners' family and friends themselves—an interesting case of how one's own network members can influence the attraction to others outside this network. Range of communication with the partner's network did not link significantly with any of the other network dimensions in friendships; in the dating group, it correlated significantly with support from the adolescents' own network (r = .40) and attraction to the partners' network (r = .44). Thus range of communication in the partner's network is not interrelated with other network factors in friendships, whereas it is among dating pairs.

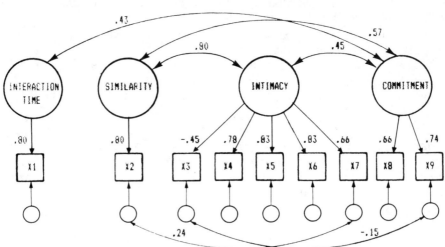

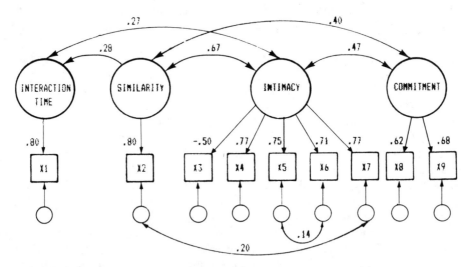

Note: Indicators: X1 = percentage of free time spent together; X2 = perceived similarity; X3 = uncertainty reduction; X4 = communication satisfaction; X5 = interpersonal solidarity; X6 = level of love; X7 = level of liking; X8 = probability of relationship continuing three or more months; X9 = probability of marriage/being friends forever.

Figure 12.3 Final submodels for dyadic relational development: adolescents' dating relationships and friendships.

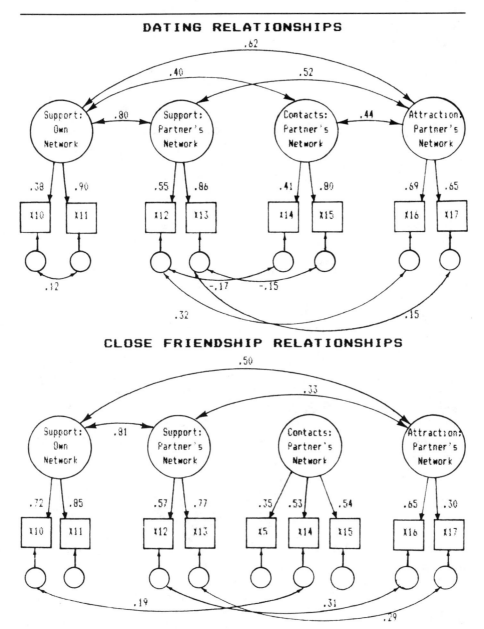

Note: Indicators: X5 = interpersonal solidarity; X10 = support: own family; X11 = support: own friends; X12 = support: partner's family; X13 = support: partner's friends; X14 = contacts: partner's family; X15 = contacts: partner's friends; X16 = attraction: partner's family; X17 = attraction: partner's friends.

Figure 12.4 Final submodels for communication network involvement: adolescents' dating relationships and friendships.

Comparing Relational Development
and Communication Network Involvement
Across Relationship Types

A LISREL analytic model for comparing across groups was used to explore if the dynamics of relational development and communication network involvement would covary in significantly different ways across relationship types. This comparative procedure involved analyzing the Phi covariance matrices (unstandardized estimates) between the eight factors in both groups.[10] Both models were entered into the LISREL V/VI program together to test the equality of parameters.[11] Although any number of invariances can be tested across groups, the tests in this study were confined to the following questions:

(1) Would the factors covary differently in the two groups, as indications thus far suggest?
(2) If so, would the dyadic relational development submodels be essentially the same as was posited?
(3) Would only the elements in the network submodel differ?
(4) Would the dynamics between relational development factors and network involvement factors differ as speculated?

The first question involved estimating the lambda and theta matrices according to the different measurement models found for each group. The phi matrix was then run as (1) invariant across the two groups, implying they were the same, and (2) free across the two groups, implying they would be different. The chi-square goodness-of-fit applied as before. Comparisons were then made between the values obtained in the two runs. These findings were:

Phi invariant: chi-square = 280.10, df = 199, p = .001
Phi matrix free: chi-square = 194.03, df = 163, p = .05
Chi-square difference = 86.07/df 36, p < .001

What this meant is that the two relationship types, besides having different measurement models, differed structurally (that is, in the variances and covariances) in statistically significant ways.

We sought next to find the parameters contributing most to the differences. This entailed three further tests across the two groups (1) constraining just the relational development elements to be invariant; (2) constraining just the network elements to be invariant; and (3) constraining only the associations among the relational development and network involvement factors. These procedures were meant to test our theoretic model: To discover if the greatest differences were in the dyadic submodel, in the network involvement submodel, or in how these two submodels interfaced across the two relationship types. In each instance, the fit of the model was much better when the parameters for each group were permitted to be free—that is, having no equality constraints placed on the phi matrix parameters, as outlined below:

(1) *Equality constraints among the dyadic parameters only:*

Equality   chi-square $= 214.03$, $df = 173$, $p = .018$
Constraints:
No constraints—   chi-square $= 194.03$, $df = 163$, $p = .05$
Phi matrix free:
Chi-square difference $= 20.00/df\ 10$, $p < .05$

These results meant the internal dynamics of friendship and dating relationships were different across the groups, but the differences were just barely significant. Thus friendships and dating relationships may differ in this respect due to chance alone at the .05 probability level.

(2) *Equality constraints among the network parameters only:*

Equality   chi-square $= 226.32$, $df = 173$, $p = .004$
Constraints:
No constraints—   chi-square $= 194.03$, $df = 163$, $p = .05$
Phi matrix free:
Chi-square difference $= 32.29/df\ 10$, $p < .001$

Additionally, these results meant that the external dynamics among the communication network involvement parameters differed significantly across the two relationship types.

(3) *Equality constraints among the parameters of relational development and network involvement only:*

Equality   Chi-square $= 248.30$, $df = 183$, $p = .001$
Constraints:
No constraints—   Chi-square $= 194.03$, $df = 163$, $p = .05$
Phi matrix free:
Chi-square difference $= 54.27/df\ 20$, $p < .001$

Finally, these findings pointed to significant differences across relationship types in how the relational development factors covaried with the network factors.

Thus the answer to all four questions posed above is that friendships and dating relationships differ significantly. They are most divergent in how communication network factors covary with relational development factors. They are a little less divergent in the dynamics among the communication network parameters only. Finally, they appear most similar in the relational development submodel.

SUMMARY AND IMPLICATIONS

Communication network involvement and personal relationship development are intricately related phenomena. Parks, Stan, and Eggert (1983) developed an initial map of the complex links among dyadic and network factors in romantic relationships among young adults. Our findings extend the boundary conditions of their model: *Communication network involvement factors covary in significantly different ways with dyadic development factors in adolescents' best friendships versus dating relationships.* These divergent patterns of associations occur among four dyadic formation factors—*interaction time, perceived similarity, intimacy,* and *commitment*—and four network involvement factors—attraction to, range of communication with, and expressed support from the partner's family and friends, and expressed support from the adolescent's own friends and family. The nature of this symmetry and asymmetry becomes evident by looking at connections with each network factor in turn.

First, previous investigators have linked *attraction* to members in the surrounding network with the similarity and/or liking between relationship partners (Granovetter, 1980; Parks, Stan, & Eggert, 1983). Our findings both support and extend this view. Attraction to the partner's network is directly associated here with the similarity between friends and dates, their emotional attachment, and commitment to each other. But liking the partner's friends and family did not correlate with how much time either friends or dates spent together. Furthermore, the ordered strength of associations differed markedly among relationship types—that is:

The greater the attraction to the partner's network, the greater the commitment, the similarity, and intimacy *in adolescents' friendships; whereas,*

The greater the attraction to the partner's network, the greater the similarity, the intimacy, and the commitment in *adolescents' dating relationships.*

The most divergent findings across relationship types occur in how the dyadic factors link with the *range of communication contacts* in the partner's network—that is, in order of strength:

The greater the range of communication contacts in the partner's network, the greater the commitment, the similarity, and the interaction time between *adolescents' best friends; whereas,*

> The greater the range of communication contacts in the partner's network,
> the greater the interaction time between *dating pairs*.

Although range of contacts correlates positively with all the dyadic elements except intimacy in friendships, it links only with the interaction time
among dating pairs. Hence, this factor varies most across relationship
types. Moreover, it is one that may change with age because it linked positively with romantic involvement among young adults (Parks, Stan, &
Eggert, 1983), but not among adolescents' dating relationships in this
study.

Many investigations focus on the *support* for a dyadic relationship from
the surrounding social network (Driscoll, Davis, & Lipetz, 1972; Lewis,
1973; Parks, Stan, & Eggert, 1983). We found mounting evidence for
direct connections between all elements of dyadic development and
expressed support, from both the partner's and the adolescents' own close
family and friends. But the strength of associations varied across the relationship types and across network sectors—that is, in order of strength
from the partner's network:

> The greater the expressed support from the partner's network, the greater
> the similarity, the commitment, the intimacy, and the interaction time in
> *adolescents' friendships;* whereas,

> The greater the expressed support from the partner's network, the greater
> the similarity, the intimacy, the commitment, and the interaction time in
> *adolescents' dating relationships*.

And, in order from the adolescents' own close family and friends:

> The greater the expressed support from the adolescents' own network, the
> greater the intimacy, the similarity, the commitment, and the interaction
> time in *adolescents' friendships;* whereas,

> The greater the expressed support from one's own network, the greater the
> similarity, the intimacy, the interaction time, and the commitment in *dat-
> ing relationships*.

Distinct contrasts emerge across relationship types when comparing
support from the two different network sectors: Generally, support from
the adolescents' own network links more strongly with friendship development, whereas support from the partner's network correlates more
strongly with romantic involvement. These findings also contrast sharply
with those of Parks, Stan and Eggert (1983). They found the strongest
links between romantic involvement and support from the subjects' own
family and friends, then from the partner's family and friends; the opposite
occurred here for adolescent dating pairs. Hence a maturational pattern

might exist: Prior to dating, adolescent same-sex friendship formation associates most strongly with support from one's own network; with dating comes a more sociocentric perspective and the adolescent's romantic involvement links more strongly with support from the partner's network; finally, with maturity and greater social exposure, one's own network support once again connects more strongly with romantic involvement. Perhaps dating relationships during adolescence serve the developmental task of achieving a sociocentric perspective and emancipation from parents and existing close friends; with maturity may come the realization that support and reinforcement from one's own social circle counts more and "isn't so out of tune after all."

Kimmel (1979) asserted that the value and relevant dimensions of personal relationships change with age, and La Gaipa (1981a) posited that the psychosocial resources exchanged would remain relatively stable in primary relationships. Findings from the analysis of the relational development submodels, and then the network submodels, illuminate these views.

First, friendships and dating relationships are most similar in the dyadic components of the two final models, thus lending some support to La Gaipa's view. Most of our findings, however, support Kimmel's assertion—asymmetry exists across the life-cycle and relationship types. Although romantic involvement is defined by a single dimension for young adults (Parks, Stan, & Eggert, 1983), it is defined here for adolescents by the four factors already mentioned. Moreover, when measured by the same indicators, these four factors were uniquely defined—most notably in the intimacy dimension. Thus we can use the same "yardsticks" to capture relationship development across adolescents' personal relationships, but when we do, the measurements will differ for friendships versus dating relationships. Furthermore, the *four relational development factors covary in significantly different ways in adolescents' best friendships and dating relationships.*[12] The connections between the interaction time and the other three factors account for one difference; also, most of these correlations have stronger, positive connections in dating relationships vis-à-vis friendships.

Second, the same four factors define patterns across both relationship types in the communication network submodel. But marked differences also occur here. When measured by the same indicators, the four dimensions are defined differently—most notably, the range of communication is reflected by interpersonal solidarity in friendships, but not in dating relationships. Furthermore, the *four communication network factors covary in significantly different ways in adolescents' best friendships and dating relationships.* The range of communication factor contributes most to this difference, linking positively with support and attraction in dating relationships, but not correlating with any other network factors in friendships.

Thus besides the differences in direct associations between dyadic development and network involvement, complex indirect associations exist among network factors like support, attraction, and range of communication—more so in dating relationships than in friendships.

To study personal relationship development as if it occurred in a vacuum is incomplete at best, and if not methodologically limited, then epistemologically flawed. Our comparisons of dyadic development in its network context across relationship types has limitations; thus we raise several concerns for future research. First, we were limited by the use of cross-sectional data, the culture of the sample, and exploring only patterns of association. Longitudinal studies are needed to ferret out these limitations and supply better evidence for causal arguments; it is also crucial to have over-time data to confirm if differences prevail across relationship types of varying duration, from initiation to demise. Alternatively, much larger sample sizes are needed to use the LISREL procedures for comparisons across mutually exclusive groups of differing relationship durations. At the same time, the findings from this study served to test the boundary conditions of an existing model of romantic involvement and social network involvement (Parks, Stan, & Eggert, 1983). However, further confirmatory evidence of the adequacy and boundary conditions of these models could be provided by reanalyzing the data from the college sample, adding a college-age sample of best friendships, and then using the LISREL comparative analytic model across all groups. Thus we would know more about life-cycle changes from middle adolescence through young adulthood and across the two relationship types.

Kandel (1978c) and others (Cohen, 1979; La Gaipa & Wood, 1981) apprise us of the existence of youth subcultures that are anticonventional or disabled in nature. Although we view the final models as representative of typical white, middle-class adolescents, and thus providing a basis for comparison, it seems especially important to test the propositions advanced in this study across special populations and subcultural groups of youth. For example, a widely held belief is that peer support groups influence youth much more than do family. Parks, Stan, and Eggert (1983) directly tested for associations between family versus peer support and romantic involvement, finding this schism did not hold. We found some evidence of shifting alliances across relationship types, from one's own versus the partner's network sectors. Obviously further research is needed here as are longitudinal data. The impact of opposition or support from family versus peer network sectors may vary across relationship types, as a function of maturity, social skills, or among subcultural youth groups, and so forth. Moreover, to get a much more complete view of the impact of life-cycle changes and developmental issues on relational development in its network context, multiple indicators of these dimensions are necessary.

Although studying the adolescent's perception of the relationship is important, the study of transitivity versus conflict and intransitivity in social bonds was limited here by using the individual as the unit of analysis. We found some small evidence of potential intransitive bonds in the friendship group—the attraction to the partner's network was much less strongly reflected by the peer network than it was in dating relationships. To test intransitivity in social bonds adequately, future studies need to collect data from the network members as well. This seems important in general given findings that judgments about feelings are largely based on nonverbal communication and impressions (Sillars et al., 1984). We do not know from our data if feelings of attraction/nonattraction were reciprocated, or if perceived support/nonsupport from the network sectors was real or a figment of the adolescents' wishful thinking. Admittedly with a 24-person network for each subject, this presents a major investment in data collection time and energy. Alternatively, we must continue constructing and evaluating tentative theories with somewhat flawed data. The LISREL programs used here are an important new tool that are valuable in this process, particularly for respecifying measurement models.

A widely held belief is that friendships during adolescence have a special value; they can help chart the course through a social world of uncertainties where the map is difficult to read and paths are not clearly marked. But scholars currently recognize that these relationships are embedded in social networks of family and friends (Duck & Gilmour, 1981b; Ridley & Avery, 1979). Moreover, Parks, Stan, and Eggert (1983) demonstrated that among youth "involvement with a romantic partner is inextricably linked to involvement with his or her social network" (p. 129). In so doing, they enriched our understanding of transitivity and the structural implications of interpersonal processes between dyads and network members.

We believe the complex system of direct and indirect connections evident in our findings lend mounting support for an interpersonal basis for transitivity. That is, personal relationships play a vital role in connecting individuals with network clusters of family and friends; the interpersonal processes inherent in this network structure constrained friendship and dating relationship development here. The bonding and barrier forces located in the cultural-normative expectations for interacting with network members; the shared activities, satisfying interactions, and reinforcement that occurred at an interpersonal level; and the relationship goals, affiliation needs, and forces driving cognitive balance in the adolescents involved—all created *interaction* between the dyads and network members. These interactions, in turn, strengthened (or weakened) dyadic relationship bonds; thus they served to create social structure. Consequently, as evidenced in the strong positive associations found in this study, adolescents' personal relationship development and communication network involvement are vitally linked. Furthermore, significantly different systems of connections exist across adolescents' personal relationships, extending our understanding of how network involvement and dyadic formation varies for the trajectories of adolescents' best friendships versus their dating relationships.

NOTES

1. Assessing the goodness-of-fit was judged by three measures: 1) the over-all chi-square with its associated degress of freedom and probability level; 2) the goodness-of-fit index (GFI) and its adjustment for degrees of freedom (AGFI); and 3) the root mean square residual (RMR). Because large chi-square values and a significant probability correspond to a bad fit, chi-square can be used as a "fit measure" rather than as a test statistic. The GFI is interpreted as a percentage where 1.00 is a perfect fit. The RMR is evaluated with respect to the variances/covariances in the sample's matrix; the smaller the value, the better the fit of the model (Herting & Costner, 1985; Joreskog & Sorbom, 1983).

2. LISREL V/VI provides several powerful diagnostic tools that were used here for evaluating the fit or detecting a lack of fit of specific parameters. Special attention was paid to the following results: 1) parameter estimates, 2) standard errors, 3) squared multiple correlations, 4) coefficients of determination, and 5) correlations of parameter estimates (Joreskog & Sorbom, 1983). Unreasonable values in any of these quantities mean the estimating model is fundamentally wrong in some parameters and requires respecification (Herting & Costner, 1985; Long, 1983).

3. Adding one dimension at a time permitted us to respecify paths and achieve a good fit for each relationship type before adding the next dimension. In this way, specific parameters contributing to the poor model were identified in nested models by paying particular attention to the five quantities mentioned above in Note 2 and the overall goodness-of-fit measures discussed in Note 1.

4. The goal was to achieve a small chi-square with p close to or $> .10$, a GFI close to or $> .90$, and a RMR as small as possible with no remaining normalized residuals larger than two in magnitude (Herting & Costner, 1985; Joreskog & Sorbom, 1983; Long, 1983).

5. Modifications also were guided by the normalized residuals, the Q-plot of these residuals and the modification indices. These are visual summaries of the "rough" left over in the data after the "smooth" has been explained by the linear relationships (Hartwig & Dearing, 1979). Nonlinearities in the Q-plot and slopes smaller than one are indicative of departures from normality or of specification errors in the model (Herting & Costner, 1985; Joreskog & Sorbom, 1983).

6. The t-values of these estimates can be obtained by dividing the parameter estimate by its standard error.

7. This is a measure of the joint strength or reliability of all the observed indicators. Thus the reliability of the total set is very high (1.0 being the highest possible value).

8. This also means that those pairs with low communication frequency would have the same structure of relations among dimensions but differ in having a lower magnitude of the coefficients from dimension to dimension (or dimension to indicator) when compared with those experiencing high communication frequency with each other.

9. This information is available from the authors upon request.

10. The comparative procedure involved analyzing the covariance matrices, because comparisons of the standardized correlation parameters are viewed as inappropriate for this task (Herting & Costner, 1985; Joreskog & Sorbom, 1983).

11. The LISREL V/VI model estimates the parameters by simultaneously calculating values that minimize the fitting function and match, as closely as possible, the observed covariance matrices of both groups. Hence, the estimation procedure does not entail averaging across the groups; nor does it perform these calculations separately for each group: rather, the estimates are obtained by achieving a simultaneous fit across the two groups (for more detail see Herting, 1985; Herting & Costner, 1985; Joreskog & Sorbom).

12. We hold this conclusion tentatively, however, because asymmetry here may be due to chance alone—differences were just barely significant ($p < .05$).

REFERENCES

Adams, J. F. (1980). *Understanding adolescence* (4th ed.). Boston: Allyn & Bacon.

Altman, I., & Taylor, D. A. (1970). *Social penetration: The development of interpersonal relationships.* New York: Holt, Rinehart & Winston.

Asher, H. B. (1976). *Causal modeling.* Beverly Hills, CA: Sage.

Befu, H. (1977). Social exchange. *Annual Reviews in Anthropology, 6,* 255-281.

Bell, R. R. (1981). *Worlds of friendship.* Beverly Hills, CA: Sage.

Bentler, P. M. (1980). Multivariate analysis with latent variables: Causal modeling. *Annual Review of Psychology, 31,* 419-456.

Berger, C. R. (1979). Beyond initial interaction: uncertainty, understanding, and the development of interpersonal relationships. In H. Giles & R. St. Clair (Eds.). *Language and social psychology* (pp. 122-144). Oxford: Basil Blackwell.

Berger, C. R. (1982, July). *Social cognition and the development of interpersonal relationships.* Paper presented at the International Conference on Personal Relationships, Madison, WI.

Berger, C. R., & Calabrese, R. J. (1975). Some explorations in initial interaction and beyond: Toward a developmental theory of interpersonal communication. *Human Communication Research, 1,* 99-112.

Berndt, R. J. (1982, July). *Why do children's friendships end: Problems with levels of analysis.* Paper presented at the International Conference on Personal Relationships, Madison, WI.

Bershied, E., & Walster, E. H. (1978). *Interpersonal attraction.* Reading, MA: Addison-Wesley.

Bigelow, B., & La Gaipa, J. J. (1980). The development of friendship values and choice. In H. C. Foot, A. J. Chapman, & J. R. Smith (Eds.), *Friendship and social relations in children* (pp. 15-44). New York: John Wiley.

Bishop, J. M. (1979). Transitivity in work relevant and sentiment-based sociograms. *Pacific Sociological Review, 22,* 185-200.

Blalock, J. R., Jr. (1969). *Theory construction.* Englewood Cliffs, NJ: Prentice-Hall.

Blalock, J. R., Jr. (1982). *Conceptualization and measurement in the social sciences.* Beverly Hills, CA: Sage.

Braiker, H. B., & Kelley, H. H. (1979). Conflict in the development of close relationships. In R. L. Burgess & T. L. Huston (Eds.), *Social exchange in developing relationships* (pp. 135-168). New York: Academic Press.

Burgess, R. L. (1981). Relationships in marriage and the family. In S. W. Duck & R. Gilmour, (Eds.). *Personal relationships 1: Studying personal relationships* (pp. 179-196). New York: Academic Press.

Burgess, R. L., & Huston, T. L. (Eds.). (1979). *Social exchange in developing relationships.* New York: Academic Press.

Burt, R. S. (1978). Cohesion versus structural equivalence as a basis for network subgroups. *Sociological Methods & Research, 7,* 189-212.

Byrne, D. (1971). *The attraction paradigm.* New York: Academic Press.

Campbell, E. Q. (1975). Adolescence: A special period. In *Socialization: Culture and personality* (pp. 32-44). Dubuque, IA: W. C. Brown.

Cohen, J. (1979). High school subcultures and the adult world. *Adolescence, 14,* 491-502.

Davis, J. (1970). Clustering and hierarchy in interpersonal relations. *American Sociological Review, 35,* 843-851.

Davis, J. (1979). The Davis/Holland/Leinhardt studies: an overview. In P. W. Holland and S. Leinhardt (Eds.). Perspectives on social network research (pp. 51-62). New York: Academic Press.

Davis, J., & Leinhardt, S. (1970). The structure of positive interpersonal relations in small groups. In J. Berger (Ed.), *Sociological theories in progress* (Vol. 2) (pp. 218-251). Boston: Houghton Mifflin.

Delia, J. G. (1980). Some tentative thoughts concerning the study of interpersonal relationships and their development. *Western Journal of Speech Communication, 44,* 97-103.

Dickens, W. J., & Perlman, D. (1981). Friendship over the lifecycle. In S. W. Duck & R. Gilmour (Eds.), *Personal Relationships 2: Developing personal relationships* (pp. 91-122). New York: Academic Press.

Douvan, E., & Adelson, J. (1966). *The adolescent experience.* New York: John Wiley.

Driscoll, R., Davis, K., & Lipetz, M. (1972). Parental interference and romantic love: The Romeo and Juliet effect. *Journal of Personality and Social Psychology, 24,* 1-10.

Duck, S. W. (1980). Personal relationships research in the 1980s: Towards an understanding of complex human sociality. *The Western Journal of Speech Communication, 44,* 114-119.

Duck, S. W., & Gilmour, R. (Eds.). (1981a). *Personal relationships. 1: Studying personal relationships.* New York: Academic Press.

Duck, S. W., & Gilmour, R. (Eds.). (1981b). *Personal relationships. 2: Developing personal relationships.* New York: Academic Press.

Duck, S. W., Lock, A., McCall, G., Fitzpatrick, M. A., & Coyne, J. C. (1984). Social and personal relationships: A joint editorial. *Journal of Social and Personal Relationships, 1,* 1-11.

Dunphy, D. C. (1963). The social structure of urban adolescent peer groups. *Sociometry, 26,* 230-246.

Ekeh, P. (1974). *Social exchange theory.* Cambridge, MA: Harvard University Press.

Erikson, E. H. (1968). *Identity, youth and crisis,* New York: Norton.

Feld, S., & Elmore, R. (1982a). Patterns of sociometric choices: Transitivity reconsidered. *Social Psychology Quarterly, 45,* 77-85.

Feld, S., & Elmore, R. (1982b). Processes underlying patterns of sociometric choice: Response to Hallinan. *Social Psychology Quarterly, 45,* 90-92.

Festinger, L. (1957). *A theory of cognitive dissonance.* Palo Alto, CA: Stanford University Press.

Gold, M., & Douvan, E. (1969). *Adolescent development: Readings in research and theory.* Boston: Allyn & Bacon.

Granovetter, M. S. (1973). The strength of weak ties. *American Journal of Sociology, 78,* 1360-1380.

Granovetter, M. S. (1980, May). *The strength of weak ties: A network theory revisited.* Paper presented at the annual convention of the International Communication Association, Acapulco, Mexico.

Griffit, W., & Veitch, R. (1974). Preacquaintance attitude similarity and attraction revisited: Ten days in a fall-out shelter. *Sociometry, 37,* 162-173.

Hallinan, M. T. (1982). Cognitive balance and differential popularity in social networks. *Social Psychology Quarterly, 45,* 86-90.

Hallinan, M. T., & Felmlee, D. (1975). An analysis of intransitivity in sociometric data. *Sociometry, 38,* 195-212.

Hays, R. B. (1984). The development and maintenance of friendship. *Journal of Social and Personal Relationships, 1,* 75-98.

Hecht, M. L. (1978). The conceptualization and measurement of interpersonal communication satisfaction. *Human Communication Research, 4,* 253-264.

Heider, F. (1946). Attitudes and cognitive organization. *Journal of Psychology, 21,* 107-112.

Heider, F. (1958). *The psychology of interpersonal relations.* New York: John Wiley.

Herting, J. R. (1985). Multiple indicator models using LISREL. In H. M. Blalock, Jr. (Ed.). *Causal models in the social sciences* (2nd ed., pp. 263-319). Chicago: Aldine.

Herting, J. R., & Costner, H. L. (1985). Respecification in multiple indicator models. In H. M. Blalock, Jr. (Ed.), *Causal models in the social sciences* (2nd ed., pp. 321-393). Chicago: Aldine.

Hill, C. T., Rubin, Z., & Peplau, L. A. (1976). Breakups before marriage: The end of 103 affairs. *Journal of Social Issues, 32,* 147-168.

Hinde, R. A. (1981). The bases of a science of interpersonal relationships. In S. W. Duck & R. Gilmour (Eds.), *Personal relationships 1: Studying personal relationships* (pp. 1-22). New York: Academic Press.

Holland, P., & Leinhardt, S. (1972). Some evidence on the transitivity of positive interpersonal sentiment. *American Journal of Sociology, 77*, 1205-1209.

Homans, G. (1950). *The human group*. New York: Harcourt Brace & World.

Homans, G. (1979). Foreword. In R. Burgess & T. Huston (Eds.), *Social exchange in developing relationships* (pp. xv-xx). New York: Academic Press.

Huston, T., & Burgess, R. (1979). Social exchange in developing relationships: An overview. In R. Burgess & T. Huston (Eds.), *Social exchange in developing relationships* (pp. 3-30). New York: Academic Press.

Joreskog, K. G., & Sorbom, D. (1983). *LISREL. Analysis of Linear Structural Relationships by the Method of Maximum Likelihood*, Versions V and VI (2nd ed.). Chicago: International Educational Resources.

Kandel, D. B. (1978a). Homophily, selection and socialization in adolescent friendships. *American Journal of Sociology, 84*, 427-436.

Kandel, D. B. (1978b). Similarity in real-life adolescent friendship pairs. *Journal of Personality and Social Psychology, 36*, 306-312.

Kandel, D. B. (1978c). On variations of adolescent subcultures. *Youth and Society, 9*, 373-384.

Kelley, J., & Thibaut, J. (1978). *Interpersonal relations: A theory of interdependence*. New York: John Wiley.

Kimmel, D. C. (1979). Relationship initiation and development: A life-span developmental approach. In R. L. Burgess & T. L. Huston (Eds.), *Social exchange in developing relationships* (pp. 351-377). New York: Academic Press.

Kon, I. S. (1981). Adolescent friendship: Some unanswered questions for future research. In S. W. Duck & R. Gilmour (Eds.), *Personal relationships 2: Developing personal relationships* (pp. 187-204). New York: Academic Press.

Kon, I. S., & Losenkov, V. A. (1978). Friendship in adolescence: Values and behavior. *Journal of Marriage & Family, 40*, 143-155.

LaGaipa, J. J. (1981a). A systems approach to personal relationships. In S. W. Duck & R. Gilmour (Eds.), *Personal relations I: Studying personal relations* (pp. 67-90). New York: Academic Press.

LaGaipa, J. J. (1981b). Children's friendships. In S. W. Duck & R. Gilmour (Eds.), *Personal relationships 2: Developing personal relations* (pp. 161-186). New York: Academic Press.

LaGaipa, J. L. (1982). Rules and rituals in disengaging from relationships. In S. W. Duck (Ed.), *Personal Relationships 4: Dissolving personal relationships* (pp. 189-210). New York: Academic Press.

LaGaipa, J. L., & Wood, D. H. (1981). Friendship in disturbed adolescents. In S. W. Duck & R. Gilmour (Eds.), *Personal relationships 3: Personal relationships in disorder* (pp. 169-190). New York: Academic Press.

Larson, R. W. (1982, July). *Adolescents' daily experience with family and friends: Contrasting opportunity systems*. Paper presented at the International Conference on Personal Relationships, Madison, WI.

Le Francois, G. R. (1981). *Adolescents* (2nd ed.). Belmont, CA: Wadsworth.

Leinhardt, S. (Ed.). (1976). *Social networks: A developing paradigm*. New York: Academic Press.

Levinger, G. (1979). A social exchange view of the dissolution of pair relationships. In R. Burgess & T. Huston (Eds.), *Social exchange in developing relationships* (pp. 169-193). New York: Academic Press.

Levinger, G., Senn, D. J., & Jorgensen, B. W. (1970). Progress toward permanence in courtship: A test of the Kerckhoff-Davis hypotheses. *Sociometry, 33*, 427-443.

Lewis, R. A. (1973). Social reaction and the formation of dyads: An interactionist approach to mate selection. *Sociometry, 36*, 409-418.

Long, J. S. (1976). Estimation and hypothesis testing in linear models containing measurement error. *Sociological Methods and Research, 5*, 157-206.

Long, J. S. (1983). *Covariance structure models: An introduction to LISREL*. Beverly Hills, CA: Sage.

Long, J. S. (1983). *Confirmatory factor analysis: A preface to LISREL*. Beverly Hills, CA: Sage.

McCall, G. J., & Simmons, J. L. (1978). *Identities and interactions: An examination of human associations in everyday life* (rev. ed.). New York: Free Press.

Milardo, R. M. (1982). Friendship networks in developing relationships: Converging and diverging social environments. *Social Psychology Quarterly, 45,* 162-172.

Milardo, R. M. (1984). Social networks and pair relationships: A review of substantive and measurement issues. *Sociology and Social Research, 68,* 1-18.

Millen, L., & Roll, S. (1977). Adolescent males' ratings of being understood by their fathers, best friends and significant others. *Psychological Reports, 40,* 1079-1082.

Miller, G. R., & Steinberg, M. (1975). *Between People.* Chicago: Science Research Associates.

Murstein, B. (1976). *Who will marry whom? Theories and research in marital choice.* New York: Springer.

Newcomb, T. M. (1968). Interpersonal balance. In R. P. Abelson, E. Aronson, W. J. McGuires, T. M. Newcomb, M. J. Rosenberg, & R. H. Tannenbaum (Eds.), *Theories of cognitive consistency: A sourcebook.* Chicago: Rand McNally.

Parks, M. R. (1978, November). *Communication correlates of perceived friendship development.* Paper presented at the annual convention of the Speech Communication Association, Minneapolis, MN.

Parks, M. R. (1982). Ideology in interpersonal communication: Off the couch and into the world. In M. Burgoon (Ed.), *Communication yearbook 5* (pp. 79-124). New Brunswick, NJ: Transaction Books.

Parks, M. R., & Adelman, M. B. (1983a). Communication networks and the development of romantic relationships: An expansion of uncertainty reduction theory. *Human Communication Research, 10,* 55-79.

Parks, M. R., Stan, C., & Eggert, L. L. (1983). Romantic involvement and social network involvement. *Social Psychology Quarterly, 46,* 116-130.

Pedazur, E. J. (1982). Introduction to linear structural relations (LISREL). In E. J. Pedazur, *Multiple regression in behavioral research* (2nd ed., pp. 636-681). New York: Holt, Rinehart & Winston.

Ridley, C., & Avery A. (1979). Social network influence on the dyadic relationship. In R. Burgess & T. Huston (Eds.), *Social exchange in developing relationships* (pp. 223-246). New York: Academic Press.

Rubin, Z. (1970). Measurement of romantic love. *Journal of Personality and Social Psychology, 16,* 265-273.

Rubin, Z. (1973). *Liking and loving: An invitation to social psychology.* New York: Holt, Rinehart & Winston.

Ryder, R., Kafka, J., & Olson, D. (1971). Separating and joining influences in courtship and early marriage. *American Journal of Orthopsychiatry, 41,* 450-464.

Schachter, S. (1974). The psychology of affiliation. In Z. Rubin (Ed.), *Doing unto others* (pp. 7-16). Englewood Cliffs, NJ: Prentice-Hall.

Schulman, N. (1975). Life-cycle variation in patterns of close relationships. *Journal of Marriage and the Family, 37,* 813-821.

Sillars, A. L., Pike, G. R., Jones, T. S., & Murphy, M. A. (1984). Communication and understanding in marriage. *Human Communication Research, 10,* 317-350.

Sullivan, J. L., & Feldman, S. (1979). *Multiple indications: An introduction.* Beverly Hills: Sage.

Thornburg, H. (Ed.). (1975). *Contemporary adolescence: Readings* (2nd ed.). Monterey, CA: Brooks/Cole.

Waller, W., & Hill, R. (1951). *The family: A dynamic interpretation.* New York: Dryden Press.

Walster, E., & Walster, G. W. (1978). *A new look at love.* Reading, MA: Addison-Wesley.

Weis, J. (1974). Styles of middle-class adolescent drug use. *Pacific Sociological Review, 3,* 251-285.

Weiss, R. S. (1974). The provisions of social relationships. In Z.Rubin (Ed.), *Doing unto others* (pp. 17-26). Englewood Cliffs, NJ: Prentice-Hall.

Wellman, B. (1981). Applying network analysis to the study of support. In B. H. Gottlieb (Ed.), *Social networks and social support* (pp. 171-201). Beverly Hills, CA: Sage.

Wheeless, L. R. (1976). Self-disclosure and interpersonal solidarity: Measurement, valida-
    tion, and relationships. *Human Communication Research, 3,* 47-61.
Wheeless, L. R. (1978). A follow-up study of the relationships among trust, disclosure, and
    interpersonal solidarity. *Human Communication Research, 4,* 143-157.
Wright, P. H. (1978). Toward a theory of friendship based on a conception of self. *Human
    Communication Research, 3,* 196-207.
Wright, P. H. (1981). Friends and parents of a sample of high school juniors: An explora-
    tory study of relationship intensity and interpersonal rewards. *Journal of Marriage and
    the Family, 43,* 559-570.

13 ● Conversational Relevance: Three Experiments on Pragmatic Connectedness in Conversation

SALLY JACKSON ●
SCOTT JACOBS ● ANA M. ROSSI

University of Oklahoma ● University of Nebraska—Lincoln

A theoretical puzzle that is achieving increasing prominence in the field of communication is the problem of coherence (Craig & Tracy, 1983; Ellis, 1982; Jacobs, 1985; McLaughlin, 1984). How can utterances or sentences fit together in meaningful ways? Coherence in discourse generally has been discussed in terms of the relevance of an utterance or sentence to prior discourse. Coherence is a global property of a whole unit; relevance is a property attributed to the elements composing the whole (McLaughlin, 1984, pp. 36-38). This much granted, just what is it that makes conversations or texts coherent and utterances or sentences relevant?

There are two approaches to thinking about these issues that have proven to be particularly beguiling. These approaches portray coherence either as the product of formal relations in discourse or as a property of the semantic content of discourse. The following sections first discuss the dangers of such approaches, then present a pragmatic alternative together with three studies that test some predictions of this alternative.

Textual Cohesion Doesn't Explain Coherence

At the most direct level, one might be tempted to search for the bases of coherence in relations among the words themselves. That is, coherence

AUTHORS' NOTE: We wish to thank John Waite Bowers, Barbara J. O'Keefe, Margaret L. McLaughlin, Robert E. Sanders, and Karen Tracy for their thoughtful and helpful commentary on issues raised in this manuscript. David Dunning and Jeffrey Philpott assisted in pilot studies not reported here.

Correspondence and requests for reprints: Sally Jackson, Department of Communication, 331 Kaufman Hall, University of Oklahoma, Norman, OK 73019.

could be equated with formal structural relations among the elements of a text or conversation that inhere in objective featues of language independently of the constructive processes of communicators. This viewpoint is most familiar in ways of talking about textual cohesion.

Cohesion is a technical term used to refer to textual linkages among words, phrases, or sentences. Sentences or utterances are said to cohere when an element of one sentence or utterance is interpreted by reference to an element in another sentence or utterance (Halliday & Hasan, 1976, p. 11). There are a variety of cohesive devices for indicating such relations (for example, anaphoric reference, ellipsis, contrast). The "denser" the clustering of these devices, the "closer" the texture and greater the interdependence of meaning; the fewer the devices, the "looser" the texture (Halliday & Hasan, 1976, p. 296). Consider the way textual relations are used to explain the coherence in examples (1) and (2):[1]

(1) (Instructions in a cookery book)
     Wash and core six cooking apples. Put them in a fire proof dish.
(2) A: Where are the pencils?
     B: They are on your desk.

Halliday and Hasan (1976) comment about (1): "It is clear that *them* in the second sentence refers back to (is ANAPHORIC to) the *six cooking apples* in the first sentence. This ANAPHORIC function of *them* gives cohesion to the two sentences, so that we interpret them as a whole" (p. 2). Similarly, Ellis (1982) describes what makes the exchange in (2) so cohesive: "It is clear that 'they' in the second utterance refers back to 'the pencils' in the first utterance. 'They' is an anaphoric mechanism and lends coherence to the two utterances so we interpret them as a whole" (p. 48). He goes on later to comment: "These parts cohere and provide a framework for processing content. The anaphoric 'they' in the above example about pencils is pure mechanics and functions as an organizational device only" (pp. 50-51).

Talking about the way in which words like *they* and *them* create cohesion by "referring back to" other words seems innocent enough, but as Morgan (1978) has pointed out this is not quite right. Words do not "refer back to" other words. In fact, words do not typically refer to *words* at all. "Them" and "they" are used above, respectively, to refer to the same six cooking apples and to the same pencils that were previously referred to by using "six cooking apples" and "the pencils." The sentences cohere not because of any formal structural relations inhering in the words themselves, but because they are used to talk about the same things.

As Morgan (1978) points out, this is not just a "niggling concern with sloppy language," but a serious objection to the underlying view of how it is that texts and conversations appear coherent (p. 109). For the question arises, how do we know what a word like *them* in (1) refers to? As Morgan argues in his response to the Halliday and Hasan analysis, we discover what "them" refers to by *assuming* coherence:

> How do we know that it refers to the apples, and not to two of the writer's bachelor uncles? We can't *know* such a thing. We can only assume that the writer is rational, and that the recipe is coherent. If it is coherent, we are justified in assuming that it is the apples that are referred to by *them*. But there is a vicious circularity here. The recipe has cohesion, is a coherent text, just in case *them* refers to the apples. But we are only justified in inferring that *them* refers to the apples if we *assume* that the text is coherent. Thus, in spite of Halliday and Hasan's claim, it is not the anaphoric facts that give rise to cohesion; rather the assumption that the text is coherent gives rise to the inference that *them* refers to the apples. (Morgan, 1978, p. 110)

What is clearly absent in the cohesion account is any acknowledgment that people have to be able to find the coherence that is assumed to be signalled by these devices. The apparent cohesive functions of words in a text or dialogue are the *product,* and not the *cause* of coherent interpretations of discourse. This can be demonstrated by showing that the presence of cohesive devices is neither necessary nor sufficient to produce coherence.

Consider first their necessity for coherent discourse. It appears that human inference can be powerful enough to create a sense of coherence without any explicit indicators whatsoever. In (3), B can be heard as giving a negative answer despite the absence of any explicit cohesive ties:

(3) A: Did you get your assignment done?
     B: The typewriter broke.

Likewise, the sentences in (4) convey a coherent description of a scene despite the absence of any explicit textual linkages.

(4) John entered the apartment. Chairs, tables, and debris were strewn everywhere. Burglars must have jimmied the window. So much for the security of deadbolt locks on front doors.

Clearly what is going on in these cases is that interpreters bring to bear a wide range of background knowledge about the world, about social conventions, and the like together with an assumption of coherence to construct a coherent understanding of what is being talked about. As the above examples show, this background knowledge can be enough to enable a coherent reading of the discourse without the presence of any cohesive devices.

Although the presence of cohesive devices may not be required for a reader or hearer to arrive at a coherent interpretation, are such devices at least sufficient when they are present? No. Without the constructive processes that bring background knowledge to bear on the interpretation of discourse, cohesive devices will not create coherent discourse—as many of the studies by Bransford and his associates have demonstrated (Bransford, 1979, pp. 129-165). Hobbs (1982, p. 225) illustrates the point nicely with the following excerpt from Edward Gorey's (1972) "The Object Lesson":

> (5) It was already Thursday, but his lordship's artificial limb could not be found; therefore, having directed the servants to fill the baths, he seized the tongs, and set out at once for the edge of the lake.

The passage contains several explicit connectives, but is strikingly incoherent. The reader has no idea of how to construct a "mental model" (Johnson-Laird, 1983) of the world being described and so has no way to assess what the connectives in the passage might connect.

The importance of a mental model in interpretation of anaphoric reference is illustrated by the contrasting pair of responses below (adapted from Waltz, 1982, p. 14).

> (6)   Q: Why did the city councilmen refuse the women a permit?
>   A1: Because they feared violence.
>   A2: Because they advocated revolution.

Clearly here, the reader connects "they" to different referents not because the word refers differently in the two cases, but because the reader applies world knowledge to construct different inferences. The idea that such devices produce coherence is difficult to reconcile with the fact that such devices are interpretable only with respect to some already-accomplished mental model.

As a final indication that cohesive devices are not sufficient to produce coherence, we may note that such devices may actually detract from the sense of coherence when the substantive relations they signal do not themselves make sense. That is, cohesive devices do not create connections, but only invite a search for connections. If background knowledge and interpretive processes "rule out" the possibility of such connections, the presence of the device reduces rather than increases the sense of coherence. Consider these pairs of examples (adapted from Brockway, 1981, pp. 65-66):

> (7a) A: Have you returned the library books?
>   B: I returned them on Friday.

(7b) A: Have you returned the library books?
      B: Anyway, I returned them on Friday.

(8a) Any mathematician should be able to add up the bill.
      Dick is a mathematician.
      Dick should be able to add up the bill.

(8b) Any mathematician should be able to add up the bill.
      Dick is a mathematician.
      Afterall, Dick should be able to add up the bill.

Anyway in (7b) and *Afterall* in (8b) are examples of a class of cohesive devices called conjunctions—one of five major classes identified by Halliday and Hasan (1976, pp. 333-338). The discourse seems perfectly coherent without the conjunctions, but this sense of coherence is visibly damaged by the insertion of the devices. (Similar results obtain for a variety of such conjunctions—insert *likewise, furthermore, alternatively,* or *yet*.) The devices invite searches for relations that are resisted by any plausible understanding of how the sentences or utterances could fit together.

It is a mistake to see cohesive devices as one of many "mechanisms" for discourse coherence akin to, say, the system of pragmatic presuppositions described by Grice's (1975) Cooperative Principle and Conversational Maxims. They are not coherence producing mechanisms at all. Cohesive devices are best seen as information-processing aids (Planalp & Tracy, 1980). They are *cues*. Cohesive devices help to activate background knowledge by inviting searches for interpretations that would be consistent with a particular class of relations. But because they invite a search for relations does not mean that they produce the relations that are found. Those relations can be found without the aid of such cues if the listener or reader has reason to bring the requisite background knowledge to bear. And those relations will not be constructed even with such cues if the available background knowledge cannot make sense of the relations that are apparently indicated. These facts may be easily overlooked and their implications lost from a formal structuralist viewpoint.

Topic Doesn't Explain Coherence

A more promising alternative to the formal structuralism invited by focusing on textual cohesion might seem to be found in the notion of a *topic*. The idea here is that what makes a text or conversation flow along as a coherent whole is that the information conveyed in a sentence or utterance is in some way "about" the same thing as the "subject matter" established in prior discourse.

At a global, intuitive level, the concept of topic is hardly objectionable. But that is because it is so ill-defined that it places no clear constraints on what a "topic" of discourse could be. We know that natural language users can reliably chunk dialogue into "topics" (Planalp & Tracy, 1980), but it remains unclear just what they are chunking. The problem is to clearly specify just what *is* a topic of discourse, so as to be able to make substantive claims about what will and what will not make a relevant contribution.

The notions of topic and topical relevance have been formulated in a wide variety of ways. Clark and Haviland (1977) see topic as a body of information "given" in memory by prior discourse; topical relevance comes about when a listener builds an inferential bridge between the referents in a sentence and those in memory. Van Dijk (1980) equates topic with "macropropositions" that summarize at various levels of abstractness the main ideas of the discourse. Schank and Abelson (1977) suggest that topical coherence involves the integration of sentences within the framework of a world model (script) activated by the discourse. Whatever the particulars of these and other theories may be, almost all represent variations on a common theme summarized by Brown and Yule (1983):

> A hypothesis underlying much of the work we shall report is that there is a specific connection between 'discourse topic' and 'discourse content.' The former can be viewed as, in some sense, consisting of the 'important' elements of the latter. If the representation of discourse content can be presented as a hierarchy of elements in the discourse, then the top-most elements are natural candidates for treatments as the 'most important' components of the discourse topic. (p. 107)

In other words, whether the informational content of a discourse topic is seen in terms of referents, concepts, propositions, or world models, topic is taken to represent the *semantic content* of discourse. Understood in this way, topic is neither necessary nor sufficient for the construction of coherent discourse.

The most obvious problem for a semantic/topic conception of discourse coherence is that it is so easy to construct coherent follow-ups to utterances or sentences grounded not in semantic content but in activities. In example 9, B responds not to the semantic content of what A says, but to the activity of teasing:

(9)   A: Boy, you sure handled that one well. Y'know I think it's really important for the junior faculty to have good role models in the department. That's why I always enjoy watching you handle problems with students. It's such a good opportunity . . . .
      B: Yeah, your mother wears Army boots.

Responses to activity-type are commonplace: complaining about complaining (instead of responding to the content of a complaint), trading compliment for compliment (instead of elaborating on the content of the compliment), taking turns telling jokes, and so on.

Bowers's (1982) analysis of "indirect answers" presents a still more serious anomaly for topic-based views of coherence. Consider this example from Bowers:

(10) A: Will you meet me at the Union for lunch about noon tomorrow?
      B: Does a duck have antlers?

B "answers" A's question only through a complicated chain of inferences that involves recognizing the response as topically *unrelated,* recognizing the response as a yes-no question whose answer is transparent, and figuring out that the intended meaning of the unrelated transparent question is that the original question has the same obvious answer (Bowers, 1982, p. 63; see Bowers, Elliott, & Desmond, 1977; Labov, 1972; Nofsinger, 1976). Whatever the connection between a question and an "indirect answer," it is not a connection between the semantic contents of the two utterances.

One might try to salvage a semantic notion of topic by arguing that these sorts of responses still amount to an indirect expression of semantically related content that "underlies" the discourse. This seems attractive at first, but it has the consequence of allowing us to analyze anything as being "on topic" just in case it is understood to be somehow relevant. But if something is topical *because* it is relevant, topicality cannot be used to determine relevance.

Nor is topical relevance in a semantic sense sufficient to produce coherent discourse. Speakers may be irrelevant despite clear connections between the semantic content of their own utterances and the semantic content of the preceding discourse. We can document this fact in many ways. As just one example, we may note that ongoing activity may change the relevance of a contribution, even when the semantic content of the contribution and its discourse context remains constant. Consider the following set of instructions for storing a phone number in a memory dialer:

(11) 1. Lift the handset. You will hear the dial tone.
      2. Press the store button. *The store button is labeled (X) in Figure 1 and is marked "S" on the keypad.*
      3. Using the keypad enter the location you want to store the number in. . . .
      6. Next—and very important—press the store button again.

Why is it that the italicized description of the store button can be relevantly placed in step 2, but would be out of place in step 6? The semantic context does not change. What does change is the presumed activity context; a reader who makes it to step 6 must already have located the button. Clearly, pragmatic considerations of the purposes for which the discourse is designed determine relevant placement. And it is also this same sort of consideration that determines whether or not semantically topical content is relevant at all (for example, "Frequency specifications for the dial tone are contained in the Appendix" would be an irrelevant digression if placed in step 1 even though it is just as semantically related to the sentences in step 1 as the italicized sentence is to the command in step 2).

So, the notion of topic conceptualized as the organization of semantic content cannot be the unifying principle behind discourse coherence. Such a principle fails to distinguish semantically connected material that is relevant from that which is irrelevant, so it is not sufficient to the task. And such a principle excludes utterances that are relevant (though not on the basis of semantic connections), so it cannot be a necessary basis for coherence either.

Coherence Is a Pragmatic Phenomenon

Of course, topic has *something* to do with the coherence of texts and conversations. Communicators do construct models of what the discourse is "about" through powerful inferential processes and use such models to piece together the elements of discourse into unified wholes (Bransford, 1979; Johnson-Laird, 1983). But something is amiss in this topic-centered conceptualization—namely, what is actually represented in the models that communicators construct.

The models that communicators construct to make sense of discourse are not limited to the referents, concepts, propositions, or states of affairs contained in the content of discourse. These semantic fields are embedded within, and structured by, pragmatic considerations such as the relation between the communicators, their purposes and plans, and the requirements of the activity being conducted by means of the discourse. Communicators do not represent this information as separate levels of coherence in discourse; the information is represented in an integrated model that incorporates discourse content into the context of activity.

That natural language users employ an integrated representation is evidenced by the facts that the same kind of knowledge is needed to understand discourse at either the semantic or the pragmatic level, and that the representation of one level influences the nature of the representation at the other level. For example, when a student tells a professor, "I didn't turn in the assignment on time because my roommate told me she couldn't find her cat," the professor doesn't use one kind of knowledge (pragmatic) to understand the student's utterance as an *excuse* and then another kind (semantic) to understand the reported utterance by the roommate as a request for help. Moreover, understanding the sense of one utterance is crucial to understanding the sense of the other. In general, the same kinds of background knowledge are brought to bear in the understanding of both the content and the performance of discourse, and these so-called "levels" interact as an integrated system.

A pragmatic conception of coherence is implicit in much communication research on discourse: Jacobs and Jackson's (1983b) outline of a rational model for the pursuit of goals in conversation, Bowers, Elliott, and Desmond's (1977) approach to analyzing the basis for pragmatically devious messages, Nofsinger's (1983) discussion of the tactical and strategic aspects of coherence, Sigman's (1983) discussion of how interactional agendas and considerations of reportability constrain topic, and Tracy's (1985) discussion of situational context as a constraint on the relevance of remarks in dialogue. In all of these approaches, the relevance of a sentence or utterance is thought to be established by the way in which it contributes to the point of the discourse—a point that is to be found in the unfolding plans and goals of the communicators.

A Pragmatic Model for Act Exchanges

A pragmatic theory of discourse coherence suggests that constraints on the relevance of utterances or sentences are structured by the point of the ongoing activity, that is, by some discursive goal or plan. The theory also suggests that relevance is a matter of degree: Those utterances that most obviously, directly, and immediately pursue the goals of the activity will create the strongest sense of relevance; those utterances that contribute ambiguously, indirectly, or in an otherwise peripheral way to some conversational plan will appear less relevant.

Although the pragmatic theory is not limited to any specific type or genre of discourse, a particularly convenient domain for an empirical test of its claims can be found in speech act exchanges. Though such exchanges enjoy no position of privilege within our theory, they happen to have several characteristics that come in handy in studying the pragmatic basis for relevance. To begin with, it is known that certain classes of speech acts are strongly associated with specifiable goals of broad, cross-contextual generality (Austin, 1962; Searle, 1969). Requests, for example, normally reflect a goal on the requestor's part to get the requestee to perform some action. The availability of satisfactory analyses of the goals associated with certain classes of acts simplifies the task of operationalizing pragmatic relevance.

Second, speech act exchanges are known to possess a hierarchical organization in which the performance of one act may call for the performance of subordinate acts (see Jacobs & Jackson, 1983a). For example, in making a request, a requestor may need to satisfy objections raised by the requestee, to modify the request to fit what the requestee is willing and able to honor, to meet conditions on compliance imposed by the requestee, to provide clarification of *what* is being requested or of the fact *that* a request is being made, and so on. Some of these subordinate acts are linked to preconditions of requesting, and others apply very generally to any communicative act. The hierarchical organization of speech act exchanges allows us to generate predictions about *degrees* of relevance for various types of response. These predictions will be concretized below, in a theoretically generated hierarchy of response types.

Finally, individual speech act types are known to differ markedly in the strength of their association with speaker goals. Not all speech acts show the strong relationship to a particular goal exhibited by requests. Statements and questions, for example, are notoriously difficult to characterize in terms of any particular goal, partly because they can serve many different types of goals, and partly because they so frequently occur as subordinate acts within some broader, more dominant, goal. The pragmatic view of relevance implies that constraints on relevance should be strongest, and judgments of relevance clearest, when actors' goals are least equivocal. Thus the variation in goal—relatedness among different speech act types allows for additional empirical predictions about perceptions of relevance.

The remainder of this paper reports the results of three experiments conducted to test various empirical implications of the pragmatic theory. Experiment 1 provides a preliminary test of the idea that relevance is a function of the way in which an utterance contributes to current interactional goals, within the context of responses to strongly goal-related speech acts. Experiment 2 provides a cross-linguistic replication of the findings of Experiment 1. Experiment 3 extends the analysis to act types whose goal-relatedness is less certain. For all three experiments, the basic experimental procedure was to present ordinary language users with experimentally manipulated dialogues, for which they were asked to judge the relevance of utterances constituting the manipulation.

EXPERIMENT 1

The most direct empirical implication of the pragmatic theory of relevance is that an utterance will be perceived as more or less relevant, depending on how it contributes to some presumed interactional goal. In Experiment 1, we analyzed perceptions of responses to three types of speech acts, all of which are closely associated with some specific speaker goal: requests, offers, and invitations. As a preliminary step, the experiment required analysis of various types of response to each act type, in terms of how the response types contribute to the goal behind the initial act. The data used to test the theory consisted of ordinary language users' perceptions of the relevance of each response type following an initial request, offer, or invitation.

METHOD

Response Types and Predicted Hierarchy

As argued above, for speech acts with strong links to specific goals, the relevance of a response should be a function of the way in which it contributes to the satisfaction (or resolution) of the goal. We can identify at least six different types of response to requests, offers, and invitations, and we can predict a specific ranking of these types based on how closely they are aligned with, or how far they are removed from, the goal behind the initiating act. Because of the predicted ordering, we shall refer to these six types as response *levels*. They also represent values of the independent variable in the experiments, as will be explained below.

Level 1: Immediate satisfaction of the goal behind the act. The most relevant response to a goal-related act is a response that satisfies the goal—direct, positive uptake of the initiating act. The idea of a "preferred second pair part" of an adjacency pair (Pomerantz, 1978; Sacks, 1973) reflects the primacy of responses that satisfy the goal of the "first pair part" (see Jacobs & Jackson, 1983b). So, for example, a Level 1 response to the request, "Can I borrow your car?" could be "Sure, go ahead"; a Level 1 response to an offer or invitation, likewise, would be an acceptance.

Level 2: Rejections, counters, or replacements for the goal. Responses at this level directly take up the pragmatic point of the initiating act, but do not satisfy the projected goal. Such replies are heard as being directly responsive to the goal, but also as being in conflict with it. So, for example, a Level 2 response to "Can I borrow your car?" could be "I was just going to ask if I could borrow yours," and a Level 2 response to an offer or invitation could be a rejection or a counteroffer.

Level 3: Expansion around the preconditions for achieving the goal. Responses as this level are less directly related to the pragmatic point established in the initiating act, because they address the goal indirectly, if at all. The preconditions for the goal are subordinate issues whose resolution is logically prior to addressing the goal itself. Furthermore, the resolution of a precondition does not necessarily resolve the main issue; that is, it is possible to resolve one precondition, only to confront another wholly independent subordinate issue. By Level 3 responses, we have in mind the sorts of responses that give rise to "expansions" of speech act sequences around the felicity conditions (Jacobs & Jackson, 1981). A Level 3 response to "Can I borrow your car?" could be "I guess I won't be needing it," which refers to one of the *Preparatory Conditions* for requesting (Searle, 1969).

Level 4: Contingent queries. Contingent queries (Garvey, 1977) raise issues of hearing and comprehension, in the slot that would normally be occupied by a level 1 or 2 response. They should be perceived as even less relevant than substantive expansions, because receiving information about what is being attempted is logically prior to using that information to evaluate whatever it is that is being attempted. For example, a Level 4 response to "Can I borrow the car?" could be "Borrow what?", which serves only to get the request repeated. Contingent queries are "holding actions" so far as the goals are concerned: Once the contingent query has been dealt with, the sequence begins again at square one, whereas the resolution of even one substantive precondition represents progress toward the goal. As Merritt (1976) put it, contingent queries "disestablish the conditional relevance" of a reply, though only temporarily.

Level 5: Challenges to the activity or speaker. Level 5 responses raise substantive interactional issues, but of a different sort than those found at Level 3. A Level 5 response calls into question the cooperative framework for conversational interaction, which is the logical precondition for taking up conversational goals at all. In this sense, Level 5 responses still have some sort of pragmatic relationship to the initiating act, but they are far removed from the goals of any act. For example, a Level 5 response to "Can I borrow your car?" could be "How dare you ask me that!"—which, among other things, indicates that the respondent is refusing out of hand to consider the other person's goal.

Level 6: Responses indifferent to the speaker's goal. Level 6 responses ignore the pragmatic point of the initiating act, extending only semantic content. They give "uptake" to the utterance, but not to the illocutionary point of the utterance. The premise behind their placement at the bottom of the hierarchy is that even a response that purposely thwarts a speaker's goal is more relevant than one that fails even to acknowledge that the utterance has a goal. The operationalization of Level 6 called for constructing remarks about persons, objects, or qualities mentioned in the initiating act; so, a Level 6 response to "Can I borrow your car?" could be "Oh! I forgot to tell you, I got a fuzz-buster for my car."

The specific hypothesis of this experiment is that responses to requests, offers, and invitations will be judged differently depending on their level, and that rank-ordering of response types will correspond to the rank-orderings of levels suggested above.

Respondents and Procedures

Respondents were 51 students, recruited on a voluntary basis, from introductory communication classes at a large midwestern university. Each respondent completed a questionnaire requiring two summary judgments of each of six two-turn dialogues. The first turn of the six dialogues was invariant within a questionnaire, and was either a request, an offer, or an invitation. This invariant initiating remark was paired with six *different* responses, one dialogue to a page, in random order. For each dialogue separately, the respondent was asked to judge *how relevant* and *how appropriate* the response was, and to indicate both judgments on 7-interval scales with scores of 1 corresponding to *relevant* and *appropriate* and scores of 7 to *irrelevant* and *inappropriate*. Relevance was defined in the instructions as "meaningfully connected to the previous remark, on topic, and to the point." Appropriateness was defined as "justified, reasonable, and polite." Only relevance ratings were of interest in testing the hypothesis.[2]

Language Samples and
Operationalization of the Hierarchy

A number of different forms of the questionnaire were created, using a wide variety of different specific message contents. The dialogues were considered to be samples from a broader language population, rather than direct operationalizations of the theorized hierarchy (following Jackson & Jacobs, 1983). Thus multiple examples of each type of response were required in order to draw valid inferences about the differences in judgments of each response level. Initially, we constructed 5 specific examples of each type of initiating act. For each of these 15 initiating remarks, 6 different responses were written, 1 at each level of the theorized hierarchy (see Table 13.1 for examples). This procedure has the effect of crossing message replications with levels of the independent variable. Each form of the questionnaire was given to 3 or 4 respondents. Due to errors in data collection, only 4 examples within the request category were actually rated; to maintain a balanced designed at the level of message replications, one example was randomly eliminated from each of the other two speech act types, entailing a loss of 6 respondents. Thus 45 raters provided 270 ratings on a total of 72 responses paired with 12 initiating remarks.

Statistical Analysis

The point of the experiment was to test the effect of response level on judgments of relevance. Initiating act type was included as a second independent variable in order to assess the consistency of the hierarchy across act types. Two levels of replications were nested within speech act types: specific message cases, and respondents (also nested within message cases). The 6 × 3 (Response Level × Act Type) design includes all effects to be tested, with all other sources of variance (messages, respondents,

Table 13.1

Examples of Initiating Acts and Responses for Experiment 1

REQUEST: I'd like to take out a loan for 300 dollars please.

(1) No problem, just sign here.
(2) Sorry, I can only loan you 100 dollars.
(3) Have you any collateral?
(4) Just a moment . . . How much did you say?
(5) Ha ha ha. You *have* to be joking.
(6) Funny, the last person wanted 300 dollars too.

OFFER: I'll take care of your dog while you're out of town.

(1) Thanks.
(2) That's already arranged.
(3) What do I have to do in return?
(4) Just the dog, or is your offer good for the turtle, too?
(5) If I need help from you, I'll ask for it.
(6) Oh, I forgot to tell you, I got a new dog — a great little Schnauzer puppy.

INVITATION: We have an extra ticket to the game — would you like to go with us?

(1) I sure would.
(2) No thanks.
(3) Maybe. Who else is going?
(4) What game is that?
(5) I'm surprised you'd even bother to ask.
(6) John had an extra ticket for me last year.

and all interactions involving either or both) representing various forms of experimental error.

As questionnaires were returned, the design was unbalanced both at the level of message cases within act types and at the level of respondents within message cases. After discarding one case each from the offers and invitations (leaving four message replications per act type), the design remained unbalanced at the level of respondents within cells, requiring unweighted means analysis of variance.[3]

RESULTS AND DISCUSSION

Act type had a small but significant effect on relevance ratings, $F(2, 9) = 5.74$, $p < .05$, $\omega^2 = .02$, but it did not interact significantly with the variable of primary interest, response level, $F(10, 45) = 0.72$. The overall effect of response level was large and significant, $F(5, 45) = 26.85$, $p < .001$, $\omega^2 = .35$. Mean ratings of relevance for each level of response were in the predicted order (see Table 13.2). The Pearson product-moment correlation between response level and mean relevance rating was .95; the rank order correlation, r_s, between predicted and observed orderings was 1.00. Mean ratings of each level of response, broken down by initiating act

Table 13.2
Mean Relevance Ratings of Response Levels for Experiment 1

Level	All Acts[a]	Requests	Offers	Invitations
1	1.53_a	1.44	1.56	1.58
2	$2.09_{a,b}$	2.06	1.81	2.40
3	2.46_b	1.75	2.56	3.06
4	2.67_b	2.69	2.06	3.25
5	4.35_c	3.56	4.56	4.94
6	5.27_d	5.19	4.63	6.00

Note: Each act type included 4 message examples rated by 3 or 4 respondents; means for each act type and across all acts are unweighted by number of respondents.
a. Means with a common subscript are not significantly different by LSD test at $p < .05$. Due to low numbers of cases within act types, comparisons of means are provided only for the combined sample.

type, confirmed the hierarchy exactly only for invitation-response dialogues (for level and rating, $r = .97$; for predicted and observed orderings, $r_s = 1.00$). Request-response and offer-response dialogues confirmed the hierarchy except for a reversal of one pair of adjacent levels in each case (Levels 2 and 3 for requests, $r = .92$, $r_s = .94$; Levels 3 and 4 for offers, $r = .89$, $r_s = .94$).

Overall, the results support two conclusions: First, people can differentiate degrees of relevance in speech act exchanges; and second, these differentiations are related to the type of relationship holding between the initiating act and the response, with goal-satisfying responses being the most relevant and responses connected only by semantic associations being the least relevant.

EXPERIMENT 2

Experiment 2 was simply a cross-linguistic replication of Experiment 1. The theoretical hierarchy underlying the experimental messages should not be bound to any particular language, because it is based on deep rational organization of discourse rather than on any surface level conventions of use. Thus replication of the main findings in languages other than English is an important source of support for the principle behind the hierarchy.

METHOD

Respondents, Procedures, and Materials

Respondents were 100 students recruited on a volunteer basis from a Brazilian university. All aspects of the procedure, including questionnaire construction and administration, were identical with Experiment 1, except that the questionnaires were written in Portuguese. The language samples used in Experiment 2 were originally written in English, then translated into Portuguese by a native speaker of Portuguese who was also a fluent speaker of English. The dialogues were given gist (rather than verbatim) translations. No case used in Experiment 1 was repeated in Experiment 2; the message samples were completely independent of those used in Experiment 1.

The same 3 speech act types were included as in Experiment 1 (requests, offers, and invitations). Originally, the message sample included 6 or 7 cases of each initiating act type, but 2 cases were randomly eliminated from the analysis to balance the design at the level of message replications. The experiment also was designed to have equal numbers of respondents nested within message cases, but 2 respondents failed to complete all ratings and had to be dropped, leaving responses of 88 raters divided among 18 message cases. As in Experiment 1, each of the 88 respondents rated 6 different responses to 1 of 18 initiating acts, so that a total of 528 ratings of relevance were included in the analysis.

The data were analyzed as a 6 × 3 (Response Level × Act Type) design with message replications nested within act type and respondents within message replications. As before, unweighted means analysis of variance was used (see note 3 for details).

RESULTS AND DISCUSSION

Neither act type nor the Response Level × Act Type interaction had any effect on ratings of relevance: For act type, $F(2, 15) = 1.02$, $\omega^2 = .00$; for the interaction, $F(10, 75) = 1.74$, $\omega^2 = .01$. But as before, response level had a substantial influence on ratings, $F(5, 75) = 41.99$, $p < .001$, $\omega^2 = .30$. Mean ratings of relevance for each level of response deviated slightly from the predicted ordering—Levels 4 and 5 reversed, but not significantly so (see Table 13.3). The correlation between level and mean rating was .96, and between predicted and observed ordering, .94.

Mean ratings of relevance for each level of response broken down by act type showed several small deviations from the predicted ordering, but a tolerably close correspondence given the small number of message replications and the difficulty of translation. Product-moment correlations between response level and mean ratings were .90 for requests, .87 for offers, and .95 for invitations; between predicted and observed orderings, the correlations were .83, .89, and 1.00, respectively.

Overall, the results of Experiment 2 deviate from the results of Experiment 1 only in minor details. Although the Portuguese messages were rated slightly differently from the English messages, these differences

Table 13.3
Mean Relevance Ratings of Response Levels for Experiment 2

Level	All Acts[a]	Requests	Offers	Invitations
1	1.71$_a$	1.70	2.05	1.40
2	2.14$_a$	2.73	1.90	1.80
3	3.04$_b$	3.73	2.78	2.60
4	4.11$_c$	3.83	4.13	4.37
5	3.69$_c$	3.47	3.64	3.97
6	5.41$_d$	5.40	6.03	4.70

Note: Each act type included 6 message examples rated by 4 or 5 respondents; means for each act type and across all acts are unweighted by number of respondents.
a. Means with a common subscript are not significantly different by LSD test at $p < .05$. Due to low numbers of cases within act types, comparisons of means are provided only for the combined sample.

showed no consistent pattern across act types that would warrant a conclusion of systematic language differences.

EXPERIMENT 3

The act types analyzed in Experiments 1 and 2 were chosen for the clarity of their connections to specified goals. The data generally confirm that such acts set up clear expectations for response. The more goal-related the response, the greater the perceived relevance. What happens when goals are less clear or less straightforward? Our pragmatic theory makes the same prediction, namely, that judgments of relevance following such acts also should depend on how goal-related the response appears to be. But the generalization of the results from Experiments 1 and 2 is not unproblematic, because difficulties in identifying goals or in evaluating goal-relatedness may make judgments of relevance less uniform and less predictable from response type alone. Speech act exchanges involving requests, offers, and invitations make for easy identification of goals, with or without additional context. But a wide range of other speech act exchanges lacks this clear association with goals, and typically depends upon context or other cues to communicate the speaker's goal. Can the pragmatic theory and hierarchy of response types derived from the theory predict judgments of relevance for less clearly goal-oriented types of speech acts?

In Experiment 3, we replicated the procedures for Experiments 1 and 2, using as initiating remarks four act types believed to bear less straightforward relationships to goals. A number of writers have pointed out difficulties in identifying the "normal" response to certain act types, including complaints (Matoesian, 1981), compliments (Pomerantz, 1978), questions (Churchill, 1978; Levinson, 1979), but especially statements (Jacobs

& Jackson, 1983b; Levinson, 1981). Examples of each act type were studied in Experiment 3.

METHOD

Response Types and Predicted Hierarchy

The theoretical hierarchy defines different response types at each level depending on differences among speech acts in illocutionary point, preconditons, and propositional content. In adapting the hierarchy to the new set of act types, Levels 1 and 2 were the most affected: for compliments, Levels 1 and 2 were operationalized as acceptances and rejections, respectively; for complaints, Level 1 responses were apologies or remedies, and Level 2 responses were contradictions; for questions, Level 1 responses were direct answers, and Level 2 responses "passed" the question to someone else or offered alternative plans for getting the answer; for statements, Level 1 and 2 responses were agreements and contradictions, respectively. Level 3, 4, 5, and 6 responses were essentially the same as those used in Experiments 1 and 2, differing only in detail to adjust to the particular type and content of the initiating act (see Table 13.4 for examples of each type).

Respondents, Procedures, and Materials

Respondents were 63 volunteers recruited from upper- and lower-division communication courses at a large midwestern university. Procedures were identical to those used in Experiment 1, except for the use of new message cases chosen to represent new act types.

Seventeen message cases were written to represent 4 act types: complaints, compliments, questions, and statements. One case was subsequently dropped, to balance the design at the level of message replications, entailing the loss of 2 subjects. A total of 61 respondents rating 6 responses to 1 of 16 initiating acts yielded 366 observations for the analysis.

The data were analyzed as a 6 × 4 (Response Level × Act Type) design, with message cases nested within act types and respondents within message cases. In all other respects, the statistical analysis was identical to that reported for Experiments 1 and 2.

RESULTS AND DISCUSSION

Neither act type nor the Response Level × Act Type interaction had any effect on relevance ratings: For act type, $F(3, 12) = .94$; for the inter-

Table 13.4
Examples of Initiating Acts and Responses for Experiment 3

COMPLAINT: Your assignment is too hard.

(1) I'm sorry it's too hard — do you need more time?
(2) It isn't too hard if you do the reading and come to class.
(3) Everyone else did it, why can't you?
(4) What part gives you problems?
(5) I don't need you to tell me how to teach my class.
(6) My assignments always have three parts.

COMPLIMENT: You look sharp today.

(1) Thank you.
(2) I haven't done anything different from any other day.
(3) Do you really like this dress?
(4) What do you mean?
(5) I'm surprised you could tell.
(6) John looked pretty sharp at the party last Friday.

QUESTION: Where's the rest room?

(1) Around the corner, on the left.
(2) There's an information center in the foyer. You can ask there.
(3) I don't know. I'm just passing through this building.
(4) Uh, sorry, but did you need the men's or the women's?
(5) Where are your manners?
(6) I hate the way some of these buildings have only men's rooms and no women's rooms.

STATEMENT: Chevys are better than Fords.

(1) They sure are.
(2) Chevys are terrible cars.
(3) What makes you say that?
(4) In what way?
(5) Yeah, like you really know something about it.
(6) Do they make Chevys in Lansing?

action, $F(15, 60) = 1.62$, $\omega^2 = .03$. Response level had a substantial main effect on ratings, $F(5, 60) = 22.56$, $p < .001$, $\omega^2 = .30$. Mean ratings of relevance for each response level were not, however, in the order predicted, the most striking deviations being a much higher level of relevance attributed to clarification questions and lower level of relevance attributed to alternative goal responses (see Table 13.5). The correlation between response level and mean rating was lower than in the other experiments, $r = .84$, as was the correlation between predicted and observed orderings, $r_s = .77$. However, the correlations remain very high overall.

Relevance ratings for each level of response to each act type showed little pattern except the predicted precedence of any goal-related response over purely semantic connections. Only compliments reproduced the ordering of means predicted; each of the other 3 act types showed some individual pattern of deviations from this ordering. Product-moment and

Table 13.5
Mean Relevance Ratings of Response Level for Experiment 3

Level	All Acts[a]	Complaints	Compliments	Questions	Statements
1	1.86$_a$	2.06	1.81	1.13	2.44
2	3.02$_b$	3.38	2.19	3.21	3.29
3	2.89$_b$	2.88	3.25	3.29	2.15
4	2.26$_{a,b}$	1.63	3.36	2.21	1.83
5	4.69$_c$	4.50	3.58	5.98	4.69
6	5.28$_c$	5.38	4.38	6.15	5.23

Note: Each act type included 4 message examples rated by 3 or 4 respondents; means for each act type and across all acts are unweighted by number of respondents.
a. Means with a common subscript are not significantly different by LSD test at $p < .05$. Due to low numbers of cases within act types, comparisons of means are provided only for the combined sample.

rank order correlations were, for complaints, .70 and .60; for compliments, .97 and 1.00; for questions, .86 and .83; and for statements, .68 and .49.

The fit between ratings of relevance and theoretical rankings of response types was much poorer in Experiment 3 than in Experiments 1 and 2. Because the hierarchy is based on the relationship between the goals expressed in each act, and because the Experiment 3 exchanges were chosen to represent act types with unclear or uncertain goals, the poorer fit was expectable. Indeed, the relative robustness of the hierarchy for even these act types is somewhat surprising. Several details of the results are noteworthy. First, as compared with Experiments 1 and 2, the relevance ratings given to Level 2 responses in Experiment 3 were quite low, averaging 3.02 across act types in Experiment 3 but 2.09 and 2.14 (where 1 is most relevant) in Experiments 1 and 2. Level 2 responses generally involve acts that thwart the goal behind the initiating act or set up a competing goal. Drawing from all 3 experiments, refusals of requests and rejections of offers, invitations, and compliments were rated between 1.8 and 2.4. Contradiction of complaints and statements and referrals of questions were rated between 3.2 and 3.4. If the goals behind the initiating acts are difficult to identify, respondents' tendencies to see goal-thwarting acts as questionably relevant are not surprising.

Second, as compared with Experiments 1 and 2, the relevance ratings given Level 4 responses were rather high, a mean of 2.26 across act types in Experiment 3, but of 2.69 and 4.11 in Experiments 1 and 2. In fact, the Experiment 3 mean would reflect still greater relevance for clarification questions (a mean of 1.89) if compliments were excluded. The increased acceptability of clarification questions in Experiment 3, like the decreased acceptability of Level 2 responses, may be seen as a predictable consequence of greater uncertainty about the speaker's goal. The most obvious differences between the results of Experiment 3 and the results of the other 2 experiments could be interpreted as indirect evidence for the principle behind the response hierarchy, even though conflicting with the details of the hierarchy itself.

The decrease in strong constraints on relevance observed with the Experiment 3 exchanges is consistent with the basic claim that relevance is a function of goal-relatedness.[4] This implies that the hierarchy of response types should work as well for these act types as for requests, offers, and invitations, if goals were made obvious through the practical or interactional context (which was not provided to respondents in these experiments). Future research should take up systematically the suggestion offered here, that speech act exchanges initiated by complaints, questions, and statements *will* show predictable constraints on relevant responding, *if* an underlying goal is clearly communicated—and otherwise not.

GENERAL DISCUSSION AND CONCLUSIONS

The experiments reported above permit two general conclusions about the nature of relevance and coherence. First, the relevance of a response or the coherence of an exchange is a judgmental issue based in interactants' understandings of what kinds of *activities* are going on, not simply in identification of formal or semantic relations in the discourse. The most consistent result across the 3 experiments was the very low perceptions of relevance for responses linked solely to propositional or referential features of initiating remarks. For every individual act type, responses based solely on extension of such content were judged the least relevant of the alternatives. The overall mean rating of such responses (unweighted by number of message cases or respondents) was 5.30, where 7 indicated maximal irrelevance.

Second, relevance of response appears to be an increasingly differentiated quality as the transparency and goal-orientation of an act increases. Our results corroborate a theoretical point made by several other authors (especially Tracy, 1984b) that relevance is a matter of degree, and that it depends on some underlying organization of participant goals. Not only in our experiments, but also in experiments reported by Tracy (1983), the acceptability of responses focused on the utterance rather than on some underlying goal or activity increased as the difficulty of identifying the goal increased. In our data, this appeared as increased acceptability of clarification questions following initiating acts with unclear points, and in Tracy's data, it appeared as increased acceptability of event extensions when no broader issue could be identified as the point of reporting the event.

An obvious question about our results is how generalizable they are. Although our intent was to test a very abstract and general position on relevance, our test procedure was limited exclusively to two-turn speech act exchanges, and further, to only seven specific types of such exchanges. We believe, however, that general conclusions are justified. Empirically, our conclusions dovetail nicely with other studies of very different types of discourse. The centrality of goals to relevance also has been corroborated by Donohue and Diez (1985) for interaction organized around conflict negotiation, by Nofsinger (1983) for casual conversation and for courtroom discourse, and by Tracy (1983, 1984a) for responses to conversational stories. Tracy (1984b) has drawn conclusions strikingly parallel to our own, based on the observation that in a wide range of situations "conversationally irrelevant" responses might be acceptable, or even preferable to extensions of the content of previous utterances. Such situations, in our view, involve a separation between conversational *content* and participants' *goals,* as for instance, in "getting to know you" conversations, in which the goal of learning about the other person does not depend upon talking *about* the other person. So what we have observed for speech act exchanges appears to be part of a very general pattern exhibited in many types of interaction, and not something peculiar to two-turn speech act exchanges or to the subset we happened to study.

But further, in principle, we would balk at an eclectic acceptance of one account of coherence for one class of phenomena, another for another class, and so on. If our conclusions fail to generalize in subsequent research on other types of discourse, we will conclude not that principles of relevance differ from domain to domain, but that our explanation for relevance in speech act exchanges is wrong, and we will search for a more fundamental principle within which unified explanations can be provided. It is this commitment to a unified theoretical account of relevance that leads us ultimately to reject both cohesion and topic as explanations not only for the cases in which they obviously fail, but also for the cases in which they apparently succeed. Unexplained empirical findings ought to be taken as indicators of something wrong with a theory, and not just as one more entry in a catalogue of limiting conditions.

NOTES

1. Examples used to develop arguments are hypothetical cases constructed by us or by other authors. Nothing in our argument hinges on whether or not such cases are actually likely to occur, because our arguments are not about behavior but about interpretation.

2. The appropriateness scale was provided to encourage respondents to separate their overall evaluative response from their judgments of relevance, because pilot testing suggested that respondents who were asked to judge only relevance would attempt to communicate other evaluative judgments anyway, leading, for example, to extremely low ratings of relevance for direct refusals of requests or for any other impolite or uncooperative act. In the main experiment, the ratings of relevance and appropriateness still correlated very highly, $r = .74$, as should be expected, because relevance is presumably one of several dimensions of appropriateness. Respondents did seem to recognize the conceptual distinction, however, as is evidenced by the fact that they tended to condemn as inappropriate acts in which

one partner thwarted the goals of the other, even though they might recognize that such acts were relevant. For example, a simple rejection of an invitation ("I called to ask you and John to come over for dinner Friday night." "Can't do it this week.") was rated inappropriate, $M = 5.00$, even though clearly relevant, $M = 2.25$.

3. None of the analysis of variance programs available with SAS (SAS, Inc., 1985), SPSS^x (SPSS, Inc., 1983), or other accessible packages perform unweighted means analysis of variance. The programs that accommodate unbalanced designs (including SAS GLM and SPSS^x ANOVA and MANOVA) take a quite different approach to unequal cell sizes, treating it as a problem of correlated factors only. This is fine when unequal cell sizes represent some sort of a fact about the population from which cases were drawn, but not when unequal cell sizes come about through wholly accidental features of data collection, subject assignment, and subject mortality. The distortions in estimates of treatment effects that can come about through unequal numbers of replications assigned to treatment levels are well known, and the method of solution is very straightforward, but the solution cannot be implemented using any of the computational options offered within any of the standard analysis of variance programs. We accomplished the unweighted means analysis of variance in a series of steps requiring hand calculations to supplement computer output. First, sums of squares for effects involving respondents were computed using SPSS^x MANOVA; second, mean ratings for each message case at each response level were obtained from SPSS^x MANOVA; third, these means, without weighting by cell sizes, were input to SAS ANOVA to get sums of squares for all remaining effects in the design, which then had only to be multiplied by the harmonic mean of the cell sizes to produce the unweighted sums of squares. F-ratios were constructed by hand, with error terms selected on the basis of statistical criteria outlined by Winer (1971) and substantive criteria suggested by Clark (1973) and by Cornfield and Tukey (1956). For the main effect of act type, the appropriate error term was the mean square for message cases within act types; for the main effect of response level and for the Response Level × Act Type interaction, the appropriate error term was the mean square for Response Level × Message Cases within Act Types.

4. Unfortunately, there is another possible explanation that we cannot rule out at this point. Reexamination of the individual dialogues revealed several problems in the operationalization of Level 4 response types within Experiment 3 (though no problems with the operationalization of Level 2 response types). A number of examples had the *form* of contingent queries, but the *function* of some higher level of response. For example, the complaint, "Your assignment is too hard," got the response, "What part gives you problems?" A reasonable interpretation of this response is that the complainee is offering to help with the hard parts, not merely trying to understand what is being said in the first turn. Likewise, in response to "You overcharged me on these groceries," the question "How much?" implies that the grocer is preparing to remedy the problem (Merritt, 1976). Because the promotion of these apparent clarification questions is accountable in terms of their implicated relationship to goals, it is unclear whether they support or contradict the pragmatic theory.

REFERENCES

Austin, J. L. (1962). *How to do things with words.* Oxford: Oxford University

Bowers, J. W. (1982). Does a duck have antlers? Some pragmatics of "transparent questions." *Communication Monographs, 49,* 63-69.

Bowers, J. W., Elliott, N. D., & Desmond, R. J. (1977). Exploiting pragmatic rules: Devious messages. *Human Communication Research, 3,* 235-242.

Bransford, J. D. (1979). *Human cognition: Learning, understanding and remembering.* Belmont, CA: Wadsworth.

Brockway, D. (1981). Semantic constraints on relevance. In H. Parret, M. Sbisà, & J. Vershueren (Eds.), *Possibilities and limitations of pragmatics: Proceedings of the conference on pragmatics, Urbino, July 8-14, 1979* (pp. 57-78). Amsterdam: John Benjamins B. V.

Brown, G., & Yule, G. (1983). *Discourse analysis.* Cambridge: Cambridge University Press.

Churchill, L. (1978). *Questioning strategies in sociolinguistics*. Rowley, MA: Newbury House.

Clark, H. H. (1973). The language-as-fixed-effect fallacy: A critique of language statistics in psychological research. *Journal of Verbal Learning and Verbal Behavior, 12*, 335-359.

Clark, H. H., & Haviland, S. E. (1977). Comprehension and the given-new contract. In R. O. Freedle (Ed.), *Discourse production and comprehension* (pp. 1-40). Norwood, NJ: Ablex.

Cornfield, J., & Tukey, J. W. (1956). Average values of mean squares in factorials. *Annals of Mathematical Statistics, 27*, 907-949.

Craig, R. T., & Tracy, K. (Eds.). (1983). *Conversational coherence: Form, structure, and strategy*. Beverly Hills, CA: Sage.

Donohue, W. A., & Diez, M. E. (1985). Directive use in negotiation interaction. *Communication Monographs, 52*, 305-318.

Ellis, D. G. (1982). Language and speech communication. In M. Burgoon (Ed.), *Communication Yearbook 6* (pp. 34-62). Beverly Hills, CA: Sage.

Garvey, C. (1977). The contingent query: A dependent act in conversation. In M. Lewis & L. A. Rosenblum (Eds.), *Interaction, conversation, and the development of language* (pp. 63-93). New York: John Wiley.

Gorey, E. (1972). *Amphigorey*. Toronto: Longmans Canada Ltd.

Grice, H. P. (1975). Logic and conversation. In P. Cole & J. L. Morgan (Eds.), *Syntax and semantics, Vol. 3: Speech acts* (pp. 41-58). New York: Academic Press.

Halliday, M., & Hasan, R. (1976). *Cohesion in English*. London: Longman.

Hobbs, J. R. (1982). Towards an understanding of coherence in discourse. In W. G. Lehnert & M. H. Ringle (Eds.), *Strategies for natural language processing* (pp. 223-244). Hillsdale, NJ: Lawrence Erlbaum Associates.

Jackson, S., & Jacobs, S. (1983). Generalizing about messages: Suggestions for the design and analysis of experiments. *Human Communication Research, 9*, 169-191.

Jacobs, S. (1986). Language. In M. L. Knapp & G. R. Miller (Eds.), *Handbook of interpersonal communication* (pp. 313-343). Beverly Hills, CA: Sage.

Jacobs, S., & Jackson, S. (1983a). Strategy and structure in conversational influence. *Communication Monographs, 50*, 285-304.

Jacobs, S., & Jackson, S. (1983b). Speech act structure in conversation: Rational aspects of pragmatic coherence. In R. T. Craig & K. Tracy (Eds.), *Conversational coherence: Form, structure, and strategy* (pp. 47-66). Beverly Hills, CA: Sage.

Johnson-Laird, P. N. (1983). *Mental models*. Cambridge, MA: Harvard University Press.

Labov, W. (1972). Rules for ritual insults. In D. Sudnow (Ed.), *Studies in social interaction* (pp. 120-169). New York: Free Press.

Levinson, S. C. (1979). Activity types and language. *Linguistics, 17*, 365-399.

Levinson, S. C. (1981). Some pre-observations on the modelling of dialogue. *Discourse Processes, 4*, 93-116.

Matoesian, G. (1981, August). *Complaining about complaining: The anatomy of a conversational device*. Paper presented at the University of Nebraska Summer Conference on Discourse Processes and Conversational Interaction, Lincoln, NE.

McLaughlin, M. L. (1984). *Conversation: How talk is organized*. Beverly Hills, CA: Sage.

Merritt, M. (1976). On questions following questions in service encounters. *Language in Society, 5*, 315-357.

Morgan, J. L. (1978). Toward a rational model of discourse comprehension. In D. L. Waltz (Ed.), *Theoretical issues in natural language processing-2* (pp. 109-114). New York: Association for Computing Machinery.

Nofsinger, R. E., Jr. (1976). On answering questions indirectly. *Human Communication Research, 2*, 172-181.

Nofsinger, R. E. (1983). Tactical coherence in courtroom conversation. In R. T. Craig & K. Tracy (Eds.), *Conversational coherence: Form, structure, and strategy* (pp. 243-258). Beverly Hills, CA: Sage.

Planalp, S., & Tracy, K. (1980). Not to change the topic but . . . : A cognitive approach to the management of conversation. In D. Nimmo (Ed.), *Communication yearbook 4* (237-258). Brunswick, NJ: Transaction Books.

Pomerantz, A. (1978). Compliment responses: Notes on the cooperation of multiple constraints. In J. Schenkein (Ed.), *Studies in the organization of conversational interaction* (pp. 79-112). New York: Academic Press.

Sacks, H. (1973). Lecture notes. Summer Institute of Linguistics, Ann Arbor, Michigan.

SAS Institute, Inc. (1985). *SAS user's guide: Statistics, version 5 edition.* Cary, NC: SAS Institute, Inc.

Schank, R. C., & Abelson, R. P. (1977). *Scripts, plans, goals and understanding: An inquiry into human knowledge structures.* Hillsdale, NJ: Lawrence Erlbaum.

Searle, J. R. (1969). *Speech acts.* London: Cambridge University Press.

Sigman. S. J. (1983). Some multiple constraints placed on conversational topics. In R. T. Craig & K. Tracy (Eds.), *Conversational coherence: Form, structure, and strategy* (pp. 174-195). Beverly Hills, CA: Sage.

SPSS, Inc. (1983). *SPSS^x user's guide* New York: McGraw-Hill.

Tracy, K. (1983). The issue-event distinction: A rule of conversation and its scope condition. *Human Communication Research, 9,* 320-334.

Tracy, K. (1984a). Staying on topic: An explication of conversational relevance. *Discourse Processes, 7,* 447-464.

Tracy, K. (1984b, May). *The obligation to be irrelevant.* Paper presented at the annual meeting of the International Communication Association, San Francisco.

Tracy, K. (1985). Conversational coherence: A cognitively grounded rules approach. In R. L. Street, Jr., & J. N. Cappella (Eds.), *Sequence and pattern in communicative behavior* (pp. 30-49). London: Edward Arnold.

van Dijk, T. A. (1982). *Macrostructures: An interdisciplinary study of global structures in discourse, interaction, and cognition.* Hillsdale, NJ: Lawrence Erlbaum.

Waltz, D. L. (1982). The state of the art in natural-language understanding. In W. G. Lehnert & M. H. Ringle (Eds.), *Strategies for natural language processing* (pp. 3-36). Hillsdale, NJ: Lawrence Erlbaum.

Winer, B. J. (1971). *Statistical principles in experimental design* (2nd ed.). New York: McGraw-Hill.

IV ● MASS COMMUNICATION

14 ● Deviance as a Predictor of Newsworthiness: Coverage of International Events in the U.S. Media

PAMELA J. SHOEMAKER ●
TSAN-KUO CHANG ● NANCY BRENDLINGER

University of Texas at Austin

T HE study of international news coverage within the United States and the flow of international news worldwide has yielded a rich body of literature describing the amount of news present from various countries in various content categories, and hypotheses have been tested about various influences on international news (for example, Galtung & Ruge, 1965; Gerbner & Marvanyi, 1977; Hart, 1966; Hester, 1971; Hicks & Gordon, 1974; Lent, 1977; Östgaard, 1965; Sande, 1971; Semmel, 1977; Smith, 1971.) A common finding has been an emphasis on bad news (for example, Bergsma, 1980; Galtung & Ruge, 1965; Kaplan, 1979; Larson, 1979; Lent, 1977) but there is little theory available to explain why this should be true.

We will attempt to go beyond the description of international news and to place it in the broader theoretical framework of social change, showing that what U.S. media define as newsworthy about world events has a direct relationship to the deviance of those events and to existing U.S. norms in particular.

Correspondence and requests for reprints: Pamela J. Shoemaker, Department of Journalism, the University of Texas at Austin, Austin, TX 78712.

Stempel (1985) shows that although the individual stories published in newspapers differ, there is considerable similarity in the kinds of topics that are appropriate or newsworthy. But what do we mean when we say an event or person is newsworthy? Definitions of newsworthiness have ranged from the pragmatic ("News is whatever the editor decides is news"; Hulteng & Nelson, 1971) to the philosophical ("The newsworthy event is one that affects or changes social, economic, political, physical, or other relationships"; Harriss, Leiter, & Johnson, 1977).

Galtung and Ruge (1965) offer a list of 12 factors affecting the coverage of international events, and most news writing textbooks offer a laundry list of news criteria. The following list is adapted from four texts: timeliness, proximity; importance, impact, or consequence; interest; conflict or controversy; sensationalism; prominence; and novelty, oddity, or the unusual (Dennis & Inmach, 1981; Harriss, Leiter, & Johnson, 1977; Izard, Culbertson, & Lambert, 1973; Stephens, 1970). Many of these indicators have been used by those studying international news content in U.S. media; yet, although such lists provide indicators of newsworthiness, they do not address the theoretical issue of explaining what underlying construct ties the indicators together into a meaningful "newsworthiness" package or of explaining why such content should be important to journalists and society.

The purpose of this chapter is to extend the study of international news coverage by showing the theoretical relationship of the newsworthiness concept to the mass media's role in social change by examining indicators of newsworthiness in the light of various conceptualizations of the construct "deviance." In brief, we will argue that an assessment of deviance underlies many of the indicators of newsworthiness. Therefore, much mass media news content elaborates the extent and direction of deviance in society and has direct implications for the mass media's impact on social change. First, we will cover five conceptualizations of the deviance construct. Second, we will show the relationship between definitions of newsworthiness and of deviance definitions. Third, we will present some empirical evidence from a pilot study that suggests that the deviance of world events is a useful predictor of whether that event is covered by the U.S. mass media or not. Fourth, we will discuss the implications of the mass media's emphasis on deviance in international news for social change.

DEVIANCE

The earliest sociological interest in deviance focused on eliminating it as an undesirable social problem, but the emphasis shifted in the early 20th century toward studying deviance as a sociological problem that had social and cultural sources (Bell, 1976). We will outline five conceptions of deviance.

The statistical definition of deviance. The simplest and perhaps most common definition of deviance is statistical: Anything that differs too much from the average is deviant (Becker, 1963). Statistical deviance is the basis for many psychological tests; if one scores too far from the mean, then one is considered deviant (Bell, 1976).

The pathological definition of deviance. The pathological conceptualization of deviance uses a medical analogy to explain deviant behaviors: Deviance is viewed as something in which no normal, healthy person would take part, and so deviant individuals are by definition not healthy. Deviance is seen as a "disease in the body of society" which must be eliminated or controlled (Hills, 1980). Many considered functionalism a "latter-day version of pathology" (Matza, 1969). Functionalism (the study of how social institutions and relationships may work to maintain or disrupt the stability of a system) may well have provided a transition between the pathological and normative conceptualizations of deviance.

The normative definition of deviance. A normative theoretical approach to deviance emphasizes behaviors that violate social norms. Behavior is de facto deviant when compared to some norm external to the individual (Wells, 1978). We could look at an infinite variety of specific norms whose breaking might be a signal of deviance, but the central issue in normative deviance is that deviance is a result of some *act,* the breaking of some norm. There is a negative connotation to normative deviance, an assumption that deviance is dysfunctional for both the individual and society (Rosenberg, Stebbins, & Turowetz, 1982), although some (including Erikson, 1966; Birenbaum & Lesieur, 1982; Scott, 1972) have suggested that deviance may in fact perform important functions for society.

The labeling definition of deviance. Early labeling theorists such as Becker (1963) and Erikson (1966) challenged the normative definition of deviance. Labeling advocates believe that an individual becomes deviant when and because someone else calls him or her deviant, not (in the extreme form) because of any inherent badness. Deviance, Erikson (1966, p. 26) says, is a quality conferred upon behavior by observers and not a quality inherent in that behavior. Becker (1963) says that the assignment of the label *deviance* is an "interaction between the person who commits an act and those who respond to it."

The self-conception definition of deviance. Our last definition of deviance is a newer, cognitive one that depends on the subjective meaning of behavior for its enactors. Behavior is *consciously* deviant to the extent that a person or group is aware that what he or she is doing is in some sense wrong or disapproved. The power to categorize a person as deviant lies entirely within that person or group (Wells, 1978). This conceptualization of deviance introduces a cognitive element to a concept that has been defined in primarily sociological terms. The individual's self-conception is not merely a function of society, as Mead would suggest, but is also affected by a series of psychological variables.

NEWSWORTHINESS

One of the mechanisms through which the mass media exert their influence on social change is in assessing the newsworthiness of people and events. Not only are deviant people and events often considered newsworthy, but deviance is itself an integral part of the newsworthiness definition.

Newsworthiness is an important criterion for publication; journalists continually emphasize discovering the new and transmitting that information to their audience members. Alexander (1981) says that the news media fulfill a normative function in society by providing ways for the society to organize and understand what happens through formulating normative explanations for what happens. Discovering instances in which norms have been broken (news) is the only way that the news media can fulfill that normative function.

Of the usual indicators of newsworthiness (timeliness;proximity; importance, impact, or consequence; interest; conflict or controversy; sensationalism; prominence; and novelty, oddity, or the unusual), the last four seem the most likely to be related to deviance, and these will be discussed as a deviance dimension of newsworthiness. Importance and interest, although related to deviance, will form a social significance dimension and timeliness and proximity will be discussed as contingent conditions.

The Deviance Dimension

Novelty. The novelty indicator has the most obvious relationship to deviance, because odd people or events are likely to be deviant, but this category also includes rare events and the unexpected, such as airplane crashes. An airplane crash is a deviant event because most planes do not crash. Heart transplants were once rare events, each earning national news coverage. Today, however, many transplant operations occur every year and so each operation is less newsworthy, less deviant in comparison to other modes of heart treatment. Today's definition of a newsworthy heart operation event is reserved for mechanical or cross-species heart transplantations. Soon even these may become commonplace and no longer deviant or newsworthy.

This conception of deviance is primarily statistical. The frequency with which an event occurs determines whether it is deviant and newsworthy or commonplace. The more frequently an event occurs, the less deviant and the less newsworthy it is. Thus even if norms are broken the novelty eventually disappears, with the ultimate result of changing the norm.

Galtung and Ruge (1965) included rare or unexpected events in their list of 12 factors affecting whether or not international events will be covered, and their concept of amplitude implies that events or things that are statistically larger or more important than the mean are most likely to be covered.

Conflict. Conflict and controversy are newsworthy because they involve changes in customs and values, social unrest, and changes in the status quo (Dennis & Inmach, 1981; Izard, Culbertson & Lambert, 1973). Many scholars have pointed out a tendency of U.S. media to publicize events dealing with conflict (such as Galtung & Ruge, 1965; Hester, 1971; Lent, 1977; and Smith, 1971).

Conflict stories include all disagreement or competition between people and groups, and deviance is possible whenever someone challenges a norm. Examples of conflict include the actions of most political groups— particularly those special interest groups that advocate social change— changes of laws or norms, changes that must be considered deviant when compared to the established order.

Sensationalism. Izard, Culbertson, and Lambert (1973) say that sensationalism is very similar to conflict, but centers on violence and crime. It is a "flaunting of basic ideas about what's important and right or wrong." Violence and crime are types of deviance—they break existing norms of behavior. Criminals break institutional norms—laws—and so come to the attention of various agents of social control, especially law enforcement officials and journalists. Sometimes the police discover a crime and report it to journalists; sometimes the reverse process occurs. Police and journalists work together—intentionally or not—to control the amount of criminal deviance in society. One punishes the deviant act through legal statutes; the other punishes the act through publicity and loss of reputation.

People and groups who challenge the status quo often must resort to conflict or sensationalism in order to get the attention of the mass media (Cobb & Elder, 1972). Because media coverage is often essential to the ability of the group to mobilize resources (Lauderdale & Estep, 1980), some groups are willing to resort to violence or crime in order to achieve their goals. Others rely on conflict to get media coverage; they often create conflict situations—media events—in order to get the media's attention. Thus although sensational activities are by definition newsworthy and deviant, they are sometimes a *reflection* of deviant attitudes and behaviors, and at other times a *strategy* for getting news coverage that may be more deviant than the group's usual activities.

Östgaard says that an emphasis on sensationalism is inherent in the news process. The result of media emphasis on sensationalism is to "give the impression that conflicts can be averted more easily by preparing for the use of force, rather than by reducing tensions by undramatic means" (Östgaard, 1965, p. 55).

Prominence. Newsworthiness also encompasses people who are celebrities or who are notorious for some reason. Galtung and Ruge (1965) say that the more elite an individual is, the more likely his or her actions are to be reported by the mass media. This can extend to the ludicrous—when the U.S. president gets a common cold, journalists interview his physician. When a successful actor marries or divorces, the event is publicized world-

wide. Such events are newsworthy not because of their inherent significance, but rather because of the nature of the people involved. Movie stars
and politicians are prominent because they are somehow *different* from the
rest of us. They are deviant when compared to norms of daily activities,
employment, money earned or inherited, and so on. It is this differentness
or deviance that makes their lives interesting reading for others. If they
were no different from the rest of us, then their activities would not be
newsworthy.

Theoretical linkage of deviance to newsworthiness. Communication is
clearly important to deviance, and an element of communication is
included in most discussions of deviance and social control (see, for example, Becker, 1963; Bell, 1976; Birenbaum & Lesieur, 1982; Gibbs, 1981;
Schur, 1980).

Yet although many deviance theorists cite the importance of communication, specifically of the mass media, they often treat the mass media as
mere channels through which passes information about deviance or about
labels that others have assigned. The type of information, even the amount
of information (Bell, 1976), is seen to be critical to deviance and social control, but there is little recognition that the mass media may themselves
transform information and affect the deviance of people and groups.

Although no integrated theory of content exists that can adequately
explain all influences on mass media content, deviance theorists may
benefit from looking at several theoretical approaches discussed by communication scholars such as Gans (1979), Gitlin (1980), Cohen and
Young (1981), and Altschull (1984). These approaches look at media content as a dependent variable, with content sometimes not mirroring reality.
The approaches can be grouped into four general categories:

(1) Content as a function of media routines. Several researchers (such
as Gans, 1979; Gitlin, 1980; Goldenberg, 1975; and Tuchman, 1973)
have studied the influences of newsgathering habits on mass media content. These studies locate the explanations for differences in media presentation and for content distortions in how news organizations gather,
process, and transmit content. Media routines such as deadlines, use of
sources, event-orientation of most stories, styles of writing, reliance on
wire services, and gatekeeping have been shown to affect the kinds of stories that are written and published or broadcast.

(2) Content as influenced by journalists' socialization and attitudes.
Researchers such as Breed (1955) and Johnstone, Slawski, and Bowman
(1972) have investigated ways in which journalists' professional socialization and personal attitudes affect the kinds of stories they write. Young
(1981) describes how journalists' professional standards may result in their
having a centrist view of the world which results in their framing reality as
divided between a consensual majority and a deviant minority. Another

approach has journalists viewing their professional roles as public educators, giving the public what it needs (Cohen & Young, 1981).

(3) Content as the result of social and institutional forces. As Gans (1979) outlines it, to understand the production of the news, one must first understand the power relationships involved between various institutions or social forces outside of the news organizations. The news is shaped by technological, economic, and cultural forces, as well as by the audience, advertisers, and news sources.

(4) Content as a function of ideological positions. In a hegemonic approach (Gramsci, 1971), the mass media are viewed as having a vested interest in the status quo, with content reflecting their interest. Although the media will criticize the status quo enough to establish their legitimacy as news organizations, they will never seriously threaten the status quo (Gitlin, 1980). Altschull (1984) has suggested another ideological approach, in which media content reflects the ideology of those who finance the mass media.

These theoretical approaches will be useful in looking at the ways in which the mass media may contribute to what Schur (1980) calls the "deviantizing" of people and groups. Although what most people know about the world comes from the mass media, there are instances in which media content presents a distorted picture of reality. It is essential that we consider ways in which the mass media may interact in the deviantizing process, such as through the determination of what is newsworthy and therefore worthy of mass media coverage.

Judgments about an event's newsworthiness are made by individual journalists, making the journalist-centered approach applicable. Yet frequently it is the executives of the news organizations who establish the organizations' definition of news, and not the reporters or low-level editors (Epstein, 1981).

News executives allocate time and resources for newsgathering according to pressures from economics, advertising, sources, special interest groups, the audience, and other social or institutional forces. This indicates that the social influence theory is probably also applicable, but the hierarchical nature of the approaches should be considered. If societal factors affect what is newsworthy, one explanation for such influence would be hegemonic. As businesspeople with a vested interest in the status quo, media owners find it functional to expose deviance. This has the simultaneous effect of giving the audience the conflict, sensationalism, prominence, and novelty it desires and of setting the boundaries of what is proper and acceptable behavior in society. Several theorists (including Birenbaum & Lesieur, 1982; Erikson, 1966; Scott, 1972) have suggested that deviance is functional for society. Deviance creates a common focus for group emotion against threats to the status quo; it clarifies the rules for everyone else without their actually testing the rules themselves; it serves as a warning of weaknesses in the system. The process of noticing and punishing or controlling deviance allows the controlling mechanisms to exhibit their power.

News is a commodity with monetary value, and the success of news organizations often rides on their ability to define what news is. Although individuals make news decisions, there is also often written or unwritten policy in the newsroom about what constitutes news to that organization. Deviance is news, and deviant events make up much of the news content for any given day. In addition, the more deviant a person or event is, the more prominently it will be covered and the more space (or time) will be allocated.

Much of the way in which newsworthiness is defined relates to deviance, and most of those deviance-newsworthiness criteria are normative. Conflict, sensationalism, and prominence are all related to departures from the usual, from societal norms, although the pathological perspective sometimes crops up too, particularly in crime news, in which the criminal may be found not guilty "by reason of insanity," or an increase in the number of transients is explained as caused by an increase in the number of mental patients released. Novelty is more a statistical conceptualization of deviance, depending on the rare or unusual event for definition.

Yet, although news organizations may use the normative, statistical, or even pathological definitions of deviance in determining what is newsworthy, we must not ignore the effects of such usage on labeling. Journalists have the power to label people as deviant through their news stories, and, when labeling occurs, it is as a result of the journalists' having used their own normative, statistical, or pathological conceptualizations of what is deviant. Labeling is, therefore, the logical result of decisions made with statistical, normative, or pathological comparisons.

The Social Significance Dimension

Hall, Chritcher, Jefferson, Clarke, and Roberts (1981, pp. 335-336) say that the most basic news value "involves an orientation to items which are 'out of the ordinary.'" Yet news organizations regularly transmit information that does not involve conflict, sensationalism, prominence, or anything unusual. The remaining four newsworthiness criteria—timeliness, proximity, importance, and interest—also influence the definition of news, and they relate to deviance in different ways.

Importance (including impact and consequence) and interest are often positively related to the four deviance criteria in that novel, controversial, sensational, and prominent situations are often inherently interesting or important. Although mechanical hearts are a novelty, they are also an important medical advance of interest to millions of people. The conflict generated by special interest groups who advocate social change is both important and interesting because of its possible consequence to society. Violent, sensational events often have important consequences for society and individuals. Prominent individuals seem always to be interesting and are sometimes important due to their social or political roles.

There are also important or interesting events that do not involve much deviance, such as meetings of legislative bodies. Meetings of public groups are often covered by the mass media as part of the media's social obligation to their communities or nations. Some newspapers pride themselves on being "newspapers of record" which document the actions of elected and appointed officials to ensure an informed citizenry. Yet being a newspaper of record may mean that accounts of such meetings are publicized regardless of whether or not the meetings result in anything important or interesting. The information is transmitted because of the long-term needs of society to have such information recorded, perhaps a form of long-term social consequence. The extent to which the media publicize a category of events, such as international events, can reveal the significance of those events to the nation (Semmel, 1977).

Such an obligatory recording of the actions of legislative bodies is likely to result in minimal, less prominent coverage, however, unless something deviant occurred in the meeting. Conflict, sensationalism, prominence, or novelty in legislative meetings will result in coverage with more space or time allocated and more prominence given to the story. So, although some socially significant events get media coverage no matter how ordinary or routine they are, the deviance of the event will affect the extent of the event's newsworthiness and the amount of space or time and prominence allocated. Deviance in the form of conflict, prominent speakers, sensational behaviors, or novel activities will increase the newsworthiness of what are otherwise ordinary and minimally newsworthy events.

Contingent Conditions

Timeliness and proximity are key criteria only for judging the newsworthiness of marginally deviant or significant events; they act as contingent conditions in the determination of whether or not such events are transmitted as news and how prominently. A boring legislative meeting may receive some perfunctory coverage by local media immediately after the meeting, and be ignored by media elsewhere. Deviant people and events—those involving conflict, sensationalism, prominence, or novelty— are often newsworthy regardless of the timeliness or proximity involved. Interest in deviant people and events is almost always high, and deviance is often important regardless of when or where it is discovered.

As Figure 14.1 points out, the publication of medium-deviance events is contingent on being either timely or proximate. Events of low deviance may be published if socially significant and either timely or proximate. This may help explain why proximity seems to influence coverage of interna-

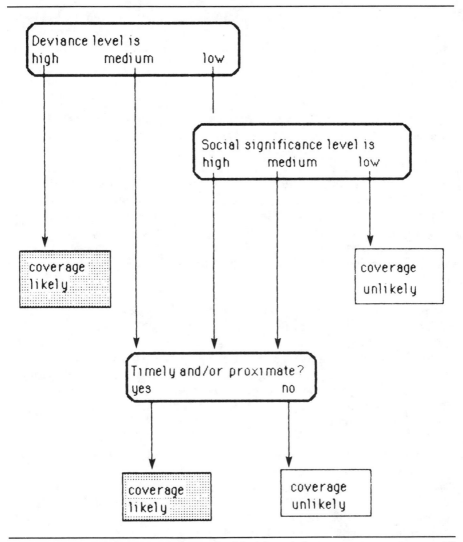

Figure 14.1 Model for predicting the likelihood that an event or issue will receive coverage.

tional events in some studies (for example, Semmel, 1977) but not in others (for example, Hicks & Gordon, 1974).

METHOD

We will test our idea that deviance is one underlying dimension of newsworthiness by studying the coverage of world events in the U.S. mass media. Our hypothesis is that the more deviant a world event is, the more likely it is to be covered in the U.S. mass media. Our assumption is that newsworthy events are more likely to be covered than nonnewsworthy events.

Deviance

Rosengren (1970) has advocated the use of extra media data in such studies, and we have adopted one of his suggested sources for our sampling frame of world events—Keesing's *Contemporary Archives: Record of World Events*. Keesing's collects information about events from world media, government, and other sources and therefore it does not provide a purely extra media data source. But, as Rosengren points out, such archives are frequently the only available way of measuring the range of world events, and, although they are not independent of mass media reports, they do provide a much larger set of world events from which to sample than we would reasonably expect any individual U.S. mass medium to cover.

We randomly sampled 179 events from the Keesing's index during the calendar year 1984. Events were selected if they occurred outside of the United States. Photocopies of the descriptions of each event were acquired, and the deviance of each event was coded independently by two of the researchers. Pearson correlation coefficients between the two coders' ratings were used to estimate intercoder reliability. Coefficients for the three scales described below were (a) statistical deviance, .74; (b) potential for social change deviance, .51 and (c) normative deviance, .84. When the coders disagreed, their average rating was used.

Deviance was rated according to three of the five definitions of deviance outlined earlier in this chapter. Labeling and self-conception deviance were not included. Although journalists may label events as deviant in their articles, there is little reason to think that labeling would be recognizable in a description of an event. Likewise, we have no entry into the psychological processes of the people involved in the events; therefore the self-conception definition does not apply to this study.

The other three definitions of deviance were integrated into the measuring scheme, with three scales used to code the deviance of each event.

Statistical deviance: the extent to which the event is unusual, given the context of how common such events are in the world. An event is coded as extremely deviant statistically if the number of times the event occurs proportionate to the number of times it could conceivably occur is extremely small. Statistical deviance is measured on a four-point scale, with the points being defined as follows: (1) The event is common. Things like this happen all of the time. (2) The event is somewhat unusual, but things like this seem to be happening more and more frequently. (3) The event is unusual, but things like this have occurred before more than once. (4) The event is extremely unusual and probably totally unexpected. Things like this have almost never been known to occur before.

Potential for social change deviance: the extent to which the event threatens the status quo in the country in which the event occurs. We have not used the medical, pathological analogy, in that we do not look at deviance as being a disease in society, but we have attempted a more functional analysis that tries to assess the extent to which the country may be changed by the event. For example, an airplane crash is statistically deviant, but would probably not change the status quo much unless the head of state was killed in the crash. Terrorism, however, might threaten change in society if it was politically motivated. Social change deviance is measured on a four-point scale, with the points being defined as follows: (1) The event is not at all threatening to the status quo. (2) The event is somewhat threatening to the status quo. It may result in changes at some future time, although change is unlikely in the near future. (3) The event is dangerous to the maintenance of the status quo. The event will probably change the status quo in some way, although not necessarily in a very serious way. (4) The event is extremely dangerous to the continued maintenance of the status quo in the country. This event will almost certainly seriously change the status quo.

Normative deviance: the extent to which the event, if it had occurred in the United States, would have broken U.S. norms. For example, terrorism would be coded as very deviant, because it violates norms of U.S. violence, even though terrorism is a usual and often expected form of violence in other countries. Modern U.S. norms (since 1950) are adopted as the reference because we are studying coverage of the events in the U.S. mass media. We assume the U.S. editors will evaluate the newsworthiness (and hence deviance) of world events based on U.S. norms. Normative deviance is measured on a four-point scale, with the points being defined as follows: (1) If the event has occurred in the United States, it would not have broken any norms. (2) If the event had occurred in the United States, it would have somewhat violated U.S. norms, but things like this seem to be occurring in the United States more often. U.S. norms on this topic may be changing. (3) If the event had occurred in the United States, it would have violated existing U.S. norms, but isolated instances like this event do occur from time to time in the United States. (4) If the event had occurred in the United States, it would have definitely broken U.S. norms. Such an event has never or almost never been known to occur in the United States.

Deviance index: to evaluate the overall assessment of an event's deviance, a deviance index was formed by summing the 3 deviance scales. The index scores ranged from 3 to 12, with higher scores denoting more deviance. Standardized item alpha for the index reliability is .81.

Event Coverage

Coverage of world events was measured by using media indexes for the *New York Times* and for U.S. television network (CBS, ABC, and NBC) news (the *Television News Index and Abstracts* from the Vanderbilt Television News Archive). These media are not assumed to be representative of U.S. media; rather, they were selected because they are as likely or more likely to cover international events than most other newspapers or television news shows, and therefore they provide a stronger test of our hypothesis than would media that regularly include less international news.

The measurement of media coverage was dichotomous—either an event sampled was listed as covered in the indexes or it was not. We assume that the events covered have been assessed as more newsworthy than events which are not covered. There is some support in the literature for this approach. As Galtung and Ruge (1965, p. 66) indicate in their discussion of newsworthiness factors, "There is a threshold the event will have to pass before it will be recorded at all."

The hypothesis predicts that events that are covered in the U.S. media studied will have a higher deviance rating than events that are not covered. A t-test was used to compare the deviance ratings of events that are covered with deviance ratings of events that are not covered. t-tests were performed for the three deviance scales individually, as well as for the deviance index. We are interested in seeing whether or not the three deviance scales and the index yield different results.

RESULTS

Although the three deviance scales are closely related (r statistical deviance, potential for change = .50; r normative deviance, statistical deviance = .70; r normative deviance, potential for social change = .58, DF = 179), they measure somewhat different parts of the deviance construct. The largest correlation coefficient is between statistical and normative deviance, possibly because norms are often based on common behaviors and attitudes (Gibbs, 1981).

The *New York Times* covered 48% of the 179 randomly selected events, whereas the three television networks together covered only 16% of the events.

The hypothesis was supported when the overall deviance index is used, although some of the three individual scales in the index are better predictors than others of whether or not an event will be covered. For both the *New York Times* and the three television networks studied, events covered by the media were more deviant than those events not covered.

Statistical deviance turned out not to be a very important predictor of coverage: Although the means are in the direction of the hypothesis, significant results were not obtained in the t-test. The scale measuring the event's potential for social change was a statistically significant predictor of event coverage in the *Times*, $t(179) = 2.78$, $p < .006$, but the t statistic just missed reaching significance at the $p < .05$ level for the television coverage, $t(179) = 1.93$, $p < .055$. This may be because of the small number of events covered by the television networks. Normative deviance was a good predictor of both newspaper $(t(179) = 2.80$, $p < .006)$ and television coverage $(t(179) = 2.40$, $p < .017)$.

Although the overall results—especially those using the deviance index—do support our hypothesis, the difference in results using the three deviance scales may be even more interesting. Statistical deviance appears to be less important than the other two scales in determining media coverage, and normative deviance appears to be the most important. The partially significant results from the social change scale may be due to the lower intercoder reliability of this scale compared to the others. Imprecise measurements may by themselves yield null results.

We also need to point out that although covered events were rated as statistically more deviant than those events not covered, there was not a huge difference between the deviance scores for covered and not-covered events. Deviance alone does not account for assessments of newsworthiness, as we pointed out earlier in this chapter. We have theorized that deviance is one—and, we believe, an important—dimension of the newsworthiness concept, but newsworthiness also includes assessments of the social significance of the event, and a consideration of contingent conditions like timeliness and proximity. These other elements in the newsworthiness concept were not measured in this study, but they clearly make an important contribution to the study of newsworthiness and should be included in future research.

SUMMARY AND IMPLICATIONS

Although studies of the role of the mass media in social control have been numerous (Comstock, 1982), few have discussed how the deviance of people and groups may affect whether the media act as controlling agents or not. Studies of international news are numerous, yet the relationship between deviance and the newsworthiness of world events has gone mostly unnoticed.

In this study, we have attempted to integrate what is already known about the newsworthiness of world events with the study of the mass media's role in social change. We have shown support for a hypothesis that world events covered by the U.S. media are more deviant than those events not covered. We assume that events that are covered have been assessed as more newsworthy than events that are not covered, thereby showing a theoretical relationship between deviance and newsworthiness.

We looked at three kinds of deviance—statistical, potential for social change, and normative—and found that statistical deviance was the least effective in distinguishing between events that were or were not covered by the mass media. This suggests that the newsworthiness indicator "novelty" is less important than the other indicators in predicting whether or not an event will be covered. In addition, statistical deviance is probably not much of a threat to the status quo by the simple virtue of its minority status. The conceptualization of statistical deviance in not ideological; it excludes any assumption of threats to change norms. Therefore it would not require much attention from those who would control the extent and direction of social change.

Social change and normative deviance are more troublesome to the status quo because they present clear challenges, the former through a kind of breakdown of normal operations, and the latter through direct ideological alternatives. Both of these types of deviance did differentiate media coverage of events, with events that were covered being less normative and presenting more opportunity for change than did events that were not covered. This suggests that conflict and sensationalism—two indicators that were related to norms and change—may be important indicators of newsworthiness.

The significance of these findings lies with the role of deviance in social change. What is the impact of the media's disproportionately covering world events that break U.S. norms and emphasize opportunities for social change within other countries?

By their very existence, deviant people and groups bring the opportunity for change. If that change seems threatening to the status quo, then its agents may act to control the direction and extent of the change. Because what is unknown cannot be controlled, the emphasis on deviance within indicators of newsworthiness is functional for the U.S. status quo. Mass media publicity of deviance in other countries is a necessary first step in controlling the threatened change.

Critics of the U.S. mass media (such as Gans, 1979; Gitlin, 1980; Lauderdale & Estep, 1980; Miliband, 1969; Paletz & Entman, 1981) have suggested that the media act as agents of social control, not by preventing the publication of new and different ideas, but rather by varying their coverage of political groups according to how different the groups are from the status quo. Miliband (1969, p. 238) says that views that do not somehow support the political consensus are brought into ideological line by ridiculing them as "irrelevant eccentricities which serious and reasonable people may dismiss as of no consequence."

Implicit in these scholars' work is the idea that deviant people and groups will be identified as such by the mass media and that stories about deviant people and groups will be qualitatively different from stories about nondeviant people and groups. If, as they say, the mass media are not mere channels for the transmission of information about deviance, then we must consider theoretical explanations for the influence that the media have on content. Of the four theoretical approaches previously mentioned, the journalist-centered approach obviously addresses the relationship between journalists' attitudes and media content. Yet these four general approaches appear to be hierarchically arrayed in terms of the social significance, level of analysis, and the ability to explain each other's effects on content. Routines of newsgathering exist because individual journalists create them. Journalists influence the news because of pressures from economic and cultural forces. Such economic and cultural forces typically work to maintain the status quo, a hallmark of hegemony. So, journalists' attitudes about deviance may be a lower-level indicator of a broader, possibly hegemonic, process at work. The tendency of the U.S. media to cover deviant events disproportionately could therefore represent part of an overall process of identifying, evaluating, and controlling threatened changes from other countries.

This approach goes beyond the descriptive approaches that are common to the study of international news. We have attempted to provide a theoretical basis for the study of newsworthiness and to place the study of news in the framework of the broader topic of social change.

Future research in this area should improve on our study. Better, more precise measures of deviance might reveal a greater difference between covered and noncovered events. Going beyond a dichotomous measurement of newsworthiness (covered versus not covered) would allow the use of interval-level statistical tests, such as multiple regression, and we could then estimate the unique contribution of each type of deviance to the events' newsworthiness. Other measures of newsworthiness could include variables such as the number of articles about an event, the number of media in which the event was covered, the prominence with which the event was displayed, or the length or time allotted to the event. Our test of the hypothesis was conservative; the dichotomous measurement of newsworthiness gave every opportunity for an event to appear in the "newsworthy" category. This may explain the small, although statistically significant, difference in deviance scores between covered and noncovered events. Continuous measurements of newsworthiness would yield a more sensitive test of the hypothesis.

Future studies should also include more events, particularly if the studies include coverage of events by television news programs. Time constraints severely limit the number of stories that may be covered by television journalists, making the researcher's task more difficult. In order to achieve a large enough number of covered events to be reliable, it is necessary to sample a very large number of events. Only one in six events in our sample was covered by the combined CBS, NBC, and ABC national news programs.

And, of course, future research must include the measurement of social significance, proximity, and timeliness variables in order to elaborate the newsworthiness concept more fully. The study of newsworthiness needs to go beyond the study of practical indicators to a fuller theoretical analysis of the role of the news in social change.

REFERENCES

Alexander, J. C. (1981). The mass news media in systemic, historical, and comparative perspective. In E. Katz and T. Szecsko (Eds.), *Mass media and social change* (pp. 17-49). Beverly Hills, CA: Sage.

Altschull, J. H. (1984). *Agents of power.* New York: Longman.

Becker, H. S. (1963). *Outsiders: Studies in the sociology of deviance.* New York: Free Press.

Becker, L. B. (1977) Foreign policy and press performance. *Journalism Quarterly, 54,* 364-368.

Bell, R. R. (1976) *Social deviance.* Homewood, IL: Dorsey Press.

Bergsma, F. (1980). News values in foreign affairs on Dutch television. In G. C. Willhoit & H. de Bock (Eds.), *Mass communication review yearbook* (Vol. 1, pp. 641-656). Beverly Hills, CA: Sage.

Birenbaum, A., & Lesieur, H. (1982). Social values and expectations. In M. M. Rosenberg, R. A. Stebbins, & A. Turowetz (Eds.),*The sociology of deviance* (pp. 97-122). New York: St. Martin's Press.

Breed, W. (1955). Social control in the newsroom: A functional analysis. *Social Forces, 33,* 326-335.

Cobb, R. W., & Elder, C. D. (1972). *Participation in American politics: The dynamics of agenda-building.* Boston, MA: Allyn & Beacon.

Cohen, S., & Young, J. (1981). Introduction. In S. Cohen & J. Young (Eds.). *The manufacture of news: Deviance, social problems and the mass media* (pp. 17-33). Beverly Hill, CA: Sage.

Comstock, G. A. (1982). Information management and mass media: Menace or myth? In J. P. Gibbs (Ed.), *Social Control* (pp. 205-227). Beverly Hills, CA: Sage.

Dennis, E. E., & Inmach, A. H. (1981). *Reporting processes and practices.* Belmont, CA: Wadsworth.

Epstein, E. J. (1981). The selection of reality. In E. Abel (Ed.) *What's news* (pp. 119-132). San Francisco, CA: Institute for Contemporary Studies.

Erikson, K. T. (1966). *Wayward puritans: A study in the sociology of deviance.* New York: John Wiley.

Fraser, R. (Ed.). (1984) *Keesing's contemporary archives: Record of world events, 30.* London: Longman Group Ltd.

Galtung, J., & Ruge, M. H. (1965). The structure of foreign news. *Journal of Peace Research, 2,* 64-91.

Gans, H. J. (1979). *Deciding what's news: A study of CBS Evening News, NBC Nightly News, Newsweek, and Time.* New York: Pantheon.

Gerbner, G., & Marvanyi, G. (1977). The many worlds of the world's press. *Journal of Communication, 27,* 52-66.

Gerth, H., & Mills, C. W. (1953). *Character and social structure.* New York: Harcourt Brace Jovanich.

Gibbs, J. P. (1981). *Norms, deviance, and social control.* New York: Elsevier.

Gitlin, T. (1980). *The whole world is watching.* Berkeley: University of California Press.

Goldenberg, E. N. (1975). *Making the papers: The access of resource-poor groups to the metropolitan press.* Lexington, MA: Lexington Books.

Gramsci, A. (1971). *Selections from the prison notebooks of Antonio Gramsci*. Q. Hoare & G. N. Smith (Eds. and Trans.). New York: International Publishers.

Hall, S., Chritcher, C., Jefferson, T., Clarke, J., & Roberts, B. (1981). The social production of news: Mugging in the media. In S. Cohen & J. Young (Eds.), *The manufacture of news* (pp. 335-367). Beverly Hills, CA: Sage.

Harriss, J., Leiter, K., & Johnson, S. (1977). *The complete reporter*. New York: Macmillan.

Hart, J. A. (1966). Foreign news in U. S. and English daily newspapers: A comparison. *Journalism Quarterly, 43*, 443-448.

Hester, A. (1971) An analysis of news flow from developed and developing nations, *Gazette, 17*, 29-43.

Hicks, R. G., & Gordon, A. (1974). Foreign news content in Israel and U. S. newspapers. *Journalism Quarterly, 51*, 639-648, 676.

Hills, S. L. (1980). *Demystifying social deviance*. New York: McGraw-Hill.

Hulteng, J. L., & Nelson, R. P. (1971). *The fourth estate*. New York: Harper & Row.

Izard, R. S., Culbertson, H.M. & Lambert, D.A. (1973). *Fundamentals of news reporting*. Dubuque, IA: Kendall/Hunt.

Johnstone, J. W. C., Slawski, E. J., & Bowman, W. W. (1972). The professional values of American newsmen. *Public Opinion Quarterly, 36*, 522-540.

Kaplan, F. L. (1979) The plight of foreign news in the U. S. mass media: An assessment. *Gazette, 25*, 233-243.

Larson, J. F. (1979). International affairs coverage in U. S. network television. *Journal of Communication, 29*, 136-142.

Lent, J. A. (1977). Foreign news in American media. *Journal of Communication, 27*, 46-51.

Lauderdale, P., & Estep, R. E. (1980). The bicentennial protest: An examination of hegemony in the definition of deviant political activity. In P. Lauderdale (Ed.), *A political analysis of deviance* (pp. 72-91). Minneapolis: University of Minnesota Press.

Matza, D. (1969). *Becoming deviant*. Englewood Cliffs, NJ: Prentice-Hall.

Miliband, R. (1969). The process of legitimation. In R. Miliband (Ed.) *The state in capitalist society* (pp. 179-264). London: Weidenfeld & Nicolson.

Östgaard, E. (1965). Factors influencing the flow of news. *Journal of Peace Research, 2*, 39-63

Paletz, D. L., & Entman, R. M. (1981). *Media, power, politics*. New York, NY: Free Press.

Rosenberg, M. M., Stebbins, R. A. & Turowetz, A. (Eds.). (1982). *The sociology of deviance*. New York. St. Martin's Press.

Rosengren, K. E. (1970). International news: Intra and extra media data. *Acta Sociologica, 13*, 96-109.

Sande, Ø. (1971). The perception of foreign news. *Journal of Peace Research, 3*, 221-237.

Schur, E. M. (1980). *The politics of deviance: Stigma contests and the uses of power*. Englewood Cliffs, NJ: Prentice-Hall.

Scott, R. A. (1972). A proposed framework for analyzing deviance as a property of social order. In R. A. Scott & J. D. Douglas (Eds.), *Theoretical perspectives on deviance* (pp. 9-35). New York: Basic Books.

Semmel, A. K. (1977). The elite press, the global system, and foreign news attention. *International Interactions, 3*, 317-328.

Smith, R. F. (1971). U. S. news and Sino-Indian relations: An extra media study. *Journalism Quarterly, 48*, 447-458, 501.

Stempel, G. H., III (1985). Gatekeeping: The mix of topics and the selection of stories. *Journalism Quarterly, 62*, 791-796, 815.

Stephens, M. (1980). *Broadcast news*. New York: Holt, Rinehart & Winston.

Tuchman, G. (1973). Making news by doing work: Routinizing the unexpected. *American Journal of Sociology, 79*, 110-131.

Wells, L. E. (1978). Theories of deviance and the self-concept. *Social Psychology 41*, 189-204.

Young, J. (1981). Beyond the consensual paradigm: A critique of left functionalism in media theory. In S. Cohen & J. Young (Eds.), *The manufacture of news* (pp. 393-421) . Beverly Hills, CA: Sage.

15 ● Attention to Local and Global Complexity in Television Messages

ESTHER THORSON ●
BYRON REEVES ● JOAN SCHLEUDER

University of Wisconsin — Madison ●
Stanford University ● *University of Texas at Austin*

ATTENTIONAL fluctuations during televison viewing are common. Some programs demand only loose monitoring, and others are quite compelling. Measuring attentional changes and relating them to the content and structure of messages has, however, proved a difficult task. The present study is one of a series that uses reaction times to intermittent cues during viewing as an index of attentional commitment. A method called the secondary task procedure is used to determine how audio and video complexity are related to viewer attention to subunits of messages.

Most television research defines attention as the selection of programs rather than as a time-dependent process that changes in intensity during viewing. When attention is defined as a process, it is usually indexed by the ability to recall or recognize program content (Anderson, Lorch, Field, & Sanders, 1981; Chaffee & Choe, 1980; Madden & Weinberger, 1982; Welch & Watt, 1982). Although some research with children has gone beyond postviewing memory measures (Anderson & Field, 1985; Krull, 1983; Watt & Welch, 1983), few adult studies have done so. The main reason, however, is probably a lack of appropriate methods rather than theoretical commitment. The developmental literature has used children's visual orientation toward the screen as an unobtrusive but accurate index of selective attention. Adults, however, orient to the screen for long periods, and consequently there is not much variation for this measure to explain.

Recently, three new methods have been used as an index of attentional change over time. A first method asks subjects to turn a dial continuously to indicate attention during viewing (Thorson & Reeves, 1986). A second method looks at physiological indices like EEG (Reeves, Thorson, Roths-

Correspondence and requests for reprints: Esther Thorson, School of Journalism and Mass Communication, University of Wisconsin, Madison, WI 53706.

child, McDonald, Goldstein, & Hirsch, 1985) or heart rate (Dimond & Farrington, 1977) as an index of attention during viewing. A third method, and the one used in the present study, asks viewers to press a reaction time (RT) button in response to an intermittent stimulus and maintain attention to the primary task of watching television. Psychologists have used this method for many years, usually to index the attentional costs of attention to primary tasks like digit naming (Wickens, 1980). Typically, such studies show that more difficult primary tasks lead to slower secondary task RTs, presumably as a result of greater attentional costs.

Recently a group of psychologists has used the secondary task paradigm to study a primary task involving a higher-order or meaning-level process, namely, reading. Britton and his associates (Britton, 1980; Britton, Glynn, Meyer, & Penland, 1982; Britton, Graesser, Glynn, Hamilton, & Penland, 1983; Britton, Holdredge, Curry, & Westbrook, 1979; Britton & Tesser, 1982; Britton, Westbrook, & Holdredge, 1978; Britton, Zieglar, & Westbrook, 1980) varied the difficulty of text passages along four dimensions: global complexity (for example, easy stories versus biological texts), structure (word choice and syntax), semantics (more versus less meaningful), and the amount of prior knowledge about the texts. Texts that were complex, had difficult syntax, more meaning, and those involving more use of prior knowledge consistently produced speeded RTs. Britton has concluded (Britton & Tesser, 1982) that this is because at a meaning level, "simple" materials engage attentional capacity more extensively, placing increased time cost on performance of a secondary task.

The secondary task has already been used in several mass communication studies. It has been used to study children's attention to ordered and jumbled versions of a TV story (Meadowcroft & Reeves, 1985), the comparative attentional cost of watching soap operas by habitual and new viewers (Ibok, 1985), the cost of understanding science stories (Shapiro, 1985), the cost of processing time-compressed television advertising (Hausknecht & Moore, 1985), and the cost of audio and video complexity in TV commercials (Thorson, Reeves, & Schleuder, 1985). Although there has been some variation in results, Meadowcroft and Reeves (1985), Hausknecht and Moore (1986), and Thorson, Reeves, and Schleuder (1985) found results similar to Britton's. Media messages that intuitively seemed more complex yielded faster RTs to a secondary task.

Although there is consistency in RT patterns for higher-order processing, and similar consistency in psychological tasks involving lower-order processing, the relation between the two remains puzzling. Watching television is surely a complex information processing task, but at any moment in time significant lower-order processing must be present. For example, lower-order processing of television messages includes object discrimination and identification, linking of information across changing frames, discrimination and identification of words, and integration into phrases and sentences.

To reconcile the opposite effects that lower-order and higher-order tasks have on secondary task RT, two components of viewer information processing (Figure 15.1) are proposed: (1) a sensory or input level involving video and audio stimulus processing and (2) a meaning processing level. The sensory level includes audio and video receptors, echoic and iconic stores, feature extraction, and pattern synthesis. The meaning level involves abstract representation of patterns, contextual, *a priori,* memorial, and other nonsensory constraints on perception, and higher-order cognitive processes like understanding, evaluating, and comparing.

The assumptions underlying this model are, first, that information handling at both the sensory and meaning levels is limited. If the limits are exceeded, the accuracy or speed (or both) of processing the information will decrease. It should be noted that although automatic processes may exist in the sensory and meaning levels and not be limited (Logan, 1979; Shiffrin & Schneider, 1977) there is no reason to expect anything but controlled processing in the tasks used here. Second, although it is assumed that the audio and video channels can work independently of each other, interaction between the channels is typical. Finally, it is assumed that sensory processing tends to integrate the flow of information only across time durations (at most a few seconds), but meaning processing integrates over longer time durations.

Before positing the influence of complexity on sensory and meaning processing, it is important to examine the concept of complexity. Message complexity is better defined in terms of people rather than of messages. In people, complexity means greater pressure on information-processing mechanisms. This greater pressure can come from many message dimensions, or from interaction between messages and people. It can come from greater amounts of information, less familiarity with the information, more complicated grammatical structures, or more complicated visual structures (cuts, dissolves, pans, zoom-ins and -outs, person and object movement, and scene changes).

Variables that influence the complexity of sensory and meaning processing are different. Processing in a sensory channel is affected by small windows or durations of program content, by activities in other sensory channels, and by the sensory modality of the secondary task. Variables that put processing pressure on sensory channels, and hence mean more complexity, are more words and/or pictures per unit time, less familiarity with those words and pictures, the number of sensory channels activated, and the channel of the secondary task. When these variables move toward greater complexity, there should be increased time cost to a secondary task.

Processing in a meaning-level channel is affected by different complexity-inducing variables. In Britton's terms, this is because materials like text and television are simpler when people have had more prior experience with

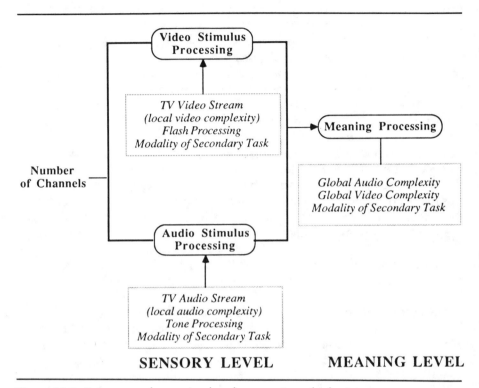

Figure 15.1 Sensory and meaning level processing of television.

them. Additional prior experience means there will be more associational links established for incoming concepts and many of these will be activated during processing. A more crowded active processing buffer will create a greater demand on attention and hence slow reaction time to a secondary task.

If this distinction between sensory and meaning processing is correct, it should be possible to produce both slowed and speeded secondary task reaction times during television viewing. Increasing the difficulty of sensory (or local) processing without affecting the meaning (or global) processing should slow reaction times. Increasing the difficulty of meaning processing without affecting sensory processing should speed reaction times.

Distinguishing local and global processing is common in psychological research, and the literature provides evidence that processing at the two levels can vary. It has been hypothesized, for example, that two attentional systems operate in visual processing (Kahneman, 1973; Neisser, 1967). A local system performs detailed analyses of content in limited visual areas. A more global system processes a wide visual array and is particularly sensitive to the presence of large features. Beck and Ambler (1974, 1973), Eichelman (1971), and Alwitt (1981) have provided evidence for independent functioning of the two systems in tasks in which letters must be detected within an array of letters (local task) or when the overall patterning of the letter array must be distinguished (global task). Pomerantz (1981, 1983) used compound letter stimuli (a large letter composed of smaller letters) to explore the same two levels of processing. He found that parts of a whole are perceived differently from the whole and concluded that the speed of perceiving wholes cannot be predicted by the speed of perceiving its parts. Navon (1977, 1981) presented subjects with pairs of geometric forms differing at either the local or global level, and also found evidence that the processing of local and global levels of information differ. Although this research involves local and global concepts, it is important to note that they deal with the integration of features at a stationary moment, rather than local and global elements within a stimulus stream changing over time.

Identification of letters in a word context has also been long identified as a global-local processing problem (Reicher, 1956; Wheeler, 1960). LaBerge and Samuels (1974) and Petersen and LaBerge (1977) explained the fact that under certain conditions people respond to whole words faster than to single letters by suggesting that reading is accomplished with a hierarchy of local feature analyzers like letter codes, spelling pattern codes, as well as a hierarchy of global feature analyzers like word codes and word-group codes. People can choose to respond on the basis of outputs from many or all of these codes. If they respond on a word-code (global) level, processing of individual letters will be slower than processing of whole words.

Although both these research streams involve only vision, the assumption that global and local processing are different and that both levels are influenced differently by processing task variables is a useful one. In the present approach, the local structural complexity of television messages was measured independently of global structural complexity. It was predicted that local complexity would slow RT to secondary tasks and that global complexity would speed RT. The predictions were tested using a data set that had been previously analyzed only for global complexity (Thorson, Reeves, & Schleuder, 1985). Three experiments from the original data set were analyzed. In the studies, subjects were presented with television commercials high and low in both global and local audio and video complexity and asked to perform a secondary task during viewing. Presentation of both the audio and video channels (AV), audio only (AO), and video only (VO) was a between-subjects manipulation. The first study used a tone as the secondary task, and local complexity was defined in terms of audio complexity. The second study eliminated the secondary task and hence provided a baseline measure of recognition performance on the primary task. The third study used a flash as the secondary task and local complexity was defined visually. Previous analyses (Thorson, Reeves, & Schleuder, 1985) had shown that global audio complexity slowed RTs when the secondary task was a flash. Global video complexity slowed RTs when the secondary task was a tone. With the tone secondary task, the presence of both the audio and video channels (AV) slowed RTs compared to presentation of only audio and video. There was no channel effect with flash as the secondary task.

The question in the present study was whether or not an independently defined local complexity factor would produce slowed rather than speeded RTs, and whether local complexity would interact with or be independent of global complexity. Additional questions concerned how local complexity would relate to the channel conditions and the modality of the secondary task.

METHODS

Subjects

A total of 180 University of Wisconsin students enrolled in an introductory advertising course participated for course credit during the 1983-1984 academic year. There were 60 students who participated in the tone secondary task—local audio complexity experiment, 60 in the flash secondary task—local video complexity experiment, and 60 in a control experiment.

Stimulus Materials

The stimulus materials, described in detail in Thorson, Reeves, and Schleuder (1985), consisted of 16 30-second television commercials representing the factorial combination of global simple and complex video complexity, and global simple and complex audio complexity (simple video-simple audio, simple video-complex audio, complex video-simple audio, complex video-complex audio).

Global video and audio complexity were judged by pretest subjects who watched and/or listened to 32 commercials. The 16 commercials receiving the most extreme ratings for the 4 factorial combinations were used in the experiment. The pretest subjects were asked to base their ratings on a previously viewed set of anchor commercials that were considered examples of either maximal or minimal audio and video complexity.

Determination of local audio complexity was based on Kintsch and van Dijk's (1978) model of propositional structure in text, as it has been applied to commercial scripts (Thorson & Snyder, 1984). In this model, idea units called *micropropositions* are integrated via grammatical rules into hierarchical orderings called *clusters*. Clusters with micropropositions in many layers of the hierarchy are more difficult for people to understand and remember (Thorson, 1983; Thorson & Snyder, 1984). Consequently, local complex audio cues were placed in these clusters. Local simple audio cues were placed in clusters containing few micropropositions in few layers. Two simple and two complex locations were chosen for each commercial, with the following restrictions: Cues were not placed during the first four seconds of a commercial and no two tones were placed closer than four seconds. It should be noted that the simple locations in complex commercials did not appear to differ from simple locations in simple commercials— there were just fewer such locations. At each of the four locations in a commercial, a tone was placed on the second audio track of the videotape. These tones were used by a computer to generate clearly audible tones for subjects and to start a reaction time clock.

Local video complexity was determined with the same coding scheme used to select the anchors presented to the pretest subjects before they rated global audio and video complexity. However, instead of counting the number of scene changes, edits, and the amount of camera, person, and object movement present in an entire message, each second of each 30-second message was coded. Those units with the fewest edits and scene changes and with the least movement were considered the most simple local video units. Units with the most edits and scene changes and with the most movement were considered the most complex local video units. Secondary-task cues were placed in the two one-second units that were most complex with the same restrictions used in placing the local audio complexity cues. The cues generated clearly visible flashes of light and also started a reaction time clock.

Of the 16 messages, 4 randomized orders, each preceded by 2 practice commercials, were dubbed to videotape for the local audio complexity experiment. Of the 16 messages, 3 randomized orders, each preceded by 2 practice commercials, were used in the local video complexity experiment.

Design and Dependent Measures

Local audio complexity and global audio and video complexity were within-subject variables for the local audio complexity experiment. Local video complexity, and global audio and video complexity were within-subject variables for the local video complexity experiment. Global video and audio complexity were within-subject variables in the control experiment. Channel complexity was a between-subjects variable in all three experiments.

The dependent variable was reaction time to a secondary task, that is, detection of a tone in the local audio complexity experiment and flash in the local video complexity experiment. In addition, responses to visual and verbal recognition tests were collected in each of three experiments. These performance tests were given to ensure that subjects paid close attention to the primary task of viewing television. Each test included six recognition questions. AO subjects, who only heard the commercials, were given six sets of four phrases. They were asked to identify the phrases that had occurred in the commercials. VO subjects, who only saw the commercials, were presented with six individual video frames and were required to identify those that had appeared in the commercial. The AV subjects received both the phrases and the video frames. The responses to the recognition tests in the audio and video local complexity experiments were compared to control experiment responses. The control experiment was identical to the local audio and video experiments in every way except for the omission of the cues that triggered either tones or flashes. Equivalence in accuracy levels for the three experiments allows direct comparison of their reaction times. Performance items for both visual and verbal recognition tests were drawn in equal number from simple and complex local places in each commercial.

Procedure. In each of the 3 experiments, 60 subjects were assigned at random to the tape orders and channel conditions. A total of 20 subjects were individually tested in each of the 3 channel conditions (AV, AO, and VO). In all conditions, subjects were presented with two practice commercials followed by 16 experimental messages. Subjects were instructed to attend closely to the messages because they would be given a recognition test immediately after each commercial. In the local audio and global complexity experiments, subjects also were instructed to press a reaction-time button as quickly as possible whenever they heard a tone (in the local audio case) or saw a flash (in the local video case) during each message.

Apparatus

Responses were made on a hand-held game paddle with reaction time button. Presentation, timing, and recording of the responses was controlled by an Apple II + microcomputer. Tones were generated by a model 2000 CDK Hewlett-Packard oscillator. Flashes were generated by a photo stimulator connected to a strobe light mounted two feet behind and five feet above the seated subject. Subjects viewed the commercials and the frame recognition test on a 19-inch Sony Trinitron television set.

RESULTS

Accuracy of Frame and Phrase Recognition

Thorson, Reeves, and Schleuder (1985) compared the performance measures collected during the local audio complexity experiment with those collected in the control experiment and found the pattern of effects identical. (In these and all succeeding analyses the .05 significance level was adopted.) An ANOVA performed on the video test responses showed no differences between AV and AO conditions in number correct. Global audio complexity had no effect, but global video-simple commercials had higher accuracy scores than did global video complex commercials, (for the local audio complexity experiment, $F(1,38) = 83.60$, $p < .01$; for the control experiment, $F(1,38) = 82.58$, $p < .01$). There were no significant differences in number correct on the global audio test between AV and AO subjects, but an audio complexity/channel condition interaction occurred for both the local audio experiment $(F(1,38) = 19.21$, $p < .01)$ and for the control experiment $(F(1,38) = 23.54$, $p < .01)$. AO subjects were more accurate for the global audio-simple commercials than the complex ones, but AV subjects showed no differences.

Reaction Times

A repeated measures ANOVA was used to test for effects of local audio complexity. Mean reaction time to tones placed in audio simple locations (collapsed across channel conditions and video and audio complexity) was significantly faster than to tones placed in complex locations, $F(1,57) = 21.24$, $p < .001$. Mean reaction times for the locally placed audio simple and complex cues were 409 and 422 msec respectively. There were no significant interactions. The panels in Figure 15.2 show RT as a function of local audio complexity and global video and audio complexity.

Complex planned comparisons (Keppel, 1982) were used to compare simple and complex local audio complexity with the levels of global and video and audio complexity for each of the three channel conditions. The panels in Figures 15.3, 15.4, and 15.5 show these results.

A local audio complexity main effect appears for the audio-video (AV) condition $(F(1,19) = 4.71$, $p < .05)$, for the audio-only (AO) condition $(F(1,19) = 7.53$, $p < .02)$, and for the video-only (VO) condition $(F(1,19) = 8.25$, $p < .008)$. As predicted, for all three viewing conditions, reaction time to cues placed in locally simple audio units was faster than reaction time to cues placed in locally complex units. Local audio complexity did not interact with number of channels on video or audio complexity in any of the analyses.

Reaction time to the global video complex messages was significantly faster $(M = 410$ msec) than to the simple messages $(M = 421$ msec), $F(1,57) = 7.61$, $p < .01$. Reaction time to the global audio complex messages $(M = 420$ msec) did not vary significantly from the simple messages $(M = 412$ msec), $F(1,57) = 3.99$, $p < .06$.

There was no significant difference in reaction time among the three viewing conditions $(F(2,27) = .02$, $p > .9)$. In an earlier analysis of these data we suspected that high between-subject variations in each condition

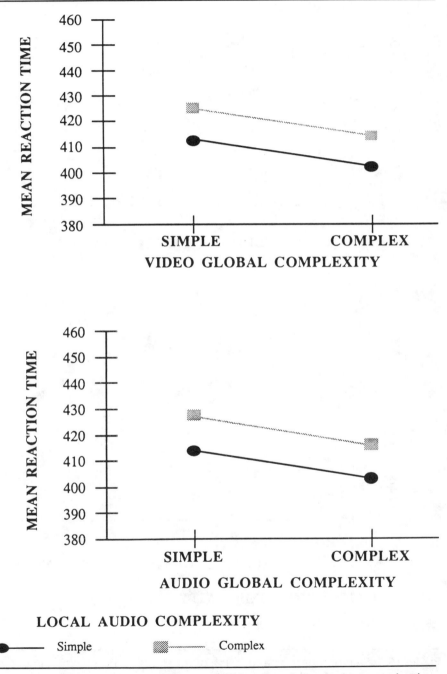

Figure 15.2 Reaction time as a function of local audio complexity and video and audio global complexity (all channel conditions).

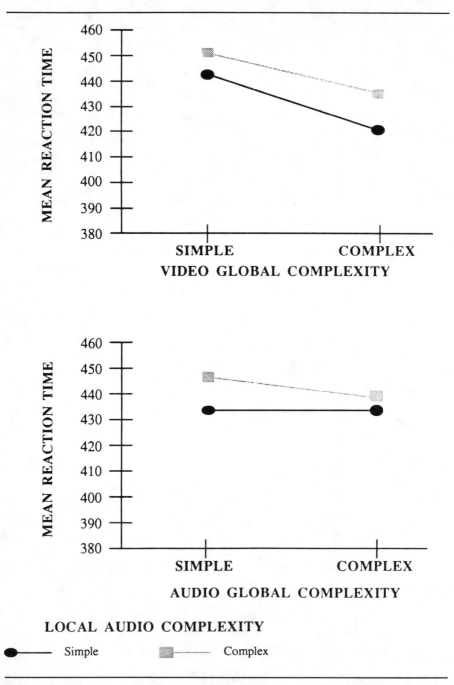

Figure 15.3 Reaction time as a function of local audio complexity and video and audio global complexity (audio-video condition).

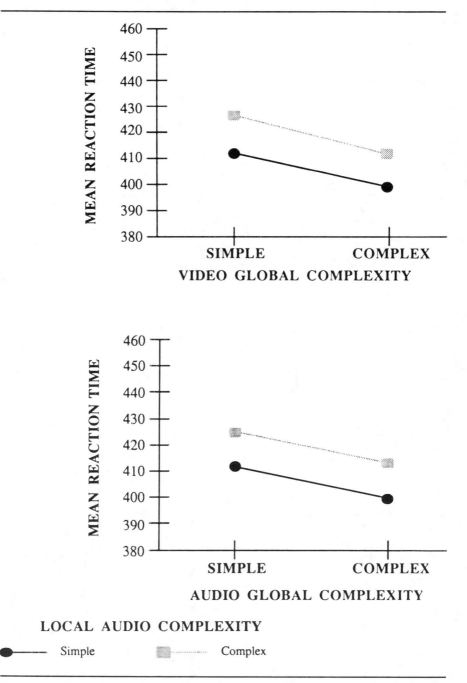

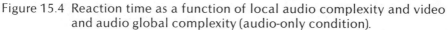

Figure 15.4 Reaction time as a function of local audio complexity and video and audio global complexity (audio-only condition).

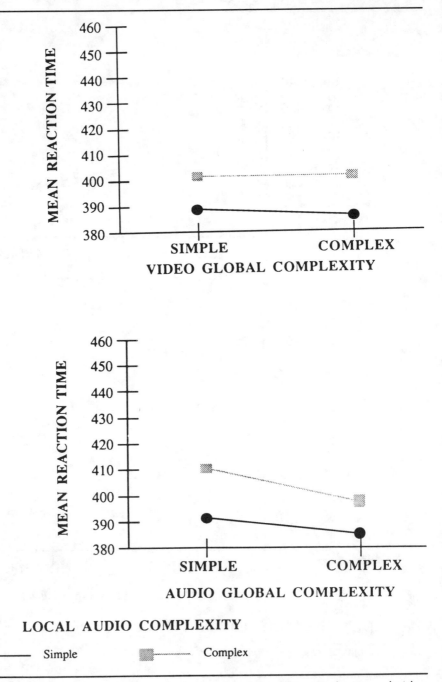

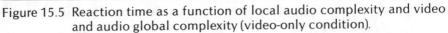

Figure 15.5 Reaction time as a function of local audio complexity and video
and audio global complexity (video-only condition).

masked the statistical differences among conditions (see Thorson, Reeves, & Schleuder, 1985). In this study, a second analysis was performed using the mean reaction time for local simple and local complex cues with each message as the unit of analysis. The analysis showed a main effect for channel condition ($F(2,30) = 24.15, p < .001$). The channel condition by local audio complexity interaction did not reach significance.

LOCAL VIDEO COMPLEXITY RESULTS

Recognition Test Responses

The pattern of results was again identical to those of the control experiment. In the visual recognition test, there were no differences in number correct between subjects in the AV and AO conditions (with a .05 criterion). Audio complexity had no significant effect, but global video-simple commercials showed higher scores than global video-complex messages ($F(1,38) = 3.99, p < .01$). Finally, there was again a significant interaction between channel condition and global audio complexity ($F(1,38) = 3.99, p < .05$). Subjects in the AO condition performed slightly better than those in the AV condition for global audio simple commercials, with no differences in the global audio-complex commercials.

Reaction Times

A repeated measures ANOVA revealed no significant differences between reaction time to cues placed locally in video simple one-second units and for cues placed in local video complex one-second units ($F(1,57) = 1.28, p > .2$). Complex planned comparisons of reaction time as a function of local complexity at each level of global video and audio complexity and each level of channel condition showed no main effects for local complexity and no interactions. The mean reaction times for locally placed video simple and complex cues in the AV condition were 408 msec and 409 msec; in the AO condition they were 401 msec and 406 msec; and in the VO condition the mean was 401 msec for simple and 409 msec for complex.

Reaction time to global audio complex messages ($M = 399$ msec) was significantly faster than to global audio simple messages ($M = 412$ msec), $F(1,57) = 7.80, p < .008$. Reaction time to global video complex messages ($M = 406$ msec) did not differ significantly from reaction time to global video simple messages ($M = 405$ msec).

Again, it was possible that a significant difference between levels of channel complexity could be masked by high between-subject variations within level. A second analysis was performed using the mean reaction time to local video simple and local complex cues within each message as the unit of analysis. There were no significant main effects or interaction.

DISCUSSION

As predicted, the local audio complexity manipulation yielded reaction time results consistent with what psychologists have found for lower-order processing. Simple locations were associated with faster RTs than were complex locations.

The analogous result for local video complexity failed to occur. Lack of difference between local video simple and complex locations may have occurred for several reasons. First, there may not have been as much stimulus difference in the local video simple and complex messages as in the audio manipulation. With an increase in the strength of the video manipulation, video effects may appear. Second, it may be that the video channel, typically associated with processing multiple inputs, is not as limited as the audio channel, which usually processes streams of successive information. Or third, it may be that video complexity effects occur only with a tone secondary task, rather than the flash secondary task used here. Choice among these alternatives awaits further research.

The difference in effects of local audio, and global audio and video is particularly important for consideration of how television is conceptualized as a stimulus. At any point in a television viewing session, it would be possible to stop the presentation at a single frame and then begin describing ever larger "windows" of the message. The smallest segment would include the structural properties of a single picture such as brightness, color, and spatial frequency, or meaningful features such as the picture content, "story," personal relevance, or aesthetic appeal. Similar descriptions could be given for increasingly larger segments. Identical features could apply to units of five seconds, five minutes, whole television programs, or even an entire viewing period. But even though the descriptions remain the same, the explanations for how the information is processed could change dramatically.

The single most important implication of this study is that different units of a television stimulus may require different explanations of how information is encoded and remembered. Even a casual review of the mass communication literature, however, shows that this distinction is often ignored. Media stimuli range from the exact onset of motion in a children's program to the study of entire genres of programming, yet often the psychological implications of these different stimulus units are explained in the same way. Concepts such as active and passive, media use, and selective attention are applied irrespective of the size of the stimulus unit considered.

This study obtained opposite results—and offered different explanations— for units of television messages that varied between 1 second (for local complexity) and 30 seconds (for global complexity). Certainly, other comparisons are possible. In a previous study (Reeves et al., 1985), viewer reactions at the exact moment when scenes change were considered, change that could take place within 1/30 of a second. The explanation for viewer reaction was taken from the literature on orienting responses that occur at the moment the visual field changes. Other processes could depend on larger or more global concepts. Processing of a story, for example, may require substantially longer stimulus units and, more important, the explanation of how stories are processed may not be derivable from the summation of the explanations for the smaller units that make up a story. Consequently, each unit may require a different level of analysis, conceptually independent of smaller and larger segments.

It might be important, however, not to tie theories strictly to stimulus definitions that depend solely on the passage of time. Some concepts that describe important processing mechanisms could operate identically but require, inconsequentially, different amounts of time. The concept of story schema might be a good example. Story schemas have been applied to segments of children's programs that last several minutes (Meadowcroft & Reeves, 1985), to television commercials that last 30 seconds (John, 1986) and to entire 30-minute programs (Roloff, 1982). Even though obvious time differences are involved, it may be possible to consider this and other meaningful elements similarly when considering psychological processing.

The explanation offered for local-global differences involves two stages— sensory and meaning processing. Although this distinction is rough, it exemplifies an approach that theories of viewing may eventually be forced to take. In the model, complexity is defined differently depending on the length of the television stimulus. For small windows (at a sensory or local level) complexity is defined as amount of material per unit time. For larger windows (meaning or global level), complexity is the number of potential associations the viewer can make with content. This complexity comes from within the viewer, rather than from the television stimulus itself. The difference in sensory and meaning complexity leads to the suggestion that additional manipulations (like number of channels to be processed and modality of secondary task) will also have different effects, depending on the level of analysis. Other possible manipulations of the television stimulus might include: compressing the time course over which information is presented, degrading the picture or sound with electronic or environmental noise, and varying the knowledge background of viewers.

REFERENCES

Alwitt, L. F. (1981). Two neural mechanisms related to modes of selective attention. *Journal of Experimental Psychology: Human Perception and Performance, 7,*(2), 324-332.

Anderson, D. R., Lorch, E. P., Field, D. E., & Sanders, J. (1981). The effects of TV program comprehensibility on preschool children's visual attention to television. *Child Development, 52,* 151-157.

Beck, J., & Ambler, B. (1972). Discriminability of differences in line slope and in line arrangement as a function of mask delay. *Perception & Psychophysics, 12,* 33-38.

Beck, J., & Ambler, B. (1973). The effects of concentrated and distributed attention on peripheral acuity. *Perception & Psychophysics, 14*, 225-230.

Britton, B. K. (1980). Use of cognitive capacity in reading: Effects of processing information from text for immediate recall and retention. *Journal of Reading Behavior, 7*, 129-137.

Britton, B. K., Glynn, S. M., Meyer, B. J. F., & Penland, M. J. (1982). Effects of text structure on use of cognitive capacity during reading. *Journal of Educational Psychology, 74*, 51-61.

Britton, B. K., Graesser, A. C., Glynn, S. M., Hamilton, T., & Penland, M. (1983). Use of cognitive capacity in reading: Effects of some content features of text. *Discourse Processes, 6*, 39-57.

Britton, B. K., Holdredge, T. S., Curry, C., & Westbrook, R. D. (1979). Use of cognitive capacity in reading identical texts with different amounts of discourse level meaning. *Journal of Experimental Psychology: Human Learning and Memory, 5*, 262-270.

Britton, B. K., & Tesser, A. (1982). Effects of prior knowledge on use of cognitive capacity in three complex cognitive tasks. *Journal of Verbal Learning and Verbal Behavior, 21*, 421-436.

Britton, B. K., Westbrook, R. D., & Holdredge, T. S. (1978). Reading and cognitive capacity usage: Effects of text difficulty. *Journal of Experimental Psychology: Human Learning and Performance, 4*, 582-591.

Britton, B. K., Zieglar, R., & Westbrook R. (1980). Use of cognitive capacity in reading easy and difficult text: Two tests of an allocation of attention hypothesis. *Journal of Reading Behavior, 7*, 23-28.

Chaffee, S. H., & Choe, S. Y. (1980, Spring). Time of decision in the Ford-Carter campaign. *Public Opinion Quarterly*, 53-69.

Dimond, S., & Farrington, L. (1977). Emotional response to films shown to the right or left hemisphere of the brain measured by heart rate. *Acta Psychologia, 41*, 255-260.

Eichelman, W. H. (1971). Changes in the relative disciminability of slant and configuration differences. *Dissertation Abstracts International, 34*, 6284B. (University Microfilms No. 71-10, 714).

Field, E. D., & Anderson, D. R. (1984). Instruction and modality effects on children's television attention and comprehension. *Journal of Educational Psychology, 77*,(1), 91-100.

Hausknecht, D. R., & Moore, D. L. (1986). The effects of time compressed advertising on brand attitude judgments. In R. J. Lutz (Ed.), *Advances in consumer research Vol. XIII* (pp. 105-110). Association for Consumer Research.

Ibok, E. (1985). *Cognitive structures and processes in recall of different types of TV programs.* Unpublished doctoral dissertation, University of Wisconsin-Madison, School of Journalism and Mass Communication.

John, D. R. (1986). The development of knowledge structures in children. In R. J. Lutz (Ed.), *Advances in consumer research Vol. XIII* (p. 648). Association for Consumer Research.

Kahneman, D. (1973). *Attention and effort.* Englewood Cliffs, NJ: Prentice-Hall.

Keppel, G. (1982). *Design & analysis: A researcher's handbook* (2nd Ed. pp. 302-332). Englewood Cliffs, NJ: Prentice-Hall.

Kintsch, W., & van Dijk, T. A. (1978). Toward a model of text comprehension and production. *Psychological Review, 85*, 363-394.

Krull, R. (1983). Children learning to watch television. In J. Bryant & D. R. Anderson (Eds.), *Children's understanding of television* (pp. 103-124). New York: Academic Press.

LaBerge, D., & Samuels, S. J. (1974). Toward a theory of automatic information processing in reading. *Cognitive Psychology, 6*, 293-323.

Logan, G. D. (1979). On the use of a concurrent memory load to measure attention and automaticity. *Journal of Experimental Psychology: Human Perception and Performance, 5*, 189-287.

Madden, T. G., & Weinberger, M. J. (1982). The effects of humor on attention in magazine advertising. *Journal of Advertising, 11*, 8-14.

Meadowcroft, J., & Reeves, B. (1985). *Children's attention to television: The influence of story schema development on allocation of cognitive capacity and memory.* Paper presented to the Speech Communication Association, Denver.

Navon, D. (1977). Forest before trees: The precedence of global features on visual perception. *Cognitive Psychology, 9,* 353-383.

Navon, D. (1981). Do attention decisions follow perception? Comment on Miller. *Journal of Experimental Psychology: Human Perception and Performance, 7,* 1175-1182.

Neisser, U. (1967). *Cognitive Psychology.* NY: Appleton-Century-Crofts.

Peterson, R. J., & LaBerge, D. (1977). Contextual control of letter perception. *Memory & Cognition, 5,* (2), 205-13.

Pomerantz, J. R. (1981). Perceptual organization in information processing. In M. Kubovy & J. R. Pomerantz (Eds.), *Perceptual organization* (pp. 141-180). Hillsdale, NJ: Lawrence Erlbaum Associates.

Pomerantz, J. R. (1983). Global and local precedence: Selective attention in form and motion perception. *Journal of Experimental Psychology: General 112,* 516-540.

Reeves, B., Thorson, E., Rothschild, M. L., McDonald, D., Goldstein, R., & Hirsch, J. (1985). Attention to television: Intrastimulus effects of movement and scene changes on alpha variation overtime. *International Journal of Neuroscience, 25,* 241-255.

Reicher, G. M. (1969). Perceptual recognition as a function of meaningfulness of stimulus material. *Journal of Experimental Psychology, 81,* 275-280.

Roloff, M. (1981). Interpersonal and mass communication scripts: An inter-disciplinary look. In G. C. Wilhoit & H. de Bock (Eds.), *Mass Communication Review Yearbook 2* (pp. 428-444). Beverly Hills, CA: Sage.

Shapiro, M. (1985, May). *Analogies, visualization and mental processing of science stories.* Paper presented at the Information Systems Division of the International Communication Association Meeting, Honolulu.

Shiffrin, R. M., & Schneider, W. (1977). Controlled and automatic human information processing: II. Perceptual learning, automatic attending, and a general theory. *Psychological Review, 84,* 127-190.

Thorson, E. (1983). Propositional determinants of memory for television commercials. In R. Martin & H. Leigh (Eds.), *Current issues and research in advertising* (pp. 139-155). Ann Arbor: University of Michigan Press.

Thorson, E., & Reeves, B. (1986). Memory effects of over-time measures of viewer liking and activity during programs and commercials. In R. J. Lutz (Ed.), *Advances in consumer research Vol. XIII* (pp. 549-553). Association for Consumer Research.

Thorson, E., Reeves, B., & Schleuder, J. (1985). Message complexity and attention to television. *Communication Research, 12*(4), 427-454.

Thorson E., & Snyder, R. (1984). Viewer recall of television commercials: Prediction from the propositional structure of commercial scripts. *Journal of Marketing Research, 21,* 127-136.

Watt, J. H., & Welch, A. J. (1983). Effects of static and dynamic complexity on children's attention and recall of televised instruction. In W. J. Bryant & D. R. Anderson (Eds.), *Children's understanding of television* (pp. 69-102). Hillsdale, NJ: Erlbaum.

Welch, A., & Watt, J. H. (1982). Visual complexity and young children's learning from television. *Human Communication Research, 8,* 133-145.

Wheeler, D. D. (1970). Processes in word recognition. *Cognitive Psychology, 1,* 59-85.

Wickens, C. D. (1980). The structure of attentional resources. In R. S. Nickerson (Ed.), *Attention and performance VIII* (pp. 239-257). Hillsdale, NJ: Lawrence Erlbaum.

16 ● Film Violence and Perceptions of Crime: The Cultivation Effect

ROBERT M. OGLES ● CYNTHIA HOFFNER

University of Wisconsin — Madison

M ASS communication researchers have raised many questions about the relationship between television use and audiences' perceptions of social reality. In the forefront are George Gerbner and his associates, who contend that heavy television viewing cultivates an exaggerated belief in a mean and scary world. Although all but a small fraction of the research evidence for cultivation is correlational, results are usually discussed in terms of television's effects on audiences. In addition, cultivation analysis has been plagued with findings that have been reversed, reduced, or eliminated altogether through the application of single or multiple control variables. Hence, the mere existence of cultivation has been the subject of heated debates.

This study's purpose was to examine the cultivation phenomenon experimentally. If cultivation is as broad and deterministic as it is often asserted to be, some evidence of its effect should be obtainable in a laboratory setting.

REVIEW OF THE LITERATURE

The social reality construct (for example, Berger & Luckmann, 1967) implies that perceptions of the world are influenced partly by actual observations and partly by expectations based on past experiences such as

AUTHORS' NOTE: Funding for this research was provided in part by National Science Foundation Grant BNS-8216772 to Edward Donnerstein and Steven Penrod. The data were collected as part of research conducted by Daniel Linz in the Department of Psychology at the University of Wisconsin—Madison. We would like to thank Dan for allowing us to include our measures in his study.

Correspondence and requests for reprints: Robert M. Ogles, Department of Communication, Purdue University, West Lafayette, IN 47907.

media use. As Gerbner's massive television content data have been interpreted, television's images are stereotypic and incongruent with the observable, measurable world. According to Gerbner's view (Gerbner, Gross, Signorielli, Morgan, & Jackson-Beeck, 1979), cultivation occurs because of (a) the repetitive, uniform nature of television content and (b) the nonselective, ritual viewing habits of the television audience. But Newcomb (1978) notes that although Gerbner's rhetoric focuses on the ritualistic function of television, he in fact discusses cultivation in terms of audience effects. These effects are attributed not only to the amount of media consumed but to specific types of media content, notably violence. In addition, Hawkins and Pingree (1981) have argued that the assumptions of uniform content and ritual viewing are not essential to cultivation; rather, they contend that the most fruitful approach to cultivation might involve examining the effects of specific types of content (such as violence or cartoons) on relevant social perceptions. It would seem, therefore, that cultivation effects could emerge as a result of extended exposure to content in any mass medium, including film (which certainly constitutes a significant portion of broadcast and cable television content).

Gerbner and his associates have amassed much support for the claim that heavy television viewing is related to fear of victimization (Gerbner et al., 1979), although other researchers have questioned the pervasiveness of the effect (Doob & MacDonald, 1979) and challenged Gerbner's methodology. Hirsch (1980, 1981), in particular, has raised a number of valid criticisms, including the definition of heavy and light viewers and the failure to distinguish between total viewing time and the amount of violence viewed as measures of television viewing. Given Gerbner's contention that the symbolic portrayal of victims and victimizers contributes heavily to the cultivation effect, it would seem that the amount of violence viewed is the more appropriate measure. This conclusion does not seem inconsistent with Gerbner's perspective, because his cultural indicators research project is primarily concerned with the amount of violence on television. Other problems associated with the correlational approach used by Gerbner and his associates include the influence of third variables and the difficulty of establishing a directional, causal link between media consumption and perceptions of social reality.

Considering the problems cited above, it seems that Gerbner's cultivation hypothesis needs to be tested in a controlled situation. Although it may not be possible to duplicate experimentally the long-term influence of heavy media use and measure cultivation directly, it is possible to vary media use experimentally (that is, treatment levels) and measure responses to questionnaire items that have been previously related to cultivation. Bryant, Carveth, and Brown (1981) took an experimental approach to the study of the relationship between television viewing and anxiety. They found that participants exposed to a heavy television diet of action-adventure programs in which transgressions went unpunished (injustice) displayed greater anxiety than either heavy viewers of programs depicting justice or light viewers. In addition, both heavy-viewing groups gave higher estimates of their likelihood of victimization than did the light-viewing group. The authors interpret their data as support for Gerbner's basic cultivation hypothesis: Heavy viewing leads to fear of victimization. This study, however, apparently was not designed to examine the impact of media violence per se. In fact, it is unclear whether or not the "transgressions" depicted in the programs were violent, although it seems likely that many of them were. With regard to the influence of media violence, Berkowitz (1984) contends that the evidence regarding the social paranoia hypothesis is inconsistent in situations where people are exposed to repeated scenes of violence in naturalistic settings. An experimental approach such as the one employed by Bryant, Carveth, and Brown should eliminate some of the interpretive problems associated with correlational data, and may be able to identify a causal influence of violence viewing on perceptions of crime and likelihood of victimization.

To this end we designed questionnaire items to tap participants' fear of victimization. These items were administered after participants had been exposed to varying amounts of film violence. We also wanted to examine how various aspects of participants' perceptions of the film content were related to their estimates of crime. Thus for each film we assessed perceptions of the amount and intensity of the violence portrayed, and enjoyment of the film. A measure of anxiety was also obtained.

METHOD

Participants

The participants were 80 male undergraduates enrolled in Introduction to Psychology at the University of Wisconsin—Madison. Students' scores on the hostility and psychoticism subscales of the Symptom Check List-90 (Derogatis, 1977), which is a self-report inventory of psychological symptoms, were used to eliminate potential participants who may have been prone to aggressive behavior. This precaution was taken because two of the conditions in the study involved viewing violent films over several days, with debriefing delayed until the final day of the study. It was thought that particularly aggressive individuals might be inclined to imitate scenes from these films. Eligible students were randomly selected from the subject pool, contacted by phone, and asked to participate in a film evaluation study. They were told that participants would be required to view films over a period of one or two weeks. The exposure condition in which they were asked to participate was randomly determined. Potential participants were

informed that the materials they would see were commercially released R-
or X-rated films that might include explicit sex and/or violence. Those who
declined to participate generally did so because of the extensive time commitment. Control participants, who did not view any of the films, were also
randomly selected from the subject pool. Of those who began the study, 4
participants in the 1-week viewing condition and 6 participants in the 2-
week viewing condition dropped out before viewing all of the films. This
left 18 one-week participants, 22 two-week participants, and 40 in the
control condition. Participants received $3.00 per film plus a bonus of
$22.00 after viewing all films and attending the debriefing session.

Materials

The following five R-rated feature films were used: *Maniac, Nightmare,
Friday the 13th, Toolbox Murders,* and *Texas Chainsaw Massacre.* Participants in the two-week condition saw the films either in the above order or
in the reverse order on Monday, Wednesday, and Friday of the first week,
and on Monday and Wednesday of the second week. Participants in the
one-week condition saw either the first two or the last two films listed above
on Monday and Wednesday of one of the weeks. The films contain many
explicit scenes of violence involving both male and female victims. The victims express fear and distress in response to the violence, which almost
always results in their deaths.

Procedure and Dependent Measures

On each viewing day, participants were met by a male experimenter
who checked to see that all students scheduled to participate were present.
Any participant who missed a viewing session was contacted immediately
and fully debriefed. The experimenter then showed a videotape of the film
stimulus on either a large-screen Sony video monitor or a Novabeam projection device. After viewing the film stimulus, participants completed the
Multiple Affect Adjective Check List (MAACL) (Zuckerman & Lubin,
1965), which produces a subscale score on anxiety. The participants were
instructed to place a check beside those items that described their feelings
"now—today." Participants also completed a number of film evaluation
items. On 7-point scales, they rated the amount and intensity of violence
portrayed in the film, and indicated the extent to which the film was enjoyable (see Ogles, 1987, for a description of these measures). Participants also
were asked to estimate the number of films like those shown in the study
that they had seen during the previous year. Participants viewed the films
in small groups. Although they also completed the questionnaires in a
group setting, their responses were made independently.

On the final day of the study (two days after viewing the last film), all
participants, including those in the control group, were asked to view a

documentary of a rape trial as part of another investigation. Prior to watching the trial, they completed a number of questionnaire items, including the dependent measure for the present study—a questionnaire dealing with perceptions of the likelihood of violent crime. These items are listed in Table 16.1. Participants in the control group were involved in this final session only.

Participants were extensively debriefed on the last day of the study. In addition, follow-up questionnaires were mailed to the participants several months after the study to confirm that they were experiencing no adverse effects. Participants also were given the phone number of someone to contact if they experienced problems related to the study.[1]

RESULTS

Responses to the eight questions were averaged to form a single Crime Perception index. Scores on this scale were analyzed in a one-way analysis of variance, with Film Exposure as the independent variable.[2] This analysis did not reach significance, $F(2, 77) = 2.22$, $p = .11$. However, a planned, one-tailed Dunn comparison revealed that the two-week exposure group perceived significantly more crime than did the one-week exposure group ($t_D(77) = 2.31$, $p < .05$, $Ms = 23.8$ and 16.1). The control group ($M = 19.8$) did not differ from either group by this procedure. The fact that the control group fell between the two experimental groups may be the result of an experimental artifact; participants in both of the violent film conditions, who may have suspected that the researchers were interested in the adverse influence of violent content on their crime estimations, could have reduced their estimates somewhat in order to demonstrate that they were not affected by such material. Hence, the interpretation of a no-film control group can present problems in a study of this type.

In addition to the problem with the control group, we thought that participants' previous exposure to violent mass media content may have mediated the effects of the experimental manipulations. A second analysis involving only the two experimental groups was conducted, with self-reported exposure during the previous year as a covariate.[3] There were higher crime estimates in the two-week exposure group ($M = 22.5$, adjusted for the covariate) than in the one-week exposure group ($M = 14.9$, adjusted for the covariate), although this analysis only approached significance, $F(1,29) = 3.15$, $p < .09$.

An interesting finding emerged when the eight scale items were analyzed in separate analyses of variance. The only question for which the analysis reached significance was the one dealing with the participants' own chances of being victims, $F(2, 77) = 3.84$, $p < .03$. Dunn comparisons revealed that those in the two-week group believed themselves more

Table 16.1
Items, Items-to-Total Correlations, and Reliability Coefficient
of the Perception of Crime Index

Perceptions of crime index items (Cronbach's alpha = .84)	Items-to-total correlations
What percentage of women in the United States were victims of a violent crime last year?	.63
What percentage of men in the United States were victims of a violent crime last year?	.68
What do you think are the chances that you will be the victim of a violent crime during the next year?	.66
What do you think are the chances that one of your family or a close friend will be the victim of a violent crime during the next year?	.68
What are the chances that a man walking alone at night in a city would be the victim of a violent crime?	.70
What are the chances that a woman walking alone at night in a city would be the victim of a violent crime?	.69
What percentage of women do you think will be raped during their lifetimes?	.49
What are the chances that a woman you know will be the victim of a rape during her lifetime?	.23

Note: All items were answered by marking a line anchored with the values of 0% and 100% and labeled at intervals of 10%. Responses were scored to the nearest labeled value.

likely to be victims ($M = 14.3_b$) than did those in either the one-week group ($M = 5.0_a$) or the control group ($M = 6.8_a$). Responses to the questions dealing with the chances that men would be victims followed the same pattern, but the analysis only approached significance, $F(2, 77) = 2.60, p = .08$ (control, $M = 19.3$; one-week, $M = 18.3$; two-week, $M = 28.0$). These results are interesting in light of participants' perceptions of the targets of violence in the films (on scales ranging from 1, not at all violent, to 7, very violent). Participants in both conditions perceived more violence directed against women than against men (one-week, $t(34) = 2.14$, $p < .025$; two-week, $t(42) = 2.99, p < .005$). The means show, however, that participants did perceive violence against men in these films. In the one-week condition, the mean degree of perceived violence against women was 5.59; for perceived violence against men, the mean was 4.31. In the two-week condition the means were 5.05 for women and 4.00 for men.

Participants' responses to the films (taken from the last viewing day) were correlated with their crime estimates, controlling for exposure to violent films during the previous year. As can be seen in Table 16.2, several

Table 16.2
Correlations with Crime Estimates

	Condition	
Item[a]	One Week	Two Week
Amount of violence	-.02	+.44**
Intensity of violence	-.04	+.13
Enjoyment	-.34	+.40*
Anxiety	-.28	-.40*
n[b]	12	17

Note: The values in the table are partial correlations, controlling for participants' exposure to violent films during the previous year.
a. For the one-week and two-week groups respectively, Cronbach's alphas for the scales were: amount of violence, .60 and .57; intensity of violence, .78 and .91; enjoyment, .88 and .59.
b. Reduction of n's is due to the fact that some participants failed to complete some scale items.
*$p = .06$,   **$p < .05$.

aspects of participants' responses to the films were related to their crime estimates, but only in the two-week condition. Most important, there was a significant positive correlation between estimates of crime victimization and perceived amount of depicted violence. In addition, crime estimates were positively correlated with participants' enjoyment of the films and negatively correlated with anxiety, although these correlations only approached significance.

DISCUSSION

The present data provide some experimental support for cultivation— participants in the two-week condition reported higher estimates of crime than participants in the one-week condition. This finding is in accord with the results obtained by Bryant, Carveth, and Brown (1981). The significant correlation between perceived violence and estimates of crime in the two-week viewing group is also consistent with the cultivation hypothesis. Although the effect of extended exposure was not large, we believe that the amount of violence viewed by our participants, even in the two-week condition, was small compared to the amount of violence people typically view over longer periods. Gerbner contends that the constant trickle of television messages over time is more important than the size of the cultivation effect at any one time. Indeed, longer exposure may be necessary to detect some of the effects of cultivation. Zillmann and Bryant (1982) examined the impact of various levels of exposure (massive, intermediate, control) to explicit sexual films over a period of six weeks. Participants in the massive exposure group viewed six erotic films each week, and those in the intermediate group viewed three per week. Zillmann and Bryant found increased estimates of the frequency of relatively common sexual behaviors among participants in both the massive and the intermediate exposure conditions. Estimates of the frequency of relatively uncommon behaviors, however, increased primarily among those in the massive exposure group. Thus with regard to media violence we believe more compelling cultivation effects may be found with intensive exposure over longer periods of time.

Furthermore, the practical significance of even small effects lies in their potential—small effects multiplied by many thousands (indeed millions) of viewers (Berkowitz, 1984). Any cultivation effect arising from five films in two weeks must be weighed against the potential effects on individuals who expose themselves to this type of media diet for longer periods of time (a likely possibility, considering the growing availability of VCRs and movie rental outlets).

The finding that extended exposure to media violence had the strongest influence on participants' estimates of their own likelihood of victimization was unexpected. Nevertheless, this outcome is not entirely inconsistent with the notion of cultivation. Although it seems that the cultivation hypothesis would generally predict stronger effects on estimates of crime against women (who were seen as victimized more often than men), Gerbner (Gerbner, Gross, Morgan, & Signorielli, 1980) also has suggested that cultivation effects may be greatest among those for whom specific media portrayals hold personal relevance ("resonance").

There are several possible explanations for the unexpected finding that extended exposure to media violence had the strongest influence on participants' estimates of their own likelihood of victimization. Although participants perceived more violence against women than men in the films, it is clear that both men and women were portrayed as victims. Participants may have attended to or processed more deeply events involving victims whom they perceived as similar to themselves (for example, men). Consistent with the availability heuristic (Tversky & Kahneman, 1973), these scenes may have come to mind later more easily than violent scenes showing women as victims. Thus it may be that violence against males in the films had a greater impact on participants' crime estimates, even though they perceived it as occurring somewhat less frequently. This conclusion is consistent with the fact that extended exposure also tended to increase participants' estimates of the percentage of men (but not women) who were victims of violent crime in the past year.

Another possible explanation is suggested by the work of Tyler and Cook (1984). In contrast to the present study, these researchers found (in study 3) that media accounts of deaths due to firearms and drunken driving increased estimates of societal risk with regard to these events, but not estimates of personal risk. Although Tyler and Cook tentatively conclude that media presentations generally have the greatest impact on societal-level judgments, they discuss several aspects of crime depictions that may influence the degree to which judgments of personal versus societal risk will be affected. They suggest that personal, but not societal, judgments of risk may be affected when an unconvincing case is made that a problem exists and the viewer perceives him- or herself as similar to the victim. We have argued already that participants may have perceived themselves to be similar to the male victims shown in our films. In addition, the crimes depicted in the films were generally violent murders committed in a random, arbitrary fashion by apparently psychotic killers. It could be argued that random murders do not present a convincing case that homicide is a serious problem in the general population, but that graphic depictions of violent death could have a strong personal impact on the viewer. This suggests that differences in the nature of the stimuli involved in the two studies—R-rated violent feature films versus articles describing the problems of gun control and drunken driving—may be another reason for the discrepant results. Although Tyler and Cook seem to focus on the objective features of the risks depicted (for example, base rates), and on the way the information is presented (for example, convincingly), it seems that the vividness associated with dramatic portrayals of victimization may also be an important factor to consider.

In sum, although the effect of violent films on participants' perceptions of personal risk is intriguing, this finding needs to be replicated in future studies before any firm conclusions can be drawn.

Also contrary to expectations was the finding that enjoyment of the films was positively correlated, and anxiety negatively correlated with estimates of victimization. Other researchers have observed the opposite relationship between anxiety and crime estimates. For example, Johnson and Tversky (1983) found that the negative mood induced by a tragic newspaper report increased estimates of all types of risks. As these authors note, much research has shown that mood can bias memory search, leading to an overestimation of events that are compatible with current mood (Bower, 1981). In the present study, however, the anxiety measure was obtained on the last viewing day, but the crime estimates were made two days later. Hence it is unlikely that the participants' moods at the time they filled out the crime estimation scales were influenced by the films.

The fear appeal literature provides some insight as to why we obtained a negative correlation between anxiety and crime estimates. The notion of "defensive avoidance," introduced by Janis and Feshbach (1953), predicts that when faced with a highly anxiety-producing event, participants will attempt to minimize or deny the threat. More recently, Beck and Frankel (1981) have argued that the effectiveness of a fear appeal depends on the degree to which the threat is portrayed as controllable. Based on this notion of threat control, Boster and Mongeau (1984) suggest that when a threat is perceived as uncontrollable, the "correlation between the amount of fear-arousing content in the persuasive message and conformity with message recommendations is expected to be negative" (p. 339). In the present study, it is possible that the stimuli caused fear in the participants, yet suggested no way to cope with the threat of random, senseless violence. For example, *Friday the 13th* and *Texas Chainsaw Massacre* conclude by suggesting that the source of the killings has not been eradicated. Thus participants who experienced greater anxiety (and less enjoyment) in response to the films may have been likely to deny the possibility that violent crime is a real risk.

It is also possible, however, that these correlations are due to the operation of a mediating variable that was not measured in the present study. Further research should attempt to determine if the observed relationship between crime estimates on the one hand, and anxiety and enjoyment on the other hand, are reliable, and if so, to explicate the underlying cognitive processes.

In conclusion, the present study provides some experimental support for Gerbner's contention that perceptions of crime are influenced by exposure to media violence. To understand the mechanisms involved more fully, future studies should systematically vary the characteristics of the violent portrayals, (for example, arbitrary versus precipitated crime) to which participants are exposed. Other studies of the influence of media crime have included such manipulations (for example, Heath, 1984) but studies of the impact of television or film violence have generally not done so. As we have argued, it is likely that vivid film portrayals may have different effects than newspaper accounts on participants' responses. The unexpected finding that participants' estimates of personal risk were most strongly influenced needs to be pursued further. In particular, the influence of film and television violence on estimates of personal risk needs to be examined more closely by devising a scale that includes many measures related to the likelihood of personal victimization (rather than just one). Obviously, experimental cultivation analysis needs to include female participants (which, unfortunately, was not possible in the present study due to the nature of the larger research program of which this analysis was a part). We believe that the ultimate result of these future experimental investigations will be a considerably better understanding of the media's effects on perceptions of social reality.

NOTES

1. A detailed description of the debriefing procedure can be found in Ogles (1987).

2. Square root transformations of the data to correct for the fact that some of the items tended to be skewed toward zero did not appreciably change the outcome of the analyses of variance.

3. Three subjects in the one-week condition and five in the two-week condition failed to answer the previous exposure item, so they could not be included in this analysis.

REFERENCES

Beck, K. H., & Frankel, A. (1981). A conceptualization of threat communications and protective health behavior. *Social Psychology Quarterly, 3,* 204-217.

Berger, P. L., & Luckmann, T. (1967). *The social construction of reality*. Garden City, NY: Anchor.

Berkowitz, L. (1984). Some effects of thoughts on anti- and prosocial influences of media events: A cognitive-neoassociation analysis. *Psychological Bulletin, 95*, 410-427.

Boster, F. J, & Mongeau, P. (1984). Fear-arousing persuasive messages. In R. N. Bostrom (Ed.), *Communication yearbook 8* (pp. 330-375). Beverly Hills, CA: Sage.

Bower, G. H. (1981). Mood and memory. *American Psychologist, 36*, 129-148.

Bryant, J., Carveth, R. A., & Brown, D. (1981). Television viewing and anxiety: An experimental examination. *Journal of Communication, 31*(1), 106-119.

Derogatis, L. R. (1977). *SCL-90: Administration, scoring and procedures manual-I, and other instruments of the psychopathology rating scale series*. Baltimore, MD: Johns Hopkins University School of Medicine, Clinical Psychometrics Research Unit.

Doob, A. N., & MacDonald, G. E. (1979). Television viewing and fear of victimization: Is the relationship causal? *Journal of Personality and Social Psychology, 37*, 170-179.

Gerbner, G., Gross, L., Morgan, M., & Signorielli, N. (1980). The "mainstreaming" of America: Violence profile no. 11. *Journal of Communication, 30*(3), 10-29.

Gerbner, G., Gross, L., Signorielli, N., Morgan, M., & Jackson-Beeck, M. (1979). The demonstration of power: Violence profile no. 10. *Journal of Communication, 29*(3), 177-196.

Hawkins, R., & Pingree, S. (1981). Uniform messages and habitual viewing: Unnecessary assumptions in social reality effects. *Human Communication Research, 7*, 291-301.

Heath, L. (1984). Impact of newspaper crime reports on fear of crime: Multimethodological investigation. *Journal of Personality and Social Psychology, 47*, 263-276.

Hirsch, P. M. (1980). The "scary world" of the nonviewer and other anomalies: A reanalysis of Gerbner et al.'s findings on cultivation analysis, part I. *Communication Research, 7*, 403-456.

Hirsch, P. M. (1981). On not learning from one's own mistakes: A reanalysis of Gerbner et al.'s findings on cultivation analysis, part II. *Communication Research, 8*, 3-37.

Janis, I. L., & Feshbach, S. (1953). Effects of fear-arousing communications. *Journal of Abnormal and Social Psychology, 48*, 78-92.

Johnson, E. J., & Tversky, A. (1983). Affect, generalization, and the perception of risk. *Journal of Personality and Social Psychology, 45*, 20-31.

Newcomb, H. (1978). Assessing the violence profile studies of Gerbner and Gross. A humanistic critique and suggestion. *Communication Research, 5*, 264-282.

Ogles, R. M. (1987). *Media-influenced estimates of crime victimization: Three empirical investigations of the cultivation hypothesis*. Unpublished doctoral dissertation, University of Wisconsin—Madison.

Tversky, A., & Kahneman, D. (1973). Availability: A heuristic for judging frequency and probability. *Cognitive Psychology, 5*, 207-232.

Tyler, T. R., & Cook, F. L. (1984). The mass media and judgements of risk: Distinguishing impact on personal and societal level judgements. *Journal of Personality and Social Psychology, 47*, 693-708.

Zillmann, D., & Bryant, J. (1982). Pornography, sexual callousness, and the trivialization of rape. *Journal of Communication, 32*(4), 10-21.

Zuckerman, M., & Lubin, B. (1965). *Manual for the Multiple Affect Adjective Check List*. San Diego, CA: Educational and Industrial Testing Service.

V ● ORGANIZATIONAL COMMUNICATION

17 ● Manager-Subordinate Control Patterns and Judgments About the Relationship

GAIL T. FAIRHURST ●
L. EDNA ROGERS ● ROBERT A. SARR

University of Cincinnati ● Cleveland State University

F OR several years researchers have asked managers and subordinates to make a variety of judgments about their work relationships, involving issues such as control, supportiveness, satisfaction, and effectiveness, among others. Obviously, social interaction plays a significant role in these relational judgments, because without interaction relationships could not exist (Cappella, 1984). Although there is a substantial body of research directed at the interrelationship of these relational assessments (for example, consideration's relationship to job satisfaction), there is considerably less work on the actual sequences and structures of manager-subordinate interactions that underpin these relational judgments. The implications of this neglect are two. First, there is an

AUTHORS' NOTE: The authors wish to thank the organization at which this research was conducted, the University Research Council of the University of Cincinnati, and the Central States Speech Association for the financial support awarded to conduct this research. We wish also to thank Roger Stuebing and Cynthia Lee for their help in the conduct of this research, and George Graen, Robert Liden, and especially Steve Green for reading earlier versions of this manuscript.

Correspondence and requests for reprints: Gail T. Fairhurst, Department of Communication, University of Cincinnati, Cincinnati, OH 45221.

overreliance on perceptual data to measure and understand relationships, and its use has been much criticized (for example, see Eden & Leviatan, 1975; Ericsson & Simon, 1980; Nisbett & Wilson, 1977; Rush, Thomas, & Lord, 1977; Schriesheim, Kinicki, & Schriesheim, 1979). Such influences as selective memory, social desirability, implicit theories, or capricious answering in response to unexpected interpretive probing can confound the measurement of relationships.

Second, and perhaps a more critical oversight for theorizing, there is a need to know more about what managers and subordinates are doing within the microstructure of their interaction that contributes to the relational states they report.[1] Given that social interaction must play a significant role in relational outcomes, then this role must be addressed empirically rather than axiomatically. Not only will we have more informed theories, but more effective interventions are possible because we can specify precisely the functional and dysfunctional interaction patterns that structure a relationship.

There have been relatively few attempts to measure social interaction directly within the organizational literature (Bales, 1950; Lewis & Fry, 1977; Putnam & Jones, 1982; Watson, 1982a), perhaps due to the large costs of social interaction analysis. In the past few years the relational communication perspective has emerged in marital and family communication research that appears to have relevance for assessing manager-subordinate interactions. This perspective assumes that the ongoing structuring of social relationships has a quality that lies beyond individuals, with the "socialness" of relationships manifested in the jointly produced behavior patterns of the interactors. Thus relational properties are constituted by the behaviors that link interactants (Bateson, 1972).

The relational communication perspective further assumes that messages convey not only referential meaning but relational meaning through which interactants define one another and their relationship vis-à-vis one another. In the ongoing stream of verbal interaction, definitions of the relationship are offered, accepted, rejected, or modified. With each interchange, patterns of relational constraint emerge. The redundancies of these stochastic processes give form or structuration (Giddens, 1982; Watson, 1982b) to the relationship.

Rogers and Farace (1975) have developed a coding scheme that focuses upon the control dimension of relationships by indexing the manner in which relational rights are established to define and direct the relationship. Interactants reciprocally define their positions in terms of three specific control moves. Messages that attempt to define the situation are coded *one up;* requests or acceptances of the other's definition of the situation are coded *one down;* and nondemanding, nonaccepting, leveling movements are coded *one across.* The combination of contiguously paired messages produces the minimum unit for describing relational structure.

Thus, in this system, dominance would be instantiated in communication every time one person asserts a definition of the situation and it is accepted by another.

Such an approach seems particularly suitable for studying manager-subordinate interactions because control within that relationship is a fundamental issue. For example, discussions range from "joint decision making" in the literature on participative management (Locke & Schweiger, 1979) to "personal control" in the performance feedback literature (Fisher, 1978; Ilgen, Fisher, & Taylor, 1979) to "autonomy" in the job design literature (Hackman & Oldham, 1975) and the marginal performers' literature (Fairhurst, Green, & Snavely, 1984), and finally to "negotiating latitude" in the leader-member exchange literature (Dansereau, Graen, & Haga, 1975). The central issue in all cases is how much the manager will prescribe rather than negotiate role expectations and other job issues for the subordinate (that is, how much the manager will dominate).

In an initial study employing a relational communication approach to the study of manager-subordinate relationships, Watson (1982a) simulated a manager-subordinate situation with 16 college student dyads. She found that "subordinates" complied with and "superiors" resisted the others' attempts to dominate the relationship, and superiors exercised a greater range of relational control maneuvers than subordinates. Watson's study illustrates the potential applicability of characterizing the microstructure of manager-subordinate interaction in terms of control patterns. Unidirectional downward influence by a manager would be reflected as dominant-submissive transactions with the managers manifesting proportionately more one-up control moves and the subordinates proportionately more one-down control moves. In contrast, reciprocal influence should reveal a more equivalent dominance pattern with manager and subordinate manifesting a similar number of combined one-up and one-down moves as well as a greater number of one-across moves (Courtright, Millar, & Rogers-Millar, 1979; Rogers, 1981; Watson, 1982b).

To summarize, we started by saying that we have many perceptions of relationship states but little insight into the interaction that underpins them. Relational communication, however, offers what appears to be a viable and relevant set of concepts and methods to begin to attack this gap in the literature. It seems clear that control or dominance is an important dimension to manager-subordinate interactions and that interactional measures of this dimension should demonstrate systematic relationships to some of the key relational judgments used in the management literature.

In the present study, the relational judgments selected were variables that are related to perceived status and power differences, namely, leader-member exchange quality, perceived "actual" and desired involvement in decision making, the manager's understanding, and the subordinate's performance rating. According to Fairhurst and Snavely (1983), perceived status and power differentials also should influence and be influenced by the tendency to accept or reject another's definition of the relationship which are proffered through the communication. Status and power differences would be minimized under conditions of reciprocal influence in which both participants offer and accept relational definitions, and maximized under conditions of unidirectional downward influence in which a subordinate acquiesces to a manager's relational definitions.

The first two relational judgments, leader-member exchange quality and decisional involvement, are closely related. Based upon the Leader-Member Exchange model, Graen and colleagues (Dansereau, Graen, & Haga, 1975; Graen & Cashman, 1975) hypothesize interactional differences among manager-subordinate dyads with high and low quality exchanges. Reacting against the notion that managers treat all subordinates alike, leader-member relationships are characterized as high or low in quality depending upon the subordinate's willingness to perform extracontractual behaviors. Influence in decision making is a frequently mentioned characteristic in that low quality leader-member exchanges are characterized by unidirectional downward influence with little negotiation by the subordinates of their role or other job issues. In contrast, high quality exchanges involve influence based upon negotiation, that is, the use of persuasion and the acceptance of counter-persuasion and the comparative infrequency of invoking status and power differentials to achieve consensus regarding role expectations and other job matters (Dansereau, Graen, & Haga, 1975; Duchon, Green, & Taber, 1986; Yukl, 1981). Yet available measures such as Graen's Leader-Member Exchange scale (Graen & Schiemann, 1978; Liden & Graen, 1980) or Duchon, Green, and Taber's (1986) sociometric alternative tap only perceptions of the overall quality of the relationship, its end state at any point in time. They do not examine interactionally what is hypothesized to contribute to the quality of the exchange.

As an interactional measure, the Rogers and Farace coding scheme codes every utterance by managers and subordinates for its control implications; thus it does not distinguish influence in decision making per se from influence in the overall relationship. Presumably, these two would be related because decision making figures prominently among a manager's activities (Yukl, 1981) and may well be the barometer for influence in the overall relationship. Given the importance ascribed to influence in decision making within the leader-member exchange construct, manager dominance should be inversely related to both perceptions of the quality of the leader-member exchange and specific perceptions of influence in decision making.

> H1: There is a negative relation between a manager's dominance of the subordinate in their communication and the perceived quality of the leader-member exchange.

H2: There is a negative relation between a manager's dominance of the subordinate in their communication and subordinate's perception of decisional involvement.

The manager's dominance also should be related to the subordinate's desire for decisional involvement. According to the leader-member exchange model, the price for organizational membership is managerial influence based upon authority (that is, unidirectional downward influence) for subordinates who do not show a willingness to go beyond their job descriptions. Thus managers would be more likely to dominate the relationship generally and the decision making specifically to the degree they perceive that a subordinate's desire for decisional involvement is low. Related work on participative management supports this view (French, Kay, & Meyer, 1966; Runyon, 1973; Vroom, 1959), suggesting the following hypothesis:

H3: There is a negative relation between a manager's dominance of the subordinate in their communication and the manager's perception of the level of the subordinate's desire for decisional involvement.

The manager's dominance also should be related to his or her understanding of the subordinate, which according to Laing, Phillipson, and Lee (1966), is viewed as the ability of the manager to predict accurately the subordinate's views on a number of important issues. When one party is dominant, as a manager is who uses his or her legitimate authority over a subordinate, there is relatively little need for that person to understand the other's position because compliance is achieved without it. Millar, Rogers-Millar, and Courtright (1979) and Courtright, Millar, and Rogers-Millar (1979) found in the marital relationship that dominance by either spouse produced a decrease in his or her understanding of the other. Further, greater participation in decision making has been found to produce greater understanding of the decision (Bass, 1970; Coch & French, 1948; Maier, 1963; Strauss, 1963). Thus the following hypothesis is posed:

H4: There is negative relation between the manager's dominance of the subordinate in their communication and the manager's understanding of the subordinate.

The performance of the subordinate also should be associated with the manager's dominance. To the extent the performance is generally poor, the manager is more likely to provide increased direction by telling the subordinate what to do, and to be less willing to provide the subordinate with such rewards as reciprocal influence opportunities (Dansereau, Graen, & Haga, 1975; Jacobs, 1971).

H5: There is a negative relation between the manager's dominance of the
subordinate in their communication and the performance rating of the
subordinate.

Finally, an additional line of research, seemingly remote from manager-
subordinate relationships, may have some relevance here. The clinical literature on family systems strongly suggests that rigid interactive structures
are predictive of many individual pathologies and family dysfunctioning
due to the system's inability to accommodate to changing situations
(Gottman, 1979; Jackson, 1959; Mishler & Waxler, 1975; Rogers &
Bagarozzi, 1983; Watzlawick, Beavin, & Jackson, 1967). In contrast,
more flexible interaction patterns contain both sufficient redundancy for
predictability in a relationship and the potential to adjust to different situations. Thus it seems worthwhile to explore the degree of rigidity in the
dominance patterns of manager-subordinate pairs. In terms of the Rogers
and Farace coding scheme, the more redundant or frequent a particular
configuration of contiguous one-up, one-down, or one-across moves, the
more rigid the interaction. Thus rigidity should be associated with the self-
report measures in this study to the degree they also serve as measures of
relationship or organizational effectiveness. Because of the exploratory
nature of this aspect of the study, however, the following is posed as a
research question:

RQ1: What are the relationships among transactional rigidity and quality of
the leader-member exchange, involvement and desired involvement
in decision making, the manager's understanding, and the subordinate's performance rating?

METHODS

Sample

The sample was initially composed of 60 manager-subordinate dyads
from a large midwestern manufacturing organization. Of the 60 dyads
whose members completed questionnaires, 48 provided taped samples of
their communication, 45 of which were usable (3 tapes were discarded due
to background noise from 1 manufacturing location). Thus 15 dyads were
eliminated for incomplete or unusable conversation data. For the remaining sample, 19 dyads, members of which ranged from hourly workers to
plant manager, came from one manufacturing location, and 26 dyads,
members of which ranged from supervisors to plant manager, came from
the other. There were 18 managers who supervised the 45 subordinates in
this study, and the average span of control was 3.75, with a range from 1 to
7 subordinates. Only 3 dyads contained females, all of whom were subor-

dinates. The average time of the participants in their present job was 3.5 years, and the average time in the organization was 12.7 years. All participants had been in their present jobs at least 6 months.

Procedures

At each plant a session was held in which the study was generally explained and questionnaire data from both managers and subordinates were collected. At that time, instructions for the taping of the conversations also were delivered. Each manager was to tape, at his convenience, normal work-related conversation with each consenting subordinate. Our intent was to capture a "slice" of their everyday on-the-job talk, assuming the information sharing, problem solving, and decision making (large and small) that goes on in the course of everyday business would create multiple influence opportunities. To reduce bias, the participants were *not* told that the specific purpose of the study was to examine the manner in which control was shared among managers and subordinates. Rather, we indicated a desire to examine typical work conversations, and the next conversation they were to have with each other that was to last more than a few minutes would be suitable. Managers were given the opportunity to tape 1 or more conversations to total 30 minutes; however, all participants chose to tape only one conversation. Most of these covered multiple topics with each subordinate. All conversations except 2 lasted 30 minutes.

Managers were then directed to mail the tapes to the investigators. The tapes were then transcribed, which resulted in over 1,400 pages of transcribed material and 11,825 individual messages to be coded.

Relational Coding

The relational approach focuses on the reciprocal process by which communicators define their positions relative to one another. The coding scheme, described more thoroughly in Rogers and Farace (1975) and Ericson and Rogers (1973), comprises three steps.

First, each message in a conversation is given a three-digit code to indicate: (1) the speaker, (2) the grammatical form of the message, and (3) the response mode relative to the previous message. The grammatical codes are as follows: (1) assertion, (2) question, (3) successful talk-over, (4) unsuccessful talk-over, (5) noncomplete, and (6) other. The response codes are as follows: (1) support, (2) nonsupport, (3) extension, (4) answer, (5) instruction, (6) order, (7) disconfirmation, (8) topic change, (9) self-direction, and (0) other. Thus communicative exchanges may be represented by a series of sequentially ordered numerical codes.

In the second step, the numerical codes are translated into control directions according to a set of rules. Messages asserting definitional rights are coded one-up (↑); accepting or requesting other's definition of the relationship are coded one down ($\downarrow$); and nondemanding, nonaccepting, leveling movements are coded one across ($\rightarrow$).

The third step pairs sequentially ordered messages. At the interact level, this produces nine transactional types: one-up, one-down complementarity ($\uparrow\downarrow$, $\downarrow\uparrow$); competitive, submissive, and neutralized symmetry ($\uparrow\uparrow$, $\downarrow\downarrow$, $\rightarrow\rightarrow$); one-up transitory ($\uparrow\rightarrow$, $\rightarrow\uparrow$); and one-down transitory ($\downarrow\rightarrow$, $\rightarrow\downarrow$). In complementary interaction the relational definition offered by one interactor is accepted by the other. With one-up complementarity ($\uparrow\downarrow$), one person asserts control and the other acquiesces, as in giving and accepting instructions. With one-down complementarity ($\downarrow\uparrow$), one person fulfills another's request to define the situation, as in questioning and answering. Competitive symmetry ($\uparrow\uparrow$) is characterized by challenge and escalation. In neutralized symmetry ($\rightarrow\rightarrow$) interactors refrain from taking a stand on the issue of control, and submissive symmetry ($\downarrow\downarrow$) involves mutual acquiescence and submission. Finally, transitory interactions ($\uparrow\rightarrow$, $\rightarrow\uparrow$, $\downarrow\rightarrow$, $\rightarrow\downarrow$) involve control leveling messages that accompany assertion or acquiescence.

The intercoder reliabilities for the three digit codes based on percentage of agreement (Guetzkow, 1950) ranged from .84 to .89 with an average of .86. When the more stringent Cohen's (1960) Kappa was used, which removes the proportion of chance agreement, the reliabilities ranged from .79 to .82 with an average of .81. These reliabilities were based on approximately 7% of the total messages coded (approximately 100 pages of transcriptions and 800 individual messages).

Although the Rogers and Farace (1975) coding scheme has been criticized on the grounds that representational validity has not been established (Folger & Sillars, 1980; Poole & Folger, 1981), recent research by Poole and Folger (1985) supports the viability of coding schemes that identify the meaning of messages on a general, conventional level. Moreover, the predictive validity of the Rogers and Farace coding scheme is well established.

Relational Control Measures

Dominance. Two operationalizations of dominance were examined.[2] The first operationalization, *comparative dominance,* is based upon the comparison between the pattern of compliance, manifested in one-up complementary transactions, versus resistance to the interactor's one-up statements, operationalized as one-up symmetrical transactions. Comparative dominance refers to the proportion between the percentages on one-up complementary ($\uparrow\downarrow$) and one-up symmetry ($\uparrow\uparrow$) (comparative dominance = %$\uparrow\downarrow$/%$\uparrow\uparrow$).

The second operationalization, *total dominance,* is based upon the percentage of statements by one person that assert a higher level of control than the subsequent statements of another. It was the percentage of one-up statements followed by one-down or one-across statements from another plus the percentage of one-across statements followed by one-down responses from another (total dominance $= \%\uparrow\downarrow + \uparrow\rightarrow + \rightarrow\downarrow$).

Dominance scores were computed not only for each participant, but for the dyad as well. The dyadic ratio for comparative dominance was calculated by dividing the manager's comparative dominance score by the subordinate's score. Thus the higher the score, the more dominant the manager *relative to the subordinate*. In a similar fashion, total dominance scores were computed for each dyad.

Table 17.1 presents the intercorrelations among the dominance measures. Because subordinate dominance scores provide only indirect evidence of the character of many of the hypothesized relationships, we chose not to present them. Despite some moderate intercorrelation among the remaining measures (for example, $r = .51$ for manager total dominance and the total dominance ratio), these will be treated as separate measures because they are conceptually distinct measures of the issues in question, and they form different relationships with the self-report measures.

Rigidity. Transactional rigidity refers to the degree of variability of the transactional patterns characterizing the manager-subordinate conversations. The fewer the number of the 9 possible transactional types used (as described in the third step of the coding procedures), the more redundant or rigid the transactional structure. Following Courtright, Millar and Rogers-Millar (1979), rigidity is operationalized as the sum of the absolute deviations from random use (that is 11%) of each of the 9 possible transaction types.

Self-Report Measures

Leader-member exchange (LMX). Quality of the leader-member exchange was assessed using the Leader-Member Exchange scale developed by Graen and his colleagues (Graen & Cashman, 1975; Liden & Graen, 1980). Following Graen, Novak, and Sommerkamp (1982), this form of the scale was lengthened from five to seven items.[3] Graen and Cashman (1975) furnish evidence of validity and reliability, although it should be noted that in a review of over 20 LMX studies, Dienesch and Liden (1986) dispute some of its psychometric properties. The seven scale items were unit weighted and summed for each respondent. Both managers (alpha $= .63$) and subordinates (alpha $= .87$) were asked to complete this scale. The higher the LMX score, the better the quality of the exchange.

Decisional involvement. This construct was measured by the Management Communication Style (MCS) scale that was developed by Richmond and McCroskey (1979) to assess the subordinate's involvement in decision making. This scale was based on Tannenbaum and Schmidt's (1958) con-

Table 17.1
Intercorrelations of Dominance Measures

		Comparative Dominance			Total Dominance		
		M	S	M/S	M	S	M/S
Comparative dominance	M	—					
	S	.32**	—				
	M/S	.44***	-.44***	—			
Total dominance	M	.47***	.20	.06	—		
	S	.20	.10	.03	.09	—	
	M/S	.05	-.01	-.01	.51****	-.72****	—

Note: M = manager, S = subordinate, M/S = manager/subordinate ratio.
*p < .10; **p < .05; ***p < .01; ****p < .001.

tinuum of leadership orientations that range from "boss centered" to "subordinate centered," which was modified by Sadler (1970) to include four steps: Tell (manager decides), Sell (manager persuades), Consult (manager solicits advice/information), Join (manager delegates).

The MCS scale is a 19-point continuum in which subjects are asked to circle the MCS under which they are working. Reliability appears to be strong (test-retest r = .85) and predictive validity with job satisfaction was established (Richmond & McCroskey, 1979).

A modification of this scale was used in the present study. Richmond and McCroskey measured the average decision style of a superior across all types of decisions. Because it seems unreasonable that managers will operate at one point on the continuum for all types of decisions (Yukl, 1981), instead of measuring "general decision style," the decisions managers make affecting subordinates were broken down into five categories: (1) work assignments, (2) budget allocations, (3) staffing and personnel issues, (4) changes in operating procedures, and (5) targets, goals, and quotas. Both managers (alpha = .80) and subordinates (alpha = .89) were asked to complete this scale with managers completing a set of scales for each subordinate. The responses to the 5 decision items by managers and subordinates were each subjected to a principal factor analysis with iterations (SAS, 1982) to arrive at a more parsimonious set of decision variables. Because this produced one main factor in both cases, the 5 items for each respondent were unit weighted and summed. The higher the score, the greater the subordinate decisional involvement.

Desired decisional involvement. This construct was measured by asking both managers and subordinates to indicate the leader-decision style subordinates prefer, using the same five scales described above. Again, for both managers (alpha = .88) and subordinates (alpha = .80) a principal factor analysis with iterations also produced one main factor in both cases; thus the items were unit weighted and summed. The higher the score, the greater the desired decisional involvement.

Understanding. Understanding was measured following Laing, Phillipson, and Lee's (1966) interpersonal perception method. With this method managers and subordinates were asked to state their own views on a number of dimensions that are expected to vary with the quality of the relationship (Schiemann & Graen, 1984). In addition, managers were asked to predict the subordinate's views on the same items. The index of items that was used was comprised of seven leader-member exchange scale items and five items measuring satisfaction with the communication and information received in the relationship. Managers' understanding was calculated using D-scores, the square root of the sum of the squared differences between the managers' prediction of the subordinates' views and the subordinates' own views (Cronbach & Gleser, 1953; Hatfield & Huseman, 1982; Parkington, Schneider, & Buxton, 1980; Wexley, Alexander, Greenwalt, & Couch, 1980). Thus the higher the score the more the manager *misunderstands* the subordinate's view of the relationship. Subordinates' understanding of the managers was also measured; however, it was used only for examining the research question.

Performance. There were two indicators of performance in this investigation. The first measure was a rating from the manager regarding the subordinate's performance. Based on Graen, Dansereau, and Minami's (1972) work, the subordinate's performance was evaluated on the following aspects: dependability, alertness, planning, know-how and judgment, overall present performance, and expected future performance. These items (scaled 1 = unsatisfactory to 7 = outstanding) were summed to create an overall performance rating (alpha = .91). The higher the score, the better the performance rating.

The second indicator of performance was the quartile rating from the company's performance appraisal system completed by each subordinate's immediate superior. It was highly correlated with the other performance measure (r = .71), and because it adds no additional information other than as a validity check, it was dropped from the analysis.

RESULTS

Conversation Descriptions

The average number of transactions (that is, contiguously paired messages) per dyad was 269 with a range from 128 to 743. The overall percentages of the 3 major transaction types and 9 subtypes are furnished in Table 17.2. Two things stand out in that table. First, only 4% of the transactions were one-up complementary (↑↓).[4] Second, nearly half of all the transactions are neutralized symmetry (→ →), greatly exceeding the percentages in the other 8 categories. Because this is the first organizational study utilizing the Rogers and Farace (1975) coding scheme, there is no established baseline with which to compare these percentages. It is interesting to note that data from 2 large studies of husbands and wives shows 12% complementarity, 33% symmetry, and 55% transition (Courtright, Millar, & Rogers-Millar, 1979; Rogers-Millar & Millar, 1979). Table 17.2 shows almost a mirror reversal of the symmetry and transition percentages for manager and subordinate interactions. It appears that conversational dynamics in the organizational setting are played out within "safer" control zones than marital conversations. The higher number of transactions in the neutralized symmetry category ($\rightarrow \rightarrow$) manifest by managers and subordinates indicate more constrained, middle-ground movement.

The message control moves reveal that approximately 65% of all messages were one across, 17% were one up, and 18% were one down. Approximately 63% of the managers' control moves were one across, 15% were one up, and 22% were one down. For the subordinates', approximately 66% of the subordinates' moves were one across, 18% were one up, and 16% were one down.

Hypotheses

Hierarchical regressions were performed to test the five hypotheses with the four dominance measures serving as the independent variables.[5] The dominance measures were entered in the following order: Managers' Comparative Dominance, Managers' Total Dominance, the Comparative Dominance Ratio, and the Total Dominance Ratio. The order was determined by the conceptual clarity and structural simplicity of the variables.[6] In order to guard against the effects of multiple tests performed on the data, alpha was set equal to .01.

An examination of the intercorrelation of the self-report measures revealed that the subordinates' perceptions of the leader-member exchange and decisional involvement are highly correlated ($r = .63, p = .001$). As suggested earlier, influence in decision making is often mentioned as contributing to the quality of the exchange. Thus these two scales were subjected to a principal factor analysis with iterations (SAS, 1982). All variables loaded cleanly on one factor that accounted for 87% of the variance. Thus the two scales were combined and Hypotheses 1 and 2 were not tested independently for subordinates. The managers' perceptions of the quality of the exchange and decisional involvement are moderately correlated ($r = .40, p = .01$), and thus those two scales were left separate.[7]

Leader-member exchange/decisional involvement (subordinates' perceptions). The total dominance ratio was the only dominance measure to have a significant effect on the combined factor containing the leader-member exchange and decisional involvement scale items ($F(1,40) =$

Table 17.2
Percentages of Transactional Types

Complementarity	Symmetry	Transition
↑↓ .04	↑↑ .02	→↑ .07
↓↑ .08	↓↓ .08	→↓ .13
Total = .12	→→ .49	↑→ .08
	Total = .52	↓→ .08
		Total = .36

5.41, $p = .02$) (see Table 17.3), although the significance level just misses the .01 level set in this investigation. This indicates that the more dominant the manager relative to the subordinate, the poorer the overall quality of the exchange and the less decisional involvement. Thus from the subordinates' data there appears to be marginal support for Hypotheses 1 and 2.

When the individual effects of the total dominance components (↑↓, ↑→, →↓) were examined, none of the components correlated significantly at conventional levels with LMX/Decisional Involvement. Thus it is their combined value that accounts for the effect.

Leader-member exchange and decisional involvement (managers' perceptions). None of the dominance measures had a significant impact on either leader-member exchange or decisional involvement. Thus from the managers' data there does not appear to be support for Hypotheses 1 or 2.

Desired decisional involvement. Managers' comparative dominance had the only significant effect on managers' perceptions of subordinates' desire for decisional involvement ($F(1,40) = 9.58$, $p = .003$) (see Table 17.4). Thus more dominant managers perceive less subordinate desire for decisional involvement lending support to Hypothesis 3.

Understanding. Managers' comparative dominance also had the only significant impact on the managers' understanding of the subordinates ($F(1,41) = 4.70$, $p = .03$) (see Table 17.5), although the alpha level did not reach the .01 level of significance. Thus Hypothesis 4 is marginally supported indicating that the more dominant the manager, the more the manager misunderstands the nature of the relationship.

Performance. Again, managers' comparative dominance had the only significant impact on the subordinates' performance rating ($F(1,43) = 6.54$, $p = .01$) (see Table 17.6). Thus Hypothesis 5 is supported by the data indicating the greater the manager's dominance, the poorer the subordinate's performance rating.

Research Question

Because of the exploratory nature of the research question, Pearson correlation coefficients were used to examine the relationships (see Table

Table 17.3
Predictors of LMX/Decisional Involvement

Variable	b(s.e.)	Total R^2	R^2 change	F	p
Mgr. comparative dominance	.05 (.16)	.00	—	.11	n.s.
Mgr. total dominance	-.15 (.18)	.02	.02	.69	n.s.
Comparative dominance ratio	-.18 (.18)	.04	.02	1.01	n.s.
Total dominance ratio	-.43 (.19)	.16	.12	5.41	.02

Table 17.4
Predictors of Subordinate Desired Decisional Involvement

Variable	b(s.e.)	Total R^2	R^2 change	F	p
Mgr. comparative dominance	-.41 (.13)	.19	—	9.58	.003
Mgr. total dominance	.05 (.16)	.20	.01	.12	n.s.
Comparative dominance ratio	-.10 (.15)	.20	0	.42	n.s.
Total dominance ratio	.32 (.21)	.25	.05	2.36	n.s.

Table 17.5
Predictors of Manager Understanding

Variable	b(s.e.)	Total R^2	R^2 change	F	p
Mgr. comparative dominance	-.27 (.13)	.10	—	4.70	.03
Mgr. total dominance	-.15	.13	.03	1.08	n.s.
Comparative dominance ratio	.04 (.14)	.13	0	.06	n.s.
Total dominance ratio	.19 (.17)	.16	.03	1.35	n.s.

Table 17.6
Predictors of Performance

Variable	b(s.e.)	Total R^2	R^2 change	F	p
Mgr. comparative dominance	-.33 (.12)	.13	—	6.54	.01
Mgr. total dominance	.16 (.14)	.16	.03	1.19	n.s.
Comparative dominance ratio	-.06 (.15)	.16	0	.16	n.s.
Total dominance ratio	-.05 (.16)	.16	0	.09	n.s.

17.4). Rigidity correlated with managers' perception of the subordinates' desired decisional involvement (r = .29, p = .06) and subordinates' understanding (r = .27, p = .08). Because rigidity refers to the degree of variability of the nine possible transaction types, it should be highly correlated with at least one of the patterns. Rigidity correlates .92 (p = .001) with neutralized symmetry (→ →). When the correlations between the above self-report measures and one-across symmetry were rerun, the latter correlated with the managers' perceptions of subordinates' desired decisional involvement (r = .36, p = .01) and subordinates' understanding (r = .26, p = .09). Thus the more one-across symmetry, the more the subordinate desired decisional involvement according to the manager, and, to a lesser extent, the more the subordinate misunderstands about the nature of the relationship.

SUMMARY AND IMPLICATIONS

The purpose of this study was to gain a better understanding of the functional and dysfunctional control patterns that underpin a variety of relational judgments made by managers and subordinates. Two dysfunctional patterns surfaced in this study, the first involving the manager's dominance of the subordinate, and the second involving the heavy use of one-across symmetry.

Manager dominance was conceptualized as both comparative and total dominance. Because comparative dominance considers the amount of resistance to one-up assertions, it may reflect a more active negotiating style. Thus the greater the manager's dominance (which reflects a higher amount of subordinate's compliance relative to the amount of resistance) the less the negotiation. It seems logical, then, that comparative dominance was associated with less understanding of the subordinate by the manager because a manager's misperceptions and unrealistic expectations cannot be corrected in the absence of challenge by the subordinate. Our findings were stronger, however, for Hypotheses 3 and 5, which showed that managers who are high in comparative dominance perceived less subordinate desire for decisional involvement and tended to give poorer performance ratings to their subordinates. Thus with interactional data we have been able to offer some support to the leader-member exchange model, which claims that the opportunity to negotiate one's role is accorded only to strong performers (Dansereau, Graen, & Haga 1975).

The managers' total dominance was negatively related to the combined leader-member exchange and decisional involvement factor for subordinates. Total dominance distinguishes itself by considering the one-across move to be a lower level of control than a one-up move but a higher level of control than a one-down move. Thus although the manager's total domi-

nance can be an obvious acquiescence to an attempt to control the defini-
tion of the situation ($\uparrow\downarrow$), it can be more subtle as when a one-across follows
a one-up move ($\uparrow\rightarrow$), or when a one-down follows a one-across move
($\rightarrow\downarrow$). The distribution of the transactional data in this study favors a more
subtle measure of total dominance. It also may be a more sensitive mea-
sure to the degree that the traditional supervisory relationship (that is,
manager asserts control and subordinate acquiesces) now assumes new
forms because of the current popularity of participatory models. Managers
are increasingly encouraged to refrain from asserting direct control and
subordinates are encouraged to contribute more. For reasons that we shall
make clear later, this makes the one-across move a more likely candidate
for use and increases the relevance of total dominance.

As expected, then, manager dominance was associated with several
negative judgments about the relationship. Our discovery of these negative consequences does not, however, obviate Graen and colleagues'
point that managers should discriminate among subordinates, forming
high quality exchanges with some and low quality exchanges with others.
Indeed the literature on participative management suggests that some subordinates actually prefer a more dominant manager (see Locke &
Schweiger, 1979), but that does not appear to be the case in the present
study. An examination of the mean and distribution of responses for subordinates' preference for decisional involvement shows that they desire a
managerial decision-making style that is midway between "Consults" and
"Joins," and the average managers' response was "Consults." More important, variance around the mean score for the managers' view of what the
subordinate wanted was three times the size of the variance around the
subordinates' responses. Subordinates' responses yielded a restricted
range, from "Consults" to "Joins," and managers' responses ranged fully
from "Tells" to "Joins."

The second dysfunctional pattern, transactional rigidity, forces us to
consider once again the possible uses of the one-across relational move, as
rigidity was highly correlated with one-across symmetry. Messages that are
classified as one-across either extend the previous message or are non-
committal (for example, "I don't know"). The data indicate that a few managers and subordinates elect to use one-across messages as much as 80%
of the time. To use one-across, control-leveling messages exclusively is to
avoid dominant-submissive interchanges altogether because neither the
manager nor the subordinate asks questions, disagrees, offers support, or
provides direction in any straightforward manner. Consequently, with this
style it is hard to imagine that any communicative goal is effectively
achieved (for example, problem solving, decision making). Moreover, the
heavy use of one-across symmetry appears specific to managers and subordinates, as this finding was not replicated among husbands and wives
(Courtright, Millar, & Rogers-Millar, 1979; Rogers-Millar & Millar, 1979).

Although the use of the "safer" one-across pattern could have been a reaction to the taping, participants within the organization confirm its heavy use. They indicated that they rarely disagree outright nor do they directly submit to another's control maneuvers for fear of appearing weak. Courtright, Millar, and Rogers-Millar (1979) report that these are the conditions under which individuals extend a conversation in the marital context.

There was also a greater use of one-across symmetry when managers perceived their subordinates to be motivated to participate in the decision making. At the time this study was conducted there was mounting pressure on the managers in the company to alter their management styles to involve the subordinates in decision making. Managers who lack the skill or self-confidence to be more participative (Maier, 1963; Yukl, 1981) and the subordinates who deserve such consideration (Anthony, 1978; Graen, Novak, & Sommerkamp, 1982) or simply prefer a more controlling style, yet also feel the pressure to change, may mask their uncertainty or their resistance to this change with a one-across pattern that subordinates likewise follow. In doing so, managers have abandoned an overtly autocratic style but they have not embraced a participative one. Unfortunately, this style is not without cost, as there was less subordinate understanding of the relationship which leaves the subordinate, in all likelihood, speculating about appropriate expectations for behavior.

As with any research effort, there are some limitations. First, because a relational analysis is time consuming and expensive, it greatly limits the ability to analyze large samples and tends to result in lower sample sizes than one typically finds in leadership research based solely on self-reports. Second, there were sampling differences between both plants. Third, the presence of the tape recorder may have affected the communication between the manager and the subordinate, although the tapes reveal that once participants begin discussing the issues at hand, awareness of the taping appears to cease. Fourth, there is no way of knowing whether or not the conversations we obtained capture the recurring patterns that historically constitute the relationship. Yet, regardless of how representative the taped conversations are, it is still actual behavior and *part* of the relationship, thus worthy of study. Fifth, the psychometric work of some of our self-reports needs further development.

Future research also needs to proceed in a number of directions. First, it would be extremely useful to compile some normative data that would allow us to determine, for example, the optimum level of one-across symmetry. One-across moves are necessary in order to assure stability within a relationship, but at what level does it become avoidance of overt dominant-submissive interaction and negatively affect the relationship? Second, less than 4% of the transactions in this study could represent the traditional supervisory relationship of subordinate yielding to managerial control attempts. If this is replicated in future research with a variety of samples, our current notions of what constitutes a traditional supervisory relationship will require change. Future research should investigate the role played by masked acquiescence and assertions of control (and thus the role of the one-across move) in traditional supervisory relationships. Third, we must continue to try to learn more about the communication behaviors that underpin the relational judgments that are reported. A further examination of the kinds of messages that fall within the one-across category and the conditions that precipitate their use is an important first step. Stochastic analyses also will reveal negotiation sequences that comparative dominance is thought to reflect. Moreover, self-report and interactional data collected over time also would contribute greatly to our understanding of perceptions of the growth and decline of relationships. Finally, a relational analysis can be a powerful feedback mechanism to managers and subordinates, and interventions designed around this type of analysis might do a lot to stimulate growth in the relationships.

The significance of this research effort (and others from a relational communication perspective) for the study of organizational communication lies in its ability to examine the ongoing structuring of manager-subordinate relationships. Because studies relying exclusively on self-reports frequently offer only global relationship descriptions and somewhat vague specifications for change, more subtle control maneuvering, such as the use of the one-across move in this study, may escape notice. Moreover, it seems amply clear that the combination of interactional and self-report data lends a richness to both sets of data that enables us to describe and understand manager-subordinate relationships more fully.

NOTES

1. See Cappella (1984) for an argument on social interaction and attraction.

2. A measure of pure dominance, defined as the proportion of all one-up statements made by a person that was followed by a one-down response from the other, was also examined. Because pure and comparative dominance scores were highly correlated (manager's score $r = .80$, manager/subordinate ratio $r = .85$) and formed similar relationships with the self-reports, it was eliminated.

3. Scale items from the LMX scale are as follows. To what extent (1) do you know how satisfied or dissatisfied your superior is with what you do, (2) does your superior understand your work problems and needs, (3) do you feel that your superior recognizes your potential, (4) would your superior be personally inclined to use his or her available power to help solve problems in your work, (5) can you count on him or her to "bail you out" at his or her expense when you really need it, and (6) do you have confidence in your superior's decisions such that you would defend and justify his or her decisions even if he or she were not present to do so? Finally, (7) how would you characterize your working relationship with your superior?

4. It is important to bear in mind that 4% complementarity represents the dyad (that is, manager or subordinate asserts dominance). The actual percentage of manager dominance would be less than 4%.

5. Although the direction of causality is likely reciprocal, for purposes of these analyses the dominance measures will be treated as the independent variables.

6. Conceptually, comparative dominance is a more straightforward measure of dominance than total dominance because the latter incorporates the one-across move that is more multifunctional than either the one-up or one-down control moves. The dyadic measures were entered last because whatever unreliability exists would be compounded by the more complex variable structure.

7. Matrices of the intercorrelations among the self-report measures, dominance, and rigidity are available from the authors.

8. A multivariate analysis of the data would be appropriate given the correlations among the self-reports; however, the small N in this study precludes this.

REFERENCES

Anthony, W. P. (1978). *Participative management*. Reading, MA: Addison-Wesley.

Bales, R. F. (1950). *Interaction process analysis: A method for the study of small groups.* Cambridge, MA: Addison-Wesley.

Bass, B. M. (1970). When planning for others. Journal of Applied Behavioral Science, 6, 151-171.

Bateson, G. (1972). *Steps to an ecology of mind.* New York: Ballantine.

Cappella, J. N. (1984). The relevance of the microstructure of interaction to relationship change. *Journal of Social and Personal Relationships, 1,* 239-264.

Cashman, J., Dansereau, F., Jr., Graen, G., & Haga, W. J.(1976). Organizational understructure and leadership: A longitudinal investigation of the managerial role-making process. *Organizational Behavior and Human Performance, 15,* 278-296.

Coch, L., & French, J. R. P., Jr. (1948). Overcoming resistance to change. *Human Relations, 1,* 512-532.

Cohen, J. (1960). A coefficient of agreement for nominal scales. *Educational and Psychological Measurement, 20,* 37-46.

Cronbach, L. J., & Gleser, G. C. (1953). Assessing similarity between profiles. *Psychological Bulletin, 50,* 456-473.

Courtright, J. A., Millar, F. E., & Rogers-Millar, L. E. (1979). Domineeringness and dominance: Replication and expansion. *Communication Monographs, 46,* 179-192.

Dansereau, F., Graen, G., & Haga, J. (1975). A vertical dyad linkage approach to leadership within formal organizations. *Organizational Behavior and Human Performance, 13,* 46-78.

Dienesch, R. M., & Liden, R. C. (1986). Leader-member exchange model of leadership: A critique and further development. *Academy of Management Review, 11,* 618-634.

Duchon, D., Green, S. G., & Taber, T. D. (1986). Vertical dyad linkage: A longitudinal assessment of antecedents, measures, and consequences. *Journal of Applied Psychology, 71,* 56-60.

Eden, D., & Leviaton, U. (1975). Implicit leadership theory as a determinant of the factor structure underlying supervisory behavior scales. *Journal of Applied Psychology, 60,* 736-741.

Ericson, P., & Rogers, L. E. (1973). New procedures for analyzing relational communication. *Family Process, 12,* 245-267.

Ericsson, K. A., & Simon, H. A. (1980). Verbal reports as data. *Psychological Review, 87,* 215-251.

Fairhurst, G. T., & Snavely, B. K. (1983). Majority and token minority group relationships: Power acquisition and communication.*Academy of Management Review, 8,* 292-300.

Fairhurst, G. T., Green, S. G., & Snavely, B. K. (1984). Face support in controlling poor performance. *Human Communication Research, 11,* 272-295.

Fisher, C. (1978). The effects of personal control, competence, and extrinsic reward systems in intrinsic motivation. *Organizational Behavior and Human Performance, 21,* 273-288.

Folger, J. P., & Sillars, A. (1980). Relational coding and perceptions of dominance. In B. Morse & L. Phelps (Eds.), *Interpersonal communication: A relational perspective* (pp. 322-333). Minneapolis: Burgess.

French, J. R. P., Kay, E., & Meyer, H. H. (1966). Participation and the appraisal. *Human Relations, 19,* 3-20.

Giddens, A. (1982). *Profiles and critiques in social theory.* London: Macmillan.

Gottman, J. M. (1979). *Marital interaction: Experimental investigations.* New York: Academic Press.

Graen, G., & Cashman, J. (1975). A role-making model of leadership in formal organizations: A developmental approach. In J. G. Hunt & L. L. Lawson (Eds.), *Leadership Frontiers* (pp. 143-165). Kent, OH: Kent State University Press.

Graen, G., Dansereau, F., & Minami, T. (1972). Dysfunctional leadership styles. *Organizational Behavior and Human Performance, 7,* 216-236.

Graen , G., Novak, M., & Sommerkamp, P. (1982). The effects of leader-member exchange and job design on productivity and satisfaction: Testing a dual attachment model. *Organizational Behavior and Human Performance, 30,* 109-131.

Graen, G., & Schiemann, W. J. (1978). Leader-member agreement: A vertical dyad linkage approach. *Journal of Applied Psychology, 63,* 206-212.

Guetzkow, H. (1950). Unitizing and categorizing problems in coding qualitative data. *Journal of Clinical Psychology, 6,* 47-58.

Hackman, J. R., & Oldham, G. R. (1975). Development of the job diagnostic survey. *Journal of Applied Psychology, 60,* 159-170.

Hatfield, J. D., & Huseman, R. C. (1982). Perceptual congruence about communication as related to satisfaction: Moderating effects of individual characteristics. *Academy of Management Journal, 25,* 349-358.

Ilgen, D. R., Fisher, C., & Taylor, M. S. (1979). Consequences of individual feedback on behavior in organizations. *Journal of Applied Psychology, 64,* 349-371.

Jackson, D. D. (1959) Family interaction, family homeostasis, and some implications for conjoint family psychotherapy. In D. H. Masserman (Ed.), *Individual and family dynamics* (pp. 122-141). New York: Grune & Stratton, Inc.

Jacobs, L. (1971). *Leadership and exchange in formal organizations.* Alexandria, VA: Human Resources Organization.

Laing, R. D., Phillipson, H., & Lee, A. R. (1966). *Interpersonal perception: A theory of method and research.* New York: Harper & Row.

Lewis, S. A., & Fry, W. R. (1977). Effects of visual access and orientation on the discovery of integrative bargaining alternatives. *Organizational Behavior and Human Performance, 20,* 75-92.

Liden, R. C., & Graen, G. (1980). Generalizability of the vertical dyad linkage model of leadership. *Academy of Management Journal, 23,* 451-465.

Locke, E. A., & Schweiger, D. M. (1979). Participation in decision making: One more look. *Research on Organizational Behavior, 1,* 265-339.

Maier, N. R. F. (1963). *Problem solving discussions and conferences: Leadership methods and skills.* New York: McGraw-Hill.

Millar, F. E., Rogers-Millar, L. E., & Courtright, J. A. (1979). Relational control and dyadic understanding: An exploratory predictive regression model. In B. D. Ruben (Ed.), *Communication Yearbook 3* (pp. 213-224). New Brunswick, NJ: Transaction Books.

Mishler, E. G., & Waxler, N. E. (1975). The sequential patterning of interaction in normal and schizophrenic families. *Family Process, 14,* 17-50.

Nisbett, R. E., & Wilson, T. D. (1977). Telling more than we can know: Verbal reports on mental processes. *Psychological Review, 84,* 231-259.

Parkington J. J., Schneider, B., & Buxton, V. M. (1980). Employee and customer perceptions of service in banks.*Administrative Science Quarterly, 25,* 252-267.

Poole, M. S., & Folger, J. P. (1981). A method for establishing the representational validity of interaction coding systems: Do we see what they see? *Human Communication Research, 8,* 26-42.

Poole, M. S., & Folger, J. P. (1985). *How shared are "shared" interpretations?* Unpublished manuscript, University of Minnesota.

Putman, L. L., & Jones, T. S. (1982). Reciprocity in negotiations: An analysis of bargaining interaction. *Communication Monographs, 49,* 171-191.

Richmond, V. P., & McCroskey, J. C. (1979). Management communication style, tolerance for disagreement and innovativeness as predictors of employee satisfaction: A comparison of single factor, two-factor, and multi-factor approaches. In D. Nimmo (Ed.), *Communication yearbook 3* (pp. 359-374). New Brunswick, NJ: Transaction Books.

Rogers, L. E. (l981). Symmetry and complementarity: Evolution and evaluation of an idea. In C. Wilder-Mott & J. H. Weakland (Eds.), *Rigor and imagination: Essays from the legacy of Gregory Bateson* (pp. 231-252). New York: Praeger.

Rogers, L. E., & Bagarozzi, D. A. (1983). An overview of relational communication and implications for therapy. In D. Bagarozzi, A. Jurich, & R. Jackson (Eds.), *Marital and family therapy: New perspectives in theory, research and practice* (pp. 48-78). New York: Human Sciences Press.

Rogers, L. E., & Farace, R. V. (1975). Relational communication analysis: New measures and procedures. *Human Communication Research, 1,* 222-239.

Rogers-Millar, L. E., & Millar, F. E. (1979). Domineeringness and dominance: A transactional view. *Human Communication Research, 5,* 238-246.

Runyon, K. E. (1973). Some interactions between personality variables and management styles. *Journal of Applied Psychology, 57,* 288-294.

Rush, M. C., Thomas, J. C., & Lord, R. G. (1977). Implicit leadership theory: A potential threat to the internal validity of leader behavior questionnaires. *Organizational Behavior and Human Performance, 20,* 93-110.

Sadler, P. J. (1970). Leadership style, confidence in management and job satisfaction. *Journal of Applied Behavioral Science, 6,* 3-19.

Scandura, T. A., & Graen, G. (1984). Moderating effects of initial leader-member exchange status on the effects of a leadership intervention. *Journal of Applied Psychology, 69,* 423-436.

Schiemann, W. A., & Graen, G. (1984). *Structural and interpersonal effects on patterns of managerial communication.* Unpublished manuscript, Opinion Research Corporation.

Schriesheim, C. A., Kinicki, A. J., & Schriesheim, J. F. (1979). The effect of leniency on leader behavior descriptions. *Organizational Behavior and Human Performance, 23,* 1-29.

Statistical analysis for the social sciences. (1982). Cary, NC: SAS Institute, Inc.

Strauss, G. (1963). Some notes on power equalization. In H. J. Leavitt (Ed.), *The social science of organizations: Four perspectives* (pp. 41-82). Englewood Cliffs, NJ: Prentice-Hall.

Tannenbaum, R., & Schmidt, W. H. (1958). How to choose a leadership pattern. *Harvard Business Review, 36,* 95-101.

Vroom, V. H. (1959). Some personality determinants of the effects of participation. *Journal of Abnormal and Social Psychology, 59,* 322-237.

Watson, K. M. (1982a). An analysis of communication patterns: A method for discriminating leader and subordinate roles. *Academy of Management Journal, 25,* 107-120.

Watson, K. M. (1982b). A methodology for the study of organizational behavior at the interpersonal level of analysis. *Academy of Management Review, 7,* 392-403.

Watzlawick, P., Beavin, J. H., & Jackson, D. D. (1967). *Pragmatics of human communication.* New York: W. W. Norton.

Wexley, K. N., Alexander, R. A., Greenwalt, J. P., & Couch, M. A. (1980). Attitudinal congruence and similarity as related to interpersonal evaluations in superior subordinate dyads. *Academy of Management Journal, 23,* 320-330.

Yukl, G. A. (1981). *Leadership in organizations.* Englewood Cliffs, NJ: Prentice-Hall.

18 ● Bridging the Parallel Organization: A Study of Quality Circle Effectiveness

CYNTHIA STOHL

Purdue University

To produce innovation more complexity is essential; more relationships, more sources of information, more angles on the problem, more ways to pull in human and material resources, more freedom to walk around and across the organization. (Kanter, 1983, p. 148)

In an attempt to cope with increasing international competition and environmental turbulence, many U.S. companies are paying greater attention to and implementing alternative organizational designs (Kanter, 1983). A primary element of these designs, the use of formalized work groups in diverse work contexts, is exemplified by an ever-increasing number of quality circle programs. Like all organizational groups, circles are influenced by their internal dynamics and positions in the formal and informal organizational structures. *The present investigation explores the relationship between communication networks and effectiveness in quality circles.*

The typical quality circle consists of 10 to 12 workers who have volunteered to meet weekly to discuss and solve problems related to quality and production. Unlike other organizational groups (for example, autonomous or self-regulating work groups) quality circles are not an integral part of the major production or administrative routines within the organizations. The groups are parallel to the regular organizational structure (Lawler & Mohrman, 1985) and members participate for only a fractional part of the work week. All workers are affiliated with larger, more primary work groups.

Since 1962 more than 6200 U.S. firms have implemented quality circles (Sealye, 1982), including over 90% of the Fortune 500 companies (Lawler & Mohrman, 1985). Circles have been heralded as the answer to everything from low productivity and poor quality control to low worker

Correspondence and requests for reprints: Cynthia Stohl, Department of Communication, Purdue University, West Lafayette, IN 47907.

morale and poor communication (Thompson, 1982). However, recent empirical data do not present such an optimistic picture. Rigorous qualitative and quantitative evaluations suggest a steady decline in program effectiveness (Lawler & Mohrman, 1985). After 12 to 18 months many quality circles suffer a serious decrease in productivity, general functioning, and organizational acceptance and support (Goldstein, 1985). Besides financial losses and the related wasted investments of time and energy by both labor and management, evidence suggests ineffective programs cultivate a sharp decline in members' attitudes that often exacerbate an already problematic situation (Stohl, 1986; Mohrman & Novelli, 1982).

The realization that circles are neither the production nor the personnel panacea they originally were thought to be has resulted in increasing attention to factors that influence the success and failure of quality circle programs. The focus of most of the work is on the implementation and administration of a quality circle program, and comparisons are made between successful and unsuccessful programs (Steel, Mento, Dilla, Ovalle, & Lloyd, 1985). The degree of organizational readiness (Bartlett, 1983), initial union support (Parker, 1985), formal recognition of the accomplishments of quality circles (Thompson, 1982), support of middle management (Steel et al., 1982), the role of facilitators and supervisors (Schuster, 1984), and differences between members and nonmembers (Dean, 1983) have been identified as salient differences between successful and unsuccessful quality circle programs across organizations.

Far less is known about why groups within the same organization vary in effectiveness. The few studies that do address this question tend to focus on small group dynamics, investigating such variables as group cohesion, leadership behavior, conflict resolution, training procedures, brainstorming, and problem-solving techniques (Cuffe & Eyo, 1984; Griffin & Wayne, 1984).

Although the importance of traditional modes of analysis is recognized, it must be stressed that phenomena at the group level are influenced not only by their internal dynamics but by their procedural, social, and psychological embeddedness in the larger organization (Putnam, 1984). The parallel structure of quality circles and the degree (or lack thereof) of their embeddedness into regular organizational routines have been suggested as inherent flaws in the design of quality circle programs.

Busche (1984) argues that in traditional manufacturing facilities the normative assumptions and procedures of the parallel structure are antithetical to the formal production organization and they cannot coexist successfully. Lawler and Mohrman (1985) suggest that a significant proportion of quality circle programs falter during the implementation stage because the circles contain, in their initial design, structural elements that lead to their elimination and demise. Many quality circles fail because "the people who are in charge of putting circle's ideas into action are not involved in the group's initial activities and therefore have little investment in them. In addition, only those individuals who develop the ideas, not those who implement them, receive recognition and rewards" (Lawler & Mohrman, 1985, p. 68). In other words, the absence of connections linking circles with the rest of the organization may produce numerous strains, tensions, and pressures that lead to program ineffectiveness. Thus to understand more fully why some circles are more effective than others we need to focus upon how they are "embedded into the larger collectivity with multiple and interlocking networks" (Putnam, 1984). This study explores the relationship between embeddedness and effectiveness in quality circles.

The general argument set forth is that quality circles that have developed linkages with organizational members/groups outside their own work area and level in the hierarchy will be more effective relative to other quality circles in the same organization lacking such linkages. The focus of this work is on the process of acquisition of resources, that is, the links created by and with the circle in pursuit of adequate information, influence, and materials relevant to goals of the circle.

Effectiveness in quality circles is based on three measures: (1) the number and percentage of solutions proposed by the circle and accepted and implemented by management, (2) perceptions of the circle's effectiveness by the members of the circle, and (3) perceptions of the quality circle's effectiveness by supervisory and managerial personnel. A fourth effectiveness measure, the continuation of the circle, was dropped from the analysis because during the eight months of the original data collection, no circles were discontinued, although individual members did drop out of circles (Stohl, 1985).

QUALITY CIRCLE PROCESSES, COMMUNICATION NETWORKS, AND GROUP EFFECTIVENESS

Kanter's (1983) descriptions of the three "basic commodities" needed to make an innovation work provide an appropriate framework for understanding the needs of quality circles: information (data, technical knowledge, political intelligence, expertise); resources (funds, materials, space, time); and support (endorsement, backing, approval, legitimacy). A circle passes through five stages to meet these needs and pursue its goals.

First, relying heavily on brainstorming within the group, the circle chooses a problem on which to work.

Second, a circle undertakes a systematic in-depth causal analysis of the problem and documents previous attempts at solution. These data, not usually available to workers, may be obtained through circle facilitators, leaders, or members contacting relevant sources outside of the meetings and/or bringing experts into the circle's meetings. Although the interactions may be established between individuals, the connections are important structurally as links between the groups and other organizational clusters (Brieger, 1982).

The third stage includes an analysis of various solutions and the determination of which solution best fits the established criteria. The viability of a solution may or may not be decided in concert with organizational members outside the circle.

After a circle has decided upon a solution, a presentation to management is prepared. This presentation includes a persuasive appeal for support and acceptance of its suggestion. The fourth stage is often the most tension-ridden. For many workers it is the first opportunity to meet and talk with a select group of senior managers (Thompson, 1982).

The fifth stage is reached only if the circle's suggestion is accepted. During this phase, the circle monitors the progress of the project to facilitate allocation of resources for implementation and evaluation. The process then begins again.

It is hypothesized that the greater the number and types of communication links quality circle members have established the (1) greater the proportion of their suggestions that will be accepted and implemented by management (solution effectiveness) (H1); (2) more positive the impression of the circle's effectiveness by its members (H2); and (3) more effective the circle will be perceived to be by supervisors, middle managers, and upper management (H3).

The first hypothesis is rooted in a resource dependence approach (Aldrich, 1979; Pfeffer & Salancik, 1978), which suggests that groups will be powerful/influential relative to other groups to the extent that they (1) can control resources needed by others and (2) can reduce their dependencies on others for resources.

It is the second component of power/influence that is of concern here. An effective quality circle must have the power to obtain cooperation and data from many sources and influence management to accept and implement its proposal. The development of alternative solutions originates with the circle, but the decision to act and commit resources to the alternative resides solely with senior management.

Clearly, if members of a circle do not create many links outside their own work area, they are more dependent upon their own supervisor and departmental manager for the relevant data and materials needed to utilize the techniques of data collection, the research skills, the analyses taught in training, and to arrive at a workable solution to the selected problem. Supervisors and middle managers are often less supportive of circle programs and more threatened by giving the circle access to information than upper management and support staff (Schuster, 1984). Thus they are less predisposed to provide the circle with the needed information. The absence of other network links may allow the supervisor to withhold information without fear of recrimination. A circle worker suggested that when they ask a supervisor for production information the supervisor is more likely to share it with the circle "if he knows if he don't tell us we will go somewhere else to get it and he will look bad for not telling us" (personal communication from a union worker, Christchurch, New Zealand).

Links with many organizational groups are expected to help circles acquire the relevant information, resources, and support that lead to acceptance of suggestions in at least two other ways. The circle's solutions are more likely to be accepted if the solutions reflect the situation accurately and take into account the diverse needs of various groups in the organization (Bartlett, 1983). Weak ties (that is, those that link the circle to new organizational segments) provide richer and more informative messages than links that do not function as bridges to new groups (Granovetter, 1983). Furthermore, if the circle can obtain the support of significant others prior to the management presentation, its presentation will be more persuasive (Ingle, 1982). Overall, it is posited that the greater the number of diverse groups from which a circle gets relevant information, resources, and support, the more influential that group will be in (1) convincing management that its proposal is sound and worthwhile, (2) gaining commitment of resources to carry out the solution, and (3) assuring implementation of the solution by those members of the organization who must carry out the new plan.

The second hypothesis posits a relationship between members' perceptions of effectiveness and involvement in networks. Prior research suggests that organizational members who are linked to many individuals develop greater commitment to the organization (Roberts & O'Reilly, 1978), have more positive orientations to their roles in the system (Albrecht, 1984), and greater job satisfaction (McDonald, 1976). The reduction of uncertainty resulting from increased communication motivates further interaction between persons (Parks & Adelman, 1983) and more influence in the organization (Albrecht, 1979). The feelings of efficacy produced by having greater involvement in the hierarchical structure are expected to result in members' feeling that membership in the circle is worthwhile and that their group is effective.

The third hypothesis associates supervisors' and managers' perceptions of the circle's effectiveness with the number of extended links and network range of the circle. In this case the individuals who may compose the extended network are the same people evaluating the circles. To the extent that these persons are communicating with the circle, there is less uncertainty about the group (Berger & Calabrese, 1975) and greater awareness and understanding of the circle process and its members, which should be related to positive perceptions of the circle. Furthermore, the links between the circles and supervisors/managers represent at least some degree of participation by the individual in the circle's decision making. Participation tends to create feelings of cohesiveness and support for the group's decision (Shaw, 1983).

METHODS

Participants

This research was part of a larger study at a manufacturing plant in New Zealand. We interviewed 180 nonsupervisory employees (75% of the work force) and 35 supervisory staff. Typical of heavy manufacturing plants both in the United States and New Zealand, the workforce was strongly unionized.

The quality circle program had been in existence for 18 months at the start of the study. The initial 8 groups were comprised of volunteers from 4 work areas. After 6 months the program had expanded into 3 other work areas. A total of 11 groups were included in the study, 8 were operating for 18 months and 3 groups were meeting for 12 months. A total of 73 members were interviewed, representing 91% of the membership in circles.

The 35 supervisory staff interviewed were 14 supervisors, 7 departmental managers, the plant manager, the industrial relations officer, and 12 support staff, including the scheduling director, scrap controller, laboratory and technical manager, head engineer, and safety officer.

Measures

Networks. During the interviews of nonsupervisory workers, respondents were asked to indicate on a 7-point scale how often they talked with each person on the roster during the previous month about their jobs, work in the plant, or the general business of the company. The roster included all 35 supervisory personnel and support staff described above.

Supervisory and managerial personnel were asked to indicate how often they talked with each quality circle about work-related or circle-related business. All 11 circles were listed with each member's name. Circle members were identified only to help the individual recall which circle he or she came from. A pilot study indicated that support staff were unable to recall the name of every worker they interacted with, but could identify which circle they were from.

A reciprocation index was used to verify or improve the validity of the circles' network listings. Of the aggregated circle links, 94% were reciprocated by the supervisor/manager. In no instance did a supervisor/manager report an unreciprocated link with a circle; for each link identified by the supervisor/manager at least one member of the circle had reported the link. In the few instances in which discrepancies were noted, the researcher went to the supervisor and asked about the missing link. In almost all cases, the interviewee indicated that he had so many interactions with workers during the month that he had simply forgotten to include that circle. Based on the high degree of agreement, all circle listings were considered when constructing the aggregated circle networks. This high rate of agreement is not surprising when we consider that detailed minutes of each circle meeting were circulated, which included a description of who was contacted for specific data and where information was obtained. Two network scores were calculated to measure the degree to which the quality circle was embedded into the organizational structure.

Network range. The range of a network describes the extent to which the links connect the group with a diversity of other actors (Burt, 1983). Range is a substantively informative attribute in that it provides a measure of the group's access to resources. Range can be measured by either counting the number of people directly connected to the circle or by the number of different status groups represented by individuals directly connected to the group. An underlying assumption of this work is that all links are not necessarily equal. Links that bridge circles to diverse groups will carry more information and influence than links to others like themselves (Granovetter, 1983). For example, five supervisory links would provide far less information regarding the long range plan of the company and how the circle solution may fit with the organizational premises than two links with the production manager and factory manager. Because links to different status groups exchange more diverse information than those to the same status group, the absolute number of links may be misleading. The range of a circle's network will be determined by assessing the number of status groups with which a circle is linked.

Extended network. Because proximity and formally required interactions may have a major effect upon network size and interaction patterns, a separate measure of extended network contact was calculated. This was done by counting the number of direct relationships with persons who were not members of the focal group's immediate workgroup (for example, their supervisor) or persons with whom the circle members normally came into contact during their required work performance. In other words, this measure reflects the extent to which circles develop relations with persons with whom they would not normally come into contact during their work activity.

Additional factors. In exploring posssible differences between the networks of effective and ineffective groups, it is important to consider what group factors may influence network composition and group effectiveness. Three compositional attributes, most often studied by small group researchers, are age and sex of group members and tenure in the organization (Shaw, 1983). These variables have been associated consistently with network development (Brass, 1985; Kanter, 1977; Tichy, 1980). However, tenure in the organization was the only compositional factor included in the study. Each group was composed entirely of men (there were no female union workers in the company); thus the sexual composition of the group is irrelevant. Furthermore, the stability of the New Zealand workforce resulted in a very strong correlation between age and tenure in the organization ($r = .86$, $p < .001$), and tenure has been more strongly associated with network development (Tichy, 1980).

Tenure. The longer a worker is part of an organization, the more he or she may know about the company and the greater the likelihood he or she has talked with more people throughout the hierarchical structure. Thus tenure may not only be related to the specific network variables studied here but also may reflect greater socialization on the part of the workers, more knowledge about the organization that could be utilized in effective decision-making, and greater insights into what persuasive strategies would be effective when dealing with management. Group tenure was determined by the average number of years the members of the circle worked for the company and ranged from seven to nine years.

Group cohesiveness also was assessed. Group cohesiveness has been frequently related to group performance (Shaw, 1981). Griffin and Wayne (1984) identified group cohesion as a key difference between effective and less effective quality circles.

Members' perceptions of group cohesiveness. Group cohesiveness is one of the most frequently and inconsistently measured group variables. Cohesion refers to the degree to which members are motivated to remain in the group. It has been related both theoretically and empirically to numerous process variables, specifically interaction quality, social influence, group productivity, and satisfaction (Shaw, 1983). Highly cohesive groups are believed to be more effective than low cohesive groups in achieving their goals (Griffin & Wayne, 1984). Thus group cohesiveness may be an important predictor of the quality circle's effectiveness. Five items measured members' perceptions of the cohesiveness of the group. Representative items include "There is a high degree of teamwork among quality circle members" and "Members of our group enjoy working with one another." Cronbach's alpha was .91 for the cohesion items.

Effectiveness. Three independent measures of effectiveness were obtained. The first measure was based on objective data whereas the last two are perceptual measures. For the two perceptual measures individual responses were averaged to compile an overall group score.

Solution effectiveness. The number of circle suggestions accepted and implemented by management is a crucial component of the circle's effectiveness. Quality circle programs are most frequently touted as mechanisms for improving quality and productivity. A primary rationale for implementing a circle program is the thousands of dollars per year a company expects to save.

An index of solution effectiveness was calculated by multiplying the number of solutions accepted by management by the percentage of solutions implemented. This measure takes into account both the absolute number of solutions generated and accepted as well as the number implemented. Many circle programs have deteriorated because of lack of followup or implementation of accepted circle suggestions (Mohrman & Novelli, 1982).

Over the 12 month period in which data were available the average number of solutions per circle accepted by management was 5.7 (range = 1-10, s.d. = 3.003). These numbers do not represent all of the circle's actions but only those that went through the formal stage of a presentation to management. Some suggestions, such as rearranging procedures for scrap pickup within a department, were implemented without formal approval by upper management. The second component of solution effectiveness reflects the rate of implementation or the percentage of accepted solutions that are actually implemented. In this study, 91% of the circles' suggestions were accepted by management whereas only 54% were actually implemented.

Members' perceptions of effectiveness. Workers' sense of the efficacy and worthwhileness of the circle as well as their satisfaction with the circle are important components of an effective circle program. Frustration and dissatisfaction with circles are often linked to declining circle programs (Bartlett, 1983).

Members' perceptions of the quality circle's effectiveness were assessed by six items designed specifically for the study. Sample items include "The time spent at quality circle meetings is well spent," "I feel my quality circle is very effective," "My circle makes a worthwhile contribution to the company." Chronbach's alpha for the six items was .89.

Supervisors' and managers' perceptions of circles' effectiveness. A crucial component of an effective quality circle program is managerial support and confidence (Lawler & Mohrman, 1985). There is some research to suggest that managers' perceptions of circles' effectiveness are associated with the support provided to the circle (Jones, 1983). Five items measured managers' and supervisors' perceptions of circles' effectiveness. These included "This quality circle is very effective," "The projects undertaken by the quality circle are worthwhile," and "The circle makes a valuable contribution to the company." Chronbach's alpha for the 5 items was .94.

ANALYSES

A hierarchical multiple regression approach to the analysis of partial variance was the primary statistical technique employed. Because the focus upon groups as the unit of analysis created an extremely small sample size (n = 11), the results must be interpreted cautiously. Findings from this study are presented as trends that warrant future research. This specific form of data analysis was chosen because the APV technique avoids many of the problems associated with analysis of covariance. Similar to the analysis of covariance, APV proceeds by initially partialling covariates from the dependent variable and then regressing the independent variables of theoretical interest on the residuals of the dependent variable. In this case tenure and group cohesion were partialled out, and the effects of network variables were regressed on three types of effectiveness.[1]

Results

Table 18.1 presents the means and intercorrelations of predictor variables and dependent effectiveness measures. Members' perceptions of effectiveness were highly correlated with solution effectiveness ($r = .72$) and supervisors/managers' perceptions of effectiveness ($r = .72$), whereas the correlation between managers' perceptions and solution effectiveness was only moderate ($r = .52$). The correlations indicate that network range is strongly related to solution effectiveness ($r = .79$) and extended network is highly correlated with managers' perceptions of effectiveness ($r = .67$).

Solution effectiveness. In this analysis tenure and group cohesion were first regressed on solution effectiveness. These covariates were not significantly related to effectiveness ($r = .44$, $r^2 = .19$), $F(2.8) = .98, p < .41$). The effect of the two network variables, extended network and network range, were entered next in the regression equation, followed by the interaction terms. Although the total regression equation did not have a significant overall F, $F(8,2) = 1.51, p < .45$, the network variables were found to account uniquely for a large and statistically significant amount of variance in group effectiveness (semipartial $r^2 = .52$), $F(2,6) = 5.37, p < .05$ (H1). Because the primary concern is with the residual variance in solution effectiveness (that is with the variance in effectiveness after partialling out the effects of tenure and group cohesion) a more appropriate index of effect size is the squared multiple partial correlation; in this case the partial $r^2 = .64$.

Members' perceptions of group effectiveness. The second analysis was identical to the first except that the measure of effectiveness was based upon members' perception of their quality circle's effectiveness. In this case, the covariates (tenure and cohesiveness) were significantly related to effectiveness ($r = .72$ $r^2 = .53$), $F(2,8) = 4.53, p < .05$. However there was not a significant overall F ratio for the total regression $F(8,2) = 3.10$, $p < .26$ and the network variables were found to account uniquely for only a very small amount of variance (partial $r^2 = .11$) (H2).

Table 18.1
Means and Intercorrelations

Variable	Mean	1	2	3	4	5	6	7
Tenure	8		.36	-.06	-.15	-.33	-.25	-.04
Cohesiveness	4.20			.64	.30	.15	.54	.59
Extended network	21.09				.41	.45	.54	.67
Network range	4.82					.79	.53	.39
Group solution effectiveness	.64						.72	.52
Members' perceptions of group effectiveness	4.37							.71
Managers' perceptions of group effectiveness	3.23							

Supervisors' and managers' perceptions of group effectiveness. In the third analysis, tenure and group cohesion were first regressed on managers' perceptions of quality circle effectiveness. The covariates were not significantly related to effectiveness ($r = .65$, $r^2 = .42$), $F(2,8) = 2.98$, $p < .11$. The effect of the two network variables, extended network and network range, were entered next in the regression equation, followed by the interaction terms. In this case the total regression equation did have a significant overall F ratio, $F(8,2) = 38.75$, $p < .025$, but the network variables alone did not account for a significant percentage of the variance in managers' perceptions of group effectiveness (partial $r^2 = .18$) (H3).

SUMMARY AND IMPLICATIONS

Although there was a very limited sample, the results of this study support Kanter's (1983) argument that the ability to produce innovation within an organization is related to the degree and flexibility of communication linkages. These data suggest that the degree to which a quality circle is embedded into the organizational network is a significant variable that has pragmatic "bottom-line" effects. Circles that transcend their parallelism and cross over into the larger organization have more of their proposals accepted and implemented. These circles are effective inasmuch as they produce innovation in the company.

Network variables, however, do not have a significant impact on members' perceptions of effectiveness; group cohesion is a far more powerful predictor of these evaluations. The evidence suggests members base their judgments on affective criteria, including how enjoyable the group is, how attractive members are, and so on.

These data are suggestive of a recent theme emerging in studies of quality circles, that is, the social needs met by this type of worker participation program are more salient than the production/work needs. An explicit managerial aim when implementing quality circle programs is to have workers identify with the program because the process itself fulfills a number of workers' desires (Parker, 1985). From this perspective the ends are not as important as the means; the outcome is not as important as the group process; external linkages are not as salient as internal linkages. Indeed, recent literature indicates the strongest reason for volunteering to participate in a circle comes from the activity of participation itself (Dean, 1983; Zahara & Lundstrom, 1984). Mohrman and Lawler (1985) also suggest that the main reason quality circles continue is because of the social satisfaction and pleasure the members experience rather than the groups' problem-solving effectiveness. Thus it may be that workers join and remain in circles because of the promised interaction within the group. The evidence from this study suggests they evaluate the circle's effectiveness by the same criterion.

Supervisors' and managers' perceptions of group effectiveness were most affected by the interaction between extended network and tenure. Those groups that were linked with the most people and were in the company the longest were perceived as most effective. A majority of supervisors/managers had been with the company at least 10 years (M = 12.6 years) and thus would tend to know of the workers who had been in the company a longer time. Although highly speculative, it may be that the more knowledge managers have of the circle and its members the more effective the group is perceived to be. Unfamiliar groups may not receive the beneficial carryover of positive impressions gained from other interactions, and may be treated with some suspicion.

Overall, the results indicate trends for future research. Despite the small sample size, when independent assessments of the dependent and independent measures were used (that is, the same people were not the source of both measures) network variables played a strong role in the prediction of circle effectiveness. A network approach is a significant departure from other explorations of circle effectiveness but one that complements the recent portrayal and critique of quality circles as a parallel organization.

Future investigations need to extend this study and examine empirically the claim that the quality circle can function effectively as a parallel structure (see Lawler & Mohrman, 1985, for a discussion of structural problems associated with quality circles). By definition, parallel groups do not intersect the larger organization but rather create a separate, unconnected structure; the evider.ce suggests that communication lines must be crossed and embedded within the larger structure if a circle is to be effective and produce change.

A network approach to the study of quality circles creates a provocative avenue of research with implications for studying effectiveness from many perspectives. Circles are praised by management for promoting organizational identification and damned by unionists as promoting promanagement thinking and undermining unionism. Parker (1985) argues strongly that circles do not empower the worker but rather makes the worker think like management and therefore not act in ways that best serve the workers' interests. He suggests the "we/they" distinction becomes "we" (circle and managers) and "they" (nonmember workers) rather than "we" (workers) and "they" (management). Network research indicates that liaisons are likely to perceive closer relationships between themselves and others because of greater contact (Albrecht, 1984). Circles with more communicative links to management may be less likely to perceive distances between management and workers. By creating new links, the effective quality circle replaces old group identities with new ones, and may give management access to worker's knowledge about the work process, gain cooperation in introducing new technology, and provide a willingness to do things for management (for example, conduct time/motion studies) that do not serve their own best interests.

Other theorists suggest that the increased linkages between management and workers that emerge from certain types of participation programs are ineffective and inefficient for the organization as well. For example, Weick (1977) argues that participation may undermine organizational adaptiveness, particularly when it involves multiple interest groups, because an emphasis on compromise and taking the perspective of the other may destroy polar responses and preferences that might be needed in changing environments. Network analysis can be a useful tool in understanding the unobtrusive power of the quality circle process. With more and more organizations implementing quality circle programs additional research on the network characteristics of effective and ineffective circles is warranted.

NOTE

1. The extremely small sample (n = 11) raises potential concerns about the statistical power of the regression analysis and effects on the beta weights. Low statistical power is of most concern with respect to committing a Type II error, that is, failing to reject the null hypothesis when there is a real relationship between variables. As reported below, however, there was a large and statistically significant relationship detected by the regression analysis. Consequently the low power of the present study caused by the small sample size was not problematic.

REFERENCES

Albrecht, T. (1979). The role of communication in perceptions of organizational climate. In D. Nimmo (Ed.), *Communication yearbook 3* (pp. 343-357). New Brunswick, NJ: Transaction Books.

Albrecht, T. (1984). An overtime analysis of communication patterns and work perceptions among managers. In R. Bostrom (Ed.), *Communication yearbook 8* (pp. 538-557). Beverly Hills, CA: Sage.

Aldrich, H. E. (1979). *Organizations and environments.* Englewood Cliffs, NJ: Prentice-Hall.

Bartlett, J. B. (1983). *Success and failure in quality circles.* Cambridge, England: Employee Relations Resource Center.

Berger, C., & Calabrese, R. (1975). Some explorations in initial interaction and beyond: Toward a developmental theory of interpersonal communication. *Human Communication Research, 1,* 99-112.

Brass, D. (1985). Men's and women's networks: A study of interaction patterns and influence in an organization. *Academy of Management Journal, 2,* 327-343.

Breiger, R. L. (1982). A structural analysis of occupational mobility. In P. V. Marsden & N. Lin (Eds.), *Social structure and network analysis* (pp. 17-31). Beverly Hills, CA: Sage.

Burt, R. (1983). Range. In R. S. Burt & M. J. Minor (Eds.), *Applied network analysis* (pp. 176-194). Beverly Hills, CA: Sage.

Busche, G. (1984, August). *Developmental trends of parallel structure interventions in unionized, manufacturing organizations: A set of propositions.* Paper presented to the Organizational Development Division, Academy of Management Convention, Boston, MA.

Cuffe, M. & Eyo, B. (1984). Conflict management styles of quality circle facilitators. *Transactions,* 96-99.

Dean, J. W., (1983). *An investigation of quality circles.* Unpublished doctoral dissertation, Carnegie Mellon University.

Goldstein, S. G. (1985). Organizational dualism and quality circles. *Academy of Management Review, 10* (3), 504-517.

Granovetter, M. (1983). The strength of weak ties: A network theory revisited. In R. Collins (Ed.), *Sociological theory* (pp. 201-233). San Francisco: Jossey-Bass.

Griffin, R. W., & Wayne, S. J. (1984, August). *A field study of effective and less effective quality circles.* Paper presented to the Organizational Behavior Division, Academy of Management Convention, Boston, MA.

Ingle, S. (1982). How to avoid quality circle failure in your company. *Training and Management Journal, 36* (6), 54-59.

Jones, W. G. (1983, May). *A study of quality circle implementation in New Zealand.* Presented at the annual conference of the New Zealand Organization for Quality Assurance, Christchurch, New Zealand.

Kanter, R. M. (1977). *Men and women of the corporation.* New York: Basic Books.

Kanter, R. M. (1983). *The Changemasters.* New York: Simon & Schuster.

Lawler, E. E., & Mohrman, S. A. (1985). Quality circles after the fad. *Harvard Business Review, 63,* 65-71.

McDonald, D. (1976). Communication roles and communication networks in formal organizations. *Human Communication Research, 4,* 365-376.

Mohrman, S. A., & Novelli, L. (1982). *Learning from a quality circles program.* Unpublished working paper, University of Southern California.

Parker, M. (1985). *Inside the circle: A Union Guide to QWL.* Boston: South End Press.

Parks, M. R., & Adelman, M. B. (1983). Communication networks and the development of romantic relationships: An expansion of uncertainty reduction theory. *Human Communication Research, 10,* 55-80.

Pfeffer, J., & Salancik, G. (1978). *The external control of organizations: A resource dependence perspective.* New York: Harper & Row.

Putnam, L. (1984). Understanding the unique characteristics of groups within organizations. In R. Cathcart & L. Samovar (Eds.), *Small group communication* (pp. 66-76). Dubuque, IA: W. C. Brown.

Roberts, K., & O'Reilly, C. (1978). Organizations as communication structures: an empirical approach. *Human Communication Research, 4,* 283-293.

Schuster, M. (1984). Supervisory attitudes toward employee participation. *Transactions,* 114-120.

Sealye, H. N. (1982). Quality circles in U. S. industry. *Quality Circles Journal, 5,* 25-28.

Shaw, M. E. (1983). *Group Dynamics: The psychology of small group behavior.* New York: McGraw-Hill.

Steel, R. P., Mento, A. J., Dilla, B. L., Ovalle, N., & Lloyd, R. F. (1985). Factors influencing the success and failure of two quality circle programs. *Journal of Management, 11,* 99-119.

Stein, B. A., & Kanter, R. M. (1980). Building the parallel organization: Creating mechanisms for permanent quality of work life. *Journal of Applied Behavioral Science, 16,* 371-388.

Stohl, C. (1986). Quality circles and changing patterns of communication. In M. McLaughlin (Ed.), *Communication yearbook 9* (pp. 511-531). Beverly Hills, CA: Sage.

Thompson, P. (1982). *Quality circles: How to make them work in America.* New York: Amacom.

Tichy, N. (1980). A social network perspective for organizational development. In T. Cummings (Ed.), *Systems theory for organizational development* (pp. 115-161). Chichester: John Wiley.

Weick, K. E. (1977). Enactment processes in organizations. In B. M. Staw & G. R. Salancik (Eds.), *New directions in organizational behavior* (pp. 267-300). Chicago: St. Clair.

Zahara, S. A., & Lundstrom, W. J. (1984). The effect of personal and organizational characteristics on participation in quality circles. *Akron Business and Economic Review, 15*(2), 33-38.

19 ● The Development and Test of a System of Organizational Participation and Allocation

KATHERINE I. MILLER ● PETER R. MONGE

Michigan State University ● University of Southern California

TWO crucial aspects of organizational functioning are making decisions and allocating rewards. Separately, these two areas have received a great deal of theoretical and empirical attention, though participation and allocation rarely have been linked conceptually. However, the way in which decisions are made in an organization can influence both the allocation methods used and employees' perceptions of allocation. Furthermore, both decision making and allocation systems can influence important individual and organizational outcomes such as satisfaction, performance, commitment, and organizational productivity.

In contrast to social scientific thinking, the link between decision making and allocation *has* been made in several practical managerial systems. For example, the Scanlon Plan and ImproShare are two managerial systems that involve both employee participation in decision making and bonuses based on organizational productivity. Advocates of these plans see both participation and allocation systems as necessary prerequisites to improved employee morale, productivity, and organizational commitment.

The research reported here will link decision making and allocation by proposing a conceptual system of the effects of participation in decision making. An important moderator variable in this model will be employees' perceptions of allocation within the organization. First, a typology of participation effects will be presented. Next, an allocational variable that has been proposed to link some of these effects will be discussed. Following this, path models will be developed that link the concepts of participation

AUTHORS' NOTE: The preparation of this manuscript was supported by a grant from the National Science Foundation (No. ISI-841276l), Peter R. Monge and Richard V. Farace, Co-Principal Investigators.

Correspondence and requests for reprints: Katherine I. Miller, Department of Communication, Michigan State University, East Lansing, MI 48824.

and allocation with organizational outcomes. These models will then be tested.

A TYPOLOGY OF EFFECTS OF PARTICIPATION

Many effects of participation have been proposed in organizational research and theory. This section will describe research investigating the (1) attitudinal, (2) cognitive, and (3) behavioral effects of participation.

Attitudinal Effects

Most research investigating participation in decision making (PDM) has considered the effects of participation on workers' attitudes. One of the most well-known early studies of participation considered an attitudinal effect. Coch and French (1948) proposed that if workers were given the opportunity to participate in decisions about the implementation of work changes, the workers would identify with the changes and be less resistant to them. Coch and French's field experiment at a garment factory in North Carolina bore out this hypothesis. Although there have been criticisms and reinterpretations of their work (Bartlem & Locke, 1981), Coch and French's research has resulted in the consideration of a number of attitudinal effects of participation.

The attitudinal variable that has received the most concentration as an effect of participation is job satisfaction. The link between PDM and job satisfaction has been derived primarily from the "Human Relations" school of management (Argyris, 1964; McGregor, 1960). The link between participation and satisfaction suggests that (1) participation in decision making is one way to satisfy higher order needs, and (2) the satisfaction of these needs will lead to greater satisfaction with work.

Research investigating the link between PDM and satisfaction has been reviewed by Locke and Schweiger (1979) and Miller and Monge (1986). Locke and Schweiger conclude that "with respect to satisfaction, the results generally favor participative over directive methods, although nearly 40 percent of the studies did not find PDM to be superior" (1979, p. 316). In a meta-analysis of the research linking PDM with job satisfaction, Miller and Monge (1986) found a relatively strong relationship ($r = .46$) between the perception of a participative climate and work satisfaction. However, there were much lower correlations between job satisfaction and (1) perceived participation on specific issues (.21) and (2) actual participation, typically involving single activities such as democratic work groups ($r = .16$).

A third attitudinal variable that has been linked to PDM is organizational commitment. The relationship between participation and commitment typically has been proposed as an indirect one through the development of cognitions about the organization (Anthony, 1978; Frost, Wakely, & Ruh,

1974). The link between participation and commitment also could be seen as mediated by the actual communicative behaviors engaged in during participation. Kiesler (1971) and Salancik (1977) suggest that organizational commitment is a function of "binding" behavioral acts that are explicit, irrevocable, public, and of free volition. Participation in organizational decision making could well involve such binding behaviors.

Cognitive Effects

The cognitive effects of participation in decision making are often proposed as intervening factors that explain more visible attitudinal and behavioral effects. In recent years, though, there have been calls for greater concentration on the importance of worker knowledge as a precursor and effect of successful participative programs (Locke & Schweiger, 1979; Lowin, 1968; Miles & Ritchie, 1971; Schuler, 1980).

There have been two major cognitive effects of participation proposed. First, it has been suggested that participation will lead to increased utilization of information from lower levels of the organizational hierarchy (Anthony, 1978; Vroom & Yetton, 1973). This line of reasoning assumes that the workers have the most complete information about how work should be done in an organization. Thus the use of participative management should utilize the knowledge of all individuals in the organization effectively.

A second proposed cognitive effect of participation is downward dissemination of information. Propositions regarding this effect have typically taken one of two forms. First, it has been proposed that participative workers will have more and better knowledge about particular decisions and thus will be better able to implement those decisions (Coch & French, 1948; Maier, 1963; Melcher, 1976; Strauss, 1963; Vroom & Yetton, 1963). It also has been proposed that participative employees will have a greater understanding of the entire organization, the marketplace, and the individual employee's part in the greater scheme of things (Bass, 1970).

Third, some researchers have proposed that PDM will lead employees to have more accurate perceptions of reward contingencies in the organization. This effect has been proposed primarily by researchers using an expectancy approach to participation (for example, Mitchell, 1973; Schuler, 1980). Finally, several researchers have argued that participation in decision making will lead to lower levels of role conflict and role ambiguity (Morris, Steers, & Koch, 1979; Schuler, 1977; Schuler, Aldag, & Brief, 1977).

Behavioral Effects

Perhaps the simplest behavioral effect of providing workers with the opportunity to participate is that employees will, indeed, engage in more communicative behaviors. The institution of a program of participation certainly does not guarantee these behaviors (for example, see research on industrial democracy in Yugoslavia by Obradovic, 1970), but communicative behavior seems more likely in a work setting that encourages participation.

Beyond this, however, the major behavioral effect of participation proposed has been individual productivity. Reviews have provided mixed conclusions about this effect. Locke and Schweiger (1979) conclude that "with respect to the productivity criterion there is no trend in favor of participative leadership as compared to more directive styles" (p. 316). A meta-analytic review of this research (Miller & Monge, 1986) found a strong effect for research setting in studies investigating participation and productivity. The correlation between participation and productivity in field studies was .27 and correlations in laboratory research were −.33 for leadership studies and −.01 for group structure studies.

In sum, then, a variety of attitudinal, cognitive, and behavioral effects of participation have been proposed. Some of these effects of participation appear to be relatively direct. For example, increases in communicative behavior, gains in knowledge, and job satisfaction are typically proposed as direct effects of participation. However, several other effects in this typology are probably less direct. For example, the effect of PDM on job performance is typically seen to be mediated by workers' knowledge, participative behavior, and motivation. The effect of participation on organizational commitment may be mediated by knowledge of the organization, self-perceptions of participative behavior, and job satisfaction.

One theoretical mechanism that has been proposed to link participation with performance and organizational commitment is Equity Theory (Adams, 1963; Walster, Walster, & Berscheid, 1978). This theoretical mechanism has been especially prevalent in work on the Scanlon Plan of participative management (Frost, Wakely, & Ruh, 1974). In particular, it has been proposed that individuals who participate in the organization will gain knowledge about the contributions and outcomes of a wide range of organizational participants. It is only when an employee sees that all participants are being equitably treated that the employee will be committed and productive. The next section of this paper will provide a brief review of theory in the area of distributive justice.

EQUITY AND DISTRIBUTIVE JUSTICE

Three important statements regarding social justice were made in the early 1960s and have influenced a great deal of theory and research in social psychology. The first of these was Homans's (1961, 1974) statement of justice in his exchange theory of social behavior. The second was Blau's

(1964) theory of exchange. Finally, Adams (1963, 1965) provided more specific elaboration of behavior in his equity theory. All three of these theories contain two notions that can be regarded as the "heart" of distributive justice theory. First, all three of these theorists propose that individuals make a comparison between what they have put into a relationship and what they are getting out of the relationship. This input/output comparison results in a conclusion regarding the "justice" or "equity" of a relationship. Second, all of these theorists agree that when there is inequity or injustice, a person will feel discomfort.

A great deal of research has followed these early theorists in distributive justice. Three important groups of scholars stand out. First, Walster and her colleagues (Walster, Berscheid, & Walster, 1973; Walster, Walster, & Berscheid, 1978) have expanded on Adam's equity theory by distinguishing between "actual equity" and "psychological equity" and by broadening the range of application of equity theory. Second, Lerner and his associates (for a review, see Lerner, 1980) have developed a line of research based on the "belief in a just world" which investigates how individuals react to people who are suffering without cause. Finally, Leventhal and his colleagues (Leventhal, 1976, 1980; Leventhal, Karuza, & Fry, 1980) have criticized the general viability of equity theory by suggesting that people use several different allocation norms rather than only considering the equitable distribution of rewards.

The work of Leventhal has led to a major debate among those studying distributive justice—the viability of the equity concept for predicting human behavior. The debate essentially comes down to whether or not justice is the only (or most crucial) norm for allocation driving human behavior. This issue typically takes two forms in the literature. The first is a consideration of whether justice—in any form—has much bearing on the way people behave. For example, Leventhal (1976) doubts that justice is even considered in many situations, and Messick and Sentis (1983) have suggested that *preferences* are more important than fairness perceptions. It also has been suggested that allocation norms other than equity are important in determining behavior. The three most prevalent allocation norms considered are (1) *equity* (or the contribution principle), in which outcomes are allocated proportionally to inputs, (2) *equality,* in which outcomes are allocated equally to all involved, and (3) *needs,* in which outcomes are allocated with the goal of meeting the needs of those involved.

A SYSTEM OF ORGANIZATIONAL
PARTICIPATION AND EQUITY

Thus far this chapter has presented several proposals about participation, equity, and organizational outcomes. First, it was proposed that the effects of participation can be divided into attitudinal, cognitive, and behavioral effects. Second, it was proposed that some of these effects were direct (communicative behavior, knowledge increases, job satisfaction) and some were indirect (performance, organizational commitment). Third, it was proposed that one theoretical mechanism that linked participation with indirect effects (particularly organizational commitment) is equity.

From this groundwork, a system of relationships can be proposed that links participation and equity with direct and indirect outcomes. This system of relationships is presented in Figure 19.1. In this model, the opportunity to participate has immediate cognitive, behavioral, and attitudinal effects. There is also an indirect attitudinal effect of participation, organizational commitment. The relationship between participation and commitment is moderated by all three of the direct effects of participation, with the behavioral and cognitive links further moderated by perceptions of allocation. As employees behave in more participative ways and learn more about the organization, they come in contact with more organizational participants and gain knowledge about the system of allocation in the organization. This will lead to perceptions of equity and organizational commitment. The next section of this paper will discuss a management system, the Scanlon Plan, which incorporates the notions of participation, equity, and outcomes for use in testing the model presented in Figure 19.1.

THE SCANLON PLAN OF
PARTICIPATIVE MANAGEMENT

The Scanlon Plan (Frost, Wakeley, & Ruh, 1974) is a system of participative management and profit-sharing designed to increase company productivity through the competent use of human resources. Although the Scanlon Plan was developed to improve company productivity, it is at heart a plan for changing the cognitions, attitudes, and behaviors of individual workers through the "Three Psychological Conditions": (1) the *identification* of the organization and employees, (2) the opportunity to *participate,* and (3) the realization of *equity*.

The psychological condition of identification suggests that employees must possess knowledge about all organizational "shareholders" (for example, customers, financial investors, management, and employees). Scanlon theorists suggest that knowledge of the company and the individual's place in it is essential for meaningful participation in the organization. The most central aspect of the identification condition is cognitive. That is, a person must have *knowledge* about the organization to participate effectively. However, an organization also must be concerned with the

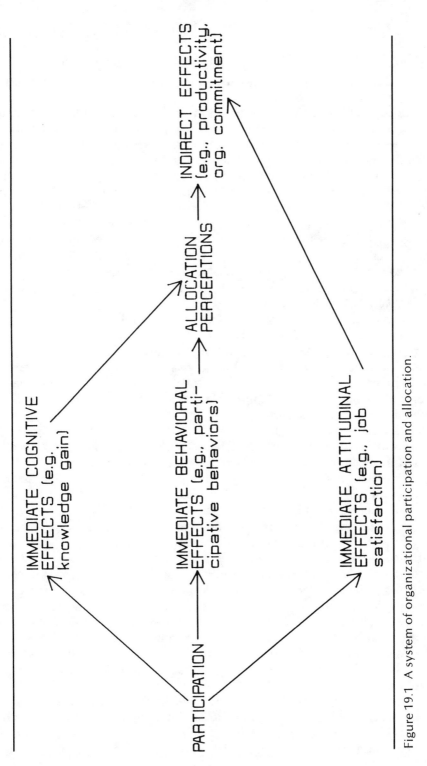

Figure 19.1 A system of organizational participation and allocation.

acquisition of knowledge. Thus Scanlon Plans often include formal mechanisms designed to facilitate the process of employees learning about the organization.

The second "psychological condition" of the Scanlon Plan, participation, is based on the notion that employees have the most complete knowledge about how a job can be accomplished. Thus employees are encouraged to make innovation suggestions. However, the content of participation is not limited to an individual's job, and employees are encouraged to participate in a wide range of organizational decisions. The major mechanism for facilitating participation in Scanlon companies is the committee. Most Scanlon companies have two types of committees: (1) production committees that encourage suggestions about the work process, and (2) screening committees that consider suggestions about companywide concerns. The Scanlon Plan also acknowledges that participation could involve channels other than the committee structure (for example, informal communication channels).

The third psychological condition of the Scanlon Plan, equity, suggests that people will continue to contribute to the organization only as long as they perceive that they are being treated equitably. Equity is defined by Scanlon advocates as the fair treatment of all shareholders in the organization. The realization of equity involves the comparison by the individual of shareholder inputs and outcomes. In practical terms, equity is realized through a profit-sharing system.

In summary, then, the three conditions proposed to be necessary for a successful Scanlon Plan are identification, participation, and equity. When these three conditions are met, Scanlon theorists suggest that a variety of outcomes will result. On the individual level these outcomes include (1) commitment, (2) satisfaction, (3) increased suggestions for innovation, and (4) increased individual productivity. These individual outcomes should then translate into company outcomes of (1) productivity, (2) profitability, and (3) a competitive edge in the marketplace.

However, research and theory on social justice strongly suggest that one of these psychological conditions, equity, may not be the driving force it is assumed to be for everyone. Rather, it may be more important for some persons to maximize their own outcomes than to see that equity is being achieved. This distinction between equity and outcome maximization can be extended to the other psychological conditions of the Scanlon Plan. That is, it is possible that norms for participation and identification also could be "individually oriented" (like outcome maximization) or "group oriented" (like equity).

These distinctions would suggest two different causal systems at work in Scanlon companies. In one, people would participate in the organization in ways advocated by the Scanlon structure, exhibit communicative behaviors commensurate with these participation channels, gain knowledge about the Scanlon system of management, and develop commitment to the organization when all shareholders in the organization are being treated equitably. In a second causal system, people would participate in the organization in individualistic ways, exhibit communicative behaviors that do not involve the formal management system, gain knowledge about how to improve individual job performance, and develop commitment to the organization when individual outcomes are maximized. Because the first system of relationships proposed above is closely tied with the management system, it will be called the *Scanlon Model*. The second system of relationships, emphasizing individual activity and outcome maximization, will be called the *Non-Scanlon Model*. These models, drawing from the general model in Figure 19.1, are presented in Figures 19.2a and 19.2b.

METHODS

This section will outline the methods used to test the Scanlon and Non-Scanlon models of allocation and participation just developed. First, the sample and procedures used in data collection will be presented. Then, the operationalization of variables will be considered. Finally, the analyses used to test the models will be discussed.

Sample

Data for this study were collected from seven Scanlon firms. All of the organizations studied were manufacturing firms, and most were located in the midwest. Company size ranged from 50 to 600 employees, with an average of 236 employees.

Research Procedures

Data for this study were collected as part of a larger research project investigating the impacts of the Scanlon Plan over time. For the research reported in this paper, data were collected from each company weekly for either 12 or 18 weeks.[1] Each week, questionnaires were sent to a contact person, who distributed them to a systematic sample of employees. Employees were asked to complete the questionnaire, seal it in an envelope, and return it to the contact person. The contact person then returned the completed questionnaires to the researchers.

Operationalization

This study required the operationalization of (1) participation channels, (2) cognitive effects (learning), (3) behavioral effects (activities), (4) attitudinal effects (job satisfaction), (5) indirect outcomes (organizational com-

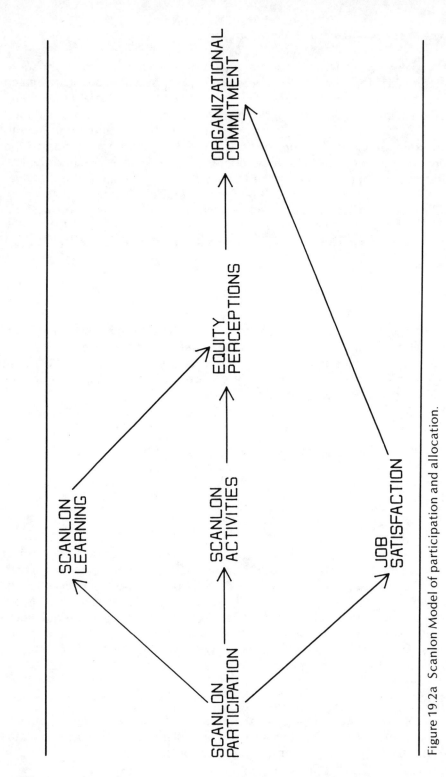

Figure 19.2a Scanlon Model of participation and allocation.

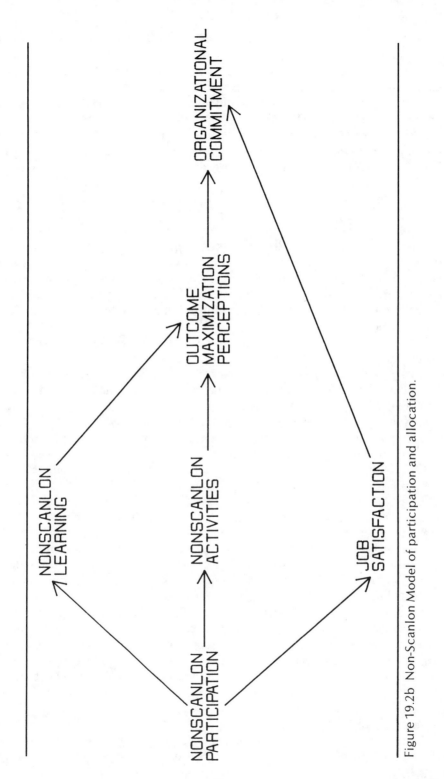

Figure 19.2b Non-Scanlon Model of participation and allocation.

mitment), and (6) perceptions about allocation. The operationalization of each of these variables is discussed below.

Participation was measured through a series of items asking employees how much they "PARTICIPATE in using the following to SOLVE PROBLEMS in meeting our company's commitments to its customers, financial investors/owners, and employees?" In order to differentiate among the Scanlon and Non-Scanlon models presented above, the subitems measuring participation included both Scanlon methods of participation (e.g., suggestions system, committee meetings) and Non-Scanlon methods of participation (e.g., other departments, my supervisor).

The *cognitive effect* of participation was operationalized by asking employees how they LEARN about the company's commitments. In order to test the Scanlon and Non-Scanlon models, the subitems in this question included both Non-Scanlon means of seeking information (for example, other employees, written reports, my supervisor) and Scanlon means for seeking information (for example, Scanlon representatives, bonus performance report).

The *behavioral effect* of participation was measured through items that asked employees about activities they use to meet company commitments. Again, both Scanlon and Non-Scanlon subitems were included. The Scanlon activities included such behaviors as volunteering for election as a Scanlon representative and encouraging other people to get involved. The Non-Scanlon activities included such behaviors as accepting almost any type of job assignment if the work needs to be done and participating in performance reviews with a supervisor.

One *immediate attitudinal outcome* of participation, job satisfaction, was considered. Job satisfaction was measured with the Satisfaction with Work subscale of the Job Descriptive Index (Smith, Kendall, & Hulin, 1969). This scale has been extensively validated and is considered a highly reliable scale. In addition, one *indirect attitudinal outcome* of participation, organizational commitment, was measured. Organizational commitment was measured with the Organization Commitment Questionnaire (Mowday, Steers, & Porter, 1979). This scale has been tested extensively for reliability and validity.

Finally, two *allocation principles* were measured: equity and outcome maximization. These were measured through two sets of items. One set of items asked employees how much organizational constituents SHOULD benefit from meeting commitments to employees and one set of items asked employees how much various organizational constituents DO benefit from meeting commitments to employees. The constituents considered were (1) our customers, (2) financial investors/owners, (3) employees, (4) myself, and (5) management.

Outcome maximization was then measured through the "Who BENEFITS" subitem of "myself." That is, those who perceived that they were benefiting to a great extent from meeting organizational commitments were seen as maximizing their own outcomes. *Equity* was computed as a function of the difference scores between "Who SHOULD BENEFIT" and "Who BENEFITS" items. Specifically, the difference between "should" and "benefit" scores for each organizational constituent was computed. The absolute value of this score was taken, as inequity could be the function of both overbenefit and underbenefit. Equity was then defined as the sum of all the individual equity scores.

Analysis

The measurement of participation, learning, and activities (discussed above) included both Scanlon and Non-Scanlon items. Confirmatory factor analysis was used to confirm a structure in which Scanlon strategies loaded on factors separate from Non-Scanlon strategies. CFA was also used to confirm the factor structure of satisfaction with work and organizational commitment scales.

The measurement models were confirmed using the PACKAGE computer program (Hunter, Cohen, & Nicol, 1982). The confirmatory factor analysis subroutine of PACKAGE allows the researcher to specify an a priori factor structure. The unidimensionality of the proposed factors can then be assessed using three criteria proposed by Hunter (1977): homogeneity of item content, internal consistency within clusters, and parallelism of items in a cluster with outside variables.

Following confirmation of the measurement models, the Scanlon and Non-Scanlon path models were analyzed using the LISREL V computer program (Joreskog & Sorbom, 1981). This program provides estimates of parameters in linear structural equations through the method of maximum likelihood. The models were evaluated with macro tests of goodness of fit and difference from the null model (Bentler & Bonett, 1980), and with micro analysis of individual causal linkages. Modification indices also were examined to identify portions of the model in which local improvements were possible. Significance for all statistical tests was set at alpha = .05.

RESULTS

Confirmatory Factor Analyses

Confirmatory factor analyses were performed to determine if the proposed scales for measuring Scanlon and Non-Scanlon Learning, Participation, and Activities were unidimensional. Factor analyses also were performed on the standard scales used to measure job satisfaction (the Job Description Index; Smith, Kendall, & Hulin, 1969) and organizational commitment (the Organizational Commitment Questionnaire; Mowday,

Steers, & Porter, 1979). The factors were evaluated in terms of item content, internal consistency, and parallelism. The combined sample from all companies used in analyses was 1,479 employees.

Several items were dropped from the scales submitted to the confirmatory factor analysis because the items did not meet the criteria of internal consistency, parallelism, and homogeneity of content. Specifically, nine items were dropped from the Job Satisfaction factor, yielding a factor with an alpha of .76. Seven items were deleted from the Organizational Commitment factor (alpha = .90), one item was dropped from the Non-Scanlon Learn factor (alpha = .80), one item was dropped from the Scanlon Participation factor (alpha = .83), and one item was dropped from the Non-Scanlon Activities factor (alpha = .69). No items were deleted from the NonScanlon Participation factor (alpha = .68), the Scanlon Learn factor (alpha = .83) or the Scanlon Activities factor (alpha = .80).[2]

Path Analysis

The scales accepted from confirmatory factor analyses were used as input for path analysis. The correlations used for path analysis, presented in Table 19.1, were corrected for attenuation due to measurement error. Because the data used in this investigation were collected over an 8 or 18 week time span (depending on the company), an analysis of variance was conducted to check on the stability of the data over time. The analytical techniques of path analysis and structural equation modeling make the assumption of cross-sectional data (Hannan & Young, 1977). Thus a check on the stability of data collected over time was necessary before these statistical techniques could be used. None of the F values was significant, and the average probability level for the stability analyses was .49. Thus it seems clear that the data are stable over time.

Path models were then analyzed using the LISREL V computer program (Joreskog & Sorbom, 1981). Models were evaluated in terms of (1) the fit of the model to the data, (2) the difference between the proposed model and the null model, and (3) the significance of individual links in the model. If the model did not fit the data well, modification indices were examined to determine if the addition of theoretically consistent links could improve the fit of the model significantly. Model fitting procedures for the Scanlon and Non-Scanlon models will be discussed separately.

Scanlon Model. The hypothesized Scanlon Model, with path coefficients and standard errors, is presented in Figure 19.3. Although this model is significantly better than the null model of no relationships (chi square difference of 2760.88 with 7 degrees of freedom), it is clear that it is not a good fit to the data. In a model-fitting procedure of this type, a nonsignificant chi square value indicates a good fit of the model to the data.

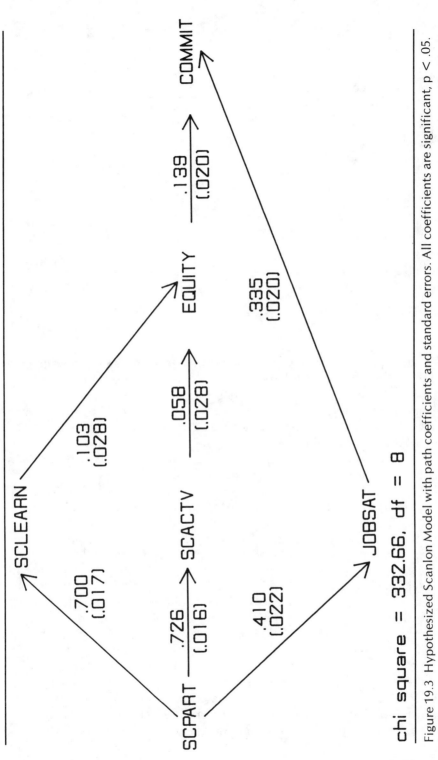

Figure 19.3 Hypothesized Scanlon Model with path coefficients and standard errors. All coefficients are significant, p < .05.

Table 19.1
Correlation Matrix Used in LISREL Path Models
(correlations corrected for attenuation; N = 1479)

	1	2	3	4	5	6	7	8	9	10	11	12
1. SCLEARN	—											
2. SCACTV	.465	—										
3. JOBSAT	.324	.400	—									
4. EQUITY	.130	.106	.153	—								
5. COMMIT	.455	.340	.463	.233	—							
6. SCPART	.700	.726	.410	.104	.393	—						
7. NSLEARN							—					
8. NSACTV							.581	—				
9. JOBSAT							.432	.433	—			
10 OUTMAX							.235	.248	.161	—		
11. COMMIT							.510	.452	.463	.325	—	
12. NSPART							.800	.749	.556	.218	.417	—

The chi square for the hypothesized model is 332.66 with 8 degrees of freedom. This value is significant, and the chi square to degrees of freedom ratio is well over five (the largest value suggested by Wheaton, Muthen, Alwin, & Summers, 1977, for a good fitting model). Thus modification indices were examined and links were added to the model in an attempt to improve its fit to the data.

Four links were added to the model. In sequence, the links added were (1) from Scanlon Learn to Commitment, (2) from Scanlon Activities to Job Satisfaction, (3) from Job Satisfaction to Equity, and (4) from Scanlon Learn to Scanlon Activities. After these four links were added, a nonsignificant link from Scanlon Activities to Equity was dropped from the model. The final model is presented in Figure 19.4. All of the path coefficients in this model are significant, and, as with the hypothesized model, this model is a significantly better fit than the null. Additionally, the chi square for this model is quite low—17.35 with 5 degrees of freedom. Although this value is still significant, the chi square to degrees of freedom ratio is less than 5, indicating a good fit of the model to the data.

Non-Scanlon Model. The hypothesized Non-Scanlon Model, with path coefficients and standard errors, is presented in Figure 19.5. Like the hypothesized Scanlon Model, the Non-Scanlon Model is significantly better than the null model (chi square difference of 3811.81 with 7 degrees of freedom). However, this model is also a poor fit to the data. The chi square value is 383.73 with 8 degrees of freedom. This value is significant, and the chi square to degrees of freedom ratio is well over five. Thus modification

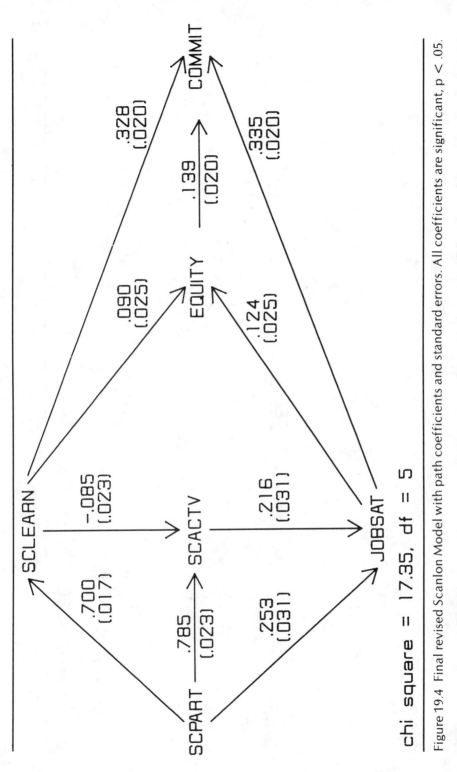

chi square = 17.35, df = 5

Figure 19.4 Final revised Scanlon Model with path coefficients and standard errors. All coefficients are significant, p < .05.

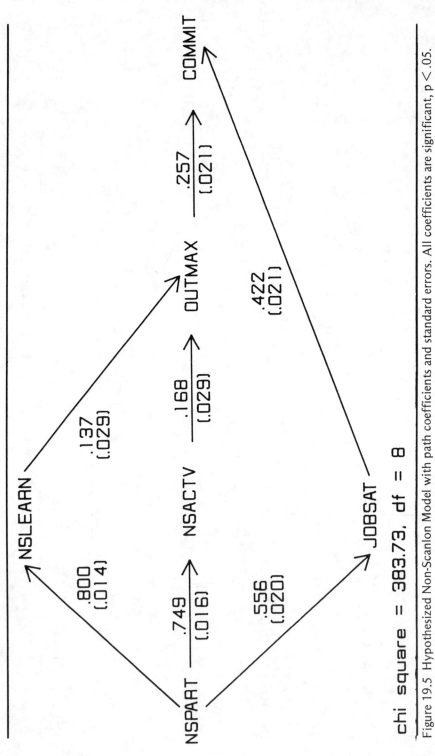

chi square = 383.73, df = 8

Figure 19.5 Hypothesized Non-Scanlon Model with path coefficients and standard errors. All coefficients are significant, p < .05.

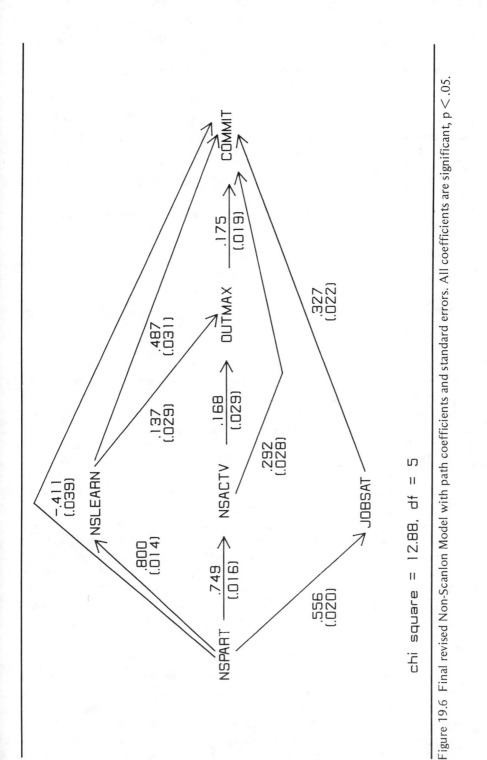

Figure 19.6 Final revised Non-Scanlon Model with path coefficients and standard errors. All coefficients are significant, p < .05.

chi square = 12.88, df = 5

449

indices were examined in an effort to improve the fit of the model to the data.

Three links were sequentially added to improve the fit of the Non-Scanlon Model. The added links were (1) from Non-Scanlon Learn to Commitment, (2) from Non-Scanlon Activities to Commitment, and (3) from Non-Scanlon Participation to Commitment. The final model is presented in Figure 19.6. All of the links in this model are significant, and the model is a significantly better fit than the null model. In addition, the chi square is very low—12.88 with 5 degrees of freedom. This value is insignificant at the .05 level, and the chi square to degrees of freedom ratio is less than three. Thus it appears that this model is a good fit to the data.

DISCUSSION

Measurement Models

The original items measuring participation channels, learning, and activities formed six factors: Scanlon Participation, Non-Scanlon Participation, Scanlon Learning, Non-Scanlon Learning, Scanlon Activities, and Non-Scanlon Activities. This finding lends considerable credence to the notion that individuals use group and Scanlon modes of participation, learning, and behaving in different ways than they use individual modes.

The measurement models for organizational commitment and job satisfaction also were interesting. The Organizational Commitment Questionnaire (Mowday, Steers, & Porter, 1979) and the Job Description Index (Smith, Kendall, & Hulin, 1969) have in recent years been considered highly reliable and valid scales. The current analysis suggests that these may not be as sound as previously believed. It is possible that these scales were not as sound as predicted because of the sample used. For example, all of the negative items in the OCQ were subsequently dropped, indicating that respondents were not interpreting these items successfully. However, this sample, a mix of white- and blue-collar workers with education typically beyond high school, is certainly not atypical of many used in organizational research. Thus it seems reasonable to suggest that more caution and careful analysis be exercised in the use of these standard scales.

Path Models

Scanlon Model. Two differences between the hypothesized Scanlon Model and the final Scanlon Model were striking. First, links were added between Scanlon Learning and Scanlon Activities and between Scanlon Activities and Job Satisfaction. The addition of these two links support Scanlon Plan theorists' (Frost, Wakely, & Ruh, 1974) contentions that the Scanlon Plan is a sequential process in which identification is necessary for participative behavior that is necessary for attitudinal outcomes. However, it should be noted that the link between Scanlon Learning and Scanlon Activities is *negative* (though small). Thus it appears that although the general effect of the opportunity to participate on participative behavior is positive, the residual effects of Scanlon learning about the organization on participative behaviors is negative.

The second striking difference between the proposed and accepted Scanlon models is the addition of a direct link between Scanlon Learning and Organizational Commitment. This link is relatively strong (.328). Thus it appears that cognitions regarding the Scanlon Plan are sufficient for developing commitment to the organization without the strong intermediate effect of an allocation variable such as equity. It should be noted that the link between Equity and Commitment is also significant, but much smaller than the link between Learning and Commitment.

Non-Scanlon Model. The most interesting feature of the final version of the Non-Scanlon path model is the multiple determinants of organizational commitment. Every variable in the model had a significant direct impact on commitment. This involved the addition of three links to the hypothesized model. A link between Non-Scanlon Learning and Commitment was added (.487) and a link between Non-Scanlon Activities and Commitment was added (.292). As with the Scanlon Model, above, the addition of these two links indicates the importance of the direct impact of behavior and cognitions on commitment, without the necessity of an intervening variable, though the link between outcome maximization and commitment also was significant.

However, the most interesting additional variable influencing commitment was Non-Scanlon Participation. This link is relatively strong and negative (-.411), but the zero-order correlation between these two variables is strong and positive (.417). Thus this path can be interpreted in the same way a partial correlation coefficient would in investigating spurious, suppressor, or interaction effects (see Bagozzi, 1980; Kenny, 1979). That is, it appears that after the direct cognitive, behavioral, and attitudinal effects of participation have been removed, the variance remaining in the relationship between participation and commitment is strongly negative. Substantively, this suggests that if employees do not receive positive cognitive, attitudinal, and behavioral benefits from participative channels, the use of these channels may well have a negative impact on commitment to the organization.

Comparison of Scanlon and Non-Scanlon models. In addition to the differences between hypothesized and final models discussed above, the general Scanlon and Non-Scanlon models can be compared in terms of the value of path coefficients in both models. For example, the coefficient between participation and learning variables in the Non-Scanlon Model (.800) is significantly larger than in the Scanlon Model (.700). The difference in the learning to commitment link is also significant, though again relatively small (.328 in the Scanlon Model versus .487 in the Non-Scanlon Model).

The largest, and perhaps most interesting, contrast between these two models is in the participation to job satisfaction link. The link between Scanlon participation and job satisfaction has a coefficient of .253 and the Non-Scanlon participation to job satisfaction link has a coefficient of .556. Thus it appears that the Non-Scanlon channels of participation (other departments in the company, my supervisor) had a much larger effect on satisfaction than the Scanlon channels of participation (work group meetings, production committee meetings, screening committee meetings). This suggests that although a complicated program of participation may be important for reaching many organizational objectives, such a program is probably not a crucial factor for improving employee attitudes. The simpler activities of talking to the supervisor and other departments had a much stronger impact on satisfaction than the complex system of committees set up by the Scanlon Plan. Thus, it may well be more important for managers to develop an atmosphere in which a variety of modes of participation are encouraged than a specific system of committees and activities for facilitating participation.

Finally, one similarity between these two models should be noted. In both models, the link between allocation perceptions (equity and outcome maximization) and commitment is relatively small, though significant. As mentioned earlier, this fact underlines the importance of direct impacts of cognitions, participative behavior, and satisfaction on commitment, and deemphasizes the importance of intervening allocation perceptions. This finding does not support the Scanlon model of the participative process in which equity is a key variable. It provides more support to Salancik's (1977) notion of commitment as a function of binding behaviors. Salancik, building on work by Kiesler (1971), has suggested that organizational commitment is the function of binding and public behaviors within the organization. Eisenberg, Monge, and Miller (1983) found support for this position in their study of participation in communication networks and organizational commitment. The direct impact of participation channels and behaviors on commitment provides further evidence for this model of organizational commitment.

LIMITATIONS AND DIRECTIONS
FOR FUTURE RESEARCH

This study had several limitations that suggest ways in which this research could be improved or extended. One clear way in which this research could be improved is in the measurement of several variables in the model. In particular, the measurement of the learning and allocation variables could be greatly improved.

The typology of participation effects developed proposed that the key cognitive effect of participation for the individual employee was increased knowledge about the organization and the individual's role in the organization. This study measured cognitive effects with a variable that considered a number of sources for information and the degree to which these sources were used by the employees. Although use of information sources may provide a rough approximation of knowledge gained through participation, a far stronger statement about cognitive effects could be made if actual knowledge gained by employees was measured.

Equity was measured in this study as the difference between how much shareholders should benefit and how much they do benefit. Although this scale is adequate for measuring allocation norms, more sophisticated measurement techniques might well provide more valuable and accurate information. For example, magnitude estimation techniques might provide a more precise measurement of perceived overreward and underreward in the organization.

In addition to better measurement of variables included in this model, our knowledge of participation and allocation norms could benefit immensely from the extension of this model to other variables. First, future research should consider indirect effects of participation other than organizational commitment. In particular, the individual productivity of workers should be considered as an outcome in this model. Second, this research could be extended usefully to consider other immediate behavioral outcomes of participative channels, particularly communicative outcomes.

Finally, this work could be extended to the study of determinants of allocation and equity norms in organizations. The path models developed clearly indicated that there are differences between equity norms and maximization norms, and that these allocational differences extend to different patterns of participation, learning, and communicative behavior. It seems reasonable to expect that there are a number of personal, situational, and cultural variables that might influence the degree to which an individual favors norms regarding equity and collectivity, or norms regarding outcome maximization and individuality.

NOTES

1. The sampling cycle for each firm was determined in part by the size of the company. An attempt was made to procure a sample of 40 employees each week from each company in the sample. However, for smaller companies, an 8- or 12-week cycle was instituted, depending on company preference. In this research, Companies 2, 3, 4, 5, and 6 were on an 8-week sampling cycle, and one full cycle of data were used in the study. Companies 1 and 7 were on longer sampling cycles and the first 18 weeks of data were used in this study.

2. Item content, factor loadings, and relevant correlation and deviation matrices for the assessment of internal consistency and parallelism are available from the senior author upon request.

REFERENCES

Adams, J. S. (1963). Toward an understanding of inequity. *Journal of Abnormal and Social Psychology, 67,* 422-436.

Adams, J. S. (1965). Inequity in social exchange. In L. Berkowitz (Ed.), *Advances in experimental social psychology* (Vol. 2, pp. 267-299). New York: Academic Press.

Anthony, W. P. (1978). *Participative management.* Reading, MA: Addison-Wesley.

Argyris, C. (1964). *Integrating the individual and the organization.* New York: John Wiley.

Bagozzi, R. P. (1980). *Casual models in marketing.* New York: John Wiley.

Bartlem, C. S., & Locke, E. A. (1981). The Coch and French study: A critique and reinterpretation. *Human Relations, 34,* 555-566.

Bass, B. M. (1970). When planning for others. *Journal of Applied Behavioral Science, 6,* 151-171.

Bentler, P. M., & Bonett, D. G. (1980). Significance tests and goodness of fit in the analysis of covariance structures. *Psychological Bulletin, 88,* 588-606.

Blau, P. M. (1964). *Exchange and power in social life.* New York: John Wiley.

Coch, L., & French, J. R. P. (l948). Overcoming resistance to change. *Human Relations, 1,* 512-532.

Eisenberg, E. M., Monge, P. R., & Miller, K. I. (1983). Involvement in communication networks as a predictor of organizational commitment. *Human Communication Research, 10,* 179-201.

Frost, C. H., Wakeley, J. H., & Ruh, R. A. (1974). *The Scanlon Plan for organization development: Identity, participation, and equity.* East Lansing: Michigan State University Press.

Hannan, M. T., & Young, A. A. (1977). Estimation in panel models: Results on pooling cross-sections and time series. In D. H. Heise (Ed.), *Sociological methodology 1977* (pp. 52-83). San Francisco: Jossey-Bass.

Homans, G. C. (1961). *Social behavior: Its elementary forms.* New York: Harcourt Brace & World.

Homans, G. C. (1974). *Social behavior: Its elementary forms* (rev. ed.). New York: Harcourt Brace & World.

Hunter, J. E. (1977). *Cluster analysis: Reliability, construct validity, and the multiple indicators approach to measurement.* Unpublished manuscript, Michigan State University, Department of Psychology.

Hunter, J. E., Cohen, S. H., & Nicol, T. S. (1982). PACKAGE:*A system of routines to do correlational analysis, including path analysis, confirmatory factor analysis, and exploratory factor analysis.* Unpublished manuscript, Michigan State University, Department of Psychology.

Joreskog, K. G., & Sorbom, D. (1981). *LISREL V: Analysis of linear structural relationships by maximum likelihood and least square methods.* Chicago: International Education Services.

Kenny, D. A. (1979). *Correlation and causality.* New York: John Wiley.

Kiesler, C. A. (1971). *The psychology of commitment: Experiments linking behavior to belief.* New York: Academic Press.

Lerner, M. J. (1980). *The belief in a just world.* New York: Plenum.

Leventhal, G. S. (1976). The distribution of rewards and resources in groups and organizations. In L. Berkowitz and E. Walster (Eds.), *Advances in experimental social psychology* (Vol. 9, pp. 91-131). New York: Academic Press.

Leventhal, G. S., Karuza, J., & Fry, W. R. (1980). Beyond fairness: A theory of allocation preferences. In G. Mikula (Ed.), *Justice and social interaction* (pp. 167-218). New York: Springer-Verlag.

Locke, E. A., & Schweiger, D. M. (1979). Participation in decision-making: One more look. *Research in Organizational Behavior, 1,* 265-339.

Lowin, A. (1968). Participative decision making: A model, literature critique, and prescriptions for research. *Organizational Behavior and Human Performance, 3,* 68-106.

Maier, N. R. F. (1963). *Problem solving discussions and conferences: Leadership methods and skills.* New York: McGraw-Hill.

McGregor, D. (1960). *The human side of enterprise.* New York: McGraw-Hill.

Melcher, A. J. (1976). Participation: A critical review of research findings. *Human Resource Management, 12-21.*

Messick, D. M., & Sentis, K. (1983). Fairness, preference, and fairness biases. In D. M. Messick and K. S. Cook (Eds.), *Equity theory: Psychological and sociological perspectives* (pp. 61-94). New York: Praeger.

Miles, R. E., & Ritchie, J. B. (1971). Participative management: Quality vs. quantity. *California Management Review, 13,* 48-56.

Miller, K. I., & Monge, P. R. (1986). Participation, satisfaction, and productivity: A meta-analytic review. *Academy of Management Journal, 29,* 727-753.

Mitchell, T. R. (1973). Motivation and participation: An integration. *Academy of Management Journal, 16,* 660-679.

Morris, J. H., Steers, R. M., & Koch, J. L. (1979).Influence of organization structure on role conflict and ambiguity for three occupational groupings. *Academy of Management Journal, 22,* 58-71.

Mowday, R. T., Steers, R. M., & Porter, L. W. (1979). The measurement of organizational commitment. *Journal of Vocational Behavior, 14,* 224-247.

Obradovic, J. (1970). Participation and work attitudes in Yugoslavia. *Industrial Relations, 9,* 161-169.

Salancik, G. R. (1977). Commitment and control of organizational behavior and belief. In B. M. Staw & G. R. Salancik (Eds.), *New directions in organizational behavior* (pp. 1-54). Chicago: St. Clair Press.

Schuler, R. S. (1977). Role conflict and ambiguity as a function of the task-structure-technology interaction. *Organizational Behavior and Human Performance, 20,* 66-74.

Schuler, R. S. (1980). A role and expectancy perception model of participation in decision making. *Academy of Management Journal, 23,* 331-340.

Schuler, R. S., Aldag, R. J., & Brief, A. P. (1977). Role conflict and ambiguity: A scale analysis. *Organizational Behavior and Human Performance, 20,* 111-128.

Smith, P. C., Kendall, L. M., & Hulin, C. L. (1969). *The measurement of satisfaction in work and retirement.* Chicago: Rand McNally.

Strauss, G. (1963). Some notes on power equalization. In H. J. Leavitt (Ed.), *The social science of organizations: Four perspectives* (pp. 39-84). Englewood Cliffs, NJ: Prentice-Hall.

Vroom, V. H., & Yetton, P. W. (1973). *Leadership and decision-making.* Pittsburgh: University of Pittsburgh Press.

Walster, E., Berscheid, E., & Walster, G. W. (1973). New directions in equity research. *Journal of Personality and Social Psychology, 25,* 151-176.

Walster, E., Walster, G. W., & Berscheid, E. (1978). *Equity: Theory and research.* Boston: Allyn & Bacon, Inc.

Wheaton, B., Muthen, B., Alwin, D. R., & Summers, A. F. (1977). Assessing reliability and stability in panel models. In D. R. Heise (Ed.), *Sociological methodology 1977* (pp. 84-136). San Francisco: Jossey-Bass.

VI ● INTERCULTURAL AND DEVELOPMENT COMMUNICATION

20 ● Cultural Dissimilarities and Uncertainty Reduction Processes

WILLIAM B. GUDYKUNST ●
ELIZABETH CHUA ● ALISA J. GRAY

Arizona State University

T HE assumption that individuals try to reduce uncertainty in initial interactions with strangers underlies uncertainty reduction theory (Berger, 1979). Uncertainty in this context refers to two phenomena: the ability to predict accurately how others will behave and the ability to explain why others behave the way they do (Berger & Calabrese, 1975). Uncertainty reduction, therefore, involves the creation of proactive predictions and retroactive explanations about others' behavior. The desire to reduce uncertainty, however, does not stop with initial interactions with strangers. Rather, as Berger (1979) argues, "the communicative processes involved in knowledge generation and the development of understanding are central to the development and disintegration of most interpersonal relationships" (p. 123).

Berger and Calabrese's (1975) initial formulation of the theory posited 7 axioms and 21 theorems specifying the interrelations among uncertainty, amount of communication, nonverbal affiliative expressiveness, information seeking, intimacy level of communication content, reciprocity, similarity, and liking. Berger (1979) elaborated the theory outlining three

Correspondence and requests for reprints: William B. Gudykunst, Department of Communication, Arizona State University, Tempe, AZ 85287.

general strategies individuals use for reducing uncertainty: passive, active, and interactive. More recently, Berger and Bradac (1982) emphasized the influence of the general similarity construct on uncertainty reduction processes, and Parks and Adelman (1983) linked shared communication networks to the reduction of uncertainty.

Cross-cultural studies suggest that the theory can be generalized to account for differences in initial interactions between Japan and the United States (Gudykunst & Nishida, 1984), as well as to explain communication in acquaintance, friend, and dating relationships in Japan, Korea, and the United States (Gudykunst, Yang, & Nishida, 1985). Recent research (Gudykunst & Hammer, in press) also reveals that the theory can elucidate ethnic differences in initial interactions between blacks and whites in the United States. Intercultural research (Gudykunst, 1985a, 1985c) further indicates that uncertainty reduction theory is useful in explaining communication between people from the United States and other cultures, as well as detailing differences in intraethnic and interethnic communication in the United States (Gudykunst, 1986).

The purpose of this chapter is to extend previous research on cultural similarity/dissimilarity and uncertainty reduction processes. This is accomplished by examining the influence of the interaction between stage of relationship development and dissimilarities along multiple dimensions of cultural variability on uncertainty reduction processes. Specifically, differences in Hofstede's (1980, 1983) four dimensions of culture (power distance, uncertainty avoidance, individualism, and masculinity) are used to operationalize cultural similarity/dissimilarity. The dependent variables examined include two interactive uncertainty reduction strategies (self-disclosure and interrogation), attraction, perceived similarity, shared communication networks, the display of nonverbal affiliative expressiveness, and attributional confidence. These variables were selected because they are central to the original theory (Berger & Calabrese, 1975) or recent elaborations (Berger, 1979; Parks & Adelman, 1983).

INFLUENCES ON UNCERTAINTY REDUCTION IN INTERCULTURAL ENCOUNTERS

Cultural Dissimilarity

Simard's (1981) research with Francophones and Anglophones in Canada revealed that both groups "perceive it as more difficult to know how to initiate a conversation, to know what to talk about during the interaction, to be interested in the other person, and to guess in which language they should talk" when communicating with someone culturally different than when communicating with someone culturally similar (p. 179). Her research also indicated that those who formed an acquaintance relationship with a culturally different person perceived this person to be as similar to them as did people who formed an acquaintance with a person who was culturally similar.

Other research is consistent with Simard's (1981) findings. Gudykunst (1983), for example, found that people make more assumptions about strangers, prefer to talk less, ask more about strangers' backgrounds, and have less attributional confidence about predicting strangers' behavior in initial intercultural encounters than in initial intracultural encounters. Similarly, in a study of Japanese and North Americans, Gudykunst and Nishida (1984) discovered that cultural similarity/dissimilarity has a multivariate effect on intent to self-disclose, interrogate, display nonverbal affiliative expressiveness, attraction, and attributional confidence. Gudykunst (1985a) also found that cultural similarity/dissimilarity has a multivariate effect on attributional confidence, self-disclosure, interrogation, deception detection, attraction, perceived attitude similarity, length of relationship, and shared communication networks. Finally, Gudykunst's (1985c) research revealed that degree of cultural dissimilarity in terms of Hall's (1976) scheme of cultural variability is related to attributional confidence and second language competence, but not information seeking.

With the exception of one study (Gudykunst, 1985c), all research to date on cultural similarity/dissimilarity has treated this variable as a dichotomy: The subjects were from either the same or different cultures. Gudykunst's (1985c) study examined low, moderate, and high cultural similarity using combinations of Hall's (1976) low- and high-context scheme (for example, low cultural similarity = one person from high-context culture and one from low-context culture). Only one dimension of cultural variability, therefore, was examined. No research has examined the effect of multiple dimensions of cultural similarity/dissimilarity on intercultural communication. One scheme of cultural variability that allows such comparisons to be made is Hofstede's (1980, 1983) dimensions of culture.

Hofstede (1980) gathered data from subsidiaries of a large multinational corporation in 40 countries. Using ecological factor analysis he extracted 4 dimensions of culture: power distance, uncertainty avoidance, individualism, and masculinity. Data from an additional 10 countries and 3 regions were added (Hofstede, 1983), yielding scores on the 4 dimensions for 50 countries and 3 regions. Differences along these 4 dimensions of culture can be used to operationalize cultural dissimilarity in order to examine its influence on uncertainty reduction processes in intercultural encounters.

Power distance is defined as "the extent to which the less powerful members of institutions and organizations accept that power is distributed unequally" (Hofstede & Bond, 1984, p. 418). This dimension relates to social inequality and the amount of authority one person has over others.

Scores on power distance ranged from a low of 11 in Austria to a high of 104 in Malaysia (M = 52, SD = 20).

Uncertainty avoidance is "the extent to which people feel threatened by ambiguous situations and have created beliefs and institutions that try to avoid these" (Hofstede & Bond, 1984, p. 419). This dimension is related to how people deal with conflict, aggression, release energy, use formal rules, and the tolerance they have for ambiguity. Uncertainty avoidance scores range from a low of 8 in Singapore to a high of 112 in Greece (M = 64, SD = 24).

The third dimension involves a bipolar continuum between individualism and collectivism. In individualistic cultures "people are supposed to look after themselves and their immediate family only," and in collectivistic cultures "people belong to in-groups or collectivities which are supposed to look after them in exchange for loyalty" (Hofstede & Bond, 1984, p. 419). People in individualistic cultures have a need for specific friendships, and people in collectivistic cultures have friendships that are predetermined by stable relationships formed early in life. Scores on this dimension range from a low of 8 in Equador to a high of 91 in the United States (M = 50, SD = 25).

The final dimension also is a bipolar continuum labeled masculinity-femininity. Masculinity involves countries "in which dominant values in society are success, money, and things," and femininity involves countries "in which dominant values are caring for others and quality of life" (Hofstede & Bond, 1984, pp. 419-420). Cultures high in masculinity have clearly differentiated sex roles, and cultures low in masculinity (high in femininity) tend to have fluid sex roles. Scores on this dimension range from a low of 5 in Sweden to a high of 95 in Japan (M = 50, SD = 20).

These dimensions should be related to uncertainty reduction processes in intercultural relationships. The rationale for uncertainty avoidance is straightforward. If individuals come from cultures that differ along this dimension they should have different needs to reduce uncertainty in intercultural relationships. Individualism also should be directly related. Gudykunst and Nishida's (1986) research suggests there are different types of uncertainty in low- and high-context cultures (Hall's, 1976, schema of cultural variability), however, they also point out that there tends to be a close association between context and individualism; that is, low-context cultures tend to be individualistic, and high-context cultures tend to be collectivistic. The link between Hofstede's other two dimensions of culture and uncertainty reduction is less straightforward, but there appears to be reason to think they too are related. Specifically, because power distance involves the degree to which inequality is viewed as natural, differences along this dimension should influence the degree to which others are perceived as similar, reciprocity in self-disclosure, and the type of relationships people establish. Finally, differences along the masculinity dimension should influence self-disclosure, the display of nonverbal affiliative expressiveness, and shared networks, to name only a few, because one end of the continuum (masculinity) emphasizes things and money, and the other end (femininity) emphasizes nurturance and caring.

Stage of Relationship

Berger (1979) argues that "the communicative process involved in knowledge generation and the development of understanding are central to the development and disintegration of most interpersonal relationships" (p. 123). The reduction of uncertainty promotes relationship development (Livingston, 1980) and plays a role in the dissolution of relationships (Harvey, Wells, & Alvarez, 1978). Most writing on interpersonal relationship development (for example, Altman & Taylor, 1973; Miller & Steinberg, 1975) similarly suggests that there should be differences in uncertainty reduction processes as relationships increase in level of intimacy. Altman and Taylor's (1973) social penetration theory, for example, gives central importance to the concept of self-disclosure and hypothesizes that interpersonal exchange gradually progresses from superficial, nonintimate areas to more specific, intimate, and central areas of the personalities of the actors in a relationship. This process is hypothesized to involve increased amounts of interpersonal exchange (breadth of penetration), as well as increasingly intimate levels of exchange (depth of penetration).

Altman and Taylor (1973) posit four stages of relationship development: orientation, exploratory affective exchange, affective exchange, and stable exchange. Exploratory affective exchange is equivalent to acquaintance relationships. This stage involves interaction at the periphery of the personality and, therefore, does not involve high levels of attributional confidence vis-à-vis the behavior of others in the relationship. The affective exchange stage, in contrast, involves friendships. Interaction at this stage is "characterized by a definite increase in communication in very private or central areas of the personality" (Altman & Taylor, 1973, p. 140). These hypothesized changes are supported by Won-Doornink's (1985) cross-cultural research, Knapp, Ellis, and Williams's (1980) and Honeycutt, Knapp, and Powers's (1983) intracultural research, as well as Gudykunst's (1985a) and Gudykunst, Nishida, and Chua's (1986) intercultural research. Given the extensive research supporting changes in patterns of communication as relationships develop, it is expected that stage of relationship development influences uncertainty reduction in intercultural relationships.

Interaction between Cultural Dissimilarity
and Stage of Relationship

Culture dissimilarity appears to have a different impact on different types of relationships. Most interpersonal relationships (that is, acquaintances, role relationships) are guided by cultural norms. Friendships, in contrast, appear to be less influenced by normative expectations. Bell (1981) argued that "the development of friendships is based upon private negotiations and is not imposed through cultural values or norms" (p. 10). This is consistent with Suttles (1970), who pointed out that friendships are the least "programmed" interpersonal relationships. Similarly, Altman and Taylor (1973) contend that in friendships "the dyad has moved to the point where interaction is relatively free in both peripheral and in more central areas of personality. Cultural stereotypy is broken down in these more intimate areas and there is a willingness to move in and out of such exchanges" (pp. 139-140). The breakdown of cultural stereotypes in friendships is consistent with Miller and Steinberg's (1975) argument that predictions are based mostly on psychological data in friendships.

If cultural stereotypes are broken down in friendships and not earlier stages, the level of cultural similarity should have a differential impact on uncertainty reduction processes in different relationships. This position is supported by Gudykunst's (1985b) research comparing intracultural and intercultural relationships and Ting-Toomey's (1981) research on Chinese-American interethnic friendships. It also is supported by Gudykunst's (1985a) study. Results of this study revealed a multivariate interaction effect between cultural similarity and type of relationship on uncertainty reduction processes, but the pattern was not exactly as would be predicted by Altman and Taylor's (1973) social penetration theory. One reason for the inconsistency proposed in the earlier study is that the relationships studied may not have been as different as need be for the interaction effect to be displayed.

Given that previous research has revealed an interaction effect, the following hypotheses are proffered: *Hypothesis 1*: Cultural dissimilarities in power distance and stage of relationship interact to influence the use of uncertainty reduction strategies, attributional confidence, attraction, perceived similarity, the display of nonverbal affiliative expressiveness, and shared networks in intercultural relationships; *Hypothesis 2:* Cultural dissimilarities in uncertainty avoidance and stage of relationship interact to influence the use of uncertainty reduction strategies, attributional confidence, attraction, perceived similarity, the display of nonverbal affiliative expressiveness, and shared networks in intercultural relationships; *Hypothesis 3:* Cultural dissimilarities in individualism-collectivism and stage of relationship interact to influence the use of uncertainty reduction strategies, attributional confidence, attraction, perceived similarity, the display of nonverbal affiliative expressiveness, and shared networks in intercultural relationships; and *Hypothesis 4:* Cultural dissimilarities in masculinity-femininity and stage of relationship interact to influence use of uncertainty reduction strategies, attributional confidence, attraction, perceived similarity, the display of nonverbal affiliative expressiveness, and shared networks in intercultural relationships.

METHODS

Respondents

Data were collected from 237 (166 males and 71 females) international students at a large southwestern university who volunteered to participate in the research. Of the males, 122 responded about relationships with other males and the other 40 responded about relationships with females. Of the females, 15 responded about relationships with males and 55 reported on relationships with other females. Because the instructions asked the respondents to answer the questions about a relationship with a member of the *same sex,* participants who responded about opposite-sex relationships were dropped from analysis. This left 177 usable responses (122 males and 55 females). Of these 177, 19 of the respondents were from cultures for which there are no data on Hofstede's (1983) four dimensions and they, therefore, had to be dropped, leaving 158 respondents.

Respondents were from 29 of the 50 countries and all 3 regions in Hofstede's (1983) analysis.[1] In order to determine if there was anything unique about this subset of cultures in terms of their scores on Hofstede's dimensions, the correlations between each pair of dimension scores were examined and are presented in Table 20.1. Hofstede's data yielded only one moderately strong correlation between the power distance and individualism dimensions (-.67, -.68). This correlation also was moderate in the present sample (-.49). The correlation between power distance and uncertainty avoidance was in the opposite direction from that obtained by Hofstede, but similar to that found in the Hofstede and Bond (1984) analysis (-.17), which was not considered problematic. No other correlation is significantly different from those in Hofstede's data. The subset of cultures represented in the present sample, therefore, appears to be a reasonable subset of the total set for which Hofstede's scores are available.

The use of international students in the United States as respondents could be problematic if culture was the independent variable. This, however, was not the case. Rather, the focus of the study was on the effects of cultural dissimilarities between the respondents' native culture and the host culture (i.e., difference scores between the respondents' native culture and the United States on Hofstede's, 1983, four dimensions was the independent variable). The respondents were all born and raised in their native culture. Anyone who travels from his or her native culture to another culture is, almost by definition, "atypical" of members of his or her native culture. While international students may not be "typical" of the people a person from the United States might meet in their native culture, they should be representative of the members of their culture who travel to the United States. There is also no reason to believe that international students (or others who travel from one culture to another) from one culture are more

Table 20.1
A Comparison of the Correlations Among the Dimensions in the
Present Sample with Hofstede's Samples[a]

Pair of Dimensions	Present Sample	Hofstede (1980)	Hofstede (1983)
Power distance X			
uncertainty avoidance	-.26	.28	.23
Power distance X			
individualism-collectivism	-.49	-.67	-.68
Power distance X			
masculinity-femininity	.14	.10	.06
Power distance X			
individualism-collectivism	-.03	-.35	-.33
Power distance X			
masculinity-femininity	.37	.12	-.03
Power distance X			
masculinity-femininity	-.04	.00	.08

a. Hofstede (1980, p. 316) correlations for 40 countries in original analysis. Hofstede (1983) for 50 countries and three regions (p. 343).

or less different from "typical" members of their culture than are international students from another culture. If there are differences, the use of broad categories of cultural dissimilarities (e.g., low, medium, high), rather than the exact quantitative difference scores, should decrease their impact. Further, the respondents who were dropped from the study (i.e., those who misread instructions and answered about an opposite-sex relationship instead of a same-sex one as requested) had been in the United States a significantly shorter time than the respondents included in the study. Their omission, therefore, should also remove any effects that might have contaminated the results due to early stages of intercultural adjustment (e.g., culture shock). The respondents in this study, therefore, appear to be reasonable subjects for the study of cultural dissimilarities on intercultural communication processes.

Measurement

All respondents completed a questionnaire in English containing the measures of the independent and dependent variables.[2] Respondents were asked to report on their interaction with a person from the United States with whom they had communicated. They were allowed to select someone they had known only a short period of time or someone with whom they had established a relationship (for example, a friend).

Cultural dissimilarity along Hofstede's (1980, 1983) dimensions of culture were operationalized by difference scores. Respondents reported the culture in which they were born and raised. They were assigned a score for each of Hofstede's four dimensions. Scores for the United States on each of these dimensions were then subtracted from the respondents' scores. The difference scores were then divided into three or four categories depending on the distribution. Because a higher or lower score than the United States on each of the dimensions makes a difference, zero (no difference along the dimension) was used as one of the dividing points for each scale. The remaining breaks were based on natural breaks in the distribution.[3] Differences in power distance yielded scores ranging from -27 to 64. It was divided into three categories: -27 to -1 = 1; 9 to 29 = 2; and 36 to 64 = 3. Uncertainty avoidance difference scores ranged from -17 to 66. It was broken down into four categories: -17 to -2 = 1; 2 to 13 = 2; 18 to 30 = 3; and 34 to 66 = 4. Differences in individualism-collectivism ranged from -83 to -2 (the United States has the highest score). These scores were divided into four categories: -83 to -71 = 1; -66 to -50 = 2; -45 to -37 = 3; and -26 to -2 = 4. Masculinity-femininity differences ranged from -54 to 33. This dimension was divided into three categories: -54 to -28 = 1; -23 to -5 = 2; and 1 to 33 = 3.

Participants labeled the type of relationship they had with their partners. Specifically, they were asked to indicate if they were relative strangers, acquaintances, friends, close friends, best friends, dates, or lovers. Dates and lovers were omitted when the opposite-sex relationships were dropped. Because of the small number of responses in the relative stranger category it was combined with acquaintances.[4] Examination of the perceived intimacy ratings of these four categories indicated that they were perceived to be significantly different, $F(3,157) = 31.14$, $p < .001$.[5] Scheffee's post hoc comparisons, however, indicated that close friends and best friends were not perceived to be significantly different in terms of intimacy. Data for close friends and best friends, therefore, were combined for purposes of analysis, resulting in three categories of relationships: (1) stranger/acquaintance, (2) friends, and (3) close/best friends. These correspond to Altman and Taylor's (1973) orientation, exploratory affective exchange, and affective exchange stages, respectively.

Five of the eight dependent variables were operationalized by responses to seven-point (strongly disagree = 1 to strongly agree = 7; items followed by (*) below were reversed for scoring) Likert-type items. The two interactive strategies were separated for purposes of analysis. Self-disclosure was measured using the five items for Wheeless's (1978) depth factor; alpha = .82. Interrogation was assessed by four items: "I have asked this person specific questions about his/her attitudes"; "I have asked specific questions about this person's values"; "I have never asked this person questions about his/her emotions/feelings" (*); and "I have asked specific questions about this person's background." Reliability for the four items was .77.

Perceived similarity was operationalized using Parks and Adelman's (1983) five- item measure. Reliability for the scale was .84. Attraction was assessed using Byrne's (1961) two-item index. Combination of the items resulted in an alpha of .77. The display of nonverbal affiliative expressiveness was measured by five items: "We touch each other often during our interactions"; "We look each other in the eye most of the time when we talk"; "We gesture frequently when we are talking"; "We do not smile much when we talk" (*); and "We speak in a pleasant tone of voice almost all of the time." The five items yielded an alpha of .72.

Shared networks was measured using Parks and Adelman's (1983) three-item index. These items assess the percentage of free time respondents and their partners had spent together in the preceding two weeks, the percentage of people that the partner knows that the respondent had met face-to-face, and the percentage of the respondent's interactions in the preceding two weeks that were with the partner's friends. Combination of the three items yielded an alpha of .75.

Finally, attributional confidence was determined using Gudykunst and Nishida's (1986) two-factor instrument. This measure is designed to take into consideration the types of uncertainty that are important in both low- and high-context cultures. Low-context attributional confidence was assessed with their first factor, which includes five of the items (#s 3, 4, 5, 6, & 7) from Clatterbuck's (1979) measure. High-context uncertainty reduction was measured with their second factor, which includes three items: "How certain are you that he/she can understand your feelings when you do not verbally express them?" "How certain are you that you understand what this person means when you communicate?" and "How confident are you that this person will make allowances for you when you communicate?" Response scales were based on zero (0; totally uncertain) to 100 (totally certain). Alpha for the low-context items was .92, and the high-context items yielded an alpha of .86.

RESULTS AND DISCUSSION

The four hypotheses were tested using multivariate analysis of variance (MANOVA). The multivariate tests were examined for each hypothesis and if this test was significant the univariate results also were examined. Not only were significant univariate results examined, but, in addition, those approaching significance (Cramer & Bock, 1966). Power for the multivariate tests was at least .72 for a small effect size of .25 (Stevens, 1980) and between .85 and .91 with a small effect size of .15 for the univariate tests (Cohen, 1977). Bartlett's test of sphericity indicated that multivariate tests of the hypotheses were warranted (108.9, 23df, p < .001).

Hypothesis 1 posited an interaction effect between differences in power distance and stage of relationship on the dependent variables. The test of this hypothesis yielded a significant effect (Hotelling's T^2 = .84, $F(32,334)$ = 2.21, p < .001). Six of the univariate tests were significant or approached significance: self-disclosure (F(4,92) = 6.62, p < .001); attraction (F = 2.37, p = .057); similarity (F = 3.90, p < .01); low-context attributional confidence (F = 5.15, p < .001); high-context attributional confidence (F = 4.89, p < .001); and shared networks (F = 2.62, p < .05). Examination of the mean scores indicates that in the early stages of relationships (that is, acquaintances) there are relatively large differences in the mean scores for the dependent variables by degree of cultural dissimilarity. For friends there are fewer differences than for acquaintances, but there is still variation in the dependent measures as a function of cultural dissimilarities. In developed relationships (that is, close/best friends) there is relatively little variation in the mean scores as a function of cultural dissimilarities.[6] To illustrate, for high-context attributional confidence the scores range from 48.75 to 61.00 for acquaintances, from 66.15 to 73.77 for friends, and from 80.44 to 81.53 for close/best friends.

The interaction effect between differences in uncertainty avoidance and stage of relationship on the dependent variables was the subject of Hypothesis 2. The test of this hypothesis resulted in a significant multivariate effect (Hotelling's T^2 = .86, F(48,500) = 1.50, p < .05). Four univariate effects were significant or approached significance: self-disclosure (F(6.92) = 4.28, p < .001); similarity (F = 2.13, p = .057); low-context attributional confidence (F = 4.37, p < .001); and high-context attributional confidence (F = 2.37, p < .05). The same pattern emerged in the mean scores as in the previous analysis.

Hypothesis 3 posited an interaction effect between differences in individualism and stage of relationship on the dependent variables. The MANOVA for this hypothesis was significant (Hotelling's T^2 = .86, F(48,500) = 1.50, p < .05). Five univariate effects were significant or approached significance: self-disclosure (F(6,92) = 4.73, p < .001); interrogation (F = 2.06, p = .065); low-context attributional confidence (F = 2.46, p < .05); and shared networks (F = 2.30, p < .05). The pattern in the means was similar to the previous two analyses.

Finally, the test of Hypothesis 4 predicting an interaction effect between differences in masculinity and stage of relationship was significant (Hotelling's T^2 = .86, F(32,334) = 2.24, p < .001). Five of the univariate tests were significant or approached significance: self-disclosure (F(4,92) = 4.52, p < .01); similarity (F = 3.68, p < .01); low-context attributional confidence (F = 7.52, p < .001); high-context attributional confidence (F = 2.26, p = .069); and shared networks (F = 3.34, p < .01). With the exception of self-disclosure, all of the variables fit the pattern in the previous analyses. For self-disclosure, there is little variation as a function of cultural dissimilarities across stages of relationship development.

The tests of the four hypotheses revealed significant interaction effects between all of Hofstede's (1980) dimensions of cultural dissimilarities and stage of relationship development. The data suggest that as relationships become more intimate, cultural dissimilarities have less effect on uncertainty reduction processes. These findings are consistent with predictions deduced from Altman and Taylor's (1973) social penetration theory. As Altman and Taylor argue, cultural stereotypy influences communication in relationships at early stages of development (orientation; strangers/ acquaintances). As relationships develop (exploratory affective exchange stage; friend), cultural stereotypy plays less of a role. When relationships reach the full affective exchange stage (close/best friendships), cultural background has very little influence on communication. These relationships, in contrast, are based on psychological data about the individual (Miller & Steinberg, 1975) and are not culturally programmed, as are relationships at earlier stages of development (Bell, 1981).

The present findings also are compatible with earlier intercultural research by Ting-Toomey (1981) on Chinese-American friendships, as well as Gudykunst's (1985b) comparison of intracultural and intercultural friendships. Finally, the present data support findings from Gudykunst, Nishida, and Chua's (1986) study of intercultural dyads. These researchers found systematic patterns in uncertainty reduction processes as relationships increase in level of intimacy.

Taken together, the tests of the hypotheses involving Hofstede's (1980, 1983) dimensions of cultural variability support Gudykunst's (in press) argument that these dimensions influence interpersonal intercultural communication. Using these dimensions, instead of comparisons of cultural similarity/dissimilarity, allows culture to be treated as a theoretical, rather than atheoretical, variable in research. For culture to constitute a theoretical variable, "a culture X and a culture Y serve to operationally define a characteristic *a*, which two cultures exhibit to different degrees" (Foschi & Hales, 1979, p. 246). Hofstede's dimensions of culture can, therefore, be used to define operationally the characteristic *a* of interest (for example, individualism-collectivism) in cross-cultural comparisons or studies of intercultural communication; that is, the characteristic *a* should involve some dimension along which cultures vary. Hofstede's theory of cultural differentiation is, at the present time, the only schema of cultural variability that is quantifiable and directly related to communication.

NOTES

1. Participants in the present study came from the following countries/regions: Belgium, Brazil, Canada, Colombia, Equador, France, West Germany, Great Britain, Greece, Hong Kong, Indonesia, India, Iran, Israel, Italy, Japan, South Korea, Malaysia, Mexico, Norway, Pakistan, Philippines, Portugal, Salvador, Spain, Taiwan, Turkey, Venezuela, Yugoslavia, East Africa, West Africa, and Arab countries.

2. Test of English as a Foreign Language (TOEFL) scores for the respondents ranged from 467 to 756, with the mean being 566. Competency in English, therefore, should not be a factor influencing responses.

3. The breaks in the variables used did not yield equal cell sizes. Dividing the variables to provide equal cell sizes would have meant that one point would have divided categories. This was deemed undesirable and, therefore, unequal cell sizes were used.

4. There were no significant differences on any of the dependent variables between relative strangers and acquaintances. They were, therefore, combined because of small cell size in the relative stranger category.

5. The question used for this analysis was worded as follows: "If zero (0) means your relationship is nonintimate and nine (9) means that it is very intimate, how intimate is your relationship?"

6. Interaction tables are omitted to conserve space. They are available from the authors on request.

REFERENCES

Altman, I., & Taylor, D. (1973). Social penetration. New York: Holt, Rinehart & Winston.

Bell, R. (1981). Worlds of friendship. Beverly Hills, CA: Sage.

Berger, C. R. (1979). Beyond initial interactions. In H. Giles & R. St. Clair (Eds.), Language and social psychology (pp. 122-144). Oxford: Basil Blackwell.

Berger, C. R., & Bradac, J. (1982). Language and social knowledge: Uncertainty in interpersonal relations. London: Edward Arnold.

Berger, C. R., & Calabrese, R. (1975). Some explorations in initial interactions and beyond. Human Communication Research, 1, 99-112.

Bradac, J., Bowers, J., & Courtwright, J. (1980). Lexical variations in intensity, immediacy, and diversity: An axiomatic theory and causal model. In R. St. Clair & H. Giles (Eds.), The social and psychological contexts of language (pp. 193-224). Hillsdale, NJ: Lawrence Erlbaum.

Byrne, D. (1961). Interpersonal attraction and attitude similarity. Journal of Abnormal and Social Psychology, 62, 713-715.

Clatterbuck, G. (1979). Attributional confidence and uncertainty in initial interactions. Human Communication Research, 5, 147-157.

Cohen, J. (1977). Statistical power analysis for the behavioral sciences (rev. ed). New York: Academic Press.

Cramer, E. M., & Bock, R. D. (1966). Multivariate analysis. Review of Educational Research, 36, 604-617.

Foschi, M., & Hales, W. M. (1979). The theoretical role of cross-cultural comparisons in experimental social psychology. In L. Eckensberger, W. Lonner, & Y. Poortinga (Eds.), Cross-cultural contributions to psychology (pp. 244-254). Lisse, Netherlands: Swets & Zeitlinger.

Gudykunst, W. B. (1985a). The influence of cultural similarity, type of relationship, and self-monitoring on uncertainty reduction processes. Communication Monographs, 52, 203-217.

Gudykunst, W. B. (1985b). An exploratory comparison of close intracultural and intercultural friendships. Communication Quarterly, 33, 270-283.

Gudykunst, W. B. (1985c). A model of uncertainty reduction in intercultural encounters. Journal of Language and Social Psychology, 4, 79-98.

Gudykunst, W. B. (1986). Intraethnic and interethnic uncertainty reduction processes. In Y. Kim (Ed.), Current research in interethnic communication. Beverly Hills, CA: Sage.

Gudykunst, W. B. (in press). Sociocultural variability and communication processes. In C. Berger & S. Chaffee (Eds.), Handbook of communication science. Beverly Hills, CA: Sage.

Gudykunst, W. B., & Hammer, M. R. (in press). The influence of ethnicity, gender, and dyadic composition on uncertainty reduction in initial interactions. Journal of Black Studies.

Gudykunst, W. B., & Nishida, T. (1984). Individual and cultural influences on uncertainty reduction. Communication Monographs, 51, 23-36.

Gudykunst, W. B., & Nishida, T. (1986). Attributional confidence in low- and high-context cultures. Human Communication Research, 12, 525-549.

Gudykunst, W. B., Nishida, T., Chua, E. (1986). Uncertainty reduction processes in Japanese-North American dyads. *Communication Research Reports, 3,* 39-46.

Gudykunst, W. B., Nishida, T., Koike, H., & Shiino, N. (1986). The influence of language on uncertainty reduction. In M. McLaughlin (Ed.), *Communication yearbook 9* (pp. 555-575). Beverly Hills, CA: Sage.

Gudykunst, W. B., Sodetani, L. L., & Sonoda, K. T. (1985, November). *Uncertainty reduction in Japanese-Caucasian relationships in Hawaii.* Paper presented at the Speech Communication Association Convention, Denver, CO.

Gudykunst, W. B., Yang, S. M., & Nishida, T. (1985). A cross-cultural test of uncertainty reduction theory: Comparisons of acquaintances, friends, and dating relationships in Japan, Korea, and the United States. *Human Communication Research, 11,* 407-454.

Hall, E. T. (1976). *Beyond culture.* New York: Doubleday.

Harvey J. H., Wells, G. L., & Alvarez, M. D. (1978). Attribution in the context of conflict and separation in close relationships. In J. Harvey, W. Ickes, & R. Kidd (Eds.), *New directions in attribution research* (Vol. 2, pp. 235-260). Hillsdale, NJ: Lawrence Erlbaum.

Hofstede, G. (1980). *Culture's consequences.* Beverly Hills, CA: Sage.

Hofstede, G. (1983). Dimensions of national cultures in fifty countries and three regions. In J. Deregowski, S. Dziurawiec, & R. Annis (Eds.), *Expiscations in cross-cultural psychology* (pp. 335-355). Lisse, Netherlands: Swets & Zeitlinger.

Hofstede, G., & Bond, M. (1984). Hofstede's culture dimensions: An independent validation using Rokeach's value survey. *Journal of Cross-Cultural Psychology, 15,* 417-433.

Honeycutt, J., Knapp, M. L., & Powers, W. (1983). On knowing others and predicting what they say. *The Western Journal of Speech Communication, 47,* 157-174.

Knapp, M. L., Ellis, D. G., & Williams, B. A. (1980). Perceptions of communication behavior associated with relationship terms. *Communication Monographs, 47,* 262-278.

Livingston, K. R. (1980). Love as a process of reducing uncertainty—cognitive theory. In K. Pope (Ed.), *On love and loving* (pp. 133-151). San Francisco: Jossey-Bass.

Miller, G. R., & Steinberg, M. (1975). *Between people: A new analysis of interpersonal communication.* Chicago: Science Research Associates.

Parks, M., & Adelman, M. (1983). Communication networks and the development of romantic relationships: An expansion of uncertainty reduction theory. *Human Communication Research, 10,* 55-80.

Simard, L. (1981). Cross-cultural interaction. *Journal of Social Psychology, 113,* 171-192.

Stevens, J. (1980). Power of the multivariate analysis of variance test. *Psychological Bulletin, 88,* 728-737.

Suttles, G. D. (1970). Friendship as a social institution. In G. McNall (Ed.), *Social relationships* (pp. 95-135). Chicago: Aldine.

Ting-Toomey, S. (1981). Ethnic identity and close friendship in Chinese-American college students. *International Journal of Intercultural Relations, 5,* 383-406.

Wheeless, L. R. (1978). A follow-up study of the relationships among trust, disclosure, and interpersonal solidarity. *Human Communication Research, 4,* 143-157.

Won-Doornink, M. J. (1985). Self-disclosure and reciprocity in conversation: A cross-national study. *Social Psychology Quarterly, 48,* 97-107.

VII ● POLITICAL COMMUNICATION

21 ● Political Alienation and Knowledge Acquisition

DIANA C. MUTZ

Stanford University

T HE term *political alienation* has been used to signify many forms of negative feeling about politics. As the popularity of the concept has increased, it also has become increasingly devoid of specific meaning. Although many scholars concur that political alienation refers to an attitude, disposition, or state of mind, there is little agreement as to the exact nature of these alienated feelings. The situation is further complicated by an abundance of cognates such as political estrangement, political cynicism, and political anomie. The existence of political alienation is also implied by the use of related antithetical terms such as political trust, diffuse political support, and political efficacy. The specific characteristics of these variations and their relationship to the more general concept of alienation are most often left undetermined.

The works of authors such as Marx, Weber, and Durkheim suggest three alternative meanings for the term *alienation* (Seeman, 1959). Alienation as *powerlessness* concerns the individual's subjective sense of control over a situation. The most frequent usage of *alienation* in social science literature deals with derivations of this particular meaning. Another form of alienation known as *meaninglessness* is said to exist when a person cannot choose with confidence among various options. Meaninglessness is high

Correspondence and requests for reprints: Diana C. Mutz, Institute for Communication Research, Stanford University, Stanford, CA 94305.

when the individual's minimum standards for decision making are not met. In addition to the perceived inability to control and the inability to choose, a third type of alienation denotes a condition of *normlessness* in which one perceives a disintegration and consequent lack of clear norms. Normlessness is generally characterized by distrust and the belief that socially inappropriate behavior is commonplace.

CONCEPTUALIZATION OF POLITICAL ALIENATION

Political alienation also has been conceptualized in a multitude of ways. These variations may be said to differ in the historical dimension of alienation from which they are derived, the implied source of the individual's political alienation, and the consequences that are expected to flow from the alienated condition.

The definitions of alienation suggested by powerlessness and normlessness are the concepts most often utilized by social scientists attempting to delineate political alienation (Finifter, 1970). Political powerlessness suggests that an individual feels that he or she cannot affect actions of the government and has no influence in such matters. The inverse of this type of alienation is the closely related concept of political efficacy. Politically powerless individuals traditionally have been identified by inefficacious responses to questions dealing with how well one thinks that he or she can understand political issues or to what extent one agrees with statements such as "People like me don't have any say about what government does."

When political alienation takes the form of political normlessness, the individual perceives that the norms or rules that are intended to govern political relations have broken down (Finifter, 1970). Politically normless individuals need not feel that the norms governing their personal behavior have disintegrated; rather, they perceive these deviations from official norms as occurring in the course of the political process. As Lane (1962, p. 162) put it, "the rules of the game are unfair, loaded, illegitimate." Believing that all politicians are nefarious crooks might fall under this category. As a dimension involving trust in government, this concept is typically viewed as ranging from high trust (low perceived normlessness) to high distrust, often referred to as political cynicism. Scales dealing with this dimension of alienation often probe attitudes toward the influence of special interest groups, the activities of local and national governments, and the amount of trust in government institutions.

In addition to differentiation based on the historical derivation of a particular species of alienation, distinct forms of the condition also may be isolated on the basis of the source from which the alienated feelings are said to flow. In early studies of political alienation, one traditionally explored a person's background and personality characteristics in order to discover sources of political alienation (Dean, 1960b). Scales were designed to measure personality traits, such as lack of faith in people, with the hypothesis that this feeling would be generalized to explain lack of faith in government. Social characteristics were also thought to be useful indicators of those most likely to be politically alienated. For instance, economic status was cited as one frequent cause of political alienation (Citrin, McClosky, Shanks, & Sniderman, 1975). Economic deprivation would supposedly result in feeling resentful and thus being more likely to reject the existing political order.

Disillusionment with this approach resulted in large part from the findings of the election studies conducted by the Survey Research Center and Center for Political Studies at the University of Michigan (Citrin, 1974). In 1958, the Survey Research Center began asking a series of "Trust-in-Government" questions in its biennial national election survey. The results of these studies indicated that social background variables were neither strong nor consistent predictors of the level of political trust. Likewise, personality variables such as personal competence and trust in people correlated weakly with political trust. Between 1964 and 1972, virtually every social group became more alienated as measured by the Michigan surveys. Because this large shift could not be attributed to social characteristics or to changes in psychological dispositions, the focus of research shifted toward alternative explanations (Citrin, 1974).

In the early 60s, Litt (1963) introduced the idea that the "political milieu" was a potentially important source of alienation in addition to the traditional personality variables. Based on his findings, he argued that viewing trust in government as a more specific instance of trust in mankind was inadequate to explain varying levels of political trust. His finding suggested that the origins of political alienation could be linked to community norms as well as to personality characteristics. Litt illustrated how such an attitude could be acquired as a part of a community's "political acculturation process." His studies in the Boston area were presented as evidence that "community-wide suspicions of 'base practices' may go hand in hand with the belief that the professional practitioner of politics will still turn an attentive ear to the plaints of his constituents" (p. 320). Thus political normlessness could exist independent of both personal mistrust and perceived powerlessness.

An analysis of the decline in public trust done by Arthur Miller (1974) also illustrated this departure from theoretical perspectives on alienation that stressed social background and personality as causal factors. Instead, Miller suggested that political factors and policy-related outcomes had a cumulative effect on the perceived legitimacy of officeholders and political institutions as a whole. The problem was viewed as essentially substantive rather than attitudinal in nature: "The disenchantment and dissatisfaction of individuals who feel politically inefficacious and cynical about the government is real, and it arises out of a reaction to real conditions of life" (p. 971). This definition of alienation was in keeping with Gamson's (1968) view of distrust as arising from dissatisfaction with the outcome of political decisions. According to Miller, politicians produced centrist policies that repeatedly disappointed an increasingly polarized public, and thus prohibited a renewal of confidence in government.

The steady decline in the level of political trust was an extremely well-documented trend in American public opinion research. However, there was a great deal of controversy surrounding its meaning and consequences. Some claimed that it signified a "radical questioning and rejection of established political institutions" (Finifter, 1970). Others maintained that it merely signified a dislike of or disappointment with incumbents that could be easily remedied through the electoral process (Abramson & Finifter, 1981).

This controversy over the significance of consequences illustrates further discrimination between types of alienation on the basis of their specific referents. Although it is quite common to describe a person simply as "alienated," use of this term always implies a referent of some sort; one must be alienated from someone or something. A primary criticism of the political trust index has involved its inability to distinguish between dissatisfaction with current government positions on issues and dissatisfaction with ongoing events and policies (Muller, Jukam, & Seligson, 1982). The implications of such a measure are obviously much greater if it reflects a basic withdrawal of support for the political system as a whole as opposed to mere dislike of the political leaders currently in power.

Miller (1974a) argued for the more apocalyptic interpretation of these data. He understood the regime to be the referent of these attitudes and suggested that the low level of trust might contribute to extralegal political behavior and a "bursting forth" of radical political change. He contended that this evidence indicated that "a situation of widespread, basic discontent exists in the U.S. today" (p. 951). An analogous interpretation of political alienation achieved popular public status in July of 1979 when President Carter delivered his "crisis of confidence" speech. Carter similarly referred to the trend suggested by public opinion data as "a fundamental threat to American democracy" (Lipset & Schneider, 1983).

In a commentary on Miller's interpretation of the alienation evidence, Citrin (1974) criticized the Trust-in-Government scale as a true indicator of political alienation on the basis of two shortcomings. First, he reiterated that the scale failed to discriminate between the truly politically alienated and those who simply mistrusted incumbent leaders. He pointed out that it was quite possible for people to distrust politicians as a class without wholly rejecting the values of the political regime and its institutions. He argued further that verbal criticisms of established institutions were more a function of ritualistic negativism than of an enduring sense of estrangement from the political regime. Citrin maintained that demeaning politics and denigrating politicians was a well-established cultural tradition in the United States. Scales with ambiguous referents composed of simple cliches about the quality of politics and politicians made it difficult to determine to what extent responses signified genuine frustration with the political regime.

The concept of diffuse support (Easton, 1979) dealt successfully with a great deal of the ambiguity surrounding specification of referents of politically alienated behavior. Diffuse support was proposed as the antithesis of alienation and implied the worth of the institution in its own right. This "orientation of good will" did not depend on the specific benefits derived; people who were not pleased with a particular policy or election outcome would still support the regime. Almond and Verba (1965) made a similarly useful differentiation using the concept of "system affect" to indicate generalized attitudes toward the system as a whole.

The many indistinct meanings of political alienation raise serious doubts concerning the utility of the existing concept for purposes of further research. There are obviously great differences of opinion as to what conditions the term *political alienation* should apply. In addition, there are differing views as to what alienation should signify once it has been identified.

The real concerns behind these empirical investigations of politically alienated attitudes are the dysfunctional implications they hold for the continued existence of the political system. Dangerous behavioral consequences are the true focus of interest in the study of alienation. Miller (1974a, p. 951) contended that "when such [diffuse] support wanes, underlying discontent is the necessary result, and the potential for revolutionary alteration of the political and social system is enhanced." Numerous examinations of political alienation similarly allude to the demise of democracy as the ultimate implication (for example, Gamson, 1968). Levels of political alienation become socially irrelevant and uninteresting unless some link exists to the actual behaviors inferred from politically alienated attitudes.

In establishing a more precise definition of political alienation, it is essential that formal relationships between various dimensions of this concept be established. The core of alienation is a negative affect toward government as exemplified by political normlessness. But distrust of government alone would likely prove an unreliable indicator of political alienation due to confounding with negative attitudes toward incumbent leaders. It is also necessary that one believe that the political system offers unacceptable and insufficient options. Adding meaninglessness as a second necessary condition ensures that the referent of disaffection is the political system as opposed to merely partisan dislike of those currently in power. If political choices are meaningless, then political participation becomes a useless conformist formality rather than a path through which to channel one's influence. Normlessness provides the necessary hostile affect toward government, and meaninglessness involves the cognitive acknowledgment that there is a narrow to nonexistent range of available choices left open to the citizen.

The role of powerlessness in identifying dysfunctional alienation is less clear, largely because alienated behavior may range from extreme apathy to radical activism. Undoubtedly, the majority of those meeting both necessary conditions of normlessness and meaninglessness would also be withdrawn from political activity, lacking the efficacy to take action (see for example, Verba & Nie, 1972). Nonetheless, a small fraction of the group meeting these criteria may pose an even greater threat to democratic stability by combining low trust with high efficacy. A number of studies have linked this combination of attitudes to "readiness to engage in acts of unconventional dissent against the state" (Muller, 1972), as well as to actual extralegal political behaviors (Paige, 1971; Schwartz, 1973; Sears & McConahay, 1973). Including powerlessness as a third necessary condition for alienation would conflict with the practical reason for concern—the dysfunctional implications that alienation holds for the political system. The sense that things are not as they should be, combined with the feeling that there are insufficient options available to correct this situation, obviates the need for the powerlessness criterion, although it is likely to coincide with this combination of attitudes.

A parsimonious definition of an alienated citizen is one who (1) does not trust the institutions of government because he or she perceives them to be corrupt or somehow outside the bounds of societal norms (normlessness); and (2) perceives the existing system as offering meaningless and unacceptable options so that even if a person did have the power to influence outcomes through the existing system, it would make no difference.

In keeping with the conceptual definition of alienation as having dysfunctional implications, the joint occurrence of meaninglessness and normlessness may be seen as a threat to democratic stability in one of two ways. Alienation from the political system could be manifested in hostility toward the political system resulting in complete withdrawal from political activity. Although these extremely apathetic individuals might be innocuous under ordinary circumstances, it has been hypothesized that latent support for oppositionist political behavior would make them highly susceptible to mobilization under the right circumstances (Kornhauser, 1959). A second dysfunctional implication is suggested by the alienated, yet politically efficacious, person who is apt to engage in regime-threatening political behavior.

This definition allows one to dispense with several political orientations commonly viewed as manifestations of political alienation. For example, political activists who express a high degree of political normlessness and manifest this through efforts at reform are most definitely not politically alienated. Although their activities may be temporarily disruptive and put stress on the system, their behavior indicates that they lack the meaninglessness criterion for political alienation. Participation within the existing institutional framework signifies that they perceive meaningful political choices that can be used to influence the political process and change social conditions.

Citizens who feel extremely powerless are often cited as evidence of political alienation as well (Dean, 1960a). However, such characteristically "powerless" behavior is not necessarily indicative of an accompanying sense of political meaninglessness or normlessness, nor is it necessarily dysfunctional for the political system. An individual may feel that the political system provides meaningful options and is operating in accordance with normative expectations, yet simultaneously feel personally ineffective. The ability to influence political events is simply not important to such a person. Perceived political powerlessness resulting in apathetic behavior also has been viewed as functional in the sense that it permits orderly maintenance of the system. Berelson, Lazarsfeld, and McPhee (1954, p. 316) suggested that these nonparticipants served to "soften and blur crippling divisions in the body politic."

OPERATIONALIZATION OF ADOLESCENT POLITICAL ALIENATION

The existence of political alienation is typically confirmed by measuring the attitudes of individuals relative to some implied standard. Most often there is no attempt to differentiate among the three dimensions of alienation discussed above. Efforts to assess these dimensions are also plagued by a lack of discriminant validity; many respondents may not differentiate between dimension-specific attitudes and will give responses indicative of the generalized, rather than the private, content of the items.

A three-wave panel of 501 Wisconsin adolescents provided an opportunity to analyze each of these three dimensions. These data were part of a larger study of political socialization during adolescence. The respondents, aged 10 to 17 at initial contact, were selected by random digit dialing techniques and interviewed during the 1980 presidential campaign year. Wave 1 took place in late January through early March, before the Wisconsin primary. Wave 2 was conducted in October, shortly before the fall election, and wave 3 took place in October through November of 1981, approximately a year later. Details on the sample and research design may be found in additional studies based on these data (Chaffee & Miyo, 1983; Chaffee & Schleuder, 1985; Chaffee & Tims, 1982; Kennamer & Chaffee, 1982). Multiple indicators of powerlessness, normlessness, and meaninglessness were available for the two waves of data collected shortly before the election and approximately a year following the election (see Appendix A). Indicators of powerlessness and normlessness were also available for wave 1 data, which were collected seven to ten months prior to the election. A total of 392 adolescents were included in all three waves and gave responses to all of the alienation items asked in each wave. Three additive scales were constructed to represent alienation dimensions at each point in time.

Using these indices, three types of relationships involving dimensions of alienation were explored. First, fluctuations in the dimensions themselves were analyzed over time. Second, the dimensions of alienation were examined as dependent variables to test traditional hypotheses relating television news viewing to alienation. Finally, the dimensions of alienation were used to construct a typology of political orientations, and these variables were examined as contingent conditions for knowledge gain. The role of communication in contributing to knowledge gain within these groups was also elaborated.

An examination of levels of the alienation dimensions over time revealed several interesting fluctuations. Feelings of political powerlessness decreased significantly in the period preceding the election ($p < .05$), and then increased back to their previous level during the postelection year ($p < .05$). In contrast, political normlessness increased significantly during the period preceding the election ($p < .05$), and then remained at an intermediate level in the period following the election. No significant differences were noted between these two dimensions when comparing the means of waves 1 and 3. Meaninglessness did not fluctuate significantly. Descriptive statistics of the alienation items and their composite dimensions indicated homogeneous variances across the three waves and no major violations of normality assumptions that would call into question the results of statistical tests.

Post hoc explanations of these variations are intuitively appealing. In the preelection period, citizens receive an unusually large amount of attention. Those exposed to political communications are being courted by politicians for their highly valued votes. In anticipation of exercising a share of political power, it is not surprising that feelings of political efficacy should increase. Even those who do not, or cannot, vote are likely to feel an increased sense of potential power over political events during this period due to the increased media attention given to people's political attitudes and preferences. After the election has passed the level of attention drops, and feelings of powerlessness rise back to their previous levels.

Changes in feelings of normlessness also may be related to the activities surrounding a presidential election year. During the course of preelection activities, normlessness increases significantly. This decline in trust is proba-

bly attributable to campaign activities and the attempts of political con-
tenders to discredit their opponents in the process of seeking office.

A factor analysis of the alienation items confirmed the existence of three
dimensions within the alienation concept as was predicted in conceptualization of the variable. When factor analyzed, the indicators chosen to represent each dimension generated three identical factors in both wave 2 and
wave 3, for which all items were available. When factor loadings of less
than .30 were omitted, the three factors reflected the initial groupings of
indicators into dimensions of normlessness, powerlessness, and meaninglessness. Questions corresponding to each dimension consistently generated factor loadings greater than .55. However, a major inconsistency was
noted in that one item in the powerlessness index loaded positively in the
wave 2 analysis and negatively in wave 3. The unreliability of the powerlessness measures further confirmed their limited usefulness for purposes
of further analysis (see Appendix B). Common sense calls into question
the face validity of an indicator of political powerlessness when measuring
adolescent attitudes, especially when the overwhelming majority of this
group is not yet able to vote. It is unlikely that such questions are meaningful to adolescents who, for all practical purposes, do not have any political
power.

The face validity of the remaining two dimensions of political alienation
appears strong in relation to the conceptualization; however, it is doubtful
that these dimensions are pure indicators of meaninglessness and normlessness. Although their content is indicative of what they purport to measure, overlap in responses to the items is quite probable due to reactions to
the generalized content and a failure to discriminate between more specific
aspects of the alienated attitude.

It is likely that the measure of each dimension consists of some generic
alienation content common to the other dimensions, as well as some
dimension-specific content. To separate these two components, regression equations were generated for each dimension using the other dimension as an independent variable. That is, an equation was generated to
indicate to what extent political meaninglessness predicted a lack of political trust, and a second equation was generated to predict the reciprocal
arrangement. Scatterplots of predicted and residual values, and normal
probability plots of observed and predicted values were used to check for
violations of regression assumptions.

From these regression equations, predicted values of the meaninglessness and normlessness dimensions were generated for each respondent.
These values were then subtracted from each person's actual score on
measurement of that particular dimension. Because the residual measures
were obtained by extracting the generalized negative affect represented in
the overlap between dimensions, these residual amounts not predicted
by the other alienation dimensions were interpreted as indicative of the

dimension-specific content generated by the measures. By eliminating the generalized alienation element, it was possible to control for the "ritualistic cynics" whose negativism and denigration of politics was more a function of habit than of a true estrangement from the political system (see Citrin, 1974). This procedure also made it possible to examine variations in each of the separate dimensions as opposed to changes confounded with generalized negative affect toward government.

POLITICAL ALIENATION AS
A DEPENDENT VARIABLE

In communication research, alienation is most commonly used as a dependent variable attributed to some outside cause. Television news viewing, in particular, has been cited as a villain contributing to a declining political morale. Robinson and colleagues (1974, 1975, 1976, 1983) have provided the bulk of the limited empirical support for this hypothesis. Robinson (1975, p. 314) coined the term "videomalaise" to describe this hypothesized effect of television news viewing on attitudes toward institutions of government. As he suggested, "Our doubts about ourselves and hostility toward our institutions would be far less severe were it not for the images we receive from the electronic media, more specifically, from network journalism." This viewpoint has been corroborated by numerous others (see for example, Graber, 1980; Lang & Lang, 1968; Levine, 1977).

When citing evidence of this relationship from research in the late 60s and 70s, it is common to question the generalizability of these results to other time periods. After all, with disillusioning events such as Vietnam and Watergate, it is not surprising that watching the evening news would destroy one's trust in government. However, as proponents of "videomalaise" are quick to point out, trends in declining voter participation and declining trust have continued without interruption since the late 50s and early 60s as television news has gained progressively larger audiences. This trend has steadily continued despite several periods of relative optimism. Although numerous other explanations have been offered to account for the decline, the television-based explanation continues to be included in the list of plausible options (Ranney, 1983).

In an effort to test the hypothesized relationship between television news viewing and political alienation dimensions, several bivariate analyses were conducted relating individual residual dimensions of political alienation measures to adolescent television news exposure and attention measures. Differences between the measures being used in this analysis and what other studies using political alienation indicators have utilized should be noted. Although many of the indicators included in this analysis have previously been used in other studies, it should be kept in mind that in purifying the dimensions and eliminating the overlapping content, the generalized negative affect toward politics was discarded. The respondents in this study are also adolescents rather than voting age adults as in many of the studies cited above. Although these differences limit the value of the study as a replication of previous findings, they enhance its capacity for identifying more specific effects as opposed to changes in generalized alienation.

Residual measures of the dimensions of alienation were correlated with attention measures and with exposure variables indicating times per week the adolescent watched evening television news. Pearson's r correlation was chosen as a suitable statistic for estimating bivariate association. One significant, although modest, correlation was noted in which meaninglessness correlated negatively with television exposure ($r = -.15$, p. $< .05$). Contrary to the expectations posited by previous hypotheses, the meaninglessness dimension of alienation corresponded to lesser amounts of television news watching. Previous political socialization studies have demonstrated consistent relationships between media exposure and political knowledge gain (Atkin & Gantz, 1975; Chaffee, Ward, & Tipton, 1971). Conway et al. (1975) also showed that exposure to television news programs was moderately associated with perceptions of policy differences between parties, a concept similar to what is addressed by the indicators of "meaninglessness" in political choices. At a stage in life in which it seems natural to doubt one's understanding of politics, it should not be surprising to find that increases in exposure to television news, and hence access to political information, decrease an adolescent's negative feelings toward the political system which result specifically from the inability to understand meaningful differences between the parties. This relationship might in fact be true for adults as well. Studies collapsing alienation dimensions into a single indicator have not permitted the analysis of how isolated dimensions are affected by media use.

A TYPOLOGY OF ADOLESCENT POLITICAL ORIENTATIONS

The preceding explication of adolescent political alienation suggests that the significance of dimensions of political alienation lies in their combination within single individuals; that is, only adolescents who have learned to distrust the political system and who perceive the options presented by the two-party system as meaningless can be considered truly alienated. Similar kinds of implications of combinations of alienated attitudes have been suggested by Finifter (1970) and Erikson, Luttberg, and Tedin (1980). Based on these examples, a fourfold typology of adolescent political orientations was constructed using the grand mean of the purified alienation measures as a dividing line between high and low levels of the dimensions. Figure 21.1 illustrates the frequencies with which adolescents fell into these four political orientations in the Wisconsin data set.

Each of the four cells in Figure 21.1 represents an orientation toward political institutions and the political process. The politically integrated adolescents trust the institutions of government to do what is appropriate, and perceive the electoral process as providing meaningful options for those wishing to influence political affairs. This combination is conducive to adolescents' becoming well integrated, "mainstream" participants in the political process. This orientation corresponds to cell #1 in the diagram.

The "loyalists" in cell #2 have been characterized aptly by the cliche "My country right or wrong" (Erikson, Luttberg, & Tipton, 1980). These adolescents trust the institutions of government to do what is right, despite feeling personally overwhelmed and confused by political affairs. In effect, loyalty is the passive orientation toward politics. Trusting the institutions of government to a great extent may even facilitate meaninglessness in the

MEANINGLESSNESS

		LOW	HIGH
N O R M L E S S N E S S	**LOW**	Cell # 1 Integrated n = 92	Cell # 2 Loyalist n = 106
	HIGH	Cell # 3 Activist n = 119	Cell # 4 Alienated n = 68

Source: Based on Finifter (1970) and Erikson et al. (1980).

Figure 21.1 Typology of adolescent political orientations.

sense that absolute trust obviates the need to master an understanding of the political process. If an adolescent perceives government as paternalistic caretaker, the inability to discriminate between political options is no longer problematic. The need to understand and to be able to influence political options is superfluous. Studies of political socialization suggest that younger adolescents have idealized conceptions of leaders and emotional allegiances to authority figures that make them likely to fall into this category (Atkin, 1981). Others have similarly suggested that it is from the onset of adolescence that distrust and cynicism begin to develop (Greenstein, 1968; Niemi & Sobieszek, 1977).

The activists in cell # 3 take an active interest in politics from more of an adversarial stance than their integrated counterparts. They are not overwhelmed by political affairs, but they seriously question the activities of government institutions and the motives of those in power. Distrust of government, combined with the perception of a meaningful range of political choices within the existing institutional framework, motivates them toward greater political involvement to alleviate the inadequacies of the system.

The alienated adolescents in cell #4 represent the most apathetic of the four hypothesized adolescent political orientations. These young people do not trust government and feel that political choices are too complicated and overwhelming to bother expending their energies. Adolescents in this orientation are probably those most likely to withdraw totally from political life at a later point in time.

EXTERNAL INDICATORS AS VALIDATORS
OF ADOLESCENT POLITICAL ORIENTATIONS

The validity of these characterizations of adolescent political orientations was tested using three external indicators measuring pride in the U.S. system of government, anticipatory socialization and levels of apathy toward political affairs. Based on the conceptualizations proposed for these various groups, one would expect the greatest amount of pride to be manifest in the integrated group in which there are positive feelings about the trustworthiness of government, in addition to feelings that meaningful options exist for citizens who wish to take part in the system. The loyalists are also likely to be strong in the relative amount of pride in the system, despite their nonparticipatory role. The "normless" activists would focus on the imperfections of the system and would most likely be less proud than the groups more trusting of government. Adolescents within the alienated orientation would probably have the least pride of all in the system of government.

Similar predictions can be made for anticipatory socialization across the various orientations. One might predict that orientations of the integrated and activist adolescents would predispose them toward anticipating future involvement in politics. The groups for which politics seemed "meaningless" would be much less likely to anticipate playing an active role as adult citizens.

Predictions of apathy levels within the groups are also facilitated by the typology of political orientations. One would expect the integrated and activist groups to be most actively interested in political affairs. From the loyalists' point of view, there is little motivation for taking an active interest in political affairs; the government essentially runs well by itself and affords them little opportunity for influence. Alienated adolescents see government institutions as untrustworthy, and the "meaninglessness" of political choices leaves them feeling politically impotent. From this perspective, one would conclude that although things are not as they should be, there is nothing one can do about it anyway. Consequently, motivation for political involvement would be lacking and high levels of apathy would result.

Three one-way analyses of variance were conducted to test differences between the mean levels of each indicator within the four political orientations. Results indicated that significant differences existed between group means across all three external indicators ($p < .05$). Comparisons of mean levels of pride, apathy and anticipatory socialization are presented in Figure 21.2.

Although these variables are fraught with the reliability problems inherent in single item indicators (the reliability estimates ranged from .39 to .49) the results largely confirm the preceding characterizations of adolescents within the four orientations. Politically integrated adolescents are characterized by a high level of anticipatory socialization, great pride in their system of government, and little apathy toward political affairs. The loyalists manifest a fairly high degree of apathy and simultaneously maintain considerable amounts of pride in the system of government. On the other hand, the activists lack pride in government relative to the other groups, yet maintain an active interest in politics and have the strongest intentions to pursue that interest through political involvement as adults. As predicted, the alienated group has the least promising responses across all three indicators.

In order to examine differences between the political orientations with respect to levels of these three variables simultaneously, a discriminant analysis was performed. Two significant discriminant functions were identified from the three discriminating variables. The location of group centroids is illustrated in Figure 21.3. Pride in the system of government is located on one dimension and the second function consists of apathy and anticipatory socialization. One of the four proposed orientations falls within each of the quadrants as originally conceptualized in Figure 21.1. The apathy/anticipatory socialization function corresponds to the meaninglessness dimension, and pride in the U.S. system of government corresponds to the trust dimension.

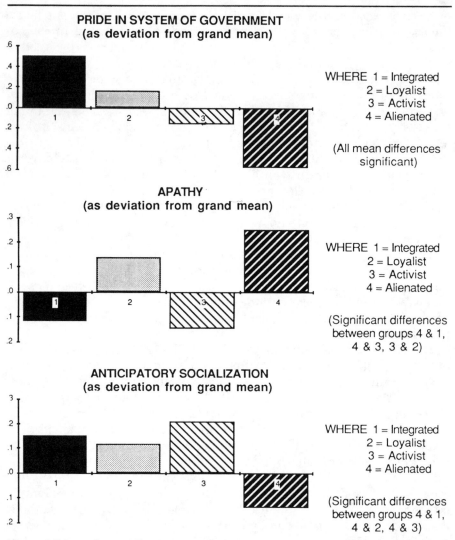

Figure 21.2 External indicators by political orientation: three one-way analyses of variance.

Note: All 3 analyses of variance were significant at the p < .05 level. Differences between group means based on Tukey method of multiple comparison (p < .05).

POLITICAL ORIENTATIONS AS CONTINGENT CONDITIONS FOR KNOWLEDGE GAIN

As previously described, the majority of research examining alienation and its dimensions has focused on alienation as an affective outcome and

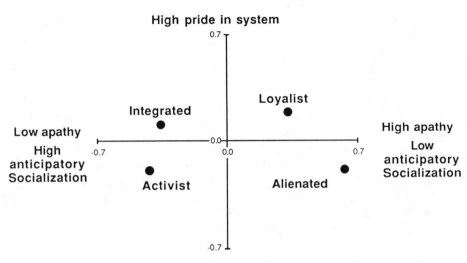

Figure 21.3 Group centroids.

Structure Matrix:	Function 1	Function 2
Pride in system of gov't	.99[a]	.09
Apathy	.25	.88[b]
Anticipatory Socialization	.09	.74[b]
Percentage of variance explained	71%	25%
Wilk's Lambda	.84	.95
Canonical correlation	.34***	.21**

Note: Entries in table are correlations between the listed variable and the rotated canonical discriminant functions; superscripts indicate strongest correlation for each variable. Only significant functions are shown.
***$p < .001$; **$p < .01$.

dependent variable related to independent variables such as television news viewing (Robinson, 1975, 1976), personality variables (see Erikson, Luttberg, & Tipton, 1980), or actual policies and political events (Miller, 1974a). Few of these approaches have consistently produced significant results.

More productive utilization of these variables involves conceptualizing them as individual differences indicative of the uniqueness of the adolescents as receivers of information. Using a functionalist perspective,
emphasis is shifted toward the adolescent's active role in the political socialization process. When adolescents are exposed to information transmitted
by mass media, they are not all affected equally in terms of knowledge
acquisition (Drew & Reeves, 1980). Figure 21.4 shows the mean knowledge of party symbols for each of the four groups across all three points in
time. Party symbol knowledge was chosen as the most appropriate indicator for this analysis because it specifically addressed knowledge of general
differences between the parties, and because these measures were available across all three waves (see Appendix C).

At time 1, there are no significant differences between the mean levels of
knowledge held by the four groups. By time 2, there is a significant gap
between the alienated and the activist groups, and between the alienated
and the integrated groups (p < .05). The loyalists are also significantly less
knowledgeable than the activist group. By time 3, these same differences
have become accentuated.

Although all groups increased their amount of knowledge over the year
and a half period, the integrated and activist groups are acquiring knowledge at a faster rate than the two groups high in meaninglessness. This suggests that a low level of meaninglessness may have primacy over a lack of
normlessness as a contingent condition for acquiring knowledge about
political affairs. The location of the activist group further suggests that perhaps a modicum of political distrust promotes knowledge acquisition by
providing greater motivation to keep up with political affairs. It is also plausible that the distrust of the activist group is simply indicative of a greater
degree of political sophistication. In the high meaninglessness conditions,
the reverse appears to be true. Low trust combined with high meaninglessness in the alienated group produces less knowledge gain than the more
trusting loyalist condition.

Extensive evidence of phenomena of this type may be found in the
knowledge gap literature; considerable disagreement exists, however, as
to what accounts for differential growth in knowledge. Using SES differences as a basis for group comparisons has little but expediency to recommend it. Although SES often demonstrates the effect adequately, it
provides no theoretically adequate explanation as to why the differential
growth might be occurring. More recent examinations of the knowledge
gap hypothesis have suggested the use of variables such as motivation and
interest as contingent conditions in lieu of differentiation based on high and
low SES levels (e.g., Ettema & Kline, 1977; Genova & Greenberg, 1979;
Lovrich & Pierce, 1984).

The results of this study commend using the more theoretically relevant
concept of political orientations as a contingent condition to explore levels

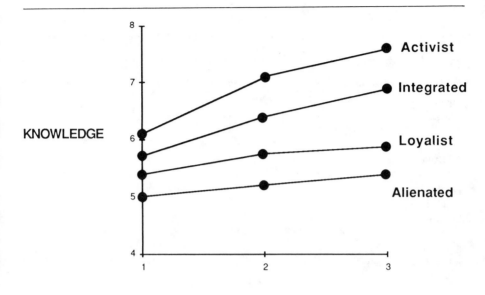

TIME

Note: Plotted points represent mean levels of party symbol knowledge at three successive times of measurement. Wave 1 measurements were obtained in late January through March, 1980. Wave 2 took place in October, 1980, shortly before the election. Wave 3 measurements were obtained in October and November of 1981. For exact content of party symbol knowledge questions, see Appendix B.

Figure 21.4 Changes in mean levels of party symbol knowledge over time.

of adolescents' political knowledge. These orientations encompass both interest and motivational aspects of adolescents' orientations toward politics. Evidence suggests that, to the extent that different audience members approach political messages with varying levels of interest and motivation, differential knowledge gains may be predicted.

PREDICTING KNOWLEDGE GAIN

A multivariate analysis of the relationships between knowledge gain and television news exposure and attention was conducted in order to examine the relative importance of various independent variables in predicting knowledge. The four political orientations served as contingent conditions, for which separate series of hierarchical regression equations were generated (see Table 21.1). Five blocks were successively entered into the

Table 21.1
Predictors of Party Knowledge by Adolescent Political Orientation
(hierarchical regression analysis)

Predictors of Knowledge at Time 3		POLITICAL ORIENTATION			
		Integrated	Loyalist	Activist	Alienated#
Equation 1:					
Age		.29	.08	.30	−.11
	Increment to R^2	(.25)	(.07)	(.23)	(.02)*
Equation 2:					
Add Autocorrelation		.38	.37	.46	.77
(Knowledge Time 1)	Increment to R^2	(.18)	(.14)	(.20)	(.48)
Equation 3:					
Add Television News		.02	−.13	.01	.06
Exposure					
	Increment to R^2	(.02)	(.01)*	(.02)	(.00)*
Equation 4:					
Add Television News		.22	.18	.18	−.10
Attention					
	Increment to R^2	(.03)	(.02)	(.03)	(.01)*
Total R^2		(.47)	(.24)	(.48)	(.51)
Interaction Term as Predictor:					
Equation 5:					
Age,		.32	.12	.32	−.08
Knowledge Time 1,		.41	.41	.46	.73
& Exposure × Attention		.16	.01	.12	−.06
Interaction					
	Increment to R^2	.02	.00*	.02	.00*
	(Total R^2)	(.45)	(.21)	(.45)	(.50)

Note: R^2 values indicate incremental variance explained in successive equations in the hierarchical regression analysis. Cell entries are standardized beta weights from final equations.
* All increments to R^2 were significant at the $p < .05$ level with these exceptions; # Caution due to small n.

equations for each of the four group contingent conditions, making a total of twenty equations.

Since considerable evidence has shown that developmental differences mediate learning processes, age was included in the first block of the hierarchical regression analysis for each contingent condition. The second block controlled for the respondent's level of knowledge at Time 1 so that later equations would test gains in knowledge between Times 1 and 3. The third block entered into the equation included the more traditional measure of exposure to television news. Equation 4 also incorporated measures of attention to television news, beyond exposure (see Appendix D). One additional equation was included to investigate the possibility that a multiplicative exposure × attention interaction term could account for greater variance than the two terms added into the equation separately (Chaffee & Schleuder, 1985).

The results of this analysis suggest that initial affective political orientations act as contingent conditions affecting the processing of new information. Comparisons of beta weights for the four different regression series suggest that knowledge levels in low and high meaninglessness groups are accounted for quite differently. Beta weights in the integrated and activist orientations are similar and the proportions of variance accounted for by each item are also equivalent.

A strikingly different situation exists in the less knowledgeable loyalist and alienated groups. For loyalists, age is a relatively weak predictor of knowledge, and for alienated youths, age becomes insignificant. Because of the stability of knowledge levels in the alienated condition, a large amount of the total variance is accounted for, but very little of this is process variance. Previous knowledge accounted for 48% of the 51% of total variance explained. This results from the fact that there was little knowledge gain to explain within this group. Caution should be exercised in interpreting the remainder of coefficients in this particular series of equations. Fluctuations in the beta weights, which occurred as additional variables were included in the equation, suggest that these figures were probably distorted due to multicollinearity.

Of general theoretical interest are the additional findings that the exposure × attention interaction variable did not account for more variance than the two items entered separately into the equations. Nonetheless, the multiplicative measures do serve to demonstrate quite clearly how knowledge gains attributable to television use may appear only under the contingent condition of an appropriate political orientation. A significant increment to R^2 could be attributed to the exposure × attention measure only under the integrated and activist conditions.

Despite the legacy of research surrounding the use of exposure measures, it is also notable that overall, the exposure variable was not as powerful a predictor of knowledge as attention. Attention accounted for an average of 2% of the variance across the four analyses compared to $1 1/4$% for the exposure measure, even though exposure was entered into the equations before attention.

Consistent knowledge gains across all groups make it appear that time itself is a sufficient condition for knowledge gain. This is not surprising because age is inevitably confounded with cumulative exposure to political information, regardless of its source. What is significant is that over time differential gains in knowledge may be predicted on the basis of the four orientations. Integrated and activist adolescents gain knowledge at a faster rate than loyalist or alienated youths.

THE ROLE OF COMMUNICATION:
EQUIVALENCE OF MEDIA USE VS.
EQUIVALENCE OF PREDICTIVE STRENGTH

Although there is clear evidence of a knowledge gap-type phenomenon, the appropriate role of communication is not well-defined. Much of
the problem in formulating a causal model stems from difficulty in specifying the role of communication. It appears that some knowledge gain
occurs almost inevitably for all groups of adolescents over time; however,
additional analyses have shown that the groupings by political orientation
are not mere surrogates for age groups. Nonetheless, adolescents within
certain orientations gain knowledge at a faster rate than those within other
groups.

A more clear understanding of what is driving this effect is needed.
Although an exhaustive elimination of alternatives was not attempted,
efforts were made to differentiate between two potential sources. McLeod
and associates (1979) suggest that uneven effects across contingent subgroups as often noted in the knowledge gap literature may be due to two
different kinds of communication "nonequivalence." In order to clarify
the source of knowledge discrepancies, they contend that answers to two
separate questions are needed. First, were information sources used
equally by all orientation groups? This aspect has been labeled *equivalence
of exposure*. Second, did particular sources produce equally strong associations with knowledge gain among the various subgroups? Assessment
of the potency of a source's impact across contingency groups was identified as *equivalence of predictive strength*. Making this distinction enables
one to determine whether differential knowledge gain among groups is
due to different amounts of exposure to various communication sources,
or to differences in the amount of influence that a given unit of exposure to
a communication medium will produce.

To execute this comparison, variables were constructed to represent
the amount of communication potentially influencing each adolescent's
knowledge gain. In order to make a comparison among media, it was
decided to use multiplicative exposure × attention measures rather than
the traditional exposure measures alone. As Chaffee and Schleuder
(1985) point out, using exposure items alone would probably underesti-
mate the potential for television's effect: "To answer a question about
'reading' a newspaper is simultaneously to report on one's exposure *and*
attention. The same does not hold for television use, however. One can
'watch' a TV news program simply because it is on, without it particularly
engaging the mind in any serious sense" (p. 33). To test equivalence of
media use, comparable measures of peoples' utilization of these sources
would need to take into account both exposure and attention to print and

broadcast media. Using a multiplicative measure allows equal expectations of knowledge gain to be assigned to low attention/high exposure to one medium as to high attention/low exposure to another. For interpersonal communication, a composite indicator of the frequency with which adolescents discussed politics with friends, family and others was used in the analysis (see Appendix D).

First, the mean levels of each of these three sources were compared across groups to test for equivalence of exposure and attention. The analyses of variance were not significant with the exception of the newspaper exposure × attention measure ($p < .05$). Student-Newman-Keuls multiple comparison tests revealed that only one pair of groups was significantly different on this measure. The mean level of newspaper exposure × attention in the integrated group was significantly higher than under the alienated contingency.

To test for equivalence of predictive strength, a regression equation controlling for the effects of age and prior knowledge was used as a basis for comparison within each orientation. The three communication sources were then entered into separate regression equations in order to obtain an increment to R^2 indicative of the predictive strength of each individual source within a contingent political orientation. The purpose of this analysis was not to maximize an overall R^2, but rather to compare the predictive strength of communication under the four contingent conditions. The results of these analyses are displayed in Table 21.2.

In combination, these results confirm the importance of a receiver-based interpretation of the observed gap. The possibility that nonequivalence of exposure and attention was responsible for differential knowledge gains was largely ruled out as a possible explanation by virtue of equivalence of exposure and attention measures between groups across almost all of the measures. A more promising possibility is suggested by the finding that the strength of any given communication source as a predictor of knowledge depends heavily on the individual's political orientation. In essence, these orientations toward politics are indicators of a motivation to focus attention on political information and thus to learn more per unit of exposure × attention. The standardized betas in Table 21.2 suggest that the higher knowledge growth rate in integrated and activist adolescents is most reasonably attributed to their efficient use of multiple sources of information. Exposure and attention to all three communication sources accounted for significant amounts of knowledge gain for activists.

The low rate of knowledge gain in the alienated group is attributable to the nonequivalence of predictive strength of communication exposure and attention measures across all sources. Standardized betas for this group reflect a radically different relationship between units of exposure × attention and knowledge gain. The lack of motivation within this group makes its members unlikely to learn despite commensurate exposure and atten-

Table 21.2
Predictors of Party Knowledge, by Adolescent Political Orientation
Using Communication Source
Exposure and Attention Interaction Measures

		POLITICAL ORIENTATION			
Predictors of Knowledge at Time 3		Integrated	Loyalist	Activist	Alienated
Baseline Equation:					
Age		.30	.17	.45	-.01
And Autocorrelation		.38	.37	.46	.74
(Knowledge Time 1)	(R² for block)	(.43)	(.21)	(.43)	(.50)
Equations 1, 2, and 3 each added *separately* to baseline equation:					
Equation 1:					
Add Television		.09	.01	.10	-.06
Exposure*Attention	(Increment to R²)	(.02)	(.00)*	(.02)	(.00)*
Equation 2:					
Add Newspaper		.02	.32	.09	-.02
Exposure*Attention	(Increment to R²)	(.00)*	(.10)	(.02)	(.00)*
Equation 3:					
Add Interpersonal		.12	-.06	.11	-.15
Communication	(Increment to R²)	(.02)	(.01)	(.01)	(.02)*

Note: R^2 values indicate incremental variance explained in equations as compared to R^2 values for baseline regression equation. Each communication source block was entered into an equation separately. Cell entries are standardized beta weights.
* All increments to R^2 were significant at the $p < .05$ level with these exceptions.

tion to potential sources of learning. Political information either is not the focus of attention or is not perceived as sufficiently important to produce recall. Because of the lesser amount of knowledge gain in this group, a large proportion of the variance is accounted for by previous knowledge.

Figure 21.5 models this contingent relationship. The parallel slopes to the left of the orientations are indicative of the baseline knowledge growth rate one might expect during adolescence. After passing through the combination of meaninglessness and normlessness composing political orientations, these angles are refracted to illustrate differential growth rates. Each orientation is associated with a differing amount of motivation to learn, which in turn produces differences among groups in how stimuli relating to political information are processed. Processing stimulated by a greater motivation to learn produces a higher knowledge growth rate than processing associated with lesser degrees of motivation. The addition of these intermediary constructs provides a fuller explanation of the causes of differential growth in knowledge among adolescents. Because exposure and attention to mass media and interpersonal sources of political information are generally equal across orientations, the potential influence of communication on all four contingencies is indicated by a single arrow. The

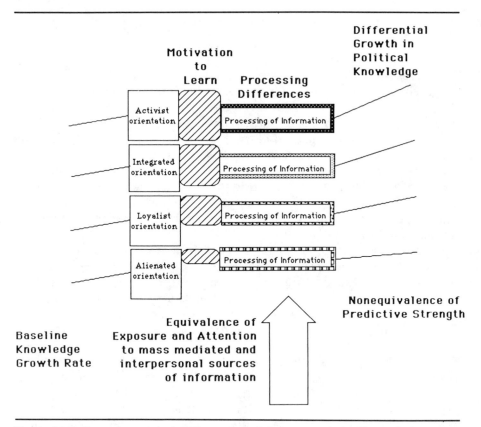

Figure 21.5 Causal model of differential adolescent political knowledge gain.

observed nonequivalence of effect depicted on the far right of Figure 21.5 is due to nonequivalence of predictive strength rather than nonequivalence of exposure and attention.

While communicative influence of some sort seems inevitably necessary for learning to occur, communication itself is not a sufficient condition for the gap effect to take place. Differing motivations to learn are also necessary for communication to exacerbate knowledge differences. The importance of a motivation-based causal interpretation was corroborated by Tichenor and associates who found that when motivations were equalized by situations of conflict, the infusion of communication into a system closed existing gaps (see Tichenor, Donahue, & Olien, 1980 for details). The conflict-knowledge hypothesis and other research relating knowledge to motivations may provide further insight into the intricacies of information processing and its subsequent effects on learning.

IMPLICATIONS FOR FUTURE RESEARCH
ON POLITICAL ALIENATION

The results of this study emphasize the importance of using additional criteria beyond traditional trust measures in identifying levels of political alienation. Because distrust may be associated with two quite different orientations toward political participation, using it as a sole criterion is likely to obscure identification of the alienated group. An analysis of the recent resurgence of trust in government between 1980 and 1984 confirms this point. Citrin and Green (1985) suggest that the close connection between attitudes toward the president and confidence in government presents strong evidence that trust in government questions are measuring attitudes toward incumbent authorities rather than alienation from the political regime.

Furthermore, the consistency with which the four political orientation groups distinguish themselves in this study recommends the use of meaninglessness as a second necessary condition to ensure that alienated attitudes are directed toward the political regime itself. Including both normlessness and meaninglessness as necessary conditions requires that alienated individuals be those who feel that neither party offers viable solutions.

The findings of this study also have clear implications for future interpretations of evidence of alienated attitudes. The driving force behind most research is the notion that alienation is inherently undesirable and dysfunctional for the political system. The knowledge levels of political orientation groups in this study suggest that a modicum of the dimension of alienation known as distrust can, in fact, be functional. Knowledge of differences between parties is essential for a politics of reason, and it is the activists who are most successful in achieving this goal. The distrust of government among members of this group apparently motivates them to acquire greater knowledge.

Loyalists are more trusting of government, and the integrated adolescents have low levels of both dimensions of alienation, but the activists are motivated to acquire knowledge at the fastest rate. Despite their awareness of government's shortcomings, they do not conclude that learning about politics is not worthwhile. On the contrary, their motivation to acquire political information from various sources appears strongest of any orientation. It is not entirely surprising to find that those adolescents who trust government only "some of the time" are among the most politically sophisticated of their peers.

Finally, these results also have implications for the political socialization of adolescents. There are basically two kinds of mistakes that can be made in cultivating political values that will ensure their political participation as adults. Adolescents can become either too eager to yield to authority, as suggested by the loyalist group, or too eager to contest it, as evidenced by the alienated group. In either case, there are also consequences for levels of political knowledge and prospects for an informed citizenry. As Sniderman (1981, p. 16) observed, "What seems in order is not blind loyalty but balanced judgment: an awareness that a democratic political order, whatever its virtues, will have shortcomings." It is likely that textbooks touting "America the Infallible" may in fact be encouraging a kind of allegiance that is a disservice to democracy.

Appendix A
Composition of Alienation Dimension Questions

Normlessness:

How often can you trust Congress to do what you think is right? (just about always, most of the time, or some of the time)

How often can you trust the U.S. Supreme Court to do what you think is right? (just about always, most of the time, or some of the time)

How often can you trust the office of the president to do what you think is right? (just about always, most of the time, or some of the time)

Meaninglessness:

Neither party stands for what I think is important. (strongly agree, agree, agree/disagree, disagree, strongly disagree)

I dislike both parties. (strongly agree, agree, agree/disagree, disagree, strongly disagree)

I don't know much about the difference between the Republican and Democratic parties. (strongly agree, agree, agree/disagree, disagree, strongly disagree)

Powerlessness:

So many people vote in the national elections that one person's vote doesn't matter. (strongly agree, agree, agree/disagree, disagree, strongly disagree)

In America, everyone who wants to does have a voice in what the government decides to do. (strongly agree, agree, agree/disagree, disagree, strongly disagree)

Note: All items were recorded so that hypothesized alienated responses to each item were represented by the highter score.

Appendix B
Reliability and Stability of Variables from Test-Retest Autocorrelations

	Reliability	T1-T2	Stability T2-T3	T1-T3
Normlessness Dimension	.65	.66	.81	.53
Powerlessness Dimension	.29	.75	.99*	.79
Meaninglessness Dimension	**	**	.81	**

* Stability > 1.0 obtained due to violation of assumptions; ** Could not be calculated since meaninglessness items were not measured at Time 1.

Appendix C
Components of Party Symbol Knowledge Index

When I read each of these names or things, which party comes most to your mind . . . the Republicans or the Democrats? If neither party comes to your mind right away, just say so and we'll go on.

A. Franklin D. Roosevelt, B. Right of center, C. Rich People, D. Liberal, E. Labor unions, F. Poor people, G. Abraham Lincoln, H. Lyndon Johnson, I. Richard Nixon, J. Conservative, K. Business, L. Left of Center, M. Elephant, N. Donkey

Scoring of Index: One point for each correct answer, zero points for any other response.

Test-Retest Reliability: .68

Appendix D
Composition of Communication
Exposure and Attention Measures

	Reliability (from test-retest autocorrelations)
Newspapers:	
How many days in the last seven did you read a newspaper?	.64
How much attention did you pay to articles in the newspaper about national politics and government? (A lot, quite a bit, some, very little, none)	.40
Interaction Term	.58
Television:	
On how many days in the past seven days did you watch the national news on television?	.49
How much attention did you pay to news on tv about national politics and government? (A lot, some, very little, none)	.37
Interaction Term	.52
Interpersonal Communication:	*
How much do you talk about national politics at home with your family? (A lot, some, very little, none)	
How much do you talk about national politics with your friends? (A lot, some, very little, none)	
How often do you usually talk with other people about national politics? (A lot, some, very little, none)	

* These variables measured in waves 2 and 3 only.

REFERENCES

Abramson, P., & Finifter, A. (1981). On the meaning of political trust. *American Political Science Review, 25,* 297-307.

Almond, G. A., & Verba, S. (1965). *The civic culture.* Boston: Little, Brown.

Atkin, C. K. (1981). Communication and political socialization. In D. D. Nimmo & K. R. Sanders, (Eds.), *Handbook of Political Communication* (pp. 229-328). Beverly Hills, CA: Sage.

Atkin, C., & Gantz, W. (1975). The role of television news in the political socialization of children. *Public Opinion Quarterly, 31,* 183-197.

Berelson, B. R., Lazarsfeld, P. F., & McPhee, W. N. (1954). *Voting.* Chicago: University of Chicago Press.

Chaffee, S. H. & Miyo, Y. (1983). Selective exposure and the reinforcement hypothesis: An intergenerational panel study of the 1980 presidential campaign. *Communication Research, 10,* 3-36.

Chaffee, S. H., & Schleuder, J. (1985, May). *Measurement and effects of attention to media news.* Paper presented at the meeting of the International Communication Association, Honolulu, Hawaii.

Chaffee, S. H., & Tims, A. T. (1982). News media use in adolescence: Implications for political cognitions. In M. Burgoon, (Ed.), *Communication Yearbook 6* (pp. 287-326). Beverly Hills, CA: Sage.

Chaffee, S. H., Ward, S., & Tipton, L. (1971). Mass communication and political socialization. *Journalism Quarterly, 47,* 647-659.

Citrin, J. (1974). Comment: The political relevance of trust in government. *American Political Science Review, 68,* 973-988.

Citrin, J., & Green, D. P. (1985). *Presidential leadership and the resurgence of trust in government.* Berkeley: University of California, Survey Research Center Working Paper Series.

Citrin, J., McClosky, H., Shanks, J. M., & Sniderman, P. M. (1975). Personal and political sources of political alienation. *British Journal of Political Science, 5,* 1-31.

Conway, M., Margaret, A., Stevens, J., & Smith, R. (1975). The relation between media use and children's civic awareness. *Journalism Quarterly, 52,* 531-38.

Dean, D. G. (1960a). Alienation: Its meaning and measurement. *American Sociological Review, 26,* 753-758.

Dean, D. G. (1960b). Alienation and political apathy. *Social Forces, 38,* 185-195.

Drew, D., & Reeves, B. (1980). Children and television news. *Journalism Quarterly, 57,* 45-54.

Easton, D. (1979). *Systems analysis of political life.* Chicago: University of Chicago Press.

Erikson, R. S., Luttbeg, N. R., & Tedin, K. L. (1980). *American public opinion: It's origins, content and impact.* New York: John Wiley.

Ettema, J. S., Brown, J. W., & Luepker, R. V. (1983). Knowledge gap effects in a cardiovascular information campaign. *Public Opinion Quarterly, 47,* 516-527.

Ettema, J. S. & Kline, F. G. (1977). Deficits, differences and ceilings: Contingent conditions for understanding the knowledge gap. *Communication Research, 4,* 179-202.

Finifter, A. W. (1970). Dimensions of political alienation. *American Political Science Review, 64,* 389-410.

Gamson, W. A. (1968). *Power and discontent.* Homewood, IL: Dorsey Press.

Genova, B. K. L., & Greenberg, B. S. (1979). Interest in news and the knowledge gap. *Public Opinion Quarterly, 43,* 79-91.

Graber, D. (1980). *Mass media and American politics.* Washington, DC: Congressional Quarterly Press.

Greenstein, F. (1968). Political socialization. In *International encyclopedia of the social sciences* New York: Macmillan.

Kennamer, D. K., & Chaffee, S. H. (1982). Communication of political information during early presidential primaries: Cognition, affect, and uncertainty. In M. Burgoon (Ed.), *Communication Yearbook 5* (pp. 627-650). New Brunswick, NJ: Transaction Books.

Kornhauser, W. (1959). *The politics of mass society.* Glencoe: Free Press.

Lane, R. E. (1962). *Political ideology.* New York: Free Press.

Lang, K., & Lang, G. E. (1968). *Politics and television.* New York: Quadrangle Books.

Levine, G. F. (1977). "Learned helplessness" and the evening news. *Journal of Communication, 27,* 100-105.

Lipset, S. M., & Schneider, W. (1983). The decline of confidence in American institutions. *Political Science Quarterly, 98,* 379-402.

Litt, E. (1963). Political cynicism and political futility. *Journal of Politics, 25,* 312-323.

Lovrich, N. P., & Pierce, J. C. (1984). Knowledge gap phenomena: Effects of situation-specific and transsituational factors. *Communication Research, 11,* 415-434.

McLeod, J. M., Bybee, C. R., & Durall, J. A. (1979). Equivalence of informed political participation: The 1976 presidential debates as a source of influence. *Communication Research, 6,* 463-487.

Miller, A. H. (1974a). Political issues and trust in government. *American Political Science Review, 68,* 851-972.

Miller, A. H. (1974b). Rejoinder to "Comment" by Jack Citrin. *American Political Science Review, 68*, 989-1001.

Muller, E. N. (1972). A test of a partial theory of potential for political violence. *American Political Science Review, 66*, 928-959.

Muller, E. N., Jukam, T. O., & Seligson, M. A. (1982). Diffuse political support and anti-system political behavior. *American Journal of Political Science, 26*, 240-264.

Niemi, R., & Sobieszek, B. (1977). Political socialization. *Annual Review of Sociology, 3*, 209-233.

Paige, J. (1971). Political orientation and riot participation. *American Sociological Review, 36*, 810-820.

Ranney, A. (1983). *Channels of power: The impact of television on American politics.* New York: Basic Books.

Robinson, M. J. (1974). The impact of the televised Watergate hearings. *Journal of Communication, 24*, 17-30.

Robinson, M. J. (1975). American political legitimacy in an era of electronic journalism: Reflections on the evening news. In D. Cater & R. Adler (Eds.), *Television as a social force* (pp. 97-113). New York: Praeger.

Robinson, M. J. (1976). Public affairs television and the growth of political malaise. *American Political Science Review, 70*, 409-432.

Robinson, M. J., & Sheehan, M. A. (1983). *Over the wire and on TV: CBS and UPI in campaign '80.* Beverly Hills, CA: Sage.

Schwartz, D. (1973). *Political alienation and political behavior.* Chicago: Aldine.

Sears, D. O., & McConahay, J. B. (1973). *The politics of violence.* Boston: Houghton-Mifflin.

Seeman, M. (1959). On the meaning of political alienation. *American Political Science Review, 24*, 783-791.

Sniderman, P. M. (1981). *A question of loyalty.* Berkeley: University of California Press.

Tichenor, P. T., Donahue, G. A., & Olien, C. A. (1980). Community conflict and citizen knowledge (pp. 139-173). In *Community conflict and the press.* Beverly Hills, CA: Sage.

Verba, S., & Nie, N. H. (1972). *Participation in America: Political democracy and social equality.* New York: Harper & Row.

22 ● A Model of Agenda Dynamics

JAROL B. MANHEIM

Virginia Polytechnic Institute and State University

OVER the decade and a half following publication of McCombs and Shaw's (1972) seminal work, the notion of agenda setting has emerged as a central focus of research in communication generally and in political communication in particular. Studies within this framework have, by and large, concentrated on the linkage between the agenda of media content and that of public concern, and their essential argument has been that public attention will, over time, be channeled to those issues or actors who occupy time or space in the mass media.

At roughly the same time that McCombs and Shaw were developing their notions of agenda *setting,* Cobb and Elder (1971, 1972) were developing some similar ideas about agenda *building,* the process by which issues emerge as legitimate concerns of the polity and its policymakers. The emphasis here is also on linkage, but in this case the linkage in question is primarily between the expression of public concerns and the targeting of formal political decision making.

Both of these conceptualizations focus on agenda development and control, and both emphasize factors that shape the context in which policy is made or implemented. Indeed, both employ distinctly similar language in describing their respective processes. But because these theoretical schema focus on seemingly disparate phenomena, with the former emphasizing primarily social-psychological events and the latter primarily institutional ones, few systematic efforts have been made yet to integrate them. The most notable exception to this generalization is Lang and Lang's (1981) critique of agenda-setting research, which calls attention to the need for a more elaborate conceptualization of the process by which issues originate and agendas are developed. Specifically, the Langs highlight the need for a framework that, among other things, distinguishes between content and salience and provides a mechanism for specifying the direction of causality in associated agenda shifts. It is the purpose of this chapter to suggest the possible outlines of such a conceptualization.

To that end, it is useful to think less of agenda setting or agenda building per se than of a comprehensive system of interactive agendas. Such a sys-

Correspondence and requests for reprints: Jarol B. Manheim, Department of Political Science, Virginia Polytechnic Institute and State University, Blacksburg, VA 24061.

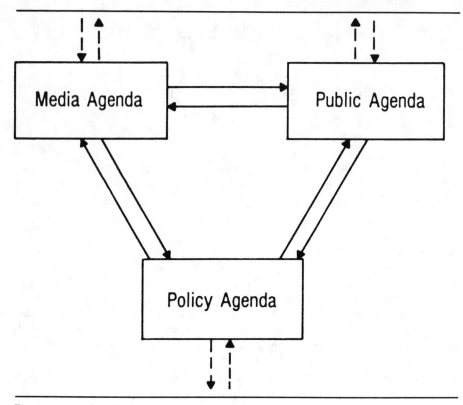

Figure 22.1 The agenda system.

tem, illustrated in Figure 22.1, is made up of three distinct agendas, those of the media, the public, and the policymakers. Each has its own character-istic internal dynamics, and each is linked to the others by one or more informational, behavioral, or institutional bridges. By exploring each of these dynamics and linkages in turn, and by adding a degree of complexity to the model represented in Figure 22.1, I shall suggest that the merger of the two conceptualizations now in the literature is both logical and poten-tially productive.

THE MEDIA AGENDA

The media agenda consists of those issues, actors, events, images and viewpoints that receive time or space in publications or broadcasts that are available to a given audience. The (political or politically relevant) content of this agenda is determined through a variety of interactions among jour-nalistic norms and behaviors, organizational structures and constraints, and exchanges between media representatives and recognized or potential newsmakers. Changes in one or more of these precursive factors are likely to be reflected in the subsequent characterization of any given agenda item (Epstein, 1973, pp. 16-18, documents two such instances).

Studies that focus on the professional norms and behaviors of journalists and their interactions with newsmakers and the public (Blumler & Gurevitch, 1981; Drechsel, 1983; Dunn, 1969; Epstein, 1973; Gans, 1979; Hess, 1981; Johnstone, Slawski, & Bowman, 1976; Roshco, 1975; Sigal, 1973; Sims, 1983; Tunstall, 1971) outline patterns of role socialization and decision making that are remarkably consistent across media and news settings. These studies make it clear that news content is often less a function of events themselves than of the professional and sociological perspectives of those whose job it is to witness and report on those events.

Still other studies (Altshull, 1984; Bennett, 1983; Cochran, 1975; Turow, 1984; see also Epstein, 1973; Gans, 1979) emphasize the commercial character of U. S. media and the importance of business decisions in limiting or even determining media content. The essential argument here is that the application of professional journalistic norms to the definition and selection of news is not unconstrained. Concerns for audience size and preferences, profitability, and the general financial well-being of media organizations create a bounded system within which journalists at varying levels of authority make decisions.

Finally, a few recent studies (Albritton & Manheim, 1983, 1985; Grunig, 1983; Hess, 1984; Manheim & Albritton, 1984; Bennett, 1983; Gans, 1979; see also Sigal, 1973) have explored the operation and influence of factors external to the media agenda but designed to encourage or constrain the selection of content. Initial evidence here suggests that such external forces are, in fact, somewhat effective in influencing the decisions that produce the media agenda.

Collectively, these studies suggest that journalistic norms and practices play a predominant role in determining the content of the media agenda, but that their influence is significantly and systematically tempered by business or other organizational requirements, by the practicability of affording complete news coverage to actors or events, and by efforts on the part of news sources to manipulate or control the flow of information. In practice, of course, this seemingly abstract confluence of forces takes a very practical form. Information is presented in the media at greater or lesser length (including total exclusion) and with greater or lesser prominence, with some number of cues as to the significance of the information for the audience, and with content that gives credence to one or another point of view or to a balance of views (DeGeorge, 1981). It is this aggregation of topics, cues, and viewpoints that constitutes the media agenda, and it is the cross-sectional or longitudinal differences in the factors that determine those topics, cues, and viewpoints that give rise to variation in their portrayal.

In an examination of the role of the media agenda in an integrated system of agenda dynamics, three dimensions of its content deserve consideration. These are illustrated in Figure 22.2 and include visibility, audience salience, and valence.

The first dimension, *visibility*, refers simply to the amount and prominence of coverage afforded by the media to any actor, event, or object. A number of studies (Behr & Iyengar, 1985; Greenberg & Garfinkle, 1963; Hvistendahl, 1968; Iyengar, Peters, & Kinder, 1982; Mehling, 1959; Powers & Kearl, 1968; Williams & Semlak, 1978; Winter & Eyal, 1981) have found that such factors as story location, the number of insertions, headline size, use of graphics, and style of presentation influence the amount of attention paid by an audience to a particular topic in the news. It follows that topics that are more visible in the media agenda are better suited for effective transfer to the public through agenda setting, and this, in turn, makes visibility an essential element of any integrative approach to agenda interactions.

The second dimension, *audience salience,* refers to the stated or implied relevance of news content to audience needs. In effect, the present formulation treats the type of content Lang and Lang (1981, pp. 451) have termed a *concern* not as an issue in its own right, but rather as an attribute that, to a greater or lesser extent, characterizes the coverage of all policy issues. Such express linkages are often the product of purposeful editorial decisions (Sharlin, 1985), and may take the form of references to social stability, economic security, or the general well-being of the audience or of its agent, the government. The function of such content is to help members of the audience to assimilate the news and, not incidentally, to market that news to them. In the present context, the function of these symbolic linkages is to integrate news content with existing cognitions (Graber, 1984a) and to enhance the perceived importance of news content among members of the public.

The third dimension of the media agenda, *valence,* refers to the general sense of favor, neutrality, or disfavor associated with the portrayal of a given object. Evidence to date does not support the effective transference of specific opinions from the media to the public agenda, but studies focused on more general attitudes (Miller, Goldenberg, & Erbring, 1979; Robinson, 1976) suggest that such transfers do occur. Indeed, Mazur (1981) has found evidence that the mere fact that an issue is included in the news may convey certain negative connotations to an audience. In at least some circumstances, then, the portrayal of issues or actors on the media agenda can influence perceptions of and judgments about those issues and actors among the public.

Within constraints arising from the characteristics of the issues themselves (their obtrusiveness or duration; see, for example, Lang & Lang, 1981, pp. 450; Zucker, 1978), the public (Winter, 1981), or even other,

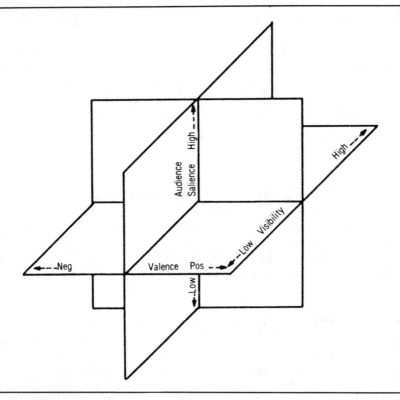

Figure 22.2 Dimensions of the media agenda.

nonagenda-related media effects (McLeod & Reeves, 1981), the three dimensions of the media agenda represented in Figure 22.2 thus work to affect the likelihood of transfer of items to the public agenda and, to a degree, the substantive content of those items that so move. Though less well documented to date, similar effects have been noted in transfers from the media to the policy agenda. Sigal (1973) and Lemert (1981, pp. 190-193) have identified several direct forms of journalistic influence in policy-making, and Paletz and Entman (1981), Cook et al. (1983), and Graber (1984b) have suggested their importance. Addressing specific themes treated in the present essay, Cobb and Elder (1972, pp. 91-92) have suggested that visibility in the media raises issues to prominence and increases the likelihood of their becoming the subject of policy action, and Gormley (1975) has found an association between media and policy agendas to occur at a general rather than a specific level. Graber (1984b, pp. 268-269) sees the media as supplying the context within which the public evaluates an issue, and suggests that balanced coverage in the media reflects and, through a recycling effect, heightens existing conflicts among policymakers.

These notions of visibility, audience salience, and valence thus find substantial grounding in the research literature to date, and together provide a useful means of viewing the internal dynamics and external linkages of the media agenda. In the sections to follow, I shall suggest the importance of corresponding dimensions in the public and policy agendas.

THE PUBLIC AGENDA

In the case of the public agenda, these corresponding dimensions include *familiarity,* or the degree of public awareness of or attention to a given topic (attitude object), *personal salience,* which incorporates such notions as involvement, interest in, or perceived relevance to one's self of the topic in question, and *favorability,* which represents a summary affective judgment of the topic. These three dimensions are illustrated in Figure 22.3.

Familiarity with an issue, actor, or event has been a central focus in studies of agenda setting from the outset (Gantz, Trenholm, & Pittman, 1976; Funkhauser, 1973; Kent & Rush, 1976; see Atkin, Galloway, & Nayman, 1976), but has not always been treated as an analytically distinct phenomenon. More often than not, the dependent variables in agenda-setting research have been defined as levels of public concern with or about an issue, a construction that fails to distinguish clearly between affects and cognitions. Indeed, in a basic formulation of the theory itself, Shaw and McCombs (1977) describe agenda setting as a cognition-based phenomenon (p. 7), then immediately and for the balance of their analysis turn their attention exclusively to the salience rather than the cognitive content of issues (pp. 7-8 et passim). For analytical purposes, however, it is useful to distinguish "what people think about" from "how important they think it is."

Accordingly, issue salience is more appropriately treated as a second dimension of the public agenda. In one form or another, salience has long been recognized as an important component of public opinion (for example, Czudnowski, 1968; Jennings & Zeigler, 1970; Lane & Sears, 1964; Verba & Nie, 1972). Of more immediate interest in the present context, however, is research that has effectively integrated this notion with the concept of agenda setting. Erbring, Goldenberg, and Miller (1980), for example, recognized the importance of the distinction between salience and familiarity, particularly in their notion of issue sensitivity, and its significance is at least implicit in other recent studies that weigh media effects against those of personal experience in assessing agenda setting (Behr & Iyengar, 1985; Einsiedel, Salomone, & Schneider, 1984; Lang & Lang,

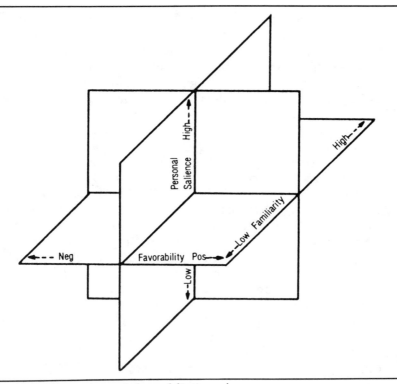

Figure 22.3 Dimensions of the public agenda.

1981, particularly in their discussion of issue thresholds). These studies focus in large measure on the *potential* media influence on individual attitudes that is delimited by the larger context of real-world activity, or, to put that another way, on the degree of susceptibility of individuals or publics to agenda-setting or other media effects.

The third dimension of the public agenda is favorability, the expressed preference of an individual or a public (depending upon one's level of analysis) with respect to an agenda item. Though evidence to date does not demonstrate agenda-setting effects on favorability comparable to those on familiarity or personal salience (an exception is Page, Shapiro, & Dempsey, 1985), such preferences are nevertheless very much a part of public opinion and very much a target of systematic attempts to influence that opinion. Indeed, Kotler (1982, pp. 56-62) characterizes politically relevant marketing procedures in precisely these terms. And Rabinowitz, Prothro, and Jacoby (1982) distinguish between salience and preferences, but suggest that the former may influence the latter significantly.

Linkage involving the public agenda might take either of two forms, that which ties it to the media agenda and that which ties it to the policy agenda.

In the first instance, the question is whether or not the presence and characterization of an item in the pubic agenda influences its presence and characterization in the media agenda. Those studies cited earlier as emphasizing the marketing of news to maximize audiences would seem to suggest the operation of bidirectional exchanges between these agendas. In examining agenda setting on several specific issues, however, Behr and Iyengar (1985, pp. 47-48) expressly rejected a public-to-media agenda effect except on one issue in which public awareness and issue salience were very high. Yet it is precisely such "mainstream" issues that market research might identify as prospective media foci, and in any event, marketing concerns of the media are less centered on issue selection than on developing attractive styles of presentation (Bennett, 1983, pp. 71-74). The answer to this first question thus appears to be that in most instances issue-specific agenda setting is unidirectional from the media to the public.

The second question addresses the nature or importance of public influence on the policy agenda. Verba and Nie (1972) have shown that issues on which there exists a high degree of consensus among politically active publics are likely to be the objects of policy action, and more recent research by Page and Shapiro (1983) demonstrates that changes in public opinion precede and are important causes of policy change, particularly when the opinion changes are large and sustained and when the issues are salient. Cobb, Ross, and Ross (1976), Bennett (1980), Erikson, Luttbeg, and Tedin (1980, pp. 235-251), and Cook and King (1982) have suggested the mechanisms through which such influence may be exercised.

THE POLICY AGENDA

The policy agenda has been defined by Cobb, Ross, and Ross (1976, p. 126) as "the list of items which decision makers have formally accepted for serious consideration." Downs (1972), Cobb and Elder (1972), Cook and King (1982), and Kingdon (1984), among others, have characterized the ways in which issues move (or are moved) on and off this agenda. Two central themes in these and related studies are (1) the likelihood that a governmental body will act on a given issue or respond to a given actor or event, and (2) the substantive nature of any policy decision or action that may emerge. Figure 22.4 illustrates these themes, labeled respectively as *support* (action more or less favorable to a given issue position or actor) and *likelihood of action*, as dimensions of the policy agenda.

Also represented in the figure is a third dimension, *freedom of action*, which refers to the range of responses or actions that is available to policymakers on a given question. Although freedom of action has not been examined extensively in the agenda-building literature per se, its significance in the policy process has long been recognized (Campbell, Converse, Miller, & Stokes, 1964; Edelman, 1964, 1971; Elder & Cobb, 1983). A

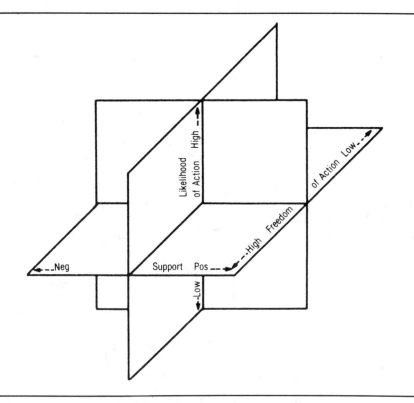

Figure 22.4 Dimensions of the policy agenda.

central argument in this literature, and particularly in Edelman's work, is that the degree of freedom of action of policymakers in general will vary directly with the quiescence of the citizenry. I am suggesting here that this argument applies not only at the level of policymaking generally, but to specific policy objects as well (see, for example, Caspary, 1970; see Almond, 1960). Figure 22.4, then, can be used to characterize issues on the policy agenda in terms of the likelihood, range, and direction of policy action. And to the extent that positioning on each of these dimensions arises from or gives rise to the positioning of issues on the media and public agendas, both of which we have, for the most part, already explored, it may be seen as a component of an integrated system of agendas and agenda transfers.

AGENDA DYNAMICS:
AN INTEGRATIVE MODEL

The nature of these interconnections is illustrated in Figure 22.5. The first point I would make with reference to this figure is that the linkage

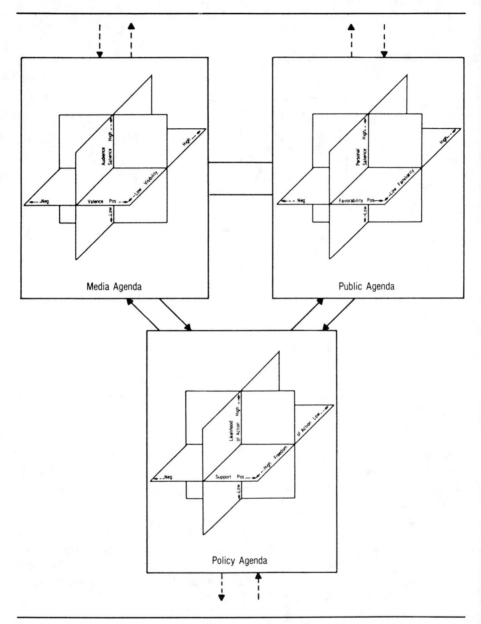

Figure 22.5 A model of agenda dynamics.

among the three agendas—the media, the public, and the policy—is considerably more complex than agenda-transfer theories presently suggest,
and, further, that this complexity takes forms that are already well docu-

mented and widely researched. Put most simply, none of these agendas is, in fact, merely a list, whether of content, opinions, or action items. Rather, each is a dynamic system in its own right, a system characterized by institutional- or individual-level patterns of behavior and by particularized structures of needs and motivations. At the same time, these separate dynamic systems are linked to one another by a flow of information, as well as by other devices. An important step forward, then, will be the successful identification of particular characteristics of that information that best serve to explain the interlocking behaviors that we can observe.

Greendale and Fredin (1977) have suggested an approach to this problem centered on topic-specific interlocks, a conceptualization that accords very closely with recent developments in "schema" theory as set forth by Axelrod (1973) and applied by Graber (1984a). In the present chapter, I have suggested a more generic strategy based on the notion that the internal and the interactive dynamics of any one agenda can influence or be influenced by the corresponding dynamics of another more or less independently of substantive content. Thus, for example, the location of a given object in the posited three-dimensional space of the media agenda has direct consequences for its subsequent positioning in the dimensioned space of the public and/or policy agendas, with perhaps the greater part of any such transfer arising from the propensities of the agenda system itself rather than from any characteristic of the issue on which it might be operating in any particular instance.

At a more general level of argument, the model illustrated in Figure 22.5 can be applied productively to organize our understanding of virtually all agenda-related inquiry. Specifically, this model can help us to identify and delineate classes of interrelated hypotheses, and to integrate seemingly disparate research findings into a unified conceptual whole. Table 22.1 illustrates one such classification scheme, one that differentiates among several basic types of hypotheses, provides a nonexhaustive listing of independent (IV) and dependent (DV) variables that might be employed in each, offers one or more citations to research or other literature in which each type of hypothesis is employed, and presents sample hypotheses suggestive of the concerns that research under each classification of the typology might address.

A unified conceptualization like that illustrated in Figure 22.5 and applied in Table 22.1 offers at least four potential advantages over present approaches to agenda setting and agenda building. First, it provides a more comprehensive and more meaningful device for characterizing the content of the media, public, and policy agendas. Second, it provides a standard of comparison for assessing the effects of both internal and external forces on the placement and movement of agenda items. Third, it provides a basis for identifying specific configurations of message (or image or issue) characteristics that facilitate or impede the development of items on

Table 22.1
A Typology of Agenda-Related Hypotheses

Type A.   Hypotheses relating to the initial location (attributes) of an item on a single agenda

A.1 Location on the media agenda

IV: events; characteristics, and operation of media decision making; efforts to influence that decision making

DV: attributes of items on the media agenda (that is, their location in the dimensioned space of Figure 22.2); temporal patterns of development

Citations: Blumler and Gurevitch (1981); Altheide (1984)

Examples: (1) The more accessible a newsworthy event, actor, or issue is to journalists, the more visible the coverage it is likely to receive.

(2) The more closely an event, actor, or issue accords with the values or preferences of news organizations, or with their perceptions of audience values or preferences, the more favorable the coverage it is likely to receive.

(3) The more interested journalists or news organizations are in influencing public perceptions of an event, actor, or issue, the more prosalience cues they will incorporate in its portrayal on the media agenda.

A.2 Location on the public agenda

IV: events; source and content of available information regarding new issues (for example, mediated versus experiential knowledge)

DV: attributes of items on the public agenda (that is, their location in the dimensioned space of Figure 22.3); temporal patterns of development.

Citation: DeGeorge (1981)

Examples: (1) The more media-dependent the image of an event, actor, or issue, the less personally salient it will be; the more experience-dependent that image, the more salient it will be.

(2) The more media-dependent the image of an event, actor, or issue, the less variability of composition it will display across individual members of the public; the more experience-dependent that image, the more variability of composition it will display.

(3) The higher the personal salience of an event, actor, or issue, the more extreme will be its favorability, whether positive or negative.

A.3 Location on the policy agenda

IV: events; development of new knowledge or expertise; changes in personnel; political processes

DV: attributes of items on the policy agenda (that is, their location in the dimensioned space of Figure 22.4); temporal patterns of development.

Citation: Kingdon (1984)

Example: Items that enter the policy agenda unexpectedly and with accompanying temporal pressures (that is, real or perceived crisis situations) are more likely to be characterized by high levels of support, high likelihood of action, and low freedom of action than are those that enter through "normal" political processes.

Type B.   Hypotheses relating to changes in the location (attributes) of an item on a single agenda.

B.1 Change in location on the media agenda

IV: events; editorial decisions; maturation processes affecting actors or events; external efforts at image manipulation; changing definitions or interpretations of journalistic norms

Table 22.1 Continued

DV: changes in attributes of items on the media agenda (that is, change of location in the dimensioned space of Figure 22.2); temporal patterns of change; resistance to change

Citation: Manheim and Albritton (1984)

Examples: (1) External control over the flow of information to news organizations, whether promotional or restrictive in character, will lead to changes in the amount and content of news coverage of specific events, actors, or issues.

(2) The effectiveness of external attempts at influencing the media portrayal of an event, actor, or issue is inversely related to the degree and duration of journalists' awareness of or sensitivity to them.

B.2 Change in location on the public agenda

IV: events; changes in underlying context of public opinion; changes in sources of information (for example, number, diversity); political socialization; maturation processes affecting actors or events

DV: changes in attributes of items on the public agenda (that is, change of location in the dimensioned space of Figure 22.3); temporal patterns of change; resistance to change; reinterpretation of existing images

Citation: Page and Shapiro (1982)

Examples: (1) As the reported ideological preferences of the public change over time, the image attributes of events, actors, or issues will change such that those perceived as most compatible with the ascendant ideology will be viewed more favorably or as more salient, and those perceived as more compatible with the descendent ideology will be viewed less favorably or as less salient.

(2) The higher the personal salience of an event, actor, or issue, the less volatile will be its favorability, whether positive or negative, over time.

B.3 Change in location on the policy agenda

IV: events; new or accumulating knowledge or information; changes in relative influence of political actors; changes in personnel occupying policymaking positions; maturation processes affecting actors or events

DV: changes in attributes of items on the policy agenda (that is, change of location in the dimensioned space of Figure 22.4); temporal patterns of change; resistance to change

Citations: Downs (1972); Cook and King (1982)

Example: Changes of administration or other superficial redistributions of political power will be accompanied or followed by short-term changes in the support and freedom and likelihood of action associated with a large number of issues, but in most instances these values will return to pre-event levels in the intermediate term. The exceptions will be those issues accorded the most salience by the beneficiaries of the redistribution (for example, their principal campaign promises), for which, at the very least, freedom of action will be maintained at lower levels than during the pre-event period.

Type C. Hypotheses relating to the movement of a given item from one agenda to another.

C.1 Media-public exchanges

IV: audience preferences or behaviors; events; initial attributes of the item; specificity or obtrusiveness of issues; economic motivations of media organizations

(continued)

Table 22.1 Continued

DV: interactive locational effects (those relating initial positioning in the dimensioned space of one agenda to subsequent positioning in the dimensioned
space of another); direction of exchanges (for example, recursiveness); temporal
characteristics of exchanges

Citations: Zucker (1978); Miller, Goldenberg, & Erbring (1979); Mazur (1981); Eyal,
Winter, & DeGeorge (1981); Lang & Lang (1981); Bennett (1983); Behr &
Iyengar (1985)

Example: An event, actor, or issue whose initial image scores high on visibility and
audience salience and is positively valenced on the media agenda will,
after a time lag, score high on familiarity and personal salience and be
viewed favorably on the public agenda, and so on. Once such images
have been established on the public agenda, however, directional
changes in favorability (public agenda) are likely to follow directional
changes in valence (media agenda) only where visibility/familiarity and
issue salience are relatively low.

C.2 Media-policy exchanges

IV: patterns of media use by policymakers; newsmaking and newsgathering behaviors; regulatory policies

DV: interactive locational effects; direction of exchanges; temporal characteristics
of exchanges

Citations: Sigal (1973); Gormley (1975); Graber (1984b)

Examples: (1) The more dependent policymakers are on mediated information for
their understanding of events, actors, or issues, the more likely the
direction and intensity of their support for a given item will be to reflect
the direction and extremity of the valence of that item on the media
agenda.

(2) To the extent that (a) journalists and policymakers receive the same
information about an event, actor, or issue at the same time, and (b) the
media portray that event, actor, or issue as highly salient, the freedom
of action of policymakers will be reduced.

(3) Items that enter independently onto the policy agenda with high likelihood of action will be more likely than those that enter with low likelihood of action to appear subsequently on the media agenda. Those
that enter the policy agenda with the greatest polarization of support
among policymakers will be accorded the highest visibility on the
media agenda.

C.3 Public-policy exchanges

IV: changes in public opinion polls on a given issue; proximity or results of elections;
public education or persuasion activities by policy actors; differential characteristics of issue publics

DV: interactive locational effects; direction of exchanges; temporal characteristics of
exchanges

Citations: Caspary (1970); Page & Shapiro (1983)

Example: The higher the familiarity and personal salience of an issue on the public
agenda, the lower the freedom of action that will characterize its location
on the policy agenda. This relationship will hold both in comparisons
across issues and longitudinally for a given issue.

Type D. Hypotheses relating to the development pattern of specific issues or images, or of general classes of issues or images

IV: specificity, obtrusiveness, instrumentality, or other characteristics of issues

Table 22.1 Continued

DV:	specific operations of the overall agenda-dynamics model from initiation of an issue through policy action
Citation:	Lang & Lang (1983)
Example:	In general, the factors affecting the location and transfer of agenda items will operate with greatest effect (that is, the agendas will be most fluid) for relatively unobtrusive events, actors or issues, and with least effect for relatively obtrusive events, actors, or issues.

Note: IV = independent variables; DV = dependent variables.

any particular agenda or their transfer from one agenda to another. And fourth, it provides a basis for characterizing more meaningfully the nature of those transfers and for differentiating among them in a systematic manner. Together, these complementary advantages will allow a much more precise specification of hypotheses related to agenda dynamics, and may themselves help to generate new comparative and interactive theories based on the attributes of agenda items.

REFERENCES

Albritton, R. B., & Manheim, J. B. (1983). News of Rhodesia: The impact of a public relations campaign. *Journalism Quarterly, 60,* 622-628.

Albritton, R. B., & Manheim, J. B. (1985). Public relations for the Third World: Images in the news. *Journal of Communication, 35,* 43-59.

Almond, G. A. (1960). *The American people and foreign policy.* New York: Praeger.

Altheide, D. L. (1984). Media hegemony: A failure of perspective. *Public Opinion Quarterly, 48,* 476-490.

Altschull, J. H. (1984). *Agents of power: The role of the news media in human affairs.* New York: Longman.

Atkin, C. K., Galloway, J., & Nayman, O. B. (1976). News media exposure: Political knowledge and campaign interest. *Journalism Quarterly, 53,* 231-237.

Axelrod, R. (1973). Schema theory: An information processing model of perception and cognition. *American Political Science Review, 67,* 1248-1266.

Behr, R. L., & Iyengar, S. (1985). Television news, real-world cues, and changes in the public agenda. *Public Opinion Quarterly, 49,* 38-57.

Bennett, W. L. (1980). Myth, ritual, and political control. *Journal of Communication, 30,* 166-179.

Bennett, W. L. (1983). *News: The politics of illusion.* New York: Longman.

Blumler, J. G., & Gurevitch, M. (1981). Politicians and the press: An essay on role relationships. In D. D. Nimmo & K. R. Saunders (Eds.) *Handbook of political communication* (pp. 467-493). Beverly Hills, CA: Sage.

Campbell, A., Converse, P. E., Miller, W., & Stokes, D. E. (1964). *The American voter.* New York: John Wiley.

Caspary, W. R. (1970). The "mood theory": A study of public opinion and foreign policy. *American Political Science Review, 64,* 536-547.

Cobb, R. W., & Elder, C. D. (1971). The politics of agenda building: An alternative perspective for modern democratic theory. *Journal of Politics, 33,* 892-915.

Cobb, R. W., & Elder, C. D. (1972). *Participation in American politics: The dynamics of agenda building.* Boston: Allyn & Bacon.

Cobb, R. W., Ross, J., & Ross, M. H. (1976). Agenda building as a comparative political process. *American Political Science Review, 70,* 126-138.

Cochran, T. C. (1975). Media as business: A brief history. *Journal of Communication, 25,* 155-165.

Cook, F. L., & King, D. S. (1982). *Toward a theory of issue decline on policy agendas* .
Paper presented at the Symposium on New Directions in the Empirical and Normative
Study of Public Policy, Northwestern University, Evanston, Illinois.

Cook, F. L., Tyler, T. R., Goetz, E. G., Gordon, M. T., Protess, D., Leff, D. R., & Molotch,
H. L. (1983). Media and agenda setting: Effects on the public, interest group leaders,
policy makers, and policy. *Public Opinion Quarterly, 47,* 16-35.

Czudnowski, M. M. (1968). A salience dimension of politics for the study of political culture. *American Political Science Review, 62,* 878-888.

DeGeorge, W. F. (1981). Conceptualization and measurement of audience agenda. In
G. C. Wilhoit & H. deBock (Eds.), *Mass communication review yearbook 2* (pp. 219-
224). Beverly Hills, CA: Sage.

Downs, A. (1972). Up and down with ecology: The "issue-attention cycle." *The Public
Interest, 28,* 38-50.

Drechsel, R. E. (1983). *Newsmaking in the trial courts.* . New York: Longman.

Dunn D. D. (1969). *Public officials and the press.* Reading, MA: Addison-Wesley.

Edelman, M. (1964). *The symbolic uses of politics.* Urbana: University of Illinois Press.

Edelman, M. (1971). *Politics as symbolic action: Mass arousal and quiescence.* Chicago:
Markham.

Einseidel, E. F., Salomone, K. L., & Schneider, F. P. (1984). Crime: Effects of media exposure and personal experience on issue salience. *Journalism Quarterly, 61,* 131-136.

Elder, C. D., & Cobb, R. W. (1983). *The political uses of symbols.* New York: Longman.

Epstein, E. J. (1973). *News from nowhere: Television and the news.* New York: Vintage.

Erbring, L., Goldenberg, E. N., & Miller, A. H. (1980). Front-page news and real-world
cues: A new look at agenda-setting by the media. *American Journal of Political Science,
24,* 16-49.

Erikson, R. S., Luttbeg, N. R., & Tedin, K. L. (1980). *American public opinion: Its origins,
content, and impact* (2nd ed.). New York: John Wiley.

Eyal, C. H., Winter, J. P., & DeGeorge, W. F. (1981). The concept of time frame in agenda
setting. In G. C. Wilhoit & H. deBock (Eds.), *Mass communication review yearbook 2*
(pp. 212-218). Beverly Hills, CA: Sage.

Funkhauser, G. R. (1973). The issues of the sixties: An exploratory study in the dynamics of
public opinion. *Public Opinion Quarterly, 37,* 62-75.

Gans, H. J. (1979). *Deciding what's news.* New York: Vintage.

Gantz, W., Trenholm, S., & Pittman, M. (1976). The impact of salience and altruism on
diffusion of news. *Journalism Quarterly, 53,* 727-732.

Graber, D. A. (1984a). *Processing the news: How people tame the information tide.* New
York: Longman.

Graber, D. A. (1984b). *Mass media and american politics* (2nd ed.). Washington, DC:
Congressional Quarterly.

Greenberg, A., & Garfinkle, N. (1963). Visual material and recall of magazine articles.
Journal of Advertising Research, 3, 30-34.

Greendale, S. C., & Fredin, E. S. (1977). Exploring the structure of national issues: Newspaper content and reader perceptions. In P. M. Hirsch, P. V. Miller, & F. G. Kline (Eds.).
Strategies for communication research (pp. 167-183). Beverly Hills, CA: Sage.

Grunig, J.E. (1983). Washington reporter publics of corporate public affairs programs.
Journalism Quarterly, 60, 603-614.

Hess, S. (1981). *The Washington reporters.* Washington, DC: Brookings.

Hess, S. (1984). *The government press connection: Press officers and their offices.* Washington, DC: Brookings.

Hvistendahl, J. K. (1968). The effect of subheads on reader comprehension. *Journalism
Quarterly, 45,* 123-125.

Iyengar, S., Peters, M. D., & Kinder, D. R. (1982). Experimental demonstrations of the
"not-so-minimal" consequences of television news programs. *American Political Science Review, 76,* 848-858.

Jennings, M. K., & Zeigler, L. H. (1970). The salience of state politics among attentive
publics. In E. C. Dreyer & W. A. Rosenbaum (Eds.). *Political opinion and behavior* (2nd
ed., pp. 257-285). Belmont, CA: Wadsworth.

Johnstone, J. W. C., Slawski, E. J., & Bowman, W. W. (1976). *The news people: A socio-logical portrait of American journalists and their work.* Urbana: University of Illinois Press.

Kent, K. E., & Rush, R. R. (1976). How communication behavior of older persons affects their public affairs knowledge. *Journalism Quarterly, 53,* 40-46.

Kingdon, J. W. (1984). *Agendas, alternatives, and public policies.* Boston: Little, Brown.

Kotler, P. (1982). *Marketing for nonprofit organizations* (2nd ed.). Englewood Cliffs, NJ: Prentice-Hall.

Lane, R. E., & Sears, D. O. (1964). *Public opinion.* Englewood Cliffs, NJ: Prentice-Hall.

Lang, G. E., & Lang, K. (1981). Watergate: An exploration of the agenda-building process. In G. C. Wilhoit & H. deBock (Eds.), *Mass communication review yearbook 2* (pp. 447-468). Beverly Hills, CA: Sage.

Lang, G. E., & Lang, K. (1983). *The battle for public opinion: The president, the press, and the polls during Watergate.* New York: Columbia University Press.

Lemert, J. B. (1981). *Does mass communication change public opinion after all?* Chicago: Nelson-Hall.

Manheim, J. B., & Albritton, R. B. (1984). Changing national images: International public relations and media agenda setting. *American Political Science Review, 78,* 641-657.

Mazur, A. (1981). Media coverage and public opinion on scientific controversies. *Journal of Communication, 31,* 106-115.

McCombs, M. E., & Shaw, D. L. (1972). The agenda-setting function of mass media. *Public Opinion Quarterly, 36,* 176-187.

McLeod, J. M., & Reeves, B. (1981). On the nature of mass media effects. In G. C. Wilhoit & H. deBock (Eds.), *Mass communication review yearbook 2* (pp. 245-282). Beverly Hills, CA: Sage.

Mehling, R. (1959). Attitude changing effect of news and photo combinations. *Journalism Quarterly, 36,* 189-198.

Miller, A. H., Goldenberg, E. N., & Erbring, L. (1979). Type-set politics: Impact of news-papers on public confidence. *American Political Science Review, 73,* 67-84.

Page, B. I., & Shapiro, R. Y. (1982). Changes in Americans' policy preferences, 1935-1979. *Public Opinion Quarterly, 46,* 24-42.

Page, B. I., & Shapiro, R. Y. (1983). Effects of public opinion on policy. *American Political Science Review, 77,* 175-190.

Page, B. I., Shapiro, R. Y., & Dempsey, G. R. (1985). *The mass media do affect policy preferences.* Paper presented at the annual meeting of the American Association for Public Opinion Research, McAfee, New Jersey.

Paletz, D. L., & Entman, R. M. (1981). *Media power politics.* New York: Free Press.

Powers, R. D., & Kearl, B. E. (1968). Readability and display as readership predictors. *Journalism Quarterly, 45,* 117-118.

Rabinowitz, G., Prothro, J. W., & Jacoby, W. (1982). Salience as a factor in the impact of issues on candidate evaluation. *Journal of Politics, 44,* 41-63.

Robinson, M. J. (1976). Public affairs television and the growth of political malaise: The case of "The Selling of the Pentagon". *American Political Science Review, 70,* 409-432.

Roshco, B. (1975). *Newsmaking.* Chicago: University of Chicago Press.

Sharlin, H. (1985). *EDB: A case study in the communication of health risk.* Report Submit-ted to the Office of Policy Analysis, U. S. Environmental Protection Agency.

Shaw, D. L., & McCombs, M. E. (1977). *The emergence of American political issues: The agenda-setting function of the press.* St. Paul, MN: West.

Sigal, L. V. (1973). *Reporters and officials: The organization and politics of newsmaking.* Lexington, MA: D.C. Heath.

Sims, R. B. (1983). *The Pentagon reporters.* Washington, DC: National Defense Univer-sity Press.

Tunstall, J. (1971). *Journalists at work.* Beverly Hills, CA: Sage.

Turow, J. (1984). *Media industries: The production of news and entertainment.* New York: Longman.

Verba, S., & Nie, N. H. (1972). *Participation in America: Political democracy and social equality.* New York: Harper & Row.

Williams, W., Jr., & Semlak, W. D. (1978). Structural effects of TV coverage on political agendas. *Journal of Communication, 28,* 114-119.

Winter, J. P. (1981). Contingent conditions in the agenda-setting process. In G. C. Wilhoit & H. deBock (Eds.), *Mass communication review yearbook 2* (pp. 235-243). Beverly Hills, CA: Sage.

Winter, J. P., & Eyal, C. H. (1981). Agenda setting for the civil rights issue. *Public Opinion Quarterly, 45,* 376-383.

Zucker, H. G. (1978). The variable nature of news media influence. In B. D. Ruben (Ed.), *Communication yearbook 2* (pp. 225-240). New Brunswick, NJ: Transaction Books.

23 ● Electoral Information Flow and Students' Information Processing: A Computerized Panel Study

SETH FINN

University of North Carolina at Chapel Hill

I N recent years, cognitive psychologists have demonstrated numerous situations in which the availability or vividness of stored information is likely to distort human judgment. Such observations should be especially salient to political communication scholars when they reflect upon the disproportionately large and continuing impact that the earliest panel studies continue to exert on popular notions of mass media effects. Certainly the Erie County (Lazarsfeld, Berelson, & Gaudet, 1944) and Elmira (Berelson, Lazarsfeld, & McPhee, 1954) studies have not been immune to criticism, either on purely methodological grounds (Maccoby, 1955; Maccoby & Hyman, 1959; Rossi, 1959) or the limitations of their empirical boundaries (Chaffee & Hochheimer, 1985; McClure & Patterson, 1974; O'Keefe, 1975, 1982). Over the years, however, these studies have maintained an unexpected vitality, their vividness enhanced, no doubt, by comparison to the pallid voter behavior studies (Campbell, Converse, Miller, & Stokes, 1960; Campbell, Gurin, & Miller, 1954) that followed them.

In the 1970s all that changed. Four major panel studies were initiated (Graber, 1984; Mendlesohn & O'Keefe, 1976; Patterson 1980; Patterson & McClure, 1976) not only to challenge the "limited effects" hypotheses that had emerged after the Erie County and Elmira studies, but to explore contemporary concerns focusing on media uses and gratifications, the informational role of television, and theories of cognitive processing. Ironically, none of these newer studies has been very successful in undermining among the general public the "milestone" status of the Lazarsfeld or Berelson studies. Although all directly challenge the notion that mass

AUTHOR'S NOTE: This investigation was supported in part by a grant from the University Research Council of the University of North Carolina at Chapel Hill.

Correspondence and requests for reprints: Seth Finn, Department of Radio, Television, and Motion Pictures, Swain Hall 044A, University of North Carolina, Chapel Hill, NC 27514.

media have only "limited effects" on voter decision making, none of them has provided a very effective antidote to the general belief that the "two-step flow" is the primary mechanism by which mass media make their influence felt in the political environment.

The Erie County Data

Chaffee and Hochheimer (1985), in their recent review of early researches in political communication, note with some exasperation that Lazarsfeld and his associates overlooked much of their own evidence in support of direct mass media effects. In particular, they cite the fact that when

> Lazarsfeld asked voters in the post-election survey what sources had pro-
> vided information that led them to arrive at their vote decisions. . . . More
> than one-half said either radio or newspapers had been the single most
> important source, but less than one-fourth cited a personal source as impor-
> tant. (pp. 272-273)

But to understand why Lazarsfeld and others chose to disregard these find-ings, one must look at what went wrong with the Erie County study—the failures in the methodology of data collection that were recognized too late.

Rossi (1959) provides perhaps the best explanation in his review 25 years ago, explaining how the researchers had created a model that equat-ed the role of the voter with that of a consumer. According to Rossi, Lazarsfeld anticipated that the "voter vacillates between one and the other candidate as propaganda from both sides filters down to him" (p. 16). The basic assumption was that the voter would record many changes of mind and that the causal connection between mass media messages and voter decision making would be easy to verify. But, as Rossi explains, that was not the case:

> The model turned out to be wrong at several crucial points. First it was dis-
> covered that on the electoral "market" there was a large number of voters
> with strong "brand loyalties". . . . Second, most voters had made up their
> minds very early in the campaign. . . . Out of 600 respondents in the main
> panel, only 54 persons were found who changed preferences during the
> study. Third, in the absence of changes in voting preferences, effects of the
> mass media and the campaign could not be clearly discerned. (p. 17)

In essence, then, the researchers' original model had overestimated the short-term direct effects of the mass media. In anticipation of numerous vote changes they had expended considerable effort in content analyzing newspapers and radio broadcast as well as obtaining careful measures of voter exposure to campaign news. All these efforts went for naught, however, when only 54 of the 600 panel members recorded changes in their voting preferences.

Given the small number of cases and the strictly inferential relationship between exposure to mass media content and changes in voting preference, it was extremely difficult to make a convincing argument about the impact of mass media. Rossi concludes that the most convincing relationships turned out to be associations between candidate preference and background variables. Furthermore, the

> homogeneity of political preference within the respondents' families, and the frequent mention of personal contacts as reasons for their changes in voting preference led to the realization that the electoral choice was more of a "group decision" than an individual one. . . . there was more evidence of the effectiveness of personal influence on voters than there was evidence for the effectiveness of mass media. (p. 19)

There is no need to repeat here the criticisms of the "two-step flow" as being a speculative finding that emerged from fragmentary data. The point that needs to be emphasized instead is that Lazarsfeld's inability to confirm the anticipated direct effects of the mass media stems not so much from countervening evidence, but methodological weaknesses in the Erie County study that only became apparent once the results were in. It is tantalizing to consider what sort of treatise *The People's Choice* might have been if 300 changes in voting preference had been recorded instead of 54.

These methodological weaknesses in the Erie County study did not escape Rossi's (1959) attention in his proposals for future research. First among them was the suggestion that researchers abandon representative samples in favor of sampling designs that would maximize the number of panel members who reported changes in voting preferences. As Rossi reasoned:

> It would make little difference in the evaluation of either the Elmira or the earlier Erie County studies if it were discovered that the samples interviewed were "unrepresentative" (but unbiased). The major interest of the analyst and the reader is not in whether the results hold for Erie County or Elmira, but in whether the differences between subgroups would hold up under replication.

> In fact, a good case can be made that the representativeness of the surveys . . . actually hindered the analysis at many points. For example, the number of changers found in both the Erie County and the Elmira study was extremely small, the variance of stability (or change) being correspondingly slight in the universes involved. How much more soundly based would be findings drawn from a larger number of changers! (Rossi, 1959, p. 45)

Rossi's suggestions seem to be at the heart of devising a panel study that effectively weighs the relative impact of mass media and interpersonal sources in voter decision making. If the "two-step flow" is a fragmentary hypothesis, then the countervening empirical evidence must be drawn from the cases of voters who have shifted their preferences. Sampling designs must be developed to optimize the number of opportunities to observe changes, and data collection methods must be employed that permit direct evidence of the sources and types of information that effected those changes.

An Exploratory Study

The 1984 North Carolina general election provided especially favorable conditions in which to pursue the type of "vote changer" study that Rossi called for. First, three major campaigns—for U.S. president, U.S. Senate, and state governor—could be monitored simultaneously. Second, the state's political environment was charged with the sorts of cross-pressures that were conducive to shifts in voter commitment.[1] And third, for first time a unique computer-based data collection and storage system (Heise & Simmons, 1985, p. 431) was available for the unobtrusive tracking of a cross-section of University of North Carolina undergraduates on an almost weekly basis. Though admittedly an unrepresentative sample of North Carolina voters, the use of primarily first-time voters was yet another factor that might heighten the probability of vote changing over the limited span of the study (O'Keefe & Liu, 1980). Even more crucial, however, was the opportunity to record—at intervals of 10 days or less—verbal self-reports of changes in voter commitment that reliably linked voting shifts to specific sources and types of campaign information.

DATA COLLECTION

The panel study was conducted using the Computer Administered Panel Study (CAPS) facility at the Institute for Research in Social Science (IRSS) at the University of North Carolina at Chapel Hill.

Sample

IRSS recruits and trains approximately 100 participants each year, who constitute a representative sample of the undergraduate student body, to complete a variety of sociological and psychological tests during 20 one-hour sessions at approximately weekly intervals from October through April. At the time of the study (October and November 1984), 94 students were participating. Of the students, 87 were U.S. citizens of voting age, and 78 were eligible to vote in North Carolina elections (9 others were eligible in other states).

Administration of Questionnaires

Three separate questionnaires were developed for the study. One questionnaire—a survey of mass media usage—was incorporated into a comprehensive background survey compiled by IRSS and administered during the first (October 8-14) wave of the panel study. Also administered for the first of four times was a second questionnaire designed specifically to poll the student participants on their support (strong, moderate, weak, or uncommitted)[2] for the Republican and Democratic candidates for the presidential, U.S. Senate, and gubernatorial contests.

Once the student's initial level of support was recorded in computer memory, each participant was prompted at approximately weekly intervals to see if there had been any change in his or her levels of commitment to voting for each candidate.[3] At subsequent interview sessions, students were asked to reconsider their previous levels of support and record any changes on a seven-point scale. Those who did were then asked to respond to two open-ended questions:

(1) "What was the new information that led you to change your opinion?"
(2) "Can you describe who told you this information or where you heard, saw, or read it?"

During the second (October 17-23), third (October 24-30), and fourth (October 31-November 6) waves, the participants' levels of support for candidates were similarly probed. As before, the use of the two open-ended questions was always contingent upon the participants' first registering an opinion-change in a particular electoral contest. Accordingly, collection of political data often constituted only a minute or two of their weekly, hour-long sessions. In comparison to the longer sociological and psychological instruments they completed at the computer console, this weekly polling was a relatively unobtrusive diversion.

During the fifth (November 7-13) wave, which began the day after the election, this procedure was slightly amended. First, as an added check on the validity of their postelection responses, participants were not prompted with previously collected data. Instead, they were asked if they had voted or not, and then given the opportunity to record their election day level of commitment or explain why they had failed to vote.[4] Because there was no prompt about previous voting levels, a stricter criterion was instituted before the normal open-ended questions about information and sources were invoked. Only if the students had not been previously committed to

any candidate in the race (that is, they had been uncommitted at the previous session) or their level of commitment had moved two or more levels
from its previous position, were they asked to describe the type and source
of information that effected the change.

ANALYSIS OF
QUANTITATIVE DATA

In gross numbers, the results were as follows. Of the 87 students, 54
(62%) registered one or more shifts in their commitment to vote for candidates during the five-week period. In fact, 26 (30%) registered two or
more changes, so that all totaled there were 91 changes made. Opinion-
changes were reflected by 25 cases in the presidential race, 29 in the U.S.
Senate race, and 37 in the North Carolina governor's race. Figures 23.1,
23.2, and 23.3 provide a graphic representation of the percentage of voters who composed each level of commitment during the time-frame of the
study. The seven bands move from the strongest level of support for the
Republican candidate at the bottom to the strongest level of support for the
Democratic candidate at the top.[5]

In Figure 23.1, aside from the overwhelming degree of support for
President Reagan, one is struck by the relative paucity of uncommitted student voters when the first wave was initiated. As one might expect the most
common change in opinion was simply the reinforcement of an earlier
commitment (44%). The movement of voters out of the ranks of the
uncommitted accounts for another 32% of the shifts (the numbers reflect
six who began uncommitted and two others who subsequently drifted in
and out of the category).

By comparison, in Figure 23.2 and especially Figure 23.3, the data
reveal much larger contingents of uncommitted voters at the start. In the
Helms-Hunt campaign, 41% of the shifts reflect changes from uncommitted to committed. Interestingly, in this controversial race, the next largest
contingent (24%) is comprised of converts from one candidate to the
other. It is in the governor's race, however, that the crystallization of opinion is most dramatic. In that race, more than 30% of the sample is uncommitted five weeks before the election, and their shifts from uncommitted to
committed account for 61% of the changes in opinion. The next largest
group, which amounts to only 16% of the recorded changes, comprises
students whose opinions have wavered, that is, their level of commitment
diminished at some point in the study.

All in all, the data document fundamental differences in the shape of the
various campaigns, suggesting not only that minds are made up earlier in
the presidential and, to some extent, the senatorial races, but that the information flow for each of these campaigns has a distinctive pattern. These
patterns took on considerably greater detail during the next phase of the

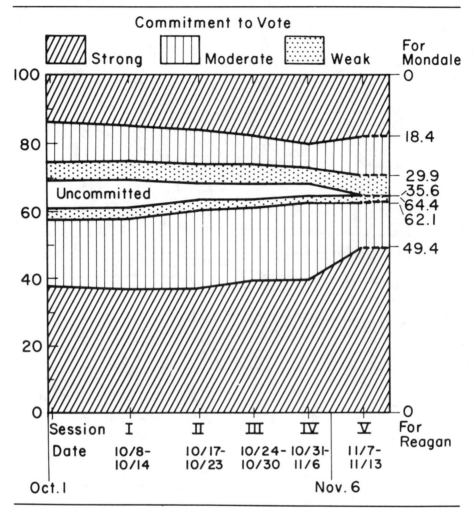

Figure 23.1 Distribution of commitment levels among panel participants (N = 87) for U.S. presidential candidates in October and November 1984.

analysis—the coding of the verbatim responses of panel members who reported shifts in voting preferences.

ANALYSIS OF
QUALITATIVE DATA

As noted above, the interviews were conducted at specially programmed computer terminals that prompted panel members with open-ended ques-

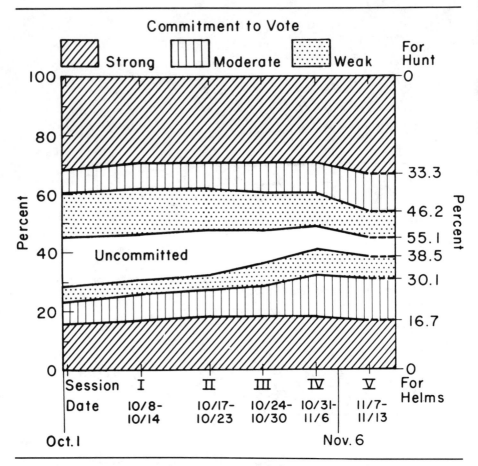

Figure 23.2 Distribution of commitment levels among panel participants (N = 78) for U.S. Senate candidates in October and November 1984.

tions only when they indicated changes in their level of commitment to voting for a specific candidate. Thus questions relating to the sources and types of political messages used in decision making were invoked only when a panel member indicated a shift in commitment—some 91 times over the course of the study.

Coding

Given the relatively small number of cases to work with, care was taken to develop rather broad categories for coding. But even more important was the realization that moving from a focus on individual voter decision making to an analysis of "vote-changes" provided a unique opportunity to

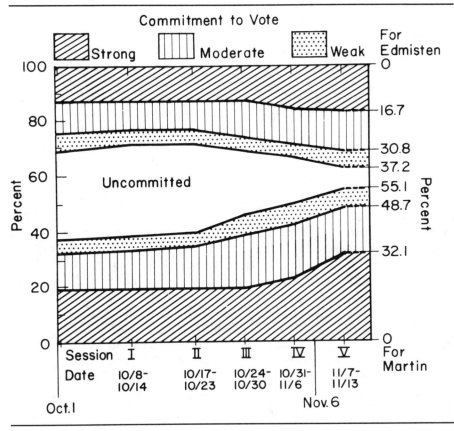

Figure 23.3 Distribution of commitment levels among panel participants (N = 78) for North Carolina gubernatorial candidates in October and November 1984.

adopt a systems level approach (Chaffee, 1975), probing for impediments to the flow of objective and relevant campaign information.

Thus the verbatim responses were analyzed with regard to five variables related to the diffusion of campaign information. First and foremost, of course, was the source: interpersonal, print, or broadcast? Next came two variables characterizing the quality of the information: Was it related to issues or images? Was it biased or impartial? And finally, the responses were analyzed with regard to the voter's depth of involvement: Was the voter actively seeking or accidentally exposed to the information? Was the degree of mental effort in processing the information high or low?

Five graduate students independently coded the verbatim responses, "sieving" each case (Guetzkow, 1950) in search of the 11 attributes that composed the five variables noted above. Although there were a few exceptional cases, the classification of a case with regard to each attribute was judged valid only if at least four of the five coders registered positive agreement for that particular attribute.[6] When the coders did not achieve a positive consensus about any attribute of a variable, then the case was judged ambiguous for that variable, and eliminated from portions of the subsequent analysis. In a few cases, coders registered a positive consensus on more than one attribute of a single variable. Those cases were treated as ambiguous for that variable also. (See the Appendix for a copy of the coding instrument.)

Primary Sources of Information

Of the 91 verbatim responses, 75 were judged classifiable with regard to the primary source of information. The results revealed that broadcast messages predominated, accounting for 45% of the total. The print media accounted for another 35%, and interpersonal messages composed the remaining 20%. Taking the election contests individually, however, there was a marked contrast between the heavy use of print media (primarily newspapers) in the governor's race, and its clearly secondary role, along with interpersonal communication, in the presidential and U.S. Senate races. Of the 37 classifiable messages in the governor's race, 43% came from print sources. The proportions dropped to 24% and 26%, respectively, for the presidential and U.S. Senate races. These differences are to some degree supported by the computation of chi-square, which approaches significance when information sources are contrasted with election contests (χ^2 (4, $N = 75$) = 7.07, $p = .13$).

Message-Related Variables

The use of information that was characterized as either issue-oriented or image-oriented turned out to be significantly related to both specific media (χ^2 (2, $N = 62$) = 7.74, $p < .05$) and particular campaigns (χ^2 (2, $N = 68$) = 6.38, $p < .05$). Both these results appear to reflect the special circumstances of the governor's race, which was marked by a substantially higher dependence upon print messages whose content was issue-oriented. Despite the small number of cases, in fact, there is a significant relationship between media source and message orientation (issue or image) within the governor's race alone (χ^2 (2, $N = 29$) = 4.05, $p < .05$). The data, therefore, suggest that image-oriented messages carried by the broadcast media tended to dominate the campaigns for the two federal offices in the last weeks of the campaign, and issue-oriented print messages played a much more important role for these student voters in the governor's race.

Within the realm of message bias, the data reveal significant relationships as well. As in the case of message orientation, message bias is significantly related to specific contests (χ^2 (2, N = 70) = 8.71, p < .05) and particular media (χ^2 (2, N = 62) = 19.23, p < .001). Furthermore, the relationships between media bias and information sources are significant within each of the three campaigns, albeit in various combinations. Although interpersonal messages were judged to be uniformly biased in all three campaigns, and print messages as somewhat more impartial, the broadcast media provided impartial messages in the presidential race and a preponderance of biased ones in the U.S. Senate and governor's races.

In retrospect, these data seem to reflect once again the heavily saturated information environment of the presidential race. Daily network news coverage plus three televized debates apparently satiated the panel participants' need for information during the last month of the campaign. However, the panel participants did not receive as heavy a dose of such impartial coverage for the U.S. Senate and governor's race. Given the leaner information environment, they tended to cite candidate-financed messages more often, whether they be TV spots, print ads, or campaign brochures.

Information-Processing Variables

The second pair of characteristics coded for each message and its source was the degree of information-seeking and depth of processing exhibited in each opinion-change situation. It is important to recognize that these two characteristics are contingent upon not only the content of the message, but also the behavior of the participants. And this additional component demonstrates itself in the data in a not unexpected way. Although the results of the coding reflect significant relationships between specific media and degree of information-seeking (χ^2 (2, N = 61) = 21.64, p < .001) and depth of processing (χ^2 (2, N = 49) = 20.07, p < .001), in neither case do significant relationships exist between these information-processing characteristics and particular campaigns. Thus it appears that voters' initiative (or passivity) can compensate for (or exacerbate) the distinctive impact of any one medium and its messages within a campaign.

Nevertheless the raw data from the content analysis are instructive about the relationship between information processing and information sources. Of the 9 classifiable voter changes that are attributed to interpersonal sources, 8 reflect accidental exposure; 9 out of 10 were characterized as requiring a low level of information processing. For the print media, the proportions are reversed. Of 23 cases, 22 reflect active information processing. Of 16 voter-change cases, 14 were judged as exhibiting a high level of mental effort. These data suggest that interpersonal messages are the result of inadvertent exposure requiring low processing effort and print messages are actively sought and require high effort.

In regard to broadcast messages, the picture is not so clear. Although processing effort was rated low in 17 of 23 classifiable cases, information-seeking was judged active in 18 out of 29 cases, 15 of those occurring in the U.S. presidential and Senate races. By way of an ex post facto accounting, one might consider the relative infrequency of broadcast coverage of the governor's race, making exposure more random. By contrast, for the presidential and U.S. Senate campaigns, the participants could seek out TV news programs and debates with a much higher degree of confidence that relevant political information would be presented.

CONCLUSIONS

When attempting to apply the results of this study to a model of voting behavior among the general public, one must proceed with due caution because of the small numbers, the use of a student sample, and the short time frame. Nevertheless, the richness of the qualitative data at hand should permit us legitimately to explore the processes observed among these student voters even if we unknowingly exaggerate their relevance to a more heterogeneous voting public.

Although early decision making in presidential races has been documented since the earliest panel surveys (Lazarsfeld, Berelson, & Gaudet, 1944; Berelson, Lazarsfeld, & McPhee, 1954), this exploratory study has provided comparative data indicating that campaign situations become relatively more fluid as one moves down the ballot. Thus the information environment in which the voter behaves is contingent upon structural limitations that reflect, for instance, the economic realities of broadcast markets (Campbell, Alford, & Henry, 1984; Luttbeg, 1983).

The content analysis of verbatim responses has suggested many interactions between the information environment, message characteristics, the status of the office, and voter information-processing. Data from the North Carolina governor's campaign in particular suggest that active information-seekers can overcome deficiencies in the information environment that occur in lower status elections by using the print media to obtain impartial information that is unavailable from either interpersonal or broadcast sources. One might also draw parallels between voter behavior in the governor's race and the problems of opinion formation in presidential primary campaigns (Kennamer & Chaffee, 1982).

Finally, one must return to the question of Lazarsfeld's two-step flow. At the aggregate level, one is struck by the relatively few times that interpersonal messages were noted as influential in this study. Even more interesting, however, are the similar characterizations ascribed to interpersonal and broadcast media. Both are characterized as image-oriented and requiring low mental effort regardless of the content. Furthermore, at the level of the governor's race, panel participants most often indicated that they had been inadvertently exposed to most broadcast and interpersonal messages, which were not only image-oriented, but also biased. In retrospect, then, we may see that the actual role of the so-called opinion leader is to translate print information into oral forms for easier processing—a role that television seems to have subsumed in the case of major electoral contests.

Overall, these results are not sufficient to support a comprehensive model. But they do provide guidance for future research. They suggest strongly that the leaner the information environment, the more interesting and the more fruitful it may be to study the campaign. Under conditions of scarce information, the voter tends to operate as a classic information-seeker, that is, in search of information in order to reduce uncertainty. But within that environment, an important trade-off occurs between information-processing costs and message bias.

Voters must weigh the high cost of securing impartial information—primarily from print sources, although broadcast media can be used selectively—against the low cost of incidental learning from interpersonal and broadcast sources. It is in such an environment that campaign strategists—given sufficient resources—may be able to shape the flow of information significantly, especially when voters are content to make decisions on the basis of biased information to which they have been accidentally exposed. To their credit, the 87 students who participated in this panel study demonstrated a high degree of active information-seeking. In that regard, however, they may be very unrepresentative of the typical American voter for whom each new bit of political information most likely exacts a strikingly higher price in terms of mental effort.

APPENDIX:
CODING THE VERBATIM RESPONSES

When we coded the verbatim student responses to the two open-ended questions, we found the replies often took on the character of a vignette rather than a fill-in-the-blank answer. To enhance validity, the coding instrument had to exploit the richness of the data (Andren, 1981). But to assure reliability, it had to provide considerable detail about the coders' judgments. Accordingly, a coding instrument was devised that listed eleven positive statements reflecting the basic attributes of the five variables under study. Coders, in turn, indicated their judgments using a five-point Likert scale.

The first section of the coding instrument was used only to identify the transcript from which the coder was working. The second section is reproduced below.

II. Please consider the following eleven statements describing the student's verbatim response. How much do you agree or disagree that these statements are accurate characterizations of the student's responses?

SA = Strongly Agree   sa = somewhat agree   un = undecided
SD = Strongly Disagree   sd = somewhat disagree

(1) The student's change in political support
     was based on relevant campaign issues.   SA   sa   un   sd   SD

(2) The student's change in political support
     was based on images of the candidate.   SA   sa   un   sd   SD

(3) The source of the information was primarily
     a friend or relative.   SA   sa   un   sd   SD

(4) The source of the information was primarily
     from the print media.   SA   sa   un   sd   SD

(5) The source of the information was primarily
     from the broadcast media.   SA   sa   un   sd   SD

(6) The information came from a biased source.   SA   sa   un   sd   SD

(7) The information came from an impartial
     source.   SA   sa   un   sd   SD

(8) The student actively sought the information
     that changed his or her mind.   SA   sa   un   sd   SD

(9) The student was accidentally exposed to the
     information that changed his or her mind.   SA   sa   un   sd   SD

(10) Consideration of the information took a
     great deal of mental effort.   SA   sa   un   sd   SD

(11) The student didn't have to pay much
     attention to understand the information.   SA   sa   un   sd   SD

As M.A. students in a mass communication department, the coders were relatively well-informed about the mechanics of the panel study and required only brief characterizations of the attributes for which they were coding. Some discussion arose about the politically biased aspects of televised debates. A consensus was reached, however, that televised debates were to be considered an impartial source of information. All other perceptions of bias or impartiality were those inferred by the coders from the verbatim transcripts.

Coefficients of agreement were computed for each set of responses using the computational method developed by Krippendorff (1980). The estimates of intercoder reliability for the successfully classified cases were 57.3% higher than chance for the "issue" attribute, 51.3% for "image," 80.2% for "interpersonal" sources, 64.6% for "print," 70.8% for "broadcast," 51.3% for bias, 60.1% for "impartial," 53.3% for "active" information-seeking, 35.8% for "accidental," 58.6% for "high" mental effort, and 53.8% for "low." None of these results was judged problematic given the rigorous character of Krippendorff's formulation, which is sensitive to the distribution of the results, and the fact that although cases were classified on the basis of positive agreement on a single attribute, these percentages reflect negative agreement among coders for the complementary attribute(s) of the same variable.

NOTES

1. Not only was the Helms-Hunt campaign to be distinguished as the most expensive U.S. Senate race in American history, but two Republican encumbents—Reagan and Helms—were seeking the support of traditionally Democratic voters, whose party had been badly split by the battle for the gubernatorial nomination (Snider, 1985).

2. These four levels ultimately resulted in a seven-point scale in which "Uncommitted" provided the center-point and "Strongly committed to voting for" either the Republican or the Democratic nominee constituted the end-points. Lazarsfeld, Berelson, and Gaudet (1944) and Berelson, Lazarsfeld, and McPhee (1954) were criticized by Maccoby (1956) for failing to quantify changes in degree of candidate support.

3. For the first wave, the participants were asked their current level of support and then questioned retrospectively to estimate their commitment levels around October 1. For the second, third, and fourth waves, no retrospective question was needed, because each participant's past level of support for the candidates was available in computer memory and automatically recalled to tailor the question to the participant's particular situation. Thus participants were told what they had indicated as their level of support for a candidate—beginning with the presidential race—at the previous session, and then asked whether or not it had remained the same. If they responded, "Yes," then the computer moved on to the U.S. Senate race for North Carolina voters or terminated the session for nonresidents. If they responded, "No," then they were asked the two open-ended questions before the computer moved on to the next race or terminated the session.

4. Of the North Carolina residents, 15 of 78 and 3 of the 9 out-of-state students failed to vote. Of the nonvoters, 10 explained that they had problems in securing absentee ballots, 4 others did not register in time, and 2 were too busy with classwork on election day. Only 2 students said they were indifferent to the results. Given the positive intentions of most of these participants, no effort was made to exclude their cases from the analysis. They account for 11 of the 91 occasions when participants recorded changes in commitment to voting for a candidate. For lack of a better indicator, their levels of commitment at the end of the fourth wave have been interpreted as their likely votes on election day.

5. Even though the subsequent analysis will disregard one-point shifts in voter commitment level that were recorded after the election, these minor changes are reflected in the final vote tallies in Figures 23.1, 23.2, and 23.3. The reader should also be aware that these charts reveal only the net effect of voter changes from period to period.

6. This turned out to be a stringent requirement. Even in a category as basic as the primary source of the information cited, there was 80% agreement for only 75 of the 91 cases, either because the panel member's response was not specific or, as a few respondents indicated, their decisions were derived from intrapersonal sources—a recounting of information stored in memory. But ultimately the stringent selection method strengthened the analysis. Although the number of missing cases may have been problematic in a basically descriptive effort, using only definitive cases helped to highlight the relationships between media and types of information this study was attempting to explore.

REFERENCES

Andren, G. (1981). Reliability and content analysis. In K. E. Rosengren (Ed.). *Advances in content analysis* (pp. 43-67). Beverly Hills, CA: Sage.

Berelson, B., Lazarsfeld, P. F., & McPhee, W. (1954). *Voting: A study of opinion formation in a presidential campaign.* Chicago: University of Chicago Press.

Campbell, A., Converse, P. E., Miller, W. E., & Stokes, D. E. (1960). *The American voter.* New York: John Wiley.

Campbell, A., Gurin, G., & Miller, W. E. (1954). *The voter decides.* Evanston, IL: Row, Peterson.

Campbell, J. E., Alford, J. R., & Henry, K. (1984). Television markets and congressional elections. *Legislative Studies Quarterly, 9,* 665-678.

Chaffee, S. H. (1975). The diffusion of political information. In S. H. Chaffee (Ed.), *Political communication: Issues and strategies for research* (pp. 85-128). Beverly Hills, CA: Sage.

Chaffee, S. H., & Hochheimer, J. L. (1985). The beginnings of political communication research in the United States: Origins of the "limited effects" model. In E. M. Rogers & F. Balle (Eds.), *The media revolution in America and Western Europe* (pp. 267-296). Norwood, NJ: Ablex.

Graber, D. A. (1984). *Processing the news: How people tame the information tide.* New York: Longman.

Guetzkow, H. (1950). Unitizing and categorizing problems in coding qualitative data. *Journal of Clinical Psychology, 6,* 47-58.

Heise, D. R., & Simmons, R. G. (1985). Some computer-based developments in sociology. *Science, 228,* 428-433.

Kennamer, J. D., & Chaffee, S. H. (1982). Communication of political information during early presidential primaries: Cognition, affect, and uncertainty. In M. Burgoon (Ed.), *Communication yearbook 5* (pp. 627-650). New Brunswick, NJ: Transaction Books.

Krippendorff, K. (1980). *Content analysis: An introduction to its methodology.* Beverly Hills, CA: Sage.

Lazarsfeld, P. F., Berelson, B., & Gaudet, H. (1944). *The people's choice.* New York: Columbia University Press.

Luttbeg, N. R. (1983). Television viewing audience and congressional district incongruity: A handicap for the challenger? *Journal of Broadcasting, 27,* 411-417.

Maccoby, E. E. (1956). Pitfalls in the analysis of panel data: A research note on some technical aspects of voting. *American Journal of Sociology, 61,* 359-362.

Maccoby, E. E., & Hyman, R. (1959). Measurement problems in panel studies. In E. Burdick & A. J. Brodbeck (Eds.), *American voting behavior* (pp. 68-79). New York: Free Press.

McClure, R. D., & Patterson, T. E. (1974). Television news and political advertising: The impact of exposure on voter beliefs. *Communication Research, 1,* 3-31.

Mendelsohn, H., & O'Keefe, G. J. (1976). *The people choose a president: Influences on voter decision making.* New York: Praeger.

O'Keefe, G. J. (1975). Political campaigns and mass communication research. In S. H. Chaffee (Ed.), *Political communication: Issues and strategies for research* (pp. 129-164). Beverly Hills, CA: Sage.

O'Keefe, G. J. (1982). The changing context of interpersonal communication in political campaigns. In M. Burgoon (Ed.), *Communication yearbook 5* (pp. 667-681). New Brunswick, NJ: Transaction Books.

O'Keefe, G. J., & Liu, J. (1980). First-time voters: Do media matter? *Journal of Communication 30(4),* 124-129.

Patterson, T. E. (1980). *The mass media election.* New York: Praeger.

Patterson, T. E., & McClure, R. D. (1976). *The unseeing eye: The myth of television power in national elections.* New York: Putnam.

Rossi, P. H. (1959). Four landmarks in voting research. In E. Burdick & A. J. Brodbeck (Eds.), *American voting behavior* (pp. 5-54). New York: Free Press.

Snider, W. D. (1985). *Helms & Hunt: The North Carolina senate race, 1984.* Chapel Hill: University of North Carolina Press.

VIII ● INSTRUCTIONAL COMMUNICATION

24 ● Popular, Rejected, and Supportive Preadolescents: Social-Cognitive and Communicative Characteristics

BRANT R. BURLESON ●
PATRICIA AMASON WALTMAN

Purdue University

I N recent years, an increasing volume of research has been devoted to identifying the characteristics of children who are either popular with or rejected by their peers. This research has been stimulated by studies indicating (a) that interaction with peers plays an important role in the development of several cognitive, emotional, and social skills during childhood (see the review of Hartup, 1983), and (b) that children rejected by peers experience significantly higher levels of personal and social maladjustment later in life (see the reviews of Burleson, 1986; Ladd & Asher, 1985). Researchers examining the correlates of acceptance by peers have found peer popularity associated with several physical and demographic characteristics (see Asher, Oden, & Gottman, 1977; Hartup, 1983). More interesting, however, are the results of studies indicating that certain cognitive and behavioral characteristics can be used to distinguish between popular and rejected children. For example, popularity with peers has been found positively associated with displaying a positive interactional style, dis-

AUTHORS' NOTE: The authors gratefully acknowledge the administration and staff of the Fayetteville, Arkansas, Public Schools, and especially Mrs. LaWanda Waltman, for their aid in the conduct of this study.

Correspondence and requests for reprints: Brant R. Burleson, Department of Communication, Purdue University, West Lafayette, IN 47907.

pensing positive reinforcement, initiating friendly approaches to other children, support giving and nurturance, and cooperative and norm-following behavior (for example, Coie & Kupersmidt, 1983; Hartup, Glazer, & Charlesworth, 1967; Ladd, 1983; Rubin & Daniels-Beirness, 1983). In contrast, rejection by peers has been found to be associated with verbal abuse and physical aggression, disruptive or off-task behavior, nega-tive reinforcement, and inappropriate initiations of interaction (Dodge, 1983; Dodge, Coie, & Brakke, 1982; Ladd, 1983; Vosk, Forehand, Parker, & Rickard, 1982).

Although extant research on the cognitive and behavioral correlates of acceptance by peers is suggestive, much of this research is limited in that only quite general assessments of interactional and/or cognitive styles have been obtained from children. For example, the "behavioral assess-ments" obtained in a number of studies have been limited to simple ratings of children's behaviors by teachers or experimenters. Obviously, such per-ceptually based data provide little information about the specific cognitive and communicative skills contributing to acceptance by peers. Similarly, the frequency counts of behavior types (for example, number of aggressive acts, number of altruistic acts) obtained in many studies generally do not provide information sufficient to identify qualitative differences in skill lev-els (see Burleson, 1984a; Renshaw & Asher, 1982).

Recently, however, researchers have begun to investigate relationships between acceptance by peers and more specific measures of children's social-cognitive and communicative skills. For example, several studies (Kurdek & Krile, 1982; Marcus, 1980; McGuire & Weisz, 1982; Rothen-berg, 1970) have found acceptance by peers positively associated with measures of affective and social role-taking ability. These studies suggest that popular children have more advanced social-cognitive skills.

Several specific communication skills also have been found related to degree of acceptance by peers. Research conducted on children's "group entry" strategies (Dodge, Schlundt, Schocken, & Delugach, 1983; Putal-laz, 1983; Putallaz & Gottman, 1981) has found that unpopular children tend to employ entry strategies that call undue attention to themselves and disrupt the ongoing activities of the group whereas popular children more frequently employ strategies reflecting an awareness of and accommoda-tion to the activities of the group. The comparatively large literature focus-ing on children's conflict management skills indicates that rejected children are more likely to perceive others as acting with hostile intentions, are more likely to become involved in conflict situations, and tend to employ aggres-sive, agonistic, and unfriendly strategies in seeking to resolve conflicts (Renshaw & Asher, 1983; Richard & Dodge, 1982; Rubin & Daniels-Beirness, 1983; see the review of Burleson, 1986). In contrast, popular children appear to have relatively large repertoires of conflict management strategies that are populated with friendly, prosocial, and cooperative tactics reflecting a concern with both the instrumental and relational aspects of conflict situations. Children's referential communication skills also appear related to acceptance by peers, particularly during early childhood; several studies (Burleson, 1985; Deutsch, 1974; Gottman, Gonso, & Rasmussen, 1975) have found referential ability and popularity moderately associated during early and middle childhood, though some research (Rubin, 1972; Tesch & Oden, 1981) suggests that referential skill and popularity are unassociated by late childhood. Burleson (1985) obtained assessments of six different communication skills (general listener-adapted communication skill, comforting skill, persuasive skill, and three types of referential skill) from a sample of first and third graders; this researcher found that his measure of comforting skill best discriminated between accepted and rejected children. Thus several distinct social-cognitive and communicative skills have been found associated with degree of acceptance by peers.

The present study represents an effort to extend in several ways prior work on the specific social-cognitive and communicative skills contributing to acceptance by peers. First, most previous work on the cognitive and communicative correlates of acceptance has studied preschoolers or children in the early elementary grades; very little research has examined the correlates of acceptance in groups of older children and adolescents. This is unfortunate because considerable research indicates that preadolescence is a particularly important developmental period. Numerous studies (Berndt, 1982; Selman, 1980; Smollar & Youniss, 1982; see the review of Serafica, 1982) have found that conceptions of and expectations for the friendship relationship exhibit major qualitative changes during the preadolescent period; whereas younger children tend to think of friendship in terms of specific behaviors and activities in which friends engage, preadolescents begin thinking of friendship as a relationship based on such psychological qualities as intimacy, trust, and mutual caring. These findings suggest that the cognitive and communicative abilities that predict acceptance by peers in preadolescence may differ from the abilities that predict acceptance in younger groups of children. Moreover, a large body of research (see the review of Hartup, 1983) indicates that during preadolescence, peers become perhaps the most important reference group and socializing agent for the child. For these reasons, then, it would seem important to determine the cognitive and communicative characteristics of accepted and rejected preadolescents. The present study thus sought to determine some of the characteristics of popular and unpopular fifth- and sixth-grade children.

The present study also sought to extend prior work by employing somewhat different measures of cognitive and communicative skills. For example, some research (for example, Rothenberg, 1970) indicates that the social perception skill of affective role-taking is a determinant of acceptance by peers. In the field of communication, researchers working with the "constructivist" theoretical perspective (see Delia, O'Keefe, & O'Keefe, 1982; O'Keefe & Delia, 1982) have argued that *all* social perception processes proceed through the application of the cognitive structures termed *interpersonal constructs*. Persons' systems of interpersonal constructs differ in the number of elements they contain, and individual differences in construct system differentiation (or "cognitive complexity") have been found associated with individual differences in several social perception skills (see the reviews of Burleson, in press; Delia, O'Keefe, & O'Keefe, 1982). Thus in order to assess the general relationship between acceptance by peers and social perception skill, the present study obtained an assessment of interpersonal cognitive complexity from the preadolescent participants.

The other social-cognitive variable assessed in the present research was "emotional empathy." Defined as the tendency to feel what another feels, emotional empathy has been hypothesized to underlie a wide range of behavioral tendencies (for example, altruism, prosocial actions) related to acceptance by peers (Zahn-Waxler, Iannotti, & Chapman, 1982). Thus far, however, no research has directly assessed the relationship between emotional empathy and acceptance by peers. Consequently, the present study included a self-report measure of empathic tendency recently developed for use with children and adolescents (Bryant, 1982).

Three different communication skills were assessed in the present research: persuasive skill, conflict management skill, and comforting skill.[1] Thus far, only one study (Burleson, 1985) has assessed the relationship between persuasive skill and status among peers; Burleson found that persuasive skills were only a marginally significant predictor of young children's (first and third graders') acceptance by peers. It remains possible, however, that the manner in which a child attempts to persuade peers to engage in various actions may influence that child's level of acceptance in the peer group; thus the present investigation sought to determine the relationship between persuasive skill and acceptance among preadolescents.

A relatively large number of studies (for example, Asher & Renshaw, 1981; Renshaw & Asher, 1983; Richard & Dodge, 1982; Rubin & Daniels-Beirness, 1983) have examined the influence of children's conflict management skills on their degree of acceptance or rejection by peers. Unfortunately, most studies assessing children's conflict management strategies have employed coding systems consisting of rather primitive and global categories (for example, "prosocial" versus "antisocial" strategies; "effective," "submissive," and "aggressive" strategies). In an effort to provide a more detailed and fine-grained analysis of children's conflict strategies, Samter and Ely (1985) developed a coding system consisting of nine hierarchically ordered categories. This system scores strategies for the extent to which proposed solutions to an interpersonal conflict accommodate the rights and legitimate interests of all conflicting parties and reflect a concern with maintaining a positive interpersonal relationship with opponents. Thus strategies seeking to resolve conflict through physical or verbal aggression (actual or threatened) are scored in the lower levels of the hierarchy; strategies attempting to resolve conflicts through simple imperatives or the invocation of relevant rules are scored in the middle levels of the hierarchy; strategies that seek resolution through offering reasons and proposing methods of integrating apparently competing interests are scored in the highest levels of the hierarchy. Clearly, children who typically resolve conflicts through the use of reasoning-oriented and integrative strategies should be better liked by peers than children who routinely employ strategies incorporating physical and/or verbal aggression. Thus we expected preadolescents' conflict management skills to be positively associated with popularity with peers and negatively associated with rejection by peers.

The third communication variable assessed in the present study was comforting skill. In the only prior study examining acceptance by peers in terms of comforting skill, Burleson (1985) found that among six different communication skills, comforting skill best discriminated between accepted and rejected children. Thus in the present research it was expected that comforting skill would be a strong determinant of status with peers. Indeed, research concerned with children's conceptions of and expectations for friendships with peers (see Serafica, 1982) indicates that preadolescents begin to view peers as major sources of comfort and support; the preadolescent period is notorious for its stresses and strains, and children who can help peers cope with their problems may be especially liked. Thus it was anticipated that comforting skill would be a particularly good predictor of status among peers.

As just noted, the preadolescent period is frequently a difficult developmental stage; youngsters at this point in life begin to encounter all the problems associated with the transition from childhood to adulthood. Physiological changes, cognitive developments, and changing social expectations present the child with new demands and new problems (Ausubel, 1954; Berndt, 1983; Fine, 1981; Hess & Goldblatt, 1960). Recent research conducted under the rubric of *social support* (Heller & Swindle, 1983; Rutter, 1983) indicates that peers provide significant aid to one another in helping cope with the stresses and problems typical of the preadolescent period. These findings have led some educators to develop training programs designed to produce "peer facilitators" or "peer counselors," children who are specially coached to help peers cope with a wide range of life problems (Anderson, 1976; Avery, Rider, & Haynes-Clements, 1981; Canning, 1983; Dougherty & Taylor, 1983; Fink, Grandjean, Martin, & Bertolini, 1978; Gray & Tindall, 1974; McCann, 1975). Although such training efforts are praiseworthy, they tend to ignore the possibility that some children may *naturally* function in the role of a "peer counselor." That is, it seems reasonable to assume that some children, because of their

relatively advanced social-cognitive and communicative skills, are spontaneously sought out by other children for support, advice, comfort, and
help in coping with various problems. We are unaware of any previous
research that has attempted to identify and determine the characteristics of
such "natural" peer counselors. Thus additional goals of the present study
included developing a method for identifying children whom peers perceive as especially important sources of social support and determining the
social-cognitive and communicative skills of these natural peer counselors.

In sum, the present study sought to determine some of the cognitive and
communicative skills of popular, rejected, and supportive preadolescents.
In general, it was expected that the social-cognitive and communicative
skills assessed in this study would be positively associated with indices of
popularity with peers and supportiveness and negatively associated with
indices of rejection by peers.

METHOD

Participants

Participants in the study were 32 fifth graders (15 males and 17 females)
and 40 sixth graders (21 males and 19 females) attending a public grammar school in a small southern community. Permission for the children to
participate in the study was obtained from both parents and school authorities. The mean age of the fifth graders was 10 years, 9 months, and the
mean age of the sixth graders was 11 years, 10 months. The children were
from middle-class backgrounds and were largely white.

General Procedures

All measures were obtained through written questionnaires administered by the child's regular classroom teacher. Children were assured of the
confidentiality of their responses, and were assigned a "secret number" to
ensure anonymity. The questionnaires were completed by the children
during the regular school day over a three-week period; the time and order
in which the questionnaires were presented were randomized. Details
regarding the specific measures obtained are presented below.

Social-Cognitive Assessments

Interpersonal Cognitive Complexity. Participants' levels of interpersonal
cognitive complexity (or construct system differentiation) were assessed
through a written, two-role version of Crockett's (1965) Role Category
Questionnaire (RCQ). Participants were asked to describe two classmates,
one whom they liked and one whom they disliked, in as much detail as

possible; they were instructed to pay particular attention to the classmates' habits, beliefs, and ways of treating others in writing their descriptions. These impressions were scored for the number of interpersonal constructs they contained according to a slightly modified version of the coding procedures detailed by Crockett, Press, Delia, and Kenney (1974). In Crockett et al.'s procedures, constructs pertaining to others' physical characteristics, social roles, and specific behaviors are not usually scored. In the present study, however, all constructs elicited by the RCQ were scored because the impressions generated by children and some adolescents often are dominated by constructs pertaining to appearance, roles, and behaviors. The total number of constructs employed in the two impressions served as the index of interpersonal cognitive complexity. For reliability purposes, the impressions produced by approximately 20% of the sample ($N = 14$) were scored by 2 independent coders; interrater reliability, as assessed by Pearson correlation, was .95. Substantial evidence supports the reliability and validity of RCQ assessments of cognitive complexity (see the review of O'Keefe & Sypher, 1981); in particular, although some researchers (for example, Beatty & Payne, 1984) have argued that RCQ measures of cognitive complexity may be confounded by "loquacity" or other general verbal traits, several studies (Burleson, Applegate, & Neuwirth, 1981; Burleson, Waltman, & Samter, in press; Sypher & Applegate, 1982) have found RCQ assessments of cognitive complexity unassociated with independent measures of loquacity, verbal fluency, verbal intelligence, and other general verbal abilities and proclivities.

Emotional Empathy. Participants' levels of emotional empathy were assessed through Bryant's (1982) adaptation of Mehrabian and Epstein's (1972) Emotional Empathy Questionnaire (EEQ). Bryant's version of the EEQ, specially tailored for use with children and adolescents, is composed of 22 seven-point Likert items tapping such aspects of empathy as susceptability to emotional contagion, emotional responsiveness, appreciation of the feelings of others, and sympathetic tendency. Bryant suggests that the total empathy score, rather than distinct factor scores, be used in analyses involving the EEQ; thus this practice was followed in the present study. In the present study, internal consistency of the 22-item EEQ, as assessed by Cronbach's *alpha,* was .76. Bryant (1982) reviews evidence supporting the reliability and validity of this measure of emotional empathy.

Communication Skill Assessments

Three different functional communication skills were assessed in this research: persuasive skill, conflict management skill, and comforting skill. In assessing each type of skill, participants were presented with two hypothetical situations and asked to write what they would say in those situations. To elicit persuasive messages, participants were asked to (a) suppose they wished to persuade a friend to attend a movie rather than go roller-skating, and (b) imagine they wished to persuade their mothers to host an overnight party for a few friends. The conflict management situations involved (a) an acquaintance changing the channel on the participant's television without asking permission when the participant was watching a program he or she enjoyed, and (b) a friend of the participant's refusing to play a card game with the participant after the participant had played a game of Monopoly in order to satisfy the friend's desires. The comforting situations involved (a) a friend being upset because he or she had not been invited to a party that the participant had been invited to, and (b) a friend being upset because he or she had received a low grade on an important test in school. Participants responded to one set of these hypothetical situations (one situation representing each communicative goal) during one test session and responded to the other set of situations during a second test session approximately two weeks later. For each of these situations, participants were instructed to write out exactly what they would say in the situation. Messages elicited by these situations were scored within an appropriate, hierarchically ordered coding system (see below); in cases in which multiple messages were produced in response to a single situation, the highest-level message was retained for purposes of analysis because the interest of the present study was in the child's level of communicative competence. The general method used in the present study to elicit and code message behavior (that is, hierarchical codings of the highest-level message produced in response to hypothetical situations) has been found to yield reliable and valid estimates of person's functional communicative competencies (see Burleson, 1984a, in press; Renshaw & Asher, 1982). Details regarding each of the three hierarchical coding systems used in scoring the messages are presented below.

Persuasive Skill. Messages elicited by the persuasion situations were scored within the nine-level hierarchical coding system developed by Delia, Kline, and Burleson (1979). Composed of three major levels with three subdivisions within each major level, this coding system scores persuasive messages for the extent to which the perspective of the message target is recognized and adapted to. Thus strategies coded within the first major level of the hierarchy failed to consider the perspective of the target by, for example, emphasizing only the needs and interests of the persuader; appeals coded within the second major level provided implicit recognition of and adaptation to the perspective of the target through, for example, refuting potential objections to the request the target might raise; and messages coded within the highest major level of the hierarchy provided explicit recognition of and adaptation to the target's perspective by, for example, showing how compliance with the request would actually benefit the target (for a more detailed description of this coding system, see Delia et al., 1979). Scores for the highest-level strategy used in response to each of these situations were averaged to provide the index of persuasive skill. Scoring reliability, assessed by having 2 independent coders each score approximately 20% of participants' messages, was .94 by Pearson correlation. The extensive evidence supporting the reliability and validity of this approach to the assessment of persuasive skill is summarized by Burleson (in press).

Comforting Skill. Messages produced in response to the two comforting situations were scored within a nine-level hierarchical coding system described by Burleson (1982, 1984b). A modified version of a coding system introduced by Applegate (1980), Burleson's system scores comforting messages for the extent to which the feelings of a distressed other are articulated, elaborated, and legitimized. Strategies coded in the bottom third of this hierarchy implicitly or explicitly denied the legitimacy of the feelings and perspective of the distressed other by, for example, telling the other how he or she *should* feel or act in response to the situation; messages coded in the middle third of the hierarchy provided implicit recognition and legitimation of the other's feelings and perspective by, for example, citing general principles or mitigating circumstances designed to "explain away" the other's feelings; and strategies coded in the top third of the hierarchy provided explicit elaboration and legitimation of the other's feelings and perspective by, for example, stating that it was understandable that the other would feel upset about the situation because most people in a similar situation also would experience similar feelings (for detailed descriptions of this coding system, see Burleson, 1982, 1984a, 1984b). Scores for the highest-level strategy produced in response to each situation were averaged to form the index of comforting skill. Two independent codings of approximately 20% ($N = 14$) of the protocols yielded an interrater reliability coefficient of .93 by Pearson correlation. Evidence supporting the reliability and validity of this approach to the assessment of comforting skill is reviewed in several sources (Burleson, 1984a, in press; Burleson & Samter, 1985).

Conflict Management Skill. Messages produced in response to the two conflict situations were coded within the nine-level hierarchy developed by Samter and Ely (1985). As noted above, this coding system scores conflict strategies for the extent to which the rights and legitimate interests of all parties are respected and integrated with a concern for maintaining a positive interpersonal relationship with one's opponent. Thus conflict strategies employing or threatening physical or verbal aggression are scored in the lowest two levels of the hierarchy; messages calling upon or threatening to call upon the intervention of a powerful external authority figure are scored at the next two levels of the hierarchy; messages invoking simple norms and rules, or containing simple requests or imperatives, are scored at levels five and six; and strategies employing polite requests, requests that include appropriate reasons or propose methods of integrating apparently competing interests are scored at levels seven, eight, and nine, respectively (for additional details pertaining to this coding system, see Samter & Ely, 1985). Scores for the highest-level strategy used in conjunction with each situation were averaged to provide an index of conflict management skill. Interrater reliability, assessed by having two independent coders each score approximately 20% of the protocols, was .87 by Pearson correlation. Data supporting the validity of this measure of conflict management skill are presented by Samter and Ely (1985); these researchers found the use of sophisticated conflict management strategies positively associated with both chronological age and an index of social-cognitive ability.

Peer-Based Assessments of Popularity, Rejection, and Supportiveness

Sociometric nomination techniques were used to produce indices of each participant's popularity, rejection, and supportiveness. Sociometric nomination techniques have been used in a large number of studies with children and have been found to exhibit high levels of reliability and validity (see the reviews of Asher & Hymel, 1981; Burleson, 1986; Hymel, 1983; Ladd & Asher, 1985). To assess relative levels of popularity with and rejection by peers, each participant was asked to name the three classmates he or she most liked to play with and the three classmates with whom he or she least liked to play. The total number of positive and negative nominations received by each child was summed to yield the indices of popularity and rejection, respectively.

Somewhat similar procedures were used to elicit nominations for supportive "peer counselors." Four situations describing common problems involving peers, parents, and teachers were presented to the participants (for example, "One of your classmates is acting like he is mad at you. This makes you very unhappy because you really like this classmate and are not sure why he might be mad at you"). For each of these problems, participants were asked to name the two classmates they would most like to talk with about the problem. The number of "peer counselor" nominations received by each child was employed as the index of supportiveness to peers.

Teacher Ratings of Peer Supportiveness and Academic Motivation

In order to assess the convergent and discriminant validity of the sociometric measure of supportiveness to peers, ratings of each child's supportiveness to peers and academic ability/motivation were obtained from the child's teacher. To assess supportiveness to peers, teachers rated each child on five seven-point semantic differential scales (sympathetic to other children/unsympathetic to other children, kind/unkind, caring/uncaring, generous/stingy, helpful/unhelpful). Teachers also rated each child on five seven-point semantic differential scales tapping aspects of the child's academic ability and motivation (motivated/unmotivated, hardworking/ lazy, studious/not studious, bright/dull, industrious/not industrious). To discourage response-set effects, the two sets of items were intermixed and the poles of every other item were reversed. All ratings were standardized for each teacher.

Principal-components factor analyses were conducted on the two sets of items; single-factor solutions were obtained for both teachers' perceptions of supportiveness to peers and teachers' perceptions of academic ability/motivation. Internal consistency for the five items tapping perceptions of supportiveness to peers, as assessed by Cronbach's *alpha*, was .96; the *alpha* coefficient for the five items tapping academic ability/motivation was .94.

The correlation between peer counselor nominations and teachers' perceptions of support to peers was $r = .22, p < .05$; the correlation between peer counselor nominations and teachers' perceptions of academic ability/motivation was $r = -.21, p < .05$. These results thus provide some support for the convergent and discriminant validity of the sociometric nomination measure of supportiveness to peers. (The correlation between the teachers' perceptions of peer support and academic ability/motivation was $r = -.57, p < .001$.)

RESULTS

A total of 10 variables were assessed in the study. There were 5 independent variables: 2 measures of social-cognitive abilities (interpersonal cognitive complexity and emotional empathy) and 3 measures of communicative abilities (conflict management skill, persuasive skill, and comforting skill). There were also 5 dependent variables: 3 peer-based measures (sociometric nominations of popularity, rejection, and supportiveness) and 2 teacher-based measures (ratings of supportiveness to peers and academic ability/motivation). To control for the potentially confounding effects of chronological age, scores on all measures were converted to Z-scores within each grade level.

Table 24.1 presents the correlations between the independent variables and the dependent variables assessed in the study. Contrary to expectations, none of the independent variables were related to popularity with peers. Conflict management skill was negatively correlated at a significant level with rejection by peers ($r = -.27, p < .01$); this correlation indicates that children with poor conflict management skills experience greater rejection by peers than children with more sophisticated conflict management skills. Interpersonal cognitive complexity was positively associated with both peer- and teacher-based measures of supportiveness to peers; level of cognitive complexity was significantly associated with the number

Table 24.1
Correlations Between the Independent and Dependent Variables

Independent Variables	Number of Positive Nominations	Number of Negative Nominations	Dependent Variables Number of Counselor Nominations	Teachers' Peer Support Ratings	Teachers' Academic Ratings
Cognitive complexity	.06	-.04	.23*	.22*	-.18
Emotional empathy	-.09	-.01	-.08	.24*	-.15
Conflict skill	.05	-.27**	.14	.15	-.16
Persuasive skill	.01	-.01	.09	.08	-.24*
Comforting skill	.00	-.01	-.05	.05	-.10

Note: $N = 72$.
*$p < .05$; **$p < .01$.

of peer counselor nominations received by the child ($r = .23, p < .05$) and with the teachers' ratings of peer support ($r = .22, p < .05$). Teachers' ratings of peer support were also positively associated with children's levels of emotional empathy ($r = .24, p < .05$). Finally, children's persuasive skills were negatively associated with teachers' perceptions of their academic ability/motivation ($r = -.24, p < .05$).

Only one of the dependent variables, teachers' perceptions of supportiveness to peers, was significantly associated with more than one of the independent variables; this dependent measure was related to both social-cognitive indices (that is, interpersonal cognitive complexity and emotional empathy). A stepwise regression analysis was carried out on this dependent variable to determine whether or not the predictors of cognitive complexity and emotional empathy collectively explained more variance in teachers' perceptions of supportiveness than either explained separately. Emotional empathy entered the regression at step one and explained a significant portion of the variance in perceptions of supportiveness to peers, $r = .24, r^2 = .06; F(1,70) = 4.40, p < .05$. After cognitive complexity was entered at the second step of the analysis, the overall regression continued to explain a significant portion of the variance in perceptions of supportiveness to peers, $R = .32, R^2 = .10; F(2,69) = 3.96, p < .02$. More important, cognitive complexity was found to explain uniquely a statistically significant portion of variance in the dependent variable, semi-partial $r = .21$, semi-partial $r^2 = .04; t(69) = 1.94, p < .05$ (one-tailed test). Thus the two predictors of emotional empathy and interpersonal cognitive complexity collectively explained significantly more variance in teachers' perceptions of supportiveness to peers than either explained individually.

SUMMARY AND IMPLICATIONS

The results of the present study contain some important findings as well as a number of surprises. Perhaps the most surprising result of the study was the complete failure of comforting skill to be associated with any of the dependent variables. In a previous investigation, Burleson (1985) found that among six different communication skills, comforting skill best distinguished between accepted and rejected children. This finding, coupled with the fact that preadolescents demonstrate an increased tendency to view friends in terms of such psychological qualities as intimacy, trust, and caring (see Serafica, 1982), led to a strong expectation that comforting skill would be positively associated with popularity with peers and negatively associated with rejection by peers. Moreover, because the role of "peer counselor" would seem to require relatively sophisticated comforting skills, it was expected that preadolescents' comforting skills would be related to indices of supportiveness to peers. Quite clearly, these expectations were not fulfilled. The failure of comforting skill to be associated with any of the dependent measures raises the possibility that this particular communication skill may be unassociated with status among peers, at least among preadolescents. However, closer inspection of the distribution of the comforting messages obtained from the participants in this study indicated that there was little variation in the sophistication of the comforting strategies produced by subjects; over 54% of the messages were scored at level four (within Burleson's [1982] nine-level hierarchy), and over 77% of the messages were scored at levels three, four, or five. Thus there was little variance in the measure of comforting skill, and the truncated distribution of scores may have been responsible for the failure of comforting skill to exhibit the expected relationships with the dependent variables. A level four comforting strategy, by far the most commonly observed strategy in the present data, seeks to provide comfort by redirecting the other's attention from the distressful situation to other, happier situations (for example, if a child is upset about not being invited to another child's party, typical level four strategies include "When I have a party, you'll be the first person I invite," and "Why don't you come over to my house and play this afternoon"). It is possible that most children of the age examined in the present study may routinely employ level four comforting strategies when dealing with such everyday hurts of others as not being invited to another child's party or failing a test; that is, individual differences in comforting skill may not be exhibited in responses to the two situations utilized by the present research. It is possible that other, more complex situations would have elicited a broader distribution of scores for comforting skill. In any event, additional research is needed to clarify the relationship between preadolescents' comforting skills and their popularity, rejection, and supportiveness.

Popularity with peers not only was unrelated to comforting skill, it was unrelated to *any* of the independent variables included in the present study. And rejection by peers was significantly and negatively related only to conflict management skill; children with comparatively poor conflict management skills are rejected more by peers than children with advanced conflict management skills. These findings are not as discouraging or as "null" as they might initially appear; indeed, they bear certain important resemblances to other findings on the correlates of acceptance and rejection by peers. For example, after reviewing numerous studies examining the behavioral correlates of peer acceptance and rejection, Hartup (1983, p. 133) concluded that "the popular child, as compared to less popular individuals, is friendly and socially adept in initiating and maintaining social interaction with other children. The rejected child is not less sociable or friendly than the nonrejected child, but displays more antisocial, disruptive, and inappropriate behaviors in interaction with other children." Of the variables assessed in the present study, only comforting skill constitutes a clear example of the positive social behaviors that might relate to popularity with peers, and there were methodological problems in the assessment of this communication skill. Persuasive skill was related to neither popularity nor rejection in the present study, and in a previous study (Burleson, 1985), was found only marginally related to acceptance by peers. Although sophisticated persuasive skills may be functional in helping children achieve various instrumental goals, they apparently have little impact on the quality of peer relationships. In retrospect, this finding is, perhaps, not too surprising; in seeking to persuade others, one is attempting to achieve one's *own* goals rather than doing something *for* another (as in comforting) or *to* another (as in conflict management). Preadolescents' conflict management skills, however, have clear implications for the quality of their peer relationships. The present findings indicate that although relatively sophisticated conflict management skills do not necessarily help a child become popular, they *do* help the child avoid becoming unpopular. This pattern of results nicely fits with Hartup's conclusions: Rejected children in the present study were more likely than their accepted counterparts to employ relatively unsophisticated strategies in seeking to manage conflicts with peers—strategies relying on physical and verbal aggression, threats, and the intervention of powerful external authorities. Viewed in conjunction with the results of prior studies (Renshaw & Asher, 1983; Richard & Dodge, 1982; Rubin & Daniels-Beirness, 1983), the present findings strongly suggest that poor conflict management skills may be a primary cause of peer rejection throughout preschool, childhood, and early adolescence.

The sociometric procedure developed to assess supportiveness to peers exhibited some degree of convergent and discriminant validity; the number of "peer counselor" nominations received by a child was positively associated with teachers' perceptions of supportiveness to peers and negatively associated with teachers' perceptions of academic ability/motivation. Given the evidence supporting the validity of this measure, it is interesting to note that the number of peer counselor nominations received by a child was positively and significantly associated with interpersonal cognitive complexity. Indeed, the relationship between cognitive complexity and number of peer counselor nominations is made even more interesting by the fact that popularity with peers and number of counselor nominations were highly associated ($r = .72$, $p < .001$), whereas peer popularity and cognitive complexity were essentially unrelated ($r = .06$). This pattern of relationships suggests that cognitive complexity is associated with that portion of the variance in peer counselor nominations that is not due to simple popularity; that is, cognitive complexity appears associated with that portion of the variance in peer counselor nominations uniquely due to the provision of social support to peers. This interpretation was supported by a partial correlation analysis: partialling out the effect of popularity with peers from the correlation between cognitive complexity and number of peer counselor nominations had the effect of *raising* the correlation from $r = .23$ to $r = .27$. Cognitive complexity has been found to be positively associated with numerous indices of advanced interpersonal functioning (see the reviews of Burleson, in press; Delia et al., 1982; O'Keefe & Sypher, 1981); presumably, preadolescents with relatively high levels of interpersonal cognitive complexity engage in forms of behavior peers find helpful, supportive, and reassuring. Unfortunately, the present results shed no light on the specific character of the "helpful" and "supportive" behaviors in which cognitively complex preadolescents presumably engage with respect to their peers.

The significant, positive association between preadolescents' levels of interpersonal cognitive complexity and teachers' ratings of supportiveness to peers further substantiates the relationship between cognitive complexity and the provision of social support to peers. Evidently, cognitively complex children not only engage in behaviors peers perceive as supportive, the behaviors these children produce are also perceived as supportive by teachers. And, as the nonsignificant negative association between children's cognitive complexity and teachers' perceptions of academic ability and motivation makes clear, the relationship between cognitive complexity and teachers' perceptions of supportiveness is not due to a mere halo effect. That is, cognitively complex children are not generally perceived as "better children" by teachers; whatever the specific character of the behaviors in which cognitively complex children engage, these behaviors are specifically relevant to the realm of interpersonal relations. Clearly, additional research should focus on the contributions of cognitive complexity to supportive, peer-related behaviors.

Teachers' ratings of supportiveness to peers were also significantly associated with children's levels of emotional empathy. Interpretation of this relationship is somewhat clouded by the fact that emotional empathy was unrelated to the peer-based measure of social support (that is, number of peer counselor nominations). Perhaps teachers perceive an emotionally empathic disposition as relevant to support of peers, whereas children do not. On the other hand, it is possible that empathic tendency is related to supportive peer-directed behaviors, but that children at this point in development are not particularly cognizant of the functions served by such empathically motivated behaviors. Additional research is needed to clarify the role of emotional empathy in peer social support, particularly with respect to the behaviors that stem from an empathic disposition.

Teachers' ratings of academic ability and motivation were related only to children's persuasive skills; preadolescents with relatively advanced persuasive skills were perceived as *less* academically able and motivated. This finding is something of an anomaly. Perhaps children with relatively advanced persuasive skills are more likely to engage in persuasive efforts with teachers; if the objects of the child's persuasive efforts focus on personal and/or social concerns, this may result in perceptions of the child as relatively unmotivated in the academic arena.

The present study was undertaken in the effort to identify some of the social-cognitive and communicative skills underlying peer popularity, rejection, and supportiveness during the preadolescent period. Few studies have examined the preadolescent period, which is unfortunate because this developmental stage is typically viewed as one characterized by changes, stresses, and problems. The results of this study indicate that the social-cognitive variable of interpersonal cognitive complexity is significantly associated with both teacher- and peer-based measures of social support; in addition, emotional empathy was related to teacher ratings of supportiveness to peers. These findings indicate that advanced social-cognitive functioning plays an important role in the provision of support to peers experiencing the strains and stresses of the preadolescent period. Additional research is needed to identify the specific character of the supportive behaviors to which advanced social-cognitive skills contribute. The results also indicated that preadolescents with poor conflict management skills are more likely to be rejected by peers than those preadolescents with relatively advanced conflict management skills. This finding underscores the significance of conflict management ability for avoiding rejection by peers, if not for gaining acceptance. None of the skills assessed in this study were related to popularity with peers; at present, then, the social-cognitive and communicative bases of popularity during preadolescence remain undetermined.

NOTE

1. Referential skills were not assessed in the present study because several previous investigations (Rubin, 1972; Tesch & Oden, 1981) have found referential ability unassociated with acceptance by peers during the preadolescent period.

REFERENCES

Anderson, R. (1976). Peer facilitation: History and issues. *Elementary School Guidance and Counseling, 9,* 16-25.

Applegate, J. L. (1980). Adaptive communication in educational contexts: A study of teachers' communicative strategies. *Communication Education, 29,* 158-170.

Asher, S. R., & Hymel, S. (1981). Children's social competence in peer relations: Sociometric and behavioral assessment. In J. D. Wine & M. D. Syme (Eds.), *Social competence.* (pp. 125-127) New York: Guilford.

Asher, S. R., Oden, S. L., & Gottman, J. M. (1977). Children's friendships in school settings. In L. G. Katz (Ed.), *Current topics in early childhood education* (Vol. 1, pp. 33-61). Norwood, NJ: Ablex.

Asher, S. R., & Renshaw, P. D. (1981). Children without friends: Social knowledge and social skill training. In S. R. Asher & J. M. Gottman (Eds.), *The development of children's friendships* (pp. 273-296). Cambridge: Cambridge University Press.

Ausubel, D. P. (1954). *Theory and problems of adolescent development.* New York: Grune & Stratton.

Avery, A. W., Rider, K., & Haynes-Clements, L. A. (1981). Communication skills training for adolescents: A five-month follow-up. *Adolescence, 16,* 289-298.

Beatty, M. J., & Payne, S. K. (1984). Loquacity and quantity of constructs as predictors of social perspective-taking. *Communication Quarterly, 32,* 207-210.

Berndt, T. J. (1982). The features and effects of friendship in early adolescence. *Child Development, 53,* 1447-1460.

Berndt, T. J. (1983). Correlates and causes of sociometric status in childhood: A commentary on 6 current studies of popular, rejected, and neglected children. *Merrill-Palmer Quarterly, 29,* 439-448.

Bryant, B. K. (1982). An index of empathy for children and adolescents. *Child Development, 53,* 413-425.

Burleson, B. R. (1982). The development of comforting communication skills in childhood and adolescence. *Child Development, 53,* 1578-1588.

Burleson, B. R. (1984a). Comforting communication. In H. E. Sypher & J. L. Applegate (Eds.), *Communication by children and adults: Social cognitive and strategic processes* (pp. 63-104). Beverly Hills, CA: Sage.

Burleson, B. R. (1984b). Age, social-cognitive development, and the use of comforting strategies. *Communication Monographs, 51,* 140-153.

Burleson, B. R. (1985, April). *Communicative correlates of peer acceptance in childhood.* Paper presented at the biennial meeting of the Society for Research in Child Development, Toronto.

Burleson, B. R. (1986). Communication skills and childhood peer relationships: An overview. In M. L. McLaughlin (Ed.), *Communication yearbook 9* (pp. 143-180). Beverly Hills, CA: Sage.

Burleson, B. R. (in press). Cognitive complexity and person-centered communication: A review of methods, findings, and explanations. In J. C. McCroskey & J. A. Daly (Eds.), *Personality and interpersonal communication.* Beverly Hills, CA: Sage.

Burleson, B. R., Applegate, J. L., & Neuwirth, C. M. (1981). Is cognitive complexity loquacity? A reply to Powers, Jordan, and Street. *Human Communication Research, 7,* 212-225.

Burleson, B. R., & Samter, W. (1985). Consistencies in theoretical and naive evaluations of comforting messages. *Communication Monographs, 52,* 103-123.

Burleson, B. R., Waltman, M. S., & Samter, W. (in press). More evidence that cognitive complexity is not loquacity: A reply to Beatty and Payne. *Communication Quarterly.*

Canning, J. (1983). Peer facilitator projects for elementary and middle schools. *Elementary School Guidance & Counseling, 18,* 124-129.

Coie, J. D., & Kupersmidt, J. B. (1983). A behavioral analysis of emerging social status in boys' groups. *Child Development, 54,* 1400-1416.

Crockett, W. H. (1965). Cognitive complexity and impression formation. In B. A. Maher (Ed.), *Progress in experimental personality research* (Vol. 2, pp. 47-90). New York: Academic Press.

Crockett, W. H., Press, A. N., Delia, J. G., & Kenney, C. J. (1974). *The structural analysis of the organization of written impressions.* Unpublished manuscript, University of Kansas, Department of Psychology.

Delia, J. G., Kline, S. L., & Burleson, B. R. (1979). The development of persuasive communication strategies in kindergarteners through twelfth graders. *Communication Monographs, 46,* 241-256.

Delia, J. G., O'Keefe, B. J., & O'Keefe, D. J. (1982). The constructivist approach to communication. In F. E. X. Dance (Ed.), *Human communication theory* (pp. 147-191). New York: Harper & Row.

Deutsch, F. (1974). Observational and sociometric measures of peer popularity and their relationship to egocentric communication in female preschoolers. *Developmental Psychology, 10,* 745-747.

Dodge, K. A. (1983). Behavioral antecedents of peer social status. *Child Development, 54,* 1386-1399.

Dodge, K. A., Coie, J. D., & Brakke, N. P. (1982). Behavior patterns of socially rejected and neglected preadolescents: The role of social approach and aggression. *Journal of Abnormal Child Psychology, 10,* 389-410.

Dodge, K. A., Schlundt, D. C., Schocken, I., & Delugach, J. D. (1983). Social competence and children's sociometric status: The role of peer group entry strategies. *Merrill-Palmer Quarterly, 29,* 309-336.

Dougherty, A. M., & Taylor, B. L. B. (1983). Evaluation of peer helper programs. *Elementary School Guidance and Counseling, 18,* 130-136.

Fine, G. A. (1981). Trends, impression management, and preadolescent behavior. In S. R. Asher & J. M. Gottman (Eds.), *The development of children's friendships* (pp. 29-52). Cambridge: Cambridge University Press.

Fink, A. M., Grandjean, P., Martin, M. G., & Bertolini, B. G. (1978). Service delivery and high school peer counseling systems. *Personnel and Guidance Journal, 57,* 80-83.

Gottman, J. M., Gonso, J., & Rasmussen, B. (1975). Social interaction, social competence, and friendship in children. *Child Development, 46,* 709-718.

Gray, H. D., & Tindall, J. (1974). Communication training study: A model for training junior high school peer counselors. *The School Counselor, 22,* 107-112.

Hartup, W. W. (1983). Peer relations. In E. M. Heatherington (Ed.), *Handbook of child psychology, Vol. 4: Socialization, personality, and social development* (pp. 103-196). New York: John Wiley.

Hartup, W. W., Glazer, J. A., & Charlesworth, R. (1967). Peer reinforcement and sociometric status. *Child Development, 38,* 1017-1024.

Heller, K., & Swindle, R. W. (1983). Social networks, perceived social support, and coping with stress. In R. D. Felner, L. A. Jason, J. N. Montisugu, & S. Farber (Eds.), *Prevention psychology: Theory, research, and practice in community intervention* (pp. 87-103). New York: Pergamon.

Hess, R. D., & Goldblatt, I. (1960). The status of adolescents in American society: A problem in social identity. In J. M. Seidman (Ed.), *The adolescent* (pp. 321-332). New York: Holt, Rinehart & Winston.

Hymel, S. (1983). Preschool children's peer relations: Issues in sociometric assessment. *Merrill-Palmer Quarterly, 29,* 237-260.

Kurdek, L. A., & Krile, D. (1982). A developmental analysis of the relation between peer acceptance and both interpersonal understanding and perceived social self-competence. *Child Development, 53,* 1485-1491.

Ladd, G. W. (1983). Social networks of popular, average, and rejected children in school settings. *Merrill-Palmer Quarterly, 29,* 283-308.

Ladd, G. W., & Asher, S. R. (1985). Social skill training and children's peer relations. In L. L'Abate & M. Milan (Eds.), *Handbook of social skills training* (pp. 219-244). New York: John Wiley.

Marcus, R. F. (1980). Empathy and popularity of preschool children. *Child Study Journal, 10,* 133-145.

McCann, B. M. (1975). Peer counseling: An approach to psychological education. *Elementary School Guidance and Counseling, 9,* 180-187.

McGuire, K. D., & Weisz, J. R. (1982). Social cognition and behavior correlates of preadolescent chumship. *Child Development, 53,* 1478-1484.

O'Keefe, B. J., & Delia, J. G. (1982). Impression formation and message production. In M. E. Roloff & C. R. Berger (Eds.), *Social cognition and communication* (pp. 33-72). Beverly Hills, CA: Sage.

O'Keefe, D. J., & Sypher, H. E. (1981). Cognitive complexity measures and the relationship of cognitive complexity to communication: A critical review. *Human Communication Research, 8,* 72-92.

Putallaz, M. (1983). Predicting children's sociometric status from their behavior. *Child Development, 54,* 1417-1426.

Putallaz, M., & Gottman, J. M. (1981). An interactional model of children's entry into peer groups. *Child Development, 52,* 986-994.

Renshaw, P. D., & Asher, S. R. (1982). Social competence and peer status: The distinction between goals and strategies. In K. H. Rubin & H. S. Ross (Eds.), *Peer relationships and social skills in childhood* (pp. 375-395). New York: Springer-Verlag.

Renshaw, P. D., & Asher, S. R. (1983). Children's goals and strategies for social interaction. *Merrill-Palmer Quarterly, 29,* 353-374.

Richard, B. A. & Dodge, K. A. (1982). Social maladjustment and problem solving among school-age children. *Journal of Consulting and Clinical Psychology, 50,* 226-233.

Rothenberg, B. B. (1970). Children's social sensitivity and the relationship to interpersonal competence, intrapersonal comfort, and intellectual level. *Developmental Psychology, 2,* 335-350.

Rubin, K. H. (1972). Relationship between egocentric communication and popularity among peers. *Developmental Psychology, 7,* 364.

Rubin, K. H., & Daniels-Beirness, T. (1983). Concurrent and predictive correlates of sociometric status in kindergarten and grade one children. *Merrill-Palmer Quarterly, 29,* 332-352.

Rutter, M. (1983). Stress, coping, and development: Some issues and some questions. In N. Garmezy & M. Rutter (Eds.), *Stress, coping, and development in children* (pp. 1-41). New York: McGraw-Hill.

Samter, W., & Ely, T. (1985, April). *Children's conflict management strategies: Assessments of individual and situational differences.* Paper presented at the Central States Speech Association convention, Indianapolis, Indiana.

Selman, R. L. (1980). *The growth of interpersonal understanding: Developmental and clinical analyses.* New York: Academic Press.

Serafica, F. C. (1982). Conceptions of friendship and interaction between friends: An organismic-developmental perspective. In F. C. Serafica (Ed.), *Social-cognitive development in context* (pp. 100-132). New York: Guilford.

Smollar, J., & Youniss, J. (1982). Social development through friendship. In K. H. Rubin & H. S. Ross (Eds.), *Peer relationships and social skills in childhood* (pp. 279-298). New York: Springer-Verlag.

Sypher, H. E., & Applegate, J. L. (1982). Cognitive complexity and verbal intelligence: Clarifying relationships. *Educational and Psychological Measurement, 49,* 537-543.

Tesch, S. A., & Oden, S. (1981, August). *Referential communication skill and peer status in third and sixth grade children.* Paper presented at the annual meeting of the American Psychological Association, Los Angeles.

Vosk, B., Forehand, R., Parker, J. B., Rickard, K. (1982). A multimethod comparison of popular and unpopular children. *Developmental Psychology, 18,* 571-575.

Zahn-Waxler, C., Iannotti, R., & Chapman, M. (1982). Peers and prosocial development. In K. H. Rubin & H. S. Ross (Eds.), *Peer relationships and social skills in childhood* (pp. 133-162). New York: Springer-Verlag.

25 ● Reducing Fear Reactions to Mass Media: Effects of Visual Exposure and Verbal Explanation

BARBARA J. WILSON ● JOANNE CANTOR

University of Louisville ● University of Wisconsin — Madison

FRIGHTENING mass media presentations have become increasingly popular in the last few years. Films such as *Halloween* and *Friday the 13th* and their numerous sequels are just a few examples of this type of content. Recent television movies such as *The Day After* and *Adam* demonstrate that frightening presentations are not limited to movie theaters.

The proliferation of this type of content has led to a growing concern over the effects of such movies on younger children. Controversy over the effects of *Gremlins* and *Indiana Jones and the Temple of Doom* on young moviegoers led the Motion Picture Association to adopt the "PG-13" rating, which indicates that a film may not be suitable for children under 13 years of age. *Silent Night, Deadly Night,* a film portraying Santa Claus as a killer, was taken out of many theaters because of parental complaints concerning its potentially upsetting content.

Recent research in this area indicates that children do seem to experience both immediate and enduring fear reactions to various media presentations (Cantor & Reilly, 1982; Cantor & Sparks, 1984; Cantor, Wilson, & Hoffner, in press; Palmer, Hockett, & Dean, 1983; Sparks, 1986; Wilson, Hoffner, & Cantor, 1986). A number of researchers have argued that more attention should be focused on techniques to prevent and reduce children's fear reactions because such fears may persist and develop into phobias

AUTHOR'S NOTE: Financial support for this study was provided by Grant MH35320 from the National Institute of Mental Health to Joanne Cantor. The authors would like to thank Eunice Warwick, Principal of Lowell Elementary School (now retired), for allowing them to conduct the study in her school. Thanks are also due to the teachers and staff at Lowell School for their cooperation. Special thanks are extended to Cynthia Hoffner for serving as one of the experimenters, to Marian Friestad for presenting the narration of the desensitization videotape, and to Quana Jew for coding the videotaped facial expressions.

Correspondence and requests for reprints: Barbara J. Wilson, Department of Communication, University of Louisville, Louisville, KY 40292.

(Graziano, DeGiovanni, & Garcia, 1979; Ollendick, 1979).

Clinical studies of children's phobias suggest that desensitization techniques that are based on gradual exposure to an actual fear stimulus may be an effective method for reducing fearful reactions. In an early study, Jones (1924) found that one of the most successful strategies for eliminating young children's fear of animals was to gradually move the animal closer to the child as the child ate a favorite food.

Most of the research on desensitization techniques with children has involved multiple treatment components. Thus the effects of gradual exposure to the frightening stimulus could not be assessed independently. For example, a number of studies have used desensitization techniques in conjunction with the modeling of nonfearful behavior (Bandura & Menlove, 1968; Roberts, Wurtele, Boone, Ginther, & Elkins, 1981). Other studies have focused on the learning of active coping behaviors during gradual exposure to the fear object (Leitenberg & Callahan, 1973; Ritter, 1968; Wallick, 1979).

The few studies that have focused primarily on gradual exposure indicate that such a technique can be used successfully to reduce children's fears. A number of case studies of younger children between the ages of 2 and 7 have reported that gradual exposure was effective in eliminating fears related to small animals (Jones, 1924; Lazarus, 1974), to loud noises (O'Reilly, 1971; Tasto, 1969), and to fire (Roberts & Gordon, 1979). In addition, studies indicate that gradual exposure techniques can be used to reduce older children's fears (Murphy & Bootzin, 1973; Wish, Hasazi, & Jurgela, 1973).

Gradual exposure techniques also have been used in conjunction with a verbal explanation of the fear stimulus. Typically, the explanation component is included as part of the exposure treatment and its independent effects on fear reduction are not assessed. The findings regarding the combination of exposure and explanation are mixed, especially in studies involving younger children. White and Davis (1974) and Machen and Johnson (1974) found that gradual presentation of dental instruments combined with an explanation of them significantly decreased anxiety behaviors during dental treatment among 4- to 8-year-old children. However, an earlier study by Johnson and Machen (1973) revealed that gradual exposure plus explanation was *not* effective in reducing preschoolers' fear reactions to such treatment. In contrast, exposure plus explanation does seem to be effective when used with older children. Oliver (1971) found that fourth graders who received lesson plans regarding mice plus actual exposure to a live mouse showed significantly less physiological arousal to the fear stimulus.

A recent study by Sheslow, Bondy, and Nelson (1983) indicates that verbal explanation and visual exposure should be assessed independently. The researchers compared three conditions in treating fear of the dark among 4- to 5-year-olds: gradual exposure to darkness, the rehearsal of verbal statements designed to decrease the threat of the dark, and the combination of these two techniques. They found that only those subjects who received gradual exposure to the dark were less fearful. The researchers suggested that the ineffectiveness of the verbal statements may have been due to the fact that the children were too young to utilize verbal coping skills.

Research on verbal explanation alone as a fear-reduction technique indicates that there may indeed be developmental differences in the ability to utilize this type of strategy. A number of studies have found that verbal explanation is not very effective with younger children (Jersild & Holmes, 1933; Jones, 1924; Lende, 1971; Rosengarten, 1961). Furthermore, recent developmental studies of fear-reduction techniques indicate that verbal explanation is more effective with older than with younger children. Cantor and Wilson (1984) found that instructions to think about the unreality of a television program when viewing it had no appreciable effect on the emotional responses of 3- to 5-year-olds to the scary scene, but significantly reduced such responses among 9- to 11-year-olds. Wilson, Hoffner, and Cantor (in press) found that older elementary school children rated the discussion of a frightening television program with a parent as a more effective fear-reduction strategy than did preschool children.

Leventhal (1984) and others (for example, Lazarus, 1984) have argued that verbal explanation techniques are designed to change the interpretation or conceptual representation of the fear stimulus. A number of studies of adults have demonstrated that providing information related to a stressful stimulus can reduce anxiety responses to it (Lazarus, Opton, Nomikos, & Rankin, 1965; Leventhal, 1984). However, virtually no attention has been given to factors that might explain the developmental differences in the effectiveness of such techniques among children.

It seems that a number of tasks or skills are required in order for a child to use and to benefit from a verbal explanation regarding a fear stimulus. First, the child must encode and comprehend the information being presented. This includes not only the ability to understand the explicit information, but also the ability to interrelate information and draw the necessary inferences regarding the degree of threat associated with the fearsome object. Studies indicate that the ability to construct and infer additional information from verbally presented narratives (see Paris & Lindauer, 1977, for brief review) and from various types of television programs (Collins, 1983) increases with age during the elementary school years.

Second, the child must store the information derived from the verbal explanation in memory. Related to this task, many studies have documented a developmental increase in functional memory capacity (Mackworth, 1976). Researchers have argued that this growing memory span is due primarily to the increased usage and efficiency of mnemonic strategies such as rehearsal, categorization, and elaboration (see Brown, Bransford, Ferrara, & Campione, 1983, for review).

Finally, the stored information must be retrieved from memory and applied to subsequent threatening situations, as the child continuously attends to the fear stimulus during these new encounters. Studies have found that children's performance on two simultaneous tasks increases with age (Manis, Keating, & Morrison, 1980; Maccoby, 1969). These findings indicate a developmental increase in the ability to allocate processing capacity effectively to multiple tasks.

Thus the relative ineffectiveness of verbal explanations with younger children could be due to developmental differences in the ability to comprehend the information, to store the information in memory, and/or to apply the stored information to a fear stimulus when simultaneously attending to it.

In contrast to verbal explanation, visual exposure can be expected to be effective at all ages because it is most likely based on fairly automatic processes such as extinction (Evans, 1973; Lomont, 1965). According to extinction theories, anxiety responses typically are conditioned responses that can be eliminated by repeated exposure to a fear stimulus in a nonthreatening manner and without any adverse consequences. This process seems to require little or no conceptual activity. The child need only attend to repeated presentations of the frightening stimulus in a nonthreatening context.

It should be noted that some researchers have advanced a more cognitive explanation of exposure techniques (Lang, 1984; Wilkins, 1971). However, it seems unlikely that exposure techniques depend on complex mental processing of information because such techniques have been found to decrease responsiveness to both fearsome and novel stimuli in animals (Wilson & Davison, 1971), in children as young as two years of age (Jones, 1924; Wallick, 1979), and in brain-damaged children (Obler & Terwilliger, 1970).

The purpose of the present research was to assess the effectiveness of desensitization as a technique to reduce children's fear reactions to mass media. The study compared two aspects of desensitization techniques—gradual exposure to a fear stimulus and verbal explanation of the fear stimulus. Children from two age groups (kindergarten and first versus second and third grade) were exposed to one of four treatment conditions: visual exposure to a fear stimulus plus a verbal explanation of it, visual exposure only, verbal explanation only, or neither exposure nor explanation. Children were then exposed to a dramatic scene involving the frightening stimulus.

The study was designed to overcome the limitations associated with prior research on desensitization with children. Nonphobic children were used and were tested in an experimental rather than a clinical setting.

Treatment components were factorially varied in order to evaluate them in a systematic fashion. Developmental differences in the effectiveness of the treatment components were examined. Finally, multiple measures of the impact of desensitization—self-report, physiological, facial, and behavioral—were assessed.

Based on the research reviewed, the following two hypotheses were advanced:

H_1: Visual exposure to the frightening stimulus will reduce fear in both younger and older children.

H_2: The verbal explanation of the fear stimulus will be more effective in reducing fear among older children than among younger children.

Because the second hypothesis involved assumptions regarding developmental differences in the ability to understand and store information, children's comprehension and recall of the verbal explanation also were assessed.

METHOD

Subjects

A total of 163 children participated in the experiment. Of the children, 82 were in kindergarten and first grade (*M* age = 6:8), and 81 were in second and third grade (*M* age = 8:9). All of the children were enrolled in an elementary school in Madison, Wisconsin.

Parental permission was obtained in writing before any child participated in the study. Within each grade, males and females separately were randomly assigned to conditions. The ratio of males to females was approximately equal in the four experimental conditions associated with each grade level.

Design

In a 2 × 2 × 2 × 2 factorial design, a desensitization videotape was created with manipulations in the video track (visual exposure, no visual exposure) and the audio track (verbal explanation, no verbal explanation). These manipulations were varied with grade (kindergarten and first versus second and third) and with sex of subject. The number of subjects in the 16 conditions was approximately equal.

Procedure

Before any testing was conducted, each classroom met with the two female experimenters for a 20-minute explanation of the research project and the physiological equipment. On the subsequent testing days, each subject was brought individually to a room at the school where the television and physiological equipment were located. The sensors associated with the heart-rate measure were connected to the subject's left hand.

Each subject viewed the videotape as his or her heart-rate responses and facial expressions were recorded. During selected pauses that consisted of black screen edited onto the videotape, the experimenter asked the subject questions about his or her reactions to the segment just viewed. The videotape session lasted approximately 22 minutes.

At the end of the viewing session, the subject was escorted to an adjoining room and was asked a series of questions related to the desensitization segment. Finally, a measure of avoidance behavior toward snakes was given. The postviewing session lasted approximately 20 minutes. Subjects were asked not to discuss the experiment with the other children until all the testing was completed.

Parents were telephoned after their child participated and were asked about typical coping techniques they used with their child.

Materials

The videotape viewed by the subjects contained eight segments. The first two segments, taken from locally produced educational programming, were selected to be relaxing and nonarousing, in order to accustom the subjects to the experimental setting.

The third segment contained the desensitization manipulation. The treatment groups viewed different versions of a Life Sciences Film entitled *Life Story of a Snake*. The color film was reedited so that it contained 12 scenes involving footage of snakes at increasingly close range. The initial scenes showed motionless snakes, at a distance, in various locations. The next scenes contained distant shots of snakes crawling and moving. The following scenes contained close-up shots of a snake's forked tongue, a baby snake hatching from an egg, a snake's skin, and a snake slithering through the grass toward the screen. The last two scenes contained rapid close-ups of many types of snakes, including poisonous ones. The entire desensitization segment was 3 minutes and 50 seconds in length.

For subjects in the three treatment groups, the experimenter introduced the desensitization segment as follows: "The next program you will see is called *Life Story of a Snake*." In the visual exposure-only condition, subjects saw the 12 scenes of snakes, prefaced by a 4-second shot of the title *Life Story of a Snake*. The soundtrack contained outdoor nature sounds of birds and crickets.

In the visual exposure-verbal explanation condition, subjects saw the same video portion of the film (including the title shot), but the soundtrack contained a narration about snakes, presented by an adult female in a calm, reassuring voice. The narration provided "neutral" facts (for example, what snakes use to smell things) and "positive" information (for example, how snakes help people by eating insects). The soundtrack also included information that attempted to reduce the perceived dangerousness of snakes. These statements indicated that black snakes may look mean but will not hurt humans or animals, and that most snakes are not poisonous.

In the verbal explanation-only condition, subjects heard the narration about snakes, and the video portion showed only the title shot of *Life Story of a Snake* for the entire segment.

Subjects in the control condition watched a Public Broadcasting Service (PBS) program about making thread and weaving cloth. The program was the same length as the desensitization segments.

The next two videotape segments were the same for all subjects. The fourth segment (2 minutes and 22 seconds) was a scene from the television program *The Courtship of Eddie's Father,* and was included in order to separate the desensitization treatment from the frightening stimulus. The fifth segment (1 minute and 35 seconds), the frightening stimulus, was the snake-pit scene from the movie *Raiders of the Lost Ark.* During the scene, the film's hero, Indiana Jones, is slowly lowered by rope into a cave containing a buried treasure. Hundreds of snakes are shown crawling around the floor of the cave. The scene ends with Indiana Jones falling to the cave floor as the rope breaks. The segment was edited in order to increase the number of shots showing close-ups of the snakes hissing and crawling around the cave.[1]

The sixth and eighth segments were neutral programs taken from educational programming. The seventh segment was a scene from the 1950s movie called *The Blob.* This segment was included as part of another study.[2]

Dependent Measures

Immediately after the *Raiders* segment, subjects were asked, "How did you feel just now, while you were watching this last program?" Responses were recorded verbatim by the experimenter. Subjects were then directly asked, "How scared did you feel? Did you feel *not at all scared* (0), *kinda scared* (1), *pretty scared* (2), or *very very scared* (3)?"[3] As these phrases were being read, subjects were shown a piece of laminated cardboard that contained ink drawings of a child's face expressing four degrees of fear, increasing in intensity from left to right, with the appropriate label below each face. Subjects could verbalize the chosen response or point to it on the board.

Heart rate was measured with a Cyborg Biolab 21 Computerized Physiological Monitoring System. The heart-rate module used a photoplethysmographic technique. A sensor was attached to the distal pad of the pointer finger with a velcro band. The computer was programmed to sample and record heart rate every second.

Facial fear was assessed using the Affex Coding Scheme (Izard, Dougherty, & Hembree, 1983). The Affex system involves the identification of appearance changes in the brow, eyes, nose, and mouth. Based on these appearance changes, the scheme permits the identification of the fear expression either in the entire face or in the upper or lower portion of the face only.[4] Fear is coded in the upper portion of the face when the eyebrows and upper eyelids are raised, the eyebrows are either straight or normal in shape, the nasal root is narrowed, and the eyes exhibit more white than normal. Fear is coded in the lower portion of the face when the mouth is open and the corners of the mouth are retracted straight back.

Coders achieved 80% reliability on the Affex training materials before any coding was conducted. One coder coded the onset and offset of emotional expressions, in tenths of a second, for all the subjects. As a measure of reliability, a second coder coded the expressions of 35 randomly selected subjects. The coders were blind to the subjects' grade level and experimental condition. Intercoder reliability was 94.4%.

In order to measure behavioral avoidance of snakes, the experimenter pulled out a covered cage at the end of the session and asked each subject if he or she would like to see a "real" snake. The experimenter recorded the subject's response.

Nine questions were used to assess recall and recognition of the information contained in the desensitization segment. Subjects in the control condition also were asked these questions in order to assess children's general knowledge of information about snakes. Six of the questions referred to neutral information about snakes (for example, "Where does a snake go when it's very cold outside?" "When baby snakes are born, what do they come out of?"). In addition, subjects were asked one question regarding positive information about snakes: "Can you tell me one way that snakes help people?"

Finally, two questions involving threatening information about snakes were asked: "Are most snakes *poisonous* or are most snakes *not poisonous?*" and "Do you think most snakes *can't* hurt people or do you think most snakes *can* hurt people?" The order of all forced-choice alternatives was systematically rotated from subject to subject.

After each child participated, his or her parent was contacted by phone. In addition to a general question regarding the child's reaction to the study, each parent was asked, "If (child's name) saw an animal or a character on TV and became upset, is there anything you think you might do to help your child not to be scared in the future?"

RESULTS

All analyses of variance included the visual exposure component of desensitization, the verbal explanation component, grade level, and sex as factors. Pairwise comparisons were made using the Scheffé procedure (p < .05). For all analyses, means or percentages having no letter in common in their subscripts are significantly different according to the appropriate post hoc test.

Self-Reports of Emotional Response

Responses to the open-ended question concerning how the subject felt were coded in two ways. First, the hedonic tone of the response was coded as negative (for example, "bad," "scared," "sad") or nonnegative (for example, "good," "happy," "normal"). Then the responses were coded for fear-related feelings. Any responses involving anxiety, worry, or fear were included in the "fear" category. All other responses were coded as "no fear." Responses were coded in these two ways because younger children are better at indicating the hedonic tone of their feelings than they are at providing specific labels for them (Izard, 1971; Wilson & Cantor, 1985). Coding was conducted by two judges who were blind to the subject's grade and experimental condition. Intercoder reliability was 90%. Disagreements were resolved by a third judge.

Four-way multidimensional contingency tables were formed for the two types of open-ended responses. Log-linear analyses were conducted on the frequencies of responses (Marascuilo & Levin, 1983). This type of analysis provides a parallel to the traditional ANOVA for nominal-level data. Both the marginal and partial tests of association were performed (Brown, 1976). Because both tests led to the same conclusions, only the partial likelihood ratio chi-squares (G^2) are reported. Post hoc comparisons were conducted using gamma (the log of the odds ratio) and the chi-square analog to the Scheffé method (p < .05).

The log-linear analysis on the frequency of negative and nonnegative feelings resulted in a significant interaction between grade level and the verbal explanation component of desensitization, G^2 (1, N = 129) = 5.85, p = .02. Pairwise comparisons revealed that for the younger subjects, there was a significantly higher proportion of negative feelings (54%$_b$) among those who heard the verbal explanation than among those who did not hear it (30%$_a$). The opposite pattern was found for the older subjects, but the difference was not significant (explanation, 44%$_{ab}$; no explanation, 59%$_b$).

The analysis of the same responses coded for mentions of fear also resulted in a significant interaction between grade level and the verbal explanation component, G^2 (1, N = 163) = 4.06, p = .04. Again, there was a higher proportion of fearful feelings among those younger subjects who heard the verbal explanation (34%) than among those who did not hear it (20%), and there was a lower proportion of fearful feelings in the explanation (24%) than in the no-explanation conditions (38%) for the older group. Although the pattern for the younger subjects was significantly different from the pattern for the older subjects, the pairwise comparisons within each age group were not significant.

An analysis of variance was performed on the forced-choice degree-of-fear responses. The analysis resulted in a main effect for the visual exposure component of desensitization that approached significance, $F(1,147) = 2.84, p = .09$. Subjects who were exposed to the video portion tended to report less fear ($M = 0.7$) than did those who were not so exposed ($M = 0.9$).

The analysis of degree of fear also revealed a significant main effect for sex, $F(1,147) = 4.63, p = .03$, and an interaction between sex and grade level that approached significance, $F(1,147) = 3.58, p = .06$. Females reported a significantly higher degree of fear ($M = 0.9$) than did males ($M = 0.7$), and this sex difference was primarily due to the older subjects. Pairwise comparisons revealed that older females reported a higher degree of fear ($M = 1.1_b$) than did older males ($M = 0.6_a$), but there was no difference in degree of fear between the younger females ($M = 0.8_a$) and males ($M = 0.8_a$).

Heart Rate

A base level for heart rate was computed using the mean response during a 19-second nonarousing videotape segment on farming that was 123 seconds into the viewing session. Analyses of covariance were conducted on the mean heart-rate responses during the entire *Raiders* scene, using the base level as a covariate.[5]

The analysis of heart-rate responses to the entire scene resulted in a main effect for the visual exposure component that approached significance, $F(1,143) = 2.75, p = .10$.[6] The two-way interaction between grade level and the verbal explanation component seemed to emerge in this analysis, although the effect did not reach conventional levels of significance, $F(1,143) = 2.57, p = .11$. The analysis also resulted in a significant two-way interaction between sex of subject and the verbal explanation component, $F(1,143) = 5.66, p = .02$.

The fact that the predicted main effect for visual exposure and the two-way interaction between grade and verbal explanation only approached significance may be due to the nature of the heart-rate response. Research indicates that heart rate may actually decrease during initial attention to a novel stimulus (Graham & Clifton, 1966; Lacey, Kagan, Lacey, & Moss, 1963). To avoid the effects of this initial orienting response, the analysis of covariance was repeated using the responses to the second half of the video-tape segment only.

The analysis of heart-rate responses to the latter portion of the scene resulted in a main effect for the visual exposure component, $F(1, 143) = 3.70$, $p = .056$. Subjects who were exposed to the video portion had lower adjusted mean heart rates ($M = 83.9$) than did those who were not exposed to the video portion ($M = 86.0$).

The analysis also revealed a two-way interaction between grade level and the verbal explanation component that approached significance, $F(1,143) = 3.24$, $p = .07$. Pairwise comparisons revealed that younger subjects who heard the verbal explanation had a significantly higher adjusted mean heart rate ($M = 86.5_b$) than did those who did not hear the explanation ($M = 83.3_a$). In contrast, the older subjects who heard the explanation had a lower adjusted mean heart rate ($M = 84.6_{ab}$) than did those who did not hear it ($M = 85.4_{ab}$), although this difference was not significant. (See Figure 25.1.)

The only other significant effect in this analysis was a two-way interaction between sex and the verbal explanation component, $F(1,143) = 6.77$, $p = .01$. Pairwise comparisons revealed that females who heard the verbal explanation had a higher adjusted mean heart rate ($M = 86.6_b$) than did those who did not hear it ($M = 82.6_a$), whereas there was no difference in the adjusted mean heart-rate responses of male subjects in these conditions (explanation: $M = 84.5_{ab}$; no explanation: $M = 86.1_b$).

Facial Expressions of Fear

Duration of the fear expression was calculated as the total number of seconds the expression occurred either in the full face or in the upper or lower portion of the face only. An analysis of variance of the duration of facial fear resulted in a significant two-way interaction between grade and the verbal explanation component of desensitization, $F(1,147) = 3.96$, $p = .05$. (See Figure 25.2). Pairwise comparisons revealed that younger subjects who heard the verbal explanation showed significantly more fear ($M = 1.3_b$) than did those who did not hear the explanation ($M = 0.1_a$). In contrast, the older subjects who heard the explanation showed less facial fear ($M = 0.3_{ab}$) than did those who did not hear it ($M = 0.7_{ab}$), although this difference was not significant.

The only other significant finding in this analysis was a two-way interaction between the visual exposure component of desensitization and sex, $F(1,147) = 4.83$, $p = .03$. Although the pairwise comparisons were not significant, females who were exposed to the video portion exhibited less fear ($M = 0.1$) than did females who were not so exposed ($M = 1.0$), whereas males exhibited more fear in the visual exposure conditions ($M = 1.1$) than in the no-exposure conditions ($M = 0.1$).

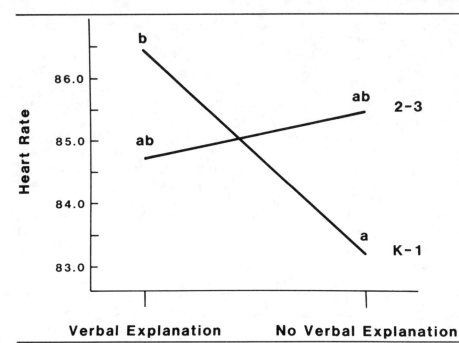

Figure 25.1 Adjusted mean heart rate to second half of the *Raiders* scene as a
           function of the verbal explanation component and grade level.
           Heart rate was measured in beats per minute. Means with no letter
           in common are significantly different at $p < .05$ using the Scheffé
           procedure.

Behavioral Responses

Only six subjects (4%) said they did not want to see the "real snake"
presented by the experimenter. An examination of the distribution of these
responses among the desensitization conditions revealed a differential
pattern as a function of grade and the verbal explanation component. A
log-linear analysis was conducted, omitting sex and the visual exposure
component as factors because of small cell frequencies. The interaction
between grade and verbal explanation was significant, G^2 $(1, N = 163) =$
$3.97, p = .05$. Both of the younger subjects who did not want to see the
snake had heard the verbal explanation, whereas three of the four older
subjects who did not want to see the snake had not heard the explanation.

Although the interaction was significant, none of the pairwise comparisons reached significance because of the low frequency of refusals to see
the snake.

Recall and Comprehension

In order to assess the differential effectiveness of the verbal explanation
for the two age groups, responses to the nine recall and comprehension

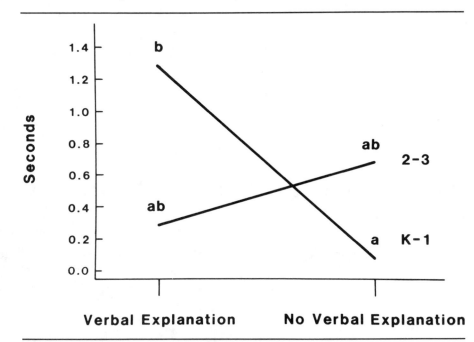

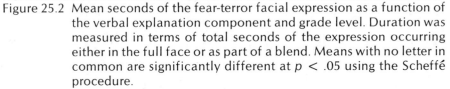

Verbal Explanation   No Verbal Explanation

Figure 25.2   Mean seconds of the fear-terror facial expression as a function of the verbal explanation component and grade level. Duration was measured in terms of total seconds of the expression occurring either in the full face or as part of a blend. Means with no letter in common are significantly different at $p < .05$ using the Scheffé procedure.

questions were analyzed separately within each grade level. Chi-square analyses were used to compare subjects who heard the verbal explanation with those who did not, in terms of the frequency of correct responses (see Table 25.1).

For five of the six items involving neutral information about snakes, the proportion of both younger and older subjects who gave correct responses was higher for those who heard the verbal explanation than for those who did not hear it. The only neutral item that showed no difference between those who heard the verbal explanation and those who did not concerned where snakes go when it is cold. Although a higher proportion of subjects in both age groups responded correctly in the verbal explanation than in the no-explanation conditions, the differences were not significant.

The analyses on the one item involving positive information resulted in a significant verbal explanation effect for both age groups. At both grade levels, a significantly higher proportion of subjects who heard the explanation than of those who did not hear it gave correct responses.

The remaining two items involved information about the danger of snakes. The analysis of the younger subjects' responses to the question regarding

Table 25.1

Subjects Giving Correct Responses to Neutral and Positive Recall Items
as a Function of the Verbal Explanation Component (in percentages)

| | Grade Level | | | | | |
| | K-1 | | | 2-3 | | |
	Verbal Explanation	No Explanation	χ^2	Verbal Explanation	No Explanation	χ^2
Neutral Items						
Do snakes climb trees?	78	54	4.39**	80	48	7.79**
What do snakes use to smell?	88	58	7.52**	85	48	11.42**
What's on a snake's body?	51	27	4.15*	88	50	11.85**
What are snakes born from?	93	76	3.29@	93	65	7.76**
How many years to adulthood?	46	12	9.96**	58	15	14.64**
Where do snakes go when cold?	66	56	0.46	88	75	1.43
Positive Item						
How do snakes help people?	73	5	37.36**	68	32	8.99**

Note: Chi-square tests were conducted on the frequencies of correct and incorrect responses within each grade level as a function of the verbal explanation. For grades K-1, $n = 82$. For grades 2-3, $n = 81$. Degrees of freedom = 1 for all chi-square values.
@ $p < .10$; * $p < .05$; ** $p < .01$.

whether most snakes can or cannot hurt people resulted in no significant difference between the verbal explanation and no-explanation conditions, χ^2 (1, n = 82) = 0.48, p = .48. The majority of the younger subjects in both conditions reported that most snakes can hurt people (explanation, 61%; no explanation, 71%). In contrast, a significantly lower proportion of older subjects who heard the verbal explanation (44%) than of those who did not (72%) said that most snakes can hurt people, χ^2 (1, n = 81) = 5.68, p = .02.

The analyses of responses to the second question, concerning whether most snakes are poisonous, resulted in a similar pattern. For the younger subjects, there was no significant difference between the verbal explana-tion (51%) and no-explanation (56%) conditions, χ^2 (1, n = 82) = 0.05, p = .82. In contrast, for the older subjects, a lower proportion of those who heard the explanation (27%) than of those who did not (48%) said that most snakes are poisonous. This difference approached significance, χ^2 (1, n = 81) = 2.87, p = .09.

Parental Coping Techniques

Parents' responses concerning coping techniques used with the child were placed into categories by two judges who agreed on 91.5% of all decisions. Disagreements were resolved by a third coder.

Only six parents (4%) mentioned a form of desensitization as a possible coping technique. These descriptions included three mentions of visual exposure to the fear object (for example, "let her see the animal in real life"), and three mentions of visual exposure plus verbal explanation (for example, "expose him to it and try to reason with him about it").

The most frequent response involved some form of discussion with the child. Of the parents, 122 (80%) mentioned a verbal discussion tech-nique. These techniques included explaining the fear object to the child, talking about special effects, or telling the child that the fear object is not real. In order to compare the reported use of this technique for the different age groups, a chi-square analysis was conducted on the frequencies of dis-cussion versus other strategies. There was no difference in the proportion of parents of younger (81%) and of older children (79%) who mentioned discussion techniques, χ^2 (1, N = 152) = 0.02, p = .90.

Summary and Implications

The results of this study provide support for the effectiveness of the visual exposure component of desensitization, and for a developmental difference in the effectiveness of the verbal explanation component. The similar patterns among the multiple measures of emotional response sug-gest convergent validity in the assessment of fear (Cronbach & Meehl, 1955).

The first hypothesis concerning visual exposure was supported by self-reported degree of fear and by heart-rate responses. Children who were exposed to the visual portion of the desensitization segment reported a lower degree of fear and had lower heart rates than did those who were not so exposed. As predicted, the effectiveness of visual desensitization was not dependent upon the child's age.

Visual exposure also influenced facial expressions of fear, although this effect interacted with sex of subject. Visual exposure reduced facial fear among females, but increased it among males. It is difficult to interpret this unusual interaction because it was not found in the self-report or heart-rate responses. Further research is needed on sex differences in facial expressivity among children.

It should be noted that the visual exposure effect was somewhat limited in these data. The effect was only marginally significant for self-reported degree of fear and for heart rate, and was limited to these two dependent measures. There are at least two possible reasons for the relative weakness of the exposure effect. First, the subjects were not preselected on the basis of phobias related to snakes. Many of the subjects were probably not very fearful of snakes to begin with. In fact, the mean degree of reported fear to the *Raiders* scene was only 0.8 on a three-point scale. Presumably the visual exposure effect would have been stronger had the study included only subjects who were frightened of snakes. Second, the exposure period was very brief in this experiment. Many of the clinical studies have involved multiple exposure periods of 20 to 30 minutes each. In contrast, the visual exposure segment in this study was only approximately 4 minutes long.

The second hypothesis was generally supported in that there was a developmental difference in the effectiveness of the verbal explanation. However, the pattern was different from that which had been predicted. The verbal explanation tended to reduce negative emotional reactions among the older subjects, but it actually *increased* such responses among the younger subjects. This pattern was found in the open-ended self-reports of negative and fearful feelings, in the heart-rate responses, in the fear expressions, and in the behavioral response of willingness to see a "live" snake.

Although the verbal explanation served to reduce negative emotional reactions among the older subjects, this effect consistently fell short of significance in the post hoc comparisons. One possible explanation for this may be that the subjects were not quite cognitively mature enough to utilize and benefit fully from the verbal explanation. Research indicates that relevant skills, such as the ability to draw inferences and the ability to perform simultaneous tasks, continually improve between the ages of 6 and 12 (Manis, Keating, & Morrison, 1980; Paris & Lindauer, 1977). Because the mean age of the older subjects in this study was only 8.8 years, the ability to utilize verbal explanations may not have been fully developed in a good portion of the subjects.

In contrast, the verbal explanation had significant and consistent negative effects on the emotional reactions of the younger subjects. Measures of recall and comprehension indicate that both younger and older subjects who heard the verbal explanation learned neutral and positive information about snakes. Thus the ineffectiveness of the verbal explanation with the younger age group was not due to a general inability to comprehend explicit information and store it in memory. However, the explanation did not significantly affect the younger subjects' views of whether or not most snakes are poisonous and whether or not most snakes can hurt people. In contrast, older children who heard the explanation were more likely to say that most snakes are not poisonous and cannot hurt people than were those who did not hear the explanation. This developmental difference could be due to the fact that the danger-related information in the verbal explanation was not as explicit as the neutral and positive information. Subjects had to infer that snakes are generally not threatening from statements that indicated that black snakes will not hurt anyone and that most snakes are not poisonous.

Another possible explanation for the ineffectiveness of the verbal explanation may be related to younger children's inability to retrieve and apply the explanation to the *Raiders* scene and simultaneously view it. However, neither the inability to infer danger-related information nor the inability to apply the information and simultaneously view the *Raiders* scene explains why the verbal explanation actually *increased* negative emotional reactions among younger subjects. Rather than having no effect, the explanation actually seems to have made the younger children more frightened.

Research on children's understanding of language is suggestive of some of the difficulties the younger children may have had with the verbal explanation. A number of studies have found that children between the ages of 4 and 7 do not fully understand comparative adjectives (for example, "less," "fewer"). For example, statements containing *less* are often interpreted as if they contained *more* (Grieve & Stanley, 1984; Palermo, 1973; Townsend, 1974), and statements containing *some* as if they meant *some and possibly all* (Smith, 1980). Research also indicates that in response to complex comparative questions, children between 3 and 6 frequently interpret only the first clause of such questions (Townsend & Erb, 1975). Finally, children below the age of 9 or 10 have been found to interpret contrastive conjunctions such as *although* and *but* as if they meant *and* (Hutson & Shub, 1975).

These various findings suggest that statements involving relative or contrastive terms are often misunderstood by younger children. Thus statements in the verbal explanation such as "although a few snakes are poisonous, most of them are not" may have been interpreted by younger subjects as suggesting that snakes are poisonous. These incorrect inferences would explain why the verbal explanation actually enhanced fear among younger subjects. It should be noted, however, that the two

danger-related comprehension items did not show that the younger subjects' perceptions actually indicated *more* danger if they heard the verbal
explanation. Further research is needed on children's comprehension of
threat-related information conveyed in a variety of forms.

The present study highlights the importance of separating visual exposure from verbal explanation in the treatment of children's fears. The study
also demonstrates the importance of adopting a developmental perspective in terms of fear-reduction techniques. Much of the research in this area
has given little attention to the multitude of developmental differences that
could interact with various treatment components.

The findings have implications for the theoretical mechanisms underlying the two fear-reduction components. Because visual exposure was
effective with children as young as 5 years of age, the process seems to be
more direct and automatic than various cognitive explanations would predict. The verbal explanation, on the other hand, was designed to alter the
interpretation of the fear stimulus. The fact that it was differentially effective
with the two age groups suggests that certain cognitive skills are involved in
the effective utilization of such information.

The research also suggests some of the potential benefits of studying
desensitization processes in the context of mass media. Mass media presentations provide an excellent vehicle for testing the effects of exposure
because such presentations can be standardized and systematically varied in terms of the type and amount of exposure to the fear stimulus. In
addition, because subjects are stationary during exposure to media presentations, their facial expressions and physiological arousal can be
continuously measured during such exposure.

Finally, the research has a number of practical implications. The systematic study of fear-reduction techniques can help therapists and parents in
alleviating children's fear reactions. For example, this study suggests that
reactions to frightening programs might be reduced by gradually exposing
the child to pictures or to educational programming related to a frightening
stimulus.

The research also indicates that parents should consider the child's age
when choosing a coping strategy. Verbal explanation, one of the techniques used most frequently by parents, may actually have negative effects
with younger children if the children draw incorrect conclusions about the
fear stimulus based on the information provided.

Future research can begin to examine the different conditions under
which exposure to a fear stimulus and explanation of a stimulus may be
effective with children of different ages. Such research will enhance our
understanding of the development of cognitive and emotional processes,
and of how such processes interact with one another.

NOTES

1. The original scene also contained a female character who exhibited extreme distress in response to the snakes in the cave. This character was edited out of the scene in order to ensure that children were reacting primarily to the snakes rather than to a character's intense fear reactions.

2. Random assignment to the experimental conditions was carried out independently for the two studies.

3. In order to obtain an equal-interval scale, eight potential modifiers for the word *scared* were rated on a six-point scale (0 = least scared, 6 = most scared) by 13 undergraduates enrolled in a communication course at the University of Wisconsin—Madison. The phrases "not at all scared" ($M = 0.1$), "kinda scared" ($M = 2.0$), "pretty scared" ($M = 3.9$), and "very very scared" ($M = 5.9$) were chosen for the scale because they received mean intensity ratings closest to the values 0, 2, 4, and 6. These phrases were also unanimously ranked in the indicated order. In a subsequent pretest, the four selected phrases were rank-ordered by 39 9- to 11-year-old children. Of the children, 90% ranked them in the correct order. Agreement on the rank ordering was highly significant (Kendall's coefficient of concordance, $W = .83, p < .01$).

4. Although 10 major emotional expressions were coded according to the Affex scheme, most of these expressions had a very low level of occurrence. Because fear was the focus of interest, only analyses associated with this emotion are reported.

5. The mean response level for heart rate was calculated based on the first 84 seconds of the *Raiders* scene. The last 11 seconds of the scene showed the main character, Indiana Jones, actually falling into the cave of snakes. Many subjects exhibited a startle reaction to this portrayal, and the body movements accompanying this reaction artificially increased the physiological responses. Therefore, responses during this latter time period were not included in the analyses. The same time period was used for the analysis of facial fear so that the two measures would coincide.

6. The data for three subjects are missing from the heart-rate analyses because of a temporary equipment problem.

REFERENCES

Bandura, A., & Menlove, F. L. (1968). Factors determining vicarious extinction of avoidance behavior through symbolic modeling. *Journal of Personality and Social Psychology, 8,* 99-108.

Brown, A. L., Bransford, J. D., Ferrara, R. A., & Campione, J. C. (1983). Learning, remembering, and understanding. In P. H. Mussen (Ed.), *Handbook of child psychology* (4th ed., pp. 77-166). New York: John Wiley.

Brown, M. B. (1976). Screening effects in multidimensional contingency tables. *Applied Statistics, 25,* 37-46.

Cantor, J., & Reilly, S. (1982). Adolescents' enduring fright reactions to television and films. *Journal of Communication, 32,* 87-99.

Cantor, J., & Sparks, G. G. (1984). Children's fear responses to mass media: Testing some Piagetian predictions. *Journal of Communication, 34,* 90-103.

Cantor, J., & Wilson, B. J. (1984). Modifying fear responses to mass media in preschool and elementary school children. *Journal of Broadcasting, 28,* 431-443.

Cantor, J., Wilson, B. J., & Hoffner, C. (1986). Emotional responses to a televised nuclear holocaust film. *Communication Research, 13,* 257-277.

Collins, W. A. (1983). Interpretation and inference in children's television viewing. In J. Bryant & D. R. Anderson (Eds.), *Children's understanding of television* (pp. 125-150). New York: Academic Press.

Cronbach, L. J., & Meehl, P. (1955). Construct validity of psychological tests. *Psychological Bulletin, 52,* 281-302.

Evans, I. M. (1973). The logical requirements for explanation of systematic desensitization. *Behavior Therapy, 4,* 506-514.

Graziano, A. M., DeGiovanni, I. S., & Garcia, K. A. (1979). Behavioral treatment of children's fears: A review. *Psychological Bulletin, 86,* 804-830.

Graham, F. K., & Clifton, R. K. (1966). Heart-rate change as a component of the orienting response. *Psychological Bulletin, 65,* 305-320.

Grieve, R., & Stanley, S. (1984). Less obscure? Pragmatics and 3-4-year-old children's semantics. *British Journal of Developmental Psychology, 2,* 95-103.

Hutson, B. A., & Shub, J. (1975). Developmental study of factors involved in choice of conjunction. *Child Development, 46,* 46-53.

Izard, C. E. (1971). *The face of emotion.* New York: Appleton-Century-Crofts.

Izard, C. E., Dougherty, L. M., & Hembree, E. A. (1983). *A system for identifying affect expressions by holistic judgments (Affex).* Newark, DE: University of Delaware, Instructional Resources Center.

Jersild, A. T., & Holmes, F. B. (1935). Methods of overcoming children's fears. *The Journal of Psychology, 1,* 75-104.

Johnson, R., & Machen, J. B. (1973). Behavior modification techniques and maternal anxiety. *Journal of Dentistry for Children, 40,* 272-276.

Jones, M. C. (1924). The elimination of children's fears. *Journal of Experimental Psychology, 7,* 382-390.

Lacey, J. I., Kagan, J., Lacey, B. C., & Moss, H. A. (1963). The visceral level: Situational determinant and behavioral correlates of autonomic response patterns. In P. H. Knapp (Ed.), *Expression of the emotions in man* (pp. 161-196). New York: International Universities Press.

Lang, P. J. (1984). Cognition in emotion: Concept and action. In C. E. Izard, J. Kagan, & R. B. Zajonc (Eds.), *Emotions, cognition, and behavior* (pp. 192-226). Cambridge: Cambridge University Press.

Lazarus, A. A. (1974). The elimination of children's phobias by deconditioning. In H. J. Eysenck (Ed.), *Experiments in behavior therapy* (pp. 467-474). New York: Pergamon.

Lazarus, R. S. (1984). Thoughts on the relations between emotion and cognition. In K. R. Scherer & P. Ekman (Eds.), *Approaches to emotion* (pp. 247-258). Hillsdale, NJ: Lawrence Erlbaum.

Lazarus, R. S., Opton, E. M., Nomikos, M. S., & Rankin, N. O. (1965). The principle of short-circuiting of threat: Further evidence. *Journal of Personality, 33,* 622-635.

Leitenberg, H., & Callahan, E. J. (1973). Reinforced practice and reduction of different kinds of fears in adults and children. *Behavior Research and Therapy, 11,* 19-30.

Lende, E. W. (1971). The effect of preparation on children's response to tonsillectomy and adenoidectomy surgery. *Dissertation Abstracts International, 32,* 3642B.

Leventhal, H. (1984). A perceptual motor theory of emotion. In K. R. Scherer & P. Ekman (Eds.), *Approaches to emotion* (pp. 271-292). Hillsdale, NJ: Lawrence Erlbaum.

Lomont, J. F. (1965). Reciprocal inhibition or extinction? *Behavior Research and Therapy, 3,* 209-219.

Maccoby, E. E. (1969). The development of stimulus selection. In J. P. Hill (Ed.), *Minnesota symposia on child psychology* (Vol. 3, pp. 68-96). Minneapolis: University of Minnesota.

Machen, J. B., & Johnson, R. (1974). Desensitization, model learning, and the dental behavior of children. *Journal of Dental Research, 53,* 83-87.

Mackworth, J. F. (1976). Development of attention. In V. Hamilton & M. D. Vernon (Eds.), *The development of cognitive processes* (pp. 111-152). New York: Academic Press.

Manis, F. R., Keating, D. P., & Morrison, F. J. (1980). Developmental differences in the allocation of processing capacity. *Journal of Experimental Child Psychology, 29,* 156-169.

Marascuilo, L. A., & Levin, J. R. (1983). *Multivariate statistics in the social sciences.* Monterey, CA: Brooks/Cole.

Murphy, C. M., & Bootzin, R. R. (1973). Active and passive participation in the contact desensitization of snake fear in children. *Behavior Therapy, 4,* 203-211.

Obler, M., & Terwilliger, R. F. (1970). Pilot study on the effectiveness of systematic desensitization with neurologically impaired children with phobic disorders. *Journal of Consulting and Clinical Psychology, 34,* 314-318.

Oliver, L. D. (1971). Desensitization of a childhood fear within a school setting. *Dissertation Abstracts International, 32,* 1222B.

Ollendick, T. H. (1979). Fear reduction techniques with children. In M. Hersen, R. M. Eisler, & P. M. Miller (Eds.), *Progress in behavior modification* (Vol. 8, pp. 127-168). New York: Academic Press.

O'Reilly, P. P. (1971). Desensitization of fire bell phobia. *Journal of School Psychology, 9,* 55-57.

Palermo, D. S. (1973). More about less: A study of language comprehension. *Journal of Verbal Learning and Verbal Behavior, 12,* 211-221.

Palmer, E. L., Hockett, A. B., & Dean, W. W. (1983). The television family and children's fright reactions. *Journal of Family Issues, 4,* 279-292.

Paris, S. G., & Lindauer, B. K. (1977). Constructive aspects of children's comprehension and memory. In R. V. Kail & J. W. Hagen (Eds.), *Perspectives on the development of memory and cognition* (pp. 35-60). New York: John Wiley.

Ritter, B. (1968). The group desensitization of children's snake phobias using vicarious and contact desensitization procedures. *Behavior Research and Therapy, 6,* 1-6.

Roberts, M. C., Wurtele, S. K., Boone, R. R., Ginther, L. J., & Elkins, P. D. (1981). Reduction of medical fears by use of modeling: A preventative application in a general population of children. *Journal of Pediatric Psychology, 6,* 293-300.

Roberts, R. N., & Gordon, S. B. (1979). Reducing childhood nightmares subsequent to a burn trauma. *Child Behavior Therapy, 1,* 373-381.

Rosengarten, M. (1961). The behavior of the preschool child at the initial dental visit. *Journal of Dental Research, 40,* 473.

Sheslow, D. V., Bondy, A. S., & Nelson, R. O. (1983). A comparison of graduated exposure, verbal coping skills, and their combination in the treatment of children's fear of the dark. *Child and Family Behavior Therapy, 4,* 33-45.

Smith, C. L. (1980). Quantifiers and question answering in young children. *Journal of Experimental Child Psychology, 30,* 191-205.

Sparks, G. G. (1986). Developmental differences in children's reports of fear induced by the mass media. *Child Study Journal, 16,* 55-66.

Tasto, D. L. (1969). Systematic desensitization, muscle relaxation and visual imagery in the counterconditioning of a four-year-old phobic child. *Behavior Research and Therapy, 7,* 409-411.

Townsend, D. J. (1974). Children's comprehension of comparative forms. *Journal of Experimental Child Psychology, 18,* 293-303.

Townsend, D. J., & Erb, M. (1975). Children's strategies for interpreting complex comparative questions. *Journal of Child Language, 2,* 271-277.

Wallick, M. M. (1979). Desensitization therapy with a fearful two-year-old. *American Journal of Psychiatry, 136,* 1325-1326.

White, W. C., & Davis, M. T. (1974). Vicarious extinction of phobic behavior in early childhood. *Journal of Abnormal Child Psychology, 2,* 25-32.

Wilkins, W. (1971). Desensitization: Social and cognitive factors underlying the effectiveness of Wolpe's procedure. *Psychological Bulletin, 76,* 311-316.

Wilson, B. J., & Cantor, J. (1985). Developmental differences in empathy with a television protagonist's fear. *Journal of Experimental Child Psychology, 39,* 284-299.

Wilson, B. J., Hoffner, C., & Cantor, J. (in press). Children's perceptions of the effectiveness of techniques to reduce fear from mass media. *Journal of Applied Developmental Psychology.*

Wilson, G. T., & Davison, G. C. (1971). Processes of fear reduction in systematic desensitization: Animal studies. *Psychological Bulletin, 76,* 1-14.

Wish, P. A., Hasazi, J. E., & Jurgela, A. R. (1973). Automated direct deconditioning of a childhood phobia. *Journal of Behavior Therapy and Experimental Psychiatry, 4,* 279-283.

26 ● The Relationship Between Selected Immediacy Behaviors and Cognitive Learning

VIRGINIA P. RICHMOND ●
JOAN S. GORHAM ● JAMES C. McCROSKEY

West Virginia University

L EARNING, particularly that which takes place in the traditional classroom setting, is an interactional process. Although curricular decisions, materials development, the organization of lectures, and the like focus primarily on the teacher's transmission of content—and student evaluation on comprehension and retention of that content—there is little disagreement that interpersonal perceptions and communicative relationships between teachers and students are crucial to the teaching-learning process.

From a theoretical standpoint, Bloom's (1956) conceptualization of learning as affective (development of a favorable or unfavorable attitude toward learning), behavioral (development of psychomotor skills or observable behavior change as a result of learning), and cognitive (comprehension and retention of knowledge) has for several decades been accepted widely as an elegant characterization of the learning construct. An interdependence among these domains of learning generally has been recognized among educators, an assumption crucial to the fact that evaluation of learning outcomes often is focused on measurement within a selected domain. Physical and vocational education skills, which are clearly observable psychomotor skills, are often assessed in the behavioral domain. Students' learning of traditional "academic subjects," for which generalization of learning to behavior outside the classroom is more difficult to assess, is generally measured via tests of recall, analysis, and synthesis, elements of the cognitive domain. Evaluation of teaching effectiveness, particularly that which is based on the ubiquitous student course evaluation form, is drawn largely from assessment of affective dimensions of teaching.

Correspondence and requests for reprints: Virginia P. Richmond, 130 Armstrong Hall, West Virginia University, Morgantown, WV 26506.

An operational definition of what constitutes good teaching has been elusive (Brim, 1958; Cyphert, 1972; Getzels & Jackson, 1963; Heath & Nielson, 1974).

> A great deal has been written lately about teaching techniques designed to help teachers engage in different types of classroom processes. Much of the literature about these classroom processes does not specify the teaching strategy necessary in order to be able to bring about desired outcomes. Often, this is because the tools for discussing the necessary teaching behaviors are not available, or not known about by the curriculum authors. Thus the desired outcome for students is discussed, but the way to get there is not.
>
> The traditional role of teacher is described by a well-known set of behaviors. Any school child playing "teacher" will produce most of the behaviors used by most teachers. Typical behaviors are: standing in the front of a group of relatively passive onlookers (a position of authority), doing most of the talking (telling), asking questions to which they already know the answers (testing), and evaluating by passing judgments. Yet, no research base indicates that these behaviors have payoff in terms of learning, and much indicates that they do not. (Simon & Boyer, 1974, p. 5)

Without a clear picture of the relationship between specific teacher behaviors and student achievement, empirically grounded prescriptions for the training and evaluation of teachers are difficult to propose. Andersen (1978, 1979) presents strong support for the centrality of nonverbal immediacy behaviors in effective teaching-learning relationships. Victoria (1970, p. 3) has noted that "nonverbal phenomena become qualitatively predominant aspects of interpersonal relationships. These interpersonal relationships are critical aspects of all learning situations." Andersen's research has focused primarily on the impact of immediacy on student affect, with recognition of its possible influence in other learning domains (Krathwohl, Bloom & Masia, 1964; Ringness, 1968).

That immediacy—which Mehrabian (1969, p. 203) defines as communicative behaviors that "enhance closeness to and nonverbal interaction with another"—is related to affective learning is intuitively comfortable: A positive interpersonal relationship developed between teachers and students would seem likely to influence the development of favorable attitudes toward the learning situation. A number of empirical studies have supported this position (see Andersen & Andersen, 1982, pp. 110-112).

Although somewhat more elusive, in light of what we know about theories of persuasion, immediacy seems likely to influence the probability of behavioral change as well. The intuitive link between cognitive learning and nonverbal immediacy is less clear. Although nonverbal communication is a relationship language, cognitive gain is generally assessed via measures of recall, synthesis, and application of information transmitted verbally. According to Mehrabian (1981, p. 3), "People rarely transmit implicitly [nonverbally] the kinds of complex information that they can convey with words; rather, implicit communication deals primarily with the transmission of information about feelings and like-dislike or attitudes. The *referents* of implicit behaviors, in other words, are emotions and attitudes or like-dislike."

The empirical evidence linking nonverbal immediacy behaviors to cognitive learning is also less clear. In Andersen's (1978, 1979) study of college students enrolled in an introductory interpersonal communication course, teacher immediacy predicted 46% of the variance in students' affect toward the instructor, 20% of the variance in students' affect toward the content of the course, and 18% of the variance in students' behavioral commitment. Cognitive learning, however, as operationalized by scores on a 50-item multiple choice test, was not significantly predicted by the teachers' immediacy. McDowell, McDowell, and Hyerdahl (1980) replicated Andersen's research in communication courses in junior and senior high schools, adding additional exploratory variables to determine whether or not measures of homophily and/or student attentiveness correlate with immediacy variables. The overall results revealed significant relationships between and among affect, behavior, immediacy, homophily, and attentiveness, but low correlation between these variables and a measure of cognitive learning. Junior high students who gave the teacher high ratings on Andersen's Behavioral Indicants of Immediacy Scale (BII)—which focuses on teachers' use of specific immediacy behaviors—reported that they enjoyed engaging in communication practices (that is, demonstrated behavioral commitment) and received higher course grades. These variables were, however, negatively correlated with the Generalized Immediacy Scale (GI), Andersen's assessment of the perceived general immediacy of the instructor. At the senior high level, significant positive relationships existed between the BII, engaging in communication practices, homophily, and attentiveness variables, but no relationship was found between these variable and cognitive learning (the course grade).

Andersen and Andersen (1982) summarize several additional studies in which examination of specific nonverbal immediacy behaviors such as eye contact (Breed, Christiansen, & Larson, 1972), vocal inflection (Coats & Smidchens, 1966), gestures (Gauger, 1952), proximity, smiling, and touch (Kleinfeld, 1973) have been positively related to various measures of cognitive gain. Taken together with the Andersen (1979) and McDowell, McDowell, and Hyerdahl (1980) studies, we are left with inconclusive and somewhat confusing data regarding the relationship of the teacher's immediacy and the cognitive domain of learning.

Krathwohl, Bloom, and Masia (1964) cite evidence that cognitive learning can occur at the expense of affective outcomes. It is equally possible that affective outcomes might occur at the expense of cognitive learning, that high affect for the teacher might, in fact, interfere with cognitive learning (Andersen, 1979). If this is true and we are concerned with achievement in the cognitive domain, we might note that highly immediate teachers produce high affect and hypothesize that less immediate teachers will thus produce high cognitive outcomes, a sort of "pain equals gain" relationship like that espoused by at least some exercise fanatics. This interpretation of mutual exclusivity is, however, incompatible not only with Bloom's taxonomy, but with Mehrabian's conceptualization of the immediacy construct. We would hypothesize that at least part of the difficulty in establishing the relationship between the teacher's immediacy and cognitive learning relates to problems in establishing valid measures of the cognitive learning variable. Andersen suggests that the single test grade entered as the cognitive learning variable in her study may have been recorded too early in the course for a relationship between performance and immediacy to have been established, or that the nature of the course, incorporating a mastery-level design, might have skewed the distributions of grades. McDowell et al. (1980) suggest that junior high students might be more motivated to study for examinations, prepare assignments, and generally strive to meet criteria for determining the course grade for teachers they wish to please. Senior high students may be less influenced by adult authority and fail to prepare for tests and assignments from which the course grade is drawn; thus long-term cognitive gain might not be reflected accurately in grades for either group. A primary concern in the design of the present study was the development of an alternative means of assessing cognitive learning that can be applied across disparate content areas and is not influenced by factors such as attendance, perceived motivation, preparation for tests or assignments, course or test design, and similar elements that are commonly reflected in assigning grades but may or may not be directly associated with perceived or actual learning.

It is important to recognize that interactions between teachers and students are characterized by both verbal and nonverbal components and that nonverbal behaviors *will* be interpreted in terms of pleasure, arousal, dominance, and liking (Mehrabian, 1981). In other words, a relationship between a teacher and a learner cannot be free of affect; the "metaphors" of approach-avoidance (or immediacy), arousal-activity, and power-status represent dimensions on which the relationship is evaluated, largely through interpretation of nonverbal cues. Furthermore, the various dimensions subsumed under "liking" (preference for versus preference against, like-dislike, positive-negative attitude) are positively correlated with those subsumed under "approach-avoidance" (physical approach versus avoidance, attention versus inattention, exploration versus lack of exploration, examination versus lack of examination, striving to get closer versus away) (Mehrabian, 1978, 1980; Mehrabian & Russell, 1974). Within Mehrabian's conceptualization of the liking/immediacy construct, then, a teacher's behavior must be characterized by some degree of immediacy.

We know that the teacher's immediacy is associated with increased student affect, and also that teachers' perceptions of success in teaching are largely associated with affective outcomes (Harootunian & Yarger, 1981). One definition of effective teaching behavior thus includes optimal use of nonverbal behaviors that enhance perceived immediacy. The prescriptive usefulness of this definition is directly associated with the degree to which nonverbal strategies can be consciously employed by teachers. It has been demonstrated (Bradley, 1979; Grant & Hennings, 1971; Karr-Kidwell, 1978; Klinzing, 1983, 1984; Nier, 1979; Nussbaum, 1984) that teachers' nonverbal behaviors can be modified through awareness and training. Because nonverbal communication is multichanneled and characterized by both intentionally and unintentionally transmitted messages, however, the totality of nonverbal behavior is difficult for teachers to monitor. Our objective in this study was thus to isolate specific nonverbal behaviors that are likely to have the greatest effect on learning. The identification of these behaviors will provide teachers and teacher educators with clearly focused behavioral objectives in their efforts to improve effectiveness in teaching.

Nonverbal Immediacy Behaviors

Mehrabian (1981) indicates that immediacy in the interaction between two people "includes greater physical proximity and/or more perceptual stimulation of the two by one another" (p. 14). Immediacy is thus characterized in part by reduced physical or psychological distances in teacher-student interaction. Hesler's (1972) study of teachers' proxemic positioning revealed that teachers who sat at, on, beside, or behind the desk were rated by students as low in both affection and inclusion and teachers who moved in front of the desk or among the students were more likely to be perceived as warm, friendly, and effective. Research has provided solid evidence that more immediacy is communicated when people face one another directly and that people assume closer positions to those they like than to strangers or those they dislike (for example, Aiello & Cooper, 1972; Andersen, Andersen, & Jensen, 1979; Byrne, Baskett, & Hodges, 1971; Mehrabian 1968, 1967; Mehrabian & Friar, 1969; Patterson & Sechrest, 1970). When social interaction takes place in close proximity, the frequency and duration of touch can be used as an indication of liking or interpersonal closeness (Andersen, Andersen, & Jensen, 1979; Fisher, Rytting, & Heslin, 1976; Henley, 1977; Jourard, 1966; Montague, 1978; Morris, 1971). Although the point at which physical proximity and, to an even greater extent, interpersonal touch become uncomfortable differs among individuals, the lack of recognition resulting from psychological distancing can negate any verbal attempts to establish interpersonal bonds. A teacher's withholding of touch, for example, may result in feelings of rejection and isolation in students (Hurt, Scott, & McCroskey, 1978).

Even when close physical proximity is not possible, direct eye contact can provide psychological closeness between teachers and students and has been shown to be an important component of both interpersonal immediacy generally and the teacher's immediacy in particular (Andersen, 1979; Andersen, Andersen, & Jensen, 1979). Hodge (1971), Bishop (1976), and others have similarly commented on the importance of the teacher's establishing eye contact with both the class as a whole and with individual students within the group. In a series of studies on the effects of teacher gaze on the attitudes of university students, Breed (1971) found that the absence of eye contact between teachers and students usually produces negative feelings in students, and that high levels of gaze at particular students makes them more attentive to the teacher. Mehrabian (1981) notes that "considerable evidence has been accumulated showing that more eye contact is associated with greater liking and more positive feelings among interactants" (p. 23). Such evidence can be found in the work of Exline and Winters (1965), Kendon (1967), Mehrabian (1968), Mehrabian and Friar (1969), and Thayer and Schiff (1974).

Beyond increasing physical and/or psychological proximity, immediacy is also characterized by behaviors that contribute to perceptual stimulation during interpersonal interaction. Smiling is one nonverbal behavior that has been associated with such perceptual stimulation, indicating both liking and arousal (Kraut & Johnston, 1979; Mehrabian, 1981). Andersen, Andersen, and Jensen (1979) classified smiling as central to the concept of immediacy. Kendon (1967) notes that smiles are reciprocal immediacy behaviors: When one person smiles, the other is likely to smile in return. Ekman (Stern, 1984) has, in fact, reported that the act of smiling "causes your involuntary nervous system to go through corresponding changes in heart rate, skin temperature and electrical resistance usually associated with the emotion and causes you to experience the feeling your face is mimicking" so that "when we see someone else smiling, we *feel* a similar sensation" (p. 113). Rosenfeld (1966) found smiling the most commonly used behavior to communicate affiliativeness; similarly, Bayes (1970) identified frequency of smiling as the single best predictor of perceived interpersonal warmth.

Perceptual stimulation is also related to body movement: A physically active teacher provides both visual and auditory sensory arousal. Subjects in Rosenfeld's (1966) study of approval-seeking increased both gestural activity and head nodding when seeking positive affect. Andersen (1979) and Andersen, Andersen, and Jensen (1979) found overall body movement positively associated with the perceived immediacy of the teacher. Mehrabian (1971) proposed that greater use of gestures by a teacher "tends to be associated with a more affiliative classroom style which in turn elicits liking and cooperation from others" (Smith, 1979, p. 649).

Beebe (1980) summarizes studies by Mehrabian (1971) and Seals and Kaufman (1975) that indicate clear differences between the kinesic patterns of effective and "average" teachers. Effective teachers moved more; student attitudes were positively correlated with increased activity by the instructor. A relaxed body posture also has been found to be related to teacher immediacy (Andersen, 1979), to be influential in eliciting opinion change (McGinley, LeFevre, & McGinley, 1975) and to be less likely when people dislike one another (Mehrabian, 1968).

A last factor related to perceptual stimulation and immediacy is the nonverbal paralinguistic or vocalic variable. Although Mehrabian (1981) demonstrates the clear relationship among vocal expressiveness, rate, and volume and both interpersonal liking and arousal, the effects of paralinguistic variables on classroom teaching have not been investigated extensively (Smith, 1979). Bayes's (1970) study of the behavioral cues of interpersonal warmth concluded that tone of voice was not a reliable indicator of affect; however, Scherer's (1972) experimentation with electronically synthesized nonverbal sounds indicated that emotional and affective cues could be communicated through changes in pitch and tempo. Andersen, Andersen, and Jensen (1979) similarly found vocal expressiveness to be an important factor in communicating immediacy. In a related study, Weineke (1981) concluded that the *delivery* as well as the content and organization of the first lecture in university classes had a significant impact on students' approach to the subject and to the teacher.

Research Questions

The studies reviewed above suggest a variety of nonverbal behaviors that teachers can employ to affect perceptions of immediacy. These include moving away from a desk or podium, facing students, touching students, establishing eye contact with students, smiling at students, moving around the room, having a relaxed posture, and being vocally expressive. All of these variables, individually and collectively, have been demonstrated to be associated with affective responses. Our concern in the present investigation, however, centered on cognitive learning. We were concerned with the degree to which these nonverbal behaviors, individually and collectively, are associated with cognitive learning in college classrooms. Specifically, our research questions were as follows:

RQ_1 To what extent are student perceptions of individual types of nonverbal behaviors of teachers associated with cognitive learning of students?

RQ_2 To what extent are student perceptions of nonverbal behaviors of teachers collectively associated with cognitive learning of students?

METHOD

Measurement

Cognitive learning. A vexing problem that has confronted previous researchers concerned with the impact of immediacy in the classroom, as well as with the impact of many other variables, is how to measure cognitive learning. Although standardized tests exist in a variety of subject matters, such tests, by their very nature, are individually restricted to a single subject area. Thus, if research is to be conducted across disciplines, such tests are not useful. Some researchers have chosen, as a result, to use grades as an indicator of cognitive learning. Unfortunately, such grades are subject to a variety of influences in addition to cognitive learning, such as attendance, participation, writing skills, and the like.

In the absence of a solid, objective measure of cognitive learning, we turned to a subjective measure. We did this with full recognition that any subjective measure would almost certainly be confounded to an unknown extent with affect. However, such confounding in measurement may be less of a problem than it may seem at first consideration, particularly among college students. Although a student may generate positive or negative affect for a course for many reasons, one very important basis for a student's affective response is whether or not the student perceives he or she "got anything out of the course." College students are adults with considerable experience in a school environment. We believe it is reasonable to expect them to estimate with considerable accuracy the amount they learn in a given class. In fact, it is likely that their estimate is at least as good as subjective grades provided by teachers in many classes or by tests administered in classes not based on clear behavioral objectives. Simply put, none of these methods is inherently superior to others in terms of validity. Rather, each probes the domain of cognitive learning in a different way and may tap it in such a way that it both overlaps with another method and captures unique information.

We asked the subjects to indicate how much they thought they learned in the classes studied. Specifically, the following scale was employed: "On a scale of 0-9, how much did you learn in the class, with 0 meaning you learned nothing and 9 meaning you learned more than in any other class you've had." Subjects were also asked, on the same scale, "How much do you think you could have learned in the class had you had the ideal instructor?" By subtracting the score on the first scale from the score on the second we created a variable labeled "learning loss" which was intended to remove some of the possible bias with regard to estimated learning that could stem from being forced to take a class in a disliked subject. As noted in the results reported below, this procedure produced results virtually identical to those of the first scale alone. The correlation between the two scores was .94.

Immediacy behaviors. Subjects were presented with a series of 14 statements describing nonverbal behaviors of teachers (see Table 26.1) that were embedded in a longer questionnaire of 39 items. The remaining items related to irrelevant (to this study) verbal behaviors. The subjects were asked to indicate (by circling "Yes" or "No") whether or not the teacher in the target class used each given behavior. If they indicated the teacher did so, they were asked to indicate how frequently the teacher did so from rarely (scored 1) to very often (scored 4). The frequency of use score was set at 0 for those subjects indicating the teacher did not use the behavior described.

The use of students to report immediacy behavior of teachers was found to be a valid method of obtaining such data in previous research by Andersen (1978). In her study Andersen found high correlations between the reports of students in classes and reports of trained observers.

A total immediacy score was generated by summing the frequency scores of the items (after reflection when necessary). The alpha reliability of the score was .87 in the first study and .80 in the second study.

Participants

Participants in both studies in this investigation were undergraduate college students in basic communication courses. Approximately half in each study were female and half male. A total of 361 persons participated in the first study and 358 in the second study.

Procedures

Study 1. The first study was designed to provide an upper estimate of the potential impact of immediacy variables on learning. Approximately half of the participants were asked to recall the "best teacher you have had in college" and complete the questionnaire concerning that teacher and the class that the subject had with the teacher. The other half did the same for the "worst teacher you have had in college."

Study 2. The second study was designed to provide a more realistic estimate of the impact of immediacy on learning. Approximately half of the participants were asked to respond to the questionnaire on the basis of a "class you took in your major or intended major last semester." The other half responded on the basis of a "class you took outside your major or intended major last semester."

In both studies the respondents were asked to participate during regular class time but were permitted to decline to participate by simply turning in a blank questionnaire. Only three blank forms were turned in. All responses were anonymous.

Table 26.1
Immediacy Behavior Items

---

*1. Sits behind desk when teaching.
 2. Gestures when talking to the class.
*3. Uses monotone/dull voice when talking to the class.
 4. Looks at the class when talking.
 5. Smiles at the class as a whole, not just individual students.
*6. Has a very tense body position when talking to the class.
 7. Touches students in the class.
 8. Moves around the classroom when teaching.
*9. Sits on a desk or in a chair when teaching.
*10. Looks at board or notes when talking to the class.
*11. Stands behind podium or desk when teaching.
 12. Has a very relaxed body position when talking to the class.
 13. Smiles at individual students in the class.
 14. Uses a variety of vocal expressions when talking to the class.

---

* Presumed to be *nonimmediate*.

Data Analyses

In both studies, simple correlations were computed between learning and learning-loss scores and both the total immediacy behavior score and the scores for the individual behavior categories. Multiple correlations were also computed in both studies with scores on the individual behavior categories serving as predictors of the learning and learning-loss scores. Discriminant analyses were conducted for the data in both studies. In the first study the classifications were "best" and "worst" teacher. In the second study, learning levels were created to serve as classifications (low = 0-3, moderate = 4-6, high = 7-9). Finally, analyses of variance were conducted in both studies with the individual behavior frequency scores and total score serving as dependent variables. In the first study the classification of the teacher was the independent variable. In the second study the independent variable was learning level of the students.

RESULTS

Table 26.1 reports the results of the correlational analyses from both studies. Correlations involving the learning and learning-loss variables were essentially similar in study 1. In both analyses, the correlation of learning with the total immediacy score indicated approximately 50% shared variance. The multiple correlations with learning indicated slightly higher shared variance.

In the second study, the correlations of the individual immediacy items with learning loss were generally somewhat higher than with learning. The correlations of the total immediacy score with learning indicated 26%

Table 26.2
Correlations of Learning and Learning-Loss Scores with
Immediacy Behavior Items and Total Immediacy Score

Immediacy Item/Score	Study 1		Study 2	
	Learning	Learning-Loss	Learning	Learning-Loss
1	−.31	.32	−.23	.29
2	.36	−.36	.09*	−.05*
3	−.58	.57	−.48	.53
4	.41	−.41	.29	−.27
5	.55	−.53	.31	−.40
6	−.37	.36	−.27	.32
7	.30	−.29	.12	−.16
8	.44	−.41	.25	−.24
9	−.12	.12	−.09*	.10*
10	−.38	.41	−.24	.34
11	−.18	.16	−.19	.25
12	.57	−.56	.26	−.39
13	.36	−.35	.18	−.20
14	.61	−.59	.40	−.45
Total	.71	.69	.51	.60
Multiple correlation	.74	.73	.57	.64

*$p > .05$.

shared variance and that with learning loss 36% shared variance. The multiple correlations indicated 32% and 41% shared variance, respectively.

Examination of the simple correlations in both studies indicated that use of vocal expressiveness, smiling at the class, and having a relaxed body position had the highest positive association with learning. Sitting on the desk when teaching and gesturing when talking demonstrated no significant relationship in the second study. In addition, touching students and smiling at individual students generated low, but positive, relationships in the second study. Moderate positive relationships were observed for looking at the class and moving around the room when teaching. Moderate negative relationships were observed for sitting behind the desk, having a tense body position, standing behind a podium or desk, and looking at the board or notes.

The discriminant analysis of the data from study 1 indicated that 95% of the participants could be classified correctly into the a priori best-teacher and worst-teacher categories. Best and worst teachers differed significantly on a linear combination of nine variables, $F(9,345) = 87.53, p < .0001$; Wilks's lambda $= .30$. Variables included in the model were numbers 3, 5, 6, 7, 8, 9, 10, 12, and 14 (see Table 26.1).

The discriminant analysis of the data from study 2 indicated that 68% of the subjects could be classified correctly into the a priori high, moderate, and low learner classifications. High, moderate, and low learners

Table 26.3
Means of Immediacy Items and Total Score by Teacher Classification

Immediacy Item/Score	Best Teacher	Worst Teacher	F-Ratio	Percentage of Variance
1	.41	1.22	33.45*	7.9
2	3.24	2.17	69.31*	14.8
3	.40	2.73	277.79*	41.4
4	3.63	2.28	119.67*	23.4
5	2.99	.91	273.64*	41.2
6	.35	1.42	60.60*	13.1
7	.71	.12	52.84*	11.8
8	2.68	1.19	113.18*	22.3
9	1.16	1.50	5.15**	1.3
10	1.09	2.29	84.99*	17.5
11	1.24	1.81	14.10**	3.5
12	3.25	1.15	275.65*	41.2
13	2.08	.99	72.16*	15.3
14	3.07	.77	400.82*	50.1
Total	41.30	22.33	546.11*	60.7

* $p < .0001$; ** $p < .05$.

could be discriminated by the teacher's scores on four immediacy variables, $F(8,656) = 11.80$, $p < .0001$; Wilks's lambda = .76. Variables included in the model were using a monotone/dull voice, looking at the class, moving around the classroom, and using vocal variety. Only use of a monotone/dull voice was a negative predictor.

A supplementary discriminant analysis involving only high and low learners indicated 92% of the subjects (N = 210) could be correctly classified into these a priori categories. Stepwise analysis yielded a six-variable model, $F(6,203) = 21.10$, $p < .0001$; Wilks's lambda = .62. Variables included in the model were gesturing when talking, using a monotone/dull voice (negative), moving around the classroom, looking at board or notes (negative), smiling at individual students, and using vocal variety.

The results of the analyses of variance for study 1 are reported in Table 26.3, those for study 2 in Table 26.4. The analyses based on the total immediacy score indicated approximately 61% of the variance was accounted for in study 1 and 21% in study 2. The individual variables on which the most variance was accounted for were those dealing with the use of voice.

An examination of the mean reported use of the individual variables in study 2 suggests that the teachers whom the students referenced in this study generally gestured and looked at the class when talking. In contrast, it appears that it was very unusual for these college teachers to touch a student and comparatively rare for the teachers to stand behind or sit on a desk or to have a tense body position when teaching.

Table 26.4
Means of Immediacy Items and Total Score by Learning Level Classification

Immediacy Item/Score	High Learner	Moderate Learner	Low Learner	F-Ratio	Percentage of Variance
1	.44	.68	1.24	7.61**	4.1
2	3.23	3.12	3.03	.89	—
3	2.67	1.15	.52	40.45*	18.6
4	3.72	3.47	3.12	12.02*	6.4
5	2.70	2.39	1.39	16.68*	8.6
6	.26	.42	1.18	13.58*	7.1
7	.40	.35	.12	1.59	—
8	2.46	2.12	1.18	12.00*	6.4
9	1.08	1.17	1.52	1.54	—
10	1.29	1.66	2.27	10.18*	5.5
11	1.58	1.81	2.33	4.18**	2.3
12	3.02	2.67	2.03	11.10*	6.1
13	1.82	1.71	1.03	5.46**	3.0
14	2.74	2.30	1.18	24.18*	12.0
Total	39.07	35.31	26.13	44.74*	21.3

* $p < .0001$; ** $p < .05$.

The total immediacy scores could range from 0 to 56; the hypothetical midpoint on the scale is 28. The observed standard deviation for the scores in study 2 was 8.22. Thus the "best" teachers in study 1 can be described as very highly immediate and the "worst" teachers probably should be described as moderately low in immediacy. Teachers of students reporting high learning in study 2 were only a little more immediate than those of students reporting moderate learning. However, both were substantially more immediate than those of students reporting low learning. An examination of a plot of the immediacy and cognitive learning scores in the second study indicated the association between the two scores clearly was nonlinear.

SUMMARY AND IMPLICATIONS

If we assume that the students in the present studies were in a position to give a reasonably accurate report of their cognitive learning and were motivated to respond truthfully to our request for that information, we may conclude from this research that immediacy behaviors are substantially associated with cognitive learning. These results suggest that across typical classrooms on the college level (study 2) the association may range from a quarter to a third of the variance. In extreme instances (study 1) the association may be quite a bit higher.

Although all of the immediacy items in our study of best and worst teachers were able to discriminate between such extreme types, it is clear that not all immediacy behaviors are of equal importance. Vocal expressiveness, smiling at the class, and having a relaxed body position appear to be most important, and looking at the class (instead of at the board or notes) and moving around the classroom rather than standing behind a desk or podium also seem to make a meaningful contribution. Although gesturing when talking made little contribution in the second study, there was a substantial correlation between gesturing and learning in the first study. The means for the gesturing item for all levels of learners were high in the second study. Consequently, it may be that most teachers actively gesture, thus providing little variance in this activity across typical classrooms. If a teacher were not to gesture, therefore, a negative impact could occur.

Whether or not these results should be generalized to lower levels of instruction must await future research at those levels. However, the present results relating to touching and smiling at individual students are unlikely to be generalizable to teaching at lower grade levels. In the studies reported here, our college student subjects indicated very few college teachers ever touch them. Observation of elementary school classrooms indicates that touch occurs on a regular basis in that environment. Similarly, because much teaching is individualized at the lower levels of education, the behavior of smiling at individual students may be much more important there than at the college level.

Our examination of the mean immediacy scores for the learning levels in the second study suggests a possible reason why previous research has not found association between cognitive learning and immediacy consistently. The present data suggest the possibility that the association between cognitive learning and immediacy is nonlinear and that most teachers may be at least moderately immediate. It seems possible that moderate immediacy is necessary for cognitive learning and low immediacy may suppress such learning. However, high immediacy may not increase cognitive learning over that generated by moderate immediacy.

In naturalistic research involving a limited number of consenting teachers, it is quite possible that the range on immediacy will be from moderate to high. The data from a study currently in progress reflect this pattern. This same pattern has been evidenced in several earlier studies in which teacher immediacy has been studied in the context of communication classes. In contrast, in experiments it would be normal to establish a clear high-low distinction. If our speculation on the nonlinearity of the relationship is correct, we would expect a low or nonsignificant relationship in the naturalistic studies but a meaningful positive relationship in the experimental studies. This expectation is consistent with the previous research in this area summarized earlier in this chapter.

The previous research relating to immediacy and affective learning, in contrast, is very consistent, and the observed relationship appears to be linear: the higher the immediacy of the teacher, the higher the affective learning of the student. Thus the composite picture of the association between teacher immediacy and learning may be drawn as follows: Teachers with low immediacy will generate lower cognitive and affective learning. Teachers with moderate immediacy will generate higher cognitive learning and moderate affective learning. Teachers with high immediacy will generate similar (to moderately immediate teachers) cognitive learning, but higher affective learning. This conclusion, of course, is speculative at this point and calls for careful research to test both the assumptions upon which it rests and the outcomes it projects.

At this point, however, we can be reasonably assured that a teacher who increases immediacy with students is likely to generate more student learning. The behaviors most likely to accomplish this objective at the college level appear to be vocal expressiveness, smiling, and having a relaxed body position.

REFERENCES

Aiello, J. R., & Cooper, R. E. (1972). Use of personal space as a function of social affect. *Proceedings of the 80th annual convention of the American Psychological Association, 7,* 207-208.

Andersen, J. F. (1978). *The relationship between teacher immediacy and teaching effectiveness.* Unpublished doctoral dissertation, West Virginia University, Morgantown, WV.

Andersen, J. F. (1979). Teacher immediacy as a predictor of teaching effectiveness. In D. Nimmo (Ed.), *Communication Yearbook 3* (pp. 543-559). New Brunswick, NJ: Transaction Books.

Andersen, P., & Andersen, J. (1982). Nonverbal immediacy in instruction. In L. Barker (Ed.), *Communication in the Classroom* (pp. 98-120). Englewood Cliffs, NJ: Prentice-Hall.

Andersen, J. F., Andersen, P. A., & Jensen, A. D. (1979). The measurement of nonverbal immediacy. *Journal of Applied Communication Research, 7,* 153-180.

Bayes, M. (1970). *An investigation of the behavioral cues of interpersonal warmth.* Unpublished doctoral dissertation, University of Miami, Miami, FL.

Beebe, S. A. (1980, November). *The role of nonverbal communication in education: Research and theoretical perspectives.* Paper presented at the annual meeting of the Speech Communication Association, New York.

Bishop, A. (1976). Actions speak louder than words. *Mathematics Teaching, 74.* 49-71.

Bloom, B. S. (Ed.). (1956). *A taxonomy of educational objectives. Handbook 1: The cognitive domain.* New York: Longmans, Green.

Bradley, B. (1979, May). *Training manual. Focused observations: Nonverbal teaching behavior.* Paper presented at the annual meeting of the International Reading Association, St. Louis. (ERIC Document Reproduction Service No. ED 196 849)

Breed, G. (1971). *Nonverbal behavior and teaching effectiveness.* Vermillion: University of South Dakota. (ERIC Document Reproduction Service No. ED 059 182)

Breed, G., Christiansen, E., & Larson, D. (1972) Effect of a lecturer's gaze direction upon teaching effectiveness. *Catalog of Selected Documents in Psychology, 2,* 115.

Brim, O. G. (1958). *Sociology and the field of education.* New York: Russell Sage Foundation.

Byrne, D., Baskett, G. D., & Hodges, L. (1971). Behavioral indicators of interpersonal attraction. *Journal of Applied Social Psychology, 1,* 137-149.

Coats, W. D., & Smidchens, U. (1966). Audience recall as a function of speaker dynamism. *Journal of Educational Psychology, 57,* 189-191.

Cyphert, F. R. (1972). An analysis of research in teacher education. *Journal of Teacher Education, 23,* 145-151.

Exline, R. V., & Winters, L. C. (1965). Affective relations and mutual glances in dyads. In S. S. Tomkins & C. Izard (Eds.), *Affect, cognition, and personality* (pp. 319-350). New York: Springer.

Fisher, J. D., Rytting, M., & Heslin, R. (1976). Hands touching hands: Affective and evaluative effects of an interpersonal touch. *Sociometry, 39,* 416-421.

French, R. L. (1970). *A study of communication events and teacher behavior: Verbal and nonverbal.* Unpublished doctoral dissertation, University of Tennessee, Knoxville, TN.

Gauger, P. W. (1952). The effect of gesture and the presence or absence of speaking on listening comprehension of eleventh and twelfth grade high school pupils. In C. W. Dow (Ed.), Abstracts of theses in the field of speech and drama. *Speech Monographs, 19,* 116-117.

Getzels, J. W., & Jackson, P. W. (1963). The teacher personality and characteristics. In N. L. Gage (Ed.), *Handbook of research on teaching* (pp. 506-582). Chicago: Rand McNally.

Grant, B. M., & Hennings, D. G. (1971). *The teacher moves: An analysis of nonverbal activity.* New York: Teachers College Press.

Harootunian, B., & Yarger, G. P. (1981). *Teachers' conceptions of their own success. Current issues.* Washington, DC: ERIC Clearinghouse on Teacher Education. (ERIC Document Reproduction Service No. ED 200 518)

Heath, R., & Nielson, M. (1974). The research basis for performance-based teacher education. *Review of Educational Research, 44,* 463-484.

Henley, N. M. (1977). *Body politics: Power, sex and nonverbal communication.* Englewood Cliffs, NJ: Prentice-Hall.

Hesler, M. W. (1972). An investigation of instructor use of space. *Dissertation Abstracts International, 33,* 3044A. (University Microfilms No. 72-30, 905).

Hodge, R. L. (1971). Interpersonal classroom communication through eye contact. *Theory Into Practice, 10,* 264-267.

Hurt, H. T., Scott, M. D., & McCroskey, J. C. (1978). *Communication in the classroom.* Reading, MA: Addison-Wesley.

Jourard, S. M. (1966). An exploratory study of body accessibility. *British Journal of Social and Clinical Psychology, 5,* 221-231.

Karr-Kidwell, P. J. (1978). *The impact of discrepant verbal-nonverbal messages in the teacher-student interaction.* (ERIC Document Reproduction Service No. ED 207 123)

Kendon, A. (1967). Some functions of gaze direction in social interaction. *Acta Psychologica, 26,* 22-63.

Kleinfeld, J. (1973). *Using nonverbal warmth to increase learning: A cross-cultural experiment.* Fairbanks: University of Alaska. (ERIC Document Reproduction Service No. ED 081 568)

Klinzing, H. G. (1983, April). *Effects of a training program on expressive nonverbal behavior.* Paper presented at the annual meeting of the American Educational Research Association, Montreal. (ERIC Document Reproduction Service No. ED 233 999).

Klinzing, H. G. (1984, April) *The effects of nonverbal behavior training on teacher clarity, interest, assertiveness, and persuasiveness during microteaching.* Paper presented at the annual meeting of the American Educational Research Association, New Orleans. (Eric Document Reproduction Service No. ED 252 519).

Krathwohl, D. R., Bloom, B. S., & Masia, B. B. (1964). *Taxonomy of educational objectives. Handbook II: The affective domain* (Chapters 1-4). New York: David McKay.

Kraut, R. E., & Johnston, R. E. (1979). Social and emotional messages of smiling: An ethological approach. *Journal of Personality and Social Psychology, 37,* 1539-1553.

McDowell, E. E., McDowell, C. E., & Hyerdahl, J. (1980, November). *A multivariate study of teacher immediacy, teaching effectiveness and student attentiveness at the junior and senior high levels.* Paper presented at the annual meeting of the Speech Communication Association, New York.

McGinley, H., LeFevre, R., & McGinley, P. (1975). The influence of a communicators' body position on opinion change in others. *Journal of Personality and Social Psychology, 31,* 686-690.

Mehrabian, A. (1967). Orientation behaviors and nonverbal attitude communication. *Journal of Communication, 17,* 324-332.

Mehrabian, A. (1968). Relationship of attitude to seated posture, orientation and distance. *Journal of Personality and Social Psychology, 10,* 26-30.

Mehrabian, A. (1969). Some referents and measures of nonverbal behavior. *Behavioral Research Methods and Instruments, 1,* 213-217.

Mehrabian, A. (1971). *Silent messages.* Belmont, CA: Wadsworth.

Mehrabian, A. (1978). Characteristic individual reactions to preferred and unpreferred environments. *Journal of Personality, 46,* 717-731.

Mehrabian, A. (1980). *Basic dimensions for a general psychological theory: Implications for personality, social, environmental and developmental studies.* Cambridge, MA: Oelgeschlager, Gunn & Hain.

Mehrabian, A. (1981). *Silent messages: Implicit communication of emotion and attitude.* Belmont, CA: Wadsworth.

Mehrabian, A., & Friar, J. T. (1969). Encoding of attitude by a seated communicator via posture and position cues. *Journal of Consulting and Clinical Psychology, 33,* 330-336.

Mehrabian, A., & Russell, J. A. (1974). *An approach to environmental psychology.* Cambridge: MIT Press.

Montague, A. (1978). *Touching: The human significance of the skin.* New York: Harper & Row.

Morris, D. (1971). *Intimate behavior.* New York: Random House.

Nier, C. J. (1979). Educational autobiographies: Explorations of affective impact. *Teacher Educator, 15,* 14-20.

Nussbaum, J. F. (1984, April). *The Montana program to systematically modify teacher communicative behavior.* Paper presented at the annual meeting of the American Educational Research Association, New Orleans. (ERIC Document Reproduction Service No. ED 243 832).

Patterson, M. L., & Sechrest, L. B. (1970) Interpersonal distance and impression formation. *Journal of Personality, 38,* 161-166.

Ringness, T. A. (1968). *Mental health in the schools* (chapter 1). New York: Random House

Rosenfeld, H. M. (1966). Instrumental affiliative functions of facial and gestural expressions. *Journal of Personality and Social Psychology, 4,* 65-72.

Scherer, K. R. (1972). *Acoustic concomitants of emotional dimensions: Judging affect from synthesized tone sequences.* Paper presented at the Eastern Psychological Association Meeting, Boston.

Seals, J. M., & Kaufman, P. A. (1975). Effects of nonverbal behavior on student attitudes in the college classroom. *Humanist Educator, 14,* 51-55.

Simon, A., & Boyer, E. G. (1974). *Mirrors for behavior III: An anthology of observation instruments.* Wyncote, PA: Communication Materials Center.

Smith, H. A. (1979). Nonverbal communication in teaching. *Review of Educational Research, 49,* 631-672.

Stern, B. L. (1984, January). When you're smiling. . . you may be saying more than you realize. *Vogue,* 113.

Thayer, S., & Schiff, W. (1974). Observer judgement of social interactions: Eye contact and relationship inferences. *Journal of Personality and Social Psychology, 30,* 110-114.

Victoria, J. (1970). *An investigation of nonverbal behavior of student teachers.* University Park: Pennsylvania State University. (ERIC Document Reproduction Service No. ED 042 724).

Weineke, C. (1981). The first lecture: Implications for students who are new to the university. *Studies in Higher Education, 6,* 85-89.

IX ● HEALTH COMMUNICATION

27 ● Patient Satisfaction with Physicians' Interpersonal Involvement, Expressiveness, and Dominance

RICHARD L. STREET, Jr. ● JOHN M. WIEMANN

Texas Tech University ● University of California, Santa Barbara

E FFECTIVE communication between medical personnel and patients is critical to the successful delivery of health care (Kreps, 1981). This premise has stimulated much research, particularly regarding physician-patient interaction. This work has generally focused on the linguistic and nonverbal behaviors (perceived or actual) exhibited by physicians and patients that lead to particular outcomes such as patients' satisfaction with health care received, understanding, and compliance with doctors' instructions (for reviews, see Pendleton & Hasler, 1983).

Unfortunately, much of this research is conducted atheoretically (Pendleton, 1983) and is frequently characterized by contradictory findings. To address these concerns, this chapter examines physician-patient

AUTHORS' NOTE: The authors gratefully acknowledge the physicians and patients of the Santa Barbara Medical Foundation Clinic for their assistance in this project. This research was supported by grants from the Santa Barbara Medical Foundation and the University of California, Santa Barbara, Academic Senate. The authors would also like to thank Don Cegala, Gary Kreps, and two anonymous reviewers for helpful comments on earlier drafts of this manuscript.

Correspondence and requests for reprints: Richard L. Street, Jr., Department of Speech Communication, Texas Tech University, Lubbock, TX 79409.

interaction from a theoretical-functional perspective, and reports (1) data examining relationships between patients' perceptions of physicians' communication and patients' satisfaction with health care received and (2) factors mediating these relationships. Also, we focus on features of communication style, or "how" individuals interact rather than "what" is said (Cegala, Savage, Brunner, & Conrad, 1982; Norton, 1983). Although the content dimensions of talk are certainly related to outcomes of medical interviews, perceptions of the relational qualities of these interactions are often more predictive of whether or not patients are satisfied with their health care and comply with physicians' recommendations (Ben-Sira, 1976, 1980; Waitzkin, 1984).

A FUNCTIONAL APPROACH TO
PHYSICIAN-PATIENT INTERACTION

By a "functional" approach to social interaction, we refer to the explication of factors (for example, personality, role expectations, intentions) influencing communication (for example, linguistic, paralinguistic, and nonverbal) and the consequences (for example, control, impression formation, partner responses, task accomplishment) of these behaviors (Patterson, 1983; Street & Cappella, 1985). Although other approaches to communication may be concerned with similar issues, the unique contribution of functional models entails the effort to group interactants' behavioral patterns according to some purpose or meaning that the pattern has for the interaction and interactants (Patterson, 1983). Specific functional categories include information exchange, coherence, expressing affect or intimacy, negotiation of social control, impression management, and task orientation (Cappella & Street, 1985; Patterson, 1983; Wiemann & Kelly, 1981).

Research on physician-patient interaction implicitly or explicitly has investigated functions such as information exchange and understanding (see Beckman & Frankel, 1984; Waitzkin & Stoeckle, 1972), affiliation (see Korsch & Negrete, 1972; Larsen & Smith, 1981), and control (see, Fisher, 1983; West, 1984). Information exchange and understanding are typically accomplished by content dimensions of interaction and thus are beyond the purview of this chapter. We organize our review of the remaining functions into two parts, interpersonal involvement and control.

Interpersonal Involvement and
Physician-Patient Interaction

The interpersonal involvement construct. Interpersonal involvement refers to the extent to which interactants are cognitively, emotionally, and behaviorally enmeshed with a topic or partner during social interaction (Cappella, 1983; Cegala et al., 1982). Cappella (1983) conceptualizes involvement behaviorally and claims it is indexed by behaviors reflecting *approach* (for example, close interpersonal distances, direct body orientations, gaze, forward lean; see Mehrabian, 1972) and *activity* (for example, gestural activity, facial expressiveness, speech rate, vocal variety; see Shrout & Fiske, 1981). Cegala (1981; Cegala et al., 1982) operationalizes interaction involvement perceptually as self- or other-reports of an interactant's perceived *attentiveness* (extent to which an individual is cognizant of stimuli in the immediate social environment), *perceptiveness* (extent to which one is aware of the meanings others assign to his or her own behavior and the meanings one ought to assign to others' behaviors), and *responsiveness* (extent to which one reacts mentally to his or her social environment and adapts by knowing what to say and when to say it). Cegala et al. (1982) have posited that highly involved conversants tend to be competent communicators (see also, Wiemann, 1977) who typically integrate feelings, thoughts, and experiences with partners in developing conversational topics. Less involved people, on the other hand, are concerned about extraneous goals or thoughts and their speech may be characterized by inattention, misunderstanding, vagueness, and inconsistency.

What is different about these formulations of involvement, with respect to related constructs of immediacy (Mehrabian, 1972) and intimacy (Patterson, 1983), is that affect is not a definitional criterion. That is, high levels of interpersonal involvement may characterize interactions viewed positively (for example, impassioned embraces between lovers), neutrally (for example, business partners in a serious discussion about an investment option), and negatively (for example, a couple in a heated argument over child custody). Of course, the affective nature of an interaction may mediate and even correlate moderately with interactants' levels of involvement; nevertheless, the two should be considered separate constructs (Cappella, 1983).

The significance of interpersonal involvement in the medical interview. In two recent reviews of physician-patient interaction, Pendleton (1983) and Waitzkin (1984) have reached independently somewhat contradictory conclusions. According to Pendleton (1983), patient satisfaction is more likely when "the doctor's manner communicates warmth, interest, and concern" (p. 39). Waitzkin (1984) concluded: "Practioners' expression of tension and an anxious tone of voice appear positively associated with patients' satisfaction" (p. 2445). The incongruity between these positions regarding whether patients prefer "warm" and "friendly" (see, Freemon, Negrete, Davis, & Korsch, 1971; Korsch, Gozzi, & Francis, 1968; Korsch, Freemon, & Negrete, 1971) or "tense," "anxious," or even "angry" physicians (see, Hall, Roter, & Rand, 1981; Lane, 1983; Larsen & Smith, 1981; Milmoe, Rosenthal, Blane, Chafetz, & Wolf, 1967) can be resolved by distinguishing patients' preferences related to the physician's *inter-personal involvement* and those additionally associated with *positive or negative affect*. The "friendliness" or "positivity" of the interaction is likely contingent on a host of factors such as the nature of the medical visit, the patient's age, and type of illness. For example, warm and friendly physicians are favorably viewed by parents of very young patients or by patients having nonserious ailments (Buller, 1986; Freemon et al., 1971; Korsch, Freemon, & Negrete, 1971). However, among chronically ill patients (for example, those suffering from diabetes, hypertension, and alcoholism), anxious and tense physicians are often preferred (Hall, Roter, & Rand, 1981; Milmoe et al., 1967). Hence, though their preferences for a physician's affect may vary situationally, patients appear to be consistently satisfied when interacting with physicians perceived to be involved interpersonally with the patient and the interaction as a whole.

Numerous studies support the claim that patient satisfaction is highest with doctors perceived as caring, concerned, interested in the patient, and who alleviate the patient's tension and anxiety (Ben-Sira, 1976, 1980; Carter, Inui, Kukull, & Haigh, 1982; Davis, 1968; DiMatteo, Prince, & Taranta, 1979; Freemon et al., 1971; Hall, Roter, & Rand, 1981; Korsch, Freemon, & Negrete, 1971; Korsch & Negrete, 1972; Lane, 1983). The studies cited have identified perceived and actual behaviors conceivably related to physicians' "perceptiveness," "attentiveness," and "responsiveness." Patients also prefer physicians' nonverbally signalling involvement through the use of close interpersonal distances, direct body orientations, gaze directed at the patient, and leaning forward during the interaction (Larsen & Smith, 1981; Smith & Larsen, 1984; Smith, Polis, & Hadac, 1981).

Physicians' expressivity and activity in the medical interview. As mentioned earlier, interpersonal involvement may also be indexed by interactants' expressivity and activity levels (Cappella, 1983). Though rarely investigated, patients' satisfaction has been associated with physicians' accuracy in expressing nonverbally different emotions (Friedman, DiMatteo, & Taranta, 1980) and to amount of time spent providing information and discussing prevention (Smith, Polis, & Hadac, 1981). Though patients may prefer relatively expressive physicians, too much animation and expressiveness may violate patients' view of physicians as professional and "businesslike" (see Hall, Roter, & Rand, 1981).

Control and Dominance In
Physician-Patient Interaction

Not surprisingly, numerous investigations have reported that control in the medical interview resides primarily with the doctor and is reflected in the fact that most of the talking, questions, directions, topics, and interruptions are produced by the physician (Coulthard & Ashby, 1975; Fisher, 1983; Frankel, 1983; Platt & McMath, 1979; West, 1984). Though few studies have examined relationships between outcomes and degree of the physician's control during the medical interview, Davis (1968) reported that patients' compliance was negatively related to the physician's degree of passivity (that is, agrees with patients, accepts passively, or complies with the patient's suggestions or requests). Although a passive doctor is least preferred, excessive control or communicative dominance by the doctor can also lead to negative reactions by the patient. Satisfaction has been diminished when physicians produced threatening utterances and numerous interruptions (Lane, 1983), used vocal tones perceived as "dominating" (Hall, Roter, & Rand, 1981), or were perceived to be dominant and argumentative (Buller, 1986).

Mediating Factors

In sum, patients' satisfaction with the physician and the medical interview appears to be related to perceptions of the physician's interpersonal involvement, expressiveness, and avoidance of excessive dominance. However, several factors may mediate these relationships including a patient's anxiety regarding the physical ailment, the physician-patient relational history, and the patient's age, sex, and education level.

Patients' anxiety. The greater the patient's anxiety about the medical problem, the more he or she prefers a physician demonstrating high interpersonal involvement and expressiveness. Implicit support for this notion comes from two studies. Ben-Sira (1980) reported that, as patients' concern about their health increased, there was a corresponding increase in the association between satisfaction with the physician and perceptions of the physician's devotion to and interest in the patient. DiMatteo, Prince, and Taranta (1979) reported significantly higher correlations between commitment to the physician and perceptions of how much the physician "cared about the patient" among hospitalized patients than among ambulatory patients. One could presume that anxiety about the ailment was greater for the former. Although patients were grouped by actual severity of the illness rather than level of anxiety, DiMatteo, Prince, and Taranta also reported slightly higher correlations between commitment to the physician and the physician's perceived concern among more as opposed to less seriously ill patients. However, the reverse held true for perceptions of how well the doctor listened to the patient. Care, concern, and interest toward an interlocutor are typically expressed nonverbally through gestures, facial expressions, and body movement. Thus we would also expect a stronger relationship between the physician's perceived level of expressiveness and satisfaction among patients highly anxious about their condition.

Patients' anxiety also may influence their satisfaction with doctors viewed to be dominating or even argumentative. Patients who are very worried about their medical conditions may tolerate, even prefer, physicians they perceive as angry (see, Hall, Roter, & Rand, 1981) or dominating (Buller, 1986; Davis, 1968). However, patients less worried about the reason for seeing a doctor will respond negatively to dominating physicians (see Buller, 1986; West, 1984).

Physician-patient relational history. Although *perceived* involvement by the physician is positively viewed by patients regardless of the number of visits to a particular doctor, relational history may mediate relationships among satisfaction and perceptions of the physician's dominance and expressiveness. nance and expressiveness.

Perceived dominance and expressiveness have a major impact on social evaluations in initial impressions that are formed when two people interact for the first time (Patterson, 1983; Shrout & Fiske, 1981; Street & Cappella, 1985; Wiemann, 1977). During future interactions nonverbal and speech styles become less salient to interpersonal judgments and previous experiences with the person assume greater import. This seems particularly true for physician-patient interaction because the relationship is typically voluntary, and the patient might not return if an experience was too negative. Thus we would expect stronger correlations between patients' satisfaction and perceptions of physicians' dominance and expressivity for patients having had few as opposed to many visits to the same physician.

Patients' sex. Though the data are sparse, women appear to elicit greater interpersonal involvement from physicians than do men. Waitzkin and his colleagues (1984; Wallen, Waitzkin, & Stoeckle, 1979) reported that female patients received more physician time, more explanations, more nondiscrepant responses, asked more questions, and talked more than did male patients. Thus females may respond more favorably to perceptions of the physician's involvement than males. Also, in nonmedical settings, women have displayed greater vocal (Ickes & Barnes, 1977; Street & Murphy, in press) and nonverbal expressiveness (Dabbs, Evans, Purvis, & Hopper, 1980; Patterson, 1983) than have males. Given that interactants usually prefer partners who have communication styles similar to their own (Cappella & Greene, 1982; Street & Giles, 1982; Warner, Kenny, & Stoto, 1979), women may report greater satisfaction with expressive than with nonexpressive doctors. Men, on the other hand, may discriminate less among physicians as a function of perceived expressivity.

Patients' education and age. Patients who have no more than a high school education often talk less, ask fewer questions, and receive less information and time from doctors than do more educated patients (Shapiro, Najman, & Chang, 1983; Waitzkin, 1984). The patient's age also is likely to influence the physician's communication. Harris, Rich, and Crowson (1985) observed that resident and staff physicians in their study had positive attitudes toward "middle-aged" and "over 65" patients but negative attitudes toward "adolescent" patients. Gray (1983), however, observed that physicians frequently have trouble interacting with elderly patients.

These differences do not necessarily mean that physicians are perceived as more involved or less dominant when interacting with more educated or middle-aged patients. It is possible that the *expectations* for interaction held by these patients are different and physicians are adapting toward them. Thus relationships among age, education levels, the physician's communication, and the patient's satisfaction deserve empirical attention.

HYPOTHESES AND RESEARCH QUESTIONS

In sum, this investigation was designed to examine the relationship of patients' satisfaction with medical care to their perceptions of physicians' involvement, expressiveness, and dominance. Factors potentially mediating these relationships also were investigated.

Based on the literature review, we expect support for the following relationships:

H_1: Patients' satisfaction with medical care is positively related to their perceptions of physicians' interpersonal involvement and expressiveness and negatively related to their perceptions of physicians' communicative dominance.

In addition, certain factors may mediate these general trends. We reasoned that patients more worried about their illnesses would prefer greater interpersonal involvement and expressiveness from physicians than patients less worried. Thus we proposed the following regarding physicians' interpersonal involvement:

H_2: Patients' anxiety significantly interacts with their perceptions of physicians' interpersonal involvement to influence their satisfaction with health care delivery. Specifically, the favorability of responses follows this pattern: highly anxious patient-involved physician > less anxious patient-involved physician = less anxious patient-uninvolved physician > highly anxious patient-uninvolved physician.

And similarly,

H_3: Patients' anxiety significantly interacts with their perceptions of physicians' expressiveness to influence their satisfaction with health care delivery. Specifically, the favorability of responses follows this pattern: highly anxious patient-expressive physician > less anxious patient-expressive physician = less anxious patient-inexpressive physician > highly anxious patient-inexpressive physician.

Finally, we proposed that worried patients would tolerate or prefer dominant physicians more than would less worried patients. Thus,

H_4: Patients' anxiety significantly interacts with their perceptions of physicians' communicative dominance to influence their satisfaction with
health care. Specifically the favorability of responses follows this pattern: highly anxious patient-nondominant physician = highly anxious
patient-dominant physician = less anxious patient-nondominant physician > less anxious patient-dominant physician.

Relative to male patients, we also anticipate that female patients respond
more favorably to a physician's involvement and expressiveness. Thus the
following hypotheses were examined:

H_5: The patient's sex significantly interacts with his or her perceptions of the
physician's interpersonal involvement to influence his or her satisfaction
with health care delivery. Specifically, the favorability of responses follows this pattern: female patient-involved physician > male patient-
involved physician > male patient-uninvolved physician > female
patient-uninvolved physician.

H_6: The patient's sex significantly interacts with perceptions of the physician's expressiveness to influence his or her satisfaction with health care
delivery. Specifically, the favorability of responses follows this pattern:
female patient-expressive physician > male patient-expressive physician = male patient-inexpressive physician > female patient-inexpressive physician.

Because of a limited empirical base for formulating a prediction for patient's
sex and the physician's perceived dominance, the following research question was posed:

RQ_1: Does the patient's sex interact with the physician's perceived communicative dominance to influence his or her satisfaction with health care
delivery?

Regarding physician-patient relational history, we propose the following
hypotheses:

H_7: The relational history of the physician and patient significantly interacts
with the patients' perceptions of the physicians' communicative dominance to influence the patients' satisfaction with health care delivery.
Specifically, favorability of responses follows this pattern: new patient
(2 visits or fewer to the physician)-nondominant physician = repeat
patient (3 or more visits to the physician)-nondominant physician =
repeat patient-dominant physician > new patient-dominant physician.

H_8: The relational history of the patient and physician significantly interacts with the patients' perceptions of the physicians' expressiveness to influence the patients' satisfaction with health care delivery. Specifically, favorability of responses follows this pattern: new patient-expressive physician = repeat patient-expressive physician = repeat patient-inexpressive physician > new patient-inexpressive physician.

Due to the paucity of research, predictions could not be made about the mediating effects of the patient's age and education. Thus the following research question was examined:

RQ_2: Do the patient's age and education interact with his or her perceptions of the physician's interpersonal involvement, expressiveness, and communicative dominance to influence the patient's satisfaction with health care delivery?

METHOD

Research Setting and Participants

Participants in this study were solicited from a large, multifaceted clinic in Santa Barbara, California. Medical departments targeted included ophthalmology (1 physician), internal medicine (13 physicians), community medicine (4 physicians), dermatology (2 physicians), oncology (2 physicians), and obstetrics-gynecology (3 physicians). The departments were chosen because they represented a wide variety of illnesses, physician-patient relationships, and types and lengths of medical examinations.

Patients' Questionnaire

The questionnaire given to patients was divided into five parts: information about the doctor, information about the patient, medical information, patient's perceptions of the doctor's communication, and the patient's satisfaction with the doctor. *Information about the doctor* included the last name of the physician just seen, whether the physician was the patient's first or second choice or was assigned by the clinic, approximately how many times the patient had seen this doctor, and approximately how many years the patient had been seeing doctors at the clinic. *Information about the patient* included items about the patient's age, sex, education, family income, and type of insurance coverage. *Medical information* included items on type of visit (initial visit, follow-up visit, routine physical or checkup, or other), time of day the patient saw the doctor, perceived seriousness of the illness, how worried the patient was about the illness or complication before and after the visit (for these scales, the wording consisted of "On a scale of 1 to 10, with 1 being NOT WORRIED AT ALL (or NOT SERIOUS AT ALL) and 10 being EXTREMELY WORRIED (or EXTREMELY SERIOUS), how worried were you about this illness (or how serious did you think this illness was) before (or after) seeing this doctor?"), approximately how much time the doctor spent with the patient, and whether or not this amount of time was adequate ("yes," "not sure," and "no.").[1]

Perceptions of the doctor's communication consisted of the Interaction Involvement Measure (Cegala et al., 1982) and Norton's (1983) Communicator Style Measure. These items were arranged in 5-point Likert Scale form. The wording of the measures was slightly modified to address a patient's perceptions of a particular doctor for a particular interaction. The *patient's satisfaction scale* was the "personal qualities" subscale of Zyzanski, Hulka, and Cassel's (1974) Medical Care Satisfaction measure and were in 7-point Likert form. The wording of this measure was also revised to elicit information about a patient's satisfaction with his or her particular doctor rather than doctors in general. The "professional competence" subscale of this measure was not included in the interests of brevity.

Procedure

The study took place during May and June of 1985. After the patient's medical visit was completed, the receptionists for each department asked the patient if he or she would be interested in filling out a questionnaire on his or her perceptions of the immediately prior interaction with the doctor. The receptionists also guaranteed that the patient's participation would be anonymous and that the physicians would not see individual responses. If he or she expressed a willingness to participate, the patient was given the questionnaire and a postage-paid envelope addressed to the researchers.

The receptionists were to continue soliciting participants until 50 questionnaires for each doctor had been distributed. Because there were some coordination problems and two participating physicians took vacation leaves, the number of questionnaires distributed per doctor ranged from 32 to 50 for a total of 982. Of these, 354 (122 were completed by males and 232 by females) were returned, or 36%. The fewest responses per doctor were 7 and the most were 32. The median number of responses per doctor was 13 and the mean was 14.2.

Statistical Analysis of Predictor and Outcome Measures

To generate perceived physician involvement, expressiveness, and dominance measures, a factor analysis with varimax rotation was performed on the Interaction Involvement Measure (Cegala et al., 1982) and the "attentive," "precise," "expressive," "dramatic," "dominant," and "argumentative" subscales of the Communicator Style Measure (Norton, 1983).[2]

Specifically, we expected the Involvement, "precise," and "attentive" items to load together, the "expressive" and "dramatic" items to load together, and the "dominant" and "argumentative" items to load together. Those items loading significantly on these dimensions were summed to produce the interpersonal involvement, expressiveness, and dominance measures, respectively. We formulated these measures using factor analytic techniques rather than on an a priori basis for two reasons. First, we wanted to reduce the number of subscales (a total of nine for both instruments) into a smaller number that would represent specific functional categories. Second, because we made minor alterations of wording to make questions relevant to medical contexts, and because some items did not readily apply to all physician-patient interactions (for example, "the doctor usually tells jokes, anecdotes, and stories when he or she communicates"), factor analytic methods allowed for identification of those items contributing meaningfully to a specific perceptual dimension.

The patient's satisfaction measure was simply a sum of Zyzanski, Hulka, and Cassel's (1974) Medical Care Satisfaction Measure.[3] Patient's anxiety was the sum of the items asking the patient to assess how "worried" he or she was about the illness/complication and how "serious" he or she thought the illness/complication was. The remaining measures were single item: relational history (that is, how many times have you seen this physician?), patient's sex, patient's age (less than 30, 30 to 50, over 50), and patient's education (high school or less, some college, college graduate/ postgraduate).

To test H_1, Pearson product-moment correlations were used. For the remaining predictions and research questions, ANOVA procedures were employed. When the physician's perceived involvement, expressiveness, and dominance were used as predictors, scores at or below the midpoint of each scale were considered "low" and scores above the midpoint were categorized as "high." Admittedly, this might create an unbalanced score distribution. For example, most physicians are likely to be perceived above the midpoint on interpersonal involvement. However, because of the number of observations ($N = 354$), we anticipated that the number of scores at the midpoint or below would be sufficient to have relatively stable variance. The midpoint of the scale was considered the appropriate boundary because we did not want to group together physicians viewed somewhat high on a communication variable with those perceived somewhat low or very low on the same variable.

For relational history, patients seeing the physician for the first or second time were considered "new" and those having had three or more visits were categorized as "repeat." For patient's anxiety, the scale midpoint was employed to decide whether patients were "highly" or "less" anxious. The response options for the single item measures represented levels for each of these measures.

RESULTS

Factor Analysis of
Patients' Perceptions of
Physicians' Communicative Behavior

Using the scree test, the factor analysis yielded a three factor solution that accounted for 51% of the variance. Although consistent with expectations, some items did not contribute significantly to any factor. The first factor was labeled *interpersonal involvement* and accounted for 32.6% of the variance among scores. This factor was comprised of all the Interaction Involvement items, three of four "attentiveness" items, and two of four "precise" items. For each subject, the measure of the physician's perceived *interpersonal involvement* was the summed score of these items.

A second factor was labeled *expressiveness;* it accounted for 9.6% of the variance. This factor consisted of three "expressiveness" items and two "dramatic" items, which summed represented the physician's perceived *expressiveness* measure.

The third factor was related to *dominance;* it consisted of three "dominance" items and two "argumentative" items. The factor accounted for 9.1% of the variance. Though the sum of highly loaded items represented physician's perceived *dominance,* the measure assessed not only dominance but also perceived argumentativeness.

In sum, the results of the factor analysis generally confirmed our expectations for a three factor solution representing interpersonal involvement, expressiveness, and dominance.

Reliabilities of Predictor
and Outcome Measures

Alpha reliabilities for physicians' perceived interpersonal involvement, expressiveness, and dominance were .88, .82, and .79, respectively. The patient's satisfaction measure was also sufficiently reliable (.86). The measure of patients' anxiety, which was computed by adding scores on the items asking the patients to assess how "worried" they were about the illness/complication and how "serious" they thought the illness/complication was, had an alpha reliability of .55.

Patients' Satisfaction and
Physicians' Perceived Interpersonal
Involvement, Expressiveness, and Dominance

Patients' satisfaction was positively related to physicians' perceived involvement ($r = .54$, $p < .0001$), expressiveness ($r = .17$, $p < .005$), and negatively to dominance ($r = -.27$, $p < .0001$). Thus the first prediction received strong support. Also, communicator image, a Communicator Style subscale related to communicative competence (Norton, 1983), was significantly correlated with patients' satisfaction ($r = .44$, $p < .0001$), which emphasizes the importance of the physician's communication to perceptions of the quality of medical care.

Factors Mediating Physicians'
Perceived Communicative Behavior
and Patients' Satisfaction

Of these analyses, the fewest observations per cell were 17. Thus though frequently different, the number of observations per cell was sufficient for ANOVA procedures. Table 27.1 reports the cell means of factors mediating patients' satisfaction with physicians' perceived communication.

Patients' anxiety. Patients' anxiety significantly interacted with physicians' perceived involvement to influence satisfaction scores, $F(1,295) = 7.85$, $p < .006$. As expected, among patients more concerned about their illnesses, perceptions of high involvement on the physician's part were associated with the highest satisfaction scores (mean $= 63.5$) and perceptions of low involvement represented the lowest satisfaction scores (mean $= 54.7$). For patients less concerned about their illnesses, low and high involvement by the physician did not affect their satisfaction (means $= 60.9$ and 62.5, respectively). Thus the second hypothesis was supported.

Regarding physician's expressiveness, $F(1,295) = 10.67$, $p < .001$, patients' satisfaction was highest among more concerned patients perceiving their doctors as expressive (mean $= 65.6$) than among similar patients judging their doctors as inexpressive (mean $= 59.1$) or among patients less concerned about their illness (means for expressive and inexpressive doctors were both 62.2). Thus the third hypothesis was substantiated.

The fourth hypothesis received partial support as the interaction of patients' anxiety and physicians' perceived communicative dominance was only marginally significant, $F(1,295) = 2.81$, $p = .09$. In essence, patients less anxious about their reasons for seeking medical care were more satisfied with nondominating physicians (mean $= 64.4$) than with more dominant doctors (mean $= 61.1$), whereas patients more anxious about their illnesses were somewhat more tolerant of both dominant (mean $= 62.0$) and nondominant physicians (mean $= 61.6$).

Patients' sex. The fifth hypothesis was supported. A significant interaction of sex of patient and physicians' perceived involvement was observed on patients' satisfaction scores, $F(1,293) = 5.52$, $p < .02$. Females were more satisfied with physicians they perceived to be more involved (mean $= 64.0$) than with those considered less involved (mean $= 58.0$). For male patients, satisfaction scores for both groups of physicians were the same (means $= 60.7$; see Table 27.1).

Table 27.1
Cell Means of Factors Mediating Patients'
Satisfaction with Physicians' Perceived Communication

Mediating Variables	Patient Satisfaction Means By:					
	Communicative Dimensions					
	Involvement		Expressiveness		Dominance	
	Low	High	Low	High	Low	High
Patient Anxiety						
Low	60.86^1_b	62.53_{ab}	62.23_b	62.19_b	64.44_a	61.10_b
High	54.65_c	63.48_a	59.11_c	65.63_a	61.63_b	62.01_{ab}
Relational History						
Unfamiliar	57.36_b	62.39_a	60.64_b	62.45_{ab}	64.36_a	60.44_b
Familiar	59.68_b	63.36_a	61.33_b	64.45_a	62.84_{ab}	62.51_{ab}
Patient Sex						
Males	60.69_b	60.74_b	61.21_b	60.14_b	61.54_b	60.42_b
Females	58.00_b	64.00_a	60.97_b	64.91_a	64.43_a	62.00_{ab}
Patient Age						
Young	60.88_{ab}	63.70_a	62.49_{ab}	64.88_a	64.65_a	62.60_{ab}
Middle-age	58.72_b	61.69_{ab}	60.94_b	62.09_{ab}	64.19_a	59.74_b
Old	58.11_b	63.20_a	61.61_b	65.64_a	63.13_a	61.34_{ab}
Patient Education						
High school	61.02_{ab}	64.32_a	62.17_{ab}	64.47_a	64.53_a	61.36_{ab}
Some college	58.60_b	62.19_{ab}	60.83_b	63.22_{ab}	63.71_a	59.87_b
College degree +	59.73_b	62.10_{ab}	60.60_b	62.93_{ab}	64.68_a	59.70_b

1. For each comparison, means sharing a common subscript were not significantly different.

There was also a significant interaction of sex of patient and physician's perceived expressiveness for patients' satisfaction, $F(1,293) = 5.61$, p < .02, thus substantiating the sixth hypothesis. As expected, female patients perceiving their physician as expressive were the most satisfied. There were no significant satisfaction differences among the other groups (see Table 27.1).

Though not interacting significantly with physicians' perceived dominance, $F(1,293) = .01$, a main effect for sex of patient emerged as females reported higher satisfaction with medical care than did males, $F(1,293) = 3.82$, p = .05.

Physician-patient relational history. The seventh hypothesis, predicting an interaction of relational history × physicians' perceived dominance on patients' satisfaction, received marginal support, F(1,295) = 2.58, p = .10. The nature of the interaction was as expected (see Table 27.1): Patients having only 1 or 2 visits to a physician were more satisfied with nondominant behavior (mean = 64.4) than with dominant behavior (mean = 60.4), whereas patients having seen a physician on three or more occasions discriminated less between dominant (mean = 62.5) and nondominant (mean = 62.8) communication styles.

The eighth prediction was not supported as relational history did not interact with physicians' perceived expressiveness to influence patients' satisfaction, $F(1,295) = .84$.

Patients' age. Patients' age did not interact significantly with physicians' perceived involvement, $F(2,292) = .43$, expressiveness, $F(2,292) = .50$, or dominance $F(2,292) = .67$, to influence patients' satisfaction (*see* Table 27.2).

Patients' education. The patient's education also did not interact significantly with physicians' perceived involvement, $F(2,292) = .01$, expressiveness, $F(2,292) = 1.22$, and dominance, $F(2,292) = .40$, to affect patients' satisfaction (*see* Table 27.1).

SUMMARY AND IMPLICATIONS

At the outset, we proposed that insights into patients' preferences for physicians' communication patterns during outpatient visits could be gained by identifying interaction functions salient to these encounters. Interaction functions refer to purposes underlying patterns of verbal and nonverbal behaviors and the meanings interactants assign to them (Cappella & Street, 1985; Patterson, 1983). Though the accomplishment of coherence in the medical interview should not be overlooked, we instead focused on two interaction functions, interpersonal involvement (and its related subconstruct, expressiveness) and dominance, which represent stylistic (Norton, 1983) and interactional features (Cappella, 1984; Cegala et al., 1982; Millar & Rogers, 1976; Wiemann & Kelly, 1981) of communication and are achieved less by "what" participants say and more by "how" the communication occurs. Using responses from patients and physicians of a large multifaceted clinic, we investigated two sets of issues: (1) relationships between patients' satisfaction with medical care and physicians' perceived communicative behaviors and (2) factors mediating these relationships. As expected, patients' judgments of physicians' behaviors coalesced along three perceptual dimensions: interpersonal involvement, expressiveness, and dominance.

Patients' Satisfaction and Physicians' Perceived Communication

Patients' satisfaction with medical care was positively related to degree of the physician's perceived interpersonal involvement and expressiveness and negatively associated with perceived communicative dominance. The apparently contradictory position of whether patients prefer "warm" and "friendly" physicians (Freemon et al., 1971; Pendleton, 1983) or "tense" and "anxious" physicians (Hall, Roter, & Rand, 1981; Waitzkin, 1984) possibly can be resolved by distinguishing interpersonal involvement from the affective valence (that is, friendly-unfriendly, happy-sad, relaxed-tense) of interactions between physicians and patients. Our findings, coupled with those of previous research (Pendleton, 1983), suggest that most patients prefer interpersonally involved physicians (that is, those appearing perceptive, responsive, precise, attentive, caring, and concerned). This perception is accomplished by behaviors such as topic extensions of partner talk (Davis, 1982), high levels of partner-directed gaze, forward lean, direct body orientation, speech matching, and back-channel responses (Cappella, 1983; Larsen & Smith, 1981; Smith et al., 1981). The affective qualities of physician-patient interactions may vary greatly depending on the patient (whether he or she is a child or an adult), type of visit (initial visit for an illness versus follow-up), and the physician's responses to patients' living, social, and dietary habits, and so on.

Admittedly, most patients probably prefer involved doctors who are also happy, friendly, and easygoing (Buller, 1986). However, the notion of interpersonal involvement appears to have greater predictive utility and encompasses physician behavior which is either warm and friendly or grave and tense. This is especially true for our data in two respects. First, perceptual measures of responsiveness, attentiveness, perceptiveness, and precision loaded as expected but none of the friendly, relaxed, and open communicator style items loaded significantly on any of the perceived communication dimensions (see Note 2). Second, of the three physicians' perceived communication variables, interpersonal involvement was the most strongly related to patients' satisfaction ($r = .54$), even more than the physicians' images as communicators ($r = .44$).

Involvement also may be indexed by conversational activity such as facial, gestural, and postural expressiveness. However, these behaviors are also related to self-presentation strategies for impression management (Giles & Street, 1985) or to conveying the meaning of utterances (Kendon, 1983). Thus, not surprisingly, subjects' responses to the "expressive" and "dramatic" items loaded as a separate factor in the factor analysis.

Although significant and positive, the correlation between the patient's satisfaction and the physician's perceived expressiveness was low ($r = .17$). Speculatively, low levels of expressiveness may reflect a lack of involvement (Cappella, 1983) and are generally viewed negatively by conversants (Shrout & Fiske, 1981). However, high levels of animation by the physician may connote insincerity, a lack of seriousness, indifference, or it may violate patient expectations for a professional and businesslike manner. Thus patients appear to prefer a *moderate* degree of expressiveness on the physician's part.

Finally, the physician's communicative dominance was negatively related to the patient's satisfaction ($r = -.27$), a finding consistent with those of Hall, Roter, and Rand (1981) and Buller (1986). The relationship may not be stronger because passive, inactive physicians also elicit negative reactions from patients (Davis, 1968). In essence, patients may seek more egalitarian interactions with physicians with both parties committed to contributing and responding to a partner's contributions rather than having the physician dominate the content and direction of the encounter. This appears true not only for the medical visit itself, but also for establishment of patients' health care programs in general (Pritchard, 1983) and is in line with expectations partners have for typical, informal social conversation (Wiemann, 1985; Wiemann & Kelly, 1981).

Mediating Factors

The patient's anxiety. The relationships between the patient's satisfaction and the physician's perceived interpersonal involvement, expressiveness, and dominance were mediated by the patient's anxiety about his or her medical condition. Specifically, patients experiencing high anxiety expressed greater satisfaction with more involved, expressive, and dominant doctors and lower satisfaction with less involved, expressive, and dominant practioners than did patients experiencing low anxiety. Our findings were consistent with those of other investigations examining the physician's perceived and actual communication behavior and either implicitly or explicitly addressing the effects of variables related to the patient's anxiety (Ben-Sira, 1980; Buller, 1986; DiMatteo et al., 1979).

Given their needs for reassurance, task commitment, and effective corrective action, worried patients probably want or expect involved and expressive physicians, are especially satisfied when they encounter them, and are very dissatisfied with physicians exhibiting little involvement or expressiveness. Also, because of their fears and the perceived threat of the illness, highly anxious patients apparently tolerate a physician's dominance more than do patients experiencing less anxiety about their medical condition.

The patient's sex. The relationships between the patient's satisfaction and the physician's perceived involvement and expressiveness were influenced by the patient's sex. Specifically, and similar to the effects of patients' anxiety, women were more satisfied with physicians perceived high in involvement and expressiveness and less satisfied with doctors viewed low on these dimensions than were men. The patient's anxiety could account for this finding if women were more worried about their ailments than men. However, the correlation between the patient's sex and anxiety was not significant ($r = -.02$). A more plausible explanation is that women generally prefer greater involvement and expressiveness from interlocutors than do men (Dabbs et al., 1980; Patterson, 1983; Shrout & Fiske, 1981; Street & Murphy, in press) and that this preference emerges in interactions between physicians and patients as well.

Relational history. The seventh and eighth hypotheses, predicting that patients having seen a particular physician three or more times would be more accepting of the physician's dominance and lack of expressiveness than patients having seen a physician fewer times, received little support. Only the relational history × perceived communicative dominance interaction approached significance (p = .10) and was in the predicted direction (see Table 27.1). Nevertheless, the relational history of the physician and patient still represents a potentially powerful mediator of patients' preferences for the physician's communication behaviors. Not only did Buller (1986) report a significant interactive effect between relational history and perceived dominance on satisfaction with health care, but other researchers have posited that, as conversants' interaction experiences increase, the impact of communication style (particularly vocal and nonverbal behaviors) on impression formation subsequently decreases (see Giles & Street, 1985; Patterson, 1983).

Patient's age and education. Patients' age and education did not significantly influence patients' satisfaction with perceptions of physician involvement, expressiveness, and dominance. These findings have at least one interesting implication, particularly for patients' education. As Waitzkin (1984) pointed out, physicians have spent less time with and provided fewer explanations and less information to poorly educated and lower class patients than to more educated patients and those with higher incomes. If the same communication patterns actually occurred between physicians and patients in this study, there was no effect on patients' satisfaction with medical care. Two possibilities may account for this finding. First, less educated patients may assume that their role during interactions with physicians is that of a passive recipient of information and/or treatment, whereas more educated patients assume the responsibility for more active participation. Second, because of the power and/or status discrepancy, less educated patients may be defensive or feel intimidated by the physician and thus talk less than more educated patients. In either case, if in this study less educated patients did talk less and/or received less information from physicians (though the perceived length of the medical visit was not correlated with patients' education, $r = -.02$), they nevertheless perceived physicians sufficiently involved, expressive, and dominant, and were even slightly more satisfied with medical care than more educated patients ($r = -.10, p = .09$).

Limitations

There are several limitations to this study. First, as with any survey, many patients did not return their response forms. Although the sample size was sufficient, there is always the possibility that the nonrespondents in some way differed from the respondents. Second, other measures of patients' anxiety and relational history need to be used or developed. The two item measure of the patient's anxiety was only moderately reliable (.55), although it was more predictive of the patient's satisfaction than either of its constituent items. Other self-report measures should be considered, as well as physiological measures of anxiety. For example, heart rate and blood pressure readings are routinely taken during medical examinations and are also indicators of arousal. With respect to relational history, other items should be included other than "How many times have you seen the physician?" For example, "How well do you know the physician?" and "How often have you seen the physician, socially or professionally, in the last month?" are possibilities.

Third, the hypotheses examined in this study should be replicated with a design offering greater experimental control. Although cell sizes were sufficient, there were many more patients perceiving physicians as involved than as uninvolved. Also, there were approximately twice as many female respondents as males. Nevertheless, the findings did generally support our predictions.

Fourth, although representing theoretically important variables, the utility of *perceived* communication behaviors must be grounded in *actual* physician-patient verbal and nonverbal behaviors and patterns. This is necessary for two reasons. One, self-reports of behavior are often distorted because of nonbehavioral factors such as psychological states, interaction goals, and expectancies. Two, the specific behaviors (for example, gaze, body orientation, language choice) or interaction patterns (for example, reciprocity) that are associated with perceptions of involvement, expressiveness, and dominance remain unanswered. In a similar vein, the study of interaction functions requires the examination of *both* participants' communicative behavior and needs to expand into the domain of physician-patient response contingencies.

Finally, multiple outcomes of interactions between physicians and patients should be examined including patients' compliance to and understanding of the physician's recommendations. Although reflective of a patient's affective response to a physician, satisfaction with the medical visit is not necessarily predictive of compliance (Speedling & Rose, 1985).

NOTES

1. Though not pertinent to this report, some of the questions on the patients' questionnaire were included because of their interest to the Clinic's administrative staff.

2. The "relaxed," "open," and "friendly" subscales of the Communicator Style Measure were not included in the factor analysis because of their questionable conceptual relationships with the constructs of involvement, expressiveness, and dominance. To verify this assumption, another factor analysis was conducted that included these items. The results indicated that none of these items significantly loaded on the involvement, expressive, or dominance dimensions.

3. Three of the items in Zyzanski, Hulka, and Cassel's (1974) Medical Satisfaction Scale were not included because of their inapplicability to a specific interaction and our

judgment that lexical modifications making these items relevant to a particular interaction were not feasible. These were "You cannot expect any doctor to be perfect," "A doctor's job is to make people feel better," and "With so many patients to see, doctors cannot get to know them all."

REFERENCES

Beckman, H. B., & Frankel, R. M. (1984). The effect of physician behavior on the collection of data. *Annals of Internal Medicine, 101*, 692-696.

Ben-Sira, Z. (1976). The function of the professional's affective behavior in client satisfaction: A revised approach to social interaction theory. *Journal of Health and Social Behavior, 17*, 3-11.

Ben-Sira, Z. (1980). Affective and instrumental components on the physician-patient relationship: An additional dimension of interaction theory. *Journal of Health and Social Behavior, 21*, 170-180.

Buller, M. K. (1986, May). *Physician communication style and health care satisfaction.* Paper presented at the annual meeting of the International Communication Association, Chicago.

Cappella, J. N. (1983). Conversational involvement: Approaching and avoiding others. In J. M. Wiemann & R. P. Harrison (Eds.), *Nonverbal interaction* (pp. 113-148). Beverly Hills, CA: Sage.

Cappella, J. N. (1984). The relevance of the microstructure of interaction to relationship change. *Journal of Social and Personal Relationships, 1*, 239-264.

Cappella, J. N., & Greene, J. O. (1982). A discrepancy-arousal explanation of mutual influence in expressive behavior for adult-adult and infant-adult interaction. *Communication Monographs, 49*, 80-114.

Cappella, J. N., & Street, R. L., Jr. (1985). A functional approach to the structure of communicative behavior. In R. L. Street, Jr. & J. N. Cappella (Eds.), *Sequence and pattern in communicative behavior* (pp. 1-29). London: Edward Arnold.

Carter, W. B., Inui, T. S., Kukull, M. S., & Haigh, J. H. (1982). Outcome-based doctor-patient interaction analysis II: Identifying effective provider and patient behavior. *Medical Care, 20*, 550-566.

Cegala, D. J. (1981). Interaction involvement: A cognitive dimension of communicative competence. *Communication Education, 30*, 109-121.

Cegala, D. J., Savage, G. T., Brunner, C. C., and Conrad, A. B. (1982). An elaboration of the meaning of interaction involvement: Toward the development of a theoretical concept. *Communication Monographs, 49*, 229-248.

Coulthard, M., & Ashby, M. (1975). Talking with the doctor. *Journal of Communication, 25*, 140-147.

Dabbs, J. M., Evans, M. S., Hopper, C. H., and Purvis, J. A. (1980). Self-monitors in conversation: What do they monitor? *Journal of Personality and Social Psychology, 39*, 278-284.

Davis, D. (1982). Determinants of responsiveness in dyadic interaction. In W. J. Ickes & E. S. Knowles (Eds.), *Personality, roles, and social behavior* (pp. 85-139). New York: Springer-Verlag.

Davis, M. (1968). Variations in patients' compliance with doctors' advice: An empirical analysis of patterns of interaction. *American Journal of Public Health, 58*, 274-288.

DiMatteo, M. R., Prince, L. M., & Taranta, A. (1979). Patients' perceptions of physician behavior: Determinants of patient commitment to the therapeutic relationship. *Journal of Community Health, 4*, 280-290.

Fisher, S. (1983). Doctor/patient talk: How treatment decisions are negotiated in doctor/patient communication. In S. Fisher & A. Todd (Eds.), *The social organization of doctor-patient communication* (pp. 135-157). Washington, DC: Center for Applied Linguistics.

Frankel, R. M. (1983). The laying on of hands: Aspects of the organization of gaze, touch, and talk in a medical encounter. In S. Fisher & A. Todd (Eds.), *The social organization of doctor-patient communication* (pp. 19-54). Washington, DC: Center for Applied Linguistics.

Freemon, B., Negrete, V. F., Davis, M., & Korsch, B. M. (1971). Gaps in doctor-patient communication: Doctor-patient interaction analysis. *Pediatric Research, 5,* 298-311.

Friedman, H. S., DiMatteo, M. R., & Taranta, A. (1980). A study of the relationship between individual differences in nonverbal expressiveness and factors of personality and social interaction. *Journal of Research in Personality, 14,* 351-364.

Giles, H., & Street, R. L., Jr. (1985). Communicator characteristics and behavior: A review, generalizations, and model. In M. L. Knapp & G. R. Miller (Eds.), *Handbook of interpersonal communication* (pp. 205-261). Beverly Hills, CA: Sage.

Gray, M. (1983). Communicating with elderly people. In D. Pendleton & J. Hasler (Eds.), *Doctor-patient communication* (pp. 193-204). New York: Academic Press.

Hall, J. A., Roter, D. L., & Rand, C. S. (1981). Communication of affect between patient and physician. *Journal of Health and Social Behavior, 22,* 18-30.

Harris, I. B., Rich, E. C., & Crowson, T. W. (1985). Attitudes of internal medicine residents and staff physicians toward various patient characteristics. *Journal of Medical Education, 60,* 192-195.

Ickes, W. J., & Barnes, R. D. (1977). The role of sex and self-monitoring in unstructured dyadic interactions. *Journal of Personality and Social Psychology, 35,* 315-330.

Kendon, A. (1983). Gesture and speech: How they interact. In J. M. Weimann & R. P. Harrison (Eds.), *Nonverbal interaction* (pp. 13-45). Beverly Hills, CA: Sage.

Korsch, B. M., Freemon, B., & Negrete, V. F. (1971). Practical implications of doctor-patient interaction: Analysis for pediatric practice. *American Journal of Disorders in Children, 121,* 110-114.

Korsch, B. M., Gozzi, E. K., & Francis, V. (1968). Gaps in doctor-patient communication. *Pediatrics, 42,* 855-871.

Korsch, B. M. & Negrete, V. F. (1972). Doctor-patient communication. *Scientific American, 227,* 66-70.

Kreps, G. (1981). Communication interaction in the future: The emerging area of health communication. *Indiana Speech Journal, 16,* 30-39.

Lane, S. D. (1983). Compliance, satisfaction, and physician-patient communication. In R. Bostrom (Ed.), *Communication yearbook 7* (pp. 772-799). Beverly Hills, CA: Sage.

Larsen, K. M., & Smith, C. K. (1981). Assessment of nonverbal communication in the patient-physician interview. *The Journal of Family Practice, 12,* 481-488.

Mehrabian, A. (1972). *Nonverbal communication.* Chicago: Aldine-Atherton.

Millar, F. E., & Rogers, L. E. (1976). A relational approach to interpersonal communication. In G. R. Miller (Ed.), *Explorations in interpersonal communication* (pp. 87-103). Beverly Hills, CA: Sage.

Milmoe, S., Rosenthal, R., Blane, H. T., Chafetz, M. E., & Wolf, I. (1967). The doctor's voice: Postdictor of successful referral of alcoholic patients. *Journal of Abnormal Psychology, 72,* 78-84.

Norton, R. (1983). *Communicator style: Theory, application, and measures.* Beverly Hills, CA: Sage.

Patterson, M. L. (1983). *Nonverbal behavior: A functional perspective.* New York: Springer-Verlag.

Pendleton, D. (1983). Doctor-patient communication: A review. In D. Pendleton & J. Hasler (Eds.), *Doctor-patient communication* (pp. 5-56). New York: Academic Press.

Pendleton, D., & Hasler, J. (Eds.) (1983). *Doctor-patient communication.* New York: Academic Press.

Platt, F. W., & McMath, J. C. (1979). Clinical hypocompetence: The interview. *Annals of Internal Medicine, 91,* 898-902.

Pritchard, P. (1983). Patient participation. In D. Pendleton & J. Hasler (Eds.), *Doctor-patient communication* (pp. 205-223). New York: Academic Press.

Shapiro, M. C., Najman, J. M., & Chang, A. (1983). Information control and the exercise of power in the obstetrical encounter. *Social Science and Medicine, 17,* 139-146.

Shrout, P. E., & Fiske, D. W. (1981). Nonverbal behaviors and social evaluation. *Journal of Personality, 49,* 115-128.

Smith, C. K., & Larsen, K. M. (1984). Sequential nonverbal behavior in the physician-patient interview. *The Journal of Family Practice, 18,* 257-261.

Smith, C. K., Polis, E., & Hadac, R. R. (1981). Characteristics of the initial medical interview associated with patient satisfaction and understanding. *The Journal of Family Practice, 12,* 283-288.

Speedling, E. J., & Rose, D. N. (1985). Building an effective doctor-patient relationship:
From patient satisfaction to patient participation. *Social Science and Medicine, 21,* 115-
120.

Street, R. L., Jr., & Cappella, J. N. (1985). Sequence and pattern in communicative
behavior: A model and commentary. In R. L. Street, Jr. & J. N. Cappella (Eds.),
Sequence and pattern in communicative behavior (pp. 243-276). London: Edward
Arnold.

Street, R. L., Jr., & Giles, H. (1982). Speech accommodation theory: A social-cognitive
approach to language and speech behavior. In M. E. Roloff & C. R. Berger (Eds.),
Social cognition and communication (pp. 193-226). Beverly Hills, CA: Sage.

Street, R. L., Jr., & Murphy, T. (in press). Interpersonal orientation and speech behavior.
Communication Monographs.

Waitzkin, H. (1984). Doctor-patient communication: Clinical implications of social scientific research. *Journal of the American Medical Association, 252,* 2441-2446.

Waitzkin, H., & Stoeckle, J. D. (1972). The communication of information about illness:
Clinical, social, and methodological considerations. *Advances in Psychosomatic Medicine, 8,* 180-215.

Wallen, J., Waitzkin, H., & Stoeckle, J. D. (1979). Physician stereotypes about female
health and illness: A study of patients' sex and the informative process during medical
interviews. *Women and Health, 4,* 135-146.

Warner, R. M., Kenny, D. A., & Stoto, M. (1979). A new round robin analysis of variance
for social interaction data. *Journal of Personality and Social Psychology, 37,* 1742-
1757.

West, C. (1984). *Routine complications: Troubles with talk between doctors and patients.*
Bloomington: Indiana University Press.

Wooley, F. R., Kane, R. L., Hughs, C. C., & Wright, D. D. (1978). The effects of doctor-
patient communication on satisfaction and outcome of care. *Social Science and Medicine, 12* (2A), 123-128.

Wiemann, J. M. (1977). Explication and test of a model of communicative competence.
Human Communication Research, 3, 195-213.

Wiemann, J. M. (1985). Interpersonal control and regulation in conversation. In R. L.
Street, Jr., & J. N. Cappella (Eds.), *Sequence and pattern in communicative behavior*
(pp. 85-102) London: Edward Arnold.

Wiemann, J. M., & Kelly, C. W. (1981). Pragmatics of interpersonal competence. In
C. Wilder-Mott & J. H. Weakland (Eds.), *Rigor and imagination: Essays from the legacy
of Gregory Bateson* (pp. 283-298). New York: Praeger.

Zyzanski, S. J., Hulka, B. S., & Cassel, J. C. (1974). Scale for the measurement of "satisfaction" with medical care: Modifications in content, format, and scoring. *Medical Care,
12,* 611-620.

28 ● Health Advertising: The Credibility of Organizational Sources

SHARON LEE HAMMOND

University of Maryland

S OURCE credibility has been studied extensively as it applies to perceptions of the credibility of individuals as sources of messages. However, little research has been conducted on the source credibility of organizations as sources of messages, especially health messages. Health organizations both public and private are putting more emphasis on behavioral and lifestyle factors in the prevention of disease. Therefore, it is important to conduct scientific research into the credibility of organizations that produce health messages and, further, the effect of this credibility on a subject's acceptance of the message and his or her behavioral intentions.

This study was designed to investigate the source credibility of organizations that advertise about health issues. The investigation sought to determine if differences exist in the credibility of an organization when it is perceived as having something to gain from the advertising (that is, making a profit), as opposed to a nonprofit organizational source. A second objective of the study was to determine if there is a change in perceived credibility as a result of a combination of profit and nonprofit organization sources in a single health advertisement.

This investigation was supported in part by the National Cancer Institute (NCI). The focus of this study was particularly relevant to the Institute because of their involvement in a recent Kellogg Company advertising campaign on nutrition and cancer. Kellogg Company recently has been advertising the benefits of their All-Bran cereal product's main ingredient— fiber. In their advertisements, Kellogg states that the National Cancer Institute has indicated that fiber has a role in reducing some kinds of cancer; therefore, people should "eat All-Bran." Other food manufacturers have approached NCI about using its name to lend credibility to their advertisements. However, NCI is concerned about the unknown effect of this col-

AUTHOR'S NOTE: I would like to acknowledge the invaluable contributions of Dr. Vicki S. Freimuth to this research and the statistical direction of Dr. Edward L. Fink. The research was funded in part by a grant from the National Cancer Institute.

Correspondence and requests for reprints: Sharon Lee Hammond, Department of Communication Arts and Theatre, University of Maryland, College Park, MD 20742.

laboration on NCI's high credibility. Will the advertisements cause NCI's credibility to drop? Kellogg's to rise? Both drop? Both rise? This study is designed to provide insight into these questions and others.

LITERATURE REVIEW

Source Credibility and Message Acceptance

The study is based on the general hypothesis put forth by Hovland, Janis, and Kelley (1953) that "when a person is perceived as having a definite *intention* to persuade others, the likelihood is increased that he will be perceived as having something to gain and, hence, as less worthy of trust" (p. 23).

Intention as a component of trustworthiness has been studied by many researchers under many names—lack of vested interest (Kelman, 1972), suspiciousness of persuasive intent (McGuire, 1969), bias (Chu, 1967), impartiality (Roberts & Leifer, 1975), and unselfishness of appeal (Walster, Aronson, & Abrahams, 1966).

Despite this variation in labels, the findings are consistent. The more impartial the source is perceived to be, the greater its ascribed credibility (Roberts & Leifer, 1975; Walster, Aronson, & Abrahams, 1966). Further, the persuasiveness of the message is also affected by the source's perceived intent (Chu, 1967; Freimuth, 1985; Hovland & Mandell, 1952; McGuire, 1969; Maccoby, 1974; Walster & Festinger, 1962). According to Chu (1967), "the persuasive effects of a communication are an inverse function of the perception of bias by an audience" (p. 248).

However, in their work on communication and persuasion, Hovland, Janis, and Kelley (1953) coined the term *dissociation* to describe a tendency on the part of the subject to "dissociate the source from the content" of the message (p. 41). Dissociation in source credibility research evolves from "attitudes and cognitive organization" research (Heider, 1946) in that under conditions in which a discrepancy exists between a person's attitude toward the source and his or her attitude toward the message, the person seeks to resolve this unbalanced state. According to Hovland, Janis, and Kelley, in this instance the person would decide to dissociate the source from the message.

Dissociation functions to reduce or eliminate the direct influence of the source on the acceptance of the message content. To the extent that the "recipient is able to dissociate source and message, *the acceptance of the message will be independent of the source*" (Hovland, Janis, & Kelley, 1953, p. 42). Therefore, if the health message is very important to the subject (that is, an advertisement for a new high blood pressure drug to a hypertensive), the research participant will be able to put aside his or her perception of the credibility of the source and accept or reject the content based on the message's own characteristics (Hovland, Janis, & Kelley, 1953; McGarry & Hendrick, 1974).

From a review of the literature on source credibility, message acceptance, and dissociation, the following four hypotheses were advanced:

> H1: A nonprofit source of health messages will be perceived as more credible than a profit source of health messages.
>
> H2: The perceived credibility of a combination of profit and nonprofit sources will be less than the perceived credibility of a nonprofit source.
>
> H3: The perceived credibility of a combination of profit and nonprofit sources will be greater than the perceived credibility of a profit source.
>
> H4: Because research participants will dissociate source from message, no significant correlation will be found between source credibility and message acceptance.

Source Credibility and Behavioral Intention

Source credibility also has been studied as it relates to behavioral intentions. However, little evidence exists in support of the assumption of a one-to-one relationship between high source credibility and positive behavioral intentions (Fishbein & Ajzen, 1975).

Intention to perform a behavior is an intermediate determinant between a person's attitude toward the behavior and his or her actual performance of that behavior. However, Ajzen and Fishbein (1980) caution that a measure of intention will not always be an "accurate predictor of behavior" (p. 42). In reality, a number of factors influence the relationship between attitude and intention to perform.

Fishbein and Ajzen (1975) suggest that a person's intention to perform a certain behavior is a function of two types of determinants: attitudinal and normative. An attitudinal determinant would be the person's attitude toward the behavior and performing the behavior. A normative determinant is a person's belief that his or her significant others would support or reject the performance of the behavior.

From a review of the research on source credibility and its effect on behavioral intentions, the following hypothesis was investigated in this study.

> H5: The higher the perception of source credibility, the greater the perceiver's reported probability of behavior change.

Credibility and Medium

This study also investigated the effect of the medium of a health message on source credibility and message acceptance. Medium is important to a study of source credibility because, as Rogers (1983) points out, "it is often difficult for individuals to distinguish between the source of a message and the channel that carries the message" (p. 197). Research has been conducted to identify differences in persuasive effects of the three media: print, radio, and television (Klapper, 1960; McGuire, 1981; U.S. Department of Health and Human Services, 1983). The findings generally show that print is more effective with complex messages, and radio and television are more effective when a message is simple.

However, little research into the direct effect of medium on source credibility or message acceptance was discovered. In a review of mass-mediated information campaigns, Atkin (1981) notes "television is generally the most influential medium in this country, followed by newspapers, radio, and magazines" (p. 277). Wade and Schramm (1969), on the other hand, report that print is more likely than television to be used as a source of knowledge about health by the public. In a recent review of persuasion studies, McGuire (1985) notes that television is regarded as more believable for people, but information and attitudes are influenced more by the print medium. Green, Kreuter, Deeds, and Partridge (1980) report that newspapers are "believed to inspire greater trust than such nonprint media as television or radio" (p. 93).

In the wake of such diverse findings, Petty and Cacioppo (1981) suggest that "no one form of [media] transmission is 'best,' but rather the most effective channel depends upon a variety of factors. These include the audience one wishes to reach; the interest value, comprehensibility, and personal relevance of the message; and the *characteristics of the source* [emphasis added]" (p. 86).

Because the literature did not assist in predicting the direction of the effect of medium on source credibility, the null hypothesis was advanced:

H6: Manipulating the medium will not affect the perceived credibility of a source of health messages.

Organizational Credibility

Most of the research on source credibility uses individuals as the source of the message. The literature contains only two studies using organizations as sources (Lynn, 1973; Lynn, Wyatt, Gaines, Pearce, & Bergh, 1978). The focus of both studies was the audience's perception of the Advertising Council, a "nonprofit organization supported financially by media, advertising agencies, advertiser associations, and donations from private firms" (Freimuth, 1985, p. 56).

Organizational credibility has been examined recently, but from a very broad perspective. McGuire (1985) cites a 1981 opinion poll that found "science, medical, and academic groups elicit a high degree of [trusted-ness], the military, police and judiciary somewhat less, followed by business and media leaders, with political officeholders and labor union officials trusted still less" (p. 263). These findings stimulate interest in organizational credibility, but empirical evidence is necessary to substantiate these general findings.

The dearth of research on organizational credibility and the untested assumption that source credibility is the same for individuals and organizations combine to argue for additional research in this area.

The following section describes the methodology used in this investigation of organizational credibility.

METHODOLOGY

Operational Definitions

Independent Variables

Two primary independent variables are manipulated in this investigation: status and medium.

Status. For the purposes of this investigation, the term *status* was used to denote perceived intention of the source. Three levels of status were studied: a profit-making source name, a nonprofit source name, and a combination source (utilizing both the profit and nonprofit organizational names).

In this investigation, perceived intent is defined as the perception that a source will make a profit from an individual adopting the advocated health behavior. This definition differentiates between organizations that make a direct profit from persuading consumers, through social advertising, to adopt an advocated health behavior from organizations that conduct social advertising solely for corporate public relations reasons. For example, the focus of the present investigation would include the advertising of a pharmaceutical firm that advocates that consumers take their medication daily regardless of whether they feel well or not. Conversely, excluded from the focus of this study would be advertisements of the tobacco association advocating that children wait until they are adults to make the decision to smoke. In the first example, the pharmaceutical firm will realize a monetary gain if a consumer heeds the advice. In the second example, the tobacco association will not directly realize a monetary gain from the advertisement but may stem the tide of adverse publicity. The results of this investigation can only be generalized to the first type of advertising.

Medium. To enhance generalizability of the results of the study and to control for any effect of an oral versus visual message on the results, identical advertisements in all three media were prepared and manipulated in the study (print, radio, and television). All three versions of the advertisement were as similar as possible in length, wording, and visuals in the case of print and television.

Dependent Variables

Three dependent variables are measured in this investigation.

Source credibility. A magnitude estimation scale was used to measure source credibility. The adjectives used in the scale were derived from the McCroskey and Jenson (1975) semantic differential scale and modified as a result of a pilot test. The alpha coefficient of the source credibility scale used in the main investigation was .94. Responses to the magnitude estimation scales were not collapsed into categories of credibility, that is, high, medium, or low. Source credibility was treated throughout as a continuous variable.

Message acceptance. The second dependent variable measured was message acceptance. To maintain consistency between the two dependent measures, a magnitude estimation scale of message acceptance also was used. Again, the scale and adjectives were modified as a result of a small sample pilot test. A reliability of .95 was achieved for the message acceptance scale used in the main investigation. The adjectives used in the modified credibility and message acceptance scales are presented in Figure 28.1.

Behavioral intention. Two questions were included in the survey to elicit from the participants any behavioral intentions resulting from the message. Previous research shows a correlation between behavioral intentions and behavior change (Ajzen & Fishbein, 1980). Therefore, information concerning behavioral intentions was collected to aid in determining the relationship between source credibility and the degree of message acceptance.

Ancillary Independent Variables

Two ancillary independent variables were included in this investigation.

Order. Each participant was asked to respond to a source credibility scale and a message acceptance scale. Both scales were included in each questionnaire along with pages of samples, instructions, and so on. The order of the source and message scales was varied within the nine versions of the questionnaire packet. For example, half of those respondents who were exposed to the print advertisement from the profit source received questionnaires containing the source scale first followed by the message scale. The remaining questionnaires contained the message scale first followed by the source scale. The manipulation was considered necessary to eliminate any effect that the order of the scales may have had on the dependent variables. Therefore, the null hypothesis was advanced:

H7: Order of the scales will not affect the participant's response to the scales.

Demographics. Although no relationships were expected between source credibility, message acceptance, and demographics, participants were asked to respond to four demographic questions: sex, age, race, and education level. Demographic data were gathered mainly to describe the sample.

Pilot Tests

Three pilot tests were conducted prior to the main investigation. The first pilot test determined the feasibility of using an existing semantic differential scale in a study of the credibility of organizations. The objective of the second pilot test was to identify fictitious organization names to be used in the health advertisements. Finally, the third pilot test evaluated the chosen measuring instrument.

Source Credibility	Message Acceptance
Reliable	Believable
Qualified	Important
Believable	Helpful
Competent	Informative
Valuable	Useful
Experienced	Persuasive
Honest	Understandable
Knowledgeable	Relevant
Helpful	Appealing
Cooperative	Effective
Professional	Uncomplicated
Concerned	Meaningful
Informed	Accurate
Organized	Convincing
Trustworthy	Unbiased
Unbiased	Necessary

Figure 28.1 Adjectives used to measure source credibility and message acceptance.

The results of the pilot tests showed that the original semantic differential scale required extensive changes in order to be applicable to organizational sources as opposed to individual sources. Therefore, a magnitude estimation scale was prepared using only the applicable adjectives as determined by the first pilot test. Two fictitious names to be used in the advertisements were selected by the respondents in the second pilot test. The "United Cancer Foundation" and "The Wellness Marketing Association" were chosen by over two-thirds of the respondents as having at least a .75 probability of being nonprofit and profit, respectively. The third pilot test was conducted to determine the reliability and validity of the magnitude estimation scales. Cronbach's alphas in excess of .90 were recorded from the small sample pilot tests of both the organization and message scales.

Experimental Design

The following illustration depicts the factorial design of this study:

R	X1	01	02
R	X2	01	02
R	X3	01	02
R	X4	01	02
R	X5	01	02
R	X6	01	02
R	X7	01	02
R	X8	01	02
R	X9	01	02

R represents the randomization of the subjects to the nine experimental groups. X1-9 represent the nine levels of treatment: X1, print profit; X2, print nonprofit; X3, print combination; X4, radio profit; X5, radio nonprofit; X6, radio combination; X7, television profit; X8, television nonprofit; X9, television combination. 01 represents the first observation of the treatment for each participant (either source scale or message scale) and 02 represents the second observation of the treatment for each participant (either source scale or message scale).

Manipulation of the Advertisement

A fictitious advertisement was prepared as part of the treatment in this investigation. The central idea of the fictitious message was that nutrition researchers have shown that increased use of fiber in our diets may reduce the risks of some kinds of cancer. The health topic, nutrition, was chosen because of its applicability to all potential subjects (as opposed to breast cancer or high blood pressure). Also, the link between high fiber and reduced risk of cancer is rooted in recent scientific research, and the effect of nutrition in preventing cancer is a highly visible health issue today. All of the above factors contributed to the realism of the experimental situation.

Nine versions of the advertisement were prepared, one for each treatment (print profit, print nonprofit, print combination, radio profit, radio nonprofit, radio combination, television profit, television nonprofit, television combination). Figure 28.2 presents the print nonprofit advertisement used in the experiment.

The 30-second television spot depicted a woman sitting at a breakfast table talking directly to the camera. At the end of the action, the name of the source was printed on the screen in white letters on black background. A voice-over also announced "This message brought to you by _____" when the name was displayed on the screen. The radio spot was produced directly from the voice track of the television spots.

Measuring Instrument

A magnitude estimation scale was used in this study to measure source credibility and message acceptance. Participants were asked to "think of an organization whose advice on health matters you would be inclined to believe most, but not necessarily all, of the time" (source scale). Respondents were then asked to assign 100 units to the organization they had in mind. This organization then became the numerical base from which all organizational comparisons were made. Participants were instructed to write the name of this base organization in a space provided.

A similar numerical base was used in the message scale. Respondents were asked to "think of an advertisement you have recently seen or heard whose message you found moderately believable." Again, participants were instructed to assign 100 units to the message they had in mind and write a brief description of the advertisement in the space provided.

A total of 18 versions of the questionnaire were prepared corresponding to the levels of the independent variables in the study. There were 3 versions of the questionnaire prepared for each type of medium. Within each type of medium, a version was prepared for each condition of the perceived intent of the source: profit, nonprofit, and combination. There were nine versions of the questionnaire prepared for the medium and status manipulations.

The remaining nine versions of the questionnaire were prepared in an attempt to control for order effects because of the inclusion of two separate scales in one questionnaire packet. Therefore, half of the total number of questionnaires were prepared with the organization scale first in the packet, and the other half of the questionnaires contained the message scale first. These manipulations resulted in 18 versions of the questionnaire.

I don't know what to believe any more, but I do know that I can believe nutrition researchers when they say I should have more fiber in my diet.

That's why I eat whole grain breads and cereals and more fresh fruits and vegetables.

They say eating foods rich in fiber may reduce the risk of some kinds of cancer.

So, am I going to change my diet?

You better believe I am!

UNITED CANCER FOUNDATION

Figure 28.2 Print nonprofit advertisement used in the investigation.

An attempt also was made to determine a respondent's intention to change behavior as a result of the acceptance of the message. An assertion was made that the respondents' perception of source and message credibility would influence their intention to change behavior in the direction of the advocated health behavior. Therefore, two questions were included at the end of the questionnaire to test the logical relationship between credibility and behavioral intentions. For example, if respondents found a source highly credible, were they then likely to attempt to change their eating behavior as a result of the message?

The final page of the questionnaire was devoted to gathering demographic data from the participants.

Description of Participants

A total of 264 participants were shown versions of the advertisement and answered the questionnaire. Substantial effort was made to use a nonstudent sample in this study. Although some of the respondents were currently enrolled in college courses, only 19 of the 264 respondents (7%) were solicited for the study through an in-session college course. The ability to use nonstudents for this study was made possible through funds provided by the National Cancer Institute.

Volunteers were solicited through offerings of donations to nonprofit organizations, that is, churches, senior citizens groups, and so on. Therefore, the experimental population was not exactly representative of the U.S. population because of the virtual self-selection of the participants. The experimental population had a higher percentage of females and whites than the population of the United States. Also, the experimental population was somewhat older than the U. S. population, possibly due to the number of religious organizations that participated in the survey. Finally, the experimental population had attained a somewhat higher level of education than the U.S. population (U.S. Bureau of the Census, 1983).

Procedure

Each audience initially was given an introductory explanation of the research including a hypothetical example to familiarize the respondents with the magnitude estimation scale. This same example was given on the first page of the survey for a second perusal by the respondent.

After the introduction, participants were randomly assigned to one of the nine treatment groups. An explanation of the procedure was given, and participants were requested not to discuss the survey or the advertisement with anyone else as the experiment was being conducted.

Each treatment group was taken separately into a private room and shown or played the 30-second advertisement. (The print version was given to participants to view for 30 seconds.) As a group, the participants then returned to their original seats to respond to the questionnaire. The procedure continued until all nine groups had been exposed to the treatment and had completed the questionnaire.

Statistical Analysis

The number of variables (both permanent and temporary) required that the statistical analysis be conducted in five phases.

The first phase of analysis was a $2 \times 3 \times 3$ analysis of variance consisting of two levels of the ancillary independent variable order (source, message; message, source), three levels of the independent variable status (profit, nonprofit, combination), and three levels of the independent variable medium (print, radio, and television), resulting in an 18-cell design.

Because the raw data did not meet the assumption of homogeneity, the statistical package *SHAZAM* (White, 1980) was used to find the optimal transformation of the data to fulfill the requirement of normal distribution. Unfortunately, the optimal transformation for the source scale could not be achieved. An appropriate transformation was found, however, and the resulting transformed data were used in the analysis of variance and *t*-tests. The *Statistical Package for the Social Sciences (SPSS)* (Nie, Hull, Jenkins, Steinbrenner, & Bent, 1975) was used to conduct the ANOVA and *t*-tests.

Because the first phase of analysis showed no main or interaction effect of order on the source credibility data (H7), this ancillary independent variable was eliminated from subsequent statistical analysis of source credibility.

During the second phase of data analysis, *t*-tests were conducted on all possible pairs of sample means for status and medium on both source credibility and message acceptance data. Hypotheses were advanced about the relationships of these comparisons (H1, H2, H3, and H6).

The third phase of analysis involved computing a correlation of the two dependent variables, source credibility and message acceptance, to determine if any relationship existed between a respondent's perception of the credibility of a source and his or her acceptance of the message (H4).

During the fourth phase of analysis, the effect of source credibility and message acceptance on behavioral intention was analyzed (H5). A correlation coefficient of the dependent variables, source credibility and message acceptance, was computed individually on each measure of the dependent variable, behavioral intention.

RESULTS

Seven hypotheses were tested in this investigation of source credibility of health organizations. A significance level of .05 was set for the ANOVA and two-tailed *t*-tests.

Of the three hypotheses that dealt specifically with source credibility of profit, nonprofit, and combination sources, two were supported and one rejected in favor of the null hypothesis. A nonprofit source and a combination of profit and nonprofit sources were perceived as significantly more credible than a profit source of health messages. The *t* value for the difference between the nonprofit source and the profit source was significant beyond the .05 level, $t(153) = -3.18$, as was the difference between the combination source and the profit source, $t(162) = -3.18$. No significant difference was found between the nonprofit source and the combination source. The total variance explained in the dependent variable, source credibility, for all main and interaction effects of status, medium, and order is 17%. Status as a main effect of source credibility accounts for 5% of the variance, medium as a main effect accounts for 3%, order as a main effect accounts for 1% of the variability, and the remaining 8% is accounted for through the interaction effects.

No significant relationship was obtained between source credibility and message acceptance, $r = -.03$, $R^2 = .00091$, $p > .05$, suggesting that some of the respondents were able to dissociate the source of the message from the message itself.

It was also hypothesized that a positive perception of source credibility would produce a positive intention to change behavior. The correlation coefficients for the relationship between source credibility and the two questions relating to intention to change behavior were, respectively, .25 ($R^2 = .02$) and .26 ($R^2 = .03$), which were significant beyond the .05 level. However, the high residual variance suggests that the relationships are not linear.

The null hypotheses predicting the effect of medium and order on the dependent variables were rejected in some tests and supported in others. Medium was found to have a significant effect on source credibility; specifically, the print advertisements were perceived as more credible than the radio advertisements, t (166) = 2.56, $p < .05$. No significant differences were obtained for the print-television and radio-television comparisons.

Order was found to have a significant effect on the message acceptance data, but not on source credibility. The F value for main effects of order on source credibility was 2.00, $p > .05$, but the F value for main effects of order on message acceptance was 6.63, $p < .05$.

SUMMARY AND IMPLICATIONS

Most of the results from this study are consistent with previous research on source credibility of individuals. However, the results suggest practical applications for organizations that advertise about health issues.

Basically, the results indicate that a nonprofit source (such as NCI) is perceived as having higher credibility than a profit source (such as Kellogg Company). However, when the two organizations combine to produce one advertisement, the combination is perceived as having almost the same credibility as a nonprofit source alone. In applying these results to NCI's concerns, one finds that Kellogg may have raised its credibility considerably by advertising with NCI. Further, NCI probably did not affect its credibility at all by advertising with Kellogg. In fact, NCI most likely saved a

Table 28.1
Three-Way ANOVA: Medium by Status by Order (Message Acceptance)

Source of Variation	Sum of Squares	df	Mean Square	F
Medium	3.33	2	1.66	1.36
Status	4.26	2	2.13	1.74
Order	8.13	1	8.13	6.63*
Medium × status	14.36	4	3.59	2.93*
Medium × order	2.45	2	1.23	1.00
Status × order	2.75	2	1.38	1.12
Medium × status × order	7.64	4	1.91	1.56
Error	292.07	238	1.23	
Total	334.99	255		

Note: Transformed data (lambda = .2); total R^2 = .017.
* $p < .05$, two-tailed.

great deal of money and gained a great deal of exposure through the advertisements, which Kellogg funded in total.

Because no correlation was found between source credibility and message acceptance, it might be construed that who produces the advertisements is inconsequential to message acceptance. On the surface, this interpretation is accurate. However, source credibility does have its effect on behavioral intentions. To return to the NCI situation, the combination of sources (NCI and Kellogg) or the nonprofit source alone (NCI) is more effective in producing an intention on the part of the respondent to change his or her behavior than the profit source alone (Kellogg).

The results of this study also suggest that the print medium is a more credible medium than the broadcast media for disseminating health information. This finding is especially important to nonprofit organizations, which frequently rely on public service announcements (PSAs) for their information dissemination. Nonprofit organizations may have more control over the placement of their print PSAs than their radio or television PSAs. Similarly, the availability of strategically targeted print outlets may assist the nonprofit organization in reaching its intended audience, that is, those at high risk for a health problem.

Even though the order of the scales within the questionnaire packet had no effect on source credibility, order of the scales did affect message acceptance. Many of those participants who responded to the source credibility scale first subsequently indicated a low acceptance of the message. This finding, although not specifically addressed by this study, may have practical applications for communication researchers in planning future surveys, and possibly for advertisers in choosing how best to design their advertisements for maximum effectiveness. For instance, a profit organization may want to consider placing its organization name at the bottom of a print advertisement or at the end of a radio or television spot, giving the viewer an opportunity to respond to the message characteristics first, prior to considering the source of the advertisement.

REFERENCES

Ajzen, I., & Fishbein, M. (1980). *Understanding attitudes and predicting social behavior.* Englewood Cliffs, NJ: Prentice-Hall.

Arkin, H., & Colton, R. R. (1963). *Tables for statisticians* (2nd ed.). New York: Barnes & Noble.

Atkin, C. K. (1981). Mass media information campaign effectiveness. In R. E. Rice & W. J. Paisley (Eds.), *Public Communication Campaigns* (pp. 265-279). Beverly Hills, CA: Sage.

Chu, G. C. (1967). Prior familiarity, perceived bias, and one-sided versus two-sided communications. *Journal of Experimental Social Psychology, 3,* 243-254.

Fishbein, M., & Ajzen, I. (1975). *Belief, attitude, intention, and behavior.* Reading, MA: Addison-Wesley.

Freimuth, V. S. (1985). Developing the public service advertisement for nonprofit marketing. In R. W. Belk (Ed.), *Advances in nonprofit marketing* (pp. 55-93). Greenwich, CT: JAI Press.

Green, L. W., Kreuter, M. W., Deeds, S. G., & Partridge, K. B. (1980). *Health education planning: A diagnostic approach.* Palo Alto, CA: Mayfield.

Heider, F. (1946). Attitudes and cognitive organization. *Journal of Psychology, 21,* 107-112.

Hovland, C. I., Janis, I. L., & Kelley, H. H. (1953). *Communication and persuasion.* New Haven: Yale University Press.

Hovland, C. I., & Mandell, W. (1952). An experimental comparison of conclusion-drawing by the communicator and by the audience. *Journal of Abnormal and Social Psychology, 47* (3), 581-588.

Kelman, H. C. (1972). Processes of opinion change. In W. L. Schramm and D. F. Roberts (Eds.), *The process and effects of mass communication* (pp. 399-425). Chicago: University of Illinois Press.

Klapper, J. T. (1960). *The effects of mass communication.* New York: Free Press.

Lynn, J. R. (1973). Perception of public service advertising: Source, message and receiver effects. *Journalism Quarterly, 50,* 673-679.

Lynn, J. R., Wyatt, R. O., Gaines, J., Pearce, R., & Bergh, B. V. (1978). How source affects response to public service advertising. *Journalism Quarterly, 55,* 716-720.

Maccoby, N. (1974). The effects of mass communication on shaping consumer and provider values in health. In L. R. Tancredi (Ed.), *Ethics of health care* (pp. 130-151). Washington, DC: National Academy of Sciences.

McCroskey, J. C., & Jenson, T. A. (1975). Image of mass media news sources. *Journal of Broadcasting, 19*(2), 169-180.

McGarry, J., & Hendrick, C. (1974). Communicator credibility and persuasion. *Memory & Cognition, 2*(1A), 82-86.

McGuire, W. J. (1969). Suspiciousness of experimenter's intent. In R. Rosenthal & R. L. Rosnow (Eds.), *Artifact in behavioral research* (pp. 13-57). New York: Academic Press.

McGuire, W. J. (1981). Theoretical foundations of campaigns. In R. E. Rice & W. J. Paisley

(Eds.), *Public communication campaigns* (pp. 41-70). Beverly Hills, CA: Sage.

McGuire, W. J. (1985). Attitudes and attitude change. In G. Lindzey & E. Aronson (Eds.), *Handbook of social psychology: Vol. II* (3rd ed., pp. 233-346). New York: Random House.

Nie, N. H., Hull, C. H., Jenkins, J. G., Steinbrenner, K., & Bent, D. H. (1975). *Statistical package for the social sciences* (2nd ed.). New York: McGraw-Hill.

Petty, R. E., & Cacioppo, J. T. (1981). *Attitudes and persuasion: Classic and contemporary approaches.* Dubuque, IA: William C Brown.

Roberts, D. F., & Leifer, A. D. (1975). Actions speak louder than words—Sometimes. *Human Communication Research, 1*(3), 257-264.

Rogers, E. M. (1983). *Diffusion of innovations.* New York: Free Press.

U. S. Bureau of the Census. (1983). *Statistical abstracts of the United States* (104th ed.). Washington, DC: Government Printing Office.

U. S. Department of Health and Human Services. (1983). *Making PSAs work* (NIH Publication No. 83-2485). Washington, DC: Government Printing Office.

Wade, S., & Schramm, W. (1969). The mass media as sources of public affairs, science, and health knowledge. *Public Opinion Quarterly, 33,* 197-209.

Walster, E., Aronson, E., & Abrahams, D. (1966). On increasing the persuasiveness of a low prestige communicator. *Journal of Experimental Social Psychology, 2,* 325-342.

Walster, E., & Festinger, L. (1962). The effectiveness of "overheard" persuasive communications. *Journal of Abnormal and Social Psychology, 65*(6), 395-402.

White, K. J. (1980). *SHAZAM: An econometrics computer program* (version 3.1.2). Houston, TX: Rice University, Social Science Computer Laboratory.

29 ● Helping People with AIDS: Mobilizing Interventionists

JIM D. HUGHEY

Oklahoma State University

Doctors need help coping with the impact of AIDS (Ricci, 1986).

BOSTON (UPI) - [Dr. Robert M. Wachter] . . . discussed the impact of AIDS on medical training in a letter in The New England Journal of Medicine.

Along with increasing the medical workload, the treatment of AIDS has forced doctors to deal with emotionally-charged issues, including homosexuality, Wachter said.

Studies show about 70 percent of the AIDS patients in the United States are homosexual or bisexual. The same percentage of physicians polled seven years ago reported discomfort in treating homosexual patients, he said.

"For the heterosexual resident, the anxiety invoked by dealing with a critically ill patient may be magnified by uneasiness with the patient's sexual orientation," Wachter wrote. . . .

Wachter says teaching hospitals across the country will increasingly feel the burden of the AIDS epidemic, which has so far been felt mainly by urban centers on the East and West coasts. . . .

"As the AIDS epidemic grows it is becoming clearer and clearer that a well-trained physician anywhere in the country will have to be comfortable taking care of these patients within five years or so," Wachter said.

Two points are illuminated by this wire-service story about doctors and AIDS. First, currently, professional health-care interventionists in high-risk states are experiencing difficulty in coming to terms with the stigma associated with AIDS patients. Second, within five years, interventionists in all areas of the country will be confronting the stigma of AIDS.

Interventionists may be professionals or volunteers who enter an ongoing system of relationship with the intention of helping the people involved (Argyris, 1970). Both professionals and volunteers are critical in any medical crisis (Gottlieb, 1981, 1983). The professional provides medical expertise. The volunteer provides psychological support as well as other services.

Correspondence and requests for reprints: Jim D. Hughey, Department of Speech Communication, Oklahoma State University, Stillwater, OK 74078.

The partnership between the volunteer helper and the person with AIDS is a joint venture in problem solving, decision making, and decision implementation. The interventions may be on the one-to-one level and rather mundane (Billie, 1985; Maves, 1985; Oklahomans for Human Rights, n.d.). The interventionist may help a person with AIDS discover ways of coping with housekeeping chores as the disease progresses, help in selecting an appropriate person to clean the house, and ensure follow through once the decision is made. Interventions may be on the system level and fairly complex. The interventionist may help people with AIDS research the prevalence of job discrimination once a person is labeled as an "AIDS victim." The helper may act as a go-between as the city council and people with AIDS formulate a policy for addressing the discrimination. Once the policy has been formulated, the interventionist may work to secure the internal commitment of the parties affected by the decision.

The need for competent interventionists is great. Between June 1, 1981, and January 13, 1986, 16,458 confirmed diagnoses of AIDS had been reported to the Centers for Disease Control (1986b). This number is expected to rise to 40,000 in 1987 (Centers for Disease Control, 1983, 1984; Kaposi's Sarcoma Research and Education Foundation, 1983). It is estimated that between 500,000 to 1,000,000 Americans have been infected with the AIDS virus and are at risk of developing the disease (Curran, Morgan, Hardy, Jaffe, Darrow, & Dowdle, 1985).

Mobilizing support for people with AIDS is compounded by the double stigma attached to people with AIDS. In addition to the stigma associated with sick people with mysterious diseases (Baker, 1983; Lapham, 1985), the person with AIDS typically belongs to groups that are often considered "socially marginal": homosexual/bisexual males, intravenous drug users, and those who have intimate relations with these individuals (Mayer & Pizer, 1983; Siegal & Siegal, 1983). As the news story in the introduction attests, even professional training offers little defense against the double stigma.

A number of articles appearing in the *American Psychologist* have described the impediments to effective interventions in the AIDS arena and have set forth a psychosocial research agenda for AIDS. Referring to AIDS as a public health and psychological emergency, Batchelor (1984) specifies how distorted images of gay men impede effective interventions. Before his death, Ferrara (1984) detailed what it is like to have AIDS and be the object of medical and psychological interventions (Ferrara, 1984). A public health perspective is furnished by Mervyn Silverman, San Francisco Director of Health (Morin, 1984). Research interventions designed to determine the psychosocial concerns of gay men are detailed by Joseph et al. (1984). Other behavioral and psychosocial factors in AIDS interventions are discussed by Martin and Vance (1984). And a call for a concerted psychosocial program of research is made by Coates, Temoshok, and Mandel (1984).

Various volunteer support programs, such as the Shanti program in San Francisco, have been described by Morin, Charles, and Malyon (1984). Currently, most volunteer interventionists have been drawn from the gay community in large metropolitan areas. Both the motivation to help and competence to help has been high in these areas (AIDS Project of Los Angeles, 1985).

As previously low-risk states with a less organized gay community are faced with more confirmed cases of the disease, it becomes prudent to discover strategies that will mobilize a population with less experience in confronting the AIDS epidemic. Indications are that the disease is spreading to low-risk states. By mid-1984, the first 4,000 cases of AIDS had been reported. Five states (New York, California, Florida, New Jersey, and Texas) accounted for most of the cases with only 17% coming from other states (Allen & Curran, 1985). In 1985, 8,072 new cases were reported (Centers for Disease Control, 1986a). Although the five states continued to account for most of the cases, 28% came from other states. Moreover, 1985 saw cases being reported from all 50 states, the District of Columbia, and three U.S. territories. As the crisis grows and affects more people in states without a strong network of indigenous support groups, the need to recruit volunteer interventionists from the general population is likely to grow.

RESEARCH QUESTIONS

This study was undertaken to explore how to broaden the pool of volunteer interventionists willing to help people with AIDS. It focuses on college students from a low-risk state and their willingness to help in the AIDS crisis.

College students, either as individuals or as members of organizations (service clubs, fraternities, and so on), donate blood during blood drives, sponsor fund-raisers for the sick or disadvantaged, and volunteer for charity work at hospitals or halfway houses. In their book on the American blood supply, Drake, Finkelstein, and Sapolsky (1982) point out that 25% or more of all blood needs are met by high schools and colleges in some regions of the nation. College students have a history of volunteering and taking active roles in civil rights, aid to the poor, and other humanitarian issues (Flacks, 1970; Kenniston, 1967; Soloman & Fishman, 1964).

A single independent variable was manipulated: type of disease. AIDS and two other diseases that have appeared during the past 10 years, Toxic-Shock Syndrome and Legionnaire's Disease, were considered for each dependent variable. These two diseases were chosen to represent non-stigmatized diseases and a baseline for comparison. However, the respondents exhibited significantly less awareness of Legionnaire's Disease than AIDS and Toxic-Shock. Consequently, the substantive comparisons reported in this paper are between AIDS and Toxic-Shock. Because AIDS affects chiefly men and Toxic-Shock affects mainly women, the issue of gender is considered also.

The study addresses five questions revolving around three dependent variables: knowledge, image, and behavioral intent.

Q1. How does perceived knowledge about AIDS compare with perceived knowledge about Toxic-Shock and Legionnaires's Disease?
Q2. How knowledgeable are the respondents about the three diseases?
Q3. How does the image of AIDS compare with the image of Toxic-Shock?
Q4. How does the behavioral intent to help people with AIDS compare with the intent to help people with Toxic-Shock?
Q5. How do factual knowledge, image dimensions of stigma, and gender relate to the willingness to help people with AIDS and Toxic-Shock Syndrome?

The answers to these questions were used to infer a preliminary set of strategies that might be useful in the recruitment of competent interventionists.

REVIEW OF THE LITERATURE

This literature review considers knowledge, image, and gender as they relate to behavior. General models are considered as well as research dealing specifically with helping behavior and stigma.

The model of the adoption process as developed by Rogers (1983) serves as a general framework for conceptualizing how knowledge, image, and behavior are related. The first three stages of the revised model are knowledge, persuasion, and decision making (followed by implementation and confirmation).

Rogers (1983) makes a strong case for the connection between knowledge and decision making. He breaks the knowledge construct into awareness-knowledge, how-to knowledge, and principles-knowledge. In terms of a decision to help a person with AIDS, awareness-knowledge occurs when attention is directed toward the disease and the adopter becomes cognizant of the general nature of the disease and people with the disease. Principles-knowledge occurs when the adopter actively searches for additional information and comes to know details about AIDS and how the disease relates to other diseases. How-to knowledge was not considered in this study but might include details about the nature of the helping duties themselves. Rogers argues that mass media play a key role in awareness-knowledge, and personal sources of information such as friends and acquaintances play a central role in developing principles-knowledge.

In the persuasion stage, the decision maker evaluates the data and weighs the pros and cons of taking action. Both attitudes and beliefs are salient in this "mental trial" stage. For instance, affective and belief components interact with the data to form an image of what it would be like to help a person with AIDS. The model postulates that a favorable image is linked with the amount of knowledge possessed by the decision maker.

In the decision stage, the choice is made to accept or reject the proposal or action. For instance, the decision maker may adopt a proposal to help a person with AIDS. On the other hand, the decision maker may actively or passively reject the proposal. Active rejection consists of considering acceptance but deciding not to adopt; passive rejection consists of never really considering acceptance of the proposal.

In the remaining stages of the model, the decision maker may or may not fully implement the decision and may ultimately reject the decision if evidence does not confirm the wisdom of the choice. For instance, a decision maker may express the intention to help a person with AIDS but may or may not actually show up to help. Even if the decision maker begins the helping process, disconfirming evidence may cause him or her to discontinue the process.

The model postulates a linear progression of stages beginning with knowledge, followed by image formation, and then by the decision to accept or reject the advocated behavior. Furthermore, Rogers (1983) presents evidence that the decision to adopt is a linear function of both knowledge and image.

However, competing models suggest that knowledge plays a different role in the adoption sequence; for example, that knowledge level may be altered as a consequence of engaging in a behavior. Krugman (1965) makes the case that the issue of "involvement" is the key to determining which model is applicable. He argues that under conditions of high involvement, where the advocated behavior touches on many spheres of personal importance, the classical model, described by Rogers (1983; Rogers & Shoemaker, 1962), is salient. Under conditions of low involvement, changes in behavior may precede changes in knowledge level.

For instance, in the case of AIDS, personal risk (the possibility of contracting the disease) may be viewed as an index of involvement. For the decision maker who sees AIDS as a personal risk for self and friends, the advocate should work to increase knowledge in order to alter the image and/or attitudes associated with the advocated behavior. Under conditions of "low involvement" where the decision maker sees little risk, Krugman argues that the advocate should work for a person to engage in the behavior. For example, as a consequence of working with a sick person on a trial basis, perceptions may change and knowledge level may increase. Festinger (1964) makes a similar point when he discusses the notion of postdecisional dissonance. Knowledge may be more critical after engaging in a behavior than before an action is taken.

But regardless of where they place knowledge and image in their models, theorists recognize the importance of the constructs in understanding the decisions made and actions taken by people. Similarly, researchers focusing on helping behavior, prosocial behavior, and/or altruism recognize the salience of knowledge and image as well as other factors.

Gottlieb (1981, 1983) stresses both the role of knowledge and favorable images in gaining volunteers to support the medically and mentally ill. Eisenberg (1982) presents and reviews a collection of studies that treat the role of cognition and affect in the development of prosocial behavior. Rushton and Sorrentino (1981) underscore the complexities of inducing altruistic behavior: The interaction of modeling and socialization, internal mediators (norms, empathy, and emotion), personality, and social constraints makes for a less than predictable outcome. These researchers acknowledge the role of knowledge and favorable images in inducing helping behavior but postulate sets of relationships that include other variables.

The literature on stigma suggests that securing a commitment to help the stigmatized is a challenge. By definition, images of the stigmatized have one or more components that are negative (Katz, 1981). Most stigmas are not addressed easily through a knowledge of the facts and resist educational and even coercive attempts. Katz (1981) uses racial stigmas to illustrate the point. He claims that, even after years of governmental intervention and countless affirmative action programs designed to achieve compliance, the stigma of being black persists.

Victims of mysterious diseases are frequently stigmatized. Sontag (1978) writes of the myths and punitive fantasies surrounding frightful diseases like cancer: The stigma of cancer evokes a sense of horror, a dread of contamination, an image of corruption and decay, and an irrationality rivaled only by the moral condemnation of leprosy in the Middle Ages. And there are indications that AIDS tops the list of diseases that are "too degrading or threatening to talk about" (Black, 1985a, 1985b; Daniels, 1985).

Goffman (1963) suggests that the stigmatized is seen as a marked person— an object of great shame. The literature suggests that sympathy, responsibility (you get what you deserve because of some moral flaw), and peril or threat (represented by fright and risk) are dimensions of stigma that lead to the global feeling of ambivalence (Jones, Farina, Hastorf, Markus, Miller, & Scott, 1984; Katz, 1981).

Stigmas may be typed in terms of the valence of their affective and belief components. The affective components of the stigma, for example, sympathy, may be either positive or negative. Similarly, the belief components, for example, responsibility/morality, may be either positive or negative. Typically, stigmas have conflicted affective and belief components. For instance, an unsympathetic reaction to a marked person may be seen as less than completely justified by the marker (Jones et al., 1984). Ambivalence arises from the negative affect and the belief that the marked person is a good person and not responsible for his or her plight. Or, positive affect (sympathy) may conflict with the belief that the marked person deserves the illness. According to Katz (1981), these stigmas also produce ambivalent feelings in the marker.

However, the most severe type of stigma occurs when the marker is unsympathetic toward the marked and believes that the marked is responsible for his or her plight and deserves the disease (Jones et al., 1984). This "negative-affect, negative-belief" stigma is based on a rigid belief system that resists facts that conflict with the stereotype. With this type of stigma the ambivalence does not arise from the inconsistency of affective and belief components of sympathy and responsibility; the affective and belief components are consonant. The ambivalence may arise from an unsympathetic view of a victim bolstered by the belief that the victim is responsible for his/her condition and the threat of the disease; for example, "This is a frightening disease that I might catch." Fear of the disease and risk of contracting the disease are two dimensions associated with threat.

Considerable research has documented the hazards of inducing helping behavior from those interacting with the stigmatized. Complex prediction models based on an ambivalence-response amplification theory advanced by Katz (1981) have been criticized by Jones et al. (1984) for their inability to forecast the direction of the behavior (for example, will help versus will not help). However, the bulk of the research on stigma seems to support the expectation that (1) stigma affects behavior and (2) stigmas may operate independent of a knowledge of the facts.

The literature suggests that females tend to score higher on indices of helping behavior than males (Dlugokinski & Firestone, 1973, 1974; Feshbach, 1982; Underwood & Moore, 1982). In his review of research of altruism in adults and children, Rushton (1980) postulates that empathy, a motivation for altruism, may provide the key to understanding why women tend to be more prosocial than men.

In summary, general models focusing on behavior or decision making support the expectation that knowledge and image influence the choices people make. However, low-involvement issues may not require a knowledge of the facts before action is taken; for instance, a person might agree to do some chores for a sick person before knowing much about the illness. In the process of helping, knowledge may be increased. Specific research on helping behavior suggests that knowledge, image, and other factors may influence the decision to help. But the stigma literature suggests stigmas may operate independent of a knowledge of the facts and that specific predictions regarding stigmatized images and behavior are risky. Also, there is evidence to support a relationship between gender and the decision to help.

PROCEDURES

A total of 126 college students participated in the study. Both male (52%) and female (48%) students enrolled in undergraduate communication courses served as respondents. A questionnaire was administered in July, 1985, to 88 respondents and in August to 38 respondents. No statistically significant differences ($p > .05$) were noted between the subgroups for any items used is subsequent analyses.

The survey consisted of items framed in an agree-disagree format and focused on AIDS, Toxic-Shock Syndrome, and Legionnaire's Disease. The items dealt with three major constructs: knowledge, image, and behavioral intent.

Knowledge was assessed by a measure of perceived knowledge for each disease, an indicator of the sources of those perceptions, and a nine-item test of factual knowledge. The perceptual items suggested: "I know very little about X," and "I know a lot about X." Respondents indicated the sources of their perceived knowledge by registering their agreement with items like, "I have heard quite a bit about X from friends and acquaintances [the mass media]."

The content of items for the knowledge test was drawn from publications furnished by the Public Health Service (1984a, 1984b, 1984c, 1984d) and the Centers for Disease Control (1983, 1984). The nine-item knowledge test formed a single-factor scale; Cronbach's coefficient alpha was .78. The test consisted of two accurate statements: "More people recover from Legionnaire's Disease than from AIDS," and "Legionnaire's Disease is easier to cure than AIDS." Four inaccurate items were included: "Both Toxic-Shock Syndrome and Legionnaire's Disease currently affect more people than AIDS," "More people die from Toxic-Shock Syndrome than from AIDS," "All three diseases are transmitted in essentially the same way," and "Like Toxic-Shock Syndrome and Legionnaire's Disease, AIDS is a bacterial infection." Three open-ended questions asked the respondents to name groups having the greatest risk of contracting Legionnaire's Disease, Toxic-Shock Syndrome, and AIDS.

The image items were based on dimensions drawn from the stigma literature: sympathy, morality, ambivalence, risk, and fright. Two items tapped the degree of sympathy felt for people with the diseases: "A person with X deserves and gets all my sympathy," and "When I hear of people who have come down with X, I cannot muster very much sympathy for them." The morality and ambivalence issues were gauged by "'Moral/Good people' seldom contract X," and "I have mixed feelings when I hear about people with X." The degree of risk and fright posed by the diseases was assessed with these statements: "It would be impossible for me or my friends to get X," and "X is the most frightening disease of our time."

Behavioral intent was measured by items taking this form: "I would eagerly help a person with X in any way that I could." Items of this nature have been demonstrated to have satisfactory validity when correlated with such indices as willingness to join an association, pay money, and allow one's name to be used for promotional purposes (r = .60 to .80); test-retest reliabilities, after a four-week period, are typically in the .60 to .70 range (Hughey, 1966).

The paired image and behavioral intent items are evaluated by *t*-tests. Discriminant analysis is used to clarify how the test of factual knowledge and the image dimensions of stigma relate to the willingness to help people with AIDS and Toxic-Shock.

FINDINGS

Q1. How does perceived knowledge about AIDS compare with perceived knowledge about Toxic-Shock and Legionnaire's Disease?

It appears that the awareness of AIDS and Toxic-Shock is higher than for Legionnaire's Disease. More than half (54%) consider themselves to be knowledgeable about AIDS with 47% aware of Toxic-Shock Syndrome. However, only 8% declare that they are knowledgeable about Legionnaire's Disease. There is no significant difference in the knowledge perceptions of AIDS and Toxic-Shock ($t(125) = 1.74$, $p > .05$), but there are large differences when AIDS and Toxic-Shock are pitted against Legionnaire's Disease ($t(125) = 14.16$, $p < .001$; $t(125) = 10.78$, $p < .001$). Other indicators suggested that about a third of the respondents had heard about AIDS and Toxic-Shock from friends and acquaintances (32% for AIDS and 31% for Toxic-Shock; $t(125) = 0.11$, $p > .05$). But only 21% had heard of Legionnaire's Disease from the mass media, whereas 83% had heard of AIDS from the media ($t(125) = 13.42$, $p < .001$).

Q2. How knowledgeable are respondents about the three diseases?

Although the majority expressed a high awareness of the AIDS issue, less than half were able to answer correctly 50% of the items on the knowledge test. There were 80 respondents who answered less than 50% of the items correctly; 46 respondents answered more than 50% of the items correctly. The sample scored lower on the test than would be expected by chance (Chi Square (1) = 9.18, $p < .002$). The mean for the test was 44% correct (SD = .27). Most of the respondents were able to name accurately a group at risk of contracting AIDS (82%) and Toxic-Shock (70%). Most were sure that AIDS, Legionnaire's Disease, and Toxic Shock are transmitted in different ways (57%). But accuracy declined for items concerning whether or not more people die from Toxic-Shock (44%) and whether or not Toxic-Shock Syndrome and Legionnaire's Disease affect more people than AIDS (31%). Accuracy fell to the 30% to 20% range for items regarding the cause of AIDS and the other diseases (29%), group at risk of Legionnaire's Disease (27%), recovery from AIDS (25%), and the ease of curing AIDS when compared with Legionnaire's Disease (21%). One of the factors contributing to the low scores on the factual test appears to be a lack of awareness of the nature of Legionnaire's Disease.

These findings suggested that Legionnaire's Disease was relatively unknown to the respondents and that further analyses including the disease would be confounded by the lack of awareness of the illness. The decision was made to focus on AIDS and Toxic-Shock in subsequent analyses because they had comparable awareness levels.

Q3. How does the image of AIDS compare with the image of Toxic-Shock?

An examination of the items associated with the image construct substantiate the expectation that AIDS is engulfed by stigma. Although 38% expressed sympathy for people with AIDS, more than three-quarters (76%) expressed sympathy for victims of Toxic-Shock, a very large and significant difference ($t(125) = 10.45$, $p < .001$). In addition, 30% asserted that "Moral people seldom get AIDS," whereas only 3% connected morality with Toxic-Shock (t (125) = 9.11, $p < .001$). Stigma sets AIDS apart from Toxic-Shock.

Ambivalence was high (73%) for AIDS but low for Toxic-Shock (7%). People with mixed feelings toward AIDS outnumbered those with mixed feelings toward Toxic-Shock at the rate of 10 to 1, a highly significant difference (t (125) = 11.76, $p < .001$).

In terms of threat, the respondents saw AIDS as a high personal risk relative to the risk of contracting Toxic-Shock, and they expressed fear of the disease. Although 66% of the respondents saw themselves or friends at risk of getting AIDS, 60% also saw themselves or friends at risk of getting Toxic-Shock. Thus the threat of getting AIDS was perceived to be high but no higher than for Toxic-Shock (t (125) = 0.04, $p > .05$). But the fright associated with AIDS was much greater. About two-thirds of the sample declared that AIDS is the most frightening disease of our time whereas the number shrank to 14% for Toxic-Shock ($t(125) = 9.41$, $p < .001$).

These findings underscore the nature of the "negative-affect, negative-belief" stigma attached to people with AIDS. These most severe stigmas occur when negative affect is coupled with a negative belief that the marked person is a morally flawed individual who deserves the disease. With this type of stigma, "negative affect is seen as totally justified" because the belief component validates the negative feeling (Jones et al., 1984, p. 9). It is postulated that the ambivalence expressed by the respondents in this study arises from the conflict between responsibility and threat. On the one hand, the respondents picture AIDS as a disease connected with an immoral life style that deserves little sympathy, but, on the other hand, the personal risk to self and friends is frightening and as real to them as the risk of Toxic-Shock.

Viewed as an index of involvement, the issue of risk is interesting. Even respondents in a low-risk state may assess the risk of contracting AIDS to be high. As a health issue, AIDS appears to be as involving as Toxic-Shock.

Q4. How does the behavioral intent to help people with AIDS compare with the intent to help people with Toxic-Shock?

In terms of behavioral intent, the sample could be described as a pool of potential volunteers. With 78% agreeing to help Toxic-Shock victims and 37% agreeing to help people with AIDS, there appears to be a high degree of willingness to help the sick. A total of 81% are willing to help with one or both of the diseases. Of course, the intent to help does not mean that the respondents would actually follow through with actual helping acts (Rogers, 1983). However, the willingness to help those suffering from AIDS is significantly less than the inclination to help those with Toxic-Shock (t(125) = 9.04, p < .001). This finding is consistent with expectations about stigmatized and nonstigmatized objects (Jones et al., 1984; Katz, 1981).

Q5. How do factual knowledge, image dimensions of stigma, and gender relate to the willingness to help people with AIDS and Toxic-Shock Syndrome?

This question was explored through a discriminant analysis and a correlational analysis. Scores from the test of factual knowledge and the image dimensions of stigma were entered into the discriminant analysis. The correlation matrix included knowledge, image, and gender variables.

The response distribution for the willingness-to-help items was partitioned into 3 groups with each group having at least 20 members. Group 1, the Helpers group, consisted of 42 respondents who agreed to help both AIDS and Toxic-Shock victims. Group 2, the TSS Helpers-AIDS Nonhelpers group, had 56 members who agreed to help people with Toxic-Shock but expressed neutrality or unwillingness to help people with AIDS. Group 3, the Nonhelpers group, was composed of 24 respondents who expressed neutrality or unwillingness to help people with either disease. Only 4 respondents expressed a willingness to help AIDS victims without agreeing to help Toxic-Shock victims; they were not included in the analysis. Consequently, the total N was reduced from 126 to 122.

The univariate analysis revealed that 9 of 11 variables discriminated among the 3 levels of behavioral intent (p < .05). Table 29.1 shows that all

9 significant variables separated Group 1, the Helpers group, from Group 3, the Nonhelpers group. Helpers scored higher on the knowledge test than nonhelpers. With the exception of 2 AIDS items (ambivalence and fright), helpers proved to be more sympathetic to victims, less likely to condemn victims on moral grounds, and more likely to see themselves or friends at risk of contracting the diseases than nonhelpers. Helpers expressed less fright of Toxic-Shock and less ambivalence toward victims than nonhelpers.

In addition, Table 29.1 shows that image variables associated with AIDS separated Group 1, the Helpers group, from Group 2, the TSS Helpers-AIDS Nonhelpers group. In this case, only the knowledge test and the fright item failed to differentiate. Moreover, the knowledge test as well as all of the image variables associated with Toxic-Shock separated Group 2, the TSS Helpers-AIDS Nonhelpers group, from Group 3, the Nonhelpers group.

Wilks's step-wise procedure was used to select an appropriate set of salient variables that maximized the separation of groups. With the criterion for entry set at F equal to or greater than one and the stipulation that the change in Lambda must exceed .01, a six-variable, two-function model was produced.

With both functions in the model, Lambda was .49 (Chi Square (2) = 83.36, p < .0000); with the first function removed Lambda was .76 (Chi Square (5) = 31.81, p < .0000). The two canonical correlations were .71 and .49; the first function had an eigenvalue of .56 and explained 64% of the variance; the second function had an eigenvalue of .31 and explained 36% of the variance.

An examination of the canonical discriminant functions evaluated at the group means suggested that Function 1 did the best job of separating Group 1 from Group 2. It was labeled "The AIDS Function" because it differentiated between those who were willing to help AIDS victims and those who were less willing to help. Function 2 was labeled "The TSS Function" because it separated those who were willing to help Toxic-Shock victims and those who were less willing to help. It did the best job of separating Groups 1 and 2 from Group 3.

Table 29.2 displays the standardized function coefficients for the six items that survived the stepwise procedure. An affective dimension, sympathy, along with measures of ambivalent reactions and the belief that AIDS poses a personal risk are most salient to the AIDS Function. Likewise, sympathy and risk play a similar role in the willingness to help Toxic-Shock victims, but the salient reaction to Toxic-Shock is degree of fright rather than ambivalence. Consistent with the expectations fostered by Rogers (1983), both affective and belief components form the bases of the images of both diseases.

Table 29.1
Means and Standard Deviations for Those Willing to Help AIDS and
TSS Victims (Group 1), Those Willing to Help TSS Victims But
Less Willing to Help People with AIDS (Group 2), and
Those Less Willing to Help People with Either Disease (Group 3)

VARIABLE (Range)*	Group 1 (n = 42) Mean (SD)	Group 2 (n = 56) Mean (SD)	Group 3 (n = 24) Mean (SD)
KNOWLEDGE Facts (0 Lo; 9 Hi)	4.21a (2.58)	4.45a (2.10)	2.29 (1.99)
AIDS Sympathy (1 Hi; 7 Lo)	2.86 (1.61)	4.84a (1.52)	4.67a (1.44)
AIDS Morality (1 Lo; 7 Hi)	5.33 (1.71)	4.43a (1.99)	3.58a (1.93)
AIDS Ambivalence (1 Hi; 7 Lo)	3.52b (1.95)	2.79a (1.58)	3.04ab (1.46)
AIDS Risk (1 Lo; 7 Hi)	5.93 (1.26)	4.77a (1.92)	4.17a (1.93)
AIDS Fright (1 Hi; 7 Lo)	2.81a (1.86)	3.00a (1.90)	3.46a (1.79)
TSS Sympathy (1 Hi; 7 Lo)	2.26a (1.20)	2.04a (1.08)	3.42 (1.09)
TSS Morality (1 Lo; 7 Hi)	6.31a (1.26)	6.61a (.91)	5.46 (1.59)
TSS Ambivalence (1 Hi; 7 Lo)	5.21a (1.60)	5.66a (1.18)	4.46 (1.32)
TSS Risk (1 Lo; 7 Hi)	5.57a (1.60)	5.16a (1.97)	4.00 (1.41)
TSS Fright (1 Hi; 7 Lo)	5.02a (1.47)	5.00a (1.45)	4.21 (.78)

Note: All means in a given row are different from each other ($p < .05$) unless marked by a or b; means sharing a common a or b are not significantly different.
* A score of 1 on the sympathy scale points to high sympathy for the victim and 7 points to low sympathy.

Consistent with the theory of Katz (1981), ambivalence is a feature of the image of AIDS. Katz contends that ambivalence is the earmark of a stigma. Fright types Toxic-Shock as a disease that evokes a nonconflicted emotional reaction—a feature of a nonstigmatized object.

Apparently, morality did not enter the model for either disease because of the redundancy created by its correlation with sympathy (AIDS, r =

Table 29.2
Standardized Discriminant Function Coefficients for the
Six Variables Meeting Wilks's Criteria for the Final Analysis
and Pooled-Within-Groups Correlations Between
Discriminating Variables and Functions for All Variables

| VARIABLE | Standardized Coefficients | | Correlations | |
	FUNC 1 AIDS	FUNC 2 TSS	FUNC 1 AIDS	FUNC 2 TSS
AIDS Sympathy	-.89	.09	-.73	-.47
AIDS Ambivalence	.35	-.16	.25	.07
AIDS Risk	.30	.16	.34	.53
TSS Sympathy	.55	-.72	.20	-.78
TSS Risk	.12	.36	.07	.57
TSS Morality			-.01	.56
KNOWLEDGE Facts			-.12	.44
TSS Ambivalence			-.18	.43
TSS Fright	-.13	.41	-.03	.42
AIDS Morality			.29	.36
AIDS Fright			-.01	.05

.48, p < .001; TSS, r = .61, p < .001). The bond between sympathy and morality is substantial. Earlier it was reported that people with AIDS are viewed with less sympathy and as more immoral. Thus AIDS seems to be the type of stigma in which negative affect and negative belief often go hand-in-hand.

The issue of involvement (Krugman, 1965), represented by the possibility of contracting the disease, enters the picture for both AIDS and Toxic-Shock. Those perceiving a greater risk are more likely to help.

The structure matrix suggests how those variables not entering the model correlated with the two functions. It is interesting to note that the knowledge test is allied with the TSS Function rather than the AIDS Function. Also salient, but not surviving the Wilks's procedure, are morality and ambivalence toward Toxic-Shock. Helpers of Toxic-Shock victims are less prone to condemn the victims of either Toxic-Shock or AIDS on moral grounds. Moreover, they are less likely to have mixed feelings about people with Toxic-Shock.

A further clarification of the relationships suggested by the discriminant analysis can be obtained from an examination of the intercorrelations among knowledge, image, behavioral intent, and gender. The image variables are represented by the casewise scores for the AIDS Function and the TSS Function.

The relationship between knowledge and the image of AIDS is a negative but nonsignificant one (r = -.17, p > .05). There is no significant correlation between behavioral intent and factual knowledge about the diseases ($r = -.02$, $p > .05$). The willingness to help a person with AIDS is related to the image of AIDS. The relationship is substantial ($r = .56$, $p < .001$). To a lesser degree, the willingness to help is related to the image of Toxic-Shock ($r = .20$, $p < .05$).

There is a substantial relationship between factual knowledge of the diseases and image of Toxic-Shock ($r = .54$, $p < .001$). Behavioral intent is also related to the knowledge of the diseases ($r = .43$, $p < .001$). The willingness to help a person with Toxic-Shock is related to the image of the disease and its victims. The relationship is substantial ($r = .54$, $p < .001$).

Knowledge appears to be configured differently for AIDS and Toxic-Shock. In the case of AIDS, there is neither a significant bond between knowledge and image nor a significant bond between knowledge and behavior. In the case of Toxic-Shock, there is a significant connection between knowledge and image as well as between knowledge and behavior. Two explanations might account for the difference in configuration.

If Toxic-Shock were a more involving issue than AIDS, one might speculate that involvement is the key to explaining the difference. Krugman (1965) posits that the connection between knowledge and image/behavior is more intimate with high involvement issues. However, the findings indicated that respondents see as much risk with AIDS as Toxic-Shock. Moreover, Table 29.2 suggests that risk plays a similar role in the image of both diseases. In terms of risk, the data offer no indication that Toxic-Shock is a more involving issue than AIDS.

A second speculation might focus on the nature of the AIDS stigma. Jones et al. (1984) contend that a "negative-affect, negative-belief" stigma operates irrespective of a knowledge of the facts. This kind of stigma is "supported by a belief system often designated as a *stereotype* because of its rigidity and unresponsiveness to ameliorating information" (Jones et al., 1984, p. 9). The data seem to portray AIDS as a "negative-affect, negative-belief" stigma. From this perspective, one might expect Toxic-Shock to exhibit the connections implied by the classical model (Rogers, 1983), whereas one might expect AIDS to exhibit an independence of knowledge and image/behavior.

Because AIDS is a disease that affects chiefly males and Toxic-Shock is a disease that affects mainly females, it is important to suggest how gender relates to the variables. Gender plays a significant role in terms of image and behavior for Toxic Shock ($r = -.34$, $p < .001$; $r = -.21$, $p < .05$) but does not appear to play a significant role for either AIDS-related variables or factual knowledge. Although Toxic-Shock may be a more involving issue for females, the valence of gender correlations is the same in all cases, indicating that females have a more sympathetic attitude toward the sick and are more inclined to help the ill regardless of the disease.

SUMMARY, CONCLUSIONS,
AND STRATEGIES

In the late summer of 1985, the respondents described in this exploratory study expressed no greater awareness of AIDS than Toxic-Shock Syndrome. However, their perceived knowledge of these two diseases was significantly greater than their perceived knowledge of Legionnaire's Disease. On a test of factual knowledge about the three diseases, the respondents answered 44% of the items correctly.

Compared with Toxic-Shock victims, people with AIDS were viewed with less sympathy and condemned more often on moral grounds. More ambivalence was expressed toward people with AIDS. Respondents expressed the belief that they and their friends were at risk of contracting AIDS as well as Toxic-Shock. However, respondents considered AIDS to be a more frightening disease than Toxic-Shock.

With 81% agreeing to help people with one or both of the diseases, the sample could be described as a pool from which volunteer helpers might be drawn. However, respondents were significantly less willing to help people with AIDS than with Toxic-Shock.

Although the willingness to help a person with AIDS was related to the image of AIDS, willingness was not related to knowledge or gender variables. Toxic-Shock variables were related to a willingness to help people with AIDS. In addition, females rather than males exhibited a more prosocial orientation toward victims of Toxic-Shock and tended to be more prosocial toward people with AIDS.

The expectation that AIDS is a deeply stigmatized disease was verified. Although the exploratory nature of the study and small sample size dictate caution in generalizing beyond the sample, the following conclusions are offered as hypotheses for future research.

(1) Sympathy and risk may represent affective and belief dimensions common to images of the stigmatized and nonstigmatized.

(2) Ambivalence may be a dimension that separates images of the nonstigmatized from the stigmatized.

(3) AIDS may be characterized as a double stigma.

(4) For a significant number of people, AIDS may represent a "negative-affect, negative-belief" stigma.

(5) AIDS may represent the kind of stigma that resists factual knowledge.

(6) AIDS as an issue may be as involving as other diseases in low-risk states.

(7) The willingness to help people with AIDS may be related to the willingness to help people with other diseases.

(8) Women may exhibit more prosocial behavior toward people with AIDS than males.

The data support the conclusion that mobilizing interventionists in low-risk states for people with AIDS is a difficult and complex undertaking. But they also suggest some provisional strategies for developing an effective mobilization campaign.

(1) Aim the campaign toward those with a general predisposition toward helping the sick. The low but significant correlation between the willingness to help people with AIDS and people with other diseases suggests that a prosocial orientation may facilitate commitment.

(2) Ask people to help. Factual knowledge about AIDS and other diseases does not appear to be a prerequisite to helping behavior. To the extent that there is an independence of AIDS knowledge, a request for help may precede efforts to build factual knowledge.

In an extensive study of the knowledge and attitudes of blood donors and nondonors (Drake, Finkelstein, & Sapolsky, 1982), it was found that one of the most salient factors separating donors from nondonors was the simple request for a donation. "Nobody asked me" was the most frequent and most salient reason cited by nondonors. Although there are obvious differences between the act of giving blood and helping people with AIDS, requesting help may facilitate the mobilization process.

Getting candidates involved in some sort of help project should be the first priority. If it is impossible to involve the candidates with an actual help project, the use of role-playing may be a viable alternative. The literature (Festinger, 1964; Marshall, Kurtz, & Associates, 1982; Wexley & Latham, 1981) supports the power of role-playing in producing commitment.

(3) Do not assume that a knowledge of the facts signals a favorable image of people with AIDS.

The news story cited in the introduction to this paper illustrates that even professional health-care interventionists with extensive factual knowledge about diseases can express negative affect toward people with AIDS. Negative affect expressed by knowledgeable interventionists is further documented by others within the psychological community.

(4) Confront the double stigma. It might be useful to separate the stigmas and deal with each as a separate issue. The findings imply that generating sympathy for a person with a deadly illness may facilitate the decision to help. People are likely to agree that AIDS is a frightening disease and that they or their friends could possibly contract the disease. The morality/responsibility issue could be confronted directly. Attacking the "just world" view may be helpful (Jones et al., 1984). Bad things do happen to good people and people do not always get what they deserve. Also, this issue could be approached through drama and modeling.

As Jones et al. (1984) point out, drama is a powerful force, along with the media, in providing examples and role models of those who have broken through a stigmatized role. Celebrities who lend their support to people with AIDS help undermine the power of the master categories. The Broadway plays *As Is* and *The Normal Heart* are examples of dramas that have portrayed the person with AIDS in a favorable light. NBC's *An Early Frost* was a television drama that depicted a gay man's efforts to cope with a diagnosis of AIDS. Some observers have labeled efforts like these as promoting a greater public understanding of "what it is like to be gay and have AIDS" (Pessin, 1985).

This list of strategies is meant to be suggestive rather than definitive. It is based on the findings from 126 respondents in one low-incidence state. Larger samples from various areas of the country are needed to cross-validate the findings.

REFERENCES

AIDS Project of Los Angeles. (1985, May). *The optimist*. Los Angeles: Author.

Allen, J. R., & Curran, J. W. (1985). Epidemiology of the acquired immunodeficiency syndrome. In J. I. Gallin & A. S. Fauci (Eds.), *Advances in host defense mechanisms: Acquired immunodeficiency syndrome*. (Vol. 5, pp. 1-27). New York: Raven.

Argyris, C. (1970). *Intervention theory and method: A behavioral science view*. Reading, MA: Addison-Wesley.

Baker, J. (1983). *AIDS: Everything you must know about acquired immune deficiency syndrome*. Saratoga, CA: Robert D. Reed.

Batchelor, W. F. (1984). AIDS: A public health and psychological emergency. *American Psychologist, 39*, 1279-1284.

Billie, D. A. (1985, May 28). AIDS hygiene: Practices and precautions. *The Advocate*, pp. 34-35.

Black, D. (1985a, March 28). Part one: The plague years. *Rolling Stone*, pp. 48-54, 114-125.

Black, D. (1985b, April 25). Part two: The plague years. *Rolling Stone*, pp. 35-45, 56-62.

Centers for Disease Control. (1983). Annual Summary 1982: Reported morbidity and mortality in the United States. *Morbidity and Mortality Weekly Report, 31*.

Centers for Disease Control. (1984). Annual Summary 1983: Reported morbidity and mortality in the United States. *Morbidity and Mortality Weekly Report, 32*.

Centers for Disease Control. (1986a). Summary—cases of specified notifiable diseases, United States. *Morbidity and Mortality Weekly Report, 34*, 782.

Centers for Disease Control. (1986b). Update: Acquired immunodeficiency syndrome—United States. *Morbidity and Mortality Weekly Report, 35*, 17-21.

Coates, T. J., Temoshok, L., & Mandel, J. (1984). Psychosocial research is essential to understanding and treating AIDS. *American Psychologist, 39*, 1309-1314.

Curran, J. W., Morgan, W. M., Hardy, A. M., Jaffe, H. W., Darrow, W. W., & Dowdle, W. R. (1985). The epidemiology of AIDS: Current status and future prospects. *Science, 229*, 1352-1357.

Daniels, J. (1985, July). The new victims: AIDS is an epidemic that may change the way America lives. *Life*, pp. 6, 12-19.

Darley, J. M., & Latané, B. (1968). Bystander-intervention in emergencies: Diffusion of responsibility. *Journal of Personality and Social Psychology, 10*, 202-214.

Dlugokinski, E. L., & Firestone, I. J. (1973). Congruence among four methods of measuring other-centeredness. *Child Development, 44*, 304-308.

Dlugokinski, E. L., & Firestone, I. J. (1974). Other-centeredness and susceptibility to charitable appeals: Effects of perceived discipline. *Developmental Psychology, 10*, 21-28.

Drake, A. W., Finkelstein, S. N., & Sapolsky, H. M. (1982). *The American blood supply*. Cambridge: MIT Press.

Eisenberg, N. (1982). *The development of prosocial behavior*. New York: Academic Press.

Ferrara, A. (1984). My personal experience with AIDS. *American Psychologist, 39*, 1285-1287.

Feshbach, N. D. (1982). Sex differences in empathy and social behavior in children. In N. Eisenberg (Ed.), *The development of prosocial behavior* (pp. 315-338). New York: Academic Press.

Festinger, L. (1964). *Conflict, decision, and dissonance.* Stanford, CA: Stanford University Press.

Flacks, R. (1970). The revolt of the advantaged. In R. Sigel (Ed.), *Learning about politics* (pp. 182-191). New York: Random House.

Goffman, E. (1963). *Stigma: Notes on the management of spoiled identity.* Englewood Cliffs, NJ: Prentice-Hall.

Gottlieb, B. H. (1981). *Social networks and social support.* Beverly Hills, CA: Sage.

Gottlieb, B. H. (1983). *Social support strategies: Guidelines for mental health practice.* Beverly Hills, CA: Sage.

Hughey, J. D. (1966). *An investigation of two selected methods of modifying credibility on the immediate and delayed effectiveness of a speaker.* Unpublished doctoral dissertation, Purdue University.

Jones, E. E., Farina, A., Hastorf, A. H., Markus, H., Miller, D. T., & Scott, R. A. (1984). *Social stigma: The psychology of marked relationships.* New York: Freeman.

Joseph, J. G., Emmons, C., Kessler, R. C., Wortman, C. B., O'Brien, K., Hocker, W. T., & Schaefer, C. (1984). Coping with the threat of AIDS: An approach to psychosocial assessment. *American Psychologist, 39,* 1297-1302.

Kaposi's Sarcoma Research and Education Foundation. (1983, March). *AIDS: A scientific and clinical bibliography.* San Francisco, CA: Author.

Katz, I. (1981). *Stigma: A social psychological analysis.* Hillsdale, NJ: Lawrence Erlbaum.

Kenniston, K. (1967). The sources of student discontent. *Journal of Social Issues, 23,* 108-135.

Krugman, H. E. (1965). The impact of television advertising: Learning without involvement. *Public Opinion Quarterly, 29,* 349-356.

Lapham, L. H. (1985, June 2). Taking the new right to task on AIDS. *New York Native,* p. 7.

Marshall, E. K., Kurtz, P. D., & Associates. (1982). *Interpersonal helping skills.* San Francisco, CA: Jossey-Bass.

Martin, J. L., & Vance, C. S. (1984). Behavioral and psychosocial factors in AIDS: Methodological and substantive issues. *American Psychologist, 39,* 1303-1308.

Maves, C. (1985, May 28). Living with AIDS. *The Advocate,* pp. 30-33.

Mayer, K., & Pizer, H. (1983). *The AIDS fact book.* New York: Bantam.

Morin, S. F. (1984). AIDS in one city: An interview with Mervyn Silverman, director of health, San Francisco. *American Psychologist, 39,* 1294-1296.

Morin, S. F., Charles, K. A., & Malyon, A. K. (1984). The psychological impact of AIDS on gay men. *American Psychologist, 39,* 1288-1293.

National Coalition of Gay STD Services. (1985, March-April). *The Official Newsletter of the National Coalition of Gay STD Services, 6.*

Oklahomans for Human Rights. (n.d.). *The AIDS crisis: Is your life on the line?* Tulsa, OK: Author.

Pessin, E. (1985, November 11). Reaction to AIDS movie. *United Press International.*

Powell, F. (1965). The effect of anxiety-arousing messages when related to personal, familial, and impersonal referents. *Speech Monographs, 32,* 102-106.

Public Health Service. (1984a, June). *Facts about AIDS.* Washington, DC.

Public Health Service. (1984b). *What everyone should know about AIDS.* South Deerfield, MA: Channing L. Bete.

Public Health Service. (1984c). *What gay and bisexual men should know about AIDS.* South Deerfield, MA: Channing L. Bete.

Public Health Service. (1984d). *Why you should be informed about AIDS: Information for health-care personnel and other care providers.* South Deerfield, MA: Channing L. Bete.

Ricci, E. (1986, January 17). Science today: Doctors need help coping with the impact of AIDS. *United Press International.*

Rogers, E. M. (1983). *Diffusion of innovations.* New York: Free Press.

Rogers, E. M., & Shoemaker, F. F. (1962). *Communication of innovations*. New York: Free Press.

Rushton, J. P. (1980). *Altruism, socialization, and society*. Englewood Cliffs, NJ: Prentice-Hall.

Rushton, J. P., & Sorrentino, R. M. (1981). *Altruism and helping behavior: Social, personality, and developmental perspectives*. Hillsdale, NJ: Lawrence Erlbaum.

Siegal, F. B., & Siegal, M. (1983). *AIDS: The medical mystery*. New York: Grove.

Solomon, F., & Fishman, J. R. (1964). Youth and peace: A psychosocial study and student peace demonstrators in Washington D. C. *Journal of Social Issues, 20*, 54-73.

Sontag, S. (1978). *Illness as metaphor*. New York: Farrar, Straus & Giroux.

Underwood, B., & Moore, B. S. (1982). The generality of altruism in children. In N. Eisenberg (Ed.), *The development of prosocial behavior* (pp. 25-52). New York: Academic Press.

West, S. G., Whitney, G., & Schnedler, R. (1975). Helping a motorist in distress: The effects of sex, race, and neighborhood. *Journal of Personality and Social Psychology, 31*, 691-698.

Wexley, K. N., & Latham, G. P. (1981). *Developing and training human resources in organizations*. Glenview, IL: Scott, Foresman.

X ● PHILOSOPHY OF COMMUNICATION

30 ● Deconstructing the Audience: Who Are They and What Do We Know About Them

BRIANKLE G. CHANG

University of Illinois at Urbana-Champaign

A UDIENCE analysis has always been one of the most active areas of mass communication research. Although specific conceptions of the audience have been challenged and subsequently modified as a result of different research findings, the category of the audience itself has never been radically problematized. Instead of trying to refine our understanding of the nature of the audience (whose composition, to make the matter more complicated, is as changing as the media, communication technologies, and research methods that target it), this chapter attempts to deconstruct (Chang, 1985; Chang, in press a; Derrida, 1976, 1978) the dominant notion of audience in mass communication research by questioning its *usefulness* as a theoretical category or concept whose supposed referent, as I will try to show, is an essentially "discursive" reality.[1] I will then propose an alternative way of viewing the familiar object previously labeled *audience* as both constitutive of and constituted by various "discursive practices" and ideological determinations involved in the social production and reproduction of meaning. Such a discursive notion of the audience might work toward displacing what I call the "psychological/sociological image" of the reader/audience implied in the sender-media-receiver model of communication process.

Correspondence and requests for reprints: Briankle G. Chang, Department of Speech Communication, 244 Lincoln Hall, 702 S. Wright St., University of Illinois at Urbana-Champaign, Urbana, IL 61801.

In so doing, the chapter shall demonstrate (1) why the conception of audience as people, as a collection of individual psychological entities, should be rejected; and (2) how the same phenomenon or entity should be rethought simultaneously as a *process* of and a *site* for decoding particular media messages within the general ideological struggle over meaning and interpretation in society. As can be seen, the chapter calls for a decentering of an anthropocentric audience as it has been operative in American mass communication research in general and in media effects research in particular; and it advocates a reconceptualization of the audience that locates it as an integral moment susceptible to all sorts of extra-media influences within the structural whole of cultural production, distribution, and consumption of meanings/messages.

"Almost every fixed inventory," Hall (1981, p. 235) once said, "will betray us," and the concept of the audience, I am afraid, has done all but that. Two requiems for mass communication have sounded over the past 15 years on both continents (Baudrillard, 1981, pp. 164-184; Schramm & Roberts, 1971, p. 191). By responding to the urgency posed by the current politics of textuality and interpretation in media research (Grossberg, 1984) through the intervention of a local topic such as "audience," a third requiem, I hope, might give birth to something new.

STRUCTURALIST APPROACH
AND THE QUESTION
OF THE SUBJECT

To illustrate how a "critical turn" in communication studies changes the direction of mass media and audience research since the mid-70s, I shall discuss *Screen*'s theory of the subject (that is, viewers, readers) in relation to text and culture as one example of the rethinking of the concept of audience. I find *Screen*'s theory illuminative for our purpose here because it represents a significant improvement over the psychological/sociological conception of audience, and at the same time it exemplifies a failure shared by other structuralist-inspired projects that depsychologize the audience only to make it unduly "textual."

Two things need to be mentioned about *Screen* at the outset: First, it is as heavily influenced by psychoanalysis (Lacan), Marxism (Althusser), and Post-Structuralism (Derrida) as it is by structural linguistics and structural anthropology. According to *Screen*'s position, the analysis of cultural productions is intimately linked with the analysis of ideology and its articulations in both cultural and artistic domains. Moreover, its analysis of ideology and its effects in different forms of representation is built upon a set of psychoanalytic processes regarded as fundamental to the psychic formation of social subjects (Heath, 1981; Metz, 1982). Second, the journal is devoted primarily to the analysis of a particular form of representation, film. Through analyzing the signifying practices of its chosen object, namely the different cinematic operations that enunciate, narrate, and finally close a filmic diegesis in relation to its spectators, writers in *Screen* undertake to reveal how ideology, embodied in its visual operators (quattrocento perspective in the Classic period, for example), pervades cinematic apparatuses to produce identifiable "effects" of representation through a particular medium (Brundson & Morley, 1978; Chang, in press b; Heath, 1981). Contrasting several approaches of cultural interpretation in contemporary critical theories, Grossberg (1984) characterizes the position of *Screen* as follows:

> Their analyses focused on the ways in which the camera functions to produce a particular series of identification for the viewer. For example, they argued that in the classic Hollywood cinema, one is positioned by the camera as if one were seeing the scene of the film from an omniscient position outside of the scene of action itself. That identification with the camera slides into the particular characters within the film, through the way in which the camera relates to the positions of the characters themselves (as agents of knowledge). Consequently, the viewer is "stitched" or "sutured" into the text. Furthermore, the camera of the Hollywood film identifies with the male protagonists and renders the female the object of the voyeuristic sight/site of the camera, the male characters, and the spectator. Alternatively, the avant-garde cinema often places the camera within the *mise-en-scene,* imposing a reflexively limited point of view on the spectator, and dispersing the viewing subject into a multiciplicity of positions, no longer claiming a privileged point of entry into or existence within the text, and thus, declaring no single access to truth. (p. 410)

The implications of this position are considerable. First of all, if the meaning-producing mechanisms in a film text work to position the subject inside the textual space in the way a close reading of its narrative structuration and particular reflection of the cinematic appratuses indicates, then perhaps other kinds of text, other modes of signifying practices, also position subjects through different mechanisms in accord with their respective representational necessity. Is it not true that a "realist" film positions its spectators much like a "realist" novel lures and then immobilizes its readers in a similar system of points of view (Rimon-Kenan, 1984; Silverman, 1983)? Although the actual "positions" into which subjects are situated might vary from one signifying system to another, the fact that the signifying practice produces the "effect" of positioning its own decoding agent seems to be a representational necessity of signification. Moreover, the positioning of the subject by the signifying practice is not just a gratuitous effect; rather it answers the demand of the dominant ideology to reproduce itself in the realm of meaning and signification. The reproduction of ideology in meaning belongs essentially to the social formation in that any social organization needs to displace its material or social contradictions onto the plane of symbolic expressions—be it graphic or verbal, visual or audio—so that they may be defused or deferred through the infinite reproducibility of signs and symbols (see Kuhn, 1982). Ideology engenders its own signifying supports, and signifying apparatuses in turn articulate meaning through diverse cultural relays that work to secure textual closures.

The structuralist position *Screen* represents provides a view of the subject of communication radically different from what we normally think of as the "sender" or "receiver" of messages. In this structuralist view, "subjects," as it were, are specific "sites," constituted by the signifying practices in a chain of signification, be it a film, a novel, or a painting (Chang, in press b). Subject-position then refers to the possibility or modality of knowing or knowledge in the cultural processes of meaning production, rather than a psychological or cognitive entity who thinks and acts as if entirely free. Discourse and subject, text and writer/reader, imply one another (Grossberg, 1982); they are moments or junctures in the temporal sliding of signs in discourse in which the signifier and the signified momentarily coincide within a "narrative space" as a result of certain psychoanalytic and textual "works" (*travail*) such as "identification" in film or the use of "pronouns" in fiction (Barthes, 1974; Metz, 1982). They are the I/eye(s) of vision and pleasure, drifting in and through the text, all the time responding to the representational priority of ideology.

There is no denying that the structuralist theory of subject formation advanced by *Screen* represents an improvement over what can be called the *psychological/sociological* construction of audience in media studies. But the *Screen* position is not without problems of its own. If the "mainstream" conception of the audience is too psychologistic or sociological, *Screen*'s redefinition of the subject in signifying productions and consumptions is too "textual." Its less than critical appropriation of semiotics and, particularly, the Lancanian psychoanalysis, as some critics have pointed out, have driven it into a too "abstract text-subject relationship" (Neale, 1977). Morley (1980) has argued that, according to *Screen*'s position,

> The subject is not conceived as already constituted in other discursive formations and social formations. Also, it is treated in relation to only one text at a time (or alternatively, all texts are assumed to function according to the rules of a single "classic realist text"). This is then explicated by references to the universal, primary psychoanalytic processes (Oedipus complex, "mirror phase," castration complex and its resolution and so on), through which, according to Lacan's reading of Freud, "the subject" is constituted. The text is understood as reproducing or replaying this primary positioning, which is the foundation of any reading. (p. 163)

The assumption of such an abstract, psychoanalytically grounded, relation between the text and subject proves to be problematic. For, apart from the difficulty of explaining "a specific instance of the text/reader relationship in terms of a universalist theory of the formation of subjects-in-general," it isolates "the encounter of text and reader from all social and historical structures *and* from other texts. Its unbalanced reliance on the functioning of 'a single, universal set of psychic mechanisms' causes the theory itself to overlook the constant intervention of other texts, discourses, and institutions that also position the subject" (p. 163). The subject envisioned by *Screen* then is a subject without histor(ies) or contradictions, if only because contradictory positions, which are always historical, have already been predetermined at the psychoanalytic level by a limited number of "primary" processes.

What the above problem means ultimately is that *Screen* theory fails to make the distinction between how the subject is constituted as a "space" and specific interpellations/interpolations that sometimes even place the subject in contradictory positions; instead, "it deduces 'subjects' from the subject positions offered by the text and identifies the two" (Morley, 1980, p. 166). This conflation between the *subject of text* and the real *social subject* forces *Screen* theory to elide constantly the concrete individual, his or her constitution as a "subject-in-and-for-discourse," and the subject position constituted by specific discursive practices and operations, thus unwittingly turning itself into the very idealist formalism it set out to undermine. Moreover, this failure to distinguish between the *subject of text* and the *social subject* also leads the theoretical discussion to slight the "nonnecessary correspondence" in the subjects/text relation; that is to say, the non-differentiation between the *abstract* subject-in-general and *concrete* social subjects oversimplifies the complex process of overdetermination through which no alignment between the text and subjects is forever fixed or causally established in a one-to-one correspondence.

Specific combinations—for example, between specific problematics and specific modes of address—may exist historically as well secured, dominant or recurring patterns in particular conjunctures in definite social formations. These may be fixed in place by the institutionalization of practices within a particular site or apparatus (for example, Hollywood cinema). Nevertheless, even these correspondences are not "eternal" or universal. . . . One can point to the practices and mechanisms which secure them and which reproduce them . . . in one text after another. Unless one is to accept that there is no ideology but the dominant ideology, which is always in its appointed place, this "naturalized" correspondence must constantly be deconstructed and shown to be *a historically concrete relation*. It follows from this argument that there must be different "realisms," not a single "classic realist text" to which all realist texts can be assimilated. And there is no *necessary* correspondence between these realisms and a particular problematic. (italics added, Morley, 1980, p. 169)

To fail to distinguish a discursive construction from concrete social subjects is to fail to maintain the specificity of different practices and institutions (for example, juridical, educational, economic, political, and so forth). No two forms of signification (for example, realist novels and documentary films) should be lumped together under one category such as "realism" without considering their respective relations to the wider cultural context. And different signifying practices should not be given equal weight in their determinations on meaning production simply because they all "position" the subject in one way or another.

SUBJECT AND
TEXT CONCRETIZED

The problems identified above may appear specific to *Screen,* but they are symptomatic of a more serious cause lying deeper in what is usually characterized as the "synchronic" outlook that plagued many early structuralist analyses of texts. Focusing on the text itself, on how the textual logic codes and invites its own consumption, the synchronic orientation tends to be oblivious to changes and the processual characteristics manifesting themselves in the text across time. This leads to a hyper-textual position, that the determining factor in the interaction between text and reader is the text itself. A film, for example, is thought to position the subject in such a way that the possible readings that subject might give of it—despite the polysemic nature of signs—are already immanent in that film's textual construction. The viewing subject then becomes a textual product. Although the structuralist approach enables media critics to reconceptualize the audience outside the demographic grid and cognitive variables, its text-centered posture eventually renders the audience passive and parasitic to the media/message(s) and their encoding design. Because of this tendency to overvalue the textual determination, many structuralist analyses were accused of being formalistic or reductionist. What is needed, rather than ignoring the diachronic determinations, is to put both subjects and texts back into history and the social context in which they exist and engage one another.

To historicize and contextualize subjects and texts means to see them, not as *given* or *complete,* but as constituted by and dependent upon the extratextual environment in which they exist. Text, for all its usefulness (as a methodological fiction), should not be understood as a finished, fixed product. Rather, it should be conceived as an achievement negotiated out of the interplay among related and often competitive reading protocols, procedures, and strategies, operative in simultaneity with it. It is the ongoing process of reading and interpretation that breathes life into texts, not the other way round.[2] For "whatever the material form or the social context in which the text reaches the reader, it does so only as already covered by a preexisting horizon of interpretive options, options which are encountered as limits, as a force that has to be reckoned with" (Bennett, 1982, p. 6). For example, Jameson (1983) has argued:

> Texts come before us as the always-already-read; we apprehend them through sedimented layers of previous interpretations, or—if the text is brand-new—through the sedimented reading habits and categories developed by those inherited interpretive traditions. (p. 58)

There are always *texts,* texts in contestation, not a single ideal text, a *Ding-an-sich* hidden behind the material surface of the empirically given text, insofar as the latter must be dissolved into the *ensemble* of its reading conjunctures and interpretations that in themselves are held in check by readings/interpretations already produced in relation to it.

No reading is, therefore, totally innocent, and the interpretations of a text can reveal to us as much about the text in question as about the extratextual milieu that makes those interpretations possible. To study texts *historically* and *contextually,* then, means to study, as Bennett (1982) calls it, "the living life of the text," by inserting the study of text into the study of social process. To do so necessarily involves studying not only the production and consumption of a text, but also the relation among different, perhaps contradictory, interpretations that are advanced, discussed, contested, and in some cases, canonized. It entails analyzing (1) how the incrustations that have been built around a text were formed and transformed in light of that text's changing inscriptions into a variety of different material, social, institutional, and ideological contexts; and (2) how a text is first activated and then given a privileged reading by a set of reading protocols in particular junctures such that the multiple destinies of the text are at once fulfilled and frustrated (Bennett, 1982; Eagleton, 1981; Macherey, 1977).[3] Parallel to the above two objectives, such an analysis alerts us, on the one hand, to the whole mobile system of signs and their circulation into which a text is inscribed and from which it cannot be separated. On the other hand, it also alerts us to that set of historically specific codes embodied in material notations that are also inscribed within different contexts and caught within an ever shifting set of relations with other texts, such that it is productive of variable effects and meanings.

What has been said of the text above applies equally to subjects; what is involved in the productivity of texts also works within the positionality of a text's writers/readers. Inasmuch as a text interacts unavoidably with other texts, any text is for that reason an *intertext.* And inasmuch as any text is an *intertext,* one needs to talk about "interlocking subjectivities" in terms of the overlaying and crisscrossing of multiple discursive influences rather than the textualized subject in abstraction. Like the text, social subjects too are caught up in a network of symbolic systems in which they always exceed the subject-in-position implied by the text, because they are also placed by a plurality of other cultural systems and are never coextensive with the subject placed by a single fragment (for example, one film) of the overall cultural text (see Morley, 1980). The subjects implicated in/implied by the text are thus always already subjects within different social practices in determinate social formations, not merely subjects in "the symbolic" in general—an important point *Screen* advocates have failed to take into account (Morley, 1980). The question of the subject then is no longer simply a question of textual relations per se; it is, more important, also a question of the politico-historical conjuncture, because "the binding of the spectator takes place [or, one might add, fails to take place] not through formal mechanisms alone but through the way social instructions impose their effectivity at given moments across the text and elsewhere" (Nowell-Smith, 1977, p. 5).

SUBJECTS, TEXTS,
AND INTERDISCOURSE

Structuralists are right to say that language and signifying practices necessarily mediate social processes and relations. But the insistence on the semiotic production of meaning should not blind us to the effectivity of social, economic, and political factors that also bear upon the production of meaning in society. For to say that language has a determining effect on social structure and individuals' experiences in it is a very different matter from saying that society is *nothing but* language and signifying practices. In fact, signifying practices and other lines of social force function *semiautonomously* in the social whole; one cannot be reduced to the other because their relative autonomy prevents themselves from having an all-inclusive effect (Althusser, 1969). It follows then that the meaning produced by the encounter of text and subject cannot be read off straight from its textual characteristics or its discursive strategies. One needs to take into consideration what Neale (1977, pp. 39-40) describes as "the use to which a particular text is put, its function within a particular conjuncture, in particular institutional spaces, and in relation to particular audiences." This means that textual analysis of meaning by itself is not sufficient and needs to be supplemented by the considerations of the extratextual interventions that don't simply "read" the text but make use strategically of certain reading(s)/interpretation(s) for purposes definitely not aesthetic.

The necessity for textual analysis to include considerations such as the use or function of the text in relation to a particular body of audiences under specific circumstances rectifies the text-centered myopia that incapacitates many early structuralist analyses of the media. The meaning(s) of a text will be constructed always through a negotiation not only of multiple discourses (knowledge, prejudices, resistances) brought to bear on the text by the reader, but also of interacting social forces and forms of determination that carry with them both political and ideological reflections, and that, although reflecting the ideology, are not in themselves purely signifying objects. These social forces (for example, class conflict) traverse myriad discourses, forming alliances with existing institutions that provide for the channels by which to disseminate ideologically charged signs. "Both the subject and the text," as Morley (1982, p. 171, italics added) rightly argues, "are constituted *in the space of the interdiscursive,*" a space involving not only that of signs but also what Foucault (1980) calls the "adjacent fields" that prey on sign processes with unmediated material forces within the grand struggle over meaning in society.

The notion of "interdiscourse" is most important in understanding the complex imbrication of the text and the social process. It represents an improvement over the notion of "intertextuality," recognizing that the social is always and already at work at the core of the textual. A text indeed bears internal relation to other texts, syntagmatically and paradigmatically, but this intertextual networking of meanings and echos of meaning dispersed in space and time cannot and does not exist in a social vacuum. In fact, textual processes are subject to changes in economics, in politics, in cultural or even intercultural relations, in law, in education, and so on, which jointly constitute a text's objective material condition of existence. Heath (1978) strives to clear a middle path between text-centered and viewer-centered positions in film theory; he argues,

> The reading of a film is neither constrained absolutely nor free absolutely but historical, that history including the determinations of the institution cinema, the conditions of the production of meanings, of specific terms of address in films, a film. The property of a film is not yours or mine, whether makers or spectators, nor its; it is in a number of instances of relations across the film's preconstruction, passage and construction that engage the spectator-subject in a multiplicity of levels of reading, reception, response. (p. 105)

Although Heath eventually locates the film text within the cinematic apparatuses, his remarks, I think, nonetheless serve well in providing a starting point that detextualizes the textual process by relating textual objects to their discursive and nondiscursive contexts. It represents a helpful formulation of the problem in that it encourages us to focus attention not just on the text or the audience, but on the mesh of variable historical determinations that mediate between and connect the two in differing and particular social and ideological relations of reading/writing.

Textual criticism must adjust not only to variable decoding positions set up by varying signifying practices but also to variable encoding forces coming from sources such as moral codes or religious teachings whose raison d'être is always more than "signification." Tracing the changing conceptions of character in literary study, Hunter (1983) has shown that "character" is not a stable concept having definite referents through time but rather a changing "rhetorical object" constructed out of describable "conditions of emergence of literary objects." The difference between the reading of *Hamlet* in the 18th century and that of the 19th century, for instance, can be shown to parallel the difference between reading a character as an element of a plausible dramatic representation (that is, the 18th-century reading protocol) and reading it as a projection or correlate of the reader's moral self and personality (that is, the 19th-century reading protocol). The emergence of the 19th-century "moral psychology" and its widespread deployment as a means of diagnosing and treating madness took no time to penetrate its contemporaneous literary domain and enwrap literary activities such as reading within a broader moral discourse of the time.

Character-ization, therefore, is not limited to literary influences alone but is also at the mercy of all sorts of nonliterary forces that invest themselves in literary objects. The condition of any literary object and, for that matter, of subject-positions too, is never one dimensional. Regardless of whatever element we focus on or from whichever viewpoint we start the analysis, we inevitably find subject, text, reading(s) already contaminated, contaminated precisely because they exist *across* heterogeneous discourses/practices, that is, *in the interdiscursive space.*

AUDIENCE AND/AS PRACTICE

In light of the previous discussion, the question we now face is how to rethink the audience *interdiscursively.* How do we modify the old conceptual framework and thus disperse any one-dimensional conception of audience into its multiple junctures and forces of formation *across* discourses? Before we do this, however, it might be helpful to stop again to ask—this time not so metaphorically—what kind of discursive space the demographically constructed audience occupies? What is that discourse that has somehow managed to enclose and determine the construction of audience in media research such that it creates and maintains—ideologically—a (forced) fit between the need of audience, media practice and policy, and those researches that are supposed to analyze the former two?

One can always recover how the audience is understood by examining how it is constructed. By tracing the way in which the "whom" was identified, surveyed, rated, analyzed, and so forth, one can in turn obtain a clearer picture of "whom" media researchers think the audience to be. As alluded to earlier, American mass communication research during the past three decades, guided by a behavioral hegemony, has always been enamoured of quantitative methodologies popularized by positivistic social sciences (Hall, 1982). Across neighboring fields, massive surveys were conducted; voluminous questionnaires were distributed, and their results displayed in graphs, charts, and numbers. It is not by accident that media analysts employed wholesale the categories of empirical sociology in their own trade. Rarely do we find audience research carried out without using variables like age, sex, income level, education, ethnic background, class, geographical location, and so on. It seems as if the audience cannot be conceptualized apart from those variables.

These variables constitute a sociological/demographic space in which relations between structural factors of societal composition and a particular cultural practice (in this case, the production and consumption of media content) are drawn. And it is within this same conceptual space that macrophenomena such as a hit TV show, violence on TV, and the like, are pared down to their microbasis, that is, to the individual viewer's psychological disposition which, in turn, can be translated back to socioeconomic positions and mapped onto a demographic grid. Through the mediation of those demographic factors, this sociological/demographic space and the socio-psychological image of audience echo and reinforce one another, thus forming the discourse of dominant media studies that legitimates certain pregiven modes and categories of analysis and ends up (self-) validating the prescribed forms of practice in predefined parameters of research.

To rethink the audience *interdiscursively* means above all to break the circular one-dimensionality of the construction of audience in the dominant media discourse. This, of course, cannot be achieved simply by abolishing all the old categories, still less by expanding the list of possibly relevant variables between media and behavior which, by the way, is theoretically infinite. What is needed, in essence, is a certain notion that allows us to conceptualize the audience *without any fixed identity*—a general notion that won't impose any grid on our perception of the decoding processes, but rather actively maps or traces the multidirectional routes by which media as well as their content are disseminated in society.

To conceptualize the audience without any fixed identity represents an attempt at antiessentialist thinking, a refusal to reify audience in terms of prescriptive characteristics (for example, demographic or cognitive variables) or some observed regularities. It also embodies a critical-structural gesture in that it rejects any psychological conception of self as an autonomous, coherent, self-identical, self-evident substratum underlying otherwise not so orderly appearances. At its most specific, this antiessentialist and critical-structural perspective suggests that the audience be viewed as "practice," or rather "bundles of practices." The idea of bundles is significant, for it suggests, on the one hand, the combination of a plurality of practices and, on the other hand, the historically changing and contextual nature of that combination at any given instance of decoding. Appropriating the text in response to the pressure generated by the differential pull amongst themselves and their relations to the broader sociocultural milieu, these bundles of practices constitute the possibility of media perception and hence materialize the effects media are thought to have.

Instead of seeing audiences as groups of people, the reconceptualization of the audience as practices insists on the primacy of interdiscursive relations and real effects of various media-related practices brought to bear by these relations on various media-centered ideological struggles over signs and meanings in a particular social formation. It is not the average people owning or sitting in front of a TV set that constitute the TV audience, but rather what they *do* with the medium and what the medium *does* to them. The fact of owning a household appliance tells us absolutely nothing about the meaning of the interaction between the owner and what is owned; nor does it indicate the implications a particular media interaction pattern and the general cultural habit of media use might have on each other. Instead of construing the receiver of communication as a unified psychological entity, the audience should be understood as the embodiment of different decoding practices, each grounded in a particular "ideological social relation of reading" (Bennett, 1982). In fact, it is the unity (or difference) of practice that unifies (or differentiates) one body of audience (from another).

In addition to avoiding the pitfalls of soft humanism, to conceive the audience as practices has other obvious advantages. Because it doesn't freeze the constantly mobile organizations and contestations over meaning in the domain of *mass media-tion,* a praxical definition of audience is able to steer clear of the difficulty in explaining the frequent coexistence of contradictory readings of an identical text at different moments, or rather similar readings of very different texts, on the part of the same audience.[4] There is no intrinsic reason why a black ghetto wage laborer cannot give the same reading as the white suburban yuppie reading of, say, *Cagney and Lacey* (Fiske, 1985) or any other text. The difference or similarity of the decoding comes not so much from their imputed class consciousness, or whatever variation of the psychological profile demographic or cognitive variables can combine to make; rather it derives from the specific changing relations of reading they bring to the text respectively, relations, by the way, not of their own choosing but determined by the social formation in which they live, feel, and work differently and in which ideology is always most swift to stretch its tentacles of seduction, persuasion, and control when it comes to "meaning" and "sense."

Now we might try to give a more precise definition of audience as *a bundle or bundles of decoding practices embedded in the social circulation/ exchange of meaning through which media texts are simultaneously constituted and consumed according to the signifying necessity of a particular framework of cultural and ideological reference at different historical moments.* As bundles of practices, the audience designates a site of ideological struggles over meaning, a locale of confrontation between competing bundles of decoding practices. These bundles are *formed,* not fixed once and for all, in the interdiscursive space: They are combinations of intersecting codes, conventions, rules, cultural habits, and all kinds of "hermeneutic operators" (Bennett, 1983) that make up the major part of what can be called the "media literacy." It is through practice that texts are produced and distributed, and quite naturally, it is in practice that an audience can be found.

Most valuable in reconceptualizing the audience as bundles of decoding practices lies in the fact that it acknowledges the discursive reality of the audience. When encountering a text, a set of decoding bundles arrests that text, freezing the textual flow momentarily and thereby giving a meaning to that text as a result of its reinscription (by those decoding practices) into the circle of meaning production and reproduction. But inasmuch as decoding practices come in bundles, the meaning(s) of a text is never stable or univocal. The instability, or rather the polysemy of a text's meaning, of course, reflects the fluid quality of the decoding bundles. But more important, it also can be seen as a direct result of what I call the "social citation" that both constrains and opens up the freedom of reading by way of a dialogic process between the text and the decoding practices.

By "social citation" I mean the reiteration of the same signs that make up a text outside that text's original context. This reiteration is necessarily social and traverses various discursive zones, because, when cited, the text falls outside the authorial control of its origin and moves into a polyphonic market of social signs, where heterogeneous decoding bundles/audiences assert and negotiate amongst themselves and each articulates its respective inscription within that arena through rhizomelike pathways of the social "heteroglossia" (Volosinov, 1983). Such a reiteration can also be understood as a form of trans-coding through which the same text undergoes appropriative interpretations as it is read and reread by different subcodes (for example, codes of the marginal, of the repressed, the code of stardom within the general code of media discourse, and so on), each of which brings its own tone to the text and cracks it for its own purpose. In fact, decoding acts can quote freely a text or fragments of it, not only because the text becomes public property once put in front of the reader, but also because changing contexts exert different hermeneutic violence on those quotes to make them fit the ideological demand of the particular instance of textual consumptions. It is an interdiscursive phenomenon, the interdiscursive fate of any text whose existence depends on being reproduced/cited continuously across space and time, that is, reiterated under ever new contexts. The meaning of a text is not merely a textual matter; instead it is intimately linked to the decoding practices that provide for the means and site of an ongoing citation, such that the text can be reenunciated whenever necessary.

Embodying bundles of decoding practices, the audience should thus be seen as the interdiscursive zone where social citations take place; where texts are "put in quotation marks" and thus appropriated by virtue of being inserted into new syntagms or discourses. Each citation signifies an insertion, and every insertion gives, in varying degrees, a new interpretation to what is cited. It is through a series of mediations that texts/messages are circulated in society, like a chain of quotations, so to speak, through which differences are created between production and consumption, and between different moments of consumption, by the intervention of the audience. What is important for audience analysis therefore is to examine those differences displayed in that process of citation: How do different decoding practices cause the text to change simply by (re-)citing it? How does the text itself (via ambiguity or other textual characteristics) resist or elicit appropriations vis-à-vis decoding forces? And, finally, how do the decoding practices stand in relation to ideology and other ideological systems of discourse functioning as forms of determination?

All these questions can and should be answered by examining the concrete discursive practices through which different readings are generated, rather than the people who, in this age of electronic media, don't seem to feel compelled to read much any more. My proposal to reconceptualize the audience in terms of practices lies in this. It encourages media critics to think seriously about the articulation between different contradictions embedded in decoding practices; about the different specificities and temporal durations through which those decoding practices operate; to think, that is to say, about the differences beyond those of sex, of class, of age, and so on. Instead of fitting societal members into abstract categories, the problem of the "audience" must be grounded in the "popular" experiences and the subtle differences among those experiences as different audience-bundles transcode constantly the culturally available messages/texts in accord with their own form of resistance, negotiation, or cooptation. We need not only a conception of the "audience," but a conception adequate to the complexity of its "referent" and the discursive relations that constitute it as such.[5] This doesn't mean, of course, that we stop using any approach that employs conventional categories or disown everything that we have learned so far through that approach. Although suffering from a "misplaced concreteness," the sociological approach should be incorporated into the critical paradigm, if only because its results often confirm the irreducible differences among audiences. After all, practice appears to be where concreteness can best be placed.

Compared to other topics, audience analysis is an overtheorized area of mass communication research. Yet the degree of critical awareness reflected in the research practices doesn't seem to match up to the apparent popularity of the subject matter and the consequent huge outpouring of research findings. Despite calls for more interpretive, critical, and cultural approaches, media studies have not yet transgressed the bounds of the behavioral hegemony described by Hall (1982) to any great extent. Tradition invariably stays unchanged, unless we say "no" to that something upon which the tradition relies for stability. About 10 years ago, a TV critic (Collins, 1976, p. 52) asked if it was possible to abolish the category of audience. I am tempted to say yes, and the purpose of this chapter is to specify in what sense one can say that. The question is not one of semantics; the answer, needless to say, can be obtained only through a change of practice.

NOTES

1. Popularized by literary critics, *deconstruction* has been an overused term as people in different fields appropriate it for their own critical purpose. A decade after its introduction into America, deconstruction has all but lost its critical specificity. When critics in communication studies use the term *deconstruction,* it doesn't seem to retain much of its original Derridean meaning that defines *deconstruction* as deeply embedded in the phenomenological tradition. See, for example, Rowland (1984). For a more precise definition of deconstruction, see Chang (1985).

2. This, of course, doesn't mean that the text exerts no determination on the possibilit(ies) of how it should be read. It does mean, however, that the capacity of the text to limit the range of its readings is itself a historically variable phenomenon. As long as we recognize that the text is above all a "meaning-object," not merely a "book" that is primarily a physical object, the discursive determination is most essential.

3. In a 1977 interview, Pierre Macherey proposed that the study of literary works involves "not just studying the text but perhaps also . . . everything which has been written *about* it, everything which has been collected on it, become attached to it—like shells on a rock by the seashore forming a whole *incrustation.* At which point the idea of 'work' loses all meaning" (italic added). Bennett's detailed analysis of the "Bond phenomenon" (1983) remains, in my opinion, the best attempt at translating Macherey's insight into concrete study.

4. The emphasis on practice not only renders visible but also makes intelligible various subcultural, marginal, or counter-cultural styles, (punk, for example) that, functioning as a representation of, and an imaginary solution to experienced contradictions, form resistance (and pose threat), through a "semiotic guerilla warfare," to the dominant ideology and its surveillance. The best example is Dick Hebdige's *Subculture: The Meaning of Style* (1979). Stuart Hall, in a recent public lecture at the University of Illinois, also talked about how a (least expected) text, the *Bible,* has been appropriated through highly creative readings by the preachers of Rastafarianism since the beginning of the movement to tell a story that fits with and answers to the history, the current predicament, and common hope, not only of the black living in the West Indies, but also of those who migrated from there to other parts of the world such as England. The same text, the *Bible,* which signifies white domination and the European presence, can be used, depending on the historical juncture and sociopolitical conditions, as an effective means in bringing about what Hall calls the "blackening" of Jamaica.

5. The tendency to view the audience as "people" is often too strong to let go. In *Key Concepts in Communication* (1983, p. 15), Fiske, Hartley, and others, known for their semiotic approach to mass communications, nevertheless define the audience as "the unknown *individuals* and groups toward whom mass communications are addressed" (italics added).

REFERENCES

Althusser, L. (1969). *For Marx.* London: Allen Lane.
Althusser, L. (1971). Ideology and ideological state apparatuses. In B. Brewster (Trans.), *Lenin and philosophy and other essays* (pp. 127-186). New York: Monthly Review Press. (Original work published 1970)

Barthes, R. (1974). *S/Z: An essay*. R. Miller (Trans). New York: Hill and Wang. (Original work published 1970)
Baudrillard, J. (1981). *For a critique of the political economy of the sign*. St. Louis: Telos Press.
Bennett, T. (1982). Text and social process: The case of James Bond. *Screen Education, 41*, 3-14.
Bennett, T. (1983). The Bond phenomenon: Theorizing a popular hero. *Southern Review, 16*(2), 195-225.
Brundson, C., & Morley, D. (1978). *Everyday television: 'Nationwide.'* London: British Film Institute.
Carey, J., & Kreiling, A. (1974). Popular culture and uses and gratifications. In J. Blumer & E. Katz (Eds.). *The uses of mass communication*. (pp. 225-248.) Beverly Hills, CA: Sage.
Chang, B. (1985). The eclipse of Being: Heidegger and Derrida. *International Philosophical Quarterly, 25*(2), pp. 113-137.
Chang, B. (in press a). Communication after deconstruction. *Studies in Symbolic Interaction, 7.*
Chang, B. (in press b). Representing representation: The visual semiotics of *Las Meninas*. *The Journal of Communication Inquiry.*
Collins, R. (1976). *Television news*. London: British Film Institute.
Derrida, J. (1976). *Of grammatology*. Baltimore: Johns Hopkins University Press.
Derrida, J. (1978). *Writing and difference*. Chicago: University of Chicago Press.
Eagleton, T. (1981). *Walter Benjamin, or towards a revolutionary criticism*. London: New Left Books.
Elliot, P. (1974). Use and gratification research: A critique and a sociological alternative. In J. Blumer & E. Katz (Eds.), *The uses of mass communication*, (pp. 249-268.) Beverly Hills, CA: Sage.
Fiske, J. (1985, April). *Cagney and Lacey: Reading character structurally and politically*. Paper delivered at the Iowa Symposium and Conference on Television Criticism, University of Iowa.
Foucault, M. (1980). *Power/knowledge: Selected interviews and other writings 1972/ 1977*. New York: Pantheon Books. (Original work published 1972)
Grossberg, L. (1982). Experience, signification and reality: The boundaries of cultural semiotics. *Semiotica, 41*, 73-106.
Grossberg, L. (1984). Strategies of Marxist cultural interpretation. *Critical Studies in Mass Communication, 1*, 372-421.
Hall, S. (1981). Notes on deconstructing "the popular." In Raphael Samuel (Ed.), *People's history and socialist theory* (pp. 227-240). London: Routledge Legan Paul.
Hall, S. (1982). The rediscovery of "ideology": Return of the repressed in media studies. In M. Gurevitch, T. Bennett, J. Curran, & J. Woolacott (Eds.), *Culture, society and the media* (pp. 56-90). London: Methuen.
Hall, S. (1985). Signification, representation, ideology: Althusser and the post-structuralist debates. *Critical Studies in Mass Communication, 2*(2), 87-90.
Heath, S. (1978). Difference. *Screen, 19*(3), 51-112.
Heath, S. (1981). *Questions of cinema*. Bloomington: Indiana University Press.
Hebdige, D. (1981). *Subculture: The meaning of style*. London: Methuen.
Hunter, I. (1983). Reading character. *Southern Review, 16*(2), 226-243.
Jameson, F. (1982). *The political unconscious*. Ithaca: Cornell University Press.
Kuhn, A. (1982). *Woman's picture: Feminism and cinema*. Boston: Routledge & Kegan Paul.
Lacan, J. (1971). *Ecrits: A selection* A. Sheridan (Trans.). New York: W. W. Norton. (Original work published 1966)
Macherey, P. (1977). Interview. *Red Letters*, (5), 7.
McQuail, D. (1983). *Mass communication theory: An introduction*. Beverly Hills, CA: Sage.
Metz, C. (1982). *The imaginary signifier*. Bloomington: Indiana University Press.
Morley, D. (1980). Texts, readers, subjects. In S. Hall, D. Hobson, A. Lowe, & P. Willis (Eds.), *Culture, media, language* (pp. 161-173). London: Hutchinson.

Morley, D. (1981). The "Nationwide" audience—a critical postscript. *Screen Education, 39*, 3-14.

Neale, S. (1977). Propaganda. *Screen, 18*(3), 9-40.

Nightingale, V. (1984). Media audience—media product? *Australian Journal of Cultural Studies, 2*(1), 23-34.

Nowell-Smith, G. (1977). Editorial. *Screen, 18*(3), 5-7.

O'Sullivan, T. et al. (1983). *Key concepts in communication*. London: Methuen.

Rimon-Kenan, S. (1984). *Narrative fiction: Contemporary poetics*. London: Methuen.

Rowland, W. D., Jr. (1984). Deconstructing American communications policy literature. *Critical Studies in Mass Communication, 1*, 423-435.

Schramm, W., & Roberts, D. (1971). *The process and effects of mass communication*. Urbana: University of Illinois Press.

Silverman, K. (1983). *The subject of semiotics*. Oxford: Oxford University Press.

Todorov, T. (1984). *Mikhail Bakhtin: The dialogical principle*. W. Godzich (Trans.) Minneapolis: University of Minnesota Press. (Original work published 1981)

Volosinov, V. N. (1983). *Marxism and the philosophy of language*. New York: Seminar Press.

31 ● Mass Media and Postmodernity: The Cultural Politics of Silencing in Jean Baudrillard

KUAN-HSING CHEN

University of Iowa

1.

Literature is communication. Communication requires loyalty. A rigorous morality results from complicity in the knowledge of Evil, which is the basis of intense communication.

Georges Bataille
(*Literature and Evil*)

With the television image—the television being the ultimate and perfect object for this new era—our own body and the whole surrounding universe become a control screen.

Jean Baudrillard
(1983e, p. 127)

Under the shadow of semiotic structuralism, current theorizing activities on popular culture have been preoccupied with meaning, signification, representation, and ideology. For instance, the *Screen* group focuses their analyses on the functionality of ideology within the text, and the ways in which the spectator (the subject) is positioned through signifying practices imposed by the text.[1] This interpretive strategy assumes the correspondence between the textual production of dominant ideology and its effectivity on the spectator; it gives full authority to the text in determining the production of meaning. Attacking *Screen's* position, the Birmingham Center for Cultural Studies shifts the focal analysis toward the question of encoding and decoding (Hall, 1980a), and argues that there is no necessary correspondence between the preferred reading and actual reading

AUTHOR'S NOTE: Larry Grossberg, John Fiske, and Hanno Hardt's comments on the earlier drafts of this chapter are gratefully acknowledged.

Correspondence and requests for reprints: Kuan-Hsing Chen, School of Journalism and Mass Communication, University of Iowa, Iowa City, IA 52242

(Morley, 1980). Obviously, the Cartesian picture provides a common matrix wherefrom both groups frame their question: subject and object, text and spectator, encoding and decoding; that is, a *linear* communication model is presupposed by both schools.[2]

To breakthrough the modernist dilemma of "transcendence," recent critical works (Bennet, 1983a; Grossberg, 1984a, 1984b, 1984c; Hall, 1983; Hebdige, 1983) of cultural politics have appropriated the French postmodernists'[3] strategic move from transcendence to immanence (Grossberg, 1982b); Foucault's (1980) archaeology-genealogy and Deleuze and Guattari's (1983b) "rhizome" have constituted a new model of analysis. This model resists the linearity of communication, and challenges the legitimacy of reading any cultural text as an isolatable object. Instead, it will read television practice, for instance, as a line or site of struggle; from this line, different intersecting lines are drawn; lines of connections are made; the emphasis is on intertextuality and effectivity rather than modernist "causality." In short, the social is read as a network working in multiple-directions and multiple-dimensions; point to point, line to line, all are interconnected without *a* common origin. The model thus constructed, we have moved from the question of "what does it mean?" to that of "what does it do?", from signification to its effectivity, from textual politics to the politics of the body, from political economy to cultural affectivity.

In what follows, I will try to read the post-1976 works of Jean Baudrillard as a "postmodernist" vision of TV culture in relation to the social machine. Baudrillard's discourse is not simply rhetorically seductive; it locates the points of configuration and offers a picture of our current (social) conditions. Based on the picture he paints, I will argue that the explosion of TV culture is constitutive of the formation of postmodernity. TV is the perfect object of postmodernity. Due to the density of Baudrillard's thinking, I will have to first reconstruct his "three orders of simulacra" so as to understand the genealogical transformation of the social machines' functioning logic and the corresponding structural law of value. I will then locate the media, TV in particular, and the "masses" within the "third order of simulacrum." This chapter will conclude by raising certain critical questions of political resistance and strategy in the age of postmodernity.

2.

The simulacrum is never that which conceals the truth—it is the truth which conceals that there is none.
The simulacrum is true.

                                        Ecclesiastes

In 1976, Baudrillard published his seminal piece, *L'Echange symbolique et la mort*. In the beginning of the text, Baudrillard declares the *intention* of this project: "To grasp the hegemony and the spectacle of the present system, we have to retrace an entire genealogy of the law of value and of successive simulacra—the structural revolution of value" (1983c, p. 56). This project postulates that the dominant mode of "social" control (of power) is no longer that of production, but that of the operational structures of codes; programmed commodity consumption (that is, the situationist's notion of the spectacle) is only a part of this coding system. More specifically, the functioning social logic has passed from commodity to sign, and the exploitation of social labor has been replaced largely by the manipulative production of meaning and information. Hence the theoretical basis of the system of power has been transferred from political economy to structuralist semiology, information theory and cybernetics.[4] To understand fully (before we can effectively overturn) the terrorism of the current coding systems, we have to analyze the entire historical process of its mutation in terms of, on the one hand, the fundamental value (ideological) structures (the law of value) which operate, in part, on the basis of the underlying episteme of different ages, and its corresponding functioning machine (the successive simulacra) on the other.[5]

On his genealogical map, Baudrillard draws "three order of simulacra." From the Renaissance to the beginning of the industrial revolution, counterfeit is the dominant mode of effectivity of the real (representation); and this first order of simulacrum is haunted by the "natural law of value." During the industrial era, production becomes the dominant scheme, and this second order of simulating machine is based on the commodity law of value. In our current system (after World War II), based on the "structural law of value," simulation has replaced production as the dominant scheme of the logic of representation as well as the functionality of machine. The map Baudrillard offers here is not intended as a universal history, but as a general picture of the changing referent (alibi) of social value and the functioning logic of society. To use contemporary terms, we shall periodize the first order as *early modernity,* the second order as *modernity,* and the third as *postmodernity.*

Within each order of simulacra a binarism, which Baudrillard implicitly designates as value/simulacrum, is in operation, and this can be understood as the structural value/structural functioning of the social machine. Structural value is a general system of value through which "we" live out "our" reality, through which "we" discern "what is" as well as "what should be" of the "social reality." The structural functioning of the social machine describes the dominant logic of power, the operational mechanism of the society during a specific historical period. This binarism is the structural basis of the social; the structural values haunt the mechanisms of the social machine; the latter in turn create new value apparatus in the next higher order of simulacra. In other words, the value apparatus of an age never captures the functioning logic of its social machine; instead, the former becomes a mystifying device to hide the objectivity of the latter. When the value apparatus discovers the machine's functioning, the machine has already transformed itself to function in a new way, which again escapes the value system. Therefore, the social machine is always ahead of our value system, and this is the secret by which the social machine protects itself from being attacked by those "crazy revolutionaries."

With these opening remarks, I propose to re-present Baudrillard's simulacra. In feudal society, prior to social problematization of representation in the Renaissance, things (representation, social status, and so on) function unequivocally. Everyone is assigned in a specific social space and social mobility is impossible. The unquestioned positioning of each individual in a social space guarantees a total transparency and clarity; a "ferocious hierarchy" prevents confusion; a reciprocal obligation operates between the lord and the servant. The order of things is total, and thus "any confusion of signs is punished" (1983a, p. 84). With the rise of the bourgeoisie, the caste order is broken through "open competition of the level of the distinctive signs" (p. 84). Here, previously unquestioned value (obligation) gets called into question: "the end of the obliged sign." We thus pass into the counterfeit: not denying the original, but extending and producing the equivalence of the original, the copy. To justify the bourgeoisie's production of the real, it claims nature as the determinant referent; the modern metaphysics is born, becoming the value apparatus of the first order. But the function simulacrum does not simply operate on the level of signification/representation, it implies "social rapport and social power" (p. 88). The nostalgia for the natural order, overturned in bourgeois value, still serves as an alibi and gives rise to the political elite of the state. A centralized strategy (an apparatus of organization) is developed to ensure the effectiveness of simulacrum. The desire for an "eternity of power" constitutes the bourgeois simulacrum as a "project of political and cultural hegemony, the fantasy of a closed mental substance—like those angels of baroque stucco whose extremities meet in a curved mirror" (p. 92). This emergent value apparatus (bourgeois value) justifies not only the power of the "new" class, but the underlying change of "form" on the social terrain: from feudal free production to the controlled production (the logic of demand/supply). *Use* value is born as the dominant form of the logic of the social machine: the production is founded on the usability and salability. For the bourgeoisie to calculate and accumulate their wealth so as to consolidate the stability of their power, they create the marketplace to sell the commodities that can be used in daily life. The primitive form of production and its exchange are taken over by bourgeois programmed production, but its basis lies still in the production of subsistence's goods. This is the early phase of capitalism haunted by the value of free competition.

With the industrial revolution, we move into the second order of simulacrum built upon a "productivist" model of simulation. Inside the social machine, signs are produced on a gigantic scale; the origin of the counterfeit becomes the technique of production. The myth of equivalence itself, of the origin, of identical objects achieves its glory by effacing the original. The metaphysical difference of being and appearance (first order) is abolished by "the absorption of appearance, or by the liquidation of the real, whichever. It establishes in any case a reality, image, echo, appearance " (1983a, p. 95). The value apparatus, in supporting the social machine, defines "production and work as potential, as force, as historical process, as generic activity: the energetic-economic myth proper to modernity" (p. 97). Convinced by this hegemonic social value, we are glad to work with the machines; we delightedly achieve the status of being able to drive the machine; but, we have become simulated by the machinic web, we are machines from now on. "Freedom from all resemblance, freed even from their [human beings'] own double, they expand like the system of production of which they are only the miniaturized equivalent" (p. 95). With the rise of technology, the nostalgia for a natural order (first order value) is abandoned; nature becomes the object of technological domination. Even though nature still serves as a dissolved alibi, as the great referent, the signified, it only operates "under the objective stamp of Science, Technology, and Production" (1975, p. 54). In short, the referent has been transformed from nature to man. From now on, man wins glory over nature so as to justify the objectivity of scientific technology.

In the early phase of the second order industrial simulacrum, when technology had not yet achieved its height of development, the production of use value and the signified are still the dominant logic of the social machine. When the industrial machine reaches its maturity, reproduction and exchange value win over production and use value, and become the dominant working logic; the production of "identical series" and of equivalence has been displaced by the nonidentical, infinite reproduction of the objects; the signifier defeats the signified. At this moment, the dominant image of the first order—theater and the stucco angel—has been replaced by the cinema and photography (Benjamin). This orgasm of the second order is precisely the point (basis) at which we "fall" into the third order of simulacrum.

When social finality is lost in the series of reproduction (second order), models take over the sacred job of directing our social functioning. Models "preceed all forms according to the modulation of their differences. Only affiliation to the model makes sense, and nothing flows any longer according to its end, but proceeds from the model, the 'signifier of reference,' which is a kind of anterior finality and the only resemblance there is" (1983a, p. 101). We are now in the third order of simulacrum, the order of models, codes, cybernetic operational configurations. "Digitality is its metaphysical principle . . . and DNA its prophet. It is in effect in the genetic code that the 'genesis of simulacra' today finds its most accomplished form" (p. 104). What haunts the functionality of models is obviously the myth of science; after God, nature and man, the rational operationality of science becomes the ultimate referent (even though the former set of terms never totally disappears). The signifier, exchange value, and theoretical pluralism justify the cold universe of the genetic code, the tactile and the digital. It is the programmed rhizome that totally governs our life; the trajectory connects points to points, lines to lines, which allow no confusion, no ambiguity. "Everything that gets inserted into the definalized space-time of the code, or tries to interfere with it, is disconnected from its own finalities, disintegrated and absorbed" (1983c, p. 57). The message, transmitted through information networks (for example, TV), is nothing but a constant testing and polling in order to make sure that the channel is still open, still under the system's random control. Programmed public opinion polls play the game of "free choice" in the form of question/answer, stimulus/response. The great referendum beautifully echos the binarism of the model. Two parties, two superpowers, center/periphery (youth, women, blacks), capitalism/communism, power/resistance; they guarantee the stability of simulacrum. Thus what Marx considered as "the nonessential" part of capital (such as advertising, media, information/communication networks, and so on) has become the "essential" sphere of simulacrum upon which "the global process of capital is founded" (1983a, p. 9).

Moreover, the radicality of the third order simulacrum lies not only in simulating everything into the network, but in its courageous abandonment of the nostalgia for the real; it thereby constitutes the "hyperrealism of simulation." Baudrillard tells us the "truth" of our new age:

> The real is hyperrealised. Neither realised, nor idealised: but hyperrealised. The hyperreal is the abolition of the real not by violent destruction, but by its assumption, elevation to the strength of the model. Anticipation, deterrence, preventive transfiguration, etc.: the model acts as a sphere of absorption of the real. (1983b, p. 84)

Having summarized Baudrillard's genealogy of simulacra, we can start to disentangle the twisting logic of the spiral of simulation. The mutation from one order to the next is not arbitrary; it is a traversal movement that can be connected with history, culture, production, technology, ideology, and so on. In the mutational process, the entire value apparatus is absorbed and recycled on a higher level of simulacra; that is, the functioning logic of a lower level becomes the alibi, the imaginary referential for the new order of value apparatus, and the social machine escapes being caught by the value apparatus.

> Each configuration of value is resumed by the following in a higher order of simulation. And each phase of value integrates into its own apparatus the anterior apparatus as a phantom reference, a puppet or simulation reference. (Baudrillard, 1983c, p. 56)

This spiral retreat to the lower order (for example, the third order's value apparatus uses the functioning logic of the second order's social machine as alibi, and at the same time, reabsorbs its own second order value) is precisely the foundation for the operation of ideology; it hides the real logic of social machines; it prevents us from seeing the cold universe operating without morality, ethics, or humanity. This logic explains the failure of Marxism: it is hopeless to combat the third order by throwing the bomb of dialectic and objective contradiction. Use value only captures the functioning logic of the first order, dialectics the second order; revolution can only counter the value apparatus of the second order; all these have already been neutralized and disarticulated by the subtlety of the third order. Hence, "you cannot beat randomness with finality, you cannot beat programmed dispersion with *prises de* conscience or dialectical transcendence, you cannot defend against the code with political economy or revolution'" (1983c, p. 57).

3.

All functions abolished in a single dimension, that of communication. That's the ecstasy of communication. All secrets, space and scenes abolished in a single dimension of information. That's obscenity.

Jean Baudrillard
(1983e, p. 131)

Two lines, but a single process, traverse throughout the simulation network: the media and the masses. In this section, I will try to describe the "mass-media" as the "subject-object" of the third order of simulacrum. In the next section, Baudrillard's notion of "a critical mass" and the strategy of resistance against the system will be discussed.

Our world has moved into the "proteinic era of networks." TV, being the ultimate and perfect object for this new era, has established a nebulous matrix to guarantee "connections, contact, contiguity, feedback and generalized interface that goes with the universe of communication" (1983e, p. 127). Hereafter, the subject, as the actor of the great social theater (first and second order), has become the terminal of multiple networks; the subject no longer projects into objects (production, consumption); the domestic universe is given up to the living satellite of spatial power. There is no longer any distinction of interiority and exteriority; the mental, the psychological, and the metaphorical are all hyperrealized and simulated on the surface. The old weapon of alienation as a defensive system to protect private individuals gives way to the obscenity of transparency and visibility; hot sexual obscenity gives way to cold communicational, functional, and contactual obscenity; the universe of passion to the universe of ecstasy and fascination.

The reinforcing agent or catalyst for the vertiginous metamorphosis (from the real to the hyperreal) is the mass media, the information network that is parallel to the technique of reproduction of the real in the second order. In the endless chains of (re)duplication from one medium to the other (from camera shooting the fact to editing), "the real is volatilized" (1983a, p. 141). The original object is destroyed, lost, and dead; "no longer object of representation, but ecstasy of denegation and of its own ritual extermination" (p. 142). The hyperreal strikes out the real, subjectivity, and moves to pure objectivity, the pure look, the surface materiality on the TV screen. The object is finally liberated from its obligation to the substance of representation. What is real now is not only its reproducibility (what can be reproduced), but the real itself is already reproduced. "The hyperreal transcends representation . . . only because it is entirely in simulation" (p. 147).

Baudrillard cites the great American event of the *Loud Family* in 1971 as an example of TV hyperrealism, as the end of perspectivism and the destruction of panopticon. What this program offered 20 million viewers, who, it was hoped, would pretend that TV camera was not there, was not only the "perverse pleasure of prying," but the joy in the "microscopic simulation which transforms the real into the hyperreal" (1983a, p. 50). With the Loud family, we discover the reversal logic of social existence: "You No Longer Watch TV, TV Watches You." It signifies the "switching over from the panoptic apparatus of surveillance to a system of deterrence, where the distinction between active and passive is abolished" (p. 53). "YOU are the model." "YOU are the majority." When the real is intermingled with the models, TV is dissolved into life, and life is dissolved into TV. No longer any transcendental space between subject and object, seeing and seen, cause and effect. The logic of immanence: "nothing separates one pole from the other, the initial form from the terminal: there is just a sort of contraction into each other, a fantastic telescoping, a collapsing of the two traditional poles into one another: an IMPLOSION—an absorption of the radiating model of causality, of the differential model of determination, with its positive and negative electricity—an implosion of meaning" (p. 57).

Without even mentioning "real" soap opera, TV news production testifies to the hyperreality. It operates entirely according to codes generated by the model of simulation. The fascinating film about the Viet Nam war can be set on the air to tell the story about the war in Central America. Does it matter whether the film is real or unreal? What we want is only the fascinating image of guerrilla warfare or the violent codes of terrorist acts. Model proceeds content; what happens will be fit into the modulation that TV has already constructed. TV—the machine of simulation.

When meaning gets imploded in the simulation machine, we enter into a new era of schizophrenia. The schizos have altered their signified from those who are segregated to a total segregation; "they" are "normalized" and "we" are "schizolized."

> The schizo is bereft of every scene, open to everything in spite of himself, living in the greatest confusion. He is himself obscene, the obscene prey of the world's obscenity. What characterizes him is less the loss of the real, the light years of estrangement from the real, the pathos of distance and radical separation, as is commonly said: but, very much to the contrary, the absolute proximity, the total instantaneity of things, the feeling of no defense, no retreat. It is the end of interiority and intimacy, the overexposure and transparence of the world which traverses him without obstacle. He can no longer produce the limit of his own being, can no longer play nor stage himself, can no longer produce himself as mirror. He is now only a pure screen, a switching center for all the networks of influence. (1983e, p. 133)[6]

In fact, MTV is precisely a concrete practice of this cultural schizophrenia. Although MTV is not the mirror of postmodernity, it is a condensed version of our world, an extreme pole of our cultural manifestation; it is a part of our cultural semiosis without signified or even signifier: the implosion of meaning. The representation of the disrupted temporality resembles the experience of schizo who cannot take the tightened pressure of capitalist production anymore: the sense of losing control and the sense of having no future. Fragmentation and nonunity become the strategies of the capitalist subject to confront the insanity of the world; the decentered subject has to find ways to fulfill the requirements of our social institutions: family, school, military, factory, and so on. (In fact, the decentered subject is not a poststructuralist theoretical construct; it has its own specificity in late capitalism in which the segmented flow of TV programming interpenetrates human subjectivity.) We are given the myth demanding that we are the subjects of humanity, whereas, in fact, we are treated as objects, the object of the capitalist machine. The obscenity (of sexuality) strips away the public/private boundary; when everything is rendered visible, the space of retreatment, of resisting alienation, disappears: either there is no longer any alienation, or it is total. The form of MTV is simulacral. The originality of MTV lies in its technique of montage, collage, segmentation with the quotation of irrelevant cultural representation. It abandons the ideology of reality principle: the original, the copy, the same, and the like are displaced by simulacrum without the nostalgia of creativity. The practice of MTV has nothing to do with truth or reality; the infinite (re-)production of fascinating image satellites the hyperreality of simulacrum.

In the third order of simulacrum, we have to relocate the masses by arguing against a sociological understanding of the masses. Because the presupposition of sociology rests on the "positive and definitive hypothesis of the social" (1983b, p. 4), and on its claim to be a "science of society," the "masses" has to be conceptualized in analyzable categories: demographers are the vanguard of the discipline. The existence of the masses in sociological reality is, after all, only the representation of codes (class, social status, sex, race, and so on) in a survey analysis. The silent majority, then, is *the* imaginary referent for the sociological/political imagination. Against a "sociological mass," Baudrillard says, "the term 'mass' is not a concept. It is a leitmotif of political demagogy, a soft, sticky, lumpenanalytical notion. . . . The mass is without attribute, predicate, quality, reference. This is its definition, or [rather,] its radical lack of definition. It has no sociological 'reality'" (pp. 4-5). To put it differently, "the mass is characteristic of our [post]modernity, as a highly implosive phenomenon" (2); the masses absorb and neutralize the energy of the social and the political; they exist in their radical silence; they are unlocatable signifieds. Baudrillard traces the functioning logic of the masses within the simulacra:

> The masses function as a gigantic black hole which inexorably inflects, bends, and distorts all energy and light radiation approaching it: an implosive sphere, in which the curvature of space accelerates, in which all dimensions curve back on themselves and "involve" to the point of annihilation, leaving in their stead only a sphere of potential engulfment. (1983b, 9)

That is, the mass is the concretization of (and in alliance with) the symbolic seduction in opposition to the simulating logic of the social machine.

The myth of the information society tells us that the democratic flow of information is to moralize better, "to socialize better, to raise the cultural level of the masses" (1980, p. 142). This is in complicity with the trap of critical thought, which "can only be exercised given the naivete and the stupidity of the masses a presupposition" (1983b. p. 99). But "the media do not bring about socialization, but just the opposite: the implosion of the social in the masses" (p. 100). For critical thought (for example, semiological analysis), the media have become the most subtle form of ideological apparatus to manipulate the masses. But for Baudrillard, these are all nonsense. The masses "resist this imperative of rational communication . . . they idolise the play of signs and stereotypes . . . they reject the 'dialectic' of meaning" (p. 10). The masses dissolve and laugh at the programmed ideology hidden behind the media. They push everything to the surface. Contrary to the will of the system, "*the mass and the media are one single process*" (p. 44): Neither side can claim priority over the other; they flow into and intersect each other. Without the media, there are no masses; without the masses, there are no "mass" media. What media analysts lose sight of is that beyond a certain point of overproduction and overexposure, meaning gets imploded and the messages do not "mean" anymore. "Media, all media, information, all information act in two directions: Outwardly they produce more of the social, inwardly they neutralise social relations and the social itself" (p. 66). That is, when the expansion of the social(ization) reaches its extreme, it reverses itself, implosively, to destroy itself. This is the beginning of simulation and the end of the social. From now on, the media slip away from the hands of power; they join the masses to accomplish the "sacred" task: "absorbing and annihilating culture, knowledge, power, the social" (p. 11).

With the end of the social, we announce the death of sociology. Although sociologists claim that the mass still manifests its statistical existence in the survey or referendum, we all know (and the masses know better) that the masses are making fun of whomever is conducting the poll or election. Beyond representation: "the masses no longer belong to the order of representation" (p. 20). Beyond ideology: "Power manipulates nothing, the masses are neither mislead nor mystified" (p. 14). We now push polls, tests, and referenda—the devices of representation—to a dimension of simulation. No longer the existence of any referent, only models with the simulating machine; beyond the subject: "It isn't a silence which does not speak, it is a silence which refuses to be spoken for in its name . . . they are no longer (a) subject . . . they can no longer be spoken for, articulated, represented . . . no longer being (a) subject, they can no longer be alienated" (p. 22).

4.

The will to power can manifest itself only against resistances; therefore it seeks that which resists it.

Nietzsche
(Will to Power, p. 346)

Entering into the third order of simulacra, the traditional forms of resistance to power, domination, exploitation, and so on have been absorbed and dissolved by the most subtle form of control: the random dispersion of the indeterminant codes. Politics, political representations are dead; at best, they are only show business performing on the side of the value apparatus to hide its triviality. What is the object any party represents? People? They lie. The social disappears; our social space of interaction has been taken over by the TV screen, by the overproduction of information and meaning. Our social machine has become an autonomous, self-regulating system without subjects. No matter who takes power, the cold machine will still function beyond (and beneath) the control of subjects. What is the difference between Reagan and Mondale? What is the difference between communism and capitalism anyway? Orwell's 1984 moves throughout our gigantic simulacrum; the fiction is realized and the real becomes fictitious: the hyperrealism of simulacra.

But, does it mean that there is no space left for struggle or resistance? In this context, we can introduce Baudrillard's notion of a critical mass. In The

Beaubourg Effect (1982a), Baudrillard reads an art center as a miniaturized model of our current system, the third order of simulacra, and the masses as "the agent of catastrophe" for the dominant culture. In traditional critical thought, art works, museums, the Beaubourg, are the devices by which the bourgeois culture produces cultural dupes, narcotizing the masses. But Baudrillard gives a counter story. When the masses stampede into the Beaubourg, they do not conform to the official culture, they transgress and destroy the myth of system. They simulate and play with the models. They do not make sense of the cultural objects, for they know there is no meaning but only simulation. With this observation, Baudrillard envisions the birth of a critical mass: "It is here that a condition of critical mass develops, surpassing that of merchandise becomes hyper-merchandise, or culture becomes hyper-culture" (1982b, p. 8). The masses, as the product of the system, as an effect of oversocialization (overexposure to the media), offer a new constitutive logic of the system that is beyond the imagination of the third order simulacra: social implosion. "The mass(es) is that space of ever greater density into which everything societal is imploded and ground up in an uninterrupted process of simulation" (p. 9). What the system designs to achieve is the "maximization of the word and the maximal production of meaning" (1983b, p. 108), whereas STOP MAKING SENSE is the strategy of resistance; nonreception, nonresponse is a "counter strategy of masses themselves in their encounter with power" (p. 104).

Hence, what the system fails to program is the silence, nonresponse, or more radically, the hypersimulation, precisely the strategy of the masses. The masses, becoming the center of implosive violence, counter the explosive/expansive violence of the system: the strategy of a destructive hypersimulation. "Subversion and violent destruction are the forms of response to a world of production. To a universe of networks, permutations and the flux, the response is reversion and implosion" (1982b, 10-11).

With the identification of this explosive/implosive logic, Baudrillard teases out the arrogance of western civilization. "We used to be a culture of liberating violence [reason]" (p. 11); the infinite expansion of territory, colonization, cultural/economic imperialism. We even intrude in another universe: moon landing. Our alibi for this violence is survival, glory, civilizing the barbarian, the release of extra energy. This explosive violence is "dialectical, energetic, cathartic;" it is also "analytic, liberating, determinate" (p. 11). But today, an implosive violence resulting from "its saturation and contraction" eludes our expansive analysis. This reversal from explosion to implosion is the effectivity of an "unlimited increase in social density, resulting from an overregulated system, from overloaded networks (of knowledge, information, power), and from hypertrophied controls that invade all the interstitial paths of facilitation" (p. 12). Even the most advanced rhizomatic analysis (Deleuze & Guattari, 1983b) is still based on the expansionist logic; schizo-analysis (Deleuze & Guattari, 1983a), after all, is only the final phase of imperialism, the great ideology of liberation.

Now a Baudrillardian (a)politics emerges. Armed with silence as their most effective weapon, the masses resist being positioned as the object and/or subject of simulacra with the strategy of hypersimulation and hyperconformity. They are beyond the imaginary control of power; they no longer operate (present themselves) on the side of value apparatus, but on the side of simulating machine. "The masses accept everything and redirect everything en bloc into the spectacular, without requiring any other code, without requiring any meaning, ultimately without resistance, but making everything slide into an indeterminate sphere that is not even that of nonsense, but that of overall manipulation/fascination" (1983b, pp. 43-44). This strategic refusal of meaning and sense, and this hyperconformist simulation of the system is the most concrete form of resistance: "it is equivalent to sending back to the system its own logic by doubling it, to reflecting, like a mirror, meaning without absorbing it" (p. 108). This strategic (counter-) intervention operates everywhere today as randomly as the system itself; it is the destiny of the system that fatally turns against itself; no one can stop it; the implosion of the system.

In primitive societies, the social functions "centripetally": a cyclic process, never expansive, centrifugal, or universal—a controlled implosion. The transformation into the explosive logic of simulacrum (even the first order) exterminates the primitive but gives birth to our modern civilization. During the golden age of our system (the second order), it survived in the form of a controlled explosion. When the infinite expansion arrives at its limit, the system (the third order) loses control. When the system's brake band is exhausted, "our culture begins to be ravaged by implosion" (p. 60). Imperialistic expansion finally reverses its direction to attack itself. Deleuze's molecular revolution and Foucault's microphysics of power only symbolize the final attempt to release the extra energy and to save the myth of explosive liberation. But it is fatal; we have to pay back the evil we do "the Other." Baudrillard gives us the final prophecy of "our" glorious civilization's fate:

> There has been no balanced transition from implosive system to explosive systems: this has always happened violently, and there is every chance that our passage towards implosion may also be violent and catastrophic. (1983b, p. 61)

Is this the end of the world? No, not necessarily. Is this the decline of "our" civilization? No, "our" civilization was never "higher" than others'. What comes after the catastrophe? We don't know. We can only wait and see if there will still be "we." It is not a tragedy. We just have to give up our mythic reality to live the hyperreal. We have lived within the universe of structural law of value by power; the system's revenge on itself is the hyperreality we must confront with courage.

5.
In truth, there is nothing left to ground ourselves on. All that is left is theoretical violence. Speculation to the death, whose only method is the radi-
calization of all hypotheses. Even the code and the symbolic are terms of
simulation—it must be possible somehow to retire them, one by one, from
discourse.

Jean Baudrillard
(1983c, p. 59)

If the task of a Baudrillardian project is to overthrow the simulacrum,
then the critical questions are: Can we oppose the third order of simulacra
by a *more* complex, *more* random practice than the system itself? Is it possible to create a higher order, to go beyond the third order of simulacra?
Even if we can break through the third order, would it still be a simulacrum?
Baudrillard offers a temporary proposal: "*Perhaps only death, the revers-
ibility of death,* is of a higher order than the code. Only symbolic disorder
can breach the code" (1983c, p. 58). What Baudrillard is proposing here is
that just as the Marxist dialectic revolution was articulated to confront the
"law of commodity and equivalence" (the second order), only the "fastidi-
ous reversion of death" can confront the "indeterminism of code and the
structural law of value" (the third order) (1983c, p. 59). When the simulacrum moves in the direction of ideal coherence, the system is moving
toward its own death, because, when a closed, or metastable, or functional,
or cybernetic system, based on a radical indeterminism, approaches its perfect operationality, all the inertia within the system works against itself: the
fatality of the cybernetic machine. At this crucial moment, "things have to
be pushed to the limit, where everything is naturally inverted and collap-
ses" (p. 58). Hence, a catastrophic strategy:

> At the peak of value, ambivalence intensifies; and at the height of their
> coherence, the redoubled signs of code are haunted by the abyss of reversal.
> The play of simulation must therefore be taken further than the system per-
> mits. Death must be played against death—a radical tautology. The system's
> own logic turns into best weapon against it. The only strategy of opposition
> to a hyperrealist system is pataphysical, a "science of imaginary solution," in
> other words, a science fiction about the system returning to destroy itself, at
> the extreme limit of simulation, a reversible simulation in a hyperlogic of
> destruction and death. (1983c, pp. 58-59)

One may say that, if Baudrillard's project is a political project, then it has
failed. Baudrillard cannot propose a more concrete strategy to overthrow
the simulacra other than standing with the masses to hypersimulate the
functioning machine. Yet, because the traditional category of the political
has vanished in our world, Baudrillard has struggled to show us that theories of production, of the unconscious, and of power/sexuality (all of them

as the determinant referent of the social machine) cannot fully grasp the functioning logic of our social machine. Our current crisis is a historical, cultural, and global one; it cannot be reduced to any single sphere: economy, politics, power, sexuality. The question, then, becomes what Baudrillard foresees as the inevitable implosion of the simulacrum. Can we do anything to redirect an uncontrollable to a controllable implosion? Is "death" something outside the simulating machine that can be used as a strategy to control the implosion? If the masses have become a part of the coding simulacrum, does the task of breaching the code result in the explosion of the whole human universe? What will happen to the masses after the death of this machinic simulacrum? If the system is inevitably imploded, why does Baudrillard even talk about the strategy of hypersimulation, or hyperconformity? To accelerate the death of the simulacrum? Baudrillard seems to have left us with all these questions unanswered.

6.

Nothing will halt the implosive process, and the only remaining alternative is between a violent catastrophic implosion, an implosion in slow motion.

Jean Baudrillard
(1983b, p. 61)

In this final section, I wish to discuss the implication of Baudrillard's strategic refusal of meaning as an alternative or a hypothesis to break through the current dilemma of cultural politics.

Within the space of Marxist cultural studies, the central concern is what Stuart Hall (1983) calls the politics of *articulation:* How to articulate a micropolitics of resistance into a macropolitics of oppositional struggle? The politics of articulation recognizes the necessity (1) to rethink the question of "the popular" (Bennet, 1983b; Fiske, 1983; Hall, 1980b), (2) to locate the site(s) of resistance, which is already taking place (Fiske, 1983, 1984; Grossberg, 1984a, 1984b; McRobbie, 1982), and (3) to capture the appropriate historical moment so as to articulate existing struggles onto the larger scope of social movement. In fact, the French postmodernist Felix Guattari (1984) has already posed the question of articulation a decade ago, but in different language:

> What now becomes essential is the linking-up of many and various molecular desires, which would have a snowball effect and lead to a large-scale confrontation. . . . An individual discourse is relevant only to the extent that it can link up with already functioning collective utterances, voices already involved in the social struggle. (1984, pp. 220-221)

What Guattari has emphasized is not so much the semiotic struggle over meaning, but the articulation of desire, intensive forces (which are beyond the realm of signification and representation) so as to oppose power structures. The line of desiring-production, or the moment of intensities, is similar to what Fiske and Watts (1985), following Barthes, discover as the moment of "jouissance" in their analysis of video arcades, and what Grossberg (1984c) calls "the affective" for the empowerment of rock and roll.

But, the unresolved dilemma is still the question of "how": How to articulate the existing forces of resistance? At this moment, I want to turn back to Baudrillard. Baudrillard seems to have offered a path, a hypothesis, to go beyond the politics of articulation: nonarticulation in conjunction with the refusal of meaning—a strategy of hypersimulation, of (non)resistance. Baudrillard's strategy is based on three presuppositions. In the first place, he challenges the possibility of articulation. In his analysis, he has shown that the masses, as the implosive postmodern forces, "can no longer be spoken for, *articulated*, represented" (1983b, p. 22). It is futile to try to articulate the silent majorities. Second, he challenges the desirability of articulation. The nonarticulation strategy is to avoid falling into (and being absorbed by) the logic of the system; the *effectivity* of power/resistance binary logic only reproduces the dominant frame of power. Whereas dominant ideology requires oppositional forces to haunt its own stability, the refusal of meaning is the refusal of ideology, and the disarticulation of coding system. This leads us to the third assumption. Baudrillard posits a logic of an inevitable implosion of the system. To resist or attack the system in an oppositional manner is only to slow down the speed of implosion. The nonreception of meaning, although positing no alternative ideology, is a strategy of nonresistance that seeks to push the system to its extreme, to accelerate the implosion process.

Although one may find Baudrillard's "logic of implosion" lacking the support of empirical evidence, one may also be frightened by the uncertainty of our future, and one may further be suspicious about a project without an alternative ideology (as Hall would argue), I do not believe that we can easily dismiss Baudrillard's challenge. Baudrillard's discourse forces us to rethink the current state of our critical activities. Are we self-reflexive enough about our critical analysis? Do we "really" understand postmodernity? Does postmodernity escape our rationalistic theorizing activities? Is the current crisis a matter of ideological struggle? As students of critical theory and practice, we have to address ourselves to these questions here and now.

NOTES

1. See for instance, Heath and Skirrow (1977).
2. Jean Baudrillard (1981) has argued that critical analyses have failed to identify the hidden ideology behind this linear model of communication, which is in complicity with the dominant ideology.

3. The "postmodern" is a floating signifier without definitive signified. I use the term *postmodernist* to designate those (anti-)theorists who see our world or culture as having moved into a new age that is radically different from modernist culture. These post-modernist thinkers include Foucault, Deleuze, and Gauttari. See Foucault (1979, 1980, 1982); Deleuze and Guattari (1983a, b); Guattari (1984). For discussions on postmodern theory and culture, see Lyotard (1984), Foster (1983), Grossberg (1982a, 1982b, 1984c), Huyssen (1984), Jameson (1983, 1984), Bernstein (1985), *New German Critique* (1981, 1984).

4. Baudrillard is not advocating this theoretical shift. His comment is partly ironical, partly descriptive.

5. I am not able to trace back the source from which Baudrillard borrows this term—simulacrum. However, I suspect that Baudrillard might have borrowed this term from Gilles Deleuze (1983). Deleuze sees simulacrum as potentially an emancipatory effect to over-throw Platonism (its nostalgia for the original, the Same, and the Like). Simulacrum is a turning away from authentic representation; it calls the original into question. Hence, Deleuze seems to use the term in a positive way. When Baudrillard uses *simulacrum,* he assigns two meanings to the word. First, in agreement with Deleuze, it is a "representa-tional" term. Second, Baudrillard uses the term *simulacrum* to describe our society as a gigantic simulating machine within which everything is positioned and programmed by preexisting models. Simulacrum in Baudrillard's enterprise is the enemy that we have to overthrow.

6. Note the difference between Deleuze and Guattari's celebration of "schizo culture" as a liberating force, and Baudrillard's use of it as a descriptive (metaphorical) device in captur-ing our current cultural situation. Baudrillard has criticized rhizomatic-molecular revolution as the final phase of the expansionist myth of liberation. See Baudrillard (1983b, pp. 58-61), for this critique.

Note also Baudrillard's difference from Jameson's use of schizo. Jameson (1983) uses schizo to describe postmodern experience of temporality and spatiality. Following Lacan, Jameson sees schizophrenia as a result of a disorder of language. For Baudrillard, if there is something literally called schizo in our world, then all of us are schizos.

REFERENCES

Baudrillard, J. (1975). *The mirror of production.* St. Louis: Telos Press.

Baudrillard, J. (1980). The implosion of meaning in the media and the implosion of the social in the masses. In Kathleen Woodward (Ed.), *The myths of information: Tech-nology and postindustrial culture* (pp. 137-147). Madison: Coda Press.

Baudrillard, J. (1981). *For a critique of the political economy of the sign.* St. Louis: Telos Press.

Baudrillard, J. (1982a). The beaubourg-effect: Implosion and deterrence. *October, (20),* 3-13.

Baudrillard, J. (1982b). Fatality or reversible imminence: Beyond uncertainty principle. *Social Research, 49*(2), 272-293.

Baudrillard, J. (1983a). The orders of simulacra. In *Simulations.* New York: Semiotext(e).

Baudrillard, J. (1983b). *In the shadow of the silent majorities or the end of the social.* New York: Semiotext(e).

Baudrillard, J. (1983c). The structural law of value and the order of simulacra. In John Fekete (Ed.), *The structural allegory: Reconstructive encounters with the new French thought.* (pp. 54-73). Minnesota Press.

Baudrillard, J. (1983d, October). What are you doing after the orgy. *Artforum,* 42-46.

Baudrillard, J. (1983e). The ecstasy of communication. In Hal Foster (Ed.), *The anti-aesthetic: Essays on postmodern culture* (pp. 126-134). Port Townsend, WA: Bay Press.

Baudrillard, J. (1984a). Clone story or the artificial child. *Z/G, (11),* 16-17.

Baudrillard, J. (1984b, September). Astral America. *Artforum,* 70-74.

Baudrillard, J. (1985). The child in the bubble. *Impulse, 11*(4).

Bennet, T. (1983a). The Bond phenomenon: theorising a popular hero. *Southern Review, 16*(July), 195-225.

Bennet, T. (1983b). Marxist cultural politics: In search of 'the popular.' *Australian Journal of Cultural Studies, 1*(2), 2-28.

Bernstein, R. (1985). (Ed.), *Habermas and modernity.*

Deleuze, G. (1983). Plato and the Simulacrum. *October,* (27), 45-56.

Deleuze, G., & Guattari, F. (1983a). *Anti-Oedipus: Schizophrenia and capitalism.* Minnesota: University of Minnesota Press.

Deleuze, G., & Guattari, F. (1983b). *On the line.* New York: Semiotext(e).

Fiske, J. (1983). Popularity and ideology: A structuralist reading of Dr. Who. *The Australian Journal of Screen Theory,* (14), 60-100.

Fiske, J. (1984). Video clippings. *Australian Journal of Cultural Studies, 2*(1), 110-114.

Fiske, J., & Watts, J. (1985). *The semiotics of video arcades.* Unpublished paper.

Foster, H. (1983) (Ed.). *The anti-aesthetic: Essays on postmodern culture* (pp. 126-134). Port Townsend, WA: Bay Press.

Foucault, M. (1979). *Discipline and punish: The birth of the prison.* New York: Vintage.

Foucault, M. (1980). *Power/knowledge: Selected interviews and other writings by Michel Foucault, 1972-1977.* New York: Pantheon.

Foucault, M. (1982). The subject and power. Printed as an afterword in H. Dreyfus & P. Rabinow *Michel Foucault: Beyond structuralism and hermeneutics* (pp. 208-226). Chicago: University of Chicago Press.

Grossberg, L. (1982a). Experience, signification, and reality: The boundaries of cultural semiotics. *Semiotica, 41*(1/4), 73-106.

Grossberg, L. (1982b). Does communication theory need intersubjectivity? *Communication Yearbook 6,* 171-205.

Grossberg, L. (1984a). The politics of youth culture: Some observations on rock and roll in American culture. *Social Text, 8*(Winter), 104-126.

Grossberg, L. (1984b). Another boring day in paradise: Rock and roll and the empowerment of everday life. *Popular Music, 4,* 225-257.

Grossberg, L. (1984c). 'I'd rather feel bad than not feel anything at all' (Rock and roll: Pleasure and power). *Enclitic, 8*(1/2), 94-111.

Guattari, F. (1984). *Molecular revolution: Psychiatry and politics.* New York: Penguin.

Hall, S. (1980a). Encoding/decoding. In S. Hall et al. (Eds.), *Culture, media, language* (pp. 15-47). London: Hutchinson.

Hall, S. (1980b). Popular-democratic vs. authoritarian populism. In A. Hunt (Ed.), *Marxism and democracy* (pp. 157-185). London: Lawrence and Wishart.

Hall, S. (1983). The problem of Ideology-Marxism without guarantees. In B. Matthews (Ed.), *Marx 100 years on* (pp. 57-86). London: Lawrence and Wishart.

Heath, S., & Skirrow, G. (1977). Television: A world in action. *Screen, 18*(2), 7-59.

Hebdige, D. (1983). Posing . . . threats, striking . . . poses: Youth, surveillance, and display. *SubStance, 37/38,* 68-88.

Huyssen, A. (1984). From counter-culture to neo-conservatism and beyond: Stages of the postmodern. *Social Science Information, 23*(3), 611-624.

Jameson, F. (1983). Postmodernism and consumer Society. In H. Foster (Ed.), *The anti-aesthetic.* (pp. 111-125). Bay Press.

Jameson, F. (1984). The cultural logic of capital. *New Left Review, 146,* 53-93.

Lyotard, J. F. (1984). *The postmodern condition: A report on knowledge.* Minnesota: University of Minnesota Press.

McRobbie, A. (1982). Jackie: An ideology of adolescent femininity. In B. Waite, T. Bennet, & G. Martin (Eds.), *Popular culture: Past and present* (pp. 263-283). London: Croom Helm.

Morley, D. (1980). *The 'Nationwide' audience: Structure and decoding.* London: British Film Institute.

New German Critique (1981). Special issue on modernism, *22*(Winter).

New German Critique (1984). Special issue on modernity and postmodernity, *33*(Fall).

Nietzsche, F. (1968). *The will to power.* New York: Vintage.

32 ● Sampling from the Museum of Forms: Photography and Visual Thinking in the Rise of Modern Statistics

FRANK BIOCCA

University of North Carolina at Chapel Hill

I N 1857, Oliver Wendell Holmes, father of the famous jurist, lifted a stereoscope to his eyes for the first time. After the initial strain, as the lenses forced his eyes to accommodate the different images only inches away, Holmes experienced two "visions." One emerged as the neurons were tricked into fusing two disparate scenes into one. The other was the brilliant flash of historical insight. Holmes verbalized it in a kind of Brechtian soliloquy:

> *Form is henceforth divorced from matter.* In fact, matter as a visible object is of no great use any longer, except as the mould on which form is shaped. Give us a few negatives of a thing worth seeing, taken from different points of view, and that is all we want of it. . . . There is only one Coliseum or Pantheon; but how many millions of potential negatives have they shed, — representatives of billions of pictures, —since they were erected! Matter must always be fixed and dear; form is cheap and transportable. We have got the fruit of creation now, and need not trouble ourselves with the core. Every conceivable object of Nature and Art will soon scale off its surface for us. Men will hunt all curious, beautiful, grand objects, as they hunt the cattle of South America, for their *skins,* and leave the carcasses of little worth. (emphasis in the original) (Holmes, 1859, p. 251f)

Holmes was examining these "carcasses" with a precision and dispassion worthy of a dean of Harvard Medical School and renowned physi-

AUTHOR'S NOTE: The author would like to acknowledge art historian and semiotician, Don Preziosi, whose enlightening discussions on the role of museums in society stimulated the writing of this chapter.

Correspondence and requests for reprints: Frank Biocca, School of Journalism, University of North Carolina, Chapel Hill, NC 27514.

ologist. Holmes, like his namesake in fiction, was peering out at the world through the analytical lens of 19th-century science. This eye of glass guided the razor edge of the scalpel. Forms distant and removed in both space and time, forms both microscopic and macroscopic would now be dissected, dessicated, and described. These "skins," etched on metal plates and negatives, would be preserved and hung to dry. The new wind blowing would not carry the stench of the "thing-in-itself," but the sterile antiseptic smell of iodine, an odor common to both 19th-century hospital and the photo developer.

Form had long been a subject of inquiry in the visual arts. Questions of "true form," "natural form," and the relation of "form and content" filled much philosophical disquisition. To questions of form and its essential locus in object, noumena, or mind have been proffered many answers, all of them bound by their history and caught within the structures of linguistic reason.

But technology asserts its own instrumental reason (Gouldner, 1976), theory manifest in creaking or humming symbol manipulators of wood, steel, or silicon. Technology is part of an instrumental reason imbedded in the texture, guided soma, and endless surface of the built environment.

As I will attempt to show in this chapter, the camera was a powerful theoretical disquisition on the nature of form, realism, and scientific vision. Information technologies like the camera operate at a number of levels. At the economic and sociological level, they alter the physical flow of information. This is the stuff of most histories of the mass media. Here, I will address this level in the real and abstract proposals for a "Museum of Forms."

But there are two other levels that are potentially more significant: the perceptual and the conceptual. In the first instance the arrival of a medium can modify the cognitive structures that guide perception. In the beginning as the pattern of diffusion spreads the technology, perceptual and conceptual change may be visible in the social strata that first come in contact with the medium and most sensitive to perturbations in the flow of perceptual information (Biocca, 1985, in press). Perception is not, as was once thought, a fixed, passive, and largely immutable process, but is in fact a profoundly cognitive phenomenon drawing on highly developed visual processing routines and developed structures of knowledge representation (Arnheim, 1969; Gollin, 1981; Gombrich, 1960, 1982; Gregory, 1970). The phylogenetic "hardware" of the sense is overlaid with an elaborate ontogenetic cognitive "software." A new information technology can redefine aspects of the cognitive structures for information by (1) increasing the range of perceptual phenomena, (2) altering the relative salience of perceptual phenomena, (3) shifting the ratio of perceptual demands made on the various senses, and (4) reorganizing the semiotic, structural, and semantic links among somatically sensitive conceptualizations.

It is in the latter case that we ascend to the level of the impact of a medium on systems of thought. Here, we are looking at the intellectual and cultural history of a medium (Czitrom, 1982; Eisenstein, 1979; Goody, 1977; Ong, 1982). When a technology invades the conceptual level it can provide working models and grand analogies for systems of thought. There are a number of examples in the history of thought such as Descartes's mechanical universe modeled after the functioning of the watch. Today, the computer is a protean and ubiquitous analogy for many concepts, but most important, for our purposes, as an analogy for perceptual and cognitive processes (Cohen & Freigenbaum, 1982; Frisby, 1979).

As we will see, it is through conceptualizations of visual thinking by the pioneer in experimental exploration of mental imagery and a key founder of modern statistics, Sir Francis Galton, that photography becomes a grand analogy for mental processes and, furthermore, nothing less than a physical *working model* for statistical processes. The camera, the scientific eye, mental imagery, and inferential statistics would be welded together in a profound and solitary vision at the birth of modern statistics. This moment in intellectual history would be possible only because of the rise of a sampling theory of reality, the photographic subjugation of visual form, and the construction of the imaginal "museum of forms."

THE CALL FOR A
MUSEUM OF FORMS

Form was now collectible. For the 19th century, just as it had been for the 17th century (Foucault, 1970), "collectibles" needed to be arranged into some physical manifestation of the classificatory logic, a *taxinomia*. Oliver Wendell Holmes, Sr., master anatomist, was by no means a stranger to the spirit of classification. Forms would be grouped into a massive library, dwarfing the similar project envisioned by Malraux (1967) in the 20th century.

> The consequence of [photography] will soon be such an enormous collection of forms that they will have to be classified and arranged in vast libraries. . . . The time will come when a man who wishes to see any object, natural or artificial, will go to the Imperial, National, or City Stereographic Library and call for its skin or form. . . . We do now distinctly propose the creation of a comprehensive and systematic stereographic library, where all men can find the special forms they particularly desire to see as artists, or as scholars, or as mechanics, or in any other capacity. . . . This is a mere hint of what is coming before long. (Holmes, 1859, p. 253)

For Oliver Wendell Holmes the collected forms were "skins" of objects to be displayed in the trophy room of the eye. Photography would give rise to a massive museum of forms, collecting *Essential Samples* of form across cultures and across time.

But Holmes's museum of forms threatened to bury the regime of the visual with an endless superfluity of the unique. The philosopher of the photographic image, Susan Sontag, provides a pithy description of this process.

> Through photographs, the world becomes a series of unrelated, free-standing particles; a history, past and present, a set of anecdotes and *faits divers*. The camera makes reality atomic, manageable, and opaque. It is a view of the world which denies interconnectedness, continuity, but which confers on each moment the character of a mystery. (Sontag, 1977, p. 70)

But Sontag fails to see that it is not the camera itself that makes these images of "reality" manageable. Paralysis came from the mesmerized eye, an eye of perfect focus but of fixed vision, a vision that does not wander but stares absorbed in the profusion of detail.

How was the community of subjects to deal with the profusion of pictorial information flooding 19th-century consciousness? One way to subdue a world of pictorial detail and cultural artifact was the museum and library. There under the guidance of language, items were classified, collected, and housed. The tradition of pictorial art suggested this solution, but already in Holmes's museum of forms there was the indication that it could not be a traditional museum. Each picture seemed like a window to a reality outside the walls of the institution. Photography resisted petrification; a kind of synthesis was necessary.

Tradition suggested other means of organizing the image. Language and numbers were portable information; they had been organized and collected in a different way. Language had been pressed into the book, numbers scrunched into the statistical table. In the early decades of photography, a profusion of books, most about travel and art, were published in honor of the new medium.

But the classificatory spirit demanded more organization than Holmes's museum of forms. How could the supervising eye collect and synthesize the "samples of reality" contained in the photograph? How could one turn the photograph into the portable information found in the word, the number, and the statistical table? This was a profoundly semiotic question. The mass of iconic information potentially amassed by the new communication medium needed to be systematized so that its rich store of data could be as relatively fluid and manipulable as our other primary means of communication. This fundamental problem has reemerged with the rise of the computer and the feverish pursuit of a sophisticated system of artificial intelligence. With standard graphic programs, the interface between the optical disk and the computer, and three-dimensional modeling, the image once again needs to be integrated with the other symbol systems, just as it integrated in the mind itself both in primary perception (Marr, 1982) and in the imaginal "medium" of the mind (Kosslyn, 1980, 1983; Paivio, 1971). There is the question of how the binary calculus of the computer can harness not just the image as a reproduction but the image as information, connotation, and icon.

At the birth of modern inferential statistics, the word, the number, and the image would be housed just briefly in one system. The camera shutter had opened upon a perception of forms that threatened to subdivide into a series of endless categories of seamless information. It is language, verbal and mathematical language, that would attempt to arrest the multiplication.

THE RISE OF THE VISUAL
SAMPLE: TRANSFORMING THE
GLANCE INTO THE GAZE

The photograph was presented as an almost self-generated "sample" of the physical continuum. This to some degree had started with painting. According to Norman Bryson (1983) and some perceptual theories of painting, one of the goals of the visual arts was the transformation of the "glance" into the "gaze." If the moment could be stopped then the desirous eye could lose itself in this endlessly repeated moment. The observant French critic of the arts, Charles Baudelaire, had remarked with elitist disdain how the possessive eye (I?) consumed the image. Mesmerized subjects stared through "a thousand hungry eyes . . . bending over the peepholes of the stereoscope, as though they were attic-windows of the infinite" (Baudelaire, 1859/1955, p. 230).

At its very moment of birth, photography began to compete with painting for the eye of the desirous subject. Photography was greeted in circles both within and outside of art with premature declarations of the death of illustration and of painting. In 1842 a poem, a tongue-in-cheek paean to the new medium, chanted over the heads of the crowds marching in front of the lens:

> Yet nothing can keep the crowd below,
> And still they mount up, stair by stair;
> And every morn, by the hurry and hum, . . .
> You fancy the "last day of drawing" has come.
> (Cruikshank, 1842, facsimile reprint in Newhall, 1956, p. 59)

These predictions were amended quickly under the attack of enraged artists like Baudelaire.

The idolatrous mob demanded an ideal worthy of itself and appropriate to its nature. . . . I believe in Nature, and I believe only in Nature. . . . I believe that Art is, and cannot be other than, the exact reproduction of Nature (a timid and dissident sect would wish to exclude the more repellent objects of nature, such as skeletons or chamber-pots). Thus an industry that should give us a result identical to Nature would be the absolute of art. A revengeful God has given ear to the prayers of the multitude. Daguerre was his Messiah. (Baudelaire, 1859/1955, p. 230)

Instead of the death of painting, an amended host of "minor deaths" of realism, naturalism, portrait painting, woodcuts, engraving, and so on, were proclaimed.

The "new" alien technology, the "industry" of vision, could be embraced so readily because it was not really new. The photograph was the culmination of the very theoretical goal of the western tradition (especially the less textual Dutch tradition, see Alpers, 1983), the reproduction of Alberti's window (1435/1972). Alberti, elaborating a theory of painting deeply influenced by the camera obscura, believed that at the moment the viewer's eye was positioned where the rays of light collected on the retina as in the original scene, the painting would dissolve into a "window" on the founding reality. The mediated perception would recreate the founding perception. Gombrich (1960) has illustrated the tendency to think through the schema of technique, the most powerful of which was the schema of technique embodied in technology. The Essential Sample of light had been the goal; the desire was to fix the image within the camera obscura and paint the back of the retina.

The desire to petrify the ephemeral arrays of light that compose the glance had been an obsession of artists for centuries. For some, the image of the camera obscura represented the ideal and found expression as Alberti's window. In 1760, almost 100 years before the invention of photography, a French utopian writer, Tiphaigne de la Roche, fantasized some future subjugation of the image:

You know that the rays of light which reflect off bodies are like an image which paints these bodies on polished surfaces, the retina of the eye, and for example, on water, and on mirrors. The elemental spirits have sought to fix these passing images. They have composed a material which is quite subtle, quite viscous which dries and hardens quickly, so that a painting is created in the blink of an eye. They utilize in this method a piece of canvas and present it to the objects they wish to paint. The first effect of this canvas is that of a mirror: one sees all nearby objects (*corps*) and those far away which the light transports.

But what a mirror cannot do, this canvas, by means of its viscous medium retains these spontaneous images (*les simulacres*). The mirror renders the objects faithfully, but retains none. Our canvases do not render them any less faithfully, but retain all of them. The impression of the images is done at the instant the canvas receives them. One removes the canvas from the easel and sets it in an obscure place; one hour later the medium is dry, and you have a painting that is more precious, and more true that no art can imitate, and which time can in no way damage.[1] (author's translation of Fournier, 1859, pp. 18-20)

In 1760 De la Roche may not have had the means to fabricate an image so clear. But it is also clear that the *camera obscura* may have fabricated the retinal object of perfection so desired by De la Roche. The Essential Sample, the ideal determined by the technology of the *camera obscura* and the mirror, was the schema for perfection internalized by those who used the technology. The painting sought by De la Roche was fashioned by the warmth of light itself, and its image haunted his vision like a succubus:

We take from their most pure source, the body of light, the colors which the painters obtain from the different materials and which time never fails to alter. The precision of line, the variety of expression, the touches more or less strong, the gradation of nuance, the rules of perspective, we abandon all of these to nature who, with its sure steps which never lie, and which trace on our canvases images which are imposing to the eye and make one doubt one's reason, so much so that that which we call reality may be nothing more than phantoms which press upon our vision, hearing, touch, and all of our senses at once. (author's translation of Fournier, 1859, p. 20ff)[2]

Once photography had come close to actualizing the fantasies of De la Roche, it rocked the very concept of the Essential Sample. Behind the retina, the new arrays of light were illuminating different regions and transforming the mental structures that guided vision.

Illustrative is the audible gasp that followed the publication and diffusion of Muybridge's study (1887) of human and animal movement. According to *Scientific American:*

The most careless observer of these figures will not fail to notice that the *conventional* figure of a trotting horse in motion does not appear in any of them, or anything like it. Before these pictures were taken no artist would have drawn a horse as a horse truly is when in motion, even if it had been possible for the unaided eye to detect his real attitude. At first sight an artist will say of many of the positions that there is absolutely no "motion" at all in them; yet after a little while the *conventional idea gives way* to Truth. (emphasis added) (Jussim, 1971, p. 230)

Even more revealing is *Century* magazine's startled reaction:

The consecutive positions of the legs in the stride of a running horse, as revealed by these photographs, seemed ludicrous and almost impossible. Indeed, it required the combination of the positions given by the reproduction of the pace in the zoetrope to convince the skeptical that the analysis of the movement was correct. . . . We are *accustomed to seeing* certain things *in a certain way*. When an attempt is made to represent them in another way our conventional natures revolt at the innovation. (emphasis added) (Jussim, 1974, p. 225)

Here was another level at which the glance had been stopped, and transformed into the paralytic fixation of the gaze. The number of forms for Holmes's museum of forms was steadily expanding. But this museum of forms was not yet housed in any location. Its present location was inside the mind of the observer of form. This expansion of forms required a recataloging of the general gestalt for form perception. The camera was joining the telescope and the microscope in expanding the range of forms. This expansion marks one phase in a two phase expansion of Holmes's museum. Later a kind of fusion was required. But first an optically transformed vision would suffer confusion under the expansion of detail.

The explosion of information that the new image represented was expressed in babbling amazement at the "detail" of the image; the discovery that issued forth from the prolonged staring within the confines of the petrified glance. Samuel F. B. Morse exclaimed at its fidelity:

The exquisite minuteness of the delineation cannot be conceived. No painting or engraving ever approached it. . . . In a view up the street, the distant sign could be perceived, and the eye could just discern that there were letters upon it. . . . By the assistance of a powerful lens which magnified fifty times . . . every letter was clearly and distinctly legible, and so also were the minutest breaks in the lines in the wall of the buildings; and the pavements of the streets. (Jussim, 1971, p. 48)

The photograph stretched the levels of *repleteness* of the image, to use a term associated with the work of Nelson Goodman (1977, 1978). As in Antonioni's movie *Blow Up,* the viewer discovers more and more in the image as detail upon significant detail is blown up into the realm of the perceivable. This stretched the very topography of meaning. Photography expands by *ratio difficilis* (Eco, 1976) the continuum of material ready for semiosis. It quotes, and it quotes profusely, and through the mere act of quoting transforms the glance into the gaze. The very act of quoting a detail suggests its significance. Holmes, Morse, and others sat mesmerized in front of the photograph and the stereoscope. Eyes devoured the details, elevating them to a new level of significance. Holmes was in rapture: "Theoretically, a perfect photograph is absolutely inexhaustible" (Holmes, 1859,

p. 247). By its practice the camera suggested at a theoretical level that the very act of seeing was semiotic.

It is here then that Holmes's museum of forms begins to expand rapidly. By the end of the 19th century, its images are housed in the art book, the travel book, and the magazine. The magazines *Life* and *Look* exemplify the portrayal of the world of experience as a visual feast. When in 1936 *Life* squeezed the image between its pages, a newborn phase of the museum of forms tumbled out before the now insatiable eye. Life itself would be drained of its pigments and slapped between glossy advertisements. The first cry of *Life* was really the triumphant shout of the regime of the camera.

> To see life; to see the world; to eyewitness great events; to watch the faces of the poor and the gestures of the proud; to see strange things—machines, armies, multitudes, shadows in the jungle and on the moon; to see man's work—his paintings, towers and discoveries; to see things hidden behind walls and within rooms, things dangerous to come to; the women that men love and many children; to see and take pleasure in seeing; to see and be amazed; to see and be instructed. (Life, 1936)

The name *Life* continued the promise of the representation of naturalism and realism, not a noumenal truth but a sensuous one. Through the inexpensive dissemination of the printed image, the arrested glance of the photographer becomes elevated into global voyeurism. By the mid-20th century Sartre (1966) could portray the existential experience of the subject as peeping through the keyhole.

In its title *Look* magazine captured the rushing expansion of the museum of images. This was more than an expression of the colonial spirit for exotica. This museum was not to be like the British Museum or the Smithsonian, a national aggrandizement of the curio cabinet. The museum of forms would become embodied in the mass media. The objects were not unique. They had no special place. They were not even moments in art. They were simply moments and little else. But must of all, they were public moments.

The publicly displayed photograph with its beckoning familiarity tinged with a subtle and novel strangeness grabs us by the sleeve and exhorts us to LOOK, to find what is significant, to construct meaning. It demands labor of the eye. It shouts like a barker at a carnival and presents all surfaces and wares and all the strange "skins" it has collected. The eye searches the details for the meaning of this quotation. The eye seeks out connotations in the first milliseconds of sight (Marcel, 1983; McCauley, Parmlee, & Sperber, 1980) it seeks to fill with metaphor. The moment within the glance expands, until for certain images it becomes bloated with meaning.

But the regime had been upset by the early discovery that the glass eye of the camera was blind. By reflecting everything it saw nothing. What it needed from the natural eye was a greater process of selection. After all, this is the function of the fovea; a global analysis of the scene leading to a careful scanning. A fovea, so dense with connections that it commands more attention from the brain than any other sense organ, needs to scan, select, and focus on the significant. The rest of the image, the countless details, are attended in the anterior room of peripheral vision waiting to be called into the central court of consciousness.

The museum of the Essential Sample with its glass eye facing a world of surfaces needed more than the linguistic librarian in the agency of word and category—it needed an editor. But for the camera everything was in focus, and herein lay a violation of truth. The mind's eye was bombarded with detail, detail that it had never before seen and that now thrust itself into focus. In the museum of forms the images would have to be summed into larger units, composites.

THE CAMERA AND THE SCIENTIFIC EYE: A SAMPLING THEORY OF REALITY

Holmes's museum of the photographic form reflects an interesting alteration of the classic Platonic concept of the noumenal form. Plato sought a transcendent noumenal form through abstraction and reflection. The inhabitants in the famous metaphor of the cave arrived at the noumenal source by breaking the spell of the shadows. In the 19th century the camera only enjoins the observer to gaze further at shadow after shadow. The Platonic notion of form was no longer noumenal but sensate.

The camera was an agent in the molding of a sampling theory of scientific reality that was battering the tower of the Cartesian and Platonic tradition from which intellectuals like Baudelaire hurled boulders. Below at the gates lay the new technology and for Baudelaire, "its natural ally," "the stupidity of the multitude."

As early as 1839, Talbot, the English inventor of photography, had predicted that the camera would guide the eye of science. For Talbot the camera was to embody the inductive method:

> This remarkable phenomena, of whatever value it may turn out in its application to the arts, will at least be accepted as a new proof of the value of inductive methods of modern science, which by noticing the occurrence of unusual circumstances . . . and by following them up with experiments, and varying the conditions of these until the true law of nature which they express is apprehended, conducts us at length to consequences altogether unexpected, remote from usual experience, and contrary to almost universal belief. (Talbot, 1839, p. 4)

In "dustbowl empiricism" induction required the patient and tedious gathering of "objective observations." The photograph would be used to collect forms, as in Holmes's museum of forms, but now the forms would be called "data." The photograph has become an extension of the scientific eye extensively used in archaeology, geology, physics, botany, chemistry, and biology, to name just a few areas of use although not including *modes* of use. The camera was considered useful to "*count, measure,* and *record* infallibly all *stationary evidence*" (Wagner, 1979).

A modern example of this in practice is a study conducted by the British government in 1972 of a number of communities. The camera was the instrument of analysis. Cameras were set up according to a "grid of coordinates" of randomly chosen public points in the community. Each camera was not run by human hands but took sample pictures of the life-space, randomly. When a human photographer was used he or she was followed by another, and then by even more photographers over the course of two years. This practical installment of a panoptic analysis of the life-space of these small English communities was designed to "effectively identify and reduce the amount of sampling error, increase intersubjective reliability of interpretation, and in some cases provide an important test of the validity of visual statements about human subjects" (Wagner, 1979, p. 148).

Although the scientific eye may have been imbued with the spirit of classification, it was also a narcissistic eye. When the camera merged its vision with the microscope, the very first picture taken was of the eye of a fly. What better image of its narcissism than for the camera to gaze at a reflection of itself: an eye that was composed of millions of details, an eye in which each cell contained one of a thousand similar images. The scopic order of the Panopticon (Dreyfus & Rabinow, 1983; Foucault, 1979) could be reduced to a portable speck and reflected in the structure of nature.

The fly speck innocence of a microscopic Panopticon is dwarfed when the sampling theory of the photo-panoptic eye gazes upon the corpus of sociology. A social world filtered and constructed through a lens can be "managed" and "guided." Here the narcissism of the scopic regime interacts with the expanding detail of the medium. The search for self-discovery gazes into a mirror divided into a multitude of small rectangular frames reflecting bits of light in all directions. The narcissistic gaze becomes lost in a profusion of points of view. This is the camera in the hands of the sociologist.

A modern sociologist writes about a regime in which the human subject is now a series of frames and a camera lens.

> In "capturing the world" we can test our ideas about each other against the photographs and the realities they represent. In "creating visual statements" we manifest our understanding of the interesting and important. Through the photographs, we increase our knowledge of each other while at the same time raise questions about how well we understand our own lives. Through

both *taking* photographs and *making* photographs, we casually participate in scientific inquiry. (Wagner, 1979, p. 12)

In our culture, thought itself is visual; one has a "perspective," a "point of view," or a "worldview." Herein lies the essence of the sampling theory of the photo-scientific eye. Vision, mediated vision, becomes scientific inquiry. One reaches an understanding of reality *through* mediated and specialized vision. The subject embodies specialized vision. One understands the shadows on Plato's cave not by turning toward the sun, the source of the forms, but by photographing all the shadows on the distorted cave wall. Understanding lies in the collection of those images.

FROM SAMPLE TO STATISTICAL COMPOSITE: RECONSTRUCTING THE ESSENCE OF THE ESSENTIAL SAMPLE

For all the photograph's striking mimesis, it was just a solitary sample of the visual reality. The true Essential Sample could not be realized in the regime of cyclopean vision. An emerging sense of reality integrated with 19th-century empiricism sought the Essential Sample in the sum of sensory samples. The arrested glance had been only an embalming of the moment.

For the scientific eye peering through the telescope, the thought that "reality" might be a collection of light samples was already the obvious operant definition. A series of articles published in 1877 in *Nature* by Sir Joseph Norman Lockyer makes the point. Lockyer was to be the first astronomer to break samples of light into its spectroscopic elements so as to measure the stars. He described how astronomers were busily gathering "120,000 times more light."

Like the camera, the telescope was "simply . . . a sort of large eye" that needed more and more samples of light for a "complete" portrait of its ancient sitter. The stronger telescope sought by Lockyer merely offered images from deeper into the past. He wrote "when we gaze at the heavens at night we are viewing the stars not as they are at the moment" (Lockyer, 1877, p. 68). This to some degree was also the function of the camera. Though it could not go deeper into the past, it collected samples of light from the past, moments of flutter in Alberti's window. But the thing-in-itself continued to elude the analytical eye; with more and more samples of light each detail of vision could be added into something more essential. Reality could be reached through patient, tireless viewing, drawing samples of the object from as many perspectives as possible. The Essential Sample would need to be triangulated and clocked.

If, as Talbot had prophesized at the very birth of photography, the camera was the embodiment of the inductive method, then the truth of the image lay in moving from particulars to more general principles. The sampling frame would need to be assembled from parts in Holmes's museum of forms, compared and merged into higher truths. One could force the merger by imposing the foreign regime of linguistic order with its preexisting categories for form and content. But if one were to remain true to the language of the image, then one could achieve general truths through the infinite comparison, composite construction, or merger of the images themselves.

The man to do this was Sir Francis Galton, cousin of Charles Darwin, paragon of 19th-century science and the inductive method. Sir Francis and his faithful student Karl Pearson (of the Pearson product moment coefficient) can be said to be founders of modern statistics (Pearson, 1897, 1900, 1920, 1930, 1978; Pearson & Hartley, 1966).[3] Their journal, *Biometrika*, developed many of the statistical techniques that guide the manipulations of the social sciences, and especially psychology (Pearson, 1938; Porter, 1981; Westergaard, 1932).

Galton, brilliant even when wrong, was the spirit of 19th-century quantification incarnate. With his friend, the astronomer Lockyer, he had gazed through the telescope of science, and searched to create Panoptic order from the chaos of random light rays. For him, everything could and should be quantified, from the flow of thoughts in his consciousness (Galton, 1878) to the ratio of pretty to unattractive women in London, Aberdeen, and Glasgow (Galton, 1908).

But in Galton, the "founder of eugenics," we also see the dark underside of 19th-century science. He sought to analyze and classify the physiological and psychological traits of man and by so doing apply this knowledge of hereditary characteristics to the perfection of the species. His camera peered out through the slits in the central tower of the panopticon. Along with other visual instruments of science, the telescope and the microscope, it would allow Galton to place mankind under glass. For thirty years, Galton labored in the tower with his "statistical camera," searching for the ultimate classification scheme and the ultimate Essential Sample.

In 1878 during a discussion with social-Darwinist Herbert Spencer, Galton was struck with the idea of somehow superimposing "longitudinal, transverse, and horizontal sections of heads" in a search for an ideal type, a new Essential Sample of classes of beings and objects. The first groups to receive his attention in this way were those who were already marginalized and classified in the real life structures of Bentham's Panopticon, prisoners of the justice system.

His first approach had been to slice pictures of heads into quadrants, fitting neat groups of them together into new arrangements all the time searching for some ideal type. The more successful method was to create a new composite photograph made by superimposing the exactly fitted images of more than one element of a class of persons (see Figure 32.1). Galton reported on his success in April of 1878 to the distinguished gathering of the Anthropological Institute:

> I submit several composites. . . . The first set of portraits are those of criminals convicted of murder, manslaughter, or robbery accompanied with violence. It will be observed that the features of the composites are much better looking than those of the components. The special villianous irregularities of the latter have disappeared and the common humanity that underlies them has prevailed. They represent not the criminal, but the man who is liable to fall to crime. (Galton, 1878, p. 98)

Criminals were to be but the beginning of a scheme of visual dissection and classification that would feature the camera in the unusual role of statistician. In Galton's vision, the statistical mind would gather the photographs classified in Holmes's museum/library of forms. Here, through scientific manipulation, each pictorial data point could be merged into something higher and more essential, the "average" image. The camera would yield what the French statistician, Quetelot (1835), had sought from his statistical computations, a physical approximation of Quetelot's "mean man." When the composite computing machine was put into action it produced not just Quetelot's mean man, but Essential Samples, and pictorial averages of not only the "ideal criminal" but the mean family member (Galton, 1879a, 1879b), "military officer" (Mahomed & Galton, 1882), "tubercular patient" (Mahomed & Galton, 1882), the average American academic (!), the average cranium for a race (Galton, 1881), the average image of historical figures from coins (Galton, 1879a, 1879b), the average philosophy student, the average George Washington, and the average "race horse" (Galton, 1881; Pearson, 1924, p. 288). Galton's composites would rip through the museum of forms distilling the essential form of all things. For Galton and many others the composite photo would "bring out what is common to all and eliminate what is exceptional" (Pearson, 1924, p. 233).

These composites were a means of filtering the light through the emerging analytical eye. This would be a means of grappling with the profusion of detail now contained in the collections of images of forms. The merged visual images, the rapid blur of thousands of forms from Holmes's imaginary museum, would be constructed according to the new sampling theory of reality. It is in this effort, the massive summing and averaging of forms, that the 19th and, to a large degree, the 20th century's version of the thing-in-itself would emerge. If criminals could be classified, then so could races as long as the classification procedure was perfectly random, scientific, and above all, statistically objective (Gould, 1981). Given Galton's interest in eugenics and our historical hindsight, it is perhaps not surprising that Gal-

Figure 32.1 Galton's early photocomposite that "calculates" the average
            image of criminals convicted for murder, manslaughter, and
            crimes of violence.
            Source: (Pearson, 1924, Plate XXVIII).

ton's composites also sought a calculus of the "Jewish type" (Galton, 1885; Jacobs, 1885).

But these pictures were not photographs as we know them. As the reader will soon see, these images were not "like" statistics, or "applications" of statistics; for the early statistical mind the composite *was* a statistical process. At the dawn of modern statistics, statistical processes were *visual* processes, which the camera and the composite simply mimicked. Galton was attempting to link psychology and physiognomy, the concept and the image. In Galton's version of the museum of forms, the librarian was not the word, not language, but the conceptual image. This essentially pictorial representation was statistical in nature. At its birth, modern statistics as it existed in the mind of Sir Francis Galton floated in a nonverbal imaginal and geometric medium. In the 30 years that Galton labored on photography, he would attempt to produce the externalized form of this statistical system, and it would be as much photographic as numerical.

To appreciate and understand fully this unusual juncture in the history of ideas, let us move backward from the photograph to Galton's mental construct of statistical processes. Galton had absorbed the notion, which as we have seen was not uncommon during this period, that the photograph was a "sample" of reality. But as others had discovered, it was not the Essential Sample, in and of itself. Rather, the Essential Sample lay in time, or somehow behind all of these images. It is clear that Galton held this notion. His description of capturing "the most probable likeness" of an individual is based on this underlying theory:

> Another use of this process is to obtain by photography a really good likeness of a living person. The inferiority of photographs to the best works of an artist, so far as resemblance is concerned, lies in their catching no more than a single expression. If many photographs of a person were taken at different times, perhaps even years apart, their composite would possess that in which a single photograph is deficient. A further use of the process would be to produce from many independent portraits of an historical personage, the *most probable likeness of him*. (emphasis added) (Galton, 1878, p. 99)

For Galton, painters already carried out such calculations in their minds, in that they painted not exactly what was seen but a mental composite image, "the most probable likeness." But the painter was a biased sampler, and according to Galton did not weigh each image equally (Galton, 1879a). The individual then was always producing composites. The composite portrait was an exemplification of a natural statistical process. According to Galton:

> Composite portraits are, therefore, much more than averages, because they include the features of every individual of whom they are composed. They

are pictorial equivalents of those elaborate statistical tables out of which averages are deduced. There cannot be a more perfect example than they afford. (Galton, 1879b, p. 167)

For Galton the composites reflected both a statistical and a mental (cognitive) process. He argued that many metaphysicians had failed to understand the subtleties of conceptual formulations such as generalizations. According to Galton, if the metaphysicians "could have seen and examined these composite portraits, and had borne in mind the well-known elements of statistical science, [they] would have written very differently" (Pearson, 1924, p. 298).

But the Essential "Mean," born of mental processes that were both photographic and statistical, required an Essential Sample to distill this generic truth. The classification process in Holmes's photographic museum of forms could yield the subject matter.

No statistician dreams of combining objects into the same generic group that do not cluster towards a common centre, no more can we compose generic portraits out of heterogenous elements, for if the attempt be made to do so the result is monstrous and meaningless. (Galton, 1879a, p. 162)

In this context we can see that the phrase *sampling frame* has an ironic double meaning and that the images in Holmes's museum of forms would cluster into natural sampling frames.

The composite photo had many of the properties of other statistical processes. The pictures were to be chosen at random from the naturally delimited sampling frame. Galton sought to prove that different pictorial samples yielded substantial agreement.

An assurance of the truth of any of our pictorial deductions is to be looked for in their substantial agreement when different batches of components have been dealt with, this being a perfect test of truth in all statistical conclusions. (Galton, 1878, p. 100)

It was important that the merger of various subcomposites also yielded similar results to the mean composite of the general population. Exposure times were calculated according to an exact formula and composites determined with great "mechanical precision." Galton also counterbalanced the order of exposure of the pictorial data points to eliminate the possibility of order effects. He agonized as to whether the composite yielded a "true average" or an "aggregate." And, finally, Galton hoped through the careful computation of pictorial family types to *predict* the appearance of various offspring (Pearson, 1924, p. 288).

I have shown thus far that in the early days of the modern statistical mind, visual-photographic processes were essentially statistical. I will now show its converse, that the statistical process, as a mental process, was essentially visual and photographic. If statistical reasoning was somehow visual or pictorial, then mathematics or at least number systems must be somehow "visual," or to put it in Galton's terms, *geometric*. In the language of modern psychology, if the cognitive processes of the early statistical mind were nonlinguistic, then they might be part of visual-spatial pattern recognition processes, or, to put it in another way, part of an essentially right brain process (Springer & Deutsch, 1985). As we will soon see, Galton argued this very point in a debate with an Oxford professor named Max Muller printed in *Nature* (Galton, 1887a, 1887b).

Galton is credited with having done some pioneering experimental work in the area of mental imagery (Kosslyn, 1980) which, almost a hundred years after Galton's study, would reemerge as a central and important subject area of research into the cognitive systems of representation (Block, 1981; Kosslyn, 1980, 1983; Paivio, 1971). In a study of the flow of his own ideas, Galton found that over 50% of them were of a visual nature (Galton, 1879c). As Galton himself made heavy use of visual nonverbal thought, he was surprised when a questionnaire on mental imagery seemed to indicate a low level of mental imagery among members of the Fellows of the Royal Society and the French Institute (Galton, 1880, 1883). There is some indication that his questionnaire may have been affected by response inhibitions in a nominalist age (Kosslyn, 1980). More recent studies have indicated the heavy use of mental imagery among the intelligent, such as Mensa members (Kosslyn, 1980; McKellar, 1965). But Galton firmly believed in the reality of nonverbal thought. This led to the debate on "Thought without Words" with professor Max Muller in the pages of *Nature* (1887a, 1887b). Here Galton argued that in his researches, he had come across many who stated they could not think, if not in pictures, and he asserted that in some persons "true thought is habitually carried on without the use of mental or spoken words" (Galton 1887a, p. 28).

It is clear that Galton perceived many thinking processes to be primarily pictorial or nonverbal, including mathematics. In his major psychological work, *Inquiries into Human Faculty* (1883), and two articles with the title of "Visualized Numerals" (1880a, 1880b), Galton put forward the thesis that many individuals, though not the majority, possessed or utilized visual number systems that he termed *number forms*. Number forms were the spatial or diagrammatic systems by which people imagined the organization of numbers. Through interviews Galton collected over 80 of these. (See Figure 32.2 for Galton's examples.) If number forms could be pictorial, then surely statistical thought itself could be pictorial, and possibly photographic. Karl Pearson, the faithful student and biographer of Galton, and unquestionably a major founder of modern statistics (see Hacking, 1984), reported his own curious blend of verbal and pictorial mental imagery in a footnote in Galton's biography (Pearson, 1924, p. 244). Galton had sought

to refine the visual representation of statistical information including stereoscopic graph images based on three dimensional models of statistical data
(Galton, 1908; Pearson, 1924). The visual representation of statistics was
an important part of statistical courses of the period (Pearson, 1938, p.
143) and the use of stereoscopic graphs was even taken up by Alexander
Graham Bell, a disciple of Galton, who once constructed and exhibited
such pictographic statistics (Second International Congress on Eugenics,
1923, plate 4).

The visual image and the photograph seem to have haunted much of the
thought, and certainly the statistical thought of Galton and some of his con-
temporaries. It can be argued that a number of aspects of Galton's models of
statistics, human faculties, and even eugenics may have been guided by
analogical reasoning directly derived from the *idea* of the photograph.

If modern models of memory and thought processes are based on computer analogies, then Galton's was clearly photographic. Galton's pictured
a mind that stared out at the world through the camera lens and absorbed
information in a flash. In the following quotation, Galton displays a tellingly
photographic concept of perception:

> A useful faculty, easily developed by practice, is that of retaining a mere reti-
> nal picture. A scene is flashed upon the eye; the memory of it persists, and
> details which escaped observation during the brief time when it was actually
> seen may be analysed and studied at leisure in subsequent vision. (Pearson,
> 1924, p. 241)

Here memory is portrayed as a series of snapshots, always available for
"study at leisure" in the photograph album of the mind. If the first traces of
visual processing led to snapshots in memory, and cerebration led to activation of these images, then might not memory be composed totally of Galton's mental versions of composite photographs? In the parallel between
psychological events and physiognomic ones, one finds not only a statistical model of photography but a composite photographic model of mental
processes.

> Whenever any group of brain-elements has been excited by a sense-
> impression, it becomes, so to speak, tender, and liable to be easily thrown
> again into a similar state of excitement. . . . Whenever a single cause throws
> different groups of brain-elements simultaneously into excitement, the result
> must be a blended memory. . . . Thus some picture of mountain and lake in
> a country which we have recollections cannot be disentangled, though gen-
> eral resemblances are recognized. . . . A generic image may be considered
> to be nothing more than a generic portrait stamped on the brain by succes-
> sive impressions made by its component images. (Galton, 1879a, p. 162)

If perception was like photography, and memory but a composite photograph, then we should not be surprised that in this visual statistical computer

EXAMPLES OF NUMBER FORMS.

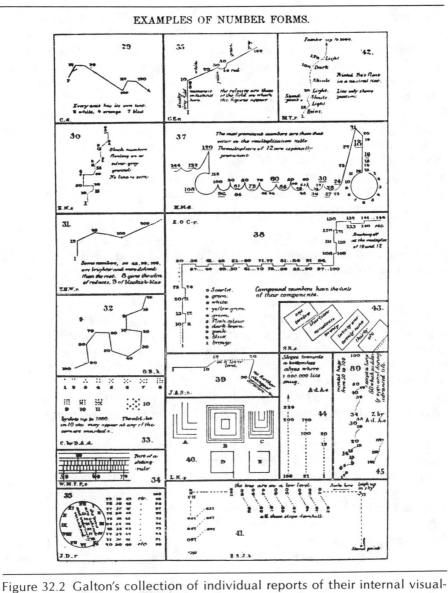

Figure 32.2 Galton's collection of individual reports of their internal visualized image of the form of pure number systems.
Source: (Pearson, 1924, Plate XXIV).

of the mind, memory recall resembled the "lantern slide" show. Galton's biographer, Pearson, was "puzzled by the large number of lantern slides in the *Galtoniana*" (collection of Galton's gadgets and devices; Pearson, 1924, p. 238). They were there to "illustrate" lectures on imagery. Given our argument until now, it follows that Galton, thinking with and through the media, should have seen imagery as an internal projection of the image through the optic nerve to the back of the retina (Galton, 1883). Therefore, if the capacity for the recall of imagery were sufficiently strong, then we might actually "see" or "project" images onto paper, or picture it in the "minds' eye." Galton wrote, "We should be able to visualize that object freely from any aspect; we should be able to project any of its images on paper and draw its outline there" (Galton, 1880b, p. 322).

But Galton worried that the mental images were blurred and lacking in clarity. "Our mental generic composites," he argued, "are rarely defined; they have that blur in excess which photographic composites have in a small degree" (Galton, 1879a, p. 169). But Galton felt that the blur of memory could be limited if that photographic-statistical apparatus of the brain could produce true "generic" composites as opposed to imperfectly sampled "general" composites.

> The criterion of the perfect mind would lie in its capacity of always creating images of a truly generic kind, deduced from the whole range of past experiences. General impressions are never to be trusted. (Galton, 1879a, p. 168)

Generalizations were the domain of metaphysicians whose composites were composed from imperfect samples. Galton felt that the "perfect mind," not surprisingly, resembled that of the visual statistician. Galton wrote, "those who are not accustomed to original inquiry entertain a hatred and horror of statistics. . . . But it is the triumph of scientific men to rise superior to such superstitions" (Galton, 1897a, p. 169).

Such then, was the structure of the statistical mind in the very early days of modern statistics—a photographic model, a great statistical program, full of graphic subroutines, to use the analogies of the present.

Galton's photographic edifice is paradigmatic, because in it we can see a complex and multifaceted interaction among a medium, perception through a medium, the concept of a medium, and the medium as grand analogy. Galton goes through all the phases mentioned at the opening of this article. For Galton the camera (1) expanded the range of what was perceptible, (2) altered the flow and collection of information, (3) interacted with and helped restructure his conceptualizations of cognitive processes and mathematical thought, (4) and finally provided a dazzling analogy for statistical and cognitive processes.

Media technology are devices for more than the manipulation of information. A medium guides perception and conceptual thought. We not only think *with* media technology and symbol systems, but *through* media technology and symbol systems. Galton may have unwittingly used the photograph as a model and analogy for thought processes just as we use the computer as an ubiquitous analogy for cognitive processes.

Though statistics and the camera would part ways once they left the spacious symbiotic environment of Sir Francis Galton's mind, both in the 20th century would carry out the agenda found in the original flash of thought escaping from Galton's statistical camera/mind late in the 19th century. The modern camera would in one of its social uses emerge as an instrument of scientific inquiry and measurement. All forms could be collected and reduced to a standard manageable size. The eye could now carry out the functions of standardization and quantification that the institution of money had carried out in the marketplace.

Holmes's great museum of forms would become an actuality. The museum of forms would never be housed in a building but would find its home in the mass media where it would permeate the culture. With the video tape, the laser disk, and the embodiment of the visual-statistical mind, the computer, everything could be captured, measured, and compared. Along with statistics it would carry out the mission of endless comparison and classification pictured in the Holmes's original vision:

> To render comparison of similar objects, or of any that we may wish to see side by side, easy, there should be a stereographic *metre* or fixed standard of focal length for the camera lens, to furnish by its multiples or fractions, if necessary, the scale of distances, and the standard of power in the stereoscopic lens. In this way the eye can make the most rapid and exact comparisons. (Holmes, 1959, p. 255)

Galton himself had devised a primitive "mechanical selector" for processing information (Pearson, 1924, p. 307). Unwittingly and through the course of events, the statistical mind of Sir Francis Galton would take shape in an environment of computers and visual media. As Galton himself once remarked when briefly straying from his eugenic creed, "The character of our abstract ideas, therefore, depends to a considerable degree on our nurture" (Pearson, 1924, p. 255).

NOTES

1. [original quotation]
Tu sais que les rayons de lumière réfléchis des différents corps font tableau et peignent ces corps sur toutes les surfaces polies, sur la retine de l'oeil, par exemple, sur l'eau, sur les glaces. Les esprits élémentaires ont cherché à fixer ces images passagères; ils on compose une matière très-subtile, très-visqueuse et très-prompte a se dessécher et à se durcir, au moyen de laquelle un tableau est fait en un clin d'oeil. Ils enduisent de cette matière une piece de toile et la présente aux objets qu'ils veulent peindre. Le premier effet de la toile est celui du miroir: on y voit tous les corps voisins et eloignes dont la lumière peut apporter l'image.

Mais ce qu'une glace ne saurait faire, la toile, au moyen de son enduit visqueux, retient les simulacres. Le mirroir vous rend fidèlement les objets, mais n'en garde aucun; nos toiles ne les rendent pas moins fidelement, mais les garde tous. Cette impression des images est l'affaire du premier instant ou la toile les recoit. On l'ôte sur-le-champ, on la place dan un endroit obscur; une heure après, l'enduit est desséché, et vous avez un tableau d'autant plus précieux, qu'aucun art ne peut l'imiter la verité et que le temps ne peut aucune manière l'endommager.

2. [original quotation]
Nous prenons dan leur source la plus pure, dan le corps de la lumière, les couleurs que le peintres tirent des different matériaux que le temps ne manque jamais d'alterer. La préci-

sion du dessin, la variété de l'expression les touches plus ou moins fortes, le gradation des nuances, les règles de la perspective, nous abandonnons tout cela à la nature qui, avec cette marche sûre qui jamais ne dementit, trace sur nos toiles des images qui en imposent aux yeux et font douter a la raison, si ce qu'on appelle réalites ne sont pas d'autre espèces de fantômes qui en imposent aux yeux, a l'ouïe, au toucher, à tous les sens à la fois.

3. At this point the distinction needs to be made between the older tradition of statistics and the modern form referred to in this paper. Statistics certainly predates Galton, but it is largely a descriptive statistics associated with government offices and the traditional accounting of "all things in the land." By modern statistics I am referring to arrival of the whole arsenal of inferential techniques used to "distill" information, test the compatability of two orders of numbers as Galton's and Pearson's product coefficients do, and the concept of probability as a means of modeling the range of potential outcomes.

REFERENCES

Alberti, L. (1972). De Pictura. London: Phaidon. (Original work published in 1435)
Alpers, S. (1983). The art of describing: Dutch art in the seventeenth century. Chicago: University of Chicago Press.
Arnheim, R. (1969). Visual thinking. Berkeley: University of California Press.
Baudelaire, C. (1955). Mirror or art, critical studies by Charles Baudelaire (Jonathan Mayne, Trans.). London: Phaidon.
Biocca, F. A. (1985, August). The pursuit of sound: Radio, perception, and the composer in the early twentieth century. Paper presented at the meeting of the Association for Education in Journalism and Mass Communication, Memphis, TN.
Biocca, F. A. (in press). Media and perceptual shifts: Early radio and the clash of musical cultures. Journal of Popular Culture.
Block, N. (1981). Imagery. Cambridge: MIT.
Bryson, N. (1983). Vision and painting. New Haven: Yale University.
Cohen P. R., & Feigenbaumb, E. A. (Eds.). (1982). The handbook of artificial intelligence (Vol. 1-3). Los Altos, CA: William Kaufmann.
Cowan, R. (1985). Sir Francis Galton and the study of heredity in nineteenth century. New York: Garland.
Cruikshank, G. (1842). Photographic phenomena and the new art of portrait painting. Omnibus London. (Reprinted in facsimile in Newhall, 1956)
Czitrom, D. J. (1982). Media and the American mind: From Morse to McLuhan. Chapel Hill: University of North Carolina Press.
Dreyfus H., & Rabinow, P. (1983). Michael Foucault: Beyond structuralism and hermeneutics. Chicago: University of Chicago.
Eco, U. (1976). A theory of semiotics. Bloomington: Indiana University Press.
Eisenstein, E. (1979). The printing press as an agent of change: Communication and cultural transformations in early- modern Europe (Vols. 1 & 2). NY: Cambridge University Press.
Foucault, M. (1970). The order of things: An archaelogy of the human sciences. London: Tavistock.
Foucault, M. (1979). Discipline and punish: The birth of the prison. (A. M. Sheridan-Smith, Trans.). New York: Random House.
Fournier, E. (1859). Le vieux-neuf, histoire ancienne des inventions et dicouvertes modernes (Vol. 1). Paris: Dentu.
Frisby, J. P. (1979). Seeing: Illusion, brain, and mind. Oxford: Oxford University.
Galton, F. (1878). Composite portraits. Nature, 18, 97-100.
Galton, F. (1879a). Generic images. Proceedings of the Royal Institution, 9, 161-170.
Galton, F. (1879b). Generic images. The Nineteenth Century, 6, 157-169.
Galton, F. (1879c). Psychometric facts. The Nineteenth Century, 6, 425-433.
Galton, F. (1880a). Statistics of mental imagery. Mind, 5, 301-308.
Galton, F. (1880b). Visualizing numerals. Nature, 26, 252-253, 323, 494-5.
Galton, F. (1880c). Visualizing numerals. Journal of the Anthropological Institute, 10, 85-102.

Galton, F. (1881, June 14). On the application of composite portraiture to anthropological purposes. *Journal and Transactions of the Photographic Society of Great Britain, 5,* 140-146.

Galton, F. (1883) *Inquiries into human faculty and its development.* London.

Galton, F. (1885). Composite photographs. *Photographic News, 29,* 243-45.

Galton, F. (1887a). Thought without words. *Nature, 36,* 28-29.

Galton, F. (1887b). Thought without words. *Nature, 36,* 100-101.

Galton, F. (1908). *Memories of my life.* London: Methuen.

Gollin, E. S. (1981). (Ed.) *Developmental plasticity: Behavioral and biological aspects of variations in development.* New York: Academic.

Gombrich, E. (1960). *Art and illusion: a study in the psychology of pictorial representation.* Princeton: Princeton University Press.

Gombrich, E. (1982). *The image and the eye.* Ithaca, NY: Cornell University Press.

Goodman, N. (1977). *Languages of art.* Indianapolis: Hackett.

Goodman, N. (1978). *Ways of worldmaking.* Indianapolis: Hackett.

Goody, J. (1977). *The domestication of the savage mind.* Cambridge: Cambridge University Press.

Gould, S. (1981). *The mismeasure of man.* New York: W. W. Norton.

Gouldner, A. (1976). *The dialectic of ideology and technology.* London: Macmillan.

Gregory, R. L. (1970). *The intelligent eye.* London: Widenfield & Nicolson.

Hacking, I. (1984). Trial by number. *Science 84, 5,* 69-70.

Holmes, O. W. (1859). The stereoscope and the stereograph. *Atlantic Monthly, 3,* 251-262.

Jacobs, J. (1885). The Jewish type, and Galton's composite photographs. *Photographic News, 29,* 268-269.

Jussim, E. (1974). *Visual communication and the graphic arts, photographic technologies in the nineteenth century.* New York: R. R. Bowker.

Kosslyn, S. M. (1980). *Image and mind.* Cambridge, MA: Harvard University.

Kosslyn, S. M. (1983). *Ghosts in the mind's machine: Creating and using images in the brain.* New York: W. W. Norton.

Life (1936). Declaration of intent. 1.

Lockyer, J. N. (1877). The modern telescope. *Nature, 26,* 66-68.

Mahomed, F. A., & Galton, F. (1882). An inquiry into the physiognomy of phthsis by the method of composite photographs. *Guy's Hospital Reports, 25.*

Malraux, A. (1967). *Museum without walls.* Garden City, NY: Doubleday.

Marcel, A. J. (1983). Conscious and unconscious perception: An approach to the relations between phenomenal experience and perceptual processes. *Cognitive Psychology, 15,* 238-300.

Marr, D. (1982). *Vision.* San Francisco: W. H. Freeman.

McCauley, C., Parmlee, C. M., & Sperber, R. D. (1980). Early extraction of meaning from pictures and its relation to conscious identification. *Journal of Experimental Psychology: Human Perception and Performance, 6,* 265-276.

McKellar, P. (1965). The investigation of mental images. In S. A. Barnett & A. McLaren (Eds.), *Penguin Science Survey.* Hammondsworth, England: Penguin.

Muybridge, E. (1887). *Animal locomotion* (Vols. 1-11). Philadelphia: University of Philadelphia.

Newhall, B. (Ed.). (1956). *On photography.* Watkins Glen, NY: Century.

Ong, W. J. (1982). *Morality and literacy: The technologizing of the word.* London: Methuen.

Paivio, A. (1971). *Imagery and verbal processes.* New York: Holt, Rinehart & Winston.

Pearson, E. S. (1938). *Karl Pearson: An appreciation of some aspects of his life and work.* Cambridge: Cambridge University Press.

Pearson, E. S. & Hartley, H. O. (Eds.). (1966). *Biometrika tables for statisticians.* Cambridge: Cambridge University Press.

Pearson, K. (1897). *The chances of death and other studies in evolution.* London: E. Arnold.

Pearson, K. (1900). *The grammar of science.* London: A. & C. Black.

Pearson, K. (1920). *On the construction of tables and interpolation, pt. 1-2.* London: Cambridge University Press.

Pearson, K. (1924). *The life, letters, and labours of Francis Galton* (Vol. 2) *Researchs of middle life*. Cambridge: Cambridge University.

Pearson, K. (Ed.). (1930). *Tables for statisticians and biometricians*. Cambridge: Cambridge University Press.

Pearson, K. (1948). *Early statistical papers*. Cambridge: Cambridge University Press.

Pearson, K. (1978). *The history of statistics in the 17th & 18th centuries against the changing background of intellectual, scientific, and religuous thought: Lectures by Karl Pearson given at University College, London, during academic sessions, 1921-1933*. London: C. Griffin.

Porter, T. M. (1981). *The calculus of liberalism: The development of statistical thinking in the social and natural sciences of the nineteenth century*. Unpublished doctoral dissertation, Princeton University.

Quetelet, A. (1835). *Sur l'homme et le development de ses facultes, ou essai de physique sociale*. Paris.

Sartre, J. P. (1966). *Being and nothingness*. New York: Washington Square.

Second International Congress of Eugenics (1923). *Eugenics, genetics and the family*. Baltimore: Williams & Wilkins.

Sontag, S. (1977). *On photography*. New York: Farrar, Stauss, & Giroux.

Springer, S., & Deutsch, G. (1985). *Left brain, right brain*. New York: Freeman.

Talbot, H. F. (1839). *Some account of the art of photogenic drawing of the process by which natural objects may be made to delineate themselves without the aid of the artist's pencil*. London: R. & J. E. Taylor.

Wagner, J. (1979). *Images of information: Still photography in the social sciences*. Beverly Hills, CA: Sage.

Westergaard, H. (1932). *Contributions to the history of statistics*. London: P. S. King & Son.

33 ● Multilevel Analysis in Critical Research

ASTRID KERSTEN

LaRoche College

O VER the past few years, the critical approach to communication has been increasingly recognized and used. In spite of the considerable differences that can be found within "the" critical approach, two common strands can be identified.

First, the position of critique can be found in most critical approaches. Described most generally as "reflection on a system of constraints which are humanly produced" (Connerton, 1978, p. 18), the position of critique questions the "naturalness" of human experience. Critique seeks to undermine "the everyday attitude that identifies what one *perceives* with what *is*" (Appelbaum & Cotiner, 1979, p. 74) and brings to the surface the underlying processes and relationships that shape and govern the surface world.

This concern with revealing deep structures and realities is combined in most critical approaches with a second common idea, namely, a conception of the social world that stresses the complexity and multiplicity of existing relationships. In emphasizing complex and multiple relationships, critical approaches seek to connect traditionally separate ideas and processes such as social structure and human agency, the material and the symbolic, and so forth.

Grossberg (1984), in a recent review, has shown the many ways in which different critical approaches conceptualize the relationship between society and culture. Although the differences in some cases are quite substantial, all critical approaches maintain conceptually the idea of an inherent *complexity* in social relationships. Extremes of structural determinism and individualistic voluntarism are avoided typically by proposing some concept that stresses processes of mutual determination and influence thought to operate between human symbolic activity on the one hand and society or social structure on the other.

Although ideas like the "duality of structure" (Giddens, 1979, 1984) or the "double articulation of social structure and human praxis" (Bhaskar,

Correspondence and requests for reprints: Astrid Kersten, LaRoche College, 9000 Babcock Blvd., Pittsburgh, PA 15237.

1983) avoid the artificial dualism characteristic of conventional social theory, the transition from theory to research and action has not been very effective to date. Studies employing the critical approach in some form or another remain relatively rare, especially in the area of organizational communication. Although there are many reasons for the paucity of critical organizational research, the issue of multilevel analysis has been one major obstacle in the development of organizational studies, posing conceptual as well as methodological problems.

This discussion will attempt to stimulate the development of critical studies of organizational communication by working through some of the aspects of the problem of multilevel analysis, or, to be more precise, the problem of making the connection, in research and action, between organizational (and intraorganizational) level phenomena and the social context. In order to focus the problem, I will begin with a brief review, describing the ways in which various authors have theorized the complex relationships between structure and agency. Next, I will describe the ways in which these theories create particular difficulties for organizational research. In the remainder of the paper I will offer some suggestions and strategies designed to facilitate the making of sound connections between the various levels of action and abstraction.

PREVIOUS FORMULATIONS:
STRUCTURALISM VERSUS INDIVIDUALISM

Previously, issues of the relationship between human interaction and social structure have been debated within the individualist/structuralist controversy. Although much of this debate concerns the issue of the level of analysis, the source of the controversy extends far beyond this into competing definitions of the nature of social reality (Pfeffer, 1982).

The individualist position holds that "social structure is nothing more than the behavior of individuals" (Collins, 1975, p. 436). Groups, organizations, and society as a whole are explained as aggregates of individuals, and individual behavior itself is explained as a function of individual values, interests, motivations, and the like.

Individualists, according to Mayhew (1980, p. 339), "assume the existence of social structures in order to study their impact on *individuals*." Structuralists, on the other hand, see it as their primary task to explain the existence of social structures.

> If one assumes the structure of society in order to examine its impact on the immediate acts, thoughts, and feelings of individuals, one has assumed most of what has to be explained in order to study a small part of human activity and experience. (Mayhew, 1980, pp. 339-340)

Structuralists clearly are not interested in studying individual human behavior. What they are interested in is the study of the "behavior of the variables which define various aspects of social organization, its population, environment, ideological and technological subsystems" (Mayhew, 1980, p. 339).

The individualist/structuralist controversy represents two incompatible theoretical positions, each disallowing the focal concern of the other. The methodological implications of each position also vary greatly. For the structuralist, the primary interest is in variations in social structure patterns that are studied and explained by linking together social level variables. Human behavior, if of interest at all, is simply viewed as a function of social structure and social structure variations. Conversely, for the individualist, variations in social structure are of interest only insofar as they are seen as the outcome of variations in individual level properties. "The relationship between man and society is one of human control, in which society is a derivative of human agency" (Dawe, 1978, p. 375; Mayhew, 1981). Individualist approaches then focus on identifying patterns in individual level variables and establishing causal relations to social level conditions.

THE CRITICAL POSITION
ON SOCIAL REALITY

The critical perspective rejects both voluntaristic individualism and deterministic structuralism on the grounds that each provides an inadequate and incomplete analysis of social reality. The alternative proposed by the critical approach offers a view of the social world that takes into account both social structure and human agency and theorizes some form of a complex relationship between the two. Generally, this is accomplished using the line of reasoning outlined below.

(1) The social world is socially produced and "reproduced in and through the everyday practices of people" (Benson, 1983, p. 332). These practices include subjective and intersubjective interpretations as well as observable enactments, resulting in objective routines, structures and conditions (Heydebrand, 1983). Once established, subjective and objective constructions become objectified, develop their own determinate tendencies, and shape future social reproductions. This establishes the social world as consisting of both objective and subjective social processes, in which social structures and human agency exist in a mutually dependent and determining relationship.

(2) The social world thus constructed is not unproblematic. It contains "contradictions," understood as opposing forces or as confrontations between opposing forms of social life. This on the one hand stresses the nonunitary nature of social constructions. On the other hand, it presents

the maintenance of social constructions as the essential problematic for investigation.

(3) Multiple levels of reality exist. Most critical positions do not confine social explanation to the level of the empirical or self-evident. Instead, using concepts such as *surface* and *deep* structure or the realms of the empirical, the actual and the real, complex, nonlinear explanations of social phenomena are formulated. Ideally, these explanations place causality in the relations between generative mechanisms and levels of reality, thus avoiding simple determinism.

(4) Social reality is systematically distorted. The way in which social reality presents itself to us is itself seen as the outcome of complex processes of mediation, generating systematic distortions that serve to maintain existing social arrangements and relations. The content of social productions is nonarbitrary, in other words, and serves to conceal, link, and distort problematic social conditions.

The above outline is obviously very general and different critical positions will take different approaches to linking structure and agency. To illustrate this, two specific examples will be reviewed next: (1) Giddens's theory of structuration and (2) Althusserian structuralism.

ONE EXAMPLE: GIDDENS'S
THEORY OF STRUCTURATION

Giddens's (1983, 1984) theory of structuration and related theories of realism (Bhaskar, 1979, 1983) provide one example of a critical attempt to sort out the connections between micro and macro levels. In an attempt to avoid a conceptual dualism between structure and agency, Giddens proposes the idea of the "duality of structure."

Social structure is seen as both the medium and the outcome of human agency, "the pre-given idioms which shape human conduct, and the reproduced results of human action" (Isaac, 1983, p. 303). Bhaskar (1983) in a related position describes the relationship as one of "double articulation" wherein social structure and human praxis are connected through relations of enablement/constraint and reproduction/transformation:

> [A] transcendental argument from intentional agency establishes the (relative) autonomy, sui generis reality and temporal pre-existence of society as a transcendentally necessary condition for it, as its means and medium. But if society is the condition of our agency, it exists and persists only through it, so that human agency is equally an existentially necessary condition for society, as it continually reproduces or transforms the latter. (Bhaskar, 1983, pp. 83-84)

Human action is "the *transformation* of pre-given materials by intentional human subjects." In other words, human agency "has social preconditions, namely the relatively *enduring relations* (e.g. husband/wife, capitalist/worker) which complexly constitute society" (Isaac, 1983, p. 303). Thus although the idea of "reproduced relations" presents actors as actively involved in the reproduction process, it also refers to historical, objective, and relatively enduring social facts: the idea that these relations "have already been *produced* in an historical sense, in order that agents are able to *reproduce* them" (Layder, 1985, p. 144).

Issues of power and domination figure central in most critical approaches and the structuration perspective is no exception. In Giddens's formulation, communication, power, and sanctions are the essential components of human interaction. These components are connected to structural properties in a fashion consistent with the position of duality. Structural properties of domination, for example, are both drawn upon and reproduced by actors in interaction and social systems are produced and reproduced through and in the combined structures of signification, domination, and legitimation.

Power remains closely tied to the idea of human agency, though, in two ways. First, Giddens sees power as relations of autonomy and dependency between actors, rather than as a structural property. Second, Giddens insists on a criterion of instanciation, whereby structures are seen as existing only *when* and *as* reproduced by actors.

In sum, the essential interest of the theory of structuration is in human practice *and* in the structural conditions of human practice, seeking to examine how the two combine in the reproduction of social systems. A different way of conceptualizing the nature of social relations is found in the critical structuralist position, represented by among others Althusser (1969, 1971) and Therborn (1980).

ANOTHER EXAMPLE: ALTHUSSER'S STRUCTURALISM AND THE STUDY OF IDEOLOGY

In this approach the particular pattern of productive and social relations in a given society, referred to as the mode of production, is seen as dependent upon a whole range of social relations and structures. Economic practices and power relations are not seen as self-sustaining, but depend for their continuation on a complex set of political, ideological, and theoretical practices, together forming "the totality of social dimensions of the productive process" (Wright, 1983, p. 83). Analysis focuses on determining the ways in which the dominant mode of production is reproduced by assessing the specific form of the relations between the various practices, thus revealing the "structure in dominance."

Essential to this approach is the idea of "structural causality":

> Once the whole of a social formation is conceived as a structured whole in which the different structures are differentiated by the domination/subordination relations that they have with each other, then we can no longer think of the whole as source or origin of the different structures which constitute the whole, nor can we suppose that the social formation itself possesses a center or essence in a particular structure from which all determinations begin. The social formation is an already-given-whole that dissimulates itself into its effects, since the effects are not outside or distinct from the structure itself. (Emerson, 1984, p. 213)

The proposed connection between social structures and human subjects shows most clearly in the concept of ideology. In the structuralist approach, ideology is said to operate in the formation and transformation of human subjectivity (Therborn, 1980). Ideology is "the medium *through which* social reality, consciousness, and meaningfulness are constructed" (Deetz & Kersten, 1983, p. 162).

Ideologies provide subjects with a *particular rendition* of social reality, specifying what is real, desirable, and possible. Through a process of "subject-qualification" individual subjectivity is formed and transformed on the basis of this particular rendition of reality. In this process, individuals are simultaneously "subjected to a particular order that favors and allows certain drives and capacities and disfavors others" and "become qualified to take up and perform the repertoire of roles given in the society to which they are born" (Therborn, 1980, p. 18). As Grossberg (1984, p. 410) describes it: "The individual becomes complicitous with his or her own insertion into the ideological production of an imaginary but lived reality."

Although ideology thus operates in the constitution of human subjectivity, ideology is also linked to objective social structures in a number of ways. One, ideological specifications are inscribed in—or evidenced in—material expressions. For an ideology to work, so to speak, it must be "backed up" by the material world. Two, ideology serves to support and sustain existing social arrangements through such processes as (1) legitimation, whereby systems of domination are sustained through a cultivated belief in their legitimacy; (2) dissimulation, which serves to conceal, deny, or misrepresent existing power relations; and (3) reification, through which existing arrangements are presented as permanent, natural, real, and independent of any human decision or participation (Thompson, 1984).

Contrary to the theory of structuration, critical structuralism seeks to emphasize the primacy of social structure in the explanation of social phenomena. Although conceptualizing human subjectivity—through ideology—the form and content of this subjectivity are ultimately understood only through the requirements of the existing mode of production.

OTHER FORMULATIONS

Giddens and Althusser represent two different critical approaches to linking social structure and human agency, each using a different emphasis. The theory of structuration, in using the criterion of instanciation, emphasizes agency as the primary factor, making structure dependent upon action. Althusser's brand of structuralism sees the complex relations between the various practices as primary, and human subjectivity as secondary.

Obviously other connections are possible. Grossberg's (1984) review organizes the different theories into (1) classical approaches, which see culture as a reflection of society and hence, propose a relatively unproblematic relationship between meaning and social structure; (2) hermeneutic approaches, which see culture as a representation of society; and (3) discursive approaches, in which "culture produces not only the structures of experience but experience itself, which functions within social structures of domination" (Grossberg, 1984, p. 418).

PROBLEMS IN CRITICAL ORGANIZATIONAL RESEARCH

Critical research in the area of organizational communication is still hard to find. Most organizational communication researchers have limited interest in the critical approach, and those that are interested have had to deal with a number of other obstacles.

The first obstacle is political in nature. Organizational research depends in part on cooperation from company management. They, however, are not likely to facilitate or finance research that may be perceived as threatening or as not serving the organizational interests.

Recently both Deetz (1985) and Riley (1985) have stressed the necessity for enhanced cooperation between organizations and researchers. The avenues suggested by them may, when implemented, solve many of the immediate, practical difficulties. Even without such increased cooperation, though, organizational research is possible. Researchers may elect to engage in differing degrees of covert research or may attempt to enter the organization at levels other than the management level.

A second reason for the paucity of organizational research is methodological in nature. Most organizational researchers have been schooled in conventional research methods and strategies that are ill-suited to critical studies. Recently, efforts have been made to clarify the relationship between critical ontology and methods (Kersten, 1985) and to provide examples of the way in which methods are used in critical research (Morgan, 1983), but more work is needed.

Third, there is the issue of multilevel analysis, which poses both conceptual and methodological difficulties. As we have seen, critical approaches typically theorize the existence of a complex set of relations between structure and agency, and between microlevel events and macrolevel arrangements. Even though the exact theories vary, the problems multilevel approaches pose for research and analysis are similar. The following section will elaborate briefly on the major conceptual and methodological problems that arise when one attempts to move from the level of theory to the level of research and action, particularly in the area of critical organizational research.

PROBLEMS OF
MULTILEVEL ANALYSIS

The first problem deals with some of the conceptual difficulties related to the micro/macro level distinction. Critical theory is typically formulated in the context of society, discussing general social mechanisms, tendencies, and phenomena. Conceptually, this creates what one might call a translation problem. Can social level concepts be "translated" to the organizational level without losing their meaning or usefulness? If the concepts can be adapted, what guidelines should be used? How is the idea of "structure-in-dominance," for example, applied at the organizational level?

The second problem concerns the way in which organizations are conceptualized. Most critical approaches are preoccupied with general social processes and phenomena and, except for a few general comments on the oppressive characteristics of modern bureaucracy, they remain silent about organizations. Are organizations, as some would argue, simply the site at which modes of production are reproduced? In this formulation, the process of reproduction is shaped by the general social relations and remains unaffected by organizational dynamics. Alternatively, we can theorize organizations as relatively self-contained. This is the position taken in the conventional organizational literature, which reasons that organizational-level phenomena are best explained by organizational-level variables, or, worse yet, by variations in individual properties. A third, more fitting, possibility is to conceptualize organizational relations as a social phenomenon, allowing for organizational level processes and dynamics, as well as for social effects. Even this approach, however, taken effectively by Clegg (1981), for example, still leaves the level of analysis problem.

This third problem—the level of analysis—creates a number of practical and methodological difficulties for the organizational researcher. Although it makes good theoretical sense to conceptualize explanatory processes and relations at both the micro- and the macrolevel, it creates confusion when it comes to collecting and interpreting data. If we use the levels sequentially, how do we determine which comes first? Or, perhaps more important, which comes last? Also, how do we preserve the theoretical relationship between the two levels, if they are separated in the process of analysis? What are the implications for the type of data collection we engage in?

On the one hand, some of these questions are questions only because we tend to prefer simple, neatly ordered programs and explanations. On the other hand, the critical approach has not really developed clear guidelines and exemplars for research and in the absence of these, the relative lack of empirical investigation becomes easier to understand, if still regrettable.

Of course, it should be kept in mind that critical methodology and analysis will never have the prescriptive, protocol character of conventional research approaches. Critical research at its best is not a series of simple, sequential steps, but rather an overall approach, "a complex of policies and strategies that permit a given problematic to be understood, analyzed, acted on, and resolved or transformed" (Heydebrand, 1983, p. 312). Ultimately, it is the phenomenon studied that dictates the particular choice of concepts, methods, and approach.

Having acknowledged this, the next sections will develop some general guidelines and suggestions that may facilitate critical organizational research. First, I will present critical research as theoretically guided, meaning that the research question itself should enable critique and acknowledge the existence of complex social relations. Second, critical research will be described as the *ongoing* development of understanding, which refers to the process of redescription or interpretation that is central in critical analysis. The issue of the direction of analysis will be addressed here also. Third, the importance of organizational and social models will be discussed. The last section will describe the issue of generalization.

ANALYSIS MUST BE
GUIDED BY THEORY

Deetz (1985, p. 15) describes the critical approach as "a theoretically guided political praxis." This description highlights the fact that in critical research the links from (and back to) theory and forward to (and back from) action are more important and more continuous than is the case in conventional approaches. Critical research is clearly theory-guided in that research questions and strategies are focused by the researcher's theoretical framework. The most important part of the connection between theory and research, however, exists in the theory's impact on the phrasing or focusing of the research interest. Two guidelines for focusing the research interest can be formulated, based on the central ideas of critique and non-linear causality.

Research Interests
Should Enable Critique

The nature of the question must reflect the idea of critique, that is, the interest in revealing contradictions and opposing forces in the existing social system. Often critique is hindered or facilitated simply by the way in which we focus our research interest. A by now well-known example of this is found in Burawoy's (1979) study of factory relations. Whereas studies of worker behavior and productivity typically phrase their interest around questions such as "Why don't workers work harder?" Burawoy was interested in the question "Why do workers work as hard as they do?" Clearly, although the first question accepts production as a natural and legitimate condition, thus thwarting the possibility of critique, the second question forces critique by viewing cooperation and production as accomplished constructions.

The study of power provides some other examples. The study of power in organizations typically has been based on, and I believe hampered by, an agency-based approach. Power and control are presented as resting in the hands of individuals who may or may not elect to exercise these powers. Obviously, power thus conceptualized obscures from examination the structural basis for power as well as the overall conditions for and effects of its existence and exercise. Studies using this approach easily accept existing structures as legitimate and become entangled in investigating individual motives and attributes. We can contrast this with Foucault's (1980) approach to power.

Foucault suggests that the study of power, broadly interpreted, has been organized from medieval times around the idea of legitimacy:

> The essential function of the discourse and technique of right has been to efface the domination intrinsic to power in order to present the latter at the level of appearance under two different aspects: on the one hand, as the legitimate rights of sovereignty, and on the other, as the legal obligation to obey it. (Foucault, 1980, p. 95)

By contrast, Foucault's very *formulation* of his own concern moves the attention away from rights as the legitimacy of power and to rights as the instrument and medium of domination, which enables as well as facilitates the critique of power relations. In studying power, Foucault wants to

> reverse the mode of analysis . . . to invert it, to give due weight that is, to the fact of domination, to expose both its latent nature and its brutality. . . .

Right should be viewed not in terms of a legitimacy to be established, but in terms of the methods of subjugation that it instigates. (Foucault, 1980, pp. 95-96)

The point here is that the quality of critical analysis is at least in part dependent upon the relationship between theory and research. Specifically, using critical theories as our guide, research questions should be conceptualized and formulated in such a way as to force and facilitate critique. The effect of this in many cases is one of shifting the interest away from the individual level and toward macro or relational levels.

Research Interests
Should Acknowledge
Complex Relations

Because the idea of complex, relational causality is so central in critical theories, it should be central also in critical research. This guideline suggests that the research questions should focus attention on *relations* and *conditions* rather than on particular, isolated expressions and manifestations.

The analysis should not concern itself with power at the level of conscious intention or decision; it should not attempt to consider power from its internal point of view and . . . it should refrain from posing the labyrinthine and unanswerable question: 'Who then has power and what has he [sic] in mind?'. . . . Instead it is a case of studying power at the point where its intention, if it has one, is completely invested in its real and effective practices. Let us not, therefore, ask why certain people want to dominate, what they seek, what is their overall strategy. Let us ask instead how things work at the level of on-going subjugation. . . . In other words, rather than ask ourselves how the sovereign appears to us in his [sic] lofty isolation, we should try to discover how it is that subjects are gradually, progressively, really and materially constituted through a multiplicity of organisms, forces, energies, materials, thoughts, etc. (Foucault, 1980, p. 97)

At the theoretical level, critical approaches remove part of the artificiality of the micro/macro distinction by conceptualizing complex and multiple relations connecting and intersecting between levels. At the research level, a first step toward carrying this through is accomplished by focusing the research interest properly, that is, making sure that the research interest reflects and accommodates both the idea of critique and idea of complex relations. The intended effect of this is to enable the researcher to *observe* — collect data and the like — a phenomenon at the microlevel, and *understand* it at the macrolevel. This idea is further developed in the next section.

RESEARCH AS THE
ONGOING DEVELOPMENT
OF UNDERSTANDING

The critical position asserts that social reality is not self-evident or self-explanatory; that explanations of social reality should not be located at the empirical level, but should instead be grounded in real generative mechanisms and tendencies; and that, as Hall (1985) has argued convincingly, no necessary correspondence exists between different practices and effects in a social formation.

Given this perspective, the idea of a linear relationship among data, analysis, and research is replaced by a concept of research as the *ongoing* process of the development of understanding, involving a continuous interaction between empirical description and theoretical explanation:

> This is not a one-sided interaction dominated by factual observations (empiricism) or by theory. Rather, there must be a continuing refinement of the (theoretical) model on the basis of more focused observations and of theoretical reflection, not simply of the facts immediately at hand but ranging across an array of accumulating knowledge of the social formation. (Benson, 1983, p. 334)

Seeing research as the ongoing development of understanding involves two questions that must be dealt with (1) the interpretive side of research and (2) the direction interpretation must take.

Research as Interpretation

The idea of research as interpretation is relevant in two ways. First, all descriptions of human conduct are hermeneutic:

> All social research involves a process of . . . the circling in and out of the forms of life that are the concern of analysis—picking up, developing, scrutinizing the mutual knowledge which is both the "means of access" to and the "research descriptions" derived from social investigations. (Giddens, 1983, p. 75-76)

Second, and more important, critical analysis in locating explanations of social phenomena in the totality of complex underlying interrelationships through "interpretative explication" (Thompson, 1984) necessarily goes "beyond the data."

> Setting the practice in relation to not just adjacent ones but to relevantly significant features of the wider social whole may lead to crucial redefinitions of

meanings and reappraisals of motives including those that formed the indispensable starting point of the research process. (Bhaskar, 1983, p. 88-89)

Critical research has been described by Benson (1983) and Outhwaite (1983) as involving two phases: a "description" phase and a "redescription" phase. The description phase involves a presentation of the phenomenon *as already defined* in everyday practice, that is, an account of the phenomenon as it exists in the social experience. The redescription phase, on the other hand, in effect recasts, redefines, and reinterprets the phenomenon "so as to bring out its complexity, i.e. the way in which it is determined by its internal and external relations as an outcome of a multiplicity of interacting tendencies" (Outhwaite, 1983, p. 328).

Thompson (1984) proposes a somewhat similar method in a three-phase process that he calls a "depth-interpretative procedure." Phase one of the procedure involves the description of the social-historical context and conditions, at micro-, meso-, and macrolevels. Phase two is discursive analysis, involving the study of situated linguistic constructions, again at different levels. Phase three finally is the interpretation phase that seeks to connect and explain the social and discursive factors and practices presented, among others, by showing how the relations between them serve to sustain relations of domination.

The idea of research as interpretation further alters the micro/macro distinction. The idea of theoretical guidance introduced earlier sought to bring about a redefinition of the social phenomenon early on in the research process, whereby phenomena are conceptualized critically and in the social context. This effect is carried through here into the actual research and analysis process. Although in the descriptive phase of research data may be collected at the microlevel, explanations or redescriptions recast the empirically based descriptions, thus eliminating exclusive micro- or macrobased understandings in favor of an understanding based on *relationships* between levels and practices.

The Direction of Analysis

As discussed above, interpretation—or redescription—changes the level at which we understand our research subject by relating it to the wider social formation. A related issue is the direction or order that this process of interpretation should take.

Here we can distinguish between ascending and descending orders of analysis. Descending analysis typically seeks to understand microlevel phenomena as effects or manifestations of macrolevel tendencies. Examples of approaches using descending analysis are Gramsci's concept of hegemony and Althusser's notions of "structure-in-dominance," "overdetermination," and "totality." For example:

If the conditions are no more than the current existence of the complex whole, they are its very contradictions, each reflecting in itself the organic relation it has with the others in the structure in dominance of the complex whole. Because each contradiction reflects in itself the structure in dominance of the complex whole in which it exists, and therefore of the current existence of this whole and therefore of its "current conditions", the contradiction is identical with these conditions: so when we speak of the "existing conditions" of the whole, we are speaking of its "conditions of existence." (Althusser, 1969, pp. 207-208)

Whereas descending analysis seeks to understand social phenomena as articulations of structural mechanisms and tendencies, ascending analysis takes a different approach. Starting at the microlevel, ascending analysis seeks to understand social phenomena both at their own relatively autonomous level and as parts of more global phenomena.

One must rather conduct an ascending analysis of power, starting, that is, from its infinitesimal mechanisms, which each have their own history, their own trajectory, their own techniques and tactics, and then see how these mechanisms of power have been—and continue to be—invested, colonised, utilised, involuted, transformed, displaced, extended etc. by ever more general mechanisms and by forms of global domination. (Foucault, 1980, p. 99)

Slack (1984, p. 11) has suggested that a combination of both approaches may be needed to "capture the interplay of power between macro- and micro-structures." Bhaskar (1983, p. 89) goes beyond that by stressing that "totalizing 'outwards' from a specific subject matter is never just a matter of drawing in further bits of knowledge; it is always potentially reciprocal." In the end, the issue of ascending versus descending analysis or some combination between the two is probably more an issue of theoretical taste than of accuracy, as each approach can accomplish the critical requirement of complex, multilevel explanation.

MAPPING OUT RELATIONS

As discussed above, critical analysis requires a "totalizing movement" that places empirical observations in relation to the core structures and tendencies of the social formation. These totalizing movements are and should be theoretically guided, in the sense that they should follow and reflect the relations indicated by the theoretical position used, allowing of course for developments and reformulations in the latter.

One of the problems, however, in critical organizational research has been that most critical literature contributes little to theorizing the organization as a social practice or as part of the larger social formation. The development, adaptation, and use of models that map out existing and potential relations within and between organizations and between organizations and society will greatly facilitate future critical organizational research.

A good example of a model, mapping out organizational and social relationships at and in terms of different levels, is provided by Clegg (1981). Starting from a definition of organizations as historically constituted, complex structures in motion, Clegg develops a class-based model of the relationship between organization and society. In this model, organizations are seen as the "sites of the social relations of production that define class structure" (p. 551). Control in organizations takes place through sedimented rule structures that operate at all levels within and outside the organization. Further, control systems themselves are seen as class conflicts, evolving from specific intra- and interorganizational relationships between parts of the organization and different levels of the societal class structure.

Clegg's model is a good example for critical organizational researchers in that it uses the idea of structural causality, based primarily on the concept of social class structure, while maintaining the idea of organizations as social formations in themselves. In doing so, the model avoids determinism, and still accounts for the power relations that exist between society and organizations.

In addition to developing new models, it is in some instances useful to "translate" or adapt social level concepts to the organizational level. Riley (1983) and Putnam (1985), for example, used Giddens's theory of structuration to study organizational processes and Kersten (1984) showed how organizations could be usefully conceptualized and studied on the basis of Althusser's interpretation of practices. Although these adaptations are of course not always possible or fruitful, in many cases they will facilitate making the micro/macro connections that are needed for critical organizational research.

MOVING BEYOND
THE SITUATION

So far the discussion has addressed problems that are encountered in making the transition back and forth between events, observed at the microlevel and in their particular form, and a theory that requires multilevel analysis. The last issue to be addressed here concerns a different type of problem, namely, how to move from the observation of particular situations and cases to a generalized understanding of the social world. The exact form of this type of move is of course determined by the particular phenomenon observed and the way it is related to the social structure at hand. However, there are a number of strategies proposed in the literature that, when used appropriately, may facilitate this part of the critical analysis.

First, there is the idea of "ideal types." The best known example of this in the critical tradition is probably Habermas's "ideal speech situation." The ideas found in most critical positions, such as the potential elimination of relations of domination or the identification of possibilities, can also be seen as ideal types. Ideal types are useful in analysis and generalization in that they provide a general standard of comparison, which is kept stable across different studies and situations, creating a basis for identifying common patterns. In addition, of course, ideal types are useful models for guiding action, as Forester (1980) demonstrates in his application of Habermas's model to the practice of community planning.

Second, there is the strategy of abstraction. Essentially what this idea emphasizes is the analysis of social situations, not with an interest in the particular details of that situation, but rather with an eye to its general features (Isaac, 1983). In Giddens's (1976) terms this involves the "methodological bracketing" of specific agents and their agency. Thus using a strategy of abstraction we may move from one case to another—allowing of course for situational variations—provided we have a sufficient understanding of which are the important general features and how they figure into the overall social formation of which both particular situations are a part. This strategy of abstraction is similar in a way to Yin's (1981) method of the case comparison approach. Yin compares this method to the craft of detective work, which emphasizes constructing plausible explanations capable of explaining different situations simultaneously.

Burawoy's (1985) work stands as an excellent example of the power of comparison. Burawoy applies his thesis that "the process of production decisively shapes the development of working class struggles" by analyzing similar conditions—shopfloor factory work—in radically different social contexts: the United States and Hungary. Not only does this type of analysis greatly contribute to understanding the relationship between the organization and the state, it also shows the pervasiveness of certain organizational conditions.

Third and last, particular situations may be understood better in relationship to others by focusing on the extremes of conditions. This is suggested among others by Foucault (1980, p. 97) who states that "one should try to locate power at the extreme points of its exercise." Bhaskar (1983, p. 91) also points out that "a long tradition in the human sciences from Marx, Durkheim, and Freud through to Garfinkel has confirmed the usefulness of the postulate of the methodological primacy of the pathological":

> Looking at failed, incompleted, bungled actions (unsuccessful species, fractured individuals, conflictual relations, contradictory systems) is not just as important; methodologically it is, if anything, more important. For in bringing out just those features of a successful action or adaptation which the very success of the action tends to elude or obscure, it guards against any reversion to a pre-Darwinian view of the world as either obvious (cf. empiricism) or numinous (cf. idealism). (Bhaskar, 1983, pp. 90-91)

CONCLUSION

Critical approaches to the study of society and organizations tend to favor theories and models that stress the complex processes of mutual determination and influence between human agency and social structure. Although these positions are theoretically stimulating, they have been difficult to apply in research studies. This chapter has been an attempt to facilitate this transition from theory to research and action by working through some of the problems and issues faced by researchers.

Obviously much work remains to be done, both in terms of dealing with the specific problems that were the concern of this chapter and in terms of related questions of method and explanation. The critical approach badly needs applications as well as examples, theoretical and practical ones. Ultimately the only protection—for any theory—against irrelevance lies in application and action. I hope the ideas suggested here will contribute to stimulating both.

REFERENCES

Althusser, L. (1969). *For Marx*. London: New Left Books.

Althusser, L. (1971). *Lenin and philosophy and other essays*. New York: Monthly Review Press.

Appelbaum, R., & Cotiner, H. (1979). Science, critique and praxis in Marxist method. *Socialist Review, 9,* 71-108.

Benson, J. K. (1983). Dialectical method for the study of organizations. In G. Morgan (Ed.), *Beyond method* (pp. 331-346). Beverly Hills, CA: Sage.

Bhaskar, R. (1979). *The possibility of naturalism: A philosophical critique of the contemporary human sciences*. Sussex: Harvester.

Bhaskar, R. (1983). Beef, structure and place: Notes from a critical naturalist perspective. *Journal for the Theory of Social Behaviour, 13,* 81-96.

Burawoy, M. (1979). *Manufacturing consent*. Chicago: University of Chicago Press.

Burawoy, M. (1985). *The politics of production*. London: Verso.

Clegg, S. (1981). Organization and control. *Administrative Science Quarterly, 26,* 545-562.

Collins, R. (1981). On the microfoundations of macrosociology. *American Journal of Sociology, 86,* 984-1014.

Collins, R. (1975). *Conflict sociology*. New York: Academic Press.

Connerton, P. (Ed.). (1978). *Critical sociology*. Harmondsworth, England: Penguin.

Dawe, A. (1978). Theories of social action. In T. Bottomore & R. Nisbet (Eds.), *A history of sociological analysis*. New York: Basic Books.

Deetz, S. (1985, May). *New sensibilities and old realities: The future of critical cultural research*. Paper presented at the International Communication Association Conference, Honolulu, Hawaii.

Deetz, S. A., & Kersten, A. (1983). Critical models of interpretive research. In L. L. Putnam and M. E. Pacanowsky (Eds.), *Communication and organizations*. (pp. 147-172). Beverly Hills, CA: Sage.

Emerson, M. (1984). Althusser on overdetermination and structural causation. *Philosophy Today, 28,* 203-214.

Forester, J. (1980). Critical theory and planning practice. *Journal of the American Planning Association, 46,* 275-286.

Foucault, M. (1980). Two lectures. In C. Gordon (Ed.), *Power and knowledge: Selected interviews and other writings 1972-1977* (pp. 78-108). New York: Pantheon.

Giddens, A. (1979). *Central problems in social theory.* Berkeley: University of California Press.

Giddens, A. (1983). Comments on the theory of structuration. *Journal for the Theory of Social Behaviour, 13,* 75-80.

Giddens, A. (1984). *The constitution of society.* Berkeley: University of California Press.

Grossberg, L. (1984). Strategies of Marxist cultural interpretation. *Critical Studies in Mass Communication, 1,* 392-421.

Hall, S. (1985). Signification, representation, ideology: Althusser and the post-structuralist debates. *Critical Studies in Mass Communication, 2,* 91-114.

Heydebrand, W. V. (1983). Organization and praxis. In D. Morgan (Ed.), *Beyond Method* (pp. 306-320). Beverly Hills, CA: Sage.

Isaac, J. (1983). Realism and social scientific theory: A comment of Porpora. *Journal for the Theory of Social Behaviour, 13,* 301-308.

Kersten, A. (1984, May). *Organizational control and the communication process.* Paper presented at the International Communication Association Conference, San Francisco, CA.

Kersten, A. (1985). Philosophical foundations for the construction of critical knowledge. In M. McLaughlin (Ed.), *Communication yearbook 9* (pp. 756-774). Beverly Hills, CA: Sage.

Layder, D. (1985). Power, structure and agency. *Journal for the Theory of Social Behaviour, 15,* 131-149.

Mayhew, B. (1980). Structuralism versus individualism, Part I: Shadowboxing in the dark. *Social Forces, 59,* 335-377.

Mayhew, B. (1981). Structuralism versus individualism, Part II: Ideological and other obfuscations. *Social Forces, 59,* 627-649.

Morgan, G. (Ed.). (1983). *Beyond method.* Beverly Hills, CA: Sage.

Outhwaite, W. (1983). Toward a realist perspective. In G. Morgan (Ed.), *Beyond method* (pp. 392-404). Beverly Hills, CA: Sage.

Pfeffer, J. (1982). *Organizations and organization theory.* Boston: Pitman.

Putnam, L. (1985, May). *Structural contradictions in a teachers' bargaining context.* Paper presented at the International Communication Association Conference, Honolulu, Hawaii.

Riley, P. (1983). A structurationist account of political culture. *Administrative Science Quarterly, 28,* 414-437.

Riley, P. (1985, May). *Critical perspectives in perspective: The use of power in organizational communication and applied settings.* Paper presented at the International Communication Association Conference, Honolulu, Hawaii.

Slack, J. D. (1984, May). *The development and rise of communication technologies: Critical issues.* Paper presented at the International Communication Conference, San Francisco.

Therborn, G. (1980). *The ideology of power and the power of ideology.* London: Verso.

Thompson, J. (1984). Ideology and the critique of domination, Part II. *Canadian Journal of Political and Social Theory, 8,* 179-196.

Wright, O. (1983). Capitalism's futures. *Socialist Review, 13,* 77-126.

Yin, R. (1981) The case study crisis: Some answers. *Administrative Science Quarterly, 26,* 58-65.

XI ● HUMAN COMMUNICATION TECHNOLOGY

34 ● The Case of the Intelligent Telephone: The Relationship of Job Category to the Adoption of an Organizational Communication Technology

RONALD E. RICE ● GEORGE G. MANROSS

University of Southern California

Instead of a one-to-one relationship between the technology and a particular organizational unit, the one-to-one relationship is between the tools and an organizational role. (Mohrman, 1982, p. 10)

Researchers are finding that the traditional process models of diffusion and implementation of computer-mediated communication technologies are occasionally inadequate for explaining why some innovations are adopted by the intended user community and others are rejected (see Berman & McLaughlin, 1978; Johnson & Rice, 1984, 1986; Rice, 1984; Rice & Rogers, 1980; Rogers, 1983; Yin, Heald, & Vogel, 1977). Thus, the search for a comprehensive adoption model continues.

The findings of a recent study by Manross and Rice (1986) involving the introduction of an "intelligent" telephone system at the West Coast offices of a Fortune 500 firm were yet another example of limitations in the traditional

AUTHORS' NOTE: We would like to thank Dr. Bill Hodge and Michael Cozzens for their input in helping us prepare this chapter.

Correspondence and requests for reprints: Ronald E. Rice, Annenberg School of Communications, University of Southern California, Los Angeles, CA 90089 model of diffusion (Rogers, 1983). Results of the prior study showed that technical and political factors were more powerful explanations of different levels of adoption than were traditional measures of attributes of the innovation and organizational innovativeness. Further, both the level of adoption and the perceived benefits of the innovation differed according to job category—whether a potential user is a manager, technician, or administrator. This chapter looks more closely at the influence of job category on perceived benefits and level of adoption of the intelligent telephone system.

RELATING ORGANIZATIONAL ROLE
TO THE ADOPTION OF
THE INTELLIGENT TELEPHONE

Tushman (1979) argues that in order to be effective in their respective missions, subunits within organizations must be able to attend to and deal with work-related uncertainty. To do this, subunits must be able to gather, process, and export information as well as receive feedback from different information sources (see also Driver & Streufert, 1969; Katz & Kahn, 1966; March & Simon, 1985; Thompson, 1967).

The types of information one needs and the manner of gathering this information differ, however, according to the role one plays within the organization. Individuals in different roles and jobs will use different media to accomplish their tasks, and use the same media differently.

The intelligent telephone may have inherent characteristics that make it one of the most appropriate communication technologies for studying differences in adoption patterns among job categories. Ithiel de Sola Pool (1983, p. 68) said the telephone "permits the operation of a complex division of labor." By this he meant that the telephone made it possible for people to stay in touch with one another without having to be in the same physical location. Perhaps of equal importance, however, is the fact that the telephone is so simple to use that it requires no special training or skills to operate. This cannot be said of such office automation technologies as a dumb terminal hooked to a mainframe computer, a personal computer, or even an electronic typewriter. An individual's job category is likely to influence the use and adoption of a new computer-mediated telephone system. Managers are likely to use a telephone to accomplish certain tasks (for example, keeping informed and maintaining control over subordinates), and clerks and secretaries use the same system to accomplish different tasks (for example, clarifying orders and staying in touch with coworkers and friends). Other types of personnel (for example, technical staff) might find the telephone an intrusive device, causing more interruptions than any other aspect of office life (Uhlig, Faber, & Bair, 1979).

Thus one's attitudes toward and usage of a given organizational medium may differ greatly for individuals in different job categories. Kerr and Hiltz

(1982) point out that although the ultimate impacts of new communication systems within an organization may be functional, dysfunctional, or neutral, they will be very different for different subgroups. They stress, therefore, that relationships between subgroups and impacts should be identified in order to ensure beneficial adoption by the intended users of such communication systems.

The next section identifies some of the aspects of innovations and organizations that influence to what extent users adopt the innovation. The subsequent section will consider how job categories and attributes of the innovation affect the levels of adoption of an intelligent telephone system.

VARIABLES INFLUENCING THE ADOPTION OF AN ORGANIZATIONAL INNOVATION

Diffusion theory, in its most familiar form, argues that potential adopters assess an innovation in order to reduce their uncertainty about the consequences and costs of adoption (Rogers, 1983). This assessment comprises five criteria: (1) its perceived relative advantage, (2) compatibility, (3) complexity, (4) trialability, and (5) observability.

Relative advantage is the degree to which a new idea is perceived by the user as being superior to the practice(s) it replaces; *compatibility*, the degree to which a new idea is perceived as being consistent with a potential adoptor's prior experience, beliefs, and values; *complexity*, the degree to which an innovation is perceived by the user as being difficult to understand; *trialability* or *divisibility*, the degree to which a new idea can be given small scale trial by a potential adopter, or the extent to which parts of the innovation may be tried; and finally, *observability* or *communicability*, the degree to which a new idea is visible to potential adopters.

Evidence about the innovation's attributes often come from observing others' uses of the innovation, and by learning more about it through various communication channels including the interpersonal channel (see Coleman, Katz, & Menzel, 1966) or mass media (see Rice & Paisley, 1981). "A system is likely to succeed if the people involved associate with it favorable — and realistic — meanings and expectations of the benefits" (Lippitt, Miller, & Halamaj, 1980).

In short, innovations that are perceived as high in relative advantage, low in complexity and high in compatibility, communicability, and divisibility have a more rapid rate of adoption. There are several additional factors that influence the ultimate success or failure of a new communication system within its intended user community.

Key actors are important factors in the adoption process. These include gatekeepers, opinion leaders, change agents, and the intended user community (Lucas, 1981; Tornatzky et al., 1980), as well as management, technical personnel, and administrative staff (Bikson, Gutek, & Mankin, 1982; Driver & Mock, 1975). Organizational forces such as power, politics, and the symbolic use of the innovation are often used or channeled by these key actors (Danzinger, Dutton, Kling, & Kraemer, 1982; Dutton, 1981; Feldman & March, 1981; Keen, 1981; Kling, 1980; Markus, 1981). The nature of one's job is likely to affect not only how influential one can be in influencing others to adopt, but also how important it is for the job incumbent to adopt the innovation.

Potential users are now recognized as a major influence on implementation efforts. Influences on adoption include the role perceived needs play (technology pull versus technology push) in the successful adoption of new technologies (Ackoff, 1967; Hopelain, 1982; Rogers, 1983); potential users' attitudes toward the system (Coe & Barnhill, 1967; Danzinger, Dutton, Kling, & Kraemer, 1982; Keen, 1981; Kling, 1980; Rice, 1980; Rice & associates, 1984); users' allegiance to some entity other than the organization (Kole, 1983; Rudawitz & Freeman, 1981); information workers' stress (Keen, 1981; Zuboff, 1982); and their amount of actual use of the new system (Hiltz & Turoff, 1981; Mohrman, 1982).

In general, in order for an office information system to be adopted by intended users, a process of "mutual adaptation" must take place. On the one hand, the work unit must understand and respond to the system's requirements. On the other hand, the information system must meet the needs and desires of the work unit and the organization. The key to this mutual adaptation is an interaction of four factors: design of the system, management support, user participation, and training.

More thorough discussions of the literature regarding the diffusion and implementation of computer-based communication technologies can be found elsewhere (Ives & Olson, 1984; Lucas, 1981; Mankin, Bikson, & Gutek, 1982; Tornatzky et al., 1983). However, this brief outline of some of the factors influencing attitudes toward and adoption of innovations such as the intelligent telephone should serve as a useful context in which to place the findings that follow.

HYPOTHESIZED MODEL OF THE INFLUENCE OF JOB CATEGORY ON PERCEIVED ADOPTION AND BENEFITS OF THE INTELLIGENT TELEPHONE

The prior discussion leads to the general hypothesis that three factors— organizational role (as measured by *job category*), *attitudes* toward the technology (as measured by perceived appropriateness of the intelligent telephone), and the amount of time one spends *using the telephone* in one's daily work pattern—are indicators of the *level of adoption* (as measured by number of functions used) immediately following introduction to the enhanced telephone system and users' *perceived benefits* of the new system. The hypothesized path model is shown in Figure 34.1. More generally stated, perceptions of benefits and use of the innovation are predicted by attitudes and behaviors. The behavior of using the phone in one's daily work is an indirect measure of information needs satisfied using that particular channel. Job category is hypothesized to play a separate part, over and above attitudes and behaviors, in explaining outcomes of the implementation process.

DATA

A high-technology Fortune 500 firm recently installed an enhanced telephone switching system—commonly known as the "intelligent telephone"—at two of its office complexes located on the West Coast near Los Angeles. Both complexes employed about 700 employees and were similarly organized and staffed. These two sites are the first of many units within the company that will eventually use an intelligent system. The firm's implementation strategy is consciously incremental. This will allow results from the early adoption efforts to be used to guide later implementation efforts. The particular intelligent switch installed in this situation provides up to 200 different functions, which is standard for most current on-site telephone switches. Some of the functions include do not disturb, executive busy override, distinctive ringing, digit translation, and automatic call distribution.

From an engineering viewpoint, of course, the intelligent telephone switching system is radically different from the regular business telephone service generally available from the local operating company. Besides the capabilities noted above, the intelligent system is capable of transmitting both voice and data simultaneously over a single pair of standard telephone wires by converting analog voice signals to digital signals (White, 1985). The intelligent switching system can also serve as a digital interface between a desktop terminal (for example, personal computer or word processor) and a mainframe computer (for example, mini-computer). As a result, data can be transported among computers via existing phone wire in order to access individual, corporate, and outside data bases, as well as communicating via electronic mail.

For individual users, these capabilities include such functions as call-forwarding, call-holding, automatic redial, conference calling, and even a "do not disturb" feature.

In addition to the user-oriented functions of the enhanced switching system, it has features designed for the system's manager. The "message reporting" feature keeps a record of each and every call, for example; "outward toll dial" tracks and records outgoing long distance calls for each

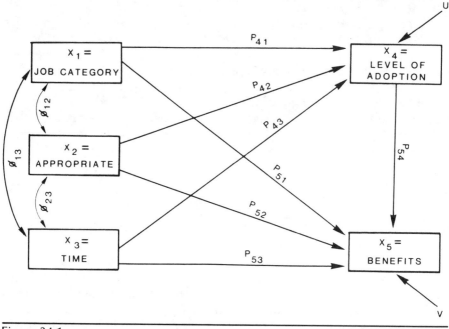

Figure 34.1

station; and "automatic billing" not only keeps a record of usage, but automatically invoices the appropriate division or department within the organization. And although the company has not yet done so, management can purchase additional software that allows telephone activity records to be stored electronically for use in preparing other kinds of reports. In short, the intelligent switching system literally turns the telephone into a hand terminal linked to a mainframe computer.

The sample for this study consisted of 7 key informants and 100 employees who had been introduced to the intelligent telephone when it was originally installed for use in the 2 office complexes. There were 50 names randomly selected from each building. Some of these individuals were no longer located in the building where they first used the enhanced phone system. However, they were still requested to participate in the study and were asked to base their input on their best recollection of their initial experience.

METHOD

Open-ended interviews were conducted with six managers involved in the decision to implement the intelligent telephone and one other person.

These seven people included the person who conducts a major portion of the user training on the new intelligent telephone system; a Senior Communications Analyst who had been watching over this project from its inception and is committed to its ultimate success; a Senior Communications Analyst who came to the corporation from one of the telephone companies, and who approaches the introduction of telephony from a more technical viewpoint; a Manager of Research; the Manager of Communications; the Operations Supervisor, who was the highest person in the management hierarchy we interviewed and who was extremely knowledgeable about the history and growth pattern of the telephone in society; and one additional person who was chosen because she had undergone the training phase of learning to use the intelligent telephone.

The 100 respondents were asked to complete a questionnaire and return it to the Communications Department (via interdepartmental mail) within 48 hours of receipt. A cover letter informed them that the study was part of an effort to analyze the intelligent telephone in order to determine whether or not it was a useful instrument for the majority of the employees at this firm. This message was personally reinforced by the respondents' immediate supervisor. All respondents were assured of the complete confidentiality of their responses; their responses were anonymous. A total of 42 people returned their questionnaires from the first of the 2 facilities and 40 employees participated from the second facility, representing an 82% response rate.

Respondents were asked to recall the number of functions used at two separate points in time.[1] The times were (1) time 1, immediately after being trained in the use of the new telephone system or about a year before; and (2) time 2, the present.

The *number of functions* from among the 200 that were available to the user was chosen as an indicator of "level of adoption" of the enhanced telephone system. It is these features that set this particular technology apart from the traditional business phone, as they are made possible by the computing power of the in-house telephone switching system. It seems reasonable to assume, therefore, that the greater the number of functions one uses from among those that are available, the more one has adopted the new technology.[2]

Respondents were also asked the percentage of time in an average working day they spent using the telephone. Other variables that compose the scales used in this analysis resulted from a series of questions designed to help identify and understand the attributes that contribute to the acceptance or rejection of the intelligent telephone. For example, several questions asked respondents to rate the system on specific measures of relative advantage, complexity, compatibility, communicability, status, reliability, innovativeness, productivity, and impacts. Finally, the measures of impacts on communication activities were variables used in a previous study of an electronic mail system (Rice & Case, 1983), which in turn were developed to replicate earlier studies (as reviewed in Rice, 1980).

The exogenous and endogenous variables were combined in a path analysis to identify significant paths corresponding to the hypothesized relations.

Path analysis is useful in making explicit the rationale of conventional regression calculations. Although path analysis is not a method for discovering causes, it is an analytical technique that can be applied to a causal model formulated by the researchers on the basis of knowledge and theoretical considerations (Duncan, 1966; Pedhazur, 1982). "It is intended to combine the quantitative information given by the correlations with such qualitative information as may be at hand on causal relations to give a quantitative interpretation" (Wright, 1934, in Pedhazur, 1982, p. 580).

RESULTS

In order to identify the underlying factors that accounted for what the users perceived as being the *attributes* and *impacts* of the enhanced telephone system, the attribute variables and the impact variables were each subjected to factor analysis. The findings, along with brief descriptions of the items, appear in Tables 34.1 and 34.2.

Perceived attributes of the intelligent telephone and the organizational context produced five factors explaining 68.4% of the variance. They were labeled (1) appropriateness, (2) complexity, (3) functionality, (4) good system, and (5) status. Perceived impacts of the new technology produced three factors explaining 66.2% of the variance. They were labeled (1) task benefits, (2) usefulness, and (3) traffic. Scales were created from these results, as explained in the notes to Table 34.1. The created scales "Appropriateness" and "Task Benefits" were used in subsequent analyses to represent attitudes and impacts.

The managerial change agents indicated in the open-ended interviews that they anticipated some differences in the acceptance level among the three categories of employees. For example, many of the firm's management and technical personnel are also scientists who operate in what some there call an "Einstein environment" (a think tank). These individuals apparently see the telephone as a necessary evil that interrupts their "think time"; thus no automated system would be seen as an improvement. Our interviewees believed that managers were therefore less willing to use the phone than other people.

The questionnaire data show lower levels of telephone usage for managers and technical personnel than for administrative personnel (14%, 11%, and 28%, respectively, of an average working day) ($F(2,78) = 12.2, p <$

Table 34.1
Factor Analysis of Impacts of Enhanced Telephone System

| | Factors | | | | |
| | | | | Good | |
Variables*	Appropriateness	Complexity	Functionality	System	Status
Status:					
Having	-0.11387	-0.04992	*0.79491*	-0.24610	0.29745
Knowing how to use	-0.06254	-0.08746	0.09005	0.23007	*0.79820*
Difficult/easy:					
System features	-0.11431	*0.85394*	0.13960	0.05279	-0.00440
Remembering codes	0.02876	*0.72619*	-0.03021	0.30168	-0.13711
Help from monitors	0.13873	*0.69740*	-0.10236	-0.00721	0.16377
Help from co-workers	0.09217	*0.51615*	-0.04068	-0.06321	0.64052
Reliability	0.09581	0.02649	-0.00322	*0.77803*	0.24453
Innovative system	-0.01949	0.11091	0.05228	*0.79771*	-0.00700
Appropriateness for:					
Exchanging info.	0.29036	0.32897	0.48333	0.56503	-0.06889
Bargaining/negotiating	*0.71287*	0.09608	0.16368	-0.03373	0.06492
Getting to know people	*0.67366*	0.10046	-0.12522	0.15522	-0.17640
Asking questions	0.38153	0.14600	*0.73087*	0.31935	-0.12568
Staying in touch	0.45463	-0.17978	*0.70987*	0.25432	-0.08192
Generating ideas	*0.79065*	0.05985	0.13268	0.07326	0.03109
Solving disagreements	*0.78752*	-0.15148	0.16252	-0.00950	0.05008
Eigenvalues	3.81	2.36	1.57	1.38	1.14
% Variance explained	25.40	15.73	10.46	9.22	7.61
Alpha reliability**	.76	.69	.68	.66	—
Nonmissing N of scale	69	67	70	79	82

* All items five-point scale except Status: Having (1 = yes, 2 = not sure, 3 = no) and Appropriateness items (1 = appropriate, 2 = not). "5" indicated "very easy," "significantly increased" or similar scale anchor on all other items.

** Scales representing factors were constructed by taking the average of variables loading at least .6 on one factor and no more than .4 on any other factor. The scale value was set to missing if more than 15% of the constituent variables had missing values. Several exceptions were intended to keep conceptually similar variables together. For example, although "exchanging info," "asking questions," and "staying in touch" loaded on a separate factor, they were added in the "Appropriateness" scale. The alpha for the four-item scale was .76; adding the three other appropriateness items raised the alpha to .83. Scale items are italicized. The status scale is only one variable, so no alpha is reported.

.001). This differential usage of the business phone—implying differential needs for the innovation (the intelligent telephone)—was associated with different levels of adoption ($r = .53$, $N = 74$, $p < .0001$). The number of functions adopted was also lower for managers than technical personnel (2.5, 3.0 and 4.2, respectively) ($F(2,71) = 4.7$, $p < .01$). However, level of perceived benefit did not differ significantly by job category (3.22, 3.14, and 3.03, respectively) ($F(2,75) = .83$, p < .45). Nor did the perceived

Table 34.2

Factor Analysis of Impacts of Enhanced Telephone System

| | Factors | | |
Variables*	Task Benefits	Usefulness	Traffic
Decrease/Increase in:			
phone usage	0.50427	0.07882	0.55844
calls received	0.35155	0.05320	0.67471
quantity of work	0.79387	−0.14944	0.12197
quality of work	0.65404	0.48689	0.20786
rate of handling info.	0.21479	0.77524	0.31791
contacts you initiate	0.67776	0.39178	0.32962
contacts others initiate with you	0.54719	0.34312	0.43838
communications from superiors	0.75016	0.29679	0.18203
communications to superiors	0.82305	0.30263	0.22549
communication with other divisions	0.74091	0.24117	0.30368
number of times leave desk	0.28830	0.53010	−0.44424
amount of after-hours work	0.72616	0.28410	−0.00862
New system helps avoid busy signals	0.09793	0.20894	0.77705
Difficult/easy to do without new phone	0.13136	0.77723	0.10412
Eigenvalues	6.72	1.41	1.14
% variance explained	47.99	10.06	8.16
Alpha reliability**	.92	.63	.68
Nonmissing N of scale	77	76	77

* All items five-point scale: "5" indicated "very easy," "significantly increased" or similar scale anchor.

** Scales representing factors were constructed by taking the average of variables loading at least .6 on one factor and no more than .4 on any other factor. The scale value was set to missing if more than 15% of the constituent variables had missing values.

appropriateness of the system vary by job category (1.55 for each) ($F(2,67)$ = .01, $p < .99$).

Three path models were analyzed[3] in order to compare the effect of each of the three job categories, telephone usage, and attitudes toward the innovation. Figures 34.2 and 34.3 show the results of the models, the first with job category as a separate, dummy variable, and the second with separate path models run for each job category.

Looking at job category separately (Figure 34.2), there is no effect of "appropriateness" and there is little effect of job category. Further, the only strong and consistent relationship was between time spent using the telephone and number of functions used (standardized *beta* coefficient = .53, .55, .51, respectively, $p < .0001$). Only the administrative position had a significant effect: Administrative personnel were significantly likely to report a lower level of benefits (*beta* = −.32, $p < .05$). Thus knowing one's job

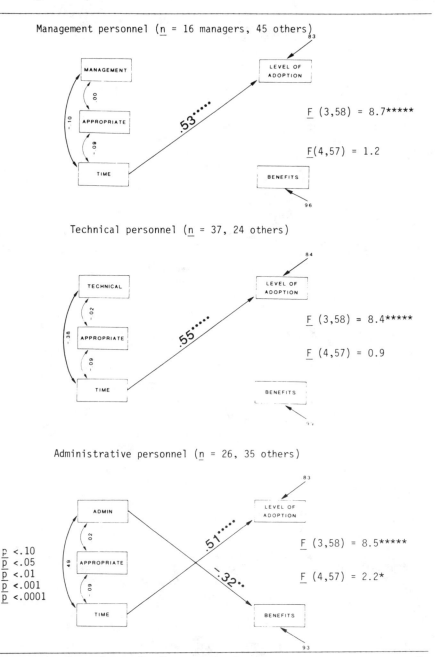

Figure 34.2 Path analysis of influence of job category, appropriateness and time spent using the telephone, on adoption and perceived benefits of using an intelligent telephone system.

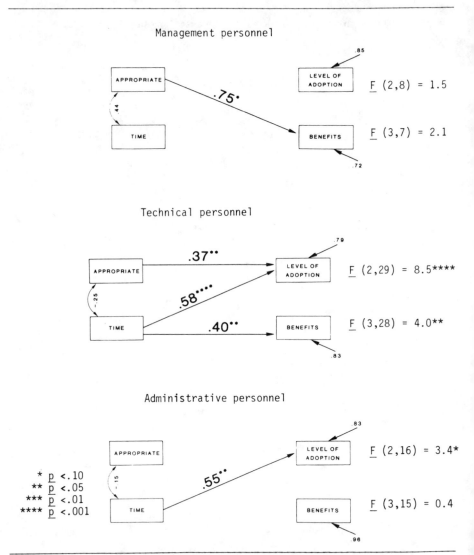

Management personnel

Technical personnel

Administrative personnel

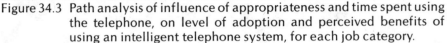

Figure 34.3 Path analysis of influence of appropriateness and time spent using the telephone, on level of adoption and perceived benefits of using an intelligent telephone system, for each job category.

category is useful in predicting only the level of adoption of the intelligent telephone by administrative personnel, who paradoxically do not report as high a level of benefits as managerial or technical staff do.

Another way of looking at job effect is to compare the model across job category samples (Figure 34.3). Clearly, the models do vary by job category, because job category differences are embedded in the "appropriateness" and "time using the telephone" variables. Managerial personnel show a relationship between attitude and benefits. Administrative personnel show a relationship between time using the phone and level of adoption. This analysis indicates that managers' responses to the innovation are strictly oriented toward attitudes and outcomes, and administrators' responses to the innovation are strictly oriented to needs and adoption behavior. Technical personnel show an interrelationship of attitudes and needs to outcomes and adoption behavior. Technical personnel are the only ones who "behave" as the general model predicted respondents would.

There is only one main factor that is independent of job category in influencing use and benefits of the system. Use of the regular business telephone—a clear basis on which to judge the relative advantage of the new system—is related to the level of adoption of the new system. That is, need leads to use. Attitudes about the appropriateness of the system are essentially not related to perceived benefits of the system, except in the model using managers only. That is, subjective assessments of the attributes of the innovation do not lead to perceived benefits of the innovation. Throughout, these two sets of relations are independent (except for the model for technical personnel only). It seems that assessments of *attributes* or *benefits* of the system do not interact with *needs* and *use* of the system. Thus evaluations of implementation strategies, adoption criteria, adoption level, and user satisfaction cannot ignore either the instrumental or the affective components. For managers and administrators, positive attitudes here are not related to adoption; real task needs are not related to subsequent perceived benefits.

Job category moderately influences the two outcome dimensions. Management and technical personnel discriminate among adoption levels (they adopt the system less) and administrative personnel seem to discriminate among the evaluation levels (they perceive fewer benefits). Perhaps management's secretarial gatekeepers decrease their direct use of the system, or management's communication norms preclude higher adoption of such an innovation. Technical personnel, taken separately, show the most relations of attitudes and needs to adoption and benefits. Perhaps due to the detailed and skeptical attitude of technical personnel toward the new system, positive attitudes and needs were far more influential than for the other positions. Administrative personnel, who use the phone twice as much as the other two positions, use the new system accordingly more, but derive significantly less benefit from the system. They "adopt" the system but do not really "accept" it. They may have more sensitive thresholds for perceived satisfaction with such innovations.

The results were then compared with the qualitative interviews with the change agents. The change agents were partially correct when they predicted differences in behavior and attitudes among the three categories of employees. They were correct when they predicted that both managers and technical personnel would probably not use the enhanced telephone system very much.

SUMMARY

The most general finding of this study was that political factors interacted with technical factors in determining the outcome of an attempt to implement an intelligent telephone system in two large divisions of a Fortune 500 company. Traditional diffusion variables such as attributes of the innovation and organizational innovation did not distinguish between the "success" and the "failure" buildings.

Job category plays a moderate part in explaining levels of adoption and perceived benefits of the intelligent telephone system.

The concept of job category as one indicator of organizational role should be included and expanded in future models of the adoption of organizational computer-based information technologies. In particular, it would help to understand just what components of job categories lead to these different outcomes, and in what ways these are separate from attitudes and use of current, related media.

Of importance to the study of the adoption of new communication technologies is that affective aspects studied in the present research—attitudes toward and benefits of the innovation—are independent of behavioral aspects—phone use and level of adoption. This absence of linkage could mean unsuccessful and unjustified implementation efforts and dissatisfied or uninterested users. Job category does not influence the relationship of affective and behavioral aspects of adoption directly, but does affect each aspect differentially. Therefore, it seems important and useful to identify this relationship, explore it further, and apply this understanding to managing the process of adopting organizational communication systems.

NOTES

1. That bias and estimation problems are present in measures of system usage based on recall is undeniable. The problem of inaccuracy in respondents' reports of their use of information systems is discussed, along with some suggested solutions, in Rice & associates (1984, p. 208). Ideally, computer-monitored usage statistics should be used (Rice & Borgman, 1983). However, such records were not available to the authors. The authors realize that the reported number of functions used nearly a year before is a weak and suspect measure of initial adoption. Further, reports of adoption at time 1 and time 2, collected at the same time, are likely to be correlated due to halo effects. The likely effect, for our purposes, is (a) to introduce measurement error, and (b) to bias time 1 reports to match time 2 reports. Both effects will operate *against* finding significant differences or correlations.

2. Although a more detailed measure of adoption would be the frequency of using specific functions such as reported, recalled measure would be even less reliable than the current indicator of adoption. Of course, the danger here is in not counting *extensive* use of *one* new function as being "adoptive" behavior.

3. The organizational role variables (job categories) are nominal and not hierarchical in nature. Therefore, in order to produce a usable path coefficient, they were each entered into the appropriate regressions in the path models by creating dummy codes for each job category. Separate path models were then run for each category. Results are shown in Figure 34.2. The alternative approach is to run each regression separately for each job category. Results are shown in Figure 34.3. The disadvantage of the first approach is that for each dummy variable the *joint* effects of the other two categories are merged in the "∅" value, possibly masking true effects of the job category being analyzed. Further, the regressions are not strictly independent as any two dummy variables share the third job category cases in the "∅" value. The advantage is that the separate effect of job category can be determined. The disadvantage of the second approach is that the sample size drops drastically, reducing the possibility of significant results. Further, the effect of the particular job category is revealed only through the "appropriateness" and "time spent using the telephone" variables. The advantage is the strict independence of models.

REFERENCES

Ackoff, R. (1967). Management misinformation systems. *Management Science, 14,* 147-156.

Berman, P., & McLaughlin, M. W. (1978). *Federal programs supporting educational change: Implementing and sustaining innovations* (Vol. 3). Santa Monica, CA: Rand Corporation.

Bikson, T. K., Gutek, B., & Mankin, E. (1982). *Implementation of information technology in office systems: Review of relevant literature.* Santa Monica, CA: Rand Corporation.

Coe, R. M., & Barnhill, E. A. (1967). Social dimensions of failure of innovations. *Human Organization, 26,* 149-156.

Coleman, J., Katz, K., & Menzel, H. (1966). *Medical innovation: A diffusion study.* New York: Bobbs-Merrill.

Danzinger, J., Dutton, W., Kling, R., & Kraemer, K. (1982). *Computers and politics: High technology in American local government.* New York: Columbia University Press.

Driver, M., & Mock. T. (1975). Human information processing, decision style theory, and accounting information systems. *The Accounting Review, 50,* 490-508.

Driver, M., & Streufert, S. (1969). Integrative complexity: An approach to individuals and groups as information-processing systems. *Administrative Science Quarterly, 14,* 272-285.

Duncan, O. D. (1966). Path analysis: Sociological examples. *American Journal of Sociology, 72,* 1-16.

Dutton, W. (1981). The rejection of an innovation: The political environment of a computer-based model. *Systems, Objectives, Solutions,* 179-201.

Feldman, M., & March, J. (1981). Information in organizations as signal and symbol. *Administrative Science Quarterly, 26,* 171-186.

Hiltz, S. R., & Turoff, M. (1981). The evolution of user behavior in a computerized conferencing system. *Communications of the ACM, 24,* 739-751.

Hopelain, D. G. (1982). Assessing the climate for change: A method for managing change in a system implementation. *Systems, Objectives, Solutions, 2,* 55-65.

Ives, B., & Olson, M. (1984). User involvement and MIS success: A review of research. *Management Science, 30,* 586-603.

Johnson, B. M., & Rice, R. E. (1984). Reinvention in the innovation process: The case of word processing. In R. E. Rice & Associates, *The new media: Communication, research and technology* (pp. 157-184). Beverly Hills, CA: Sage.

Johnson, B. M., & Rice, R. E. (1986). *Managing organizational innovation: The evolution from word processing to office information systems.* New York: Columbia University Press.

Katz, D., & Kahn, R. (1966). *The social psychology of organizations.* New York: John Wiley.

Keen, P. (1981). Information systems and organizational change. *Communications of the ACM, 24,* 24-33.

Kerr, E. B., & Hiltz, S. R. (1982). *Computer-mediated communication systems: Status and evaluation.* New York: Academic Press.

Kling, R. (1980). Social analyses of computing: Theoretical perspectives in recent empirical research. *Computing Surveys, 12,* 61-110.

Kole, M. A. (1983). A non-developmental MIS strategy for small organizations. *Systems, Objectives, Solutions, 3,* 31-39.

Lippitt, M., Miller, J., & Halamaj, J. (1980). *Patterns of use and correlates of adoption of an electronic mail system.* Las Vegas, NV: The American Institute of Decision Sciences Proceedings.

Lucas, H. C. (1981). *Implementation: The key to successful information systems.* New York: Columbia University Press.

Mankin, D., Bikson, T. K., & Gutek. B. (1982). The office of the future: Prison or paradise? *The Futurist, 16,* 33-37.

Mankin, D., Bikson, T. K., & Gutek, B. (1983). Factors in successful implementation of computer-based office information systems: A review of the literature with suggestions for OBM research. Submitted to *Journal of Organizational Behavior Management,* August.

Manross, G. G., & Rice, R. E. (1986). Don't hang up! Organizational diffusion of the intelligent telephone. *Information and Management, 10*(3), 161-175.

March, J. G., & Simon, H. A. (1985). *Organizations.* New York: John Wiley.

Markus, L. (1981) Implementation politics: Top management support and user involvement. *Systems, Objectives, Solutions, 1,* 203-215.

Mohrman, A. (1982, July). *The impact of information processing technologies on office roles.* Paper presented at the annual meeting of the World Futures Society, Washington, D. C.

Pedhazur, E. (1982). *Multiple regression in behavioral research* (2nd ed.). New York: Holt, Rinehart & Winston.

Pool, I. de Sola (1983). *Forecasting the telephone: A retrospective technology assessment.* Norwood, NJ: Ablex Publishing Corporation.

Rice, R. E., & Associates (1984). *The new media: Communication, research and technology.* Beverly Hills, CA: Sage.

Rice, R. E. (1980) Impacts of organizational and interpersonal computer-mediated communication. In M. Williams (Ed.), *Annual Review of Information Science and Technology: Vol. 15* (pp. 221-249). White Plains, NY: Knowledge Industry Publications.

Rice, R. E. (1984). Evaluating new media systems. *New Directions in Program Evaluation, 23,* 52-67.

Rice, R. E., & Borgman, C. (1983). The use of computer-monitored data in information science and communication research. *Journal of the American Society for Information Science, 34,* 247-256.

Rice, R. E., & Case D. (1983). Computer-based messaging in the university: A description of use and utility. *Journal of Communication, 33,* 131-152.

Rice, R. E., & Paisley, W. (Eds.). (1981). *Public communication campaigns.* Beverly Hills, CA: Sage.

Rice, R. E., & Rogers, E. M. (1980). Re-invention in the innovation process. *Knowledge: Creation, Diffusion, Utilization, 1,* 499-514.

Rogers, E. M. (1983). *Diffusion of innovations.* New York: Free Press.

Rudawitz, L. M., & Freeman, P. (1981). Client-centered design: Concepts and experience. *Systems, Objectives, Solutions, 1,* 21-32.

Thompson, J. D. (1967). *Organizations in action.* New York: McGraw-Hill.

Tornatzky, L., Eveland, J. D., Boylan, M. G., Hetzner, E. C., Johnson, D., Roitman, D., & Schneider, J. (1983). *The process of technological innovation: Reviewing the literature.* Washington DC: National Science Foundation.

Tushman, M. L. (1979). Work characteristics and subunit communication structure: A contingency analysis. *Administrative Science Quarterly, 24,* March, 82-98.

Uhlig, R., Faber, D., & Bair, J. (1979). *The office of the future.* New York: North-Holland.

White, E. (1985, September 16). The digital dilemma: 'Smart phones' can be long term money savers, but adjusting to them can be frustrating. *The Wall Street Journal,* p. 38.

Yin, R. K., Heald, K. A., & Vogel, M. E. (1977). *Tinkering with the system: Technological innovations in state and local services.* Lexington, MA: Lexington Books.

Zuboff, S. (1982). New worlds of computer-mediated work. *Harvard Business Review, 20,* 142-152.

35 ● A Typology for Interactive Media

JEROME T. DURLAK

York University

THE original idea for this topic began as a response to remarks by advocates for new communication technologies and mass media reporters who called Telidon and the QUBE cable system "interactive" media and took it for granted that everyone shared a common meaning for the term.[1] The implication was that the "interactivity" of these media represented revolutionary breakthroughs that would radically improve human communication. Although both these media were potentially interactive (that is, they had the potential to allow mutual discourse through an electronic mail or conferencing service, and so on), their actual implementation (the user could only select once from a single group of options) was reactive or "pseudointeractive" at best.

Friendly discussions of ideas of media "interactivity" among media professionals or academics in communications, computer science, sociology, and psychology often became heated debates. Few of us consider the same set of variables and, therefore, few of us had the same meaning for "interactive" media. The object of this chapter, then, is to present a more comprehensive as well as provocative typology for determining the extent to which a medium is "interactive" in the hope of encouraging a more enlightened dialogue.[2]

CONTEXT

To set the boundaries for the discussion of the typology it would be useful to state a number of givens, which are listed below.

(1) Interactive media systems include the telephone; "two-way television; audio conferencing systems; computers used for communication; electronic mail; videotext; and a variety of technologies that are used to exchange information in the form of still images, line drawings, and data."[3]

Correspondence and requests for reprints: Jerome T. Durlak, Mass Communication Programme, York University, 4700 Keele Street, North York, Ontario, Canada M3J 1PB3.

(2) The emergence of the above media means that the discrete distinctions among intrapersonal, interpersonal, and mass-mediated communication is giving way to a continuum of communication behaviors.

(3) Until now the ideal means of interactive communication has been face-to-face communication.

(4) Face-to-face communication is held up as the model because the sender and receiver use all their senses, the reply is immediate, the communication is generally closed circuit, and the content is primarily informal or "ad-lib" (Bretz, 1983, pp. 22-23).

(5) Fully interactive media imply that the sender and receiver roles are interchangeable; they imply that there be a response from A to B based on B's response to A's first initiation (Bretz, 1983, p. 13).

(6) A or B does not have to be human.

(7) Interactive media always include at least two channels facing in opposite directions, or a single channel that is reversible (for example, telephone and a push-to-talk intercom).

(8) Joining a computer (on a continuum from microprocessor to mainframe) to a medium or transmission system enables interactivity among the system components, as well as A's and/or B's control over the pace, structure, and content of the communication (Rice, 1984, p. 35).[4]

(9) For this chapter "a medium is a technological system for conveying messages, operating intermediately between sender(s) and receiver(s), when they are separated in space, time, or both."[5]

(10) Communication means or tools are the ways we have of forming messages and communication media are used to transmit such means.

(11) Finally, "the quality and effectiveness of a message depend on how well the message is expressed by the sender and understood by the receiver, and usually only secondarily on the characteristics of the medium that transmits or records it" (Bretz, 1983, p. 26).

We begin our account by examining the intentions of designers of interactive media systems, an area that is usually overlooked by communication researchers. Interactive media designers pursue three general goals. The first is to simulate, within the limitations of the medium, the experiences of face-to-face communications. An example is the **MISAR II** video conferencing system. When two people speak simultaneously, the voice controlled system produces a split-screen composite of the two shots so that both people are shown at once, life-size. The second involves maintaining the illusion. In the words of Alan Kay, an *Apple* Fellow: "You have to have immediacy, that is what maintains the user illusion, the involvement with the task itself rather than being distracted by the equipment. Any lag at all breaks the fantasy." The third element of the design process is to go beyond the possibilities of face-fo-face meetings and develop new possibilities for communication. In other words, the media system becomes an intelligence, fantasy or creativity amplifier (Kay & Goldberg, 1977; Licklider & Taylor, 1968). In the **MISAR II** system, continuing the above example, all the participants have a ten-button "Image Pad" to select manually additional camera targets such as blackboard and other graphic devices, slides, videotape, and so on. The first design goal "characterizes particularly the voice-based media, and the third is an objective mainly of computer designers" (Bretz, p. 174). For the typology, then, the three main objectives of the design process are

(1) SIMULATING FACE-TO-FACE COMMUNICATION
(2) MAINTAINING THE ILLUSION
(3) MIND AMPLIFICATION

COMPONENTS OF AN INTERACTIVE MEDIA SYSTEM

For the typology, the components that make up a media system include in most cases the **HARDWARE** (equipment), **SOFTWARE** (ranging from a computer algorithm to a schedule for a teleconference), **TOOLS** (the applications) and **PEOPLE[WARE]** (the creative, integrative, and technical people involved in production and operation). One of the difficulties in focusing on "interactivity" is that it is becoming more difficult to find out where, for example, hardware ends and software/tools or people begin. For example, the MacIntosh desktop computer contains two ROM chips (hardware) with 64K bytes of handcrafted system software that, besides performing traditional operating system functions such as memory and file management (software), contains a Quickdraw package [tool] and a User-Interface Toolbox to help programmers (people) develop applications (tools) that share a consistent, advanced user interface. So, for this discussion there are the four components as well as the common boundaries between software and hardware and software and tools:

I II III IV V VI
Hardware / Software / Tools / People

I. **Hardware** is broken down into the following three variables.
(1) Sensory richness. The amount of sensory (speech, hearing, sight, touch, smell) apparatus (for example, television camera, speech synthesizer, voice recognition, and so on) that work in concert with each other "in order to represent or recognize human intentions accurately and to output responses in a human vocabulary, one not limited to verbal languages" (Bolt, 1984, p. xiii). A video teleconference, if done well, represents the sight and sounds of the participants accurately, whereas a computer conference depends on written text.

(2) Spatial management. How the medium manages the actual interaction of people and machines in space including the physical location of people as well as a variety of visual and written messages. The Media Room at MIT's Architecture Machine Group laboratory is probably the most interactive setting for managing data between a person and a machine medium and MISAR II for managing people and data in a teleconference.

(3) Responsiveness or power (amount and speed of memory, processing power and the size of the data path). How much and how quickly a machine mediated interactive encounter can be "played back" and "massaged" to facilitate reaching objectives. A computer conference usually has the means for easy and quick playback, manipulation, and search of text. A radio or video teleconference usually does not have quick "random access."

II. **Hardware/Software** contains six elements.

(1) Social presence. How does one sense that the communicative act is "person-oriented" or that the message conveys some of the person's "presence?" In terms of social presence interactive media can be distinguished by their ability to convey nonverbal (both proxemic and kinesic) dimensions of a personal conversation, the potential of immediate, two-way exchange, as well as the context in which they are used. Andrew Lippman, a designer and researcher at the Electronic Publishing Group of the Media Lab at the Massachusetts Institute of Technology, suggests that social presence is characterized by simultaneity, memory (people actively processing information all the time by listening and composing their next response) and interruptability (Lippman, 1985, p. 10). In addition, the redundancy of the medium as well as the public-private quality of the media also affects social presence (Rice, 1984, pp. 59-60). In the future, social presence may be affected also by artificial intelligence researcher Marvin Minsky's work with "telepresence" or Bretz's work with the "telehandshake."

(2) Personalization (machine as intimate friend). The extent to which a machine looks, feels, and sounds friendly. This includes simulating those qualities that make interaction with other people enjoyable. For example, the medium's informal conversational style could make interaction in certain contexts more comfortable. "In its first encounter it might be somewhat hesitant and unassuming, but as it came to know the user it would progress to a more relaxed and intimate style. The machine would not be a passive participant but would add its own suggestions, information and opinion; it would sometimes take the initiative in developing or changing the topic and would have a personality of its own" (Frude, 1983, p. 23).

(3) Transparency. The quality of a specific media system configuration (not the medium itself) in which the user ignores the presence of the media systems components (such as a microphone or camera) and is able to *see through* the system to concentrate wholly on the ultimate receiver to whom he or she is communicating.

(4) User friendliness. A silly name for a serious thing. One purpose is usually easily understood: to make the person comfortable with the machine. This relates to personalization. The concern here, however, is with the more ambitious goal of attempting to make media (especially computers) an "effortlessly exercised lever of human thought" ("Man Meet Machine," 1984,p. 95). In other words (using computers as the illustration), how do we bring computers into close contact with the persons whose thinking they are supposed to amplify? For example, the Apple Macintosh uses four principal devices for mediating between the user and the computers: menus, icons, windows, and a mouse.

(5) Machine metaphors. Simulating the interaction between the mind and the real world. A recent metaphor is the desktop. The screen shows several different applications at the same time: the one you are working on displayed prominently, others tucked away (only corners showing). If you want to work on something else, you pull the semihidden application into view just as you would pull out a piece of paper from a pile on your desk.

(6) Graphics. Dynamic visual representations. Our well developed two- and three-dimensionally oriented eye-brain pattern recognition mechanism allows us to perceive and process many types of data very rapidly and efficiently if the data are presented pictorially. High resolution screens, screen-control techniques called bit mapping, in which each of the small elements (pixels) that make up the pictures can be individually controlled, plus techniques of motion dynamics (objects can be moved and tumbled with respect to a stationary observer or vice versa) and update dynamics (actual change of the shape, color, or other properties of the objects being viewed) allow us to achieve "much higher bandwidth person-machine communication" and therefore greater interactivity (Foley & Van Dam, p. 6).

III. **Software:** The software of an interactive media system, whether it is the Reading, Pennsylvania, Community TV station, Dataland of the Nicholas Negroponte group at MIT, or the "collaborative soap opera" on the Electronic Information and Exchange System of NJIT, is probably the most important dimension of interactive media.

Software is divided into eight levels (Seeley, 1980, p. 7).

(1) Reactive. The users may vote or select only once from a single group of options such as with Telidon, the QUBE system, or most electronic voting systems and computer assisted instruction. For all intents and purposes these are passive rather than active systems.

(2) Selective. The user looks for some particular information, for example, the weather, and may search for it using menu-trees. The easiest example is the restaurant guide in TELEGUIDE. Once again this use of Telidon is a passive relationship between the user and a data base and its "knowledge." In terms of Sherry Arstein's, "A Ladder of Citizen Participation," reactiveness and selectivity would be considered either nonparticipation or tokenism.

(3) Provision. The user may provide actual content to the data base, teleconference, community bulletin board, and so on. For example, if TELE-GUIDE operated at this level, a person who used the restaurant guide to choose the location of their evening's meal would afterward have the opportunity to add his or her comments to the restaurant listing.

(4) Dialogue. The user actively controls the flow of interaction and is not bound by a preprogrammed sequence, but can select instructions as he or she wishes. Probably the best example is the Feedback Dialog system of John D. C. Little and others of the Operations Research Center of MIT. Operations researchers developed computerized models of complex policy decisions that were based on real data of two forthcoming policy decisions: higher education tuition and secondary school financing. Based on historical data, a time-sharing computer could be queried by remote terminal to point out the consequences of choosing various policy options. Interested citizen groups were given access to terminals and the software. The experiment illustrates how citizen groups might be given access to the same kinds of advanced policy formation tools once reserved for elites. In this case, the groups had access to a computer analysis, could put in their own assumptions and proposed actions, and could evaluate the results for themselves (Laudon, 1977, pp. 34-35). "User-oriented programs should empower users, not control (allow, permit, etc.) them" (Seeley, 1980, p. 47).

(5) Structure. Users can tell the software media system how items are to be categorized. For example, the electronic Community Memory system developed in Berkeley encouraged free association in organizing their files. Another example is the Adventure Construction Set for the Apple computer. It contains six "miniadventures," a full length adventure and the adventure construction set. The software provides the user not only the opportunity to change the adventures constructed himself or herself, but any other adventure on the disk. When you are ready to construct your adventure, you have the option of incorporating any of 250 different locations, 500 creatures, and more than 5,000 things, including buildings, weapons, magical what-nots, and music. When you are ready to build your own world map you decide where to put the mountains, rivers, forests, and doorways in subregions and towns. If there is some sort of building or other icon one needs in the world-picture that is not on the master list, the player can either draw what he or she needs or modify an existing picture. Everyone has an opportunity to build his or her own worldview.

(6) Access structure. Users can interlink message categories in any way that they choose, because the access structure is open to different processes or styles of inquiry. The software does not impose one style of inquiry. One example might be the Conference Tree Program that is available for computer bulletin board systems. The program, as its name suggests, is designed like a tree with its many branches. It is a data base of messages, designed to

be accessed according to different subjects and "subjects within subjects" rather than in a linear fashion. Another example is the software/hardware voice and gesture recognition system designed by the Architecture Machine Group at MIT that allows the user to **Put That There**. You sit in a chair, and the entire wall in front of you is a rear-projection screen that is initially clear or bears some simple backdrop such as a map. Against this background the user, through voice or gesture, calls items into existence, moves them about, replicates objects, alters their attributes, and then may order the objects to vanish (Bolt, 1984, p. 44). The user says, "Create a blue cruise ship," and the system says, "Where?" and the user says, "There." You just talk to the system and point your arm in space. You then might say "Move the blue cruise ship there" and so on.

(7) Functional freedom. Users can expand the system's "repertoire of operations" by using a workbench of programming tools. The USER-INTERFACE TOOLBOX for the Macintosh computer is a collection of various managers and services to help a programmer develop a wide variety of applications that conform to the Macintosh standard user interface.

(8) Knowledge dialogues. "Artificial intelligence" researchers and knowledge engineers are working on software that will enable machines to learn and change as a result of experience as humans do. Currently the commercial software that is available consists of expert system software that is stripped of its knowledge component, "leaving only a shell—the linguistic and reasoning mechanisms that interpret and draw conclusions from knowledge" (Kinnucan, 1985, p. 16). Computer programs have been developed that, for example, "interpret text in the way that a dispassionate observer might interpret it. But we are far from approaching the kind of deep-level understanding that is typical of an understanding that is truly empathetic" (Schank, 1984, p. 47) In the future software may understand some micro-universe of discourse, which means it would implicitly be using a model of how the world works. A knowledge-dialogue would be a discussion that is a synthesis of the world understood by the intelligent media and the user.

IV. **Software/Tools:** Although machine mediated interactive communication is increasing with several different media, it is computer communication that is growing most rapidly. Although it is unlikely that any single method of computer communication will predominate, there are two approaches getting attention, because they are the tools that humans use to absorb most of their information: graphics and natural language. Natural language for computers is how the most efficient and complicated human communications are made. However, the qualities that make natural language a subtle instrument for human communication also make it a nightmare for computers. The experience of the world is what the computer lacks. As we stated above, the central effort of artificial intelligence research is to find a way to represent knowledge in a computer and enable the machine to make inferences from it. If software/tool developers are able to develop even a limited fluency in English or French the computer can become a more interactive tool in its user's hands.

There are three main stages that computers go through to analyze an English or French sentence: syntactics, semantics, and pragmatics. Computers perform syntactical analysis by applying rules to determine possible structure. Today's machines can parse more than 90% of natural language sentences. It is in trying to understand the semantics of a sentence and especially its meaning context (pragmatics) that machines falter. "But if the world the computer must bring to bear in interpreting a sentence is made far smaller and better defined than the real world, machines can understand natural language requests ("As She Is Spoke," 1984, pp. 96-97). The program *Intellect,* which is now running at 250 companies, is designed for middle managers. A manager might ask: "How many managers in our company have training in communications?" *Intellect* works because the world it has to know (a single company's) is relatively small and the organization of knowledge in the data base is thoroughly understood. Each company writes a lexicon so the software will know the company's jargon.

The work on natural language is also related to machine-assisted translation systems that are on the verge of becoming routine. For example, Meteo II, which is linked to the Canadian Meteorological Centre's nationwide communications network, translates reports from English directly into French. All output runs past human translators on a screen and the translators change only about 6% of what passes them on a screen. Similar software/tools are now well enough developed in a number of cases to be run on small table top computers.

Another important software/tool that facilitates interactive machine mediated communication is the effort to "integrate" the computer's functions so that conversations from a communication program on a personal computer can be transferred immediately from the user's screen to a word processing or data base program. Three approaches are being tried. The program *Symphony* extends the spreadsheet metaphor-rows and columns of interactive cells to all the machine's applications. An alternative program, *Framework,* relies on the "nesting" of applications programs one inside the next. The third technique, exemplified by the *Apple* utility program *Switcher,* allows two to four applications programs to be loaded into memory simultaneously. The Macintosh literally switches among these applications by either clicking with the mouse on an arrow symbol or by pressing two keys.

In summary, there are three software/tools that have a large potential impact on media interactivity:

(1) Natural language. Currently almost all natural language programs are running on large computers. The main aim of current research is to

increase the size of the grammars available to a machine and to create systems that are increasingly independent of the structure and content of the data base. When these efforts are successful the limited world that natural language systems can deal with will be enlarged. However, enlarging it to the size of the real world will take a long time.

(2) *Machine translation.* Although full-scale systems are at least 10 years down the road, the race has begun. Last year the chief executive of Japan's NEC announced at the world Telecommunication Forum in Geneva that they were developing an English-to-Japanese (and vice versa) computer-based translating telephone system. An interesting proposition is that control over who can say what to whom across national boundaries will break down when voice translation is a practical possibility ("Japan Devising Translating Telephone," 1984, pp. 5-6).

(3) *Integration.* The integration of software and hardware is beginning to expand rapidly. For example, by the end of this year we should see desk top computers being integrated with digital laser discs and digital TV sets. In terms of software, the real breakthroughs will begin sometime in 1987 when 32-bit chips will become available. This will put vastly more power at the disposal of personal computer designers, enough for them to give each user considerable flexibility in deciding how the hardware and software should run.

V. **Programmable Tools:** In setting out the context for this chapter, it was mentioned that one of the general goals of designers was to go beyond the possibilities of face-to-face meetings and develop new possibilities for communication. Researchers learned, for example, that teleconferencing was accepted and effective for tasks involving information exchange, routine decision making, or cooperative problem solving, but not as good for getting to know people, bargaining and negotiation, and tasks involving serious conflict (Svenning & Ruchinskas, 1984). However, some tasks, including generating ideas, decision making, resolving disagreements, and bargaining do not seem as inappropriate to experienced computer users as they do to the casual, novice, or nontechnical user (Rice, 1984, p. 9). As people become experienced the potential range of uses for interactive computer communication expands.

"Computers have introduced something new into life; some of their power to aid people would be lost if they were treated as nothing more than an electronic means for doing the familiar" ("Man Meet Machine," 1984, p.95). The rate at which software tools help individuals to make an intuitive leap and "go beyond the information given" is beginning to expand rapidly. The new software tools allow us to ask "what if" questions, assist us in making educated guesses, facilitate the generation of ideas, and encourage visual thinking, visual problem solving, and visual expression. For parsimony we call these tools:

(1) speculation
(2) idea generation
(3) visualization

Examples of these tools are below.

Visicalc, the computer spreadsheet, became one of the great software tool successes by accident. Its designers thought it would be used the way a paper ledger sheet is. But once users learned how it works, they ignored the electronic spreadsheet accountancy functions and began to make imaginative "what-if" business projections, a use that had no counterpart in the noncomputer world.

TK!Solver is a unique alternative to traditional programming for the solution of systems of equations. With TK!Solver no variable is prespecified as input or output, and it is easy to solve equations for variables on either side of the equation (that is, it lets an individual backsolve). It also solves problems via an iterative process best exemplified by the adage: "If at first you do not succeed, try, try again." The user supplies the first guess and the maximum number of iterations desired; the program does the rest.

ThinkTank is an idea processor. It lets the user enter his or her thoughts quickly as they surface in an impulsive fashion and organizes them into a logical format. **ThinkTank** can be useful for "electronic brainstorming" and overcoming writer's cramp.

MacPaint allows the user to think visually and relate visuals to verbals with a facility not readily available before. It is also the equivalent of an artist's canvas in video. The amateur or professional artist can choose a wide variety of tools in an almost limitless number of combinations and create images that are easy to create and distribute (Benzon, 1985, p. 116).

Filevision was created with the concept of a visual data base. The program offers a completely new way to organize data. One begins with a visual problem. What will your flower garden look like on August 15th? After drawing a diagram of the garden the user enters data about each plant. The program could then search through the data base and highlight all the plants that are in bloom in mid-August. "Using this visual map for reference, you might decide to buy an additional rosebush, transplant the azaleas, or uproot some forsythia to make sure the garden is in bloom with flowers of a particular color" (McGolgrick, 1985, p. 6).

VI. **People:** There are many people in information occupations whose work either makes possible, facilitates, or increases the potential of interactive media. For our purposes seven kinds of information workers immediately come to mind:

(1) Animators
(2) Creators

(3) Dispatcher-Mediators
(4) Group Leader(s)
(5) Technician(s)
(6) Programmer(s)
(7) Weaver(s)

The jobs of most of these people require no further explanation. A **dispatcher-mediator** is a person and/or machine in a computer conference or network that serves as a dispatcher, mediating the distribution of messages. If the human dispatcher grows tired of forwarding the same kinds of messages to the same list of people he or she can program the computer to distribute well-defined messages automatically. So, in the above contexts, both human and computer dispatchers are likely to emerge in interactive information networks, with computers handling the routine cases and humans called on to handle difficult ones.

A **weaver** is a person in a computer conference or network who keeps a list of people interested in particular contacts. If a user wants to send a message to all people who have an interest in a particular subject, but does not know who they are, the user in this case turns to the weaver to send the message to the appropriate people.

SUMMARY AND CONCLUSIONS

Figure 35.1 is an attempt to classify the variables of "interactivity" into cells with the components of an interactive media system on the horizontal axis and the three design goals placed on the vertical axis. Although the classification of the variables is based on intuitive rather than objective criteria, the typology suggests several relationships that can lead to a better conceptual understanding of the complexity that exists among variables of "interactivity" and components of media systems and goals of interactive media designers. The typology also puts us in a better position to plan strategic empirical studies that will increase our knowledge of "interactivity" and interactive media.

Examining the figure from right to left several comments are in order.

(1) The hardware variables are nominal yet fit into different design goals. The sensory richness variable has been studied in teleconferencing studies, and research on responsiveness and spatial management is taking place mainly in computer science.

(2) Social presence has been examined by communication researchers, but relatively little research has been done on the other variables, with the exception of personalization, which is currently being studied by artificial intelligence researchers.

Components of an Interactive
Media System

Designer Goals

	HARDWARE		SOFTWARE	TOOLS	PEOPLE
SIMULATING FACE-TO-FACE	Sensory Richness	Social Presence		Natural Language	Group Leader
				Translation	Animateur
MAINTAINING THE ILLUSION	Responsiveness	Transparency			Technician
				Integration	
		Personalization			
			Reactive		
			Selective		
			Access		
			Structure		Programmer
			Dialog		
		User	Provision		Dispatcher-
		Friendliness			Mediator
MIND AMPLIFICATION	Spatial Management		Structure	Speculation	
		Metaphor			Weaver
			Functional	Idea	
		Graphics	Freedom	Generation	
					Creator
			Knowledge	Visualization	
			Dialog		

Figure 35.1 Toward a typology for interactive media.

(3) The software variables can be rank ordered and separated into different design goals. They should be relatively easy to operationalize and this would certainly be a fruitful area for research. For example, the French videotex system has over a million subscribers and it would be worthwhile to explore what services are successful and why.

(4) The software/tools variables are certainly important in the study of the computer as a medium of communication, but there are certain technical problems such as limited speech recognition vocabularies and computer memory that make research difficult. Substantial communication research in this area is still probably several years away. Integration is an important variable and a hot topic in the personal computer area, but it is difficult to operationalize in a way that gets at the essence of the problem.

(5) The tool variables fit into only one design goal. There has been sub-

stantial research on visualization and idea generation in psychology, but relatively little research on the speculation variable, although Visicalc and related "what if" programs have probably been the main reason several hundred thousand people have bought table top computers.

(6) There is a substantial amount of research in the teleconferencing literature on group leaders and animators, but there is a substantial need for research on the role of dispatcher-mediators (who have some of the characteristics of gatekeepers but also substantially different characteristics) and weavers because of the rapid growth of computer networking.

(7) Overall it appears that most of the research on interactive media has focused on the simulation of face-to-face interaction and has not dealt with the dimensions of maintaining the illusion and mind amplification.

(8) As a person examines the typology it also becomes clear that the conceptual categories are not black and white, but rather shades of grey. For example, there is a distinction that can be made between systems in which the user has some small measure of control and those that are interactive. Andrew Lippman, in *Imaging and Interactivity,* considers the "threshold" of interactivity. It is too bad that we don't have more interesting methodologies that would let us explore these shades of grey as well as the overlaps among variables. It might be a good idea for researchers in this area to explore the methodological possibilities of "fuzzy logic," an idea of Lofti Zadeh at the University of California at Berkeley (Zadeh, 1984, pp. 26-32). There have been several thousand papers written on fuzzy sets and their mathematical and statistical applications.[6]

(9) Finally, the computer is speeding up the process of improving both the fidelity and quality of rendition of interactive media systems through bandwidth compression, word processing, image processing, signal restoration, and so on. It is entering into the communicative process as an active agent, a mediator of content as well as quality. The distinctions among technologies, techniques, and applications are also becoming "fuzzy."

Developments in the interactivity of data bases, electronic networks, community bulletin boards (CBBs) transmission systems, and the messages themselves deserve more attention than they can be given here. In passing we might note:

> The 21 volume, 9 million word Grolier encyclopedia takes up only 110 megabytes of the several hundred megabytes available on a 4 3/4 inch optical CD-ROM disk, and almost half of that is the word retrieval index which means that any word or combination of words can be the target of a diskwide search. ("CD-ROM: Megabytes into Minispace," 1985, p. 28)

> **Megawars III** has more than 1,000 participants (as well as more than 100 players at a time) on *Compuserve,* and *Compuserve* itself has over 250,000 on line subscribers.

Usenet on the private *Unix* network has over 250 bulletin boards or discussion groups, and the number of public CBBs in North America has grown from 200 in 1980 to over 2000 in 1985.

INet from Bell Canada Enterprises, which acts as a universal communications protocol interpreter between different data bases and different computers, is now in commercial use.

Interactive fiction is becoming popular with personal computer users. Douglas Adams, author of *The Hitchhiker's Guide to the Galaxy*, currently one of the most popular pieces of interactive fiction on personal computers, explains why.

We started by developing a kind of horizontal and vertical branching network. It would have been pointless to do a linear trot through the book. Once you start to think in the strange logic we set up, you can begin to negotiate your way around the game pretty easily. There's no necessarily correct answer at any point, and all your previous choices influence what you can do. So not only is there no absolutely correct route, there is no way that you will follow the same path twice. (Young, 1985, p. 150.)

The problem we all face in studying interactive media is that the concepts and methodologies that evolved for studying traditional modes of expression and communication are being stretched to the limits of capacity to cover new situations, and the new media themselves, as well their services and uses, are in constant evolution.

NOTES

1. An earlier version of some of the ideas expressed here was prepared for the Canadian Communication Association in May, 1985.

2. The typology is an analogy based on the classic article by Arnstein (1969, May).

3. Taken from the program description of The Interactive Telecommunications Program at New York University.

4. Rice (1984) states that "computer conferencing is not only interactive in the sense that participants may exchange comments with other participants in real or delayed time, but the system used is a product of interaction with the systems designers, programmers, and conference moderators as they create a communication environment."

5. Definition of Bretz (1983, pp. 22-23) as opposed to a wider ranging definition such as that of Lias (1982, pp. 1-12)

6. Briefly, "whereas a conventional or 'crisp' set has sharp boundaries (such as the set of all numbers greater than 2), the transition between membership and nonmembership in a fuzzy set is gradual rather than sharp, the degree of membership is specified by a number between 1 (full member) and 9 (full nonmember)," so that one could ask questions such as "Does media system one have much more social presence than media system two?" Indeed, fuzzy sets and fuzzy logic are finding application in a broad range of problem solving from expert systems to pattern recognition. See, for example, the *International Journal of Fuzzy Sets and Systems*, published by North Holland, and the *Bulletin of Fuzzy Sets and Their Applications*, published in France.

REFERENCES

Arnstein, S. (1969, May). A ladder of citizen participation. *Journal of the American Institute of Planners, 35*, 216-224.

As she is spoke (1984, October 27). *The Economist*, 96-97.

Benzon, B. (1985, January). *Byte, 10* (1) 113-130.

Bolt, R. (1984). *The human interface.* Belmont, CA: Lifetime Learning.

Bretz, R. (1983). *Media for interactive communication.* Beverly Hills, CA: Sage.

CD-ROM: Megabytes in minispace (1985, September 23). *Infoworld*, 27-30.

Foley, J., & Van Dam (1983). *Fundamentals of interactive graphics.* Boston, MA: Addison Wesley.

Frude, N. (1983, December). The affectionate machine. *Psychology Today*, pp. 22-23.

Japan devising the translating telephone (1984). *Intermedia, 12*(6), 96-97.

Kay, A., & Goldberg, A. (1977, March). Personal dynamic media. *Computer*, 31-41.

Kinnucan, P. (1985, March). Software tools speed expert system development. *High Technology*, 16.

Laudon, K. (1977). *Communication technology and citizen participation.* New York, NY: Praeger.

Lias, E. (1982). *Future mind.* Boston, MA: Little, Brown.

Licklider, J., & Taylor, R. (1968, April). The computer as a communication device. *Science and Technology*, pp. 21-31.

Lippman, A. (1985). *Imaging and interactivity.* Cambridge, MA: The Media Lab.

Man meet machine. (1984, October 27). *The Economist*, 94-96.

McGolgrick, N. (1985, January). Filevision: A database in pictures. *Macworld*, 62-71.

Rice, R, & Associates (1984). *The new media.* Beverly Hills, CA: Sage.

Schank, R. (1984). *The cognitive computer.* Boston, MA: Addison Wesley.

Seeley, D. (1980). The ecology of information or avoiding the pollution of reality in the information age. In Durlak J. & Roosen-Runge (Eds.). Toronto, ON: York University.

Svenning, L., & Ruchinskas, J. (1984). Organizational teleconferencing. In R. Rice & Associates, *The new media* (pp. 217-249). Beverly Hills, CA: Sage.

Young. J. (1985, May). *MACWORLD*, 148-153.

Zadeh, L. (1984, August). Making computers think like people. *IEEE Spectrum*, 26-32.

XII ● POPULAR CULTURE

36 ● Media and Folklore as Intertextual Communication Processes: John F. Kennedy and the Supermarket Tabloids

S. ELIZABETH BIRD

University of Iowa

F OLKLORE, the orally transmitted traditions of any given group of people, has rarely been considered by communications scholars, remaining the province of anthropologists and specialized folklorists. Yet the transmission and maintenance of folk traditions are clearly complex communication processes that are important in constituting the worldview of any culture. According to Bascom (1954), in a classic statement on the functions of folklore, folklore serves to educate, to validate culture, to maintain conformity, and to serve as an outlet for wish fulfillment.

Through folklore, such as tales, jokes, legends, and rumor, a culture reaffirms its values and offers answers to perplexing questions. Rodgers (1985), one of the few communications scholars to look closely at folklore as communication, offers an explanation for the importance of "urban legends"— the usually apochryphal tales that circulate orally about phantom hitchhikers, cats in microwaves, celebrities in unusual situations, and so on. Drawing on the work of Brunvand (1981) and others, Rodgers explains the importance of such legends in constituting and reconstituting a culture's worldview, a worldview that often appears unscientific, distrustful of government and technology, and reliant on stereotypical views of gender and different ethnic groups. Brunvand's study of urban legends points out that

Correspondence and requests for reprints: S. Elizabeth Bird, School of Journalism and Mass Communication, University of Iowa, Iowa City, IA 52242.

although the tales are told as entertainment, they depend on a degree of plausibility and authentication, confirming and revitalizing existing fears and stereotypes by articulating these in narrative form. The legends will continue to circulate in different, ever-changing variants as long as there is a reason to tell them. Almost all make some overt or implicit point; a lesson is learned in the telling.

Rodgers argues for the importance of analyzing oral tradition as popular communication, pointing out that folklore is a thriving process in contemporary, urban communities. For although communications scholars would no doubt accept the important role of folklore in constituting culture in less technologically based societies (see, for example, Basso, 1984), many neglect this same process in contemporary society. It is left to folklorists such as Dundes (1982) to point out that "the folk" are urban Americans as well as rural peasants.

Rodgers's work is unusual in bringing folklore into the realm of communication study. In general there has been virtually no contact between folklorists, with their emphasis on oral transmission, and media scholars, with their emphasis on mediated transmission. Increasingly, folklorists are having to look at media, but the approach is usually to identify folkloric motifs that appear in the media—folklore in literature, folklore in television, and so on. Several researchers, such as Brunvand (1981) and Hobbs (1978), have shown how newspapers sometimes pass on urban legends, but the idea seems to be that this is somehow accidental, that newspapers are primarily concerned with "facts," but sometimes they get duped.

Thus Degh and Vazsonyi point out, "there is no doubt that media draws heavily on folklore and vice versa," (1973, p. 36), but they go on to distinguish between "genuine folk tradition" and the media contribution to it. Even those folklorists who study urban cultures will often ignore the fact that these contemporary "folk" are surrounded by messages from many sources other than face-to-face contact. For the sake of disciplinary convenience they continue to separate genres and sources in a way that misrepresents the actual cultural context.

Meanwhile, media researchers have viewed newspapers and other media as active transmitters that act upon passive consumers, in a one-way transmission process. The result has been a tradition in American media research that emphasizes effect rather than process, and the discovery of the uniqueness of media messages rather than their cultural context (Kepplinger, 1979). With both disciplines defending the uniqueness of oral versus media communication processes, there has been little opportunity for dialogue. Donald Allport Bird (1976) was one of the first to question this state of affairs, challenging folklorists to take a broader view of media:

> Folklore and mass communications share common frameworks of defined situations, structure, function, and tradition. Communication—whether folk-

loric or mass—frequently takes place through media and contains verbal and non-verbal expressive forms and common symbols that are often ritualistic and ceremonial. Mass communication in itself is a social, cultural phenomenon worthy of study by the folklorist. (pp. 285-286)

The crucial point here is the assertion that mass communication in itself is worthy of study—not just the way folkloric themes sometimes filter into the media, but the process of the media message itself, taking into account the interaction of the consumer in receiving and interpreting the message.

This study attempts to draw together some of the approaches of folklore and media research to show that oral transmission and media transmission may not be as distinct in kind as the interdisciplinary barriers would suggest. The case study chosen is an analysis of the "image" of President John F. Kennedy in "supermarket tabloid" newspapers. This shows how that image draws on orally transmitted "legends," but also how media accounts themselves work like urban legends in restructuring diffuse beliefs, uncertainties, and stereotypes in narrative form. The image of Kennedy can be seen to derive from many sources, oral and mediated; to divide these up into entirely different processes, worthy of study by entirely different specialists, is artificial and unproductive. People construct a view of reality from all the culturally embedded messages they encounter, whether these are oral, written, or electronic. Furthermore, the media themselves, as part of culture, develop their themes and tell their stories in ways that are not unlike the process of oral transmission.

KENNEDY AND
THE TABLOIDS

Several folklorists have pointed out the way supermarket tabloids, such as the *National Enquirer, Star, Globe, National Examiner,* and others have picked up folkloristic stories, including Kennedy legends. Blaustein (undated) has looked in a more general sense at the way the *National Enquirer* restates the folk theme of "rags-to-riches" by constantly retelling it through specific stories. His approach is, I believe, more fruitful than simply pointing out appearances of clearly identifiable urban legends in print. Rather, we look for some kind of cumulative themes that emerge from the papers over time.

These themes are clear, and have been listed by a writer who has made a living in the tabloids market (Holden, 1979). They include celebrity gossip, rags-to-riches stories, self-improvement through diet and exercise (often with an almost magical component), and the handicapped overcoming terrible odds. A special category includes what have variously been called "Gee whiz" or "Hey Martha" stories—the kind that make people look up and say,

"Hey Martha, did you know that. . . ." These are the quintessential tabloid stories (McDonald, 1984).

Kennedy's role as tabloid hero began to emerge only after his death. Tabloids generally ignore politics and politicians, and it was his developing status as a popular hero rather than as a president as such that turned him into a tabloid staple. The growth of that status was rapid, and dependent on the assassination. Just before the 1960 New Hampshire primary, the *National Enquirer* (in a brief, soon-to-be dropped "political" column) reported that Kennedy's biggest drawback as a presidential candidate was "the vagueness of his popularity with the voters" (*National Enquirer*, 1960, p. 15), and in April of that year it commented: "He fears that his youthful appearance will cost him a good deal of support" (1960, p. 10). As Edwards writes, "Kennedy was not elected by image; he was chiefly elected because the suspicions of him were outweighed by the suspicions of Nixon" (1984, p. 410). Even the assassination itself was ignored in 1963 by the *National Enquirer*, which presumably was not anticipating the growth of a "legend."

However, not long after Kennedy's death, and especially following doubts raised by the Warren Commission findings, the "legend" was under way:

> Suddenly, the dead Kennedy became what he had been for relatively few in life—the hope for the future, the promise of advancement for the underdog, the notion of grace and magic, the hero, the Prince of youth . . . it was also the age-old horror of the slaying of the priest-king, which Kennedy had not been until he fell. (Edwards, 1984, p. 413)

By 1983, the 20th anniversary of the assassination, Kennedy's status was well established, both in the tabloids and elsewhere. Analysis of tabloid texts from several papers in 1983 and 1984 reveals some clear themes.[1] Perhaps the most striking, and certainly the most paralleled in identifiable oral legends, is the "Kennedy-is-alive" story.

This legend is still circulating orally, and was first documented in the folklore literature in the late 1960s. De Caro and Oring (1969) detail tales collected from oral tradition that describe Kennedy as alive in a "vegetable-like state" in Athens, Greece, and the marriage of Jacqueline Kennedy to Aristotle Onassis as a carefully arranged fake, with sources often offering psychic Jean Dixon as authority for the story. Rosenberg (1976) gives oral variants in which Kennedy is in Parkland Hospital in Dallas or at Camp David.

Rosenberg also discusses the circulation of the story, attributed to Truman Capote, in the *Milwaukee Metro-News* and the *National Informer*, a now-defunct Chicago-based tabloid, again including an explanation for Jacqueline Kennedy's marriage. Baker (1976) offers a variant reported in the *National Tattler* in 1971—Kennedy on a Greek island owned by Onassis. His widow is supposed to have married Onassis only so she can visit the island without suspicion. The story also appeared in a Montreal-based tabloid (*Midnight,* Oct. 18, 1969, pp. 14-15). According to a former staff member of that publication, the story, which included photographs, was elaborately fabricated and staged in light of the widely known legends circulating orally at the time.[2]

The most recent printed version appeared in the *National Examiner* (July 26, 1983, p. 23). In this variant, Kennedy is being kept closely guarded at a retreat in the Swiss Alps. He has regained some of his mental functions, and on good days he has the abilities of an 11-year-old. The story is reminiscent both of urban legends and of mainstream news accounts in its attention to detail and insistence on attribution to reliable sources. In this case the authority is a Swedish psychic, Sven Petersen, "who contributes to para-psychology newsletters around the world and is especially respected for his experiments in communication with the dead." Throughout the story his expertise is stressed: "a reputation as one of the world's most skilled mediums," "a considerable reputation for accuracy and veracity." The story also quotes a Dr. Chandra Singh, "a political scientist at the University of Calcutta," who maintains that these circumstances would explain the many discrepancies in accounts of what happened to Kennedy after the shooting. In this version, it is pointed out that Jacqueline Kennedy was not party to the secret, a point that indicates the way she has been gradually cut out of the picture over the years as the image of J.F.K. himself has assumed prominence.

The story, of course, rests on the assumption that *National Examiner* readers have a great deal of faith in psychics, an assumption that pervades all tabloid narratives and that also underlies other stories that have developed the "Kennedy-is-alive" theme. In these cases, Kennedy has been reincarnated, first in the form of a 7-year-old German boy (*Sun,* July 3, 1984). "Psychics have confirmed that they can communicate with the spirit of J.F.K. through Klaus Zimmerman," the account claims, adding that a U.S. government official "shook his head in amazement" when he interviewed the boy. Again, the details: "He even recalls a 1962 conversation between little Caroline Kennedy and the ambassador of Niger." Psychics quoted in the account predict that Klaus will grow up to be a great leader who will reunite East and West Berlin—echoes of "Ich bin ein Berliner," perhaps.

A month later, a 10-year-old Indian girl is "hailed by scientists and religious leaders as incredible proof of reincarnation" (*National Examiner,* Aug. 4, 1984). Dr. Chandra Murakajee, "a world-respected parapsychologist and professor of antiquities," is quoted as saying, "there is little doubt that Sharda lived before as President Kennedy." Like Klaus, she suffers headaches that are her recollections of the assassination.

As Rosenberg (1976) points out, the notions of a dead mythic hero (or villain) being alive and ready to return, or returning in the form of another person, are widespread heroic motifs. Tied closely to the idea of Kennedy's return is the theme of a conspiracy that killed him: Perhaps he is dead, but it took almost superhuman powers to kill him, a motif also discussed by Rosenberg (1976). This old motif was probably fueled further by the genuine controversy over the Warren Commission's conclusions, and the uncertainties surrounding responsibility for the murder. Ambiguity and unsatisfactorily explained circumstances traditionally provide fertile ground for the growth of legend and rumor (Mullen, 1972).

Thus the *Globe* (Nov. 29, 1983, p. 7) reports that "he died because a Buddhist curse guided three independent assassination teams to Dallas on that fateful day, claim two top psychics and a veteran investigator." The curse was invoked in November, 1963, by a group of Buddhist monks who blamed J.F.K. for the assassination of the president of Vietnam and his brother. The curse set in motion all three forces opposing Kennedy—the Guardians, a clandestine group of international arch-conservatives, some C.I.A. elements who said he was a threat to national security, and the Mafia, whose feud with the Kennedys dated back to the 1920s. Kennedy apparently knew he was doomed, but like Jesus and other heroes, "he calmly accepted that, and played the role fate had assigned him." The narrative effect sought here, as throughout the tabloid treatment of Kennedy, has been described by Hernstein Smith (1981, p. 225) as "resonance." The story is intended to evoke in the reader a complex of responses and emotions associated with the cultural heritage of "doomed hero" conventions.

The *National Enquirer,* in a special issue commemorating the assassination (Nov. 22, 1983), throws a new group into the conspiracy. "Working with top experts on the assassination" (p. 30), it identifies the assassins as French terrorists who apparently hated J.F.K. because of his speeches supporting Algerian independence. The *Enquirer's* cover photograph for its special issue was clearly chosen for its resonant qualities, showing Kennedy kneeling, hands folded in prayer, eyes gazing heavenward. In the same issue, the *Enquirer* develops the mystique supposedly surrounding the assassination with "a long list of people associated with the J.F.K. slaying who have died mysteriously and often violently since then" (p. 35).

As a kind of subplot, the "Kennedy curse" continues to haunt the family, and is cited as a major factor in such tragedies as the death of David Kennedy (*National Enquirer,* May 15, 1984, pp. 30-35; *National Examiner,* May 15, 1984, p. 11; *Star,* May 15, 1984, pp. 16-17). A strange echo of the living Kennedy theme appears in a *National Examiner* story that asks, "Was David Kennedy buried alive?" (Nov. 20, 1984, p. 27).

A final main theme is the prowess of Kennedy with women, an aspect that has grown to heroic proportions since his death. News of Kennedy's womanizing was suppressed by the media during his life (Gans, 1980, p. 484) and many mainstream media have continued to play it down, preferring to present Kennedy as a more sanitized hero. In the popular worldview, however, Kennedy's sexuality has become a major part of the legend, and even in more mainstream media this aspect of Kennedy's image has come more to the fore, in spite of the scruples of "responsible" writers:

> We've heard all this before in the National Enquirer and elsewhere, but it says something about our culture that it can appear as well in a biography whose title declares it celebratory. This, then, is yet another of the roles Kennedy played: Don Juan. Accompanied by winks, it too has become part of the myth-verification that the hero of World War II and the Cuban missile crisis was, in the same macho terms, heroic in bed as well. (Hochschild, 1984, p. 56)

For, as Owen Jones writes, "A hero is a man whose deeds epitomize the masculine attributes most highly valued within a society" (1971, p. 341), and prowess with women is certainly one of these. The tabloids are tireless in their listing of the women Kennedy supposedly seduced, including Judy Garland, Veronica Lake, Angie Dickinson, and Gene Tierney. The various affairs described provide not only a vivid picture of the "heroic" male role ascribed to Kennedy but also of conventional images of female sexuality, from helpless innocent, through insatiable slut, to untouchable princess. Most of the affairs share a feature that raises Kennedy's prowess to a mystical level; the women involved could not help themselves, but fell completely under his spell, although he remained always in control. They were conquests to him, but he was the love of their lives.

Thus Veronica Lake "would have given up Hollywood in a flash for the chance to be his bride," and Gene Tierney "succumbed to J.F.K.'s charm and fell very much in love" (Globe, Nov. 29, 1983, p. 4). Marielle Novotny was said to be an 18-year-old Soviet spy who was ordered to seduce Kennedy and obtain state secrets. "But the Russian scheme backfired when Novotny succumbed to J.F.K.'s charms and fell madly in love with him." According to her husband, "J.F.K. was her first and probably her only true love" (Globe, Nov. 29, 1983, p. 4). Florinda Bolkan, a Brazilian actress, was said to be Kennedy's last lover. "He was handsome, young, rich, intelligent, and at the height of his power. He could have had any woman he wanted" (Globe, Dec., 1983). Bolkan is quoted: "We were so close in that short time before his death that I believe he has watched over me ever since. There was something strange, almost supernatural, in our meeting. . . . He was my first love, and my last."

Rather different is the treatment given to Kennedy's reported relationship with Marilyn Monroe, herself a perennial tabloid favorite. According to the National Examiner, Monroe had sexual relations with both John and Robert Kennedy, and was pregnant by Robert when she died (National Examiner, July 3, 1984, p. 1; Oct. 23, 1984, p. 35). She was also used by the Soviet Union, who extracted "pillow talk" secrets from her through a spy who became her lover and eventually murdered her. She is portrayed as a woman who had numerous lovers, most of whom used her. It is almost the mirror image of the portrayal of Kennedy, and is a clear example of the "double standard" at work.

One woman, however, was apparently special—the woman who in the tabloids has become a mythic princess comparable to Kennedy's prince, and who seems to represent the other side of Monroe's sad nymphomaniac. Both the *National Examiner* and the *Globe* report on the secret romance between J.F.K. and Princess Grace of Monaco. Like all women, "Grace fell almost immediately under the sway of the president" (*Globe,* Nov. 29, 1983, p. 7). In recurring verbal formulae, Kennedy is compared to Prince Rainier: "Kennedy at the height of his power and glamor, was almost embarrassingly superior in every way to the paunchy Prince of a tiny country devoted to gambling and vacations." According to the *Examiner,* "he was at the height of his power—the most powerful man in the world and one who had brought a message of hope and peace for all" (Sept. 13, 1983).

According to the *Globe,* Kennedy traveled secretly to Nice to meet Grace seven times, although there was some question as to whether the relationship was sexual. The *Examiner* is more specific: "Grace, of course, was too principled ever to launch into an affair with Kennedy, but who's to say if her heart was ever her own, or Rainier's, after this momentous meeting" (Sept. 13, 1983). On Kennedy's part, "who could blame him if for an instant, it crossed his mind that she would have been the perfect wife to reign with him in Camelot" (Sept. 13, 1983).

Kennedy's actual wife, Jacqueline, seems to have almost disappeared from the tabloids, apart from occasional appearances in gossip round-ups and as peripheral to stories about the other Kennedys. One rather odd exception is a story describing how J.F.K. installed listening devices (bugs) in his wife's brassieres so that he could hear her conversations with aides (*National Examiner,* Sept. 4, 1984, p. 1). Kennedy's total control over women, including his own wife, seems to reach an absurd level in this account.

IMPLICATIONS

From this brief summary of tabloid stories, we have a picture of Kennedy as a mythic hero, potent both politically and sexually. He can only die as a result of treachery and in the face of exceptional odds, and his charisma transcends death itself.

An important question that arises is whether or not the tabloid media create an image and then foist it upon their readership, as mass media effects research would tend to suggest, or, conversely, whether or not tabloids merely passively reflect the image of the world already held by their readers. The answer is, I believe, more complex than such simplistic models would suggest.

The image of Kennedy that emerges from the tabloids is not unique to them, but includes elements that appear both in oral tradition and in other mass media (see, for example, Epstein, 1975). In addition, specific stories about Kennedy are often resonant with association that goes beyond him as an individual. Rather than plucking the stories out of thin air, it appears that the tabloids pick up on their readers' (and others') existing ideas and beliefs, restating them in narrative form, performing much the same function as the teller of an urban legend. It is likely that some readers will then pass them on orally through conversation and gossip. This is not to say that reading a tabloid is identical to hearing an oral legend, but if with Hernstein Smith we agree that narrative of all kinds is a "social transaction" (1981, p. 228) involving frames of reference shared by teller and audience, we may see them as comparable processes.

Even more than newspapers, tabloids place much emphasis on reader response and involvement. The *National Enquirer* alone receives over one million letters a year, and uses them to gauge audience interest. *Enquirer* publisher Generoso Pope has said that every story he runs must interest more than 50% of his readers (McDonald, 1984), although he does not explain how this is determined. It seems unlikely that the tabloids themselves have to create a belief in reincarnation, psychics, and the like—only to rearticulate it. The readers then pass on these beliefs, probably not in the form of detailed urban legends, but in gossip and rumor. As Rosnow and Fine (1976) have pointed out, the media often act as brokers of such rumor, the audience and media existing in a symbiotic relationship.

Like traditional storytellers, journalists often work by taking general themes and structuring them into a coherent narrative, using established formulae. Like the purely oral storytellers described by Lord (1971) in his classic analysis of formulaic oral composition, journalists have to work quickly and efficiently, slotting new information into frameworks that are clearly understood by both teller and audience. These constructed narratives then fragment back into oral tradition, only to be restructured by another storyteller later, in a continuing, cyclical process.

The effect of themes that recur over and over again in a slightly different form is noted by Lord:

> This common stock of formulas gives the traditional songs a homogeneity which strikes the listener or reader as soon as he has heard or read more than one song, and creates the impression that all singers know all the same formulas. (Lord, 1971, p. 49)

News is often similar. Graber (1984) observes that "most stories are simply minor updates of previous news or new examples of old themes" (p. 61), and Rock (1981) comments:

> The content may change, but the forms will be enduring. Much news is, in fact, ritual. It conveys an impression of endlessly repeated drama whose themes are familiar and well-understood. (p. 68)

Folkloric communication and mass communication are, therefore, not the entirely different processes that both folklorists and mass communications researchers have implied. Tabloid journalism is a particular type of highly stylized communication that tends to represent the worldview of certain parts of the population, a worldview that may rest on attribution to psychics and celebrities as well as to the more conventional "authorities." However, all journalism is the construction of reality, and as process it belongs on the same continuum with oral tradition. Journalism, particularly of the "human interest" kind, is by nature storytelling, a fact that has only recently been fully recognized in the communications literature. From this view, journalism is not merely the objective reporting of facts, but the construction of narratives that conform to the expectations of reader and writer (Barkin, 1984; Bird & Dardenne, 1986; Eason, 1981).

Cohen (1973) observed the interrelationship between oral and print communication when analyzing 19th-century ballad and newspaper stories of a murder, both of which "distorted facts to accommodate a shared pattern of storytelling" (p. 4). Her assumption was that "these formulae are shared also by large numbers of the reading and listening public who accept and preserve these narratives" (pp. 4-5).

Darnton (1975) argues that this relationship is also a contemporary one. Storytelling codes provide techniques that still guide the construction of many news stories, involving the "manipulation of standardized images, cliches, angles, slants, and scenarios, which will call forth a conventional response in the minds of editors and readers" (p. 189). Recalling his experience as a *New York Times* reporter, he describes the way journalists could obtain quotes for particular, standard stories:

> When I needed such quotes I used to make them up, as did some of the others . . . for we knew what the bereaved mother and the mourning father should have said, and possibly even heard them speak what was in our minds rather than in theirs. (p. 190)

This being said, it should also be stressed that writing or reading newspapers is not the same as telling or listening to a story. The news is obviously mediated not only through the journalist, but also through the institutional structures of the newspaper and of society at large. Thus Hall (1975) acknowledges the social transaction between newspapers and readers, commenting "successful communication in this field depends to some degree on a process of mutual confirmation between those who produce and those who consume" (p. 22). He cautions, however, that "at the same time, the producers hold a powerful position vis-à-vis their audiences"

(p. 22) and thus will tend to set the agenda. As Nord (1980) points out, formulaic popular genres are a product not only (or primarily in his view) of mutually understood frameworks. They are also a product of economic forces that make formulaic potboilers easy and profitable to turn out.

Nevertheless, a purely economic view begs the question of where the formulae came from in the first place, and the answer, reinforced by the evidence of folklore and popular culture, is that they are not imposed from above. Slater (1982), in one of the few specific studies that compares media and folkloric communication, argues that media framings are in large part determined by an awareness on the part of journalists of existing folk schemata. She quotes a writer of the popular "literatura de cordel" in Brazil, which has some clear similarities to tabloids:

> It does no good to write about a child who was born with two heads if there is not already a rumor to the effect, if people are not already talking about it in the streets. (p. 53)

Similarly, tabloid writers tend to write stories that pick up on tales and images of Kennedy that already exist, in turn helping to keep these alive and circulating.

Young (1981), although agreeing that both economic considerations and maintenance of a dominant ideology are fundamental to the functioning of modern mass media, argues that particularly those media that must sell to working-class audiences must to a great extent represent the culture of their audiences. As Carey (1975) writes, news may be seen not so much as information-giving, but as ritual or play, as social values are defined and celebrated through the telling of stories that lay out cultural codes. Indeed, Bascom's (1954) functions of folklore (mentioned above) could just as accurately be applied to news. The power of media's "ideological effect" as discussed by Hall (1977) and others derives not from coercion and forcing audiences to consume a product they dislike, but from using familiar narrative structures to frame stories in ways that reinforce hegemony.

According to Cawelti's discussion of "artistic matrices," face-to-face oral transmission might belong to the "communal matrix," in which "there is a lack of distance between its elements and the absence of mediating figures within the system" (1978, p. 296). Closely related to this is the "mythological matrix" that "resembles the communal model in that there is a high degree of identification between creator-performer and audience, and the genres are a communal possession rather than individual creations" (p. 298). Through this matrix, a culture's values and beliefs are dramatized in such media as news and other popular culture, but with the "myth-maker" retaining control over the product. A dialectical relationship exists between symbolic systems and society so that, as Geertz (1973) notes, these symbolic systems are both a model of and a model for society, both reflecting and re-presenting value systems. It is here that media such as tabloids are situated, as they pick up existing folk ideas, re-presenting them as story, and helping to reinforce and reshape the folk worldview.

The folk worldview of tabloid readers is not always shared by the culture as a whole. In fact, tabloids may be an example of what Young (1981) calls "the accommodative culture" of the working class, a culture that, although accommodated within the dominant ideology, may be at odds with that ideology:

> This is evident, for example, in the language of newspapers directed to the working class involving the distinctly non-bourgeois world of fate, luck, inequality and cynicism. (p. 41)

Tabloids, with their emphasis on the unexplained and the mystical, as reflected in many aspects of the Kennedy myth, represent aspects of the folk worldview of their targeted audiences, just as mainstream newspapers, with their emphasis on official sources, scientific explanation and so on, represent the folk worldview of theirs (with a considerable overlap between the two, of course). Although much of the mystical view did permeate the "quality" press and other media, it dominated the tabloids, which dealt exclusively in his personality and charisma, responding to their primarily working-class readers (Perpich and Lehnert, 1984). We see clearly the "paradox of charisma," as Geertz (1983) has termed it.

> [Although] charisma is rooted in the sense of being near to the heart of things . . . a sentiment that is felt most characteristically and continuously by those who in fact dominate social affairs . . . its most flamboyant expressions tend to appear among people at some distance from the center, indeed often enough at a rather enormous distance, who want to be closer. (pp. 143-144)

Of course, there is no neat cause-and-effect relationship such that only people who read "quality" papers hold "nonmystical" images of Kennedy, or that only tabloid readers have heard that Kennedy is alive. Most people are exposed to information from myriad sources. The point is simply that in a world where mass media and oral transmission go hand-in-hand, people's perceptions derive from communication processes of all kinds. As Blaustein (undated) points out:

> The folklorist is essentially a student of human communication. In contemporary American society, the folklorist must take account of the bewilderingly complex mesh of communication channels through which our culture is generated, transmitted and perpetuated. (p. 2)

Distinctions between communication channels and genres, important as they may be to folklorists and communication scholars, are not as relevant to the "folk" in constructing a particular view of the world. Smith (1984) argues that generic distinctions between, for example, legend and rumor may be counterproductive; his argument may be extended profitably to mass communication channels:

> Irrespective of whether, as folklorists, we wish to draw the line and say this is legend and this rumour, to everyone else in the world that line does not exist. Instead the narrative content is simply information which can be derived from a variety of sources each using different forms of communication. . . . We cannot afford to use the easy option of avoiding forms of contemporary legends which occur in what we define as non-traditional modes. (pp. 212-213)

Johnson (1983) echoes this argument in his discussion of the interdisciplinary, intermedia approach of cultural studies:

> Texts are encountered promiscuously; they pour in on us from all directions in diverse, coexisting media, and differently-paced flows. In everyday life, textual materials are complex, multiple, overlapping, co-existent, juxta-posed, in a word, 'inter-textual' (p. 41)

Journalism and folklore are not only related on the occasions when newspapers report an "urban legend" as fact. Media, particularly such media as tabloids, are not merely good sources of folklore. Rather, media and oral tradition are comparable, though not identical, communication processes, during which narratives are constructed from familiar themes that repeat themselves over time. People do not necessarily transmit folklore and attend to media in different ways and for different purposes—both are part of the complex way in which cultural "reality" is constructed. The "truth" about John F. Kennedy differs among people, but whatever that perceived truth or image might be, it is a dynamic one that is fed by communication processes of all kinds, oral and mass-mediated among them.

NOTES

1. The texts studied appeared in several weekly tabloids from July, 1983, through 1984. Some stories were obtained in the form of photocopies from publishers' offices; in these cases, page references are unavailable.
2. Interview with Mary Perpich, former staff writer for *Midnight,* Aug. 6, 1985, Memphis, TN.

REFERENCES

Baker, R. L. (1976). The influence of mass culture on modern legends. *Southern Folklore Quarterly, 40,* 367-376.

Barkin, S. M. (1984). The journalist as storyteller: An interdisciplinary perspective. *American Journalism, 1*(2), 27-33.

Bascom, W. R. (1954). Four functions of folklore. *Journal of American Folklore, 67,* 333-349.

Basso, K. H. (1984). Stalking with stories: Names, places, and moral narratives among the Apache. In E. M. Bruner (Ed.), *Text, play and story: The construction and reconstruction of self and society* (pp. 19-55). WA: American Ethnological Society, 19-55.

Bird, D. A. (1976). A theory for folklore in mass media: Traditional patterns in the mass media. *Southern Folklore Quarterly, 40,* 285-305.

Bird, S. E., & Dardenne, R. W. (1986). *Myth, chronicle, and story: Exploring the narrative qualities of news.* Revised, unpublished version of paper presented in Qualitative Studies Division, Association for Education in Journalism and Mass Communication, Memphis, TN, 1985.

Blaustein, R. (Undated). *Horatio Alger is alive and well: The rags to riches syndrome and the reaffirmation of belief in the National Enquirer.* Unpublished manuscript, Indiana University, Indiana Folklore Archive.

Brunvand, J. H. (1981). *The vanishing hitchhiker.* New York: W. W. Norton.

Carey, J. (1975). A cultural approach to communication. *Communication, 2,* 1-22.

Cawelti, J. G. (1978). The concept of artistic matrices. *Communication Research, 5*(3), 283-305.

Cohen, A. (1973). *Poor Pearl, poor girl: The murdered girl stereotype in ballad and newspaper.* Austin, TX: Publications of the American Folklore Society Memoir Series, 58.

Darnton, R. (1975). Writing news and telling stories. *Daedalus, 104*(2), 175-194.

De Caro, F. A., & Oring, E. (1969). J.F.K. is alive: A modern legend. *Folklore Forum, 2*(2), 54-55.

Degh, L., & Vazsonyi, A. (1973). The dialectics of legend. Bloomington: Indiana University Folklore Preprint Series 1(6).

Dundes, A. (1982). *Interpreting folklore.* Bloomington: Indiana University Press.

Eason, D. L. (1981). Telling stories and making sense. *Journal of Popular Culture, 15*(2), 125-129.

Edwards, O. D. (1984). Remembering the Kennedys. *Journal of American Studies, 18*(3), 405-423.

Epstein, E. J. (1975). *History as fiction. In between fact and fiction: The problem of journalism.* New York: Vintage Books.

Gans, H. J. (1980). *Deciding what's news: a study of CBS Evening News, NBC Nightly News, Newsweek, and Time.* New York: Vintage Books.

Geertz, C. (1973). *The interpretation of cultures.* New York: Basic Books.

Geertz, C. (1983). Centers, kings, and charisma: Symbolics of power. In *Local knowledge: Further essays in interpretive anthropology.* New York: Basic Books.

Globe (1983, Nov. 29). Series of stories on John F. Kennedy, 4-7.

Globe (1983, December). I was J.F.K.'s last lover, page unknown.

Graber, D. A. (1984). *Processing the news: How people tame the information tide.* New York: Longman.

Hall, S. (1975). Introduction. In A. C. H. Smith, *Paper voices: The popular press and social change 1935-1965.* London: Chatto & Windus.

Hall, S. (1977). Culture, the media and the ideological effect. In J. Curran, M. Gurevitch, & J. Woolacutt (Eds.), *Mass communication and society* (pp. 315-348). London: Edward Arnold.

Hernstein Smith, B. (1981). Narrative versions, narrative theories. In W. J. T. Mitchell (Ed.), *On narrative,* (pp. 209-232). Chicago: Chicago University Press.

Hobbs, S. (1978). The folktale as news. *Oral History, 6*(2), 74-86.

Hochschild, A. (1984, February-March). Would J.F.K. be a hero now? *Mother Jones,* 56-57.

Holden, L. (1979, July). The incredibly rich tabloid market. *Writers Digest.* 19-22.

Johnson, R. (1983). *What is cultural studies anyway?* Birmingham University, Centre for Contemporary Cultural Studies General Series SP 74.

Kepplinger, H. M. (1979). Paradigm change in communication research. *Communication, 4*(2), 160-171.

Lord, A. B. (1971). *The singer of tales.* Cambridge, MA: Harvard University Press.
McDonald, D. M. (1984). *Supermarket tabloids.* Paper presented at 14th Annual Convention of the Popular Culture Association, Toronto, Canada.
Midnight (1969, October 18). Photos show JFK alive on Skorpios, 14-15.
Mullen, P. B. (1972). Modern legend and rumor theory. *Journal of the Folklore Institute, 9,* 95-109.
National Enquirer. (1960, Jan. 15). Political Notebook, 15. (1960, April 3). Political Notebook, 10.
        (1983, Nov. 22). Special Section on John F. Kennedy, 30-35.
        (1984, May 15). Special Section on David Kennedy, 30-35.
National Examiner. (1983, July 23). J. F. K. is alive!, 23.
        (1983, Sept. 13). Grace and J.F.K.'s love secrets, page unknown.
        (1984, May 15). Kennedy curse: who's next?, 11.
        (1984, July 3). Marilyn was pregnant with Kennedy baby, 1.
        (1984, Aug. 7). I lived before as J.F.K., page unknown.
        (1984, Sept. 4). J.F.K. bugged Jackie's bra, 1.
        (1984, Oct. 23). Marilyn Monroe seduced J.F.K. and Bobby for reds, 35.
        (1984, Nov. 20). Was David Kennedy buried alive?, 27.
Nord, D. P. (1980). An economic perspective on formula in popular culture. *Journal of American Culture, 3,* 17-31.
Owen Jones, M. (1971). (PC + CB) × SD (R + I + E) = Hero. *New York Folklore Quarterly, 27,* 243-260.
Perpich, M. J., & Lehnert, E. (1984). *An attitude segmentation study of supermarket tabloid readers.* Paper presented at 14th Annual Convention of the Popular Culture Association, Toronto, Canada.
Rodgers, R. S. (1985). *Popular legend and urban folklore as popular communication.* Paper presented in Popular Communication Interest Group, Annual Convention of International Communication Association, Honolulu, HI.
Rock, P. (1981). News as eternal recurrence. In S. Cohen & J. Young (Eds.), *The manufacture of news: Social problems, deviance and the mass media* (pp. 64-70). London: Constable.
Rosenberg, B. A. (1976). Kennedy in Camelot: The Arthurian legend in America. *Western Folklore, 25*(1), 52-59.
Rosnow, R. L., & Fine, G. A. (1976). *Rumor and gossip: The social psychology of hearsay.* New York: Elsevier.
Slater, C. (1982). The hairy leg strikes: The individual artist and the Brazilian literatura de cordel. *Journal of American Folklore, 95,* 51-89.
Smith, P. (1982). *On the receiving end: When legend becomes rumour.* Paper presented at the Perspectives on Contemporary Legend Conference, Sheffield, England.
Star (1984, May 15). Guilt-ridden David Kennedy's anguish, 16-17.
Sun (1984, July 3) Boy, 7, is reincarnation of J.F.K., page unknown.
Young, J. (1981). Beyond the consensual paradigm: a critique of left functionalism in media theory. In S. Cohen & J. Young (Eds.), *The manufacture of news: Social problems, deviance and the mass media* (pp. 393-421). London: Constable.

37 ● Behaving Oneself: The Place of Manners in Contemporary American Culture

KARI WHITTENBERGER-KEITH

The University of Texas at Austin

MANNERS are a big business in contemporary American society ("Minding our manners again," 1984). Manners camps and classes are popular for children and adults alike. Books about manners, ranging from the proper wedding etiquette to manners in the office, are at the top of the bestsellers lists. Popular magazines count columns on manners among their most popular features. Americans generally seem to be much more concerned about social behavior than they have been in the recent past.

The leader of the 1980s manners movement would have to be Judith Martin, former dance and theater critic for the *Washington Post.* Writing under the pseudonym of Miss Manners, Martin has made manners, and general concern with social behavior, popular again. Her "Miss Manners" column started in 1978, after she convinced a dubious editorial board at the *Post* that a manners column could be popular. Her success has gone beyond anyone's wildest dreams. The column, first syndicated to only 3 newspapers, is now featured in almost 200 newspapers nationwide. Martin receives over 10,000 letters a year in response to the column, from readers of all ages, posing various questions about manners. Her first book, *Miss Manners' Guide to Excruciatingly Correct Behavior* (1982), was on the bestseller lists for several months, and her second book, *Miss Manners' Guide to Rearing Perfect Children* (1984), has been issued in a first printing of 200,000 copies. Obviously, manners, especially in the form of Miss Manners, sells.

AUTHOR'S NOTE: The author wishes to extend grateful thanks to William Keith, David Payne, and Roderick Hart for incisive comments on drafts of this manuscript. This study is part of a larger historical study of the rhetorical functions of manners in the United States, results of which can be obtained from the author.

Correspondence and requests for reprints: Kari Whittenberger-Keith, Department of Speech Communication, the University of Texas at Austin, Austin, TX 78712.

Perhaps more important, Miss Manners signifies something of a break from the traditional approach to manners, the one commonly associated with Emily Post (1934) and Amy Vanderbilt (1952). Manners, more commonly termed *etiquette,* comprised a set of iron-clad, unbending rules that had to be followed regardless of circumstances. Traditional books about manners tended to consist of lists of prescriptions meant to be learned by heart and followed unfailingly (Beery, 1949; Holt, 1921; Post, 1934, Vanderbilt, 1952). Martin, in the person of Miss Manners, introduces a different approach to manners, in which a system of manners functions as a form of communication and a method of regulating and simplifying social interaction. This "new style" of manners has been adopted by other etiquette books as well, reflecting a seeming "humanization" of social behavior processes (Baldridge, 1984; Ford, 1983; Post, 1984).

My purpose in this chapter is to examine the nature of manners in contemporary American culture as exemplified by Judith Martin's *Miss Manners.* Although a discussion of Martin's work certainly does not exhaust what can be said about American manners, her work is nevertheless quite instructive. In order to divine the relationship of manners to communication, I will first argue that, in essence, Martin's approach to manners takes a rhetorical view of the world and a correspondingly rhetorical view of the place and function of social behavior. I will contend that the "Miss Manners" approach represents a significant, though not total, break with some established American traditions of etiquette. Second, I will identify the social and rhetorical dimensions along which manners function, according to Martin. Next, I will determine some of the ways manners may be used in contemporary American society. Finally, I will speculate as to why, after the "people as people" decade of the 60s, and the fabled "Me" decade of the 70s American society seems to have returned once again to a concern with social, "other-directed" behavior in the form of manners.

MISS MANNERS AS
A RHETORICAL ARTIFACT

Rhetoric can be broadly defined as the communication techniques and strategies for achieving social ends. Rhetorical artifacts are those that embody instrumental, behaviorally oriented strategic means for accomplishing a goal. From a rhetorical point of view, talk is purposeful, and manners (or codes of social behavior) are just as purposeful. They serve specific ends for both the individual and the social system in which he or she participates (Burke, 1969, pp. xiv, 208). The essence of Martin's definition of manners is clearly seen in her thoughts on "white" lies:

Miss Manners does not like the term "white lie," because it suggests that it is sometimes right to lie. What it actually attempts to name, however, is the skill of interpreting and responding to a complex exchange of ideas and feelings in polite society, without which civilization could not exist. . . . Responding to conventional phrases and situations in terms of *what they really mean,* rather than what they are on the surface, is [civilized behavior]. (italics added) (Martin, 1984, p. 323)

For Martin, manners serve as a rhetorical tool for achieving ends for the individual and at the same time providing a "glue" for the social fabric. She goes on to define manners as "having to do with the appearance of things, rather than with total reality" (Martin, 1982, p. 13).

To answer the question "Would you like to see some pictures of my grand-children?" with the direct literal truth—"No! Anything but that!"—would be cruel. But is that the real question? The question, if one has any sensitivity to humanity, is "Would you be kind enough to let me share some of my senti-ments, and reassure me that they are important and worthwhile?" To which a decent person can only answer, "I'd love to." (Martin, 1984, p. 303)

Probably unintentionally, Martin here touches on one of the key concepts that has delimited rhetoric since antiquity, that rhetoric deals with how peo-ple perceive the world, rather than with "reality." Martin defends an essen-tially rhetorical role for manners in human interaction and focuses on that role throughout her writings.

From what has been said so far it might seem that Martin urges two sepa-rate principles: On the one hand individuals are to accomplish their goals by being mannerly, and on the other, society as a whole is supposed to bene-fit from mannerly behavior. Although there seems to be a conflict between achievement of individual goals and social goals, Martin's conception of manners resolves this apparent contradiction. Martin's view of manners insists that mannerly or polite behavior preserves a certain *appearance.* What defines mannerly or polite behavior in a given context is the appear-ance of complete *goodwill* on the part of all concerned. In order to deter-mine what polite behavior is (for a given context), one asks oneself "How would I act if I had only goodwill and the best in mind for this person?" In the examples given later we will see that no actual goodwill is required for this; the point is that the polite person never acts as if he or she didn't have goodwill to others. This principle provides the consistency and flexibility lacking in some earlier etiquette authors, who composed long lists of rules, seemingly for the express purpose of maintaining the proper class distinc-tions. In Martin's system, the dichotomy between helping the self and help-ing society does not arise.

This rhetorical approach to manners lies at the base of the "new" style of manners Martin proposes. Her view of manners as a means of achieving ends, of accomplishing goals, and of serving individual purposes reflects a very different perspective than one that views manners as a set of unbreakable laws to be followed diligently by anyone who wishes to be considered upper class or as having good taste. As we shall see, it is this rhetorical approach to manners that may have once again made manners relevant, and important, to American culture.

THE DIMENSIONS OF
MISS MANNERS' RULES
FOR SOCIAL BEHAVIOR

Judith Martin represents a substantive break with older traditions of American manners/etiquette, such as those exemplified by etiquette writers like Emily Post. The distinctiveness of Martin's approach is highlighted most clearly in contrast to the standing tradition of etiquette books, of which Post is the chief representative. Although an authority such as Emily Post defined etiquette as a way of teaching "Good Taste" to the masses of people (Post, 1934, pp. 2-3) Martin believes these rules are essential to the functioning of the social system; "manners are the basis of civilized society" (Martin, 1984, p. 3). Manners act as the glue that holds a social system together, with people from various backgrounds, social classes, and educational levels all being bound by similar basic standards of behavior. Manners are not, in Martin's mind, a tool used by the elite to shame the lower classes, but rather a method of making the system function as smoothly as possible for all members (Martin, 1982, pp. 4-5).

In addition, Martin differs from other etiquette writers in terms of the approach she takes to learning and using manners. Although for Post and others, manners represented a set number of rules to be mastered and then applied unthinkingly (Post, 1934, pp. 2-3), Martin sees manners as a perspective by which one views life's events (Martin, 1984, p. 287). This perspective can (and must) be taught and practiced with thought and with care; it requires active involvement rather than passive reaction.

As we have seen, Martin's approach to manners differs significantly on a "philosophical" level from the etiquette "experts" of the past. Martin's approach also differs in terms of the dimensions along which manners function. Although Post and others would probably identify manners as working only on a superficial social level, Martin sees three levels on which manners fulfill needs—the level of the individual, of the society, and of the culture.

The Individual and
the Use of Manners

As noted above, Martin sees etiquette as a system within which people participate to achieve individual goals. Martin acknowledges that each person functions within a different social situation with different goals in mind, and she sets out to construct a system that will allow individuals to accomplish their goals in the most effective way possible. Within that system, there is only one unbreakable rule—do not be rude. (And perhaps it is not even a rule—it is really a definition of politeness—a very flexible one.) All goals must be achieved within the context of politeness; as Miss Manners notes, "[even] the rudeness of others [can be] conquered by politeness" (Martin, 1982, p. 4). Outside of that injunction, means are determined on the basis of an analysis of the actual situation, the possible outcomes, and the individual actor's desires and goals. (Bitzer, 1968, sounds a very similar theme in his description of the rhetorical situation.) Etiquette is not simply making other people feel "comfortable"; etiquette *can* be used to make other people feel uncomfortable (which, therefore, is not necessarily rude):

> If you are rude to your ex-husband's new wife at your daughter's wedding, you will make her feel smug. Comfortable. If you are charming and polite, you will make her feel uncomfortable. Which do you want to do? (Martin, 1982, p. 7)

Etiquette can also be used to prove a point or to take a stand, or respond to the rudeness of others:

> A gentleman of Miss Manners' acquaintance dislikes being honked at by impatient drivers for not starting his automobile quickly enough when a traffic signal turns to green. Instead of honking back, he puts on his emergency brake, emerges from his car, presents himself to the honker in the vehicle behind, and inquires politely, "Did you summon me?" (Martin, 1982, p. 4)

Martin also acknowledges that individuals use manners to accomplish their own goals. She discusses at length, for example, the appropriate behavior for a houseguest, not only in terms of pleasing the host, but also in terms of receiving attractive rewards:

> The perfect houseguest is often dishonest, in touch with others' feelings, able to refrain from communicating his own needs . . . such behavior can be quite pleasureable to those who indulge in it, and leads to fulfillment, happiness and invitations to beach condominiums, shooting parties, and yachts. (Martin, 1982, p. 228)

Martin wants to allow *all* individuals in a situation to gain the best possible results (and at the same time accomplish their unique ends) through a system that is flexible enough to accommodate individual differences. She allows for situational analysis and action based on that analysis, as well as upon the general rules of etiquette for broad categories of situations. For Martin, the rights and duties of the individual become a primary focus of her behavioral system.

The Use of Manners
Within the Social System

Martin does not focus solely on the individual in developing her system of rules for social behavior; she also recognizes the role of manners in the smooth functioning of society itself. Manners, in Martin's view, are necessary simply because individuals must live within a social system. A social system consists of a hierarchical system based on the power of each individual, and manners provide a basis through which these dimensions of power are exploited (Burke, 1969). Martin sees manners as both the great social equalizer and as the separator of people. For example, Martin subscribes to the theory that as *Americans,* all people in this country are deserving of equal respect and recognition of their human dignity; unlike previous writers on etiquette, Martin abhors the use of manners to make others feel socially inferior (Martin, 1984, p. 108). On the other hand, Martin also believes that a person with good manners will triumph over a person with bad manners— the American work ethic as adapted to manners (Martin, 1982, p. 7). Therefore, a person may treated badly by his or her boss, but in the end, he or she will be rewarded by acting politely:

> Dear Miss Manners:
> The other night, a young woman asked me where I worked and was very impressed when I told her the name of the prestigious institution. She immediately wanted to know what I did there and when I said I was a secretary, you would have thought I'd just come down with a terminal disease. Even worse were the words, "well even though you're just a secretary, it must be an interesting place to work." Can you suggest a way to avoid this situation?
>
> Gentle Reader:
> You know Miss Manners does not allow her readers to answer rudeness with rudeness. But you might say with polite pride, "Oh, no, you're mistaken. I started out as just-a-secretary, but now I'm a full secretary." (Martin, 1982, p. 173)

As illustrated by this example, Martin believes good manners are the basis of true power, the power of the individual to control his or her own destiny and survive within the social system. The secretary responds as if she took the remark in all goodwill and was merely trying to be informative. This is only polite, and any shame felt by the other person is based on personal knowledge of his or her own unpleasant intentions.

Martin also recognizes the nature of human interaction, not as the complete revelation of the self to whomsoever might be within earshot, but as the thoughtful and selective perception of others and actions of oneself. Certain situations are structured so that personal opinions and tastes are not at all to the point:

Dear Miss Manners:
You wrote about visiting newborn babies, but you didn't say what the visitor should say if the baby is a mess. I mean really ugly. . . . Can you suggest something for people who don't want to lie and say the baby is beautiful?

Gentle Reader:
It is not a lie. All babies and all brides are beautiful by definition. That is a fact of nature. (Martin, 1982, p. 41)

The person who thinks that there ought to be a polite way of telling someone that their baby is unattractive has misunderstood the situation: No one involved wants to hear that person's "real" opinion. Martin's seemingly absolute prescription here merely means that she cannot imagine a situation in which a person of goodwill would want to say that a bride or baby is ugly. Hypocrisy is a "virtue," not a curse, because hypocrisy involves the evaluation of others and a rhetorical analysis of the situation at hand (Martin, 1984, p. 85). Hypocrisy involves the sparing of feelings, always a virtue and never a sin—the only mannerly way to behave.

Therefore, Martin sees manners as providing a system of rules that allows a person to fit relatively comfortably and with a minimum of trouble into his or her social system. One might compare Martin's view of manners with the (more or less uniform) system of parliamentary procedure that in America guides all official decision-making bodies. Parlimentary procedure is democratic in that everyone has an equal voice, and it is in everyone's (personal and collective) best interest to conform to the rules. But as anyone who has ever tried to use parliamentary procedure knows, the skillful can use the rules to their advantage—in much the same vein as Martin's politely-making-others-uncomfortable. However *any* member could use the rules that way, and, whatever the defects of such a system, each member has both an individual and collective stake in the continuance of the system. Manners function similarly: Whether through an exercise of power, or the use of hypocrisy to help other people, manners allow an individual a method for dealing with his or her society.

Manners as Cultural Continuity

Finally, Martin views manners as the thread that connects a culture's past and future. In her view, the rituals people learn under the rubric of manners provide the basis for cultural identification (Martin, 1984, p. 12). Further, manners provide a basis from which an individual can interpret and come to grips with cultural and social change. In the world of Miss Manners, one finds that some things never change:

Dear Miss Manners,
Don't you think that nowadays, in modern life, the old fashioned custom of condolence calls is out of date?

Gentle Reader:
Why is that? Is it because people don't die anymore, or is it because the bereaved no longer need the comfort of their friends? Miss Manners is always interested in hearing about how life has been improved by modern thinking. (Martin, 1982, p. 700)

In Martin's world, some things, like death, taxes, and common courtesy, will never change, and so provide continuity within an inevitably changing world.

On the other hand, Martin also sees manners as a vehicle by which social change can be assisted (or at least not obstructed). Through the use of common courtesy and the consideration of people as individuals regardless of their race, creed, or belief system, manners can be used to open minds and acclimate people to a changing, yet still stable, world. Certain things are always irrelevant to mannerly behavior:

Dear Miss Manners:
What am I supposed to say when I am introduced to a homosexual couple?

Gentle Reader:
How do you do? How do you do? (Martin, 1982, p. 67)

Through the use of manners as a connection with the past, in this case common courtesy to people regardless of their sexual preference, society can be acclimated to changing standards and mores, such as the acknowledgement of the existence of homosexual couples, or biracial marriages, or different belief systems. In an egalitarian (even if imperfectly so) culture such as that of the United States, mannerly behavior seems to require a wide tolerance of diversity.

In addition, Martin concentrates on the role of manners in the education of youth as to the standards and traditions of their culture.

Manners are the basis of civilized society, and passing on civilization to the young, so that they do not run around in a natural and savage state but can live easily and comfortably within the accumulated traditions and standards of their society, is what child-rearing is all about. (Martin, 1984, p. 3)

Martin views manners as a tool of cultural transmission, as well as an artifact through which the essence of the culture can be discovered. As Europeans will happily explain, regardless of superficial similarities, American manners are quite distinctively American. Manners allow a person to maintain a sense of the past and accommodate him- or herself to the future. In other words, manners are one of the methods by which change is effected in a relatively stable social system.

Martin's treatment of manners isolates three basic levels at which manners function: the individual, the societal, and the cultural. Within each of these areas, the rules for social behavior serve a different purpose; each level embodies a tension between the individual and the larger society and/ or culture. The existence of this tension leads to the question of how manners are used in contemporary American society, particularly this "new" form of manners proposed by Judith Martin and others.

HOW MANNERS ARE USED
IN AMERICAN SOCIETY

Norbert Elias, in his excellent study of the development of manners in the Middle Ages, concludes that the purpose of rules for social behavior in any society is to preserve order and preserve the structure of hierarchy within that system (Elias, 1978, 1982, 1983). In Elias's view, manners developed from the need of the upper or ruling class to differentiate itself from the lower or peasant classes (1982). Manners provided a method of differentiation that could be easily and readily recognized by members of the elite class. As strict rules of social behavior developed, then, manners also provided a means by which individuals could, with some practice and some good fortune (usually in the form of cash), rise through the class structure— if one acted like a member of the ruling class, one might gain entrance to the ranks of the ruling class. Thus the standardization of a system of behavioral rules worked to preserve the social and hierarchical structure, by differentiating members of the respective classes and at the same time providing the opportunity for upward mobility, at least to a limited degree.

Elias's analysis of the purpose of manners in the Middle Ages provides a solid basis on which to analyze the current situation. I shall claim any study of manners in contemporary America eventually confronts the need to resolve some basic tensions within American society; manners and the desire for "polite behavior" lie at the intersection of some traditional contradictions of American life. The essential tensions of American society seem to revolve around the need to assimilate and the need to differentiate, on individual, societal, and cultural levels. America, land of the individual yet a nation of communities, has struggled with this tension throughout its existence. Manners now seem to be used to help resolve this tension, by balancing the needs of the individual, at whatever level, against the needs of the larger system. In order to gain a clearer understanding of this function, I shall deal with each of these levels separately.

The Tension Within the Self

It is evident, both in daily experiences and in the writings of Judith Martin, that to some extent individuals participate in the social order to accomplish their own goals (the fabled "pursuit of happiness"). Sometimes a person wants to align himself or herself with the system and cooperate with the hierarchy to achieve his or her own ends; conformity can bring success. At other times, a person might wish to differentiate himself or herself from the system as completely as possible, to divide and conquer in a sense, to reach his or her individual goals; uniqueness can also bring success. Thus there is a constant tension between the individual and the larger system over the interpretation of the self—to suit the society or to achieve individual ends. People are multifaceted and it is unlikely that any individual will interpret himself or herself, or be interpreted by others, the same way in all contexts. The individual is constantly wrestling with the problems of identification, both in terms of the preservation of the self and in terms of accomplishing personal goals that require the cooperation of (and so concessions to) others.

Although these tensions no doubt exist within any system, they seem to be exacerbated within the American social system. American society constantly balances the rights of individuals and the requirements of community. As a nation founded on the ideas of freedom, self-determination, and independence, America has struggled self-consciously with questions of the rights of individuals versus the benefits to the system as a whole, whether it be in laws or rules for behavior. The struggle to preserve the individual in the face of the social system is constant and ongoing.

The new style of manners addresses the self-society conflict by proposing a balance between the needs of the individual (through the instrumental and flexible nature of manners) with the needs of the social system as a whole (by holding politeness and mannerly behavior paramount in any human interaction). What emerges from this set of guidelines is a picture of a social individual, one who behaves according to a set of standards, but who within those standards is allowed (and indeed expected) to exercise a broad range of behavioral options, depending on the characteristics of the social situation. Manners seem to provide a way of adjudicating this basic individual-versus-society tension in such a way that both the individual and the social system can continue to operate with a minimum of disruption.

The Tension Within the Society

In much the same way the individual is constantly at odds with the social system as a whole, groups within the social system compete for a place in the social hierarchy. Martin discusses this problem at length, noting that America is, by definition at least, a classless society—or, perhaps, a middle-class society—yet people want to set their group apart from the indistinguishable middle class. As Martin says:

> There are three social classes in America: upper middle class, middle class, and lower middle class. Miss Manners has never heard of an American owning up to being in any other class. However, if there is one thing that all

Americans agree upon, no matter what their background, it is that the middle class is despicable. (Martin, 1982, pp. 7-8)

Americans by definition belong to the middle class, yet are dissatisfied with that classification. Martin further observes that all classes have traditionally treated one another badly, and those in the middle-middle class have had the opportunity to abuse those both above and below them in the class structure (for being too rich and too poor, respectively). The end result is that, in America, though no one wants to be average, everyone is supposed to be average.

Manners can provide a way for individuals to transcend class distinctions as such. In a sense, manners permit an individual to assimilate to his or her class and his or her social system and at the same time differentiate himself or herself from the "masses" (rudeness, of course, knows no class distinctions). No one wants to be *merely* a member of the middle-middle class and manners permit one to gloss over distinctions between the various forms of the middle-classness, distinctions that have to do with monetary differences rather than with levels of civility. Martin, in particular, sees politeness as a feature common to any social group, with class distinctions having no impact on how polite or impolite an individual should be.

On the other hand, manners may constitute a means by which an individual can move through the social system. Through a knowledge and appropriate application of the rules of social behavior, an individual can adopt the "look" of another group in the social system. Manners provide a common substance by which to judge the appropriateness of behavior (the "goodwill" test), thus unifying social groups; at the same time manners highlight distinctions between the groups (specific norms, such as those regarding swearing), allowing each group to set itself apart from the social system as a whole. In other words, manners in America reflect class or social distinctions, and at the same time provide the opportunity or possibility of jumping classifications. Therefore, manners on a societal level serve to both assimilate social groups under a general rubric of appropriate social behavior and at the same time differentiate the groups as to group-specific appropriate behavior (Goffman, 1959, 1971). Manners thus help to preserve the power structures of the society and at the same time provide a vehicle by which individuals can move through the hierarchy.

The Tensions Within the Culture

Finally, manners help the culture as a whole deal with both the preservation of tradition and the necessity of change. Manners aid an individual in coping with the changes going on in society, by providing a context for classifying changing conditions and a set of structures by which to act. At one and the same time, manners enable people to cling to the familiar, in the form of traditions, and to open themselves up to the idea of change, at least within the context of previously mannerly behavior.

In this sense, the very purpose of manners seems to have changed in recent years. Contrary to popular belief, manners have not died out (though formalized etiquette to a large extent has). Manners now serve a somewhat altered purpose within the social system, and have changed to fill that role. Manners now appear more situational, not in the sense of absolute relativity of behavior (after all, even Martin has some absolute principles), but in the sense of applying the standards differently according to the social situation in which they occur. Manners are less a commodity reserved for use at parties and formal occasions than a set of behavioral rules and standards that permeate every facet of life.

This "new look" for manners may not be readily recognizable to people who were raised with strong formal standards (usually centering around the use of forks). But there are standards for behavior and there are rules for application—and it seems typically American that the standards have become more flexible and the rules situationally applied. America, as the melting pot of cultures, needs such flexibility in a way that older, more "traditional" societies do not. Manners have developed into a tool through which people can interpret and adjust to an ever-changing society; a tool that allows a grounding in the traditions of the past and at the same time provides the flexibility needed to face the future. Continuity thus may be maintained by manners, and the tension between change and stasis is resolved.

Manners, then, seem to perform a number of functions within contemporary American society. First, they provide a way for the individual to resolve the tension between his or her need to be an individual and, at the same time, the need to be a member of the social system. Second, manners provide a method by which social groups can resolve their tensions and conflicts, both by being drawn together with similar basic mannerly standards, and being differentiated through the application of these standards to different situational contexts. Finally, manners help the culture resolve the tension between the pull of tradition and the need to change by providing basic standards that have the capacity to accommodate situational differences. Manners serve very real purposes in American society, purposes rarely acknowledged. The recognition of these purposes brings us full circle in our discussion then—the question now becomes why has American society turned back toward manners? Why have manners become big business? In other words, why manners, and why now?

THE RISE OF
MANNERS IN AMERICA

Having looked at the general functions of manners in American society, it seems worthwhile to speculate on possible reasons for the current interest in manners, as exemplified by the many books now being published on that subject. The era of the 1980s may well represent a synthesis of the variety of cultural experiences in recent times. People who have lived through both the 60s and the 70s, and the extremes they represented, now seem to feel a pressure to find their place within the social system. This nostalgic view of conformity is known as "Getting Back To Traditional Values."

The interest in manners in the 1980s may reflect an attempt to synthesize these experiences and arrive at a workable resolution. The "new manners" of Martin and others combine components from both eras, as well as some of the traditions of past etiquette, into a usable set of standards. The experiences of the 1960s are reflected in a concern over how to treat people who have "thrown away tradition" by living together, marrying across races, or taking on nontraditional roles. According to Martin, one deals with these situations by remembering that other people's sexual and relationship preferences are nobody else's business: For the purpose of making introductions, people who are not married are "good friends," and no other details (sexual habits, living arrangements, and so on) are required. At the same time the theme of individuality so prevalant in the 1970s is reflected in the increasingly situational focus of manners, with the individual analyzing the situation and acting on his or her wishes—the common notion of "assertiveness." Note what Miss Manners says about salespeople:

> The less scrupulous of those who sell funeral services try to embarrass people with the suggestion that anyone who cares about the recently deceased will "spare no expense" in the burial, an emotional non sequitur if ever there was one. The same tactic has been adopted by other professions. The whole posture of what is termed, in the vernacular, "snooty" is cultivated by some headwaiters, real estate salespeople, boutique clerks, and others who hope to embarrass honest customers into spending more than they wish to spend. . . . This should be seen as a commercial ploy, not a challenge of manners. It is perfectly good manners to check over one's bill and ask for an explanation if it seems to be wrong; it is good manners to spend what one wishes to spend and not what one doesn't want to or cannot afford; and it is good manners to ask for what is coming to one if it does not seem to be forthcoming. (Martin, 1982, pp. 10-11)

According to Martin, "manners" do not have to mean deference and turning the other cheek; the new manners provide a way of coping with change on all levels: change in roles, change in technology, change in traditions.

Further, the consumers of these new manners, insofar as they can be classed simply as the adults born during the "baby boom," may well need these new standards. As the children of a relatively prosperous world, untouched by the Great Depression or the Great War, these people are the essence of the great and indistinguishable middle class. These persons are having to adjust, after having revolted in the 60s, to membership in the middle class, often as the vice presidents of companies with homes in the suburbs. At the same time, they want very much to keep their sense of self and individuality in a seemingly group-oriented society. They have turned to manners as a way of balancing these opposing desires, as a method of achieving their own ends within the social system. In this way, manners may provide a vehicle by which these tensions can be and are being resolved. This desire, for a means by which to solve problems and reach goals, more than anything else may have laid the groundwork for Americans' revived interest in the seemingly old-fashioned subjects of manners and etiquette.

CONCLUSION

In the past, the study of manners has too often shared the same fate as the study of rhetoric and communication in the intellectual community at large. Both subjects have been perceived as too shallow and too irrelevant to command serious scholarly attention. Yet, as we have seen, manners and etiquette are much more than the superficial trappings of social situations. Because manners operate in everyday contexts, in every social interchange, mannerly behavior and values exert great influence over the form and content of communication. What makes American culture idiosyncratic, among other things, is that Americans transact their social business in a unique way. The study of manners gives us direct access both to social interaction, communication, and culture, and the ways in which these are interdependent.

REFERENCES

Baldridge, L. (1984). *Amy Vanderbilt's complete book of etiquette*. New York: Doubleday.
Beery, M. (1949). *Manners made easy*. New York: Whittlesey House.
Bitzer, L. (1968). The rhetorical situation. *Philosophy and Rhetoric, 1*, 1-13.
Burke, K. (1969). *A rhetoric of motives*. Berkeley: University of California Press. (Original work published 1954)
Carson, G. (1966). *The polite Americans*. New York: William Morrow.
Elias, N. (1978). *The civilizing process: The history of manners* (E. Jephcott, Trans.). New York: Urizen Press. (Original work published 1939)
Elias, N. (1982). *The civilizing process: Power and civility* (E. Jephcott, Trans.). New York: Pantheon. (Original work published 1939)
Elias, N. (1983). *The court society* (E. Jephcott, Trans.). New York: Pantheon. (Original work published 1969).
Ford, C. (1980). *Charlotte Ford's book on modern manners*. New York: Simon & Schuster.
Goffman, E. (1959). *The presentation of self in everyday life*. New York: Doubleday.
Goffman, E. (1971). *Relations in public*. New York: Harper Torch Books.
Holt, E. (1921). *Encyclopedia of etiquette: A book of manners for everyday use*. Oyster Bay, NY: Doubleday.
Martin, J. (1982). *Miss Manners' guide to excruciatingly correct behavior*. New York: Warner.
Martin, J. (1984). *Miss Manners' guide to rearing perfect children*. New York: Antheneum.
Mazzei, G. (1983). *The new office etiquette: A guide to getting along in the corporate age*. New York: Poseidon.

Merser, C. (1983). *Honorable intentions: The manners of courtship in the 80's*. New York: Antheneum.

Minding our manners again. (1984, November). *Time*, 62-70.

Post, E. (1984). *Emily Post's etiquette*. New York: Funk & Wagnalls.

Post, E. P. (1934). *Etiquette: The blue book of social usage*. New York: Funk & Wagnalls.

Robertson, J. O. (1980). *American myth, American reality*. New York: Hill & Wang.

Schlesinger, A. M., Sr. (1947). *Learning how to behave*. New York: Macmillan.

Vanderbilt, A. (1952). *Complete book of etiquette: A guide to gracious living*. Garden City, NJ: Doubleday.

38 ● The Portrayal of Conversation in "Cathy" Cartoons: A Heuristic Tool for Rules Research

SUSAN B. SHIMANOFF

San Francisco State University

S INCE its debut on November 22, 1976, the popularity of the comic strip "Cathy," created by Cathy Guisewite, has mushroomed. Beginning as illustrated letters to her mother, it now appears in over 400 newspapers and is ranked as first or second in popularity in several readership polls. The strip has been lauded for having "universal appeal," has been compared favorably to other comic giants like "Peanuts," "Doonesbury," and Woody Allen, and has been highlighted in several popular magazines (Alter, 1984; "Cathy Guisewite," 1977; Guisewite, 1982, 1983, 1984; Harayda, 1978; Harrison, 1981; James, 1982; Koris, 1982; Krupp, 1982; Millner, 1983; Robotham, 1982). The strip's main character, Cathy, has been described as "exactly like somebody everybody knows," and as one who "strikes a responsive chord in us because of her humanness and vulnerability" (Peter, 1979, p. 68).

Typically, "Cathy" is characterized as embodying the conflicts of a contemporary working woman as she chooses between traditional values and emerging new ones (Alter, 1984; Harrison, 1981; Koris, 1982; Krupp, 1982; Peter, 1979; Robotham, 1982). Admittedly, this is a major theme of the strip, but the present analysis is concerned with another issue, namely Guisewite's portrayal of conversational rules. References to communication are abundant in the "Cathy" cartoons. This abundance may be due, in part, to the cartoonist's background. Ms. Guisewite holds a B.A. degree in English and was a highly successful vice president of an advertising firm, two endeavors in which, like cartooning, effective communication is paramount. In addition to the presence of abundant commentaries by a skilled practitioner, there are other reasons why Guisewite's "Cathy" cartoons may be of interest to communication scholars.

Correspondence and requests for reprints: Susan B. Shimanoff, Department of Speech and Communication Studies, San Francisco State University, San Francisco, CA 94132.

Cartoons are for several reasons an excellent resource for identifying cultural conceptions of what constitutes typical and ideal communication. Cartoons "draw heavily from the experiences of the society which produces them" (Turner, 1977, p. 28) and thus they "serve as revealing reflectors of popular attitudes, tastes, and mores" (Inge, 1979, p. 631). In addition to reflecting cultural values, cartoons "invite us to think about its [culture's] constituent parts and their meaning for our own lives" (DeSousa & Medhurst, 1982, p. 83). Thus they can become "equipment for living" (Turner, 1977, p. 28) or, in this case, guides for communicating. Cartoons also reflect the insights of a sensitive observer (the cartoonist), and thus may provide richer data than those produced by the untrained informants in typical social science research (Coser, 1963).

Further, cartoons frequently make cultural values transparent by violating accepted practices. In fact, Suls (1983) argues that humor "seems to require that some rules are violated . . . humor presents extreme divergencies from what is expected" (pp. 53-54). Although all of the above characteristics make cartoons a rich source for identifying communication rules, it is the propensity of cartoons to deviate from rules, and at the same time reflect common behaviors, that makes them especially valuable to communication scholars.

Sometimes implicit rules are only made visible to researchers when the rules are violated and engender some form of metacommunication (messages about messages (for example, alignment talk, repair, or explicit criticism; see Morris & Hopper, 1980; Shimanoff, 1980) or produce a negative outcome. Because the preference for rule conformity over rule deviation is reinforced by positive and negative sanctions, observers of naturally occurring discourse may have difficulty finding a sufficient number of deviations from which to infer rules. In addition, unless a deviation is of a sufficient magnitude to exceed the hearer's "tolerance threshold" (Boynton, 1979), the social injunctions against drawing attention to the errors of others may decrease further the available evidence for implicit rules in everyday conversations. In contrast to everyday conversations, the abundance of demonstrative deviations and sanctions in cartoons makes them an ideal resource for identifying probable rules. Once such rules are hypothesized, the task of verifying them with naturally occurring discourse should be much easier than if one were to examine such discourse "blindly."

Other researchers (Hugenberg & Schaefermeyer, 1983; Kougl, 1983) have demonstrated that fiction can be used to generate heuristic propositions regarding interpersonal communication. In a similar fashion, the present study sought to determine if the portrayal of conversation in "Cathy" cartoons could serve as a heuristic tool for rules research. To be valuable as heuristic tools, the cartoons should meet three criteria: (1) reflect the assessments of several native speakers, (2) mirror established research findings on conversational behavior, and (3) highlight aspects of conversation not typically studied and/or indicate fruitful directions for rules research.

Meeting the first criterion would increase the probability that the inferred rules would be applicable to a reasonably large speech community, and meeting the second criterion would increase the probability that any additional rules inferred from the cartoons actually operate in everyday conversations. To meet the third criterion the analysis need not produce "earthshattering" revelations, but it should complement other rules research by providing further confirmation of preliminary findings and speculations, or by drawing attention to topics largely neglected by current research. Because "Cathy" cartoons are very popular, and critics, as well as readers, consider them accurate reflections of everyday life, it seems likely that they meet the first criterion. Therefore, the present analysis sought to determine whether or not these cartoons met the other two criteria.

METHOD

In particular, the present investigation examined portrayals of conversational ideals as they appear in Guisewite's books: *Another Saturday Night of Wild and Reckless Abandon* (1982), *A Mouthful of Breath Mints and No One to Kiss* (1983), and *Men Should Come with Instruction Booklets* (1984).[1] The main characters in the strips include: the heroine, Cathy, who is a career woman and single; Irving, Cathy's principal boyfriend; Cathy's parents; Andrea, Cathy's closest female friend; Charlene, the receptionist in Cathy's office; and Mr. Pinkley, Cathy's boss.

Because positive and negative sanctions are indicative of prescriptive[2] rules (Shimanoff, 1980), the cartoons used in the analysis included those in which communication was evaluated (verbally, nonverbally, or in a thought bubble), those in which a positive or negative outcome was attributed to a communication practice, and those in which utterances within one strip were incongruous with each other. These cartoons were then repeatedly examined in an effort to locate recurring themes. Similarities and differences were noted among those communication behaviors that prompted evaluations or incongruities and those that were presented as producing positive or negative outcomes. As the cartoons were grouped and regrouped into various classification schemes, it became apparent that one coherent way of presenting the patterns observed in the cartoons was to compare them to Grice's (1975) conversational maxims.

Language philosopher H. Paul Grice (1975) argued that conversants generally assume that four basic conversational rules or maxims are operative: (1) quality (tell the truth and don't talk about things for which one does not have adequate evidence), (2) quantity (provide all necessary information, but no more), (3) relation (make one's remarks relevant), and (4) manner (avoid obscurity and ambiguity, and be brief and orderly).[3] Grice's primary purpose in articulating these maxims was to demonstrate that they could be used to account for conversational implicatures or inferences, but he also indicated that in general communicators are expected to observe these maxims to avoid producing utterances that are "conversationally unsuitable" (1975, p. 45). Grice admitted that there are other conversational rules and maxims, but he chose to elaborate only on the four stated above.

The "Cathy" strips were rich with examples of various conversational practices as they relate to these maxims. Each cartoon was examined to assess the degree to which it was consistent with Grice's conversational maxims. The results of these comparisons are presented below. Cartoons that were clear reflections of the maxims are presented first, followed by cartoons that seemed to be an extension of the maxims as articulated by Grice (that is, cartoons that suggested additional rules not acknowledged by Grice and yet consistent with the principles he identified). Finally, some cartoons suggested that there may be mitigating circumstances that rendered the maxim inoperative or that some rules superseded others. These cartoons are explicated in a section entitled "Qualification" for each maxim for which such cartoons occurred. Whenever Guisewite's portrayal of conversational practices and rules reflected issues also contained in other scholarly writings on naturally occurring conversations, the relevant research was compared to the cartoon portrayals.

CARTOON PORTRAYAL OF
CONVERSATIONAL MAXIMS AND RULES

Quality Maxim

Like other conversants, the characters in the "Cathy" strips generally proceeded on the assumption that their conversational partners were telling the truth. Listeners rarely challenged the truth of speakers' claims, even in those cases in which the speaker is in fact lying. For example, Andrea believed Cathy when Cathy claimed to have gotten the best possible price for her own car even though she undersold it (1982, p. 70) as well as when she told Andrea that she had completed her tax forms when she had not even opened the envelopes (1984, p. 107). Cathy also lied about herself, dating other men, the frequency with which she lost her keys, Irving's strengths, getting a present for Irving, and getting a raise (1982, p. 18, 47, 101, 111, 118, 126; 1983, p. 119; 1984, p. 7, 72).

In each case the lies were not challenged initially by the hearer. Further, even if a lie was eventually revealed to the hearer, lying itself was rarely negatively sanctioned. Instead, typically the speaker was criticized for the behavior that prompted the lie (for example, Andrea criticized Cathy for buying

Irving a present, but not for lying about it) or the lie led to other types of negative consequences (for example, Cathy's checks bounced and her apartment was a mess because rather than doing these chores, as she claimed,
she was secretly dating several men simultaneously). Further, although
hearers rarely criticized lies, speakers were sometimes critical of their own
fabrications and the consequences.

Messages aimed at manipulating the hearer, by saying what the speaker
assumes the hearer wants to hear (that is, half-truths), seemed to be more
readily detected by cartoon characters than outright lies. For the most part
these messages failed because the hearer recognized the manipulation or
the manipulation was transparent. For example, when Irving gushed with
affection for Cathy over the telephone, insisting that he must see her, Cathy
recognized his sneaky but eloquent effort to get invited over to use her air
conditioner (1984, p. 37). In other strips Cathy tried to impress her dates
by saying what she thought they wanted to hear, but they recognized her
motives and tried to get her to express her own opinion (1982, p. 107;
1984, p. 60).

If the manipulation was immediately detected, then negative sanctions
were usually limited to the hearer exposing the speaker's insincerity. However, if the hearer later discovered that he or she had been manipulated by
one of these messages, then the negative sanctions were more severe. For
example, Cathy became visibly angry when Ed's behavior made it apparent that he had behaved like a gentleman so he could seduce her (1983,
p. 22), and when Irving revealed that he had feigned emotional expressiveness to gain her affection (1984, p. 35).

In the few instances manipulative messages were successful in the strip,
the hearer wanted to believe the speaker and never recognized the manipulation. For example, Cathy decided to buy a car from a salesman, even
though he told her that the car would lose all its resale value within three
years and the costs of maintaining it would go up. Based on this disclosure
Cathy decided to buy from him because "he seemed so honest"; because
he told Cathy what she already believed, whatever else he said was viewed
as truthful (1982, p. 70). Cathy's mother was eager to believe a misrepre-
sentation of Cathy's breakup with Brian because she then was able to fulfill
her role as a comforting mother (1983, p. 124), and when Irving pretended
to express sincere emotional distress, Cathy welcomed his expression of vulnerability and intimacy by embracing and comforting him (1983, p. 103).

In summary, then, Guisewite's characters generally assumed that their
conversational partners were telling the truth. These portrayals are consistent with Grice's quality maxim. Although there were relatively few deviations from this maxim, these deviations typically either went undetected by
the hearers or, if detected, were criticized only mildly, if at all. It was only
when the lie resulted in the hearer being manipulated that violations of the
honesty maxim were considered serious breaches of the maxim.

Extensions

In addition to telling the truth, the quality maxim holds that one should not speak if one lacks adequate evidence. The adequate-evidence maxim typically is discussed in terms of a speaker's assertions, and often is associated with rumor or gossip. There was only one conversation in which speakers were criticized for gossiping, and in this case it was not the absence of evidence, but rather the potential use of the information that was questioned (1984, p. 16). Thus there were no clear violations of this maxim from the speaker's perspective. However, when hearers expressed their interpretations of previous utterances, their articulated responses frequently reflected exaggerations or misinterpretations that were based on inadequate or even contradictory evidence.

Guisewite's characters have a propensity to hear what they want to hear (1982, p. 24, 25, 46, 81, 119; 1983, p. 63, 71, 103, 118, 119, 123; 1984, p. 19, 20, 28, 30, 38, 57, 65, 94, 98). For example, when a woman telephoned Irving and described him as an "inconsiderate pig . . . self-centered scum . . . miserable despicable worm . . . clod!" he gleefully announced, "At last . . . a woman called me!!" (1984, p. 19). In another strip, Grant delivers a lengthy speech admonishing Cathy for assuming they have a relationship. He told her that although they had two great dates, they may or may not go out again, and that in the meantime he was not going to kiss the ground she walks on or feel guilty because he was not dancing through life with her! With a broad smile, Cathy summarized his speech as "Great dates. Go out again. Kiss and dance" (1983, p. 71). Cathy had a similar experience when she tried to dump Brian. She told him that she only dated him because she needed to boost her ego "in the most superficial way," needed to remind herself not to be tempted by a cute face or egomaniac again, and needed to practice being honest with someone she doesn't like. When asked if he understood, Brian exclaimed "You need me!!" (1983, p. 123).

The cartoons also exposed how the conversants sometimes assumed a more negative interpretation than was warranted by the available information (1982, p. 108, 118; 1983, p. 8, 104, 126; 1984, p. 6, 22, 29, 52, 55, 66, 85, 91, 120, 121). For example, merely because Cathy and Irving were not conversing as they drove back from dinner, Irving concluded that Cathy was mad, bored, hated him, and if she hated him "who needs her?" (1984, p. 52). Cathy was equally capable of this kind of paranoia. In response to a simple compliment about her briefcase, Cathy responded, "Oh sure. Today you think it's a great-looking briefcase. Tomorrow you'll be screaming at me because we're having frozen dinners again and I took a business call at home!! Who needs it??!" (1984, p. 85).

The incongruities among messages within these strips draws the reader's attention to a communication problem. Regardless of whether the respondent errs in a positive or negative direction when articulating interpretations, the cartoon's humor is dependent upon the reader's recognition that such interpretations are not warranted. What is significant about these particular cartoons is that they demonstrate that the responses of hearers, as well as initial utterances by speakers, are governed by rules. Although these rules do not usually determine precisely how one must respond (Jacobs, 1985), they do render some responses illegitimate. One might argue that an ideal communicator (hearer) would seek adequate information to make accurate interpretations rather than faulty or exaggerated ones, but as shall be demonstrated in the section on manner, other conversational constraints do not always make it as easy to achieve this goal as one might assume.

Qualifications

Although lying produced little in the way of negative sanctions, telling the truth (that is, abiding by the honesty maxim) often produced dramatically negative consequences (1982, p. 7, 19, 65, 73, 77, 97, 100, 123; 1983, p. 7, 21, 29, 77, 89, 94, 121; 1984, p. 28, 33, 35, 42, 45, 59, 78, 99, 111, 117, 121). For example, after being prompted by the other to talk about their feelings, Cathy and Irving freely disclosed their attraction to other people. These disclosures led to negative responses. In one strip, Irving walked out on Cathy as she said, "I knew you wouldn't understand" (1982, p. 19), and in another, Cathy dumped a bucket of chicken on Irving's head, prompting him to exclaim, "I fail to see how this is bringing us any closer, Cathy" (1982, p. 73).

Because telling the truth can be troublesome, characters sometimes avoided being completely honest about their attitudes and needs. In other words, they failed to be assertive. Cathy periodically announced that she should be assertive, and Andrea constantly encouraged her in that direction. However, Cathy often found it difficult to be assertive, particularly when it came to initiating, maintaining, or rejecting romantic relationships (1982, p. 5, 7, 16, 27, 29, 32, 52, 55, 82, 88, 92, 95, 103, 107, 124; 1983, p. 19, 33, 36, 39, 94; 1984, p. 15, 32, 86, 106). In fact, Cathy claimed that the only men with whom she could be really honest were those she never wanted to speak to again (1982, p. 71).

Cathy was sometimes so evasive that she made an unpleasant message sound positive. For example, she told Andrea that she was furious with Irving, that he confused her, and was driving her nuts. When Andrea asked her if she had told Irving that, she replied, "Sort of . . . I told him no man has ever made me feel this way before" (1984, p. 15). The extreme incongruity between Cathy's feelings and her words leads to laughter, but her behavior is not unlike that found in naturally occurring conversations. Shimanoff (1985b) reported that speakers tend to downgrade unpleasant emotions regarding the hearer and to speak more frankly when that person is not present. Such downgrades probably occur in part because a full expression of unpleasant emotions would be considered less polite (Brown & Levinson, 1978; Shimanoff, 1985a, 1985b).

Guisewite appears to be less certain than Grice about the advisability of telling others the truth. Lying was negatively sanctioned when it threatened the face-needs of the hearer (that is, when the message threatened the hearer's need for approval or for autonomy; Brown & Levinson, 1978), but so was telling the truth under those conditions. Guisewite generally appears to agree less with Grice and more with linguist Robin Lakoff (1975), who wrote: "When the crunch comes, the rules of politeness will [should] supersede the rules of conversation: better to be unclear than be rude" (p. 74). Conversants seem to be caught in a double bind between two sets of incompatible rules: (1) be assertive and truthful versus (2) be tactful and be discreet. The cartoons reflected a preference for the second set of rules. Native speakers reported similar conflicts and preferences in their expression of emotions (Shimanoff, 1985a). Future research on other types of conversational behavior may reveal that the preferences of Guisewite's characters are the preferences of native speakers in other contexts as well.

Quantity Maxim

Grice (1975) argued that if conversants are cooperative they will provide all necessary information without giving extraneous information. Several of the strips dealt with the amount of information disclosed and its effects. Most of these dealt with purposeful evasion or unwarranted verbosity rather than messages that were inadvertently insufficient. However, this latter error did appear in one strip. Cathy was unsuccessful in communicating her attraction to a man because he failed to infer her interest when she purposefully touched his arm with her elbow (1983, p. 29).

Most typically the absence of adequate information was attributed to purposeful evasion rather than to an accidental omission (1982, p. 93; 1983, p. 21, 50, 118; 1984, p. 84, 92). Purposeful evasion was common in Cathy's relationship with her mother. For example, when Cathy delivered a philosophical "oration" about the merits of her class reunion, rather than revealing the gossip she had acquired, her mother complained, "Come on, Cathy . . . get to the good stuff" (1982, p. 93). When her mother asked her about her job, apartment, Irving, and having children, Cathy responded to each question in turn by saying that each was a "gray area" (1984, p. 84). Evasion between Cathy and her mother was common, but it occurred between other characters as well.

In fact, Cathy was sometimes the recipient of such messages. For example, Irving tried to avoid telling Cathy he had another woman in his apartment by using the rather transparent pronoun "it." He managed to keep up this evasion for three turns-at-talk, but finally he said "she." Cathy began cheering, "She! Ahah! Ahah!! I got you to say 'She'!" She then realized the ramifications of the message and wondered, "What am I celebrating for?" (1983, p. 21). Sometimes less information, just like less than the complete truth, is better.

At other times characters criticized each other for being too verbose (1982, p. 32, 48; 1983, 11, 51; 1984, p. 117, 121). Many of these strips reflected a double standard: It is not all right for you to talk at length, unless you say positive things about me, but it is acceptable for me to take the floor for long periods of time. Lengthy speech also was criticized for two other reasons: (1) If one discloses too much too early in a relationship it removes all the excitement (1982, p. 48), and (2) it is too costly to be verbose when placing personal advertisements in the newspaper (1984, p. 117).

Cathy told Andrea that after only three dates she could not get excited about going out with Jeff again because they have "already told each other all the good stuff" (1982, p. 48). Cathy knew experientially what communication researchers have demonstrated empirically: that complete and immediate disclosure is not always wise (Bochner, 1982). Guisewite also demonstrated how a financial motive can cut through all the excess to the core of one's message. Cathy's want ad, which started out as "Dynamic woman wishes to establish emotional harmony with man who has seen *The Big Chill* more than three times . . . Watches *Cheers* every week . . . Knows all the words to 'Yesterday' . . . and is counting the days until 'Doonesbury' returns" was reduced to "Child of the media seeks same."

Qualification

Although Grice (1975) argued that providing too little information may be more problematic than providing too much, the cartoon characters were more critical of receiving too much information than not enough. This observation is consistent with Jackson and Jacobs's (1980) claim that in conversations there is a preference for being underinformative rather than being overinformative. One reason for this preference is that the turn-taking mechanism in conversation makes it easier to repair an error of too little information than one of too much information.

In addition, the likelihood that the speaker will threaten his or her own face (image) or the hearer's face typically becomes greater as the amount of information increases, and this may further contribute to the preference for being underinformative. It is evident, for example, that Cathy's vague description of her anger toward Irving was less threatening than a more direct and detailed description would have been. When speakers were evasive in responding to questions about themselves they sometimes frustrated and misled their hearers, but in most cases the reader is encouraged to sympathize with the speaker more than the hearer, because the hearer was shown prying into personal matters. Evasive answers helped to maintain the speaker's privacy and image. The tendency in the cartoons to avoid revealing information that might dishonor the hearer (that is, avoiding total honesty) or speaker is consistent with Keenan's (1976) finding that in Madagascar information that might bring shame is not disclosed. The cartoons suggest that a similar tendency, even if not as strong, may exist in the United States.[4]

Relevance Maxim

Grice (1975) argued that conversants require that their conversational partners demonstrate the relevance of their utterance to the preceding remark. There were no cartoons in which subsequent remarks were totally unrelated to the preceding ones. There were, however, various other ways in which respondents viewed utterances as irrelevant, or at least inappropriate in light of preceding discourse.

There are several cartoons in which Cathy's subsequent remarks were in one sense technically relevant, but nonetheless were viewed as irrelevant and totally baffling to her conversational partner. These apparent violations of the relevance maxim occurred because the preceding utterances, which would have made the relevance of the subsequent remark clear, were not accessible to the hearer. The preceding remarks were contained either in a conversation with another person (1982, p. 96, 103; 1983, p. 47; 1984, p. 70) or in an internal (intrapersonal) conversation (1982, p. 52, 75, 86; 1983, p. 44, 71; 1984, p. 23, 66, 83) rather than in a conversation in which the current hearer was present. If the conversational partner had been privy to these preceding remarks, the utterances would have been perceived as relevant; however, without access to this information, confusion and negative evaluations of the speaker often resulted.

For example, in one conversation with her mother, Cathy used a pond metaphor to illustrate what happens when couples ignore unpleasant aspects of their relationship. Irving arrived at Cathy's apartment door in the middle of this conversation. When Cathy opened the door, rather than a usual greeting Cathy shouted, "PRAY FOR RAIN, MY DARLING. OUR POND IS EVAPORATING!!" Totally disoriented, Irving responded, "Huh? Aach! Huh? What?" (1984, p. 70).

On another occasion when by herself, Cathy worried that Irving might have a new girlfriend. She got so worked up that in her mind Irving and this hypothetical girlfriend had fallen in love and might be moving away. Irving was not privy to any of Cathy's anxieties, so when she finally spoke and said, "MY DARLING! I WOULD FOLLOW YOU TO THE OCEAN TO WIN YOU BACK!", Irving thought to himself, "I hate coming in after the movie starts" (1984, p. 83). The behavior of the conversational partners in these strips is typical of that found in other cartoons; the speaker understands the relevance of the utterance while the hearer is baffled and negatively sanctions the speaker.

Extensions

Typically there is a large range of responses that would be considered topically relevant. In fact this latitude is frequently so large that scholars have argued that topical relevance is not found in a single utterance, but in the interaction between utterances (Litton-Hawes, 1977; Schank, 1977). Still some responses will be judged as more appropriate (more relevant) than others. In addition to topical relevance with the preceding utterance, the cartoons demonstrated that several other factors affect these judgments: (1) cultural expectations, (2) the focal point of the preceding discourse, (3) the tone or mood of the preceding discourse, (4) time and place, (5) prior conversations, and (6) the audience.

Cultural expectation. The humor of several cartoons was dependent upon violations of common expectations regarding the kinds of utterances that follow other utterances. In creating these expectations Guisewite drew upon various linguistic and cultural rituals. For example, Guisewite capitalized on expectations concerning the phrase "three little words." When Cathy telephoned Irving to tell him that she was thinking about him and "those three little words that mean so much to both of us," Irving responded with "I have company" (1984, p. 23). In another strip, Cathy offered another meaning for that common phrase. When she was distraught because Irving had not called in a week and she asked her mother what to say to Irving, her mother recommended, "Just . . . say those three magic little words." Cathy then shouted into the phone, "IS SHE SKINNY?!" (1983, p. 100). In each case the "three little words" expressed were topically relevant but nonetheless unexpected. These deviations were associated with embarrassment, anger, and fear.

Of further significance to the relevance maxim is the fact that to be humorous Cathy's responses could not be totally irrelevant to the preceding utterances. Suls (1983) pointed out that to be funny the incongruity in humor "must be perceived to fit in some fashion with the earlier premise of the joke" (p. 53). The cartoons would not be as funny with just any response (for example, "The dog ran " instead of "Is she skinny?" for "three little words"). Thus even when deviating from probable responses the cartoonist was constrained by relevancy conventions.

Focal point. In addition to violating specific expectations, conversants sometimes failed to address the essence of preceding remarks. For example, in one strip Cathy's date made several sexual overtures when he explained how car seats, couches, and chairs are all like beds. Cathy failed to acknowledge the sexual message and instead, after each of his descriptions, commented on how each object reminded her of food (for example, chocolate color, oreo pattern, hue of milk duds). Although both conversants were discussing the same pieces of furniture, the remarks of each appeared to be irrelevant given the comments of the other (1983, p. 64).

Guisewite's exploitation of these kinds of expectations illustrates a principle of conversational relevance that has been the focus of recent research. In a series of studies, Tracy and Moran (1983) demonstrated that it is not enough for speakers to make their utterances relevant to just any element in preceding discourse; to be a more competent speaker one must address the main issue. Although the responses in the above cartoons were related tangentially to the preceding discourse, they are humorous because they fail to address the presumed issue.

The preceding tone. Topical relevance alone may not be enough for an utterance to be considered an appropriate or relevant conversational next-turn. Guisewite demonstrated that for an utterance to be perceived as a competent next-turn, the utterance also may need to incorporate the primary tone of previous utterances. For example, when Cathy got a raise and was celebrating with Irving, she announced that she wanted "to savor this moment forever!!" Irving provided minimal recognition of Cathy's news and then informed Cathy that he got laid off. With his disclosure Cathy's enthusiasm evaporated and she revealed that she had hoped "forever" was going to be longer than that (1983, p. 17). In another strip, a group of women had a "bitch-session" in which one by one they took another drink as they denounced the evil deeds of a man. However, when Charlene deviated from this tone and toasted "sweet, adorable Frank, who asked me to be his bride!!", the group became quite disgruntled (1983, p. 55). To the present author's knowledge, researchers of naturally occurring conversations have not investigated rules regarding maintaining or changing the tone or mood of previous discourse.

Time and place. Some utterances in the strips were not technically irrelevant given preceding discourse, but they were nonetheless negatively evaluated because of when or where they occurred; that is, the characters indicated that such utterances would be more appropriate or relevant at another time. For example, when Irving told Cathy that he loved her over the telephone just before he boarded a flight, Cathy screamed, "WHY DON'T YOU EVER SAY YOU LOVE ME WHEN YOU'RE STANDING IN MY LIVING ROOM?!!" (1983, p. 6).

In another strip, as Irving kissed Cathy she asked him, "What color are you going to paint your living room?" When Irving seemed baffled by Cathy's behavior, she explained that she was initiating small talk because it is supposed to remove the pressure associated with a romantic moment. But Irving found Cathy's explanation unsatisfactory, and he emphatically denounced her sense of timing: "I'M KISSING YOU AND YOU'RE PLANNING SMALL TALK?? YOU'RE NUTS!!" (1983, p. 112). Irving's comment is consistent with Watzlawick, Beavin, and Jackson's (1967) observation that when communicators violate another's sense of what is appropriate (that is, rules), they are perceived as "mad or bad."

Prior conversations. Guisewite also illustrated an aspect of conversational relevance that has been noted by only a few conversational researchers, namely that conversants must demonstrate they have taken into account all preceding discourse, including previous conversations. This means that previous conversational partners are expected to share some "taken-for-granteds" and to reflect that knowledge as they construct relevant remarks (Hopper, 1981; Sigman, 1983). The poignancy of this expectation (rule) was evident when Cathy asked Jeff questions she had already asked on their previous date and was inaccurate in her recall of information they had discussed at length. Cathy was embarrassed by her repeated failure to remember these taken-for-granteds, and the pressure of this obligation was reflected in her thoughts: "I hate second dates" (1982, p. 46).

The audience. At times Guisewite's characters were topically relevant, but their utterances were nonetheless considered defective because they were addressed to an inappropriate or irrelevant audience (1982, p. 127; 1983, p. 17; 1984, p. 31, 36, 72, 110, 123). For example, Cathy told Andrea that she told the cleaning lady she loved Irving, Irving that she wanted a raise, her boss that she admired her mother, and her mother that the cleaning lady did a terrible job. When asked why she did that, Cathy responded that she got "the joy of expression without the repercussions" (1984, p. 110).

In another strip, Cathy revealed that when it came to conversations about relationships, Bill talked to her about Shirley, Irving talked to her about Brenda, she talked to Grant about Bill and Irving, and Grant talked to her about Sue. She then described these circumspect exchanges as "meaningful conversations with the wrong people" (1984, p. 31). In each of these cartoons metacommunication was used to comment on the appropriateness of the message for a particular audience, but metacommunication was not used to correct the situation.

The cartoons expressed a clear preference for messages that are in the proper context, whether that context was the topic or tone of the preceding remark, the content of previous conversations, the appropriate time and place, or the audience. Deviations from these preferences were among those most emphatically criticized by the cartoon characters. Still, in practice characters often failed to produce relevant remarks. The most probable cause for "irrelevant" messages in the cartoons was portrayed as a failure to take the perspective and needs of the hearer into account. On the other hand, failures to address appropriate audiences were attributed to an effort to avoid repercussions. In this latter case, the message was similar to that for the honesty maxim in that one is caught in a bind: One should address the most relevant audience, but it may be safer socially (less threatening to the speaker or to the hearer's face) to address another audience.

Manner Maxim

Grice (1975) maintained that conversants expect each other to avoid obscurity and ambiguity, and to be brief and orderly. There would appear to be some overlap between the quantity and manner maxims. That is, if one is evasive or otherwise underinformative, one has violated the quantity maxim by not providing enough information, and the manner maxim by being obscure. On the other hand, if one is verbose, one has violated the quantity maxim by providing too much information and the manner maxim by not being brief. Therefore, all the cartoons on evasion of information and too much information, discussed above under the quantity maxim, are relevant to the manner maxim as well. There were no cartoons that were concerned with violating the proper order of utterances; this absence suggests that Guisewite's characters typically did not find the order of messages troublesome. What remains to be discussed in this section are cartoons that were concerned with ambiguity.

Guisewite's characters commented on the ambiguity and confusion that exists when one receives contradictory messages (1982, p. 109, 113, 124, 363; 1984, p. 5, 102). Particularly frustrating were messages that created a double bind: "Damned if you do and damned if you don't." For example, Cathy indicated that her mother was driving her crazy because she encouraged her to be assertive, independent, and to get more sleep, and then criticized her for making a scene, not coming over often enough, and for not getting her thank-you notes done (1984, p. 102). In another strip, Cathy berated Irving for inconsistencies between what he said and did, for making her guess his thoughts and then criticizing her for being wrong, and for treating her like the most important thing in his life one moment and then like she is from Mars the next. Given these conflicting messages Cathy screamed, "WHAT ARE YOU TRYING TO DO TO ME, IRVING?!!" (1984, p. 5). Clearly, Guisewite's characters consider contradictory messages inappropriate.

Extensions

Although the ambiguity maxim encourages speakers to be clear, the cartoons also revealed that hearers are prohibited from constantly questioning the meaning of the speaker's remarks. Occasionally Guisewite's characters asked speakers to elaborate on the intended meaning of their remarks (1982, p. 28, 106; 1983, p. 25, 85, 87, 123; 1984, 5, 50, 69). All but one of these strips dealt in one way or another with romantic relationships, and most of them concerned choosing between the opposite extremes of acceptance or rejection (for example, does he love or hate me? [1984, p. 69]; does "I hope we can still be friends" mean "I will always love you" or "I never want to see your disgusting face again"? [1983, p. 123]; and does "you're a riot" mean "I love you" or "we just broke up"? [1984, p. 50]). Cathy's reactions to these quandaries were to ask the men directly and to assert that "men should come with instruction booklets" (1984, p. 50). But she also willingly acknowledged her tendency to generate these extreme possibilities in statements like "one mind, one thousand misinterpretations" (1983, p. 123), and "Irving, which part of our date should I be blowing out of proportion?" (1984, p. 69).

Cathy never succeeded in her attempts to clarify what is meant. In fact, her hearers often treated her questions as anomalies. Their negative responses to her questions about the meanings of utterances are consistent with what researchers have suggested about naturally occurring conversations. Typically, conversants take it for granted that hearers share the same meaning for utterances; conversants who do not make this assumption and constantly question the meaning of symbols are perceived as teasing, belligerent, sick, ignorant, or for some other reason, noncooperative (Bach & Harnish, 1979; Garfinkel, 1967; Hopper, 1981; Shimanoff, 1980). They are considered deviants and their questioning behavior is rejected as inappropriate.

Guisewite's treatment of potentially ambiguous messages illustrates an interesting paradox for conversants. Cathy's questions expose how much we take for granted, how potentially ambiguous much of communication is, and thus how easily we can err in the assumptions we make. On the other hand, it is easy to sympathize with the frustration of Cathy's conversational partners. Their responses make it clear how important these taken for granteds are to conversations, for without them very little information would be exchanged because it would take an inordinate amount of time. What is amazing is that in most conversations we handle this balancing act quite well. It is only when communication fails that we realize there are times when we assume too much and other times too little. Metacommunication is one way of identifying the proper balance for a particular situation, but as these cartoons illustrate, such messages have their own risks.

SUMMARY

Guisewite's portrayal of conversational practices and ideals is largely consistent with Grice's conversational maxims. For the most part speakers who deviate from these maxims are subject to negative sanctions. Guisewite's portrayals also reveal other aspects of conversational behavior not highlighted by Grice's maxims.

For example, she demonstrates that hearers, as well as speakers, are constrained by conversational rules (for example, one's interpretation of utterances must be reasonably consistent with the available evidence, and one must not constantly question the meaning of utterances). The cartoons also indicate that conversational rules may be hierarchically ordered (for example, tact before honesty, brevity before verbosity), and that rules governing the relevance of an utterance are concerned with much more than mere topical relevance with the preceding utterance. Figure 38.1 presents a sum-

Grice's Maxims	Guisewite's Rules
Tell the truth.	Do not tell obvious lies.
	Do not tell the truth about others if it threatens their self-esteem or your relationship, unless you do not want to interact with them again.
Do not speak without adequate evidence.	
	Do not express an exaggerated (positive or negative) interpretation for which there is inadequate evidence.
Provide all, and only the necessary information.	Err in the direction of providing too little information rather than being verbose.
Be relevant.	Provide background information necessary to understand the relevance of an utterance; initial utterances to hearers should not be taken from the middle of conversations with others or from "mental" monologues.
	Address the main issue of preceeding remarks rather than tangential elements.
	Make one's remarks consistent with the tone or mood of the preceding comments.
	Reflect knowledge of the entire discourse history, not merely the preceding comment.
	Address one's remarks to a relevant audience, unless it threatens the hearer's self-esteem.
Avoid obscurity and ambiguity.	Do not send contradictory messages.
	Do not repeatedly question the meaning of an utterance.
Be orderly.	

* A blank line indicates that this maxim was not directly portrayed in Guisewite's cartoons.

Figure 38.1 Grice's maxims and Guisewite's portrayal of conversational rules.

marized comparison of Grice's maxims and conversational rules as portrayed by Guisewite; it illustrates the ways in which Guisewite's portrayal both conforms to and extends Grice's maxims.

CONCLUSIONS AND IMPLICATIONS

Overall, Guisewite appears to be a rather astute observer of conversational behavior. As noted throughout this chapter, Guisewite's cartoon portrayal of conversational rules and behavior is strikingly similar to observations made by several scholars of naturally occurring conversations (for example, Bach & Harnish, 1979; Bochner, 1982; Brown & Levinson, 1978;

Garfinkel, 1967; Grice, 1975; Hopper, 1981; Jackson & Jacobs, 1980; Keenan, 1976; Lakoff, 1975; Shimanoff, 1985a, 1985b; Sigman, 1983; Tracy & Moran, 1983; Watzlawick, Beavin, & Jackson, 1967). Further, although social scientists typically focus on individual aspects of conversational behavior, Guisewite illuminates not one, but several conversational rules through the cartoon medium, thus facilitating comparisons among different rules.

The isomorphism between the cartoons and everyday communication probably contributes to the popularity of the strip; indeed, Hewison (1977) reported that the "How true!" or "Ah-ha!" response is the most common reaction to popular cartoons. It is certainly also true that Guisewite presents exaggerated portrayals of everyday interactions, but for cartoons to be effective the "exaggeration must first be based on a collective perception that the cartoon reflects some inner truth" (DeSousa & Medhurst, 1982, p. 87).

In addition to providing a picture of conversational ideals and practices, Guisewite also reflects some common attitudes about metacommunication. In the strips, metacommunication was used to criticize the communication of others, but not to compliment. Although it was used to point out problems, it was not used to suggest constructive solutions. Further, it was frequently shown not only as failing to achieve its goals, but as even making matters worse. This finding is consistent with Wilmot's (1985) observation that metacommunication may be taboo in many relationships "because people have not seen productive uses of metacommunication in action" (p. 11).

Given the consistency between Guisewite's portrayals and communication research, the cartoons meet the second criterion for being heuristic. The third, and final, criterion is whether or not the cartoons point to aspects of communication not typically addressed in conversational research. The present analysis demonstrated that the cartoons do in fact meet this criterion.

Guisewite's portrayals point to both macroscopic and microscopic issues that are not typically discussed in conversational research. For example, the cartoons make conflicts between competing rules explicit. Conversational researchers have given very little attention to explicating rule conflicts and resolutions. Further, in investigating conversational rules most researchers have focused exclusively on the behavior of the speaker. Several of Guisewite's cartoons make it clear that conversational rules exist for hearers as well. On a more specific level, the cartoons indicate that other factors (for example, consistency within the overall conversational tone) may be at least as important as topical consistency in judging the appropriateness of an utterance.

The cartoons also suggest that the frequency and intensity with which types of behaviors are praised or blamed may provide one method of identifying those behaviors that communicators find more or less troublesome. For example, Guisewite's characters seem to have more trouble with parts of the quality and relevance maxims than with the quantity and manner maxims. The characters also demonstrated a preference for tact over truth, and a preference for too little information over too much. Although these observations are about fictional characters, the categories and types of comparisons made here could be employed profitably in analyses of nonfictional conversations. When the number of commentaries varies significantly from one maxim or rule to another, additional research will be needed to determine whether or not the difference is due to the number of violations or whether or not compliance with one rule over another is more important.

The present analysis has demonstrated that an examination of conversational ideals and practices as they are portrayed in popular cartoons can be a heuristic tool for rules research. Certainly, analyses of cartoons cannot substitute for careful investigations of actual conversations, but they can be used to identify profitable directions for studying the role of rules in everyday conversations. The present analysis indicates that a research agenda for conversational rules might benefit from including further explications of competing rules, hierarchical rules, rules for hearers as well as speakers, and more elaborated rules for the relevance (appropriateness) of subsequent remarks.

Because the bulk of this chapter has explicated the benefits of cartoons to rules research, it seems only fitting that it end by briefly recognizing the contribution of rules to cartoons. Although rule violations serve as a primary source of humor in cartoons, rules also render some violations baffling or rude rather than humorous. Thus although cartoonists may violate certain rules, they must conform to other rules (for example, in the "three little words" examples). In addition, because cartoons are inherently brief, cartoonists frequently employ enthymematic messages (Turner, 1977) that depend upon rules to fill in the missing information. Cartoonists can then rely on these rules to prompt readers to formulate particular expectations that can be violated. Of further interest to the communication scholar is the fact that humor in cartoons often depends on incongruity created by manipulating linguistic ambiguity and rules (Pepicello & Weisberg, 1983; Suls, 1983). Cartoons and communication rules, then, share a symbiotic relationship, with rules giving cartoons life, and cartoons exposing rules that might otherwise go unnoticed.

NOTES

1. These books were selected for analysis because they shared several features. All 3 books are about 125 pages long, all cartoons are black and white drawings with 4 frames per strip, all 3 books were intended for adult audiences, and they are the only books of this type that are still in print. The 3 books contained a total of 1,107 strips.

2. The adjective *prescriptive* is used here to distinguish the rule perspective taken in this chapter as compared to other uses of the term "rule." For example, Pearce and Cronen (1980) use the concept "rule" to describe how communicators construct meaning: "rules are descriptions of how persons process information" (p. 139). Rather than a description, *rule* is conceptualized in this chapter as a "prescription that indicates what behavior is obligated, prohibited, or preferred in certain contexts" (Shimanoff, 1980, p. 57).

3. Although these categories are not exhaustive of all communication portrayals in the cartoons, they did encompass most of the observations about communication in the "Cathy" cartoons, and no other major patterns emerged from those cartoons that could not be compared to these maxims.

Because there is some potential overlap between maxims, it is appropriate that some distinctions be specified, particularly regarding the meaning of utterances. When assigned meanings or inferences are unwarranted, ambiguous, or nonexistent, they are all in one sense related to insufficient information. However, cartoons regarding unwarranted inferences contained inadequate or contradictory evidence, and because that is a concern of the quality maxim, those cartoons were included in that section. Ambiguity is a stated concern of the manner maxim, and thus cartoons regarding these types of inferences were discussed under that maxim. Nonexistent inferences, when one was intended, seemed most clearly and appropriately attributed to insufficient information, so cartoons regarding such inferences were included in the quantity maxim. Although these distinctions are admittedly somewhat arbitrary, they were chosen because they seemed to be the most consistent with Grice's original categories.

4. Keenan (1976) demonstrated that in some cases information that Americans would readily share is withheld by Malagasy villagers. This suggests that information may be restricted even more severely in Madagascar than in the United States. However, it may be profitable to explore further the kinds of restrictions Americans place on the flow of information.

REFERENCES

Alter, J. (1984, October 1). Comics in yuppiedom: The "Doonesbury" strip returns to funny pages far different from the sedate, safe days of "Blondie." *Newsweek, 104,* pp. 76-79.

Bach, K., & Harnish, R. M. (1979). *Linguistic communication and speech acts.* Cambridge: MIT Press.

Bochner, A. (1982). On the efficacy of openness in close relationships. In Burgoon (Ed.), *Communication Yearbook 5* (pp. 109-124). New Brunswick, NJ: Transaction Books.

Boynton, K. R. (1979). Deviation: A communication perspective. *Central States Speech Journal, 30,* 83-95.

Brown, P., & Levinson, S. (1978). Universals in language usage: Politeness phenomena. In E. N. Goody (Ed.), *Questions and politeness: Strategies in social interaction* (pp. 56-289). Cambridge: Cambridge University Press.

Cathy Guisewite. (1977, December 19). *People, 8,* p. 82.

Coser, L. A. (1963). *Sociology through literature.* Englewood Cliffs, NJ: Prentice-Hall.

DeSousa, M. A., & Medhurst, M. J. (1982). Political cartoons and American culture: Significant symbols of campaign 1980. *Studies in Visual Communication, 8,* 83-98.

Garfinkel, H. (1967). *Studies in ethnomethodology.* Englewood Cliffs, NJ: Prentice-Hall.

Grice, H. P. (1975). Logic and conversation. In P. Cole & J. L. Morgan (Eds.), *Syntax and semantics: Speech acts* (Vol. 3, pp. 41-58). New York: Academic Press.

Guisewite, C. (1982). *Another Saturday night of wild and reckless abandon.* Kansas City: Andrews & McMeel.

Guisewite, C. (1983). *A mouthful of breath mints and no one to kiss.* Kansas City: Andrews & McMeel.

Guisewite, C. (1984). *Men should come with instruction booklets.* Kansas City: Andrews, McMeel & Parker.

Harayda, J. (1978, July). Talking with Cathy Guisewite. *Glamor, 76,* p. 84.

Harrison, R. P. (1981). *The cartoon: Communication to the quick.* Beverly Hills, CA: Sage.

Hewison, W. (1977). *The cartoon connection: The art of pictorial humor as seen by William Hewison.* North Pomfrey, VT: Hamish Hamilton.

Hopper, R. (1981). The taken-for-granted. *Human Communication Research, 7,* 195-211.

Hugenberg, L. W., Sr., & Schaefermeyer, M. J. (1983). Soliloquy as self-disclosure. *Quarterly Journal of Speech, 69,* 180-187.

Inge, M. T. (1979). The comics as culture: Introduction. *Journal of Popular Culture, 12,* 631-639.

Jackson, S., & Jacobs, S. (1980). Structure of conversational argument: Pragmatic bases for the enthymeme. *Quarterly Journal of Speech, 66,* 251-265.

Jacobs, S. (1985). Language. In M. L. Knapp & G. R. Miller (Eds.), *Handbook of interpersonal communication* (pp. 313-343). Beverly Hills, CA: Sage.

James, M. (1982, July 13). Cathy and her mom. *Woman's Day, 96,* p. 96.

Keenan, E. O. (1976). The universality of conversational postulates. *Language in Society, 5,* 67-80.

Koris, S. (1982, July 5). Cartoons are no laughing matter for Cathy Guisewite. *People, 18,* pp. 90-91.

Kougl, K. M. (1983). Novels as a source for heuristics about interpersonal communication. *Communication Quarterly, 31,* 282-290.

Krupp, C. (1982, August). Becoming rich and famous. *Glamor, 80,* pp. 323.

Lakoff, R. (1975). *Language and woman's place.* New York: Harper & Row.

Litton-Hawes, E. M. (1977). A foundation for the study of everyday talk. *Communication Quarterly, 25,* 2-11.

Millner, C. (1983, May). How cartoonist Cathy Guisewite makes us laugh at life's little frustrations. *Seventeen, 42,* pp. 42-43.

Morris, G. H., & Hopper, R. (1980). Remediation and legislation in everyday talk: How communicators achieve consensus. *Quarterly Journal of Speech, 66,* 266-274.

Pearce, W. B., & Cronen, V. E. (1980). *Communication, action and meaning: The creation of social realities.* New York: Praeger.

Pepicello, W. J., & Weisberg, R. W. (1983). Linguistics and Humor. In P. E. McGhee & J. H. Goldstein (Eds.), *Handbook of humor research: Basic issues* (Vol. I, pp. 59-84). New York: Springer-Verlag.

Peter, L. J. (1979, January). Sketches of cartoon Cathy's creator. *Human Behavior, 8,* p. 68.

Robotham, R. (1982, September). Funny females in the funny pages. *Life, 5,* p. 90.

Schank, R. C. (1977). Rules and topics in conversations. *Cognitive Science, 1,* 421-441.

Shimanoff, S. B. (1980). *Communication rules: Theory and research.* Beverly Hills, CA: Sage.

Shimanoff, S. B. (1985a). *Emotional expressiveness among acquaintances and best friends.* Unpublished manuscript.

Shimanoff, S. B. (1985b). Expressing emotions in words: Verbal patterns. *Journal of Communication, 35,* 16-31.

Sigman, S. J. (1983). Some constraints placed on conversational topics. In R. T. Craig & K. Tracy (Eds.), *Conversational coherence: Form, structure, and strategy* (pp. 174-195). Beverly Hills, CA: Sage.

Suls, J. M. (1983). Cognitive processes in humor appreciation. In P. E. McGhee & J. H. Goldstein (Eds.), *Handbook of humor research: Basic issues* (Vol. I, pp. 39-58). New York: Springer-Verlag.

Tracy, K., & Moran, J. P. III. (1983). Conversational relevance in multiple-goal settings. In R. T. Craig & K. Tracy (Eds.), *Conversational coherence: Form, structure, and strategy* (pp. 116-135). Beverly Hills, CA: Sage.

Turner, K. J. (1977). Comic strips: A rhetorical perspective. *Central States Speech Journal, 28,* 24-35.

Watzlawick, P., Beavin, J. H., & Jackson, D. J. (1967). *Pragmatics of human communication: A study of interactional patterns, pathologies and paradoxes.* New York: W. W. Norton.

Wilmot, W. W. (1985, February). *Metacommunication in interpersonal relationships.* Paper presented to the Western Speech Communication Association Convention, Fresno, CA.

XIII ● PUBLIC RELATIONS

39 ● Interorganizational Networks via Shared Public Relations Firms' Centrality, Diversification, Media Coverage, and Publics' Images

JAMES A. DANOWSKI ● GEORGE A. BARNETT ● MATTHEW H. FRIEDLAND

University of Illinois at Chicago ● State University of New York at Buffalo

PROBLEM FOCUS

In the early treatments of organizational environments two main approaches were apparent. One conceptualized environmental features primarily in individual-level psychological terms, emphasizing perceived environmental uncertainty (Emery & Trist, 1965, Terryberry, 1968; Thompson, 1967). The other approach took a more relational, macro, network view, conceptualizing environments in terms of interorganizational relationships (Clark, 1965; Etzioni, 1960; Hage and Aiken, 1969; Levine & White, 1961; Litwak & Hylton, 1962; Warren, 1967; Wigand, 1979). Since these seminal studies, the interorganizational network approach continues to be actively pursued. More sensitive structural analysis of interorganizational relations has been developed and linked to a range of variables (for a review see Eisenberg et al., 1985).

A dominant approach has been "interlocking directorates" research (Burt, Christman, & Kilburn, 1980; Sonquist & Koenig, 1975). Investigators have defined network links as the extent to which corporations share individual members of boards of directors. Although the validity of such relations for communication research can be questioned, this work has

Correspondence and requests for reprints: James A. Danowski, Department of Communication and Theatre, University of Illinois at Chicago, Chicago IL 60680.

been useful in focusing theoretical attention on interorganizational network structures.

A key problem that arises in this area of research is the linking of network position variables with the domain of effects. In particular, it would be useful theoretically to explore how interorganizational network structures are associated with the message content and form projected about organizations into societal media systems. Also of interest is how these media representations affect audience members' cognitive schemata, how these images affect the activation of interpersonal communication networks among audience members, and in turn how such networks penetrate the interorganizational network domain. By considering the three domains— interorganizational relations, mass media representations, and audience effects—it is expected that theories of interorganizational relations and communication can be advanced.

When examining the links of interorganizational structures to media representations and audience effects it may be fruitful to define organizational interactions in ways other than through shared individual members of boards of directors. In particular, relationships defined by shared communication behaviors, and at levels of observation higher than the individual, may have greater conceptual validity for the problem at hand.

Nevertheless, it can be counterargued that individuals on boards of directors do indeed communicate as representatives of organizations, and also that they serve as symbols or signals of higher-order interorganizational linkage. But such communication is a limited slice of the wider range and there is little evidence that boards of directors interactions affect communication in other areas of the organizations.

Moreover, when questions concern how interorganizational network structures are associated with media use by organizations and with the effects on images that audiences hold about these organizations, no persuasive evidence has been presented in the literature as to why interlocking directorates might explain these processes. More conceptually compelling would be theories that include variables tapping organizations' public relations activities as definers of interorganizational relationships.

Consider that public relations processes are the formalized bridge between the organization and its environment. Through this bridge organizations seek to accomplish a number of goals. One is to communicate purposively with other organizations through the mass and specialized media (Adler, 1986). Organizations also use public relations processes to communicate with publics such as investors, constituencies of political actors who can control the organization, political actors directly, and various diffuse publics whose activation (Grunig, 1982) can affect the organization and its environment.

The larger the organization, the more likely that it retains public relations firms (agencies) to aid in managing external communication activities. From an organizational roles perspective, these firms reduce transaction costs for organizations (Aldrich, 1979). Public relations firms are likely to help plan and execute proactive campaigns to achieve strategic public relations goals efficiently.

On the other hand, the client's internal public relations managers, in addition to liaison with retained firms, are more likely to react to day-to-day information needs from the environment, such as requests for information from reporters, preparation of routine news releases, and handling of ritualized press relations. As well, internal staff are likely to be responsible for employee communication programs.

In sum, given the important roles of public relations firms in the management of large organizations' external communication, they may be useful as a basis for representing interorganizational relations. Consider that Mitchell (1973) argued that interorganizational relations be defined in terms of the exchange of content and of goods and services. Accordingly, in this study the content exchanged concerns communication with an organization's publics. The services exchanged are public relations assistance to the organization in accomplishing its communication objectives. Thus the relations are not only communicative, they are metacommunicative. Another theoretically relevant aspect of this type of relation is its positioning in Eisenberg et al.'s (1985) distinction among representative, interpersonal, and institutional types of interorganizational relations. Because we conceptualized relations in this research as the sharing of public relations firms among organizations our approach was "institutional."

More abstractly, our approach is consistent with Breiger's (1974) representation of relations among nodes defined on attribute similarity. The N × N matrix of node relations is the square transformation of the N × M node by attribute matrix, where N is an array of organization nodes and M is an array of public relations firms they share. The transformation of N × M results in an N × N matrix of frequencies of shared relations among all pairs of organizations.

The interorganizational network so defined is, therefore, an indirect one. The organizations sharing the same public relations firms may not communicate directly. In other words, the public relations firms may not tell one client formally what they are doing with another. Our assumption is, however, that the relationship defined among organizations is transitive. If A is related to B, and B is related to C, then A is indirectly related to C. Hence, structural equivalence (Burt, 1982) among the organizations can be identified and tested for its predictive validity.

Moreover, to the extent that particular public relations firms have their own style of doing business, the similarity relationship among clients is amplified. They are more alike in the kinds of public relations activities they implement. In more abstract terms, this notion can be represented by interaction effects on the original node matrix of structural equivalencies. These arise from an M × O matrix of public relations firms (M) by stylistic attributes (O). As the M × O matrix is transformed into its M × M matrix, structural equivalencies in that matrix may interact through the N × M matrix with the structural equivalences in the N × N matrix. Thus indirectly, public relations firms' styles of operation can multiplicatively increase the coherence of structural equivalence effects at the interorganizational level defined according to sharing of public relations firms.

Besides the reasons already noted for our choosing to define interorganizational linkage as the sharing of public relations firms, there were also other theoretical motives. We are interested in tying organizational theory with mass communication theory. Most organizational theory has not recognized uses of mass media by organizations, and most mass communication theory has focused on the audience at the individual level and has not treated organizational characteristics of media systems or their sources.

Nevertheless, public relations activities in practice bridge organizations with publics, often via dissemination of information about the organization or its issue positions to external publics through the mass and specialized media, and by gathering information about publics. Thus to the extent that theory ought to be rooted in practice, attempts to link organizational and mass communication theory should not ignore public relations activities. Rather, they may be usefully placed in the conceptual foreground.

In particular, theoretical progress in the organizational and mass communication interface should probably address questions such as the following:

- How do organizations' positions in interorganizational networks account for the amount and kind of media coverage about them?
- What are effects of media coverage on audiences' cognitive schemata about organizations?
- How do cognitive schemata changes activate interpersonal communication structures?
- How do activations of interpersonal communication networks affect interorganizational network structures?

In this research we take some initial steps toward addressing the first two questions. Based on the results we also suggest hypotheses for subsequent research.

Some of the highlights of our approach include:

- investigating macrolevel units of analysis in mass communication research, not just individual audience members,
- tying organizational variables to mass communication variables,
- defining interorganizational relations with a link that is itself at the organizational, not individual, level: sharing services of public relations organizations.

HYPOTHESES

Prior organizational research suggests the following hypotheses:

H1: The greater the organization's centrality in interorganizational networks, the greater the organizational diversification.

The rationale for this hypothesis is that organizations seek to reduce their environmental uncertainty in order to maintain stability in their internal structures and in environmental conditions affecting them (Katz & Kahn, 1978; Thompson, 1967). One way to manage environmental uncertainty is to diversify organizational activities, such as by maintaining operations in different product/service sectors. Then as economic and other market conditions affect these sectors differentially, the organization can buffer fluctuations and maintain a more steady state. This is a strategy of optimizing risk by lowering it at the aggregate level (Cyert, Feigenbaum, & March, 1959; Pfeffer & Salancik, 1978).

Another approach to diversification is not moving into entirely different product/service areas, but differentiating and integrating within a narrower set. For example, a publishing company acquires computer software firms, media production firms, training companies, market research firms, and other communication service providers to businesses. In the case of petroleum firms, the concept of "vertical integration" from resource exploration through retail sales is an example of this type of diversification. In short, rather than acquiring unrelated businesses, the organization adds units that serve different areas of the same broader market. Such processes are like what Thompson (1967) described as the creation of "buffers" between the organization's "core technology" and the environment.

As organizations are diversified in either of the two basic ways, we hypothesized that they are more central in information flow networks. Conceptually, centrality was defined as increasing as an inverse function of the average minimum path distance for a node to reach all other nodes in the network through direct or indirect links. An underlying premise is that nodes become more similar to one another through the exchange of more common information (Danowski, 1974; Rogers & Kincaid, 1981). Conversely, as nodes exchange more diverse information they become more different from one another. Given the "strength of weak ties" aspects of networks (Granovetter, 1973), nodes in more central positions are linked with more diverse nodes and hence process more diverse information. To encode and decode more diverse information requires a more structurally diverse internal system (Ashby, 1956). In this study, diversification was defined as the number of different kinds of businesses the organization operated.

H2:   The greater the organizational centrality, the more the media coverage
in business-oriented publications.

Organizations that are more central in the interorganizational network defined
by shared public relations firms were hypothesized to receive more media
coverage. One reason may be that the organization seeks out public relations firms that can get it more coverage. Those public relations firms serving more centrally in interinstitutional networks may be perceived as being
more successful at obtaining coverage, although this has not been empirically verified.

Another reason may be that more central organizations are more able, if
they choose, to control their communication environments. Organizations
that are structurally more independent have been found to engage in more
boundary-spanning activity (Kapp & Barnett, 1983). As a particular type
of boundary-spanning, organizations or their agents may be more able to
influence media organizations to cover them. Alternatively, media reporters
and editors may on their own initiative give more coverage to more central
organizations, because media practitioners perceive their audiences to be
more interested in them. Hence their public service and their profit motives
may lead journalists to pay more attention to central organizations.

In this research we first sought to establish whether or not there was a relationship between organizational centrality and amount of media coverage.
If there was, then the reasons for this could be investigated in later research.
Also, before we would take on the complex and more labor-intensive task
of measuring the qualitative features of the media content, we wanted to
start by seeing whether or not there was support for our hypothesis that
centrality is associated with the volume of media coverage.

Supporting the start with media coverage quantity rather than quality is
evidence that amount of coverage is a more important determinant of audience effects than the quality of coverage. More broadly, the mass media
agenda-setting research suggests that the "media tell people what to think
about, not what to think." Amount of coverage of issues predicts later public perceptions of issue importance, whereas qualitative features of coverage may have less effect on publics' positions on the issues (McCombs &
Shaw, 1976).

H3:   The more central the organization in interorganizational networks, the
more favorable the public image of the organization.

This proposition is grounded on several assumptions. One is that organizations seek favorable images among publics to support product/service promotion, avoid harmful legislation, increase stock value, blunt political and
social opposition groups, and demonstrate social responsibility, among other
motives. Another assumption is that some public relations firms are more

successful than others in aiding the nurturance of favorable organizational images. More successful service firms are able to reduce more cost effectively the client's transaction costs in communicating with publics (Aldrich, 1979; Aldrich & Whetten, 1981). These assumptions taken together suggest that organizations more central in interorganizational networks have more favorable images among publics.

In the current research we examined organizational image among members of one key public: investors. One of the public relations objectives of publicly held firms is to enact (Weick, 1979) a favorable climate for investment. The organization's image among members of the investment community is an important element in this enactment process. Expectations of future performance are key determinants of stock prices (Abel, 1980) rather than exclusively the past financial performance of the organization. Expectations can be understood as cognitive schemata that evolve as information is processed from the environment. These schemata are superimposed on projections of future value.

Accordingly, in this study we considered as a surrogate variable for organizational image factors among the investment community the relative change in an organization's common stock value. This was based on the assumption that stock prices are tied to corporate financial performance as well as to perceptions of nonfinancial factors.

For example, investment analysts talk about a stock being "undervalued" or "overvalued." This means that the stock price is either lower than or higher than the financial data alone would warrant. Image factors can be considered to account for under and over valuation of an organization's common stock. In addition, the financial data itself contributes to the images that investors hold about an organization. These financial and nonfinancial image factors can be assumed to influence directly the prices of stocks traded. Thus within the investment community relative increases in stock price are indicants of more favorable images of the organization, and relative decreases in stock price are indicants of more negative images of the organization.

Questions about image effects of interorganizational network position are also of interest with publics other than investors. The mass public may also have images that are linked to institutional network structures. We are interested in examining relationships with mass publics, but this is beyond the scope of the current study. Future research may profitably investigate multidimensional corporate images held by mass and other publics as a function of interorganizational network structures. Schema-based information processing approaches (Graber, 1984) may be useful, particularly if the message content that audiences process is treated with a relational analysis system such as network analysis. In the discussion section we give an example of such an analysis.

METHODS

Sample

We selected the "Fortune 100" industrial corporations for the research. Our reasons included the fact that this sample has been used in earlier interorganizational research and hence our use contributes to the "cumulative knowledge" value of scientific research. In addition, pilot coding revealed that our resources would allow for analysis of a rather small data set. A sample size of 100, however, would provide for adequate statistical testing.

Operational Definitions

Links. The basic relation of shared public relations firms was indexed as follows. *O'Dwyer's Directory of Public Relations Firms* (1985) includes a listing by client organization as to which public relations agencies are retained. We used this list to define links. Each pair of industrial organizations was examined for how many public relations firms they used in common. The greater the number of shared firms, the higher the link strength.

Organizational diversification. Organizations were examined for the number of different products/services they offered. This information was based on counting the number of different two-digit Standard Industrial Codes (SICs) listed in entries for organizations in the *Corporate Affiliations Directory* (1985). The number of organization units was indexed by counting the number of different divisions, subsidiaries, member firms, and units listed for each organization in the same directory.

Media coverage. Two business-oriented newspapers were measured for amount of coverage: the *Wall Street Journal* and the *New York Times*. The number of stories appearing in 1984 were counted by tabulating stories listed for each of the organizations in the respective annual indexes of the newspapers. In addition, to cover the more trade-oriented media, we counted stories for the organizations as indexed in *Business Periodicals Index* for August 1983 through July 1984, the closest time frame to that for the two other media indexes. This index covers over 295 different trade and professional publications.

In addition to number of stories, we computed an index of story length for the *Wall Street Journal*. It was the only publication of the three whose index was appropriately organized. We measured the number of columns of story listings in the indexes. Some stories have only one line entries, such as "Mr. X promoted to CEO of Y Corporation," or "Y Corporation's profits in the third quarter were z." On the other hand, some entries were a paragraph long. These represented more lengthy and detailed stories in the newspapers about the organization. So, as a measure of average story length, an indicator of depth of coverage, we divided the number of index columns for an organization by the number of stories.

Image. We indexed image favorability within the investment community. The variable used was percentage change in common stock value. The greater the common stock price increase, the more favorable the image of the organization in the investment community. Data on the percentage increases in common stock prices from January 2, 1979, to January 2, 1985, were obtained from *Forbes* (January 14, 1985). These data were chosen as a matter of convenience. The five-year time frame prior to that of the 1984 public relations firm data suggests that we must assume that firm retention patterns of 1984 are autocorrelated from 1979 through 1984, if an effect on stock prices over that period is attributable to shared public relations firms networks and not to some rival explanation. It would be useful in future research to examine a fine-grained time-series of price data before and after the time frame for defining the interorganizational network so that various explanations can be tested.

Analysis

Organizations were network analyzed using the NEGOPY computer program (Rice & Richards, 1981). Parameters settings for group detection and other basic program operations were set at default values, except scan radius which was set at 200. (Given the results, default values would have yielded the same structure.) Strengths of 1 or more were analyzed without weighting.

For the 100 nodes, the total number of links was 897. Average link strength (number of shared public relations firms) was 1.2, with a range of 1 to 5. Organizations that shared 5 common public relations firms were Dart & Kraft and General Foods. Those sharing 4 common firms were: ITT and Dart & Kraft, ITT and Coca-Cola, ITT and Phillip Morris, and Phillip Morris and Coca-Cola. Sharing 3 common firms were 23 pairs of organizations. Table 39.1 lists the node pairs at the top 3 strength levels. Figure 39.1 shows the network of relations among the 23 organizations sharing 3 or more firms.

Several public relations firms were more often involved in shared use by pairs of organizations. We tabulated the number of times that firms were shared among pairs with 3, 4, and 5 firms in common. These firm frequencies appear in Table 39.2. It shows that the most shared firm was Burson-Marsteller, followed by Hill and Knowlton, then several others used by two firms.

To place the data on shared firms into context, we computed descriptive statistics on all firms retained by organizations. The range was 0 to 17 firms per organization, with a mean of 5.9 and a standard deviation of 4.7. The median number of firms was 5. Given an average number of shared firms of 1.3, this indicates that Fortune 100 organizations share 22% of their public relations firm links with other such organizations.

Table 39.1
Shared Public Relations Firms

Organizations with Most Shared PR Firms	Number
Dart & Kraft and General Foods	5
ITT and Coca-Cola	4
ITT and Phillip Morris	4
Phillip Morris and Coca-Cola	4
Mobil and Dart & Kraft	3
A T & T and Dupont	3
A T & T and Dart & Kraft	3
A T & T and Johnson and Johnson	3
A T & T and IC Industries	3
Westinghouse and United Technologies	3
ITT and Allied	3
ITT and Pepsi	3
ITT and Bristol Myers	3
Westinghouse and Rockwell International	3
Phillip Morris and Union Carbide	3
Phillip Morris and Ralston Purina	3
Dart & Kraft and Beatrice	3
Dart & Kraft and Monsanto	3
Dart & Kraft and Johnson & Johnson	3
Dart & Kraft and American Home Industries	3
Dart & Kraft and IC Industries	3
Dart & Kraft and Allied Corp.	3
General Foods and Bristol Myers	3
Johnson & Johnson and TRW	3
Johnson & Johnson and American Home Products	3
TRW and Bristol Myers	3
Control Data and Pillsbury	3

Turning to the network structure defined by all shared firms, we observed that total system connectedness was .18, indicating rather low structural density. One large group was identified with 89 nodes, with 11 nodes peripherally positioned outside the group. These included 5 fully isolated nodes, 3 nodes with only 1 link, 2 isolated dyad members, and 1 tree node.

For the group of 89, connectedness was .22, indicating rather low structural density within the group. Group members' centrality varied from a minimum average path distance between nodes of 1.4 links steps to 3.0. The ten most central nodes were: ITT, Draft & Kraft, Bristol-Myers, Coca-Cola, Dupont, AT&T, Phillip Morris, Mobil, Monsanto, and Allied Corporation. The ten least central group nodes were: Goodyear, N. A. Philips, SOHIO, Consolidated Foods, Firestone, Boeing, General Dynamics, Caterpillar Tractor, and Burroughs. Table 39.3 lists the centrality scores for the most and least central group nodes.

The nongroup nodes, peripherals in the network were: Phillips Petroleum, Unocal, Amereda Hess, Georgia-Pacific, W. R. Grace, Digital

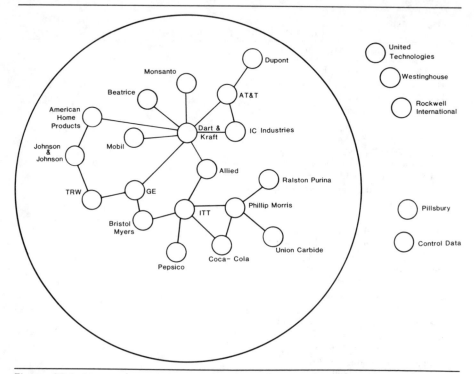

Figure 39.1 Network among organizations sharing three or more public relations firms.

Equipment Corporation, Bethlehem Steel, Colgate-Palmolive, Archer-Daniels-Midland, International Harvester, and Agway.

Test of H1

Because this research is the first of this sort to be conducted, we set a significance level of .10, the traditionally accepted value for such research. To test the hypothesis that centrality in the interorganizational network is associated with more organizational diversification, a t-test was performed between the 10 most central group members and the 10 least central group members plus the 9 peripheral organizations. First, the dependent variable tested was number of different product/service areas, as indexed by the number of different Standard Industrial Codes (SICs) considering the first two digits.

The mean number of two-digit SICs for the most central group was 12.1 with a standard deviation of 5.4, and for the most peripheral group it was 7.7 with a standard deviation of 4.5. This difference was significant (t (28) = 2.34, $p < .02$).

Table 39.2
Public Relations Firms of Organizations Sharing Four and Five Firms

Firm	Frequency
Burson-Marsteller	5
Hill and Knowlton	3
Cushman	3
Ruder, Finn and Rotman	2
Epply	2
Ogilvy & Mather	1
Byoir	1
Manning, Savage & Lee	1
Lewis, Gilman & Kynett	1
Kuhn	1
Wiener	1

The second test was with the number of organizational units. The mean number of units for the central group was 33.7 with a standard deviation of 30.0. For the peripheral group the mean was 18.1 with a standard deviation of 18.1. The difference was significant (t (28) = 1.78, $p < .05$).

To see if the number of organization units itself was significantly different, controlling for the number of SIC codes, we divided the number of units by the number of SICs and ran a t-test using the resulting value as the dependent variable. The mean for the central group was 2.6 with a standard deviation of 1.5, and for the peripheral group the mean was 2.2 with a standard deviation of 1.0. This difference was not significant (t (28) = .79, $p < .22$).

In sum, hypothesis one was supported. More central organizations were diversified both in terms of number of organizational units and the number of different product/service areas. Both more units and more product/service areas are necessary for greater centrality. Having more units controlling for number of product/services was not tied to centrality.

Test of H2

To test the hypothesis that organizational centrality is associated with more media coverage, we first ran t-tests on the number of stories appearing in the *Wall Street Journal*. The mean number of stories for the central group was 85.3 with a standard deviation of 64.5. For the peripheral group the mean was 46.5 with a standard deviation of 38.3. This difference was significant (t (28) = 2.07, $p < .03$).

Using story length as a variable resulted in a mean of .03 columns of index summary per story with a standard deviation of .01 for the central group. For the peripheral group the mean was .04 with a standard deviation of .01. The difference was not significant, although more central nodes tended to have slightly shorter stories, meaning that reporters and editors

Table 39.3
Fortune 100 Public Relations Firm Network:
Most and Least Central Group Nodes and Peripheral Nodes

Node	Centrality[a]
CENTRAL GROUP NODES	
ITT	−1.71
Dart & Kraft	−1.61
Bristol-Myers	−1.47
Coca-Cola	−1.44
Dupont	−1.30
A T & T	−1.30
Phillip Morris	−1.27
Mobil	−1.20
Monsanto	−1.20
Allied Corp.	
PERIPHERAL GROUP NODES	
Goodyear	1.26
N. A. Philips	1.54
SOHIO	1.70
Consolidated Foods	1.77
Firestone	1.91
Boeing	1.91
General Dynamics	2.38
Caterpillar	2.58
Burroughs	2.89
PERIPHERAL NONGROUP NODES	
Phillips Petroleum	
Unocal	
Amerada Hess	
Georgia-Pacific	
W. R. Grace	
Digital Equipment Corp.	
Bethlehem Steel	
Colgate-Palmolive	
Archer-Daniels-Midland	
International Harvester	
Agway	

a. These are standardized scores of average minimum link path distances to all other group nodes.

may tend to cover less important matters in the more central organizations ($t (27) = -.87, p < .2$). Because using index abstracts constrains "true" variation in the source materials, more direct analysis of news stories would be in order. Perhaps then the magnitudes of difference would be statistically significant.

Tests were also run for the number of stories appearing in the *New York Times*. The mean number of stories for the central group was 15.4 with a standard deviation of 11.6, and for the peripheral group the mean was 8.8 with a standard deviation of 7.3. This difference was significant ($t (28) = .91, p < .04$).

The number of stories indexed in the *Business Periodicals Index* was a mean of 43.4 with a standard deviation of 77.9 for the central group and a mean of 16.4 with a standard deviation of 23.4 for the peripheral group. This difference was significant (t (28) = 1.45, p < .08).

In sum, hypothesis 2 was relatively strongly supported for the *Wall Street Journal* and the *New York Times* and weakly supported for the *Business Periodicals Index*. The greater the organizational centrality the greater the media coverage, particularly in the New York-based business and professionally oriented newspapers.

Test of H3

The third hypothesis was that more central interorganizational network nodes would have more favorable images within the investing public, as indexed by relative change in common stock values. Table 39.4 shows that the mean percentage change for the central nodes was +79% with a standard deviation of 59%, and for the peripheral nodes the change was +44% with a standard deviation of 60%. This difference was significant (t (28) = 1.43, p < .08). More central groups had a higher increase in stock prices, indicating in part that their images may be more positive among the investment community.

SUMMARY AND IMPLICATIONS

Support was found for three hypotheses linking organizations' positions in interorganizational networks defined by shared public relations firms. More central organizations were more diversified in number of product/service areas and organizational units. Central organizations also received more media coverage in the *Wall Street Journal, New York Times,* and publications indexed in *Business Periodicals Index*. Indicating that more central organizations had more favorable images within the investing public was that their stock values from 1979 to 1985 showed significantly higher increases than did peripheral nodes'.

Rival Explanations

Some rival explanations for the link found between stock price increases over a 5-year period through 1984 and network centrality revolve around the following notions. For price increases over this time period to be associated with interorganizational network position defined by the shared firms pattern in 1984 suggests that to some extent a similar pattern may have been in existence in previous years. Media coverage in these years that was stimulated by organizations' public relations firms would account for the finding. A rival explanation, however, is that organizations choose public

Table 39.4
Network Position, Number of News Stories, and Stock Prices

Medium	Node	Mean	SD	T	P
A. Number of Stories					
Wall Street Journal					
central group		85.3	64.5		
periph. nodes		46.5	38.3	2.07	.03
New York Times					
central nodes		15.4	11.6		
periph. nodes		8.8	7.3	1.91	.04
Business Periodicals Index					
central nodes		43.4	77.9		
periph. nodes		16.4	23.4	1.45	.08
B. Stock Price Changes-5 yrs.					
central nodes		+79%	59%		
periph. nodes		+44%	60%	1.43	.08

relations and perhaps other service firms based on the organizations' fiscal health. When it is improving, organizations may choose more expensive firms. These firms are perhaps more central in the M × M transformation of the N × M matrix, where N is organization nodes and M is public relations firms. Testing to rule out this explanation is beyond the scope of the present study.

For the findings tying centrality positively to media coverage, a rival explanation could be that the divestiture of AT&T, one of the central organizations, occurred during the time period of media content analysis. This divestiture created a substantial amount of media coverage. Because it could be considered that the organizational change was largely due to an external set of forces and not due directly to the actions of AT&T, one might want to exclude this organization from the analysis and determine if the same results occurred.

To determine whether or not this rival explanation could be ruled out, we removed AT&T from the t-test group and reran the analysis. Differences were still in the same direction and were significant at less than the .10 level. If a larger range of organizations beyond the top 100 were used, it is possible that this relationship would be stronger. Also, if more years were content analyzed for media coverage, the variances probably would be more stable. Then, even with the present small subsamples, the same magnitude of mean difference might be more statistically significant. In sum, even with AT&T removed from the analysis, the hypotheses were supported ($p < .10$).

Considering the basic findings of this research, questions arise as to causal sequences. Do organizations that are already more central in other ways also choose public relations firms that maintain centrality within that particular network? Or is it possible that if a peripheral organization hires the same set of public relations firms used by more central organizations that the previously marginal organization will become more successful in media coverage and image formation among publics? Such questions about the direction of causal sequencing of the relationships found have not only theoretical value but practical force.

The findings about media coverage are also causally problematic. Do more central organizations receive more coverage due to public relations activities that their agents initiate? Or is it more the case that media reporters and editors themselves seek out information on more central organizations or are more willing to publish source-initiated content? If so, to what extent are journalists motivated by audience interests or more circumscribed professional norms? May there be an indirect causal flow from public relations activities that directly communicate with publics through controlled media and avoid mass media? Organizations may increase publics' interests directly. In turn, do media practitioners detect this increased salience and then due to circulation, profit, and prestige motives decide to cover the organizations more?

These various causal questions about interorganizational network structures, mass media coverage, and audience processes can be addressed empirically without extreme difficulty, although depending on the scope and nature of the analysis such research can be time consuming. The kinds of data useful in testing relationships over time are readily available in archives. Illustrated in this research, rich information can be obtained from sources such as directories, indexes, and financial records. By setting up time-series analyses using data such as these, researchers can precisely estimate relative causal flows among sets of variables. This was beyond the scope of the present research, which set out first to see if there were any cross-sectional findings that would merit more extensive time-series analysis. But now such investigation appears warranted.

Further research on media coverage also may benefit from adding analysis of the qualitative features of news stories to the measurement of amount of coverage. Even though media agenda-setting research suggests quantity overrides quality, empirical investigation in the context of the questions addressed here is warranted. Techniques are being developed to use network analysis models to represent the structure of what is communicated in news stories (Danowski & Andrews, 1985), treating words as nodes in a network. By using the same analytical model for measuring interorganizational relationships and media content internal validity of research should be higher.

To illustrate such an approach we performed a limited version of this kind of analysis, treating the interorganizational network represented in news stories about a particular organization. More full application of network analysis to media content would include not only organizations comentioned in stories, as in the example, but the full text of the words describing the organizations. This would enable analysis of the images projected about the organizations. Then the structures of these representations could be linked with audiences' schemata to account for differential effects of messages on the images audiences retain, on other variables such as recall, and so on.

To frame the current more limited illustration, we took the most central organization identified in the interorganizational analysis presented in this paper—ITT. We then selected the media vehicle that had the highest magnitude of relationship to the interorganizational structure—the *Wall Street Journal*. We coded all stories appearing about ITT in 1984 in this newspaper for comentions of organizations in the stories. Each time more than one organization was mentioned in a story, the pairs of all such organizations were given a score. These were aggregated across all stories. Note that all comentions were aggregated, some of which included conflictual as well as cooperative and other sorts of relations. We did not distinguish these relations in the current analysis. Future research might do so profitably, depending on the theoretical focus and the hypotheses to be tested.

Network analysis using NEGOPY was performed on the organizational comentions with ITT in the news stories. Group detection algorithms were set at default values and strengths of 1 or more were used unweighted. Across the 117 stories, 76 organizations were mentioned along with ITT. So ITT's media representation field of interorganizational relations has a field size of 76. Figure 39.2 shows the network structure among these organizations. Note that all nodes have a link to ITT, but that graphing each link would muddle the figure. Only links among the organizations other than ITT are shown.

In this network, the organizations above the median in centrality were (in order): GTE, Army, Standard Telephone and Cable (Britain), MCI, Plessy (Britain), Southern Tel, AT&T, Rockwell International, TDX Systems, Virginia, NEC, and Malaysia. Table 39.5 lists the organizations with highest centrality and their scores. It is interesting to examine to what extent the sheer frequency of comentions is associated with centrality, or conversely, to note whether or not network structure gives any additional information beyond mere number of comentions. The raw number of mentions for those organizations with group centrality scores appears in Table 39.5 along with the centrality information. We correlated the frequency values for the organizations in Tables 39.4 and 39.5 with the centrality values. The correlation coefficient was $-.08$ ($p < .32$). This suggests that there is no relationship between raw frequency of mention and the actual position centrality of a node in the network.

Figure 39.2 Organizations cooccurring in news stories about ITT in the *Wall Street Journal* in 1984.

Note: Organizations noted with an asterisk co-appeared only with ITT and to facilitate readability do not appear here.

1 ITT
* 2 Qume
* 3 U.S. Army
* 4 United Telecommunications
5 Nigeria
6 International Monetary Fund
7 Mobil Oil
* 8 Mediscience
9 U.S. Air Force
*10 Spain Telephone
*11 Chase Manhattan Bank
*12 British Telecom
13 Turkey
*14 Teletas
15 Texas Instruments
*16 EDS
*17 Times Mirror Corp.
*18 Times Mirror Microwave
*19 Chernow Communications
20 Malaysia
21 GTE
22 NEC
23 Fujitsu
24 LM Ericsson
25 Seimens AG
26 Central Intelligence Agency
27 US Government
*28 California Public Utilities Comm
29 Pacific Telesis
30 MCI
*31 Spain
*32 IBM
*33 Coins Group
34 Britain
*35 Standard Oil of Ohio
*36 Treego Bina PTY, Ltd
*37 Bell Telephone Manufacturing
*38 Federal Communications Commission

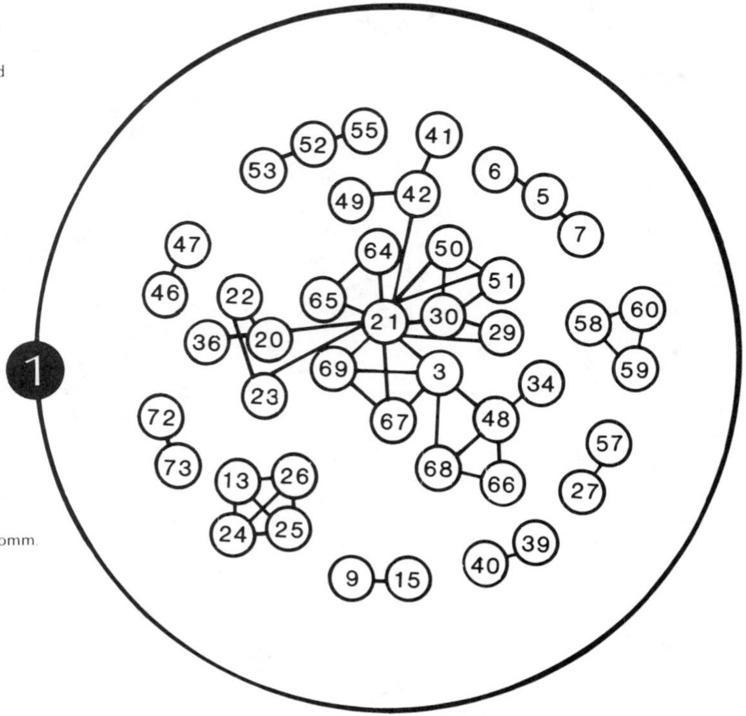

39 Laxard Freres and Co.
40 Golman Sachs and Co
41 General Electric
42 AT&T
* 43 Federal Trade Commission
* 44 On-Line Software International
* 45 Securities and Exchange Commission
46 West Germany
47 Hungary
48 Standard Telephone and Cables plc
49 Virginia
50 Southern Tel
51 TDX Systems
52 Ralston Purina
53 Moody's
54 U.S. Navy
55 Standard and Poors
56 Deutsche Bank
57 Soviet Government
58 Christian Rovsing As
59 Denmark PKA Pension Fund
60 Handelsbank Copenhagen
* 61 Fortune
* 62 Forbes
* 63 Screenplay, Inc.
64 Bellsouth
65 Allnet Communications
66 Plessy Co plc
67 Thomas sa
68 Rockwell International
69 Raytheon
*70 Nippon Telephone and Telegraph
*71 New American Library
72 Compushop. Inc
73 MBank of Dallas
*74 New York Stock Exchange
*75 Sonat Exploration Co.

825

Table 39.5
Frequency of Organization Comentions with ITT
in Wall Street Journal in 1984 and Network Centrality

Organization	Frequency	Centrality
Air Force	6	0.50
GTE	5	-2.07
Turkey	4	0.66
Ralston Purina	4	0.34
Army	3	-0.62
Malaysia	3	-0.14
SEC	3	3.00
Standard Tele. & Cables	3	-0.46
Qume	2	3.00
Teletas	2	3.00
TI	2	0.50
U.S. Government	2	0.50
Britain	2	0.34
A T & T	2	-0.30
TDX Systems	2	-0.14
Moody's	2	0.50
S & P	2	0.50
MCI	3	-0.46
Plessy Co.	1	-0.30
Southern Tel.	1	-0.30
Rockwell International	1	-0.14
Virginia	1	-0.14
NEC	1	-0.14
Allnet Communications	1	0.02
Bellsouth	1	0.02
General Electric	1	0.02
Pacific Telesis	1	0.02
Fujitsu	1	0.02
MBank of Dallas	1	0.50
Compushop	1	0.50
Soviet Government	1	0.50
Treego Bina	1	0.50
Thomas SA	1	1.45
Raytheon	1	1.93

In short, this illustration of using network analysis approaches to analyze media content representations of interorganizational relations shows that the same analytical framework can be applied to both interorganizational relations as "objectively" defined and as represented in the mass media. As well, the same network analysis approach can be applied to measuring audiences' cognitive schemata for the same symbolic domain.

The audience effects part of the equation, here indirectly indexed through stock values, offers potential for investigating mass media phenomena that adds a missing link to the literature. Traditionally only the audience was studied. More recently the media organization has been added to the process. Subsequently, the media's source organizations may be monitored as to how they link to mass media-audience dynamics. The current research is a case in point. An obvious extension of this research is to obtain audience image data directly through survey research and represent it in a network model.

To illustrate how this may be done and what the results are like, we gathered image data from a sample of five experts, stock brokers. Each was asked what kinds of images come to mind when they think of ITT. Then, each pair of attributes mentioned by a respondent was given a comention score. These were aggregated and network analyzed. Results are presented in Figure 39.3. The technique can be used with large samples as well. Note that the darker nodes in the figure had a frequency of two or more activations of that semantic region of the network across the sample.

Future research can test hypotheses about the structural correspondence of audience cognitive schemata and message representational networks as predictors of effects on schema change, awareness, activation, and interpersonal network structures. Similarly, networks can be examined for tests of hypothesized relationships across interpersonal and interorganizational domains, and across interorganizational and media representational domains. Statistical tests are available for determining the significance of differences of networks (Baker & Hubert, 1981).

Testing such theories of interorganizational relations, media coverage, and audience effects is perhaps more reliably done using network analysis as a common analytical framework across the three domains. Error due to misalignment of meta-analytical structures may be reduced. Future research can determine to what extent this is the case.

From a broader view, the present research has demonstrated that it is possible to frame research questions at and use methods at macrolevels when concerned with mass media-related processes. Most mass media research has been conducted at the individual level. This is despite the fact that media management is organized on the more macro "market" level, that researchers focus more on media organizations' impact on audiences, and that these organizations communicate with source organizations via public relations processes.

This research also shows that interorganizational relations can be defined institutionally using communication-based relationships such as sharing public relations firms. The interlocking directorate research focusing on sharing individual boards of directors members has dominated the literature. That approach is limited in providing conceptual rationale for communication effects across organizations and their environments.

Future interorganizational research may fruitfully examine the sharing of other services, such as advertising, accounting, legal, and others. Examining more such relationships would increase the external validity of inter-

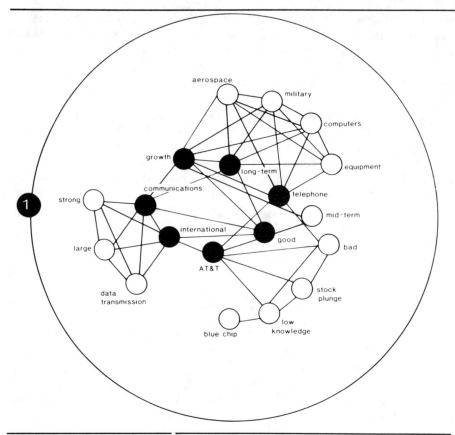

Figure 39.3 Cognitive network about ITT Corp. held by stockbrokers.

organizational network analysis as representing more generic structures that may cut across those for the particular service domain. How correspondent public relations-based networks are to others could be determined as well. In fact, we have begun a similar but more detailed analysis of the shared advertising agency links among the Fortune 500 and the largest financial, insurance, retail, transportation, and utilities organizations. We are testing hypotheses that more structurally equivalent organizations communicate more similar advertisements.

Institutional or corporate advertising also may be interesting to examine along with mass media coverage in elite and other press. Does such paid-for communication with publics serve to compensate for inadequate press coverage, or do the two forms of communication more often parallel one another?

Merger and acquisition phenomena also may be analyzable with methods such as those used in the present research. By acquiring or merging with firms in a particular position in interorganizational networks, does the new organization acquire the media and image profile of those it subsumes, or are there synthetic effects? Based on the present research, one may consider that acquiring firms with a particular position within the shared public relations network may have predictable consequences for media coverage and audience images.

On a broader plane, this research demonstrates that public relations firms play a role in organizations' linkages through the media to their publics. Although practitioners operate from this premise, social research has yet to gauge the effects of public relations using empirical methods. Organizational communication research, an area in which one would expect naturally to find treatment of public relations processes, has seen very little mention of these phenomena in its literature. Previously decoupled areas of organizational and mass communication appear integratible into a broader theoretical architecture framed by public relations.

REFERENCES

Abel, A. (Ed.). (1980). *The collected papers of Franco Modigliani.* Cambridge: MIT Press.

Adler, I. (1986). *Uses and effects of mass media in a large bureaucracy: A case study in Mexico.* Unpublished doctoral dissertation, University of Wisconsin-Madison.

Aldrich, H. (1979). Organizations and environments. Englewood Cliffs: NJ: Prentice-Hall.

Aldrich, H., & Whetten, D. A. (1981). Organization-sets, action-sets, and networks: Making the most of simplicity. In P. C. Nystrom & W. H. Starbuck (Eds.), *Handbook of organization design* (Vol. 2, pp. 385-408). New York: Oxford University Press.

Ashby, H. R. (1956). Variety, constraint, and the law of requisite variety. In An Introduction to Cybernetics (pp. 202-209). London: Chapman & Hall.

Baker & Hubert (1981). The analysis of social interaction data. *Sociological Methods and Research, 9,* 339-361.

Breiger, R. L. (1974). The duality of persons and groups. *Social Forces, 53,* 181-190.

Burt, R. S. (1982). *Toward a structural theory of action.* New York: Academic Press.

Burt, R. S., Christman, K. P. & Kilburn, H. C. (1980). Testing a structural theory of corporate cooptation: Interorganization directorate ties as a strategy for avoiding marketing constraints on profits. *American Sociological Review, 45,* 821-841.

Clark, B. R. (1965). Inter-organizational patterns in education. *Administrative Science Quarterly, 9,* 70-90.

Corporate affiliations directory (1985). Wilmette, IL: National Register Publishing Co.

Cyert, R. M., Feigenbaum, E. A. & March, J. G. (1959). Models in a behavioral theory of the firm. *Behavioral Science, 4,* 82-83.

Danowski, J. A. (1974). *An information processing model of organizations: A focus on environmental uncertainty and communication network structuring.* Paper presented to the International Communication Association.

Danowski, J. A., & Andrews, J. R. (1985). *An automated word-network analysis method.* Paper presented to the Social Networks Conference.

Danowski, J. A. (1986). Interpersonal network radiality and non-mass media use. In G. Gumpert & R. Cathcart (Eds.), *Intermedia* (3rd ed.). New York: Oxford University Press.

Eisenberg, E. M., Farace, R. V., Monge, P. R., Bettinghaus, E. P., Kurchner-Hawkins, R., Miller, K. I. & Rothman, L. (1985). Communication linkages in inter-organizational systems: Review and synthesis. In B. Dervin (Ed.), *Advances in communication science* (pp. 231-261). Norwood, NJ: Ablex.

Emery, S. E. & Trist, E. L. (1965). The causal texture of organizational environments. *Human Relations, 18,* 21-32.

Etzioni, A. (1960). New directions in the study of organizations and society. *Social Research, 27,* 223-228.

Forbes. (1985 January 14).

Graber, D. A. (1984). *Processing the news: How people tame the information tide.* New York: Longman.

Granovetter, M. S. (1973). The strength of weak ties. *American Journal of Sociology, 73,* 1361-1380.

Grunig, J. E. (1982). The message-attitude-behavior relationship: Communication behaviors of organizations. *Communication Research, 9,* 163-200.

Hage, J., & Aiken, H. (1969). Routine technology, social structure, and organizational goals. *Administrative Science Quarterly, 14,* 366-377.

Kapp, J. E., & Barnett, G. A. (1983). Predicting organizational effectiveness from communication activities: A multiple indicator model. *Human Communication Research, 9,* 239-254.

Katz, D., & Kahn, R. (1978). *The social psychology of organizations.* New York: John Wiley.

Levine, S., & White, P. E. (1961). Exchange as a conceptual framework for the study of inter-organizational relationships. *Administrative Science Quarterly, 5.* 583-601.

Litwak, E., & Hylton, L. F. (1962). Inter-organizational analysis: A hypothesis on coordinating agencies. *Administrative Science Quarterly, 6,* 397-420.

McCombs, M. E., & Shaw, D. E. (1976). Structuring the unseen environment. *Journal of Communication, 26,* 18-28.

Mitchell, J. C. (1973). Networks, norms and institutions. In J. Boissevain & J. C. Mitchell (Eds.), *Network analysis* (pp. 15-35). Hague, Netherlands: Mouton.

O'Dwyer, J. (1985). *O'Dwyer's directory of public relations firms.* New York: J. R. O'Dwyer Co.

Pfeffer, J., & Salancik, G. R. (1978). *The external control of organizations.* New York: Harper & Row.

Rice, R., & Richards, W. D., Jr. (1981). NEGOPY network analysis program. *Social Networks, 3,* 215-223.

Rogers, E. M., & Kincaid, D. L. (1981). *Communication networks: Toward a new paradigm for research.* New York: Free Press.

Sonquist, J., & Koenig, T. (1975). Interlocking directorates in the top U.S. corporations: A graph theory approach. *Insurgent Sociologist, 5,* 196-229.

Terryberry, S. (1968). The evolution of organizations environments. *Administrative Science Quarterly, 12,* 590-613.

Thompson, J. (1967). *Organizations in action.* New York: McGraw-Hill.

Warren, R. L. (1967). The inter-organizational field as a focus for investigation. *Administrative Science Quarterly, 12,* 396-419.

Weick, K. E. (1979). *The social psychology of organizing* (2nd ed.). Reading, MA: Addison-Wesley.

Wigand, R. T. (1979). A model of interorganizational communication among complex organizations. In K. Krippendorff (Ed.), *Communication and control in society.* New York: Gordon & Breach Science Publishers.

40 ● Public Relations in Trade and Professional Associations: Location, Model, Structure, Environment, and Values

SALLY J. McMILLAN

University of Wisconsin — Eau Claire

PROBLEM STATEMENT

Location

Trade and professional associations traditionally have established national offices in New York City or Chicago. Several studies (Adler, 1972; Bower, 1979; Clarke, 1967; "Why Associations Move," 1972) suggest that the many mass media outlets in New York make that city a favorite location of associations that attempt to gain media exposure for their members, and that Chicago, because of its central location, is valued by associations that wish to maintain contact with members who live in many different areas of the United States.

In the 1960s and 1970s, observers (Collins, 1961; "Washington Attracts More Trade Groups," 1976) noted a new trend developing as many associations moved their national headquarters to Washington, D.C. Though a variety of reasons for a Washington headquarters are cited, Miles (1964) states that reacting to and with the government is the reason for being of most public relations practice in Washington.

Grunig and Hunt (1984) identify the public affairs activities often practiced in Washington as fact-finding; liaison work that includes attending hearings, interviewing officials, and entertaining; interpretation of government action to management or members; information giving—that is,

AUTHOR'S NOTE: This chapter is based on a master's thesis prepared for the University of Maryland College of Journalism. The author gratefully acknowledges the assistance of James E. Grunig, Ray E. Hiebert, Roger Yarrington, and James E. Fields for review and comments on drafts of this chapter.

Correspondence and requests for reprints: Sally J. McMillan, P.O. Box 1029, Eau Claire, WI 54702.

preparing information for government officials; and advocacy, commonly referred to as lobbying.

Public affairs activities are only one type of public relations practiced in trade and professional associations. Studies of association public relations (Abbott, 1965; American Society of Association Executives, 1975; Havas, 1969; Mortenson, 1975) identify the following other activities as public relations functions of associations: write newsletters, bulletins, trade and technical publications; provide industry or product information to members; promote products or services; furnish advertising materials to members; sponsor umbrella consumer promotions; conduct public service campaigns; promote interindustry cooperation; gain public acceptance of industry, trade, or profession; conduct mass media relations; combat adverse publicity; prepare educational materials; speak at conventions, seminars, and meetings; conduct conventions, meetings, and workshops; promote trade exhibits and shows; affect government regulation; inform members of relevant government activities; change attitudes, actions, ethics of the industry, trade, or profession; promote industry standards or certification programs; sponsor competitions and awards; increase membership; engage in two-way communication with members; and conduct market surveys, opinion polls, and other research.

Models

Grunig's (1983) four models of public relations provide a theoretical base for examining the public relations activities of associations. The four models are defined by variation along two independent dimensions: asymmetric versus symmetric goals and one-way versus two-way nature of communication. Grunig and Hunt (1984) suggest that, in addition to the asymmetric/symmetric goal and the nature of communication, the purpose and role of public relations and the nature of research also help define the models.

The goal of public relations in the press agentry model is control of the environment. Communication flows from the organization to its publics in an attempt to persuade. Organizations practicing the press agentry model perceive the purpose of public relations to be propaganda. The role of the public relations practitioner is to serve as advocate for the organization. Public relations research is seldom conducted by organizations practicing the press agentry model.

Organizations practicing the public information model of public relations have adaptive goals. The organizations do not seek to control their environment, nor do they attempt to understand the environment. The flow of communication is from the organization to the public. The purpose of the public information model is dissemination of information. In organizations practicing the public information model, the role of the public relations practitioner is that of a disseminator. Research is limited in this model to readability tests that establish the suitability of written messages and readership studies to determine who is reading the messages.

The goal of public relations in organizations practicing the two-way asymmetric model is control of the environment. Communication flows both to and from the organization, but the communication from publics is used to aid the organization in controlling the environment. The purpose of public relations in this model is scientific persuasion and the role of the practitioner is an advocate who aids the organization in planning programs that will persuade publics. Research is important in the two-way asymmetric model. Research is the means by which organizations establish the two-way flow of communication.

The goal of organizations practicing the two-way symmetric model of communication is adaptation. Two-way communication between the organization and its publics aids the organization in obtaining this goal. The purpose of public relations in organizations exhibiting two-way symmetric public relations behavior is mutual understanding. The practitioner serves as a mediator between management and publics and thus helps the organization and its publics achieve mutual understanding. Formative research indicates how the public perceives the organization and determines what consequences the organization has for the public. Evaluative research measures the effectiveness of a public relations program by determining if management and publics have improved their understanding of one another.

Grunig (1983) suggests that an organization does not necessarily practice one model to the exclusion of others. An organization may practice all four of the models depending on specific needs. As indicated above, association public relations needs cover a wide spectrum ranging from member relations to government relations.

Hypothesis 1: Associations will practice mixed models of public relations behavior.

Grunig and Hunt (1984) note that associations are usually not highly structured. Members of associations often join to obtain information. This low-structure and high-information need suggests that member communication in associations should follow the two-way symmetric model. Grunig and Hunt also suggest that association members actively seek information that will help them meet specialized work situations. This active communication-seeking also suggests the need for use of the two-way models. Abbott (1965) and Ebel (1981) indicate that member support is important in associations with headquarters in a city other than Washington.

Hypothesis 2: Associations with headquarters in cities other than Washington, D.C., will, because of their emphasis on member support, exhibit predominantly two-way symmetric public relations behavior.

The literature on public relations behaviors of associations in Washington, D.C. (Bower, 1979; Grunig & Hunt, 1984; Harrison, 1977; Hattal, 1967a, 1967b, 1968, 1973; Miles, 1964; Quiggle & Elliott, 1982) suggests that associations with headquarters in the nation's capital stress government relations and public affairs activities. The literature on public affairs and government relations in associations (Abbott, 1965; Bonsib, 1979; Cray, 1978; Ebel, 1981; Fulmer, 1972; Havas, 1969; Rosenbloom, 1967) focuses primarily on lobbying activities.

Grunig and Hunt (1984) suggest that when organizations involved in public affairs activities focus on advocacy (lobbying), the two-way asymmetric model works well for achieving public affairs goals. The literature (Bevevino, 1966; Harrison, 1977; Havas, 1969; McCormick, 1957) indicates that most Washington-based associations employ two-way communications techniques in order to achieve control over the legislative process.

Hypothesis 3: Associations with headquarters in Washington, D.C., will, because of their emphasis on government relations, exhibit predominantly two-way asymmetric public relations behavior.

Organizational Structure

Grunig (1976) suggests that the public relations behaviors of practitioners are largely determined by the structure of the organization and the practitioner's role in that structure. Grunig and Hunt (1984) indicate that the vertical structure of an organization distributes the decision-making power in an organization. The more that power is located at the top levels of management, the more structured the organization will be.

Hage (1974) identifies four variables in the vertical structure of organizations that have an impact on communication: complexity, centralization, stratification, and formalization. The higher the level of centralization, stratification, and formalization and the lower the level of complexity, the more rigid the vertical structure will be. Grunig and Hunt (1984) suggest that these four structural variables help predict the public relations model practiced by an organization. They indicate that organizations with a rigid vertical hierarchy will practice the one-way models: press agentry and public information. Organizations with a flexible vertical hierarchy will practice the two-way models: two-way asymmetric and two-way symmetric.

Practitioners in the one-way models have little need for input into the organization. They routinely produce communications messages and do not usually feel constrained by the rigid vertical hierarchy that limits their autonomy, decision-making power, and ability to communicate with managers. Practitioners in the two-way models, however, have a greater need for autonomy, decision-making power, and access to managers in higher levels of the vertical structure. The tasks they perform are shaped by the changing needs of publics. The two-way flow of communication between the organization and its publics must be interpreted by the public relations practitioners. A more flexible vertical hierarchy enables practitioners to perform these tasks. Grunig and Hunt (1984) identify associations as highly autonomous organizations that cannot be constrained by centralized or formalized structure.

> *Hypothesis 4:* Associations with low complexity, high centralization, high stratification, and high formalization will practice one-way models of public relations.
>
> *Hypothesis 5:* Associations with high complexity, low centralization, low stratification, and low formalization will practice two-way models of public relations.
>
> *Hypothesis 6:* The two-way models of public relations will be dominant in associations.

Environmental Variables

In the context of organizational theory, environment consists of "external influences on organizational structure and performance" (Hage, 1980, p. 379). In his 1983 work, Grunig suggests that environmental variables should be better predictors of public relations behavior than structural variables because "Both structure and public relations behavior depend upon the environment of the organization" (p. 15).

Hage and Aiken (1970) indicate that structural characteristics of organizations are affected by the amount of change in the environment. When the environment is dynamic, organizations have the following structural characteristics: high complexity, low centralization, low stratification, and low formalization. When the environment is static, organizations have the following structural characteristics: low complexity, high centralization, high stratification, and high formalization. Grunig (1983) suggests that structure also affects the way in which organizations cope with the environment. Organizations use one of two methods for dealing with the environment: seeking to control the environment or adapting to the environment.

Grunig's 1983 work indicates that public relations behaviors of organizations are affected by the environment because the public relations department of an organization helps other subsystems within the organization communicate with the part of the environment assigned to that subsystem. As the environment of subsystems stabilizes or changes, the public relations behavior must either stabilize or it must change to meet the needs of those subsystems of the organization.

Grunig and Hunt (1984) identify four variables that explain the relationship between environment and public relations behavior: scale of demand, knowledge complexity, constraints, and uncertainty. Scale of demand and knowledge complexity are related to the product/service environment of organizations. Constraints and uncertainty are in the political/regulatory environment.

The product/service environment is composed of those external influences that affect organizations' products or services. Hage and Hull (Hage, 1980; Hage & Hull, 1981; Hull & Hage, 1981) identify four organizational niches based on scale and complexity: traditional, mechanistic, organic, and mixed mechanistic/organic organizations. Demand for products or services is measured in terms of scale. Knowledge complexity has to do with the level and range of knowledge that are necessary to prepare the products or services of the organization. Traditional organizations have low knowledge complexity and small scale of demand. Mechanistic organizations have low knowledge complexity and large scale of demand. Organic organizations have high knowledge complexity and small scale of demand. Mixed mechanistic/organic organizations have high knowledge complexity and large scale of demand.

Grunig (1983) suggests that the Hage-Hull typology should explain how organizations use public relations to support the marketing of products and services. Traditional organizations would be most likely to use the press agentry model to make the public aware of the products or services offered by the organization. Mechanistic organizations do not need to make the public aware of their products and services because of the large stable demand for the outputs of the organization. These organizations would be likely to practice the public information model to give consumers or users factual information about products or services. Organic organizations would be expected to use the two-way symmetric model to help them adapt to their complex, changing product/service environment. Mixed mechanistic/organic organizations would be likely to mix the models of public relations that they practice. They may use the two-way asymmetric model for marketing their complex products or services. The two-way symmetric model may be used to help them adapt to their changing environment.

> *Hypothesis   7:* The public relations behaviors of traditional associations will follow the press agentry model.
>
> *Hypothesis   8:* The public relations behaviors of mechanistic associations will follow the public information model.
>
> *Hypothesis   9:* The public relations behaviors of organic associations will follow the two-way symmetric model.
>
> *Hypothesis 10:* The public relations behaviors of mixed mechanistic/ organic associations will be a mix of the two-way asymmetric and two-way symmetric models.

Grunig (1983) warns, however, that "The product/service environment explains only part of an organization's public relations behavior. . . . Relationships with publics, pressure groups, and governments—in the political/ regulatory environment—generate separate models of public relations behavior" (p. 21). Grunig suggests that constraints and uncertainty are the factors that determine the nature of the political/regulatory environment.

Environmental constraints affect the asymmetric/symmetric goals that determine public relations models. When constraints are low, public relations behavior is asymmetric. At this level, organizations desire to demonstrate social responsibility. When an organization faces a medium level of constraints, public relations behavior is symmetric. At this level, activists have asked for regulation and the organization seeks to avoid regulation. When constraints on an organization reach a high level, public relations behavior once again becomes asymmetric as the organization fights to eliminate regulation.

Uncertainty affects the one-way/two-way nature of communication in the public relations models. When uncertainty is low, communication will be one way. When uncertainty is high, organizations will use two-way communication in their public relations behavior.

Hypothesis 11: When environmental constraints are low and environmental uncertainty is low, the public relations behavior of associations will follow the press agentry model.

Hypothesis 12: When environmental constraints are low and environmental uncertainty is high, the public relations behavior of associations will follow the two-way asymmetric model.

Hypothesis 13: When environmental constraints are at a medium level and environmental uncertainty is low, the public relations behavior of associations will follow the public information model.

Hypothesis 14: When environmental constraints are at a medium level and environmental uncertainty is high, the public relations behavior of associations will follow the two-way symmetric model.

Hypothesis 15: When environmental constraints are high and environmental uncertainty is low, the public relations behavior of associations will follow the press agentry model.

Hypothesis 16: When environmental constraints are high and environmental uncertainty is high, the public relations behavior of associations will follow the two-way asymmetric model.

Values

J. E. Grunig (personal communication, March 2, 1984) suggests that the values of management in reference to political/regulatory issues may affect the public relations behavior of the organization. If managers hold conservative political values and believe that government regulation is unnecessary, the public relations behaviors of the organization are likely to be asymmetric. If managers are politically liberal and believe that the organization should take responsibility for adapting to the needs of its publics, public relations behaviors of the organization are likely to be symmetric.

Hypothesis 17: When managers have conservative political/regulatory values, the public relations behaviors of the organization will
follow one of the asymmetric models.

Hypothesis 18: When managers have liberal political/regulatory values,
the public relations behaviors of the organization will follow one of the symmetric models.

Dominant Models

Grunig's 1983 study revealed that organizations practice more than one
model of public relations. He suggests that this is because of different needs
in product/service and political/regulatory environments. The dominant
model of public relations in an organization will be determined by the dominance of the product/service or political/regulatory environment. However, both types of environment affect organizations, so public relations
strategies must address both product/service and political/regulatory factors. The nondominant portion of the environment may be addressed by a
public relations model different from the dominant model.

As noted earlier, associations in Washington, D.C., seem to place more
emphasis on government relations than do associations located elsewhere.
In the analysis of the product/service environment versus the political/
regulatory environment, it seems that government relations would logically fall into the domain of the political/regulatory environment.

Hypothesis 19: Associations located in Washington, D.C., will be more
likely to have a dominant public relations model that
responds to the political/regulatory environment than will
associations located elsewhere.

METHODOLOGY

To test the predicted relationships among location, models, structure,
environment, and values in the public relations behavior of associations, it
was necessary to gather data relative to the public relations goals, purposes, roles, communication, research, and behaviors of associations as
well as information about the structure of the associations and the environments in which they operate. To gather these data, a survey questionnaire
was mailed to 600 associations drawn at random from the 5 applicable sections of the *Encyclopedia of Associations: National Organizations of the
United States* (EOA).

Table 40.1 indicates the number of associations sampled from each of
the relevant sections of the EOA: trade associations; legal associations; scientific, engineering, and technical associations; education associations; and
health and medical associations. Table 40.1 also indicates the number of

Table 40.1
Associations Sampled in Each EOA Section
Indicating Washington and Non-Washington Location

Section	Number sampled	Percent of total sample	Washington location	Non-Washington location
1—Trade	336	56	84	252
3—Legal	17	3	2	15
4—Scientific, engineering, technical	115	19	24	91
5—Educational	104	17	24	80
8—Health, medical	28	5	6	22
Totals	600	100	140	460
Percentage of sample			23	77

respondents from Washington and non-Washington zip codes. The sampling procedure did not include any method for selecting quotas of Washington or non-Washington associations. The proportions of associations from each location are the result of the random sample of the universe of 6,154 trade and professional associations listed in the EOA.

The size of the sample from each section was proportionate to the size of that section in relationship to the total number of associations in the universe. For example, the section listing trade associations is numbered sequentially from 1 to 3,494. These 3,494 associations account for approximately 56% of the 6,154 trade and professional associations listed in the EOA. Therefore, 56%, or 336, of the sample of 600 associations was selected from this section of the EOA. A computer-generated list of 336 random numbers between 1 and 3,494 was used to select the sample of trade associations.

The survey was addressed to executive directors of associations with instructions that they personally answer the questionnaire. In similar studies testing the four models of public relations, Grunig (1983) found that when several individuals in an organization were interviewed in reference to the public relations behaviors of the organization, high-level personnel had more representative perceptions than did low-level personnel.

Responses to the survey represented 30.4% of the actual sample after adjusting for questionnaires returned by the post office because of noncurrent address and by associations because the association did not fit the descriptions of a trade or professional association.

Table 40.2 indicates the number of respondents from trade, legal, scientific, engineering, technical, education, health, and medical associations and indicates whether the respondent was from a Washington-based association or an association based elsewhere. Associations with headquarters in or near Washington, D.C., accounted for 23% of the sample but 39% of

Table 40.2
Respondents from Each EOA Section
Indicating Washington and Non-Washington Location

Section	Number of respondents	Percent of total sample	Washington location	Non-Washington location
1—Trade	80	51	31	49
3—Legal	7	4	2	5
4—Scientific, engineering, technical	36	23	14	22
5—Educational	28	18	13	15
8—Health, medical	7	4	2	5
Totals	158	100	62	96
Percentage of sample			39	61

the return. This high return rate from Washington associations may have been due to the proximity of the University of Maryland to Washington, D.C. The questionnaire identified the author's affiliation with the University of Maryland.

FINDINGS

As hypothesized, associations did mix public relations models. However, data derived from the survey did not support hypotheses 2 and 3, which predicted that associations located in Washington would practice the two-way asymmetric model and associations located elsewhere would practice the two-way symmetric model.

Geographical location was not found to have any significant relationship to the model of public relations practiced by associations. The press agentry model was dominant in all locations in contradiction to hypothesis 6 which predicted that the two-way models of public relations would be dominant in associations.

Lack of a clear definition of association public relations may help to explain the dominance of the press agentry model. Public relations in associations is difficult to define. Some observers identify all association activities as public relations. Yet, 64% of the respondents indicated that their association has no public relations department. However, in many of those associations, public relations tasks are performed by several different departments such as media relations, legislative activities, and member relations.

The press agentry model is the oldest form of public relations. The other three models have evolved as organizations have recognized public relations needs that cannot be met by the press agentry model. The fact that so

many associations do not recognize public relations as a specialized function, requiring a department to perform public relations tasks, may reflect a
lack of recognition of public relations needs of associations. It is possible
that respondents equated the terms *media relations* and *public relations*
thus indicating that the press agentry model is the dominant model of public relations in the association.

Associations practicing the one-way models were expected to show negative correlation with complexity and positive correlation with centralization, stratification, and formalization. The survey showed that complexity,
as measured by education of members, had a significant negative correlation with press agentry ($r = -.16$). This provides limited support for the
hypothesized relationship between structure and the one-way models. No
positive correlations were found between one-way models and centralization, stratification, or formalization. Instead, significant negative correlations were found between press agentry and stratification (status) ($r =
-.15$) and formalization (rules) ($r = -.19$), and between public information
models and formalization (employee) ($r = -.20$).

Associations practicing two-way models were expected to correlate positively with complexity and negatively with centralization, stratification, and
formalization. Centralization was found to have a significant negative correlation ($r = -.17$) with the two-way symmetric model, but no other significant hypothesized relationships were obtained.

Environmental variables were no more reliable as predictors of the model
of public relations practiced by associations than were location and organizational structure. An examination of the zero-order correlations among
Hage's four organizational types, which define the product/service environment, and the four models of public relations indicates that the only
significant positive correlation is between mechanistic organizations and
the two-way symmetric model ($r = .16$). This was not a hypothesized
relationship.

Correlations among the levels of change and constraint and the public
relations models were calculated. Both two-way models correlated positively with the environmental condition that exists when political change
and environmental constraints are both at a high level: for high/high and
two-way asymmetric, r was .14; for high-high and two-way symmetric, r
was .12 ($p < .05$ for both rs). The high/high environmental condition was
predicted to result in two-way asymmetric public relations behavior. No
other hypothesized relationships between environment and model were
supported by the data.

Correlations between values and the four public relations models appear
in Table 40.3. It is interesting to note that all four models showed significant positive correlations with the item that suggests that the association
benefits if it changes to meet the demands of the publics. Only the public
information and two-way symmetric models were predicted to show such

Table 40.3
Pearson Correlations Between Political/Regulatory Values
of Respondents and Four Models of Public Relations

Political/ regulatory values	Press agentry	Public information	Two-way asymmetric	Two-way symmetric
(1) Government regulation is needed when organizations are irresponsible.	-.06	-.05	.07	.02
(2) Publics are better off if our association can persuade them to its point of view.	.06	.06	.27***	-.04
(3) Society benefits when government has an active role in the economy.	.00	.04	-.07	-.01
(4) The association benefits if it changes to meet demands of publics.	.20**	.13*	.18**	.24**
(5) Most of the executives of this association are politically conservative.	.10	.03	.14*	.08

$* \ p < .05; ** \ p < .01; *** \ p < .001.$

correlation. The predicted positive correlation was found between the two-way asymmetric model and the following statements: "Publics are better off if our association can persuade them to its point of view," and "Most of the executives of this association are politically conservative." However, liberal values (items 1, 3, and 4 on Table 40.3) did not consistently correlate with two-way models nor did conservative values (items 2 and 5 on Table 40.3) consistently correlate with one-way models.

Because no significant correlations were found between location and the dominant public relations model, the hypothesized relationships among location, dominant public relations model, and responsiveness to the political/regulatory or product/service environment could not be tested.

CONCLUSIONS

Although the findings did not support many of the predicted relationships among location, model, structure, environment, and values of associations, the data do not permit the conclusion that geographic location has no effect on the public relations function of associations. The hypothesized relationships between model and location were based on the expected emphasis of public relations programs in Washington and non-Washington locations. Lobbying activities in Washington seemed to employ the goals and communications methods of the two-way asymmetric model. The member support emphasis of non-Washington associations seemed to employ the goals and communications methods of the two-way symmetric model. But Grunig and Hunt (1984) have noted that lobbying can be performed according to the principles of all four models of public relations. Member support activities also can be practiced according to the principles of all four models.

Associations located in Washington may emphasize lobbying more than do associations located elsewhere, but they will not necessarily practice the two-way asymmetric model. Non-Washington associations may perform more member support service than their Washington counterparts, but they will not necessarily practice the two-way symmetric model.

The political/regulatory values of management may help explain the lack of support for hypotheses about the relationship among structure, environment, and models. The relationships among structure, environment, and model predicted in this study describe the organizational structure and public relations behavior that would best enable organizations to achieve equilibrium with the environment in which they exist. But, as Hage (1980) indicates, organizations may be out of equilibrium with their environments. Grunig (1983, pp. 25-26) suggested that a primary reason for this disequilibrium may be that the powerful people who manage the organization, the "dominant coalition," do not understand or value public relations.

SUGGESTIONS FOR
FURTHER RESEARCH

The lack of support for some of the hypotheses of this study suggests the need for further research on public relations in associations, and on the relationship among public relations models, organizational structure, environments, and the values of those who have decision-making power in organizations.

A possible reason for the lack of support for many of the hypotheses about the public relations function in associations may be the fact that public relations is not recognized as a specialized department in many associations. A need seems to to exist for descriptive research of the public relations function in associations to determine what activities associations perceive as part of the public relations function and how those activities are performed.

The four models of public relations did not illuminate any difference in the emphasis of public relations programs in Washington and associations located elsewhere. This suggests that location is not a significant factor in this public relations theory. Location does not seem to be related to the factors used to describe or predict models of public relations.

This study examined structural variables in terms of the structure of associations. The environment was examined in terms of the product/service or political/regulatory environment of member organizations. Lack of significant correlations between either structural variables and model or environmental variables and model may be related to this mixed testing of associations and member organizations. Studies examining structure and environment of either association or member organizations—but not both—may find more significant correlations among structure, environment, and the model of public relations practiced.

The two factors that seem to hold promise for predicting the model of public relations practiced in associations are the political/regulatory values of management and the values of the dominant coalition. Both of these factors need to be studied in greater detail. Variables used to test the political/regulatory values of managers need to be reworded and expanded. Variables need to be designed to test the relationship between values of the dominant coalition and the public relations behaviors of associations. The relationship between public relations behavior and the presence or absence of a public relations representative in the dominant coalition also should be examined.

The political/regulatory values of managers and the values of the dominant coalition may explain low correlations between structural and environmental factors and the public relations model practiced by associations.

REFERENCES

Abbott, K. E. (1965). Public relations programs of organizations in eleven professions whose members are licensed by the ten most populous states (Master's thesis, Ohio State University, 1964). *Journalism Abstracts, 3,* 40-41.

Adler, W. (1972). Public relations in a membership organization. *Public Relations Quarterly, 16*(4), 19-21.

Akey, D. S. (Ed.). (1984). *Encyclopedia of associations: National organizations of the United States* (18th ed., Vols. 1, 2). Detroit: Gale Research Co.

American Society of Association Executives (1975). *Principles of association management.* Washington, DC: Author.

Bevevino, C. R. (1966). A perspective on lobbying with selective examples from the American Retail Federation and members of its Central Council of National Retail Associations which are headquartered in Washington, DC (Master's thesis, American University, 1966). *Journalism Abstracts, 4,* 44-45.

Bonsib, L. W. (1971, February). Washington Focus. *Public Relations Journal,* p. 1.

Bower, S. S. (1979, June). Watch out, Washington, here come the trade associations. *National Journal,* pp. 956-957.

Clarke, C. C. (1967). Setting the record straight. *Public Relations Quarterly, 12*(2), 7-23.

Collins, F. W. (1961, April 23). Another Potomac army: The lobbyists. *New York Times Magazine,* pp. A13, 99, 100.

Cray, J. L. (1978). Public relations programs of the American Dental Association related to government activities—A case study (Master's thesis, Northern Illinois University, 1981). *Journalism Abstracts, 19,* 39.

Ebel, R. G. (1981). A study of predicted member-support behavior involving association public relations (Master's thesis, Northern Illinois University, 1981). *Journalism Abstracts, 19,* 39.

Fulmer, R. W. (1972). *Managing associations for the 1980s.* Washington, DC: American Society of Association Executives.

Grunig, J. E. (1976). Organizations and public relations: Testing a communication theory. *Journalism Monographs, 46.*

Grunig, J. E. (1983, August). *Organizations, environments, and models of public relations.* Paper presented at the meeting of the Association for Education in Journalism and Mass Communication, Corvallis, OR.

Grunig, J. E., & Hunt, T. (1984). *Managing public relations.* New York: Holt, Rinehart & Winston.

Hage, J. (1974). *Communication and organizational control: Cybernetics in health and welfare settings.* New York: Wiley-Interscience.

Hage, J. (1980). *Theories of organizations: Form, process, and transformation.* New York: Wiley-Interscience.

Hage, J., & Aiken, M. (1970). *Social change in complex organizations.* New York: Random House.

Hage, J., & Hull, F. (1981). *Determinants of organizational structure and the consequences for industrial innovation* (Working Paper No. 1). College Park: University of Maryland, Center for the Study of Innovation, Productivity & Strategy in cooperation with the Research Program for Innovation and Productivity Strategies, Rutgers University, Newark, NJ.

Harrison, E. B. (1977, November). Washington focus. *Public Relations Journal,* p. 2.

Hattal, A. M. (1967a, April). Washington focus. *Public Relations Journal,* p. 4.

Hattal, A. M. (1967b, July). Washington focus. *Public Relations Journal,* p. 2.

Hattal, A. M. (1968, May). Washington focus. *Public Relations Journal,* p. 6.

Hattal, A. M. (1973, August). Washington focus. *Public Relations Journal,* p. 4.

Havas, J. M. (1969). Counseling the trade association. *Public Relations Quarterly, 14*(2), 7-14.

Hull, F. & Hage, J. (1981). *Beyond Burns and Stalker: Multiple kinds of organic and mechanical organization* (Working Paper No. 2). College Park: University of Maryland, Center for the Study of Innovation, Productivity & Strategy in cooperation with the Research Program for Innovation and Productivity Strategies, Rutgers University, Newark, NJ.

McCormick, R. L. L. (1957). The anatomy of public relations in Washington. *Public Relations Quarterly, 2*(1), 1-8.

Miles, T. W. (1964). Public relations practice in Washington. *Public Relations Quarterly, 9*(3), 7-15.

Mortenson, C. (1975). *Association evaluation: Guidelines for measuring organizational performance.* Washington, DC: American Society of Association Executives.

Quiggle, J., & Elliott, C. D. (1982, May 17). Associations migrate to DC. *The Washington Business Review,* p. 10.

Rosenbloom, M. V. (1967). Effective public relations with Washington. *Public Relations Quarterly, 12*(2), 7-23.

Washington attracts more trade groups as government eyes business closely. (1976, December 17). *The Wall Street Journal,* p. 1.

Why associations move to Washington. (1972, September). *Association Management,* pp. 50-54.

NAME INDEX

ABOUT THE EDITOR

MARGARET L. McLAUGHLIN (Ph.D., University of Illinois, 1972) is Professor in the Department of Communication Arts and Sciences at the University of Southern California. She is the author of *Conversation: How Talk Is Organized* (Sage, 1984), the editor of *Communication Yearbook 9* (Sage, 1986), and the editor of *Communication Monographs*. Her research interests include interpersonal communication, conversational analysis, and communication and the sexes.

ABOUT THE AUTHORS

G. BLAKE ARMSTRONG (Ph.D., Michigan State University, 1986) is Assistant Professor of Communication at Marist College in Poughkeepsie, New York. His research interests include media effects on social perceptions and cognitive processing, the structure of social and cultural attitudes, and the process of attitude change. His work has appeared in *Development and Change* and *Human Communication Research*.

GEORGE A. BARNETT (Ph.D., Michigan State University, 1976) is Associate Professor at the State University of New York at Buffalo. His research focuses on mathematical modeling and the role of communication in cognitive and sociocultural change. He has written articles in organizational and intercultural communication as well as the diffusion of communication technologies and their impact upon organizations.

BENJAMIN J. BATES (Ph.D., University of Michigan, 1986) is Visiting Lecturer in the Communication Studies Program at the University of California, Santa Barbara. His research interests focus on the social and economic effects of communication policy and the structure of communication systems.

FRANK BIOCCA is Assistant Professor in the School of Journalism at the University of North Carolina, Chapel Hill. His research interests focus on the areas of visual communication and cognition. Specifically, he is interested in the interaction of technological and semiotic structures with perceptual and cognitive processes.

S. ELIZABETH BIRD (Ph.D., cultural anthropology; M.A., journalism and folklore) teaches courses in anthropology, journalism, and folklore at the University of Iowa. Her research interests include popular culture/folklore, media and society, and cultural studies. She has published in several journals; her most recent publications appeared in *Folklore, Journalism Quarterly,* and the *Journal of Communication Inquiry*. She is currently researching a book examining American weekly tabloid newspapers from a cultural studies perspective.

JAMES J. BRADAC (Ph.D., Northwestern University, 1970) is Professor of Communication Studies at the University of California, Santa Barbara.

He has published widely in the areas of interpersonal communication, language behavior, and language attitudes. Currently, his research focuses on communication and cognition, language and power, and message variation.

DAVID A. BRENDERS (Ph.D., Purdue University, 1983) is an Assistant Professor in the Department of Speech Communication at Indiana University. His research interests include the general areas of interpersonal and health communication, with special emphases in pragmatic approaches to interpersonal influence and the ways in which a variable belief in perceived control affects the processes and outcomes of interpersonal situations.

NANCY BRENDLINGER is a Ph.D. student at the University of Texas at Austin. Her research interests include communications in Third World countries, mass media and social change, and the role of news values in satisfying audience information needs.

BRANT R. BURLESON (Ph.D., University of Illinois at Urbana-Champaign, 1982) is an Associate Professor of Communication at Purdue University. His research interests include comforting communication, the development of communication competencies, the social cognitive foundations of communication skills, and the social outcomes associated with individual differences in communication skills. His recent research reports have appeared in *Human Communication Research, Communication Yearbook, Communication Monographs, Communication Education, Child Development, Journal of Language and Social Psychology,* and *Written Communication.* He has also authored chapters for several edited books, including Sypher and Applegate's *Communication by Children and Adults,* Sigel's *Parental Belief Systems,* Ellis and Donohue's *Contemporary Issues in Language and Discourse Processes,* and McCroskey and Daly's *Personality and Interpersonal Communication.*

JOANNE CANTOR (Ph.D., Indiana University, 1974) is Professor in the Department of Communication Arts at the University of Wisconsin—Madison. Her research interests are in the effects of the mass media, particularly the social and psychological effects of television and films on children. Her recent publications investigate relationships between cognitive development and affective responses to mass media.

JOAN L. CASHION is a doctoral candidate in the Department of Communication Arts and Sciences at the University of Southern California. She is an Assistant Professor in the Department of Communication Studies at California State University, Los Angeles. Her research interests include gender and communication, language behavior, and ethics and communication.

BRIANKLE G. CHANG is an Instructor in the Department of Communication, Rutgers University. He is currently completing his doctorate from the University of Illinois, Urbana-Champaign. He has published articles in *International Philosophical Quarterly, Studies in Symbolic Interaction, Current Perspectives in Social Theory,* and other journals. His research interests include philosophy of communication, cultural studies, rhetorical theory and criticism, and film theory.

TSAN-KUO CHANG is an Assistant Professor in the Department of Communication at Cleveland State University. His research interests are in the areas of mass media and politics, media and society, and international communication. His current research deals with the mass media and foreign policy in the United States.

KUAN-HSING CHEN is a Ph.D. candidate in the School of Journalism and Mass Communication, University of Iowa. He is currently writing his dissertation on postmodernism and mass media.

MILTON CHEN (Ph.D., Stanford University, 1986) is an Assistant Professor at the Harvard Graduate School of Education. He has worked at Children's Television Workshop since 1972, conducting research for TV series in science, mathematics, and reading. His research interests address the educational uses and effects of television and computer-based media and include evaluation research, equity issues, and educational innovation. He is the coeditor of *Children and Microcomputers: Research on the Newest Medium* (with William Paisley; Sage, 1985) and was a contributor to *Communication Yearbook 8*.

ELIZABETH CHUA completed her M.A. in communication at Arizona State University. Her major research interests are in the area of culture and conflict. She is currently writing a book, *Interpersonal Communication Across Cultures,* with William B. Gudykunst (for Sage).

JAMES A. DANOWSKI (Ph.D., Michigan State University, 1975) is an Associate Professor in the Department of Communication, University of Illinois at Chicago. His research interests focus on testing hypotheses linking communication networks across organizational, media, and cognitive domains. Accordingly, his publications appearing in *Communication Yearbooks 5* and *6, Human Communication Research, Journalism Quarterly, Communication Research,* and numerous books have treated media behaviors of individuals with different personal network structures; cohort effects on political information seeking and process and content gratifications; communication network structures and attitudinal uniformity; effects of crisis on organizational electronic mail networks; and relationships of work-network structures with who-to-whom and cognitive networks, using methods he developed for network analysis of natural language texts of messages.

JEROME T. DURLAK has degrees from Notre Dame, Stanford University, and Michigan State University. He has a broad interdisciplinary background in communications research, environmental design, and urban planning, and is an Associate Professor in the Mass Communications Programme and the Graduate Faculty of Environmental Studies at York University in Toronto, Canada. His teaching revolves around the social impact and implementation of new communications technologies and services and his research specializes in the evaluation of communication, transportation, and community development projects. Currently, he is completing a book on the emergence of computers as communications media rather than as number crunchers or symbol manipulators.

LEONA L. EGGERT (Ph.D., speech communications, University of Washington, 1984) is an Assistant Professor of Psychosocial Nursing at the University of Washington. Her research has focused on the dynamics of relationship development and maintenance within personal communication networks, therapeutic communication in nurse/client relationships, and social support intervention programs for adolescent drug users/abusers. She has published several articles on individual and group work with adolescents and their families, the psychosocial development of adolescents, and therapeutic communication.

GAIL T. FAIRHURST (Ph.D., University of Oregon, 1978) is an Associate Professor of Communication at the University of Cincinnati. Her research interests include manager-subordinate communication and controlling ineffective performance. Her research has appeared in *Human Communication Research, Communication Yearbooks 8* and *9, Organizational Behavior and Human Decision Processes, Academy of Management Journal,* and *Academy of Management Review*. She is also a consultant to a number of organizations.

EDWARD L. FINK (Ph.D., University of Wisconsin) is an Associate Professor in the Department of Communication Arts and Theatre at the University of Maryland, College Park, having previously taught at the universities of Wisconsin, Notre Dame, and Michigan State. He has taught and conducted research in the areas of formal theory construction, measurement, research design and data analysis, persuasion and attitude change, interaction, social cognition, and humor. His most recent publications reflect this; his mathematical or structural models have appeared in *Communication Monographs, Behavioral Science, Human Communication Research, Communication Research, Journal of Communication,* and *Communication Yearbooks 6* and *8*. His discussions of research methods have appeared in *Sociological Methods and Research, Progress in Communication Sciences 8,* and *Communication Yearbook 7*.

SETH FINN is an Assistant Professor in the Department of Radio, Television, and Motion Pictures at the University of North Carolina at Chapel Hill. After completing his M.A. in broadcasting and film at Stanford University in 1973, he worked as a writer and news producer at KRON-TV San

Francisco. In 1979, he returned to Stanford to complete a Ph.D. in communication theory and research before coming to Chapel Hill in 1982. Although North Carolina has provided a particularly interesting political environment in which to study the diffusion of information in election campaigns, his primary research interest continues to be the role of arousal and mental effort in the processing of print and broadcast news stories.

MATTHEW H. FRIEDLAND (M.A., State University of New York at Buffalo, 1986) is currently a doctoral student at SUNY, focusing on organizational communication.

HOWARD GILES (Ph.D., University of Bristol, 1971) is Professor of Social Psychology and Director of the Centre for the Study of Communication and Social Relations at the same institution. He is founding editor of the *Journal of Language and Social Psychology* and a number of book series; he has published widely in areas such as language attitudes and intergroup communication. Currently, his prime research interests are in the relationships among intergenerational communication, health, and social identity.

JOAN S. GORHAM (Ed.D., Northern Illinois University, 1983) is an Assistant Professor in the Department of Communication Studies at West Virginia University. She is a member of the Executive Council of the Eastern Communication Association and former chair of the Instructional Practices Interest Group of ECA. Her major research interests include instructional, interpersonal, and nonverbal communication.

ALISA J. GRAY completed her B.A. in communication at Arizona State University. She is currently working as an intercultural communication trainer.

JOHN O. GREENE (Ph.D., University of Wisconsin—Madison, 1983) is an Assistant Professor of Communication at Purdue University. His primary interests include interpersonal communication and communication theory, with special emphasis upon cognitive science as an approach toward these domains of inquiry. His current work concerns developing and testing models of the cognitive structures and processes underlying the production of verbal and nonverbal behaviors. Publications representative of his work have appeared in a number of scholarly journals, including *Human Communication Research, Communication Monographs, Quarterly Journal of Speech, Journal of Language and Social Psychology, Language and Speech, Journal of Nonverbal Behavior, Western Journal of Speech Communication,* and *Communication Quarterly,* as well as in a number of edited volumes.

WILLIAM B. GUDYKUNST (Ph.D., University of Minnesota, 1977) is a Professor of Communication at Arizona State University. His research focuses on uncertainty reduction processes across cultures and between people from different cultures. His most recent book is *Intergroup Com-*

munication (published by Edward Arnold). Currently he is writing *Interpersonal Communication Across Cultures* (with E. Chua, for Sage) and *Strangeness and Similarity: A Theory of Interpersonal and Intergroup Communication* (for Multilingual Matters), as well as coediting *The Handbook of Intercultural Communication*, 2nd ed. (with M. Asante, for Sage), *Current Research on Intercultural Adaptation* (with Y. Kim, for Sage), and *Theoretical Perspectives on Intercultural Communication* (with Y. Kim, for Sage).

SHARON LEE HAMMOND is a doctoral student in public communication at the University of Maryland and a part-time lecturer at the University of Maryland University College campus. Her research interests include health communication and the mass media, health survey research, and spatial models of the cognitive structures of health concepts. She is currently writing a book chapter for the National Cancer Institute describing the mass media promotion efforts of the Cancer Information Service. She has more than twelve years' professional experience as a management analyst and public affairs officer at the Food and Drug Administration, Washington, D.C.

RODERICK P. HART is the F. A. Liddell Professor of Communication at the University of Texas at Austin. He received his B.A. degree from the University of Massachusetts and his M.A. and Ph.D. degrees from the Pennsylvania State University. His areas of special interest include political communication, rhetorical criticism, and contemporary persuasive movements. The author of *Public Communication, The Political Pulpit, Verbal Style and the Presidency,* and *The Sound of Leadership,* he has published in such journals as *Quarterly Journal of Speech, Human Communication Research, Philosophy and Rhetoric, Communication Monographs,* and *Journal of Communication*.

CYNTHIA HOFFNER (M.A., University of Wisconsin—Madison, 1984) is a doctoral candidate in the Department of Communication Arts at the University of Wisconsin—Madison. Her research involves cognitive and emotional responses to mass media.

JIM D. HUGHEY is a Professor of Speech Communication at Oklahoma State University. He has investigated the relationship between communication responsiveness and instructor/student variables; his recent results have been published in *Communication Education*. His current research focuses on the media and public perceptions of health issues.

YOUICHI ITO is Professor in the Institute for Communications Research at Keio University in Tokyo. He received his degrees from Keio University, School of Public Communication at Boston University, and the Fletcher School of Law and Diplomacy at Tufts University. His recent major English-language publications include "Telecommunication and Industrial Policies in Japan: Recent Developments" (in M.S. Snow, ed., *Telecommunications Regulation and Deregulation in Industrial Democracies;* Longman/Annenberg, 1986); "The 'Johoka Shakai' Approach to the Study of Communication in Japan" (in G. C. Wilhoit and H. de Bock, eds., *Mass Communication Review Yearbook,* Vol. 2; Sage, 1981); "Mass Communications in Japan" (in A. S. Tan, ed., *Alternative Mass Communication Systems: The Third World, China and Japan;* Erlbaum, forthcoming); and "Cable Television in Japan: Empirical Research Findings" (in W. Dutton et al., eds., *Shaping the Future of Communication: National Visions and Wired City Ventures;* forthcoming).

SALLY JACKSON (Ph.D., University of Illinois, 1980) is Assistant Professor of Communication at the University of Oklahoma. Her research interests are in the areas of interpersonal argumentation and discourse analysis. She has received the SCA Golden Anniversary Prize Monograph Award, the AFA Daniel M. Rohrer Award for Research in Argumentation, and the CSSA Federation Prize. She has published in *Human Communication Research, Communication Monographs, Quarterly Journal of Speech, Journal of Child Language,* and elsewhere.

SCOTT JACOBS (Ph.D., University of Illinois, 1982) is Assistant Professor of Communication at the University of Oklahoma. His research interests are in the areas of discourse processes, conversational argument, and the ethnography of speaking. He has received the SCA Golden Anniversary Prize Monograph Award, the AFA Daniel M. Rohrer Award for Research in Argumentation, the SCA Outstanding Dissertation Award, and the Karl R. Wallace Memorial Award for his work in these areas. He has published in *Quarterly Journal of Speech, Communication Monographs, Human Communication Research, Journal of Child Language,* and elsewhere.

SUSAN JARBOE (Ph.D., University of Wisconsin) is an Assistant Professor of Communication Arts and Sciences at California State University, Fresno. Her research interests are focused on small group communication, including problem solving, conflict management, group effectiveness, and research methods.

PATRICIA JOHNSON received her Ph.D. in social psychology from the University of Bristol in 1984. Her research interests (which have focused on Welsh-English relations) have been in the relationships between language and ethnic identity, ethnolinguistic values, language attitudes, and speech accommodation theory.

STAN A. KAPLOWITZ (Ph.D., University of Michigan, 1971) is Professor of Sociology at Michigan State University. Among his publications are articles on the interaction of moral and instrumental thinking (*Journal of Conflict Resolution*), on the social psychology of power attribution (*Social Psychology Quarterly*), and on the detection of falsified data (*Public Opin-*

ion Quarterly). His current research interests are in the areas of attitude change, public opinion, and formal theory construction. He and E. L. Fink are collaborating on a theory of attitude change and cognition, and parts of their research have appeared in *Communication Yearbooks 6* and *8*, *Communication Monographs*, and *Behavioral Science*.

KATHY KELLERMANN (M.A., Wake Forest University, 1979; M.S., Northwestern University, 1982; Ph.D., Northwestern University, 1983) conducts research in interaction analysis, with specific interests including conversational structure, the relationship between cognition and communication, social cognition, discourse analysis, and mathematical modeling of conversational behavior. She is an Assistant Professor of Communication at Michigan State University.

ASTRID KERSTEN is an Assistant Professor in the Division of Administration and Management of La Roche College, Pittsburgh, Pennsylvania. She has published a number of articles on critical organizational analysis in edited essay volumes, including *Communication Yearbook 9*. Her current research interests include the development of research strategies for critical analysis and research, the application of critical theory in organizational analysis, the role of ideology in organizational control, and the development of alternative systems of organization, including worker democracy.

JAROL B. MANHEIM (Ph.D., Northwestern University, 1971) is Associate Professor of Political Science at Virginia Polytechnic Institute and State University. He is author of five books, including *The Politics Within* and *Empirical Political Analysis* (with Richard C. Rich). His database index, *DataMap*, was designated an American Library Association "Outstanding Reference Source of 1984." He has contributed articles to leading journals in political science and communication studies, including the *American Political Science Review, Journal of Politics, British Journal of Political Science, Journal of Communication, Journalism Quarterly*, and *Political Communication and Persuasion*, and has served as Associate Editor of *Journal of Politics*, Literature Review Editor and Editorial Board Member of *Policy Studies Journal*, and Editor of the Longman series Professional Studies in Political Communication and Policy. His research interests include the domestic and international uses of political public relations techniques and the characteristics of information flows among political leaders, the media, and the public.

GEORGE G. MANROSS is a Ph.D. candidate at the Annenberg School of Communications, University of Southern California, and president of a marketing research and political campaign management firm. His research interests include adoption of innovations and political communication.

JAMES C. McCROSKEY (Ed.D., Pennsylvania State University, 1966) is Professor and Chairperson, Department of Communication Studies, West

Virginia University. He is a Fellow of ICA, former Editor of *Human Communication Research,* and a former member of the ICA Board of Directors. He is Past President of the Eastern Communication Association and Vice-President of the World Communication Association.

SALLY J. McMILLAN is currently an Instructor in the Department of Journalism at the University of Wisconsin—Eau Claire, Co-Director of Interfaith Caregivers Coalition, Inc., and operator of an independent communication consulting business. Her current research interests include descriptive analysis of the public relations function in nonprofit associations, and analysis of pedagogical methods for the teaching of mass media writing.

KATHERINE I. MILLER (Ph.D., University of Southern California, 1985) is Assistant Professor of Communication at Michigan State University. She has had recent publications in *Human Communication Research* and *Academy of Management Journal.* Her current research interests include the modeling of organizational and group decision-making systems, the role of work and social support in the experience of stress in the workplace, and the dynamics of interpersonal relationships in organizational settings.

PETER R. MONGE (Ph.D., Michigan State University, 1972) is Professor of Communication at Annenberg School of Communications, University of Southern California. He is the current Editor of *Communication Research* and has had recent publications in *Management Science, Academy of Management Journal,* and *Human Communication Research.* His current research interests include the study of participative processes in organizations and inter- and intraorganizational communication networks, particularly in relationship to organizational outcomes such as worker satisfaction and productivity.

DONALD DEAN MORLEY (Ph.D., University of Iowa, 1982) is an Assistant Professor of Communication at the University of Colorado at Colorado Springs. His current research interests are in the areas of persuasion and organizational communication. His recent publications have presented a theory of persuasion and focused on the influence of gender, communication apprehension, and conflict preferences on individual and organizational outcomes.

ANTHONY MULAC (Ph.D., University of Michigan, 1969) is Professor of Communication Studies at the University of California, Santa Barbara. He has published widely in the areas of gender-linked language behavior and language attitudes. Currently his research is focusing upon gender-linked verbal and nonverbal differences in interpersonal communication and speech accommodation.

DIANA C. MUTZ is a doctoral candidate in the Department of Communication and Institute for Communication Research at Stanford University. Her research interests include political communication, public opinion research, and communication and social cognition.

KIMBERLY A. NEUENDORF (Ph.D., Michigan State University, 1982) is Assistant Professor of Communication at Cleveland State University and Visiting Assistant Professor at University of Maryland (fall 1986). Her research interests include cognitive processes of and affective reactions to mass media, the cultural correlates of media use, and measurement issues as related to media studies. Her publications include work in *Journal of Communication, Journalism Quarterly, Journal of Broadcasting, Media Information Australia, Review of Religious Research,* and *Religious Communication Today.*

ROBERT M. OGLES (Ph.D., University of Wisconsin—Madison, 1986) is an Assistant Professor in the Department of Communication at Purdue University. His research interests are focused on social psychological effects of mass communication, especially media-influenced constructions of social reality.

MALCOLM R. PARKS (Ph.D., human communications, Michigan State University, 1976) is currently Associate Professor of Speech Communication at the University of Washington. His research has focused on the development and dissolution of friendships, premarital romantic relationships, and marital relationships, with a special concern for the dynamics of communications networks. He has also conducted research on related topics, such as communicative competence, shyness, alienation, marital interaction, matchmaking, and privacy/disclosure dialectics. His work has appeared in *Human Communication Research, Communication Monographs, Communication Yearbook,* and *Social Psychology Quarterly,* as well as numerous edited volumes.

BYRON REEVES is Professor of Communication at Stanford University. His Ph.D. is in communication from Michigan State University. His research interests include children and television and processing of media messages.

RONALD E. RICE is Assistant Professor at the Annenberg School of Communications, University of Southern California, and currently Chair of ICA's Human Communication Technology Interest Group. His research areas include communication networks, diffusion of innovations, social impacts of telecommunications, and organizational communication. He is coeditor or coauthor of *Public Communications* (Sage, 1981), *The New Media* (Sage, 1984), and *Managing Organizational Innovation* (Columbia University Press, 1987).

VIRGINIA P. RICHMOND (Ph.D., University of Nebraska, 1977) is Professor and Coordinator of Graduate Studies in the Department of Communication Studies at West Virginia University. She is Vice-President of the Eastern Communication Association and Editor of *Communication Research Reports.* Her major research areas include instructional, interpersonal, and organizational communication.

L. EDNA ROGERS (Ph.D., Michigan State University, 1972) is a Professor of Communication at Cleveland State University. Her research interests include relational communication and marital and family communication. Her research has been published widely in communication periodicals, including *Human Communication Research* and *Communication Monographs*, as well as several book chapters. She is also on the editorial board for several journals.

ANA M. ROSSI (M.S., Florida State University) is a doctoral candidate and instructor at the University of Nebraska—Lincoln. Formerly a Brazilian attorney, she is currently a stress management and biofeedback therapist and is developing a training program to deal with acute anxiety in public speaking.

ROBERT A. SARR (M.B.A., Stanford University, 1966) is an Internal Management Consultant in the Industrial Relations Division of the Procter & Gamble Company. His current work focuses primarily on organizational development.

JOAN SCHLEUDER is Assistant Professor of Journalism at the University of Texas at Austin. She holds a Ph.D. in journalism and mass communication from the University of Wisconsin—Madison. Her research focuses on the processing of media messages.

SUSAN B. SHIMANOFF (Ph.D., University of Southern California, 1978) is Assistant Professor, Department of Speech and Communication Studies, San Francisco State University. Her research has focused on identifying and explicating the role of communication rules in everyday interactions. The theoretical foundations for this research appeared in her book, *Communication Rules: Theory and Research* (Sage, 1980). Her more recent research has been concerned primarily with rules for expressing emotions, small group interaction, and choosing between presumed synonyms. Her research has been published (or is scheduled to appear) in a variety of journals and books, including *Communication Monographs, Communication Quarterly, Journal of Communication, Small Group Communication,* and *Western Journal of Speech Communication.*

PAMELA J. SHOEMAKER (Ph.D., University of Wisconsin—Madison) is an Assistant Professor in the Department of Journalism, University of Texas at Austin, and Director of the Office of Survey Research for the College of Communication. Her research interests include theory building, deviance, social change, and influences on media content. She is the author of a monograph entitled "Building a Theory of News Content: A Synthesis of Current Approaches" (*Journalism Monographs* 103) forthcoming in June 1987. Her other publications deal with how the media treat deviant political groups, political group legitimacy, ethnic media use and political behaviors, and the communication of deviance.

RUTH C. SMITH is a doctoral candidate and Assistant Lecturer in the Department of Communication Arts and Sciences, University of Southern California. Her research areas include organizational communication, interpersonal communication, and language behavior. Her present focus is on the social and cognitive functions of figurative language in everyday talk.

SANDI W. SMITH (Ph.D., University of Southern California, 1986) is Assistant Professor of Communication at Purdue University. Her research interests include social cognition and information processing in both interpersonal and organizational contexts.

CYNTHIA STOHL (Ph.D., Purdue University, 1982) is an Assistant Professor of Communication at Purdue University. Her research focuses upon the relationships among formal and emergent features of social networks, worker participation programs, and the development of organizational competence.

RICHARD L. STREET, Jr. (Ph.D., University of Texas at Austin) is Associate Professor and Chairperson of the Department of Speech Communication at Texas Tech University in Lubbock, Texas. He has published over 30 articles and book chapters in such outlets as *Human Communication Research, Communication Monographs, Journal of Language and Social Psychology, Communication Yearbook,* and *The Handbook of Interpersonal Communication.* He is coeditor (with Joe Cappella) of *Sequence and Pattern in Communicative Behavior.* His research interests entail the study of communicative patterns and outcome in various interaction contexts, including physician-patient communication, interviews, social conversation, and adult-child talk.

ESTHER THORSON is Associate Professor of Journalism and Mass Communication at the University of Wisconsin—Madison. She holds a Ph.D. in psychology from the University of Minnesota. Her research focuses on how consumers process television advertising.

FRANK TUTZAUER holds degrees in both mathematics (B.S., Southwestern, 1981) and communication studies (M.A., Northwestern, 1984; Ph.D., Northwestern, 1985), and he is currently an Assistant Professor of Interpersonal and Public Communication at Bowling Green State University. His most recent articles are "Bargaining as a Dynamical System" (*Behavioral Science,* April 1986) and "Toward a Theory of Disintegration in Communication Networks" (*Social Networks,* September 1985). His research interests include bargaining and negotiation, network analysis, and mathematical theories of human behavior. His current research project involves a game-theoretic investigation of fractionated bargaining.

PATRICIA AMASON WALTMAN (M.A., University of Kentucky, 1983) is a doctoral candidate in communication at Purdue University. Her major research interests include communicative development, communication and social support networks, and training children and adolescents in communication skills. She has recently presented papers at conventions of the International Communication Association and the Speech Communication Association.

KARI WHITTENBERGER-KEITH is currently completing her Ph.D. in communication studies at the University of Texas at Austin. Her dissertation examines 100 years of American etiquette books, focusing on the changes in etiquette as reflections of changes in Americans' perceptions of themselves. Her research interests include all facets of political communication, as well as the relationship of rhetoric to the analysis of social and cultural history. She is currently Assistant to the Director, Learning Research and Development Center, University of Pittsburgh.

JOHN M. WIEMANN (Ph.D., Purdue University) is Associate Professor of Communication Studies at the University of California, Santa Barbara. His research interests include communicative competence, nonverbal behavior, communication problems involved with health care and aging, and conversation structure and strategy. He is coeditor of *Nonverbal Interaction* (Sage, 1983), *Communication Strategies* (Erlbaum, forthcoming), and *Rethinking Communication Research* (Sage, forthcoming), and coauthor of *Communicative Competence: A Theoretical Analysis* (Edward Arnold, forthcoming). He is coeditor of the Sage Annual Reviews of Communication Research series (Vols. 16-21). His research appears in journals and book chapters in the disciplines of communication, social psychology, and education. He has been a W. K. Kellogg Foundation National Fellow (1980-1983) and a Fulbright-Hayes Senior Research Scholar (1985) in residence at the Department of Psychology, University of Bristol (UK).

BARBARA J. WILSON (Ph.D., University of Wisconsin—Madison, 1985) is Assistant Professor in the Department of Communication, University of Louisville. Her research focuses on developmental differences in children's cognitive and emotional reactions to mass media.